Architectural Alternatives for Exploiting Parallelism

David J. Lilja

1951-1991

IEEE Computer Society Press
Los Alamitos, California

Washington • Brussels • Tokyo

IEEE COMPUTER SOCIETY PRESS TUTORIAL

Library of Congress Cataloging-in-Publication Data

Lilja, David J.
    Architectural alternatives for exploiting parallelism
        p.   cm.
    Includes bibliographical references.
        ISBN 0-8186-2640-2 (p). -- ISBN 0-8186-2641-0 (m/f). -- ISBN
    0-8186-2642-9 (case).
    1. Parallel computers. 2. Computer architecture I. Title QA76.58.L55 1992
004' .35--dc20   CIP 91-33298

Published by the
IEEE Computer Society Press
10662 Los Vaqueros Circle
PO Box 3014
Los Alamitos, CA 90720-1264

IEEE Computer Society Press Order Number 2642
Library of Congress Number 91-33298
IEEE Catalog Number 91EH0348-3
ISBN 0-8186-2641-0 (microfiche)
ISBN 0-8186-2642-9 (case)

Additional copies can be ordered from

IEEE Computer Society Press Customer Service Center 10662 Los Vaqueros Circle PO Box 3014 Los Alamitos, CA 90720-1264	IEEE Service Center 445 Hoes Lane PO Box 1331 Piscataway, NJ 08855-1331 Technical Editor: Joydeep Ghosh	IEEE Computer Society 13, avenue de l'Aquilon B-1200 Brussels BELGIUM	IEEE Computer Society Ooshima Building 2-19-1 Minami-Aoyama Minato-ku, Tokyo 107 JAPAN

Editorial production: Robert Werner
Technical editor: Joydeep Ghosh
Copy editor: Phyllis Walker
Cover designed by Joseph Daigle/Schenk-Daigle Studios
Printed in the United States of America by Braun-Brumfield, Inc.

**The Institute of Electrical and
Electronics Engineers, Inc.**

Preface

In Euclidean geometry, lines that never intersect are said to be "parallel." In computer architecture, computational tasks that are independent are said to be "executed in parallel" when they are run concurrently on different functional units or processors. The instantaneous number of these independent tasks from a single program that can be executed simultaneously is the parallelism available in that program at that instant in time. Since the number of independent tasks available to be executed varies over the course of a program's execution, a program's average parallelism may be much lower than its maximum instantaneous parallelism. Several studies have shown that there can be a significant amount of parallelism in many scientific and engineering application programs, but it remains an open question as to what type of processor architecture can best exploit this parallelism. As a result, an incredible variety of parallel computer architectures have been proposed and implemented. This tutorial surveys

- The fine-grained parallel architectures that attempt to exploit the parallelism available at the instruction-set level;
- The coarse-grained parallel architectures that exploit the parallelism available at the loop and subroutine levels; and
- The single-instruction stream, multiple-data stream (SIMD), massively parallel architectures that exploit parallelism across large data structures.

After studying the papers reprinted in this tutorial, the reader should have a clear understanding of the variety of architectures that are available for exploiting parallelism, as well as some idea of the trade-offs involved in using each of the architectures.

This tutorial is divided into four chapters, each with an introduction followed immediately by a list of relevant references. (In the reference lists, references that appear as reprints in this tutorial are marked with an asterisk.) These lists of references are necessarily incomplete, but they should provide a good starting point for anyone wishing to study a particular topic in greater depth. The introduction to Chapter 1 discusses the potential of parallel processing for reducing the execution time of a single program, beginning with Amdahl's conjecture that parallel speedup is limited ultimately by the inherently sequential component of the program. Reprinted in Chapter 1 are several papers that examine the controversial topic of how much parallelism actually is available in application programs.

The four sections in Chapter 2 present processor architectures that attempt to exploit parallelism at the instruction level. The first section provides an introduction to pipelined processors. The second section describes multiple instruction-issue architectures. The decoupled access/execute architectures discussed in the third section combine some aspects of both pipelining and multiple-instruction issuing. The last section of Chapter 2 introduces the dataflow concept, which potentially allows for a high degree of fine-grained parallelism.

Architectures that try to extract parallelism at higher levels, such as at the loop level and at the subroutine level, are presented in Chapter 3, along with an introduction to the massively parallel SIMD architectures. The first section in Chapter 3 discusses shared-memory multiprocessors, in which many identical processors are connected to a common memory. While communication among processors in this type of system is limited to the sharing of variables through the common memory structure, the distributed-memory multicomputer systems presented in the second section of Chapter 3 communicate using explicit messages. Also, a reprinted paper in this section presents a survey of systems that hide the message passing from the programmer by implementing a virtual shared memory on top of a distributed system. The last section of Chapter 3 presents several SIMD, massively parallel architectures in which a single sequence of instructions performs the same operation simultaneously on several thousand different data elements.

The parallel architectures presented in this tutorial have significant differences in synchronization overhead, instruction-scheduling constraints, memory latencies, and implementation details, making it difficult to determine which architecture is best able to exploit the parallelism available in a given application. Chapter 4 includes several studies that compare the performance of some of the different architectures.

v

Intended Audience

This tutorial is aimed at computer architects, system designers, researchers, and students who are interested in a guide for surveying and comparing the broad field of general-purpose parallel computer architectures. It also should serve as a valuable reference source for all computer professionals. Some basic knowledge of computer architecture and design will be helpful when reading this tutorial. The level of this tutorial is appropriate for graduate students and advanced undergraduate students, as well as practicing engineers.

Acknowledgments

The result of an effort such as preparing this tutorial text is as much a function of the environment in which the author finds himself as it is of the author's individual effort. Recognizing this synergism, I would like to thank all of my colleagues at the Center for Supercomputing Research and Development at the University of Illinois at Urbana-Champaign for helping to create an intellectually stimulating environment in which to research some of the problems in parallel processing. I would particularly like to thank Pen-Chung Yew for providing me with the freedom to pursue this project. I also would like to acknowledge the support of Mos Kaveh, my department head at the University of Minnesota, Minneapolis, in providing me with the time to complete this text.

Thanks to Rao Vemuri, editor-in-chief of the IEEE Computer Society Press, who helped track down this manuscript when it went astray during a change of personnel. As the coordinator of the referee process for this manuscript, Joydeep Ghosh provided some excellent reviews that significantly improved the quality of the presentation, particularly in the sections on dataflow processors, distributed-memory multicomputers, and reconfigurable and massively parallel architectures. I would also like to thank Bob Werner, Phyllis Walker, and Henry Ayling of the IEEE Computer Society Press for their invaluable assistance in editing and producing this tutorial. I hope the final result proves useful to the computer community.

David J. Lilja
Minneapolis, Minnesota
December 27, 1991

Table of Contents

Chapter 1: Introduction

The past several decades have seen exponential improvements in the performance of computer systems, mostly due to increases in single-processor performance. These increases have been possible because, as a fundamental limit has been approached in one technology, a new technology has been introduced to supplement or replace the old. For example, the frequent introduction of new logic families has helped reduce supercomputer cycle times by a factor of two every four or five years over the last 30 years.[1] However, as semiconductor technologies have matured, growth in single-processor performance has shown signs of slowing. To continue to obtain the expected improvements in system performance, computer architects are incorporating more parallel processing technology into new computer designs.

In contrast with the technique of speeding up a single processor by using new semiconductor technology to produce faster logic, parallel processing attempts to increase performance by dividing a program into independent tasks that can be executed concurrently on several functional units or processors. The size of the computational tasks, called the "granularity" of the parallelism, can have a significant impact on the performance of a parallel system, since there may be some parallelism accessible at one task size, but not at another. The papers selected for this tutorial survey several classes of parallel computer architectures:

- Those that attempt to exploit the fine-grained parallelism available at the instruction-set level,
- Those that exploit the coarser-grained parallelism at the loop level and the subroutine level, and
- Those that exploit data parallelism by performing the same operation simultaneously on several thousand different data elements.

To obtain an idea of the potential performance gains of using a parallel architecture, consider a program that executes in time T_1 on a single processor. If α is the dynamic fraction of all operations in the program that must be executed sequentially, the time required to execute this part of the program on a single processor (when the single processor is part of a multiprocessor) is αT_1. The remaining fraction of the operations in the program, $(1 - \alpha)$, are said to be "perfectly parallel" and so can be executed p times faster on a multiprocessor with p processors, giving a parallel execution time of $(1 - \alpha)(T_1/p)$. The total execution time T_p is the sum of these serial and parallel times, $T_p = \alpha T_1 + (1 - \alpha)T_1/p$, and the speedup S_p for the multiprocessor is the ratio of the single-processor execution time T_1 to the multiprocessor execution time T_p, as shown in the following equation:

$$S_p = \frac{T_1}{T_p} = \frac{T_1}{\alpha T_1 + \dfrac{(1-\alpha)T_1}{p}} = \frac{1}{\dfrac{1}{p} + \alpha\left(1 - \dfrac{1}{p}\right)} \qquad \qquad 1$$

Ideally, the sequential component is negligible (that is, $\alpha \approx 0$), making the speedup the same as the number of processors: $S_p \approx p$. However, for $\alpha > 0$, the limit as $p \to \infty$ in Equation 1 is $S_p \to 1/\alpha$. This result, known as Amdahl's Law,[2] says that no matter how many processors are used to execute a program, the maximum speedup is limited by the program's inherently sequential component, α. For example, if 10 percent of the total operations executed in a program must be executed sequentially (that is, $\alpha = 0.1$), the maximum speedup S_p for the program is $1/0.1 = 10$. There have been some reports of obtaining speedups greater than p when using p processors,[3-5] but it appears[6*] that the causes of these reports are attributable to such factors as overhead reductions, cache size effects, memory latency hiding, and the use of randomized algorithms.

There are arguments that, as more processors are added to a system, the system is more effectively used by solving a larger version of a problem in the same amount of time than by trying to reduce the execution time of a fixed-size version of the problem. This approach defines a new concept, called "scaled speedup,"[7,8*] in which the value of α is reduced by increasing the number of operations in the parallel part of the program. In addition, there are many enhancements to and variations of Amdahl's Law that incorporate more details into the system models than the simple one used here[9,10] and that relate efficiency and speedup.[11-14]

The actual parallelism available in an application program is limited by its dependences.[15] A dependence between two computational tasks is a conflict that prevents the tasks from executing simultaneously. That is, a dependence from one task to another implies that the first task must complete its execution before the dependent task can begin executing. Dependences can be categorized into the following three types:

(1) Resource dependences are a physical limitation imposed by the architecture and the hardware of the particular machine on which the program is to be executed. This type of dependence occurs when two tasks need to use the same resource at the same time, forcing one to wait for the other to complete its execution. Any real machine has a limited number of functional units and limited memory bandwidth, for example, which may prevent exploiting all of the parallelism available in an application.

(2) Control dependences, in which a statement cannot execute until the result of an earlier conditional statement has been resolved, are a function of the algorithm and of the programming language used to implement the algorithm.

(3) Data dependences, also known as "hazards,"[16] are read-write conflicts between two operations that prevent the operations from executing concurrently. In a flow dependence (read-after-write hazard), the result of one operation is read by a subsequent operation. An output dependence (write-after-write hazard) exists between two statements when they both write to the same variable. Two statements are said to have an "antidependence" (write-after-read hazard) when a later statement writes to a variable that is read by an earlier statement. Output dependences and antidependences occur when variables and registers are reused by the programmer or the compiler; given a sufficient number of temporary storage locations, many of these two kinds of dependences can be eliminated by renaming variables.

Available parallelism

The question of how much parallelism is available in application programs is somewhat controversial. Table 1 summarizes the results of several studies that show that there is a wide range of potential parallelism in actual application programs. This wide range is due partly to the significantly different architectural assumptions made in each of the simulation studies and partly to actual differences in inherent parallelism. These assumptions include differences in memory delays, functional unit latencies, register and memory conflicts, synchronization costs, specific application programs tested, compiler quality, and other such implementation details. However, it appears that when basic block boundaries are ignored — so that the entire program is available for exploiting parallelism — engineering and scientific programs can exhibit a high level of inherent parallelism. (A "basic block" is a sequence [or block] of instructions in a program that has no branches into or out of the block.) Computation that is less numeric than that in "typical" scientific and engineering application programs has relatively little parallelism, even when basic block boundaries are ignored. While compiler transformations and algorithm changes may significantly increase the available parallelism in an application,[29] limiting parallelism extraction to a basic block limits speedups to a maximum of about two to four.

Table 1. Reported speedup values.

Researchers	Speedup Mean[a]	Speedup Range	Programs tested	Functional units	Basic blocks?
Kumar (1988)[21*]	1400	475-3500	4 scientific	∞	No
Arvind et al. (1988)[18]	590	463-745	2 scientific	∞	No
Butler et al. (1991)[19*]	171	17-1165	9 mixture	∞	No
Riseman and Foster (1972)[24]	37	7.8-120.5	7 mixture	∞	No
	1.66	1.22-2.98	7 mixture	∞	Yes
Nicolau and Fisher (1984)[23*]	28	3-988.5	22 scientific	∞	No
	2.2	1.37-5.58	22 scientific	∞	Yes
Wall (1991)[27*]	24	6.5-60.4	19 mixture	∞	No
	2.7	1.3-17.5	19 mixture	∞	Yes
Lilja and Yew (1991)[22]	8.7	1.5-646	20 scientific	∞	No
Acosta et al. (1986)[17]	2.79	NA[b]	Livermore loops	∞	Yes
Smith et al. (1989)[25]	2.5	NA	13 nonscientific	—[c]	No
	4.1	NA	13 nonscientific	—[d]	No
Jouppi and Wall (1989)[20*]	2.2	1.6-3.2	8 mixture	8	Yes
Tjaden and Flynn (1970)[26]	1.86	1.2-3.2	31 mixture	∞	Yes
Weiss and Smith (1984)[28*]	1.6	1.2-2.0	Livermore loops	—[e]	Yes

a. This value is either the mean reported in the study, or the geometric mean calculated from the reported values.

b. NA stands for "not available."

c. One of each type of functional unit; limited instruction look-ahead.

d. One of each type of functional unit; limited instruction look-ahead; flow dependences only.

e. Cray-1 functional units.

Based on the studies summarized in Table 1, it is not apparent what type of architecture can best exploit the available parallelism nor even how much parallelism exists. As a result, an incredible variety of architectures has been proposed to try to exploit whatever parallelism is available. Pipelined processors and multiple instruction-issue processors, discussed in Chapter 2, exploit the fine-grained parallelism available at the instruction-set level. The multiprocessors presented in the first two sections of Chapter 3 exploit coarse-grained parallelism by distributing independent loop iterations and subroutines to different processors. In addition, massively parallel single-instruction stream, multiple-data stream (SIMD) architectures discussed in the last section of Chapter 3 exploit the fact that — in some problems — the same operation is repeated many times over a large array of data. In these SIMD machines, a single instruction-sequencer controls the simultaneous operation of thousands of identical processors, with each processor acting on a different data element.

The parallel architectures presented in this tutorial use significantly different techniques for synchronizing, scheduling instructions, reducing memory delay, and implementing the hardware, making it difficult to determine which architecture is best able to exploit the parallelism available in a given application. By presenting a few studies that compare the performance potential of several of the different parallel architectures, Chapter 4 provides some insight into making this determination.

References (Chapter 1)

An asterisk following a reference citation below indicates the inclusion of that paper in this tutorial.

Available parallelism

1. J. Worlton, "Some Patterns of Technological Change in High-Performance Computers," *Supercomputing '88*, 1988, pp. 312-320.

2. G.M. Amdahl, "Validity of the Single Processor Approach to Achieving Large Scale Computing Capabilities," *AFIPS Conf. Proc., Spring Joint Computer Conf.*, Apr. 1967, pp. 483-485.

3. K. Li, "IVY: Shared Virtual Memory System for Parallel Computing," *Int'l Conf. Parallel Processing, Vol. II: Software*, 1988, pp. 94-101.

4. B.R. Preiss and V. C. Hamacher, "Semi-Static Dataflow," *Int'l Conf. Parallel Processing, Vol II: Software*, 1988, pp. 127-134.

5. J. Sanguinetti, "Performance of Message-Based Multiprocessor," *Computer*, Vol. 19, No. 9, Sept. 1986, pp. 47-55.

6.* D.P. Helmbold and C.E. McDowell, "Modeling Speedup (n) Greater Than n," *IEEE Trans. Parallel and Distributed Systems*, Vol. 1, No. 2, Apr. 1990, pp. 250-256.

7. J.L. Gustafson, G.R. Montry, and R.E. Benner, "Development of Parallel Methods for a 1024-Processor Hypercube," *SIAM J. Scientific and Statistical Computing*, Vol. 9, No. 4, July 1988, pp. 609-638.

8.* J.L. Gustafson, "Reevaluating Amdahl's Law," *Comm. ACM*, Vol. 31, No. 5, May 1988, pp. 532-533.

9. X. Zhou and J. Staudhammer, "New Speedup Function for Supercomputing," *Proc. Int'l Symp. Mini and Microcomputers*, Dec. 1988.

10. X. Zhou, "Bridging the Gap Between Amdahl's Law and Sandia Laboratory's Results," *Comm. ACM*, Vol. 32, No. 8, Aug. 1989, pp. 1014-1015.

11. M.L. Barton and G.R. Withers, "Computing Performance as a Function of the Speed, Quantity, and Cost of the Processors," *Proc. Supercomputing '89*, 1989, pp. 759-764.

12. D.L. Eager, J. Zahorjan, and E.D. Lazowska, "Speedup Versus Efficiency in Parallel Systems," *IEEE Trans. Computers*, Vol. 38, No. 3, Mar. 1989, pp. 408-423.

13. A.H. Karp and H.P. Flatt, "Measuring Parallel Processor Performance," *Comm. ACM*, Vol. 33, No. 5, May 1990, pp. 539-543.

14. J.R. Zorbas, D.J. Reble, and R.E. VanKooten, "Measuring the Scalability of Parallel Computer Systems," *Proc. Supercomputing '89*, 1989, pp. 832-841.

15. D.J. Kuck, *The Structure of Computers and Computations*, John Wiley and Sons, New York, N.Y., 1978, pp. 135-141.

16. P.M. Kogge, *The Architecture of Pipelined Computers*, Hemisphere, New York, N.Y., 1981, p. 220.

17. R.D. Acosta, J. Kjelstrup, and H.C. Torng, "An Instruction Issuing Approach to Enhancing Performance in Multiple Functional Unit Processors," *IEEE Trans. Computers*, Vol. C-35, No. 9, Sept. 1986, pp. 815-828.

18. Arvind, D.E. Culler, and G.K. Maa, "Assessing the Benefits of Fine-Grain Parallelism in Dataflow Programs," *Proc. Supercomputing '88*, Nov. 1988, pp. 60-69.

19.* M. Butler et al., "Single Instruction Stream Parallelism is Greater Than Two," *Int'l Symp. Computer Architecture*, 1991, pp. 276-286.

20.* N.P. Jouppi and D.W. Wall, "Available Instruction-Level Parallelism for Superscalar and Superpipelined Machines," *Third Int'l Conf. Architectural Support Programming Languages and Operating Systems*, Apr. 1989, pp. 272-282.

21.* M. Kumar, "Measuring Parallelism in Computation-Intensive Scientific/Engineering Applications," *IEEE Trans. Computers*, Vol. 37, No. 9, Sept. 1988, pp. 1088-1098.

22. D.J. Lilja and P.-C. Yew, "The Performance Potential of Fine-Grain and Coarse-Grain Parallel Architectures," *Hawaii Int'l Conf. System Sciences, Vol. I: Architecture*, 1991, pp. 324-333.

23.* A. Nicolau and J.A. Fisher, "Measuring the Parallelism Available for Very Long Instruction Word Architectures," *IEEE Trans. Computers*, Vol. C-33, No. 11, Nov. 1984, pp. 968-976.

24. E.M. Riseman and C.C. Foster, "The Inhibition of Potential Parallelism by Conditional Jumps," *IEEE Trans. Computers*, Vol. C-21, No. 12, Dec. 1972, pp. 1405-1411.

25. M.D. Smith, M. Johnson, and M.A. Horowitz, "Limits on Multiple Instruction Issue," *Third Int'l Conf. Architectural Support Programming Languages and Operating Systems*, Apr. 1989, pp. 290-302.

26. G.S. Tjaden and M.J. Flynn, "Detection and Parallel Execution of Independent Instructions," *IEEE Trans. Computers*, Vol. C-19, No. 10, Oct. 1970, pp. 889-895.

27.* D.W. Wall, "Limits of Instruction-Level Parallelism," *Fourth Int'l Conf. Architectural Support Programming Languages and Operating Systems*, Apr. 1991, pp. 176-188.

28.* S. Weiss and J.E. Smith, "Instruction Issue Logic in Pipelined Supercomputers," *IEEE Trans. Computers*, Vol. C-33, No. 11, Nov. 1984, pp. 1013-1022.

29. D.J. Kuck et al., "The Effects of Program Restructuring, Algorithm Change, and Architecture Choice on Program Performance," *Int'l Conf. Parallel Processing*, 1984, pp. 129-138.

Available parallelism

Modeling Speedup (*n*) Greater than *n*

DAVID P. HELMBOLD AND CHARLES E. McDOWELL

Abstract—We present a simple model of parallel computation which is capable of explaining speedups greater than *n* on *n* processors. We derive necessary and sufficient conditions for these exceptional speedups from the model. Furthermore, we resolve several of the contradictory previous results relating to parallel speedup by using the model.

Index Terms—Parallel processing, performance model, speedup, superlinear, superunitary.

I. INTRODUCTION

The speedup of a parallel processor with n processing elements (written $S(n)$) is defined to be the ratio of the total execution time on a uniprocessor to the total execution time on the parallel processor. The term "superlinear speedup" has been used to describe a computation using n processors which is more than n times faster than the same computation performed on a uniprocessor. In many cases, the choice of the word "superlinear" is inappropriate because the speedup may actually be linear and still be greater than n on n processors.

Manuscript received April 21, 1989; revised December 11, 1989. This work was supported in part by the IBM Corporation under Contract SL 88096.
The authors are with the Board of Studies in Computer and Information Sciences, University of California at Santa Cruz, Santa Cruz, CA 95064.
IEEE Log Number 8934125.

In this paper, we use the following hierarchy of terms adapted from [17].

- Superlinear speedup: $\lim_{n \to \infty} S(n)/n = \infty$.
- Linear superunitary speedup: $\lim_{n \to \infty} S(n)/n$ is finite and greater than 1.
- Unitary speedup: $\lim_{n \to \infty} S(n)/n = 1$.
- Linear subunitary speedup: $0 < \lim_{n \to \infty} S(n)/n < 1$.
- Sublinear speedup: $\lim_{n \to \infty} S(n)/n = 0$.

When considering the speedup over a finite range of n (rather than in the limit) we use the terms *superunitary, unitary*, and *subunitary* speedup when $S(n) > n$, $S(n) = n$, and $S(n) < n$, respectively.

Hypothesized upper bounds on speedup have ranged from $O(\log(n))$ [16] to unbounded [15]. The controversy continues, with recent papers claiming either that superunitary speedup is possible [18] or that superunitary speedup is impossible [6], [4]. While Minsky's $\log(n)$ bound made overly restrictive assumptions about the amount of parallelism in a program, the reports of superunitary and unbounded speedup are based on comparisons to sequential algorithms that are not the best known. Recently, there have been reports of superunitary speedups in simulations and even in real programs [20], [8], [11], [19], [12], [2]. In addition, formal analysis has been used to argue that superunitary speedup can occur [10], [13], [15], [14]. In this paper, we attempt to unify the previous reports and results in two ways. First we present a simple unified model that includes the necessary parameters to describe the various results. Second we illustrate how different assumptions are responsible for the apparently contradictory results.

It is often convenient to divide the work into *real* work and *overhead*. The *real* work includes all operations explicitly called for in the algorithm. The *overhead* includes all other work such as scheduling and synchronization in the parallel processor. The determination of what is *real* work and what is *overhead* is not universally agreed upon. Regardless of how much work is *real* and how much is *overhead*, we have the following obvious fact.

Superunitary speedup ($S(n) > n$) is possible only when the total amount of work performed (i.e., units of processor time consumed) by the n processors is *strictly less* than the total work performed by the single processor.

Notice that if the *real* work decreases for the parallel version then the uniprocessor version can always reduce its *real* work and increase its *overhead* via timeslicing. If a parallel algorithm is demonstrating dramatic (i.e., superunitary) speedup then it probably makes sense to pay some overhead in the sequential version to mimic the parallel version. Furthermore (as noted in [23]), in most real environments processors are already timeshared; hence, the overhead is already being (at least partially) paid. Thus, in many cases we would expect a negligible increase in overhead from any additional timeslicing.

Reports of superunitary speedup fall into the following general categories:

1) Observed in a real system [11], [8].
2) Observed in a simulation [19].
3) Shown analytically [10], [13], [23], [15].

The superunitary speedups that have been shown analytically can be further categorized as follows.

- The sequential algorithm is somehow constrained to use an inferior method. Allowing the sequential version to use the "same" algorithm as the parallel version(s) eliminates the superunitary performance.

0-8186-2642-9/92 $3.00 © 1990 IEEE

- The problem is NP-hard and the best known algorithm is a randomized search. Furthermore, for *any input* most random choices lead quickly to a solution but there are a few bad choices which force the algorithm to run for an extremely long time. (In [23] it is stated that "while. . .possible, we know of no practical algorithms for which it has been observed.") When multiple choices are explored in parallel, the chance that all of the choices lead to lengthy executions goes down exponentially. Therefore, the expected execution time drops quickly as the number of processors increases.[1]

In Section II, we present a general model that can be used to unify all but the probabilistic results with regard to speedup. In Section III, we present a necessary and sufficient condition for achieving speedups greater than n. In Section IV, we apply this model to several previously reported results.

II. The Multiprocessor Model

The multiprocessor model used in the following analysis is very general. An implementation of an algorithm on a particular multiprocessor will be composed of various types of operations. These could be low level operations such as register to register operations, local memory reads, remote memory reads, and synchronization operations; or they could be high level operations such as sort, merge, inner product, etc. The total work W^n is defined to be the total *number* of operations that must be executed when the algorithm is run on an n processor system. To compute the total time taken by the algorithm, the number of operations must be weighted by the time taken per operation. In addition, W^n does not include any implicit delays that might occur due to memory latency or synchronization. The value represented by W^n is simply the number of operations performed.

The various types of operations performed by the algorithm may require different amounts of time. Therefore, we usually partition W^n into disjoint subscripted components. Each W_i^n is the number of times operations of type i are performed. Associated with each operation i is a cost function $C_i(n)$ indicating the total amount of processor time (in some appropriately scaled unit) used by all processors in order to perform one operation of type i in an n processor system (if this total varies for a given type, then $C_i(n)$ is the average amount of processor time used). For example, if one processor can complete an operation in 2 s (while the other processors are performing other operations) then the cost of the operation $C_i(n)$, is 2 processor-seconds. Alternatively, if all n processors must work together for 5 s to perform an operation, the cost of the operation is $5n$ processor-seconds.

Computing speedups using the time taken by the "optimal" sequential algorithm poses a number of pitfalls. Even the best known algorithm for a particular problem may be improved on by future researchers. Furthermore, although one algorithm may have a superior worst case performance, another may tend to perform better on the data of interest. A natural compromise is to insist that, in some sense, the "same" algorithm is used on both the sequential and multiprocessor system. We consider two algorithms to be the same if they require the same number of each type of operation. Note, however, that the *costs* of the work types can, and often do, vary depending on the size of the multiprocessor.

III. A Necessary Condition for Superunitary Speedup

Throughout the paper, we use W_s^n to represent the number of serial operations in the n-processor version of the algorithm,[2] and

---

[1] These results may also fit into the first category since a uniprocessor system can obtain a similar improvement in expected running time by aborting long computations and restarting using a different set of random choices.

[2] For notational simplicity, the algorithm under consideration is assumed and will be clear from the context.

$C_s(n)$ to represent the cost (i.e., number of processor time-units) for computing a single serial operation on an n processor system. We assume throughout that in sequential mode one processor is working and the other $n - 1$ are idle; therefore, $C_s(n) = nC_s(1)$. For notational convenience (and without loss of generality) we define the duration of a basic serial operation to be one "unit" of processor time, i.e., $C_s(1) = 1$.

If the kinds of work undertaken by a parallel algorithm can be divided into those which must be executed sequentially and those which can execute with at least n-fold parallelism, then the following theorem holds.

Theorem 1: Let

$$W^n = W_s^n + \sum_{i \in P} W_i^n$$

where P is the set of parallel work types that exhibit n-fold parallelism. Then $S(n) > n$ if and only if

$$W_s^1 C_s(1) + \sum_{i \in P} W_i^1 C_i(1) > W_s^n C_s(n) + \sum_{i \in P} W_i^n C_i(n).$$

(3.1)

Proof:

$$T(1) = W_s^1 C_s(1) + \sum_{i \in P} W_i^1 C_i(1)$$

$$nT(n) = W_s^n C_s(n) + \sum_{i \in P} W_i^n C_i(n)$$

$$S(n) = \frac{n \left(W_s^1 C_s(1) + \sum_{i \in P} W_i^1 C_i(1) \right)}{W_s^n C_s(n) + \sum_{i \in P} W_i^n C_i(n)}.$$

Thus, $S(n) > n$ if and only if

$$\frac{W_s^1 C_s(1) + \sum_{i \in P} W_i^1 C_i(1)}{W_s^n C_s(n) + \sum_{i \in P} W_i^n C_i(n)} > 1$$

from which the theorem immediately follows. $\square$

If the sequential and parallel versions use the same algorithm then the operation counts should be the same regardless of the number of processors. Formally, $W_i^1 = W_i^n$ for each $i \in P \cup \{s\}$. When this holds, we can omit the superscript on W and Theorem 1 becomes

Corollary 1: $S(n) > n$ if and only if

$$\sum_{i \in P} W_i(C_i(1) - C_i(n)) > (n - 1)W_s C_s(1) \qquad (3.2)$$

where P is the set of worktypes that exhibit n-fold parallelism and W_s is the number of operations that must be performed sequentially.

IV. Application of the Model to Previous Results

In this section, we show how our model can be used to generate several previous results.

A. Superunitary Speedup is Impossible

Under certain assumptions it is indeed true that superunitary speedup is impossible [6]. Corollary 1 clearly states the conditions necessary for superunitary speedup. If other assumptions about the parallel machine guarantee that inequality (3.2) is never satisfied then no superunitary speedup is possible. Early models assumed that adding processing elements to a parallel machine was essentially the same as adding ALU's. In particular they did not consider the effects of additional memory and cache space associated with the "processors" in many parallel computers. (See Section IV-C for an example of superunitary speedup based on increasing cache size.)

If we let W_p and $C_p(n)$ be the amount and cost of work that exhibits n-fold parallelism then the standard argument against superunitary speedup can be stated as follows (again W_s and C_s are the number and cost of sequential operations):

$$W = W_s + W_p$$

$$C_s(n) = n$$

$$C_p(n) = 1.$$

Equation (3.2) then becomes $W_p(C_p(1) - C_p(n)) > (n-1)W_s$, and since the left-hand side is 0, superunitary speedup is impossible. In fact, if W_s is positive, then the speedup equation becomes

$$S(n) = \frac{W_s + W_p}{W_s + \dfrac{W_p}{n}} \leq 1 + \frac{W_p}{W_s}$$

and we obtain Amdahl's law [1].

This idea has been extended by Flatt [5] to show that $S(n)$ is bounded under certain assumptions on the overhead incurred by parallel processing. Here we derive a weaker result using the assumption that there is a monotonically increasing positive overhead cost when using increasing numbers of processors. This is formulated in our model by adding W_o and $C_o(n)$ which represent the number of operations incurring this overhead and their cost.[3]

$$W = W_s + W_p + W_o$$

$$C_s(n) = n$$

$$C_p(n) = 1$$

$$C_o(n) = \text{Oh}(n)$$

where $\text{Oh}(n)$ is the required overhead function. Equation (3.2) now becomes

$$W_o(\text{Oh}(1) - \text{Oh}(n)) > (n-1)W_s$$

which is clearly never true, because the overhead function $\text{Oh}(n)$ is nondecreasing.

If $W_s = 0$, but W_o is some fixed fraction of the total work and $\text{Oh}(n)$ is unbounded, then even linear subunitary speedup is impossible.[4] In this case the speedup equation becomes

$$S(n) = \frac{n(W_o \, \text{Oh}(1) + W_p)}{W_p + W_o \, \text{Oh}(n)}.$$

In order to achieve linear subunitary speedup in the limit, $S(n)$ must be greater than ϵn for some fixed $0 < \epsilon < 1$. Thus,

$$n(W_o \, \text{Oh}(1) + W_p) \geq \epsilon n(W_p + W_o \, \text{Oh}(n))$$

$$\frac{W_p}{W_o} \geq \frac{\epsilon \, \text{Oh}(n) - \text{Oh}(1)}{1 - \epsilon}.$$

[3] We assume that these increasing-cost operations can be executed in parallel.

[4] We actually show that linear subunitary speedup is impossible in the limit. As long as the speedup is positive, it is possible to find an $\epsilon > 0$ for any fixed n so that $S(n) > \epsilon n$.

Since the $\text{Oh}(n)$ is unbounded, the right side of the last inequality becomes arbitrarily large while the left side remains constant.

B. Superunitary Speedup Due to Reduced Overhead

Some operations, for example those related to resource management, may require an amount of time that depends on the number of processes which reside on a processor. Superunitary speedup has been reported in a simulation of a (semi-static) dataflow model called "Queue Machines" [19]. Their basic explanation is that the cost (i.e., processor time) of some kernel calls on an n processor machine will actually be only $1/n$th of the cost on a single processor. They justify this by noting that each processor in the parallel machine deals with only $1/n$th of the processes that the uniprocessor must manage.

In our model this corresponds to the following:

$$W = W_s + W_p + W_k$$

$$C_s(n) = n$$

$$C_p(n) = 1$$

$$C_k(n) = c\left(1 + \frac{P}{n}\right)$$

where P is the number of processes, W_p is the number of parallel user mode operations plus fixed time kernel calls,[5] and W_k is the number of kernel calls with variable execution time.

From Corollary 1, $S(n) > n$ if and only if

$$W_p(C_p(1) - C_p(n)) + W_k(C_k(1) - C_k(n)) > (n-1)W_s$$

which simplifies to

$$\frac{W_k}{W_s} > \frac{n}{c \cdot P}.$$

This shows that superunitary speedup occurs whenever the number of variable time kernel calls exceeds the number of sequential user mode operations by more than a factor of n/P times some constant. The size of the constant c is determined by the relative cost of kernel calls and basic user mode operations. Even if the cost function for the variable time kernel calls is reduced to

$$C_k(n) = c\left(1 + \log\left(\frac{P}{n}\right)\right)$$

superunitary speedup can still occur. (This cost function appears more reasonable because the time to access large data structures in a well-designed system is more likely to be logarithmic rather than linear in the size of the data structure.) Using the modified cost function and Corollary 1,

$$S(n) > n \text{ if and only if } \frac{W_k}{W_s} > \frac{n-1}{c \log(n)}.$$

The validity of the premise used in the preceding analysis, (i.e., the cost of some kernel calls on an n processor machine will actually be only a fraction of the cost on a uniprocessor machine) is debatable and depends upon the specific system. Given sufficient memory, the uniprocessor should be capable of running multiple versions of the kernel and partition the processes between them. However, there may

[5] All kernel calls are assumed to be independent and therefore can execute in parallel.

be other considerations: the cost of the memory, the cost of a system redesign if the uniprocessor cannot accommodate the additional memory, the cost of programming, the cost of additional context switching, etc. Our goal is to isolate and clarify those assumptions that are responsible for the apparently contradictory claims.

C. Superunitary Speedup Due to Increasing Cache Size

The appearance of superunitary speedup can occur when each processor contains a local cache. In this case, not only does the number of ALU's increase with n, but so does the amount of cache.[6]

Consider the following model of a shared memory multiprocessor with local caches. Tasks are assigned to processors from a global pool of ready tasks. If the algorithm uses m logical processes with $m > n$ and there is some form of synchronization that prevents running each task to completion before running the next task, then the following model can be used:

$$W = W_s + W_p + W_m + W_{\text{sync}}$$

$$C_s(n) = n$$

$$C_p(n) = 1$$

$$C_m(n) = 1 + \alpha_n \, \text{miss}\,(n)$$

$$C_{\text{sync}}(n) = 1 + \beta_n \, switch$$

where W_m is the number of (parallelizable) memory reference operations, W_{sync} is the number of communication/synchronization operations, and W_p is the number of nonmemory, nonsynchronization parallel operations.

In the above, α_n is the fraction of memory references that are not satisfied by the cache. The amount of processor time needed to process a miss on an n processor system is miss (n). Note that α_n will be a function of n as described below.

We use β_n for the fraction of times a task must stop at a synchronization operation when there is something else for the processor to do. The amount of processor time needed for a context switch is *switch*. As with the cache hit ratio, β_n will be a function of n.

The cache miss ratio α_n may decrease as n increases [21]. This may occur because the number of different tasks that will execute on a particular processor decreases as the number of processors increase. For this example we further assume that the cache is not flushed on context switches within a single job and all tasks within the same job share the same virtual address space. When there is one processor per process the cache only needs to hold those memory locations that are referenced by that particular process, which is presumably smaller than the entire address space of the job and exhibits better locality of reference.

Similarly β_n may decrease as n increases. In the serial case every synchronization operation may cause a context switch to a different process. In the ideal case with all processes being of equal size and running at equal speed, it is remotely possible that no synchronization operations would block, and therefore no context switches would occur. In this latter case, there would still be blocking for the serial sections of code but this is accounted for in C_s.

---

[6] Whether or not a processor's local cache should be considered part of the processor depends upon what is being measured. It is not generally reasonable to assume that the cache size of the uniprocessor can be increased to match that of the multiprocessor.

From Corollary 1, $S(n) > n$ if and only if

$$W_s(n-1) < W_m(\alpha_1 \cdot \text{miss}\,(1) - \alpha_n \cdot \text{miss}\,(n))$$

$$+ W_{\text{sync}}(\beta_1 \cdot \text{switch} - \beta_n \cdot \text{switch}).$$

D. Superunitary Speedup by Hiding Latency

We describe two ways to hide some of the latency in a communication or an interconnection network. It must be recognized that these latency hiding techniques can be used on a uniprocessor, and therefore are optimizations rather than sources of true superunitary speedup. We include these techniques because they help explain observed behavior and help demonstrate the versatility of our model.

The first technique uses an excess of process level parallelism (i.e., the number of processes greatly exceeds the number of processors) in order to hide the latency in remote operations. Notice that a uniprocessor running a parallel program via timeslicing typically has extra process level parallelism, making this technique suitable. If a second process is available, then it can be executed while the first process is waiting for the remote operation to return. This reduces the induced idle time of the remote operation at the expense of some additional context switching. This type of latency hiding may be beneficial whenever it is possible to perform a context switch between the initiation of the remote operation and the completion of the operation.

The second technique for latency hiding exploits parallelism within a single process during a remote operation. If the processor (possibly with some help from the compiler) is capable of inserting other operations between the initiation and completion of the remote operation, the latency can be partially or completely hidden. This exploits additional parallelism within a single process, beyond that explicitly described by the algorithm.

The Denelcor HEP [22] was designed to exploit the first technique for hiding latency. Each processor included an eight-stage pipeline in the main datapath. Each stage in the pipeline was occupied by an instruction from a different process. This essentially provided a zero cost context switch every clock cycle between the (up to 50) processes in the processor's active queue. When there is only a single process using the processor, each stage of the datapath is idle 7/8ths of the time. Therefore, considering only local operations, the processor would exhibit eightfold speedup if the problem could be split into at least eight independent processes.

To explain the reported superunitary speedup [7] it is necessary to consider how the HEP handles split phase memory operations. When the main datapath detects a memory operation, the process is moved to a queue of processes waiting for memory fetches. This queue is maintained by a separate functional unit of the processor. Again this switching from the active datapath queue to the memory processing queue is done in hardware at the cost of 1 cycle through the pipeline. Because the memory fetch hardware is used by both the sequential and parallel algorithms, we choose not to count it as an additional processor (see the comments at the end of this section). This effectively eliminates any delays due to memory latency if there are enough processes to keep the eight-stage pipeline full.

The superunitary behavior was observed on the HEP when a program was executed with increasing numbers of processes (not processors). This occurs because a single process can only have a single instruction in the pipeline at any one time. Therefore, a single process uses only 1/8th of the pipeline. The "parallel" version with eight or more processes can have eight instructions in the pipeline, utilizing all of the hardware. Adding processes in the HEP thus has an effect similar to adding processors in other models. In our model of the HEP we will treat each 1/8th of the pipeline as a separate processor.

11

Therefore, $T(1)$ is the time to execute the program when constrained to use only 1/8th of the datapath capability, and $T(8)$ is the time to execute the program when running eight or more processes, thus fully utilizing the datapath. In our model, the HEP can be described by the following:

$$W = W_a + W_m + W_{\text{sync}}$$

$$C_a(1) = C_a(8) = 8$$

$$C_m(1) = C_m(8) = 8 + latency$$

$$C_{\text{sync}}(1) = 8$$

$$C_{\text{sync}}(8) = 8 + idle$$

where W_m is the number of unsynchronized memory reference operations, W_{sync} is the number of synchronized memory references using full/empty bits, and W_a is the number of basic ALU operations. Notice that for this example there is no serial work W_s.

The corresponding execution times for one and eight processors[7] is then

$$T(1) = 8W_a + (8 + latency)W_m + 8W_{\text{sync}}$$

$$T(8) = \frac{8W_a + (8 + latency)W_m + (8 + idle)W_{\text{sync}}}{8}.$$

First notice that there is no context switching overhead. Context switching is done in hardware for zero run-time cost. As given above there is still no superunitary speedup. Superunitary speedup occurs as a result of the following observation. If there is sufficient parallelism (i.e., substantially more than eight processes ready to run at any time) then the latency in the computation of $T(8)$ is completely masked (i.e.. there is no induced delay of a processor). Furthermore, *idle* will be zero since there are assumed to be sufficient ready tasks to keep the main datapath pipeline full. Given these assumptions the speedup is

$$S(8) = \frac{8(8W_a + (8 + latency)W_m + 8W_{\text{sync}})}{8W_a + 8W_m + 8W_{\text{sync}}}$$

which reduces to

$$S(8) = 8 + latency \frac{W_m}{W_a + W_m + W_{\text{sync}}}.$$

This analysis is intended to explain observed results and should not be construed as a claim that the HEP architecture exhibits superunitary speedup. The HEP contains a "hidden" I/O processor that is prevented from executing in parallel with the main pipeline for single process programs. This same I/O processor is assumed to execute in parallel with the main pipeline when significantly more than eight processes are executing in parallel. Any speedup claims must account for the extra heterogeneous processor in the HEP system.

E. Accounting for Latency Hiding

In order to account for the "hidden" I/O processor in the previous section the model must support at least two types of processors. Consider a very simple model where W_p is the amount of non-I/O parallel work and W_I is the amount of I/O work. If C_p and C_I are the corresponding cost functions, then

$$T(1) = W_p C_p + W_I C_I.$$

This assumes there is no overlap between the I/O operations. If we now add a second processor capable of performing the I/O operations, and we further assume that the distribution of work is such that either the I/O processor or the non-I/O processor are 100 percent utilized then

$$T(2) = \max(W_p C_p, W_I C_I).$$

This leads to the following for a system with $n-1$ non-I/O processors and one I/O processor:

$$T(n) = \max\left(\frac{W_p C_p}{n-1}, W_I C_I\right).$$

If we assume that all I/O is overlapped[8] then $W_I C_I \leq W_p C_p / (n-1)$ and

$$S(n) = \frac{W_p C_p + W_I C_I}{\dfrac{W_p C_p}{n-1}}$$

$$= n - 1 + \frac{(n-1)}{W_p C_p} W_I C_I$$

$$\leq n - 1 + \frac{(n-1)}{W_p C_p}\left(\frac{W_p C_p}{n-1}\right)$$

$$\leq n.$$

Applying this modified model to the HEP will eliminate the apparent superunitary speedup in the previous section. Assuming the synchronization is always hidden (even with only one processor), and assuming as before the latency can be hidden, then the HEP is now modeled as

$$T(1) = 8W_a + (8 + latency)W_m$$

$$T(2) = \max(8(W_a + W_m), latency \cdot W_m)$$

$$T(9) = \max((W_a + W_m), latency \cdot W_m)$$

$$latency \cdot W_m \leq W_a + W_m$$

$$S(9) = \frac{8(W_a + W_m) + latency \cdot W_m}{W_a + W_m}$$

$$= 8 + \frac{latency \cdot W_m}{W_a + W_m}$$

$$\leq 9.$$

F. Superunitary Speedup in Randomized Algorithms

Randomized algorithms have been studied for use in reducing the solution time for some problems. A parallel randomized algorithm can simultaneously pursue several randomized solutions to the same problem. If the solution time has a sufficiently high variance, then the expected time for the first finish of n random attempts is less than $1/n$th the expected time for a single attempt. This seems to indicate a potential for superunitary speedup. The work equation for this case is

$$W^n = W_s^n + W_p^n$$

where W_p^n is the (expected) number of parallel operations before the first of n different attempts finishes. As always, W_s^n is the amount of sequential work required.

---

[7] Each processor is actually 1/8th of the HEP pipeline capacity.

[8] Any other assumption will only give lower speedups.

It is possible that the fastest sequential algorithm also pursues multiple random solutions via timeslicing. In this case, the extra context switching overhead will determine the degree to which the parallel version exceeds unitary speedup. This leads to the assumption that the same number of solutions, m, are pursued by all processor configurations, and the model becomes

$$W = W_s + W_p^m$$

$$C_s(n) = n$$

$$C_p^m(n) = 1 + \text{Oh}^m(n)$$

where $\text{Oh}^m(n)$ is the overhead for timesharing m processes on n processors. A suitable overhead function will satisfy the following:

$$\text{Oh}^m(n) = \frac{switch}{Q(n)} \text{ when } n \leq m$$

$$\frac{1}{Q(n)} = \frac{m-n}{(m-1)Q(1)}$$

where $switch$ is the context switch time and $Q(n)$ is the average time per timeslice on an n processor system. We have defined the quantum $Q(n)$ so that $Q(1)$ is a constant and $Q(m)$ is infinite, which is precisely the effect (i.e., no context switches) when there is one process per processor.

Assuming $n = m$ and using Corollary 1, $S(n) > n$ if and only if $W_p^n(switch/Q(1)) > (n-1)W_s$. The actual speedup when $n = m$ is

$$S(n) = n + \frac{n\left(W_p^n \dfrac{switch}{Q(1)} - W_s(n-1)\right)}{nW_s + W_p^n}.$$

V. Scaled Speedup

In the previous sections we considered how much faster a given problem can be solved on increasing amounts of hardware. Another approach considers a revised speedup measure where both the amount of hardware and the problem size are increased [3], [9]. We define the *scaled speedup* $S'(n)$ to be the ratio of the uniprocessor execution time to the parallel processing time (on n processors) for a problem of size n.

In this section, $W_s^n(m)$ and $W_p^n(m)$ represent the number of sequential and parallel operations required to solve a problem of size m on an n processor system. It is natural to think of $W_s^n(m)$ and $W_p^n(m)$ as nondecreasing functions, although this is not assumed by our analysis. As before, we use $C_s(n)$ and $C_p(n)$ for the units of processor time consumed when performing a sequential or parallel operation on an n processor system. We also define $T(n, m) = (W_s^n(m)C_s(n) + W_p^n(m)C_p(n))/n$, the time taken by an n processor system to solve an instance of size m. For the following analysis, we assume that the number of operations called for by the algorithm is independent of the number of processors (note that the costs will still vary with the number of processors). Therefore, $W_s^1(m) = W_s^n(m)$ and $W_p^1(m) = W_p^n(m)$, which we abbreviate $W_s(m)$ and $W_p(m)$, respectively.

The scaled speedup on an n processor system is the ratio of the time to solve a problem of size n on a uniprocessor to the time to solve the same problem on an n processor system. This is expressed as

$$S'(n) = \frac{T(1, n)}{T(n, n)} = \frac{W_s(n)C_s(1) + W_p(n)C_p(1)}{\dfrac{1}{n}(W_s(n)C_s(n) + W_p(n)C_p(n))}.$$

Assuming $C_p(n) = 1$ and $C_s(n) = n$ as before, this simplifies to

$$S'(n) = \frac{n(W_s(n) + W_p(n))}{nW_s(n) + W_p(n)}.$$

Since $W_s(n) + W_p(n)$ is always less than $nW_s(n) + W_p(n)$ (assuming $W_s(n) \neq 0$), unitary scaled speedup is impossible. However, linear subunitary scaled speedup does occur in the limit when $W_s(n) + W_p(n)/nW_s(n) + W_p(n) \geq \epsilon$ for some positive constant ϵ. Working from this inequality, we get that

$$\frac{W_p(n)}{W_s(n)} \geq \frac{\epsilon n - 1}{1 - \epsilon}$$

is a necessary and sufficient condition for linear subunitary scaled speedup. In other words, the amount of parallel work must grow roughly n times faster than the amount of sequential work in order to achieve linear scaled speedups.

Note that we have not specified how quickly the total work grows as a function of the problem size. For example, if $W_p(n)/W_s(n) = n^{1/2}$ then we can make it appear that linear subunitary scaled speedup is possible by redefining the problem size, so that $W_p'(n) = W_p(n^2)$ and $W_s'(n) = W_s(n^2)$. Whenever the ratio $W_p(n)/W_s(n)$ is unbounded, the appearance of linear subunitary scaled speedup can be created by changing the problem size metric.

A common reason for considering scaled speedups is an interest in how large a problem can be solved within some fixed amount of time, rather than in how quickly a given problem can be solved. From this reasoning, it is reasonable to assume that the total work grows no faster than $O(n)$, i.e., $W_s(n) + W_p(n) \leq cn$. Under this assumption, $W_s(n)$ must be bounded by a constant to achieve a speedup of ϵn, as shown below.

$$W_s(n) \leq cn - W_p(n)$$

$$W_s(n) \leq cn - W_s(n)\frac{\epsilon n - 1}{1 - \epsilon}$$

$$W_s(n) \leq \frac{(1 - \epsilon)}{\epsilon}\frac{cn}{(n-1)}.$$

This analysis shows that linear subunitary scaled speedup is possible even in the presence of sequential work. This contrasts sharply with the corresponding nonscaled case, where $S(n)$ is always bounded by a constant in the presence of sequential work (as noted by Gustafson [9]).

Once $W_p(n)$ and $W_s(n)$ are known, we can fix the problem size m for the (unscaled) speedup and plot the curves (see Fig. 1) $S(n) = n(W_p^m + W_s^m)/(W_p^m + nW_s^m)$ and $S'(n) = n(W_p(n) + W_s(n))/(W_p(n) + nW_s(n))$. The two curves intersect where $S(n) = S'(n)$, or

$$(W_p^m + W_s^m)(W_p(n) + nW_s^m) = (W_p(n) + W_s(n))(W_p^m + nW_s^m)$$

$$(n-1)W_p^m W_s(n) = (n-1)W_p(n)W_s^m$$

$$\frac{W_p^m}{W_s^m} = \frac{W_p(n)}{W_s(n)}.$$

Thus, if $W_p(n)/W_s(n)$ is constant, then the curves are identical. In any case, the curves intersect at $n = m$ and[9] $n = 1$. If the ratio $W_p(n)/W_s(n)$ is an increasing function of n, then $S(n) > S'(n)$ for $1 < n < N$ and $S(n) < S'(n)$ for $n > N$. Conversely, if $W_p(n)/W_s(n)$ decreases as n increases, then $S'(n)$ lies above $S(n)$ for $1 < n < m$, but below it when $n > m$. This is to

[9] We divided through by $n - 1$, and $S(1) = S'(1) = 1$.

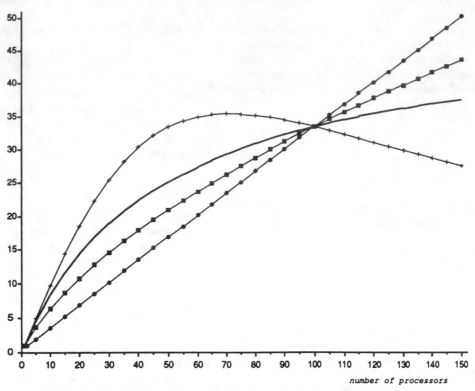

speedup

number of processors

Fig. 1. Normal and scaled speedups. The heavy line is the normal speedup curve $S(n)$ with $W_p = 98$ and $W_s = 2$. The boxes indicate the scaled speedup curve $S'(n)$ where $W_s(n) = \sqrt{n}/5$, the dots indicate $S'(n)$ where $W_s(n) = 2$, and the crosses indicate $S'(n)$ where $W_s(n) = n^2/(n+4900)$. In the three scaled curves, $W_p(n) = n - W_s(n)$. Note that the four curves were chosen to have the same amounts of parallel and sequential work at $n = 100$.

be expected from the relative percentages of parallel work in the formulas for $S(n)$ and $S'(n)$.

VI. CONCLUSIONS

We have presented a model that is simple and yet sufficiently powerful to explain several apparently contradictory claims about the performance of parallel machines. A necessary and sufficient condition for superunitary speedup was presented based on the model. The model was then applied to several previously reported results.

ACKNOWLEDGMENT

The authors gratefully acknowledge the many useful comments from the anonymous referees.

REFERENCES

[1] G. Amdahl, "Validity of the single processor approach to achieving large scale computing capabilities," in *Proc. AFIPS Comput. Conf.*, vol. 30, 1967, pp. 483–485.
[2] J. Barton, "Superlinear performance of the SAXPY kernel on the Silicon Graphics 4D120/GTX," Personal commun., 1988.
[3] R. E. Benner, J. L. Gustafson, and R. E. Montry, "Development and analysis of scientific application programs on a 1024-processor hypercube," Tech. Rep. SAND 88-0317, Sandia National Laboratories, Albuquerque, NM, Feb. 1988.
[4] D. L. Eager, J. Zahorjan, and E. D. Lazowska, "Speedup versus efficiency in parallel systems," *IEEE Trans. Comput.*, vol. 38, pp. 408–423, Mar. 1989.
[5] H. P. Flatt, "Further comments on a model for parallel processing," Tech. Rep. IBM PASC G320-3503, 1987.
[6] V. Faber, P. M. Lubeck, and A. B. White, Jr., "Superlinear speedup of an efficient sequential algorithm is not possible," *Parallel Comput.*, vol. 3, pp. 259–260, 1986.
[7] D. H. Grit and J. R. McGraw, "Programming divide and conquer for a MIMD machine," *Software Pract. Exp.*, vol. 15, no. 1, pp. 41–53, Jan. 1985.
[8] E. F. Gehringer, D. P. Siewiorek, and Z. Segall, *Parallel Processing, the Cm* Experience*. Bedford, MA: Digital Press, 1987.
[9] J. L. Gustafson, "Reevaluating Amdahl's law," *IEEE Trans. Comput.*, vol. 37, no. 5, pp. 532–533, May 1988.
[10] W. A. Kornfeld, "Combinatorially implosive algorithms," *Commun. ACM*, vol. 25, no. 10, pp. 734–738, Oct. 1982.
[11] K. Li, "IVY: A shared virtual memory system for parallel computing," in *Proc. 1988 Int. Conf. Parallel Processing*. 1988, pp. 94–101.
[12] J. Lipkis, "Superlinear performance of a monte carlo code on the NYU Ultracomputer," Personal commun., 1988.
[13] T. Lai and S. Sahni, "Anomalies in parallel branch-and-bound algorithms," *Commun. ACM*, vol. 27, no. 6, pp. 594–602, June 1984.
[14] G.-J. Li and B. W. Wah, "Coping with anomalies in parallel branch-and-bound algorithms," *IEEE Trans. Comput.*, vol. C-35, pp. 568–573, June 1986.
[15] R. Mehrotra and E. F. Gehringer, "Superlinear speedup through randomized algorithms," in *Proc. 1985 Int. Conf Parallel Processing*, 1985, pp. 291–300.
[16] M. Minsky, "Form and content in computer science," ACM Turing Lect., *J. ACM*, vol. 17, pp. 197–215, 1970.
[17] E. Miya, "Suggestion on superlinear speed up terminology," *Network News Posting*, Dec. 1988.
[18] D. Parkinson, "Parallel efficiency can be greater than unity," *Parallel Comput.*, vol. 3, pp. 261–262, 1986.
[19] B. R. Preiss and V. C. Hamacher, "Semi-static dataflow," in *Proc. 1988 Int. Conf. Parallel Processing*, 1988, pp. 127–134.
[20] J. Sanguinetti, "Performance of a message-based multiprocessor," *IEEE Comput. Mag.*, vol. 19, no. 9, pp. 47–55, Sept. 1986.
[21] C. B. Stunkel and W. K. Fuchs, "Analysis of hypercube cache performance using address traces generated by TRAPEDS," in *Proc. 1989 Int. Conf. Parallel Processing*, 1989, pp. I-33-I-40.
[22] B. J. Smith, "Architecture and applications of the HEP multiprocessor computer," in *Real-Time Signal Processing IV*, vol. 298. Bellingham, WA: SPIE, 1981, pp. 241–248.
[23] B. W. Weide, "Modeling unusual behavior of parallel algorithms," *IEEE Trans. Comput.*, vol. C-31, pp. 1126–1130, Nov. 1982.

REEVALUATING AMDAHL'S LAW

JOHN L. GUSTAFSON

At Sandia National Laboratories, we are currently engaged in research involving massively parallel processing. There is considerable skepticism regarding the viability of massive parallelism; the skepticism centers around *Amdahl's law*, an argument put forth by Gene Amdahl in 1967 [1] that even when the fraction of serial work in a given problem is small, say, *s*, the maximum speedup obtainable from even an infinite number of parallel processors is only $1/s$. We now have timing results for a 1024-processor system that demonstrate that the assumptions underlying Amdahl's 1967 argument are inappropriate for the current approach to massive ensemble parallelism.

If N is the number of processors, *s* is the amount of time spent (by a serial processor) on serial parts of a program, and *p* is the amount of time spent (by a serial processor) on parts of the program that can be done in parallel, then Amdahl's law says that speedup is given by

$$Speedup = (s + p)/(s + p/N)$$
$$= 1/(s + p/N),$$

where we have set total time $s + p = 1$ for algebraic simplicity. For $N = 1024$ this is an unforgivingly steep function of *s* near $s = 0$ (see Figure 1).

The steepness of the graph near $s = 0$ (approximately $-N^2$) implies that very few problems will experience even a 100-fold speedup. Yet, for three very practical applications ($s = 0.4$–0.8 percent) used at Sandia, we have achieved speedup factors on a 1024-processor hypercube that we believe are unprecedented [2]: *1021* for beam stress analysis using conjugate gradients, *1020* for baffled surface wave simulation using explicit finite dif-

ferences, and *1016* for unstable fluid flow using flux-corrected transport. How can this be, when Amdahl's argument would predict otherwise?

The expression and graph both contain the implicit assumption that *p* is independent of *N*, which *is virtually never the case*. One does not take a fixed-sized problem and run it on various numbers of processors

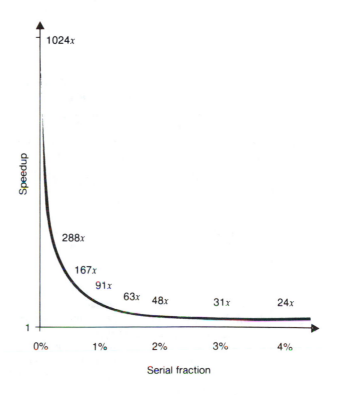

FIGURE 1. Speedup under Amdahl's Law

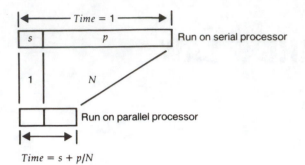

$$Scaled\ speedup = (s + p \times N)/(s + p)$$
$$= s + p \times N$$
$$= N + (1 - N) \times s.$$

In contrast with Figure 1, this function is simply a *line*, and one with a much more moderate slope: $1 - N$. It is thus much easier to achieve efficient parallel performance than.is implied by Amdahl's paradigm. The two approaches, fixed sized and scaled sized, are contrasted and summarized in Figure 2a and b.

Our work to date shows that it is *not* an insurmountable task to extract very high efficiency from a massively parallel ensemble, for the reasons presented here. We feel that it is important for the computing

FIGURE 2a. Fixed-Sized Model for *Speedup* = 1/(s + p/N)

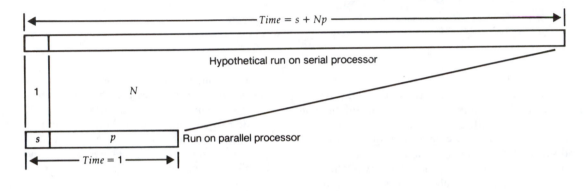

FIGURE 2b. Scaled-Sized Model for *Speedup* = s + Np

except when doing academic research; in practice, *the problem size scales with the number of processors*. When given a more powerful processor, the problem generally expands to make use of the increased facilities. Users have control over such things as grid resolution, number of time steps, difference operator complexity, and other parameters that are usually adjusted to allow the program to be run in some desired amount of time. Hence, it may be most realistic to assume *run time*, not *problem size*, is constant.

As a first approximation, we have found that it is the *parallel* or *vector* part of a program that scales with the problem size. Times for vector start-up, program loading, serial bottlenecks, and I/O that make up the s component of the run do *not* grow with problem size. When we double the number of degrees of freedom in a physical simulation, we double the number of processors. But this means that, as a first approximation, the amount of work that can be done in parallel *varies linearly with the number of processors*. For the three applications mentioned above, we found that the parallel portion scaled by factors of 1023.9969, 1023.9965, and 1023.9965. If we use s and p to represent serial and parallel time spent on the *parallel* system, then a serial processor would require time $s + p \times N$ to perform the task. This reasoning gives an alternative to Amdahl's law suggested by E. Barsis at Sandia:

research community to overcome the "mental block" against massive parallelism imposed by a misuse of Amdahl's speedup formula; speedup should be measured by scaling the problem to the number of processors, not by fixing problem size. We expect to extend our success to a broader range of applications and even larger values for N.

REFERENCES
1. Amdahl, G.M. Validity of the single-processor approach to achieving large scale computing capabilities. In *AFIPS Conference Proceedings*, vol. 30 (Atlantic City, N.J., Apr. 18–20). AFIPS Press, Reston, Va., 1967, pp. 483–485.
2. Benner, R.E., Gustafson, J.L., and Montry, R.E. Development and analysis of scientific application programs on a 1024-processor hypercube. SAND 88-0317, Sandia National Laboratories, Albuquerque, N.M., Feb. 1988.

CR Categories and Subject Descriptors: C.1.2 [Processor Architectures]: Multiple Data Stream Architectures (Multiprocessors)—*parallel processors*
General Terms: Theory
Additional Key Words and Phrases: Amdahl's law, massively parallel processing, speedup

Author's Present Address: John L. Gustafson, Sandia National Laboratories, Albuquerque, NM 87185.

Single Instruction Stream Parallelism Is Greater than Two

Michael Butler, Tse-Yu Yeh, and Yale Patt
Department of Electrical Engineering
and Computer Science
The University of Michigan
Ann Arbor, Michigan 48109-2122

Mitch Alsup, Hunter Scales, and Michael Shebanow
Motorola Incorporated
Microprocessor and Memory Technology Group
6501 William Cannon Drive West
Austin, Texas 78735

Abstract

Recent studies have concluded that little parallelism (less than two operations per cycle) is available in single instruction streams. Since the amount of available parallelism should influence the design of the processor, it is important to verify how much parallelism really exists. In this study we model the execution of the SPEC benchmarks under differing resource constraints. We repeat the work of the previous researchers, and show that under the hardware resource constraints they imposed, we get similar results. On the other hand, when all constraints are removed except those required by the semantics of the program, we have found degrees of parallelism in excess of 17 instructions per cycle. Finally, and perhaps most important for exploiting single instruction stream parallelism now, we show that if the hardware is properly balanced, one can sustain from 2.0 to 5.8 instructions per cycle on a processor that is reasonable to design today.

1 Introduction

The increasing density of VLSI circuits has motivated research into ways to utilize large numbers of logic elements to improve computational performance. One way to use these elements is to replicate multiple functional units on a single chip. This technique is effective only if the amount of instruction–level parallelism present in real applications warrants it. Early studies[3, 5, 14, 15, 16] suggested that this was in fact the case. More recently, some researchers[1, 2] have concluded that insufficient parallelism exists in real, non-scientific applications to support processors that will execute more than two instructions per cycle.

Since the amount of available parallelism should influence the design of the processor, it is important to verify how much parallelism exists. To do this, we have undertaken a study of available parallelism in optimized, compiled code. We have used nine of the ten programs in the SPEC suite,[1] a set of real applications that have become the de facto standard in compute-bound performance benchmarks. We have measured the performance of these benchmarks on several execution models, including those studied by Patt and Hwu[3, 5] and by Smith and Johnson[1] and Jouppi[2]. We have also measured the performance of these benchmarks on an unconstrained execution model in order to quantify how much parallelism exists in these benchmarks that could be exploited if the artifacts of the processor did not prevent it.

Our results show that, with undue constraints on the processor, it is difficult to sustain parallel execution of more than two instructions per cycle. On the other hand, when all constraints are removed except those required by the semantics of the program, we have found degrees of parallelism in excess of 17 instructions per cycle. Finally, we show that when the hardware is properly balanced, one can sustain an execution rate of 2.0 to 5.8 instructions per cycle on a processor that is reasonable to design today.

This paper is organized in six sections. Section 2 discusses restricted data flow, an abstract execution model that allows available instruction stream parallelism to be exploited. Section 3 describes our experiments: the simulator, the benchmarks, and the machine configurations tested. Section 4 reports the results of our simulations and discusses the influence of various machine features on performance. The model used by Smith and Johnson[1], the unconstrained case, and several machines which are realistic to implement today, are all identified. Section 5 presents a brief discussion of implementation issues. Section 6 offers some concluding remarks and discusses the future work we have planned.

---

[1] The Nasa7 benchmark was not simulated because this benchmark consists of seven independent loops. Due to time constraints, we omitted these loops.

2 The RDF Model of Execution

To exploit whatever parallelism exists in the instruction stream, one needs an execution model devoid of artifacts that limit the utilization of that parallelism. The abstract restricted data flow (RDF) paradigm is such a model. It is characterized by three parameters: window size, issue rate, and instruction class latencies.

Processing consists of systematically issuing instructions from a program's dynamic instruction stream, converting those instructions into a dynamic data flow graph, scheduling instructions for execution when their flow dependencies have been resolved, and retiring those instructions after execution has completed. The dynamic instruction stream is created by an omniscient branch predictor that always knows the way a conditional branch will execute. Instructions are issued in the order they appear in the dynamic instruction stream.

The window size is the maximum number of instructions from the dynamic instruction stream that can be present in the dynamic data flow graph at any instant of time. (Instructions can be issued as long as the number of instructions in the window is less than the window size.) The issue rate is the maximum number of instructions that can be removed from the dynamic instruction stream and entered into the window in a single cycle. We call the group of instructions that can be brought into the machine in one cycle a packet. The instruction class latencies specify the set of operations and the latency associated with each operation. In the RDF model, the number of functional units is unbounded, each can perform every desired operation, and the latency associated with each operation is specified.

The RDF model was first defined because its parameters correspond to some important practical constraints on cpu design [3]. The RDF restriction on window size corresponds to a practical limitation on the amount of buffering that can be supported. The restriction on issue rate corresponds to the limitation on instruction memory bandwidth.

Clearly, the RDF model specified above, with its omniscient branch prediction and unbounded functional units, is not realizable. Nonetheless several variations of the RDF model are interesting to study. For example, if in addition to the functional units, the window size and issue rate are also unbounded, we have an execution unit that presents no impediment to exploiting all the parallelism present in the application. We call this model an unrestricted data flow (UDF) machine. It specifies all the parallelism available in the instruction stream.

On the other hand, if we restrict the various parameters of the RDF model, we obtain upper bounds on the level of performance that is possible. For example, the RDF model gives an upper bound on the performance of a machine that can support a specific window size and issue rate if function unit capability and branch prediction were not a problem. If we couple the RDF model to a real branch predictor, we obtain an upper bound on the performance of a machine that can support a specific window size and issue rate if functional unit capability were not a problem. Finally, if we further restrict our RDF model to a functional unit configuration that is implementable, we have an execution model that corresponds to a realizable machine that efficiently exploits the available parallelism in a single instruction stream.

We first specified a realizable implementation of the RDF model, the High Performance Substrate (HPS) in 1985 [3]. HPS was originally developed as a speedup mechanism for complex instruction set architectures, although we quickly discovered its applicability to the implementation of all architectures. Today, it is continually being refined by our research group in an effort to improve its performance and reduce its cost of implementation. Its ultimate objective, emulating an (optimal) RDF machine, has not changed.

In this paper, we are concerned with the influence of the RDF parameters on the performance of the SPEC benchmarks. We will identify several implementable RDF models, with differing values for window size, issue rate, and functional unit capability.

3 Experiments

3.1 Benchmarks

The results presented in this paper are for nine integer and floating point programs from the SPEC suite: eqntott, espresso, gcc, li, doduc, fpppp, matrix300, spice2g6, and tomcatv, compiled for and run under the M88000 instruction set architecture. The benchmarks were compiled using the Green Hills FORTRAN 1.8.5 compiler or the Diab Data C Rel. 2.4 compiler with all optimizations turned on. (A particular compiler was selected for a given benchmark if that compiler produced the most efficient object code (i.e. shortest run time) when run on an MC88100–a conventional scalar processor.) All benchmarks were run unchanged with the following exceptions: cpp is not called in eqntott, gcc was run without cpp and used the output of the preprocessor as the input file. Due to time limitations, each benchmark was simulated for ten million instructions.

Table 1 shows instruction classes and their simulated execution latencies. Each instruction class is listed with its abbreviation (A for floating point add, M for floating point and integer multiply, L for memory loads, etc.), its execution latency (in cycles), and a description of the instructions that belong to that class. The latencies for all but one machine were taken from Smith and Johnson[1]. We know of several machines with smaller floating point latencies, however, so in order to investigate the effect of shorter latencies, we simulated one

Instruction Class	Execution Latency	Description
(A) FP Add	6	FP add, sub, and convert
(M) Multiply	6	FP mul and INT mul
(D) Divide	12	FP div and INT div
(L) Mem Load	2	Memory loads
(S) Mem Store	-	Memory stores
(B) Branch	1	Control instructions
(T) Bit Field	1	Shift, and bit testing
(I) Integer	1	INT add, sub and logic OPs

Table 1: Instruction Classes and Latencies

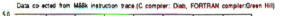

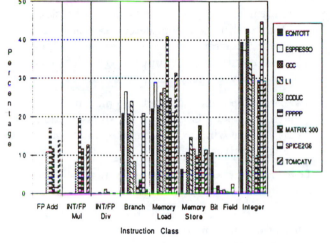

Figure 1: Benchmark Code Analysis

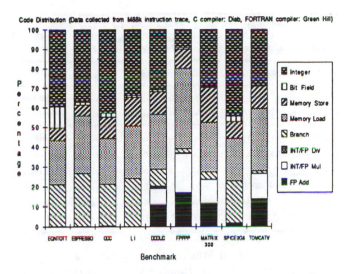

Figure 2: Instruction Class Distribution in Benchmarks

configuration using floating point latencies of 3, 3, and 8 for floating point add, multiply, and divide, respectively.

Figure 1 shows histograms of the dynamic frequency of each instruction class for each of the nine benchmarks. Within each instruction class, the nine vertical bars correspond respectively to the nine benchmarks listed at the right of the figure. As can be seen, approximately 33 percent of instructions are simple integer ALU operations: loads and branches comprise another 28 and 15 percent respectively. Figure 2 presents a stack chart of the same data organized by benchmark.

3.2 Machine Configurations

The instruction class frequency is particularly important for examining performance of machines such as the ones we simulated. Machine resources must reflect the instruction frequency if we are to achieve efficient utilization of functional units. Also, since issue is dependent on functional unit configuration (only one instruction can be issued to each functional unit each cycle), the machine configuration contributes to the upper bound on execution throughput.

The machine configurations simulated are listed in Figure 3. Each machine is specified by its set of functional units, branch prediction mechanism, issue rate, retirement mechanism, the size of an instruction packet (i.e. a group of instructions that are issued in a single cycle), and the characteristics of the load/store pipes and instruction prefetch buffer.

With respect to its functional unit configuration, each set of parentheses corresponds to a single functional unit, and the letters within the parentheses indicate the instruction classes that the functional unit is capable of executing. In the Smith/Johnson machines, each functional unit is capable of executing only one class of instructions, so each set of parentheses contains only one letter. The UDF and RDF.I8 machines can be described as machines with an unbounded number of functional units, each of which is capable of executing all instruction classes. The remaining machines have functional units that are capable of handling multiple instruction classes. For example (see Figure 3) the machine identified as 4F2M has four functional units. One of these functional units can execute instructions from the classes A, M, D, and I, one can execute instructions from B and I, and two can execute instructions from classes L, S, T, and I.

In choosing machine configurations an effort was made to match functional unit capabilities to instruction class frequencies. In addition, the relative cost of adding functionality was considered. If infrequently used functional units could be made to service an additional (frequently used) class of instructions at nominal increase in hardware cost, the resultant machine performance would be enhanced. For example, integer ALUs service the most frequently occurring instructions and can be implemented at a nominal cost relative to the rest of the machine. As such, all functional units are

Machine Name	Functional Unit Configuration	Branch Prediction	Packet Issue Rate	Retire Mech.	# of Inst./Packet	Load / Store	Inst. Prefetch Buffer
S&J 4	(A)(M)(D)(L)(S)(B)(T)(I)(I)(L)	85% Syth.	4	Out of Order	1	Sequential	Aligned 4 words
UDF	∞(A,M,D,L,S,B,T,I)	100%	Infinite	Out of Order	1	Out of Order	Unaligned Fetch
RDF.I8	∞(A,M,D,L,S,B,T,I)	100%	8	Out of Order	1	Out of Order	Unaligned Fetch
4F2M	(A,M,D,I)(B,I) 2(L,S,T,I)	100%	1	In Order	4	Out of Order	Unaligned Fetch
4F2M.B85	(A,M,D,I)(B,I) 2(L,S,T,I)	85% Syth.	1	In Order	4	Out of Order	Unaligned Fetch
6F3M	(A,I)(M,D,I)(B,I) 3(L,S,T,I)	100%	1	In Order	6	Out of Order	Unaligned Fetch
8F3M	(A,I)(M,I)(D,I)(T,I)(B,I) 3(L,S,T,I)	100%	1	In Order	8	Out of Order	Unaligned Fetch
8F3M.B85	(A,I)(M,I)(D,I)(T,I)(B,I) 3(L,S,T,I)	85% Syth.	1	In Order	8	Out of Order	Unaligned Fetch
8F3M.RB	(A,I)(M,I)(D,I)(T,I)(B,I) 3(L,S,T,I)	Real BP	1	In Order	8	Out of Order	Unaligned Fetch

Figure 3: Simulated Machine Configurations
With respect to its functional unit configuration, each set of parentheses corresponds to a single functional unit, and the letters within the parentheses indicate the instruction classes that the functional unit is capable of executing. A number appearing before a set of parentheses indicates that multiple copies of the functional unit exist. In the case of our abstract machines, UDF and RDF.I8, an unbounded number of functional units are present.

capable of executing simple integer operations (except in the simulations of Smith and Johnson's machines).

3.3 Simulation Process

The simulator is capable of modeling a wide range of machines as well as execution models. The simulation process works as follows:

An instruction level simulator for the MC88100 (ISIM) reads in the object code and simulates execution, producing an instruction trace. Our RDF simulator reads in a configuration file which describes the machine to be simulated and then begins processing the dynamic instruction stream produced by ISIM. The simulator performs data dependency analysis and scheduling, and gathers execution rate statistics.

Our simulator makes several simplifying assumptions:

- Register renaming is performed. Renaming eliminates anti and output dependencies and is critical for achieving high performance with the models of execution we simulated.

- No memory renaming is performed. In the early stages of the simulator, we supported memory renaming at the byte granularity level, but found that renaming occurred so infrequently, either because of the algorithms or the actions of the compilers, that renaming did not noticeably improve performance.

- No caches are explicitly modeled in the current version of the simulator. We assume 100 percent hit rates for both I and D caches.

- No bank conflicts are modeled.

- All machines modeled are capable of performing store/load forwarding if stores and loads to the same memory location are both resident in the window. We found that this forwarding occurs very infrequently.

- All functional units are fully pipelined (i.e. able to initiate a new operation each cycle) and are mutually independent.

- Instructions are removed from the window (i.e. "retired") in whole packet units after all instructions in that packet have completed execution. This assumption corresponds to our use of checkpointing [6] as a mechanism for supporting both branch prediction miss recovery and precise interrupts.

- When a trap is encountered, the machine being simulated must stop issue, wait for all instructions currently in the window to complete, and then execute the trap instruction.

There are several key parameters that define execution in the simulator.

- Window size - This parameter limits the total number of instructions that can exist in the machine at any one time. An instruction is considered in the machine, and thus occupying space in the window, from the time it is issued until it is retired. Instructions can be in one of four states: waiting for operands, ready but waiting for the assigned functional unit to become free, executing, or waiting for retirement. Window size is given in the number of issue packets.

- Packet Issue Rate - This parameter indicates the number of packets that can be issued per cycle. A packet consists of a group of instructions that are brought into the machine in a single cycle. Normally the packet issue rate is set to one and the number of instructions issued per cycle is determined solely by the machine configuration.

- Prefetch Buffer Configuration - An instruction prefetch buffer may be modeled with specified size and refill characteristics. This was used only in the Smith/Johnson machines in order to match their configurations.

- Functional Unit Configuration - The number and capabilities of all functional units are specified in the configuration file. Each functional unit is defined by the instruction classes it is capable of executing.

- **In/Out of Order Execution** - This flag indicates whether instructions can be executed out-of-issue order for each functional unit. In-order execution still allows for slip to occur between functional units — i.e. operations are executed in-order within each functional unit, but out-of-order with respect to other functional units.

- **Branch Prediction** - There are two types of branch prediction supported - synthetic and real[11]. With synthetic branch prediction, the branch prediction accuracy is specified in the machine configuration file. As branches are encountered in the dynamic instruction stream, a random number is generated to determine whether the branch is predicted correctly or not. This is the mechanism used by Smith/Johnson [1]. With real branch prediction, an actual prediction is made and then compared to the real outcome as determined by the trace. If a prediction fails, issue is stalled until the branch is resolved. This models the performance of a checkpointing mechanism.

- **Instruction Class Latency** - These latencies describe the number of clock cycles required to execute a given type of instruction. The latencies we used are given in table 1. The only exception to these latencies is the machine model with the "SF" suffix. This machine used smaller floating point latencies of 3, 3, and 8 for floating point add, multiply, and divide respectively.

- **Unbounded Functional Units** - This flag allows the simulator to model a machine with an unbounded number of functional units. With this machine, there are effectively as many functional units as are needed in any given cycle.

- **Instruction Issue Constraint** - This flag indicates whether instructions are assigned to a particular functional unit at issue time (with at most one instruction going to each functional unit), or whether they are issued to a common window. The consequence of assigning instructions at issue time is that issue is constrained to match each instruction to a unique functional unit. Thus if an instruction can not be assigned to a functional unit capable of executing it, that instruction and all instructions following it cannot be issued in that cycle.

4 Simulation Results

Each benchmark was simulated under three sets of machine configurations: (1) a model faithful to the previous work of Smith and Johnson[1], (2) a model representing no artificial constraints on the processor, and (3) realizable machines obtained by restricting the values

for parameters of the unconstrained machine. We will discuss the simulation results for each set of machine models in turn.

4.1 Previous Work

For each of the nine benchmarks (Figures 4 through 12), the curve labeled SJ4 presents the results of modeling the assumptions and machine configuration of Smith and Johnson's machine 4[1]. (All four machine configurations were simulated, but only SJ4 results are presented for clarity in the figures. SJ4 was selected because it demonstrated the highest performance of the four Smith/Johnson machine models.) In this model, a four instruction wide prefetch buffer is filled with memory words aligned on a four-instruction-word boundary. Thus, as many as 3 of the 4 instructions in the prefetch buffer may not be required. Instruction issue, the act of bringing instructions into the machine, is not constrained by functional unit configuration. Thus, for example, more than one integer instruction can be placed in the window in a cycle even though there is only a single integer ALU (The integer instructions will of course be scheduled for different cycles). The functional units execute instructions in data-dependent order and instructions are removed from the window upon completion. Loads and stores are executed in order and store instructions are executed only after all previously issued instructions have completed. Branch prediction accuracy is 85 percent (synthetic) as in [1].

While a direct comparison is not possible due to different instruction set architectures and different compilers, one notes from Figures 4 through 12, that the results of our simulations are consistent with results published by Smith and Johnson. Our simulations show performance between 1.7 and 2.1 IPC for the integer benchmarks, and between 1.4 and 3.1 IPC across the floating point benchmarks. Smith and Johnson show performance in terms of speedup over a scalar processor, and report the harmonic mean for their entire benchmark suite. To provide a rough comparison between our results and those published by Smith and Johnson, the IPC of the superscalar machine executing a particular benchmark is divided by the IPC of a scalar machine.

Several details of the Smith/Johnson machines impede high performance unnecessarily. The most obvious limit to achieving high performance is the issue rate of four. The machine is comprised of nine independent, pipelined functional units, allowing for a peak execution rate of nine IPC. However, since a maximum of four instructions are issued per cycle, peak execution has been reduced to four IPC.

Aside from the four instruction wide fetch limit, there are three additional machine characteristics that limit performance: a poorly balanced machine configuration, an overly-constrained prefetch buffer, and a sequential load/store execution constraint.

A significant source of performance degradation in the Smith/Johnson machines is an imbalance in the machine configurations. The scarcity of integer units gives rise to a performance bottleneck. If integer operations comprise nearly 38 percent of the instructions in the integer benchmarks and the machine contains only one integer unit, then it is unreasonable to expect a speedup of much greater than two simply because the integer ALU will be saturated. This is in fact what happens in our simulations — the integer units are constantly busy and the execution time for the program is determined largely by contention for the integer ALU resource.

Another bottleneck to performance is the behavior of the prefetch buffer. Because the buffer is aligned with respect to memory, any branch targets in the middle of cache lines will reduce the number of useful instructions fetched. Assuming a uniform distribution and small basic blocks, on average only 2.5 useful instructions will be fetched per cycle by such a prefetch buffer. As discussed in [1], if the prefetch buffer were expanded to fetch two lines from the i-cache, and perform alignment so as to produce four useful instructions (in the absence of the end of basic blocks), performance would improve. Another shortcoming of the prefetch buffer is that it is only refilled when completely empty. If, for instance, the buffer contains four instructions but can only issue two due to a full window, the prefetch buffer does not attempt to fetch new instructions into the empty buffer space. The next cycle, regardless of the available window space, the prefetch buffer can only issue two instructions. This inefficiency can be eliminated at the cost of a more complex prefetch controller by prefetching anytime there is room in the prefetch buffer. These two features unnecessarily limit the ability of the machine to issue instructions and thus impede execution throughput.

Finally, in the Smith/Johnson model, execution of loads occur strictly in sequential issue order with respect to other loads, and stores are executed only after all previous instructions (i.e. instructions issued before the store) have been executed. These constraints are applied in order to maintain a consistent state in the memory system. This is unnecessary, however, with the support of a checkpointed write buffer as described in [6].

When all of the changes suggested above are implemented in a machine model, the improvements have a synergistic effect and performance improves significantly. For instance, removing the sequential load/store constraint allows for greater performance to be gained from the addition of extra load/store pipes. The result of implementing all of these is a performance increase of 30 to 50 percent (.6 to 1.0 IPC) over the Smith/Johnson model, across the four integer benchmarks tested (gcc, li, eqntott, and espresso).

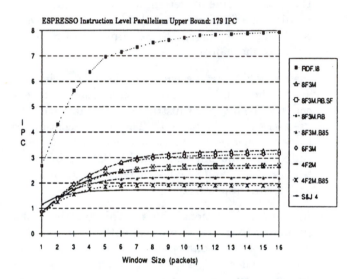
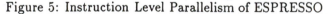

Figure 4: Instruction Level Parallelism of EQNTOTT

Figure 5: Instruction Level Parallelism of ESPRESSO

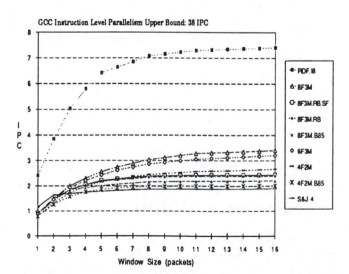

Figure 6: Instruction Level Parallelism of GCC

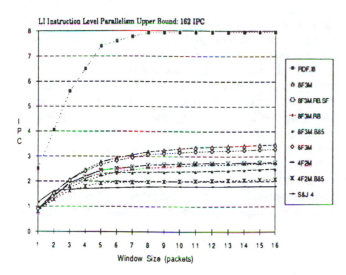

Figure 7: Instruction Level Parallelism of XLISP

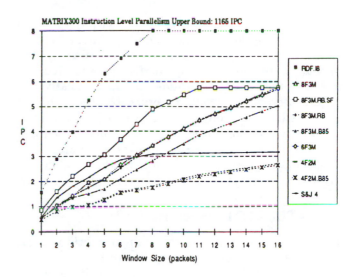

Figure 10: Instruction Level Parallelism of MATRIX300

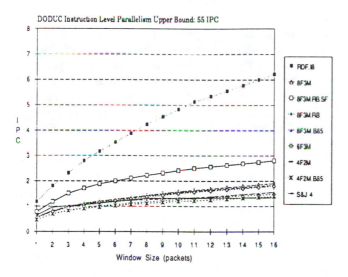

Figure 8: Instruction Level Parallelism of DODUC

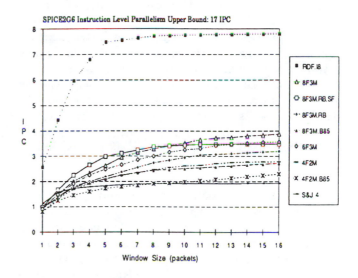

Figure 11: Instruction Level Parallelism of SPICE2G6

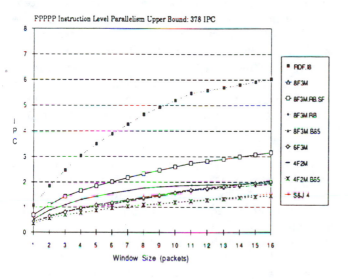

Figure 9: Instruction Level Parallelism of FPPPP

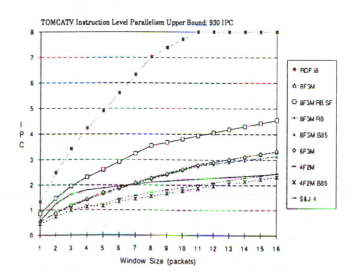

Figure 12: Instruction Level Parallelism of TOMCATV

We also note that we have simulated models based on the assumptions of Jouppi[2] and obtained results similar to his published data (less than two IPC). The primary impediments to high performance for Jouppi's machine are in-order execution and no speculative execution beyond branches. In-order execution imposes a serious limitation on performance by effectively introducing false dependencies between an instruction and all instructions that precede it in the I-stream. Lack of speculative execution limits the machine's ability to utilize parallelism to that which is within a basic block.

4.2   The RDF Machine

For each of the nine benchmarks, Figures 4 through 12, the highest performance curve shows the performance of a restricted dataflow machine with an issue rate of eight instructions per cycle. This abstract machine issues eight instructions each cycle regardless of instruction class, until the window is full. Functional units, each capable of executing any type of instruction, remove instructions from the window out-of-order as they complete execution. No other restrictions are placed on execution. Branch prediction is omniscient. Clearly this is an unrealizable machine model. However, the simulation results provide an upper bound for machines that approximate the RDF model with an issue rate of eight. Note that performance approaches an asymptote of eight IPC.

If we do not restrict window size or fetch rate, the simulator provides an absolute upper bound for that particular benchmark. This is the Unrestricted Data Flow Machine (UDF). In this case, execution is constrained only by true dependencies. This value, reported at the top of each of graph, ranges from 17 to 1165 IPC and indicates all the parallelism that exists in the program segments traced.

4.3   The Middle Ground

4.3.1   Configurations

For each of the nine benchmarks, Figures 4 through 12, the middle curves show the performance of a series of machine configurations under various assumptions. The assumptions that drove the selection of this set of machine configurations were based on a desire to pick configurations that are implementable, coupled with an interest in knowing the effect of better branch prediction schemes. Consequently, each of the machine configurations combines a realistic window size, issue rate, and set of functional units with one of the following branch predictors: 100 percent accurate, 85 percent accurate (synthetic), and a real branch predictor.

The model of execution simulated in these experiments differs from the Smith/Johnson model in that instructions are entered and removed from the window in issue packet units, only after all instructions in the packet have been completed, and in the order in which the packets were issued. This is in contrast to the Smith/Johnson model where instructions are removed out-of-order as soon as the instruction has completed execution. This constraint, required by the mechanism we chose for implementing checkpointing, reduces the effective window size. While this is not significant for the integer benchmarks, it impacts the performance of the floating point benchmarks. As seen in the figures, the Smith/Johnson machine performs better than our machines on the floating point intensive benchmarks for smaller window sizes because it makes more effective use of the window.

4.3.2   Results

Four-functional-unit machines with two memory units and either 85 percent or 100 percent branch prediction accuracy are shown to demonstrate the performance advantages of a properly balanced machine with no prefetch buffer constraints. Performance of the machine with 100 percent branch prediction ranges from 2.7 to 2.9 IPC for the integer benchmarks and 1.5 to 2.8 IPC for the floating point benchmarks. Performance of the machine with 85 percent branch prediction ranges from 1.9 to 2.2 IPC (integer) to 1.4 to 2.7 IPC (floating point).

A six-functional-unit configuration with three memory units is presented with 100 percent branch prediction. Performance ranges from 3.2 to 3.6 IPC for the integer benchmarks and from 1.8 to 5.7 for the floating point benchmarks.

Several eight functional unit machines with three memory units are also presented. These machines each have different branch prediction characteristics: 100 percent synthetic, 85 percent synthetic, and real branch prediction. The real mechanism predicts the outcome of a branch based on the history of that branch in conjunction with dynamically gathered branch characteristics of the running program. Performance of these machines suffers from the one branch per cycle limitation we assumed for the issue mechanism. The average size of basic blocks (five) limits the advantage of additional functional units. Performance ranges from approximately 2.2 to 2.9 IPC for the integer benchmarks using 85 percent branch prediction, and from 1.6 to 5.0 for the floating point benchmarks. With the real branch predictor, performance of between 2.4 and 3.4 (integer), and 1.9 and 5.8 (floating point) is obtained. Because of the significant impact of floating point latencies on the performance of the floating point benchmarks, and the existence of several machines with smaller latencies, we repeated the experiment for the eight functional unit machine using smaller latencies. With the real branch predictor, the performance of the smaller latency machine ranges from 2.8 to 5.8 on the floating point benchmarks. The performance on the integer benchmarks remains unchanged.

4.3.3 Analysis

Performance, measured in instructions executed per clock cycle, can be modeled as:

$$ipc = I * \mu * \delta$$

where I is the maximum issue rate in instructions per clock cycle, μ is the *static issue efficiency* factor, and δ is the *dynamic execution efficiency* factor. Both μ and δ range between zero and one inclusive.

The maximum issue rate I is determined by the designer and establishes an upper bound on performance. The static issue efficiency factor μ is determined by the dynamic instruction stream (which is program/data dependent) and by the issue restrictions of the machine. For example, a restriction of at most one branch per clock cycle and no instructions issued beyond a branch will reduce the number of instructions that can be issued in a single clock below the maximum value I unless the dynamic instruction stream has one branch every I instructions. Other restrictions, such as those caused by functional unit conflicts (e.g., only one multiply issue per clock due to the presence of only one multiplier) will further reduce μ. Clearly, μ can be improved through compiler assistance. A compiler for a superscalar machine could reorganize code such that issue restriction effects are minimized. It should be emphasized that for the results presented, no superscalar optimizations were performed.

The effects of the static issue efficiency factor can be clearly seen in the results by comparing the performance levels of the RDF.I8 machine to that of the 8F3M machine. The RDF machine is limited only by window size and operation latencies. The 8F3M machine adds issue restrictions, such as one branch per issue cycle and only 3 memory ports. Otherwise, for any given window size, and with the exception of retirement policy, both machines are identical. The range for this factor is approximately .33 to .72.

The dynamic execution efficiency represents the fraction of clock cycles in which instructions were effectively issued. This is determined by four factors: instruction pointer availability, instruction availability, branch misprediction losses, and full window frequency. In a pure RDF model, the first three factors play no part since unbounded instruction bandwidth and branch prediction omniscience is assumed. In a real machine however, these factors have a major effect on performance.

In certain circumstances, the location from which to fetch instructions may not be known. For example, in machine architectures which permit a jump to a location stored in a register, the jump cannot be performed until the register value is known. The machine must stall issue from the time the jump is issued until the register value is known. We define this condition as a lack of instruction pointer availability.

Lack of instruction availability will reduce the number of instructions that can be issued. This can arise because of instruction cache misses, memory bank conflicts, etc. We point out that there is a dichotomy between instruction traffic and data traffic in Von Neumann machines. It is possible to buffer against data cache misses. For example, we can allow a subsequent memory load to access the data cache even after a prior memory load has missed the cache (lock-up free). There is no corresponding way to deal with instruction cache misses. This condition was not modeled in our simulations.

Branch misprediction effectively causes issue stalls. From the time a mispredicted branch is issued until it is determined that it has been mispredicted, all instructions issued after the branch must be discarded. From the point of view of being able to retire instructions, this is equivalent to having stalled instruction issue after the mispredicted branch instead of predicting it. There are two remedies for this effect. First, reduce the frequency of misprediction by either eliminating branches or by using a better branch prediction algorithm. Second, reduce the latency of branch issue to branch execute. This has the effect of reducing the number of instructions discarded after a mispredicted branch.

The effect of branch misprediction is clearly visible in figures 4, 5, 6, 7, and 11. It is most notable in gcc (figure 6) for the 8F3M machines: the performance of the 8F3M machine with omniscient branch prediction is almost 50 percent greater than the 8F3M.RB machine.

Finally, full window effects arise when *instruction lifetime* exceeds the window size. Instruction lifetime is measured as the time from issuance of an instruction into the window until it is removed from the window by retirement. At a minimum, instruction lifetime is equal to its latency. This time can be increased if the instruction must wait for operands after it is issued. This effect can be minimized by either having the compiler attempt to schedule code so that operands are likely to be available as an instruction is issued or by increasing the window size. The effect of window overflow can be seen in figures 4-12 at small window sizes. Once the window size increases beyond some point, other factors such as static issue efficiency, branch misprediction losses, etc. dominate.

However, there are code fragments for which code reorganization or window size increases will have little effect. Consider the Livermore Loops kernel #5:

```
DO 10 i = 2,n
    X(i)= Z(i)*(Y(i) - X(i-1))
10  CONTINUE
```

This simple recurrence relation will require at least two loads, a floating point subtract, a floating point multiply, a store, and an increment, compare and branch: perhaps 8 instructions per iteration. On a superscalar degree 8 machine, it takes just one clock to issue each iteration. However, each iteration will take a minimum of 12 clocks to execute using the latencies given in Table 1. Since each iteration is dependent on the prior iteration, a full window condition will quickly arise. For large 'n', the number of iterations, the machine will achieve steady state at an issue rate of one clock out of twelve. Inside this loop, the dynamic execution efficiency δ is only .08! The only remedy for such situations is to reduce the latencies of the executed instructions or recode the loop. The doduc and fpppp benchmarks exhibit this type of latency induced problem.

5 Implementation Issues

Several aspects of implementing a superscalar machine based on RDF principles are not trivial. Among these difficult issues are instruction delivery and multiple simultaneous data accesses.

Instruction delivery is the problem of determining what instructions must be fetched, fetching them, and delivering them to the proper function units for execution. Aside from bandwidth issues, branches and machine issue restrictions (e.g., only one floating point multiplier issue per clock) make instruction delivery difficult. We briefly address these issues here.

Given a fetch address, the technique as proposed in [1], that of fetching several cache lines simultaneously, is a good way of providing the raw bandwidth necessary to issue several instructions in one clock. For example, for a superscalar degree four engine, assuming that each cache line holds four instructions, fetching two sequential cache lines guarantees that four instructions can be delivered regardless of the alignment of the fetch address within the first cache line.

Once a group of instructions has been fetched, the difficulty lies in quickly determining where to fetch the next packet. Issue constraints determine how many instructions can be issued, and thus what the next fetch address should be. These constraints, however, are not resolved until after decode. Furthermore, the presence of branches in the packet determine the end of the packet as well as a possibly non-sequential next address. The branch needs to be predicted and the branch target calculated in time to perform the next fetch. These problems can be circumvented through the use of a decoded instruction cache (DIC) [10, 3]. Rather than caching undecoded instructions in an instruction cache, an instruction packet can be predecoded and stored in the DIC. The DIC, in addition to storing decoded instructions, can store branch prediction information,

branch target addresses, and packet sizes.

Another implementation problem is that of providing multiple memory accesses per machine cycle. We briefly describe two techniques which can be used to provide the necessary memory bandwidth. First, a small fully associative cache backed by a conventional cache can be used. The small cache would be implemented with multiple access ports. Its small size would make the cost of the multiple ports less prohibitive. Another organization uses one, single ported cache per memory request unit. Standard cache consistency techniques can be used to keep the caches consistent with each other in the presence of memory stores.

6 Concluding Remarks

This paper is only a beginning in the demonstrated viability of a single instruction stream processor capable of delivering execution rates in excess of the two instructions per cycle limit stated in [1, 2]. Our simulation results have shown performance up to more than 3 instructions per cycle on large integer applications on processors that are reasonable to implement today.

Note that, in the interests of producing data that is consistent with the software and hardware mechanisms available today, we have imposed limitations on the performance that can be achieved. When these limitations are removed, the performance of single instruction stream processors will improve substantially.

For example, we have required that instructions be removed from the window in whole packet increments. Packets are removed only in the order in which the packets were issued, and only after all instructions in the packet have completed execution. In this way, completed instructions consume valuable window space while waiting to be removed. With a different implementation of checkpointing, it is possible to eliminate this inefficiency and make better use of the window, thus improving performance.

Second, we have assumed only one branch per cycle, and no instructions following the branch being issued in the same cycle with the branch. This limits the available parallelism to the average size of a basic block. Allowing multiple branches per cycle would increase the amount of available parallelism.

Furthermore, our results of 2.0 to 5.8 instructions per cycle come from a restricted data flow engine that has a limited window size and issue rate, consistent with what is reasonable today. As levels of integration and bandwidth capabilities increase, window sizes and issue rates will increase correspondingly. In the limit, our unbounded window size and issue rate machine (the UDF) shows instructions per cycle in the 17 to 1165 range. While we are not suggesting that this is possible (yet), we expect numbers well in excess of 5 instructions per cycle.

Finally, and perhaps most importantly, it is worth re-emphasizing that all of our results have been obtained using compilers not optimized for superscalar issue. With architecture-specific compiler assistance to perform code motion to provide higher issue density, performance can be expected to increase further. With compiler support to produce larger granularity execution units [12], performance should increase still further.

The bottom line is that processors can be implemented today that deliver more than twice the performance suggested in [1, 2], and the limits to what will be deliverable tomorrow by single instruction stream processors is still an open question.

References

[1] M.D. Smith, M.Johnson, and M.A. Horowitz, "Limits on Multiple Instruction Issue", *Proceedings of the Third International Conference on Architectural Support for Programming Languages and Operating Systems*, (April 1989), pp.290-302.

[2] N.P. Jouppi, and D. Wall, "Available Instruction-Level Parallelism for Superscalar and Superpipelined Machines.", *Proceedings of the Third International Conference on Architectural Support for Programming Languages and Operating Systems*, (April 1989), pp.272-282.

[3] Y.N. Patt, W. Hwu, and M. Shebanow, "HPS, A New Microarchitecture: Rationale and Introduction.", *Proceedings of the 18th Annual Workshop on Microprogramming*,(December 1985), pp.103-108.

[4] Y.N. Patt, W. Hwu, and M. Shebanow, "Critical Issues Regarding HPS, A High Performance Microarchitecture.", *Proceedings of the 18th Annual Workshop on Microprogramming*,(December 1985), pp.109-116.

[5] Y.N. Patt, and W. Hwu, "HPSm, a High Performance Restricted Data Flow Architecture Having Minimal Functionality.", *Proceedings of the 13th Annual Symposium on computer Architecture*, (June 1986), pp.297-307.

[6] W.W. Hwu and Y.N. Patt, "Checkpoint Repair for Out-of-order Execution Machines", *IEEE Transactions on Computers*, (December 1987), pp.1496-1514.

[7] W.M. Johnson, "Super-Scalar Processor Design", Technical Report No. CSL-TR-89-383, Stanford University, (June 1989).

[8] Norman P. Jouppi, "The Nonuniform Distribution of Instruction-Level and Machine Parallelism and Its Effect on Performance", *IEEE Transactions on Computers*, Vol. 38, No. 12, (December 1989), pp.1645-1658.

[9] G. S. Sohi and S. Vajaperyam, "Instruction Issue Logic for High-Performance Interuptable Pipelined Processors.", *Proceedings of the 14th Annual Symposium on Computer Architecture*, (June 1987), pp. 27-34.

[10] D. R. Ditzel, A. D. Berenbaum and H.R. McLellan, "The Hardware Architecture of the CRISP Microprocessor.", *Proceedings of the 14th Annual Symposium on Computer Architecture*, (June 1987), pp. 309-319.

[11] Tse-Yu Yeh, "Adaptive Training Branch Prediction ", Technical Report, University of Michigan, (1991).

[12] Steve Melvin and Yale Patt, "Exploiting Fine-Grained Parallelism Through Combined Hardware and Software Techniques", *Proceedings of the 18th Annual Symposium on Computer Architecture*, (May 1991)

[13] Robert Colwell, Robert Nix, John O'Donnell, David Papworth, and Paul Rodman, "A VLIW Architecture for a Trace Scheduling Compiler.", *IEEE Transactions on computers* , (August 1988), 967-979.

[14] Alexandru Nicolau and Joseph Fisher, "Measuring the Parallelism Available for Very Long Instruction Word Architectures", *IEEE Transactions on computers C-33, 11*, (November 1984), 968-976.

[15] Edward M. Riseman and Caxton C. Foster, "The Inhibition of Potential Parallelism by Condition Jumps.", *IEEE Transactions on computers C-21, 12*, (December 1972), 1405-1411.

[16] D. J. Kuck, Y. Muraoka, and S-C. Chen, "On the Number of Operations Simultaneously Executable in Fortran-Like Programs and Their Resulting Speedup", *IEEE Transactions on computers C-21, 12*, (December 1972), 1293-1310.

[17] G. S. Tjaden and M. J. Flynn, "Detection and Parallel Execution of Independent Instructions", *IEEE Transactions on computers C-19, 10*, (October 1970), 889-895.

Measuring Parallelism in Computation-Intensive Scientific/Engineering Applications

MANOJ KUMAR, MEMBER, IEEE

Abstract—A software tool for measuring parallelism in large scientific/engineering applications is described in this paper. The proposed tool measures the total parallelism present in programs, filtering out the effects of communication/synchronization delays, finite storage, limited number of processors, the policies for management of processors and storage, etc. Although an ideal machine which can exploit the total parallelism is not realizable, such measures would aid the calibration and design of various architectures/compilers. The proposed software tool accepts ordinary Fortran programs as its input. Therefore, parallelism can be measured easily on many fairly big programs. Some measurements for parallelism obtained with the help of this tool are also reported. It is observed that the average parallelism in the chosen programs is in the range of 500–3500 Fortran statements executing concurrently in each clock cycle in an idealized environment.

Index Terms—Maximum/total parallelism, measurement of parallelism, parallelism in Fortran programs, parallelism in scientific/engineering applications, upper bound on parallelism.

I. INTRODUCTION

THE VIABILITY of a parallel processing system depends heavily on the presence of parallelism in the application programs expected in the workload of that system. Since the scientific/engineering applications domain has been designated as the primary beneficiary of parallel processing, there have been several attempts to make parallel machines targeted for scientific/engineering applications [1]–[3], [6], [7]. In each case, the claim for the viability/optimality of the machine design (and often for its superiority over all other machine designs) is based on the assumptions about the amount of parallelism present in the applications (number of concurrently performable operations, averaged over time) and its nature (fine grain, coarse grain, vectorial, etc.).

The ensuing debate on the advantages, disadvantages, and efficiency of these different machine designs has been inconclusive, and often confusing, because researchers differ on the extent and nature of parallelism found in scientific/engineering applications. The differences have arisen because of several reasons, some of which are addressed below.

Traditionally, the investigation of parallelism in large scientific/engineering applications has been restricted to measuring the parallelism that can be exploited by some particular machine. Studies have been conducted to measure parallelism exhibited by vector machines such as Cray and Cyber, SIMD

Reprinted from *IEEE Transactions on Computers*, Vol. 37, No. 9, September 1988, pages 1088–1098. Copyright © 1988 by The Institute of Electrical and Electronics Engineers, Inc. All rights reserved.

machines such as ILLIAC-IV and MPP, and MIMD machines such as Intel-Hypercube and RP3 [2], [8], [9]. Usually these experiments report only part of the parallelism present in the program, the part which can be exploited effectively by the machine on which the program is executed. For example, studies conducted on the vector machines ignore the parallelism present in the unstructured portions of the program, which cannot be vectorized. Similarly, the MIMD machines do not exploit, and the experiments run on these machines do not report, the low-grained parallelism which cannot be exploited effectively on MIMD machines.

To add to the reigning confusion, when parallelism is measured on a particular machine, the reported parallelism is diluted with the synchronization, communication, and resource management overheads required to exploit it. Furthermore, measurements are usually taken on a few small programs because in the absence of good tools, the measurement of parallelism is quite difficult and time consuming. Finally, no serious attempt has been made to characterize parallelism. Most measurements report only the reduction in finish time (for a few programs) as a function of the number of processors used.

A more reliable measure of parallelism is needed to aid the development and evaluation of future parallel processors, a measure that captures the parallelism in a program irrespective of whether this parallelism can be detected by any existing/promised compiler, and whether it can be effectively exploited by any available/promised parallel processing system. Machine dependent overheads incurred in moving the data, scheduling the computation, and managing the processor and memory resources, should be filtered out from the measurements because these overheads change from machine to machine. For similar reasons, machine dependent limitations such as the effect of finite number of processors and finite storage should also be filtered out. Parallelism measured according to these guidelines will be called total parallelism.

Some early measurements of parallelism in Fortran programs are reported by Kuck *et al.* in [4]. These measurements were obtained by analyzing the programs (statically) and determining which statements can execute in parallel. Since the programs were not executed and the actual execution path of the programs could not be determined, the parallelism available in a program was estimated by taking the average of the parallelism found on each trace in that program. Parallelism was measured at the level of primitive operations. Compiler transformations such as tree height reduction and forward substitution were used to expose additional parallelism in the program, beyond what was actually present.

As noted by Kuck *et al.* in [4], taking the average of the parallelism in each trace gives a conservative estimate for the total parallelism. Although many programs were analyzed in [4], each individual program was relatively small. Larger computation-intensive problems might have more parallelism than that observed in [4]. Furthermore, static analysis of programs tends to give a conservative estimate for available parallelism because flow of a value between two operations has to be assumed whenever the absence of this flow cannot be proved analytically.

A software tool developed for measuring the total parallelism in Fortran programs and characterizing it is described in this paper. It was named COMET, an abbreviation for "concurrency measurement tool." Parallelism in a program is obtained by actually executing the program, monitoring the statements executed and the flow of values between them, and then deducing the maximum concurrency possible. This approach avoids most of the shortcomings inherent in the approaches mentioned earlier.

The measurements obtained from COMET would aid the evaluation of various parallel processing systems by providing the right set of assumptions for the extent of parallelism present in applications. These measurements can also be used to gauge the efficiency of various compilers and machine architectures. The characterization of parallelism is a more difficult task and is handled at a cursory level at present. In the current implementation of COMET, concurrency in any chosen section(s) of a computation can be monitored over desired intervals. However, work is in progress to refine this characterization.

To measure the parallelism in a Fortran program, the program is modified/extended by including a set of shadow variables (one for each variable in the original program) and a set of statements that initialize and manipulate the shadow variables. The statements of the original program are called the core statements and the newly added statements are called tracking statements. The shadow variables and the tracking statements are inserted automatically by COMET. Therefore, there is no need to understand the application or change it in any other way.

The modified/extended program is compiled and executed (using the available input data sets). During the execution of the program, the tracking statements trace the dynamic execution sequence of the core statements. For each core statement in this sequence, the corresponding tracking statements also compute the earliest time at which this core statement would execute if the program was executed on a machine capable of exploiting all the parallelism present in the program without incurring any overheads, i.e., an ideal parallel machine.

The shadow of a variable (storage cell) is used to record the time at which the current value of this variable was computed. The earliest time at which a core statement can execute is determined by using the values of the appropriate shadow variables. This "earliest time" is used to update a table which, at the termination of the program, contains a profile of parallelism observed in the program.

The programs analyzed for parallelism are fairly large

applications. Under ideal conditions, the average parallelism observed in the chosen programs is in the range of 500–3500 Fortran statements executing concurrently in each clock cycle. Furthermore, parallelism is fairly uneven in most applications. There are phases during the execution of the program when the instant parallelism is several orders of magnitude above/below the average parallelism.

While modifying/extending a program to monitor the parallelism, the original computation is not transformed in any way. The operations performed and the flow of operands between them (the computation graph) remain unchanged. Various compiler transformations (such as scalar expansion/renaming, tree height reduction, and various loop-oriented optimizations), which can increase the amount of parallelism exhibited by the program, were not used. In fact, COMET can measure the effectiveness/importance of these transformations by comparing the parallelism observed in the original and the transformed program.

The next section of this paper states the metric used for measuring parallelism. A hypothetical machine called the "ideal parallel machine" is defined to simplify this discussion. A brief overview of the approach used for measuring parallelism is given in Section III. In this approach, the program to be analyzed is modified. The required modifications/extensions are illustrated in Section IV. The measurements taken on some large programs with the help of COMET are reported in Section V. In Section VI, extensions needed in COMET to allow the measurement of parallelism in storage-oriented architectures are described (here write after read/write synchronizations must be observed). The impact of assuming *a priori* knowledge of how the data flow between various statements of a program (a characteristic of the ideal parallel machine) is discussed in Section VII. Suggestions for further research in this direction are outlined in Section VIII, and finally, the summary and conclusions of this paper are given in Section IX.

II. The Ideal Parallel Machine

Our objective is to measure the total parallelism present in a Fortran program. This total parallelism can be observed if the program is executed on a machine which has unlimited processors and memory, does not incur any overhead in scheduling tasks and managing machine resources, does not incur any communication and synchronization overheads, and detects and exploits all the parallelism present in the program. The ideal parallel machine defined in this section is a hypothetical machine which possesses the above mentioned qualities. Parallelism in a program is defined as the activity observed in this hypothetical machine when it is executing that program.

In the following discussion, it is important to differentiate the terms "variables" and "values," A variable is a storage cell or any array of storage cells accessible by a program. A value is a particular scalar intermediate result, computed during the execution of the program. Values are assigned to (stored in) variables. Thus, the sequence of statements "$A = 5; A = B; A = \cos (B) \cdots$" assign three different values to the same variable.

The ideal parallel machine exhibits the following behavior.

1) It executes one Fortran statement in unit time. All the memory access and logic/arithmetic operations involved in executing this statement are completed within this unit time.

2) A statement S is executed as soon as

- all the conditional branches that precede S in the sequential execution of the Fortran program, and whose outcome affects the decision whether to execute S or not, have been resolved,
- all the input data values required by S are available.

3) It has a complete knowledge of how the data flow between the statements of a program during the program's execution. When a data value is produced by some statement, the ideal parallel machine can infer which successor statements will ultimately use that value.

4) The output value produced by a Fortran statement is available forever after the execution of that statement (even after the variable to which that value was assigned, has been reassigned with a different value). Therefore, there is no need for write after read/write synchronization in the ideal machine.

Perhaps, the last two points need further clarification. In Fortran, if a statement A assigns a value to a variable V and a successor statement B requires the value associated with variable V as an input, one cannot conclude that the value produced by A and the value required by B are the same until one verifies that the sequence of statements executed between A and B do not modify the variable V. However, we will assume that the ideal parallel machine can foresee the sequence of statements to be executed in the future for the restricted purpose of enumerating the successor statements that will use the currently computed result as one of the required inputs.

The above mentioned situation is illustrated in Fig. 1. A subcomputation consisting of four statements is shown in this figure. Assume that the subcomputation is initiated at time (t = 1), the value of Y is 2, i.e., the true branch of the conditional statement is taken, and that the value of Y is available at time (t = 10). The value of t shown in parenthesis next to each statement in Fig. 1 indicates the time at which the statement can be executed. Statements 1 and 2 will execute at times 1 and 10, respectively, according to the first two rules mentioned above. In practice, one would expect the execution of statement 4 to be delayed at least until the condition in statement 2 is evaluated, because until then it is not known whether the value of variable A to be used by statement 4 is the value created by statement 1 or the one created by statement 3. Unfortunately, there is no simple method for determining all the necessary delays of this kind without being overrestrictive. So the ideal machine will ignore the delays of this kind and execute statement 4 at time (t = 2). By observing/respecting all the true data dependencies [5], one can incorporate all the necessary delays at the cost of including some unnecessary ones. This approach and its limitations are discussed further in Section VII.

There was a motive for ignoring the write after read/write synchronizations. The need for such synchronizations arises primarily because Fortran presents a storage-oriented model

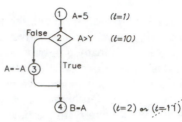

Fig. 1. Assumption about the advance knowledge of how the data flows between the statements of a program.

of computation, and application programmers have a tendency to minimize the storage requirement by reusing storage. Thus, the need for write after read/write synchronizations is usually not inherent in the application, but imposed by the programmer. This need can often be avoided by renaming the variables that create the need.

The repercussions of ignoring the write after read/write synchronizations are illustrated in Fig. 2. Once again, assume that the subcomputation consisting of four statements is initiated at time (t = 1), and that the value of Y is available at time (t = 10). Then the first three statements of the subcomputation will execute at times (t = 1), (t = 10), and (t = 11), respectively. In storage-oriented machines, state 4 (which assigns a new value to variable A) cannot execute until statement 3 (which uses the previous value of A) completes execution. Thus, the earliest time at which the execution of statement 4 can be initiated is (t = 12).

In machines that allow several values associated with the same variable to coexist (such as dynamic data flow machines [3]), a new value can be created for a variable before all the uses of the previous value assigned to the same variable are complete. Thus, statement 4 can define a new value for variable A before statement 3 completes execution, and therefore it can be executed at time (t = 2). Although the ideal parallel machine ignores the write after read/write synchronizations, they can be incorporated easily, and one method for incorporating them is discussed in Section VI.

III. METHOD FOR MEASURING PARALLELISM

To measure the parallelism that a Fortran program P will exhibit while executing on the ideal parallel machine, the program P is extended/modified to produce another Fortran program P'. The program P' thus obtained is compiled and executed, using one or more input data sets intended to be used with the original program P. The output obtained on executing P' consists of the results expected from the execution of P and a histogram of the parallelism observed in the program. The modifications/extensions are used for monitoring the computation. The original computation is not altered or transformed in any way. The extensions/modifications required in P, and their role in the measurement of parallelism, is discussed in this section. The key extensions are the following.

Shadow variables: For each variable accessible in P, a shadow variable is added in P'. The shadow of an N-dimensional array is an N-dimensional array with matching dimensions. Thus, for each scalar element of an array, there is a scalar shadow element in the shadow array. The shadow of a scalar variable or an array element holds the time at which the

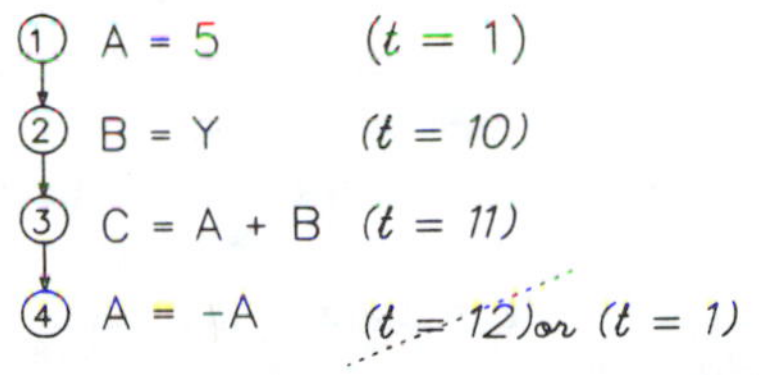

Fig. 2. Repercussions of ignoring the write after read and write after write dependencies.

value of the associated scalar element (a storage cell which can be a scalar variable or an array element) was computed.

Control variables: An array CVAR is added to P' so that for each statement S in P, there is a control variable CVAR(S) defined in P'. CVAR(S) marks the time at which one can conclude that S must execute. Tracking statements associated with the conditional branch and loop control statements keep the value of the CVAR() variables consistent. For example, if a statement S is executed only if a particular branch is taken from a conditional branch statement C, then one cannot decide whether S must execute or not until C is executed. In fact, the execution of S has to be delayed until the last conditional branch statement C', which precedes S and controls its execution in the above mentioned manner, has been executed. The CVAR variable for statement S is set by the tracking statements associated with C'.

Statements for updating shadow variables: For each assignment statement S in P, tracking statements are added to P' to update the shadow of the scalar element being modified by S. The time at which the execution of S can be initiated is determined by taking the maximum of CVAR(S) and the shadows of the scalar elements required to execute S. This is the earliest time at which we know that S must execute and that all the input values required by S are available. The time required to execute S is assumed to be one cycle, but one can substitute more realistic values for this time such as the height of the expression tree being evaluated or the number of nodes in the expression tree. The time at which the new value of the scalar element being updated by S is available is obtained by adding the time required to execute S and the time at which the execution of S can be initiated. The shadow of the updated variable is modified to reflect this time.

Statements for updating control variables: Conditional branch statements (arithmetic and logical "IF's," "DO" loops, and computed and assigned "GO TO's") are split into two statements. The first statement evaluates the condition and updates a Boolean variable, and is treated like an assignment statement. A tracking statement is generated for it as mentioned in previous paragraph. The second statement makes the branch based on the value of this Boolean variable. Tracking statements are inserted on each target of the branch. For each branch target, these tracking statements modify the CVAR variables of the successor statements which are reachable from this branch target but are not reachable from all the targets of this branch statement.

The array PROFILE: A one-dimensional array "PRO-FILE" is added in P'. It is initialized at the beginning of P'. Every time a core statement S executes in P', the time T at which its execution completes (determined by the associated

tracking statements) is used to increment PROFILE(T) by one. For each statement in P, a tracking statement is added in P' to perform this increment operation. At the termination of P', the contents of this array are printed out. The array "PROFILE" essentially gives the parallelism that will be observed in the program, if the program is executed on the ideal parallel machine.

The conversion from P to P' is automatic. The Fortran program is scanned (lexically) to produce the symbol table and the control flow graph. The symbol table is used to generate the declarations of the shadow variables. (Special consideration is given to "COMMON" declarations and equivalence statements.) The tracking statements that modify the CVAR variables are generated by analyzing the control flow graph, and those associated with the assignment statements are generated by enumerating all the scalar elements accessed by the assignment statement.

IV. CREATING MODIFIED/EXTENDED FORTRAN PROGRAMS

This section illustrates how the modifications/extensions mentioned in the previous section can be incorporated in Fortran programs. A small program consisting of 11 Fortran statements is shown in Appendix A. The extended/modified version of the same program is shown in Appendix B. These two programs will serve as an example to show the required modifications/extensions. These extensions/modifications can be placed in three broad categories, namely, the declaration and initialization of shadow variables, addition of tracking statements (associated with assignment statements) to update the shadow variables and the histogram for parallelism, and addition of tracking statements (associated with conditional branch and loop control statements) to update the CVAR variables.

Declaration and initialization of shadow variables: The names of shadow variables are obtained by prefixing the variable names with "$". Thus, the shadow for $A(I)$ is $$A(I)$. All shadow variables are declared implicitly as integers (line 1). However, the shadow variables for arrays have to be declared explicitly, and this is done at the beginning of the program (line 3). Next, all shadow variables are initialized to 1 (lines 4–6), since it is assumed that the initial values of all variables are available at time ($t = 1$). DO loops are inserted to initialize the shadows of arrays (lines 7–8). The variables in COMMON blocks are initialized in a separate subroutine created specifically for this purpose, and called at the beginning of the main program.

Updating the shadow variables and the histogram for parallelism: Line 25 in Appendix B illustrates how shadows are updated. To execute statement 6, the array element $A(N - I)$ is required. However, to compute the index of the array element, we need the variables I and N. Variable I is also needed to index the location where the result computed by statement 6 is stored. The variables $A(N - I)$, N, and I are available at ($t = $A(N - I)$), ($t = N), and ($t = I), respectively. Furthermore, CVAR(6), set by the tracking statements of statement 5 (in line 20), indicates the earliest time at which it is known that statement 6 must execute. Therefore, the maximum of CVAR(6), $A(N - I)$, N, and

31

I indicates the earliest time at which statement 6 can execute. The time at which the new value for $A(I)$ is available is obtained by adding 1 (the time to compute statement 6) to the time at which execution of statement 6 is initiated. The shadow of $A(I)$, which is $\$A(I)$, is updated to reflect this time.

Every time a new value is assigned to some variable, in addition to updating the shadow of that variable, a subroutine is called (subroutine $MK1\$$ in this example) to update the histogram for parallelism (lines 17, 26, and 30). This histogram is initialized at the beginning of the program by the subroutine $MKINIT$ (line 13). At the termination of the program, this histogram is printed out by the subroutine PRINT\$ (line 38).

Modifying the CVAR array: It is assumed that the main program is started at time step 1. Therefore, on entry to the main program, the CVAR values of all statements that are guaranteed to execute on invocation of the main program are initialized to 1 as shown in lines 9–12 of Appendix B. The CVAR values of statements that are enclosed within loops or conditional sections, and thus may be executed repeatedly or not at all, are set within the program itself as discussed next.

Lines 19–24 illustrate how a conditional branch introduced by a "logical IF" statement (statement 5 in Appendix A) is handled. Statement 8 is executed if and only if the branch is taken. Statements 6 and 7 are executed if and only if the branch is not taken. All other statements reachable from the conditional branch statement are executed irrespective of whether the branch is taken or not. Therefore, if the branch is taken, then before jumping to the target of the branch (statement 8) the CVAR variable for statement 8 is updated. If the branch is not taken, then before executing statements 6 and 7, their CVAR variables are updated.

DO loops are viewed (thought of) as two assignment statements and a logical branch statement. One assignment statement is needed to initialize the loop induction variable, and the other is needed to update and check the loop induction variable in each loop iteration. Lines 14 and 32 in Appendix B are the tracking statements required to update the shadow of the loop induction variable on each update of the loop induction variable. Lines 34–36 update the CVAR variables of those statements within the loop whose execution is guaranteed in each new iteration.

When there are multiple exits from a loop, the CVAR variables of statements, which can be reached from the normal exit (the loop closing statement) but not from all loop exits, are updated immediately after the loop closing statement.

The loop statements are treated differently in programs written in Fortran-66, and in Fortran-77. The fact that zero trip DO loops are not allowed in the former version is taken into account. The method of handling arithmetic IF statements and computed and assigned "go to" statements is similar to that of handling logical IF statements. The essential change is in the number of branch targets allowed.

The execution of a subroutine or a function subprogram is started as soon as it is known that the subroutine call statement or the statement invoking a user-defined function (say statement x) must execute, i.e., at the time indicated by CVAR(x).

(It is assumed that system-defined functions return their results in unit time.) On entering a subroutine or a function subprogram, the CVAR values of all statements that are guaranteed to execute on entry are initialized to CVAR(x). The CVAR values of the remaining statements (those enclosed by "DO" loops or conditional sections) are set within the called routine in the same manner as for the main program. The value of CVAR(x) is passed from the calling routine to the called routine as a parameter. The interprocedural true data dependencies are observed by adding to the parameter list the shadows of all the values to be exchanged between the calling and the called routine. Thus, the called routine can infer when it can start executing and when the values of its global variables and formal parameters become available.

As a result of the above mentioned modifications, the number of statements in the Fortran program increases by a factor of 4–5. The storage required to hold shadow variables, control variables, and other information required to track the execution of the program is between 1 and 1.5 times the data storage required for the original program. The execution time of the program increases by a factor of roughly 10.

V. EXPERIMENTS

Some measurements taken with the help of COMET are discussed in this section. Different aspects of parallelism were observed in four large Fortran programs. The programs analyzed are SIMPLE, VA3D, Discrete Ordinate Transport (SNEX), and Particle-in-Cell (WAVE). In this section, the parallelism in a program is expressed as a function of time, over the interval between the start time and the finish time of a program (when executed on the ideal parallel machine). For a given time instance in this interval, parallelism is equal to the number of Fortran statements that would be executing concurrently on the ideal parallel machine at that time instance.[1] Average parallelism, obtained by dividing the total number of Fortran statements executed in the program by the execution time of the program on the ideal parallel machine, is also reported. This number can also be interpreted as the speedup of the ideal parallel machine over an ideal sequential machine which executes a Fortran program sequentially at the rate of one statement per cycle.

The SIMPLE code models the hydrodynamic and thermal behavior of plasma. The bulk of the computation in this code is performed in the single outermost loop. Each iteration of this loop calculates the changes in the hydrodynamic and thermal properties of the plasma over an incremental time step. Each iteration of this loop consists of two main parts, the hydrodynamic calculations and the heat-conduction calculations. The hydrodynamic equations are solved using an explicit method and the heat-conduction equations are solved using an alternating direction implicit (ADI) method. The mesh size is 32 × 32.

The parallelism observed in a single iteration of the

---

[1] The number of points on each parallelism plot is under 3000 (limitations of the plotting software). For programs whose execution time exceeds 3000 cycles, the execution time is divided into subintervals (less than 3000). The average number of statements executed per cycle within a subinterval is plotted for each subinterval.

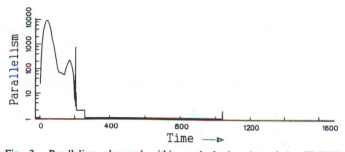

Fig. 3. Parallelism observed within a single iteration of the SIMPLE program.

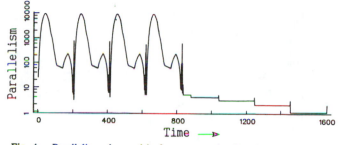

Fig. 4. Parallelism observed in four consecutive iterations of SIMPLE.

outermost loop of the SIMPLE program (one pass through the hydro and conduction phases) is illustrated in Fig. 3. The activity outside the loop has been filtered out from the measurements so that the one-time computation performed for setting up the program (noniterative part) is not reflected in the measurements. This was accomplished by initializing the PROFILE array just before the loop was entered, changing the loop test so that precisely one iteration was performed, and printing the contents of the PROFILE array immediately after the loop exit. The parallelism in four consecutive iterations of SIMPLE was measured in a similar way and the results are shown in Fig. 4.

It can be readily seen that the bulk of the computation in each iteration is performed in the first 200 time steps of the iteration, and substantial parallelism is present in this phase. The average parallelism observed in these 200 cycles is about 2350 Fortran statements/cycle. However, a small amount of computation (roughly 800 statements) is absolutely sequential. This part of the program computes the total internal energy by summing up the internal energy of each grid element. A single variable is used to accumulate the partial sums and hence the sequential behavior (32 × 32 numbers are added in sequence). Thus, each iteration spans a little over 1000 time steps. The average parallelism over the entire iteration is about 475 Fortran statements/iteration.

One can readily see in Fig. 4 that most of the activities of two consecutive iterations of the SIMPLE program do not overlap in time. Still, the second iteration starts much before the first iteration is over, because the second iteration does not depend on the total internal energy computed in the first iteration. In other words, the sequential part of the computation within an iteration of the outer loop can be overlapped with the sequential computations of preceding and subsequent iterations, but the parallel computation within one iteration can not be overlapped with the parallel computation of other iterations.

The breakup of parallelism between the hydro and conduction phases within a single iteration is shown separately in Fig. 5. A substantial part of the computation performed in the conduction phase cannot be overlapped with the hydro phase because the former uses the velocities, pressures, and densities computed in the latter. Furthermore, the conduction phase has less parallelism than the hydro phase perhaps because the former uses an implicit technique for solving the PDE's while the latter uses an explicit method.

The VA3D program solves the 3-D Euler equations, which are thin layer approximations to the compressible Navier-

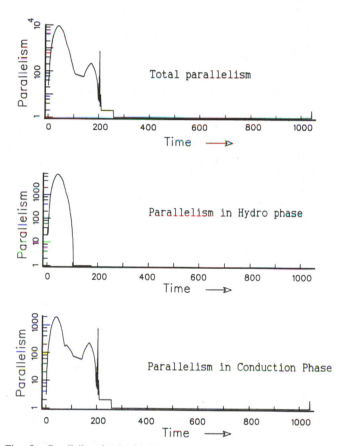

Fig. 5. Parallelism in the hydrodynamic and heat-conduction phases of SIMPLE, within one iteration.

Stokes equations, on a small three-dimensional grid of size 30 × 21 × 30. Viscous effects are simulated only along one direction.

The parallelism observed in a single iteration of the outermost loop of the VA3D program is shown in Fig. 6. The average parallelism in this case is about 2200 Fortran statements/cycle. How this parallelism overlaps with the parallelism in the subsequent iterations of this loop can be observed in Fig. 7, which shows the parallelism in three consecutive iterations of the loop. It can be seen in Fig. 7 that the work done in the outermost loop can be divided in two parts. The computation belonging to first part can be overlapped with the same computation from other iterations of this loop while the computation belonging to the second part cannot be overlapped with the same computation in preceding iterations of this loop. However, substantial parallelism exists within each iteration of the loop.

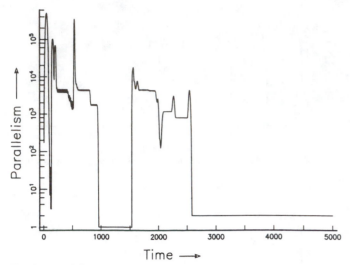

Fig. 6. Parallelism observed in a single iteration of the outermost loop of the VA3D program.

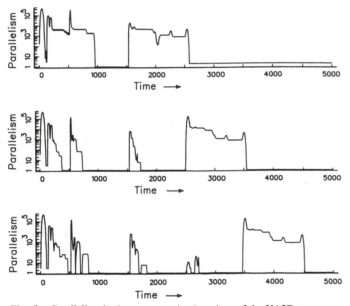

Fig. 7. Parallelism in three consecutive iterations of the VA3D program.

The program SNEX provides numerical solution for the monoenergetic discrete ordinate equations in hydrodynamics, plasma, radiative transfer, and neutral and charged particle transport applications. It generates the exact solution for the linear transport equations in one-dimensional plane, cylindrical, and spherical geometries. The overall parallelism observed in this application is shown in Fig. 8. The average parallelism exhibited by this program is about 3500 Fortran statements/cycle.

Finally, WAVE is a two-dimensional particle-in-cell code used primarily to study the interaction of intense laser lights with plasmas. It solves the Maxwell equations and particle equations of motion on a Lagrangian mesh. The overall parallelism observed in this program is shown in Fig. 9, and the average parallelism is about 1180 Fortran statements/cycle.

In almost all measurements, there is an initial burst of very high level of parallelism. This happens because the control structures of the computation, especially the loops, unfold rather rapidly while the computation within the loops does not proceed as rapidly because of data dependencies. The initial burst of parallelism is created by this unfolding of the loops.

VI. INCORPORATING THE EFFECT OF WRITE AFTER READ/WRITE SYNCHRONIZATIONS

In the preceding discussion, the write after read and write after write synchronizations were ignored. Howevei, in storage-oriented architectures and in machines with restricted storage, these synchronizations are necessary. The parallelism present in the programs (or the loss of parallelism incurred) when these synchronizations are observed can be measured by modifying COMET in the following manner.

Two shadow variables are now associated with each program variable instead of one, the read shadow and the write shadow. The read shadow keeps track of the time at which the associated variable was last read after being written. The write shadow keeps track of the time at which the associated variable was last written. The tracking statements associated with each assignment statement of the original program are changed and new tracking statements are added as shown in Fig. 10. In this figure AW, BW, CW and AR, BR, CR are the write and read shadow variables for A, B, and C.

The earliest time at which a statement S can be executed is found by taking the earliest time at which 1) the variable being updated by S has been written and read by all statements that precede X in the sequential execution of the program and access this variable, 2) S can be executed on the ideal parallel machine. The earliest time at which both these requirements are met is found by taking the maximum of CVAR(S), the write shadows of all the variables being accessed by S (both on the left- and right-hand sides of S), and the read shadow of the scalar variable or array element being updated.

The read shadow of each variable accessed by S for obtaining an input value is modified by the tracking statements associated with S to reflect the latest time at which this value is accessed by S or its sequential predecessor. It is assumed that an input value required by S must be available until the execution of S completes. Therefore, the latest time at which S and its predecessors read this input value can be obtained by taking the maximum of the time at which S reads the input value and the latest time at which the predecessors of S read this input value.

For the SIMPLE program, the loss in parallelism incurred on incorporating the effect of write after read/write synchronizations is shown in Fig. 11. These synchronizations were observed for all variables except the loop control variables (the variables occurring in the DO statements). The consecutive iterations of the outer loop in the program start with a stride of roughly 200 cycles when the write after read/write synchronizations are ignored. The stride increases to roughly 5000 cycles when the above mentioned synchronizations are incorporated. However, it should be recalled that an old and unmodified Fortran program is being monitored. By using compiler transformations such as scalar/array renaming/ expansion, and clever storage management policies, most of the parallelism lost because of write after read/write synchronizations can be recovered.

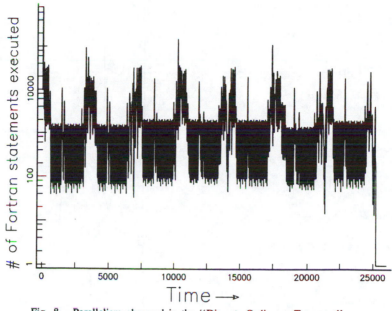

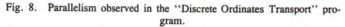

Fig. 8. Parallelism observed in the "Discrete Ordinates Transport" program.

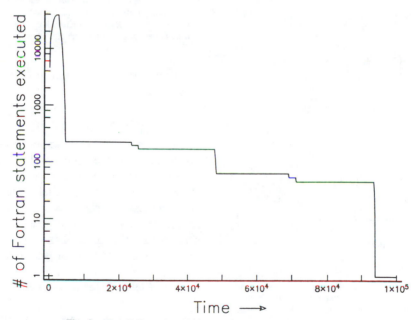

Fig. 9. Parallelism observed in the "Particle-in-Cell" program.

VII. RELAXING THE ASSUMPTION ABOUT *A PRIORI* KNOWLEDGE OF DATA FLOW

As discussed in Section II, by assuming the complete knowledge of the data flow between statements, the ideal parallel machine can initiate the execution of a statement much earlier than a realistic machine. Hence, the reported parallelism in this paper is an upper bound or an optimistic estimate of the parallelism exploitable by any realistic machine. This inaccuracy can be reduced to a certain extent by analyzing the data dependencies in the program [5], and using the information to delay the execution of statements when necessary. This section briefly discusses an approach to avoid the assumption that the ideal parallel machine has complete knowledge of the data flow between statements, and the limitations of this approach.

The true data dependencies can be used to enumerate, for each statement A in the program, the list $L(A)$ of all predecessor statements which can possibly provide an input value for A. This list can be used to determine the set $S(A)$ of statements such that the result of executing any statement in the set either provides the last input value required by A or determines that no other statements from $L(A)$ will execute before A. Then the execution of A in a parallel machine can be initiated as soon as some statement in $S(A)$ is executed.

The difficulty with this approach is that the true data dependencies generated at compile time are usually conserva-

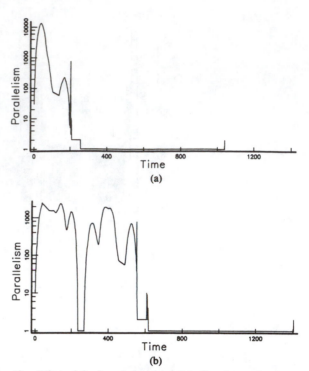

Fig. 12. Effect of the knowledge about data flow between statements on observed parallelism. (a) All knowledge about data flow between statements known *a priori*. (b) Knowledge about data flow generated at compile time (superset of actual data flow that occurs during execution).

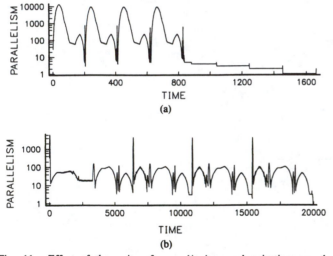

Fig. 10. Modifications required in COMET to incorporate the costs of write after read/write synchronizations.

$AW = Compute Time +
    MAX(CVARS(i), $BW, $CW, $AW, $AR)

$BR = MAX($BR, $AW)

$CR = MAX($CR, $AW)

Fig. 11. Effect of the write after read/write synchronizations on the parallelism observed in the SIMPLE program. (Four consecutive iterations of the outermost loop monitored). (a) Write after read/write synchronization ignored. (b) Write after read/write synchronization incorporated.

tive (superset of the arcs that indicate the actual flow of data during the execution of the program), because techniques for interprocedural data flow analysis, analysis of complex subscript expressions, etc., have not been perfected yet. Hence, the parallelism observed in the program, when the above mentioned approach is used to initiate the execution of statements, will be a conservative estimate of the total parallelism available.

The parallelism observed in the SIMPLE program on using the approach discussed in this section is shown in Fig. 12(b). For comparison, the parallelism observed when the complete knowledge of data flow between statements is known *a priori* is shown in Fig. 12(a). It should be remembered that the algorithms used for analyzing data dependencies in this experiment are perhaps less sophisticated than those available with the leading vendors of vectorizing compilers.

VIII. SUGGESTIONS FOR FURTHER RESEARCH

The main objectives of implementing the COMET software are to measure the total parallelism present in the Fortran programs, characterize this parallelism, and to evaluate the efficiency of various parallel machine organizations. While the paper has focused primarily on measurement of the total parallelism, this section summarizes the efforts underway to characterize the parallelism, to evaluate various machine organizations, and to improve COMET's usability and applicability.

Since COMET actually executes a program and monitors the flow of operands between various Fortran statements, it can be used to detect storage/network bottlenecks and processor idling in various machine organizations with a finite number of processors and specific memory organization. If the algorithms which assign computation to processors and values/variables to memory modules are specified, the number of operations performed on each processor, the number of memory accesses to each storage module, and the number of operands moved on each network link can be counted to determine whether a processor, memory module, or a memory link is overutilized. COMET can also serve as a testbed for evaluating these resource management algorithms and various scheduling algorithms in the finite processor case.

The characterization of parallelism, which was handled at a cursory level in this paper, is perhaps the most deserving topic for further investigation. COMET can be used to determine whether the parallelism present in programs is fine grained or coarse grained or both. Measurements of parallelism at the level of operations, statements, and subroutines have been obtained with the help of COMET software. However, further refinements and measurements are required before meaningful characterization of parallelism can be provided.

The characterizations of parallelism that have a bearing on the resource management algorithms for parallel machines are of special interest. Given a partitioning of the program into tasks, the parallelism exhibited by each task and how the parallel execution of two tasks overlaps in time can be observed. This could lead to more effective partitioning of the program. Facilities are provided in COMET to allow dynamic specification of tasks (at run time).

Another useful characterization of parallelism is its dependence on the size of the input problem and internal data structures. For a given problem, such dependence could be observed by simply running the problem repeatedly for different input data (grid size or convergence limit, etc.).

COMET generates a tremendous amount of information during the execution of a large program, which in its totality is definitely not fit for human consumption. During the development of COMET and its subsequent use in measuring parallelism, the need for user-friendly editing facilities to digest the raw information and reproduce it in a more palatable form became quite obvious. These editing facilities are needed for taking a detailed look at the parallelism observed in some part of a big program, or that observed in the entire program during a small time window.

COMET is geared to analyze source programs written in Fortran. This choice was made because most major scientific/ engineering applications are written in this language. One can easily reimplement COMET to accept another source language. This would require the rewriting of the scanner which creates the program graph and symbol table from the input program, and the output routines which generate the modified/ extended program. Such a reimplementation would perhaps be substantially easier than the original effort because most languages are better structured than Fortran.

IX. SUMMARY AND CONCLUSIONS

In this paper, we described a software tool for measuring parallelism in large programs, and reported some measurements obtained with the help of this tool. An important feature of this tool is its ability to accept ordinary Fortran programs (without any modifications) as its inputs. Thus, parallelism can be measured over many large programs to get a reasonably accurate idea about the presence of parallelism in scientific engineering applications.

While only four programs were analyzed for parallelism, each of these programs is a complete and fairly large application. A few hundred million Fortran statements are executed in one run of each application (except SIMPLE, where the number is about 500 000). Under ideal conditions (the environment of the ideal parallel machine), the average parallelism observed in the chosen programs is in the range of 500–3500 Fortran statements executing concurrently in each clock cycle.

An important conclusion to be drawn from this paper is that

parallelism is fairly uneven in most applications, i.e., there are phases during the execution of the program when the instant parallelism is several orders of magnitude higher than the average parallelism, and then there are times when the instant parallelism is several orders of magnitude lower than the average.

APPENDIX A

The program to be analyzed:

```
        IMPLICIT LOGICAL (F)          ⟨Statement  1⟩
        INTEGER A(10), I, N           ⟨           2⟩
        DO 2 I = 1, N                 ⟨           3⟩
        FV1 = I.LE.N/2                ⟨           4⟩
        IF (FV1) GO TO 1              ⟨           5⟩
        A(I) = A(N − I)               ⟨           6⟩
        GO TO 2                       ⟨           7⟩
1       A(I) = 1                      ⟨           8⟩
2       CONTINUE                      ⟨           9⟩
        STOP                          ⟨          10⟩
        END                           ⟨          11⟩
```

APPENDIX B

Extended/modified version of the program in Appendix A:

```
        IMPLICIT INTEGER ($), LOGICAL (F)  ⟨Line  1⟩
        INTEGER CVAR(1000)                 ⟨      2⟩
        INTEGER $A(10), A(10), I, N        ⟨      3⟩
        $I = 1                             ⟨      4⟩
        $N = 1                             ⟨      5⟩
        $FV1 = 1                           ⟨      6⟩
        DO 9997 IV1$ = 1, 10               ⟨      7⟩
9997    $A(IV1$) = 1                       ⟨      8⟩
        DO 9996 IV1$ = 3, 5                ⟨      9⟩
9996     CVAR(IV1$) = 1                    ⟨     10⟩
        DO 9995 IV1# = 9, 10               ⟨     11⟩
9995     CVAR(IV1$) = 1                    ⟨     12⟩
        CALL MKINIT                        ⟨     13⟩
        $I = 1 + MAX0(CVAR(3),$N)          ⟨     14⟩
        DO 9998 I = 1, N                   ⟨     15⟩
        $FV1 = 1 + MAX0(CVAR(3),$N,$I)     ⟨     16⟩
        CALL MK1$ (4, $FV1)                ⟨     17⟩
        FV1 = I.L.E.N/2                    ⟨     18⟩
        IF (FV1) GO TO 9994                ⟨     19⟩
        DO 9993 IV1$ = 6, 7                ⟨     20⟩
9993     CVAR(IV1$) = $FV1                 ⟨     21⟩
        GO TO 9999                         ⟨     22⟩
9994    CVAR(8) = $FV1                     ⟨     23⟩
        GO TO 1                            ⟨     24⟩
9999    $A(I) = 1 +
          MAX0(CVAR(6),$N,$A(N − I),$I)    ⟨     25⟩
        CALL MK1$ (6, $A(I))               ⟨     26⟩
        A(I) = A(N − I)                    ⟨     27⟩
        GO TO 2                            ⟨     28⟩
1       $A(I) = 1 + MAX0(CVAR(8),$I)       ⟨     29⟩
        CALL MK1$ (8, $A(I))               ⟨     30⟩
        A(I) = 1                           ⟨     31⟩
2       $I = 1 + MAX0(CVAR(9),$N,$I)       ⟨     32⟩
        CALL MK1$ (9, $I)                  ⟨     33⟩
```

```
       DO 9992 IV1$ = 3, 5                    〈    34〉
9992     CVAR(IV1$) = $I                       〈    35〉
         CVAR(8) = $I                          〈    36〉
9998 CONTINUE                                  〈    37〉
     CALL PRINT$                               〈    38〉
     STOP                                      〈    39〉
     END                                       〈    40〉
```

ACKNOWLEDGMENT

I would like to thank K. Ekanadham and R. Cytron for their valuable assistance and helpful suggestions. The algorithm used to find which control variables are modified by a conditional statement was implemented by K. Ekanadham.

REFERENCES

[1] J. Beetem, M. Denneau, and D. Weingarten, "The GF11 supercomputer," in *Proc. 12th Annu. Symp. Comput. Architecture,* June 1985, pp. 108–113.

[2] W. Crowther *et al.*, "Performance measurements on a 128-node butterfly parallel processor," in *Proc. 1985 Conf. Parallel Processing,* Aug. 1985, pp. 531–540.

[3] J. R. Gurd, C. C. Kirkham, and I. Watson, "The Manchester prototype dataflow computer," *Commun. ACM,* vol. 28, pp. 34–52, Jan. 1985.

[4] D. J. Kuck *et al.*, "Measurements of parallelism in ordinary FORTRAN programs," *Computer,* vol. 7, pp. 37–46, Jan. 1974.

[5] D. A. Padua, D. J. Kuck, and D. H. Lawrie, "High-speed multiprocessors and compilation techniques," *IEEE Trans. Comput.,* vol. C-29, pp. 763–776, Sept. 1980.

[6] G. F. Pfister *et al.*, "The IBM research parallel processor prototype (RP3): Introduction and architecture," in *Proc. 1985 Conf. Parallel Processing,* Aug. 1985, pp. 764–771.

[7] C. L. Seitz, "The cosmic cube," *Commun. ACM,* vol. 28, pp. 22–33, Jan. 1985.

[8] K. So, F. Darema-Rogers, D. A. George, V. A. Norten, and G. F. Pfister, "PSIMUL-A system for parallel simulation of the execution of parallel programs," IBM Res. Rep. RC-11674 (52414), Jan. 86.

[9] E. Williams and F. Bobrowicz, "Speedup predictions on large scientific parallel programs," in *Proc. 1985 Conf. Parallel Processing,* Aug. 1985, pp. 541–543.

Manoj Kumar (S'79–M'83) received the B. Tech. degree from the Indian Institute of Technology, Kanpur, in 1979, and the M.S. and Ph.D. degrees in electrical engineering from Rice University, Houston, TX, in 1981 and 1984, respectively.

Since 1983 he has been a Research Staff Member at the IBM T. J. Watson Research Center, Yorktown Heights, NY. His research interests include computer architecture, parallel processing systems, and interconnection networks for parallel processing systems.

Measuring the Parallelism Available for Very Long Instruction Word Architectures

ALEXANDRU NICOLAU AND JOSEPH A. FISHER

Abstract —Long instruction word architectures, such as attached scientific processors and horizontally microcoded CPU's, are a popular means of obtaining code speedup via fine-grained parallelism. The falling cost of hardware holds out the hope of using these architectures for much more parallelism. But this hope has been diminished by experiments measuring how much parallelism is available in the code to start with. These experiments implied that even if we had infinite hardware, long instruction word architectures could not provide a speedup of more than a factor of 2 or 3 on real programs.

These experiments measured only the parallelism within basic blocks. Given the machines that prompted them, it made no sense to measure anything else. Now it does. A recently developed code compaction technique, called trace scheduling [9], could exploit parallelism in operations even hundreds of blocks apart. Does such parallelism exist?

In this paper we show that it does. We did analogous experiments, but we disregarded basic block boundaries. We found huge amounts of parallelism available. Our measurements were made on standard Fortran programs in common use. The actual programs tested averaged about a factor of 90 parallelism. It ranged from about a factor of 4 to virtually unlimited amounts, restricted only by the size of the data.

An important question is how much of this parallelism can actually be found and used by a real code generator. In the experiments, an oracle is used to resolve dynamic questions at compile time. It tells us which way jumps went and whether indirect references are to the same or different locations. Trace scheduling attempts to get the effect of the oracle at compile time with static index analysis and dynamic estimates of jump probabilities. We argue that most scientific code is so static that the oracle is fairly realistic. A real trace-scheduling code generator [7] might very well be able to find and use much of this parallelism.

Index Terms —Memory antialiasing, microcode, multiprocessors, parallelism, trace scheduling, VLIW (very long instruction word) architectures.

I. INTRODUCTION

IN this paper we describe experiments we have done to empirically measure the maximum parallelism available to *very long instruction word* (VLIW) architectures. The most familiar examples of VLIW architectures are *horizontally microcoded CPU's* and some very popular specialized *scientific processors*, such as the floating point systems AP-120b and FPS-164.

Very long instruction word architectures take advantage of fine-grained parallelism to speed up execution time.

However, in contrast to vector machines and traditional multiprocessors, no currently available machines use this architecture for great amounts of parallelism. A user in any practical environment is doing well if he obtains a factor of 2 or 3 speedup over sequential execution. Why are these machines not dramatically more parallel? One probable reason is that the popular wisdom has it that a factor of 2 or 3 is all the fine-grained parallelism that is there to exploit. A chief contributor to this belief was a set of experiments done in the early 1970's. They measured the fine-grained parallelism available under the hypothesis that there was *infinite hardware available* to execute whatever parallelism was found. Unfortunately, all they could find was a factor of 2 or 3.

We believe these experiments, done for a somewhat different domain than VLIW architectures, were far too pessimistic. We will explain why shortly. In this paper we report on experiments we have done which we think more directly address this question for VLIW architectures.

A. Very Long Instruction Word Architectures

The defining properties of VLIW architectures are: 1) there is one central control unit issuing a single wide instruction per cycle; 2) each wide instruction consists of many independent operations; 3) each operation requires a small statically predictable number of cycles to execute. Operations may be pipelined.

Restrictions 1) and 3) distinguish these from typical multiprocessor organizations.[1]

Since it is nearly impossible to tightly couple very many highly complex operations, the underlying sequential architecture of a VLIW will invariably be a *reduced instruction set computer* or *RISC* [16]. Thus, the instruction set will typically consist of register to register operations, with memory references being simple loads/stores without complex addressing modes. This will greatly simplify the scheduling part of the compiler.

VLIW machines might have large numbers of identical functional units. When they do, we do not require that they be connected by some regular and concise scheme such as shuffles or cube connections. A tabular description of the somewhat ad hoc interconnections suffices for our purposes.[2] This makes the use of VLIW machines very different from machines with regular interconnection structures and/or complex hardware data structures.

---

[1] VLIW architectures do not fit neatly into many of the taxonomies of parallel processor organization.

[2] We rely heavily on the compiler to schedule data movements and (when feasible) parallel memory fetches as well as operation execution. Thus, the interconnections between the various processing units need not be very regular, as we expect only the compiler (not humans) to have to deal with them.

Reprinted from *IEEE Transactions on Computers*, Vol. C-33, No. 11, November 1984, pages 968-976. Copyright © 1984 by The Institute of Electrical and Electronics Engineers, Inc. All rights reserved.

A VLIW machine, the ELI (enormously long instructions), is being designed and built at Yale University. The machine has instruction words in excess of 1000 bits, and has the ability to take advantage of considerable fine-grained parallelism. A detailed discussion of VLIW architectures and the ELI machine can be found in [9].

1) Why Have these Machines Not Been Built for Massive Parallelism? We believe that the following statements, valid or not, characterize the feelings most architects have about VLIW architecture machines. We feel this has limited the amount of parallelism that has been built into VLIW architectures.

1) Hand coding machines even as wide as those built today is nearly impossible. Hand coding significantly wider machines is out of the question. (By wider, we mean having more instruction level parallelism, thus more instruction word bits.)

2) The machines are very irregular and inelegant. It is nearly impossible to prove anything about them or algorithms for them. This has probably contributed to a lack of academic interest in them, and has led to a general lack of knowledge about them.

3) Code generation is impossible or very difficult, inhibiting the use of reasonable high level languages.

4) Experiments have indicated a general lack of available parallelism.

We agree fully with reasons 1) and 2). Coding VLIW machines is a horrible task (ask anyone who has tried). And they are not very pretty to look at.

But we disagree with points 3) and 4). We attempt to demonstrate in this paper that the earlier experimental measures should not be taken as upper bounds on available parallelism. And we feel that *trace scheduling* [8], a recently developed global code generation technique, has allowed an effective VLIW machine compiler to be built. Code generation for VLIW machines differs from the ordinary in that it does large scale code rearrangement in order to pack operations efficiently into wide instructions. If this process, called *compaction,* is not done, the code will usually be intolerably slow.

B. What Were the Earlier Experiments?

Tjaden and Flynn [18] and Foster and Riseman [10] did the following.

• They took actual machine language execution streams from normal programs running on various IBM/CDC machines.

• They broke the streams up into basic blocks.

• They asked: Given infinite hardware (they were thinking in terms of an infinite number of CDC/IBM functional units), how much faster would the programs have been executed? We may assume that instruction issue is instantaneous.

When one considers the hardware that inspired these experiments, this is quite a reasonable question to ask. These machines use run time hardware scheduling, assigning operations to functional units, to take advantage of fine-grained parallelism. The hardware really cannot know what to do in the face of a conditional jump. It has to play safe, not being able to do a data flow analysis of the program, and it has to

wait until the conditional jump settles before writing variables with possibly incorrect values.

Various machines, including the IBM STRETCH, 360/95, and the Manchester MU-5 [14], attempted some amount of calculation past jumps, but they did not do anything irreversible until the jump settled. This seemed a limited benefit.

But what would one do if one *really* had infinite hardware? One would have been running the same program on two identical machines, and whenever a conditional jump came along, one would let the two of them take different paths. One would then just throw out the wrong one when the test settled. In a companion to one of the above experiments, that is exactly what was measured [17]. Although they found extensive speedups might be available, they dismissed the exploitation of parallelism by bypassing conditional jumps as impractical. They note that obtaining even a tenfold speedup mandated that one would have to start with $o(2^{16})$ machines, a rather unacceptable hardware cost.

C. So What Was Wrong with these Experiments?

There are several problems with the above experiments. To start with, they were all heavily biased towards hardware oriented schemes of identifying parallelism. As such, they spent a great deal of effort in adapting their model to closely emulate the idiosyncrasies of the particular hardware which motivated their experiments, reducing the generality of the results as measures of parallelism available in ordinary programs. Even more important, this approach effectively limited the measured parallelism to basic blocks. Dynamically overcoming basic block boundaries on a large scale was deemed completely unrealistic and they did not foresee any possibility of bypassing large numbers of conditional jumps *statically* at compile time. Given the unavailability of good global compaction methods at the time, their attitude was quite natural.

The domain from which the sample programs were taken further reduces the utility of these results for our purposes. All experiments dealt with seemingly randomly chosen programs from several applications areas. Most of them appear to be heavily data-driven (e.g., compiler, sorter, string matching), some with complex flow of control. Such algorithms are not likely to be amenable to effective compile time global compaction techniques, and thus are of limited interest from our perspective. Furthermore the data-dependent nature of control flow in these programs negatively affects the practicality of the results.

D. Other Previous Experiments

Many suggestions for improved parallelism location have been reported in the literature, often accompanied by empirical measures of effectiveness. Important work done by D. Kuck's group at the University of Illinois [3], [5], [11], has measured the actual parallelism obtainaorable by such algorithm transformations as recurrence solution and tree height reduction. In particular, in [12] it is shown that using the compilation techniques developed as part of the Parafrase project at the University of Illinois, 16 or more processors could be kept busy. However these measurements involve efficiency and practical considerations which are quite different from the *bounds* we are discussing here.

E. Trace Scheduling

People who hand code similar architectures would not consider restricting themselves to basic blocks while doing code rearrangements. It is commonly possible to move an operation up past a jump, making one branch shorter at the expense of the other. Similarly, operations may move down into one or both branches. These operations may be done "for free" in unused fields of the target instruction.

Trace scheduling is a technique for replacing the block-by-block compaction of code with the compaction of long streams of code, possibly thousands of instructions long. The major characteristics of trace scheduling are the following.

1) Dynamic information is used at compile time to select streams with the highest probability of execution.

2) Pre- and postprocessing allows the entire stream to be compacted as if it were one basic block. *This is the key feature of trace scheduling. By using good scheduling heuristics on long streams, large quantities of far reaching parallelism may be efficiently identified.* Thus, we avoid a case by case search for code motions, which would be far too expensive on such large streams and would be unlikely to yield much parallelism.

3) Preprocessing is done to prevent the scheduler from making absolutely illegal between block code motions, i.e., those that would clobber variables which are live off the trace. The constraints on code motion are encoded into the data precedence graph via edges from the conditional jump off the trace to any later operation that could clobber the variable. This makes those constraints look just like the usual data precedence constraints that a basic block scheduler would have to cope with. The scheduler is then permitted to behave just as if it were scheduling a single basic block. It pays no attention whatsoever to block boundaries.

4) After scheduling has been completed on a stream, the scheduler has made many code motions which, while potentially legal, will not correctly preserve jumps from (or rejoins to) the stream to the outside world. To make these code motions actually legal, a postprocessor inserts new code at the stream exits and entrances to recover the correct machine state outside the stream. Without this ability, available parallelism would be unduly constrained by the need to preserve jump boundaries.

5) The most frequently executed code beyond the stream, including the new state recovery code, is then compacted as well, possibly producing more state recovery code.

Eventually, this process works its way out to code with little probability of execution, and more mundane compaction methods are used which do not cause the possible code growth of the state recovery operations.

Trace scheduling will not do well on code which is dominated by highly unpredictable jumps (e.g., parsing loops or tree searches). Experience with scientific code (our target domain) shows, however, that one can make a good guess at the direction of most jumps in this type of code. These guesses may be derived using a tool to run debugged code on samples of data, or may be programmer supplied.

Inner loops of code present a special opportunity for code compaction. *Software pipelining* is a technique used by hand coders to increase parallelism. It involves rewriting a loop so that pieces of several consecutive original iterations are done simultaneously in each new iteration. Although interesting work has been done towards automating software pipelining [11], [13], the techniques do not seem to lend themselves well to more complex types of loops. Trace scheduling, on the other hand, may be trivially extended to do software pipelining on any loop. It is sufficient to simply unroll the loop for many iterations. This will yield a stream, which may be compacted as above. All the intermediate loop tests will now be conditional jumps in the stream; they require no special handling beyond that always given conditional jumps. While that may be somewhat less space efficient than is theoretically necessary, it can handle arbitrary flow of control within each old loop iteration, a major advantage in attempting to compile real code. The extra space is not of major importance here. A detailed description of trace scheduling can be found in [8], while an overall discussion of its actual implementation as part of the Bulldog compiler (a compiler for VLIW machines developed at Yale University) is given in [7].

F. Using an Oracle to Measure Available Parallelism

Given trace scheduling, it is clear that the restriction to basic blocks is not realistic. How may we obtain a more reasonable empirical upper bound on what we could do with very cheap hardware? A reasonable attack is to assume that an *oracle* is present to guide us at every conditional jump, telling us which way the jump will go each reference, and resolving all ambiguous memory references.

Loosely speaking, the parallelism found by the oracle is equivalent to the execution of an idealized data flow machine (assuming infinite resources, a language which resolves ambiguities, and no resources/synchronization induced constraints on parallelism). In fact, trace scheduling attempts to achieve *at compile time* an effect similar to that of data-flow processors [2], [6].

1) True Data Precedence and the Oracle: Another limitation of the earlier experiments of Tjaden and Riseman is that they used register assignments to determine data precedence. This is unrealistic since these assignments are done by a compiler to sequential streams, and impose artificial data-precedence relations.[3] Data precedence should be based upon *actual uses of values*. To handle this, the *single identity principle,* used in many parallel processing applications, should be followed. It mandates that even though a programmer may have reused a variable name (programmers do that for clarity and for storage allocation), we give the new use of the variable a new name if the two definitions never reach any common use.

Arrays present very special data-precedence considerations. A topic of general interest in parallel processing is the disambiguation of indirect memory references [4].[4] For example, in the loop

---

[3]Register allocation techniques for trace scheduling compilers is a subject of current research.

[4]This is a problem only when scheduling at compile time. At runtime no ambiguous references can exist.

```
    for I := 2 to N do
        A(I) := A(I − 1) + tot;
        A(I + 2) := A(I + 1) + tot;
        tot := tot + B(I)
    end
```

we would need to know that $A(I)$, $A(I − 1)$, $A(I + 1)$, and $A(I + 2)$ were different from each other to have proper code motion freedom. A hand coder would not think twice about permuting the first two lines. More sophisticated memory disambiguation involves an analysis of the possible range of a variable's values, and the solution of diophantine equations. The situation is made more complex in the presence of conditional jumps. Such a disambiguator has been implemented at Yale as part of the Bulldog compiler.

Since we are finding an empirical upper bound on available parallelism, we also ask our oracle to resolve all indirect references. That means that code which chases down pointers, say, would have a lot of parallelism exposed that we would never be able to find in any practical environment. But, once again, the static nature of the scientific code we are considering makes this not such an unrealistic assumption. In any event, it is an upper bound on available parallelism that we are seeking here.

While we ask our oracle to overcome many of the limitations to parallelism, the obstacle that we do not eliminate is that of data precedence. We are forced to wait until values have been calculated before we use such values. Naturally, we could again ask our oracle for the value of all computed variables, but that would be much less realistic than the tasks we have asked the oracle to do so far. That would also trivialize our results since we could just ask for all output variables at the outset, and do all our computation in one step!

II. THE DESIGN OF THE EXPERIMENT

In the process of designing our experiment several decisions had to be made.

• We needed to choose a *language level* at which the parallelism would be found.

• *Sample programs* within which to find parallelism had to be chosen.

• We had to devise an *oracle* that would eliminate the inhibition of parallelism due to conditional jumps and ambiguous memory references.

A. Experimental Language Level

For the purpose of our experiment we have dealt with programs represented in a language we call N-ADDRESS CODE or NADDR. NADDR is being used as the intermediate language for several code compaction projects at Yale University, and may be compiled from several high level languages. Similar to the 3-address codes used as compiler intermediate languages [1], NADDR is at the right level for this type of experimentation. A higher level language would not have presented enough granularity for our purposes. A specific assembly language would have burdened the experiment with unnecessary detail and might have biased our results by losing some of the parallelism in the binding to machine constructs.

1) NADDR Code: An instruction in NADDR is written as an operator, followed by one or more operands. The meaning and number of the operands are determined by the operator. There are no expressions in NADDR, so in compiling from high level languages, temporaries are introduced to buffer intermediate operands. For example, the Fortran statement $A = B * (C + D)$ would appear as shown in Fig. 1. Fig. 2 shows (a) a sample Fortran program and (b) its equivalent *n*-address version. NADDR contains only one-dimensional arrays, multidimensional arrays being linearized by our translator. Some of the directives in the figure are obscure, and meant for the interpreter's eyes only.

In order to simplify the bookkeeping required by our measurements, we have assumed that each instruction takes exactly one time unit to execute. This assumption avoids the need to deal with specific complex architectures; it's removal would have a minimal effect on our results.

B. The Sample Programs and How They Were Chosen

In our experiment we have focused on numerical analysis applications, although a few other programs have been included for comparison purposes. Numerical applications were selected because they are a logical application of the compaction techniques that suggested this experiment.

• Numerical analysis programs are very CPU intensive and could greatly benefit from any achievable speedup. In real time applications, the speedup may allow the execution of certain programs which would otherwise not be feasible.

• Since good compaction methods are expensive to run, they are most useful in cases where the programs compacted have relatively large life spans. Many numerical analysis programs fall into these categories.

• Numerical analysis programs as a group lend themselves well to global compaction techniques. Conditional transfers of control and pointer chasing are the main inhibitors of parallelism. In this respect, numerical applications do well since the control structures of these programs tend to be relatively simple and the conditional jumps are heavily biased towards one of the possible paths. Most array references are found within loops in which the index is a simple increment or something equally tractable. These may be successfully analyzed for potential parallelism at compile time. In short, numerical code is typically not very data driven.

Another advantage comes with the non-data-driven property of most scientific code. The available parallelism we measured is not greatly affected by the data we happened to choose. Most of these programs will execute nearly the same streams of instructions no matter what the data. Thus, we did not have to fear biasing our results by the use of atypical data.

Table I contains a list of the programs we used. Most of these were chosen as being typical numerical analysis code in everyday use. The only modification made to the original programs was the replacement of I/O statements with reads from and writes to array buffers. This is a standard method for dealing with I/O in parallel applications, removing the need to deal with the intrinsic sequentiality of these operations. In some applications these factors might dominate the running time, but those are not the applications we are interested in.

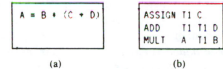

A = B * (C + D)	ASSIGN T1 C ADD T1 T1 D MULT A T1 B
(a)	(b)

Fig. 1. Example of NADDR code representation. (a) Fortran statement. (b) NADDR code representation.

```
(DCL L7 LONG 1 (3 0))
(DCL CON1 LONG 1 (1))
(LASSIGN L7 CON1)
(DCL S-8 INT 1 (0))
(DCL CON5 INT 1 (5))
(IASSIGN S-8 CON5)
(LABEL L5)
(ISUB S-8 S-8 CON1)
(DCL CON0 INT 1 (0))
(DCL T1 INT 1 (0))
(ILT T1 S-8 CON0)
(TRUEGO T1 L6)
(LABEL L1)
(DCL T2 INT 1 (0))
(INT-LONG T2 L7)
(DCL CON-1 INT 1 (-1))
(DCL T3 INT 1 (0))
(IADD T3 T2 CON-1)
(DCL L8 REAL 5 (0 0 0 0 0))
(DCL T4 DOUBLE 1 (0))
(DOUBLE-LONG T4 L7)
(DASSIGN (OFFSET L8 T3) T4)
(LADD L7 L7 CON1)
(GOTO L5)
(LABEL L6)
(DCL L9 REAL 1 (0))
(DCL CON0D0 REAL 1 (0 0))
(DASSIGN L9 CON0D0)
(LASSIGN L7 CON1)
(IASSIGN S-8 CON5)
(LABEL L11)
(ISUB S-8 S-8 CON1)
(DCL T5 INT 1 (0))
(ILT T5 S-8 CON0)
(TRUEGO T5 L12)
(LABEL L10)
(DCL T6 INT 1 (0))
(INT-LONG T6 L7)
(DCL T7 INT 1 (0))
(IADD T7 T6 CON-1)
(DCL T8 DOUBLE 1 (0))
(DADD T8 (OFFSET L8 T7) L9)
(DASSIGN L9 T8)
(LADD L7 L7 CON1)
(GOTO L11)
(LABEL L12)
(LABEL L1)
```

```
Dimension A(5)
DO 10 I = 1,5
10    A[I] = I

SUM = 0

DO 20 I = 1,5
   SUM = SUM/5
STOP
END
```

(a)   (b)

Fig. 2. Sample program. (a) Input Fortran program. (b) NADDR output of the translator.

TABLE I
SAMPLE PROGRAM DESCRIPTIONS

Program Name	Description
RFALS1	Calculates roots of scalar functions using the Regula Falsi method
RFALS2	Calculates roots of scalar functions using the Regula Falsi method, with check
EXPNT	Sample numerical analysis computation. Computes a negative exponent using two methods
GRAM	Stabilized Gram-Schmidt orthogonalization
ODE4	Solves the differential equation Y' = Y on the interval [0, 10], using an implicit two step method
EXTRAP	Evaluates the derivative of a given function at a given point using extrapolation
BISECT	Computes a root of a polynomial using the bisection method
NEWT1	Computes the root of a polynomial using Newton's method
NEWT2	Computes the root of a polynomial using Newton's method (similar to NEWT1, but higher precision)
JACOBI	Solves a system of linear equations using the Jacobi iteration method
FIXPT	Calculates a fixed point approximation for a given function
ROFERR1	Sample numerical analysis computation (Exemplifies the influence of round-off errors)
EULER	Approximate solution to the initial value problem $Y'=Y$, $Y_0=1$ on the unit interval using Euler's method
GAUS	Solves a linear equations system using the Gauss-Seidel iteration Method
CHEBY	Finds a maximum point for a polynomial with evenly spread roots, on the interval [-1, 1]
SINFFT	Computes a one dimension sine transform using a one dimensional complex fast Fourier transform
SPOFA1	Factors a real symmetric positive definite matrix (Choleski) Input size(20x20)
SPOFA2	Same as above but for a larger input matrix (50x50)
RS	Input size (10x10)
SQRDC	QR factorization Input size(40x20)
SSVDC	Singular value decomposition of a real matrix. Input size(8x8)
SGEFA	Factors a real matrix by Gaussian elimination. Input size(4x4)

C. Optimal Scheduling Using the Oracle

1) What the Oracle Had to Do: In this experiment, operations are scheduled in cycles at compile time in such a way that true data precedence is the only constraint to parallelism. The conceptual model we used for resolving dynamic questions at compile time involves an oracle. The oracle allows us to always know, while scheduling, which way a jump would go. It allows us to completely unwind the code, and it tells us what locations all indirect references are to, so that we may do code motions without being unsafe.

In order to simulate such an oracle we used two major modules: an interpreter and a scheduler. The interpreter accepts the NADDR generated from high-level code and executes it, instruction by instruction. The stream produced is passed to the scheduler which places each instruction at the earliest possible level for execution, based on the dependencies between the current instruction and the previously scheduled ones. The "two pass" nature of this process gives us our oracle. When an instruction is ready to be scheduled, the code has executed all the way up through that instruction. Thus, all branches have been determined, and all earlier indirect memory references have been resolved. The ability to "know" which way jumps go with 100 percent accuracy enables the oracle to create an optimal schedule for the run. This is a result of only scheduling the operations that are actually executed (no operations from the unused branches are ever scheduled by the oracle).

Both the interpreter and the scheduler were compiled MACLISP running on a DEC-20 under TOPS-20.

2) Coping with Very Large Instruction Streams: It was still necessary to follow data-dependency constraints. To do this, many scheduling schemes use a DAG (directed acyclic graph) representation of the program, in which the vertices represent instructions and the edges express the dependency relation between them. However, we were experimenting with rather large programs, and were scheduling entire execution traces, not just basic blocks. Building a full DAG to represent the dependency relations would have required far too much space.

Fortunately, such a representation was not necessary for our purposes. In our model, in which the only dependencies are data dependencies, it suffices to build a symbol table to keep track of the schedule level at which a variable was last read/written. Then when an instruction is considered for placement in the schedule, the variables read and written by the instruction are checked against the stored information. The instruction is scheduled at the first level consistent with all the data dependencies of the instruction. The infinite resources hypothesis guarantees that the instruction may be legally scheduled there, and data precedence assures that it may not be scheduled any earlier. Thus, the bound we obtain is optimal in the sense of this experiment. The space overhead required to store last read/last written information in this scheme is minimal since we keep in effect only a "front line" of the DAG, which is dynamically updated in the process of building the schedule. The details of the scheduling algorithm which achieves this are given in Fig. 3, together with the rules for legal references of data-dependent variables. Another advantage of this approach is that instructions can be scheduled on the fly, without the need to keep the whole schedule in memory. The only information required to establish the level of an instruction is provided by the last read/written levels of the variables used by the instruction. Besides not keeping the entire DAG in memory, there was no reason to keep the schedule itself. We simply waited until the end, and noted the largest cycle number at which any variable had been written. That was the length of the schedule.

III. RESULTS

A. What was Measured

For the programs in our database, each running a single set of data, we measured the following.

• *Speedup ratio* — The ratio between the number of cycles required for the sequential execution of the program, and the number of cycles required for the parallel execution of the compacted version of the program. This is the measurement we were most interested in.

• *Average speedup per basic block* — Defined exactly as above, except with compaction limited to inside basic blocks. This was measured for comparison to earlier experiments

done by others, who measured only this. We also wanted to see the difference between global and local available parallelism in our domain.

• *Number of added variables* — The number of variables introduced in the process of renaming. Renaming may be used to allow some calculations to proceed beyond a conditional jump, and be conveniently thrown away when the jump goes the "wrong way." This enhances parallelism by removing some artificial dependencies. Our code did this even when it was clear that it would not provide added parallelism, so this is an upper bound measurement.

• *Maximal level width* — The maximal number of computational resources (e.g., adders, multipliers, etc.) used by the most resource intensive cycle of the compacted schedule. Since no attempt was made to even out the use of resources, this is very much an upper bound measurement.

The last two measurements were added for interest; we did not attempt to draw any conclusions from them.

B. Potential Global Speedup Ratio

Looking at Table II, we see that *the available global speedups found by our experiment ranged from below 4 to 988 times increase in execution speed.*

Many of the programs were limited only by the size of their data[5] (e.g., programs 17 and 18 in Table II). If anything, the data we usually picked were smaller than those encountered in realistic applications since we had to simulate the code.

Several of these programs (1, 2, 3, 5, 11, 12, 13 in Table II) are rather sequential in nature. Thus, one would expect less potential parallelism, and that is the case. This is probably parallelism that a compacting compiler could take advantage of, though, since it does not generally involve disambiguating memory references.

The programs that exhibit the largest parallelism (4, 6, 17, 18, 22 in Table II) operate on arrays. Intuitively, array processing presents greater opportunities for parallelism, and these results bear this out. The magnitude of the speedups clearly indicates that they do not result from the parallelization of trivial parts of the programs (such as the initialization of arrays), but rather that the parallelism is intrinsic to the whole computation process. Here the disambiguation of memory references is particularly important, so it is more problematical whether practical compaction methods will be able to approach the upper bound. However, the amount of available parallelism is large enough to encourage the development of sophisticated (and costly) disambiguation techniques.

C. Basic Block Compaction

We found that when compaction was limited to basic blocks only, the available speedup was almost always less than a factor of 2.5. This is consistent with earlier experiments [10], [18]. The difference between this measure and the global speedup is dramatic enough by itself to account for a large measure of the pessimism that has been felt about VLIW architectures. If trace scheduling, or some other global compaction technique, can recover a large share

---

[5]While the program control flow was not influenced greatly by the data contents, size made a difference in the amount of parallelism available.

(a) Rules for the Preservation of Data Dependency:

1. An operation **reading** variable V_i, can be scheduled for execution no earlier than the next cycle after the one in which V_i was last written. That is, if V_i was last written at cycle L_j, it could be read at cycle L_j+1 at the earliest.

2. An operation **writing** variable V_i, can be scheduled for execution no earlier than the cycle in which V_i was last read. That is, if V_i was last read at cycle L_j, it could be written at cycle L_j at the earliest. Note that if renaming is used, this rule becomes superfluous.

(b) Inner Loop of Scheduling Algorithm:

```
Read(operation)
WHILE operation # EOF DO BEGIN

    FOR V  IN Read-List(operation) DO BEGIN

        L   = Cycle-Last-Written(V ) + 1. /* By rule 1 above */
        Cycle-List  = Cycle-List || L .      /* Add L  to possible
                                                    cycle list */
        END.


    FOR V  IN Write-List(operation) DO BEGIN

        L   = Cycle-Last-read(V ).        /* By rule 2 above */
        Cycle-List  = Cycle-List || L .      /* Add L  to possible
                                                    cycle list */
        END.


    Max-Cycle   = MAX(Cycle-List).            /* Find earliest possible
                                                    Cycle */

    Insert-in-Schedule(operation,Max-Cycle).  /* Schedule operation at
                                                    earliest safe cycle */

    /* Peset last read/written information for all variables in operation */
    FOR V  IN Read-List(operation) DO
        Update-Last-Read(V , Max-Cycle).

    FOR V  IN Write-List(operation) DO
        Update-Last-Written(V , Max-Cycle).

    Read(operation).
    End.
```

Fig. 3.   Instruction scheduling. (a) Data dependency rules. (b) Algorithm.

TABLE II
RESULTS

	1 RFALS1	2 RFALS2	3 EXPNT	4 GRAM	5 ODE4	6 EXTRAP	7 BISECT	8 NEWT1	9 NEWT2	10 JACOBI	11 FIXPT	12 RFALS1	13 RFALS2	14 EXPNT	15 GRAM	16 ODE4	17 EXTRAP	18 BISECT	19 NEWT1	20 NEWT2	21 JACOBI	22 FIXPT
STREAM LENGTH	2047	841	9042	40530	1983	1859	1477	4605	696	480	201	1375	31111	460	50000	3822	3219	17634	23225	19784	32877	1333
MIN SCHED LENGTH	190	205	3015	41	324	28	70	103	18	23	76	52	5394	23	1436	22	28	58	1557	501	805	26
MAX LEVEL WIDTH	258	30	4	3234	238	198	80	1503	288	58	6	123	20	56	4293	292	479	2669	1518	3203	3118	192
TEMPS ADDED	1934	735	7026	33955	1630	1501	1376	4373	633	348	162	1148	23953	348	39986	3127	2419	13519	18963	16089	25631	862
NUMBER OF BLOCKS	62	77	2009	5238	310	275	62	202	32	26	32	212	7138	26	9998	5.18	498	2718	2874	2328	5014	268
AVG BLOCK LENGTH (BEFORE)	33.02	10.92	4.5	7.74	6.40	6.76	23.82	22.80	21.75	18.46	6.28	6.49	4.36	17.69	5.00	7.38	6.46	6.48	8.08	8.49	6.55	4.97
AVG BLOCK LENGTH (AFTER)	13.35	6.69	3.0	3.95	3.60	3.56	11.35	6.44	6.13	3.31	3.38	4.73	2.86	7.95	3.06	3.71	2.03	2.00	3.61	3.28	3.44	2.64
SPEEDUP PER BLOCK	2.47	1.63	1.5	1.96	1.78	1.90	2.10	3.54	3.55	5.58	1.86	1.37	1.53	2.22	1.64	1.99	3.18	3.23	2.24	2.58	1.90	1.88
POTENTIAL GLOBAL SPEEDUP	10.77	4.10	3.0	988.5	6.12	66.39	21.1	44.72	38.67	20.87	2.65	26.44	5.77	20	34.82	173.73	114.96	304.03	14.91	39.49	40.84	51.26

of this difference, then there is real hope for using VLIW architectures for significant parallelism.

IV. CAN THIS PARALLELISM BE EXPLOITED?

In these experiments we have endeavored to find an upper bound on the available parallelism, which may be obtained by simple program rearrangement. As such these results are very encouraging with respect to the potential for fine-grained parallelism exploitation on VLIW architectures. Still, since we were finding a bound, we assumed an oracle and a hardware model which were unrealistic in several respects. We will now discuss the extent to which the bound can be approached by a trace scheduling compiler for a real-life VLIW machine.

A. Hardware Limitations

Although it does not directly involve the oracle, the most unrealistic aspect of the model is the assumption of unlimited hardware resources. Clearly, the parallelism ultimately used will be only as large as permitted by the width of the real-life machine.

Even though the resources required by any given program are obviously not infinite, and are even reasonable, they tend to vary widely and are often dependent on the size of the data. Thus, we are not likely, for efficiency reasons, to build machines which will accommodate the largest possible requirements we may envision. As a result, we are bound to run into programs whose potential parallelism far exceeds that of the available hardware. In these cases, however, VLIW machines can be expected to offer extremely graceful degradation of performance because of the fine granularity of the parallelism used by these machines and because of the ability of trace scheduling to naturally deal with resource conflicts (by encoding them as data dependencies). This is a major advantage of our approach over other methods of parallelism exploitation (e.g., vector machines).

B. How Unrealistic is the Oracle?

Riseman and Foster demonstrated that a straightforward hardware mechanism which obtained even a small portion of the available parallelism would engender an unacceptable hardware cost. The only viable alternative is to try to statically exploit parallelism by compile time global scheduling. The oracle we have postulated did just that, but used two unrealistic assumptions.

• We can *always* predict which way conditional jumps will branch.

• We can *always* predict whether two memory references collide.

While a compiler cannot possibly hope to do this, the real question is: Can it do well enough to exploit a sizable fraction of the exposed parallelism?

1) Trace Scheduling as a Conditional Jump Predictor: Trace scheduling by its very nature attempts to approximate the oracle's prediction of conditional jump directions. The underlying assumption for the success of this process is that almost all jumps branch in a predictable direction almost all of the time. As we mentioned previously, programs in our target domain (scientific computation) have simple and mostly data-independent flow of control, with conditional jumps often biased towards one branch. Parallelism enhancement transformations (e.g., loop unwinding) will only tend to increase this effect. Because of this, we can expect a trace scheduling compiler to come close to the oracle in its branch predictions.

For other types of code (e.g., Systems) containing highly unpredictable flow of control, trace scheduling could not hope to approximate the oracle's predictions. Because of this, we did not include any such programs in our samples since the potential parallelism, however large, would have been meaningless for our approach.

2) Memory Disambiguation as a Reference Conflict Predictor: Our compiler uses conventional and unconventional flow analysis techniques in an attempt to prespecify as accurately as possible at compile time which indirect references access the same address location during the execution of the program. Of course, disambiguation cannot hope to achieve good results (i.e., come close to the oracle's predictions) on references that are very data dependent. For example, pointer chasing down a linked list or dereferencing involving input parameters are often intractable using static disambiguation.[6] The ineffective memory antialiasing of such references will result in spurious data dependencies, and inhibit parallelism.

Fortunately, though, indirect memory references in scientific code are almost always array references, with relatively simple indexes.[7] As a result, the antialiasing system is usually able to disambiguate them effectively, making the oracle predictions quite realistic. As in the case of trace scheduling, parallelism enhancing techniques will not interfere with memory disambiguation. In fact, the potential for successful disambiguation may increase. For example, in the case of loop unwinding, indirect references are generated which differ only by a constant and which are therefore trivial to disambiguate.

C. Substantiating our Claims

As reported upon in [7], J. Ellis, J. Ruttenberg, and the authors of this paper have implemented a trace scheduling compiler at Yale University. Based on our experience with it, we informally divide a test suite of source programs[8] into three broad classes.

Type P1 — Those which (we believe) stand a chance of obtaining significant parallel speedups using an ordinary multiprocessor or a vector machine.[9] Examples of these include an FFT, convolution, and matrix multiply.

Type P2 — Those which appear on the surface to have potential parallelism but are too irregular or interwoven to fit into Type P1. These include a prime number sieve and LU-decomposition.[10]

---

[6]Sometimes indirect references can be seen not to conflict even when unpredictable parameters are involved in the index calculations.

[7]This property of scientific code has been recognized and used by many other researchers. See, for example, the work of D. Kuck and U. Banerjee.

[8]Somewhat different from the set of programs reported upon here.

[9]Doing so might still require significant programmer effort.

[10]A small algorithmic transformation makes LU-decomposition suitable for a vector processor. We use the straightforward statement of the algorithm. It evidently took years before people in the scientific programming community noticed this transformation, even though this code was the subject of much attention.

Type S — Those which seem too sequential to allow any significant speedup due to parallelism. Examples of these include various series summations, dot products, iterative solvers, etc. This is a place where both vector machines and the Bulldog compiler may be helped by the work of D. Kuck's group at the University of Illinois [15]. Their source transformer can probably solve the recurrence and improve performance on these types of programs.

We believe that Types P2 and S are much more common in real life than Type P1. Since Type P1 is also found in the inner loops of programs of Types P2 and S, it might seem sufficient (e.g., for signal processing) to only handle Type P1. But we believe that even among most applications with Type P1 code in the inner loops, not enough of the running time is in the inner loops to justify special hardware. For example, if 80 percent of the code fits very well, and even if parallelism reduces that nearly to zero, the maximum possible speedup is under a factor of 5.

The general results we obtained on the test bed of programs we currently run through the Bulldog compiler are as follows.

Type P1 — We find all the parallelism the hardware will allow, *without the programmer having to alter the natural expression of the algorithms,* as is customary for with other approaches.

Type P2 — We again find all the parallelism the hardware will allow. We find it even if the inner loops contain conditional flow of control and data-precedence between loop iterations. We find it even with widely scattered references to array elements.[11]

Type S — We generally get a factor of 5 or more speedup. These are programs that we believe would be impossible to speedup at all with other processors.

V. CONCLUSIONS

We have shown that a large degree of functional unit parallelism exists in scientific code. Some code has dramatic speedup potential (approaching a factor of 1000) available. A sizable fraction of this parallelism can be exploited by a trace scheduling compiler in conjunction with a smart antialiasing mechanism.

Raw hardware cost has now become the inexpensive component in computing systems. This reality has spawned much research into the problem of formulating algorithms to use parallel hardware effectively. VLIW architectures present a form of parallelism not usually considered in parallel processing studies. This is true partly because of the pessimistic results of early basic block experiments. We hope that our experiments constitute a strong rebuttal of that pessimism. They clearly demonstrate that fine-grained VLIW type parallelism deserves much more attention than it has received.

---

[11]Our individual control over memory accesses, and our ability to differentiate the banks being referenced, allow us to maintain a high memory bandwidth in situations that would reduce other processors to uniprocessor speed. This is perhaps the most encouraging fact about VLIW's and the Bulldog compiler.

REFERENCES

[1] A. V. Aho and J. D. Ullman, *Principles of Compiler Design.* Reading, MA: Addison-Wesley, 1977.

[2] Arvind and V. Kathail, "A multiple processor data flow machine that supports generalized procedures," in *Proc. 8th Annu. Symp. Comput. Arch. ACM (SIGARCH),* May 1981, vol. 9, no. 3, pp. 291–302.

[3] U. Banerjee, S. C. Chen, D. J. Kuck, and R. A. Towle, "Time and parallel processor bounds for Fortran-like loops," *IEEE Trans. Comput.,* vol. C-28, pp. 660–670, Sept. 1979.

[4] U. Banerjee, "Speedup of ordinary programs," Dep. Comput. Sci., Univ. Illinois, Urbana, IL, Tech. Rep. UIUCDS-R-79-989, Oct. 1979.

[5] S. C. Chen and D. J. Kuck, "Time and parallel processor bounds for linear recurrence systems," *IEEE Trans. Comput.,* vol. C-24, pp. 701–717, July 1975.

[6] J. B. Dennis and D. P. Misunas, "A preliminary architecture for a basic data-flow processor," in *Proc. 2nd Annu. ACM–IEEE Symp. Comput. Arch.,* 1974, pp. 126–132.

[7] J. A. Fisher, J. R. Ellis, J. Ruttenberg, and A. Nicolau, "Parallel processing: A smart compiler and a dumb machine," to be published.

[8] J. A. Fisher, "Trace scheduling: A technique for global microcode compaction," *IEEE Trans. Comput.,* vol. C-30, pp. 478–490, July 1981.

[9] ——, "Very long instruction word architectures and the ELI-512," Dep. Comput. Sci., Yale Univ., New Haven, CT, Tech. Rep. 253, 1982; see also, *Proc. 10th Annu. Int. Arch. Conf.,* Stockholm, June 1983.

[10] C. C. Foster and E. M. Riseman, "Percolation of code to enhance parallel dispatching and execution," *IEEE Trans. Comput.,* vol. C-21, pp. 1411–1415, Dec. 1972.

[11] D. J. Kuck, Y. Muraoka, and S. -C. Chen, "On the number of operations simultaneously executable in Fortran-like programs and their resulting speedup," *IEEE Trans. Comput.,* vol. C-21, pp. 1293–1310, Dec. 1972.

[12] ——, "Measurements of parallelism in ordinary FORTRAN programs," *Computer,* vol. 7, pp. 37–46, 1974.

[13] L. Lamport, "The parallel execution of DO loops," *Commun. ACM,* vol. 17, pp. 83–94, Feb. 1974.

[14] J. K. F. Lee and A. J. Smith, "Branch prediction strategies and branch target buffer design," *Computer,* vol. 17, pp. 6–22, Jan. 1984.

[15] D. A. Padua, D. J. Kuck, and D. H. Lawrie, "High speed multiprocessors and compilation techniques," *IEEE Trans. Comput.,* vol. C-29, pp. 763–776, Sept. 1980.

[16] D. A. Paterson and C. H. Sequin, "A VLSI RISC," *Computer,* vol. 15, pp. 8–21, Sept. 1982.

[17] E. M. Riseman and C. C. Foster, "The inhibition of potential parallelism by conditional jumps," *IEEE Trans. Comput.,* vol. C-21, pp. 1405–1411, Dec. 1972.

[18] G. S. Tjaden and M. J. Flynn, "Detection and parallel execution of independent instructions," *IEEE Trans. Comput.,* vol. C-19, pp. 889–895, Oct. 1970.

Alexandru Nicolau received the B.A. degree in computer science from Brandeis University, Waltham, MA, in 1980 and the M.S. and Ph.D. degrees from Yale University, New Haven, CT, in 1981 and 1984, respectively.

He is currently an Assistant Professor in the Department of Computer Science, Cornell University, Ithaca, NY. His research interests include parallel computation, computer systems architecture, and optimizing compilers.

Joseph A. Fisher received the A.B. degree in mathematics from New York University, New York, NY, in 1968, and the M.S. and Ph.D. degrees in computer science from the Courant Institute of Mathematical Sciences, New York University, in 1976 and 1979, respectively.

He has been at Yale University, New Haven, CT, since 1979, where he is an Associate Professor. His research interests include very long instruction word architectures, parallel processing, automated design of computers, and microprogramming.

Dr. Fisher was the Program Chairman of the ACM–IEEE Fifteenth Annual Workshop on Microprogramming in 1982, and a Board Member of the IEEE Computer Society from 1981 to 1982. He recently received the Presidential Young Investigator Award.

Limits of Instruction-Level Parallelism

David W. Wall

Digital Equipment Corporation
Western Research Laboratory

Abstract

Growing interest in ambitious multiple-issue machines and heavily-pipelined machines requires a careful examination of how much instruction-level parallelism exists in typical programs. Such an examination is complicated by the wide variety of hardware and software techniques for increasing the parallelism that can be exploited, including branch prediction, register renaming, and alias analysis. By performing simulations based on instruction traces, we can model techniques at the limits of feasibility and even beyond. Our study shows a striking difference between assuming that the techniques we use are perfect and merely assuming that they are impossibly good. Even with impossibly good techniques, average parallelism rarely exceeds 7, with 5 more common.

1. Introduction

There is growing interest in machines that exploit, usually with compiler assistance, the parallelism that programs have at the instruction level. Figure 1 shows an example of this parallelism.

r1 := 0[r9]	r1 := 0[r9]
r2 := 17	r2 := r1 + 17
4[r3] := r6	4[r2] := r6
(a) parallelism=3	*(b) parallelism=1*

Figure 1. Instruction-level parallelism (and lack thereof).

The code fragment in 1(a) consists of three instructions that can be executed at the same time, because they do not depend on each other's results. The code fragment in 1(b) does have dependencies, and so cannot be executed

in parallel. In each case, the parallelism is the number of instructions divided by the number of cycles required.

Architectures to take advantage of this kind of parallelism have been proposed. A superscalar machine [1] is one that can issue multiple independent instructions in the same cycle. A superpipelined machine [7] issues one instruction per cycle, but the cycle time is set much less than the typical instruction latency. A VLIW machine [11] is like a superscalar machine, except the parallel instructions must be explicitly packed by the compiler into very long instruction words.

But how much parallelism is there to exploit? Popular wisdom, supported by a few studies [7,13,14], suggests that parallelism within a basic block rarely exceeds 3 or 4 on the average. Peak parallelism can be higher, especially for some kinds of numeric programs, but the payoff of high peak parallelism is low if the average is still small.

These limits are troublesome. Many machines already have some degree of pipelining, as reflected in operations with latencies of multiple cycles. We can compute the degree of pipelining by multiplying the latency of each operation by its dynamic frequency in typical programs; for the DECStation 5000,[*] load latencies, delayed branches, and floating-point latencies give the machine a degree of pipelining equal to about 1.5. Adding a superscalar capability to a machine with some pipelining is beneficial only if there is more parallelism available than the pipelining already exploits.

To increase the instruction-level parallelism that the hardware can exploit, people have explored a variety of techniques. These fall roughly into two categories. One category includes techniques for increasing the parallelism within a basic block, the other for using parallelism across several basic blocks. These techniques often interact in a way that has not been adequately explored. We would like to bound the effectiveness of a

---

[*] DECStation is a trademark of Digital Equipment Corporation.

"Limits of Instruction-Level Parallelism" by D.W. Wall from *International Conference on Architectural Support for Programming Languages and Operating Systems*, 1991, pages 176-188. Copyright © 1991 by The Association for Computing Machinery, Inc., reprinted with permission.

technique whether it is used in combination with impossibly good companion techniques, or with none. A general approach is therefore needed. In this paper, we will describe our use of trace-driven simulation to study the importance of register renaming, branch and jump prediction, and alias analysis. In each case we can model a range of possibilities from perfect to non-existent.

We will begin with a survey of ambitious techniques for increasing the exploitable instruction-level parallelism of programs.

1.1. Increasing parallelism within blocks.

Parallelism within a basic block is limited by dependencies between pairs of instructions. Some of these dependencies are real, reflecting the flow of data in the program. Others are false dependencies, accidents of the code generation or results of our lack of precise knowledge about the flow of data.

Allocating registers assuming a traditional scalar architecture can lead to a false dependency on a register. In the code sequence

$$r1 := 0[r9]$$
$$r2 := r1 + 1$$
$$r1 := 9$$

we must do the second and third instructions in that order, because the third changes the value of r1. However, if the compiler had used r3 instead of r1 in the third instruction, these two instructions would be independent.

A smart compiler might pay attention to its allocation of registers, so as to maximize the opportunities for parallelism. Current compilers often do not, preferring instead to reuse registers as often as possible so that the number of registers needed is minimized.

An alternative is the hardware solution of *register renaming*, in which the hardware imposes a level of indirection between the register number appearing in the instruction and the actual register used. Each time an instruction sets a register, the hardware selects an actual register to use for as long as that value is needed. In a sense the hardware does the register allocation dynamically, which can give better results than the compiler's static allocation, even if the compiler did it as well as it could. In addition, register renaming allows the hardware to include more registers than will fit in the instruction format, further reducing false dependencies. Unfortunately, register renaming can also lengthen the machine pipeline, thereby increasing the branch penalties of the machine, but we are concerned here only with its effects on parallelism.

False dependencies can also involve memory. We assume that memory locations have meaning to the programmer that registers do not, and hence that hardware renaming of memory locations is not desirable. However, we may still have to make conservative assumptions that lead to false dependencies on memory. For example, in the code sequence

$$r1 := 0[r9]$$
$$4[r16] := r3$$

we may have no way of knowing whether the memory locations referenced in the load and store are the same. If they are the same, then there is a dependency between these two instructions: we cannot store a new value until we have fetched the old. If they are different, there is no dependency. *Alias analysis* can help a compiler decide when two memory references are independent, but even that is imprecise; sometimes we must assume the worst. Hardware can resolve the question at run-time by determining the actual addresses referenced, but this may be too late to affect parallelism decisions. If the compiler or hardware are not sure the locations are different, we must assume conservatively that they are the same.

1.2. Crossing block boundaries.

The number of instructions between branches is usually quite small, often averaging less than 6. If we want large parallelism, we must be able to issue instructions from different basic blocks in parallel. But this means we must know in advance whether a conditional branch will be taken, or else we must cope with the possibility that we do not know.

Branch prediction is a common hardware technique. In the scheme we used [9,12], the branch predictor maintains a table of two-bit entries. Low-order bits of a branch's address provide the index into this table. Taking a branch causes us to increment its table entry; not taking it causes us to decrement. We do not wrap around when the table entry reaches its maximum or minimum. We predict that a branch will be taken if its table entry is 2 or 3. This two-bit prediction scheme mispredicts a typical loop only once, when it is exited. Two branches that map to the same table entry interfere with each other; no "key" identifies the owner of the entry. A good initial value for table entries is 2, just barely predicting that each branch will be taken.

Branch prediction is often used to keep a pipeline full: we fetch and decode instructions after a branch while we are executing the branch and the instructions before it. To use branch prediction to increase parallel execution, we must be able to execute instructions across an unknown branch *speculatively*. This may involve maintaining shadow registers, whose values are not committed until we are sure we have correctly predicted the branch. It may involve being selective about the instructions we choose: we may not be willing to execute memory stores speculatively, for example. Some of this may be put partly under compiler control by designing an instruction set with explicitly squashable instructions.

Each squashable instruction would be tied explicitly to a condition evaluated in another instruction, and would be squashed by the hardware if the condition turns out to be false.

Rather than try to predict the destinations of branches, we might speculatively execute instructions along *both* possible paths, squashing the wrong path when we know which it is. Some of our parallelism capability is guaranteed to be wasted, but we will never miss out by taking the wrong path. Unfortunately, branches happen quite often in normal code, so for large degrees of parallelism we may encounter another branch before we have resolved the previous one. A real architecture may have limits on the amount of fanout we can tolerate before we must assume that new branches are not explored in parallel.

Many architectures have two or three kinds of instructions to change the flow of control. Branches are conditional and have a destination some specified offset from the PC. Jumps are unconditional, and may be either *direct* or *indirect*. A direct jump is one whose destination is given explicitly in the instruction, while an indirect jump is one whose destination is expressed as an address computation involving a register. In principle we can know the destination of a direct jump well in advance. The same is true of a branch, assuming we know how its condition will turn out. The destination of an indirect jump, however, may require us to wait until the address computation is possible. Little work has been done on predicting the destinations of indirect jumps, but it might pay off in instruction-level parallelism. This paper considers a very simple (and, it turns out, fairly accurate) jump prediction scheme. A table is maintained of destination addresses. The address of a jump provides the index into this table. Whenever we execute an indirect jump, we put its address in the table entry for the jump. We predict that an indirect jump will be to the address in its table entry. As with branch prediction, we do not prevent two jumps from mapping to the same table entry and interfering with each other.

Loop unrolling is an old compiler optimization technique that can also increase parallelism. If we unroll a loop ten times, thereby removing 90% of its branches, we effectively increase the basic block size tenfold. This larger basic block may hold parallelism that had been unavailable because of the branches.

Software pipelining [8] is a compiler technique for moving instructions across branches to increase parallelism. It analyzes the dependencies in a loop body, looking for ways to increase parallelism by moving instructions from one iteration into a previous or later iteration. Thus the dependencies in one iteration can be stretched out across several, effectively executing several iterations in parallel without the code expansion of unrolling.

Trace scheduling [4] was developed for VLIW machines, where global scheduling by the compiler is needed to exploit the parallelism of the long instruction words. It uses a profile to find a *trace* (a sequence of blocks that are executed often), and schedules the instructions for these blocks as a whole. In effect, trace scheduling predicts a branch statically, based on the profile. To cope with occasions when this prediction fails, code is inserted outside the sequence of blocks to correct the state of registers and memory whenever we enter or leave the sequence unexpectedly. This added code may itself be scheduled as part of a later and less heavily executed trace.

2. This and previous work.

To better understand this bewildering array of techniques, we have built a simple system for scheduling instructions produced by an instruction trace. Our system allows us to assume various kinds of branch and jump prediction, alias analysis, and register renaming. In each case the option ranges from perfect, which could not be implemented in reality, to non-existent. It is important to consider the full range in order to bound the effectiveness of the various techniques. For example, it is useful to ask how well a realistic branch prediction scheme could work even with impossibly good alias analysis and register renaming.

This is in contrast to the 1989 study of Jouppi and Wall [7], which worked by scheduling static program executables rather than dynamic instruction traces. Since their compiler did scheduling only within basic blocks, they did not consider more ambitious scheduling.

The methodology of our paper is more like that of Tjaden and Flynn [14], which also scheduled instructions from a dynamic trace. Like Jouppi and Wall, however, Tjaden and Flynn did not move instructions across branches. Their results were similar to those of Jouppi and Wall, with parallelism rarely above 3, even though the two studies assumed quite different architectures.

Nicolau and Fisher's trace-driven study [11] of the effectiveness of trace scheduling was more liberal, assuming perfect branch prediction and perfect alias analysis. However, they did not consider more realistic assumptions, arguing instead that they were interested primarily in programs for which realistic implementations would be close to perfect.

The study by Smith, Johnson, and Horowitz [13] was a realistic application of trace-driven simulation that assumed neither too restrictive nor too generous a model. They were interested, however, in validating a particular realistic machine design, one that could consistently exploit a parallelism of only 2. They did not explore the range of techniques discussed in this paper.

We believe our study can provide useful bounds on the behavior not only of hardware techniques like branch prediction and register renaming, but also of compiler techniques like software pipelining and trace scheduling.

Unfortunately, we could think of no good way to model loop unrolling. Register renumbering can cause much of the computation in a loop to migrate backward toward the beginning of the loop, providing opportunities for parallelism much like those presented by unrolling. Much of the computation, however, like the repeated incrementing of the loop index, is inherently sequential. We address loop unrolling in an admittedly unsatisfying manner, by unrolling the loops of some numerical programs by hand and comparing the results to those of the normal versions.

3. Our experimental framework.

To explore the parallelism available in a particular program, we execute the program to produce a trace of the instructions executed. This trace also includes data addresses referenced, and the results of branches and jumps. A greedy algorithm packs these instructions into a sequence of pending cycles.

In packing instructions into cycles, we assume that any cycle may contain as many as 64 instructions in parallel. We further assume no limits on replicated functional units or ports to registers or memory: all 64 instructions may be multiplies, or even loads. We assume that every operation has a latency of one cycle, so the result of an operation executed in cycle N can be used by an instruction executed in cycle N+1. This includes memory references: we assume there are no cache misses.

We pack the instructions from the trace into cycles as follows. For each instruction in the trace, we start at the end of the cycle sequence, representing the latest pending cycle, and move earlier in the sequence until we find a *conflict* with the new instruction. Whether a conflict exists depends on which model we are considering. If the conflict is a false dependency (in models allowing them), we assume that we can put the instruction in that cycle but no farther back. Otherwise we assume only that we can put the instruction in the next cycle after this one. If the correct cycle is full, we put the instruction in the next non-full cycle. If we cannot put the instruction in any pending cycle, we start a new pending cycle at the end of the sequence.

As we add more and more cycles, the sequence gets longer. We assume that hardware and software techniques will have some limit on how many instructions they will consider at once. When the total number of instructions in the sequence of pending cycles reaches this limit, we remove the first cycle from the sequence, whether it is full of instructions or not. This corresponds

to retiring the cycle's instructions from the scheduler, and passing them on to be executed.

When we have exhausted the trace, we divide the number of instructions by the number of cycles we created. The result is the parallelism.

3.1. Parameters.

We can do three kinds of *register renaming:* perfect, finite, and none. For perfect renaming, we assume that there are an infinite number of registers, so that no false register dependencies occur. For finite renaming, we assume a finite register set dynamically allocated using an LRU discipline: when we need a new register we select the register whose most recent use (measured in cycles rather than in instruction count) is earliest. Finite renaming is normally done with 256 integer registers and 256 floating-point registers. It is also interesting to see what happens when we reduce this to 64 or even 32, the number on our base machine. To simulate no renaming, we simply use the registers specified in the code; this is of course highly dependent on the register strategy of the compiler we use.

We can assume several degrees of *branch prediction.* One extreme is perfect prediction: we assume that all branches are correctly predicted. Next we can assume a two-bit prediction scheme as described before. The two-bit scheme can be either infinite, with a table big enough that two different branches never have the same table entry, or finite, with a table of 2048 entries. To model trace scheduling, we can also assume static branch prediction based on a profile from an identical run; in this case we predict that a branch will always go the way that it goes most frequently. And finally, we can assume that no branch prediction occurs; this is the same as assuming that every branch is predicted wrong.

The same choices are available for *jump prediction.* We can assume that indirect jumps are perfectly predicted. We can assume infinite or finite hardware prediction as described above (predicting that a jump will go where it went last time). We can assume static prediction based on a profile. And we can assume no prediction. In any case we are concerned only with indirect jumps; we assume that direct jumps are always predicted correctly.

The effect of branch and jump prediction on scheduling is easy to state. Correctly predicted branches and jumps have no effect on scheduling (except for register dependencies involving their operands). Instructions on opposite sides of an incorrectly predicted branch or jump, however, always conflict. Another way to think of this is that the sequence of pending cycles is flushed whenever an incorrect prediction is made. Note that we generally assume no other penalty for failure. This assumption is optimistic; in most real architectures, a failed prediction causes a bubble in the pipeline, resulting in one or more cycles in which no execution whatsoever can occur. We will return to this topic later.

We can also allow instructions to move past a certain number of incorrectly predicted branches. This corresponds to architectures that speculatively execute instructions from both possible paths, up to a certain *fanout limit*. None of the experiments described here involved this ability.

Four levels of *alias analysis* are available. We can assume perfect alias analysis, in which we look at the actual memory address referenced by a load or store; a store conflicts with a load or store only if they access the same location. We can also assume no alias analysis, so that a store always conflicts with a load or store. Between these two extremes would be alias analysis as a smart vectorizing compiler might do it. We don't have such a compiler, but we have implemented two intermediate schemes that may give us some insight.

One intermediate scheme is *alias by instruction inspection*. This is a common technique in compile-time instruction-level code schedulers. We look at the two instructions to see if it is obvious that they are independent; the two ways this might happen are shown in Figure 2.

$$
\begin{array}{ll}
r1 := 0[r9] & r1 := 0[fp] \\
4[r9] := r2 & 0[gp] := r2 \\
(a) & (b)
\end{array}
$$

Figure 2. Alias analysis by inspection.

The two instructions in 2(a) cannot conflict, because they use the same base register but different displacements. The two instructions in 2(b) cannot conflict, because one is manifestly a reference to the stack and the other is manifestly a reference to the global data area.

The other intermediate scheme is called *alias analysis by compiler* even though our own compiler doesn't do it. Under this model, we assume perfect analysis of stack and global references, regardless of which registers are used to make them. A store to an address on the stack conflicts only with a load or store to the same address. Heap references, on the other hand, are resolved by instruction inspection.

The idea behind our alias analysis by compiler is that references outside the heap can often be resolved by the compiler, by doing dataflow analysis and possibly by solving diophantine equations over loop indexes, whereas heap references are often less tractable. Neither of these assumptions is particularly defensible. Many languages allow pointers into the stack and global areas, rendering them as difficult as the heap. Practical considerations such as separate compilation may also keep us from analyzing non-heap references perfectly. On the other

side, even heap references are not as hopeless as this model assumes [2,6]. Nevertheless, our range of four alternatives provides some intuition about the effects of alias analysis on instruction-level parallelism.

The *window size* is the maximum number of instructions that can appear in the pending cycles at any time. By default this is 2048 instructions. We can manage the window either *discretely* or *continuously*. With discrete windows, we fetch an entire window of instructions, schedule them into cycles, and then start fresh with a new window. A missed prediction also causes us to start over with a full-size new window. With continuous windows, new instructions enter the window one at a time, and old cycles leave the window whenever the number of instructions reaches the window size. Continuous windows are the norm for the results described here, although to implement them in hardware is more difficult. Smith, Johnson, and Horowitz [13] assumed discrete windows.

	lines	dynamic instructions	remarks
Livermore	268	22294030	Livermore loops 1-14
Whetstones	462	24479634	Floating-point
Linpack	814	174883597	Linear algebra [3]
Stanford	1019	20759516	Hennessy's suite [5]
sed	1751	1447717	Stream editor
egrep	844	13910586	File search
yacc	1856	30948883	Compiler-compiler
metronome	4287	70235508	Timing verifier
grr	5883	142980475	PCB router
eco	2721	26702439	Recursive tree comparison
ccom	10142	18465797	C compiler front end
gcc1	83000	22745232	pass 1 of GNU C compiler
espresso	12000	135317102	boolean function minimizer
li	7000	1247190509	Lisp interpreter
fpppp	2600	244124171	quantum chemistry
doduc	5200	284697827	hydrocode simulation
tomcatv	180	1986257545	mesh generation

Figure 3. The seventeen test programs.

3.2. Programs measured.

As test cases we used four toy benchmarks, seven real programs used at WRL, and six SPEC benchmarks. These programs are shown in Figure 3. The SPEC benchmarks were run on accompanying test data, but the data was usually an official "short" data set rather than the reference data set. The programs were compiled for a DECStation 5000, which has a MIPS R3000[*] processor. The Mips version 1.31 compilers were used.

---

[*] R3000 is a trademark of MIPS Computer Systems, Inc.

4. Results.

We ran these test programs for a wide range of configurations. The results we have are tabulated in the appendix, but we will extract some of them to show some interesting trends. To provide a framework for our exploration, we defined a series of five increasingly ambitious models spanning the possible range. These five are specified in Figure 4; the window size in each is 2K instructions. Many of the results we present will show the effects of variations on these standard models. Note that even the Fair model is quite ambitious.

	branch predict	jump predict	reg renaming	alias analysis
Stupid	none	none	none	none
Fair	infinite	infinite	256	inspection
Good	infinite	infinite	256	perfect
Great	infinite	infinite	perfect	perfect
Perfect	perfect	perfect	perfect	perfect

Figure 4. Five increasingly ambitious models.

	branches			jumps		
	infinite	finite	static	infinite	finite	static
Linpack	96%	96%	95%	99%	99%	96%
Livermore	98%	98%	98%	19%	19%	77%
Stanford	90%	90%	89%	69%	69%	71%
Whetstones	90%	90%	92%	80%	80%	88%
sed	97%	97%	97%	96%	96%	97%
egrep	90%	90%	91%	98%	98%	98%
yacc	95%	95%	92%	75%	75%	71%
met	92%	92%	92%	77%	77%	65%
grr	85%	84%	82%	67%	66%	64%
eco	92%	92%	91%	47%	47%	56%
ccom	90%	90%	90%	55%	54%	64%
li	90%	90%	90%	56%	55%	70%
tomcatv	99%	99%	99%	58%	58%	72%
doduc	95%	95%	95%	39%	39%	62%
espresso	89%	89%	87%	65%	65%	53%
fpppp	92%	91%	88%	84%	84%	80%
gcc	90%	89%	90%	55%	54%	60%
mean	92%	92%	92%	67%	67%	73%

Figure 5. Success rates of branch and jump prediction.

4.1. Branch and jump prediction.

The success of the two-bit branch prediction has been reported elsewhere [9,10]. Our results were comparable and are shown in Figure 5. It makes little difference whether we use an infinite table or one with only 2K entries, even though several of the programs are more than twenty thousand instructions long. Static branch prediction based on a profile does almost exactly as well as hardware prediction across all of the tests;

static jump prediction does a bit better than our simple dynamic prediction scheme. It would be interesting to explore how small the hardware table can be before performance starts to degrade, and to explore how well static prediction does if the profile is from a non-identical run of the program.

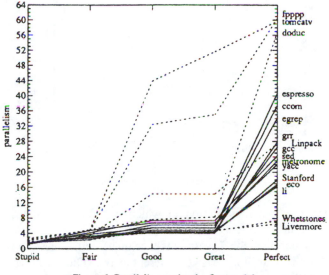

Figure 6. Parallelism under the five models.

4.2. Parallelism under the five models.

Figure 6 shows the parallelism of each program for each of the five models. The numeric programs are shown as dotted lines. Unsurprisingly, the Stupid model rarely gets above 2; the lack of branch prediction means that it finds only intra-block parallelism, and the lack of renaming and alias analysis means it won't find much of that. The Fair model is better, with parallelism between 2 and 4 common. Even the Great model, however, rarely has parallelism above 8. A study that assumed perfect branch prediction, perfect alias analysis, and perfect register renaming would lead us down a dangerous garden path. So would a study that included only fpppp and tomcatv, unless that's really all we want to run on our machine.

It is interesting that Whetstones and Livermore, two numeric benchmarks, do poorly even under the Perfect model. This is the result of Amdahl's Law: if we compute the parallelism for each Livermore loop independently, the values range from 2.4 to 29.9, with a median around 5. Speeding up a few loops 30-fold simply means that the cycles needed for less parallel loops will dominate the total.

4.3. Effects of unrolling.

Loop unrolling should have some effect on the five models. We explored this by unrolling two benchmarks by hand. The normal Linpack benchmark is already unrolled four times, so we made a version of it unrolled

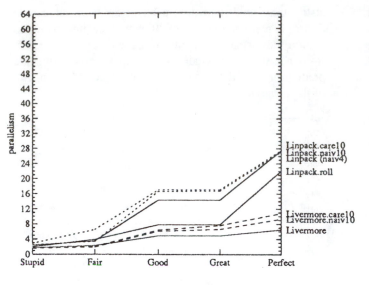

Figure 7. Unrolling under the five models.

ten times, and a version in which we rolled the loops back up, removing the normal unrolling by four. We also unrolled the Livermore benchmark ten times. We did the unrolling in two different ways. One is *naive* unrolling, in which the loop body is simply replicated ten times with suitable adjustments to array indexes and so on. The other is *careful* unrolling, in which computations involving accumulators (like scalar product) are reassociated to increase parallelism, and in which assignments to array members are delayed until after all the calculations are complete, so that false memory conflicts do not interfere with doing the calculations in parallel.

Figure 7 shows the result. The dotted lines are the 10-unrolled versions. Unrolling helps both Livermore and Linpack in the more ambitious models, although unrolling Linpack by 10 doesn't make it much more parallel than unrolling by 4. The difference between unrolling by 4 or 10 disappears altogether in the Perfect model, because the *saxpy* routine, which accounts for 75% of the executed instructions, achieves a parallelism just short of our maximum of 64 in each case. The aggregate parallelism stays lower because the next most frequently executed code is the loop in the *matgen* routine. This loop includes an embedded random-number generator, and each iteration is thus very dependent on its predecessor. This confirms the importance of using whole program traces; studies that considered only the parallelism in *saxpy* would be quite misleading.

Naive unrolling actually hurts the parallelism slightly under the Fair model. The reason is fairly simple. The Fair model uses alias analysis by inspection, which is not always sufficient to resolve the conflict between a store at the end of one iteration and the loads at the beginning of the next. In naive unrolling, the loop body is simply replicated, and these memory conflicts impose the same rigid framework to the dependency

structure as they did before unrolling. The unrolled versions have slightly less to do within that framework, however, because 3/4 or 9/10 of the loop overhead has been removed. As a result, the parallelism goes down slightly. Even when alias analysis by inspection is adequate, unrolling the loops either naively or carefully sometimes causes the compiler to spill some registers. This is even harder for the alias analysis to deal with because these references usually have a different base register than the array references.

Loop unrolling is a good way to increase the available parallelism, but it is clear we must integrate the unrolling with the rest of our techniques better than we have been able to do here.

4.4. Effects of window size.

Our standard models all have a window size of 2K instructions: the scheduler is allowed to keep that many instructions in pending cycles at one time. Typical superscalar hardware is unlikely to handle windows of that size, but software techniques like trace scheduling for a VLIW machine might. Figure 8 shows the effect of varying the window size from 2K instructions down to 4. Under the Great model, which does not have perfect branch prediction, most programs do as well with a 32-instruction window as with a larger one. Below that, parallelism drops off quickly. Unsurprisingly, the Perfect model does better the bigger its window. The Good model is not shown, but looks almost identical to the Great model.

4.5. Effects of using discrete windows.

A less ambitious parallelism manager would get a window full of instructions, schedule them relative to each other, execute them, and then start over with a fresh window. This would tend to have less parallelism than the continuous window model we used above. Figure 9 shows the same models as Figure 8, except assuming discrete windows rather than continuous. Under the Great model, discrete windows do nearly as well as continuous when the window is 2K instructions, but the difference increases as the window size decreases; we must use discrete windows of 128 instructions before the curves level off. If we have very small windows, it might pay off to manage them continuously; in other words, continuous management of a small window is as good as multiplying the window size by 4. As before, the Perfect model does better the larger the window, but the parallelism is only two-thirds that of continuous windows.

4.6. Effects of branch and jump prediction.

We have several levels of branch and jump prediction. Figure 10 shows the results of varying these while register renaming and alias analysis stay perfect. Reduc-

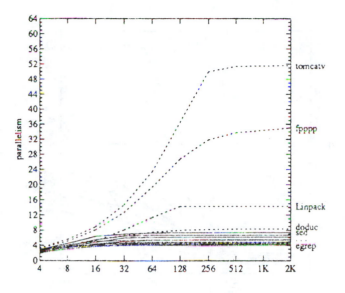

Figure 8(a). Size of continuous windows under Great model.

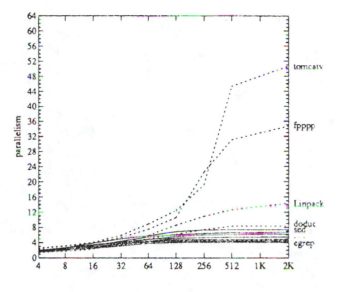

Figure 9(a). Size of discrete windows under Great model.

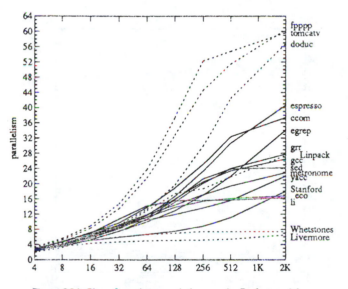

Figure 8(b). Size of continuous windows under Perfect model.

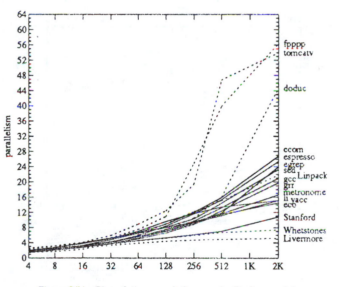

Figure 9(b). Size of discrete windows under Perfect model.

ing the level of jump prediction can have a large effect, but only if we have perfect branch prediction. Otherwise, removing jump prediction altogether has little effect. This graph does not show static or finite prediction: it turns out to make little difference whether prediction is infinite, finite, or static, because they have nearly the same success rate.

That jump prediction has little effect on the parallelism under non-Perfect models does not mean that jump prediction is useless. In a real machine, a jump predicted incorrectly (or not at all) may result in a bubble in the pipeline. The bubble is a series of cycles in which no execution occurs, while the unexpected instructions are fetched, decoded, and started down the execution pipeline. Depending on the penalty, this may have a serious effect on performance. Figure 11 shows the degradation

of parallelism under the Great model, assuming that each mispredicted branch or jump adds N cycles with no instructions in them. If we assume instead that *all* indirect jumps (but not all branches) are mispredicted, the right ends of these curves drop by 10% to 30%.

Livermore and Linpack stay relatively horizontal over the entire range: They make fewer branches and jumps, and their branches are comparatively predictable. Tomcatv and fpppp are above the range of this graph, but their curves have slopes about the same as these.

4.7. Effects of alias analysis and register renaming.

We also ran several experiments varying alias analysis in isolation, and varying register renaming in isolation.

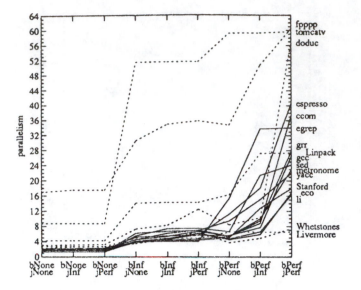

Figure 10. Effect of branch and jump prediction with perfect alias analysis and register renaming

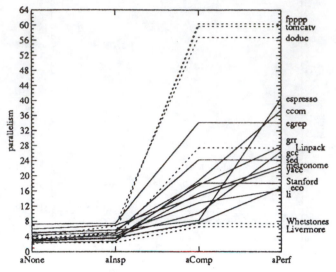

Figure 12(a). Effect of alias analysis on Perfect model.

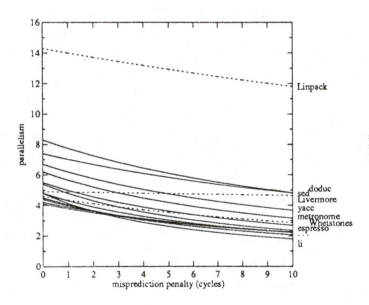

Figure 11. Effect of a misprediction cycle penalty on the Great model.

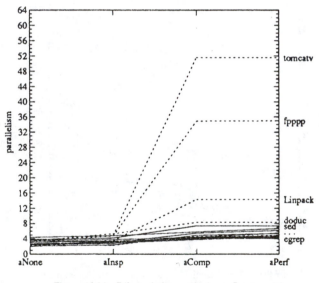

Figure 12(b). Effect of alias analysis on Great model.

Figure 12 shows the effect of varying the alias analysis under the Perfect and Great models. We can see that "alias analysis by inspection" isn't very powerful; it rarely increased parallelism by more than 0.5. "Alias analysis by compiler" was (by definition) indistinguishable from perfect alias analysis on programs that do not use the heap, and was somewhat helpful even on those that do. There remains a gap between this analysis and perfection, which suggests that the payoff of further work on heap disambiguation may be significant. Unless branch prediction is perfect, however, even perfect alias analysis usually leaves us with parallelism between 4 and 8.

Figure 13 shows the effect of varying the register renaming under the Perfect and Great models. Dropping from infinitely many registers to 256 CPU and 256 FPU registers rarely had a large effect unless the other parameters were perfect. Under the Great model, register renaming with 32 registers, the number on the actual machine, yielded parallelisms roughly halfway between no renaming and perfect renaming.

4.8. Conclusions.

Good branch prediction by hardware or software is critical to the exploitation of more than modest amounts of instruction-level parallelism. Jump prediction can reduce the penalty for indirect jumps, but has little effect on the parallelism of non-penalty cycles. Register

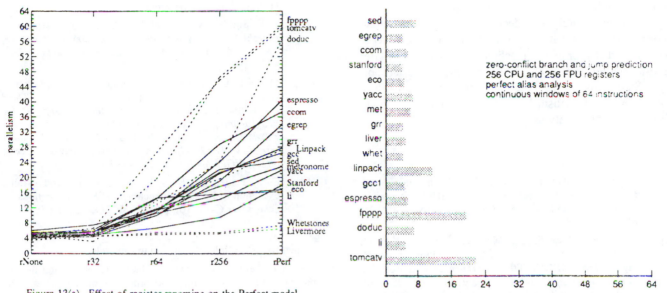

Figure 13(a). Effect of register renaming on the Perfect model.

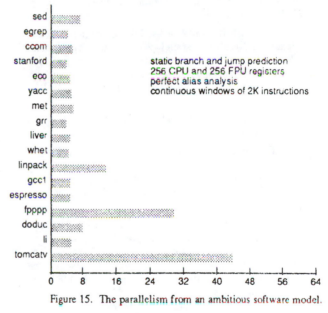

Figure 14. The parallelism from an ambitious hardware model.

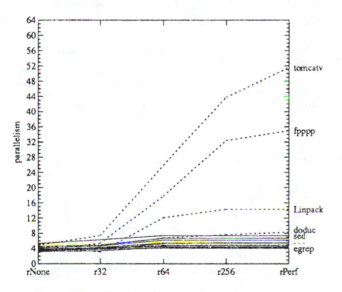

Figure 13(b). Effect of register renaming on the Great model.

Figure 15. The parallelism from an ambitious software model.

renaming is important as well, though a compiler might be able to do an adequate job with static analysis, if it knows it is compiling for parallelism.

Even ambitious models combining the techniques discussed here are disappointing. Figure 14 shows the parallelism achieved by a quite ambitious hardware-style model, with branch and jump prediction using infinite tables, 256 FPU and 256 CPU registers used with LRU renaming, perfect alias analysis, and windows of 64 instructions maintained continuously. The average parallelism is around 7, the median around 5. Figure 15 shows the parallelism achieved by a quite ambitious software-style model, with static branch and jump prediction, 256 FPU and 256 CPU registers used with LRU renaming, perfect alias analysis, and windows of 2K instructions maintained continuously. The average here

is closer to 9, but the median is still around 5. A consistent speedup of 5 would be quite good, but we cannot honestly expect more (at least without developing techniques beyond those discussed here).

We must also remember the simplifying assumptions this study makes. We have assumed that all operations have latency of one cycle; in practice an instruction with larger latency uses some of the available parallelism. We have assumed unlimited resources, including a perfect cache; as the memory bottleneck gets worse it may be more helpful to have a bigger on-chip cache than a lot of duplicate functional units. We have assumed that there is no penalty for a missed prediction; in practice the penalty may be many empty cycles. We have assumed a uniform machine cycle time, though adding superscalar capability will surely not decrease the cycle time and may in fact increase it. We have assumed uniform technology, but an ordinary machine may have a shorter time-to-market and therefore use newer, faster technology. Sadly, any one of these considerations could reduce our expected parallelism by a third; together they could eliminate it completely.

References

[1] Tilak Agarwala and John Cocke. High performance reduced instruction set processors. IBM Thomas J. Watson Research Center Technical Report #55845, March 31, 1987.

[2] David R. Chase, Mark Wegman, and F. Kenneth Zadeck. Analysis of pointers and structures. *Proceedings of the SIGPLAN '90 Conference on Programming Language Design and Implementation*, pp. 296-310. Published as *SIGPLAN Notices 25* (6), June 1990.

[3] Jack J. Dongarra. Performance of various computers using standard linear equations software in a Fortran environment. *Computer Architecture News 11* (5), pp. 22-27, December 1983.

[4] Joseph A. Fisher, John R. Ellis, John C. Ruttenberg, and Alexandru Nicolau. Parallel processing: A smart compiler and a dumb machine. *Proceedings of the SIGPLAN '84 Symposium on Compiler Construction*, pp. 37-47. Published as *SIGPLAN Notices 19* (6), June 1984.

[5] John Hennessy. Stanford benchmark suite. Personal communication.

[6] Neil D. Jones and Steven S. Muchnick. A flexible approach to interprocedural data flow analysis and programs with recursive data structures. *Ninth Annual ACM Symposium on Principles of Programming Languages*, pp. 66-74, Jan. 1982.

[7] Norman P. Jouppi and David W. Wall. Available instruction-level parallelism for superscalar and super-pipelined machines. *Third International Symposium on Architectural Support for Programming Languages and Operating Systems*, pp. 272-282, April 1989. Published as *Computer Architecture News 17* (2), *Operating Systems Review 23* (special issue), *SIGPLAN Notices 24* (special issue). Also available as WRL Research Report 89/7.

[8] Monica Lam. Software pipelining: An effective scheduling technique for VLIW machines. *Proceedings of the SIGPLAN '88 Conference on Programming Language Design and Implementation*, pp. 318-328. Published as *SIGPLAN Notices 23* (7), July 1988.

[9] Johnny K. F. Lee and Alan J. Smith. Branch prediction strategies and branch target buffer design. *Computer 17* (1), pp. 6-22, January 1984.

[10] Scott McFarling and John Hennessy. Reducing the cost of branches. *Thirteenth Annual Symposium on Computer Architecture*, pp. 396-403. Published as *Computer Architecture News 14* (2), June 1986.

[11] Alexandru Nicolau and Joseph A. Fisher. Measuring the parallelism available for very long instruction word architectures. *IEEE Transactions on Computers C-33* (11), pp. 968-976, November 1984.

[12] J. E. Smith. A study of branch prediction strategies. *Eighth Annual Symposium on Computer Architecture*, pp. 135-148. Published as *Computer Architecture News 9* (3), 1986.

[13] Michael D. Smith, Mike Johnson, and Mark A. Horowitz. Limits on multiple instruction issue. *Third International Symposium on Architectural Support for Programming Languages and Operating Systems*, pp. 290-302, April 1989. Published as *Computer Architecture News 17* (2), *Operating Systems Review 23* (special issue), *SIGPLAN Notices 24* (special issue).

[14] G. S. Tjaden and M. J. Flynn. Detection and parallel execution of parallel instructions. *IEEE Transactions on Computers C-19* (10), pp. 889-895, October 1970.

Appendix. Parallelism under many models.

On the next two pages are the results of running the test programs under more than 100 different configurations. The columns labelled "Livcu10" and "Lincu10" are the Livermore and Linpack benchmarks unrolled carefully 10 times. The configurations are keyed by the following abbreviations:

bPerf	perfect branch prediction, 100% correct.
bInf	2-bit branch prediction with infinite table.
b2K	2-bit branch prediction with 2K-entry table.
bStat	static branch prediction from profile.
bNone	no branch prediction.
jPerf	perfect indirect jump prediction, 100% correct.
jInf	indirect jump prediction with infinite table.
j2K	indirect jump prediction with 2K-entry table.
jStat	static indirect jump prediction from profile.
jNone	no indirect jump prediction.
rPerf	perfect register renaming: infinitely many registers.
rN	register renaming with N cpu and N fpu registers.
rNone	no register renaming: use registers as compiled.
aPerf	perfect alias analysis: use actual addresses to decide.
aComp	"compiler" alias analysis.
aInsp	"alias analysis "by inspection."
aNone	no alias analysis.
wN	continuous window of N instructions, default 2K.
dwN	discrete window of N instructions, default 2K.

config	gcc	espresso	li	fpppp	doduc	tomcat	sed	egrep	ccom	eco	yacc	met	grr	Stan	Whet	Liv	Livcul0	Lin	Lincul0
bPerf jPerf rPerf aPerf	26.5	40.6	16.3	60.4	56.8	59.7	24.2	34.1	37.4	16.8	22.0	22.9	27.8	18.0	7.4	6.5	10.8	27.4	27.5
bPerf jPerf rPerf aPerf w512	23.4	30.7	15.7	51.5	42.5	54.8	23.9	22.0	32.4	16.1	15.6	19.4	24.0	11.1	7.4	5.4	8.5	21.8	24.1
bPerf jPerf rPerf aPerf w256	20.5	23.3	15.6	44.6	29.9	52.3	21.3	17.0	25.1	15.4	13.6	17.1	20.1	8.8	7.4	5.2	8.0	18.7	22.2
bPerf jPerf rPerf aPerf w128	16.0	16.7	15.5	32.8	19.7	37.4	15.8	12.9	18.9	13.8	11.9	14.4	15.2	7.5	7.0	5.1	7.5	17.4	17.5
bPerf jPerf rPerf aPerf w64	11.9	11.7	14.2	21.6	13.3	23.8	11.2	10.0	13.8	11.2	11.9	11.9	10.7	6.7	6.6	5.0	6.5	12.9	13.0
bPerf jPerf rPerf aPerf w32	8.6	8.1	10.7	13.4	9.2	14.7	9.0	7.5	9.7	8.4	8.9	9.2	7.5	5.9	6.0	4.7	5.2	8.7	9.0
bPerf jPerf rPerf aPerf w16	6.2	5.8	7.0	8.3	6.4	8.9	7.2	5.3	7.1	5.8	6.7	6.1	5.2	5.1	5.1	4.3	4.3	5.4	5.9
bPerf jPerf rPerf aPerf w8	4.1	3.9	4.6	5.2	4.3	5.6	4.8	3.8	4.8	4.1	4.1	4.0	3.5	3.9	3.7	3.5	3.3	3.2	3.6
bPerf jPerf rPerf aPerf w4	2.6	2.5	2.9	3.2	2.8	3.3	2.9	3.0	2.9	2.7	2.5	2.5	2.4	2.6	2.5	2.5	2.4	2.0	2.2
bPerf jPerf rPerf aPerf dw	21.0	25.4	15.1	56.4	44.7	54.0	23.3	24.0	26.8	14.5	15.1	16.6	19.8	10.8	7.4	5.2	7.7	21.8	23.9
bPerf jPerf rPerf aPerf dw512	13.2	15.3	13.4	39.9	16.0	46.8	14.4	11.8	15.9	11.4	11.1	11.6	12.4	6.7	6.7	4.9	6.8	15.1	18.2
bPerf jPerf rPerf aPerf dw256	9.7	11.6	11.7	24.9	10.5	19.4	10.3	9.3	12.0	9.0	9.4	9.5	8.8	6.1	5.9	4.7	6.1	12.2	14.0
bPerf jPerf rPerf aPerf dw128	7.4	8.4	9.6	10.9	7.4	12.4	8.1	7.1	8.9	7.0	8.0	7.5	6.6	5.3	5.2	4.4	5.1	9.0	9.9
bPerf jPerf rPerf aPerf dw64	5.7	5.9	7.0	7.5	5.5	8.9	6.6	5.2	6.7	5.5	6.5	5.6	5.0	4.6	4.5	3.9	4.2	6.1	6.6
bPerf jPerf rPerf aPerf dw32	4.3	4.2	5.3	5.3	4.2	5.6	5.2	3.8	5.1	4.3	4.8	4.1	3.7	3.6	3.6	3.3	3.5	3.7	4.1
bPerf jPerf rPerf aPerf dw16	3.3	3.0	3.8	3.9	3.3	4.1	4.0	2.8	3.8	3.3	3.3	3.4	2.8	2.9	2.9	2.7	2.3	2.3	2.5
bPerf jPerf rPerf aPerf dw8	2.5	2.2	2.8	3.1	2.7	3.2	2.7	2.0	2.8	2.5	2.3	2.4	2.1	2.3	2.3	2.2	2.2	1.7	1.9
bPerf jPerf rPerf aPerf dw4	1.9	1.7	2.0	2.4	2.2	2.6	2.0	1.5	2.0	1.9	1.7	1.8	1.7	1.7	1.9	1.7	1.8	1.5	1.6
bPerf jPerf rPerf aComp	10.1	8.2	12.8	60.4	56.8	59.7	24.2	34.1	18.7	7.6	14.6	15.3	17.5	18.0	7.4	6.5	10.8	27.4	27.5
bPerf jPerf rPerf aInsp	4.2	5.6	4.8	4.8	6.7	4.9	5.0	7.4	2.7	3.6	3.7	3.4	3.7	5.7	3.5	2.4	2.1	3.5	6.7
bPerf jPerf rPerf aNone	3.3	5.1	3.1	3.4	3.9	3.5	4.4	7.3	2.7	2.7	6.0	2.9	3.0	4.9	5.5	2.3	1.8	3.4	6.0
bPerf jPerf r256 aPerf	21.3	24.1	15.6	46.6	24.2	45.8	22.1	19.0	28.8	15.6	14.2	17.6	21.0	9.5	5.5	5.2	6.9	19.6	23.6
bPerf jPerf r64 aPerf	11.5	10.9	14.6	19.6	12.9	26.6	11.4	10.0	14.4	11.4	10.6	11.8	10.0	6.7	5.4	5.0	6.5	13.9	14.7
bPerf jPerf r32 aPerf	5.1	4.8	6.2	5.4	5.1	6.6	7.5	5.7	5.7	5.8	5.8	5.8	4.4	4.9	4.6	4.5	5.0	3.2	4.6
bPerf jPerf rNone aPerf	4.6	4.0	4.0	3.5	4.5	6.0	6.0	5.5	4.5	4.8	5.3	4.9	4.3	4.3	3.5	3.6	3.2	4.8	5.8
bPerf jPerf rNone aNone	2.8	3.1	2.8	2.6	3.1	3.0	3.4	4.3	2.3	2.5	3.9	2.5	2.5	2.8	3.5	3.6	1.8	3.4	4.0
bPerf jInf rPerf aPerf	7.7	18.1	6.6	50.8	10.3	59.3	21.5	33.8	8.8	5.9	15.1	10.0	9.5	12.8	4.9	6.5	10.8	27.3	27.5
bPerf jNone rPerf aPerf	5.6	11.2	4.7	34.8	8.4	59.2	6.6	15.3	5.5	4.5	9.4	5.4	5.3	5.0	3.7	6.5	10.8	16.3	20.9
bPerf jNone rNone aNone	2.5	3.0	2.4	2.6	3.0	3.0	3.1	4.3	2.0	2.3	3.8	2.3	2.4	3.1	2.2	2.2	1.7	3.4	4.0
bInf jPerf rPerf aPerf	5.7	5.7	6.2	35.9	12.5	51.7	7.5	4.1	6.7	6.1	6.9	7.0	4.7	4.4	6.6	4.9	7.6	17.1	17.1
bInf jInf rPerf aPerf	4.8	5.5	4.8	35.0	8.3	51.6	7.4	4.1	5.4	4.5	6.7	6.2	4.4	4.2	4.6	4.9	7.6	14.3	17.0
bInf jInf rPerf aPerf w512	4.8	5.5	4.8	33.8	8.3	51.4	7.4	4.1	5.4	4.5	6.7	6.2	4.4	4.2	4.6	4.9	7.6	14.3	17.0
bInf jInf rPerf aPerf w256	4.8	5.5	4.8	31.9	8.2	50.0	7.4	4.1	5.4	4.5	6.7	6.2	4.4	4.2	4.6	4.9	7.6	14.3	16.6
bInf jInf rPerf aPerf w128	4.8	5.4	4.8	26.8	8.0	36.5	7.4	4.1	5.4	4.5	6.7	6.2	4.3	4.2	4.6	4.9	7.3	14.3	14.4
bInf jInf rPerf aPerf w64	4.7	5.4	4.8	19.4	7.5	23.5	7.3	4.0	5.4	4.5	6.7	6.2	4.3	4.1	4.6	4.9	6.4	14.3	11.6
bInf jInf rPerf aPerf w32	4.6	5.0	4.7	12.7	6.6	14.7	7.0	4.0	5.3	4.4	6.5	6.2	4.2	4.1	4.6	4.7	8.1	11.4	8.4
bInf jInf rPerf aPerf w16	4.3	4.4	4.3	8.1	5.5	8.9	6.4	3.7	5.1	4.2	5.5	4.8	3.8	4.0	4.4	4.2	5.2	8.4	5.7
bInf jInf rPerf aPerf w8	3.4	3.4	3.7	5.1	4.1	5.6	4.5	3.1	4.1	3.5	3.8	3.7	3.0	3.4	3.4	3.4	4.3	5.2	3.6
bInf jInf rPerf aPerf w4	2.5	2.3	2.7	3.2	2.8	3.3	2.9	2.0	2.7	2.5	2.4	2.4	2.2	2.5	2.5	2.4	3.3	3.2	2.2
bInf jInf rPerf aPerf dw	4.8	5.5	4.8	34.7	8.3	50.7	7.4	4.1	5.4	4.5	6.7	6.2	4.4	4.2	4.6	4.9	7.4	14.3	17.0
bInf jInf rPerf aPerf dw512	4.8	5.4	4.8	31.1	8.3	45.3	7.3	4.1	5.4	4.5	6.4	6.1	4.3	4.1	4.6	4.8	7.4	12.6	15.2
bInf jInf rPerf aPerf dw256	4.7	5.3	4.8	22.6	7.4	19.2	7.3	4.1	5.3	4.4	6.1	6.0	4.3	4.0	4.6	4.7	6.7	10.9	12.9
bInf jInf rPerf aPerf dw128	4.6	5.1	4.8	10.6	6.2	12.4	6.9	4.0	5.2	4.4	5.6	5.6	4.2	4.0	4.4	5.0	6.0	8.6	9.4
bInf jInf rPerf aPerf dw64	4.3	4.4	4.4	7.5	5.0	8.9	5.8	3.8	4.9	4.1	5.5	4.8	3.8	3.8	4.1	4.4	5.0	8.6	6.4
bInf jInf rPerf aPerf dw32	3.6	3.6	4.0	5.3	4.1	5.9	5.0	3.1	4.2	3.7	4.4	3.8	3.2	3.3	3.4	3.8	4.2	5.9	4.1
bInf jInf rPerf aPerf dw16	2.9	2.7	3.3	3.9	3.3	4.1	3.9	2.5	3.5	3.0	3.3	2.9	2.6	2.7	2.7	3.3	3.4	3.6	2.5
bInf jInf rPerf aPerf dw8	2.3	2.1	2.6	3.1	2.6	3.2	2.7	2.0	2.7	2.4	2.3	2.3	2.0	2.2	2.2	2.8	2.8	2.3	1.9
bInf jInf rPerf aPerf dw4	1.8	1.7	2.0	2.4	2.1	2.6	1.9	1.5	2.0	1.9	1.7	1.8	1.7	1.7	1.9	2.2	1.7	1.4	1.6
bInf jInf rPerf aComp	4.0	4.4	4.3	34.9	8.3	51.6	7.4	4.1	4.9	3.8	5.8	5.5	4.3	4.2	4.6	4.9	7.6	14.3	17.0
bInf jInf rPerf aInsp	3.1	3.8	3.3	4.7	5.3	4.9	4.2	3.4	2.4	2.9	4.8	3.0	2.8	3.3	3.0	2.3	2.1	3.5	6.5
bInf jInf rPerf aNone	2.7	3.6	2.5	3.4	3.4	3.5	3.8	3.4	2.1	2.4	4.4	2.6	2.4	3.1	2.5	2.3	1.8	3.4	5.9

	gcc	espresso	li	fpppp	doduc	tomcat	sed	egrep	ccom	eco	yacc	met	grr	Stan	Whet	Liv	Livcul0	Lin	Lincul0
bInf jInf r256 aPerf	4.8	5.5	4.8	32.4	7.6	43.8	7.4	4.1	5.4	4.5	6.7	6.2	4.4	4.2	4.2	4.9	6.4	14.3	17.0
bInf jInf r256 aPerf w512	4.8	5.5	4.8	32.2	7.6	43.8	7.4	4.1	5.4	4.5	6.7	6.2	4.4	4.2	4.2	4.9	6.4	14.3	17.0
bInf jInf r256 aPerf w256	4.8	5.5	4.8	31.6	7.6	43.3	7.4	4.1	5.4	4.5	6.7	6.2	4.4	4.2	4.2	4.9	6.4	14.3	16.6
bInf jInf r256 aPerf w128	4.8	5.4	4.8	26.8	7.5	32.9	7.4	4.1	5.4	4.5	6.7	6.2	4.3	4.2	4.2	4.9	6.3	14.2	14.3
bInf jInf r256 aPerf w64	4.7	5.4	4.7	19.4	7.0	21.8	7.3	4.1	5.4	4.5	6.7	6.2	4.3	4.1	4.2	4.8	6.3	11.4	11.6
bInf jInf r256 aPerf w32	4.6	5.0	4.3	12.7	6.3	14.0	7.0	4.0	5.3	4.4	6.5	6.0	4.2	4.1	4.2	4.5	5.2	8.1	8.4
bInf jInf r256 aPerf w16	4.3	4.4	3.7	8.1	5.4	8.9	6.4	3.7	5.1	4.2	5.5	4.8	3.8	4.0	4.1	4.1	4.3	5.2	5.7
bInf jInf r256 aPerf w8	3.4	3.4	2.7	5.1	4.0	5.6	4.5	3.1	4.1	3.5	3.8	3.7	3.0	3.4	3.3	3.3	3.3	3.2	3.6
bInf jInf r256 aPerf w4	2.5	2.5	2.7	3.2	2.7	3.3	2.9	2.0	2.7	2.5	3.8	2.4	2.2	2.4	2.4	2.5	2.4	2.0	2.2
bInf jInf r256 aComp	4.0	4.4	4.3	32.4	7.6	43.8	7.4	4.1	4.9	3.8	5.8	5.5	4.3	4.2	4.2	4.9	6.4	14.3	17.0
bInf jInf r256 aInsp	3.1	3.8	3.3	4.7	5.0	4.8	4.2	3.4	2.4	2.9	4.8	3.0	2.8	3.3	2.8	2.3	2.1	3.5	6.5
bInf jInf r256 aNone	2.7	3.6	2.5	3.4	3.3	3.4	3.8	3.4	2.1	2.4	4.4	2.6	2.4	3.0	2.3	2.2	1.8	3.4	5.9
bInf jInf r64 aPerf	4.7	5.3	4.8	17.8	6.8	25.9	7.4	4.1	5.4	4.5	6.7	6.2	4.3	4.2	4.2	4.9	6.3	12.1	12.5
bInf jInf r64 aComp	4.0	3.8	4.3	17.8	6.8	26.8	7.4	4.1	4.9	3.8	5.8	5.5	4.2	4.2	4.2	4.9	6.3	12.1	12.5
bInf jInf r64 aInsp	3.1	3.1	3.3	4.7	4.6	7.4	4.1	3.4	2.4	2.9	4.8	3.0	2.8	3.3	2.3	2.3	2.1	3.1	4.5
bInf jInf r32 aPerf	3.9	3.8	4.2	5.4	4.6	7.4	6.3	3.8	4.3	4.1	4.9	4.7	3.4	3.8	3.8	4.0	4.9	3.1	4.5
bInf jInf r32 aComp	3.4	3.2	3.9	5.4	4.6	7.5	6.3	3.8	4.1	3.6	4.5	4.3	3.4	3.8	3.8	4.0	4.9	3.1	4.5
bInf jInf r32 aInsp	2.9	3.0	3.2	3.9	3.9	4.4	3.8	3.2	2.4	2.8	3.9	2.9	2.6	3.2	2.6	2.3	2.1	2.7	3.6
bInf jInf rNone aPerf	3.5	3.3	3.9	3.4	4.2	4.9	5.3	3.8	3.6	3.7	4.5	4.2	3.2	3.5	3.3	3.6	3.2	4.6	5.6
bInf jInf rNone aComp	3.2	2.9	2.9	3.4	4.2	4.9	5.3	3.8	3.5	3.3	4.3	4.0	3.2	3.5	3.6	3.6	4.6	4.6	5.6
bInf jInf rNone aInsp	2.8	2.8	3.1	3.2	3.7	3.8	3.5	3.3	2.3	2.7	3.8	2.7	2.5	3.0	2.6	2.2	1.9	3.4	4.2
bInf jStat rPerf aPerf	4.8	5.4	5.2	34.3	8.8	51.6	7.4	4.1	5.5	4.8	6.6	5.8	4.4	4.2	4.8	4.9	7.6	14.3	17.0
bInf jNone rPerf aPerf	4.1	5.2	3.9	30.6	7.3	51.5	5.5	4.1	4.5	3.9	6.2	4.5	3.8	3.8	3.5	4.9	7.6	14.1	16.8
bInf jNone r256 aPerf	4.1	5.2	3.9	29.5	6.8	43.7	5.5	4.1	4.5	3.9	6.2	4.5	3.8	3.8	3.3	4.9	6.4	14.1	16.8
bInf jNone r256 aComp	3.6	3.6	3.7	29.5	6.8	43.7	5.5	4.1	4.2	3.5	5.5	4.3	3.7	3.8	3.3	4.9	6.4	14.1	16.8
bInf jNone r256 aInsp	2.9	3.7	3.0	4.7	4.8	4.8	3.6	3.4	2.2	2.8	4.6	2.7	2.6	3.2	2.7	2.3	2.1	3.4	6.5
b2K j2K rPerf aPerf	4.6	5.4	4.8	32.4	8.2	51.6	7.4	4.1	5.3	4.4	6.7	6.2	4.3	4.2	4.6	4.9	7.6	14.3	17.0
b2K j2K r256 aPerf	4.6	5.4	4.8	30.5	7.5	43.8	7.4	4.1	5.3	4.4	6.7	6.2	4.3	4.2	4.2	4.9	6.4	14.3	17.0
b2K j2K r256 aComp	3.9	3.8	4.3	30.5	7.5	43.8	7.4	4.1	4.8	3.8	5.8	5.5	4.2	4.3	4.2	4.9	6.4	14.3	17.0
b2K j2K r256 aInsp	3.1	3.1	3.3	4.7	5.0	4.8	4.2	3.4	2.4	2.9	4.8	3.0	2.8	3.3	2.8	2.3	2.1	3.5	6.5
b2K j2K r64 aPerf	4.5	5.3	4.8	17.6	6.8	26.3	7.4	4.1	5.3	4.4	6.7	6.2	4.3	4.2	4.2	4.9	6.3	12.1	12.5
b2K j2K r32 aPerf	3.8	3.8	4.2	5.3	4.5	7.5	6.3	3.8	4.3	4.1	4.9	4.7	3.4	3.8	3.8	4.0	4.9	3.1	4.5
b2K j2K rNone aPerf	3.5	3.3	3.9	3.4	4.1	4.9	5.3	3.8	3.6	3.6	4.5	4.2	3.2	3.5	3.3	3.6	3.2	4.6	5.6
bStat jInf rPerf aPerf	4.7	5.0	4.8	31.6	8.2	51.4	7.4	4.3	5.4	4.4	5.3	6.1	4.0	4.0	4.8	4.9	7.6	13.6	16.6
bStat jInf r256 aPerf	4.7	5.0	4.8	29.8	7.5	43.7	7.4	4.3	5.4	4.4	5.3	6.1	4.0	4.0	4.2	4.9	6.4	13.6	16.6
bStat jStat rPerf aPerf	4.8	5.0	5.2	31.6	8.7	51.4	7.4	4.3	5.5	4.7	5.3	5.7	4.0	4.0	4.9	4.9	7.6	13.6	16.6
bStat jStat r256 aPerf	4.8	5.0	5.2	29.7	8.0	43.7	7.4	4.3	5.5	4.7	5.3	5.7	4.0	4.0	4.4	4.9	6.4	13.6	16.6
bNone jPerf rPerf aPerf	1.8	1.7	2.1	17.5	3.2	8.7	1.7	1.3	2.3	2.0	1.3	1.9	1.8	1.6	2.6	2.7	4.1	4.2	5.5
bNone jPerf rNone aNone	1.5	1.5	1.6	2.5	2.0	2.7	1.5	1.2	1.6	1.5	1.3	1.5	1.4	1.5	1.8	1.7	1.6	2.4	2.9
bNone jInf rPerf aPerf	1.8	1.8	2.0	17.5	3.1	8.7	1.7	1.3	2.2	1.9	1.3	1.9	1.8	1.6	2.6	2.7	4.1	4.2	5.5
bNone jInf r256 aComp	1.7	1.6	2.0	17.0	3.1	8.7	1.7	1.3	2.2	1.9	1.3	1.9	1.8	1.6	2.5	2.5	3.8	4.2	5.5
bNone jInf r256 aInsp	1.6	1.5	1.8	4.5	2.7	3.9	1.6	1.3	1.7	1.5	1.3	1.6	1.6	1.5	2.0	1.8	2.0	2.6	4.2
bNone jNone rPerf aPerf	1.5	1.5	1.5	3.3	2.1	8.7	1.5	1.3	2.1	1.9	1.3	1.8	1.4	1.6	1.8	1.8	1.7	2.5	4.0
bNone jNone rPerf aNone	1.8	1.7	1.9	16.9	3.0	8.7	1.6	1.3	2.1	1.9	1.3	1.8	1.8	1.6	2.2	2.5	3.8	4.2	5.5
bNone jNone r256 aPerf	1.7	1.6	1.9	16.4	3.0	8.7	1.6	1.3	2.1	1.9	1.3	1.8	1.7	1.6	2.2	2.5	3.8	4.2	5.5
bNone jNone r256 aComp	1.6	1.5	1.7	16.4	3.0	8.7	1.6	1.3	1.6	1.8	1.3	1.8	1.7	1.6	2.2	2.5	3.8	4.2	5.5
bNone jNone r256 aInsp	1.5	1.5	1.5	4.4	2.7	3.9	1.5	1.3	1.5	1.6	1.3	1.5	1.4	1.5	2.0	1.8	2.0	2.6	4.2
bNone jNone r256 aNone	1.5	1.5	1.5	3.3	2.1	3.0	1.5	1.3	2.1	1.8	1.3	1.8	1.5	1.5	1.8	1.8	1.7	2.0	3.6
bNone jNone rNone aPerf	1.7	1.7	1.9	3.3	2.4	4.1	1.6	1.2	2.1	1.6	1.3	1.8	1.7	1.5	2.1	2.4	2.7	2.8	3.6
bNone jNone rNone aComp	1.7	1.6	1.9	3.1	2.3	3.3	1.5	1.3	1.6	1.6	1.3	1.5	1.5	1.5	2.1	1.7	2.7	2.8	3.6
bNone jNone rNone aInsp	1.6	1.6	1.7	3.1	2.3	3.3	1.5	1.3	1.6	1.6	1.3	1.5	1.5	1.5	1.8	1.7	1.8	2.5	3.0
bNone jNone rNone aNone	1.5	1.5	1.5	2.5	2.0	2.7	1.4	1.2	1.5	1.4	1.3	1.4	1.4	1.4	1.8	1.7	1.6	2.4	2.9

Chapter 2: Fine-Grained Parallel Architectures

Fine-grained parallel architectures exploit parallelism by finding independent instructions to execute concurrently, using both static (compile-time) and dynamic (run-time) dependence checking. Some architectures — such as pipelined processors — time-multiplex the use of functional units, while others — such as multiple instruction-issue architectures — replicate the functional units. These different approaches are not mutually exclusive, and some architectures incorporate several techniques.[1,2*,3]

Pipelining

Pipelining — in which the execution of many different instructions overlaps — has been used extensively to exploit parallelism.[4-8] Given an m-stage pipeline and an ideal instruction stream of I_d instructions (that is, a stream in which there are no dependences that could prevent a new instruction from issuing each cycle), it will take m cycles to fill the pipeline. After the pipeline has been filled, a new instruction will complete execution every cycle, so that the total execution time is $T_m = m + (I_d - 1)$ cycles. (The same instruction stream can be executed on a nonpipelined processor with the same functionality in $T_1 = mI_d$ cycles, because each operation takes m cycles to complete.) The speedup of this ideal pipelined processor is

$$S_m = \frac{T_1}{T_m} = \frac{mI_d}{m + I_d - 1} = \frac{m}{\frac{m}{I_d} + 1 - \frac{1}{I_d}}$$

2

As more instructions are executed (that is, $I_d \rightarrow \infty$), the ideal speedup approaches the number of pipeline stages, m. In a real instruction stream, there are dependences that prevent a new instruction from issuing every cycle, and branches can disrupt the flow of instructions in the pipeline,[9*] so that the actual speedup is less than m. There are a variety of static and dynamic dependence-checking techniques that can be used by the instruction-issuing logic in a pipelined processor to determine when to issue the next instruction.[10-20,21*,22*]

Multiple-instruction issuing

The issuing logic of a typical processor can restrict performance by limiting the issue rate to one instruction per cycle. To break this "Flynn bottleneck,"[23] the processor can be designed to issue multiple instructions in a single cycle. If there are no dependences in the instruction stream, an ideal processor that can issue j instructions per cycle has a maximum speedup of $S_j = j$. As with pipelined processors, dependences in multiple instruction-issue processors can be checked statically by the compiler, as is done in very long instruction word (VLIW) machines, or dynamically by the hardware, as is done in superscalar processors.

In VLIW machines, the compiler packs several independent operations into one instruction word that is several hundred bits long, so that all of the operations are issued simultaneously. Trace scheduling[24] and software pipelining[25*] are compilation techniques for VLIW machines such as the ELI-512,[26] the Multiflow computer,[27] and the processing elements in the Warp computer.[28*,29] The IMPACT project[30] has examined and further extended some of these VLIW compilation techniques. The polycyclic architecture[31,32] is a wide instruction word architecture that provides some additional hardware features to simplify the compiler's instruction-scheduling task. Some of these hardware features have been implemented in the Cydrome Cydra-5 computer.[33-35,36*] Another VLIW architecture[37-40] speeds up nonnumeric applications by simultaneously evaluating the results of taking several different branch paths and throwing away all but the result of the single branch path that turns out to be valid.

VLIW and superscalar processors are similar in that both try to issue multiple operations in a single cycle. In VLIW machines, independent operations are determined at compile-time; in superscalar machines, the issuing hardware dynamically examines the instruction stream at run-time, looking for independent instructions that can be issued simultaneously.[1,41*,42-47,48*,49] This ability to dynamically examine the instruction stream potentially allows a superscalar processor to be instruction-level compatible with other, possibly nonparallel, processors. A VLIW processor may have poorer code density than a superscalar processor, since unused operations in the VLIW instruction word must be filled with no-ops. This difference between VLIW and superscalar processors may reduce the effectiveness of a VLIW processor's instruction cache when compared to an equivalently sized instruction cache in a superscalar processor. However, because each functional unit in a VLIW processor has a corresponding field in the instruction word, instruction issuing is simpler in the VLIW than in the superscalar processor. As a result, VLIW and superscalar processors probably have about the same ability to exploit parallelism in an application program.

Decoupled access/execute architectures

The work performed by a processor can be partitioned into an access process and an execute process.[50] The access process performs those actions required to access memory and the execute process performs the real work of the program. Several architectures that take advantage of this decoupling have been proposed[51*-54] and a number of machines incorporating the idea of decoupling these two processes have been built.[2*,55-58] These machines use the compiler to divide the instructions into the two processes, and the functional units for each process usually are pipelined with dynamic dependence checking so that multiple operations can execute concurrently. In addition, as far as dependences permit, the access process can run ahead of the execute process and thus hide the delay to access memory.

Dataflow processors

Conceptually, dataflow processors[59*,60*-69,70*-73,74*-78] can take advantage of all of the parallelism available in a program, since, in a dataflow processor, execution is driven only by the availability of operands at the inputs to the functional units. There is no need for a program counter in this architecture, and its parallelism is limited only by the actual data dependences in the application program. While the dataflow concept offers the possibility of high performance, the performance of an actual implementation of a dataflow processor can be restricted by resource dependences, such as a limited number of functional units, limited memory bandwidth, and the need to associatively match pending operations with available functional units. These restrictions are especially troublesome for loops, and there have been proposals to include coarser-grained iterative instructions in dataflow processors.[75,79,80]

Some researchers have argued that the dataflow concept should not be built into the hardware, but rather is better applied to higher, more conceptual levels. For example, the dataflow concept could be used to partition a program into coarse-grained independent tasks and to schedule these tasks onto a coarse-grained parallel machine.[81] Others have argued that it is more appropriate to combine the dataflow concept with a traditional von Neumann architecture.[70*,82-85] The high performance substrate (HPS) architecture,[83-85] for example, combines the dataflow concept with a von Neumann architecture by applying dataflow techniques to a small section of a program, thereby exploiting only local parallelism. It is left to higher levels, such as the compiler, to exploit the available global parallelism. The concept of dataflow is a powerful one, but more research is needed to determine how to best utilize the potential of dataflow for exploiting parallelism.

References (Chapter 2)

An asterisk following a reference citation below indicates the inclusion of that paper in this tutorial.

1. K. Murakami et al., "SIMP (Single Instruction Stream/Multiple Instruction Pipelining): A Novel High-Speed Single-Processor Architecture," *Int'l Symp. Computer Architecture*, 1989, pp. 78-85.

2.* J.E. Smith, "Dynamic Instruction Scheduling and the Astronautics ZS-1," *Computer*, Vol. 22, No. 7, July 1989, pp. 21-35.

3. M.R. Thistle and B.J. Smith, "A Processor Architecture for Horizon," *Proc. Supercomputing '88*, Nov. 1988, pp. 35-41.

Pipelining

4. S.S. Chen, J.J. Dongarra, and C.C. Hsiung, "Multiprocessing Linear Algebra Algorithms on the CRAY X-MP-2: Experiences with Small Granularity," *J. Parallel and Distributed Computing*, Vol. 1, No. 1, Aug. 1984, pp. 22-31.

5. J. Hennessy et al., "The MIPS Machine," *IEEE Digest of Papers-CompCon*, Feb. 1982, pp. 2-7.

6. P.M. Kogge, *The Architecture of Pipelined Computers*, Hemisphere, New York, N.Y., 1981.

7. D.A. Patterson, "Reduced Instruction Set Computers," *Comm. ACM*, Vol. 28, No. 1, Jan. 1985, pp. 8-21.

8. N.P. Topham, A. Omondi, and R.N. Ibbett, "On the Design and Performance of Conventional Pipelined Architectures," *J. Supercomputing*, Vol. 1, 1988, pp. 353-393.

9.* D.J. Lilja, "Reducing the Branch Penalty in Pipelined Processors," *Computer*, Vol. 21, No. 7, July 1988, pp. 47-55.

10. D.W. Anderson, F.J. Sparacio, and R.M. Tomasulo, "The IBM System/360 Model 91: Machine Philosophy and Instruction-Handling," *IBM J. Research and Development*, Vol. 11, No. 1, Jan. 1967, pp. 8-24.

11. D. Bernstein, "An Improved Approximation Algorithm for Scheduling Pipelined Machines," *Int'l Conf. Parallel Processing, Vol. I: Architecture*, 1988, pp. 430-433.

12. D.S. Coutant, C.L. Hammond, and J.W. Kelly, "Compilers for the New Generation of Hewlett-Packard Computers," *IEEE Digest of Papers-CompCon*, Feb. 1986, pp. 48-61.

13. J. Hennessy et al., "Hardware/Software Tradeoffs for Increased Performance," *Int'l Conf. Architectural Support Programming Languages and Operating Systems*, Mar. 1982, pp. 2-11.

14. P.Y.-T. Hsu and E.S. Davidson, "Highly Concurrent Scalar Processing," *Int'l Symp. Computer Architecture*, 1986, pp. 386-395.

15. N.P. Jouppi, "Architectural and Organizational Tradeoffs in the Design of the MultiTitan CPU," *Int'l Symp. Computer Architecture*, 1989, pp. 281-289.

16. A.R. Pleszkun et al., "WISQ: A Restartable Architecture Using Queues," *Int'l Symp. Computer Architecture*, 1987, pp. 290-299.

17. G. Radin, "The 801 Minicomputer," *IBM J. Research and Development*, Vol. 27, No. 3, May 1983, pp. 237-246.

18. R.M. Russell, "The CRAY-1 Computer System," *Comm. ACM*, Vol. 21, No. 1, Jan. 1978, pp. 63-72.

19. G.S. Sohi and S. Vajapeyam, "Instruction Issue Logic for High-Performance, Interruptible Pipelined Processors," *Int'l Symp. Computer Architecture*, 1987, pp. 27-34.

20. G.S. Sohi, "Instruction Issue Logic for High-Performance, Interruptible, Multiple Functional Unit, Pipelined Computers," *IEEE Trans. Computers*, Vol. 39, No. 3, Mar. 1990, pp. 349-359.

21.* S. Weiss and J.E. Smith, "Instruction Issue Logic in Pipelined Supercomputers," *IEEE Trans. Computers*, Vol. C-33, No. 11, Nov. 1984, pp. 1013-1022.

22.* S.R. Kunkel and J.E. Smith, "Optimal Pipelining in Supercomputers," *IEEE Int'l Symp. Computer Architecture*, 1986, pp. 404-411.

Multiple-instruction issuing

23. M.J. Flynn, "Very High-Speed Computing Systems," *Proc. IEEE*, Vol. 54, No. 12, Dec. 1966, pp. 1901-1909.

24. J.A. Fisher, "Trace Scheduling: A Technique for Global Microcode Compaction," *IEEE Trans. Computers*, Vol. C-30, No. 7, July 1981, pp. 478-490.

25.* M. Lam, "Software Pipelining: An Effective Scheduling Technique for VLIW Machines," *Proc. SIGPLAN '88 Conf. Programming Language Design and Implementation*, June 1988, pp. 318-328.

26. J.A. Fisher, "Very Long Instruction Word Architectures and the ELI-512," *Int'l Symp. Computer Architecture*, 1983, pp. 140-150.

27. R.P. Colwell et al., "A VLIW Architecture for a Trace Scheduling Compiler," *IEEE Trans. Computers*, Vol. 37, No. 8, Aug. 1988, pp. 967-979.

28.* M. Annaratone et al., "The Warp Computer: Architecture, Implementation, and Performance," *IEEE Trans. Computers*, Vol. C-36, No. 12, Dec. 1987, pp. 1523-1538.

29. R. Cohn et al., "Architecture and Compiler Tradeoffs for a Long Instruction Word Microprocessor," *Third Int'l Conf. Architectural Support Programming Languages and Operating Systems*, Apr. 1989, pp. 2-14.

30. P.P. Chang et al., "IMPACT: An Architectural Framework for Multiple-Instruction-Issue Processors," *Int'l Symp. Computer Architecture*, 1991, pp. 266-275.

31. B.R. Rau and C.D. Glaeser, "Some Scheduling Techniques and an Easily Schedulable Horizontal Architecture for High Performance Scientific Computing," *Ann. Microprogramming Workshop*, Oct. 1981, pp. 183-198.

32. B. R. Rau, C.D. Glaeser, and R.L. Picard, "Efficient Code Generation for Horizontal Architectures: Compiler Techniques and Architectural Support," *Int'l Symp. Computer Architecture*, 1982, pp. 131-139.

33. J.C. Dehnert, P.Y.-T. Hsu, and J.P. Bratt, "Overlapped Loop Support in the Cydra 5," *Third Int'l Conf. Architectural Support Programming Languages and Operating Systems*, Apr. 1989, pp. 26-38.

34. B.R. Rau, "Cydra 5 Directed Dataflow Architecture," *IEEE Digest of Papers-CompCon*, Feb. 1988, pp. 106-113.

35. B.R. Rau, M.S. Schlansker, and D.W.L. Yen, "The Cydra 5 Stride-Insensitive Memory System," *Int'l Conf. Parallel Processing, Vol I: Architecture*, 1989, pp. 242-246.

36.* B.R. Rau et al., "The Cydra 5 Departmental Supercomputer," *Computer*, Vol. 22, No. 1, Jan. 1989, pp. 12-35.

37. K. Ebcioglu, "A Compilation Technique for Software Pipelining of Loops with Conditional Jumps (Preliminary Version)," *Proc. Ann. Workshop on Microprogramming*, Dec. 1987, pp. 69-79.

38. K. Ebcioglu, "A Wide Instruction Word Architecture for Fine-Grain Parallelism," *CONPAR*, Cambridge Univ. Press, Cambridge, Mass., 1988.

39. K. Ebcioglu, "Some Design Ideas for a VLIW Architecture for Sequential-Natured Software," *Proc. IFIP WG 10.3 Working Conf. Parallel Processing*, Apr. 1988, pp. 3-21.

40. K. Ebcioglu and A. Nicolau, "A Global Resource-Constrained Parallelization Technique," *Int'l Conf. Supercomputing*, 1989, pp. 154-163.

Superscalar processors

41.* R.M. Tomasulo, "An Efficient Algorithm for Exploiting Multiple Arithmetic Units," *IBM J. Research and Development*, Vol. 11, No. 1, Jan. 1967, pp. 25-33.

42. R.D. Acosta, J. Kjelstrup, and H.C. Torng, "An Instruction Issuing Approach to Enhancing Performance in Multiple Functional Unit Processors," *IEEE Trans. Computers*, Vol. C-35, No. 9, Sept. 1986, pp. 815-828.

43. H.B. Bakoglu and T. Whiteside, "RISC System/6000 Hardware Overview," *IBM RISC System/6000 Technology*, Austin, Texas, 1990, pp. 8-15 (order no. SA23-2619).

44. R.D. Groves and R. Oehler, "RISC System/6000 Processor Architecture," *IBM RISC System/6000 Technology*, Austin, Texas, pp. 16-23 (order no. SA23-2619).

45. C.B. Hall and K. O'Brien, "Performance Characteristics of Architectural Features of the IBM RISC System 6000," *Fourth Int'l Conf. Architectural Support Programming Languages and Operating Systems*, Apr. 1991, pp. 303-309.

46. R.W. Horst, R.L. Harris, and R.L. Jardine, "Multiple Instruction Issue in the NonStop Cyclone Processor," *Int'l Symp. Computer Architecture*, 1990, pp. 216-226.

47. W. Mangione-Smith, S.G. Abraham, and E.S. Davidson, "Architectural vs. Delivered Performance of the IBM RS/6000 and the Astronautics ZS-1," *Hawaii Int'l Conf. System Sciences, Vol. I: Architecture*, 1991, pp. 397-408.

48.* C. Stephens et al., "Instruction Level Profiling and Evaluation of the IBM RS/6000," *Int'l Symp. Computer Architecture*, 1991, pp. 180-189.

49. G.S. Tjaden and M.J. Flynn, "Detection and Parallel Execution of Independent Instructions," *IEEE Trans. Computers*, Vol. C-19, No. 10, Oct. 1970, pp. 889-895.

Decoupled access/execute architectures

50. D.W. Hammerstrom and E.S. Davidson, "Information Content of CPU Memory Referencing Behavior," *Int'l Symp. Computer Architecture*, 1977, pp. 184-192.

51.* A.R. Pleszkun and E.S. Davidson, "Structured Memory Access Architecture," *IEEE Int'l Conf. Parallel Processing*, 1983, pp. 461-471.

52. G.S. Sohi and E.S. Davidson, "Performance of the Structured Memory Access (SMA) Architecture," *Int'l Conf. Parallel Processing*, 1984, pp. 506-513.

53. A.R. Pleszkun et al., "Features of the Structured Memory Access (SMA) Architecture," *IEEE Digest of Papers-CompCon*, Feb. 1986, pp. 259-263.

54. J.E. Smith, "Decoupled Access/Execute Computer Architectures," *ACM Trans. Computer Systems*, Vol. 2, No. 4, Nov. 1984, pp. 289-308.

55. E.U. Cohler and J.E. Storer, "Functionally Parallel Architecture for Array Processors," *Computer*, Vol. 14, No. 9, Sept. 1981, pp. 28-36.

56. J.R. Goodman et al., "PIPE: A VLSI Decoupled Architecture," *Int'l Symp. Computer Architecture*, 1985, pp. 20-27.

57. W. Lichtenstein, "The Architecture of the Culler 7," *IEEE Digest of Papers-CompCon*, Feb. 1986, pp. 467-470.

58. J.E. Smith et al., "The ZS-1 Central Processor," *Second Int'l Conf. Architectural Support Programming Languages and Operating Systems*, Oct. 1987, pp. 199-204.

Dataflow processors

59.* Arvind and K.P. Gostelow, "The U-Interpreter," *Computer*, Vol. 15, No. 2, Feb. 1982, pp. 42-49.

60.* Arvind and R.A. Iannucci, "Two Fundamental Issues in Multiprocessing," *Proc. DFVLR Conf. Parallel Processing Science and Eng.*, 1987.

61. Arvind, D.E. Culler, and G.K. Maa, "Assessing the Benefits of Fine-Grain Parallelism in Dataflow Programs," *Proc. Supercomputing '88*, Nov. 1988, pp. 60-69.

62. Arvind, D.E. Culler, and K. Ekanadham, "The Price of Asynchronous Parallelism: An Analysis of Dataflow Architectures," *CONPAR*, Cambridge Univ. Press, Cambridge, Mass., 1988, pp. 541-555.

63. A.L. Davis and R.M. Keller, "Data Flow Program Graphs," *Computer*, Vol. 15, No. 2, Feb. 1982, pp. 26-41.

64. J.B. Dennis, "Data Flow Supercomputers," *Computer*, Vol. 13, No. 11, Nov. 1980, pp. 48-56.

65. J.B. Dennis, G.-R. Gao, and K.W. Todd, "Modeling the Weather with a Data Flow Supercomputer," *IEEE Trans. Computers*, Vol. C-33, No. 7, July 1984, pp. 592-603.

66. V.G. Grafe et al., "The Epsilon Dataflow Processor," *Int'l Symp. Computer Architecture*, 1989, pp. 36-45.

67. J.R. Gurd and I. Watson, "A Practical Dataflow Computer," *Computer*, Vol. 15, No. 2, Feb. 1982, pp. 51-58.

68. J.R. Gurd, C.C. Kirkham, and I. Watson, "The Manchester Prototype Dataflow Computer," *Comm. ACM*, Vol 28, No. 1, Jan. 1985, pp. 34-52.

69. J.R. Gurd, C.C. Kirkham, and A.P. Bohm, "The Manchester Dataflow Computing System," in *Experimental Parallel Computing Architectures*, J.J. Dongarra, ed., Elsevier Science Publishing Company, Inc., New York, N.Y., 1987, pp. 177-219.

70.* R.A. Iannucci, "Toward a Dataflow/von Neumann Hybrid Architecture," *IEEE Int'l Symp. Computer Architecture*, 1988, pp. 131-140.

71. Y. Inagami and J.F. Foley, "The Specification of a New Manchester Dataflow Machine," *Int'l Conf. Supercomputing*, 1989, pp. 371-380.

72. L.M. Patnaik, R. Govindarajan, and N.S. Ramdoss, "Design and Performance Evaluation of EXMAN: An Extended Manchester Dataflow Computer," *IEEE Trans. Computers*, Vol. C-35, No. 3, Mar. 1986, pp. 229-243.

73. B.R. Preiss and V.C. Hamacher, "Semi-Static Dataflow," *Int'l Conf. Parallel Processing, Vol II: Software*, 1988, pp. 127-134.

74.* S. Sakai et al., "An Architecture of a Dataflow Single Chip Processor," *Int'l Symp. Computer Architecture*, 1989, pp. 46-53.

75. T. Shimada et al., "Evaluation of a Prototype Data Flow Processor of the SIGMA-1 for Scientific Computations," *Int'l Symp. Computer Architecture*, 1986, pp. 226-234.

76. V.P. Srini, "An Architectural Comparison of Dataflow Systems," *Computer*, Vol. 19, No. 3, Mar. 1986, pp. 68-87.

77. P. Treleaven, B.R. David, and P.R. Hopkins, "Data Driven and Demand Driven Computer Architectures," *Computing Surveys*, Vol 14, No. 1, Mar. 1982, pp. 93-143.

78. T. Yuba et al., "Dataflow Computer Development in Japan," *Int'l Conf. Supercomputing*, 1990, pp. 140-147.

79. A.P.W. Bohm and J. Sargeant, "Code Optimization for Tagged-Token Dataflow Machines," *IEEE Trans. Computers*, Vol. 38, No. 1, Jan. 1989, pp. 4-14.

80. A.P.W. Bohm and J.R. Gurd, "Iterative Instructions in the Manchester Dataflow Computer," *IEEE Trans. Parallel and Distributed Systems*, Vol. 1, No. 2, Apr. 1990, pp. 129-139.

81. D.D. Gajski et al., "A Second Opinion on Data Flow Machines and Languages," *Computer*, Vol. 15, No. 2, Feb. 1982, pp. 58-69.

82. R. Buehrer and K. Ekanadham, "Incorporating Data Flow Ideas into von Neumann Processors for Parallel Execution," *IEEE Trans. Computers*, Vol. C-36, No. 12, Dec. 1987, pp. 1515-1522.

83. W. Hwu and Y.N. Patt, "HPSm, a High Performance Restricted Data Flow Architecture Having Minimal Functionality," *Int'l Symp. Computer Architecture*, 1986, pp. 297-306.

84. W.W. Hwu and Y.N. Patt, "Design Choices for the HPSm Microprocessor Chip," *Hawaii Int'l Conf. System Sciences*, 1987, pp. 329-336.

85. Y.N. Patt, W. Hwu, and M.C. Shebanow, "HPS, a New Microarchitecture: Rationale and Introduction," *Ann. Workshop on Microprogramming*, 1985, pp. 103-108.

Reducing the Branch Penalty in Pipelined Processors

David J. Lilja

University of Illinois at Urbana-Champaign

Reprinted from *Computer*, Vol. 21, No. 7, July 1988, pages 47-55.

Pipelining improves computer performance by overlapping the execution of several different instructions. If no interactions exist between instructions in the pipeline, then several instructions can be in different stages of execution simultaneously.

However, dependencies between instructions—particularly branch instructions—prevent the processor from realizing its maximum performance. In a pipeline with sequential prefetching, for example, the processor must flush instructions executing in the pipeline after a successful branch (since they were incorrectly prefetched and loaded) and fetch instructions from the new path. This flushing and refilling reduces processor performance.

This article develops a probabilistic model to quantify the performance effects of the branch penalty in a typical pipeline. The branch penalty is analyzed as a function of the relative number of branch instructions executed and the probability that a branch is taken. The resulting model shows the fraction of maximum performance achievable under the given conditions. Techniques to reduce the branch penalty include static and dynamic branch prediction, the branch target buffer, the delayed branch, branch bypassing and multiple prefetching, branch folding, reso-

> **Branch dependencies between instructions penalize pipelined processors. Several simple techniques can restore some of the lost performance.**

lution of the branch decision early in the pipeline, using multiple independent instruction streams in a shared pipeline, and the Prepare-to-branch instruction.

Branch types

A branch instruction requires two pieces of information that the processor must determine before executing the instruction: whether the branch is to be taken and the branch target address. The three basic types of branches in a traditional proces-

sor are unconditional, conditional (such as decisions), and loop control. (Loop control branches are often special cases of conditional branches optimized for the regularity of loop structures.) The three methods used to determine the branch target address are absolute address, computed address, and indirect address.

An *unconditional* branch always alters the sequential program flow. The target address is part of the instruction itself and is known when the program is compiled or loaded. Consequently, the processor can treat an unconditional branch like a sequential program flow, except that the program counter is loaded with a new value rather than being incremented by one. Unconditional branches jump around data blocks, jump to the start of a program, branch to a subroutine, jump around the else block of an if-then-else construct, etc.

In a *conditional* branch, the processor must make some decision before it can determine the correct execution path. The decision usually derives from some condition code (such as a binary test on the result of a previous operation) and results in selecting either the instruction at the branch target address or the next sequential instruction. The target address typically is known at compile time. An

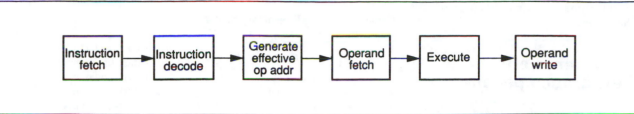

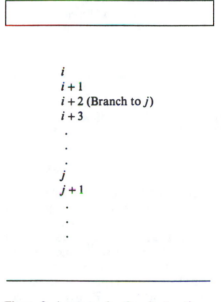

Figure 1. An example of a processor pipeline.

i
$i+1$
$i+2$ (Branch to j)
$i+3$
.
.
.
j
$j+1$
.
.
.

Figure 2. An example of an instruction stream.

example of a conditional branch is the if-then construct.

The branch in a *loop-control* statement is usually taken and the target address is known when the program is compiled or loaded. The branch usually leads back to the top of the loop and is executed a fixed or data-dependent number of times. The number of iterations of the loop may depend on the size of a data structure (such as a for loop indexing through all of the values of an array) or the value of some data element (such as a while loop iterating through a series of calculations until some error parameter reduces to an acceptable level). A loop-control branch may be a type of conditional branch or a special hardware instruction.

The processor must determine the branch target address before executing any

of these branch types. Some branch instructions provide the *absolute* address of the target instruction. Thus, fetching the next instruction requires no computation or additional memory accesses.

A slightly more complicated method *computes* the branch target address. An example of a computed target address is a hardware implementation of a case statement where control can pass to any of several different addresses. A more common example is the register-relative branch. In this case, an offset added to the contents of the given register produces the branch target address. The register is frequently the program counter, making the branch "program counter-relative." Relocatable object code uses this method.

The last method of determining the target address uses an *indirect* pointer. The processor uses the contents of a register as the address of a location in memory that contains the desired target address. A common example is the Return-from-subroutine instruction, in which the processor does not know the target address at compile time but can find it on the return address stack before executing the instruction. This method uses the stack pointer for an indirect memory access to obtain the branch target address.

Branch penalty

To analyze the effects of these branch instructions on the performance of a pipelined processor, consider the pipeline in Figure 1. The first stage of the pipeline fetches the next instruction from memory. The next stage decodes the instruction, and the third stage generates the addresses of the required operands (assuming that at least one operand is in memory). The fourth stage fetches the operands. The last two stages perform the actual execution

and store the results. If the instruction is a conditional branch, the resolution of the branch decision occurs in the Execute segment of the pipe.

Figure 2 shows a code fragment to be executed in this pipeline. Instructions i, $i+1$, and $i+2$ execute sequentially. Instruction $i+2$ is a branch instruction that can either jump to instruction j if the branch is taken or fall through to instruction $i+3$ if the branch fails.

Figure 3 shows the flow of this fragment through the pipeline. Instruction i enters the pipeline during cycle 1. The other segments of the pipeline are empty and the processor produces no results for the first five cycles. This unproductive time is called the *start-up latency*. The first instruction completes at the end of cycle 6 and subsequent instructions complete every cycle. Thus, the maximum throughput of the pipeline is one instruction per cycle.

During cycle 7, the branch instruction, $i+2$, enters segment 5. The segment executes the instruction and resolves the branch decision at the end of the cycle. Consequently, assuming the branch decision is taken, the processor fetches instruction j during cycle 8 and flushes from the pipeline the instructions ahead of j ($i+3$ to $i+6$). Thus, no instructions complete during cycles 9 through 12. These wasted cycles constitute the branch penalty.

The penalty may be greater in processors using a cache. With a forward branch, the cache typically does not contain the branch target instruction, increasing the penalty due to the subsequent cache miss. Loop instructions, on the other hand, typically branch backwards by several instructions, and a loop typically executes several times. Thus, the cache normally contains the branch target and the penalty consists only of the time taken to drain and refill the pipe. In the interest of simplicity, the following discussion ignores cache effects. The discussion of the branch table buffer extends the model to include the effects of cache misses.

Performance effect of the branch penalty

The branch penalty described above affects processor performance whenever a branch is taken. That is, performance fails to reach its maximum value of one instruction per cycle whenever a nonsequential branch is taken in the program.

Each branch has two possible outcomes: taken or not taken. If the branch is taken, execution continues at the branch target address and incurs the branch penalty. If it is not taken, execution continues with the next sequential instruction and there is no penalty. For simplicity, assume that the branch target address is available when the branch is resolved. Other than the branch itself, assume the pipeline contains no dependencies, so each instruction advances one stage in the pipeline for each cycle. Also, the pipeline contains only one unresolved branch during any cycle. Assume the following parameters:

p_b = the probability that a particular instruction is a branch

p_t = the probability that a branch is taken

b = the branch penalty (that is, the number of cycles wasted when a branch is taken)

T_{ave} = the average number of cycles required per instruction

After the start-up latency, a nonbranch instruction completes every cycle. Thus, each nonbranch instruction requires one cycle to complete. For a branch instruction, there are two cases to consider. If the branch is not taken, the time to execute the instruction is one cycle. If the branch is taken, however, execution time is one cycle plus b cycles due to the branch penalty. The average number of cycles per instruction is then

$$T_{ave} = (1 - p_b)(1) + p_b[p_t(1 + b) + (1 - p_t)(1)] \quad (1)$$

which reduces to

$$T_{ave} = 1 + bp_bp_t \quad (2)$$

Equation 2 shows that the average number of cycles required to execute an instruc-

tion is one plus a fraction of b, the branch penalty. Let this fraction be p_e, where $p_e = p_bp_t$. For the simple pipeline model presented here, this fraction is determined by the percentage of branch instructions executed and the probability that the branch is taken. Think of it as the effective fraction of the branch penalty incurred by the instructions.

Maximum performance occurs when the branch penalty is zero and one instruction completes every cycle. Thus, with no branch penalty, the average number of cycles per instruction is one. Define F_b as the number of cycles required to execute an instruction in the maximum performance case (that is, one cycle) divided by the average number of cycles required to execute an instruction when the branch penalty is included. Then

$$F_b = \frac{1}{1 + bp_e} \quad (3)$$

Figure 4 uses F_b, interpreted as the fraction of maximum performance realized by the pipeline due to the effects of the branch penalty, as the vertical axis. The horizontal axis is the effective probability that an instruction is a taken branch (p_e). The curves represent values of b ranging from one to six.

Lee and Smith analyzed branching behavior from the traces of 26 programs totaling more than 94 million instructions.[1] The programs consisted of a mix of compiler, business, scientific, and operating system programs run on an IBM System/370; a typical mix of educational programs run on a PDP-11-70; and several scientific programs run on a CDC 6400. These programs showed the average p_b to be approximately 0.1 to 0.3 and the average p_t to be approximately 0.6 to 0.7. That is, about 10 percent to 30 percent of the instructions executed in a typical program are branch instructions, of which the branch is taken about 60 percent to 70 percent of the time. Thus, the average effective probability that an instruction is a taken branch is 0.06 to 0.21. Referring to Figure 4, if $p_b = 0.2$, $p_t = 0.65$, and $b = 4$, for example, then $p_e = 0.13$ and the branch instructions cause the pipeline to execute at about 66 percent of its maximum rate.

Note that the range of F_b is $0 < F_b \leq 1$. The upper bound (one) occurs whenever any of the terms in the denominator of Equation 3 are zero. That is, the processor executes at the maximum rate of one instruction per cycle when the branch penalty is zero, when there are no branch instructions, or when the branches are never taken. The processor approaches the

Cycle	Pipeline segment #						
	1	2	3	4	5	6	
1	i	-	-	-	-	-	(Start-up latency)
2	$i+1$	i	-	-	-	-	(Start-up latency)
3	$i+2$	$i+1$	i	-	-	-	(Start-up latency)
4	$i+3$	$i+2$	$i+1$	i	-	-	(Start-up latency)
5	$i+4$	$i+3$	$i+2$	$i+1$	i	-	(Start-up latency)
6	$i+5$	$i+4$	$i+3$	$i+2$	$i+1$	i	Instruction i finished
7	$i+6$	$i+5$	$i+4$	$i+3$	$i+2$	$i+1$	Instruction $i+1$ finished
8	j	$i+6$	$i+5$	$i+4$	$i+3$	$i+2$	Instruction $i+2$ finished
9	$j+1$	j		$i+6$	$i+5$	$i+4$	$i+3$	(Branch penalty)
10	.	$j+1$	j		$i+6$	$i+5$	$i+4$	(Branch penalty)
11	.	.	$j+1$	j		$i+6$	$i+5$	(Branch penalty)
12	.	.	.	$j+1$	j		$i+6$	(Branch penalty)
13	.	.	.	.	$j+1$	j	Instruction j finished
14	.	.	.	.	.	$j+1$	Instruction $j+1$ finished

Figure 3. Instruction flow in the example pipeline showing the branch penalty.

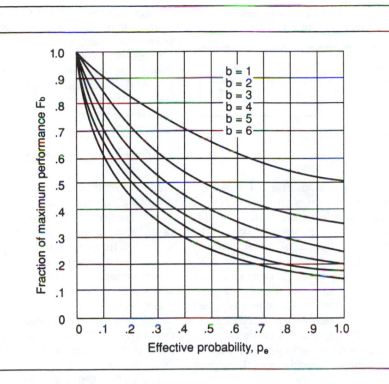

Figure 4. Fraction of maximum performance as a function of the effective probability and the branch penalty b.

lower bound of zero asymptotically when there is a nonzero probability that a branch exists and is taken and the branch penalty b becomes very large. Between these limits, processor performance degrades rapidly for even small values of b and p_e. These curves demonstrate the significant effect branches can have on the performance of a pipelined processor.

Branch prediction

Branch prediction reduces performance degradation due to branch instructions. A pipeline with branch prediction uses some additional logic to guess the outcome of a branch decision before it is determined. The pipeline then begins prefetching the instruction stream from the predicted path. (Note that the predicted path may be the normal sequential path.) Thus, a correct prediction eliminates wasted cycles due to the branch penalty.

If the branch is predicted to be taken, the branch target address also must be predicted. The branch target address may be explicitly encoded into the instruction or it may be predicted, for example, to be the same target address as the last execu-

tion of the instruction.

The processor may predict the branch path either statically or dynamically. In the static case, the processor makes a presumptive decision as to whether the branch is likely to be taken. Whenever the instruction executes, the processor prefetches from the same predicted path. In the dynamic case, the hardware maintains some past information on the branch instruction being executed. The processor then uses this information to predict the branch decision according to some prediction algorithm.

Static branch-prediction mechanisms. The simplest form of static prediction predicts that all branches are always taken or never taken. A typical pipelined computer fetches instructions sequentially, even after a branch has been decoded. This sequential fetching is equivalent to statically predicting that branches are never taken. Alternatively, we could design a pipeline to begin fetching from the branch target path whenever it encounters a branch instruction. This method is equivalent to predicting that branches are always taken. Studies analyzing program behavior have shown that branches are

taken more than 50 percent of the time,[1] so if the cost of prefetching from either path is the same, then always prefetching from the branch target address should give better performance than always prefetching from the sequential path.

Another form of static prediction is based on the op-code of the branch instruction. The hardware assumes that the branch will be taken for certain branch op-codes and not for others. When the instruction is decoded, the op-code implicitly determines the branch-prediction decision. This mechanism allows prediction accuracies of greater than 75 percent.

A slightly more complicated form of static prediction uses a likely/not-likely bit within the instruction. The hardware prefetches the branch target instruction if the bit is set; otherwise, it prefetches the next sequential instruction. The compiler determines the setting depending on the apparent use of the branch within the program, or using some intelligent heuristic algorithm. For example, it would set loop-control branches to likely and branches that exit a loop to not likely. Accuracy depends on the compiler's ability to predict the branch decision. Using a set of benchmark programs, Ditzel and McLellan reported prediction accuracies of 74 percent to 94 percent for the AT&T CRISP processor, which uses this prediction mechanism.[2]

Another method of determining the setting for the likely bit involves tracing the execution of a program using several different data sets and recording the outcomes of all of the branch decisions. The likely bit is then set to the outcome that occurred most often for that particular branch instruction. By simulating this technique, McFarling and Hennessy[3] found a correct prediction rate of 85 percent averaged over several benchmark programs. Furthermore, the correct prediction rate fell only slightly when significantly different input data sets were used.

Dynamic branch-prediction mechanisms. In dynamic prediction techniques, the processor uses history information about branch instructions that have executed to predict the outcome of the branch the next time it executes. For example, the processor can maintain a small table for recently executed branch instructions with several bits in each entry. It can access the table associatively like a data cache, or by using the low-order bits of the branch instruction's address. The processor then uses the bits to make a prediction decision with some heuristic algorithm. The hardware costs of this mechanism will be influenced by the number of entries in the history table, the number of history bits maintained, the set-associativity of the table, and other such cache-related issues.

Lee and Smith[1] analyzed several different schemes for predicting the branch outcome using the stored history bits. Using a single history bit yielded prediction accuracies ranging from about 80 percent to 96 percent on the previous mix of instruction traces. Accuracy increased as the number of history bits increased. Using five bits resulted in prediction accuracies ranging from 84 percent to 98 percent. Another study resulted in dynamic prediction accuracies of 83 percent averaged over three smaller benchmark programs.[3]

Consider the following example of a prediction algorithm based on history bits. A finite-state machine implements this algorithm with two bits in each table entry. If the last two branches for the given instruction have taken the same path, the prediction is to take that path again. If the prediction is wrong, it remains the same the next time the instruction executes. If the prediction is wrong again, however, the prediction will be to select the opposite path the next time. Thus, the algorithm requires two consecutive wrong predictions to change the predicted path; if a branch executes an unusual direction once, the prediction will be wrong only once. This type of branching behavior is common for loops executing within another loop.

The S-1 computer uses a dynamic prediction technique. The processor has a jump bit and a wrong bit associated with each branch instruction.[1] The jump bit is set to indicate that the branch is predicted to be taken, while the wrong bit is set to indicate that the last prediction was wrong. Two consecutive wrong predictions toggle the jump bit. This mechanism is similar to the one described above. The Mitsubishi M32 microprocessor, developed as part of the Japanese TRON project,[4] also uses a dynamic prediction mechanism.

Performance effects of branch prediction

A simplified model using the pipelined processor in Figure 1 as an example provides a feel for how branch prediction may reduce the performance degradation of

Table 1. Branch penalties (in cycles) for predicted and actual outcomes.

| | Actual | |
Prediction	Not taken	Taken
Not taken	0	b
Taken	c	d

branch instructions. Table 1 shows the four combinations of predicted and actual branch outcomes along with the performance penalty of each outcome. The actual performance of the processor is determined as follows.

If the prediction is that the branch will not be taken, then the first row of the table applies and the average number of cycles required to execute the instructions is the same as in Equation 2. However, if the prediction is that the branch will be taken, then from the second row of the table,

$$T_{ave} = 1 + cp_b(1 - p_t) + dp_bp_t \quad (4)$$

An incorrect prediction calls for c additional cycles, and a correct prediction, d additional cycles.

Assume that the penalty of a correctly predicted taken branch in Figure 1 is zero ($d = 0$). Also, assume that the penalty for an incorrect prediction is the same regardless of whether the actual outcome is taken or not taken (that is, $c = b$). Under these circumstances, the average number of cycles required to execute an instruction is

$$T_{ave} = 1 + bp_bp_w \quad (5)$$

where p_w is the probability of a wrong prediction. Thus, the b branch penalty cycles are wasted only when the prediction is wrong.

This performance equation is essentially the same as the one developed for the branch penalty. Thus, we can use Figure 4 to determine the fraction of maximum performance realized by using $p_e = p_bp_w$. For example, if 20 percent of the instructions are branches and the prediction algorithm is correct 80 percent of the time, then $p_e = 0.04$. Using a branch penalty of $b = 4$, we find from Figure 4 that the processor will operate at about 86 percent of its maximum value.

By predicting the branch outcomes with an accuracy better than the probability of a branch being taken ($p_w < p_t$), a processor using branch prediction can outper-

form one without it. While this model is a simplification, it helps explain the effectiveness of branch prediction. However, the potential increase in processor performance must be balanced against the actual cost of the extra hardware, the software costs, and the real performance cost of an incorrect prediction.

Branch target buffer

In a typical pipelined processor, the processor consumes new instructions faster than the main memory can deliver them. Consequently, instructions are prefetched from the sequential instruction stream into a prefetch buffer. When the processor needs the next instruction, it is available from the prefetch buffer without delay. When a nonsequential branch occurs, however, the required instruction most likely is not in the prefetch buffer. To alleviate this problem, we can use a *branch target buffer*.

The BTB is a special, selective cache memory associated with the instruction-fetch portion of the pipeline. Each entry in the BTB consists of the address of a branch instruction that has already executed and the target instruction itself. The BTB may also store the next few instructions after the branch target instruction.

When the pipeline decodes a branch instruction, it associatively searches the BTB for the address of that instruction. If it is in the BTB, the instruction is supplied directly to the pipeline and prefetching begins from the new path. If the instruction is not in the BTB, however, the pipeline is stalled while it fetches the new instruction stream. The processor then selects an entry in the BTB for replacement and stores the new target instruction in the BTB.

The BTB also can be called a loop buffer. In many cases, a loop may be small enough to completely fit within the BTB. Thus, the pipeline can execute the loop directly out of this special-purpose instruction cache. Loop buffers have been successfully implemented in the Cray-1, IBM System/360 Model 91, and Mitsubishi M32.[4]

The Advanced Micro Devices Am29000 microprocessor also incorporates a BTB to increase performance due to repeated branches.[5] In this implementation, a 512-byte cache is divided into 128 32-bit words (each instruction uses one word). Two-way set-associative mapping is used, and a random-replacement strategy resolves collisions between entries that map to the same location. Each entry in this BTB consists of four sequential instruction words for a total of 32 unique branch targets in the entire BTB. When a nonsequential instruction fetch occurs, the BTB is searched simultaneously with the address translation in the memory management unit. If the target instruction is in the BTB, it is passed to the pipeline along with the next three instructions. The instruction prefetch unit then begins prefetching from this new path.

We can extend the performance model developed for the branch penalty to include the effects of adding a BTB to the pipeline model in Figure 1. Assume that the sequential program path is always being prefetched and that no extra cycles are required to fetch the branch target instruction from the BTB on a hit. Let b' be the number of branch penalty cycles and c be the number of cycles required to fetch the branch target instruction on a BTB miss. Then, the average number of cycles required to execute an instruction is

$$T_{ave} = 1 + (b' + cp_m)p_bp_t \qquad (6)$$

where p_m is the probability of a BTB miss.

In this model, the effective probability is $p_e = p_bp_t$, while the effective branch penalty is the normal branch penalty, b', plus a fraction of the number of cycles required for a BTB miss. In terms of Equation 3 and Figure 4, $b = b' + cp_m$. For example, in a processor with 20 percent branch instructions, of which 65 percent are taken, $p_e = 0.13$. With a BTB miss ratio of 25 percent, a branch penalty of $b' = 4$, and $c = 2$ cycles required to service a miss, the effective branch penalty is $b = 4.5$ cycles. Interpolating with Figure 4, or using Equation 3 directly, the processor will realize approximately 63 percent of its maximum possible performance.

To determine the effectiveness of the BTB, Lee and Smith examined the hit ratios for several different workloads.[1] (The hit ratio is the probability that the desired instruction will be in the BTB when fetched, which is $1 - p_m$.) Using a two-way set-associative BTB with 16 entries and a least-recently-used replacement strategy, the hit ratio was approximately 27 percent. When the BTB size increased to 64 entries, the hit ratio increased to approximately 47 percent. A BTB size of 256 entries resulted in a hit ratio of 72 percent. Using a direct-mapped scheme and a different workload mix, McFarling and

The compiler for a processor with delayed branches detects dependencies in the instruction stream.

Hennessy found average hit ratios of 47 percent, 83 percent, and 93 percent for a BTB with 16, 64, and 256 entries, respectively.[3] They attributed their higher results to different workload characteristics.

Delayed branch

In an architecture using a delayed branch, some number of instructions after the branch execute regardless of whether the branch is taken. In particular, let instruction i be a branch to instruction j. A processor with a branch delay of b will execute the instructions in the sequence i, $i + 1, \ldots, i + b, j, \ldots$ if the branch is taken. If the branch is not taken, instruction $i + b$ is followed by $i + b + 1$. Thus, the b instructions after the branch always execute.

The compiler for a processor with delayed branches detects dependencies in the instruction stream and rearranges the code to insert useful instructions in the delay slots. For example, the compiler can determine that the program dependencies allow a few of the instructions preceding the branch to be moved into the delay slots after the branch. Then, when the branch executes, these instructions will always execute, whether the branch is taken or not. The effect is the same as if the instructions executed in their original order, except that the branch penalty decreases. Other, more complicated, code rearrangement schemes are also possible. In many cases, however, some or all of the b instructions after the branch must be filled with no-ops.

Gross and Hennessy developed an algorithm for optimizing delayed branches in the compiler for the MIPS project.[6] For a series of small benchmark programs, this compiler filled the first delay location after a branch with a useful instruction more

than half of the time. Subsequent delay locations were increasingly more difficult to fill. The compiler for the IBM 801 minicomputer[7] filled the single delay slot in that processor with a useful instruction approximately 60 percent of the time. The Am29000[5] and several other computers have also successfully used the delayed branch scheme.

To simplify reordering the instruction stream, the delayed branch in the Hewlett-Packard Precision architecture[8] includes a nullification or canceling feature, allowing a branch instruction to dynamically force the next instruction after the branch to be a no-op, depending on the outcome of the branch itself. This feature is commonly used in a loop-control branch at the bottom of a loop. For example, in a processor with a branch delay of one, the instruction after the branch can be a copy of the first instruction at the top of the loop. The branch target then is the second instruction of the loop. When the branch fails and the loop is exited, the instruction after the branch is nullified and execution continues sequentially.

Hsu and Davidson have proposed an extension of the nullification concept using the idea of guarded instructions, in which a Boolean-valued guard expression is added to a Store instruction or a conditional branch.[9] If the guard expression evaluates to false, it inhibits the Store or branch operation, converting the instruction to a no-op.

For example, consider a Store instruction that is the target of a conditional branch. It should execute only if the branch is taken. Most processors with a delayed branch cannot move this instruction into a delay slot due the instruction's dependence on the outcome of the branch. However, a guard expression that is a function of the branch condition allows the processor to move the Store instruction into a delay slot by ensuring that the Store will be inhibited if the branch is not taken.

Using this technique and a decision-tree scheduling heuristic, Hsu and Davidson achieved performance speedups for the memory scheduler from the Unix kernel of 1.7 to 4.6 times over a conventional pipelined processor.[9] In this study, the branch penalty was much larger than that of the example pipeline in Figure 1. Consequently, using the guarded instruction scheme in this pipeline would result in smaller speedups than those achieved by Hsu and Davidson.

As before, we can modify the performance model of the branch penalty to include the effects of using a delayed branch architecture. In a processor with b delay slots and without the nullification feature, the average number of cycles required to execute an instruction is

$$T_{ave} = 1 + bp_bp_{nop} \qquad (7)$$

Notice that since the b delay cycles execute whether or not the branch is taken, the probability p_t is not involved in this equation. Instead, the equation uses the fraction of the b delay slots filled with no-ops, p_{nop}. If f_i is the probability that delay slot i is filled with a useful instruction, then

$$p_{nop} = 1 - \frac{f_1 + f_2 + \ldots + f_b}{b} \qquad (8)$$

Thus, p_{nop} shows the fraction of the delay slots that do no useful work and thereby add to the branch penalty.

Again, the form of the equation for T_{ave} allows us to use Figure 4 to estimate the fraction of maximum performance in this pipeline. In this case, $p_e = p_bp_{nop}$. For example, assume that a processor with a branch delay of four can fill the first delay slot with a useful instruction 60 percent of the time, and the second delay slot only 10 percent of the time. The last two delay slots are never used. Using these values for f_i, $p_{nop} = 0.825$. With $p_b = 0.2$, $p_e = 0.165$, resulting in 60 percent of the processor's maximum performance being realized.

In a processor with this feature, nullifying the instructions in the delay slots wastes b cycles on the branch. If the processor resolves the branch so the instructions can execute, however, the branch penalty is only bp_{nop} additional cycles. Consequently, the average number of cycles required to execute an instruction is

$$T_{ave} = 1 + bp_b[p_{nop}(1 - p_{null}) + p_{null}] \qquad (9)$$

The term p_{null} is the probability that the instructions in the delay slots are nullified. This probability equals the probability that the branch is taken, p_t, if the instruction is of the Nullify-on-branch-taken type. Otherwise, $p_{null} = (1 - p_t)$. In this model, the effective probability is

$$p_e = p_b[p_{nop}(1 - p_{null}) + p_{null}] \qquad (10)$$

Since the nullification scheme allows the instructions in the delay slots to execute only when the branch is in a particular

---

> **The processor can fetch both paths and throw away the incorrect one when the branch is resolved.**

---

direction, the compiler can more effectively put useful instructions in the delay slots. Consequently, it is likely that the fraction of delay slots filled with no-ops, p_{nop}, will be smaller than in a processor that does not use nullification. Or, equivalently, we can assume that the probability of a useful instruction filling a delay slot i (f_i) will be larger than in the no-nullification case.

For instance, in a processor with nullification and $b = 4$, assume that $f_1 = 0.8$, $f_2 = 0.3$, $f_3 = 0.1$, and $f_4 = 0$, which gives $p_{nop} = 0.70$. Assuming that nullification occurs when the branch is not taken, $p_{null} = (1 - p_t) = 0.35$. The effective probability is then $p_e = 0.161$, which, using Figure 4, results in the processor executing at 61 percent of its maximum performance. Notice that with these parameters, the performance of the processor with nullification is only about one percent better than the previous example without nullification.

Branch bypass and multiple prefetch

To eliminate the need to predict which path will be taken after a branch, the processor can fetch both paths and throw away the incorrect one when the branch is resolved. This technique is called *branch bypassing* or *multiple prefetching*. A pipeline that can contain only one branch instruction at any given time must prefetch two execution paths. Similarly, a processor that can contain two unresolved branches must prefetch four paths. Two of the paths are from the taken/not-taken choices of the first branch, while two are from the taken/not-taken choices of the second. The pipeline must prefetch all four paths until the branches are resolved. In general, if the pipeline can contain j

unresolved branches at the same time, then it must prefetch 2^j execution paths.

The performance advantage of prefetching all of the execution paths is that the processor has already fetched the correct path from memory when it finally resolves a branch. If the hardware does this without executing the paths, there will be some performance penalty as the pipeline flushes and refills as it resolves the branches. However, we can design hardware that actually executes more than one of the paths, perhaps using the guarded execution scheme mentioned above. In terms of the previous performance models, we can reduce the branch penalty b to almost zero at the expense of sufficiently complicated hardware.

To determine the theoretical maximum speedup from bypassing a number of branches, Riseman and Foster[10] simulated the performance of a hypothetical machine with infinite storage and an infinite number of functional units. Performance in this machine is limited only by data and branch dependencies. They discovered that performance increases proportional to $\sqrt{j}$, where j levels of unresolved branches exist. For example, a processor maintaining the possible outcomes of 16 branches theoretically runs twice as fast as one maintaining four outcomes, which runs twice as fast as one maintaining only one outcome. This relation seems to hold for values of j up to 32. Since the number of paths to be maintained grows as 2^j, but the performance grows as $\sqrt{j}$, this technique is unreasonable beyond very small values of j.

Branch folding

The AT&T CRISP processor[2] uses a technique called *branch folding* that can reduce the branch penalty to zero. In this processor, the pipeline is broken into a fetch-and-decode unit and an execution unit. The *fetch-and-decode* unit reads encoded instructions from memory and places the decoded instructions into a special instruction cache. Each decoded instruction has an associated next-address field that is the address of the next instruction to be executed. Thus, each instruction can be an unconditional branch instruction in addition to its normal operation.

The fetch-and-decode unit recognizes when an unconditional branch instruction follows a nonbranch instruction and "folds" the branch instruction into the nonbranch instruction, effectively eliminating the branch instruction from the execution pipeline.

Conditional branch instructions maintain an alternate next-address field along with the normal next-address field. When a folded conditional instruction executes, the execution unit selects one of the two next-address paths. The address of the other path proceeds down the pipeline with the executing instruction. When the pipeline finally resolves the branch, it either throws away the alternate path address or flushes itself and restarts execution at the alternate address.

Since no explicit branch instructions exist in the execution pipeline, the branch penalty becomes zero for unconditional branches. The performance for conditional branches is the same as that in the first performance model with p_b replaced by the probability of an instruction being a conditional branch. The cost of this technique is significantly more complicated hardware.

Early branch resolution

As shown in the performance model of the branch penalty, processor performance degrades by a fraction of the branch penalty when a branch instruction is taken. The fraction of maximum performance realized by the processor increases as the branch penalty decreases. For example, if the branch decision is resolved in the first stage of the pipeline in Figure 1, the branch penalty can be reduced to zero. No degradation of processor performance due to a taken branch exists in this case. However, effectively resolving branches early in the pipeline may require a significant amount of hardware. In fact, this additional hardware may increase the critical path delay and thus the processor's cycle time, potentially reducing overall performance.

In the Tandem VLX computer system,[11] the processor uses extra logic to test the branch condition before the branch executes. By anticipating the branch direction, the processor can fetch instructions from the target address into the cache and immediately load the new instruction stream into the pipeline. Of course, the processor may not always be able to determine the branch condition early enough, in which case the pipeline must wait. The increased performance in executing branch instructions offsets the cost of the extra logic.

Multiple independent instruction streams in a shared pipeline

Most high-performance processors are multiprogrammed, with several independent processes sharing execution time on a single processor. We can eliminate dependencies within the pipeline by interleaving the execution of these processes so each stage of the pipeline has a different process.

For example, an n-stage pipeline executes n different processes simultaneously. Each stage of the pipeline executes an instruction from one of the n different processes. Since each process is independent, no branch dependencies exist between instructions in the pipeline. Consequently, execution of a branch instruction carries no performance penalty. Of course, each process runs at a fraction of $1/n$ times its maximum possible performance. The advantage is that the pipeline is completely used, thereby increasing overall system performance (as measured by the number of instructions executed per unit of time).

Shar and Davidson[12] discussed this concept of multistreaming, and it was incorporated into the design of the Denelcor HEP computer system.[13] The HEP system broke programs into several independent, cooperating processes. Each process experienced a performance degradation of $1/n$, but the entire distributed program ran at the maximum performance allowed by the pipeline.

Prepare-to-branch instruction

The techniques discussed so far implicitly assume that the branch target address is immediately available or that it can be calculated in parallel with the resolution of the branch decision. Thus, determining the target address was assumed to have no effect on pipeline performance. However, the instruction-fetch logic may need some advance warning about a branch to begin prefetching from the appropriate instruction stream. For example, the Texas Instruments ASC computer[14] uses the Prepare-to-branch instruction to give the control hardware advance warning that a branch instruction is going to execute. This warning passes the branch target address to the control unit so that the unit can begin instruction prefetching from that address. The useful-

ness of the Prepare-to-branch instruction depends on the ability of the compiler or programmer to insert the instruction at the appropriate point in the instruction stream.

Extensive use of pipelining has increased the parallelism, and thus the performance, of high-speed processors. The first model in this article showed how branch dependencies between instructions in the segments of a pipelined processor reduce processor performance. The different techniques presented can reduce the performance effects of branch instruction execution. While the performance models developed for these techniques are somewhat simplified, they provide a useful method of comparing the performance effects of various architectural alternatives.

Not all of the techniques will be useful for every processor. The choice of which techniques to use depends on the performance requirements and cost constraints of the particular processor design. The simplicity of some of the techniques, however, suggests that almost any pipelined processor could benefit from one of the methods. □

Acknowledgments

I wish to thank Edward S. Davidson for his helpful comments on an early version of this article. In addition, the thoughtful comments provided by the reviewers have significantly enhanced the quality of this presentation.

This paper was written while I was supported by the Center for Supercomputing Research and Development under the following grants: National Science Foundation MIP-8410110, US Department of Energy DE-FG02-85ER25001, and the IBM Donation.

References

1. J.K.F. Lee and A.J. Smith, "Branch-Prediction Strategies and Branch Target Buffer Design," *Computer*, Jan. 1984, pp. 6-22.

2. D.R. Ditzel and H.R. McLellan, "Branch Folding in the CRISP Microprocessor: Reducing Branch Delay to Zero," *Proc. 14th Ann. Symp. Computer Architecture*, 1987, pp. 2-9.

3. S. McFarling and J. Hennessy, "Reducing the Cost of Branches," *Proc. 13th Ann. Symp. Computer Architecture*, 1986, pp. 396-403.

4. T. Yoshida and T. Enomoto, "The Mitsubishi VLSI CPU in the TRON Project," *IEEE Micro*, Apr. 1987, p. 24.

5. M. Johnson, *Am29000 User's Manual*, Advanced Micro Devices, Sunnyvale, Calif., 1987.

6. T.R. Gross and J.L. Hennessy, "Optimizing Delayed Branches," *Proc. IEEE Micro-15*, Oct. 1982, pp. 114-120.

7. G. Radin, "The 801 Minicomputer," *IBM J. Research and Development*, May 1983, pp. 237-246.

8. M.J. Mahon et al., "Hewlett-Packard Precision Architecture: The Processor," *Hewlett-Packard J.*, Aug. 1986, pp. 4-21.

9. P.Y.T. Hsu and E.S. Davidson, "Highly Concurrent Scalar Processing," *Proc. 13th Ann. Symp. Computer Architecture*, 1986, pp. 386-395.

10. E.M. Riseman and C.C. Foster, "The Inhibition of Potential Parallelism by Conditional Jumps," *IEEE Trans. Computers*, Dec. 1972, pp. 1,405-1,411.

11. Anon., "Tandem Makes a Good Thing Better," *Electronics*, Apr. 14, 1986, pp. 34-38.

12. L.E. Shar and E.S. Davidson, "A Multiminiprocessor System Implemented Through Pipelining," *Computer*, Feb. 1974, pp. 42-51.

13. B.J. Smith, "Architecture and Applications of the HEP Multiprocessor Computer System," *Real-Time Signal Processing IV, Proc. SPIE*, 1981, pp. 241-248. Reprinted in *Supercomputers: Design and Applications*, Kai Hwang, ed., Computer Society Press, Silver Spring, Md., pp. 231-238.

14. W.J. Watson, "The TI ASC—A Highly Modular and Flexible Supercomputer Architecture," *Proc. AFIPS Fall Joint Computer Conf.*, Vol. 41, AFIPS Press, Montvale, N.J., Dec. 1972, pp. 221-228.

David J. Lilja is a doctoral candidate in the Department of Electrical and Computer Engineering and a graduate research assistant in the Center for Supercomputing Research and Development at the University of Illinois at Urbana-Champaign. His main research interests are in computer architecture and parallel processing.

Lilja received a BS in computer engineering from Iowa State University and an MS in electrical engineering from the University of Illinois. He is a member of Tau Beta Pi, Eta Kappa Nu, and Phi Kappa Phi, a student member of the Computer Society, and a registered Professional Engineer in California.

Readers may write to Lilja at the Center for Supercomputing Research and Development, University of Illinois at Urbana-Champaign, 305 Talbot Laboratory, 104 S. Wright St., Urbana, IL 61801-2932.

Instruction Issue Logic in Pipelined Supercomputers

SHLOMO WEISS AND JAMES E. SMITH, MEMBER, IEEE

Abstract — Basic principles and design tradeoffs for control of pipelined processors are first discussed. We concentrate on register–register architectures like the CRAY-1 where pipeline control logic is localized to one or two pipeline stages and is referred to as "instruction issue logic." Design tradeoffs are explored by giving designs for a variety of instruction issue methods that represent a range of complexity and sophistication. These vary from the CRAY-1 issue logic to a version of Tomasulo's algorithm, first used in the IBM 360/91 floating point unit. Also studied are Thornton's "scoreboard" algorithm used on the CDC 6600 and an algorithm we have devised. To provide a standard for comparison, all the issue methods are used to implement the CRAY-1 scalar architecture. Then, using a simulation model and the Lawrence Livermore Loops compiled with the CRAY Fortran compiler, performance results for the various issue methods are given and discussed.

Index Terms — CDC 6600 scoreboard, control logic, CRAY-1, IBM 360/91, instruction issue logic, performance simulation, pipelined computers, supercomputers, Tomasulo's algorithm.

I. INTRODUCTION

ALTHOUGH modern supercomputers are closely associated with high-speed vector operation, it is widely recognized that scalar operation is at least of equal importance, and pipelining [9] is the predominant technique for achieving high scalar performance. In a pipelined computer, instruction processing is broken into segments and processing proceeds in an assembly line fashion with the execution of several instructions being overlapped. Because of data and control dependencies in a scalar instruction stream, interlock logic is placed between critical pipeline segments to control instruction flow through the pipe. In register–register architectures like the CDC 6600 [12], the CDC 7600 [3], and the CRAY-1 [6], [7], [11], most of the interlock logic is localized to one segment early in the pipeline and is referred to as "instruction issue" logic.

It is the purpose of this paper to highlight some of the tradeoffs that affect pipeline control, with particular emphasis on instruction issue logic. The primary vehicle for this discussion is a simulation study of different instruction issue methods with varying degrees of complexity. These range from the simple and straightforward as in the CRAY-1 to the complex and sophisticated as in the CDC 6600 and the IBM 360/91 floating point unit [13]. Each is used to implement the CRAY-1 scalar architecture, and each imple-

mentation is simulated using the 14 Lawrence Livermore Loops [10] as compiled by the Cray Research Fortran compiler (CFT).

A. Tradeoffs

We begin with a discussion of design tradeoffs that centers on four principle issues: 1) clock period, 2) instruction scheduling, 3) issue logic complexity, and 4) hardware cost, debugging, and maintenance. Each of these issues will be discussed in turn.

Clock Period: In a pipelined computer, there are a number of segments containing combinational logic with latches separating successive segments. All the latches are synchronized by the same clock, and the pipeline is capable of initiating a new instruction every clock period. Hence, under ideal conditions, i.e., no dependencies or resource conflicts, pipeline performance is directly related to the period of the clock used to synchronize the pipe. Even with data dependencies and resource conflicts, there is a high correlation between performance and clock period.

Historically, pipelined supercomputers have had shorter clock periods than other computers. This is in part due to the use of the fastest available logic technologies, but it is also due to designs that minimize logic levels between successive latches.

Scheduling of Instructions: Performance of a pipelined processor depends greatly on the order of the instructions in the instruction stream. If consecutive instructions have data and control dependencies and contend for resources, then "holes" in the pipeline will develop and performance will suffer. To improve performance, it is often possible to arrange the code, or schedule it, so that dependencies and resource conflicts are minimized. Registers can also be allocated so that register conflicts are reduced (register conflicts caused by data dependencies cannot be eliminated in this way, however). Because of their close relationship, in the remainder of the paper we will group code scheduling and register allocation together and refer to them collectively as "code scheduling."

There are two different ways that code scheduling can be done. First, it can be done at compile time by the software. We refer to this as "static" scheduling because it does not change as the program runs. Second, it can be done by the hardware at run time. We refer to this as "dynamic" scheduling. These two methods are not mutually exclusive.

Most compilers for pipelined processors do some form of static scheduling to avoid dependencies. This adds a new dimension to the optimization problems faced by a compiler, and occasionally a programmer will hand code inner loops in

Reprinted from *IEEE Transactions on Computers*, Vol. C-33, No. 11, November 1984, pages 1013-1022. Copyright © 1984 by The Institute of Electrical and Electronics Engineers, Inc. All rights reserved.

Assembly language to arrive at a better schedule than a compiler can provide.

Issue Logic Complexity: By using complex issue logic, dynamic scheduling of instructions can be achieved. This allows instructions to begin execution "out-of-order" with respect to the compiled code sequence. This has two advantages. First, it relieves some of the burden on the compiler to generate a good schedule. That is, performance is not as dependent on the quality of the compiled code. Second, dynamic scheduling at issue time can take advantage of dependency information that is not available to the compiler when it does static scheduling. Complex issue logic does require longer control paths, however, which can lead to a longer clock period.

Hardware Cost, Debugging, and Maintenance: Complex issue methods lead to additional hardware cost. More logic is needed, and design time is increased. Complex control logic is also more expensive to debug and maintain. These problems are aggravated by issue methods that dynamically schedule code because it may be difficult to reproduce exact issue sequences.

B. Historical Perspective

It is interesting to review the way the above tradeoffs have been dealt with historically. In the late 1950's and early 1960's there was rapid movement toward increasingly complex issue methods. Important milestones were achieved by STRETCH [4] in 1961 and the CDC 6600 in 1964. Probably the most sophisticated issue logic used to date is in the IBM 360/91 [1], shipped in 1967. After this first rush toward more and more complex methods, there was a retreat toward simpler instruction issue methods that are still in use today. At CDC, the 7600 was designed to issue instructions in strict program sequence with no dynamic scheduling. The clock period, however, was very fast, even by today's standards. The more recent CRAY-1 and CRAY X-MP [8] differ very little from the CDC 7600 in the way they handle scalar instructions. The CDC CYBER205 [5] scalar unit is also very similar. At IBM, and later at the Amdahl Corporation, pipelined implementations of the 360/370 architecture have replaced the complex issue methods of the 360/91 with simpler ones that issue instructions strictly in order.

As for the future, both the debug/maintenance problem and the hardware cost problem may be significantly alleviated by using VLSI where logic is much less expensive and where replaceable parts are such that fault isolation does not need to be as precise as with SSI. In addition, there is a trend toward moving software problems into hardware, and code scheduling seems to be a candidate. Consequently, tradeoffs are shifting and instruction issue logic that dynamically schedules code deserves renewed study.

C. Paper Overview

The tradeoffs just discussed lead to a spectrum of instruction issue algorithms. Through simulation we can look at the performance gains that are made possible by dynamic code scheduling. Other issues like clock period and hardware

cost and maintenance are more difficult and require detailed design and construction to make quantitative assessments. In this paper, we do discuss the control functions that need to be implemented to facilitate qualitative judgements. Section II examines one endpoint of the spectrum: the CRAY-1. The CRAY-1 uses simple issue logic with a fast clock and static code scheduling only. Section III examines the other end point of the spectrum: Tomasulo's algorithm. Tomasulo's algorithm is capable of considerable dynamic code scheduling via a complex issue mechanism. Sections IV and V then discuss two intermediate points. The first is a variation of Thornton's "scoreboard" algorithm used in the CDC 6600. Thornton's algorithm is also used to implement the CRAY-1 scalar architecture. The second is an algorithm we have devised to allow dynamic scheduling while doing away with some of the associative compare logic required by the other methods that perform dynamic scheduling. Each of the four CRAY-1 implementations is simulated over the same set of benchmarks to allow performance comparisons. Section VI contains a further discussion on the relationship between software and hardware code scheduling in pipelined processors, and Section VII contains conclusions.

II. THE CRAY-1 ARCHITECTURE AND INSTRUCTION ISSUE ALGORITHM

A. Overview of the CRAY-1

The CRAY-1 architecture and organization are used throughout this paper as a basis for comparison. The CRAY-1 scalar architecture is shown in Fig. 1. It consists of two sets of registers and functional units for 1) address processing and 2) scalar processing. The address registers are partitioned into two levels: 8 A registers and 64 B registers. The integer add and multiply functional units are dedicated to address processing. Similarly, the scalar registers are partitioned into two levels: 8 S registers and 64 T registers. The B and T register files may be used as a programmer-manipulated data cache, although this feature is largely unused by the CFT compiler. Four functional units are used exclusively for scalar processing. In addition, three floating point functional units are shared with the vector processing section (vector registers are not shown in Fig. 1).

The instruction set is designed for efficient pipeline processing. Being a register–register architecture, only load and store instructions can access memory. The rest of instructions use operands from registers. Instructions for the B and T registers are restricted to memory access and copies to and from register files A and S, respectively.

The information flow is from memory to registers A (S), or to the intermediate registers B (T). From file A (S) data are sent to the functional units, from which they return to file A (S). Then data can be further processed by functional units, stored into memory, or saved in file B (T). Block transfers of operands between memory and registers B and T are also available, thus reducing the number of memory access instructions.

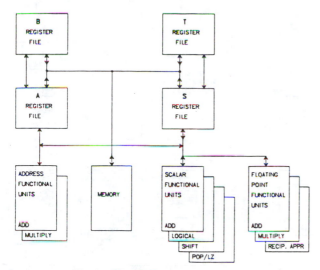

Fig. 1. The CRAY-1 scalar architecture.

B. CRAY-1 Issue Logic

Instructions are fetched from instruction buffers at the rate of one parcel (16 bits) per clock period. Individual instructions are either one or two parcels long. After a clock period is spent for instruction decoding, the issue logic checks interlocks. If there is any conflict, the issue is blocked until the conflict condition goes away.

For scalar instructions, the following are the primary interlock checks made at the time of instruction issue.

1) Registers: Both the source and destination registers must not be reserved (there must be no currently executing instruction that will modify them).

2) Result bus: The A and S register files have one bus each over which data can be written into the files. Based on the completion time of the particular instruction, a check is made to determine if the bus will be available at the clock period when the instruction completes.

3) Functional unit: Due to vector instructions, a functional unit may be busy when a scalar instruction wishes to use it. Since we are considering scalar performance only, this type of conflict will not occur. The memory system can also be viewed as a functional unit; it can occasionally become busy due to a memory bank conflict, but for scalar code this is a very infrequent occurrence and does not affect performance in any appreciable way.

If all its interlocks pass, an instruction issues and causes the following to take place.

1) The destination register is reserved: This reservation is removed only when the instruction completes.

2) The result bus is reserved for the clock period when the instruction completes.

Memory accesses have one further interlock to be checked: memory bank busy. This must be delayed until the indexing register is read and the effective address is computed. Hence, the bank busy check is performed two clock periods after a load or store instruction issues. If the bank happens to be busy, the memory "functional unit" is busied, and no further loads or stores can be issued. Because all loads and stores are two parcels long, they can issue at a maximum rate of one

every two clock periods. This means that a bank busy blockage catches a subsequent load or store before it is issued. After a load instruction passes the bank busy check, it places its reservation for the appropriate result bus. A load can only conflict for the bus with a previously issued reciprocal approximation instruction, so the additional interlocking done at that point is minimal.

C. CRAY-1 Performance

In this paper performance is measured by simulating the first 14 Lawrence Livermore Loops. These are excerpts from large Fortran programs that have been judged to provide a good measure of large scale computer performance. The loops were compiled using the CFT compiler, and instruction trace tapes were generated. These were then simulated with a performance simulator written in C, running on a VAX11/780. With bank busies and instruction buffer misses modeled, the simulator agrees exactly with actual CRAY-1 timings, except when there is a difference in the way a loop fits into the instruction buffers. This particular difference is a function of where the loader chooses to place a program in memory, and for practical use has to be viewed as a nondeterminism.

Since we are interested in scalar performance, the CFT compiler was run with the "vectorizer" turned off so that no vector instructions were produced. When the vectorizer is on, half of the 14 loops contain a substantial amount of vector code, and half remain scalar.

For the simulations reported here, we have made the following simplifications. 1) There are no memory bank conflicts. 2) All loops fit in the instruction buffers.

One reason for this simplification was to simplify the simulator design for the alternative CRAY-1 issue methods to be given later; as mentioned earlier our original CRAY-1 simulator is capable of modeling bank conflicts and instruction buffers. Also, this allows us to concentrate on the performance differences caused by issue logic and to filter the "noise" introduced by other factors (e.g., instruction buffer crossings). Table I shows the scalar performance of the CRAY-1 for the first 14 Lawrence Livermore Loops.

III. TOMASULO'S ALGORITHM

The CRAY-1 forces instructions to issue strictly in program order. If an instruction is blocked from issuing due to a conflict, all instructions following it in the instruction stream are also blocked, even if they have no conflicts. In contrast, the scheme in this section allows instructions to begin execution out of program order. It is a variation of the instruction issue algorithm first presented in [13]. Although the original algorithm was devised for the floating point unit of the IBM 360/91, we show how it can be adapted and extended to control the entire pipeline structure of a CRAY-1 implementation.

Fig. 2 illustrates the essential elements of a tag-based mechanism for issue of instructions out-of-order. Fig. 3 illustrates the full CRAY-1 implementation.

TABLE I
CRAY-1 EXECUTION TIMES FOR THE 14 LAWRENCE LIVERMORE LOOPS. ONE PARCEL INSTRUCTION IS ISSUED IN ONE CYCLE; TWO PARCEL INSTRUCTIONS ARE ISSUED IN TWO CYCLES.

Loop	# instructions executed	# clock cycles
1	7217	18046
2	8448	18918
3	14015	38039
4	9783	22198
5	8347	21707
6	9350	23045
7	4573	10361
8	4031	7841
9	4918	10146
10	4412	10230
11	12002	30011
12	11999	29999
13	8846	18858
14	9915	22391

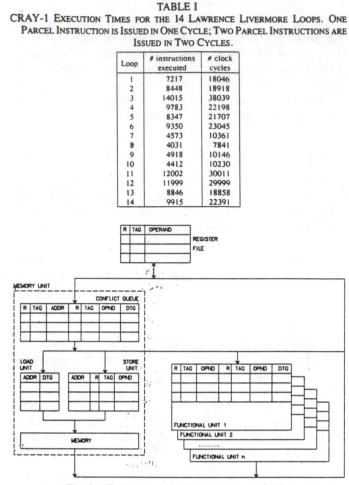

Fig. 2. Tag-based mechanism to issue out-of-order.

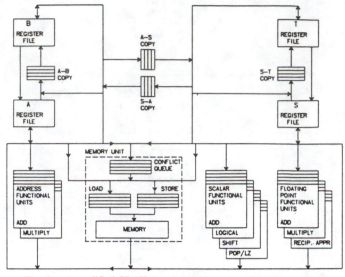

Fig. 3. A modified CRAY-1 scalar architecture to issue instructions out-of-order.

Each register in the A and S register files is augmented by a *ready* bit (R) and a *tag* field. Associated with each functional unit is a small number of *reservation stations*. Each reservation station can store a pair of operands; each operand has its own tag field and ready bit. A reservation station also holds a *destination tag* (DTG). When an instruction is issued, a new tag is stored into DTG (see Fig. 2).

New destination tags are assigned from a "tag pool" that consists of some finite set of tags. These are associated with an instruction from the time the instruction is issued to a reservation station until the time it produces a result and completes. The tag is returned to the pool when an instruction finishes. In the original Tomasulo's algorithm, the tags were in 1-to-1 correspondence with the reservation stations. This particular way of assigning tags is not essential, however. Any method will work as long as tags are assigned and released to the pool as described above.

We treat the register files B and T as a unit, with one *busy* bit per file since it is not practical to assign tags to so many registers. When one of these registers awaits an operand, the whole file is set to busy.

To facilitate transfer of operands between the register files, special copy units ($AS, SA, AB,$ and ST) are introduced. These are treated as functional units, with reservation stations and execution time of one clock cycle. These reservation stations (and some others, e.g., reciprocal approximation) have only one operand.

The memory unit appears to the issue logic as a (somewhat more complex) functional unit. Instead of one set of reservation stations, the memory unit has three: *Load* reservation stations, *Store* reservation stations, and a *Conflict Queue*. When a new memory instruction I_i is issued, its effective address (if available) is checked against addresses in the Load and Store reservation stations and the Conflict Queue. If there is a conflict with instruction I_j, I_i is issued and queued in the Conflict Queue. When I_j is eventually processed and the conflict disappears, I_i is transferred from the Conflict Queue to a Load or Store reservation station. If I_i uses an index register that is not ready, or there is any member of the Conflict Queue whose index register is not ready, an effective address is unknown, and there is no way to check for conflicts. In this case, I_i is stored in the Conflict Queue, where it waits for its index register to become ready.

Therefore, instructions from the Load and Store units can be processed asynchronously since they never conflict with each other (no two instructions in these units have the same effective address). On the other hand, instructions from the Conflict Queue are processed in the order of arrival. This guarantees that two instructions with the same effective address are processed in the right order. The above mechanism takes care of any read after write, write after read, or write after write hazards. The Conflict Queue is the only unit in the system in which instructions are strictly processed in the order of their arrival. This is a simpler mechanism that the one employed by the IBM 360/91 Storage System [2]. The latter has a similar queue for resolving memory conflicts, but instructions stored in this queue can be processed out of order; only two or more requests for a particular address are kept in sequence.

The tag mechanism described above allows decoded instructions to issue to functional units with little regard for dependencies. There are three conditions that must be checked before an instruction can be sent to a functional unit, however.

1) The requested functional unit must have an available reservation station.

2) There must be an available tag from the tag pool. In Tomasulo's implementation, conditions 1) and 2) are equivalent.

3) A source register being used by the instruction must not be loaded with a just-completed result during the same clock period as the instruction issues to a reservation station. This hazard condition is often neglected when discussing Tomasulo's algorithm. If it is not handled properly, the source register contents and the instruction that uses the source register will both be transferred during the same clock period. Because the instruction is not in the reservation station at the time of the register transfer, the register's contents will not be correctly sent to the reservation station. When this hazard condition is detected, instruction issue is held for one clock period.

In our simulations, each functional unit had 8 reservation stations. The reason we had a relatively large number of reservation stations was to monitor their usage; in fact, most of them were not required. Few functional units need more than one or two reservation stations. Those that need more, usually because they wait for instructions with long latency, such as load or floating point multiply and add, would do very well with 4 reservation stations. Although in our scheme reservation stations are statically allocated to each functional unit, it is possible to reduce their number and optimize their usage by clustering them in a common pool and then allocating them as needed.

When an instruction is issued, the following actions take place.

1) The instruction's source register(s) contents are copied into the requested functional unit's reservation station.

2) The instruction's source register(s) ready bits are copied into the reservation station.

3) The instruction's source register(s) tag fields are copied into the reservation station.

4) A tag allocated from the tag pool is placed in the result register's tag field (if there is a result), the register's ready bit is cleared, and the tag is written into the DTG field of the reservation station.

Thus, if a source register's ready bit is set, the reservation station will hold a valid operand. Otherwise, it will hold a tag that identifies the expected operand.

In order for an instruction waiting in a reservation station to begin execution, the following must be satisfied.

1) All of its operands must be ready.

2) It must gain access to the required functional unit; this may involve contention with other reservation stations belonging to the same functional unit that also have all operands ready.

3) It must gain access to the result bus for the clock period when its result will be ready; again, this may involve contention with other instructions issuing to the same or any other functional unit that will complete at the same time.

When an instruction begins execution, it does the following.

1) It releases its reservation station.

2) It reserves the result bus for the clock period when it will complete. Reserving the bus in advance avoids the implementation problems of stopping the pipeline if the bus is busy. An alternative is to request the bus a short time before the end of execution and to provide buffering at the output of the functional unit [13].

3) It copies its destination tag into the functional unit control pipeline because the destination tag must be attached to the result when the instruction completes.

When either a load or functional unit instruction completes, its result and corresponding destination tag appear on the result bus. (In a practical implementation, the tag will probably precede the data by one clock period.) The data are stored in all the reservation stations and registers that have the ready bit clear and a tag that matches the tag of the result. Then the ready bit is set to signal a valid operand.

Because instruction issue takes place in two phases (the first moves an instruction to a reservation station and the second moves it on to the functional unit for execution) we assume that each phase takes a full clock period. In the CRAY-1 there is only a one clock period delay in moving an instruction to a functional unit. We recognize the one clock period difference in our simulation model, so that the minimum time for an instruction to complete is one clock period greater than in the CRAY-1. This takes into account some of the lost time due to the more complex control decisions that are required. The primary factor that may lead to longer control paths is the contention that takes place among the reservation stations for functional units and buses when more than one are simultaneously ready to initiate an instruction.

When branches are taken, issue is held for at least 5 clock cycles. Since branches test the contents of register $A0$ for the condition specified in the branch instruction, $A0$ should not be busy in the previous 2 cycles. These assumptions are in accord with the CRAY-1 implementation and the assumptions made to produce Table I.

A. Performance Results

Table II shows the results of simulating the CRAY-1 implemented with Tomasulo's algorithm. The total speedup achieved was 1.43. We recognize that these are in a sense, "theoretical maximum speedups"; any lengthening of the clock period due to longer control paths will diminish this speedup.

We noticed while doing the simulations that limiting instruction fetches to the maximum rate of one parcel per clock period appeared to be restricting performance. Hence, we modified the implementation so that a full instruction could be fetched and issued to a reservation station each clock period. This would be slightly more expensive to implement, but for Tomasulo's algorithm it gives a significant performance improvement over one parcel per clock period.

To keep comparisons fair, we first went back and modified the original CRAY-1 simulation model so that it, too, could issue instructions at the higher rate. Table III gives the results of these simulations, and compares them to the one parcel per clock period results given earlier. Here, the performance improvement is small. This is an interesting result in itself, and shows the wisdom of opting for simpler instruction fetch logic in the original CRAY-1.

Because the higher instruction fetch rate does appear to

TABLE II
PERFORMANCE WITH TOMASULO'S ALGORITHM: ONE PARCEL ISSUED PER CLOCK PERIOD

Loop	# clock cycles on CRAY-1	# clock cycles for Tomasulo's algorithm	speedup
1	18046	10838	1.67
2	18918	14102	1.34
3	38039	30017	1.27
4	22198	16534	1.34
5	21707	16925	1.28
6	23045	15042	1.53
7	10361	6513	1.59
8	7841	6780	1.16
9	10146	8238	1.23
10	10230	7421	1.38
11	30011	20006	1.50
12	29999	20000	1.50
13	18858	12314	1.53
14	22391	12780	1.75
total	281790	197510	1.43

TABLE III
COMPARISON OF THE 14 LAWRENCE LIVERMORE LOOPS ON THE CRAY-1; ONE INSTRUCTION PER CLOCK PERIOD VERSUS ONE PARCEL PER CLOCK PERIOD

Loop	# clock cycles 1 parcel/cp	# clock cycles 1 instr/cp	speedup
1	18046	17244	1.05
2	18918	17717	1.07
3	38039	37037	1.03
4	22198	21163	1.05
5	21707	20709	1.05
6	23045	22045	1.05
7	10361	10241	1.01
8	7841	6874	1.14
9	10146	9744	1.04
10	10230	9430	1.08
11	30011	28013	1.07
12	29999	28001	1.07
13	18858	17957	1.05
14	22391	22087	1.01
total	281790	268262	1.05

TABLE IV
PERFORMANCE OF TOMASULO'S ALGORITHM; ONE INSTRUCTION ISSUED PER CLOCK PERIOD

Loop	# clock cycles on CRAY-1	# clock cycles for Tomasulo's algorithm	speedup
1	17244	8832	1.95
2	17717	11062	1.60
3	37037	28012	1.32
4	21163	15418	1.37
5	20709	16898	1.23
6	22045	12956	1.70
7	10241	5069	2.02
8	6874	5195	1.32
9	9744	6332	1.54
10	9430	5318	1.77
11	28013	17871	1.57
12	28001	16001	1.75
13	17957	9364	1.92
14	22087	11713	1.89
total	268262	170041	1.58

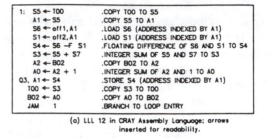

(a) LLL 12 in CRAY Assembly Language; arrows inserted for readability.

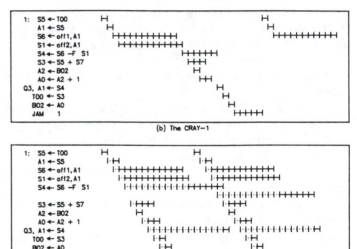

(b) The CRAY-1

(c) Tomasulo's algorithm

Fig. 4. Timing diagrams for Lawrence Livermore Loop (LLL) 12. (a) LLL 12 in CRAY assembly language, arrows inserted for readability. (b) The CRAY-1. (c) Tomasulo's algorithm.

improve the efficiency of Tomasulo's algorithm, we incorporated it into the model for the studies to follow, and used the CRAY-1 results of Table III (1 instruction per clock period) as a basis for further comparisons.

Table IV shows simulation results for Tomasulo's algorithm with one instruction issued per clock period. The speedup achieved is in the range 1.23–2.02 (total 1.58). In three out of the four loops whose speedup was less than 1.5 (i.e., loops 3, 4, and 8) issue was halted due to a busy T file. With an architecture that does not have the large number of registers the CRAY-1 has, it would be possible to use tags for all the registers, thus increasing the speedup of the above loops.

B. Example

Fig. 4 shows a timing diagram of Tomasulo's algorithm compared to that of CRAY-1, both executing loop 12. On the left-hand side appear the instructions as generated by the CFT compiler. The timing for two consecutive loop iterations are shown next to each other. Each "⊢" represents one clock period. From the standpoint of issue logic, when store instructions are initiated they go to memory and are no longer considered. Therefore, stores are shown to execute only for the clock period they are initiated. Solid lines indicate that the respective instruction is in execution. For Tomasulo's algorithm, a dotted line shows that an instruction has been issued to a reservation station, and is waiting for operand(s).

With the original CRAY-1 issue algorithm, all instructions in a loop must begin execution and a loop-terminating condi-

tional branch instruction must complete before the next loop iteration can begin. With Tomasulo's algorithm, loop iterations can be "telescoped"; a second loop iteration can begin after all instructions have been sent to reservation stations and the conditional branch is completed. The instructions belonging to the first loop iteration do not necessarily need to begin execution. One could also view this as dynamic rescheduling of the branch instruction. Obviously, the branch instruction is one instruction that cannot be moved earlier in the loop as would have to be the case with static rescheduling. The significant speedup of Tomasulo's algorithm for this loop (1.75, see Table IV) is due mainly to the overlap of the loading of registers $S6$ and $S1$ with the floating point difference ($-F$) which uses $S6$ and $S1$ as operands. Although $-F$ cannot be executed until the operands return from memory, it can be issued to a reservation station; this allows following instructions to proceed. On the other hand, the CRAY-1 executes the load of $S1$ and the floating point difference strictly in order.

One can see from the timing diagrams that with Tomasulo's algorithm only 2 reservation stations are used for more than 1 clock period. The store instruction needs a reservation station that is released a short period of time before the next store is issued. Another reservation station is used extensively by the floating point difference instruction.

IV. THORNTON'S ALGORITHM

Tomasulo's algorithm leads to complex issue logic and may be quite expensive to implement. Therefore, in this section and in the next section, we consider ways to reduce the cost. One major cost is the associative hardware needed to match tags. When an operand and its attached tag appear on a bus, register files A and S and all the reservation stations have to be searched simultaneously. The operand is stored in any register or reservation station with a matching tag.

In this section, we implement the CRAY-1 scalar architecture with an issue method that is a derivative of Thornton's "scoreboard" algorithm used in the CDC 6600. Here, control is more distributed (there is no global scoreboard), and reservation stations have been added to functional units. The primary difference between Thornton's algorithm and Tomasulo's is that instruction issue is halted when the destination of an instruction is a register that is busy. This simplifies the issue logic hardware in the following ways.

1) The associative compare with the register file tags is eliminated.

2) Tag allocation and deallocation hardware is eliminated because the result register designator acts as the tag.

Fig. 5 illustrates the algorithm. Most reservation stations hold two operands (although some need only one, depending on the functional unit) and the address of the destination register (DR). Attached to each operand is the source register designator (SR) and a ready flag (R). Also, attached to each register in the register file is a ready bit (R). (These are logical complements of the reserved bits used in the original CRAY-1 control.)

The following operations are performed when an instruction is issued.

1) A reservation station of the requested functional unit, if available, is reserved. Otherwise, issue is blocked.

2) If a source register is ready, it is copied into the reservation station and the ready bit is set. Otherwise, the ready bit is cleared and the source register's designator is stored into the SR field.

The conditions for moving an instruction from a reservation station to begin execution are the same as given for Tomasulo's algorithm in the previous section. When a functional unit is finished with an instruction the result register designator is matched against all the SR fields in the reservation stations, and the result is written into the reservation stations where there is a match. The corresponding operand ready bits are then set. The result is also stored into the destination register, and it is set ready.

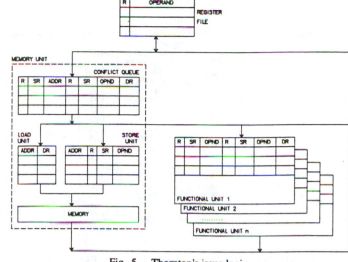

Fig. 5.   Thornton's issue logic.

Although the above is derived from Thornton's original algorithm, there are some differences. The functional units of the CDC 6600 do not have reservation stations (one could say that they have reservation stations of depth 1 that are not able to hold operands, only control information). This imposes some additional restrictions. An instruction to be executed on a particular functional unit can be issued even if its source registers are not ready, but a second instruction requiring the same functional unit will block issue until the first one is done. On the other hand, with reservation stations, several instuctions can wait for operands at the input of the functional unit. For example,

$$S1 \leftarrow S2 *F S3$$

$$S4 \leftarrow S5 *F S6$$

with the CDC 6600 scoreboard the second instruction will block, while with the algorithm here it will be issued.

Another restriction of the scoreboard is the following. In this example,

$$S1 \leftarrow S2 *F S3$$

$$S2 \leftarrow S4 + 1$$

we assume that $S2$ and $S4$ are ready, while $S3$ is not (e.g., it awaits an operand from memory). The second instruction will be completed before the first one, but on the CDC 6600 the result cannot be stored into $S2$ since it serves as a source register for the first instruction. Therefore, the add functional unit will remain busy until the first instruction completes as well. On the other hand, with the algorithm we have given, $S2$ has been copied into the floating point multiply reservation station when the first instruction was issued, and therefore the second instruction can complete before the first one.

A. Performance Results

We originally planned to simulate the scoreboard as designed by Thornton, but decided that it would lead to a more interesting comparison if multiple reservation stations were allowed. The results of the simulation are shown in Table V. The total speedup is 1.28. We discuss ways this can be improved by static code scheduling in Section VI.

TABLE V
PERFORMANCE OF THORNTON'S ALGORITHM; ONE INSTRUCTION ISSUED PER CLOCK
PERIOD

Loop	# clock cycles on CRAY-1	# clock cycles for Thornton's algorithm	speedup
1	17244	12434	1.39
2	17717	13500	1.31
3	37037	28020	1.32
4	21163	19578	1.08
5	20709	17030	1.22
6	22045	18370	1.20
7	10241	8671	1.18
8	6874	6381	1.08
9	9744	8634	1.13
10	9430	7820	1.21
11	28013	18001	1.56
12	28001	16003	1.75
13	17957	14870	1.21
14	22087	20273	1.09
total	268262	209585	1.28

V. AN ISSUE METHOD USING A DIRECT TAG SEARCH

In this section we propose an alternative issue algorithm that is related to Tomasulo's algorithm, but which eliminates the need for associative tag comparison hardware in the reservation stations. This algorithm instead uses a direct tag search (DTS), and will be referred to as the "DTS" algorithm. The DTS algorithm imposes the restriction that a particular tag can be stored only in one reservation station. This is easily implemented by associating with each tag in the tag pool a *used* bit. Whenever a register that is not ready is accessed for the first time, its tag is copied to the respective reservation station and the used bit is set. A second attempt to use the same tag will block issue.

The DTS algorithm allows implementation of the tag search mechanism by a table indexed by tags (Fig. 6), rather than associative hardware. For each tag there is one entry in the table that stores the address of a reservation station. The table is small since there are few tags (we used 5 bits for each tag; there are 32 tags).

A. Performance Results

A comparison of the results for the DTS algorithm with Tomasulo's algorithm reveals that for 9 out of the 14 loops the DTS algorithm achieves speedup similar to Tomasulo's algorithm. This shows that the restriction imposed by the DTS algorithm, namely that a tag can be in no more than one reservation station at a given time, has only a limited effect on performance. The reason is that the following pattern is quite common:

$$S1 \leftarrow off1, A1$$

$$S2 \leftarrow off2, A1$$

$$S3 \leftarrow S1 *F S2$$

$$S5 \leftarrow S3 + F S4$$

That is, two registers are loaded and are sent to a functional unit whose result is input to another functional unit, and so on. The DTS algorithm is able to process such code at full speed.

On the other hand, if a register is used as an input to a functional unit and at the same time has to be stored (in the memory, or temporarily in the T or B file), then the register

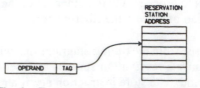

Fig. 6. Tag search table for DTS algorithm.

and its tag, have to be used twice, so the DTS algorithm blocks issue. Such cases account for the lower speedup of 5 out of 14 loops.

VI. FURTHER COMMENTS ON CODE SCHEDULING

For all the various issue logic simulations, we used as input the object code generated by the CRAY-1 optimizing Fortran compiler, without any changes. Therefore, the level of code optimization and scheduling is realistic for the CRAY-1. Tomasulo's algorithm is less sensitive to the order of the instructions since it does a great deal of dynamic scheduling. It is also capable of dynamic register reallocation so it is not as susceptible to the compiler's register allocation method. On the other hand, static scheduling and register allocation has a significant impact on the performance of the DTS issue logic and Thornton's algorithm. Since we have not reorganized the code for the latter two schemes, many dependencies and resource conflicts that appear in the compiled code contribute to lower performance as compared to Tomasulo's algorithm.

Fig. 7 illustrates an example, extracted from Lawrence Livermore Loop 4. The instruction "$T02 \leftarrow S5$" saves register $S5$ for use during the next pass through the loop. For the DTS issue logic, this instruction has to be blocked since it attempts to use register $S5$ as a source for the second time (register $S5$ is not ready and was used for the first time by the previous instruction). However, neither $S5$ nor $T02$ is used before the branch instruction, so this interlock could be postponed by moving instruction "$T02 \leftarrow S5$" down, just before the branch. The 4 clock cycles thus saved, multiplied by the number of iterations through the loop, result in a 4 percent performance improvement.

Fig. 8 shows another example, extracted from loop 1. Registers $S2$, $S6$, $S1$, $S3$, and $S4$ are designated as destination registers for the first time in the upper half of the loop, and then for the second time, almost in the same order, in the lower half of the loop. The second usage of $S2$ ($S2 \leftarrow S4 *R S6$) as a destination register causes an immediate blockage for Thornton's algorithm since $S2$ is still busy from the previous load instruction ($S2 \leftarrow off1, A1$). Any independent instruction inserted just before instruction "$S2 \leftarrow S4 *R S6$" will execute for free. There are three such instructions before the branch

$$A2 \leftarrow B02$$

$$A0 \leftarrow A2 + 1$$

$$B02 \leftarrow A0$$

TABLE VI
PERFORMANCE OF DTS ISSUE LOGIC

Loop	# clock cycles on CRAY-1	# clock cycles for the DTS algorithm	speedup
1	17244	8832	1.95
2	17717	11083	1.60
3	37037	28020	1.32
4	21163	20534	1.03
5	20709	17690	1.17
6	22045	17027	1.29
7	10241	5069	2.02
8	6874	5361	1.28
9	9744	6732	1.45
10	9430	8518	1.11
11	28013	17871	1.57
12	28001	16001	1.75
13	17957	14356	1.25
14	22087	17421	1.27
total	268262	194515	1.38

```
      do 175 l = 7,107,50
      lw = 1
      do 4 j = 30,870,5
      x(l − l) = x(l − l) − x(lw)*y(j)
4     lw = lw + 1
      x(l − l) = y(5)*x(l − l)
175   continue
```

(a)

```
LOOP4:      S6  ←  T00
            S1  ←  T01
            A3  ←  S1
            A2  ←  S6
            S3  ←  off2,A3      .x(lw)
            S5  ←  off3,A2      .y(j)
            S4  ←  S5 *R S3
            S3  ←  T02
            S5  ←  S3 − F S4
            S4  ←  S1 + S2
            A1  ←  B02
            S3  ←  S6 + S7
      off4,A7  ←  S5            .x(1 − 1)
            T02 ←  S5
            T01 ←  S4
            A0  ←  A1 + 1
            T00 ←  S3
            B02 ←  A0
            JAM    LOOP4
```

(b)

Fig. 7. Example of interlock for DTS issue logic. (a) Fortran code for Lawrence Livermore Loop 4 (banded linear equations). (b) Compiled object code (the inner loop) extracted from Lawrence Livermore Loop 4.

This simple rescheduling gives a performance improvement of 10.7 percent.

Since there is a large gap between Tomasulo's and Thornton's algorithms for loop 1 (1.95 versus 1.39), we tried to see if this gap could be closed by reallocating registers for Thornton's algorithm. The following code does the processing of loop 1, except for index and address calculations:

$$S1 \leftarrow off1, A1$$

$$S2 \leftarrow off2, A1$$

$$S4 \leftarrow S1 *F S3$$

$$S6 \leftarrow S2 *F S5$$

```
      q = 0.0
      do lk = 1,400
1     x(k) = q + y(k)*(r*z(k + 10) + t*z(k + 11))
```

(a)

```
LOOP1:      S5  ←  T00
            A1  ←  S5
            S2  ←  off1,A1      .z(k + 10)
            S6  ←  off2,A1      .z(k + 11)
            S1  ←  T02
            S3  ←  S1 *R S2
            S4  ←  T01
            S2  ←  S4 *R S6
            S6  ←  off3,A1
            S1  ←  S2 + F S3
            S4  ←  S6 *R S1
            S3  ←  S5 + S7
            A2  ←  B02
            A0  ←  A2 + 1
      off4,A1  ←  S4
            T00 ←  S3
            B02 ←  A0
            JAM    LOOP1
```

(b)

Fig. 8. Example of interlock for Thornton's algorithm. (a) Fortran code for Lawrence Livermore Loop 1 (hydro excerpt). (b) Assembly code extracted from Lawrence Livermore Loop 1.

$$S7 \leftarrow S4 + F S6$$

$$S8 \leftarrow off3, A1$$

$$S9 \leftarrow S7 *F S8$$

$$off4, A1 \leftarrow S9$$

Since registers are not reused during the same pass through the loop, Thornton's algorithm would run as fast as Tomasulo's. But we need 9 scalar registers, more than are available on the CRAY-1. The high speedup achieved by Tomasulo's algorithm demonstrates the importance of its ability to reallocate registers dynamically.

VII. SUMMARY AND CONCLUSIONS

We have discussed design tradeoffs for control of pipelined processors. Performance of a pipelined processor depends greatly on its clock period and the order in which instructions are executed. Simple control schemes allow a short clock period and place the burden of code scheduling on the compiler. Complex control schemes generally require a longer clock period, but are less susceptible to the order of the instructions generated by the compiler. The latter are also able to take advantage of information only available at run time and "dynamically" reschedule the instructions. Additional factors to be considered are hardware cost, debugging, and maintenance.

We have presented a quantitative measure of the speedup achievable by sophisticated issue logic schemes. The CRAY-1 scalar architecture is used as a basis for comparison. Simulation results of the 14 Lawrence Livermore Loops executed on 4 different issue logic mechanisms show the performance gain achievable by various degrees of issue logic complexity. Tomasulo's algorithm gives a total speedup of 1.58. The direct tag search (DTS) algorithm introduced in this paper allows dynamic scheduling while eliminating the need for associative tag comparison hardware. The DTS issue logic achieves a total speedup of 1.38, and thus retains much of the performance gain of Tomasulo's algorithm. A derivative of Thornton's algorithm gives a total gain of 1.28.

In our model, the large intermediate register files of the CRAY-1 (B and T) are treated as a unit since it is not practical to assign tags to so many registers. With Tomasulo's algorithm, this was the cause of a relatively low performance for three loops. With an architecture that does not have the large number of registers the CRAY-1 has, it would be possible to use tags for all the registers, thus increasing the speedup of the above loops.

Finally, we have discussed the impact of code scheduling on the simulation results. Tomasulo's algorithm is less sensitive to the order of the instructions since it does a great deal of dynamic scheduling and register reallocation. On the other hand, static scheduling has a significant impact on the performance of the DTS and Thornton's algorithms. We gave specific examples how the performance of the latter two algorithms can be improved even by simple code scheduling.

ACKNOWLEDGMENT

The authors would like to thank N. Pang for the CRAY-1 simulators used for generating the results in Tables I and III.

REFERENCES

[1] D. W. Anderson, F. J. Sparacio, and F. M. Tomasulo, "The IBM System/360 model 91: Machine philosophy and instruction-handling." *IBM J.*, vol. 11, Jan. 1967.
[2] L. J. Boland, G. D. Granito, A. U. Marcotte, B. U. Messina, and J. W. Smith, "The IBM System/360 model 91: Storage system," *IBM J.*, vol. 11, Jan. 1967.
[3] P. Bonseigneur, "Description of the 7600 computer system," *Comput. Group News*, pp. 11–15, May 1969.
[4] *Planning a Computer System*. W. Bucholz, Ed. New York: McGraw-Hill, 1962.
[5] *CDC CYBER 200 Model 205 Computer System Hardware Reference Manual*, Control Data Corp., Arden Hills, MN, 1981.
[6] "The CRAY-1 Computing System," Cray Research, Inc., Chippewa Falls, WI, Pub. 2240008 B, 1977.
[7] *CRAY-1 Computer Systems, Hardware Reference Manual*, Cray Research, Inc., Chippewa Falls, WI, 1979.
[8] *CRAY X-MP Computer Systems Mainframe Reference Manual*, Cray Research, Inc., Chippewa Falls, WI, 1982.
[9] P. M. Kogge, *The Architecture of Pipelined Computers*. New York: McGraw-Hill, 1981.
[10] F. H. McMahon, "FORTRAN CPU performance analysis," Lawrence Livermore Laboratories, Livermore, CA, 1972.
[11] R. M. Russell, "The CRAY-1 Computer System," *Commun. ACM*, vol. 21, pp. 63–72, Jan. 1978.
[12] J. E. Thornton, *Design of a Computer—The Control Data 6600*. Glenview, IL: Scott, Foresman and Co., 1970.
[13] R. M. Tomasulo, "An efficient algorithm for exploiting multiple arithmetic units," *IBM J.*, vol. 11, Jan. 1967.

Shlomo Weiss received the B.S.E.E. degree (cum laude) from the Technion–Israel Institute of Technology, Haifa, Israel, in 1973, and since 1981 has been a Ph.D. student at the University of Wisconsin, Madison, WI.

Previously, he has held positions with the Israel Aircraft Industry, Koor Systems, Ltd., and Motorola Israel, Ltd. He spent the summer of 1982 with Xerox Palo Alto Research Center, Palo Alto, CA. His research interests include high-performance computing and computer-aided design for VLSI systems.

James E. Smith (S'74–M'76) received the B.S., M.S., and Ph.D. degrees from the University of Illinois at Urbana-Champaign, Urbana, IL, in 1972, 1974, and 1976, respectively.

Since 1976, he has been on the faculty of the University of Wisconsin, Madison, WI, where he is currently an Associate Professor in the Department of Electrical and Computer Engineering. He spent the summer of 1978 with the IBM T. J. Watson Research Center, Yorktown Heights, NY, and from September 1979 until July 1981 he took a leave of absence to work for the Control Data Corporation (CDC), Arden Hills, MN. While at CDC he participated in the design of the CYBER 180/990. He is currently working for the Astronautics Corporation of America on the design of a medium-scale scientific computer system.

OPTIMAL PIPELINING IN SUPERCOMPUTERS

Steven R. Kunkel and James E. Smith

Department of Electrical and Computer Engineering
University of Wisconsin-Madison
Madison, Wisconsin 53706

Abstract

This paper examines the relationship between the degree of central processor pipelining and performance. This relationship is studied in the context of modern supercomputers. Limitations due to instruction dependencies are studied via simulations of the CRAY-1S. Both scalar and vector code are studied. This study shows that instruction dependencies severely limit performance for scalar code as well as overall performance.

The effects of latch overhead are then considered. The primary cause of latch overhead is the difference between maximum and minimum gate propagation delays. This causes both the skewing of data as it passes along the data path, and unintentional clock skewing due to clock fanout logic. Latch overhead is studied analytically in order to lower bound the clock period that may be used in a pipelined system. This analysis also touches on other points related to latch clocking. This analysis shows that for short pipeline segments both the Earle latch and polarity hold latch give the same clock period bound for both single-phase and multi-phase clocks. Overhead due to data skew and unintentional clock skew are each added to the CRAY-1S simulation model. Simulation results with realistic assumptions show that eight to ten gate levels per pipeline segment lead to optimal overall performance. The results also show that for short pipeline segments data skew and clock skew contribute about equally to the degradation in performance.

1. Introduction

Pipelining is an essential element of modern supercomputer design. Each new supercomputer generation has used a higher degree of pipelining than its predecessor. Furthermore, pipelining is becoming important in other, lower performance computer systems. Pipelining is a very appealing design technique because it offers a theoretical speedup of N when N pipeline stages are used. There are, however, practical constraints that limit the performance increases that are possible. These are:

(1) **Instruction dependencies** that cause the pipeline to be less than 100 percent utilized;

(2) **Latch overhead** that tends to aggravate the effects of instruction dependencies, as well as placing some fundamental limitations on the clock frequency (and the degree of pipelining) that can be used;

(3) **Control path limitations** that force a minimum amount of logic to be placed between pipeline segments.

In this paper, we study the relationship between the theoretical linear speedup that pipelining offers and the practical limitations. One goal is to determine the ultimate performance improvements that are possible through pipelining. Another goal is to study optimal latching and clocking methods in pipelined computers. In order to increase its usefulness, this study is made in the context of current supercomputer technology, design techniques, architectures, and compilers.

1.1. Instruction Dependencies

Instruction dependencies, involving both data and control information, limit performance because they reduce the amount of the potential parallelism that is actually realized. Such dependencies are a very important practical limitation, and are a property of the algorithms, programs, and compilers. Hence, in order to arrive at meaningful results we study them using simulation of a state-of-the-art pipelined computer system, the CRAY-1S. [1]

1.2. Latch Overhead

There are three main components to latch overhead.

(1) **Propagation delay** through storage elements can cause extra pipeline latency. Careful latch design can significantly reduce this component of latch overhead, and we discuss such latch designs in Section 3.

(2) **Data skew** is the difference between the maximum and minimum signal propagation times through combinational logic between pipeline stages, and in the latches that separate the stages. This skew occurs even if the clock signal to the latch is perfectly controlled, and it forces constraints on the clock period in order to ensure reliable latching of data.

(3) **Clock skew**, due primarily to differences between maximum and minimum delays in clock fanout logic, causes an unintentional variation in the arrival time of the clock at succeeding latches in a pipeline. This unintentional skew increases the clock period necessary to ensure reliable latching of data.

1.3. Control Path Limitations

Control information must pass down the stages of a pipelined computer, just as the data does. It is often more difficult to sub-divide control operations than data operations, however. For example, control logic is required to interlock pipeline stages. These interlocking operations can not be sub-divided while maintaining an execution rate of one instruction per clock period.

Consider the instruction issue logic in the CRAY-1S. At the time an instruction is issued to the execution units, any register that the instruction uses must not be reserved for a result by an earlier instruction. If the operand registers are all available for use, the current instruction reserves its result register as it issues. In order to issue an instruction every clock period, however, checking the register reservations and reserving the result register must both be performed in the same clock period. Because of the indivisibility of this operation, there is a minimum logic delay that limits the clock period that can be used.

Control path limitations are a very important design consideration. The best solution is a clean architecture; those designed by S. Cray are excellent examples. Because a study of control path limitations would involve architectural and detailed logic design alternatives that are beyond the scope of this paper, we will not consider them.

---

[1] Although the CRAY-1S is older than the CRAY X-MP and CRAY-2, the major differences between a CRAY-1S cpu and the newer models are in the gate and packaging technology, not the cpu architecture and logic design techniques.

1.4. Previous Research

The problem of detecting and utilizing independent instructions in a single instruction stream has been studied previously [RIS72, FOS72, TJA70, SHA77, NIC84]. In most of these studies, however, pipelining was not specifically studied, and an infinite hardware machine was assumed so an upper limit on the available parallelism could be determined. Hence, these studies are more theoretical than ours.

In the area of latch timing, Cotten [COT65] developed some basic timing constraints, and looked at maximum clocking rates in 1965. Hallin and Flynn [HAL72] developed timing constraints for the Earle latch (to be described later) without considering clock skew or data skew. Later Fawcett [FAW75] expanded these timing constraints to account for these skews. A summary of Fawcett's work is given later along with additional analysis.

Some of the practical limitations on pipelining caused by control paths are discussed in [AND67]. There is also some interesting discussion about design of highly-overlapped computer systems in [THO70].

1.5. Paper Overview

Section 2 describes the simulation method and pertinent assumptions. Section 3 is a simulation study of the importance of instruction dependencies; latch overhead is neglected. Section 4 discusses latch overhead due to propagation delays in latches. Latch designs that minimize latch propagation delays are discussed. Section 5 discusses latch overhead due to data skew; the clock is assumed to be perfectly controlled. Unintentional clock skew is studied in Section 6, and there is a further simulation study with clock skew included. Section 7 contains a summary and conclusions.

2. Simulation Method

We use the CRAY-1S, CFT FORTRAN Compiler (version 111g) and the first 14 Lawrence Livermore Loops [MCM72]. The CFT compiler is a mature compiler that accurately represents the state-of-the-art, at least for the specific workload we are using. The Lawrence Livermore Loops are chosen because they are small enough to be simulated for a large number of cases, are representative of a class of real programs, and are widely used for comparing the performance of pipelined computer systems. Furthermore, by using a set of standard benchmarks with a well-documented computer, our experiments are repeatable by other researchers. The simulator used is described in [PAN83].

In the initial part of our study, we neglect latch overhead. We first calculate the total lengths of the various pipelines in the CRAY-1S, measured in gate levels. These base numbers are derived using the fact that there are eight levels of gates between latches in the CRAY-1S. The pipeline lengths in clock periods are given in the CRAY-1S hardware reference manual [CRA79].

If a pipelined operation requires n clock periods, we estimate that between $8n$ and $8(n-1)+1 = 8n - 7$ gate levels are needed. The minimum number comes about because if one fewer gate level is used, i.e. $8(n-1)$, then one fewer pipeline segment can be used. For example, the floating point adder in the CRAY-1S is six clock periods long and the number of gates per clock period is eight. Therefore the maximum number of gate levels possible is 48 and a reasonable minimum is 41. Because there is an uncertainty in the number of gate levels, it is possible to calculate a range of performance levels. Continuing with the example of the floating point adder, suppose the clock frequency is changed so that there are four gate levels in each segment. Using the maximum number of gate levels, 48, the new adder has 12 segments. But, using the minimum number of gates levels, 41, the adder has only 11 segments. In our study, we simulated both endpoints of the range to yield a maximum and minimum performance.

We simulated pipeline segments varying in length from two gate levels to 16 gate levels at even numbered intervals and 32 gate levels. In all the simulations, we used code exactly as it is scheduled for the CRAY-1S. Because the ratios of the pipeline lengths remain the same, the code schedule is of the same quality in virtually all the cases. The only exceptions occur because of scheduling conflicts involving the result buses that feed into the register files. In these very few cases,

some of the code runs slightly faster when a larger number of gate levels is used (giving a slightly longer pipeline) than when a smaller number of gate levels is used.

Seven of the 14 Lawrence Livermore loops are vectorized by the CFT compiler. Because the operations that flow down a vector pipeline are by definition independent, one would expect significantly better performance on vector code than on scalar code. For this reason we give separate performance numbers for the vectorizable loops, the scalar loops, and the combination.

To measure performance, first the computation rate in Millions of Floating Point Operations per Second (MFLOPS) was generated for each loop. These numbers were used to compute the harmonic mean MFLOPS. The harmonic mean was chosen because it is a much more meaningful measure than the more common arithmetic mean [WOR84].

Informally, to compute the harmonic mean one should first compute the time, T_i, it takes to execute exactly F (F can be arbitrarily chosen) floating point operations in each of the loops L_i. Then the harmonic mean performance for m loops is $\dfrac{mF}{\sum\limits_{i=1}^{m} T_i}$. If the MFLOPS rate for loop i is M_i, it can be shown that the harmonic mean also equals $\dfrac{m}{\sum\limits_{i=1}^{m} \dfrac{1}{M_i}}$.

3. Instruction Dependencies

An instruction may be dependent on an earlier instruction for either data or control. A data dependency occurs, for example, if one instruction computes a result that is used as an input operand by another. A control dependency occurs in the case of a conditional branch where the execution of an instruction following the branch is dependent on the branch outcome. More complete discussions of the types of instruction dependencies that can occur are given in [KUC78].

Instruction dependencies limit the efficiency of a pipelined system. For example, in a straightforward pipeline design if two consecutive instructions passing down the pipeline are dependent, then the second must wait for the first to complete before the second can begin. Pipelining is wasted because instruction execution is not overlapped and pipeline segments sit idle.

The effects of dependencies can be handled to some extent by the compiler, and/or clever pipeline design. For example, the compiler can schedule the instructions so that consecutive instructions tend to be independent. There are limits, however, to the number of independent instructions that can be found. Conditional branches pose a particular problem because the possibilities for scheduling them are much more limited than for other instructions.

For a high degree of pipelining, the theoretical peak throughput is increased, but the pipeline may be used inefficiently because there are not enough independent instructions to keep it full. Conversely, if there is a low degree of pipelining, it is relatively easy to keep the pipeline full, but its peak throughput is reduced. This tradeoff is of course dependent on the problem, algorithm, program, and even the programming language. Hence, we study instruction dependencies through simulation with realistic computers and programs.

3.1. Simulation Results

The results of the first set of simulations which neglect latch overhead are shown in Table 1. The results are all normalized to the performance for the combined loops when eight gate levels are used (the same as in the CRAY-1S). In the tables and graphs that follow there is a minimum and maximum performance given that bounds the range of possible performances. This arises because of uncertainty in the number of pipeline segments as described in section 2. Obviously, the maximum performance is achieved when the minimum number of pipeline segments is used for a given number of gate levels per segment.

The data in Table 1 shows that the performance for scalar and combined code is significantly less than the performance that would be

gate levels per segment	7 scalar loops		7 vector loops		14 combined loops	
	max	min	max	min	max	min
2	0.78	0.67	11.90	11.20	1.47	1.27
4	0.70	0.65	7.03	6.90	1.28	1.18
6	0.65	0.59	5.04	4.94	1.15	1.05
8	0.57	0.57	3.88	3.88	1.00	1.00
10	0.55	0.52	3.18	3.15	0.93	0.89
12	0.50	0.47	2.68	2.66	0.84	0.80
14	0.45	0.43	2.33	2.30	0.76	0.73
16	0.40	0.40	2.04	2.04	0.66	0.66
32	0.23	0.23	0.94	0.94	0.37	0.37

Table 1. Normalized performance with no latch overhead.

theoretically predicted if there were no data dependencies. For example, the performance with two gate levels should theoretically be four times the performance with eight gate levels. However, the results show a maximum increase in performance of 23% over this interval. This deviation from the theoretical peak becomes larger as the number of gate level becomes smaller. The gain achieved in going from eight to four gates per segments is only about two thirds of that achieved in going from sixteen to eight gates per segment. Performance for the seven loops that vectorize does not deviate as significantly from the theoretical as it does for the scalar loops.

For vector code, the performance increases almost linearly with the increasing clock frequency. When the scalar loops and vector loops are combined the curve more closely resembles that of scalar loops by themselves because of the well-known dominance of the slower code [WOR81].

4. Latch Propagation Delay

This section is the first of three that study latch overhead. We separate the three components of latch overhead in order to measure the contribution of each to performance degradation. Our discussion concentrates on latch designs that minimize the effects of latch propagation delay.

4.1. The Earle Latch

Latch propagation delay occurs in gates used to construct latches. A distinguishing characteristic of propagation delay is that it would be present even with skewless gates, i.e. all gates have exactly the same propagation delay. A latch typically has a propagation delay from clock to output of at least two gate delays. While this may be insignificant in some systems, it is a major concern in pipelined systems when the clock period becomes very short. To reduce its significance, J. G. Earle introduced a latch that was used in carry-save adders for the IBM360/91 [EAR65]. The so-called Earle latch can be used for any combinational logic function, however, not just carry-save addition.

Fig. 1a is a simple Earle latch; the NAND gate equivalent is, of course, more commonly used in practice. This latch performs two levels of useful logic as well as the latching function. There is no added propagation delay beyond that needed to perform the useful function. This enables the overhead due to propagation delay through latches to be essentially eliminated. As an example of the way a combinational function can be built into an Earle latch, Fig. 1b is a 2-to-1 multiplexer/latch.

4.2. The Polarity Hold Latch

The polarity hold latch is a simplified form of the Earle latch (see Fig. 2). It does not use the center AND gate that protects against a logic hazard. This logic hazard can be avoided by intentionally skewing the C and $\bar{C}$ signals properly. In practice, this reduction in gate usage is attractive not only because it is cheaper but also because it reduces fan-in at the output gate. Polarity hold latches are used in

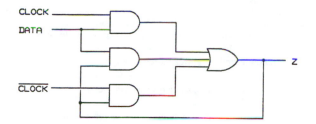

a) Basic Earle latch

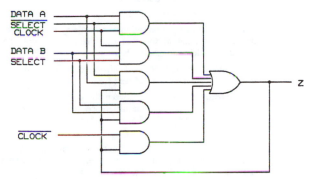

b) Earle latch with built-in multiplexer

Fig. 1. Earle latches

pipelined CPUs designed at CDC, Cray Research, and the Amdahl Corporation. As we shall see, however, clock skew constraints are tighter for polarity hold latches than for Earle latches in order to avoid logic hazards.

Because Earle and polarity hold latches can eliminate propagation delay, we assume their use throughout the rest of this paper. Other causes of latch overhead are examined in the context of Earle and polarity hold latches.

5. Data Skew

Data skew occurs because gates used to implement latches and combinational logic between latches have different propagation delays. In order to isolate the effects of data skew, we assume the logic used for clock fanout has no unintentional skew due to gate delay differences. That is, clock signals reaching the latches are perfectly controlled.

The distinction we are making between intentional skew and unintentional skew should be carefully noted. It is often necessary to intentionally skew clock signals. This is done in the case of multiphase clocks, and in controlling the C and $\bar{C}$ signals to avoid hazards. Unintentional skew is due to imperfections in the clock distribution network and fanout logic. While unintentional clock skew is ignored in this section, it is the primary topic of the next section.

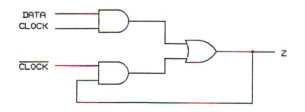

Fig. 2. Polarity hold latch

A basis for the analysis given here for the Earle latch is presented in [FAW75]. As shown in Fig. 1, the Earle Latch actually has two clock signals, one is the complement of the other. Our analysis assumes that the width of the C_{high} pulse is the same as the width of the $\overline{C}_{low}$ pulse.

We now introduce Fawcett's terminology.

t_{max} -   maximum propagation delay time for a logic gate (NAND gate)

t_{min} -   minimum propagation delay time for a logic gate (NAND gate)

C_{high} -   the duration of C = 1 (clock high)

C_{low} -   the duration of C = 0 (clock low)

P_{max} -   maximum delay time on the maximum delay path from the output of a latch to input of next latch. This does not include any delay for the latch itself.

P_{min} -   minimum delay time on the minimum delay path from the output of a latch to input of next latch.

$S(X,Y)$ -   This quantity is the skew between the edges X and Y and is always positive. It is the difference between the arrival of edge X and edge Y. If Y arrives before X, the quantity is zero.

$AS(X,Y)$ -   This quantity is the algebraic skew between the edges X and Y and can be positive or negative. It is the difference between the arrival of edge X and edge Y. If Y arrives before X, the quantity is negative.

U_X -   This quantity is the uncertainty of X. It represents the quantity such that X lies in the interval $(X - U_X, X + U_X)$.

5.1. Timing Constraints on Earle Latches

Repeating the work of Fawcett, we give four timing constraints on the clock signal. These constraints are discussed only briefly; we regret that space does not permit a more complete explanation of Fawcett's work. The first constraint is on the minimum width of the clock pulse C_{high}. The pulse has to be wide enough to ensure that valid data is stored in the latch. That is, it must be wide enough to allow data to propagate from the D input to the latch output, then to feed back around to be latched. This gives

$$C_{high} \geq 3t_{max} - t_{min} + S(C_{rise}, \overline{C}_{fall}). \tag{1}$$

The second timing constraint is on the maximum width of the clock pulse C_{high}. Obviously, the clock width must be shorter than the minimum propagation delay from the input of one latch to the input of the next, assuming no intentional clock skew. Two other terms must be added to allow for skewed clocks. The precise constraint is

$$C_{high} + AS(C_{i-1,rise}, C_{i,rise}) \leq 2t_{min} + P_{min} - S(\overline{C}_{fall}, C_{rise})$$
$$- \max[0, t_{max} - t_{min} + AS(C_{rise}, \overline{C}_{fall})]. \tag{2}$$

Fawcett's third constraint is on the minimum clock period, $C_{high} + C_{low}$. This constraint arises because the latch can not be clocked until the data from the previous latch has arrived. Thus the minimum clock period must be longer than the maximum propagation delay from the input of one latch to the input of the following latch. The complete expression derived by Fawcett is

$$C_{high} + C_{low} + AS(C_{i-1,rise}, C_{i,rise}) \geq 2t_{max} + P_{max} + S(C_{rise}, \overline{C}_{fall}) \tag{3}$$

Fawcett combined the three constraints to arrive at an alternative lower bound on the clock period:

$$C_{high} + C_{low} \geq \ P_{max} - P_{min} + 5t_{max} - 3t_{min}$$
$$+ 2S(C_{rise}, \overline{C}_{fall}) + S(\overline{C}_{fall}, C_{rise}) \tag{4}$$
$$+ \max[0, t_{max} - t_{min} + AS(C_{fall}, \overline{C}_{rise})].$$

This concludes our initial summary of Fawcett's work. What follows in this subsection and in succeeding subsections are extensions and further analysis of the timing constraints.

Fawcett's work allows for the possibility of multi-phase clocks. We will consider both single and multi-phase clocks. The pipelined computers produced by Cray Research, CDC, and Amdahl all use single phase clocks. We do not consider C and $\overline{C}$ going to a single latch as a multi-phase clock. In a typical supercomputer system, a single clock waveform is generated and distributed to the logic chips (modules in the case of the CRAY-1S). On each chip, there is a "clock shaper" circuit that, among other things, produces both the C and $\overline{C}$ signals.

If we restrict ourselves to an ideal, single phase-clock then $C_{i-1,rise} = C_{i,rise}$. Also, (3) gives a minimum clock period if the clock signals can be controlled so that $\overline{C}_{fall}$ precedes C_{rise}, making the last term zero. Thus for an ideal, single phase clock we can derive a lower bound on the clock period using (3).

Clock Period Bound: Earle Latch, Single Phase Clock

$$C_{high} + C_{low} \geq 2t_{max} + P_{max}, \quad provided \ AS(C_{rise}, \overline{C}_{fall}) \leq 0. \tag{5}$$

For a multi-phase clock, we can derive a lower bound on the clock period using (4).

Clock Period Bound: Earle Latch, Multi-Phase Clock

$$C_{high} + C_{low} \geq P_{max} - P_{min} + 6t_{max} - 4t_{min}, \tag{6}$$

$$provided \ -(t_{max} - t_{min}) \leq AS(C_{fall}, \overline{C}_{rise}) \leq 0$$

5.2. Timing Constraints on Polarity Hold Latches

Because the polarity hold latch is an Earle latch with the hazard gate removed, the clock signals must be intentionally skewed to ensure proper operation of the latch. This additional constraint can be expressed as

$$AS(C_{rise}, \overline{C}_{fall}) \leq -(t_{max} - t_{min}). \tag{7}$$

Applying (7) makes some of the terms in (1), (2), and (3) zero, simplifying them to (8), (9), and (10) given below.

$$C_{high} \geq 3t_{max} - t_{min}. \tag{8}$$

$$C_{high} + AS(C_{i-1,rise}, C_{i,rise}) \leq 2t_{min} + P_{min} - S(\overline{C}_{fall}, C_{rise}). \tag{9}$$

$$C_{high} + C_{low} + AS(C_{i-1,rise}, C_{i,rise}) \geq 2t_{max} + P_{max} \tag{10}$$

For an ideal, single phase clock $C_{i-1,rise} = C_{i,rise}$, which reduces (10) to the following lower bound on the clock period.

Clock Period Bound: Polarity Hold Latch, Single Phase Clock

$$C_{high} + C_{low} \geq 2t_{max} + P_{max}, \tag{11}$$

$$provided \ AS(C_{rise}, \overline{C}_{fall}) \leq -(t_{max} - t_{min}).$$

For the case in which a multi-phase clock is used, the same optimization technique that Fawcett used can be performed on (8), (9), and (10) yielding,

$$C_{high} + C_{low} \geq P_{max} - P_{min} + 5t_{max} - 3t_{min} + S(\overline{C}_{fall}, C_{rise}). \tag{12}$$

Considering (7), (12) can be reduced to a lower bound clock period for multi-phase clocks.

Clock Period Bound: Polarity Hold Latch, Multi-Phase Clock

$$C_{high} + C_{low} \geq P_{max} - P_{min} + 6t_{max} - 4t_{min}, \tag{13}$$

$$provided \ AS(C_{rise}, \overline{C}_{fall}) \leq -(t_{max} - t_{min}).$$

We have shown that the Earle latch and the polarity hold latch have the same lower bound on the clock period for both single and multiple phase clock. The difference is that the constraint on the intentional clock skew is more restrictive for the polarity hold latch if the bound is to be met. This implies that more careful control over the clock signals is required.

5.3. Latch Overhead

We are now ready to analyze the latch overhead due to data skew. We emphasize single phase clocks with polarity hold latches because they are commonly used in practice. Some discussion of multi-phase clocks and Earle latches is also included, however.

Let n be the number of gate levels between latches (this does not include the two gate levels in the latch, itself). Considering that useful logic can be performed in the latches, there are a total of $n+2$ useful gate levels in each pipeline segment. We assume an equal number of gate levels on all paths. The generalization to different length paths is straightforward. Equal length paths tend to allow shorter clock periods, however. For example, note the importance of $P_{max} - P_{min}$ in (4).

Let r be the ratio of the minimum gate delay to the maximum. Then $t_{min} = rt_{max}$. For simplicity, we begin by assuming all delays are concentrated in gates, not in wires between gates. In practice, one can add wire delay following a gate to the gate, itself. Later, when we need to intentionally add extra delay to paths, we do consider separate wire delays.

Because delays are assumed to be in the gates, $P_{max} = nt_{max}$, and $P_{min} = nt_{min} = nrt_{max}$.

5.3.1. Polarity Hold Latch; Single Phase Clock

For a single phase clock, (11) becomes

$$C_{high} + C_{low} \geq (n + 2)t_{max} \qquad (14)$$

For a single phase clock, however, any clock period lower bound is subject to a lower bound on P_{min} that comes from combining (8) and (9) to eliminate C_{high}. The resulting inequality can be rearranged to yield $P_{min} \geq 3t_{max} - 3t_{min} + S(\overline{C}_{fall}, C_{rise})$. Further restricting the condition that gives the lower bound clock period as determined in (11) to $AS(\overline{C}_{fall}, C_{rise}) = t_{max} - t_{min}$, yields

$$P_{min} \geq 4(t_{max} - t_{min}). \qquad (15)$$

Substituting rt_{max} for t_{min} and nrt_{max} for P_{min} and rearranging yields

$$n \geq \frac{4}{r} - 4 \qquad (16)$$

That is, for a single phase clock there must be at least $n \geq \frac{4}{r} - 4$ gate levels for proper operation. If the number of gate levels is fewer, then some extra intentional delay pad must be added. This can either be in the form of gates or wires.

5.3.2. Delay Padding

If intentional delay is added with gates, then $\frac{4}{r} - 4 - n$ gate delays must be added to the path so that (16) is satisfied. This yields:

$$C_{high} + C_{low} \geq (n + 2)t_{max} + (\frac{4}{r} - 4 - n)t_{max}$$
$$\geq \frac{4}{r}t_{max} - 2t_{max} \qquad (17)$$

In the first line of (17), the $(n + 2)t_{max}$ term accounts for the delay for performing useful logic; two levels in the latch and n levels between latches. The $(\frac{4}{r} - 4 - n)t_{max}$ term is overhead. Also note that the final form of (17) is independent of n. Thus, if gates are used for delay padding, there is no advantage to using fewer than $\frac{4}{r} - 4$ gates between latches.

We now consider using wire delays for padding. First consider that without padding P_{min} is nrt_{max}. P_{min} must be at least $4(t_{max} - rt_{max})$, however. Hence, an additional pad of $4(t_{max} - rt_{max}) - nrt_{max}$ must be added. This yields

$$C_{high} + C_{low} \geq (n + 2)t_{max} + 4(t_{max} - rt_{max}) - nrt_{max}$$
$$\geq (n + 2)t_{max} + (4 - (n + 4)r)t_{max} \qquad (18)$$

In (18) the wire delay overhead is $(4 - (n + 4)r)t_{max}$. We now compare this overhead with that in (17). The gate pad overhead is easily shown to be $\frac{1}{r}$ times the wire pad overhead. By definition

$\frac{1}{r} \geq 1$. Hence, a wire delay pad potentially leads to a shorter clock period than a gate pad.

5.3.3. Polarity Hold Latch; Multi-phase Clock

For a multi-phase clock, (13) easily reduces to (18). For multi-phase clocks, (18) holds for all values of n. When $n \leq \frac{4}{r} - 4$ the "overhead" term in (18) is positive, and the minimum clock period is the same for both a single and multi-phase clock. Hence, for very short clock periods, there is no performance advantage to using a multi-phase clock.

On the other hand, when $n > \frac{4}{r} - 4$ the "overhead" term in (18) is negative, and the multiphase clock period can be less than the single phase clock period. Note that for the case of a multi-phased clock there is no limit on P_{min} because the phase of the clocks can be shifted using (2) and (9) to accommodate any value of P_{min}.

5.3.4. Earle Latches

A similar line of reasoning to the above can be used to calculate a minimum for P_{min} in the Earle latch using (1) and (2). This also yields (14) through (18), provided $-(t_{max} - t_{min}) \leq AS(C_{fall}, \overline{C}_{rise}) \leq 0$ which is slightly more restricting than the minimum condition for (3).

5.4. Simulation Results

We now use simulation to evaluate the performance of a single phase clock and polarity hold latches under some realistic assumptions. A survey of the currently available, high performance TTL and ECL parts [MOT82, FAI84] indicates values of r in the range of .3 to .4. It is quite possible that r could be increased by screening of the chips, however. Also wire delays added to gate outputs tend to increase the effective value of r. A survey of ECL gate arrays, [FAI85, APP85] indicates larger values of r, up to .6. Hence a realistic value for our simulations is $r = .5$.

The simulation results with data skew overhead added are given in Table 2. The performance results are again normalized with respect the combined loop performance with eight useful gate levels. These results show the best scalar and combined performance occurs at about six useful gates levels per pipeline segment. A substantial performance improvement can be achieved by increasing the clock frequency on vectors. No peak appears as the performance seems to continue to increase as the clock frequency increases.

6. Unintentional Clock Skew

The results in the previous section are based on an assumption of a perfectly controlled clock. When designing real processors, however, there is always some uncertainty in the clock. To model this, it is necessary to add uncertainty terms to the clocking constraints.

As done by Fawcett, we assume there can be unintentional skew between the C and $\overline{C}$ signals (denoted as $U_{C,\overline{C}}$) and between clock signals reaching different latches (U_{C_{i-1},C_i}). Expressions with

useful gates levels per segment	7 scalar loops		7 vector loops		14 combined loops	
	max	min	max	min	max	min
2	0.39	0.34	5.95	5.60	0.74	0.64
4	0.56	0.52	5.62	5.52	1.02	0.95
6	0.65	0.59	5.04	4.94	1.15	1.05
8	0.57	0.57	3.88	3.88	1.00	1.00
10	0.55	0.52	3.18	3.15	0.93	0.89
12	0.50	0.47	2.68	2.66	0.84	0.80
14	0.45	0.43	2.33	2.30	0.76	0.73
16	0.40	0.40	2.04	2.04	0.66	0.66
32	0.23	0.23	0.94	0.94	0.37	0.37

Table 2. Normalized performance with data skew overhead.

uncertainty terms added are derived in a manner very similar to (1) through (18). For brevity, we give only the most significant ones. A complete set of expressions is given in the appendix.

6.1. Basic Clocking Constraints

The uncertainties not only affect the clock inequalities, but they affect the intentional clock skew constraints that give minimum clock periods. The four lower bound expressions follow.

Clock Period Bound: Earle Latch, Single Phase Clock

$$C_{high} + C_{low} \geq 2t_{max} + P_{max} + U_{C_{i-1},C_i} \qquad (5^*)$$

provided $AS(C_{rise}, \overline{C}_{fall}) \leq -U_{C,\overline{C}}$.

Clock Period Bound: Earle Latch, Multi-Phase Clock

$$C_{high} + C_{low} \geq P_{max} - P_{min} + 6t_{max} - 4t_{min} + 2U_{C_{i-1},C_i} + 2U_{C,\overline{C}} , \qquad (6^*)$$

provided $-(t_{max} - t_{min}) - U_{C,\overline{C}} \leq AS(C_{rise}, \overline{C}_{fall}) \leq -U_{C,\overline{C}}$

Clock Period Bound: Polarity Hold Latch, Single Phase Clock

$$C_{high} + C_{low} \geq 2t_{max} + P_{max} + U_{C_{i-1},C_i} , \qquad (11^*)$$

provided $AS(C_{rise}, \overline{C}_{fall}) \leq -(t_{max} - t_{min}) - U_{C,\overline{C}}$

Clock Period Bound: Polarity Hold Latch, Multi-Phase Clock

$$C_{high} + C_{low} \geq P_{max} - P_{min} + 6t_{max} - 4t_{min} + 2U_{C_{i-1},C_i} + 2U_{C,\overline{C}} , \qquad (13^*)$$

provided $AS(C_{rise}, \overline{C}_{fall}) = -(t_{max} - t_{min}) - U_{C,\overline{C}}$

As before, the Earle latch and the polarity hold latch have the same lower bound on the clock period for both single and multiple phase clock. The only difference is in the required constraint on the intentional clock skew.

6.1.1. Latch Overhead due to Unintentional Clock Skew

Once again, we assume n gates between latches, and a ratio t_{min} to t_{max} of r. This gives $P_{max} = nt_{max}$, and $P_{min} = nt_{min} = nrt_{max}$. We begin with a single phase clock and polarity hold latch.

For a single phase clock,

$$C_{high} + C_{low} \geq (n+2)t_{max} + U_{C_{i-1},C_i} \qquad (14^*)$$

When $AS(C_{fall}, \overline{C}_{rise}) = -(t_{max} - t_{min}) - U_{C,\overline{C}}$, a lower bound on P_{min} is

$$P_{min} \geq 4(t_{max} - t_{min}) + U_{C_{i-1},C_i} + 2U_{C,\overline{C}} . \qquad (15^*)$$

Substituting rt_{max} for t_{min} and nrt_{max} for P_{min} and rearranging yields

$$n \geq \frac{4}{r} - 4 + \frac{U_{C_{i-1},C_i} + 2U_{C,\overline{C}}}{rt_{max}} \qquad (16^*)$$

Equation (16*) bounds the number of gate levels necessary for proper operation with a single phase clock. As before, if the number of gate levels is fewer, then some extra intentional delay pad in the form of either gates or wires must be added.

If intentional delay is added with gates, then

$$C_{high} + C_{low} \geq \frac{4}{r}t_{max} - 2t_{max} + \frac{(r+1)}{r}U_{C_{i-1},C_i} + \frac{2U_{C,\overline{C}}}{r} \qquad (17^*)$$

Equation (17*) is independent of n. Thus, if gates are used for delay padding, there is no advantage to using fewer than indicated by (16*).

If wire delays are used for padding, then

$$C_{high} + C_{low} \geq (n+2)t_{max} + (4 - (n+4)r)t_{max}$$
$$+ 2U_{C_{i-1},C_i} + 2U_{C,\overline{C}} \qquad (18^*)$$

As we did earlier, it can be shown that a wire delay pad leads to a shorter clock period than a gate pad.

To determine the overhead due to unintentional clock skew, we compare the above results with those in the previous section. When

$$n \geq \frac{4}{r} - 4 + \frac{U_{C_{i-1},C_i} + 2U_{C,\overline{C}}}{rt_{max}}, \qquad (14^*)$$ indicates that unintentional clock skew adds additional overhead of U_{C_{i-1},C_i}. When

$$n < \frac{4}{r} - 4 + \frac{U_{C_{i-1},C_i} + 2U_{C,\overline{C}}}{rt_{max}}, \qquad (18^*)$$ indicates that unintentional clock skew adds an additional overhead of $2U_{C_{i-1},C_i} + 2U_{C,\overline{C}}$.

For a multi-phase clock, the clock period bound is the same as in (18*). This means that the minimum clock period is the same for both a single and multi-phase clock when

$$n \leq \frac{4}{r} - 4 + \frac{U_{C_{i-1},C_i} + 2U_{C,\overline{C}}}{rt_{max}}.$$

Otherwise, the multi-phase clock may be faster.

For the Earle latch, the same results as above can be derived. As has typically been the case, however, the intentional clock skew constraints are reduced. In particular, minimum clock periods are achieved when $-(t_{max} - t_{min}) - U_{C,\overline{C}} \leq AS(C_{fall}, \overline{C}_{rise}) \leq -U_{C,\overline{C}}$.

6.2. Simulation Results

We continue our simulations to determine the effect of unintentional clock skew under realistic conditions. To do this, we must estimate values of unintentional skews. We first observe that $U_{C,\overline{C}}$ is relatively easy to control, because both signals feeding a particular latch are formed on the same printed circuit module (CRAY-1S) or on the same chip (CYBER205) from a single master clock signal.

If one gate is used to generate $\overline{C}$, then

$$U_{C,\overline{C}} = \frac{1}{2}(t_{max} - t_{min}).$$

When $r = .5$, $U_{C,\overline{C}} = .25t_{max}$.

If two logic levels are used to fanout the clock, then

$$U_{C_{i-1},C_i} = 2t_{max} - 2t_{min}.$$

When $r = .5$, the uncertainty becomes $U_{C_{i-1},C_i} = t_{max}$. If the fanout logic is extended to four levels, the uncertainty doubles and $U_{C_{i-1},C_i} = 2t_{max}$.

The performance when clock uncertainty is added to the latch overhead is shown in Tables 3 and 4. Comparing these results with those obtained without unintentional clock skew shows that peak performance moves to a larger number of gate levels per segment. Also vectors alone now have a peak; they do not continue to increase as the number of gate levels decreases. As expected, for a larger uncertainty, a larger number of gate levels per segment is needed to achieve peak performance. This can be seen by comparing the two-level fanout results to the four-level fanout results. For the two-level clock fanout, scalar code has the best performance at eight to ten gate levels per segment while vectors peak at four gate levels per segment. Scalars dominate when the two are combined to give a peak at eight to ten gate

useful gate levels per segment	7 scalar loops		7 vector loops		14 combined loops	
	max	min	max	min	max	min
2	0.29	0.25	4.35	4.09	0.54	0.46
4	0.45	0.41	4.45	4.37	0.81	0.75
6	0.55	0.49	4.22	4.14	0.97	0.88
8	0.57	0.57	3.88	3.88	1.00	1.00
10	0.59	0.56	3.43	3.40	1.01	0.96
12	0.55	0.51	2.93	2.92	0.92	0.87
14	0.50	0.48	2.58	2.55	0.84	0.81
16	0.44	0.44	2.28	2.28	0.74	0.74
32	0.27	0.27	1.08	1.08	0.43	0.43

Table 3. Normalized performance with data skew and unintentional clock skew; two-level clock fanout.

useful gate levels per segment	7 scalar loops		7 vector loops		14 combined loops	
	max	min	max	min	max	min
2	0.27	0.23	4.03	3.79	0.50	0.43
4	0.43	0.39	4.25	4.18	0.78	0.72
6	0.53	0.48	4.14	4.06	0.95	0.86
8	0.57	0.57	3.88	3.88	1.00	1.00
10	0.63	0.60	3.65	3.62	1.07	1.02
12	0.62	0.58	3.30	3.28	1.04	0.98
14	0.57	0.54	2.93	2.90	0.95	0.92
16	0.50	0.50	2.61	2.61	0.85	0.85
32	0.31	0.31	1.27	1.27	0.50	0.50

Table 4. Performance with data skew and unintentional clock skew; four-level clock fanout.

levels per segment. The same is true for a four-level clock fanout which peaks at ten gate levels per segment for both scalars and scalars combined with vectors.

7. Summary and Conclusions

Our first set of simulations with no latch overhead show that data dependencies alone place rather severe limits on pipeline performance. Performance always improves as pipeline segments are shortened, however.

When data skew is considered, our analysis shows that multiphase and single phase clocks have the same lower bound clock periods when few gate levels are used. For longer pipeline segments, however, multiphase clock periods can be shorter than single phase clock periods. Earle and polarity hold latches give the same lower bound clock periods, but constraints on clock skew to achieve these clock periods are tighter with polarity hold latches.

When pipeline segments are extremely short, it becomes necessary to pad with intentional delay. For this purpose, we have shown that wire pads lead to better performance than gate pads.

Our simulation results with realistic data skews added to our simulation model show that overall performance peaks at about six gate levels per pipeline segment. When unintentional clock skew is added to the model, overall performance peaks at eight to ten gate levels per segment.

To get an idea of the relative importance of the primary causes of latch overhead, we have combined the data in Tables 1, 2, and 3 into graphs; one each for scalar, vector, and combined performance. Originally, each of the tables was normalized with respect to a different data point. Consequently, before combining the results from the different tables, we have first re-normalized all the data with

respect to eight gate level performance for the combined loops with all skews included (this value comes closest to a real pipelined computer).

These graphs are Figs. 3, 4, and 5. They clearly show the points of optimal performance we pointed out earlier. They also show that for relatively long pipeline segments, adding data skew does not affect performance. For short pipeline segments, however, its effects become increasingly significant. For short pipeline segments, clock skew adds about the same amount of additional degradation as data skew. For longer segments, there is still some small degradation due to clock skew.

8. Acknowledgement

This is material based upon work supported by the National Science Foundation under Grant ECS-8207277.

9. References

[AND67] D. W. Anderson, F. J. Sparacio, and R. M. Tomasulo, "The System/360 Model 91: Machine Philosophy and Instruction Handling," *IBM Journal*, Vol. 11, No. 34, pp. 8-24, January 1967.

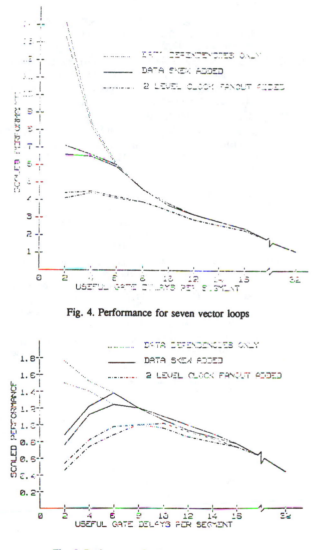

Fig. 4. Performance for seven vector loops

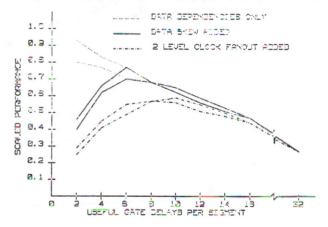

Fig. 3. Performance for seven scalar loops

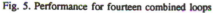

Fig. 5. Performance for fourteen combined loops

[APP85] Applied Micro Circuits Corp., *Q1500 Series Design Guide*, 1985.

[COT65] L. W. Cotten, "Circuit Implementation of High-Speed Pipeline Systems", *AFIPS Fall Joint Computer Conference*, pp. 489-504, 1965.

[CRA79] *CRAY-1 Computer Systems, Hardware Reference Manual*, Cray Research, Inc., Chippewa Falls, WI, 1979.

[EAR65] J. G. Earle, "Latched Carry-Save Adder", *IBM Technical Disclosure Bull.*, Vol. 7, pp. 909-910, March 1965.

[FAI84] Fairchild, *Fast Fairchild Advanced Schottky TTL*, 1984.

[FAI85] Fairchild, *FGE Series Design Manual*, Vol. II, 1985.

[FAW75] B. K. Fawcett, "Maximal Clocking Rates for Pipelined Digital Systems", M.S. Thesis, Dept. Elec. Eng., University of Illinois at Urbana-Champaign, 1975.

[FLY66] M. J. Flynn, "Very High-Speed Computing Systems," *Proceedings of the IEEE*, Vol. 54, No. 12, pp. 1901-1909, December 1966.

[FOS72] C.C. Foster and E. M. Riseman, "Percolation of Code to Enhance Parallel Dispatching and Execution", *IEEE Trans. Computers*, Vol. C-21, No. 12, pp. 1411-1415, December 1972.

[HAL72] T.G. Hallin and M. J. Flynn, "Pipelining of Arithmetic Functions", *IEEE Trans. Computers*, Vol. C-21, No. 8, pp. 880-886, August 1972.

[KUC78] D. J. Kuck, *The Structure of Computers and Computations, vol. 1*, John Wiley and Sons, New York, 1978.

[MCM72] F. H. McMahon, "FORTRAN CPU Performance Analysis", Lawrence Livermore Laboratories, 1972.

[MOT82] Motorola, Inc., *MECL Device Data*, 1982.

[NIC84] A. Nicolau, and J. A. Fischer, "Measuring the Parallelism Available for Very Long Instruction Word Architectures," *IEEE Trans.* Vol. C-33, No. 11, November 1984, pp. 968-976.

[PAN83] N. Pang and J. E. Smith, "CRAY-1 Simulation Tools", Tech. Report ECE-83-11, University of Wisconsin-Madison, Dec. 1983.

[RIS72] E. M. Riseman and C. C. Foster, "The inhibition of Potential Parallelism by Conditional Jumps", *IEEE Trans. Computers*, Vol. C-21, No. 12, pp. 1405-1411, December 1972.

[SHA77] H. D. Shapiro, "A Comparison of Various Methods for Detecting and Utilizing Parallelism in a Single Instruction Stream", *1977 International Conference on Parallel Processing*, pp. 67-76, Aug. 1977.

[THO70] J. E. Thornton, *Design of a Computer - The Control Data 6600*, Scott, Foresman and Co., Glenview, IL, 1970.

[TJA70] G. S. Tjaden and M. J. Flynn, "Detection and Parallel Execution of Independent Instructions", *IEEE Trans. Computers*, Vol. C-19, No. 10, pp. 889-895, October 1970.

[WOR81] J. Worlton, "The Philosophy Behind the Machines," *Computer World*, Nov. 9. 1981.

[WOR84] J. Worlton, "Understanding Supercomputer Benchmarks", *Datamation*, Vol. 30, No. 9, pp. 121-130, September 1, 1984.

Appendix

Complete set of equations with unintentional clock skew.

$$C_{high} \geq 3t_{max} - t_{min} + S(C_{rise} + U_{C,\bar{C}}, \bar{C}_{fall}) \tag{1*}$$

$$C_{high} + AS(C_{i-1,rise}, C_{i,rise}) \leq 2t_{min} + P_{min}$$
$$- S(\bar{C}_{fall} + U_{C,\bar{C}}, C_{rise}) - U_{C_{i-1},c_i}$$
$$- \max[0, t_{max} - t_{min} + U_{C,\bar{C}}$$
$$+ AS(C_{rise}, \bar{C}_{fall})] \tag{2*}$$

$$C_{high} + C_{low} + AS(C_{i-1,rise}, C_{i,rise}) \geq 2t_{max} + P_{max} + U_{C_{i-1},c_i}$$
$$+ S(C_{rise} + U_{C,\bar{C}}, \bar{C}_{fall}) \tag{3*}$$

$$C_{high} + C_{low} \geq P_{max} - P_{min} + 5t_{max} - 3t_{min} + 2U_{C_{i-1},c_i}$$
$$+ 2S(C_{rise} + U_{C,\bar{C}}, \bar{C}_{fall}) + S(\bar{C}_{fall} + U_{C,\bar{C}}, C_{rise}) \tag{4*}$$
$$+ \max[0, t_{max} - t_{min} + AS(C_{rise}, \bar{C}_{fall}) + U_{C,\bar{C}}]$$

$$C_{high} + C_{low} \geq 2t_{max} + P_{max} + U_{C_{i-1},c_i} \tag{5*}$$

$$provided\ AS(C_{rise}, \bar{C}_{fall}) \leq -U_{C,\bar{C}}$$

$$C_{high} + C_{low} \geq P_{max} - P_{min} + 6t_{max} - 4t_{min} + 2U_{C_{i-1},c_i} + 2U_{C,\bar{C}},$$
$$provided\ -(t_{max} - t_{min}) - U_{C,\bar{C}} \leq AS(C_{rise}, \bar{C}_{fall}) \leq -U_{C,\bar{C}} \tag{6*}$$

$$AS(\bar{C}_{rise}, C_{fall}) \geq t_{max} - t_{min} + U_{C,\bar{C}} \tag{7*}$$

$$C_{high} \geq 3t_{max} - t_{min} \tag{8*}$$

$$C_{high} + AS(C_{i-1,rise}, C_{i,rise}) \leq 2t_{min} + P_{min} - U_{C_{i-1},c_i}$$
$$- S(\bar{C}_{fall} + U_{C,\bar{C}}, C_{rise}) \tag{9*}$$

$$C_{high} + C_{low} + AS(C_{i-1,rise}, C_{i,rise}) \geq 2t_{max} + P_{max} + U_{C_{i-1},c_i} \tag{10*}$$

$$C_{high} + C_{low} \geq 2t_{max} + P_{max} + U_{C_{i-1},c_i}, \tag{11*}$$
$$provided\ AS(\bar{C}_{rise}, C_{fall}) \geq t_{max} - t_{min} + U_{C,\bar{C}}$$

$$C_{high} + C_{low} \geq P_{max} - P_{min} + 5t_{max} - 3t_{min}$$
$$+ S(\bar{C}_{fall} + U_{C,\bar{C}}, C_{rise}) + 2U_{C_{i-1},c_i} \tag{12*}$$

$$C_{high} + C_{low} \geq P_{max} - P_{min} + 6t_{max} - 4t_{min} + 2U_{C_{i-1},c_i} + 2U_{C,\bar{C}},$$
$$provided\ AS(C_{rise}, \bar{C}_{fall}) = -(t_{max} - t_{min}) - U_{C,\bar{C}} \tag{13*}$$

$$C_{high} + C_{low} \geq (n+2)t_{max} + U_{C_{i-1},c_i} \tag{14*}$$

$$P_{min} \geq 4(t_{max} - t_{min}) + U_{C_{i-1},c_i} + 2U_{C,\bar{C}} \tag{15*}$$

$$n \geq \frac{4}{r} - 4 + \frac{U_{C_{i-1},c_i} + 2U_{C,\bar{C}}}{rt_{max}} \tag{16*}$$

$$C_{high} + C_{low} \geq \frac{4}{r}t_{max} - 2t_{max} + \frac{(r+1)}{r}U_{C_{i-1},c_i} + \frac{2U_{C,\bar{C}}}{r} \tag{17*}$$

$$C_{high} + C_{low} \geq (n+2)t_{max} - (nr+4r-4)t_{max}$$
$$+ 2U_{C_{i-1},c_i} + 2U_{C,\bar{C}} \tag{18*}$$

Multiple-instruction issuing

R. M. Tomasulo

An Efficient Algorithm for Exploiting Multiple Arithmetic Units

Abstract: This paper describes the methods employed in the floating-point area of the System/360 Model 91 to exploit the existence of multiple execution units. Basic to these techniques is a simple common data busing and register tagging scheme which permits simultaneous execution of independent instructions while preserving the essential precedences inherent in the instruction stream. The common data bus improves performance by efficiently utilizing the execution units without requiring specially optimized code. Instead, the hardware, by 'looking ahead' about eight instructions, automatically optimizes the program execution on a local basis.

The application of these techniques is not limited to floating-point arithmetic or System/360 architecture. It may be used in almost any computer having multiple execution units and one or more 'accumulators.' Both of the execution units, as well as the associated storage buffers, multiple accumulators and input/output buses, are extensively checked.

Introduction

After storage access time has been satisfactorily reduced through the use of buffering and overlap techniques, even after the instruction unit has been pipelined to operate at a rate approaching one instruction per cycle,[1] there remains the need to optimize the actual performance of arithmetic operations, especially floating-point. Two familar problems confront the designer in his attempt to balance execution with issuing. First, individual operations are not fast enough* to allow simple serial execution. Second, it is difficult to achieve the fastest execution times in a universal execution unit. In other words, circuitry designed to do both multiply and add will do neither as fast as two units each limited to one kind of instruction.

The first step toward surmounting these obstacles has been presented,[2] i.e., the division of the execution function into two independent parts, a fixed-point execution area and a floating-point execution area. While this relieves the physical constraint and makes concurrent execution possible, there is another consideration. In order to secure a performance increase the program must contain an intimate mixture of fixed-point and floating-point instructions. Obviously, it is not always feasible for the programmer to arrange this and, indeed, many of the programs of greatest interest to the user consist almost wholly of floating-point instructions. The subject of this paper, then, is the method used to achieve concurrent execution of floating-point instructions in the IBM System/360 Model 91. Obviously, one begins with multiple execution units, in this case an adder and a multiplier/divider.[1]

It might appear that achieving the concurrent operation of these two units does not differ substantially from the attainment of fixed-floating overlap. However, in the latter case the architecture limits each of the instruction classes to its own set of accumulators and this guarantees independence.* In the former case there is only one set of accumulators, which implies program-specified sequences of dependent operations. Now it is no longer simply a matter of classifying each instruction as fixed-point or floating-point, a classification which is independent of previous instructions. Rather, it is a question of determining each instruction's relationship with all previous, incompleted instructions. Simply stated, the objective must be to preserve essential precedences while allowing the greatest possible overlap of independent operations.

This objective is achieved in the Model 91 through a scheme called the common data bus (CDB). It makes possible maximum concurrency with minimal effort (usually none) by the programmer or, more importantly, by the compiler. At the same time, the hardware required is small and logically simple. The CDB can function with any number of accumulators and any number of execution units. In short, it provides a hardware algorithm for the automatic, efficient exploitation of multiple execution units.

---

* During the planning phase, floating-point multiply was taken to be six cycles, divide as eighteen cycles and add as two cycles. A subsequent paper[2] explains how times of 3, 12, and 2 were actually achieved. This permitted the use of only one, instead of two, multipliers and one adder, pipelined to start an add cycle.

---

* Such dependencies as exist are handled by the store-fetch sequencing of the storage bus and the condition code control described in the following paper.[2]

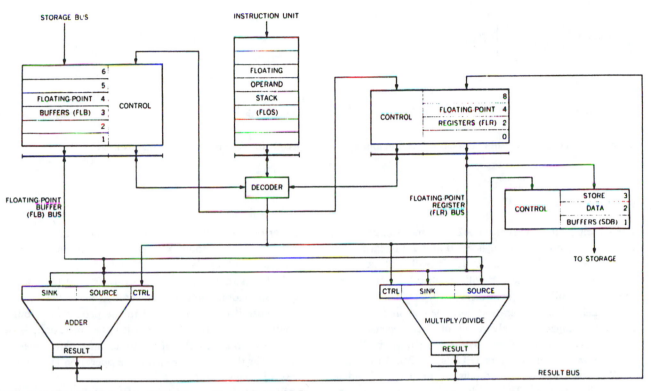

Figure 1 Data registers and transfer paths without CDB.

The next section of this paper will discuss the physical framework of registers, data paths and execution circuitry which is implied by the architecture and the overall CPU structure presented in a previous paper.[1] Within this framework one can subsequently discuss the problem of precedence, some possible solutions, and the selected solution, the CDB. In conclusion will be a summary of the results obtained.

Definitions and data paths

While the reader is assumed to be familiar with System/360 architecture and mnemonics, the terminology as modified by the context of the Model 91 organization will be reviewed here. The instruction unit, in preparing instructions for the floating-point operation stack (FLOS), maps both storage-to-register and register-to-register instructions into a pseudo-register-to-register format. In this format R1 is always one of the four floating-point registers (FLR) defined by the architecture. It is usually the *sink* of the instruction, i.e., it is the FLR whose contents are set equal to the result of the operation. Store operations are the sole exception* wherein R1 specifies the *source* of the operand to be placed in storage. A word in

storage is really the sink of a store. (R1 and R2 refer to fields as defined by System/360 architecture.)

In the pseudo-register-to-register format "seen" by the FLOS the R2 field can have three different meanings. It can be an FLR as in a normal register-to-register instruction. If the program contains a storage-to-register instruction, the R2 field designates the floating-point buffer (FLB) assigned by the instruction unit to receive the storage operand. Finally, R2 can designate a store data buffer (SDB) assigned by the instruction unit to store instructions. In the first two cases R2 is the *source* of an operand; in the last case it is a sink. Thus, the instruction unit maps all of storage into the 6 floating-point buffers and 3 store data buffers so that the FLOS sees only pseudo-register-to-register operations.

The distinction between source and sink will become quite important during the discussion of precedence and should be fixed firmly in mind. All of the instructions (except store and compare) have the following form:

R1	op	R2	⟶ R1
Register		Register	Register
		or	
		buffer	
source		source	sink

---

* Compares do not, of course, alter the contents of R1.

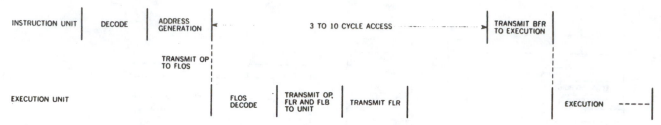

Figure 2 Timing relationship between instruction unit and FLOS decode for the processing of one instruction.

For example, the instruction AD0, 2 means "place the double-precision sum of registers 0 and 2 in register 0," i.e., R0 + R2 → R0. Note that R1 is really both a source and a sink.* Nevertheless, it will be called the sink and R2 the source in all subsequent discussion.

This definition of operations and the machine organization taken together imply a set of data registers with transfer paths among them. These are shown in Fig. 1. The major sets of registers (FLR's, FLB's, FLOS and SDB's) have already been discussed, both above and in a preceding paper.[1] Two additional registers, one sink and one source, are shown feeding each execution circuit. Initially these registers were considered to be the internal working registers required by the execution circuits and put to multiple use in a way to be described below. Later, their function was generalized under the reservation station concept and they were dissociated from their "working" function.

In actually designing a machine the data paths evolve as the design progresses. Here, however, a complete, first-pass data path will be shown to facilitate discussion. To illustrate the operation let us consider, in turn, four kinds of instructions—load of a register from storage, storage-to-register arithmetic, register-to-register arithmetic, and store. Let us first see how each can be accomplished *in vacuo*; then what difficulties arise when each is embedded in the context of a program. For simplicity double-precision (64-bit operands) will be used throughout.

Figure 2 shows the timing relationship between the instruction unit's handling of an instruction and its processing by the FLOS decode. When the FLOS decodes a load, the buffer which will receive the operand has not yet been loaded from storage.† Rather than holding the decode until the operand arrives, the FLOS sets control bits associated with the buffer which cause its content to be transmitted to the adder when it "goes full." The

adder receives control information which causes it to send data to floating-point register R1, when its source register is set full by the buffer.

If the instruction is a storage-to-register arithmetic function, the storage operand is handled as in load (control bits cause it to be forwarded to the proper unit) but the floating-point register, along with the operation, is sent by the decoder to the appropriate unit. After receiving the buffer the unit will execute the operation and send the result to register R1.

In register-to-register arithmetic instructions two floating point registers are transmitted on successive cycles to the appropriate execution unit.

Stores are handled like storage-to-register arithmetic functions, except that the content of the floating-point register is sent to a store data buffer rather than to an execution unit.

Thus far, the handling of one instruction at a time has proven rather straightforward. Now consider the following "program":

Example 1

LD   F0   FLB1   LOAD register F0 from buffer 1

MD   F0   FLB2   MULTIPLY register F0 by buffer 2

The load can be handled as before, but what about the multiply? Certainly F0 and FLB2 cannot be sent to the multiplier as in the case of the isolated multiply, since FLB1 has not yet been set into F0.* This sequence illustrates the cardinal precedence principle: No floating-point register may participate in an operation if it is the sink of another, incompleted instruction. That is, a register cannot be used until its contents reflect the result of the most recent operation to use that register as its sink.

The design presented thus far has not incorporated any mechanism for dealing with this situation. Three functions must be required of any such mechanism:

(1) It must recognize the existence of a dependency.

---

* Note that the program calls for the product of FLB1 and FLB2 to be placed in F0. This hints at the CDB concept.

98

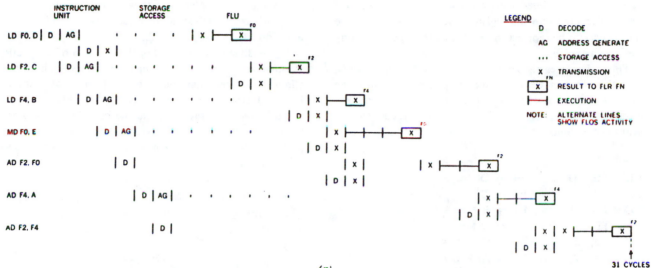

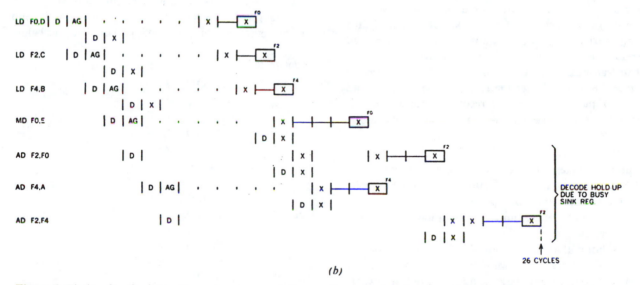

Figure 3 Timing for the instruction sequence required to perform the function A + B + C + D * E : (a) without reservation stations, (b) with reservation stations included in the register set.

(2) It must cause the correct sequencing of the dependent instructions.

(3) It must distinguish between the given sequence and such sequences as

    LD   F0, FLB1
    MD   F2, FLB2

Here it must allow the independent MD to proceed regardless of the disposition of the LD.

The first two requirements are necessary to preserve the logical integrity of the program; the third is necessary to

meet the performance goal. The next section will present several alternatives for accomplishing these objectives.

Preservation of precedence

Perhaps the simplest scheme for preserving precedence is as follows. A "busy" bit is associated with each of the four floating-point registers. This bit is set when the FLOS decode issues an instruction designating the register as a sink; it is reset when the executing unit returns the result to the register. No instruction can be issued by the FLOS if the busy bit of its sink is on. If the source of a register-to-register instruction has its busy bit on, the FLOS sets control bits associated with the source register. When a result is entered into the register, these control bits cause the register to be sent via the FLR bus to the unit waiting for it as a source.

This scheme easily meets the first two requirements. The third is met with the help of the programmer; he must use different registers to achieve overlap. For example, the expression $A + B + C + D * E$ can be programmed as follows:

Example 2

LD	F0,	D	$F0 = D$
LD	F2,	C	$F2 = C$
LD	F4,	B	$F4 = B$
MD	F0,	E	$F0 = D * E$
AD	F2,	F0	$F2 = C + D * E$
AD	F4,	A	$F4 = A + B$
AD	F2,	F4	$F2 = A + B + C + D * E$

The busy bit scheme should allow the second add and the multiply to be executed simultaneously (really, in any order) since they use different sinks. Unfortunately, the timing chart of Fig. 3a shows not only that the expected overlap does not occur but also that many cycles are lost to transmission time. The overlap fails to materialize because the first add uses the result of the multiply, and the adder must wait for that result. Cycles are lost to control because so many of the instructions use the adder. The FLOS cannot decode an instruction unless a unit is available to execute it. When an assigned unit finishes execution, it takes one cycle to transmit the fact to the FLOS so that it can decode a waiting instruction. Similarly, when the FLOS is held up because of a busy sink register, it cannot begin to decode until the result has been entered into the register.

One solution that could be considered is the addition of one or more adders. If this were done and some programs timed, however, it would become apparent that the execution circuitry would be in use only a small part of the time. Most of the lost time would occur while the adder waited for operands which are the result of previous instructions. What is required is a device to collect operands (and control information) and then engage the execution circuitry when all conditions are satisfied. But this is precisely the function of the sink and source registers in Fig. 1. Therefore, the better solution is to associate more than one set of registers (control, sink, source) with each execution unit. Each such set is called a *reservation station.* * Now instruction issuing depends on the availability of the appropriate kind of reservation station. In the Model 91 there are three add and two multiply/divide reservation stations. For sim-

---
* The fetch and store buffers can be considered as specialized, one-operand reservation stations. Previous systems, such as the IBM 7030, have in effect employed one "reservation station" ahead of each execution unit. The extension to several reservation stations adds to the effectiveness of the execution hardware.

plicity they are treated as if they were actual units. Thus, in the future, we will speak of Adder 1 (A1), Adder 2 (A2), etc., and M/D 1 and M/D 2.

Figure 3b shows the effect of the addition of reservation stations on the problem running time: five cycles have been eliminated. Note that the second AD now overlaps the MD and actually executes before the first AD. While the speed increase is gratifying and the busy bit method easy to implement, there remains a dependence on the programmer. Note that the expression could have been coded this way:

Example 3a

LD	F0,	E
MD	F0,	D
AD	F0,	C
AD	F0,	B
AD	F0,	A

Now overlap is impossible and the program will run six cycles longer despite having two fewer instructions. Suppose however, that this program is part of a loop, as below:

Example 3b

LOOP 1	LD	F0,	Ei
	MD	F0,	Di
	AD	F0,	Ci
	AD	F0,	Bi
	AD	F0,	Ai
	STD	F0,	Fi
	BXH i, −1, 0, LOOP 1 (decrease i by 1, branch if i > 0)
LOOP 2	LD	F0,	Ei
	LD	F2,	Ei + 1
	MD	F0,	Di
	MD	F2,	Di + 1
	AD	F0,	Ci
	AD	F2,	Ci + 1
	AD	F0,	Bi
	AD	F2,	Bi + 1
	AD	F0,	Ai
	AD	F2,	Ai + 1
	STD	F0,	Fi
	STD	F2,	Fi + 1
	BXH i, −2, 0, LOOP 2

Iteration $n + 1$ of LOOP 1 will appear to the FLOS to depend on iteration n, since the instructions in both iterations have the same sink. But it is clear that the two iterations are, in fact, independent. This example illustrates a second way in which two instruction sequences can be independent. The first way, of course, is for the two strings to have different sink registers. The second way is for the second string to begin with a load. By its definition a load launches a new, independent string because it instructs the computer to destroy the previous contents of the specified register. Unfortunately, the busy bit scheme does not recognize this possibility. If overlap is to be achieved with this scheme, the programmer must write LOOP 2. (This technique is called *doubling* or *unravelling*. It requires twice as much storage but it runs faster by enabling two iterations to be executed simultaneously.)

Attempts were made to improve the busy bit scheme so as to handle this case. The most tempting approach is the expansion of the bit into a counter. This would appear to allow more than one instruction with a given sink to be issued. As each is issued, the FLOS increments the counter; as each is executed the counter is decremented. However, major difficulty is caused by the fact that storage operands do not return in sequence. This can cause the result of instruction $n + 1$ to be placed in a register before that of n. When n completes, it erroneously destroys the register contents.

Some of the other proposals considered would, if implemented, have been of such logical complexity as to jeopardize the achievement of a fast cycle.

The Common Data Bus

The preceding sections were intended to portray the difficulties of achieving concurrency among floating-point instructions and to show some of the steps in the evolution of a design to overcome them. It is clear, in retrospect, that the previous algorithms failed for lack of a way to uniquely identify each instruction and to use this information to sequence execution and set results into the floating-point registers. As far as action by the FLOS is concerned, the only thing unique to a particular instruction is the unit which will execute it. This, then, must form the basis of the common data bus (CDB).

Figure 4 shows the data paths required for operation of the CDB.* When Fig. 4 is compared with Fig. 1 the following changes, in addition to the reservation stations, are evident: Another output port has been added to the buffers. This port has been combined with the results from the adder and multiplier/divider; the combination is the CDB. The CDB now goes not only to the registers but also to the sink and source registers of all reservation stations, including the store data buffers but excluding the floating-point buffers. This data path will enable loads to be executed without the adder and will make the result of any operation available to all units without first going through a floating-point register.

Note that the CDB is fed by all units that can alter a register and that it feeds all units which can have a register as an operand. The control part of the CDB enumerates the units which feed the CDB. Thus the floating-point buffers 1 through 6 are assigned the numbers 1 through 6; the three adders (actually reservation stations) are numbered 10 through 12; the two multiplier/dividers are 8 and 9. Since there are eleven contributors to the CDB, a four-bit binary number suffices to enumerate them. This number is called a *tag*. A tag is associated with each of the four floating-point registers (in addition to the busy bit*), with both the source and sink registers of each of the five reservation stations and with each of the three Store Data Buffers. Thus a total of 17 four-bit tag registers has been added, as shown in Fig. 4.

Tags also appear in another context. A tag is generated by the CDB priority controls to identify the unit whose result will next appear on the CDB. Its use will be made clear shortly.

Operation of this complex is as follows. In decoding each instruction the FLOS checks the busy bit of each of the specified floating-point registers. If that bit is zero, the content of the register(s) may be sent to the selected unit via the FLR bus, just as before. Upon issuing the instruction, which requires only that a unit be available to execute it, the FLOS not only sets the busy bit of the sink register but also sets its tag to the designation of the selected unit. The source register control bits remain unchanged. As an example, take the instruction, AD F0, FLB1. After issuing this instruction to Adder 1 the control bits of F0 would be:

BB	TAG
1	1010 (A1)

So far the only change from previous methods is the setting of the tag. The significant difference occurs when the FLOS finds the busy bit on at decode time. Previously, this caused a suspension of decoding until the bit went off. Now the FLOS will issue the instruction and update the tag. In so doing it will not transmit the register contents to the selected unit but it will transmit the "old" tag. For example, suppose the previous AD was followed by a second AD. At the end of the decode of this second AD, F0's control bits would be:

BB	TAG
1	1011 (A2)

One cycle later the sink tag of the A2 reservation station would be 1010, i.e., the same as A1, the unit whose result will be required by A2.

Let us look ahead temporarily to the execution of the first AD. Some time after the start of execution but before the end,[†] A1 will request the CDB. Since the CDB is fed by many sources, its time-sharing is controlled by a central

---

*The FLB and FLR busses are retained for performance reasons. Everything could be done by a slight extension of the CDB but time would be lost due to conflicts over the common facility.

*The busy bit is no longer necessary since its function can be performed by use of an unassigned tag number. However, it is convenient to retain it.

†Since the required lead time is two cycles, the request is made at the start of execution for an add-type instruction.

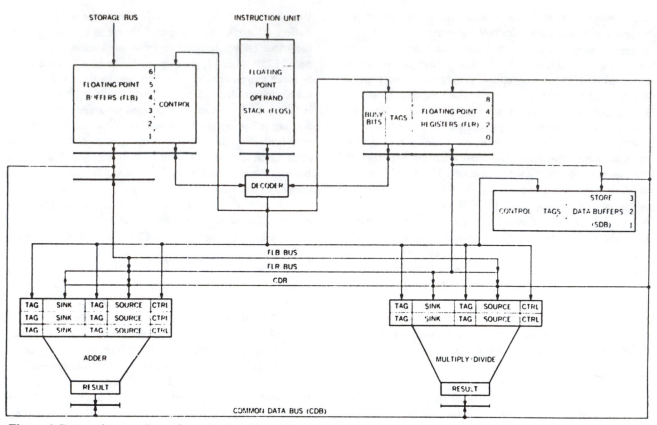

Figure 4 Data registers and transfer paths, including CDB and reservation stations.

priority circuit. If the CDB is free, the priority control signals the requesting adder, A1, to outgate its result *and* it broadcasts the tag of the requestor (1010 in this case) to all reservation stations. Each active reservation station (selected but awaiting a register operand) compares its sink and source tags to the CDB tag. If they match, the reservation station ingates the data from the CDB. In a similar manner, the CDB tag is compared with the tag of each *busy* floating-point register. All busy registers with matching tags ingate from the CDB and reset their busy bits.

Two steps toward the goal of preserving precedence have been accomplished by the foregoing. First, the second AD cannot start until the first AD finishes because it cannot receive both its operands until the result of the first AD appears on the CDB. Secondly, the result of the first AD cannot change register F0 once the second AD is issued, since the tag in F0 will not match A1. These are precisely the desired effects.

Before proceeding with more detailed considerations let us recapitulate the essence of the method. The floating-point register tag identifies the last unit whose result is destined for the register. When an instruction is issued that requires a busy register the tag is sent to the selected

unit in place of the register contents. The unit continuously compares this tag with that generated by the CDB priority control. When a match is detected, the unit ingates from the CDB. The unit begins executing as soon as it has both operands. It may receive one or both operands from either the CDB or the FLR bus; the source operand for storage-to-register instructions is transmitted via the FLB bus.

As each instruction is issued the existing tag(s) is (are) transmitted to the selected unit and then the sink tag is updated. By passing tags around in this fashion, all operations having the same sink are correctly sequenced while other operations are allowed to proceed independently. Finally, the floating-point register tag controls the changing of the register itself, thereby ensuring that only the most recent instruction will change the register. This has the interesting consequence that a loop of the following kind:

Example 5

```
LOOP   LD    F0,  Ai
       AD    F0,  Bi
       STD   F0,  Ci  STORE
       BXH   i,  −1,  0,  LOOP
```

102

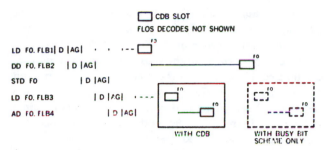

Figure 5 Timing sequence for Example 6, showing effect of CDB.

may execute indefinitely without any change in the contents of F0. Under normal conditions only the final iteration will place its result in F0.

As mentioned previously, there are two ways of starting an independent instruction string. The first is to specify a different sink register and the second is to load a register. The CDB handles the former in essentially the same way as the busy bit scheme. The load, which had been a difficult problem previously, is now very simple. Regardless of the register tag or busy bit, a load turns the busy bit on and sets the tag equal to the floating-point buffer which the instruction unit had assigned to the load. This causes subsequent instructions to sequence on the buffer rather than on whatever unit may have identified the register as its sink prior to the load. The buffer controls are set to request the CDB when the storage operand arrives. The following example and Fig. 5 show this clearly.

Example 6

```
LD     F0, FLB1
DD     F0, FLB2      DIVIDE
STD    F0, A
LD     F0, FLB3
AD     F0, FLB4
```

Note that the add finishes before the divide. The dashed line portion of Fig. 5 shows what would happen if the busy bit scheme alone were used. Figure 6 displays the sequences followed under the two schemes. This figure graphically illustrates the bottleneck caused by using a single sink register with a busy bit scheme. Because all data must pass through this register, the program is reduced to strictly sequential execution, steps 1 through 7. With the CDB, on the other hand, the sink register hardly appears and the program is broken into two independent, concurrent sequences. This facility of the CDB obviates the need for loop doubling.

The CDB makes it possible to execute some instructions in, effectively, no time at all. In the above example the

store took place during the CDB cycle following the divide. In a similar fashion a register-to-register load of a busy register is accomplished by moving the tag of the source floating-point register to the tag of the sink floating-point register. For example, in the sequence

```
AD     F0,  FLB1
LDR    F2,  F0      move F0 to F2
```

the tag of F0 will be 1010 (A1) at the time the LDR is decoded. The decoder simply sets F2's tag to 1010. Now, when the result of the AD appears on the CDB both F0 and F2 will ingate since the CDB tag of 1010 will match the tag of each register. Thus, no unit or extra time was required for the execution of the LDR.

A number of details have been omitted from this discussion in order to clarify the concept, but really only two are of operational significance. First, every unit must request the CDB two cycles before it finishes execution. (These two cycles are required for propagation of the request to the CDB controls, the establishment of priority among competing units, and propagation of a "select" signal to the chosen unit.) This limits the execution time of any instruction to a two-cycle minimum. (Of course, the faster the execution the less the need for, or gain from, concurrency.) It also adds one* cycle to the access time for loads. Because of buffering and overlap, this does not usually cause an increase in problem running time.

The second point is concerned with mixed precision. Because the architectural definition causes the low-order part of an FLR to be preserved during single-precision operation, an error can occur in the following kind of program:

```
LD     F0,   FLB1
AD     F0,   FLB2
AE     F0,   FLB3
```

Since only the last instruction, which is single-precision, will change F0, the low order result of the double-precision AD will be lost. This is handled by associating a bit with each register to indicate whether a particular register is the sink of an outstanding single- or double-precision instruction. If this bit does not match the "length" of the instruction being decoded, the decode is suspended until the busy bit goes off. While this stratagem† solves the logic problem, it does so at the expense of performance. Unfortunately, no way has been found to avoid this. Note, however, that all-single- or all-double-precision programs run at the maximum possible speed. It is only the interface between single- and double-precision to the *same* sink register that suffers delay.

---

* It does not add two cycles since storage gives one cycle prenotification of the arrival of data.
† Further complications arise from the fact that single-precision multiply produces a double-precision product. This is handled separately but with the same time penalty as above.

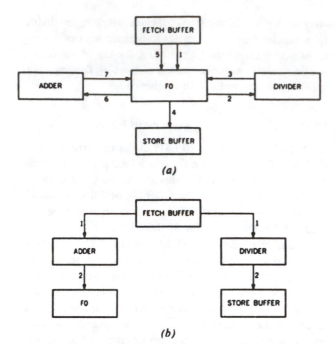

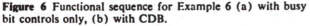

(a)

(b)

Figure 6 Functional sequence for Example 6 (a) with busy bit controls only, (b) with CDB.

Conclusions

Two concepts of some significance to the design of high-performance computers have been presented. The first, reservation stations, is simply an expeditious method of buffering, in an environment where the transmission time between units is of consequence. Because of the disparity between storage access and circuit speeds and because of dependencies between successive operations, it is observed (given multiple execution units) that each unit spends much of its time waiting for operands. In effect, the reservation stations do the waiting for operands while the execution circuitry is free to be engaged by whichever reservation station fills first.

The second, and more important, innovation, the CDB, utilizes the reservation stations and a simple tagging scheme to preserve precedence while encouraging concurrency. In conjunction with the various kinds of buffering in the CPU, the CDB helps render the Model 91 less sensitive to programming. It should be evident, however, that the programmer still exercises substantial control over how much concurrency will occur. The two different programs for doing A + B + C + D * E illustrate this clearly.

It might appear that the CDB adds one cycle to the execution time of each operation, but in fact it does not. In practice only 30 nsec of the 60-nsec CDB interval are required to perform all of the CDB functions. The remaining time could, in this case, be used by the execution unit to achieve a shorter effective cycle. For example, if an add requires 120 nsec, then add plus the CDB time required is 150 nsec. Therefore, as far as the add is concerned, the machine cycle could be 50 nsec. Besides, even without the CDB, a similar amount of time would be required to transmit results both to the floating-point registers and back as an input to the unit generating the result.

The following program, a typical partial differential equation inner loop, illustrates the possible performance increase.

```
LOOP    MD      F0,  Ai
        AD      F0,  Bi
        LD      F2,  Ci
        SDR     F2,  F0
        MDR     F2,  F6
        AD2     F2,  Ci
        STD     F2,  Ci
        BXH     i,  -1,  0,  LOOP
```

Without the CDB one iteration of the loop would use 17 cycles, allowing 4 per MD, 3 per AD and nothing for LD or STD. With the CDB one iteration requires 11 cycles. For this kind of code the CDB improves performance by about one-third.

Acknowledgments

The author wishes to acknowledge the contributions of Messrs. D. W. Anderson and D. M. Powers, who extended the original concept, and Mr. W. D. Silkman, who implemented all of the central control logic discussed in the paper.

References

1. D. W. Anderson, F. J. Sparacio and R. M. Tomasulo, "The System/360 Model 91: Machine Philosophy and Instruction Handling," *IBM Journal* 11, 8 (1967) (this issue).
2. S. F. Anderson, J. Earle, R. E. Goldschmidt and D. M. Powers, "The System/360 Model 91 Floating-Point Execution Unit," *IBM Journal* 11, 34 (1967) (this issue).

Received September 16, 1965.

Software Pipelining:
An Effective Scheduling Technique for VLIW Machines

Monica Lam

Department of Computer Science
Carnegie Mellon University
Pittsburgh, Pennsylvania 15213

Abstract

This paper shows that software pipelining is an effective and viable scheduling technique for VLIW processors. In software pipelining, iterations of a loop in the source program are continuously initiated at constant intervals, before the preceding iterations complete. The advantage of software pipelining is that optimal performance can be achieved with compact object code.

This paper extends previous results of software pipelining in two ways: First, this paper shows that by using an improved algorithm, near-optimal performance can be obtained without specialized hardware. Second, we propose a *hierarchical reduction* scheme whereby entire control constructs are reduced to an object similar to an operation in a basic block. With this scheme, all innermost loops, including those containing conditional statements, can be software pipelined. It also diminishes the start-up cost of loops with small number of iterations. Hierarchical reduction complements the software pipelining technique, permitting a consistent performance improvement be obtained.

The techniques proposed have been validated by an implementation of a compiler for Warp, a systolic array consisting of 10 VLIW processors. This compiler has been used for developing a large number of applications in the areas of image, signal and scientific processing.

The research was supported in part by Defense Advanced Research Projects Agency (DOD) monitored by the Space and Naval Warfare Systems Command under Contract N00039-87-C-0251, and in part by the Office of Naval Research under Contracts N00014-87-K-0385 and N00014-87-K-0533.

1. Introduction

A VLIW (very long instruction word) machine [5, 11] is similar to a horizontally microcoded machine in that the data path consists of multiple, possibly pipelined, functional units, each of which can be independently controlled through dedicated fields in a "very long" instruction. The distinctive feature of VLIW architectures is that these long instructions are the machine instructions. There is no additional layer of interpretation in which machine instructions are expanded into micro-instructions. While complex resource or field conflicts often exist between functionally independent operations in a horizontal microcode engine, a VLIW machine generally has an orthogonal instruction set and a higher degree of parallelism. The key to generating efficient code for the VLIW machine is global code compaction, that is, the compaction of code across basic blocks [12]. In fact, the VLIW architecture is developed from the study of the global code compaction technique, trace scheduling [10].

The thesis of this paper is that software pipelining [24, 25, 30] is a viable alternative technique for scheduling VLIW processors. In software pipelining, iterations of a loop in a source program are continuously initiated at constant intervals without having to wait for preceding iterations to complete. That is, multiple iterations, in different stages of their computations, are in progress simultaneously. The steady state of this pipeline constitutes the loop body of the object code. The advantage of software pipelining is that optimal performance can be achieved with compact object code.

A drawback of software pipelining is its complexity; the problem of finding an optimal schedule is NP-complete. (This can be shown by transforming the problem of resource constrained scheduling problem [14] to the software pipelining problem). There have been two approaches in response to the complexity of this problem: (1) change the architecture, and thus the characteristics of the constraints, so that the problem becomes tractable, and (2) use heuristics. The first approach is used in the polycyclic [25] and Cydrome's Cydra architecture; a specialized crossbar is used to make optimizing loops without data dependencies between iterations tractable. However, this hardware feature is expensive; and, when inter-iteration dependency is present in a loop, exhaustive search on the strongly connected components of the data flow graph is still necessary [16]. The second approach is used in the FPS-164 compiler [30]. Software pipelining is applied to a restricted set of loops, namely those containing a single Fortran statement. In other words, at most one inter-iteration data dependency relationship can be present in the flow graph. The results were that near-optimal results can be obtained cheaply without the specialized hardware.

This paper shows that software pipelining is a practical, efficient, and *general* technique for scheduling the parallelism in a VLIW machine. We have extended previous results of software pipelining in two ways. First, we show that near-optimal results can often be obtained for loops containing both intra- and inter-iteration data dependency, using software heuristics. We have improved the scheduling heuristics and introduced a new optimization called modulo variable expansion. The latter implements part of the functionality of the specialized hardware proposed in the polycyclic machine, thus allowing us to achieve similar performance.

Second, this paper proposes a *hierarchical reduction* scheme whereby entire control constructs are reduced to an object similar to an operation in a basic block. Scheduling techniques previously defined for basic blocks can be applied across basic blocks. The significance of hierarchical reduction is threefold: First, conditional statements no longer constitute a barrier to code motion, code in innermost loops containing conditional statements can be compacted. Second, and more importantly, software pipelining can be applied to arbitrarily complex loops, including those containing conditional statements. Third, hierarchical reduction diminishes the penalty of short loops: scalar code can be scheduled with the prolog and epilog of a pipelined loop. We can even software pipeline the second level loop as well. The overall result is that a consistent speed up is obtained whenever parallelism is available across loop iterations.

Software pipelining, as addressed here, is the problem of scheduling the operations within an iteration, such that the iterations can be pipelined to yield optimal throughput. Software pipelining has also been studied under different contexts. The software pipelining algorithms proposed by Su et al. [27, 28], and Aiken and Nicolau [1], assume that the schedules for the iterations are given and cannot be changed. Ebcioglu proposed a software pipelining algorithm to generate code for a hypothetical machine with infinitely many hardware resources [7]. Lastly, Weiss and Smith compared the results of using loop unrolling and software pipelining to generate scalar code for the Cray-1S architecture [31].

However, their software pipelining algorithm only overlaps the computation from at most two iterations. The unfavorable results obtained for software pipelining can be attributed to the particular algorithm rather than the software pipelining approach.

The techniques described in this paper have been validated by the implementation of a compiler for the Warp machine. Warp [4] is a high-performance, programmable systolic array developed by Carnegie Mellon and General Electric, our industrial partner. The Warp array is a linear array of VLIW processors, each capable of a peak computation rate of 10 million floating-point operations per second (10 MFLOPS). A Warp array typically consists of ten processors, or cells, and thus has an aggregate bandwidth of 100 MFLOPS.

Each Warp cell has its own sequencer and program memory. Its data path consists of a floating-point multiplier, a floating-point adder, an integer ALU, three register files (one for each arithmetic unit), a 512-word queue for each of the two inter-cell data communication channels, and a 32 Kword data memory. All these components are connected through a crossbar, and can be programmed to operate concurrently via wide instructions of over 200 bits. The multiplier and adder are both 5-stage pipelined; together with the 2 cycle delay through the register file, multiplications and additions take 7 cycles to complete.

The machine is programmed using a language called W2. In W2, conventional Pascal-like control constructs are used to specify the cell programs, and asynchronous computation primitives are used to specify inter-cell communication. The Warp machine and the W2 compiler have been used extensively for about two years, in many applications such as low-level vision for robot vehicle navigation, image and signal processing, and scientific computing [2, 3]. Our previous papers presented an overview of the compiler and described an array level optimization that supports efficient fine-grain parallelism among cells [15, 20]. This paper describes the scheduling techniques used to generate code for the parallel and pipelined functional units in each cell.

This paper consists of three parts: Part I describes the software pipelining algorithm for loops containing straight-line loop bodies, focusing on the extensions and improvements. Part II describes the hierarchical reduction approach, and shows how software pipelining can be applied to all loops. Part III contains an evaluation and a comparison with the trace scheduling technique.

2. Simple loops

The concept of software pipelining can be illustrated by the following example: Suppose we wish to add a constant to a vector of data. Assuming that the addition is one-stage pipelined, the most compact sequence of instructions for a single iteration is:

```
1    Read
2    Add
3
4    Write
```

Different iterations can proceed in parallel to take advantage of the parallelism in the data path. In this example, an iteration can be initiated every cycle, and this optimal throughput can be obtained with the following piece of code:

```
1    Read
2    Add     Read
3            Add     Read
4 L:Write            Add     Read    CJump L
5            Write           Add
6
7                            Write
```

Instructions 1 to 3 are called the *prolog*: a new iteration is initiated every instruction cycle and execute concurrently with all previously initiated iterations. The *steady state* is reached in cycle 4, and this state is repeated until all iterations have been initiated. In the steady state, four iterations are in progress at the same time, with one iteration starting up and one finishing off every cycle. (The operation **CJump L** branches back to label **L** unless all iterations have been initiated.) On leaving the steady state, the iterations currently in progress are completed in the *epilog*, instructions 5 through 7. The software pipelined loop in this example executes at the optimal throughput rate of one iteration per instruction cycle, which is four times the speed of the original program. The potential gain of the technique is even greater for data paths with higher degrees of pipelining and parallelism. In the case of the Warp cell, software pipelining speeds up this loop by nine times.

2.1. Problem statement

Software pipelining is unique in that pipeline stages in the functional units of the data path are not emptied at iteration boundaries; the pipelines are filled and drained only on entering and exiting the loop. The significance is that optimal throughput is possible with this approach.

The objective of software pipelining is to minimize the interval at which iterations are initiated; the *initiation interval* [25] determines the throughput for the loop. The basic units of scheduling are minimally indivisible sequences of micro-instructions. In the example above, since the result of the addition must be written precisely two cycles after the computation is initiated, the add and the write operations are grouped as one indivisible sequence. While the sequence is indivisible, it can overlap with the execution of other sequences. The minimally indivisible sequences that make up the computation of an iteration are modeled as nodes in a graph. Data dependencies between these sequences are mapped onto precedence constraints between the corresponding nodes; associated with each node is a resource reservation table indicating the resources used in each time step of the sequence. To ensure a compact steady state, two more constraints are imposed: the initiation interval between all consecutive iterations must be the same, and the schedule for each individual iteration must be identical. In other words, the problem is to schedule the operations within an iteration, such that the same schedule can be pipelined with the shortest, constant initiation interval.

The scheduling constraints in software pipelining are defined in terms of the initiation interval:

1. *Resource constraints.* If iterations in a software pipelined loop are initiated every sth cycle, then every sth instruction in the schedule of an iteration is executed simultaneously, one from a different iteration. The total resource requirement of every sth instructions thus cannot exceed the available resources. A modulo resource reservation table can be used to represent the resource usage of the steady state by mapping the resource usage of time t to that of time $t \bmod s$ in the modulo resource reservation table.

2. *Precedence constraints.* Consider the following example:

```
FOR i := 1 TO 100 DO
BEGIN
     a := a + 1.0;
END
```

The value of **a** must first be accessed before the store operation, and the store operation must complete before the data is accessed in the second iteration. We model the dependency relationship by giving each edge in the graph two attributes: a minimum iteration difference and a delay. When we say that the minimum iteration difference on an edge (u,v) is p and the delay is d, that means node v must execute d cycles after node u from the pth previous iteration. Let $\sigma : V \to N$ be the schedule function of a node, then

$$\sigma(v) - (\sigma(u) - s \cdot p) \geq d, \quad \text{or} \quad \sigma(v) - \sigma(u) \geq d - s \cdot p,$$

where s is the initiation interval. Since a node cannot depend on a value from a future iteration, the minimum iteration difference is always nonnegative. The iteration difference for an intra-iteration dependency is 0, meaning that the node v must follow node u in the same iteration. As illustrated by the example, inter-iteration data dependencies may introduce cycles into the precedence constraint graph.

2.2. Scheduling algorithm

The definition of scheduling constraints in terms of the initiation interval makes finding an approximate solution to this NP-complete problem difficult. Since computing the minimum initiation interval is NP-complete, an approach is to first schedule the code using heuristics, then determine the initiation interval permitted by the schedule. However, since the scheduling constraints are defined in terms of the initiation interval, if the initiation interval is not known at scheduling time, the schedule produced is unlikely to permit a good initiation interval.

To resolve this circularity, the FPS compiler uses an iterative approach [30]: first establish a lower and an upper bound on the initiation interval; then use binary search to find the smallest initiation interval for which a schedule can be found. (The length of a locally compacted iteration can serve as an upper bound; the calculation of a lower bound is described below). We also use an iterative approach, but we use a linear search instead. The rationale is as follows: Although the probability that a schedule can be found generally increases with the value of the initiation interval, schedulability is not monotonic [21]. Especially since empirical results show that in the case of Warp, a schedule meeting the lower bound can often be found, sequential search is preferred.

A lower bound on the initiation interval can be calculated from the scheduling constraints as follows:

1. *Resource constraints*. If an iteration is initiated every s cycles, then the total number of resource units available in s cycles must at least cover the resource requirement of one iteration. Therefore, the bound on the initiation interval due to resource considerations is the maximum ratio between the total number of times each resource is used and the number of available units per instruction.

2. *Precedence constraints*. Cycles in precedence constraints impose delays between operations from different iterations that are represented by the same node in the graph. The initiation interval must be large enough for such delays to be observed. We define the delay and minimum iteration difference of a path to be the sum of the minimum delays and minimum iteration differences of the edges in the path, respectively. Let s be the initiation interval, and c be a cycle in the graph. Since

$$\sigma(v) - \sigma(u) \geq d(e) - s \cdot p(e)$$

we get:

$$d(c) - s \cdot p(c) \leq 0.$$

We note that if $p(c)=0$, then $d(c)$ is necessarily less than 0 by the definition of a legal computation. Therefore, the bound on the initiation interval due to precedence considerations is

$$\max_c \left\lceil \frac{d(c)}{p(c)} \right\rceil, \quad \forall \text{ cycle } c \text{ whose } p(c) \neq 0.$$

2.2.1. Scheduling acyclic graphs

The algorithm we use to schedule acyclic graphs for a target initiation interval is the same as that used in the FPS compiler, which itself is derived from the list scheduling algorithm used in basic block scheduling [9]. List scheduling is a non-backtracking algorithm, nodes are scheduled in a topological ordering, and are placed in the earliest possible time slot that satisfies all scheduling constraints with the partial schedule constructed so far. The software pipelining algorithm differs from list scheduling in that the modulo resource reservation table is used in determining if there is a resource conflict. Also, by the definition of modulo resource usage, if we cannot schedule a node in s consecutive time slots due to resource conflicts, it will not fit in any slot with the current schedule. When this happens, the attempt to find a schedule for the given initiation interval is aborted and the scheduling process is repeated with a greater interval value.

2.2.2. Scheduling cyclic graphs

In adapting the scheduling algorithm for acyclic graphs to cyclic graphs, we face the following difficulties: a topological sort of the nodes does not exist in a cyclic graph; precedence constraints with nodes already scheduled cannot be satisfied by examining only those edges incident on those nodes; and the maximum height of a node, used as the priority function in list scheduling, is ill-defined. Experimentation with different schemes helped identify two desirable properties that a non-backtracking algorithm should have:

1. Partial schedules constructed at each point of the scheduling process should not violate any of the precedence constraints in the graph. In other words, were there no resource conflicts with the remaining nodes, each partial schedule should be a partial solution.

2. The heuristics must be sensitive to the initiation interval. An increased initiation interval value relaxes the scheduling constraints, and the scheduling algorithm must take advantage of this opportunity. It would be futile if the scheduling algorithm simply retries the same schedule that failed.

These properties are exhibited by the heuristics in the scheduling algorithm for acyclic graphs. A scheduling algorithm for cyclic graphs that satisfies these properties is presented below.

The following preprocessing step is first performed: find the strongly connected components in the graph [29], and compute the closure of the precedence constraints in each connected component by solving the all-points longest path problem for each component [6, 13]. This information is used in the iterative scheduling step. To avoid the cost of recomputing this information for each value of the initiation interval, we compute this information only once in the preprocessing step, using a symbolic value to stand for the initiation interval [21].

As in the case of acyclic graphs, the main scheduling step is iterative. For each target initiation interval, the connected components are first scheduled individually. The original graph is then reduced by representing each connected component as a single vertex: the resource usage of the vertex represents the aggregate resource usage of its components, and edges connecting nodes from different connected components are represented by edges between the corresponding vertices. This reduced graph is acyclic, and the acyclic graph scheduling algorithm can then be applied.

The scheduling algorithm for connected components also follows the framework of list scheduling. The nodes in a connected component are scheduled in a topological ordering by considering only the *intra-iteration* edges in the graph. By the definition of a connected component, assigning a schedule to a node limits the schedule of all other nodes in the component, both from below and above. We define the *precedence constrained range* of a node for a given partial schedule as the legal time range in which the node can be scheduled, without violating the precedence constraints of the graph. As each node is scheduled, we use the precomputed longest path information to update the precedence constrained range of each remaining node, substituting the symbolic initiation interval value with the actual value. A node is scheduled in the earliest possible time slot within its constrained range. If a node cannot be scheduled within the precedence constrained range, the scheduling attempt is considered unsuccessful. This algorithm possesses the first property described above: precedence constraints are satisfied by all partial schedules.

As nodes are scheduled in a topological ordering of the intra-iteration edges, the precedence constrained range of a node is bounded from above only by inter-iteration edges. As the initiation interval increases, so does the upper bound of the range in which a node is scheduled. Together with the strategy of scheduling a node as early as possible, the range in which a node can be scheduled increases as the initiation interval increases, and so does the likelihood of success. The scheduling problem approaches that of an acyclic graph as the value of the initiation interval increases. Therefore, the approach also satisfies the second property: the algorithm takes advantage of increased initiation interval values.

2.3. Modulo variable expansion

The idea of modulo variable expansion can be illustrated by the following code fragment, where a value is written into a register and used two cycles later:

```
Def (R1)
op
Use (R1)
```

If the same register is used by all iterations, then the write operation of an iteration cannot execute before the read opera-

tion in the preceding iteration. Therefore, the optimal throughput is limited to one iteration every two cycles. This code can be sped up by using different registers in alternating iterations:

```
Def (R1)
  op        Def (R2)
L:Use (R1)  op        Def (R1)
            Use (R2)  op        Def (R2) CJump L
                      Use (R1)  op
                                Use (R2)
```

We call this optimization of allocating multiple registers to a variable in the loop *modulo variable expansion*. This optimization is a variation of the variable expansion technique used in vectorizing compilers [18]. The variable expansion transformation identifies those variables that are redefined at the beginning of every iteration of a loop, and expands the variable into a higher dimension variable, so that each iteration can refer to a different location. Consequently, the use of the variable in different iterations is thus independent, and the loop can be vectorized. Modulo variable expansion takes advantage of the flexibility of VLIW machines in scalar computation, and reduces the number of locations allocated to a variable by reusing the same location in non-overlapping iterations. The small set of values can even reside in register files, cutting down on both the memory traffic and the latency of the computation.

Without modulo variable expansion, the length of the steady state of a pipelined loop is simply the initiation interval. When modulo variable expansion is applied, code sequences for consecutive iterations differ in the registers used, thus lengthening the steady state. If there are n repeating code sequences, the steady state needs to be *unrolled n* times.

The algorithm of modulo variable expansion is as follows. First, we identify those variables that are redefined at the beginning of every iteration. Next, we pretend that every iteration of the loop has a dedicated register location for each qualified variable, and remove all *inter-iteration* precedence constraints between operations on these variables. Scheduling then proceeds as normal. The resulting schedule is then used to determine the actual number of registers that must be allocated to each variable. The lifetime of a register variable is defined as the duration between the first assignment into the variable and its last use. If the lifetime of a variable is l, and an iteration is initiated every s cycles, then at least $\lceil \frac{l}{s} \rceil$ number of values must be kept alive concurrently, in that many locations.

If each variable v_i is allocated its minimum number of locations, q_i, the degree of unrolling is given by the lowest common multiple of $\{q_i\}$. Even for small values of q_i, the least common multiple can be quite large and can lead to an intolerable increase in code size. The code size can be reduced by trading off register space. We observe that the minimum degree of unrolling, u, to implement the same schedule is simply $\max_i q_i$. This minimum degree of unrolling can be achieved by setting the number of registers allocated to variable v_i to be the smallest factor of u that is no smaller than q_i, i.e.,

$$\min n, \text{ where } n \geq q_i \text{ and } u \bmod n = 0.$$

The increase in register space is much more tolerable than the increase in code size of the first scheme for a machine like Warp.

Since we cannot determine the number of registers allocated to each variable until all uses of registers have been scheduled, we cannot determine if the register requirement of a partial schedule can be satisfied. Moreover, once given a schedule, it is very difficult to reduce its register requirement. Indivisible micro-operation sequences make it hard to insert code in a software pipelined loop to spill excess register data into memory.

In practice, we can assume that the target machine has a large number of registers; otherwise, the resulting data memory bottleneck would render the use of any global compaction techniques meaningless. The Warp machine has two 31-word register files for the floating-point units, and one 64-word register for the ALU. Empirical results show that they are large enough for almost all the user programs developed [21]. Register shortage is a problem for a small fraction of the programs; however, these programs invariably have loops that contain a large number of independent operations per iteration. In other words, these programs are amenable to other simpler scheduling techniques that only exploit parallelism within an iteration. Thus, when register allocation becomes a problem, software pipelining is not as crucial. The best approach is therefore to use software pipelining aggressively, by assuming that there are enough registers. When we run out of registers, we then resort to simple techniques that serializes the execution of loop iterations. Simpler scheduling techniques are more amenable to register spilling techniques.

2.4. Code size

The code size increase due to software pipelining is reasonable considering the speed up that can be achieved. If the number of iterations is known at compile time, the code size of a pipelined loop is within three times the code size for one iteration of the loop [21]. If the number of iterations is not known at compile time, then additional code must be generated to handle the cases when there are so few iterations in the loop that the steady state is never reached, and when there are no more iterations to initiate in the middle of an unrolled steady state.

To handle these cases, we generate two loops: a pipelined version to execute most of the iterations, and an unpipelined version to handle the rest. Let k be the number of iterations started in the prolog of the pipelined loop, u be the degree of unrolling, and n be the number of iterations to be executed. Before the loop is executed, the values of n and k are compared. If $n < k$, then all n iterations are executed using the unpipelined code. Otherwise, we execute $n-k \bmod u$ iterations using the unpipelined code, and the rest on the pipelined loop. At most $\lceil \frac{l}{s} \rceil$ iterations are executed in the unpipelined mode, where l is the length of an iteration and s is the initiation interval. Using this scheme, the total code size is at most four times the size of the unpipelined loop.

A more important metric than the total code length is the length of the innermost loop. An increase in code length by a factor of four typically does not pose a problem for the machine storage system. However, in machines with instruction buffers and caches, it is most important that the steady state of a pipelined loop fits into the buffers or caches. Although software pipelining increases the total code size, the steady state of the loop is typically much shorter than the length of an unpipelined loop. Thus, we can conclude that the increase in code size due to software pipelining is not an issue.

3. Hierarchical reduction

The motivation for the *hierarchical reduction* technique is to make software pipelining applicable to all innermost loops, including those containing conditional statements. The proposed approach schedules the program hierarchically, starting with the innermost control constructs. As each construct is scheduled, the entire construct is reduced to a simple node representing all the scheduling constraints of its components with other constructs. This node can then be scheduled just like a simple node within the surrounding control construct. The scheduling process is complete when the entire program is reduced to a single node.

The hierarchical reduction technique is derived from the scheduling scheme previously proposed by Wood [32]. In Wood's approach, scheduled constructs are modeled as black boxes taking unit time. Operations outside the construct can move around it but cannot execute concurrently with it. Here, the resource utilization and precedence constraints of the reduced construct are visible, permitting it to be scheduled in parallel with other operations. This is essential to software pipelining loops with conditional statements effectively.

110

3.1. Conditional statements

The procedure for scheduling conditional statements is as follows: The THEN and ELSE branches of a conditional statement are first scheduled independently. The entire conditional statement is then reduced to a single node whose scheduling constraints represent the union of the scheduling constraints of the two branches. The length of the new node is the maximum of that of the two branches; the value of each entry in the resource reservation table is the maximum of the corresponding entries in the tables of the two branches. Precedence constraints between operations inside the branches and those outside must now be replaced by constraints between the node representing the entire construct and those outside. The attributes of the constraints remain the same.

The node representing the conditional construct can be treated like any other simple node within the surrounding construct. A schedule that satisfies the union of the constraints of both branches must also satisfy those of either branch. At code emission time, two sets of code, corresponding to the two branches, are generated. Any code scheduled in parallel with the conditional statement is duplicated in both branches. Although the two branches are padded to the same length at code scheduling time, it is not necessary that the lengths of the emitted code for the two branches be identical. If a machine instruction does not contain any operations for a particular branch, then the instruction simply can be omitted for that branch. The simple representation of conditional statements as straight-line sequences in the scheduling process makes it easy to overlap conditional statements with any other control constructs.

The above strategy is optimized for handling short conditional statements in innermost loops executing on highly parallel hardware. The assumption is that there are more unused than used resources in an unpipelined schedule, and that it is more profitable to satisfy the union of the scheduling constraints of both branches all the time, so as not to reduce the opportunity for parallelism among operations outside the conditional statement. For those cases that violate this assumption, we can simply mark all resources in the node representing the conditional statements as used. By omitting empty machine instructions at code emission time, the short conditional branch will remain short. Although this scheme disallows overlap between the conditional statement and all other operations, all other forms of code motion around the construct can still take place.

3.2. Loops

The prolog and epilog of a software pipelined loop can be overlapped with other operations outside the loop. This optimization can again be achieved by reducing a looping construct to a simple node that represents the resource and precedence constraints for the entire loop. Only one iteration of the steady state is represented. The steady state of the loop, however, should not be overlapped with other operations. To prevent this, all resources in the steady state are marked as consumed.

3.3. Global code motions

Once conditional statements and loops are represented as straight-line sequences of code, scheduling techniques, formerly applicable only to basic blocks, such as software pipelining and list scheduling, can be applied to compound control constructs. Global code motions automatically take place as the enclosing construct is scheduled according to the objective of the scheduling technique.

The significance of hierarchical reduction is to permit a consistent performance improvement be obtained for all programs, not just those programs that have long innermost loops with straight-line loop bodies. More precisely, hierarchical reduction has three major effects:

1. The most important benefit of hierarchical reduction is that software pipelining can be applied to loops with conditional statements. This allows software pipelining to be applied to all innermost loops. Overlapping different iterations in a loop is an important source of parallelism.

2. Hierarchical reduction is also important in compacting long loop bodies containing conditional statements. In these long loop bodies, there is often much parallelism to be exploited within an iteration. Operations outside a conditional statement can move around and into the branches of the statement. Even branches of different conditional statements can be overlapped.

3. Hierarchical reduction also minimizes the penalty of short vectors, or loops with small number of iterations. The prolog and epilog of a loop can be overlapped with scalar operations outside the loop; the epilog of a loop can be overlapped with the prolog of the next loop; and, lastly, software pipelining can be applied even to an outer loop.

4. Evaluation

To provide an overall picture of the compiler's performance, we first give the statistics collected from a large sample of user programs. These performance figures show the effect of the software pipelining and hierarchical reduction techniques on complete programs. To provide more detailed information on the performance of software pipelining, we also include the performance of Livermore loops on a single Warp cell.

4.1. Performance of users' programs

The compiler for the Warp machine has been in use for about two years, and a large number of programs in robot navigation, low-level vision, and signal processing and scientific computing have been developed [2, 3]. Of these, a sample of 72 programs have been collected and analyzed [21]. Table 4-1 lists the performance of some representative programs, and the performance of all 72 programs is graphically presented in Figure 4-1.

Task All images are 512×512	Time (ms)	Mflops
100×100 matrix multiplication	25	79.4
512×512 complex FFT (1 dimension)	164	71.9
3×3 convolution	70	65.7
Hough transform	2113	42.2
Local selective averaging	406	39.2
Shortest path Warshall's algorithm (350 nodes, 10 iterations)	104	24.3
Roberts operator	192	15.2

Table 4-1: Performance on Warp array

All application programs in the experiment have compile-time loop bounds, and their execution speeds were determined statically by assuming that half of the data dependent branches in conditional statement were taken. All the programs in the sample are homogeneous code, that is, the same cell program is executed by all cells. Except for a short setup time at the beginning, these programs never stall on input or output. Therefore, the computation rate for each cell is simply one-tenth of the reported rate for the array.

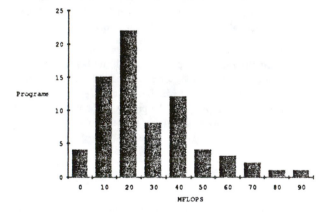

Figure 4-1: Performance of 72 users' programs

To study the significance of software pipelining and hierarchical reduction, we compare the performance obtained against that obtained by only compacting individual basic blocks. The speed up is shown in Figure 4-2. The average factor of increase in speed is three. Programs are classified according to whether they contain conditional statements. 42 of the 72 programs contain conditional statements. We observe that programs containing conditional statements are sped up more. The reason is that conditional statements break up the computation into small basic blocks, making code motions across basic blocks even more important.

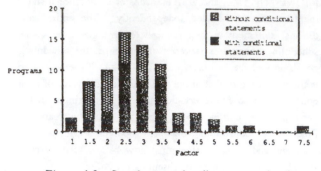

Figure 4-2: Speed up over locally compacted code

In this sample of programs, 75% of all the loops are scheduled with an initiation interval matching the theoretical lower bound. 93% of the loops containing no conditional statements or connected components are pipelined perfectly. The presence of conditional statements and connected components make calculating a tight lower bound for the initiation interval and finding an optimal schedule difficult. In particular, branches of a conditional statement are first compacted as much as possible, with no regard to the initiation interval of the loop. Software pipelining is then applied to the node representing the conditional statement, treating its operations as indivisible. This approach minimizes the length of the branches to avoid code explosion, but increases the minimum initiation interval of the loop. Of the 25% of the loops for which the achieved initiation interval is greater than the lower bound, the average efficiency is 75% [21].

4.2. Livermore loops

The performance of Livermore loops [23] on a single Warp cell is presented in Table 4-2. The Fortran programs were translated manually into the W2 syntax. (The control constructs of W2 are similar to those of Pascal.) The translation was straightforward except for kernels 15 and 16, which required the code be completely restructured. The INVERSE and SQRT functions expanded into 7 and 19 floating-point operations, respectively. The EXP function in loop 22 expanded into a calculation containing 19 conditional statements. The large numbers of conditional statements made the loop not pipelinable. In fact, the scheduler did not even attempt to pipeline this loop because the length of the loop (331 instructions) was beyond the threshold that it used to decide if pipelining was feasible. Loops 16 and 20 were also not pipelined, because the calculated lower bound on the initiation interval were within 99% of the length of the unpipelined loop.

Kernel	MFLOPS	Efficiency (lower bound)	Speed up
1	6.2	1.00	8.25
2*	2.5	0.75	3.25
3	1.4	1.00	2.71
4*	1.4	1.00	2.71
5	0.6	0.94	1.12
6*	1.4	1.00	2.86
7	7.9	1.00	6.00
8*	8.2	1.00	2.29
9	7.7	1.00	4.27
10	3.4	0.85	5.31
11	0.5	0.90	1.30
12	1.7	1.00	4.00
13	2.0	1.00	2.63
14**	2.2	1.00	3.32
15	5.9	0.85	5.50
16	0.3	1.00	1.00
17	0.8	1.00	1.20
18	7.5	0.97	3.70
19	0.7	1.00	1.24
20	0.9	0.99	1.00
21	3.0	1.00	6.00
22***	1.1	0.56	1.00
23	1.1	1.00	1.10
24	0.4	1.00	1.33
H-Mean	1.2		

*   Compiler directives to disambiguate array references used
**   Multiple loops were merged into one
*** EXP function expanded into 19 IF statements

Table 4-2: Performance of Livermore loops

The MFLOPS rates given in the second column are for single-precision floating-point arithmetic. The third column contains lower bound figures on the efficiency of the software pipelining technique. As they were obtained by dividing the lower bound on the initiation interval by the achieved interval value, they represent a lower bound on the achieved efficiency. If a kernel contains multiple loops, the figure given is the mean calculated by weighing each loop by its execution time. The speed up factors in the fourth column are the ratios of the execution time between an unpipelined and a pipelined kernel. All branches of conditional statements were assumed to be taken half the time.

The performance of the Livermore loops is consistent with that of the users' programs. Except for kernel 22, which has an extraordinary amount of conditional branching due to the particular EXP library function, near-optimal, and often times, optimal code is obtained. The MFLOPS rates achieved for the different loops, however, vary greatly. This is due to the difference in the available parallelism within the iterations of a loop.

There are two major factors that determine the maximum achievable MFLOPS rate: data dependency and the critical resource bottleneck.

1. Data dependency. Consider the following loop:

```
FOR i := 0 TO n DO BEGIN
    a := a * b + c;
END;
```

Because of data dependency, each multiplication and addition must be performed serially. As additions and multiplications are seven-stage pipelined, the maximum computation rate achievable by the machine for this loop is only 0.7 MFLOPS.

2. Critical resource bottleneck. A program that does not contain any multiplication operations can at most sustain a 5 MFLOPS execution rate on a Warp cell, since the multiplier is idle all the time. In general, the MFLOPS achievable for a particular program is limited by the ratio of the total number of additions and multiplications in the computation to the use count of the most heavily used resource.

Inter-iteration data dependency, or recurrences, do not necessarily mean that the code is serialized. This is one important advantage that VLIW architectures have over vector machines. As long as there are other operations that can execute in parallel with the serial computation, a high computation rate can still be obtained.

5. Comparison with trace scheduling

The primary idea in trace scheduling [10] is to optimize the more frequently executed traces. The procedure is as follows: first, identify the most likely execution trace, then compact the instructions in the trace as if they belong to one big basic block. The large block size means that there is plenty of opportunity to find independent activities that can be executed in parallel. The second step is to add compensation code at the entrances and exits of the trace to restore the semantics of the original program for other traces. This process is then repeated until all traces whose probabilities of execution are above some threshold are scheduled. A straightforward scheduling technique is used for the rest of the traces.

The strength of trace scheduling is that all operations for the entire trace are scheduled together, and all legal code motions are permitted. In fact, all other forms of optimization, such as common subexpression elimination across all operations in the trace can be performed. On the other hand, major execution traces must exist for this scheduling technique to succeed. In trace scheduling, the more frequently executed traces are scheduled first. The code motions performed optimize the more frequently executed traces, at the expense of the less frequently executed ones. This may be a problem in data dependent conditional statements. Also, one major criticism of trace scheduling is the possibility of exponential code explosion [17, 19, 22, 26].

The major difference between our approach and trace scheduling is that we retain the control structure of the computation. By retaining information on the control structure of the program, we can exploit the semantics of the different control constructs better, control the code motion and hence the code explosion. Another difference is that our scheduling algorithm is designed for block-structured constructs, whereas trace scheduling does not have similar restrictions. The following compares the two techniques in scheduling loop and conditional branching separately.

5.1. Loop branches

Trace scheduling is applied only to the body of a loop, that is, a major trace does not extend beyond the loop body boundary. To get enough parallelism in the trace, trace scheduling relies primarily on source code unrolling. At the end of each iteration in the original source is an exit out of the loop; the major trace is constructed by assuming that the exits off the loop are not taken. If the number of iterations is known at compile-time, then all but one exit off the loop are removed.

Software pipelining is more attractive than source code unrolling for two reasons. First, software pipelining offers the possibility of achieving optimal throughput. In unrolling, filling and draining the hardware pipelines at the beginning and the end of each iteration make optimal performance impossible. The second reason, a practical concern, is perhaps more important. In trace scheduling, the performance almost always improves as more iterations are unrolled. The degree of unrolling for a particular application often requires experimentation. As the degree of unrolling increases, so do the problem size and the final code size.

In software pipelining, the *object* code is sometimes unrolled at code emission time to implement modulo variable expansion. Therefore, the compilation time is unaffected. Furthermore, unlike source unrolling, there is an optimal degree of unrolling for each schedule, and can easily be determined when the schedule is complete.

5.2. Conditional statements

In the case of data dependent conditional statements, the premise that there is a most frequently executed trace is questionable. While it is easy to predict the outcome of a conditional branch at the end of an iteration in a loop, outcomes for all other branches are difficult to predict.

The generality of trace scheduling makes code explosion difficult to control. Some global code motions require operations scheduled in the main trace be duplicated in the less frequently executed traces. Since basic block boundaries are not visible when compacting a trace, code motions that require large amounts of copying, and may not even be significant in reducing the execution time, may be introduced.

Ellis showed that exponential code explosion can occur by reordering conditional statements that are data independent of each other [8]. Massive loop unrolling has a tendency to increase the number of possibly data independent conditional statements. Code explosion can be controlled by inserting additional constraints between branching operations. For example, Su et al. suggested restricting the motions of operations that are not on the critical path of the trace [26].

In our approach to scheduling conditional statements, the objective is to minimize the effect of conditional statements on parallel execution of other constructs. By modeling the conditional statement as one unit, we can software pipeline all innermost loops. The resources taken to execute the conditional statement may be as much as the sum of both branches. However, the amount of wasted cycles is bounded by the operations within the conditional statement.

6. Concluding remarks

This paper shows that near-optimal, and sometimes optimal, code can be generated for VLIW machines. We use a combination of two techniques: (1) software pipelining, a specialized scheduling technique for iterative constructs, and (2) hierarchical reduction, a simple, unified approach that allows multiple basic blocks to be manipulated like operations within a basic block. While software pipelining is the main reason for the speed up in programs, hierarchical reduction makes it possible to attain consistently good results on even programs containing conditional statements in innermost loops and innermost loops with small numbers of iterations. Our experience with the Warp compiler is that the generated code is comparable to, if not better than, handcrafted microcode.

The Warp processors do not have any specialized hardware support for software pipelining. Therefore, the results reported here are likely to apply to other data paths with similar degrees of parallelism. But what kind of performance can be obtained if we scale up the degree of parallelism and pipelining in the architecture? We observe that the limiting factor in the performance of Warp is the available parallelism among iterations in a loop. For those loops whose iterations are independent, scaling up the hardware is likely to give a similar factor of increase in performance. However, the speed of all other loops are limited by the cycle length in their precedence constraint graph. The control of all functional units by a central sequencer makes it difficult for VLIW architectures to exploit other forms of parallelism other than the parallelism within a loop. This suggests that there is a limit to the scalability of the VLIW architecture. Further experimentation is necessary to determine this limit.

Acknowledgments

The research reported in this paper is part of my Ph.D. thesis. I especially want to thank my thesis advisor, H. T. Kung, for his advice in the past years. I would like to thank all the members in the Warp project, and in particular, Thomas Gross for his effort in the W2 compiler. I also want to thank Jon Webb, C. H. Chang and P. S. Tseng for their help in obtaining the performance numbers.

References

1. Aiken, A. and Nicolau, A. Perfect Pipelining: A New Loop Parallelization Technique. Cornell University, Oct., 1987.

2. Annaratone, M., Bitz, F., Clune E., Kung H. T., Maulik, P., Ribas, H., Tseng, P., and Webb, J. Applications of Warp. Proc. Compcon Spring 87, San Francisco, Feb., 1987, pp. 272-275.

3. Annaratone, M., Bitz, F., Deutch, J., Harney, L., Kung, H. T., Maulik P. C., Tseng, P., and Webb, J. A. Applications Experience on Warp. Proc. 1987 National Computer Conference, AFIPS, Chicago, June, 1987, pp. 149-158.

4. Annaratone, M., Arnould, E., Gross, T., Kung, H. T., Lam, M., Menzilcioglu, O. and Webb, J. A. "The Warp Computer: Architecture, Implementation and Performance". *IEEE Transactions on Computers C-36*, 12 (December 1987).

5. Colwell, R. P., Nix, R. P., O'Donnell, J. J., Papworth, D. B., and Rodman, P. K. . A VLIW Architecture for a Trace Scheduling Compiler. Proc. Second Intl. Conf. on Architectural Support for Programming Languages and Operating Systems, Oct., 1987, pp. 180-192.

6. Dantzig, G. B., Blattner, W. O. and Rao, M. R. All Shortest Routes from a Fixed Origin in a Graph. Theory of Graphs, Rome, July, 1967, pp. 85-90.

7. Ebcioglu, Kemal. A Compilation Technique for Software Pipelining of Loops with Conditional Jumps. Proc. 20th Annual Workshop on Microprogramming, Dec., 1987.

8. Ellis, John R. *Bulldog: A Compiler for VLIW Architectures*. Ph.D. Th., Yale University, 1985.

9. Fisher, J. A. *The Optimization of Horizontal Microcode Within and Beyond Basic Blocks: An Application of Processor Scheduling with Resources*. Ph.D. Th., New York Univ., Oct. 1979.

10. Fisher, J. A. "Trace Scheduling: A Technique for Global Microcode Compaction". *IEEE Trans. on Computers C-30*, 7 (July 1981), 478-490.

11. Fisher, J. A., Ellis, J. R., Ruttenberg, J. C. and Nicolau, A. Parallel Processing: A Smart Compiler and a Dumb Machine. Proc. ACM SIGPLAN '84 Symp. on Compiler Construction, Montreal, Canada, June, 1984, pp. 37-47.

12. Fisher, J. A., Landskov, D. and Shriver, B. D. Microcode Compaction: Looking Backward and Looking Forward. Proc. 1981 National Computer Conference, 1981, pp. 95-102.

13. Floyd, R. W. "Algorithm 97: Shortest Path". *Comm. ACM 5*, 6 (1962), 345.

14. Garey, Michael R. and Johnson, David S.. *Computers and Intractability A Guide to the Theory of NP-Completeness*. Freeman, 1979.

15. Gross, T. and Lam, M. Compilation for a High-performance Systolic Array. Proc. ACM SIGPLAN 86 Symposium on Compiler Construction, June, 1986, pp. 27-38.

16. Hsu, Peter. *Highly Concurrent Scalar Processing*. Ph.D. Th., University of Illinois at Urbana-Champaign, 1986.

17. Isoda, Sadahiro, Kobayashi, Yoshizumi, and Ishida, Toru. "Global Compaction of Horizontal Microprograms Based on the Generalized Data Dependency Graph". *IEEE Trans. on Computers c-32*, 10 (October 1983), 922-933.

18. Kuck, D. J., Kuhn, R. H., Padua, D. A., Leasure, B. and Wolfe, M. Dependence Graphs and Compiler Optimizations. Proc. ACM Symposium on Principles of Programming Languages, January, 1981, pp. 207-218.

19. Lah, J. and Atkin, E. Tree Compaction of Microprograms. Proc. 16th Annual Workshop on Microprogramming, Oct., 1982, pp. 23-33.

20. Lam, Monica. Compiler Optimizations for Asynchronous Systolic Array Programs. Proc. Fifteenth Annual ACM Symposium on Principles of Programming Languages, Jan., 1988.

21. Lam, Monica. *A Systolic Array Optimizing Compiler*. Ph.D. Th., Carnegie Mellon University, May 1987.

22. Linn, Joseph L. SRDAG Compaction - A Generalization of Trace Scheduling to Increase the Use of Global Context Information. Proc. 16th Annual Workshop on Microprogramming, 1983, pp. 11-22.

23. McMahon, F. H. Lawrence Livermore National Laboratory FORTRAN Kernels: MFLOPS.

24. Patel, Janak H. and Davidson, Edward S. Improving the Throughput of a Pipeline by Insertion of Delays. Proc. 3rd Annual Symposium on Computer Architecture, Jan., 1976, pp. 159-164.

25. Rau, B. R. and Glaeser, C. D. Some Scheduling Techniques and an Easily Schedulable Horizontal Architecture for High Performance Scientific Computing. Proc. 14th Annual Workshop on Microprogramming, Oct., 1981, pp. 183-198.

26. Su, B., Ding, S. and Jin, L. An Improvement of Trace Scheduling for Global Microcode Compaction. Proc. 17th Annual Workshop in Microprogramming, Dec., 1984, pp. 78-85.

27. Su, B., Ding, S., Wang, J. and Xia, J. GURPR – A Method for Global Software Pipelining. Proc. 20th Annual Workshop on Microprogramming, Dec., 1987, pp. 88-96.

28. Su, B., Ding, S. and Xia, J. URPR – An Extension of URCR for Software Pipeline. Proc. 19th Annual Workshop on Microprogramming, Oct., 1986, pp. 104-108.

29. Tarjan, R. E. "Depth first search and linear graph algorithms". *SIAM J. Computing 1*, 2 (1972), 146-160.

30. Touzeau, R. F. A Fortran Compiler for the FPS-164 Scientific Computer. Proc. ACM SIGPLAN '84 Symp. on Compiler Construction, June, 1984, pp. 48-57.

31. Weiss, S. and Smith, J. E. A Study of Scalar Compilation Techniques for Pipelined Supercomputers. Proc. Second Intl. Conf. on Architectural Support for Programming Languages and Operating Systems, Oct., 1987, pp. 105-109.

32. Wood, Graham. Global Optimization of Microprograms Through Modular Control Constructs. Proc. 12th Annual Workshop in Microprogramming, 1979, pp. 1-6.

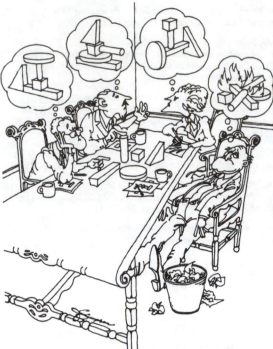

The Cydra 5 Departmental Supercomputer

Design Philosophies, Decisions, and Trade-offs

Reprinted from *Computer*, Vol. 22, No. 1, January 1989, pages 12-35. Copyright © 1989 by The Institute of Electrical and Electronics Engineers, Inc. All rights reserved.

B. Ramakrishna Rau, David W.L. Yen,
Wei Yen, and Ross A. Towle
Cydrome, Inc.

The Cydra 5 Departmental Super-computer targets small work groups or departments of scientists and engineers.[1] It costs about the same as a high-end superminicomputer ($500,000 to $1 million), but it can achieve about one-third to one-half the performance of a supercomputer costing $10 to $20 million. This results from using high-speed, air-cooled, emitter-coupled logic technology in a product that includes many architectural innovations.

The Cydra 5 is a heterogeneous multiprocessor system. The two types of processors are functionally specialized for the different components of the work load found in a departmental setting. The Cydra 5 numeric processor, based on the company's directed-dataflow architecture,[2] provides consistently high performance on a broader class of numerical computations than do processors based on other architectures. It is aided by the high-bandwidth main memory system with its stride-insensitive performance. The interactive processors offload all nonnumeric work from the numeric processor, leaving it free to spend all its time on the numerical application. Lastly, the I/O processors permit high-bandwidth I/O transactions

To meet price-performance targets for a new minisupercomputer, a team of computer scientists conducted an exhaustive—and enlightening—investigation into the relative merits of available architectures.

with minimal involvement from the interactive or numeric processors.

A version of this article appeared in *Proc. 22nd Hawaii Int'l Conf. on Systems Sciences*, Jan. 3-6, 1989, Kailua-Kona, Hawaii.

The Cydra 5 grew from eight years of research and development dating back to work done at TRW Array Processors and at ESL (a subsidiary of TRW). The polycyclic architecture[3] developed at TRW/ESL is a precursor to the directed-dataflow architecture developed at Cydrome starting in 1984. The common theme linking both efforts is the desire to support the powerful and elegant dataflow model of computation with as simple a hardware platform as possible.

The driving force behind the development of the Cydra 5 was the desire for increased performance over superminis on numerically intensive computations, but with the following constraint: The user should not have to discard the software, the set of algorithms, the training, or the techniques acquired over the years. As a result, the user would be able to move up in performance from the supermini to the minisuper in a transparent fashion. This transparency is important for a product such as the Cydra 5, which is aimed at the growth phase of the minisupercomputer market. Such a product must cater to a broader and less forgiving user group than the pioneers and early adopters who purchased first-generation minisupercomputers. Ideally, a departmental supercomputer will display none of the idiosyncrasies of typical supercomputers and minisupercomputers and, in fact, will project the "feel" of a conventional minicomputer, except for its much higher performance on numerically intensive tasks.

Cydra 5 system architecture

From the outset we were determined not to build an attached processor. The clumsiness of the host processor/attached processor approach leads to difficulty of use and loss of performance. The programmer must manage two computer systems, each with its own operating system and its own separate memory. The programmer must explicitly manage the movement of programs and data back and forth between the two systems. Since the data transfer path is slow relative to the processing speed of both computers, it becomes a performance bottleneck. Program development tools for the attached processor, such as compilers and linkers, run on the host. To avoid an unhealthy dependence on a single brand of host computer, this software must be maintained on multiple brands of host computer.

A self-sufficient, stand-alone computer has none of these problems. On the other hand, it assumes the burden of performing all of the general-purpose, nonnumeric work—such as networking, developing programs, and running the operating system—in addition to the numerically intensive jobs for which it was originally intended. As we will show later, the tradeoffs made in designing a supercomputer and a general-purpose processor are often diametrically opposed. As a result, each ends up being the most cost effective for a different class of jobs. Whereas a supercomputer may have 20 to 30 times the performance of a general-purpose processor on numerically intensive tasks, it may have only three or four times the performance on general-purpose tasks. When price is considered as well, the supercomputer ends up having poorer cost-performance than the general-purpose processor on nonnumeric tasks, since its expensive floating-point hardware is irrelevant.

We wanted the Cydra 5 to be not only a stand-alone computer but also a departmental supercomputer. By this we mean a number of things. It should be affordable to a small group or department of engineers or scientists, which means an entry-level price under $500,000. It should be easy to use by such a group and not require a "high priesthood" of skilled systems analysts catering to the idiosyncrasies of the machine. Lastly, it should be designed to handle *all* of the work load created by a department, not just the numerical tasks. As noted, this includes tasks such as compiling, text editing, executing the operating system kernel, and networking—tasks for which a supercomputer architecture is not cost effective.

These goals led to one of the key decisions regarding the Cydra 5: to have a numeric processor, highly optimized for numerical computing, and a tightly integrated general-purpose subsystem that would handle the nonnumeric work load. In other words the Cydra 5 was to be a heterogeneous multiprocessor, with each processor functionally specialized for a different, but complementary, class of jobs.

Initially, we planned to acquire a general-purpose processor on an original-equipment-manufacturer basis and integrate into it a numeric processor of our own design. We had determined that we needed about 10 million instructions per second of computation capability from the general-purpose processor to handle the I/O load imposed by the application running on the numeric processor, as well as the rest of the general-purpose work load. We soon discovered that a superminicomputer in this performance range would itself have a list price of about $500,000—the targeted price for the entire Cydra 5! We found consistently that lower priced general-purpose computation engines whose performance and price were closer to what we wanted had underdeveloped I/O capability by departmental supercomputer standards. This situation remains unchanged, if you examine the current crop of workstations and super-workstations. The only workable scheme that met both our cost and performance constraints was to design our own general-purpose subsystem consisting of multiple microprocessor-based processors.

Following a careful evaluation, we chose the as yet unannounced Motorola 68020 microprocessor. The various RISC (reduced instruction set computer) microprocessors were only on the drawing boards at the time. Around the 16-MHz 68020 we designed a fast interactive processor incorporating a 16-Kbyte, zero-wait-state cache. A scheme developed by two of the authors[4] maintained cache coherency in this multiprocessor environment.

We could not afford to develop an operating system from scratch, so we selected Unix, the only nonproprietary operating system available. Every workstation and minisupercomputer vendor has had to make the same choice for the same reason. As a result, Unix has become the de facto standard operating system for the engineering and scientific community. The more difficult choice was between the two competing flavors of Unix: Berkeley 4.2 and AT&T System V. Although Berkeley 4.2 was clearly dominant in 1984-85, we believed that with the addition of virtual memory and networking, and with AT&T's more aggressive support, System V would pull ahead by the time Cydra 5 was introduced. Accordingly, we took a deep breath and jumped on the System V bandwagon.

Although Cydrix, Cydrome's implementation of Unix, complies with the System V interface definition, it does contain a number of extensions, primarily for performance reasons. For use with a supercomputer, Unix is a rather low-performance, uniprocessor operating system. We rewrote the kernel significantly to symmetrically (not in a master-slave fashion) distribute it over multiple interactive processors so that one or more processors could be simultaneously executing in kernel mode. This allowed us to bring the aggregate computing capability of multiple processors to bear on the task of supporting the I/O for the numeric processor application. The file and I/O systems also received numerous enhancements.

As a consequence of this series of design decisions, the Cydra 5 Departmental Supercomputer is two computers in one: a numeric processor that is the functional equivalent of other minisupercomputers, and a general-purpose multiprocessor that plays the role of a front-end system (Figure 1). However, these two subsystems are very tightly integrated. They share the same memory system and peripherals and are managed by the same operating system. Because of this, the Cydra 5 with Cydrix presents the illusion of a simple uniprocessor system to the user who does not wish to be bothered with what is inside the black box.

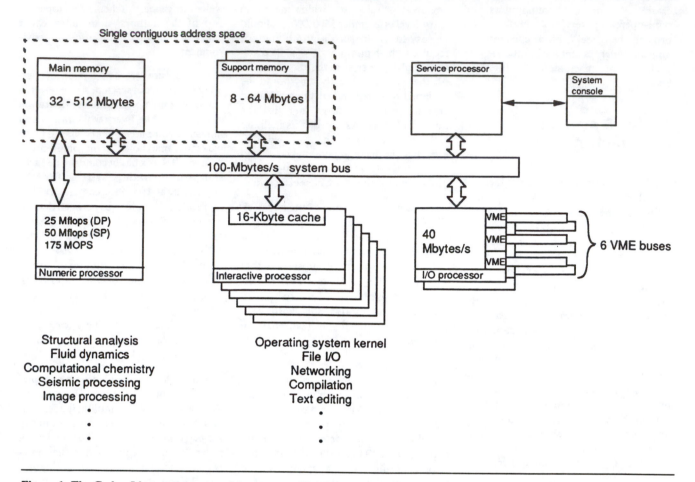

Figure 1. The Cydra 5 heterogeneous multiprocessor. The general-purpose subsystem consists of up to six interactive processors, up to 64 Mbytes of support memory, one or two I/O processors, and the service processor/system console connected over a 100-Mbyte/s system bus. Each I/O processor handles up to three VME buses, to which the peripheral controllers are attached. Also connected to the system bus, via a 100-Mbyte/s port, is the pseudorandomly interleaved main memory. The numeric processor has three dedicated ports into the main memory, each providing 100-Mbyte/s bandwidth. One of these is for instructions; the other two are for data. The main memory and support memory share a common address space and are both accessible from any processor.

The directed-dataflow architecture

Assuming the use of the fastest reasonable technology, any further increase in performance requires the effective exploitation of parallelism in one form or another.

Fine-grained versus coarse-grained parallelism. There are two major forms of parallelism: coarse-grained and fine-grained. Coarse-grained parallelism, popularly referred to as parallel processing, means multiple processes running on multiple processors in a cooperative fash-

ion to perform the job of a single program. In contrast, fine-grained parallelism exists within a process at the level of the individual operations (such as adds and multiplies) that constitute the program. Vector, SIMD (single-instruction, multiple-data), and the attached-processor, or VLIW (very long instruction word), architectures are examples of architectures that use fine-grained parallelism.

Coarse-grained parallelism is complementary to fine-grained parallelism in that they can be used in conjunction. However, coarse-grained parallelism is not user transparent, since state-of-the-art compilers cannot, except in limited situations, take a sequential program written in a lan-

guage such as Fortran and automatically partition it into multiple parallel processes. The user must explicitly restructure the program to capitalize on this type of parallelism. Since this did not satisfy our criteria for ease of use, we focused on the exploitation of fine-grained parallelism.

A bottom-up perspective. The final objective is to minimize the execution time of any given program. We can express this execution time T as

$$T = N \times C \times S$$

where N is the total number of instructions that must be executed, C is the average number of processor cycles per instruction, and S is the number of seconds per processor cycle. To a first approximation, N, C, and S are affected primarily by the compiler's optimization capability, the instruction set architecture, and the implementation technology, respectively. However, the picture is more complicated, and decisions that decrease one factor may end up increasing another.

The techniques used to minimize T have been many and varied. For general-purpose processors, the traditional approach was to reduce N at the expense of a smaller increase in C. The general thrust was to better utilize the micro-parallelism present in horizontally microcoded machines by defining more complex instructions with more internal micro-parallelism in the hope that N would decrease more sharply than C would increase. This approach is now termed CISC (complex instruction set computer). By contrast, the RISC approach focuses on the use of very simple, hardwired, pipelined instructions exclusively to reduce C and S. The resulting increase in N is minimized by the use of code optimization techniques in the compiler for an overall reduction in T. Although both approaches have been successful at different times and under different circumstances, they are not sufficient to meet the performance objectives of supercomputers.

The emphasis in supercomputers is on execution of arithmetic (particularly floating-point) operations. The starting point for all supercomputer architectures is multiple, pipelined, floating-point functional units, in addition to any needed for integer operations and memory accesses. The fundamental objective is to keep them as busy as possible. Assuming this will be achieved, the hardware must be equipped to provide two input operands per functional unit and to accept one result per functional unit per cycle. Furthermore, since the results of one operation will be required as inputs to subsequent operations, some form of interconnection is needed between the result and input buses. Finally, since results are not always used immediately after generation, storage in the form of one or more register files is needed. Figure 2a shows the data paths of a generic supercomputer. The details, of course, vary from one machine to the next; the number and types of functional units, the number of register files, and the structure of the interconnect can all be different.

Interesting and rather fundamental

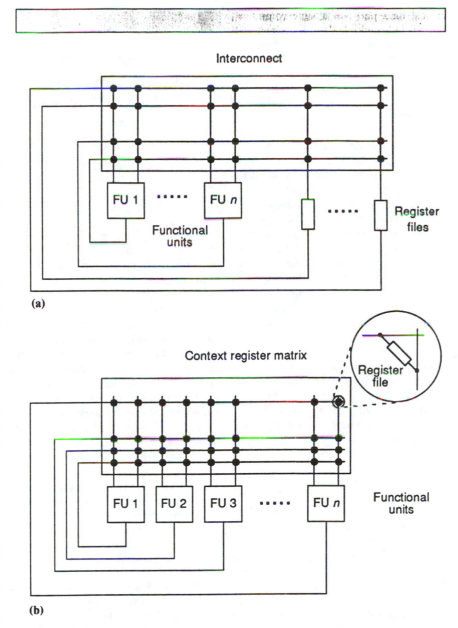

(a)

(b)

Figure 2. (a) Generic supercomputer data paths. (b) Generic directed-dataflow-processor data paths. Each row of cross-point register files in the context register matrix can be written into by only a single functional unit, and all register files in a single row have identical contents. Since each of the register files in a row can be read in parallel, each row is logically equivalent to a single multiported register file capable of one write and multiple reads per cycle. Each of the cross-point register files can be written to by only a single functional unit and can be read by only a single input of a single functional unit—the one associated with that column of cross-point register files. This, along with the property that each register file is capable of one read and one write each cycle, guarantees conflict-free access to the context registers for every functional unit for inputs as well as outputs.

differences exist between the data paths of a scalar processor and those of a supercomputer. In the scalar processor the critical data paths consist of the circuit from the general-purpose registers (GPRs), through the integer arithmetic-logic unit or the cache, and back to the GPRs. This makes it relatively easy to keep the physical distances small, the pipelining moderate, and the cycle time short. In contrast, critical data paths in a supercomputer must include multiple floating-point pipelines, large numbers of register files, and a complex interconnect. The physical distances are necessarily larger, and there are more electrical loads to be driven on each bus. Both factors cause a larger fraction of the cycle to be consumed in merely transferring data from one point to another. This makes it necessary to increase the depth of pipelining to avoid compromising the cycle time. Thus the trade-off is short pipeline latencies and better sequential performance versus multiple, deep pipelines and better parallel performance.

All the hardware in a supercomputer can be justified only if it is kept well utilized. But keeping all these pipelines busy requires that multiple operations be issued (as opposed to being in execution) at every cycle. This is impossible in conventional scalar architectures, since a maximum of one instruction is issued per cycle.

Two styles of uniprocessor architecture have been developed to circumvent this bottleneck. One is the vector architecture, which attempts to reduce N by the use of very complex instructions—vector instructions—where a single vector instruction does the work of multiple, identical scalar operations. Once a few vector operations have been launched, multiple operations are issued per cycle, one each by every vector operation that is active. This is philosophically akin to the CISC approach and suffers from the standard problem of complex instructions: They work well when they exactly fit the job that must be done, but they are useless if the task differs even slightly.

The second, more flexible, approach is an architecture in which multiple operations can be issued in a single instruction.[2,3,5-7] We can view this as an extension of the SIMD architecture; instead of the same opcode's being applied to all the pairs of input data, as in SIMD, distinct opcodes are used. The formal name for such an architecture might be single instruction, multiple operation, multiple data (SIMOMD), or MultiOp for short. Other terms used for such an architecture include horizontal[3] or very long instruction word (VLIW).[5] We can also view this as a generalization of the RISC architecture, where C is reduced to less than 1 by issuing multiple operations (or multiple instructions, from a scalar processor point of view) per cycle.

When we started in 1984, MultiOp execution was used in a number of attached-processor products—for example, the

FPS-164.[6] Expert programmers were able to coax much better sustained performance out of these products than could be achieved with vector processors having the same peak performance. But programming these products for high performance had all the complexities associated with microprogramming, and some more besides.[3,8] The problem resulted from the processors' having been designed entirely from a bottom-up, hardware perspective, with no thought to how they were to be programmed or the obstacles the compiler writer would face. While we felt it constituted a step in the right direction, it was clear to us that the attached-processor architecture was unacceptable. Although the general hardware structure of the directed-dataflow architecture was dictated by the considerations discussed above, the subtler aspects resulted from a top-down thought process driven by our model of computation.

The model of computation. Although there is a tendency to categorize architectures superficially by their hardware attributes (pipelined or VLIW, for example), we believe that the underlying models of computation and usage are what really matter. They determine the context within which all of the design decisions are made, and they lead to architectural features that, though subtle, have a major impact on the performance and breadth of a product's applicability. Just as pipelining has been applied to a number of quite different architectures, so too we find that the ability to issue multiple operations per cycle has been used in at least three types of architectures with quite distinct underlying models of computation: the microprogrammed attached-processor architectures, the VLIW architecture, and the directed-dataflow architecture.

The attached processors borrowed their model of computation from micropro-

gramming, where the perspective is very bottom-up. In microprogramming, the hardware is viewed as a collection of functional units and buses, and the task of the microprogrammer is to determine on a cycle-by-cycle basis which functional unit inputs and outputs connect to which buses. The microprogram is generally viewed as a sequence of micro-operations, and any parallelism needed to exploit a horizontal microarchitecture is exposed on a localized, "peephole" basis. Microprograms for instruction set interpretation put very little emphasis on iterative constructs (loops) but a lot on branching. When an architecture with these underlying assumptions is adopted for numerical processing (where the emphasis is on loops), a great deal of programming complexity results if one wishes to fully exploit the opportunities for parallelism.[3]

Although the VLIW school of thought, too, has its roots in microprogramming, the VLIW architecture is properly viewed as the logical extension to the scalar RISC architecture. The underlying model is one of scalar code to be executed, but with more than one operation issued per cycle. The obstacle to good performance is the high frequency of branches in typical programs, a problem common to microprogramming. Consequently, trace scheduling,[9] originally developed for microprogramming, is used with VLIW processors. No special consideration—beyond the standard scalar processing compiler technique of loop unrolling—is given to loops in software, and none whatsoever is given in hardware. Using trace-scheduling techniques, VLIW can provide good speedup on scalar code, and when loop unrolling is used, some further speedup on iterative computations occurs as' well. However, given the lack of architectural emphasis on loops, VLIW does not do as well on vectorizable computations as a vector processor does.

A supercomputer architecture must do well on all types of numerical computation it might encounter. This includes straight-line or sequential code as well as branching scalar code; but clearly of equal or greater importance are the iterative constructs that constitute the heart of numerical computations. Loops, whether they are vectorizable or of the type that contains recurrences, conditional branching, or irregular references to memory, must get explicit support in the hardware. The vector architecture provides hardware support, but only for a limited subset of loops (those without recurrences and conditional branches), reflecting a restrictive model of computation. If greater generality is required in the capabilities of the architecture, a more general model of computation is needed, one that does well not only on scalar and vector code like the VLIW and vector architectures, respectively, but also on the important class of loops that possess parallelism but are not vectorizable.

The dataflow model of computation. By making execution of an operation contingent only on its inputs' being available and a functional unit's being free to execute the operation, the dataflow model of computation exposes and exploits every bit of parallelism in the computation regardless of its form.[10] Thus it provides an excellent basis for a fine-grained parallel architecture of broad applicability.

However, most dataflow research assumes that the program is written in a dataflow or functional language, whereas we had to face the real world of Fortran programs. Consequently, we had to base our architecture on an extended dependency graph model that included the concept of memory and the corresponding memory read and write operations. This, in turn, required that the model include the concept of antidependency and output dependency,[11] in addition to that of data dependency. Also, to reflect the rather unstructured nature of Fortran control constructs, we had to include a richer control dependency model that went beyond nested IF-THEN-ELSEs. Nevertheless, the basic philosophy was unchanged; an operation is a candidate for execution as soon as all its incoming dependencies, of all types, have been satisfied. Notwithstanding the differences between the dataflow model of computation and our dependency graph model, we will, for the sake of convenience, refer to our model of computation as a dataflow model.

The dataflow model has the richness needed to yield parallelism on both scalar and iterative computation. In scalar code, parallelism is restricted by the presence of conditional branches and their associated control dependencies. Dataflow gets around this problem with a mode of operation known as *eager execution*, which causes operations to be executed before it is certain that their execution is needed (Figures 3a-3f). This is equivalent to selectively removing certain control dependence arcs to increase the parallelism.

In iterative computations, dataflow dynamically unrolls a loop the same num-

> ## The dataflow model has the richness needed to yield parallelism on both scalar and iterative computation.

ber of times that the loop was supposed to be executed.[10] This generates the maximum parallelism possible, limited only by the inherent dependencies in the computation. (The amount of this parallelism actually used depends on the number of functional units present.) The dataflow architecture's ability to exploit whatever parallelism exists in all of these constructs makes it the architecture best able to exploit all of the fine-grained parallelism existing in programs. Furthermore, since parallelism is achieved without having to make any algorithmic changes to the program, the dataflow architecture delivers performance increases transparently. For these reasons the dataflow architecture serves as the basis for the Cydra 5.

Directed dataflow. The directed-dataflow architecture is also significantly influenced by another philosophy, one of moving complexity and functionality out of hardware and into software whenever possible; this is the cornerstone of the RISC concept as well. The benefits of this philosophy are reduced hardware cost and often the ability to make better decisions at compile time than can be made at runtime. In the directed-dataflow architecture, the compiler makes most decisions regarding the scheduling of operations at compile time rather than at runtime—but with the objective of emulating faithfully the manner in which a hypothetical dataflow machine with the same number of functional units would execute a particular program.

The compiler takes a program and first creates the corresponding dataflow graph. It then enforces the rules of dataflow execution, with full knowledge of the execution latency of each operation, to produce a schedule that indicates exactly when and where each operation will be performed. While scheduling at compile time, the compiler can examine the whole program,

in effect looking forward into the execution. It thus creates a better schedule than might have been possible with runtime scheduling. An instruction for the directed-dataflow machine consists of a time slice out of this schedule, that is, all operations that the schedule specifies for initiation at the same time. Such an instruction causes multiple operations to be issued in a single instruction.

So far, this is the same as any other VLIW processor. However, more than the ability to issue multiple operations per cycle is needed to efficiently support the dataflow model of computation in a compiler-directed fashion, especially when executing loops. Specifically, the directed-dataflow architecture provides two architectural features: the context register matrix and conditional scheduling control.

The context register matrix. Unlike the generic structure shown in Figure 2a, a directed-dataflow machine combines the register storage and the interconnect between functional unit outputs and inputs into a single entity known as the context register matrix, as shown in Figure 2b. In general the interconnect structure can be viewed as a sparse crossbar with certain cross-points absent but with a register file at each cross-point present. The context register matrix guarantees conflict-free access to the context registers for every functional unit. This in turn guarantees that once a schedule has been prepared by the compiler, it will not be rendered infeasible because of contention in getting data into or out of the context registers, which is one of the fundamental problems with the attached-processor architectures.[3]

When executing loops in a maximally parallel dataflow fashion, each iteration is viewed as a distinct computation executing in parallel with the other iterations. As with similar situations where the same code is being executed by distinct parallel computations, each iteration must have its own context so that when two iterations apparently refer to the same variable or, in this case, the same register (since they are both executing the same code), the physical locations actually accessed are distinct. When concurrent processes are forked, this is achieved by providing each process with a duplicate name space. In the case of recursive invocations of the same procedure, this is handled by providing separate stack frames. Each invocation's reference to a particular local variable is in the context of its own stack frame. Like-

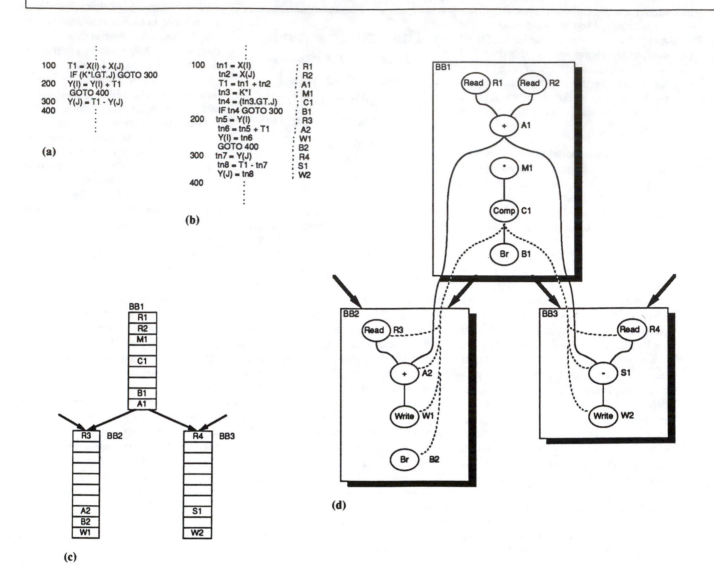

Figure 3. (a) A fragment of Fortran code. (b) Expansion of the code into individual operations with a label on the right-hand side for each operation. The scalar variables K, I, and J are assumed to be in registers already. (c) Sequential code schedule assuming a seven-cycle latency for memory reads and a two-cycle latency for all other operations. The code fragment consists of three basic blocks. BB2 and BB3 can be entered from BB1 as well as from elsewhere. A traversal of this code fragment takes 19 cycles. Note the scheduling of operations in the delay slots of the delayed branch. (d) The dataflow graph for this code fragment. Solid arcs are data dependencies. Dashed arcs are control dependencies that enable or disable operations, depending on the Boolean result of the comparison C1. Note that branch operations have no role in the dataflow model of computation. (e) Schedules resulting from the execution of the dataflow graph (assuming the ability to initiate two memory operations and one other operation per cycle). Operation A1 from BB1 is initiated in parallel with the execution of either BB2 or BB3. The extent of the overlap between the execution of BB1 with the execution of either BB2 or BB3 is determined by the control dependency from C1 to R3 or R4, which determines whether BB2 or BB3 should be executed. (f) Eager execution of R3 or R4 results from the removal of the control dependency from C1. Now both R3 and R4 are initiated before it has been determined whether BB2 or BB3 is to be executed. As a result the total execution time is reduced. (g) Directed-dataflow code that achieves the same effect as in (e). Operation A1 has been moved from BB1 into both BB2 and BB3. However, to preserve the original semantics, it should be executed only if BB2 or BB3 was entered from BB1. Therefore, both copies of A1 have the predicate corresponding to BB1 even though they are in BB2 and BB3. (h) Directed-dataflow code that performs the eager execution of R3 and R4 by moving them up into BB1. (They must also be copied into all basic blocks from which they can be entered.) The total execution time for this fragment of code is now 12 cycles.

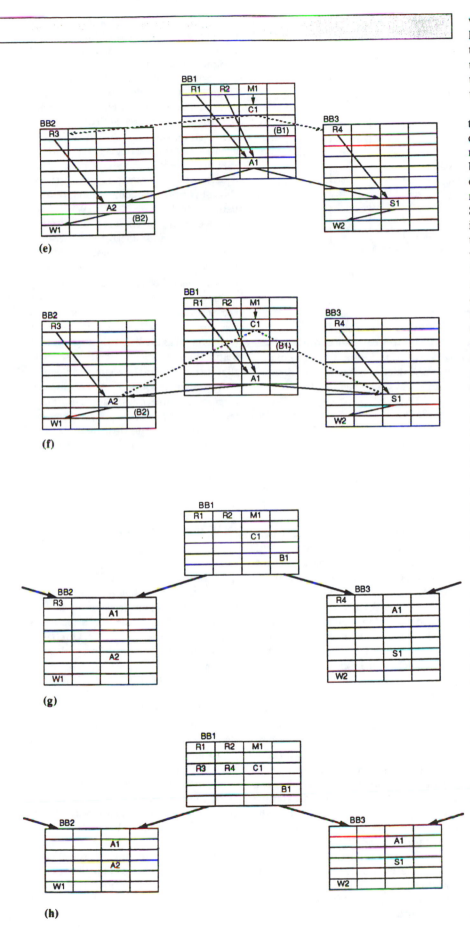

(e)

(f)

(g)

(h)

wise, the maximally parallel execution of loop iterations requires that each iteration's register references be within the context of the corresponding *iteration frame*, that is, a set of registers allocated to a particular iteration.

The directed-dataflow architecture has the architectural facilities needed to dynamically allocate iteration frames at runtime and the requisite addressing capabilities to reference registers in both the current iteration frame and, in the case of recurrences, in previous iteration frames. Surprisingly, these architectural facilities incur only a modest hardware cost, namely the ability to reference the context registers with an instruction-specified displacement from a base register containing the *iteration frame pointer* (IFP). Since the IFP is decremented each time a new iteration is initiated, each iteration of the loop accesses a distinct set of physical registers. Any result computed during the same or a previous iteration can be accessed by using the appropriate displacement from the current value of the IFP. This displacement can be computed by the compiler, since it knows the difference between the current value of the IFP and the value at the time the result was generated, as well as the original displacement from that value of the IFP. Some interesting register allocation techniques in the compiler are central to the efficient use of the context registers, but they are beyond the scope of this article and will be reported elsewhere.

Conditional scheduling control. In a sequential model of computation, the program consists of a set of basic blocks, each containing a list of instructions. Only one basic block is active at any one time. The equivalent dataflow view is that a program consists of a set of basic blocks, each consisting of a dependency graph of operations executed in a parallel fashion. Conceptually, any given operation has two types of incoming dependencies: the data (input operands) dependencies, which determine *when* the operation can be issued, and a control dependency from an operation—in another basic block—that computes the predicate. The predicate determines whether the operations in a basic block are to be issued at all. The predicate is true and the operations are issued if and only if control would have flowed to that basic block in the corresponding sequential program.

Since an operation can be executed as soon as its data and control dependencies

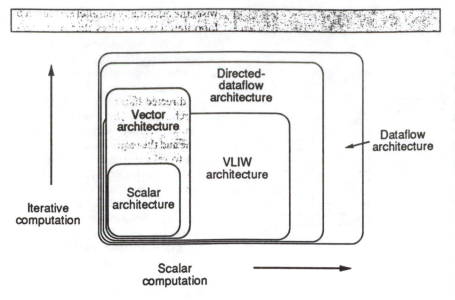

Figure 4. Relationship between various uniprocessor architectures. On vectorizable loops, directed-dataflow is slightly better than the vector architecture, which is better than VLIW, which in turn is better than the scalar architecture. On sequential code, directed dataflow is at least as good as VLIW, which is better than both the vector and scalar architectures. On nonvectorizable loops, directed dataflow is significantly better than all three architectures.

have been satisfied, it is possible to have multiple basic blocks active at the same time (Figures 3e and 3f), particularly in the case of loops, whether they have conditional branching within the body of the loop or not. This generates the desired parallelism but is possible only because dataflow can have multiple loci of control active simultaneously. The directed-dataflow architecture has the goal of achieving the same effect as dataflow, but with a single locus of control. This is achieved by including in each basic block operations from other basic blocks that should be executing in parallel (Figures 3g and 3h). This is a form of code motion, in this case for enhancing the parallelism in the program.

An explicit predicate is unnecessary in the sequential model of computation, since all operations in a single basic block, by definition, have the same predicate. This predicate is implied by the fact that the program branched to this basic block; that is, it decided that this basic block was to be executed. Thus the predicate's being true and the flow of control's arriving at the basic block are synonymous.

But these two concepts must be decoupled in the case of directed dataflow, since a basic block can contain operations that

in the sequential program would have been in another basic block, and thus under a different predicate. Consequently, each operation is provided with a third input—the predicate—in addition to the two normal ones. An operation is issued only if control flows to its basic block and the predicate is true. The predicate input specifier specifies a register in a Boolean register file, which, for historical reasons, is termed the iteration control register (ICR) file. Boolean values, which result from compare operations, may be transferred into the ICR. In loops, each iteration generates predicates corresponding to the conditional branches (including the loop exit conditional) within the loop body. Therefore, the ICR too must support the capability for allocating iteration frames.

With hardware support in the form of the context register matrix and conditional scheduling control, the compiler can generate code for the directed-dataflow machine that retains the parallelism of the dataflow architecture. At the same time, it capitalizes on the efficiencies of moving scheduling from runtime to compile time. It is this architectural support for the dataflow model of computation that sets directed dataflow apart from other VLIW architectures.

Comparison with other fine-grained architectures. Figure 4 shows the relationship between various architectures that exploit fine-grained parallelism. It uses two criteria: performance on iterative computations and performance on scalar code. At opposite ends of the spectrum are the (dynamically scheduled) dataflow architecture, which can exploit all the parallelism, and the scalar architecture, which exploits none of it. The vector architecture is better than the scalar on the restricted class of vectorizable computations, but no better on scalar code. The VLIW architecture does better than the scalar architecture on scalar code and much better on iterative computations, but it does not do as well as the vector architecture on vectorizable loops. This is because the loop-unrolling techniques that it uses can yield only short vector performance levels. On scalar codes the directed-dataflow architecture is at least as good as the VLIW architecture and better than the vector architecture. It is slightly better than the vector architecture on vectorizable loops, since strip mining (Figure 5) is unnecessary, and it is far better on nonvectorizable loops. Directed dataflow, as a result of its architectural support for dataflow, is better than the VLIW architecture on iterative computations.

Numeric processor decisions and trade-offs

Technology selection. The choice of implementation technology was perhaps the most important decision we had to make, since it fundamentally affected all other decisions and trade-offs. Our back-of-the-envelope calculations indicated that the same architecture could be implemented in TTL/CMOS at two-fifths the performance of an emitter-coupled logic (ECL) implementation and two-thirds the cost (a 100-nanosecond rather than a 40-nanosecond cycle). If cost and performance had been the only considerations, it would have been a simple decision, since our corporate objective was to serve the high end of the departmental supercomputer market. However, we realized that opting for an ECL implementation would preclude the use of VLSI floating-point chips such as the Weitek chips and that it would require the design of more logic and more boards, as well as more development time—hence, more nonrecurring expenditures.

Also, some people at that time believed ECL was a doomed technology, that CMOS would catch up in performance—and at a fraction of the cost. Although this belief was, and still is, incorrect, there was tremendous pressure from the investment community to build a TTL/CMOS product and even to discard some of the functionality and build a subset of what we were planning. However, we were convinced that the low end of the market would be very crowded with minisupercomputers and array processor products. (This has, in fact, come to pass, except that superworkstations have replaced array processors as the threat at the low end.) We wanted to be above the general melee, so we decided to stick with our business plan and implement an ECL product. We now feel vindicated in that decision, since more and more computer vendors are currently moving to this technology. At a 40-nanosecond cycle time, this yielded a processor with a peak performance of 25 million floating-point operations per second (Mflops) with 64-bit operands, 50 Mflops with 32-bit operands, and 175 million operations per second overall.

In the interest of reducing the nonrecurring development costs and the development risk, we made another important decision: By and large, we would use off-the-shelf ECL components. Gate arrays would be used only in certain performance-critical parts of the design, and even so, not for control logic. Since this was the first implementation of a directed-dataflow processor, the decision, even in retrospect, was correct. But it had many unpleasant consequences. The 1985 vintage of standard ECL logic was at a very low level of integration. This meant that the numeric processor would occupy a lot of real estate. Since manufacturing considerations limited us to boards of roughly 18 inches on a side, the numeric processor would have to be spread out over a large number of boards. This led to a snowballing effect; large amounts of buffer logic were required to drive signals between the many boards. This in turn increased the total amount of logic even further. If we had had the option of implementing the numeric processor entirely with gate arrays, we could have reduced its size by a factor of three or four.

Number of functional units. Our performance goal was to be able to initiate one floating-point add and one floating-point multiply every 40-nanosecond cycle, using two separate pipelined functional units.

Additional functional units were required to support these two floating-point pipelines. The first issue was the number of ports to memory that were needed. Our thinking here was influenced by the fact that our model of computation was dataflow and not vectors. We viewed the entire body of the loop as a single entity rather than as a number of separate vector operations. Thus we required memory reads and writes only for the array inputs and outputs, not for the scalar temporaries, which on a vector machine would be converted to vector temporaries. This reduced the relative number of memory operations needed on our machine (Figure 5).

Our program statistics indicated that within innermost loops the balance between memory bandwidth and floating-point computation capability was between one and three memory operations per pair of floating-point operations. Although certain important computations such as SAXPY (the addition of one vector to another one that has been multiplied by a scalar) require one and a half memory operations per floating-point operation, we felt that this was an expensive luxury in hardware and that the need was not statistically frequent enough to warrant the expense. Also, half a memory operation per floating-point operation seemed entirely inadequate. So, given the existence of two floating-point functional units, we decided to have two ports to memory. Since it is necessary to compute an address for each memory operation, typically to increment an index into an array, this implied the presence of two address (unsigned integer) adders. Also, to facilitate dope vector calculations for random references into multidimensional arrays, we provided an address multiplier.

Within loops there are also, typically, a certain number of integer operations. Since we did not wish to have these operations steal cycles from the floating-point units, we added an integer functional unit. This left us with a grand total of eight pipelined functional units. A subsequent crisis caused by the burgeoning amount of logic required a reduction in the size of the numeric processor. As a result of this exercise, we eliminated the integer unit and the address multiply unit as separate pipelines and merged them with the floating-point adder and address adder units, respectively.

Very early in the project, we constructed a prototype scheduler that would generate schedules for programs written in a low-

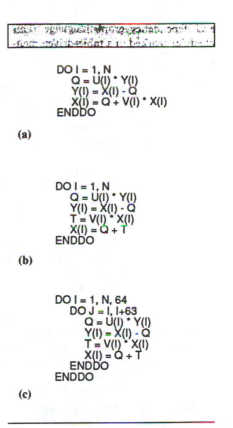

```
DO I = 1, N
    Q = U(I) * Y(I)
    Y(I) = X(I) - Q
    X(I) = Q + V(I) * X(I)
ENDDO
```

(a)

```
DO I = 1, N
    Q = U(I) * Y(I)
    Y(I) = X(I) - Q
    T = V(I) * X(I)
    X(I) = Q + T
ENDDO
```

(b)

```
DO I = 1, N, 64
    DO J = I, I+63
        Q = U(I) * Y(I)
        Y(I) = X(I) - Q
        T = V(I) * X(I)
        X(I) = Q + T
    ENDDO
ENDDO
```

(c)

Figure 5. (a) Fortran code for a loop. (b) Fortran loop rewritten with just one floating-point operation per statement. Each statement would become a vector floating-point operation. Using registers in a scalar machine would result in only six memory operations (four reads and two writes) per iteration. A memory-to-memory vector processor would require 12 memory operations per iteration (two reads and one write per statement). (c) Using vector registers can bring the memory operations back down to six per iteration, but because of the finite length of the vector register (assumed to be 64 in this example), strip mining must be used. The loop is transformed into a doubly nested loop. The inner loop handles 64 long chunks of the vector; the outer loop sequences through all chunks that make up the vector. (For simplicity, N is assumed to be a multiple of 64.) Strip mining limits the length of vector operations to no more than the vector register length, thus reducing performance. In the directed-dataflow architecture, since registers are continuously deallocated from iterations that have completed and allocated to new iterations, the number of memory operations per iteration is six, yet there is no restriction on the length of the vector operation.

level dependency graph language. This scheduler worked in a table-driven manner, using for this purpose a machine description file. By modifying this machine description file, we were able to estimate the relative performance of the numeric processor while varying the number of pipelines, the depth of the pipelines, and the assignment of opcodes to functional units. One of the alternatives we experimented with was the number of floating-point functional units, bearing in mind that computational balance required a memory port and an address unit for each floating-point unit. We found that the increase in performance with the number of floating-point units was quite sublinear, while the increase in cost and complexity was most definitely superlinear. We opted, therefore, to stay with two floating-point units and to design them to run as fast as possible instead of providing many slow units. Given a certain target performance level, the compiler needs to find less parallelism in the program in a processor with a few fast units than in one with many slow units.

At this point we had six pipelined functional units (including the two memory ports), each requiring two input operands and generating a result. Complete connectivity between all outputs and all inputs would have required a 6×12 crossbar with a register file at each cross-point. This was infeasible from an implementation viewpoint. And yet, with our understanding of the problems of programming Floating Point Systems' AP-120B, we were unwilling to eliminate cross-points in an ad hoc manner. Some underlying scheme having conceptual integrity and relevance from the viewpoint of the compiler writer was essential.

We partitioned the functional units on the basis of data versus addresses, placing the two floating-point units, the integer unit, and the two memory ports in the data cluster and the remaining functional units in the address cluster. This immediately reduced the number of cross-points by half. The final structure of the numeric processor's data paths is shown in Figure 6.

Another major constraint, especially in the context of an interconnection-rich architecture such as this, was the amount of board I/O. Obviously, the choice of data path width had a major impact on the number of signals crossing board boundaries. With 32-bit data paths we found ourselves up against a wall even with the use of fairly aggressive connector technol-

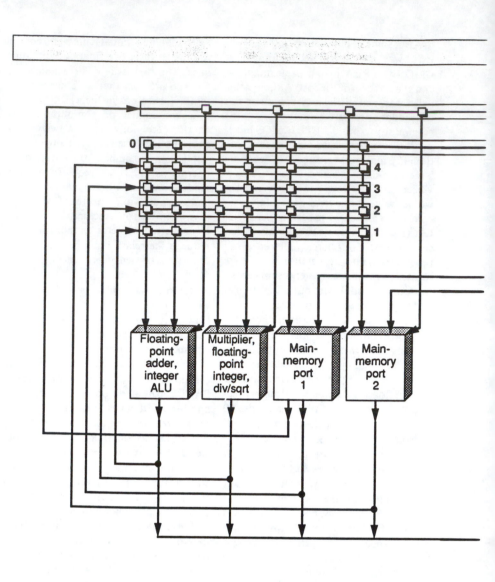

Figure 6. Major numeric processor data paths. The numeric processor E-unit contains two major parts: the data cluster and the address cluster. The data cluster consists of four functional-unit pipelines interconnected by the data context register matrix. These four pipelines are (1) the floating-point adder/integer ALU (four-cycle latency), (2) the floating-point/integer multiplier (five-cycle latency) and divider, as well as the square-root unit, (3) memory data port 1 (17-cycle latency), and (4) memory data port 2 (17-cycle latency). The address cluster consists of two address adder pipelines (three-cycle latency) interconnected by the address context register matrix. In addition, the first pipeline provides a bit-reverse capability, while the second provides an integer multiply capability. The context register

ogy. A move to 64-bit data paths would have required the use of exotic and expensive connectors. The rule of thumb we had developed indicated that 64-bit data paths instead of 32-bit data paths would increase 64-bit performance by 50 percent and 32-bit performance not at all. Discretion being the better part of valor, we elected to use 32-bit data paths.

Register storage. The context register matrix provides the architectural facilities needed to dynamically allocate iteration frames at runtime. Since each iteration initiated is allocated an iteration frame, and since the total number of registers in the context register matrix is fixed, the iteration frames for past iterations must be deallocated at the same rate that new ones

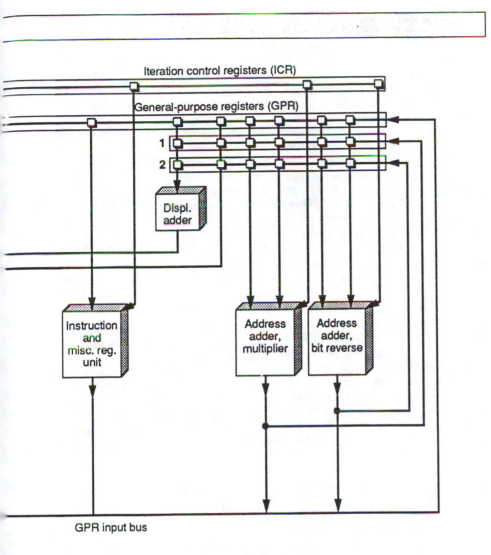

Iteration control registers (ICR)

General-purpose registers (GPR)

1

2

Displ. adder

Instruction and misc. reg. unit

Address adder, multiplier

Address adder, bit reverse

GPR input bus

---

matrix (CRM) provides simultaneous, conflict-free access to all functional-unit inputs and outputs. Also, by virtue of the iteration frame pointer relative addressing into it, the CRM supports overlapped execution of loops. Each functional unit has three inputs. Two of these are the conventional operand inputs sourced by either the CRM or the general-purpose registers (GPR). The third input is a Boolean value from the iteration control register (ICR) used to conditionally control the issuance of operations. The output of each functional unit can go either to its row in the CRM or to the GPR. Like the CRM, the GPR and ICR consist of as many carbon-copy register files as there are inputs that can source them.

are allocated. While this is exactly what is desired for loop variants (values computed by each iteration), it poses a problem for loop-invariant values that are used, but never computed, within the loop. Unless they are continuously copied from one iteration frame to the next, they will be overwritten. To avoid the significant overhead of copying loop invariants, we

provided a register file that is global to all iterations and does not possess the iteration frame capabilities. With considerable originality, we called this the *general-purpose register* file. In a single cycle it can be read by any number of functional unit input ports simultaneously and at distinct locations, just like a row in the context register matrix, and it can be written to by the

output port of any functional unit, but only one at a time.

One of the more ad hoc decisions we made was choosing the number of registers per register file. The problem we faced was a lack of directly relevant statistics on the effect of this parameter on performance in the context of a directed-dataflow style of execution. So we plucked the decision out of thin air. Our collective intuition told us that 32 registers per register file was too few, and 128 registers looked difficult from an implementation viewpoint. Thus we settled on 64 registers per register file. Comforted by the lack of alternatives, we moved on.

The capacity of the iteration control register (ICR) was determined by two opposing considerations. Since each predicate would be used as input to operations scheduled to execute at times separated by rather long intervals, we expected the lifetime of these values to be long. This implied more capacity in the ICR than in the register files in the context register matrix. On the other hand, the number of bits available in the instruction format to address the ICR was at a premium. We finally decided to provide an ICR capacity of 128.

Opcode repertoire. The basic philosophy in the directed-dataflow architecture is to work with atomic operations that can be scheduled with maximum flexibility. So, we have no operations of the CISC type that read from memory (two operands), perform an operation, and write the result back to memory. To our way of thinking, this is actually four different operations packaged together, usurping the compiler's ability to achieve optimal scheduling. Except for the memory Read and Write opcode class, no other opcodes access memory. Their inputs and outputs are predominantly either the context register matrix or the GPR file. Also, with a few exceptions, the opcode repertoire is the normal set of integer, logical, floating-point, and memory operations. The few exceptions relate to supporting the directed-dataflow model of computation. The opcode repertoire reflects the numerical bias; while there is extensive support for floating-point operations, there is none for binary-coded decimal arithmetic or string operations. Except in the case of (bitwise) logical operations, where it would be redundant, opcodes are provided for both single-precision (32-bit) and double-precision (64-bit) operations. The data types supported by the execution unit hardware are 32-bit and 64-bit IEEE floating point, 32-bit and 64-bit 2's complement integers, 32-bit unsigned in the address cluster, and 32-bit logical.

The data paths, as well as the registers in the numeric processor, are 32 bits wide. We believed that register allocation in the compiler would be simplified if the two halves of a 64-bit datum could be independently assigned to unrelated registers. This meant we would need four source-register specifiers and two destination-register specifiers for a 64-bit operation. Since we have 32-bit data paths, it takes two cycles to provide the input operands for a 64-bit operation. Consequently, in the schedule as well as in the code, no operation can immediately follow a 64-bit operation. We decided to use this dead cycle to provide two source specifiers and one destination specifier. The rest of the specifiers are provided in the previous instruction (the one initiating the 64-bit operation).

The memory opcode repertoire includes opcodes to read and write 32-, 16-, and 8-bit data. The 16-bit reads and writes have signed as well as unsigned versions. With the 16-bit reads, this determines whether the 16-bit datum is interpreted as a signed or an unsigned integer. This in turn determines whether the sign is extended or zeros are inserted in the high-order 16 bits of the 32-bit destination register. All integer arithmetic is carried out thereafter on 32-bit data. When a 16-bit datum is written back to memory, use of the signed or unsigned opcode determines whether or not the 32-bit quantity in the register can be treated as a 16-bit quantity without overflow. If an overflow occurs, it is reported at the time of the 16-bit write. The 32-bit Exchange Read opcode exchanges the contents of the specified register and memory location as an indivisible operation. This opcode supports synchronization between asynchronous parallel processes.

Although the opcode repertoire is identical for both memory ports, an asymmetry results because of insufficient instruction word bits to go around. Memory port 1 can specify the memory address as an instruction-specified displacement off a base register. Memory port 2 cannot specify a displacement.

The numeric processor has two special opcodes to support loop execution: *brtop* and *nexti*. Two types of actions must be performed to control loops. One is to determine whether another iteration is to be executed and, if so, to allocate a new iteration frame. This is done by the nexti

opcode. The other action is to actually branch back to the top of the loop if another iteration is to be executed. The brtop opcode does this in addition to everything the nexti opcode does. If it were not for the long, three-cycle branch latency, the nexti operation would be unnecessary. But in certain very small loops, the interval between the initiation of successive iterations can be less than the branch latency. If not for the nexti opcode, this would pose an unnecessary upper bound on performance of one iteration every three cycles. But with the nexti opcode, it is possible to initiate new iterations in the delay slots of the brtop operation. This allows up to three iterations per brtop executed and the initiation of up to one new iteration every cycle.

Instruction format. The data paths of the numeric processor can initiate six operations every cycle. Therefore, the MultiOp instruction format (Figure 7a) must be able to issue six operations on the six functional units, plus an additional one to control the instruction unit and other miscellaneous operations. A MultiOp instruction consists of seven partitions, one for each operation; each instruction looks like a conventional RISC instruction except for the existence of a predicate specifier. The typical format for each operation partition consists of an opcode, two source-register specifiers, one destination-register specifier, and one predicate-register specifier (Figure 7b).

The data cluster has four context register matrix rows and the GPR to select among for a source, and one row plus the GPR to select between for the destination. Similarly, the address cluster has two context register matrix rows and the GPR to select among for a source, and one row plus the GPR to select between for the destination. Assuming an average of five or six bits in the opcode field, 64 registers in each register file, and 128 locations in the ICR, this implies roughly 40 bits per operation partition or 240 bits per instruction. To avoid the need for complex instruction fetch logic, we were determined that the instruction word width would be a power of 2. Thus 256 bits appeared to be a reasonable target. Furthermore, since an instruction word width of 512 bits would have caused a considerable increase in the cost and complexity of the instruction unit, 256 bits seemed the only option available. This rigid constraint required a number of trade-offs, which are discussed below.

In portions of the program where significant parallelism exists, including but not limited to innermost loops, the MultiOp format is very effective. However, because it gobbles up 32 bytes every 40 nanoseconds, we were worried about the effect on instruction cache performance and capacity should the MultiOp format be used indiscriminately, even in portions of the code where little parallelism exists. With this in mind, we created the UniOp instruction format (Figure 7c), which allows only a single operation to be initiated per instruction, making it possible to fit multiple UniOp instructions in each 256-bit container. The opcode repertoire available in the UniOp format is identical to that in the MultiOp format. While executing UniOp instructions, the numeric processor is similar to other scalar architectures that have no pipeline interlocks in hardware.

The UniOp instruction must contain not only all the information contained in the corresponding MultiOp partition, but also a few additional bits to indicate which functional unit is being tasked. The longest partition in the MultiOp format is for memory port 1, which contains a literal field for specifying an address displacement or a data literal. This partition is 44 bits long. If each UniOp instruction is at least 44 bits, it is possible to fit at most five instructions per instruction container, for an average instruction width of 51 bits. We felt that this would dilate the size of the compiled code to an uncomfortable extent. As a compromise we decided to forgo the predicate capability in UniOp, reasoning that the UniOp sections of code were not supposed to be performance critical anyway. Now it was possible to fit six UniOp instructions per container. Any more than six per container would have required us to reduce the 16-bit address displacement field size. Since we felt that 16 bits was barely adequate, we were unwilling to reduce it further. The 40-bit UniOp format also permitted us to provide a 24-bit program address literal.

The MultiOp format contained 18 context register matrix or GPR specifiers and six ICR specifiers. Increasing the number of registers per register file from 64 to 128 would have required 18 additional instruction bits in MultiOp, which were not available. This helped us realize that adding more registers was not an option. Decreasing the number of ICR locations from 128 to 64 would have saved six MultiOp instruction bits—not enough to make an appreciable difference elsewhere.

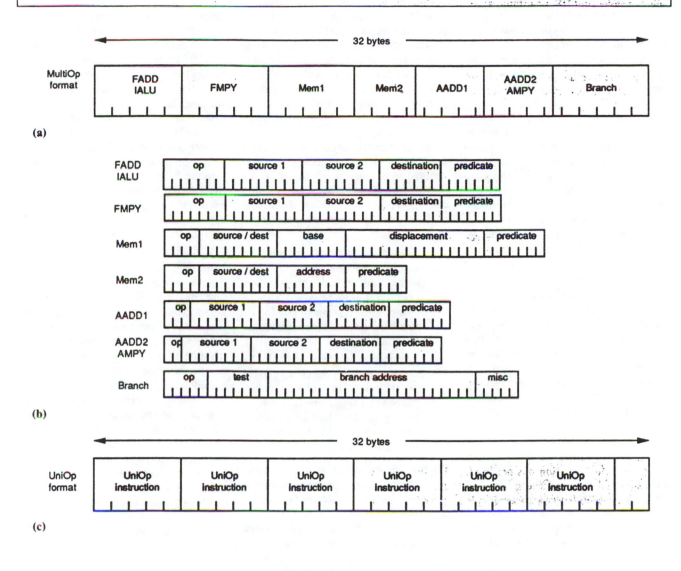

(a)

(b)

(c)

Figure 7. Numeric processor instruction formats. (a) The MultiOp format is 32 bytes long and permits seven operations to be issued during each 40-nanosecond cycle. (b) The structure of each partition in the MultiOp format. (c) The UniOp format allows six instructions to fit into a 32-byte container. Each instruction can issue only one operation per 40-nanosecond cycle.

Exception handling. Exceptions and interrupts pose a special challenge to architectures such as directed dataflow, where the execution sequence is so carefully and rigidly choreographed. The basic problem in handling an exception is *schedule tearing*, which means the carefully crafted computation schedule is being drastically altered by inserting the computation corresponding to the exception handler into the middle of the original computation. The compiler-generated schedule is literally torn apart to allow the

exception handler to execute. This can cause two types of problems: first, the conflicting usage of scheduled resources, and second, the violation of implicit dependencies between operations.

Avoidance of resource conflicts is achieved by flushing all pipelines during transition between the user program and the exception handler. This is done by aborting operations in progress, by allowing them to execute to completion, or by saving and subsequently restoring their state of partial execution. Conceptually,

the last alternative is the simplest. It is also the costliest in terms of hardware requirements, so it is the solution of last resort. Aborting operations is extremely complicated, since those operations will need to be reissued after exception handling, which means the program counter and the processor state must be backed up. Allowing operations that have been issued to go to completion is the best technique overall, except in certain cases. Clearly, if the exception is due to an operand page fault occurring in the course of executing a memory operation, the memory operation cannot complete until the page fault exception has been handled and the page has been brought into physical memory. In this case the best alternative is to save the state of that portion of the memory pipeline extending through the virtual address translation and to restore it after exception handling.

If special care is not taken, schedule tearing can result in the violation of required dependencies between operations. It can cause an operation scheduled to finish after a second one has started to actually finish *before* the second one starts. This will lead to incorrect results if the first operation writes to the same register the second one reads, and if the second operation expects to get the contents that existed prior to the register's having been overwritten. Such a situation is prevented by a compiler convention that decrees a register to be "in use" from the beginning of the operation that writes to it until the latest completion time of all operations using that value. With this convention in place, two operations that overlap each other's execution intervals will have to use different source and destination registers, thereby avoiding the problem.

Clearly, handling an exception requires that no further instructions (operations) be issued once the exception has occurred. But this can contradict the strategy of executing to completion an operation in progress if the information corresponding to that operation is distributed across multiple instructions. This is often the case in microprogramming-style architectures, where, instead of providing the opcode, the source specifiers, and the result specifiers at the same time, the architecture provides the result specifier many instructions later than the opcode, reflecting the time when each item of information is actually needed.

The problem is that when the exception occurs, not all of the information needed by the operation to execute to completion has been issued; that is, the operation is in a partially issued state. For the operation to execute to completion, further instructions must be issued, which in turn would cause further operations to be issued whose completion would require the issuance of still more instructions, and so on. The only solution would be to issue further instructions selectively in a way that would prevent the issuance of new operations until the operations already in progress had received all the information they need

to execute to completion. After the exception has been handled, instruction issuance would have to begin with the first instruction initiating an operation that was not issued prior to exception handling, while taking care to selectively mask out operations issued previously. Because this is so messy, it is highly desirable that all information pertaining to a single operation be specified at the same time in the same instruction.

In the numeric processor, however, double-precision operations are distributed over two consecutive (in time) instructions. Thus, at least to a limited extent, the problems described above must be dealt with. Two measures accomplish this:

(1) The one instruction issued after the exception (since it may contain the second half of a double-precision operation) must be issued with all "new" (that is, single-precision or first half of double-precision) operations disabled.

(2) The opcode for the second half of a double-precision operation should be such that in isolation (when viewed as a single-precision operation or the first half of a double-precision operation) it will be interpreted as a no-op.

The first requirement allows the appropriate functional unit to get the information it needs to allow a double-precision operation issued in the previous cycle to execute to completion. The second requirement makes it simple to resume issuing instructions after handling the exception. Since they are interpreted as no-ops, second halves of double-precision operations will automatically "mask" themselves out.

However, the first requirement cannot be met when the second half of a double-precision operation lies in a different page from that in which the first half lies and if the instruction fetch for the second half generates a page fault. In this case the double-precision operation must be aborted and restarted by resuming instruction issuance with the last instruction actually issued. For this to be possible, the inputs to operations issued in the instruction to be restarted must not have been modified. This will be true if another compiler convention is observed: The registers that are sources to an operation in a particular instruction should be viewed as "busy" through the end of the issuance of all double-precision operations whose first halves are in the same instruction.

PC history queue. One consequence of very deep pipelines is that between the issuance of an operation and its completion, it is possible to have executed multiple branch operations. If an operation generates an exception, the deep pipelining makes it extremely difficult for a debugger to figure out the program counter value for the instruction that initiated the offending operation. To solve this problem, we included a circular 256-entry *PC history queue* (PCHQ). During normal operation the current PC value is written into the PCHQ on every cycle. The state of the PCHQ is frozen when an exception occurs. Knowing the latency of the offending operation, the debugger can index back into the PCHQ by that amount to locate the PC value for the corresponding instruction.

Although this was the original motivation for the PCHQ, it was soon pressed into service for an additional function. Again due to the depth of the pipelines, between the time an exception occurs and the time all pipelines have been flushed, many operations complete that can generate additional exceptions. These operations will not be reissued after exception handling, so the exceptions must all be recorded and handled en masse. Since this exception logging process occurs only after the first exception has occurred, and since the PCHQ has stopped recording PC values at this point, we decided to switch the PCHQ from the task of recording PC values to the task of recording exception records at the time the first exception occurs.

The main memory system

The ideal memory system for a supercomputer would provide large capacity at a low price and extremely high bandwidth with very low access time. Furthermore, the bandwidth and access time would be insensitive to the size of the data sets being operated on, the manner in which the data are placed in memory, and the order in which they are referenced. Needless to say, such a memory system has never been built. Each computer architect must decide which of these attributes are essential and which can be compromised.

Data cache anomalies. General-purpose computing almost invariably employs caches. Assuming locality of reference and

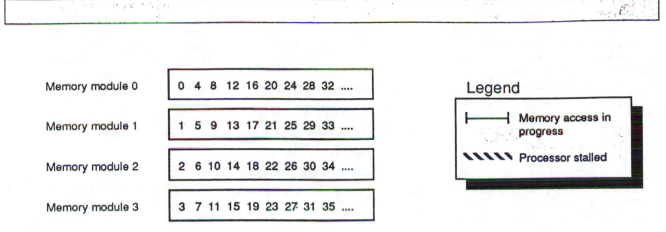

(a)

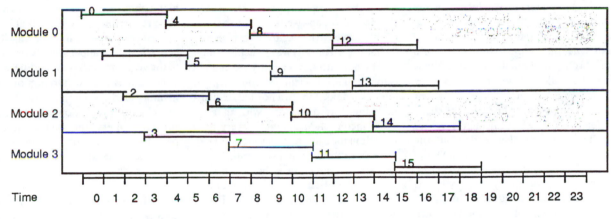

(b)

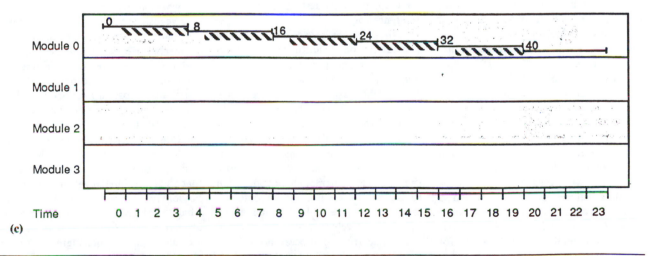

(c)

Figure 8. Sequentially interleaved memory. (a) The conventional assignment of memory locations to memory modules in a sequentially interleaved memory system with four modules. A memory module is busy for four cycles when handling a request. Thus, the peak bandwidth is one request per cycle. **(b)** With a sequential request stream, perfect operation takes place. No request ever encounters a busy module, and the peak bandwidth is achieved. **(c)** For a request stream with a stride of eight, every request is directed to the same module. Every request encounters a busy module, the processor must halt three cycles for each cycle it advances, and the achieved bandwidth is one request per four cycles.

hence a high hit rate, the cache provides the desired high bandwidth and, on the average, low access time, while the main memory provides large capacity at a low price. Whereas the assumption of good locality is usually true with general-purpose work loads, it can be wildly wrong in numerically intensive computing. Often, numerical applications sweep through large arrays such that a particular element is rereferenced only after all other elements have been referenced. Except in the case of toy problems, the arrays tend to be comparable to the main memory in physical size and considerably larger than any realistic cache. Consequently, each word is displaced from the cache before it is next referenced, resulting in a low hit ratio.

The processor is now working directly out of the main memory, which typically is underdesigned for this situation, since the design assumption was that only a small fraction of the references would come through to the main memory. Worse yet, if the stride with which the processor is referencing memory is equal to or greater than the cache line size, the cache will fetch an entire line for each reference that the processor makes, and all but one word of the line is wasted. Far from helping the situation, the cache is now compounding the problem by amplifying the request rate to an already underdesigned main memory. This phenomenon has been researched and reported by Abu-Sufah and Mahoney.[12]

In the case of a really high-performance processor, a further problem makes using a data cache difficult. In addition to the bandwidth needed for instruction fetching, it is necessary to perform two or three data references per processor cycle to keep memory bandwidth in balance with the processor's computational capability. This requires the use of either an interleaved cache or multiple caches, along with a cache coherency mechanism. At extremely fast clock rates, both alternatives present formidable obstacles. In view of these considerations, we elected not to use a cache for data references. We provided a 32-Kbyte cache for instructions, since cache performance for instruction references is not qualitatively different for numerical programs.

Sequentially interleaved memory architectures. The full operand request rate now had to be handled by the main memory, and we were back to the problem of providing a consistently high bandwidth

> The ideal
> memory system
> for a supercomputer
> would provide large
> capacity, low price,
> high bandwidth, and
> very low access time.

and low access time using main-memory technology. In the context of a departmental supercomputer price objective, this meant that using fast, static, ECL RAM was precluded, and we had to use the relatively inexpensive but slow MOS DRAM technology. The only way to achieve high bandwidth with slow memory technology is to use multiple memory modules in an interleaved fashion. In a normal, sequentially interleaved memory, with an interleave factor of M modules, every Mth word is in the same memory module (Figure 8a). In the case of a sequential reference stream, this ensures high bandwidth, since all modules are referenced before the same module is referenced again (Figure 8b). If the degree of interleaving is large enough compared with the ratio of the memory cycle time to the processor cycle time, the memory module will be ready to handle another request by the time it is referenced again.

Although interleaved memories can provide the bandwidth requirements of high-performance processors, they do not address the desire for short access times. Without the use of a cache, the access time, even under the best of circumstances, can be no less than the access time of the memory technology used in the main memory. Since in numerically intensive computations processor performance is more rigidly linked to memory bandwidth than to memory access time, supercomputer architectures have evolved in such a way as to be relatively insensitive to memory access time. In vector processors the memory access time contributes only to the vector start-up penalty, not to the vector execution rate. Likewise, in the dataflow and directed-dataflow architectures, a longer access time is handled by scheduling the memory access earlier than it is needed.

general-purpose processors are better "MIPS engines" than supercomputers running at the same clock speed. In general-purpose computing the emphasis is less on iterative computations and memory bandwidth and more on branching, procedure calls and returns, and memory access time. This makes cache memories indispensable. Without its cache memory, a high-speed scalar processor would slow down to a crawl.

The stride problem. In well-designed supercomputer architectures, the trade-off is always in the direction of ensuring consistently high memory bandwidth, even at the expense of increased access time. However, conventional, sequentially interleaved memories cannot guarantee even high bandwidth. They break down badly if the references have a stride that is a multiple of the degree of interleaving (Figure 8c). When this happens, every reference is to the very same memory module, and the bandwidth is degraded to that of a single memory module. The processor's performance drops proportionately. On existing supercomputers, the magnitude of this penalty is so large[13] that the user is forced to contort the algorithm to avoid this stride problem.

Pseudorandomly interleaved memory architecture. We found this situation unacceptable and developed an interleaved memory architecture that is impervious to the stride problem. Instead of assigning every Mth word to the same memory module, we assigned the memory locations to the memory modules in a carefully engineered pseudorandom fashion such that every reference sequence likely to occur in practice would be as uniformly distributed across the memory modules as would a truly random request sequence (Figure 9a). To someone familiar with the folklore of interleaved memory design, this might seem like exactly the wrong thing to do. It is a popularly held belief that an M-way interleaved memory with a random request sequence will only achieve a bandwidth proportional to $\sqrt{M}$ modules instead of getting the full benefit of the M modules. This is true (Figure 9b) if the memory system does not have the facilities to queue-up references to busy modules.[14] With sufficient buffering (Figure 9c), the full bandwidth of M modules can be achieved.[15] Furthermore, since every request sequence, whether sequential, of stride M, or totally scrambled, appears

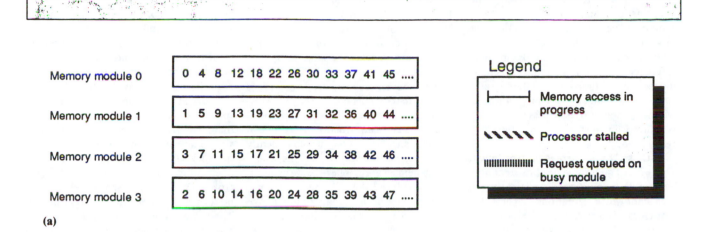

(a)

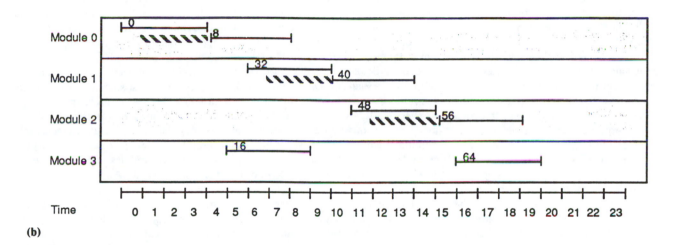

(b)

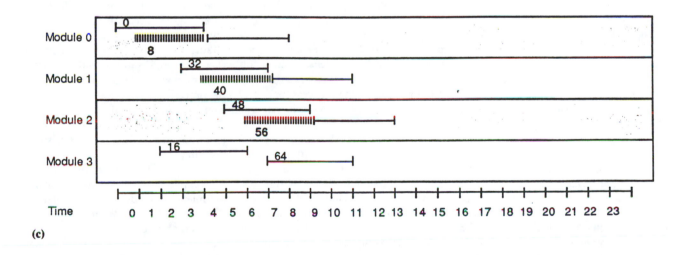

(c)

Figure 9. Pseudorandomly interleaved memory. (a) The assignment of memory locations to four memory modules in a pseudorandomly interleaved memory. (b) Even with a stride of eight, eventually the requests are evenly distributed across all four memory modules. However, every so often requests will encounter a busy module. If no buffering is provided at the memory modules, the processor must halt until the module is no longer busy. (c) Although individual requests might have to wait even with buffering, the processor need not. It can continue to issue a request every cycle, yielding full bandwidth.

equally random to the interleaved memory, this high bandwidth is consistently achieved. The only exception is a situation in which the same location is repeatedly referenced (for instance, a scalar memory reference in a loop). Standard, machine-independent optimizations in the compiler get rid of such situations. Thus, high bandwidth is guaranteed regardless of how data is placed in memory and how it is referenced.

But, as always, there is no free lunch. The price of guaranteeing consistent high bandwidth is an increase in access time in high-bandwidth situations. When the request rate is high (close to the maximum bandwidth the memory system is designed for), the randomness of the pseudorandomized request sequence will cause queues to form every so often on busy modules. A request arriving at such a queue will experience a delay equal to the memory chip access time plus the time spent waiting in line. Thus, the access time perceived by the processor increases. Also, this increase in access time is a stochastic quantity, and the overall access time for a request now lies within a range of values. Whereas the limits on the range can be predicted, the exact value (within that range) for the access time of a specific request cannot. Moreover, this range shifts, depending on the request rate of the processor. Under light load conditions (as when executing scalar code), one can expect little queueing delay, but when the request rate increases (within innermost loops), so will the queueing delay.

The memory latency register. In and of itself, the increased access time is not a major problem; the second-order penalty due to the increased access time is more than compensated for by the first-order benefit of guaranteeing high bandwidth. (This does, however, cause a further polarization between a well-designed general-purpose processor and a well-designed supercomputer.) What *is* of concern is the nondeterministic nature of the access time in the context of a processor architecture in which every operation is rigidly scheduled at compile time and in which the latency of every operation, including the memory operations, must be deterministic. The way other architectures that use compile-time scheduling normally handle this is to "fake" a deterministic access time.[6] If the memory access occurs sooner than expected, the data can be buffered internally to the memory system and delivered to the processor at exactly the right

time. If, on the other hand, the data takes longer than expected, the processor is "frozen" until the data is available, so that in the processor's "virtual time" the request always takes the same amount of time.

Yet another delicate trade-off exists here. If the compiler consistently underestimates the access time, the processor will spend a significant fraction of its time in a frozen state. If the compiler consistently overestimates the access time, the schedules generated at compile time are unnecessarily dilated. At either extreme, performance is less than optimal. We addressed this issue by simulating the memory system at various request rates and plotting performance against the nominal (assumed) memory latency. As expected, we found that for each request rate the curve peaked at a certain value of memory latency. In the vicinity of this optimum memory latency, performance was not particularly sensitive to the value of the memory latency. On the other hand, the value of the optimum memory latency was very sensitive to the request rate. This made us nervous about hardwiring the nominal memory latency value into the compiler and the hardware.

We solved this problem by incorporating a memory latency register. The MLR is a programmatically writable register that always holds the value of the memory latency assumed by the compiler when scheduling the currently executing code. The memory system uses the value in this register to decide whether the datum is early or late and, consequently, whether the datum should be buffered or the processor frozen. When executing scalar code with little parallelism and a low request rate, the MLR is set to the minimum possible memory access time of 17 numeric processor cycles (each cycle is 40 nanoseconds). When the program is in an innermost loop, the MLR is set to the optimum value of 26 cycles to reflect the expected delay due to the higher request rate. The MLR allows the compiler to treat memory accesses as having a deterministic latency but to use different values for the latency in different portions of the code so as to always deliver near-optimal performance.

Compiler-scheduled memory modules. One of the alternatives we considered, and decided against, very early in the design process was to place the memory modules under the explicit scheduling control of the compiler (much like the adder and mul-

tiplier) instead of treating the memory system like a black box. Ideally, in such a scheme the compiler must know *at compile time* whether or not a set of references are to distinct memory modules. It can then schedule the initiation of the memory requests in such a way that the referenced memory module is no longer busy by the time the request is made. This would eliminate the need for any buffering. Also, with knowledge of the (deterministic) memory latency that exists in the absence of queuing, operations that use the data from memory can be scheduled to occur no sooner than when the data is available. The processor would never need to be frozen, nor would access times need to be overestimated. Presumably, the hardware would be simpler and less expensive with no buffering facilities. Thus, near-optimal performance could be achieved if the appropriate information were known at compile time.

But commonly occurring program constructs can defeat such a strategy. In the case of references to $X(I)$ and $X(J)$, the manner in which the variables I and J are computed may be such as to preclude the compiler's being able to determine whether the modules referenced are distinct or the same. Another problem lies with subscripted-subscript references to arrays, such as $X(JA(I))$, where the index into one array, $X()$, is determined by reading the contents of another array, $JA(I)$. Since the contents of $JA()$ are determined at runtime, the compiler is once again unable to predict which module will be referenced. In such circumstances the compiler must either assume the worst and serialize all such references or assume that no conflict exists and count on the presence of some hardware mechanism that will freeze the processor if a request is submitted to a busy module. With the latter approach, the $\sqrt{M}$ law becomes applicable. In either case the program experiences a sizable drop in performance.

As we see it, the most serious drawback of compile-time scheduling of memory modules is that it does nothing to address the stride problem. With a bad stride, whether compile-time memory disambiguation works or not, the memory bandwidth collapses. Memory disambiguation merely confirms the bad news at compile time. Using pseudorandom interleaving to solve the stride problem would make the task of compile-time disambiguation next to impossible. So eventually the trade-off was one of simpler hardware, more complex software, and a reduced average access time versus a guaranteed, consistently high bandwidth. In view of our central objective of providing a product with minimal difficulty of use, we chose the latter.

Reflections

While developing this product, we became aware of certain broad truths, and we have tried to convey them in this article. The most important of these is that the behavior of general-purpose and numerically intensive work loads can be drastically different. In nonnumeric programs the emphasis is on branching and procedure calls; in numeric programs it is on loops. General-purpose jobs tend to access their data with a high degree of locality. This is not always so with numerically intensive jobs.

Consequently, the design decisions and trade-offs steadily push the well-designed scalar processor and the well-designed numeric processor apart. In a scalar processor the emphasis is on short pipeline latencies rather than on extensive parallelism. In a numeric processor the emphasis is on multiple, parallel pipelines even at the expense of very deep pipelines and, hence, reduced scalar performance. Whereas the use of caches for data is virtually mandatory for good performance in a scalar processor, it is far less beneficial, and sometimes even detrimental, to the performance of a numeric processor. A numeric processor is more sensitive to memory bandwidth and less so to access time. The opposite is true for a scalar processor. Thus it remains as difficult now as it has been in the past to design a single machine that is best for both numeric and nonnumeric work loads.

Much has been said over the past few years about the relative merits of RISC and CISC approaches to hardware design. We feel that the same issue could well be raised regarding software, specifically compiler software. With the headlong rush to move complexity out of hardware and into software, compilers are beginning to groan under the burden of newly acquired responsibilities. It is possible to go too far and to end up increasing the total complexity of the hardware-software system. The designers' responsibility is to minimize overall complexity, not just that of the hardware. In the Cydra 5 we decided not to transfer complexity from hardware to software in some areas such as the context

register matrix, conditional scheduling control, and hardware-scheduled memory modules. To paraphrase Einstein, "Hardware should be as simple as possible, and no simpler."

Designing and developing a product of this performance level and with these capabilities necessitated a break with architectures of the past so that we could incorporate a more powerful model of computation. This meant that we often had to fly by the seat of our pants, there being little experience or data on which to base our decisions. Fortunately, we have not yet discovered any major blunders, although it is quite possible that the machine has been overdesigned in various places because of our tendency to err on the safe side. These areas of overdesign will reveal themselves slowly as we build up our experience in the use of this new architecture.

T oday, a number of Cydra 5 systems are in use at customer sites. The performance of these systems has met our expectations. On widely quoted industry-standard benchmarks such as Linpack[16] and the Livermore Fortran Kernels,[17] the Cydra 5 delivers 15.4 Mflops and 5.8 Mflops, respectively. This is the highest performance of any minisupercomputer (even those whose peak performance is twice that of the Cydra 5) and about one-third the performance of a Cray X-MP supercomputer, which has nine times the Cydra 5's peak performance. On the 24 Livermore Fortran Kernels taken as a group, the Cydra 5 can achieve 23 percent of its peak performance as opposed to 15 percent and 8 percent for VLIW and vector processors, respectively. On Linpack, which is considerably more vectorizable, the Cydra 5 achieves 60 percent of its peak performance. The VLIW and vector processors achieve only 40 percent and 20 percent, respectively.

On other, less vectorizable, benchmarks, such as ITPack[18] (an iterative sparse-matrix solver), the Cydra 5 achieves half the performance of the Cray X-MP. We have even encountered a couple of extremely nonvectorizable applications in which the Cydra 5 has actually achieved parity with the Cray X-MP. In general, across a spectrum of applications, the Cydra 5 can achieve between one-fourth and two-thirds the performance of a Cray X-MP, depending on the extent to

which the application is vectorizable. However, there is still room for improvement, since the compiler has not yet peaked in its ability to wring performance out of code. □

Acknowledgments

The Cydra 5 owes its existence to the group of bright and dedicated individuals who make up Cydrome. Each has left his or her mark on this machine. We wish to acknowledge the especially important contributions of Stimson Ho, Gary Beck, Joe Bratt, Ed Wolff, Mike Schlansker, and John Brennan.

References

1. "Cydra 5 Departmental Supercomputer Product Summary," Cydrome, Inc., Milpitas, Calif., 1988.

2. B.R. Rau, "Cydra 5 Directed Dataflow Architecture," *Proc. Compcon Spring 88*, No. 828, Computer Society Press, Los Alamitos, Calif., pp. 106-113.

3. B.R. Rau, C.D. Glaeser, and R.L. Picard, "Efficient Code Generation for Horizontal Architectures: Compiler Techniques and Architectural Support," *Proc. Ninth Ann. Int'l Symp. Computer Architecture*, M411 (microfiche), Computer Society Press, Los Alamitos, Calif., 1982, pp. 131-139.

4. W.C. Yen, D.W.L. Yen, and K.S. Fu, "Data Coherence Problem in a Multicache System," *IEEE Trans. Computers*, Vol. C-34, No. 1, Jan. 1985, pp. 56-65.

5. J.A. Fisher, "Very Long Instruction Word Architectures and the ELI-512," *Proc. 10th Ann. Int'l Symp. Computer Architecture*, M473 (microfiche), Computer Society Press, Los Alamitos, Calif., 1983, pp. 140-150.

6. A.E. Charlesworth, "An Approach to Scientific Array Processing: The Architectural Design of the AP-120B/FPS-164 Family," *Computer*, Vol. 14, No. 9, Sept. 1981, pp. 18-27.

7. Y.N. Patt, W.-M. Hwu, and M. Shebanow, "HPS, a New Microarchitecture: Rationale and Introduction," *Proc. 18th Ann. Workshop Microprogramming*, M653 (microfiche), Computer Society Press, Los Alamitos, Calif., 1985, pp. 103-108.

8. D. Cohen, "A Methodology for Programming a Pipeline Array Processor," *Proc. 11th Ann. Workshop Microprogramming*, M204 (microfiche), Computer Society Press, Los Alamitos, Calif., 1978, pp. 82-89.

9. J.R. Ellis, *Bulldog: A Compiler for VLIW Architectures*, MIT Press, Cambridge, Mass., 1986.

10. Arvind and K.P. Gostelow, "The U-Interpreter," *Computer*, Vol. 15, No. 2, Feb. 1982, pp. 42-49.

11. D.J. Kuck, *The Structure of Computers and Computation*, John Wiley and Sons, New York, 1978.

12. W. Abu-Sufah and A.D. Mahoney, "Vector Processing on the Alliant FX/8 Multiprocessor," *Proc. Int'l Conf. Parallel Processing*, M724 (microfiche), Computer Society Press, Los Alamitos, Calif., 1986, pp. 559-563.

13. J.M. van Kats and A.J. Van der Steen, "Minisupercomputers, a New Perspective?" Report TR-24, Academisch Computer Centrum Utrecht, University of Utrecht, Utrecht, Netherlands, May 1987.

14. H. Hellerman, *Digital Computer System Principles*, McGraw-Hill, New York, 1967, pp. 228-229.

15. F.A. Briggs and E.S. Davidson, "Organization of Semiconductor Memories for Parallel-Pipelined Processors," *IEEE Trans. Computers*, Vol. C-25, Feb. 1977, pp. 162-169.

16. J.J. Dongarra, "Performance of Various Computers Using Standard Linear Equations Software in a Fortran Environment," Tech. Memo No. 23, Argonne National Laboratory, Argonne, Ill., Jan. 1988.

17. F. McMahon, "The Livermore Fortran Kernels," National Technical Information Service, Ann Arbor, Mich., Dec. 1986.

18. T.C. Oppe and D.R. Kincaid, "The Performance of ITPACK on Vector Computers for Solving Large Sparse Linear Systems Arising in Sample Oil Reservoir Simulation Problems," *Comm. Applied Numerical Methods*, Vol. 3, 1987, pp. 23-29.

B. Ramakrishna Rau is a cofounder and the chief technical officer of Cydrome, Inc. He is the chief architect of Cydrome's Cydra 5 minisupercomputer based on the company's directed-dataflow architecture. Previously he held positions at Elxsi and TRW, and he taught electrical engineering at the University of Illinois, Urbana-Champaign. His research interests include parallel architectures, compiler techniques for high-performance computing, and analytical methods for computer performance evaluation and prediction.

Rau received a B.Tech. degree in electrical engineering from the Indian Institute of Technology, Madras, in 1972 and MS and PhD degrees in electrical engineering from Stanford University in 1973 and 1977, respectively. He is a member of the IEEE, the IEEE Computer Society, and the Association for Computing Machinery.

David W.L. Yen cofounded Cydrome, a minisupercomputer manufacturer, in 1984. He contributed to the Cydra 5 architecture design and project planning and served as director of hardware development. He joined Sun Microsystems in October 1988. In addition, Yen has engaged in research and design for the IBM San Jose Research Laboratory, TRW Array Processors, and the Coordinated Science Laboratory at the University of Illinois. His interests include computer architecture, special processors for high-performance requirements, computer-aided design automation, and product development.

Yen received a BS from National Taiwan University in 1973 and MS and PhD degrees from the University of Illinois, Urbana-Champaign, in 1977 and 1980, respectively, all in electrical engineering. He is a member of Phi Kappa Phi and Eta Kappa Nu, and he served as secretary of the IEEE Computer Society's Computer Standards Committee from 1983 to 1984.

Wei Yen is vice president for development, in charge of engineering, at Cydrome. He is the primary system architect for the Cydra 5 minisupercomputer and was extensively involved in the design and development of Cydrome's operating system and compilers. He has also worked on development projects at the Fairchild Advanced R&D Laboratory and Hewlett-Packard Laboratories. His technical interests include multiprocessor systems, distributed systems, programming environments, and dataflow compiler design.

Yen received a PhD in electrical engineering from Purdue University in 1981. He is a member of Phi Kappa Phi, Sigma Xi, and the Association for Computing Machinery.

Ross A. Towle is cofounder and president of Apogee Software, a company specializing in compilers for RISC and VLIW architectures. He was also a cofounder of Cydrome, where he served as manager of languages. His interests include global optimization, parallelization, and instruction scheduling.

Towle received BS and MS degrees in mathematics and a PhD in computer science, all from the University of Illinois, Urbana-Champaign.

The authors can be contacted through B. Ramakrishna Rau at 159 Belvue Dr., Los Gatos, CA 95032.

Instruction Level Profiling and Evaluation of the IBM RS/6000 *

Chriss Stephens   Bryce Cogswell   John Heinlein   Gregory Palmer †
John P. Shen

Center for Dependable Systems
Department of Electrical and Computer Engineering
Carnegie Mellon University
Pittsburgh, PA 15213
shen@ece.cmu.edu

Abstract

This paper reports preliminary results from using *goblin*, a new instruction level profiling system, to evaluate the IBM RISC System/6000 architecture. The evaluation presented is based on the SPEC benchmark suite.

Each SPEC program (except gcc) is processed by *goblin* to produce an instrumented version. During execution of the instrumented program, profiling routines are invoked which trace the execution of the program. These routines also collect statistics on dynamic instruction mix, branching behavior, and resource utilization. Based on these statistics, the actual performance and the architectural efficiency of the RS/6000 are evaluated. In order to provide a context for this evaluation, a comparison to the DECStation 3100 is also presented. The entire profiling and evaluation experiment on nine of the ten SPEC programs involves tracing and analyzing over 32 billion instructions on the RS/6000.

The evaluation indicates that for the SPEC benchmark suite the architecture of the RS/6000 is well balanced and exhibits impressive performance, especially on the floating-point intensive applications.

1 Introduction

1.1 Instruction Level Profiling

Instruction level profiling techniques are becoming increasingly important in the design and analysis of modern computer architectures [1, 2, 3, 4, 5]. These techniques provide efficient generation and analysis of very long address traces which are necessary for analyzing very large cache designs [3]. They also provide precise information about execution behavior, such as branching statistics, and detailed information about resource utilization, such as register working sets.

Traditionally, much of the information that instruction level profiling provides has been obtained via simulation. However, because profiling runs several orders of magnitude faster than simulation, it becomes feasible to collect this information for much larger programs. As CPU designs grow more complex, their behavior becomes harder and more time consuming to simulate. Profiling, however, can be used to directly evaluate and quantify the performance gains of such architectural features as multiple instruction dispatch and branch prediction. Further, the information profiling provides can be used to evaluate compiler scheduling techniques and improve compiler generated code. Thus an instruction level profiler is truly a computer architect's multipurpose tool.

For these reasons, and to provide an empirical evaluation of IBM's new RISC System/6000 superscalar architecture [6], an instruction level profil-

---

*This work was supported in part by NSF Contract MIP9007678.

†Supported in part by an NSF Fellowship.

ing system, *goblin*, has been designed and implemented. This paper presents a discussion of the development of the *goblin* system, and some of the preliminary results that have been collected using this system. These results have been collected on an IBM RS/6000 Model 530 running at 25MHz with 64 Mbytes of main memory. All programs have been compiled with either version 1.01 of the XL-FORTRAN compiler or version 1.01 of the XL-C compiler. These initial results are interesting for several reasons: they demonstrate the capabilities of the *goblin* system, they demonstrate a new technique for implementing instruction level profiling, and they provide an interesting quantitative analysis of the RS/6000 architecture, the first system to incorporate a superscalar processor. They also provide an interesting quantitative characterization of the Systems Performance Evaluation Cooperative (SPEC) benchmark suite [7], the set of programs analyzed. This set of programs has been drawn from engineering and scientific applications and attempts to approximate the typical workload on engineering and scientific workstations.

For each SPEC program, the following sets of statistics are generated using *goblin*: branching statistics along with an evaluation of IBM's branch prediction strategy, dynamic instruction mix, execution unit utilization, and register working set sizes. This paper only presents our initial results concerning the performance of the RS/6000; further data collection and analysis is still in progress.

1.2 RS/6000 Architecture

The IBM RS/6000 is a second generation RISC, superscalar processor [6, 8]. The distinguishing feature of a superscalar processor is its ability to issue and execute multiple independent instructions per clock cycle [1]. The RS/6000 is the first widely available workstation to incorporate such a processor, and is intended for engineering and scientific applications.

As illustrated in Figure 1, the RS/6000 has parallel execution resources: a single fixed point pipeline (FXU) and a single floating point pipeline (FPU). In addition to these pipelines, instructions may be executed by the branch processor. Thus in a single cycle the RS/6000 can execute a maximum of four independent instructions: a fixed point instruction, a floating point instruction, a condition register instruction, and a branch. The condition register instructions are executed within the branch processor. A more detailed description of the RS/6000 may be found in a special issue of the *IBM Journal of Research and Development* [6].

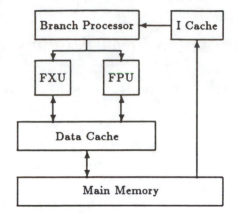

Figure 1: IBM RS/6000 Superscalar Architecture

2 Goblin Profiling System

The design of the *goblin* profiling system employs a combination of features from the *pixie* profiling system for MIPS machines [9], and ideas from the link-time code modification work of Wall et al. at DECWRL [2]. In order to extract an exact instruction level profile of a program during execution, all three systems rely on a technique best described as *invasive profiling* of the compiled code. This type of profiling inserts additional instructions into the object code of the program being profiled. These instructions, called *instrumentation code*, provide the mechanism whereby data can be collected about the execution of the program. The routines that are invoked by instrumentation code to collect and analyze the data are referred to as the *profiling code*.

2.1 Existing Profiling Systems

Prior to the implementation of *goblin*, the only profiling system available on the IBM RS/6000 was the Unix profiling system *prof/gprof* [10]. This system relies on limited invasive techniques coupled with *statistical profiling* techniques. In statistical profiling, interrupts are triggered at precise intervals during program execution. The profiling routines then log the location in the program where the interrupts occur. From this execution histogram, it is possible to estimate how frequently each part of the program is executed.

The *prof/gprof* system requires that the compiler insert additional code to call the profiling routines on entry to each procedure. Thus a complete trace of the program at the procedure level is recorded by this system. The statistical part of this system is used to determine how much time is spent in each procedure as a percentage of the total execution time of the program. Such information is useful for directing program optimization efforts by providing feedback on program bottlenecks. The advantage of such a system is that it has lower overhead as compared to a more invasive system like *goblin*. However, such a system cannot provide accurate instruction level information, and so is not effective as an architecture analysis tool.

The *pixie* profiling system is more suitable as an analysis tool. This system modifies the object code of a program directly to create a new instrumented version. It can produce several different instrumented versions including one which collects the execution trace and one which collects a trace of all memory references.

2.2 Implementation of Goblin

The *goblin* profiling system uses invasive profiling techniques exclusively. It applies these techniques at the basic block level[1], and can therefore extract fine grain execution behavior. The goblin approach is illustrated in Figure 2, and differs slightly from the systems described in [2, 9, 10]. The differences are dictated partially by circumstance and partially by design. The *goblin* system does not rely on the compiler to insert instrumentation code, and does not make any attempt to insert instrumentation code directly into the object file of the program. Instead, goblin generates an assembly level version of the program being profiled, and inserts the instrumentation code at this same level (see Figure 2). This approach is similar to using the compiler to insert the instrumentation code, but it permits greater flexibility. A single profiling system can be used with the output of multiple compilers, and development of the profiling system can proceed independent of compiler development.

2.3 Profiling Libraries

In order to provide maximum flexibility, the profiling routines are not included in the instrumented assembly version of the program. Rather, these routines are contained in a library file and are added to the instrumented program during the link phase. To date, two different profiling libraries have been implemented and tested. The simpler of these libraries, the `trace` library, generates a basic block trace of the instrumented program. This trace can then be used by a variety of applications including trace driven simulators and the analysis program.

---

[1] A basic block is a sequence of instructions which has a single entry point and a single exit.

This program is part of the *goblin* system and extracts simple statistics from the trace.

One drawback to the `trace` library is that the trace of the entire program execution is explicitly generated and stored for subsequent analysis. This explicit generation and storage can take a prohibitively long time and large amount of space for large programs. In order to avoid this penalty when profiling programs, a second library, the `otftrace` (on-the-fly) library, has been implemented. This library collects and computes the statistics during program execution, and avoids the problems involved in storing and manipulating large address traces. In the current implementation, it also provides approximately an order of magnitude increase in the speed of execution of the instrumented program as compared to the `trace` library. This library is the one used to profile and generate the results for the SPEC programs.

3 Profiling Experiments

This section describes the set of programs analyzed, and the methods used to collect and analyze the data for each program.

3.1 Program Set

The results presented in this paper are based on our analysis of the SPEC benchmark suite which is becoming a standard for reporting performance of engineering and scientific workstations [7]. This suite attempts to provide a program workload that is representative of typical engineering and scientific applications. Table 1 presents a short description of each program along with the number of instructions traced and analyzed for each program. These programs are used because they represent an accepted standard, the results for a wide variety of other architectures have been reported and provide a source for comparison, and the sources and input data sets are widely available.

We have successfully instrumented and profiled nine of the ten SPEC programs. The gcc program has presented difficulties due to its large static code size: it causes the current version of the RS/6000 assembler to fail. Without modification, the assembler cannot handle the extremely large assembly file produced by instrumenting gcc.

3.2 Experimental Method

In order to generate the various statistics reported below, the following procedure is used. Each SPEC

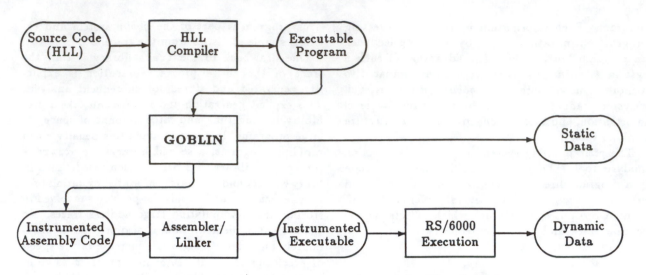

Figure 2: The *Goblin* Instrumentation and Profiling Procedure

Program	Description	Characteristics	Dynamic instrs
doduc	Monte Carlo simulation of nuclear reactor	FORTRAN, floating point	1060×10^6
eqntott	boolean equation to truth table translator	C, integer	979×10^6
espresso	logic minimization package	C, integer	2180×10^6
fpppp	quantum chemistry simulation	FORTRAN, floating point	1040×10^6
li	XLISP interpreter solving 8 queens problem	C, integer	5779×10^6
matrix300	matrix operations on 300x300 matrices	FORTRAN, floating point	1110×10^6
nasa7	seven floating-point kernels from NASA	FORTRAN, floating point	4860×10^6
spice2g6	device level circuit simulator	FORTRAN, floating point	14780×10^6
tomcatv	vectorized mesh generation	FORTRAN, floating point	744×10^6
gcc	GNU C compiler	C, integer	N/A

Table 1: The SPEC Programs

program is compiled with the options supplied by IBM for use with the SPEC suite. During this step, a compiler option is used to append symbol table information to the object module, as required by *goblin*. Each program is then executed to verify that its unprofiled behavior produces results identical to those supplied with the SPEC suite. During this stage the execution time of each program is obtained. From these data the SPECratio for each program is computed. Figure 3 plots the SPECratio for each program and the geometric mean of the entire set of programs, the subset of floating point intensive programs, and the subset of integer programs. The geometric mean of the SPECratio for each program is the SPECmark for the machine. The measured SPECmark value is slightly higher than the published value [7] because gcc has been omitted from this measurement.

Once a working, optimized version of a SPEC program has been generated, an optimized, instrumented version of each program is generated following the procedure outlined in Section 2. This instrumented version is then executed on the RS/6000, and

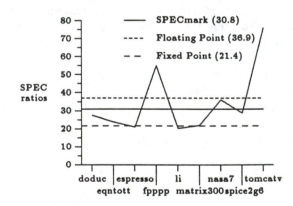

Figure 3: Summary of Measured SPEC Ratios

the results are verified to make sure they are identical to the results supplied by SPEC. This step assures that the instrumentation and profiling routines have not changed the semantics of the program.

The addition of instrumentation code causes the static code size of the SPEC programs to increase by a factor of three, on average, over the size of the original static code. The increase in execution time due to the overhead of the instrumentation code and the profiling library can be measured for each of the profiling libraries independently. A lower bound on the execution cost of profiling is obtained by replacing the context swap code with a return instruction. With this modification the only additional code executed by the instrumented version of the program is the instrumentation code. Averaged across the nine SPEC programs (excluding gcc), instrumentation alone increases the runtime by a factor of three.

The cost of using the otftrace library, the library used to profile the SPEC programs, increases linearly with the number of instructions profiled. The cost of profiling a single instruction is approximately $11\mu s$ which represents a slowdown of program execution by a factor of 275. The majority of this cost is associated with collecting register utilization information as described in Section 4.4. For this preliminary study no attempt has been made to minimize this cost.

3.3 Register Working Set

The average size of the register working set (RWS) for each program is presented in Section 4.4. This information has been collected as follows. The RWS at instruction i is defined to be the set of registers which are *live* during instruction i's execution. A register is *live* for those instructions between a register write and the read directly prior to the next write. Thus, a register is considered *live* when it holds a value which later read. The lifetime of this value is defined to be the number of instructions between the first write of the register and the last read of the register. If a register is never read then it is defined to have a lifetime of zero.

We define the size of the RWS at instruction i as:

$$| RWS_i | = \sum_{j=1}^{\# \text{ regs}} P_i(j),$$

where $P_i(j) = \begin{cases} 1 & \text{if register } j \text{ is live in instr } i \\ 0 & \text{otherwise} \end{cases}$

Determining the RWS at each instruction requires one to maintain long traces of program execution, which becomes impractical for large programs. We therefore simplify the problem by computing only the average RWS size as follows:

$$average \mid RWS \mid = \frac{\sum_{i=1}^{n} \mid RWS_i \mid}{n} = \frac{\sum_{i=1}^{n} \sum_{j=1}^{\# \text{ regs}} P_i(j)}{n}$$

where n is the total number of instructions in the program. The two summations in the above equation are independent and so may be interchanged. This allows the live regions for each register to be computed independently. The live region is found by scanning the instruction stream, and maintaining a table indicating the last instruction at which each register was read and written. When a subsequent write to that register is encountered, the number of instructions between the previous write and read is accumulated. The average |RWS| is then easily computed by summing the lifetimes of each individual register and dividing by the total number of instructions.

3.4 Branching Statistics

The branching statistics are collected by noting the following: each branch that is profiled terminates a basic block. Therefore, immediately after each branch the profiling routine is entered, and the direction taken by that branch can be determined. In order to handle an arbitrary n-way branch, such as the register indirect branch typically used to implement a *switch* statement in C, it is sufficient to associate a list of successor addresses with each basic block.

4 Results and Evaluation

The total number of instructions executed for each SPEC program is summarized in Table 1. The execution of dynamically linked library calls and operating system calls is not currently profiled, so the numbers in Table 1 represent a lower bound on the total number of instructions executed by each program. However, it has been determined, by using the *prof/gprof* system described earlier, that the percentage of time each program spends in library routines is less than one percent of its total execution time. Thus omitting the library routines does not significantly distort the results.

4.1 Instruction Mix

Figures 4 and 5 present the dynamic instruction mix for each of the programs. In Figure 4, instructions are classified based on the unit in which they are executed. For this classification, floating point loads and stores are counted as fixed point unit operations. In Figure 5, instructions are classified based on execution latency. Since many instructions have variable latencies and the exact latency is difficult to determine, the latency assigned to an instruction represents a worst case value. For instance, conditional branches may execute in zero to three cycles, but they are all classified as instructions with a latency of three cycles. Instructions with data dependent latencies, i.e. the string operations, are considered to have a minimum latency of four cycles. The only other instructions with latency of four or greater are floating point divide and integer multiply. Integer multiply has a worst case latency of five cycles. Normal fixed point instructions have a latency of one cycle, and normal floating point instructions (add, multiply) have a latency of two cycles.

In order to approximate the capability of the RS/6000's parallel instruction dispatching, the *potential issuing parallelism* (PIP) can be computed from the data in Figure 4. The PIP is calculated based upon the following two optimistic assumptions: there are no data dependencies among the instructions and the instructions which execute on different units are evenly distributed throughout the program. Given these assumptions, the instruction mix data of Figure 4 exactly determine how many instructions on average may be issued in parallel each cycle, e.g. if there are 50% floating point instructions and 50% fixed point instructions then the PIP will be equal to two. On the RS/6000, the SPEC programs exhibit a PIP of between 1.21 on li and 2.00 on tomcatv. The condition code unit (CCU) instructions have been ignored in these calculations so the maximum possible PIP is equal to three.

To aid in the interpretation of the data presented in Figure 5, the average degree of superpipelining (ADS) [11] has been computed. The ADS is computed by multiplying the latency of an instruction class by the frequency of that class and averaging over all instruction classes. For the SPEC programs running on the RS/6000, the ADS ranges from 1.65 on espresso to 2.01 on matrix300.

The product of PIP and ADS, the *potential machine parallelism* (PMP), reflects the amount of resource parallelism visible to a particular program. For the program to fully utilize the PMP, the instruction level parallelism (ILP) inherent in the program must be greater than or equal to the PMP.

4.2 Basic Block Statistics

Table 2 presents the average basic block sizes for each program. The sizes are measured in number of instructions. This number is computed by dividing the total number of instructions executed by the total number of basic blocks executed. The fpppp program is machine generated and has some abnormally large basic blocks. This accounts for its high average basic block size. The dynamic basic block

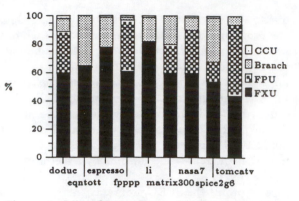

Figure 4: Mix of Instr Types by Execution Unit

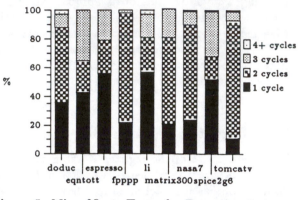

Figure 5: Mix of Instr Types by Execution Latency

size for the eqntott program is extremely small due to the large percentage of branches executed by this program. This program spends 95% of its execution time sorting using the quicksort algorithm.

Program	Static Average	Dynamic Average	Avg. Branch Distance
doduc	7.48	5.61	10.59
eqntott	3.58	2.09	2.86
espresso	3.96	3.40	4.81
fpppp	14.56	33.40	58.35
li	4.02	3.92	6.05
matrix300	6.43	5.00	5.05
nasa7	7.53	9.72	10.72
spice2g6	6.26	4.34	3.27
tomcatv	5.25	10.90	16.28

Table 2: Average Basic Block Sizes, Branch Distances

4.3 Branching Characteristics

Table 2 also presents the average distance between branches for each program. Distance is defined to be the number of instructions executed between branches, including the branch instruction. These data are related to but not identical to the average basic block sizes since basic blocks need not be separated by a branch instruction. The program fpppp again exhibits a large distance between branches because it executes large basic blocks, and eqntott again executes a mere three instructions between branches because of its small basic blocks.

Figure 6 presents the results of the branch behavior analysis of the SPEC programs. Branches are broken down into the following four types: unconditional branches, taken conditional branches, not taken conditional branches, and register indirect jumps.

The RS/6000 attempts to minimize the effect of branches on the execution pipelines. It is able to do this for several types of branches: unconditional branches, conditional branches that are not taken, and loop closing branches implemented with a decrement and branch instruction. Table 3 summarizes the percentage of these types of branches in the programs. These branches are resolved early enough by the branch processing unit to avoid pipeline breaks. Three of the programs, matrix300, tomcatv and nasa7, contain a very high percentage of these types of branches: the vast majority of these are loop closing branches executed while processing large matrices. With the exception of li, the percentages for the rest of the programs remain high, and provide evidence that this branch resolution mechanism works well for a large variety of scientific programs.

Program	% Branches Resolved
doduc	93.9%
eqntott	98.5%
espresso	97.9%
fpppp	94.5%
li	88.7%
matrix300	99.9%
nasa7	97.8%
spice2g6	97.5%
tomcatv	99.9%

Table 3: Branches Resolved Without Delay Penalty

are assigned to bucket 2^n. These buckets are plotted along the x-axis in the figures. The fraction of total lifetimes is plotted on the y-axis using a log scale. These values have been averaged over all of the SPEC programs. Also plotted in both figures are the read distances. These correspond to the distance between the last write or write and a read. These data give some indication of the frequency of access to a variable stored in a register.

From Figure 7 it can be seen that values stored in fixed point registers tend to be live for between 1 and 32 instructions, while these values are accessed between every 1 to 16 instructions. Figure 8 shows the majority of floating point lifetimes to be small: 1 to 32 instructions. However, there are some odd peaks in the data near the high end of the scale. These peaks are primarily due to the anomalous floating point behavior of li and espresso. These integer intensive programs make use of the floating point registers at widely separated points in the program which gives rise to extremely long lifetimes.

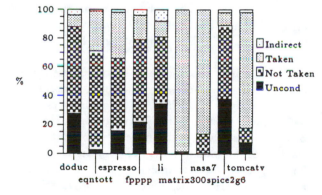

Figure 6: Mix of Branch Instruction Types

4.4 Register Utilization

Figures 7 and 8 present results of the register lifetime analysis, (see Section 3.3 for a definition of lifetime). The otftrace library collects this information while determining the register working set (see Section 3.3). In both graphs, the register lifetimes have been assigned to "buckets" as follows: all lifetimes between 2^n and $2^{n+1} - 1$ instructions

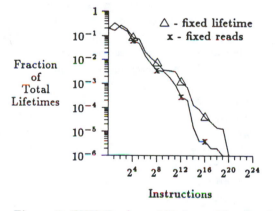

Figure 7: FXU Register Lifetimes Distribution

Figures 9 and 10 present the average number of registers live for each program. These statistics have been collected as described in Section 3.3. Several interesting questions can be asked about register usage. The most straightforward one, "are there

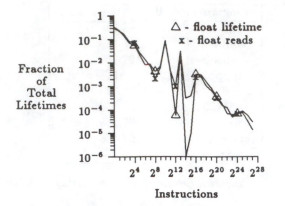

Figure 8: FPU Register Lifetimes Distributions

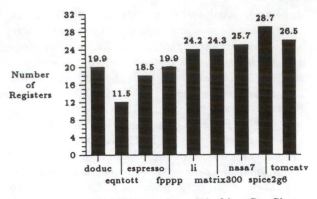

Figure 9: Average FXU Register Working Set Sizes

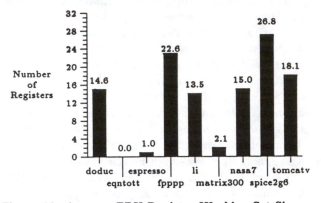

Figure 10: Average FPU Register Working Set Sizes

enough registers?", is, unfortunately, hard to answer. The average RWS, however, provides some insights since it represents a lower bound on how many registers are required. In Figures 9 and 10, it is apparent that for most of the SPEC programs the fixed point register file is well utilized, and that with fewer than 32 registers the RS/6000 would probably suffer a decrease in performance.

The eqntott program does not make use of a large number, on average, of fixed point registers. This is probably due to the small basic blocks in this program and the amount of time it spends executing branches (see Section 4.2). This type of behavior can make register allocation very difficult for the compiler which in turn can decrease the register working set.

The average floating point RWS data tell a similar story. The use of floating point registers by the espresso and li programs is essentially irrelevant as described above. For the programs which execute useful floating point instructions, the working sets again provide a lower bound on the number of registers needed for this level of performance. The matrix300 program is an interesting exception because its performance is not determined by the number of available registers. The majority of the execution of this program is spent in a single inner loop (saxpy) which performs a multiply accumulate. On the RS/6000, the execution of this loop is limited by the available memory bandwidth. Only two registers are required, one for each operand, to achieve maximum performance.

4.5 Locality Analysis

Figures 11 and 12 present the results of a locality analysis performed on the programs. The results in Figure 11 are obtained as follows: the contribution of each basic block to the total number of instructions

executed is computed; the dominant basic blocks are then sorted from largest contributor to smallest and plotted. Figure 12 illustrates the same results, but instead of basic blocks, the static number of instructions contained in the dominant basic blocks is plotted.

Code locality is important in system design because it dictates necessary instruction cache size. Code locality is quantified in the *goblin* system by determining the number of instructions and/or basic blocks in the static program responsible for a given fraction of the total number of instructions executed. This is, in effect, a graphical representation of the popular 90%/10% rule. Figures 11 and 12 show the number of basic blocks and instructions, respectively, which account for a given fraction of total executed instructions.

Locality analysis shows that for five of the nine programs, 90% of the executed instructions depend on less than 1000 unique instructions (see Figure 12). The instruction cache on the RS/6000 is 8 Kbytes and can easily capture the critical working set of these programs. The other programs show a wide variation in locality.

Looking at the number of basic blocks contributing to total execution also shows a wide spectrum, yet the total number is still fairly small for most programs. It should be noted that programs with small basic block counts are excellent candidates for specialized optimization.

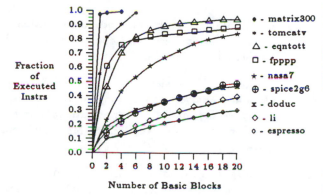

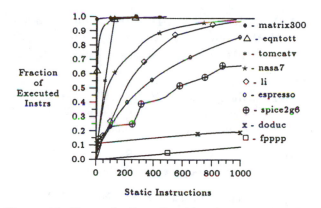

Figure 11: Dynamic Contribution of Dominant Basic Blocks

Figure 12: Dynamic Contribution of Instructions in Dominant Basic Blocks

5 Comparison & Conclusions

To provide perspective on the evaluation of the RS/6000, similar experiments have been repeated on a DECStation 3100. This machine has a MIPS R2000 CPU running at 16.6MHz and 24 Mbytes of main memory. The data for this machine have been collected with the aid of the *pixie* [9] profiling program. Only six of the SPEC programs have been successfully profiled on the DS3100 due to problems with both the *pixie* system and the FORTRAN compiler.

Table 4 presents the measured cycles per instruction (CPI) obtained per program for both machines. Note that the data for the DS3100 include the library functions. Also presented for each machine is the number of instructions executed per program (IPP).

	CPI		IPP	
Program	DS3100	RS/6000	DS3100	RS/6000
doduc	1.99	1.61	1.6B	1.1B
eqntott	1.25	1.15	1.3B	1.0B
espresso	1.31	1.21	3.4B	2.2B
fpppp	2.53	1.33	2.9B	1.0B
li	N/A	1.34	N/A	5.8B
matrix300	2.98	4.66	4.7B	1.1B
nasa7	N/A	2.89	N/A	4.9B
spice2g6	N/A	1.41	N/A	14.8B
tomcatv	2.19	1.18	2.1B	0.7B

Table 4: DS3100 and RS/6000 Comparison

It is interesting to note that the RS/6000 achieves a lower CPI on every comparable program except matrix300. As mentioned previously, the vast majority of the instructions executed in matrix300 are in a single tight loop. On both machines, the performance of this loop is limited by the data memory bandwidth, but the DS3100 executes 21 instructions in this inner loop while the RS/6000 executes only 5 instructions. Thus, while performing an equivalent amount of work, the DS3100 executes four times as many instructions as the RS/6000. The RS/6000 achieves this compact inner loop by encoding a multiply-add operation as a single instruction and by encoding update forms of load and store operations as single instructions [12].

By combining the PIP and the ADS (see Section 4.1), it is possible to approximate the cycles per instruction (CPI) [5] for each program. The first approximation is based on the pessimistic assumption that there is a data dependency between *every* two consecutive instructions. Under this assumption, PIP instructions can be dispatched every ADS cycles so the pessimistic approximation for CPI is $CPI_{pes} = ADS/PIP$. On the other hand, $1/PIP$ can be used as the optimistic approximation, CPI_{opt}, i.e. PIP number of instructions can always be issued in every cycle. These two CPI values can be averaged to give the best estimated CPI, CPI_{est}, see Table 5.

By comparing the measured CPI to the estimated CPI it is possible to determine how efficiently the RS/6000 is executing instructions. The measured CPI values which include both cache and operating system effects, are very close to CPI_{exp} for every program except matrix300. For matrix300, the measured CPI is not close to the estimate because the assumptions behind the estimate do not take memory latency into account. These data indicate that overall the RS/6000 is a very efficient architecture.

Program	CPI_{pes}	CPI_{opt}	CPI_{est}	CPI_{meas}
doduc	1.10	0.63	0.87	1.62
eqntott	1.25	0.65	0.95	1.51
espresso	1.30	0.79	1.04	1.21
fpppp	1.11	0.62	0.86	1.33
li	1.36	0.83	1.10	1.34
matrix300	1.21	0.60	0.90	4.66
nasa7	1.13	0.61	0.87	2.89
spice2g6	0.99	0.55	0.77	1.41
tomcatv	0.98	0.50	0.74	1.18

Table 5: Estimated and Measured CPI Values for the RS/6000

6 Future Directions

The *goblin* system has been used to successfully instrument and profile nine of the ten SPEC program. While this system provides a rich set of information for the computer architect to work with, there are several areas where its capabilities can be extended. The most obvious extension is the addition of a data address trace collection mechanism. *Goblin* is being modified to include this feature. When the modification is complete, *goblin* will be able to add instrumentation code to collect a complete memory reference trace. A new profiling library is also being designed which will provide on-the-fly analysis of these traces. This library will also provide an efficient interface to a cache simulator.

Given that an instruction level profiling system now exists for both the IBM RS/6000 as well as the DS3100, a detailed architectural comparison between these two machines can now be performed.

In summary, the *goblin* system provides the basic instruction level profiling mechanisms necessary to make it a valuable tool to computer architects, engineers, and application programmers. We plan to place the goblin system in the public domain in the near future. More information is available from the authors.

7 Acknowledgments

We would like to thank John A. Derringer and Paul Bassett of IBM-STD for providing the RS/6000 system, Martin Hopkins of IBM-TJW and Bill Brantley of IBM-AWD for their discussions, assistance and encouragement, Alan DeWitt of IBM-Pittsburgh for his assistance in installing and maintaining our RS/6000 system, and Trung Diep of CMU for assistance in debugging early versions of *goblin*.

References

[1] M. Johnson, *Superscalar Microprocessor Design*. Englewood Cliffs, NJ: Prentice-Hall, Inc., 1991.

[2] D. W. Wall. "Link-time code modification,". Digital Western Research Laboratory, Research Report 89/17, Sep. 1989.

[3] A. Borg, R. E. Kessler, and D. W. Wall, "Generation and analysis of very long address traces," in *Proceedings of the 17th International Symposium on Computer Architecture*, May 1990, pp. 270–279.

[4] A. Borg, R. E. Kessler, G. Lazana, and D. Wall. "Long address traces from RISC machines: Generation and analysis,". Digital Western Research Laboratory, Research Report 89/14, 1989.

[5] J. L. Hennessy and D. A. Patterson, *Computer Architecture A Quantitative Approach*. San Mateo, CA: Morgan Kaufmann Publishers, Inc., 1989.

[6] P. S. Hauge, ed., *IBM Journal of Research and Development*. IBM Corporation, Jan. 1990. Special Issue on the RS/6000.

[7] "SPEC newsletter,". Systems Performance Evaluation Cooperative, Spring 1990.

[8] M. Misra, ed., *IBM RISC System/6000 Technology*. IBM Corporation, 1990. IBM Publication SA23-2619.

[9] "MIPS language programmer's guide,". MIPS Computer Systems, Inc., 1986.

[10] *IBM RISC System/6000, XL C User's Guide*. IBM Corporation, 1990. IBM Publication SC09-1259.

[11] N. P. Jouppi, "The nonuniform distribution of instruction-level and machine parallelism and its effect on performance.," *IEEE Transactions on Computers*, vol. 38, pp. 1645–1658, Dec. 1989.

[12] C. B. Hall and K. O'Brien, "Performance characteristics of architectural features of the IBM RISC system/6000," in *Proceedings of ASPLOS-IV*, 1991.

Decoupled access/execute architectures

STRUCTURED MEMORY ACCESS ARCHITECTURE

A. R. Pleszkun
Department of Computer Science
University of Wisconsin
1210 W. Dayton St.
Madison, WI 53706

E. S. Davidson
Coordinated Science Laboratory
University of Illinois
1101 W. Springfield Ave.
Urbana, IL 61801

ABSTRACT

Conventional von Neumann architectures generate addresses for referencing memory by transferring addressing information from the memory to the CPU, by performing computations on addressing information, and by fetching and executing address bookkeeping instructions. Memory wait time is increased by computing operand addresses just before executing instructions which use those operands. These phenomena result in the von Neumann bottleneck at the CPU-memory interface. This work investigates one method of reducing the von Neumann bottleneck.

Program referencing behavior is determined by analyzing dynamic address traces. The Structured Memory Access (SMA) architecture developed in this work uses a computation processor (CP) and a decoupled memory access processor (MAP) with special hardware for efficient accessing of program and data structures and for effective branch and loop management.

Prototypical SMA machines are compared to conventional VAX-like machines. For a set of benchmark programs, the SMA machine reduces the number of memory references to between 1/5 and 2/5 of those required by a VAX. Actual performance is very sensitive to memory bandwidth and the amount of unoverlapped computation; however, SMA machines perform significantly better than conventional machines with the same parameter values. The SMA architecture reduces addressing overhead and improves system performance by (1) efficiently generating operand requests, (2) making fewer memory references, and (3) maximizing computation and access process overlap.

1. INTRODUCTION

This paper concerns the interactions between the central processing unit (CPU) and the memory of a computer system, modeled as shown in figure 1 [Hamm77]. Work performed by the CPU is partitioned into an access process and a computation process. The access process generates a stream of addresses for read and write requests to be serviced by the memory. Write data can originate from either process. The memory responds to read requests by generating a stream of data and instructions which returns to the CPU. Some portions of these data and instructions, returned to the access process,

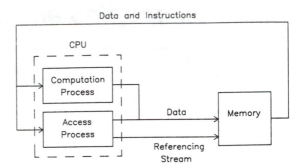

Figure 1. CPU-memory model

contain information for generating more references; the remaining portion is used by the computation process to produce its output data. In our view, the computation process performs the desired work of the system, while the work done by the access process represents overhead which should be reduced.

In conventional von Neumann architectures, the CPU interacts with only 1 memory, over 1 bus, and receives only 1 word per memory access. The computation and access processes compete for access to the memory over this single, narrow path, the so-called "von Neumann bottleneck."

A great deal of computing is performed solely for the generation of addresses. Hammerstrom [Hamm77] calculated the addressing overhead and the entropy of the stream of computation references by analyzing the address traces of several programs executed on an IBM 360. By measuring addressing overhead in bits input to the access process per computation process reference, he found that for a Gaussian elimination program and an eigenvalue-finding program, the addressing overhead was, respectively, 17.2 and 17.0 bits per computation reference. For a symbol manipulation program, the addressing overhead was 24.1 bits per computation process instruction fetch or memory data reference. These results represent a large percentage of the total number of bits input to the CPU from the memory.

The inefficiency of the conventional access process is exposed further when the addressing overhead is compared to the entropy of the stream of computation references. The entropy of the computation reference stream is likewise measured in bits per computation reference and is interpreted as the average number of bits needed to select among the possible successor references, i.e., to choose the particular next reference address given the current reference address. If the current and the possible successor reference addresses are

This work was supported by Navelex under contract N00039-80-C-0556: Reliable, High-Performance VHSIC Systems.

known, Hammerstrom found that for the programs he analyzed, between .845 and 1.86 bits of information per computation reference are needed to select among the possible successor reference addresses. These values can be treated as lower bounds on the number of bits which would be needed to specify a successor reference. Comparing these values to the addressing overhead, we find that they differ by at least an order of magnitude. Thus significantly more bits than necessary are being transferred between the memory and the access process during the execution of a program.

This access overhead and hence the von Neumann bottleneck can be reduced if the activities of the access process can be (1) modified to reduce the number of times the memory is accessed and (2) overlapped with those of the computation process. This paper introduces a Structured Memory Access (SMA) machine organization which includes mechanisms to take explicit advantage of a program's structure and of the regular patterns in which data structures are referenced. A more detailed presentation of the SMA architecture is found in [Ples82]. This architecture shares some goals and implementation characteristics with Smith's decoupled access/execute (DAE) architecture [Smit82], notably the decoupling of and separate processors for access and execution. The SMA, however, has explicit mechanisms for reducing the bookkeeping overhead for data and program structure references. SMA executes a single instruction stream, whereas DAE requires two.

The SMA "access mechanisms" eliminate most of the accessing overhead for well-structured computations. Previous attempts with conventional architectures, i.e., adding new address modes and including vector data types, have less effect. Use of cache memory actually increases accessing overhead both in time and in costly cache management hardware. Cache memory must be fast enough, and hence expensive, to overcome this overhead and provide improvement. By adding just one additional VLSI processor chip to run the access process, SMA achieves high performance with conventional slow memory. Effective access prediction tolerates slow memory if adequate interleaving is provided; eliminating overhead references can allow SMA to outperform a conventional processor with fast cache memory.

The SMA also includes a "loop mode" which eliminates the need to refetch instructions for each iteration of short loops. Finally, by physically separating the two processes into a memory access processor (MAP) and a computation processor (CP) and allowing them to be loosely coupled, memory wait time is reduced and significant process overlap is achieved. Compilation of SMA programs is straightforward and well suited to the capabilities of conventional compilers.

Little use is made of program structure to reduce addressing overhead in conventional machines. Our preliminary studies [Ples81] have indicated that a substantial amount of structure can be ascertained directly from a mechanical analysis of a program's address stream. Knowing, or at least accurately predicting, possible successor memory references is very important in achieving an efficient access process and can significantly reduce the addressing overhead of a program. Additionally, exploiting this predictability leads to a more nearly autonomous operation of the access process and the computation process, thus permitting an overlapped execution of the two processes and a reduction of memory wait time.

2. STRUCTURED MEMORY ACCESS MACHINE (SMA) ARCHITECTURE

From the analysis of program address traces, it is possible to determine the control and data structures of a program and the mechanisms by which data structures are accessed. Instructions can be divided into blocks such that blocks are entered only at the first instruction and execution always proceeds sequentially to the last instruction. A block may have one, two, or more successor blocks. The control structure of a program is well identified by a graph in which nodes are blocks and arcs point to successor blocks. This control structure can be found by mechanically analyzing the dynamic address trace of a program. Furthermore, if an instruction in a static listing always references the same memory location for its operand, e.g., with a direct addressing mode, that reference is called a scalar data reference; if more than one location is referenced by that operand reference as it recurs in a dynamic address trace, e.g., by using an index mode where the index value varies, the reference is called a data structure reference. This behavioral definition of scalar and structure tends to correspond in practice to common definitions. A sequential pattern of accessing through a data structure, as required for successive executions of a data structure reference, e.g., a row major scan of the upper triangle of a matrix, is called an access mechanism. Scalar data, data structures, and access mechanisms can likewise be found mechanically from trace analysis.

The Structured Memory Access (SMA) architecture uses this structural information to reduce access process overhead. Access process overhead exists in two forms. Address specification overhead refers to the increasing number of address bits needed to address a memory location as the address space becomes large. Most of these bits are redundant, given knowledge about possible address sequences. The second and more costly form of overhead, address calculation overhead, refers to address calculations explicitly performed by the CPU. Address calculation overhead involves some combination of extra instructions, parts of instructions, registers, memory accesses, and computation time. Both types of overhead are greatly reduced by the SMA architecture. Consider, for example, branch target addresses and operand references.

In the SMA machine, the complete branch target address is specified in a branch instruction. However, since the SMA machine provides instruction buffers to capture repeatedly executed instruction blocks, the number of times the branch instruction and its target address are accessed is reduced. The instruction buffer effectively limits the number of bits fetched from memory to specify branch target addresses.

To reference scalars, the SMA machine provides a base register. A scalar reference specification is simply an offset to be summed with the contents of the base register to form an entire scalar address. Traces we have analyzed reference few distinct scalars for the computation process and a few bits are sufficient for the offset.

The referencing of data structures is the prime cause of address calculation overhead. Conventional machines use bookkeeping scalars and instructions to manage iterative sequencing through data structures. To reduce this overhead, the SMA architecture uses special hardware to generate data structure references with minimal input to the access process from the memory.

The SMA machine implements the function of index registers by using a hardware stack. This stack tracks the active indices of inner loops during program execution, and all data structure references are made by using a subset of these index values. To reduce access process input, tables in the SMA processor are used to store the base address of each data structure and other information necessary to generate an entire address from indices. These tables must be loaded before any instruction which uses them is executed. Depending on the amount of hardware allocated for the tables, the number of data structures, and their access mechanisms, the tables may only have to be loaded once at the beginning of program execution. The tables may also be loaded during the execution of the program. A data structure reference specification is thus a set of pointers to table entries. Such a scheme provides the necessary flexibility for generating access mechanisms while maximizing the rate of address generation through the use of pipelining techniques.

Generally, the value of an index only needs to be associated with the access process. Thus, the stack containing indices, the tables for generating data structure references, and the address generation portion of the CPU may be separated from the computation-oriented portions of the CPU. This partition divides the computer system into two processors: a computation processor (CP) and a memory access processor (MAP). The CP is used strictly for the computation process, i.e., the useful computations of the system; while the MAP is responsible for the access process, i.e., generating all addresses for data and instructions. The index stack and the associated access tables mentioned above are kept in the MAP. Since only the MAP generates addresses, it controls all transactions with the memory.

There is no address bus between the CP and the memory since all memory requests are generated and controlled by the MAP. Also, since the CP is not responsible for addressing, the instructions sent to the CP contain no addressing information. Thus, the instructions are short and contain little more than opcodes and register tags. The CP is strictly devoted to performing computations and contains the ALU of the system; instructions and data are streamed into the CP by the MAP. The CP may receive entire blocks of instructions which it then holds in an internal instruction buffer. The CP may execute in loop mode by iterating over one or more blocks of instructions in its buffer without refetching. The CP also has a set of registers for holding the scalars used by an instruction block. The internal instruction buffer and the registers are provided to eliminate some repeated memory accessing and its associated time and load on the MAP.

The MAP, as shown in figure 2, has an internal Operand-Instruction Buffer (OIB) to hold its instructions and the operand specifications of CP instructions. The MAP can also operate in a loop mode fashion. Operation of the MAP is, to a great extent, independent of the CP. When the MAP begins receiving instructions, it forwards the MAP instructions and the operand specification portions of CP instructions to its OIB. The opcode and register tag portions of CP instructions are forwarded to the CP instruction buffer. The MAP immediately begins generation of operand addresses. The operand addresses are then placed on the read or write queue of outstanding memory requests. Write data is produced in the same order as corresponding write addresses. Thus when write data is produced, it is paired with the appropriate queued write address. As soon as a read request is serviced, the operand returned by that request is forwarded to the CP or to the MAP tables. With such a scheme, reads are performed early, writes are done late, the CP concentrates on the useful calculations of a program, and the MAP is left with the important, but overhead-related, generation of addresses.

The MAP accesses instruction blocks, scalars, and data structures with special hardware. Special instructions initialize and control the access mechanisms used for address generation. An SMA program thus contains a mixture of MAP and CP instructions. The data type of each operand is explicitly specified in each instruction. This extra information found in SMA instructions requires that the compiler must be capable of distinguishing loop control (index) branching from data dependent branching, and scalars from data structures.

Super computers and vector machines also contain special hardware for array referencing; however, the programming of these machines quite often requires rearranging of an algorithm to suit the hardware, and program compilation is difficult. Furthermore, their structured data access mechanisms are usually limited to a single vector of the structure at a time, i.e., "a constant stride" or constant step-size access mechanism with one index. Also, the same operation must be executed on each element of the vector, few vectors can be active at once, and access mechanisms are not easily suspended and resumed when more complex program loops are executed. The TI-ASC offers somewhat more flexibility by providing both inner and outer loop control for stepping though a matrix, i.e., two active indices.

The SMA machine provides more flexibility in the accessing of matrices since it offers more index levels by providing a stack on which to store indices. In our observations, even a 2-dimensional structure can require 3 levels of loop nesting for controlled rescan. Extra levels of nesting are also useful for providing nonconstant strides.

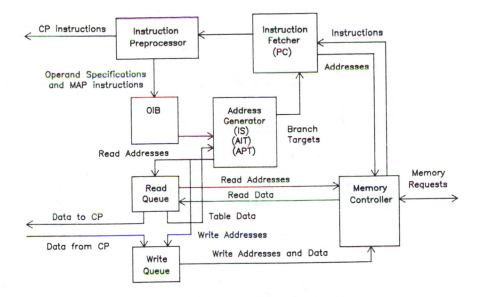

Figure 2. MAP internal organization

In vector machines, the vector access mechanisms are explicitly coded into instructions and then recognized and set up during execution time. The SMA architecture is designed so that data structure access mechanisms are recognized as early as possible. Some accesses mechanisms can be set up as early as compile time or load time. This early recognition can lead to reduced run-time overhead.

In conventional systems, the ALU makes branch decisions. In the SMA, two types of branch decisions are distinguished: decisions based on program data, which are made by the CP, and those based on indices used for referencing data, which are made by the MAP.

The SMA thus reduces the serial dependence which exists between the access process and the computation process. Since the MAP makes branch decisions based on index values during the execution of a loop, the MAP can generate memory requests for operands before the CP is ready to execute the instructions requiring those operands. In fact, the MAP should normally stay ahead of the CP so as to minimize the amount of time that the CP waits for data from memory. The MAP must wait for the CP when the MAP's read data queue is full or when the CP must resolve a computation-dependent branch. The CP must wait for the MAP when the MAP's write data queue is full, when the read data queue is empty, or when the CP instruction buffer does not contain the next instruction.

The SMA organization described above is used to reduce the addressing overhead primarily by improving the accessing of data structures through efficient access mechanisms and prefetching. The process of accessing instructions can likewise be improved if information concerning the instruction block structure of a program, which is apparent in high-level source code, is kept with the program as it is translated down to machine level. Retaining the block structure of a program can be used advantageously to cause the CP to enter and leave loops.

In conventional machines, loop mode control is generated dynamically during execution. Upon recognizing a short backwards branch, it is assumed that the second iteration of a loop is about to begin. The instructions of the loop are refetched and trapped in the loop buffer where they remain for repeated execution until the loop ending branch is unsuccessful.

The loop buffers in the CP and the MAP also trap loop instructions. However, loop mode control is set up at compile time. Loop structures are quite explicit and obvious in the high-level language source code available at compile time. If the instruction blocks which form the body of a loop are sufficiently short, they may all be stored in the instruction buffer at the same time. The processors thus are able to trap the body of a loop the first time the loop is executed. The loop buffers eliminate the need for repeated memory accesses for the same instructions during the execution of a loop. In any case, repetition requires no data-dependent branch and no wait time. Execution continuation after the loop is also efficient when the successor block is known, since it can be prefetched by the MAP during loop execution.

This structured prefetching by the MAP from a conventional slow memory with small processor buffers and without overhead references is felt to be superior to the unstructured use of a costly cache memory with attendant miss penalties, superfluity problems, and access overhead reference cycles.

3. AN SMA IMPLEMENTATION

3.1. Data Types

In this implementation, the SMA distinguishes among four types of operands: (1) immediate operands, (2) scalar operands, (3) data structure operands, and (4) index operands. Immediate operands are data whose values are embedded in an instruction. Scalar and data structure operands are defined as above. An index operand is one of the current indices found on the index stack. The index operand is used only to read a current index value from the index stack and transfer its value to the CP. An index operand differs from a scalar operand primarily in that the index operand originates from the MAP while the scalar operand originates from the memory. The operand type may be specified in a subfield of an instruction's operand field or it may be implicitly associated with a particular instruction. Additionally, an indirect addressing mode is provided specifically for use in the calling of subroutines and in the accessing of data items from structures such as linked lists. As with operand type specification, indirect addressing may be specified in a variety of ways.

At some time it may be desirable to distinguish explicitly among several types of data structures. Instead of having a data structure operand, one may wish to have an array operand, a linked list operand, a binary tree operand, etc. For each operand type, some special accessing mechanisms would be provided to improve the speed with which an operand address is generated. Accessing mechanisms as implemented allow the instruction code to reference structured data simply by pointing to the mechanism, which then references the next data in the established pattern.

3.2. Scalar Data

Scalar data is treated in the manner of a vector rather than as a set of disassociated items. The specification for a scalar operand includes a specification of a MAP base register and a displacement into a scalar data area in memory. The MAP can have more than one scalar base register to aid in the accessing of local and global variables, such as during subroutine calls. Such a base register can be used as the argument pointer set during a subroutine call. For the programs we studied, the number of simultaneously active scalars is relatively small, particularly in an SMA program.

3.3. Index Operations

The SMA's memory access processor has special mechanisms to track indices for data structure computations. These indices are used to generate the addresses for specific items of the data structure to be referenced. An index is specified by its current value, final value, step-size and indexing level. When the index is first established, the current value is equal to its initial value. At any time, several indices may be active; and the level, or nesting, of these indices is dictated by the time at which they were instantiated, or set up. In the SMA, the current value, final value, and step-size of an index are kept on a LIFO stack structure known as the index stack (IS). Each stack position is numbered sequentially, with the bottom of the stack numbered level 1. This convention provides a convenient way of referring to the current value of any active index because the bottom of stack entry corresponds to the outermost level of nesting, i.e., level 1. Stack continuation in memory can be provided for overflow.

When a "setup index" instruction is executed by the MAP, the initial value, final value, and step-size are pushed onto the stack. To change the current value of an index, an "increment index" instruction is used. This instruction must specify three items: the level of the index which is being incremented, and two initial addresses of blocks which are the targets of a branch outcome. If the current value of the index is less than the final value, control is transferred to the first block which is specified. If, on the other hand, the current value equals or exceeds the final value, control is transferred to the second specified block.

By checking the index value early, during each increment index instruction, and by having the branching information available, the next instruction can start being accessed while the CP is still performing the final computations of a loop. Furthermore, no guess is made about which direction an index-based branch will take, thus no time is wasted in fetching potentially unnecessary blocks of instructions from the main memory.

When the current value of the index has reached its final value, that index should be at the top-of-stack and it is removed (popped) from the stack. Two other methods of removing indices from the stack are (1) the "remove index" instruction which removes the highest level current index from the top of the stack and (2) a "clear all indices" instruction which removes all indices from the stack.

To save loading of index instruction parameters from memory, The MAP is loaded with a set of templates for these values at the start of program execution. A template is a specification of the values needed to initialize an index on the index stack. Templates are loaded into an index template table. When an index is set up in the IS, the IS is loaded directly from the index template table. For a particular program, the number of distinct templates could be fairly small. For example, analysis of a Gaussian elimination program shows that 995 dynamic index setups are required, representing 16 static index setups, but only 8 templates are needed. Each index activated with a particular initial specification can use the same entry from the index template table. Even if the number of templates exceeds the table size, judicious reloading limits overhead.

3.4. Data Structure Accessing

To access data structures in the SMA, one must combine index values to form a data address. In the SMA, information for forming proper combinations is stored in two data tables within the MAP. As with some of the other repeatedly used information, the contents of the tables may be loaded when the program begins execution. The two tables are the access pattern table (APT), which indicates the index levels to be used, and the access information table (AIT), which contains information about data structures.

Each line of the APT is divided into several dimension fields. Each dimension field is divided into 2 subfields. The index level subfield indicates which level of the index stack (IS) is associated with that dimension field. The offset sub-field contains the value of a small positive or negative offset to be added to the index before the index is used. This feature is useful since quite often the index of a data structure access is an existing presently active index, plus or minus a small constant. An entry in the APT may be used by more than one data structure since the information is not altered during execution and does not depend on accessing a specific data structure.

For each data structure currently being used by the program, there is an entry in the AIT. If the number of data structures in a program is sufficiently small, the AIT need only be loaded at the beginning of program execution. Each entry of the AIT is composed of three types of values: (1) the base address of the data structure, (2) a displacement for each dimension of the data structure, and (3) an upper bound for each dimension of the data structure.

A data structure reference may be made by specifying an entry in the APT and an entry in the AIT. A data structure address is generated by summing the base address in the AIT entry and the index terms for each dimension. Each term is formed by adding the offset in the APT entry to the index value identified by the level in the APT entry and multiplying by the displacement in the AIT entry. Bounds checking can be performed by comparing the index terms with the bound in the AIT entry.

While this computation may be tedious to perform for each data structure access, hardware must be present in the MAP to perform this computation at least occasionally. Once the hardware is present, it can be pipelined at little additional cost to allow the straightforward solution of performing this computation for every data structure reference. Pipelining allows a high rate of address generation; effective prediction overcomes the pipeline delay and allows the MAP to remain ahead of the CP.

3.5. Control Issues

The instruction fetcher in the MAP is responsible for generating instruction requests. The instruction fetcher sends the instructions it receives from the memory to the instruction preprocessor. The instruction preprocessor forwards portions of instructions to the CP with operand specifications replaced by buffer tags. MAP instructions and operand specifications are placed in the Operand-Instruction Buffer (OIB). The address generation unit steps through the MAP instructions and operand specifications found in the OIB, executes MAP instructions, generates operand addresses, and forwards each operand address to the read or write queue. When the memory returns the data associated with addresses in the read queue, that data is sent to a FIFO buffer in the CP. The CP sends data to the MAP for the write queue. Addresses in the write queue which have received their associated data are serviced by the memory.

The CP has an instruction buffer to hold the instructions it receives from the MAP. An execution unit in the CP steps through the instruction buffer, executing instructions one by one. If an instruction needs a data item from memory, that data is found at the head of the FIFO buffer. If the buffer is empty, execution is suspended until a data item is received from the MAP. Along with each data item, the CP receives an additional bit from the MAP which is used as an end-of-data signal. Assertion of the end-of-data signal in loop mode indicates that execution of the current instruction loop is to terminate and that the CP should begin execution of another block found in its instruction buffer, or wait until a new instruction block arrives from the MAP. The CP generates write data and signals the MAP regarding success or failure of CP tests for data-dependent branches performed in the MAP.

A program begins execution by having the monitor or operating system jump to the beginning of the program; that is, the operating system sets the program counter (PC) to the starting address of the program. In the SMA machine, the PC is located in the instruction fetcher of the MAP. When the PC is set to the beginning of the program, the instruction fetcher generates requests for instructions from the memory. Instruction requests are generated until the end of a block is encountered. If the instruction at the end of a block is a branch instruction, the instruction fetcher suspends operation until the branch is resolved. An end-of-block bit, attached to each instruction, indicates the last instruction of each block. The starting address of each block, as found in the PC, is saved to be used later when checking whether a block loops upon itself or branches to some other block in the OIB (and in the CP instruction buffer).

With the information stored in the OIB, the address generation unit can generate all the data requests required by a program. As the OIB is loaded, the address generator can begin executing MAP instructions and generating operand addresses by stepping through the entries of the OIB with its own internal program counter.

The addresses in the read and write queues are kept in the order that they were generated so that the CP receives read operands in the expected order and the MAP receives write data in the proper order. If write data is soon read back from memory, it is possible that the address of that data item will appear in both queues at the same time. Each time a read address is placed on the read queue, the write queue must be checked for an outstanding write to that address in order to prevent the reading of invalid data. If a match occurs, the read must not be permitted to occur before the write; otherwise, reads have priority over writes.

3.6. Branching

When the instruction fetcher of the MAP reaches the end of a block and the instruction is a branch, the instruction fetcher suspends further sequential instruction requests. If the branch depends on a condition in the CP, a signal must be received from the CP before the instruction fetcher and the address generator can resume operation. This signal indicates the success or failure of the branch. If the branch, however, depends on the value of an index in the index stack, the branch is resolved in the MAP. Thus, if the result of an index-dependent branch requires executing a new block of instructions, the instruction fetcher can begin fetching the instructions of the new block while the CP is performing calculations on the data for a previous block. The address generator can even begin making data requests for the new block while the previous block is still executing in the CP.

At any one time, the CP's instruction buffer may contain the CP instructions for more than one instruction block. The OIB in the MAP must, at the same time, be capable of holding the accessing information and MAP instructions corresponding to the instruction blocks in the CP buffer. The CP's instruction buffer and the MAP's OIB, while they hold information for the same number of blocks, are not necessarily the same size since corresponding CP and MAP blocks themselves differ in size. Monitoring the amount of information held by both the buffers is the responsibility of the instruction preprocessor since the instruction preprocessor fills the OIB and forwards CP instructions to the CP.

When a branch is resolved, there is a chance that the target block of the branch is already resident in the OIB and the CP's instruction buffer. The address generator checks for this situation by comparing the branch target address against the saved first address of each block currently found in the OIB. If there is a match, the address generator can immediately begin generation of data addresses for the new block. If, on the other hand, the information for the block is not in the OIB, the instruction fetcher is signaled by the address generator that a new block must be fetched. In such a case, the address generator must wait until new MAP instructions arrive in the OIB. When a branch is resolved, the MAP must signal the CP which one of the following three branch options the CP should take: (1) continue repeated execution of the currently executing block, (2) execute some other block found in the CP's instruction buffer, or (3) expect to receive a new instruction block from the MAP. When an entire block does not fit in the instruction buffer, it may be streamed through, but loop mode is not possible.

Normally, the CP is in a loop mode type of operation and expects a stream of data from the MAP. That is, if the end of the currently executing block is not a branch which depends on data in the CP, the execution unit of the CP will re-execute the currently executing block as long as the CP receives data from the MAP and the end-of-data signal is not set. This mode of operation is especially well-suited for executing an instruction block which operates on an array. Since the number of times such a loop is executed depends on the size of the array and the value of indices in the IS, branches will occur in the MAP based on values in the IS. The only effect these branches have on the CP is that data continues to be supplied to the CP until the loop terminates.

If the MAP determines that branch options 2 or 3 are to be followed, an active end-of-data flag is sent to the CP on the read data queue after the last data item associated with the currently executing block. The value of the data word sent with an active end-of-data signal informs the CP whether option 2 or option 3 is followed. One data value is reserved to indicate that the CP should expect a new block from the MAP (option 3). Any other data value is a pointer to a block in the CP's instruction buffer (option 2). Thus, program execution in the CP is controlled through the read data stream and the CP checks for the end-of-data signal on each read data queue access.

When the CP performs the test for a data-dependent branch, the MAP ceases prefetching data until the branch is resolved. This wait time incurred by the MAP is undesirable when such a test is executed frequently and a particular outcome is expected. Instead, the wait time could be used to prefetch the data for the likely branch target. The end-of-data signal provides a convenient way of disposing of data wrongly prefetched by the MAP. A reserved data value, sent with the end-of-data signal, could signal the CP to purge all buffered and incoming data until the next end-of-data signal. Such a reserved value would be written by the MAP into its read buffer whenever the MAP continued prefetching data and received a wrong-way branch indication from the CP. This signaling capability would be allowed only by special CP branch instructions whose opcodes would instruct the CP to purge data upon a wrong-way branch. All data in the CP read buffer is then purged up to the "purge" end-of-data signal and all following data is purged up to the next end-of-data signal. Prefetching instructions in such a case has no purge problem since the next end-of-data signal after the "purge" end-of-data signal indicates which instruction block to execute next.

The methods for communication between the MAP and the CP are designed to limit the number of interruptions in execution due to branching. Branches which depend on data in the MAP may occur many times without interrupting the operation of the CP; therefore, once the CP has a block of instructions in its buffer, the MAP can keep a stream of data flowing into the CP.

3.7. Subroutine Calls

The SMA uses a control stack for handling subroutine calls. A stack pointer, frame pointer, and an argument pointer are used as in the Digital Equipment VAX system. These pointers are maintained in the MAP, and MAP instructions are provided to access the pointers and to push and pop the SP.

4. SMA EVALUATION

The effectiveness of the SMA machine in reducing addressing overhead has been evaluated by comparing an SMA machine's performance to that of a VAX-like machine, primarily with respect to the execution of a Gaussian elimination algorithm (GAUSS). Some other evaluations are mentioned briefly. GAUSS, written in FORTRAN, is taken from [SSPP68]. From the high-level program source, the program is compiled into assembly language for a VAX running the UNIX operating system and for the example SMA machine. To compile the program into SMA assembly language, the VAX assembly listing is modified only with respect to the way data referencing occurs. That is, when a matrix is being accessed, SMA instructions are added to setup the indices for the matrix and to increment these indices. These SMA instructions, however, eliminate the need for some of the variables used and calculations performed by the VAX. Care is taken not to give either machine any special advantages. Thus, the code produced for the SMA by this transformation of VAX machine code is not hand optimized to any extent.

4.1. Number of Memory References Generated

A program's instruction blocks can be identified from the high-level source. Figure 3 is a diagram of the control flow for GAUSS in terms of instruction blocks. For GAUSS, only two of the branches are probabilistic in the sense that they are truly data dependent. Each of the other branches in the program are determined by the value of an index. These and the unconditional branches are handled very well by the MAP of the SMA machine.

The results of a static analysis of GAUSS are shown in Table 1. In the SMA version, GAUSS requires fewer than half the instructions needed in

$$[A]_{nxn} \; [X]_{nx1} = [B]_{nx1} \;, \; \text{solve for X}$$

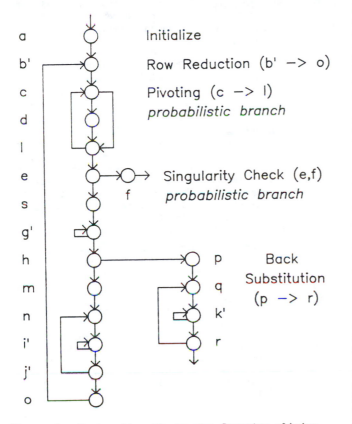

Initialize

Row Reduction (b' -> o)

Pivoting (c -> l)
probabilistic branch

Singularity Check (e,f)
probabilistic branch

Back Substitution (p -> r)

Figure 3. Instruction blocks for Gaussian elimination

Table 1. Statistics from a static analysis of GAUSS, EIGEN, and QSORT.

Number of	GAUSS		EIGEN		QSORT	
	VAX	SMA	VAX	SMA	VAX	SMA
instruction blocks	19	19	61	61	14	18
distinct scalars	16	6	36	23	8	8
distinct data structures	2	2	3	3	1	1
access patterns	11	11	19	19	1	1
instructions	123	50	534	251	68	59
data references	84	40	446	319	61	62
scalar	62	13	386	251	54	53
data structure	22	22	60	60	7	7
index	0	3	0	8	0	2

the VAX version. When counting the SMA instructions, MAP instructions are also included in the total number of instructions. The difference in the number of data references is as dramatic as the difference in the number of instructions. Since the VAX and the SMA versions of GAUSS make the same number of data structure references, the difference in data referencing is due to the scalar references. The SMA programs have fewer distinct scalars than the VAX programs due to overhead reduction; thus, the VAX program not only has more scalars but also performs overhead instructions to operate on these scalars.

The static differences between the VAX and the SMA versions of GAUSS translate directly into substantial differences in the dynamic count of the number of memory references for each program. To obtain this dynamic count for GAUSS, the number of memory references generated by each block is calculated as a function of n, the matrix size. For data dependent branches, successors are chosen to produce a path with the largest number of instructions and data references. Thus in GAUSS, pivoting is always done and a singular matrix is not encountered. Therefore, this is a worst case dynamic memory reference analysis.

In this analysis, it is also desirable to see what effects loop mode has on the number of data references. Thus for each machine there are two cases: one with loop mode and one without loop mode. For GAUSS, blocks (n, i', j'), blocks (q, k', r), and blocks (c, d, l) are considered inner loops for loop mode execution. To hold each set of these blocks in a loop buffer, a hypothetical VAX with loop mode added would need to provide a buffer of 24 instructions, while the SMA needs a buffer of only 8 instructions.

Figure 4 shows a plot of the dynamic count of the total number of memory references required by the GAUSS program for a VAX and an SMA machine with and without loop mode as a function of n. The SMA machine always makes fewer memory references than the VAX, even if the VAX has a loop mode. The number of memory references needed by an SMA machine running the GAUSS program on a 100 x 100 matrix is only 20% of the number of memory references made by the VAX without loop mode. Thus the SMA with slow memory can easily outperform a VAX with a 1 clock cache cycle.

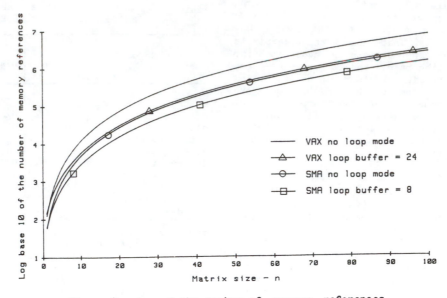

Figure 4. Log of the number of memory references
for GAUSS for an nxn matrix

A similar analysis was performed on an eigenvalue-finding algorithm (EIGEN), and a quick-sort algorithm (QSORT). EIGEN is written in FOR-TRAN and is the HQR routine from the Eispack sub-routine package [Smit74]. QSORT is a recursive program written in PASCAL and based on an algorithm from Horowitz and Sahni [Horo76].

In a static count, the SMA version of EIGEN requires fewer than half the instructions and only approximately 75% of the data references of the VAX version. A dynamic analysis indicates the SMA machine without loop mode generates approximately the same number of memory references as the VAX with loop mode. For the EIGEN program operating on a 100 x 100 matrix, the SMA with and without loop mode makes only 30.5% and 47.2%, respectively, of the references made by the VAX without loop mode. In this analysis an "instruction" represents an opcode or a memory reference. Thus a VAX instruction with two memory reference operands would count as three of these simple instructions.

A static analysis of QSORT reveals little difference between the VAX and SMA versions. Nevertheless, the SMA machine reduces dynamic memory references for QSORT approximately as much as for EIGEN.

4.2. An Estimate of Relative Performance

A program's execution time can be partitioned into 1) time spent accessing memory and 2) time spent computing. The execution time is reduced by overlapping these two quantities. Generally, it is not possible to overlap all of the computation time with memory referencing activity. We call unover-lapped computation time the computational overhead. By allocating a portion of this computational over-head to each memory reference, the execution time of a program can be expressed as:

$$T = M (1/v + c)$$

where M is the number of memory references, c is computational overhead, and the term $1/v$ is the effective amount of time needed per memory access. The variable v is the memory bandwidth and is included as a parameter so that comparisons can be made between machines whose memory speeds differ. A larger v represents a faster memory and, there-fore, a reduced memory access time. If the memory is interleaved, v takes the interleaving factor into account. The same algorithm executed on dif-ferent machines will yield a different execution time because the term M will vary from machine to machine, as will the term c.

The computational overhead, c, is difficult to measure. It varies from one program to another and also from one machine to another. Due to machine dependencies, different models of even the same machine will have different values of c. The value of c is also a function of the memory bandwidth v. As memory access time decreases (increasing v), less computation time can be overlapped with memory accesses, causing c to increase. Due to these dependencies, c is treated as a parameter in our comparison of performance.

The performance of a machine is given by the inverse of the execution time. We calculated the performance of conventional machines and an SMA machine for c ranging from 0 to 2 and for v taking on values of 1, 2, 4, and 8. The computational overhead is in units of standard memory cycle times per memory reference, as is the term $1/v$. The fac-tor M is taken from the dynamic analysis of GAUSS run on a 100 x 100 matrix. To aid in comparing one machine with another, performance is normalized to the performance of a conventional machine with no computational overhead (c=0) and a memory bandwidth of one (v=1).

The normalized performance for GAUSS is shown in figure 5. Machines with and without loop mode are treated separately because the presence of loop mode affects the number of memory accesses required

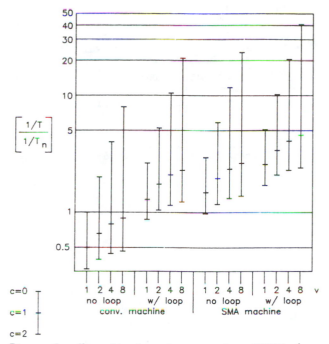

Figure 5. Normalized performance for GAUSS (v = memory bandwidth, c = computational overhead, T = run time)

by the program. Once loop mode is established, memory requests for the instructions of the loop are not needed.

Each vertical line of the graph represents the relative performance of a machine with a particular memory bandwidth and with the computational overhead ranging from 0 to 2. A conventional machine with no loop mode, v=1, and c=1 would require approximately twice as much time to run a Gaussian elimination program on a 100 x 100 matrix as the machine with c=0. At the other extreme, a c=0 SMA machine with loop mode and a memory bandwidth of 8 would perform approximately 42 times better than the base machine: conventional, no loop, v=1, and c=0.

The performance of the base machine was also compared to an SMA machine running EIGEN and QSORT. In this comparison, there is a great improvement in performance when an SMA machine is used; however, the improvement is not as dramatic as for GAUSS.

For all of the three programs and a given memory bandwidth, a conventional machine with loop mode and an SMA machine without loop mode perform almost equally. Furthermore, performance is sensitive to changes in computational overhead, especially when c varies from 0 to 1. Different machines should not simply be compared with the same value for c.

5. CONCLUSIONS

5.1. Summary of Results

Due to the von Neumann bottleneck, inefficiencies exist in the way address generation is performed in most conventional machines. The research presented here has studied the access process to discover where the access inefficiencies lie and how they can be reduced.

From a detailed analysis of program address traces [Ples82] we determined the types of features that should be included in a machine designed to generate memory references efficiently. The proposed Structured Memory Access (SMA) machine contains these features. The SMA machine is divided into a computation processor (CP) and a memory access processor (MAP). As their names imply, the CP is responsible for the desired computations of the system, while the MAP generates all the memory references for a program. The SMA machine reduces addressing overhead by providing special access mechanisms in the MAP to generate references efficiently for blocks of instructions and several data types. The storing of bounds information permits bounds checking to occur automatically in hardware when data structures are accessed. Because of the system's organization, the CP and MAP can operate relatively independently of one another. In particular, prefetching of instructions and data, and index-dependent loop control are inherent features of the SMA machine.

The operation of the MAP and its interactions with the CP were discussed as were the types of access mechanisms which reside in the MAP. The machine's ability to reduce addressing overhead was then evaluated. A comparison was made between a hypothetical SMA machine and a VAX-like machine with respect to the number of memory references generated by a set of programs. Depending on the program, the SMA machine reduces the number of memory references to between 1/5 and 2/5 of those required by a conventional VAX.

The performance of the SMA machine was then evaluated. A machine's performance was parameterized by the memory bandwidth and the computational overhead. It was found that performance is very sensitive to these parameters; however, an SMA machine performs significantly better than a conventional machine with the same parameters. Now that the SMA concept has been justified, more detailed performance evaluation and design modifications are being carried out in our continuing research.

REFERENCES

[Hamm77a]   D. W. Hammerstrom and E. S. Davidson, "Information Content of CPU Memory Referencing Behavior," Fourth Annual Symposium on Computer Architecture, March 1977, pp. 184-192.

[Hamm77b]   D. W. Hammerstrom, "Analysis of Memory Addressing Architecture," Tech. Report R-777, Coordinated Science Lab., Univ. of Illinois, Urbana, IL July 1977.

[Horo76]   E. Horowitz and S. Sahni, The Fundamentals of Data Structures, Computer Science Press, Inc., 1976, p. 347.

[Ples81]   A. R. Pleszkun, B. R. Rau, and E. S. Davidson, "An Address Prediction Mechanism for Reducing Processor-Memory Address Bandwidth," _Proc. 1981 IEEE Workshop on Computer Architecture for Pattern Analysis and Image Database Management_, Nov. 11, 1981, pp. 141-148.

[Ples82]   A. R. Pleszkun, "A Structured Memory Access Architecture", Computer Systems Group Report CSG-10, Coordinated Science Lab., Univ. of Illinois, Urbana, IL Oct. 1982.

[Smit74]   B. J. Smith, J. M. Boyle, B. S. Garbow, Y. Ikebe, V. C. Klema, and C. B. Moler, _Lecture Notes in Computer Science, Volume 6: Matrix Eigensystem Routines - EISPACK Guide_, Springer-Verlag, 1974.

[Smit82]   J. E. Smith, "Decoupled Access/Execute Computer Architectures," _Ninth Annual Symp. on Computer Architecture_, April 1982, pp. 112-119.

[SSPP68]   _1130 Scientific Subroutine Package Programmer's Manual_, International Business Machines Corp., 1968, p. 115.

Dynamic Instruction Scheduling and the Astronautics ZS-1

James E. Smith

Astronautics Corporation of America

Reprinted from *Computer*, Vol. 22, No. 7, July 1989, pages 21-35.
Copyright © 1989 by The Institute of Electrical and Electronics
Engineers, Inc. All rights reserved.

Pipelined instruction processing has become a widely used technique for implementing high-performance computers. Pipelining first appeared in supercomputers and large mainframes, but can now be found in less expensive systems. For example, most of the recent reduced instruction set computers use pipelining.[1,2] Indeed, a major argument for RISC architectures is the ease with which they can be pipelined. At the other end of the spectrum, computers with more complex instruction sets, such as the VAX 8800,[3] make effective use of pipelining as well.

The ordering, or "scheduling," of instructions as they enter and pass through an instruction pipeline is a critical factor in determining performance. In recent years, the RISC philosophy has become pervasive in computer design. The basic reasoning behind the RISC philosophy can be stated as "simple hardware means faster hardware, and hardware can be kept simple by doing as much as possible in software." A corollary naturally follows, stating that instruction scheduling should be done by software at compile time. We refer to this as *static instruction scheduling*, and virtually every new computer system announced in the last several years has followed this approach.

> **Dynamic instruction scheduling resolves control and data dependencies at runtime. This extends performance over that possible with static scheduling alone, as shown by the ZS-1.**

Many features of the pioneering CDC 6600[4] have found their way into modern pipelined processors. One noteworthy exception is the reordering of instructions at runtime, or *dynamic instruction scheduling*. The CDC 6600 *scoreboard* allowed hardware to reorder instruction execution, and the memory system *stunt box* allowed reordering of some memory references as well. Another innovative computer of considerable historical interest, the IBM 360/91,[5] used dynamic scheduling methods even more extensively than the CDC 6600.

As the RISC philosophy becomes accepted by the design community, the benefits of dynamic instruction scheduling are apparently being overlooked. Dynamic instruction scheduling can provide performance improvements simply not possible with static scheduling alone.

This article has three major purposes:

(1) to provide an overview of and survey solutions to the problem of instruction scheduling for pipelined computers,

(2) to demonstrate that dynamic instruction scheduling can provide performance improvements not possible with static scheduling alone, and

(3) to describe a new high-performance computer, the Astronautics ZS-1, which uses new methods for implementing dynamic scheduling and which can outperform computers using similar-speed technologies that rely solely on state-of-the-art static scheduling techniques.

0-8186-2642-9/92 $3.00 © 1989 IEEE

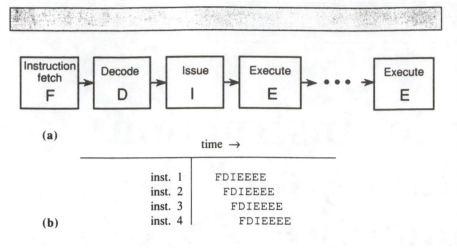

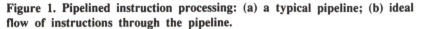

inst. 1	FDIEEEE
inst. 2	FDIEEEE
inst. 3	FDIEEEE
inst. 4	FDIEEEE

(b)

Figure 1. Pipelined instruction processing: (a) a typical pipeline; (b) ideal flow of instructions through the pipeline.

R1 ← (Y)	Load register R1 from memory location Y
R2 ← (Z)	Load register R2 from memory location Z
R3 ← R1 +f R2	Floating add registers R1 and R2
(X)← R3	Store the result into memory location X
R4 ← (B)	Load register R4 from memory location B
R5 ← (C)	Load register R5 from memory location C
R6 ← R4 *f R5	Floating multiply registers R4 and R5
(A)← R6	Store the result into memory location A

(a)

time →

R1 ← (Y)	FDIEEEE
R2 ← (Z)	FDIEEEE
R3 ← R1 +f R2	FD...IEEE
(X)← R3	F...D..IEEEE
R4 ← (B)	F..DIEEEE
R5 ← (C)	FDIEEEE
R6 ← R4 *f R5	FD...IEEE
(A)← R6	F...D..IEEEE

(b)

Figure 2. Pipelined execution of X=Y+Z and A=B*C: (a) machine code; (b) pipeline timing.

Introduction to pipelined computing

Pipelining decomposes instruction processing into assembly line-like stages. Figure 1 illustrates a simple example pipeline. In Figure 1a, the pipeline stages are:

(1) Instruction fetch -- for simplicity assume that all instructions are fetched in one cycle from a cache memory.

(2) Instruction decode -- the instruction's opcode is examined to determine the function to perform and the resources needed. Resources include general-purpose registers, buses, and functional units.

(3) Instruction issue -- resource availability is checked and resources are reserved. That is, pipeline control interlocks are maintained at this stage. Assume that operands are read from registers during the issue stage.

(4) Instruction execution -- instructions are executed in one or several execution stages. Writing results into the general-purpose registers is done during the last execution stage. In this discussion, consider memory load and store operations to be part of execution.

Figure 1b illustrates an idealized flow of instructions through the pipeline. Time is measured in clock periods and runs from left to right. The diagram notes the pipeline stage holding an instruction each clock period. F denotes the instruction fetch stage, D denotes the decode stage, I denotes the issue stage, and E denotes the execution stages.

In theory, the clock period for a p-stage pipeline would be $1/p$ the clock period for a nonpipelined equivalent. Consequently, there is the potential for a p times throughput (performance) improvement. There are several practical limitations, however, on pipeline performance. The limitation of particular interest here is instruction dependencies.

Instructions may depend on results of previous instructions and may therefore have to wait for the previous instructions to ˙ complete before they can proceed through the pipeline. A *data dependence* occurs when instructions use the same input and/or output operands; for example, when an instruction uses the result of a preceding instruction as an input operand. A data dependence may cause an instruction to wait in the pipeline for a preceding instruction to complete. A *control dependence* occurs when control decisions (typically as conditional branches) must be made before subsequent instructions can be executed.

Figure 2 illustrates the effects of dependencies on pipeline performance. Figure 2a shows a sequence of machine instructions that a compiler might generate to perform the high-level language statements $X = Y + Z$ and $A = B * C$. Assume load and store instructions take four execution clock periods while floating-point additions and multiplications take three. (These timing assumptions represent a moderate level of pipelining. In many RISC processors fewer clock periods are needed. On the other hand, the Cray-1 requires 11 clock periods for a load, and floating-point additions take six. Cray-2 pipelines are about twice the length of the Cray-1's.)

Figure 2b illustrates the pipeline timing. A simple in-order method of instruction issuing is used; that is, if an instruction is blocked from issuing due to a dependence, all instructions following it are also blocked. The same letters as before are used to denote pipeline stages. A period indicates that an instruction is blocked or "stalled" in a pipeline stage and cannot proceed until either the instruction ahead of it proceeds, or, at the issue stage, until all resources and data dependencies are satisfied.

The first two instructions issue on consecutive clock periods, but the add is dependent on both loads and must wait three clock periods for the load data before it can issue. Similarly, the store to location X must wait three clock periods for the add to finish due to another data dependence. There are similar blockages during the calculation of A. The total time required is 18 clock periods. This time is measured beginning when the first instruction starts execution until the last starts execution. (We measure time in this way so that pipeline "fill" and "drain" times do not unduly influence relative timings.)

Instruction scheduling

An important characteristic of pipelined processors is that using equivalent, but reordered, code sequences can result in performance differences. For example, the code in Figure 3a performs the same function as that in Figure 2a except that it has been reordered, or "scheduled," to reduce data dependencies. Furthermore, registers have been allocated differently to eliminate certain register conflicts that appear to the hardware as dependencies. Figure 3b illustrates the pipeline timing for the code in Figure 3a. Note that there is considerably more overlap, and the time required is correspondingly reduced to 11 clock periods.

The above is an example of *static instruction scheduling*, that is, the sched-

R1 ← (Y)	Load register R1 from memory location Y
R2 ← (Z)	Load register R2 from memory location Z
R4 ← (B)	Load register R4 from memory location B
R5 ← (C)	Load register R5 from memory location C
R3 ← R1 +f R2	Floating add X and Y
R6 ← R4 *f R5	Floating multiply B and C
(X) ← R3	Store R3 to memory location X
(A) ← R6	Store R6 to memory location A

(a)

```
                          time →

R1 ← (Y)              FDIEEEE
R2 ← (Z)               FDIEEEE
R4 ← (B)                FDIEEEE
R5 ← (C)                 FDIEEEE
R3 ← R1 +f R2             FD.IEEE
R6 ← R4 *f R5             F.D.IEEE
(X) ← R3                   F.DIEEEE
(A) ← R6                    FD.IEEEE
```

(b)

Figure 3. Reordered code to perform X=Y+Z and A=B*C: (a) machine code; (b) pipeline timing.

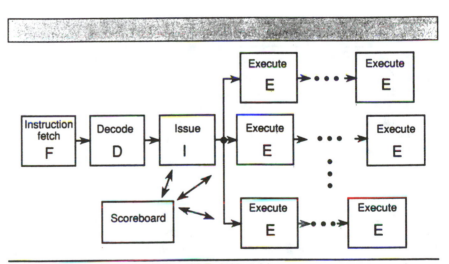

Figure 4. Block diagram of the CDC 6600-style processor.

uling or reordering of instructions that can be done by a compiler prior to execution. Most, if not all, pipelined computers today use some form of static scheduling by the compiler. Instructions can also be reordered after they have entered the pipeline, which is called *dynamic instruction scheduling*. Used in some high-performance computers over 20 years ago, it is rarely used in today's pipelined processors.

Dynamic instruction scheduling: scoreboards. The CDC 6600[4] was an early high-performance computer that used dynamic instruction scheduling hardware. Figure 4 illustrates a simplified CDC 6600-type processor. The CDC

161

```
                    time  →

R1 ← (Y)         FDIEEEE
R2 ← (Z)          FDIEEEE
R3 ← R1 +f R2      FDI...EEE
(X)← R3             FDI.....EEEE
R4 ← (B)             FDIEEEE
R5 ← (C)              FDIEEEE
R6 ← R1 *f R2          FDI...EEE
(A)← R6                 FDI.....EEEE
```

Figure 5. Pipeline flow in a CDC 6600-like processor.

R1 ← (Y)   Load register R1 from memory location Y
R2 ← (Z)   Load register R2 from memory location Z
R3 ← R1 +f R2   Add registers R1 and R2
(X)← R3   Store the result into memory location X
R1 ← (B)   Load register R1 from memory location B
R2 ← (C)   Load register R2 from memory location C
R3 ← R1 *f R2   Multiply registers R1 and R2
(A)← R3   Store the result into memory location A

(a)

```
                    time  →

R1 ← (X)         FDIEEEE
R2 ← (Y)          FDIEEEE
R3 ← R1 +f R2      FDI...EEE
(X)← R3             FDI.....EEEE
R1 ← (B)             FDIEEEE
R2 ← (C)              FDIEEEE
R3 ← R1 *f R2          FDI...EEE
(A)← R3                 FDI.....EEEE
```

(b)

Figure 6. Pipelined execution of X=Y+Z and A=B*C using Tomasulo's algorithm: (a) minimal register machine code; (b) timing for pipeline flow.

6600 was pipelined only in the instruction fetch/decode/issue area. It used parallel execution units (some duplicated) to get the same overlapped effect as pipelining. In addition, parallel units allowed instructions to complete out of order, which, in itself, is a simple form of dynamic scheduling.

The CDC 6600 had instruction buffers for each execution unit. Instructions were issued regardless of whether register input data were available (the execution unit itself had to be available, however). The instruction's control information could then wait in a buffer for its data to be produced by other instructions. In this way, instructions to different units could issue and begin execution out of the original program order.

To control the correct routing of data between execution units and registers, the CDC 6600 used a centralized control unit known as the *scoreboard*. The scoreboard kept track of the registers needed by instructions waiting for the various functional units. When all the registers had valid data, the scoreboard issued a series of "go" signals to cause the data to be read from the register file, to send data to the correct functional unit, and to start the unit's execution. Similarly, when a unit was about to finish execution, it signaled the scoreboard. When the appropriate result bus was available, the scoreboard sent a "go" signal to the unit, and it delivered its result to the register file.

The original CDC 6600 scoreboard was a rather complicated control unit. In recent years, the term "scoreboard" has taken on a generic meaning: any control logic that handles register and result bus reservations, including methods that are not as sophisticated as the 6600's scoreboard.

Figure 5 illustrates the example of Figure 2 executed with a pipeline using scoreboard issue logic similar to that used in the CDC 6600. The pipeline latencies are the same as those in previous examples. The add instruction is issued to its functional unit before its registers are ready. It then waits for its input register operands. The scoreboard routes the register values to the adder unit when they become available. In the meantime, the issue stage of the pipeline is not blocked, so other instructions can bypass the blocked add. Performance is improved in a way similar to the static scheduling illustrated in Figure 3. Here, it takes 13 clock periods to perform the required operations.

Developed independently, and at roughly the same time as the CDC 6600, the IBM 360/91 floating-point unit[6] used a similar but more elaborate method of dynamically issuing floating-point instructions. Instructions were issued to *reservation stations* at the inputs of the floating-point units. The reservation stations held not only control information, but also operand data. The operands were given *tags* that associated the data buffers in the reservation stations with functional units that would supply the data. The data would then be automatically routed via a common data bus to the appropriate reservation stations as they became available. Any instruction in a reservation station that had received all its input operands was free to issue.

Tomasulo's algorithm,[6] used in the IBM 360/91, differed from the CDC 6600 method in two important ways:

(1) There were multiple reservation stations at each unit so that more than one instruction could be waiting for operands. The first one with all its input operands could proceed ahead of the others.

(2) The use of tags, rather than register designators, allowed a form of dynamic register reallocation, as well as instruction reordering. This feature was particularly important in the 360/91 because the IBM 360 architecture had only four floating-point registers.

Figure 6 shows the example of Figure 2 with a minimal register allocation. The pipeline timing with Tomasulo's algorithm appears in Figure 6b. Here, the timing is essentially the same as with the CDC 6600 scoreboard in Figure 5. Note, however, that the registers are automatically reassigned by the hardware. If the CDC 6600 were given the same code as in Figure 6, its timing would be similar to the slower timing shown in Figure 2 because it would be unable to reassign registers "on-the-fly" as the 360/91 does.

Control dependencies. It may appear from the previous examples that, while the dynamic scheduling methods are very clever, a compiler could be used to arrange the code as well as the hardware can (see Figure 3). One need only consider programs containing conditional branches, especially loops, to see that this is not the case.

For static code scheduling, instruction sequences are often divided into *basic blocks*. A basic block is a sequence of code that can only be entered at the top and exited at the bottom. Conditional branches and conditional branch targets typically delineate basic blocks. To phrase it differently, control dependencies break programs into basic blocks. Dynamic scheduling allows instruction reordering beyond machine-code-level basic-block boundaries. This ability to schedule past control dependencies is demonstrated in later examples.

Some advanced static scheduling methods are also directed at minimizing the effects of control dependencies. Loop unrolling and vectorizing start with high-level language basic blocks and produce machine-code-level basic blocks con-

taining more operations. Performance is improved by reducing the number of control dependencies, but static scheduling still cannot look beyond the larger machine-code-level blocks. Dynamic scheduling can be used in conjunction with loop unrolling and vectorizing to further enhance performance by looking beyond the remaining control dependencies.

Trace scheduling[7] is based on statically predicting conditional branch outcomes. These predictions are based on compile-time information deduced from the source code or from compiler directives. Instructions can then be reordered around control dependencies, but instructions must also be inserted to "undo" any mistaken static branch predictions. Incorrect branch predictions result in:

(1) instructions executed that should not be,
(2) additional instructions to undo the mistakes, and
(3) execution of the correct instructions that should have been done in the first place.

With dynamic resolution of control dependencies, there are no mistakes, and no "undoing" is necessary.

Some types of control constructs inherently make certain static scheduling techniques extremely difficult. For example, "while" loops (in Fortran, Do loops with early exit conditions) severely restrict loop unrolling and vectorizing techniques because the exact number of loop iterations is only discovered at the time the loop is completed.

As the following example illustrates, however, there are other advantages to dynamic resolution of control dependencies associated with ordinary Fortran Do loops. Figure 7 shows a Fortran loop and a compilation into machine instructions. The loop code has been statically scheduled. Its execution for two iterations on a standard pipelined machine is shown in Figure 7c (left pipeline flow), and its execution with a Tomasulo-like dynamic hardware scheduler is shown in Figure 7c (right pipeline flow).

Performance with the dynamic scheduling algorithm is improved because the conditional branch at the end of the loop issues and executes before some of the preceding instructions have begun execution. After the conditional branch is out of the way, instructions following the

branch instruction can also be fetched and executed before all the instructions from the previous basic block(s) have executed.

Note that, in the above example, no special techniques are used to improve the performance of the conditional branch instruction. That is, there is no branch prediction or delayed branching. Only after the branch is executed can instruction fetching of the target instruction begin. Dynamic scheduling reduces the delay between the branch and preceding instructions. Therefore, performance improvements for conditional branches accrue regardless of whether a particular branch is taken or not. More advanced branching methods tend to improve performance after the branch execution by reducing the hole in the pipeline between the branch and the following instruction. Consequently, special branching techniques can be successfully used to supplement a dynamic scheduling algorithm.

Quantitatively, with static scheduling only, each loop iteration in Figure 7 executes in 18 clock periods. With dynamic scheduling it takes only 11 clock periods. This is an improvement of about 60 percent. A more complete performance comparison can be found in Weiss and Smith,[8] where the Cray-1 architecture is used as a common base for comparing various instruction issue methods, including Tomasulo's algorithm. Instructions are statically scheduled prior to the performance analysis, and Tomasulo's algorithm is shown to provide a 60-percent performance improvement beyond that provided by static scheduling.

Data dependencies. Techniques (both static and dynamic) that reduce the performance impact of control dependencies tend to expose data dependencies as the next major performance obstacle.

(1) Dynamic scheduling around control dependencies causes instructions in the basic block following a branch to be eligible for issue and execution before all the instructions in the previous block have finished. Instructions from the two different basic blocks may have data dependencies that a static scheduler cannot resolve.

(2) Static scheduling methods that increase basic block size, such as trace scheduling and loop unrolling, increase the scheduling possibilities within the

(a)

```
      Do 1 I = 1,100
  1     A(I) = B(I) + C(I)*D(I)
```

(b)

```
            R1 ← 100
            R2 ← 1
      loop: R3 ← (C + R2)
            R4 ← (D + R2)
            R5 ← (B + R2)
            R6 ← R3 *f R4
            R7 ← R6 +f R5
            (A + R2) ← R7
            R2 ← R2 + 1
            Br loop; R2 ≤ R1
```

(c)

```
                                  static scheduling only                    dynamic scheduling

R3 ← (C + R2)        FDIEEEE                                 FDIEEEE
R4 ← (D + R2)         FDIEEEE                                 FDIEEEE
R5 ← (B + R2)          FDIEEEE                                 FDIEEEE
R6 ← R3 *f R4           FD..IEEE                                FDI..EEE
R7 ← R6 +f R5            F..D..IEEE                              FDI....EEE
(A + R2) ← R7             F..D..IEEEE                             FDI......EEEE
R2 ← R2 + 1                F..DIE                                  FDIE
Br loop; R2 ≤ R1            FDIE                                     FDIE
R3 ← (C + R2)                  FDIEEEE                                  FDIEEEE
R4 ← (D + R2)                   FDIEEEE                                  FDIEEEE
R5 ← (B + R2)                    FDIEEEE                                  FDIEEEE
R6 ← R3 *f R4                     FD..IEEE                                 FDI..EEE
R7 ← R6 +f R5                      F..D..IEEE                               FDI....EEE
(A + R2) ← R7                       F..D..IEEEE                              FDI......EEEE
R2 ← R2 + 1                          F..DIE                                   FDIE
Br loop; R2 ≤ R1                      FDIE                                      FDIE
```

Figure 7. Loop execution with and without dynamic instruction scheduling: (a) Fortran loop; (b) machine instructions; (c) pipeline flows.

basic block. Indeed, this is a major justification for using such methods. In the process, however, the number and variety of data dependencies is increased as well.

Data dependencies may involve data held either in registers or memory. There are three varieties of data dependencies[9]:

(1) flow dependencies, when a result operand of one instruction is used as a source operand for a subsequent one,

(2) output dependencies, when a result operand of one instruction is also used as a result operand for a subsequent one, and

(3) antidependencies, when a source operand of one instruction is used as a result operand for a subsequent one.

All three types of data dependencies can occur for either register data or memory data. Flow dependencies are inherent in the algorithm and cannot be avoided. Within a basic block, output and antidependencies involving registers can be avoided by static methods, specifically by reallocating registers (assuming that enough registers are available). However, dynamic scheduling of branch instructions may result in situations where output and antidependencies involving register instructions in

different basic blocks must be resolved. For example, in Figure 7, one can conceive of dynamic issuing methods where the load from memory into R3 is ready to issue for the second loop iteration before the instruction using the old value of R3 (i.e., $R6 = R3$ *f $R4$) has issued in the first loop iteration. (While this may at first seem farfetched, the dynamic issuing method used by the ZS-1 frequently causes such a situation.) Dynamic register reallocation such as that provided by Tomasulo's algorithm can effectively deal with such situations.

Probably more difficult to deal with than dependencies involving registers are memory data dependencies. All three forms of data dependencies that can occur with registers can also occur with memory data. For example, a load instruction following a store to the same memory address is a flow dependence, and the load may not be reordered ahead of the store instruction. On the other hand, if the load and store are to different addresses, there is no problem with reordering them.

Load and store instructions to scalar variables produce dependencies that are relatively simple to resolve. Furthermore, data dependencies involving scalars can often be removed by optimizing compilers.

Memory dependencies involving arrays and other data structures are much more difficult to schedule. The major problem with scheduling such memory dependencies lies in detecting them. Accesses involving arrays and other data structures use index values that can change at runtime, so complete information regarding the index values may be difficult or impossible for the compiler to discern. This is because the only address information available to the compiler is in symbolic form (such as array subscript expressions expressed in a high-level language).

Trace scheduling and loop unrolling combine high-level language basic blocks into larger machine-language ones. Significant performance advantages accrue if operations from the original basic blocks can be "blended" together as the instructions are scheduled. A good schedule tends to have load instructions near the top of a basic block with functional operations (adds and multiplies) in the middle and stores near the bottom. To achieve this with trace scheduling or loop unrolling, load instructions must often be scheduled ahead of stores belonging to different loop iterations. Consequently, the ability to determine data dependencies involving loads and stores from different HLL basic blocks is of critical importance. In the trace scheduling method, this process, known as *memory disambiguation*,[10] is a very important component. Memory disambiguation manipulates array subscript expressions in the form of systems of integer equations and inequalities to determine if load and store addresses to the same array can ever coincide in such a way that it is unsafe to interchange the load and store instructions.

Vectorizing compilers also concentrate on this kind of dependence, using very similar methods.[11] In fact, resolving memory data dependencies involving array references is a primary feature of vectorizing methods. Because of the excellent literature available on vectorizing compilers, the remaining discussion on memory data dependencies is phrased in terms of vectorizing compilers.

If the loop statement $A(I) = A(I) + C(I)$ is vectorized,

(1) the elements of $A(I)$ are loaded as a vector,
(2) the elements of $C(I)$ are loaded as a vector,
(3) there is a vector add of $A(I)$ and $C(I)$, and
(4) $A(I)$ is stored as a vector.

The vector load of the $A(I)$ followed later by the vector store amounts to a massive reordering of the loads and stores. That is, loads from $A(I)$ for later loop iterations are allowed to pass stores for earlier iterations. The loop $A(I) = A(I-1) + C(I)$ cannot be vectorized as just described, however, because the loads of $A(I-1)$ involve values just computed during the previous loop iteration. (Some simple linear recurrences may vectorize on certain computers that have special recurrence instructions. Throughout, this article uses simple examples for illustrative purposes; more complex linear and nonlinear recurrences could just as easily be used to prove the point.)

In two important classes of problems the static data dependence analysis done by compilers cannot achieve performance as high as dynamic runtime analysis. The first class involves analyses of such complexity that the compiler cannot safely determine if the subscripts are independent. These are referred to as *ambiguous subscripts*. The second class consists of code that has true load/store conflicts, but only for a few iterations of a loop.

An example of ambiguous subscripts is shown below:

```
         NL1=1
         NL2=2
         Do 1 I=1,N
         Do 2 J=1,N
2        A(J,NL1)=A(J-1,NL2)+B(J)
         NTEMP=NL1
         NL1=NL2
1        NL2=NTEMP
```

In the above example, the array A is split into two halves; old values in one half are used to compute new values in the other. When this process is finished, the two halves are switched (by interchanging $NL1$ and $NL2$). This kind of construct can be found in many Fortran programs. In fact, the original program from which Lawrence Livermore Kernel 8[11] was extracted used this kind of technique. A vectorizing compiler must determine that $NL1$ is never equal to $NL2$ to vectorize the loop. It is doubtful that any current vectorizing compiler has this capability. (However, a compiler might compile the example code as both vector and scalar and use a runtime test whenever the loop is encountered to determine which version should be used.) In general, $NL1$ and $NL2$ could be arbitrarily complex functions of any number of variables. This suggests the theoretical undecidability of vectorizable loops.

As another example, consider array references that frequently occur when handling sparse matrices. For example, $A(MAP(I)) = A(MAP(I)) + B(I)$, where MAP is an integer array of indices. This code can be vectorized (with vector gather/scatter instructions) if the compiler can determine that none of the $MAP(I)$ are equal. In most cases this is beyond a vectorizing compiler's capabilities.

As mentioned above, the second important class of problems where static analysis is inferior to dynamic analysis occurs when loops have true data dependencies, but for relatively few of the loop iterations. For example, consider the following nested loop:

```
         DO 1 J=1,N
         DO 1 I=1,N
1        X(I) = X(J) + Y(I)
```

For a particular execution of the inner loop, the value of $X(J)$ changes partway through, when $I=J$. The store into $X(I)$ when $I=J$ must follow all the loads of $X(J)$ for preceding inner loop iterations. This store must precede all subsequent loads of $X(J)$.

Another example is the case where subscripted subscripts are used; for example, the inner loop statement $X(M(K)) = X(N(K)) + W(K)$, where M and N have a small nonempty intersection. In this case, many, but not all, of the loads may pass stores. (The ones that may not pass occur when $M(I1) = N(I2)$ for $I2 < I1$.)

Dynamic scheduling: stunt boxes. The IBM 360/91 memory system[12] al-

```
      DO 1 J=1,N
      DO 1 I=1,N
 1    X(I) = X(J) + Y(I)
```

(a)

R3 ← (R1)	FDIEEEE
R4 ← (Y + R2)	FDIEEEE
R6 ← (Y+1 + R2)	FDIEEEE
R5 ← R3 +f R4	FDI..EEE
(X + R2) ← R5	FDI....EEEE
R7 ← (R1)	FDI....EEEE
R8 ← R6 +f R7	FDI.......EEE
(X+1 + R2) ← R8	FDI.........EEEE
R2 ← R2 + 1	FDIE
Br loop; R2 ≤ R1	FDIE
R3 ← (R1)	FDI....EEEE
R4 ← (Y + R2)	FDI....EEEE
R6 ← (Y+1 + R2)	FDI....EEEE
R5 ← R3 +f R4	FDI......EEE
(X + R2) ← R5	FDI........EEEE
R7 ← (R1)	FDI........EEEE
R8 ← R6 +f R7	FDI..........EEE
(X+1 + R2) ← R8	FDI............EEEE
R2 ← R2 + 1	FDIE
Br loop; R2 ≤ R1	FDIE

(b)

	no memory conflicts	with memory conflict
R3 ← (R1)	FDIEEEE	FDIEEEE
R4 ← (Y + R2)	FDIEEEE	FDIEEEE
R6 ← (Y+1 + R2)	FDIEEEE	FDIEEEE
R5 ← R3 +f R4	FDI..EEE	FDI..EEE
(X + R2) ← R5	FDI....EEEE	FDI....EEEE
R7 ← (R1)	FDIEEEE	FDI....EEEE
R8 ← R6 +f R7	FDI...EEE	FDI.......EEE
(X+1 + R2) ← R8	FDI.....EEEE	FDI'.........EEEE
R2 ← R2 + 1	FDIE	FDIE
Br loop; R2 ≤ R1	FDIE	FDIE
R3 ← (R1)	FDIEEEE	FDIEEEE
R4 ← (Y + R2)	FDIEEEE	FDIEEEE
R6 ← (Y+1 + R2)	FDIEEEE	FDIEEEE
R5 ← R3 +f R4	FDI..EEE	FDI..EEE
(X + R2) ← R5	FDI....EEEE	FDI....EEEE
R7 ← (R1)	FDIEEEE	FDIEEEE
R8 ← R6 +f R7	FDI...EEE	FDI...EEE
(X+1 + R2) ← R8	FDI.....EEEE	FDI.....EEEE
R2 ← R2 + 1	FDIE	FDIE
Br loop; R2 ≤ R1	FDIE	FDIE

(c)

Figure 8. The effects of load/store reordering: (a) a nonvectorizable loop with a memory hazard; (b) pipeline execution without dynamic memory reordering; (c) pipeline execution with dynamic memory reordering.

lowed load instructions to pass store instructions after they had been issued. The memory system allowed the dynamic reordering of loads and stores as long as a load or a store did not pass a store to the same address. Store instructions could issue before their data were actually ready. There was a queue for store instructions waiting for data. Load instructions entering the memory system had their addresses compared with the waiting stores. If there were no matches, the loads were allowed to pass the waiting stores. If a load matched a store address, it was held in a buffer. When the store data became available, they were automatically bypassed to the waiting load as well as being stored to memory.

The CDC 6600 memory system was simpler than in the IBM 360/91 and allowed some limited reordering of memory references to increase memory throughput in a memory system that used no cache and had a relatively slow interleaved main memory. In the CDC 6600, the unit used for holding memory references while they were waiting for memory was called the *stunt box*. The CDC 6600 stunt box did not actually allow loads to pass waiting stores, but just as the term "scoreboard" has taken on a more general meaning than the way it was used in the 6600, the term "stunt box" has come to mean any device that allows reordering of memory references in the memory system.

Figure 8a shows a Fortran loop, unrolled twice, that has a memory data dependence that inhibits vectorization. Because of this, the compiler is restricted from moving certain loads above stores that may potentially be to the same address. Figure 8b shows pipeline usage with dynamic scheduling but with no provision for loads to pass stores via a stunt box. Figure 8c shows pipeline usage with dynamic scheduling and a memory stunt box. The left pipeline flow is for a sequence of code where $I<J$ so there are no dependencies involving $X(I)$ and $X(J)$. The right pipeline flow includes the case where I "passes" J so that there is temporarily a memory hazard preventing a load from $X(J)$ from passing a store to $X(I)$ when $I=J$. This results in a temporary glitch in the execution of memory instructions, but there is no overall time penalty as the code sequence continues past the point where $I=J$. By inspecting the timing diagrams, the pipeline without dynamic load/store reordering can execute one loop iteration

(two iterations in the original rolled loop) every 17 clock periods. With dynamic load/store reordering, it executes an iteration every 13 clock periods. Without any dynamic scheduling at all, each loop iteration takes 25 clock periods (this case is not illustrated). Using full dynamic scheduling results in an almost two-times performance improvement over static scheduling alone.

The viability of dynamic scheduling

As pointed out, dynamic scheduling was used in large-scale computers in the 1960s and has not been used to any appreciable extent since. One can only speculate about the reasons for abandonment of dynamic scheduling in production high-performance machines. Following are some of the possible reasons:

(1) Increased difficulty in hardware debugging: a hardware failure can cause errors that are highly dependent on the order of instruction issuing for many clock periods prior to the actual detection of the error. This makes error reproducibility difficult. The fault diagnosis problem was compounded in the IBM 360/91 and CDC 6600 because discrete logic was used, and diagnostic resolution had to be very fine.

(2) Longer clock period: dynamic instruction issuing can lead to more complex control hardware. This carries with it potentially longer control paths and a longer clock period.

(3) Advances in compiler development: initially, dynamic scheduling permitted simple compilers that required relatively little static scheduling capability. However, improved compilers with better register allocation and scheduling could realize some (but certainly not all) of the benefits of dynamic issuing.

Why consider dynamic scheduling today, when it was passed by years ago? First, very large scale integration parts and extensive use of simulation in today's computers alleviate many of the debugging and diagnosis problems present 20 years ago. Simulation can be used to find design errors, and hardware faults need only be located to within a (large) replaceable unit. That is, if a fault is detected in a CPU's instruction issue logic, the entire CPU, or at least a large part of it, can be replaced; there is no

need for extensive and detailed fault location methods.

Second, it is possible to use methods that selectively limit the generality of dynamic scheduling so that significant performance benefits can be realized while keeping the control logic simpler than in the CDC 6600 and IBM 360/91. Techniques of this type have been successfully used in the ZS-1 and are described in later sections.

Third, both compiler scheduling and processor design are much more mature, and most of the big performance gains in these areas have probably been made. Consequently, the gains achievable by dynamic scheduling may appear more attractive today than they did 20 years ago.

The ZS-1

The Astronautics ZS-1 is a recently developed, high-speed computer system targeted at scientific and engineering applications. The ZS-1 central processor is constructed of transistor-transistor logic-based technology and has no vector instructions, but makes extensive use of dynamic instruction scheduling and pipelining to achieve one-third the performance of a Cray X-MP1.

A block diagram of a ZS-1 system is shown in Figure 9. The ZS-1 is divided into four major subsystems: the central processor, the memory system, the I/O system, and the interconnection network. In its maximum configuration, the ZS-1 contains one gigabyte of central memory, and an I/O system consisting of up to 32 input-output processors. Unix is the primary operating system.

The ZS-1 uses a decoupled architecture[13] that employs two instruction pipelines to issue up to two instructions per clock period. One of the instruction streams performs the bulk of fixed-point and memory addressing operations, while the other performs floating-point calculations.

To support the two instruction streams, the decoupled architecture of the ZS-1 provides two sets of operating registers. A set of thirty-one 32-bit A registers is used for all memory address computation and accessing, and a second set of thirty-one 64-bit X registers is used for all floating-point operations. The A and X registers provide fast temporary storage for 32-bit integers and 64-bit floating-point numbers, respectively.

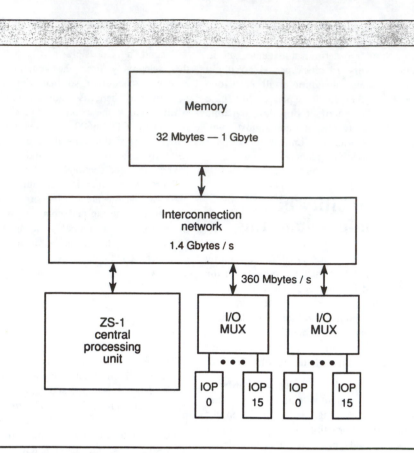

Figure 9. Overall diagram of the ZS-1 system.

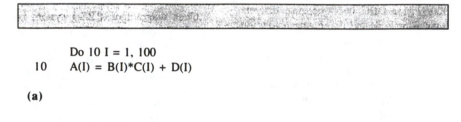

```
        Do 10 I = 1, 100
10      A(I) = B(I)*C(I) + D(I)
```

(a)

```
S1:         A5 ← 0                  .loop count
S2:         A6 ← A - 8              .load initial pointer to A
S3:         A7 ← B - 8              .load initial pointer to B
S4:         A8 ← C - 8              .load initial pointer to C
S5:         A9 ← D - 8              .load initial pointer to D
S6: loop:   A5 ← A5 + 1             .increment A5
S7:         B, A0 ← (A5 == 100)     .compare =, set Branch Flag
S8:         XLQ ← (A7 = A7 + 8)     .load next element of B
S9:         XLQ ← (A8 = A8 + 8)     .load next element of C
S10:        XLQ ← (A9 = A9 + 8)     .load next element of D
S11:        X2 ← XLQ                .copy B element into X2
S12:        X3 ← X2 *f XLQ          .multiply B and C
S13:        XSQ ← XLQ +f X3         .add D; result to XSQ
S14:        (A6 ← A6 + 8) = XSQ     .store result into A
S15:        Br loop; B==0           .branch on false to "loop"
```

(b)

**Figure 10. A Fortran loop and its ZS-1 compilation: (a) Fortran source;
(b) machine language version of the loop.**

A distinctive feature of the ZS-1 is the use of architectural queues for communication with main memory. There are two sets of queues. One set consists of a 15-element A load queue (ALQ) and a 7-element A store queue (ASQ). These A queues are used in conjunction with the 32-bit A registers. The other set of queues consists of a 15-element X load queue (XLQ) and a 7-element X store queue (XSQ). These X queues are used in conjunction with the 64-bit X registers.

Instructions. Instruction formats are reminiscent of those used in the CDC 6600/7600 and Cray-1. There is an opcode, and operands specified by i, j, and k fields. The j and k fields typically specify input operands and the i field specifies the result. The i, j, and k operands may be either general-purpose registers or queues. A designator of 31 in the j or k field indicates that the first element of the load queue is used as a source operand. A designator of 31 in the i field indicates that the result is placed into the store queue. In this way, queue operands can be easily intermixed with register operands in all instruction types. The opcode determines whether A registers and queues or X registers and queues are to be operated upon.

The ZS-1 architecture is best understood by examining a sequence of machine code. Figure 10a contains a simple Fortran loop, and Figure 10b contains a compilation into ZS-1 machine instructions. The instruction $S1$ initializes fixed-point register $A5$, which is used as the loop counter. Then instructions $S2$ through $S5$ initialize $A6$ through $A9$ to point to the arrays accessed in the loop. The pointers are offset by -8 because byte addressing is used, and the load and store instructions use pre-autoincrementing.

In the loop body, instructions $S6$ and $S7$ increment the loop counter and test it to see if it has reached the upper limit. The test is done by a compare instruction, which generates a Fortran Boolean result that is placed in $A0$ (because $A0$ is defined to always hold constant 0, this is equivalent to discarding it), and it also sets the architectural branch flag, B, to the result of the comparison. The branch flag will be tested by the conditional branch instruction that terminates the loop.

Instructions $S8$ through $S10$ load the elements from arrays B, C, and D. These memory operands are automatically

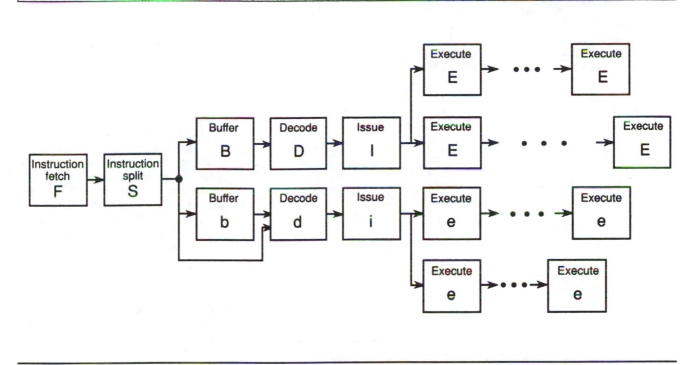

Figure 11. The ZS-1 processor pipelines.

placed in the XLQ. Because the destination of the load instructions are queues implied by the opcode, the i field of load and store instructions may be used to specify a result register for the effective address add. This makes autoincrementing memory operations particularly easy to implement.

Then instructions $S11$ through $S13$ copy the memory data from the XLQ and perform the required floating-point operations. These are generic floating-point instructions with register designator 31 used wherever there is a queue operand. The floating-point add is of particular interest because it not only uses the XLQ as its j operand, but it also uses the XSQ for its result. The store instruction, $S14$, generates the store address in array A.

Decoupled implementation

A simplified block diagram of the ZS-1 CPU pipelines is shown in Figure 11. The pipeline segments include an instruction fetch stage where instruction words are read from a 16-kilobyte in-

struction cache. An instruction word may contain either one 64-bit instruction (used for conditional branches and loads and stores with direct addressing) or two 32-bit instructions (by far the most common case). The next pipeline segment is the "splitter" stage, where instruction words are split into instructions and sent to the two instruction pipelines. In one cycle, the instruction word is examined by the A instruction pipeline and the X instruction pipeline to see whether it contains one or two instructions and to determine whether the instructions are:

(1) X unit instructions,
(2) A unit instructions,
(3) branch instructions or system call/return instructions.

Branch and system call/return instructions are held and executed in the splitter stage. Instructions belonging to the first two classes are sent to an instruction buffer at the beginning of the appropriate instruction pipeline. Up to two instructions are forwarded to the instruction pipelines per clock period.

The instruction buffer in the X instruc-

tion pipeline can hold 24 instructions. The buffer in the A instruction pipeline is four instructions deep and can be bypassed. The very deep X instruction buffer allows the A instruction pipeline to issue many instructions in advance of the X instruction pipeline. The A instruction buffering is intended to reduce blockages of the splitter. The bypass allows instructions to move quickly up the A pipeline when it is empty; for example, following some branches.

In the instruction pipelines, pipeline segments are:

(1) the buffer stage where instructions are read from the instruction buffers,
(2) the decode stage where instructions are decoded, and
(3) the issue stage where instructions are sent to functional units for execution.

At the issue stage a simple Cray-1-like issuing method allows instructions to begin execution in strict program sequence. For example, if an instruction uses the result of a previously issued, but unfinished, instruction, it waits at the

```
 1:  A5 ← A5 + 1              FSdie
 2:  B, A0 ← (A5 == 100)      FSbdie
 3:  XLQ ← (A7 = A7 + 8)       FSbdieeee
 4:  XLQ ← (A8 = A8 + 8)       FS.bdieeee
 5:  XLQ ← (A9 = A9 + 8)        FS.bdieeee
 6:  X2 ← XLQ                   FSBD...IE
 7:  X3 ← X2 *f XLQ              FSB...DIEEE
 8:  XSQ ← XLQ +f X3            FS....BD..IEEE
 9:  (A6 ← A6 + 8) = XSQ         FSbdi........eeee
10:  Br  loop;B==0                FS
11:  A5 ← A5 + 1                    FSdie
12:  B, A0 ← (A5 == 100)            FSbdie
13:  XLQ ← (A7 = A7 + 8)             FSbdieeee
14:  XLQ ← (A8 = A8 + 8)             FS.bdieeee
15:  XLQ ← (A9 = A9 + 8)              FS.bdieeee
16:  X2 ← XLQ                         FSBD...IE
17:  X3 ← X2 *f XLQ                    FSB...DIEEE
18:  XSQ ← XLQ +f X3                   FS.B...D..IE
19:  (A6 ← A6 + 8) = XSQ                FSbdi......eeee
20:  Br  loop;B==0                       FS
```

Figure 12. The processing of two iterations of the loop in Figure 10.

issue register until the previous instruction completes.

At the time an instruction is issued from one of the pipelines, operand data are read from the appropriate register files and/or queues. After issue, the instruction begins execution in one of the parallel functional units. The primary functional units for the fixed-point A instructions are: a shifter, an integer adder/logical unit, and an integer multiplier/divider. The primary functional units for the floating-point X instructions are: an X logical unit, a floating-point adder, a floating-point multiplier, and a floating-point divider. Data can be copied between A and X registers via the copy unit.

The ZS-1 uses several dynamic scheduling techniques:

(1) The architectural instruction stream is split in two, with each resulting stream proceeding at its own speed. This not only permits the ZS-1 to sustain an instruction issue rate of up to two instructions per clock period, but it allows the memory access instructions to dynamically schedule ahead of the floating-point instructions. In addition, the scoreboard issue logic at the end of each

of the instruction pipelines remains as simple as in the Cray-1; no instruction reordering is done within a single pipeline.

(2) Branch instructions are held and executed at the splitter. This is accomplished by decomposing branch operations into their two fundamental components: comparing register values and transferring control. Compare instructions are detected in the splitter and set the branch flag to "busy" as they pass through. If a branch instruction encounters a "busy" branch flag, it waits in the splitter until the flag is set by the compare instruction. Compare instructions are subsequently issued from the appropriate instruction pipeline, depending on whether fixed- or floating-point data are tested. A comparison sets the branch flag when it completes. Consequently, branch instructions do not directly read register values, they simply test the branch flag. This mechanism allows branches to be executed dynamically ahead of instructions that precede them in the instruction stream. Furthermore, executing branches very early in the pipeline reduces, and in some cases eliminates, any resulting "hole" in the pipeline.

(3) Using queues for memory oper-

ands provides an elastic way of joining the memory access and floating-point functions. This elasticity allows the memory access function to schedule itself dynamically ahead of the floating-point operations. This can also be viewed as a way of achieving dynamic register allocation. That is, each load or store instruction dynamically allocates a new value of "register" 31.

(4) Store instructions merely generate store addresses; they do not wait for the store data before issuing. In the memory system is a stunt box containing two queues, one for load addresses and the other for store addresses. Store addresses wait in their queue until a corresponding data item appears in a store data queue (one for fixed-point data, one for floating-point). Load addresses may pass store instructions that are waiting for their data. Memory hazards are checked by comparing load and store addresses so that loads do not pass stores to the same address.

Figure 12 illustrates the processing of two iterations of the loop in Figure 10. As in earlier examples, only the instructions within the loop body are shown. Many of the pipeline stages are the same as in previous examples, and there are two new stages. One of the new stages is the splitter stage, the other is the buffer stage at the beginning of each of the instruction pipelines (although the buffer in the fixed-point pipeline can be bypassed). Because there are actually two distinct instruction pipelines following the splitter, for all stages after the splitter lowercase letters are used to denote fixed-point instructions, and uppercase letters are used for floating-point instructions. Pipeline lengths are the same as in the previous examples to more clearly demonstrate the principles at work. To summarize, the letters labeling pipeline stages have the following meanings:

F denotes the instruction is in the fetch stage,

S indicates the instruction word is processed at the splitter,

B or b indicates the instruction is read from an instruction buffer,

D or d indicates the instruction is decoded,

I or i indicates the instruction is issued for execution,

E or e indicates the instruction is executed.

The first instruction ($A5 = A5 + 1$) is split at time 0, decoded at time 1 (the buffer is bypassed), issued at time 2, and executed at time 3.

The second instruction is split at the same time as the first and is read from the buffer at time 1. Note that this second instruction sets the branch flag. The next three instructions follow a similar sequence for processing.

The sixth instruction is the first X instruction. It is split at time 2, is read from the X instruction buffer at time 3, and is decoded at time 4. It must then wait for data from the XLQ before continuing.

The seventh and eighth instructions perform the required floating-point operations in sequence, with the eighth putting its result in the XSQ for storage to memory.

The ninth instruction generates the store address for the preceding one. It is an A instruction that issues at time 7. It passes through four clock periods of execution while the address is generated and translated. It then waits while the preceding floating-point addition completes. Then the result is stored to memory.

The tenth and final instruction in the loop body is the conditional branch. It is detected and executed in the splitter stage. Note that, in this example, all but one of the clock periods required for the conditional branch are hidden; instruction issuing proceeds without interruption in the fixed-point pipeline.

The second loop iteration follows the first in Figure 12, and all subsequent loop iterations are similar to it. In this example, steady state performance is determined by the rate at which the fixed-point operations can be issued. In cases where floating-point dependencies are more severe, steady state performance is determined by the floating-point pipeline.

By extrapolating data from the diagram we can see that up to three iterations of the loop are in some phase of processing simultaneously. This is a clear example of the ability of dynamic scheduling to fetch and execute instructions beyond basic-block boundaries. During many clock periods eight or more instructions are processed in parallel (not counting those blocked in the pipeline).

The example just given is intended to illustrate dynamic scheduling aspects of the ZS-1 implementation. In fact, the ZS-1 compilers automatically unroll loops. The degree of unrolling is a function of

```
A5 ← A5 + 1                 FSdie
B, A0 ← (A5 == 100)         FSbdie
XLQ ← (A1)                   FSbdieeee
XLQ ← (A2 + 8)             FS.bdieeee
XLQ ← (A2 + 8)              FS.bdieeee
X1 ← XLQ                    FSBD...IE
XSQ ← X1 +f XLQ              FSB...DIEEE
X2 ← XLQ                    FS....BDIE
(A3 + 8) ← XSQ               FSbdi.....eeee
XLQ ← (A1)                  FS.bdieeee
XSQ ← X2 +f XLQ              FS...BD.IEEE
(A3 + 8) ← XSQ               FS.bdi......eeee
Br loop;B==0                  FS
A5 ← A5 + 1                 FSdie
B, A0 ← (A5 == 100)         FSbdie
XLQ ← (A1)                   FSbdieeee
XLQ ← (A2 + 8)             FS.bdieeee
XLQ ← (A2 + 8)              FS.bdieeee
X1 ← XLQ                    FSBD...IE
XSQ ← X1 +f XLQ              FSB...DIEEE
X2 ← XLQ                    FS....BDIE
(A3 + 8) ← XSQ               FSbdi.....eeee
XLQ ← (A1)                  FS.bdieeee
XSQ ← X2 +f XLQ              FS...BD.IEEE
(A3 + 8) ← XSQ               FS.bdi......eeee
Br loop;B==0                  FS
```

Figure 13. ZS-1 execution of a nonvectorizable loop.

the size of the loop; for a simple loop as illustrated in Figure 12, the Fortran compiler unrolls the loop body eight times. When this is done, and instructions are rescheduled using the resulting larger basic blocks, vector levels of performance can be achieved. For example, if the loop of Figure 12 is unrolled for the ZS-1, a load or store instruction issues during 94 percent of the clock periods. In other words, the memory path is busy 94 percent of the time. Many vector processors, including the Cray-1 and Cray-2, have their vector performance limited by their ability to perform only one load or store operation per clock period. For practical purposes, this is the same bottleneck that ultimately limits ZS-1 performance, and vector instructions would provide no significant performance benefit.

On the other hand, when faced with loops like those in Figure 8 that do not vectorize, the ZS-1 can achieve vector performance levels. This is illustrated in Figure 13, where the loop is unrolled two times to permit comparison with the earlier example.

This example illustrates the iterations

where no memory conflict exists. When $I=J$ and there is a memory conflict, a slight perturbation that lasts for only two loop iterations occurs. The delays caused by this perturbation are completely hidden by the dynamic scheduling, however. The total time to execute an inner loop in this example is nine clock periods. Because this loop is not vectorizable, we saw earlier that it would take a static-scheduled Cray-1-like machine 17 clock periods to execute the inner loop once. Note also that this example illustrates a situation where instruction issuing in the fixed-point pipeline is completely uninterrupted by the conditional branch executed at the splitter.

ZS-1 performance

All the examples in this article have used a fixed set of pipeline lengths to make comparisons possible. The production ZS-1 models operate at a 45-nanosecond clock period and use VLSI floating-point chips that provide pipeline lengths of three clock periods for 64-bit floating-point multiplication and addition. (The prototype systems described in an earlier work[14] used standard TTL-based floating-point units with latencies about twice as long. In addition, the production systems use a true divide algorithm as opposed to the reciprocal approximation method described in that work.[14]) The memory pipeline is conservatively designed and consumes eight clock periods for data found in the 128-kilobyte data cache. The decision to use a data cache was made relatively late in the design process. Consequently, the cache was added in series with the address translation unit, with a board-crossing between. A more parallel address translation/cache system would probably have only half the latency, or about four clock periods.

For performance comparisons, we use the 24 Livermore Kernels[11] because they are extracted from real programs and contain a realistic mix of both vector and scalar code. To summarize performance in millions of floating-point operations per second (Mflops), we use the harmonic mean, which is the total number of operations (scaled to be the same for each kernel) divided by the total time. For the 24 double-precision kernels, using the original Fortran (with no added compiler directives, as are often used to assist vector machines), the ZS-1 performs at 4.1 Mflops.

The Multiflow Trace 7/200[10] is constructed of similar-speed technology (about 3.5 nanoseconds per gate) as the ZS-1 and uses state-of-the-art trace scheduling compiler technology. On the 24 Livermore Kernels the Multiflow Trace operates at 2.3 Mflops. As a final comparison, the Cray X-MP can execute the Livermore Kernels at 12.3 Mflops.[11]

Of course, all the above performance numbers are very much a function of the compiler used. It is expected that later compiler versions for any of the machines, including the ZS-1, could lead to improved performance.

Dynamic instruction scheduling improves performance by resolving control and data dependencies at runtime using real data.

Static scheduling must rely on predictions or worst-case assumptions made at compile time. Consequently, there will always be situations where runtime scheduling can outperform static scheduling.

It is generally true that simple, streamlined instruction sets reduce hardware control complexity and tend to produce faster pipelined implementations than complex instruction sets. However, it does not logically follow that less hardware control complexity leads to better performance. When complexity is directed toward greater instruction functionality, performance often does suffer, but carefully chosen control complexity can also be directed toward greater performance.

There is a performance/complexity trade-off curve, but it is not clear that the maximum performance point occurs at the minimal complexity end of the curve. It may very well be that some additional control complexity can be effectively used to increase performance. The risk, of course, in increasing control complexity is that performance advantages can be offset by slower control paths and an increased clock period. The ZS-1 is a successful attempt at achieving improved performance levels by using an architecture that naturally leads to multiple instruction streams and dynamic instruction scheduling. Despite using dynamic scheduling, the ZS-1's 45-nanosecond clock period is the fastest we know of for standard TTL-based machines.

The result is an architecture that can achieve vector levels of performance on highly parallel, vectorizable code. Furthermore, and more importantly, similar performance levels can be achieved with many less parallel, nonvectorizable codes. This is done by mixing advanced static scheduling techniques, based on loop unrolling (and simple forms of trace scheduling), with advanced dynamic scheduling techniques. It is important to note the "orthogonality" of advanced static scheduling techniques and dynamic scheduling. Static scheduling can go a long way toward high performance, but this article has shown that dynamic scheduling can extend performance beyond that achievable with static scheduling alone.

A final observation is that compiler complexity and compilation times are often considered to be of little consequence when discussing hardware control complexity/performance trade-offs. This is not absolutely true, however. Mature compilers take considerable time to construct, and in many program development environments compilation times using advanced static scheduling methods can become excessively long. Using dynamic scheduling provides good performance on nonoptimum code. This means that immature compilers, or very fast compilers with reduced optimization, can come close to achieving the full potential of a computer that uses dynamic scheduling methods. □

Additional reading on dynamic instruction scheduling

The book by Thornton[4] describing the CDC 6600 is a classic, but unfortunately it is out of print. Considerable detail on the scoreboard design can be found in the Thornton and Cray patent, U.S. patent no. 3,346,851. The IBM 360/91 is described in a series of papers in the January 1967 issue of the *IBM Journal of Research and Development*. A recent book by Schneck[15] contains a discussion of several pipelined machines, including both the CDC 6600 and the IBM 360/91. The book by Kogge[16] is another excellent reference. Recent research in pipelined computers has concentrated on static scheduling, rather than dynamic scheduling. A notable exception is work being undertaken by Hwu and Patt[17] that contains interesting enhancements to Tomasulo's algorithm.

Acknowledgments

The ZS-1 has resulted from the hard work of many people; only a few are acknowledged here. The original architecture was specified by Greg Dermer, Tom Kaminski, Michael Goldsmith, and myself. The processor design was completed by Brian Vanderwarn, Steve Klinger, Chris Rozewski, Dan Fowler, Keith Scidmore, and Jim Laudon. Other principals in the hardware design effort were Bob Niemi, Harold Mattison, Tom Staley, and Jerry Rabe. In the software area, Don Neuhengen managed the operating system development, Greg Fischer managed compiler development, and Kate Murphy managed applications development. Finally, I would like to acknowledge the constant interest and encouragement provided by Ron Zelazo, president of the Astronautics Corporation of America.

References

1. J. Hennessy, "VLSI Processor Architecture," *IEEE Trans. on Computers*, Vol. 33, Dec. 1984, pp. 1,221-1,246.

2. D.A. Patterson, "Reduced Instruction Set Computers," *Comm. ACM*, Vol. 28, Jan. 1985, pp. 8-21.

3. D.W. Clark, "Pipelining and Performance in the VAX 8800 Processor," *Proc. 2nd Int'l Conf. Architectural Support for Programming Languages and Operating Systems* (ASPLOS II), Oct. 1987, pp. 173-177.

4. J.E. Thornton, *Design of a Computer -- The Control Data 6600*, Scott, Foresman and Co., Glenview, Ill., 1970.

5. D.W. Anderson, F.J. Sparacio, and R.M. Tomasulo, "The IBM System/360 Model 91: Machine Philosophy and Instruction-Handling," *IBM J. Research and Development*, Jan. 1967, pp. 8-24.

6. R.M. Tomasulo, "An Efficient Algorithm for Exploiting Multiple Arithmetic Units," *IBM J. Research and Development*, Jan. 1967, pp. 25-33.

7. J.A. Fisher, "Trace Scheduling: A Technique for Global Microcode Compaction," *IEEE Trans. Computers*, Vol. C-30, July 1981, pp. 478-490.

8. S. Weiss and J.E. Smith, "Instruction Issue Logic in Pipelined Supercomputers," *IEEE Trans. Computers*, Vol. C-33, Nov. 1984, pp. 1,013-1,022.

9. D.A. Padua and M.J. Wolfe, "Advanced Compiler Optimizations for Supercomputers," *Comm. ACM*, Vol. 29, Dec. 1986, pp. 1,184-1,201.

10. R.P. Colwell et al., "A VLIW Architecture for a Trace Scheduling Compiler," *IEEE Trans. Computers*, Vol. 37, Aug. 1988, pp. 967-979.

11. F.H. McMahon, "The Livermore Fortran Kernels: A Computer Test of the Numerical Performance Range," Research Report, Lawrence Livermore Laboratories, Dec. 1986.

12. L.J. Boland et al., "The IBM System/360 Model 91: Storage System," *IBM J.*, Jan. 1967, pp. 54-68.

13. J.E. Smith, S. Weiss, and N. Pang, "A Simulation Study of Decoupled Architecture Computers," *IEEE Trans. Computers*, Vol. C-35, Aug. 1986, pp. 692-702.

14. J.E. Smith et al., "The ZS-1 Central Processor," *Proc. ASPLOS II*, Oct. 1987, pp. 199-204.

15. P.B. Schneck, *Supercomputer Architectures*, Kluwer Acacemic Publishers, Norwell, Mass., 1988.

16. P.M. Kogge, *The Architecture of Pipelined Computers*, McGraw-Hill, New York, 1981.

17. W. Hwu and Y.N. Patt, "HPSm, a High Performance Restricted Data Flow Architecture Having Minimal Functionality," *Proc. 13th Ann. Symp. Computer Architecture*, June 1986, pp. 297-307.

James E. Smith has been with the Astronautics Corporation Technology Center in Madison, Wis., since 1984. He is system architect for the ZS Series of computer systems and has performed research and development activities primarily directed toward the ZS-1, a large-scale scientific computer system. He is currently involved in the specification and design of follow-on products.

Smith received BS, MS, and PhD degrees from the University of Illinois in 1972, 1974, and 1976, respectively. Since 1976, he has been on the faculty of the University of Wisconsin at Madison, where he is an associate professor (on leave) in the Department of Electrical and Computer Engineering. He is a member of the IEEE Computer Society, IEEE, and ACM.

Readers may contact the author at Astronautics Corp. of America, Technology Center, 4800 Cottage Grove Rd., Madison, WI 53716-1387.

Dataflow processors

By giving a unique name to every activity generated during a computation, the U-interpreter can provide greater concurrency in the interpretation of data flow graphs.

The U-Interpreter

Reprinted from *Computer*, Vol. 15, No. 2, February 1982, pages 42-49. Copyright © 1982 by The Institute of Electrical and Electronics Engineers, Inc. All rights reserved.

Arvind
MIT

Kim P. Gostelow
General Electric

The usual method of interpreting data flow graphs assumes a finite token capacity (usually one) on each arc. This unnecessarily limits the amount of parallelism that can be easily exploited in a program. The U-interpreter is a method for assigning labels to each computational activity as it is dynamically generated during program execution. The U-interpreter assigns and manipulates labels in a totally distributed manner, thus avoiding a sequential controller, which can be a bottleneck in the design of large multiple-processor machines.

Motivation

Suppose we want to integrate a function $f(x)$ from $x=a$ to $x=b$. If the interval from a to b is divided into n equal parts of size $h=(b-a)/n$, then according to the trapezoidal rule the integral is

$$\sum_{i=1}^{n} (f(x_i) + f(x_{i-1}))*h/2$$

$$= ((f(x_0)+f(x_n))/2 + \sum_{i=1}^{n-1} f(x_i))*h$$

where $x_i = a + i*h$.

On a multiple-processor machine we would like to evaluate concurrently as many f's as the number of processors in the machine permits. There are several ways of exposing parallelism in a problem, and in the following paragraphs we discuss some of these methods briefly.

The most common method for exposing parallelism is to write the program in a conventional language like Fortran and then detect the opportunities for parallel execution by a compiler. Such a compiler can be quite complex because it has to check against side effects permitted by the language. In the trapezoidal rule example, if function f is (textually) large and uses common storage for parameters, the compiler may fail to detect that all f's can be executed concurrently. Generally, clever coding of an algorithm for a sequential computer obscures the inherent parallelism of a problem. The greatest advantage of using Fortran is that existing programs only have to be recompiled for new high-performance architectures. This has been the most popular approach in the past. State-of-the-art analytical techniques for detecting parallelism and compiling suitable code are represented by the Parafrase system of Kuck.[1]

Another method for exposing parallelism is to extend an existing programming language with explicit parallel constructs: vector operators, and constructs such as DOALL are examples of extensions suggested in the past (e.g., Fortran for Burrough's scientific processor).[2-4] The theoretical weakness of this approach is that programs with parallel constructs are not necessarily well formed; a program may show unintended nondeterministic behavior and thus produce wrong results. Detection of such errors complicates the compiler considerably, and this approach, though quite old, has not been widely practiced. (Languages such as Concurrent Pascal are intended to express *nondeterministic* behavior of concurrent processes, and thus are not relevant to the discussion of expressing parallelism in deterministic computation.)

It has been pointed out many times during the last 15 years that it is easier to detect parallelism in functional languages than in imperative languages.[5-7] Parallelism in functional programs can be detected without a global analysis of programs.[8,9] Function f in the trapezoid rule example remains a pure function when coded in a functional language. Therefore, a compiler, without examining the body of f, can deduce that all instances of f are permitted to execute concurrently.

One way to execute functional languages is to translate them into data flow graphs suitable for execution on a multiple-processor machine.[10,11] Some functional languages (e.g., Val)[12] have also incorporated parallel constructs such as FORALL to provide further opportunities for optimization. (The FORALL construct in Val does not destroy the determinacy property of its programs.) Functional languages, in addition to expressing parallelism, seem to offer opportunities for writing more modular, reliable, and verifiable programs. Interest in functional languages has increased dramatically in recent years. However, their acceptance has been slow because of incompatibility with existing systems and a lack of good implementations.

In this article we present a different approach to exploiting parallelism in functional language programs. It does not involve special compile time analysis, nor does it rely on special constructs to specify parallelism explicity. We interpret programs in such a way that during execution any two computations not dependent on each other for data are automatically eligible for concurrent execution. The U-interpreter has this property and can be used for any functional language that can be compiled into the usual data flow graphs. Such a compiler for the high-level language Id (Irvine data flow) is already in use.

An efficient implementation of the U-Interpreter requires special hardware structures. In fact, the original motivation for developing the U-interpreter was to define some appropriate basis for a highly parallel multiple-processor machine.[13] Results of the simulation of a U-interpreter machine have been reported by Gostelow and Thomas,[14] and a multiple-processor machine that implements the U-interpreter is being designed at the MIT Laboratory for Computer Science.[15]

Assigning labels to computational activities

Consider the following Id program that integrates function f by the trapezoidal rule:

```
(initial s←(f(a) +f(b))/2;
    x←a+h;
  for i from 1 to n−1 do
    new s←s+f(x) ;
    new x←x+h;
  return s) *h
```

A translation of this program into a data flow graph appears in Figure 1. In order of understand the translation, note that a token is replicated when it encounters a fork, and a SWITCH operator switches the data input token to one of the output arcs according to the boolean value of the control input token.[10] For the moment, treat operators L, L^{-1}, D, and D^{-1} as identity operators. Now, if we assume that each arc in the graph has a capacity to hold only one token, then the output arc of an operator must be empty before each firing of that operator. In the graph of Figure 1 this assumption severely limits the amount of concurrency that is possible. Suppose that function f, relative to $+$, takes a long time to execute. Then f will soon block the firing of the middle switch, which in turn will block the firing of the loop predicate. Essentially, not much will happen until f completes its first execution.

Now assume that arcs in the graph have unbounded token capacity. This will not change the outcome of the program and will greatly improve execution speed, but it will require very different hardware structures for implementation. Consider again the movement of tokens on the graph of Figure 1. Since the loop predicate $i \leq n-1$ does not depend on $f(x)$, the production of the $n-1$ values for x over the range $a+h$ to b proceeds relatively quickly. Hence it is possible that even before f completes its first execution, the next $n-2$ input values for f pile up on the input arc to f. Under such circumstances, $n-2$ true tokens followed by one false token will accumulate on the control input of the leftmost switch, and a single token will sit on the first input arc of the $+$ operator. Every time f produces an output, one token from the control input of the switch will be removed. However, the U-interpreter will actually start $n-1$ executions of f by dynamically assigning a different label to each instance of f. (In data flow graphs an operator or a function does not have internal memory; hence, theoretically, several may execute concurrently as long as all inputs are available.) A computation activity with a label can execute (proceed) as soon as its inputs are available.

Note that when concurrent invocations of f are permitted, the correctness of results must be ensured even if the second instance of f completes before the first. In our particular example this issue is of no consequence—if one assumes that $+$ is an associative operator. However, in order to make the U-interpreter completely general, we don't assign any specific interpretation to noncontrol operators; whether an operator is arithmetic or relational, commutative or associative is immaterial to the U-interpreter. Each operator is assumed to produce exactly one output token for each set of input tokens and is considered "strict" in all its inputs. (A function f is said to be strict with respect to input x if divergence, or nontermination, of the computation of x implies divergence of f.) Thus, in the trapezoidal program, the U-interpreter adds the outputs of f in the correct order even if the second instance completes before the first.

An *activity* is a single execution of an operator. The U-interpreter gives a unique name to every activity generated during a computation, and each token (value) in the machine carries the name of its destination activity. An activity accepts all, but only, those tokens that carry its destination *activity name*. An activity name comprises four fields: u, c, s, and i.

- u is the context field, which uniquely identifies the context in which a code block is invoked. The context field is itself an activity name, so the definition is recursive.
- c is the code block name. In Id, every procedure and loop is given a unique code block name by the compiler.

- s is the instruction number within the code block.
- i is the initiation number, which identifies the loop iteration in which this activity occurs. (This field is 1 if the activity occurs outside a loop.)

Since the destination operator may require more than one input, each token also carries the number of its destination port. In the following we represent a token by $<u.c.s.i, \text{data}>_p$ where p is the port number. (We often omit the port number when there is no ambiguity.) Note that fields c, s, and p of an activity name specify that the token is moving along an arc of the program graph connected to input port p of the operator in instruction s of code block c. This implies, of course, that the operator that produced the token is a predecessor of instruction s in code block c consistent with the static structure of the program. Fields u and i, on the other hand, must be consistent with the dynamics of program execution. For example, a token that has been generated during the ith iteration of a loop carries value i in its initiation number field.

Rules for manipulating activity names

Generating unique activity names for each computational activity is easy if one does not insist on performing this task in a distributed manner. A trivial scheme uses an integer counter that is read and incremented every time a new activity name is needed. This scheme will generate activity names sequentially, requiring only simple coordination among activities that generate tokens for the same destination activity.

The scheme employed by the U-interpreter generates new activity names based solely on the activity names carried by input tokens and a description of the code block. Thus no centralized name generator need be involved. At this point we describe the activity-name generation mechanism for a set of base language operators sufficient to implement a language with conditional, loop, and recursive procedure constructs.

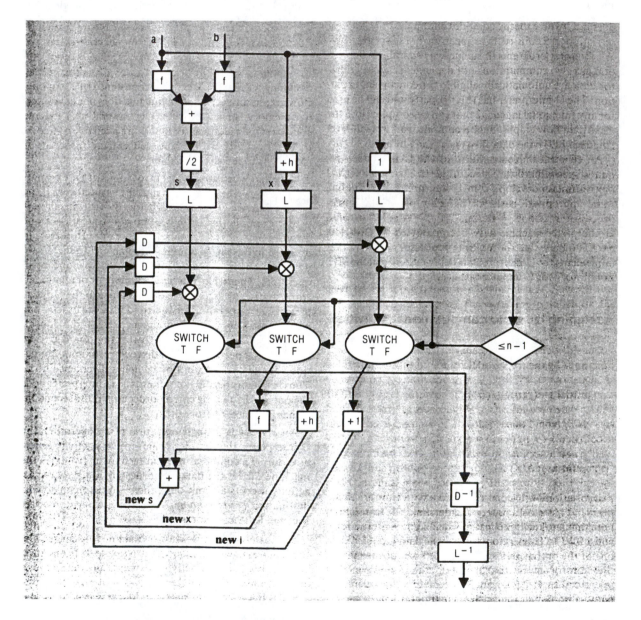

Figure 1. Translation of the trapezoidal program.

Functions and predicates. This class of operators includes all arithmetic, boolean, and relational operators, as well as select and append operations on data structures. If the operator in instruction s of code block c performs the (binary) function f, and if instruction t is the destination of s, then we have

$$\text{input token set} = \{<u.c.s.i, x>_1, <u.s.c.i, y>_2\}$$
$$\text{output token set} = \{<u.c.t.i, f(x,y)>_p\}$$

If an output of s forks to n distinct inputs, then the output part of s will produce n distinct tokens, one for each input. Note that an acyclic base-language program (i.e., an Id block expression) composed of any number of interconnected function and predicate operators has the property that the ith set of input tokens produces the ith set of output tokens. This is true for any expression in the base language that is formed by composition of blocks, conditionals, loops, and procedure schemas. The activity-name generation rule given here does not require multiple initiations of a block to initiate or terminate in any particular order. In fact, activities corresponding to each initiation can execute independently of each other.

Conditionals. The SWITCH operator needed to implement the conditonal schema (Figure 2) may be described by

$$\text{input} = \{<u.c.s.i, x>_{\text{data}}, <u.c.s.i, b>_{\text{control}}\}$$
$$\text{output} = \textbf{if } b = \textbf{true then } \{<u.c.s_T.i, x>\}$$
$$\textbf{else if } b = \textbf{false then } \{<u.c.s_F.i, x>\}$$
$$\textbf{else undefined}$$

Exactly one of the successor instructions s_T or s_F receives a token. The total number of successors need not be the same on both sides of the switch. Since the iteration counts of the tokens going into f and g will be mutually exclusive for valid f and g, the iteration counts of the tokens on the output arcs of f and g will also be mutually exclusive. Hence, merging of outputs of f and g using $\otimes$ will not cause any activity names to be duplicated. Note that an *if*-expression behaves as a function box from input to output; the ith set of input tokens produces the ith set of output tokens.

Loops. A simplified loop schema is shown in Figure 3, for which the corresponding Id expression is

$$(\textbf{while } p(x) \textbf{ do}$$
$$\text{new } x \leftarrow f(x)$$
$$\textbf{return } x)$$

A loop uses operators D, D^{-1}, L, and L^{-1}, as well as SWITCH. None of these operators affect the data portion of the tokens passing through. An execution of a loop expression can receive information only from tokens explicitly input to it because Id loops have no memory (i.e., no leftover tokens). Thus, in the case of nested loops it is quite possible that the input tokens for several instantiations of an inner loop may be available at the same time. It is the L operator (in conjunction with the L^{-1} operator) that capitalizes on this by creating a new context u' for each instantiation of a loop. An L operator is described by

$$\text{input} = \{<u.c.s.i, x>\}$$
$$\text{output} = \{<u'.c'.t'.1, x>\}$$

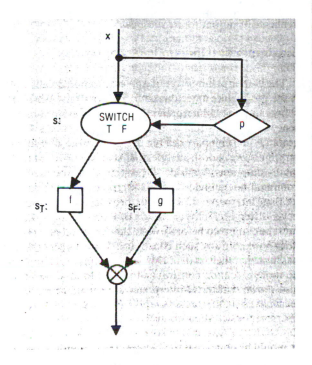

Figure 2. Translation of the if *p(x)* then *f(x)* else *g(x).*

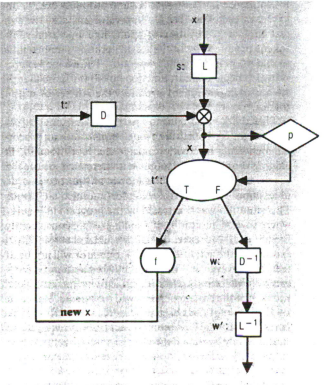

Figure 3. A loop schema.

where $u' = (u.c.s,i)$ and c' is the code block name of the invoked loop.

The initiation number of a token in a loop must be incremented every time a token goes around the loop. Corresponding to every **new** x-type variable in a loop, a D operator accomplishes this as follows:

$$input = \{<u'.c'.t.j, x>\}$$
$$output = \{<u'.c'.t'.j+1, x>\}$$

If after $n-1$ iterations the loop predicate p becomes false, the switch sends the last token with initiation number n to the D^{-1} operator, which changes the initiation number n to 1:

$$input = \{<u'.c'.w.n, x>\}$$
$$output = \{<u'.c'.w'.1, x>\}$$

The L^{-1} operator sends its input token to an activity whose context and initiation number are identical to those of the activity that initiated this loop:

$$input = \{<u'.c'.w'.1, x>\}$$
$$output = \{<u.c.s'.i, x>\}$$

where $c.s'$ is the successor of instruction $c'.w'$ (i.e., the L^{-1} operator) and $u' = (u.c.s.i)$.

Note that the L operator generates exactly one set of input tokens (with initiation number 1) for a loop expression in a given context ($u' = (u.c.s.i)$). Therefore, the input arcs of f, D, p, and SWITCH receive tokens with unique activity names, provided f is a valid expression. Clearly the D^{-1} operator never receives more than one token; hence L^{-1} also receives and produces exactly one token on each line. The L^{-1} operator unstacks the context part stacked by the corresponding L operator, so the tokens produced by L^{-1} have an iteration number equal to that of the input to the L operator. Thus, a loop expression also behaves like a function box in the sense that the ith set of input tokens produces the ith set of output tokens.

All activities belonging to a particular instantiation of a loop are said to constitute a *loop domain* and can proceed independent of activities outside the loop domain, including those of nested loops. It is interesting to note that tokens need not go around a loop in any particular order unless constrained by the need for intermediate results. This situation was illustrated by the program in Figure 1 where several initiations of f could execute concurrently. Even if the $j+1$st execution of f terminates before the jth execution, the activities of the $+$ operator will not be affected. However, in Figure 1, the $j+1$st activity of the $+$ can take place only after its jth activity has completed because of the data dependency of s on **new** s. Hence the $j+1$st output of f has been produced and absorbed by the jth activity of the $+$. Automatic unraveling of loops, constrained only by data dependencies that are actually present, greatly increases the concurrency within programs, many of which would otherwise be considered completely sequential.

We have analyzed the behavior of the graph in Figure 1 assuming that f took considerable time to compute relative to a $+$. In passing we note that if f were some trivial operation and took only as long as the $+$ operator, probably no effective unfolding of this loop program would take place. In other words, the programmer need not know the relative timing of operators in order to write a parallel program. The fewer the data dependencies implied in a program, the more concurrent activities will be generated by the U-interpreter.

Procedure application. A procedure application is implemented using two operators: A and A^{-1}. As shown in Figure 4, each procedure is prefixed by a BEGIN operator and suffixed by an END operator. The A operator must create a new context u' within which the procedure whose code block name arrives on arc q may execute, and it must pass the argument value on line a to that context. The A operator is described by:

$$input\ token\ set = \{<u.c.s_A.i, q>_{proc}, <u.c.s_A.i, a>_{arg}\}$$
$$output\ token\ set = \{<u'.c_q.begin.1, a>\}$$

where $u' = (u.c.s_T.i)$ and s_T is the number of the A^{-1} operator corresponding to the A operator in s_A.

That is, the "return address" $u.c.s_T.i$ is stacked, and u' becomes the new context in which procedure q is executed. The output of A goes to the BEGIN operator, which simply replicates tokens for each fork in its output line. The END operator is more complex. It returns the result to the caller by unstacking the return address:

$$input\ token\ set = \{<u'.c_q.end.1, b>\}$$

where $u' = (u.c.s_T.i)$

$$output\ token\ set = \{<u.c.s_T.i, b>\}$$

Finally, the A^{-1} operator is straightforward, since, just like the BEGIN operator, it also serves only to replicate its output for its successors.

Maximum parallelism in a program

The U-interpreter is free of implementation details and is therefore quite amenable to formal analysis. We have shown that the U-interpreter does provide more concurrency than the usual way of interpreting data flow graphs.[16] To compare the relative parallelism of two interpreters, we choose a model that is independent of timing assumptions. Consider a program P involving two computations, x and y. We call interpreter I1 more parallel than interpreter I2 if results produced by I1 and I2 never differ, and if the execution of P on I2 implies that x must be computed before y while the execution of P on I1 does not imply any such constraint. Thus, in general, I1 has more parallelism than I2 if for all programs I1 implies no more execution constraints than I2. In fact, we have also shown that the U-interpreter finds maximum parallelism in an uninterpreted graph[16] (i.e., a graph in which operators other than control operators SWITCH, D, D^{-1}, L, L^{-1}, A, and A^{-1} are not assigned any meaning). It should be noted that the U-interpreter cannot improve on the graph itself; any unnecessary data dependencies will remain even if the graph is executed using the

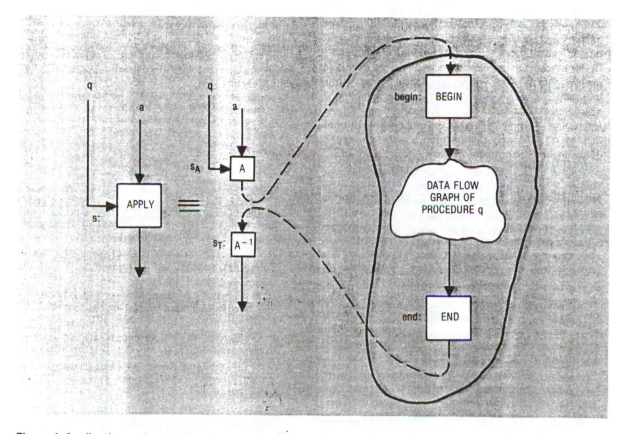

Figure 4. Application and execution of procedure *q*.

U-interpreter. The most common situation involving extraneous data dependencies arises in data structure operations. For example, the computation $a+x[2]$ depends on a and the 2nd element of x. However, the semantics of the particular high-level language may require the compiler to generate data flow graphs that cause all elements of x to be computed before $x[2]$ can be used.[8]

A formal definition of termination is often needed to resolve questions about how fast the final results will be produced. Program termination under the U-interpreter can be defined as the situation in which no activity is enabled or executing. The graphs produced for Id are "self-cleaning": on termination no tokens remain in the graph except on the output arcs. Our definition of termination is, in some sense, at odds with the notion of termination of a sequential program. In a sequential program the production of results and program termination occur simultaneously. On the other hand, if the "results" of a parallel program are the history of tokens on the output arcs, then results may be produced long before a program terminates. Thus, until the data flow program terminates, there is a possibility of producing more results. There is, however, no possibility of changing results that have already been produced. (The history of an arc is *monotonic*.) It should be noted that in order to assert that all output tokens that will be produced actually *are* produced, even if the computation does not terminate, one has to assume only a *fair* scheduling of activities: no enabled activity waits indefinitely.[16]

If function f in the trapezoidal rule example is some trivial function, not much is gained by unfolding the loop

for concurrent execution. As we pointed out earlier, the U-interpreter would automatically avoid unfolding the loop in that case. However, if each instance of f requires a lot of computation, then too much unfolding may take place. This would pose the practical problem of managing limited processing and memory resources.

We have described labeling of activities for graphs of deterministic computations. The U-interpreter is easily extended to deal with nonstrict as well as nondeterministic operators. The Id language has *resource managers*, which can be used to describe the nondeterministic interaction between processes that share objects. The labeling scheme for these constructs has been discussed elsewhere.[10] We believe the U-interpreter that incorporates nondeterministic and nonstrict operators, and that treats conventional sequential programs as primitive nodes of a graph, may help in structuring distributed systems.

Implications for computer architecture

Dynamic and explicit labeling of activities by an interpreter can increase the asynchrony and parallelism of any functional language. However, it seems that the practical benefits of dynamic labeling can best be exploited only by building special hardware structures. The benefits of the U-interpreter have been measured on a simulated machine and reported by Gostelow and Thomas.[14] A prototype for a thousand-processor machine based on the U-interpreter is currently being designed at MIT.[15]

A group at the University of Manchester in England independently discovered the idea of explicitly labeling computational activities for parallel execution. An experimental computer in which tokens carry long labels (56 bits) is currently under construction at Manchester.[17,18] In this machine a number of mechanisms for manipulating labels are provided for the language designer, without imposing *a priori* a specific set of label manipulation rules. Since the U-interpreter is an abstract model for interpreting data flow programs, it can probably be implemented on the Manchester machine, which is also capable of supporting the nondeterministic constructs of Id.[19]

A machine to implement the U-interpreter must provide an efficient mechanism for matching tokens with identical labels. In the Manchester machine, one waiting-matching store with 16K token capacity is provided. The matching is done by hashing and searching.[18] The tagged-token data flow machine under construction at MIT provides one small (32- or 64-token) waiting-matching store per processing element. The processing element is selected by hashing part of the label on the token,[14,15] and then the waiting-matching section is searched accordingly. This machine has a much smaller waiting-matching store because, unlike the Manchester machine, tokens for data-structure storage operations do not go through the waiting-matching section.

Logically, activity names can become arbitrarily long because the context field is recursive. For terminating computations, names can be kept within bounds by proper encoding of the information. One proposed scheme[15] works as follows: Suppose processing elements of a machine are (logically) partitioned into groups of various sizes called *physical domains*. Given the size of a processing element and a physical domain, there must be a maximum number (n) of loop and procedure invocation (i.e., *logical domains*) that can be concurrently executed. (One may draw analogy with an elevator that has a maximum capacity of 10 people or 2000 lbs.) We assign n "tickets" to such a physical domain. A new loop or procedure invocation is started in a physical domain only if a ticket is available. For example, an L operator will have to get a ticket from a finite ticket pool for the new context $u' = (u.c.s.i)$ and then send the current context associated with this ticket on a special dummy token directly to the corresponding L^{-1} operator. With the help of the dummy token, the L^{-1} operator will be able to generate the proper activity names for the output tokens and release the ticket for further use. If all the tickets are in use, then execution of an L operator will be delayed until a ticket is freed. Similar behavior holds for A and A^{-1} operators. This scheme does imply a degree of sequentiality in securing a ticket. It remains to be shown that disadvantages of this type of sequentiality are more than compensated for by an even distribution of activities on processing elements. A complete discussion of this and other architectural issues is beyond the scope of this paper.

The notion of labeling computational activities as used in the U-interpreter, coupled with an understanding of the rules for manipulating the activity names, should help to enhance the parallelism of programs written in any functional language. This implies the need to build special hardware structures to exploit the practical benefits of the method. ∎

Acknowledgment

This research was done by the authors at the University of California, Irvine, and was partially supported by NSF grant MCS76-12460.

References

1. D. J. Kuck, R. H. Kuhn, D. A. Padua, B. Leasure, and M. Wolfe, "Dependence Graphs and Compiler Optimizations," *Proc. ACM Symp. Principles of Programming Languages,* Jan. 1981, pp. 207-218.

2. N. E. Abel, et al., "TRANQUIL: A Language for an Array Processing Computer," *AFIPS Conf. Proc.,* Vol. 34, 1969 SJCC, pp. 57-73.

3. D. H. Lawrie, T. Layman, D. Baer, and J. M. Randel, "GLYPNIR—A Programming Language for Illiac IV," *Comm. ACM,* Vol. 18, No. 3, Mar. 1975, pp. 157-164.

4. R. E. Millstein, "Control Structures in Illiac IV Fortran," *Comm. ACM,* Vol. 6, No. 10, Oct. 1973, pp. 621-627.

5. L. G. Tesler and H. J. Enea, "A Language Design for Concurrent Processes," *AFIPS Conf. Proc.,* Vol. 32, 1968 SJCC, pp. 403-408.

6. J. B. Dennis, "First Version of a Data Flow Procedure Language," (in) *Lecture Notes in Computer Science, Volume 19: Programming Symp.: Proc. Colloque sur la Programmation,* B. Robinet (ed.), Springer-Verlag, 1974, pp. 362-376.

7. J. Backus, "Can Programming be Liberated from the von Neumann Style? A Functional Style and its Algebra of Programs," *Comm. ACM,* Vol. 21, No. 8, Aug. 1978, pp. 613-641.

8. W. B. Ackerman, "Data Flow Languages," *Computer,* this issue.

9. A. L. Davis and R. M. Keller, "Data Flow Program Graphs," *Computer,* Vol. 15, No. 2, Feb. 1982, pp. 26-41.

10. Arvind, K. P. Gostelow, and W. Plouffe, "An Asynchronous Programming Language and Computing Machine," Tech. Report TR114a, Department of Information and Computer Science, University of California, Irvine, Dec. 1978.

11. R. M. Keller, G. Lindstrom, and S. S. Patil, "A Loosely-Coupled Applicative Multiprocessing System," *AFIPS Conf. Proc.,* Vol. 48, 1979 NCC, pp. 613-622.

12. W. B. Ackerman and J. B. Dennis, "VAL—A Value-Oriented Algorithmic Language: Preliminary Reference Manual," Tech. Report TR-218, Laboratory for Computer Science, MIT, Cambridge, Mass., June 1979.

13. Arvind and K. P. Gostelow, "A Computer Capable of Exchanging Processors for Time," *Proc. IFIP Congress 77,* Aug. 1977, pp. 849-853.

14. K. P. Gostelow and R. E. Thomas, "Performance of a Simulated Dataflow Computer," *IEEE Trans. Computers,* Vol. C-29, No. 10, Oct. 1980, pp. 905-919.

15. Arvind and V. Kathail, "A Multiple Processor Dataflow Machine That Supports Generalized Procedures," *8th Ann. Symp. Computer Architecture,* May 1981, pp. 291-302.

16. Arvind and K. P. Gostelow, "Some Relationships Between Asynchronous Interpreters of a Dataflow Language," (in) E. J. Neuhold (ed.), *Formal Description of Programming Languages,* North-Holland Publ. Co., New York, 1977.

17. J. Gurd and I. Watson, "Data Driven System for High Speed Parallel Computing—Part 2: Hardware Design," *Computer Design,* Vol. 19, No. 7, July 1980, pp. 97-106.

18. I. Watson and J. R. Gurd, "A Practical Data Flow Computer," *Computer,* Vol. 15, No. 2, Feb. 1982, pp. 51-57.

19. A. J. Catto and J. R. Gurd, "Resource Management in Dataflow," *Proc. Conf. Functional Programming Languages and Computer Architecture,* Portsmouth, NH, Oct. 1981, pp. 77-84.

Kim P. Gostelow is currently with the General Electric Research and Development Center in Schenectady, New York. His interests include operating systems, machine architecture, and the semantics of programming languages. From 1972 to 1974 he did work on network modeling at the Stichting Academisch Rekencentrum Amsterdam, The Netherlands. From 1974 to 1980 he was assistant, and then associate professor of information and computer science at the University of California, Irvine. He received the BS and MS degrees in engineering and the PhD in computer science from the University of California, Los Angeles, in 1966, 1968, and 1971, respectively.

Arvind is a guest editor of this issue of *Computer.* His biography appears on p. 13.

Two Fundamental Issues in Multiprocessing

Arvind

Robert A. Iannucci

Abstract

A general purpose multiprocessor should be scalable, *i.e.*, show higher performance when more hardware resources are added to the machine. Architects of such multiprocessors must address the loss in processor efficiency due to two fundamental issues: long memory latencies and waits due to synchronization events. It is argued that a well designed processor can overcome these losses provided there is sufficient parallelism in the program being executed. The detrimental effect of long latency can be reduced by instruction pipelining, however, the restriction of a single thread of computation in von Neumann processors severely limits their ability to have more than a few instructions in the pipeline. Furthermore, techniques to reduce the memory latency tend to increase the cost of task switching. The cost of synchronization events in von Neumann machines makes decomposing a program into very small tasks counter-productive. Dataflow machines, on the other hand, treat each instruction as a task, and by paying a small synchronization cost for each instruction executed, offer the ultimate flexibility in scheduling instructions to reduce processor idle time.

Key words and phrases: caches, cache coherence, dataflow architectures, hazard resolution, instruction pipelining, LOAD/STORE architectures, memory latency, multiprocessors, multi-thread architectures, semaphores, synchronization, von Neumann architecture.

1. Importance of Processor Architecture

Parallel machines having up to several dozen processors are commercially available now. Most of the designs are based on von Neumann processors operating out of a shared memory. The differences in the architectures of these machines in terms of processor speed, memory organization and communication systems, are significant, but they all use relatively conventional von Neumann processors. These machines represent the general belief that processor architecture is of little importance in designing parallel machines. We will show the fallacy of this assumption on the basis of two issues: *memory latency* and *synchronization*. Our argument is based on the following observations:

1. Most von Neumann processors are likely to "idle" during long memory references, and such references are unavoidable in parallel machines.

2. Waits for synchronization events often require task switching, which is expensive on von Neumann machines. Therefore, only certain types of parallelism can be exploited efficiently.

We believe the effect of these issues on performance to be fundamental, and to a large degree, orthogonal to the effect of circuit technology. We will argue that by designing the processor properly, *the detrimental effect of memory latency on performance can be reduced provided there is parallelism in the program*. However, techniques for reducing the effect of latency tend to increase the synchronization cost.

In the rest of this section, we articulate our assumptions regarding general purpose parallel computers. We then discuss the often neglected issue of quantifying the amount of parallelism in programs. Section 2 develops a framework for defining the issues of latency and synchronization. Section 3 examines the methods to reduce the effect of memory latency in von Neumann computers and discusses their limitations. Section 4 similarly examines synchronization methods and their cost. In Section 5, we discuss multi-threaded computers like HEP and the MIT Tagged-Token Dataflow machine, and show how these machines can tolerate latency and synchronization costs provided there is sufficient parallelism in programs. The last section summarizes our conclusions.

1.1. Scalable Multiprocessors

We are primarily interested in *general purpose parallel computers*, *i.e.*, computers that can exploit parallelism, when present, in any program. Further, we want multiprocessors to be *scalable* in such a manner that adding hardware resources results in higher performance without requiring changes in application programs. The focus of the paper is not on arbitrarily large machines, but machines which range in size from ten to a thousand processors. We expect the processors to be at least as powerful as the current microprocessors and possibly as powerful as the CPU's of the current supercomputers. In particular, the context of the discussion is not machines with millions of one bit ALU's, dozens of which may fit on one chip. The design of such machines will certainly involve fundamental issues in addition to those presented here. Most parallel machines that are available today or likely to be available in the next few years fall within the scope of this paper (*e.g.*, the BBN Butterfly [36], ALICE [13] and now FLAGSHIP, the Cosmic Cube [38] and Intel's iPSC, IBM's RP3 [33], Alliant and CEDAR [26], and GRIP [11]).

If the programming model of a parallel machine reflects the machine configuration, *e.g.*, number of

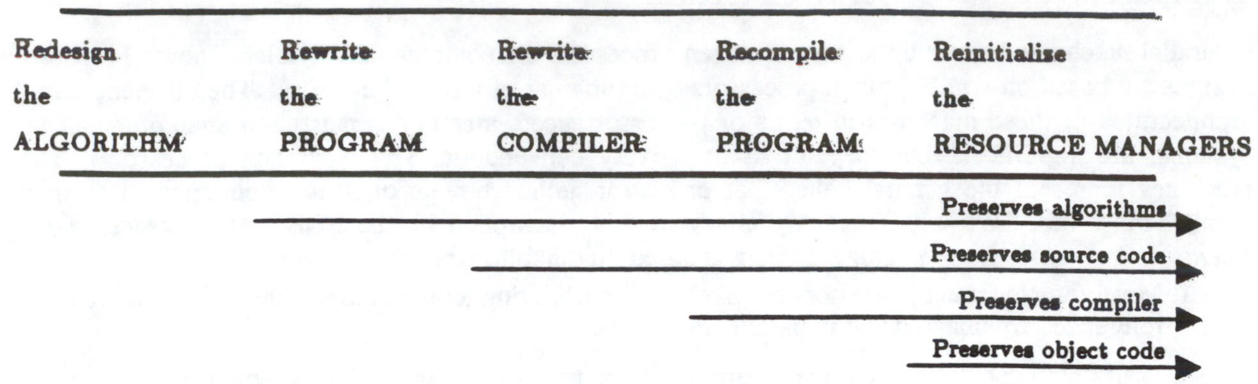

Redesign the ALGORITHM	Rewrite the PROGRAM	Rewrite the COMPILER	Recompile the PROGRAM	Reinitialise the RESOURCE MANAGERS

Preserves algorithms →

Preserves source code →

Preserves compiler →

Preserves object code →

Figure 1: The Effect of Scaling on Software

processors and interconnection topology, the machine is not scalable in a practical sense. Changing the machine configuration should not require changes in application programs or system software; updating tables in the resource management system to reflect the new configuration should be sufficient. However, few multiprocessor designs have taken this stance with regard to scaling. In fact, it is not uncommon to find that source code (and in some cases, algorithms) must be modified in order to run on an altered machine configuration. Figure 1 depicts the range of effects of scaling on the software. Obviously, we consider architectures that support the scenario at the right hand end of the scale to be far more desirable than those at the left. It should be noted that if a parallel machine is not scalable, then it will probably not be fault-tolerant; one failed processor would make the whole machine unusable. It is easy to design hardware in which failed components, e.g., processors, may be masked out. However, if the application code must be rewritten, our guess is that most users would wait for the original machine configuration to be restored.

1.2. Quantifying Parallelism in Programs

Ideally, a parallel machine should speed up the execution of a program in proportion to the number of processors in the machine. Suppose $t(n)$ is the time to execute a program on an n-processor machine. The speed-up as a function of n may be defined as follows:[1].

$$speed-up(n) = \frac{t(1)}{t(n)}$$

Speed-up is clearly dependent upon the program or programs chosen for the measurement. Naturally, if a program does not have "sufficient" parallelism, no parallel machine can be expected to demonstrate dramatic speedup. Thus, in order to evaluate a parallel machine properly, we need to characterize the inherent or potential parallelism of a program. This presents a difficult problem because the amount of parallelism in the source program that is exposed to the architecture may depend upon the quality of the compiler or programmer annotations. Furthermore, there is no reason to assume that the source program cannot be changed. Undoubtedly, different algorithms for a problem have different amounts of parallelism, and the parallelism of an algorithm can be obscured in coding. The problem is compounded by the fact that most programming languages do not have enough expressive power to show all the

---

[1]Of course, we are assuming that it is possible to run a program on any number of processors of a machine. In reality often this is not the case.

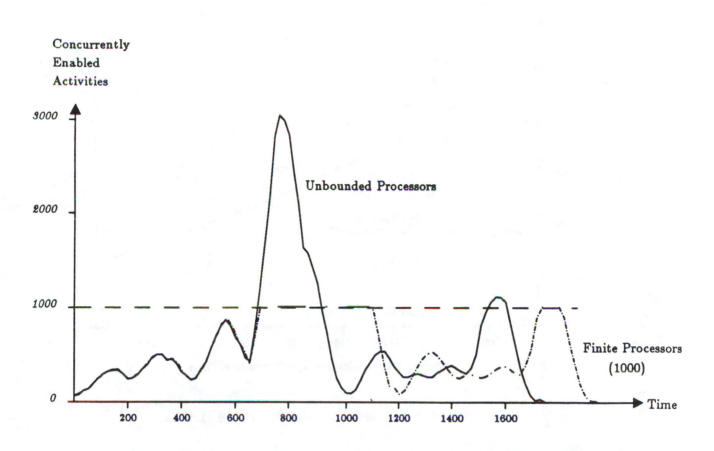

Concurrently
Enabled
Activities

Figure 2: Parallelism Profile of SIMPLE on a 20×20 Array

---

possible parallelism of an algorithm in a program. In spite of all these difficulties, we think it is possible to make some useful estimates of the potential parallelism of an algorithm.

It is possible for us to code algorithms in Id [30], a high-level dataflow language, and compile Id programs into dataflow graphs, where the nodes of the graph represent simple operations such as fixed and floating point arithmetic, logicals, equality tests, and memory loads and stores, and where the edges represent only the *essential* data dependencies between the operations. A graph thus generated can be executed on an interpreter (known as GITA) to produce results and the *parallelism profile*, $pp(t)$, *i.e.*, the number of concurrently executable operators as a function of time on an idealized machine. The idealized machine has unbounded processors and memories, and instantaneous communication. It is further assumed that all operators (instructions) take unit time, and operators are executed as soon as possible. The parallelism profile of a program gives a good estimate of its "inherent parallelism" because it is drawn assuming *the execution of two operators is sequentialized if and only if there is a data dependency between them*. Figure 2 shows the parallelism profile of the SIMPLE code for a representative set of input data. SIMPLE [12], a hydrodynamics and heat flow code kernel, has been extensively studied both analytically [1] and by experimentation.

The solid curve in Figure 2 represents a single outer-loop iteration of SIMPLE on a 20×20 mesh, while a typical simulation run performs 100,000 iterations on 100×100 mesh. Since there is no significant parallelism between the outer-loop iterations of SIMPLE, the parallelism profile for N iterations can be obtained by repeating the profile in the figure N times. Approximately 75% of the instructions executed involve the usual arithmetic, logical and memory operators; the rest are miscellaneous overhead

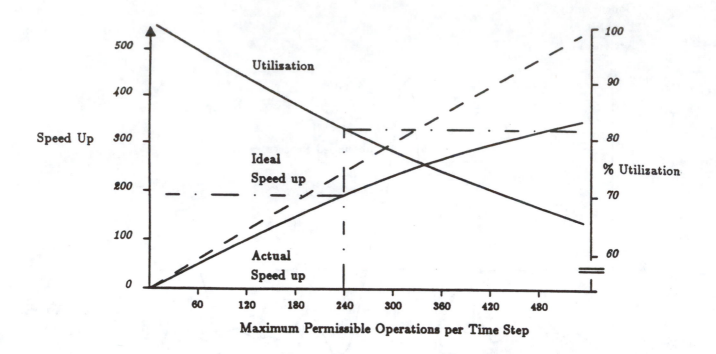

Figure 3: Speed Up and Utilization for 20×20 SIMPLE

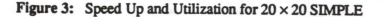

operators, some of them peculiar to dataflow. One can easily deduce the parallelism profile of any set of operators from the raw data that was used to generate the profile in the figure; however, classifying operators as overhead is not easy in all cases.

The reader may visualize the execution on n processors by drawing a horizontal line at n on the parallelism profile and then "pushing" all the instructions which are above the line to the right and below the line. The dashed curve in Figure 2 shows this for SIMPLE on 1000 processors and was generated by our dataflow graph interpreter by executing the program again with the constraint that no more than n operations were to be performed at any step. However, a good estimate for $t(n)$ can be made, very inexpensively, from the ideal parallelism profile as follows. For any τ, if $pp(\tau) \le n$, we perform all $pp(\tau)$ operations in time step τ. However, if $pp(\tau) > n$, then we assume it will take the least integer greater than $pp(\tau)/n$ steps to perform $pp(\tau)$ operations. Hence,

$$t(n) = \sum_{\tau=1}^{T_{MAX}} \lceil \frac{pp(\tau)}{n} \rceil$$

where T_{MAX} is the number of steps in the ideal parallelism profile. Our estimate of $t(n)$ is conservative because the data dependencies in the program may permit the execution of some instructions from $pp(\tau+1)$ in the last time step in which instructions from $pp(\tau)$ are executed.

In our dataflow graphs the number of instructions executed does not change when the program is executed on a different number of processors. Hence, $t(1)$ is simply the area under the parallelism profile. We can now plot *speed-up(n)=t(1)/t(n)* and *utilization(n)=t(1)/n×t(n)*, for SIMPLE as shown in Figure 3. For example, in the case of 240 processors, *speed-up* is 195, and *utilization* is 81%. One way to understand *utilization(n)* is that a program has n parallel operations for only *utilization(n)* fraction of its total $t(n)$ duration.

It can be argued that this problem does not have enough parallelism to keep, say, 1000 processors fully utilized. On the other hand, if we cannot keep 10 processors fully utilized, we cannot blame the lack of parallelism in the program. Generally, under-utilization of the machine in the presence of massive parallelism stems from aspects of the internal architecture of the processors which preclude exploitation of certain types of parallelism. Machines are seldom designed to exploit inner-loop, outer-loop, as well as instruction-level parallelism simultaneously.

It is noteworthy that the potential parallelism varies tremendously during execution, a behavior which in our experience is typical of even the most highly parallel programs. We believe that any large program that runs for a long time must have sufficient parallelism to keep hundreds of processors utilized; several applications that we have studied support this belief. However, a parallel machine has to be fairly general purpose and programmable for the user to be able to express even the class of partial differential equation-based simulation programs represented by SIMPLE.

2. Latency and Synchronization

We now discuss the issues of latency and synchronization. We believe latency is most strongly a function of the physical decomposition of a multiprocessor, while synchronization is most strongly a function of how programs are logically decomposed.

2.1. Latency: The First Fundamental Issue

Any multiprocessor organization can be thought of as an interconnection of the following three types of modules (see Figure 4):

1. **Processing elements (PE):** Modules which perform arithmetic and logical operations on data. Each processing element has a single *communication port* through which all data values are received. Processing elements interact with other processing elements by sending messages, issuing interrupts or sending and receiving *synchronizing signals* through shared memory. PE's interact with memory elements by issuing LOAD and STORE instructions modified as necessary with atomicity constraints. Processing elements are characterized by the rate at which they can process instructions. As mentioned, we assume the instructions are simple, *e.g.*, fixed and floating point scalar arithmetic. More complex instructions can be counted as multiple instructions for measuring instruction rate.

2. **Memory elements (M):** Modules which store data. Each memory element has a single communication port. Memory elements respond to requests issued by the processing elements by returning data through the communication port, and are characterized by their total capacity and the rate at which they respond to these requests[2].

3. **Communication elements (C):** Modules which transport data. Each nontrivial communication element has at least three communication ports. Communication elements neither originate nor receive synchronizing signals, instructions, or data; rather, they retransmit such information when received on one of the communication ports to one or more of the other communication ports. Communication elements are characterized by the rate of transmission, the time taken per transmission, and the constraints imposed by one transmission on others, *e.g.*, blocking. The maximum amount of data that may be conveyed on a *communication port* per unit time is fixed.

Latency is the time which elapses between making a request and receiving the associated response. The

---

[2]In many traditional designs, the "memory" subsystem can be simply modeled by one of these M elements. Interleaved memory subsystems are modeled as a collection of M's and C's. Memory subsystems which incorporate processing capability can be modeled with PE's, M's, and C's. Section 4.3 describes one such case.

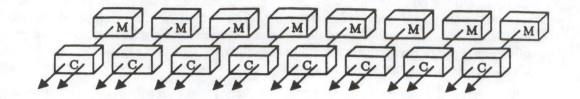

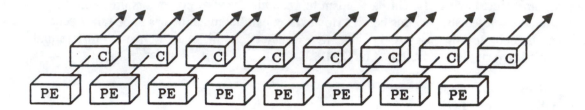

Figure 4: Structural Model of a Multiprocessor

above model implies that *a PE in a multiprocessor system faces larger latency in memory references than in a uniprocessor system* because of the transit time in the communication network between PE's and the memories. The actual interconnection of modules may differ greatly from machine to machine. For example, in the BBN Butterfly machine all memory elements are at an equal distance from all processors, while in IBM's RP3, each processor is closely coupled with a memory element. However, we assume that the average latency in a well designed n-PE machine should be $O(log(n))$. In a von Neumann processor, memory latency determines the time to execute memory reference instructions. Usually, the average memory latency also determines the maximum instruction processing speed. When latency cannot be hidden via overlapped operations, a tangible performance penalty is incurred. We call the cost associated with latency as the total *induced processor idle time* attributable to the latency.

2.2. Synchronization: The Second Fundamental Issue

We will call the basic units of computation into which programs are decomposed for parallel execution *computational tasks* or simply *tasks*. A general model of parallel programming must assume that tasks are created dynamically during a computation and die after having produced and consumed data. Situations in parallel programming which require task synchronization include the following basic operations:

1. *Producer-Consumer*: A task produces a data structure that is read by another task. If producer and consumer tasks are executed in parallel, synchronization is needed to avoid the *read-before-write* race.

2. *Forks* and *Joins*: The *join* operation forces a synchronization event indicating that two tasks which had been started earlier by some *forking* operation have in fact completed.

3. *Mutual Exclusion*: Non-deterministic events which must be processed one at a time, *e.g.*, serialization in the use of a resource.

The minimal support for synchronization can be provided by including instructions, such as atomic TEST-AND-SET, that operate on variables shared by synchronizing tasks[3]. However, to clarify the true cost

---

[3]While not strictly necessary, atomic operations such as TEST-AND-SET are certainly a convenient base upon which to build synchronization operations. See Section 4.3.

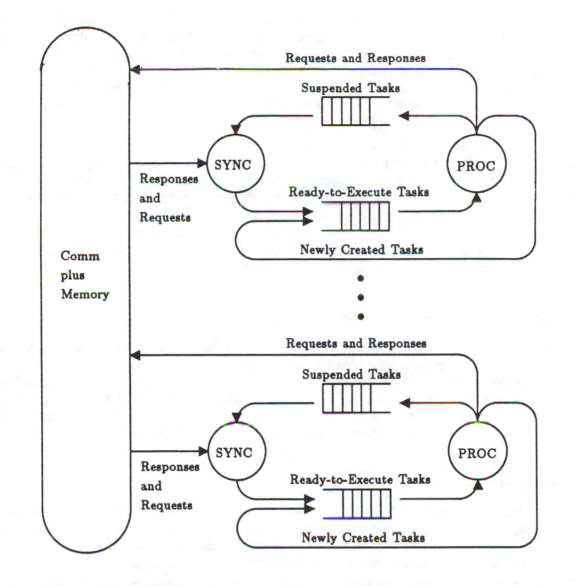

Figure 5: Operational Model of a Multiprocessor

---

of such instructions, we will use the *Operational Model* presented in Figure 5. Tasks in the operational model have resources, such as registers and memory, associated with them and constitute the smallest unit of independently schedulable work on the machine. A task is in one of the three states: *ready-to-execute*, *executing* or *suspended*. Tasks ready for execution may be queued locally or globally. When selected, a task occupies a processor until either it completes or is suspended waiting for a synchronization signal. A task changes from *suspended* to *ready-to-execute* when another task causes the relevant synchronization event. Generally, a suspended task must be set aside to avoid deadlocks[4]. The cost associated with such a synchronization is *the fixed time to execute the synchronization instruction plus the time taken to switch to another task.* The cost of task switching can be high because it usually involves saving the processor state, that is, the *context* associated with the task.

---

[4]Consider the case of a single processor system which must execute *n* cooperating tasks.

There are several subtle issues in accounting for synchronization costs. An event to enable or dispatch a task needs a *name*, such as that of a register or a memory location, and thus, synchronization cost should also include the instructions that generate, match and reuse identifiers which name synchronization events. It may not be easy to identify the instructions executed for this purpose. Nevertheless, such instructions represent overhead because they would not be present if the program were written to execute on a single sequential processor. The hardware design usually dictates the number of names available for synchronization as well as the cost of their use.

The other subtle issue has to do with the accounting for *intra-task synchronization*. As we shall see in Section 3, most high performance computers overlap the execution of instructions belonging to one task. The techniques used for synchronization of instructions in such a situation (*e.g.*, instruction dispatch and suspension) are often quite different from techniques for inter-task synchronization. It is usually safer and cheaper not to put aside the instruction waiting for a synchronization event, but rather to idle (or, equivalently, to execute NO-OP instructions while waiting). This is usually done under the assumption that the idle time will be on the order of a few instruction cycles. We define the synchronization cost in such situations to be the *induced processor idle time* attributable to waiting for the synchronization event.

3. Processor Architectures to Tolerate Latency

In this section, we describe those changes in von Neumann architectures that have directly reduced the effect of memory latency on performance. Increasing the processor state and instruction pipelining are the two most effective techniques for reducing the latency cost. Using Cray-1 (perhaps the best pipelined machine design to date), we will illustrate that it is difficult to keep more than 4 or 5 instructions in the pipeline of a von Neumann processor. It will be shown that every change in the processor architecture which has permitted overlapped execution of instructions has necessitated introduction of a cheap synchronization mechanism. Often these synchronization mechanisms are hidden from the user and not used for inter-task synchronization. This discussion will further illustrate that reducing latency frequently increases synchronization costs.

Before describing these evolutionary changes to hide latency, we should point out that the memory system in a multiprocessor setting creates more problems than just increased latency. Let us assume that all memory modules in a multiprocessor form one global address space and that any processor can read any word in the global address space. This immediately brings up the following problems:

- The time to fetch an operand may not be constant because some memories may be "closer" than others in the physical organization of the machine.

- No useful bound on the worst case time to fetch an operand may be possible at machine design time because of the scalability assumption. This is at odds with RISC designs which treat memory access time as bounded and fixed.

- If a processor were to issue several (pipelined) memory requests to different remote memory modules, the responses could arrive out of order.

All of these issues are discussed and illustrated in the following sections. A general solution for accepting memory responses out of order requires a synchronization mechanism to match responses with the destination registers (*names* in the task's context) and the instructions waiting on that value. The ill-fated Denelcor HEP [25] is one of the very few architectures which has provided such mechanisms in the von Neumann framework. However, the architecture of the HEP is sufficiently different from von Neumann architectures as to warrant a separate discussion (see Section 5).

3.1. Increasing the Processor State

Figure 6 depicts the modern-day view of the von Neumann computer [9] (*sans* I/O). In the earliest computers, such as EDSAC, the *processor state* consisted solely of an accumulator, a quotient register, and a program counter. Memories were relatively slow compared to the processors, and thus, the time to fetch an instruction and its operands completely dominated the instruction cycle time. Speeding up the Arithmetic Logic Unit was of little use unless the memory access time could also be reduced.

The appearance of multiple "accumulators" reduced the number of operand fetches and stores, and index registers dramatically reduced the number of instructions executed by essentially eliminating the need for self-modifying code. Since the memory traffic was drastically lower, programs executed much faster than before. However, the enlarged processor state did not reduce the time lost during memory references and, consequently, did not contribute to an overall reduction in cycle time; the basic cycle time improved only with improvements in circuit speeds.

3.2. Instruction Prefetching

The time taken by instruction fetch (and perhaps part of instruction decoding time) can be totally hidden if prefetching is done during the execution phase of the previous instruction. If instructions and data are kept in separate memories, it is possible to overlap instruction prefetching and operand fetching also. (The IBM STRETCH [7] and Univac LARC [16] represent two of the earliest attempts at implementing this idea.) Prefetching can reduce the cycle time of the machine by twenty to thirty percent depending upon the amount of time taken by the first two steps of the instruction cycle with respect to the complete cycle. However, the effective throughput of the machine cannot increase proportionately because overlapped execution is not possible with *all* instructions.

Instruction prefetching works well when the execution of instruction n does not have any effect on either the choice of instructions to fetch (as is the case in a BRANCH) or the content of the fetched instruction (self-modifying code) for instructions $n+1$, $n+2$, ..., $n+k$. The latter case is usually handled by simply outlawing it. However, effective overlapped execution in the presence of BRANCH instructions has remained a problem. Techniques such as prefetching both BRANCH targets have shown little performance/cost benefits. Lately, the concept of *delayed* BRANCH instructions from microprogramming has been incorporated, with success, in LOAD/STORE architectures (see Section 3.4). The idea is to delay the effect of a BRANCH by one instruction. Thus, the instruction at $n+1$ following a BRANCH instruction at n is always executed regardless of which way the BRANCH at n goes. One can always follow a BRANCH instruction with a NO-OP instruction to get the old effect. However, experience has shown that seventy percent of the time a useful instruction can be put in that position.

3.3. Instruction Buffers, Operand Caches and Pipelined Execution

The time to fetch instructions can be further reduced by providing a fast instruction buffer. In machines such as the CDC 6600 [40] and the Cray-1 [37], the instruction buffer is automatically loaded with n instructions in the neighborhood of the referenced instruction (relying on spatial locality in code references), whenever the referenced instruction is found to be missing. To take advantage of instruction buffers, it is also necessary to speed up the operand fetch and execute phases. This is usually done by providing *operand* caches or buffers, and overlapping the operand fetch and execution phases[5]. Of course, balancing the pipeline under these conditions may require further pipelining of the ALU. If successful, these techniques can reduce the machine cycle time to one-fourth or one-fifth the cycle time of an unpipelined machine. However, overlapped execution of four to five instructions in the von Neumann

---

[5]As we will show in Section 4.4, caches in a multiprocessor setting create special problems.

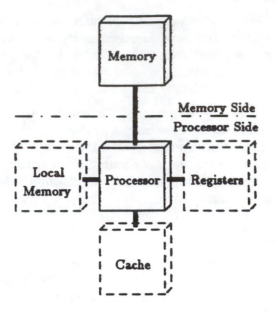

Figure 6: The von Neumann Processor (from Gajski and Peir [20])

framework presents some serious conceptual difficulties, as discussed next.

Designing a well-balanced pipeline requires that the time taken by various pipeline stages be more or less equal, and that the "things", *i.e.*, instructions, entering the pipe be independent of each other. Obviously, instructions of a program cannot be totally independent except in some special trivial cases. Instructions in a pipe are usually related in one of two ways: Instruction *n* produces data needed by instruction *n+k*, or only the complete execution of instruction *n* determines the next instruction to be executed (the aforementioned BRANCH problem).

Limitations on hardware resources can also cause instructions to interfere with one another. Consider the case when both instructions *n* and *n+1* require an adder, but there is only one of these in the machine. Obviously, one of the instructions must be deferred until the other is complete. A pipelined machine must be temporarily able to prevent a new instruction from entering the pipeline when there possibility of interference with the instructions already in the pipe. Detecting and quickly resolving these *hazards* is very difficult with ordinary instruction sets, *e.g.*, IBM 370, VAX 11 or Motorola 68000, due to their complexity.

A major complication in pipelining complex instructions is the variable amount of time taken in each stage of instruction processing (refer to Figure 7). Operand fetch in the VAX is one such example: determining the addressing mode for each operand requires a fair amount of decoding, and actual fetching can involve 0 to 2 memory references per operand. Considering all possible addressing mode combinations, an instruction may involve 0 to 6 memory references in addition to the instruction fetch itself! A pipeline design that can effectively tolerate such variations is close to impossible.

3.4. Load/Store Architectures

Seymour Cray, in the sixties, pioneered instruction sets (CDC 6600, Cray-1) which separate instructions into two disjoint classes. In one class are instructions which move data *unchanged* between memory and high speed registers. In the other class are instructions which operate on data in the registers. Instructions

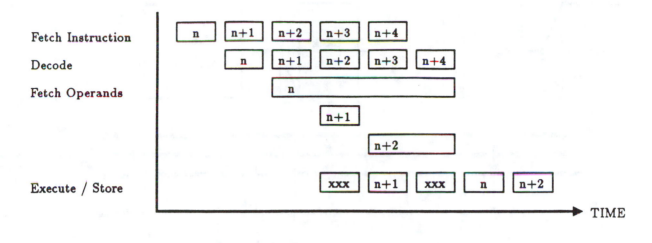

Figure 7: Variable Operand Fetch Time

---

of the second class *cannot* access the memory. This rigid distinction simplifies instruction scheduling. For each instruction, it is trivial to see if a memory reference will be necessary or not. Moreover, the memory system and the ALU may be viewed as parallel, noninteracting pipelines. An instruction dispatches exactly one unit of work to either one pipe or the other, but never both.

Such architectures have come to be known as LOAD/STORE architectures, and include the machines built by Reduced Instruction Set Computer (RISC) enthusiasts (the IBM 801 [34], Berkeley's RISC [32], and Stanford MIPS [22] are prime examples). LOAD/STORE architectures use the time between instruction decoding and instruction dispatching for hazard detection and resolution (see Figure 8). The design of the instruction pipeline is based on the principle that if an instruction gets past some fixed pipe stage, it should be able to run to completion without incurring any previously unanticipated hazards.

LOAD/STORE architectures are much better at tolerating latencies in memory accesses than other von Neumann architectures. In order to explain this point, we will first discuss a simplified model which detects and avoids hazards in a LOAD/STORE architecture similar to the Cray-1. Assume there is a bit associated with every register to indicate that the contents of the register are undergoing a change. The bit corresponding to register R is set the moment we dispatch an instruction that wants to update R. Following this, instructions are allowed to enter the pipeline only if they don't need to reference or modify register R or other registers reserved in a similar way. Whenever a value is stored in R, the reservation on R is removed, and if an instruction is waiting on R, it is allowed to proceed. This simple scheme works only if we assume that registers whose values are needed by an instruction are read before the next instruction is dispatched, and that the ALU or the multiple functional units within the ALU are pipelined to accept inputs as fast as the decode stage can supply them[6]. The dispatching of an instruction can also be held up because it may require a bus for storing results in a clock cycle when the bus is needed by another instruction in the pipeline. Whenever BRANCH instructions are encountered, the pipeline is effectively held up until the branch target has been decided.

Notice what will happen when an instruction to load the contents of some memory location M into some register R is executed. Suppose that it takes k cycles to fetch something from the memory. It will be

---

[6]Indeed, in the Cray-1, functional units can accept an input every clock cycle and registers are always read in one clock cycle after an instruction is dispatched from the Decoder.

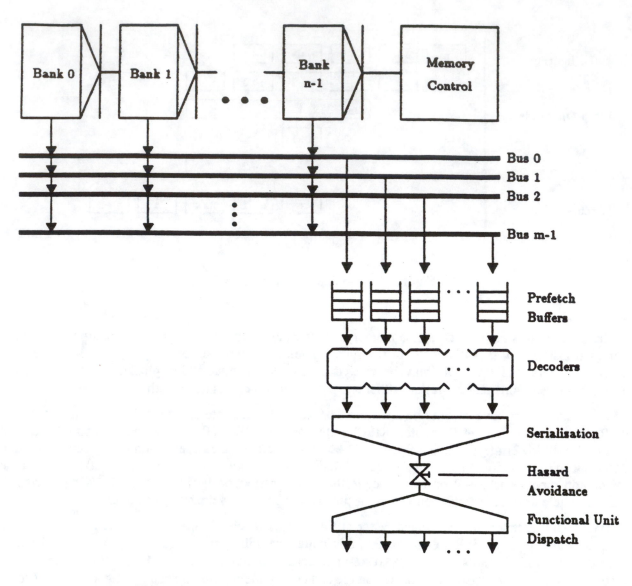

Figure 8: Hazard Avoidance at the Instruction Decode Stage

---

possible to execute several instructions during these k cycles as long as none of them refer to register R. In fact, this situation is hardly different from the one in which R is to be loaded from some functional unit that, like the Floating Point multiplier, takes several cycles to produce the result. These gaps in the pipeline can be further reduced if the compiler reorders instructions such that instructions consuming a datum are put as far as possible from instructions producing that datum. Thus, we notice that machines designed for high pipelining of instructions can hide large memory latencies provided there is local parallelism among instructions[7].

From another point of view, latency cost has been reduced by introducing a cheap synchronization mechanism: reservation bits on processor registers. However, the number of *names* available for

---

[7]The ability to reorder two instructions usually means that these instructions can be executed in parallel.

synchronization, *i.e.*, the size of the task's processor-bound context, is precisely the number of registers, and this restricts the amount of exploitable parallelism and tolerable latency. In order to understand this issue better, consider the case when the compiler decides to use register R to hold two different values at two different instructions say, i_n and i_m. This will require i_n and i_m to be executed sequentially while no such order may have been implied by the source code. *Shadow registers* have been suggested to deal with this class of problems. In fact, shadow registers are an engineering approach to solving a non-engineering problem. The real issue is *naming*. The reason that addition of explicit and implicit registers improves the situation derives from the addition of (explicit and implicit) *names* for synchronization and, hence, a greater opportunity for tolerating latency.

Some LOAD/STORE architectures have eliminated the need for reservation bits on registers by making the compiler responsible for scheduling instructions, such that the result is guaranteed to be available. The compiler can perform hazard resolution only if the time for each operation *e.g.*, ADD, LOAD, is known; it inserts NO-OP instructions wherever necessary. Because the instruction execution times are an intimate part of the object code, *any* change to the machine's structure (scaling, redesign) will at the very least require changes to the compiler and regeneration of the code. This is obviously contrary to our notion of generality, and hinders the portability of software from one generation of machine to the next.

Current LOAD/STORE architectures assume that memory references either take a fixed amount of time (one cycle in most RISC machines) or that they take a variable but predictable amount of time (as in the Cray-1). In RISC machines, this time is derived on the basis of a cache hit. If the operand is found to be missing from the cache, the pipeline stops. Equivalently, one can think of this as a situation where a clock cycle is *stretched* to the time required. This solution works because, in most of these machines, there can be either one or a very small number of memory references in progress at any given time. For example, in the Cray-1, no more than four independent addresses can be generated during a memory cycle. If the generated address causes a bank conflict, the pipeline is stopped. However, any conflict is resolved in at most three cycles.

LOAD/STORE architectures, because of their simpler instructions, often execute 15% to 50% more instructions than machines with more complex instructions [34]. This increase may be regarded as synchronization cost. However, this is easily compensated by improvements in clock speed made possible by simpler control mechanisms.

4. Synchronization Methods for Multiprocessing

4.1. Global Scheduling on Synchronous machines

For a totally synchronous multiprocessor it is possible to envision a master plan which specifies operations for every cycle on every processor. An analogy can be made between programming such a multiprocessor and coding a horizontally microprogrammed machine. Recent advances in compiling [18] have made such code generation feasible and encouraged researchers to propose and build several different synchronous multiprocessors. Cydrome and Multiflow computers, which are based on proposals in [35] and [19], respectively, are examples of such machines. These machines are generally referred to as *very long instruction word*, or VLIW, machines, because each instruction actually contains multiple smaller instructions (one per functional unit or processing element). The strategy is based on maximizing the use of resources and resolving potential run-time conflicts in the use of resources at compile time. Memory references and control transfers are "anticipated" as in RISC architectures, but here, multiple concurrent threads of computation are being scheduled instead of only one. Given the possibility of decoding and initiating many instructions in parallel, such architectures are highly appealing when one realizes that the fastest machines available now still essentially decode and dispatch instructions one at a time.

We believe that this technique is effective in its currently realized context, *i.e.*, Fortran-based computations on a small number (4 to 8) of processors. Compiling for parallelism beyond this level, however, becomes intractable. It is unclear how problems which rely on dynamic storage allocation or require nondeterministic and real-time constraints will play out on such architectures.

4.2. Interrupts and Low-level Context Switching

Almost all von Neumann machines are capable of accepting and handling interrupts. Not surprisingly, multiprocessors based on such machines permit the use of inter-processor interrupts as a means for signalling events. However, interrupts are rather expensive because, in general, the processor state needs to be saved. The state-saving may be forced by the hardware as a direct consequence of allowing the interrupt to occur, or it may occur explicitly, *i.e.*, under the control of the programmer, via a single very complex instruction or a suite of less complex ones. Independent of *how* the state-saving happens, the important thing to note is that each interrupt will generate a significant amount of traffic across the processor - memory interface.

In the previous discussion, we concluded that larger processor state is good because it provided a means for reducing memory latency cost. In trying to solve the problem of low cost synchronization, we have now come across an interaction which, we believe, is more than just coincidental. Specifically, in very fast von Neumann processors, the "obvious" synchronization mechanism (interrupts) will only work well in the trivial case of infrequent synchronization events or when the amount of processor state which must be saved is *very small*. Said another way, reducing the cost of synchronization by making interrupts cheap would generally entail increasing the cost of memory latency.

Uniprocessors such as the Xerox Alto [42], the Xerox Dorado [27], and the Symbolics 3600 family [29] have used a technique which may be called *microcode-level context switching* to allow sharing of the CPU resource by the I/O device adapters. This is accomplished by duplicating programmer-visible registers, in other words, the processor state. Thus, in one microinstruction the processor can be switched to a new task without causing any memory references to save the processor state[8]. This dramatically reduces the cost of processing certain types of events that cause frequent interrupts. As far as we know, nobody has adapted the idea of keeping multiple contexts in a multiprocessor setting (with the possible exception of the HEP, to be discussed in Section 5) although it should reduce synchronization cost over processors which can hold only a single context. It may be worth thinking about adopting this scheme to reduce the latency cost of a nonlocal memory references as well.

The limitations of this approach are obvious. High performance processors may have a small programmer-visible state (number of registers) but a much larger implicit state (caches). Low-level task switching does not necessarily take care of the overhead of flushing caches[9]. Further, one can only have a small number of independent contexts without completely overshadowing the cost of ALU hardware.

4.3. Semaphores and the Ultracomputer

Next to interrupts, the most commonly supported feature for synchronization is an *atomic operation* to test and set the value of a memory location. A processor can signal another processor by writing into a location which the other processor keeps reading to sense a change. Even though, theoretically, it is possible to perform such synchronization with ordinary read and write memory operations, the task is much simpler with an atomic TEST-AND-SET instruction. TEST-AND-SET is powerful enough to implement

---

[8]The Berkeley RISC idea of providing "register windows" to speed up procedure calls is very similar to multiple contexts.

[9]However, solutions such as multicontext caches and multicontext address translation buffers have been used to advantage in reducing this task switching overhead, (*c.f.*, the STO stack mechanism in the IBM 370/168).

all types of synchronization paradigms mentioned earlier. However, the synchronization cost of using such an instruction can be very high. Essentially, the processor that executes it goes into a *busy-wait* cycle. Not only does the processor get blocked, it generates extra memory references at every instruction cycle until the TEST-AND-SET instruction is executed successfully. Implementations of TEST-AND-SET that permit non-busy waiting imply context switching in the processor and thus are not necessarily cheap either.

It is possible to improve upon the TEST-AND-SET instruction in a multiprocessor setting, as suggested by the NYU Ultracomputer group [17]. Their technique can be illustrated by the atomic FETCH-AND-<OP> instruction (an evolution of the REPLACE-ADD instruction). The instruction requires an address and a value, and works as follows: suppose two processors, i and j, simultaneously execute FETCH-AND-ADD instructions with arguments (A, v_i) and (A, v_j) respectively. After one instruction cycle, the contents of A will become $(A)+v_i+v_j$. Processors i and j will receive, respectively, either (A) and $(A)+v_i$, or $(A)+v_j$ and (A) as results. Indeterminacy is a direct consequence of the race to update memory cell A.

An architect must choose between a wide variety of implementations for FETCH-AND-<OP>. One possibility is that the processor may interpret the instruction with a series of more primitive instructions. While possible, such a solution does not find much favor because it will cause considerable memory traffic. A second scheme implements FETCH-AND-<OP> in the memory controller (this is the alternative chosen by the CEDAR project [28]). This typically results in a significant reduction of network traffic because atomicity of memory transactions from the memory's controller happens by default. The scheme suggested by the NYU Ultracomputer group implements the instruction *in the switching nodes of the network.*

This implementation calls for a *combining* packet communication network which connects *n* processors to an n-port memory. If two packets collide, say FETCH-AND-ADD(A, v_i) and FETCH-AND-ADD(A, v_j), the switch extracts the values v_i and v_j, forms a new packet (FETCH-AND-ADD(A, v_i+v_j)), forwards it to the memory, and stores the value of v_i temporarily. When the memory returns the old value of location A, the switch returns two values $((A)$ and $(A)+v_i)$. The main improvement is that some synchronization situations which would have taken $O(n)$ time can be done in $O(logn)$ time. It should be noted, however, that one memory reference may involve as many as $log_2 n$ additions, and implies substantial hardware complexity. Further, the issue of processor idle time due to latency has not been addressed at all. In the worst case, the complexity of hardware may actually increase the latency of going through the switch and thus completely overshadow the advantage of "combining" over other simpler implementations.

The simulation results reported by NYU [17] show quasi-linear speedup on the Ultracomputer (a shared memory machine with ordinary von Neumann processors, employing FETCH-AND-ADD synchronization) for a large variety of scientific applications. We are not sure how to interpret these results without knowing many more details of their simulation model. Two possible interpretations are the following:

1. Parallel branches of a computation hardly share any data, thus, the costly *mutual exclusion* synchronization is rarely needed in real applications.

2. The synchronization cost of using shared data can be acceptably brought down by judicious use of cachable/non cachable annotations in the source program.

The second point may become clearer after reading the next section.

4.4. Cache Coherence Mechanisms

While highly successful for reducing memory latency in uniprocessors, caches in a multiprocessor setting introduce a serious synchronization problem called *cache coherence.* Censier and Feautrier [10] define the problem as follows: *"A memory scheme is coherent if the value returned on a LOAD instruction is always the value given by the latest STORE instruction with the same address.".* It is easy to see that this may be difficult to achieve in multiprocessing.

Suppose we have a two-processor system tightly coupled through a single main memory. Each processor has its own cache to which it has exclusive access. Suppose further that two tasks are running, one on each processor, and we know that the tasks are designed to communicate through one or more shared memory cells. In the absence of caches, this scheme can be made to work. However, if it happens that the shared address is present in both caches, the individual processors can read and write the address and *never* see any changes caused by the other processor. Using a store-through design instead of a store-in design does not solve the problem either. What is logically required is a mechanism which, upon the occurrence of a STORE to location x, invalidates copies of location x in caches of other processors, and guarantees that subsequent LOADs will get the most recent (cached) value. This can incur significant overhead in terms of decreased memory bandwidth.

All solutions to the cache coherence problem center around reducing the cost of detecting rather than avoiding the possibility of cache incoherence. Generally, *state* information indicating whether the cached data is private or shared, read-only or read-write, etc., is associated with each cache entry. However, this state somehow has to be updated after each memory reference. Implementations of this idea are generally intractable except possibly in the domain of bus-oriented multiprocessors. The so-called *snoopy bus* solution uses the broadcasting capability of buses and purges entry x from all caches when a processor attempts a STORE to x. In such a system, at most one STORE operation can go on at a time in the whole system and, therefore, system performance is going to be a strong function of the snoopy bus' ability to handle the coherence-maintaining traffic.

It is possible to improve upon the above solution if some additional state information is kept with each cache entry. Suppose entries are marked "shared" or "non-shared". A processor can freely read shared entries, but an attempt to STORE into a shared entry immediately causes that address to appear on the snoopy bus. That entry is then deleted from all the other caches and is marked "non-shared" in the processor that had attempted the STORE. Similar action takes place when the word to be written is missing from the cache. Of course, the main memory must be updated before purging the private copy from any cache. When the word to be read is missing from the cache, the snoopy bus may have to first reclaim the copy privately held by some other cache before giving it to the requesting cache. The status of such an entry will be marked as shared in both caches. The advantage of keeping shared/non-shared information with every cache entry is that the snoopy bus comes into action only on cache misses and STOREs to shared locations, as opposed to all LOADs and STOREs. Even if these solutions work satisfactorily, bus-oriented multiprocessors are not of much interest to us because of their obvious limitations in scaling.

As far as we can tell, there are no known solutions to cache coherence for non-bussed machines. It would seem reasonable that one needs to make caches partially visible to the programmer by allowing him to mark data (actually addresses) as shared or not shared. In addition, instructions to flush an entry or a block of entries from a cache have to be provided. Cache management on such machines is possible only if the concept of shared data is well integrated in the high-level language or the programming model. Schemes have also been proposed explicitly to interlock a location for writing or to bypass the cache (and flush it if necessary) on a STORE; in either case, the performance goes down rapidly as the machine is scaled. Ironically, in solving the latency problem via multiple caches, we have introduced the synchronization problem of keeping caches coherent.

It is worth noting that, while not obvious, a direct trade-off often exists between decreasing the parallelism and increasing the cachable or non-shared data.

5. Multi-Threaded Architectures

In order to reduce memory latency cost, it is essential that a processor be capable of issuing multiple, overlapped memory requests. The processor must view the memory/communication subsystems as a logical pipeline. As latency increases, keeping the pipeline full implies that more memory references will have to be in the pipeline. We note that memory systems of current von Neumann architectures have very little capability for pipelining, with the exception of array references in vector machines. The reasons behind this limitation are fundamental:

1. von Neumann processors must observe instruction sequencing constraints, and

2. since memory references can get out of order in the pipeline, a large number of identifiers to distinguish memory responses must be provided.

One way to overcome the first deficiency is to interleave many threads of sequential computations (as we saw in the very long instruction word architectures of Section 4.1). The second deficiency can be overcome by providing a large register set with suitable reservation bits. It should be noted that these requirements are somewhat in conflict. The situation is further complicated by the need of tasks to communicate with each other. Support for cheap synchronization calls for the processor to switch tasks quickly and to have a non-empty queue of tasks which are ready to run. One way to achieve this is again by interleaving multiple threads of computation and providing some intelligent scheduling mechanism to avoid busy-waits. Machines supporting multiple threads and fancy scheduling of instructions or processes look less and less like von Neumann machines as the number of threads increases.

In this section, we first discuss the erstwhile Denelcor HEP [25, 39]. The HEP was the first commercially available multi-threaded computer. After that we briefly discuss dataflow machines, which may be regarded as an extreme example of machines with multiple threads; machines in which each instruction constitutes an independent thread and only non-suspended threads are scheduled to be executed.

5.1. The Denelcor HEP: A Step Beyond von Neumann Architectures

The basic structure of the HEP processor is shown in Figure 9. The processor's data path is built as an eight step pipeline. In parallel with the data path is a control loop which circulates process status words (PSW's) of the processes whose threads are to be interleaved for execution. The delay around the control loop varies with the queue size, but is never shorter than eight pipe steps. This minimum value is intentional to allow the PSW at the head of the queue to initiate an instruction but not return again to the head of the queue until the instruction has completed. If at least eight PSW's, representing eight processes, can be kept in the queue, the processor's pipeline will remain full. This scheme is much like traditional pipelining of instructions, but with an important difference. The inter-instruction dependencies are likely to be weaker here because adjacent instructions in the pipe are always from *different processes*.

There are 2048 registers in each processor; each process has an index offset into the register array. Inter-process, *i.e.*, inter-thread, communication is possible via these registers by overlapping register allocations. The HEP provides FULL/EMPTY/RESERVED bits on each register and FULL/EMPTY bits on each word in the data memory. An instruction encountering EMPTY or RESERVED registers behaves like a NO-OP instruction; the program counter of the process, *i.e.*, PSW, which initiated the instruction is not incremented. The process effectively *busy-waits* but without blocking the processor. When a process issues a LOAD or STORE instruction, it is removed from the control loop and is queued separately in the Scheduler Function Unit (SFU) which also issues the memory request. Requests which are not satisfied because of improper FULL/EMPTY status result in recirculation of the PSW within the SFU's loop and also in reissuance of the request. The SFU matches up memory responses with queued PSW's, updates registers as necessary and reinserts the PSW's in the control loop.

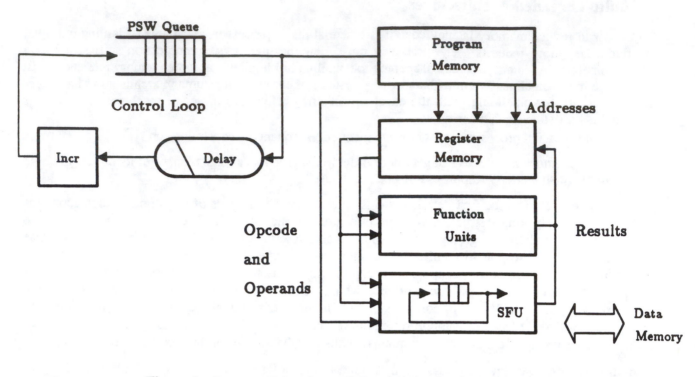

Figure 9: Latency Toleration and Synchronization in the HEP

Thus, the HEP is capable up to a point of using parallelism in programs to hide memory and communication latency. At the same time it provides efficient, low-level synchronization mechanisms in the form of presence-bits in registers and main memory. However, the HEP approach does not go far enough because there is a limit of *one* outstanding memory request per process, and the cost of synchronization through shared registers can be high because of the loss of processor time due to *busy-waiting*. A serious impediment to the software development on HEP was the limit of 64 PSW's in each processor. Though only 8 PSW's may be required to keep the process pipeline full, a much larger number is needed to name all concurrent tasks of a program.

5.2. Dataflow Architectures

Dataflow architectures [2, 15, 21, 23] represent a radical alternative to von Neumann architectures because they use dataflow graphs as their machine language [4, 14]. Dataflow graphs, as opposed to conventional machine languages, specify only a partial order for the execution of instructions and thus provide opportunities for parallel and pipelined execution at the level of individual instructions. For example, the dataflow graph for the expression a*b + c*d only specifies that both multiplications be executed before the addition; however, the multiplications can be executed in any order or even in parallel. The advantage of this flexibility becomes apparent when we consider that the order in which a, b, c and d will become available may not be known at compile time. For example, computations for operands a and b may take longer than computations for c and d or *vice versa*. Another possibility is that the time to fetch different operands may vary due to scheduling and hardware characteristics of the machine. Dataflow graphs do not force unnecessary sequentialization and dataflow processors schedule instructions according to the availability of the operands.

The instruction execution mechanism of a dataflow processor is fundamentally different from that of a

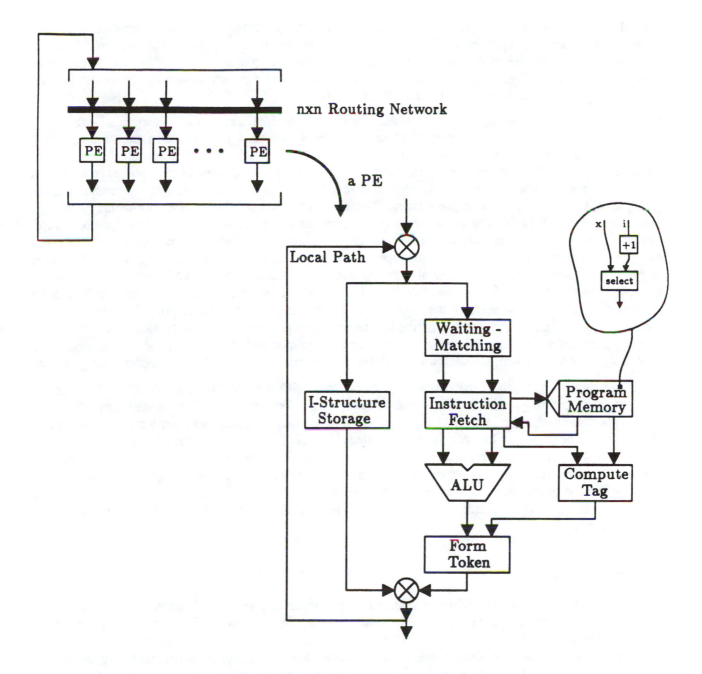

Figure 10: The MIT Tagged-Token Dataflow Machine

von Neumann processor. We will briefly illustrate this using the MIT Tagged-Token architecture (see Figure 10). Rather than following a *Program Counter* for the next instruction to be executed and then fetching operands for that instruction, a dataflow machine provides a low-level synchronization mechanism in the form of *Waiting-Matching* section which dispatches only those instructions for which data are already available. This mechanism relies on *tagging* each datum with the address of the instruction to which it belongs and the context in which the instruction is being executed. One can think of the instruction address as replacing the program counter, and the context identifier replacing the frame base register in traditional von Neumann architecture. It is the machine's job to match up data with the same tag and then to execute the denoted instruction. In so doing, new data will be produced, with a new tag indicating the successor instruction(s). Thus, each instruction represents a synchronization operation. Note that the number of synchronization names is limited by the size of the tag, which can easily be made much larger than the size of the register array in a von Neumann machine. Note also that the processor pipeline is non-blocking: given that the operands for an instruction are available, the corresponding instruction can be executed without further synchronization.

In addition to the waiting-matching section which is used primarily for dynamic scheduling of instructions, the MIT Tagged-Token machine provides a second synchronization mechanism called *I-Structure Storage*. Each word of I-structure storage has 2 bits associated with it to indicate whether the word is empty, full or has pending read-requests. This greatly facilitates overlapped execution of a producer of a data structure with the consumer of that data structure. There are three instructions at the graph level to manipulate I-structure storage. These are *allocate* - to allocate *n* empty words of storage, *select* - to fetch the contents of the ith word of an array and *store* - to store a value in a specified word. Generally software concerns dictate that a word be written into only once before it is deallocated. The dataflow processor treats all I-structure operations as *split-phase*. For example, when the *select* instruction is executed, a packet containing the tag of the destination instruction of the select instruction is forwarded to the proper address, possibly in a distant I-structure storage module. The actual memory operation may require waiting if the data is not present and thus the result may be returned many instruction times later. The key is that the instruction pipeline need not be suspended during this time. Rather, processing of other instructions may continue immediately after *initiation* of the operation. Matching of memory responses with waiting instructions is done via tags in the waiting-matching section.

One advantage of tagging each datum is that data from different contexts can be mixed freely in the instruction execution pipeline. Thus, instruction-level parallelism of dataflow graphs can effectively absorb the communication latency and minimize the losses due to synchronization waits. We hope it is clear from the prior discussion that even the most highly pipelined von Neumann processor cannot match the flexibility of a dataflow processor in this regard. A more complete discussion of dataflow machines is beyond the scope of this paper. An overview of executing programs on the MIT Tagged-Token Dataflow machine can be found in [6]. A deeper understanding of dataflow machines can be gotten from [2]. Additional, albeit slightly dated, details of the machine and the instruction set are given in [3] and [5], respectively.

6. Conclusions

We have presented the loss of performance due to increased latency and waits for synchronization events as the two fundamental issues in the design of parallel machines. These issues are, to a large degree, independent of the technology differences between various parallel machines. Even though we have not presented it as such, these issues are also independent of the high-level programming model used on a multiprocessor. If a multiprocessor is built out of conventional microprocessors, then degradation in performance due to latency and synchronization will show up regardless of whether a shared-memory, message-passing, reduction or dataflow programming model is employed.

Is it possible to modify a von Neumann processor to make it more suitable as a building block for a parallel machine? In our opinion the answer is a qualified "yes". The two most important characteristics of the dataflow processor are split-phase memory operations and the ability to put aside computations (*i.e.*, processes, instructions, or whatever the scheduling quanta are) without blocking the processor. We think synchronization bits in the storage are essential to support the producer-consumer type of parallelism. However, the more concurrently active threads of computation we have, the greater is the requirement for hardware-supported synchronization names. Iannucci [24] and others [8] are actively exploring designs based on these ideas. Only time will tell if it will be fair to classify such processors as von Neumann processors.

The biggest appeal of von Neumann processors is that they are widely available and familiar. There is a tendency to extrapolate these facts into a belief that von Neumann processors are "simple" and efficient. A technically sound case can be made that well designed von Neumann processors are indeed very efficient in executing sequential codes and require less memory bandwidth than dataflow processors. However, the efficiency of sequential threads disappears fast if there are too many interruptions or if idling of the processor due to latency or data-dependent hazards increases. Papadopoulos [31] is investigating dataflow architectures which will improve the efficiency of the MIT Tagged-Token architecture on sequential codes without sacrificing any of its dataflow advantages. We can assure the reader that none of these changes are tantamount to introducing a program counter in the dataflow architecture.

For lack of space we have not discussed the effect of multi-threaded architectures on the compiling and language issues. It is important to realize that compiling into primitive dataflow operators is a much simpler task than compiling into cooperating sequential threads. Since the cost of inter-process communication in a von Neumann setting is much greater than the cost of communication within a process, there is a preferred process or "grain" size on a given architecture. Furthermore, placement of synchronization instructions in a sequential code requires careful planning because an instruction to wait for a synchronization event may experience very different waiting periods in different locations in the program. Thus, even for a given grain size, it is difficult to decompose a program optimally. Dataflow graphs, on the other hand, provide a uniform view of inter- and intra-procedural synchronization and communication, and as noted earlier, only specify a partial order to enforce data dependencies among the instructions of a program. Though it is very difficult to offer a quantitative measure, we believe that an Id Nouveau compiler to generate code for a multi-threaded von Neumann computer will be significantly more complex than the current compiler [41] which generates fine grain dataflow graphs for the MIT Tagged-Token dataflow machine. Thus dataflow computers, in addition to providing solutions to the fundamental hardware issues raised in this paper, also have compiler technology to exploit their full potential.

Acknowledgment

The authors wish to thank David Culler for valuable discussions on much of the subject matter of this paper, particularly Load/Store architectures and the structure of the Cray machines. Members of the Computation Structures Group have developed many tools, without which the analysis of the Simple code would have been impossible. In particular, we would like to thank Ken Traub for the ID Compiler and David Culler and Dinarte Morais for GITA. This paper has benefited from numerous discussions with people both inside and outside MIT. We wish to thank Natalie Tarbet, Ken Traub, David Culler, Vinod Kathail and Rishiyur Nikhil for suggestions to improve this manuscript.

References

1. Arvind and R. E. Bryant. Design Considerations for a Partial Equation Machine. Proceedings of Scientific Computer Information Exchange Meeting, Lawrence Livermore Laboratory, Livermore, CA, September, 1979, pp. 94-102.

2. Arvind and D. E. Culler. "Dataflow Architectures". *Annual Reviews of Computer Science 1* (1986), 225-253.

3. Arvind, D. E. Culler, R. A. Iannucci, V. Kathail, K. Pingali, and R. E. Thomas. The Tagged Token Dataflow Architecture. Internal report. (including architectural revisions of October, 1983).

4. Arvind and K. P. Gostelow. "The U-Interpreter". *Computer 15*, 2 (February 1982), 42-49.

5. Arvind and R. A. Iannucci. Instruction Set Definition for a Tagged-Token Data Flow Machine. Computation Structures Group Memo 212-3, Laboratory for Computer Science, MIT, Cambridge, Mass., Cambridge, MA 02139, December, 1981.

6. Arvind and R. S. Nikhil. Executing a Program on the MIT Tagged-Token Dataflow Architecture. Proc. PARLE, (Parallel Architectures and Languages Europe), Eindhoven, The Netherlands, June, 1987.

7. Block, E. The Engineering Design of the STRETCH Computer. Proceedings of the EJCC, 1959, pp. 48-59.

8. Buehrer, R. and K. Ekanadham. Dataflow Principles in Multi-processor Systems. ETH, Zurich, and Research Division, Yorktown Heights, IBM Corporation, July, 1986.

9. Burks, A., H. H. Goldstine, and J. von Neumann. "Preliminary Discussion of the Logical Design of an Electronic Instrument, Part 2". *Datamation 8*, 10 (October 1962), 36-41.

10. Censier, L. M. and P. Feautrier. "A New Solution to the Coherence Problems in Multicache Systems". *IEEE Transactions on Computers C-27*, 12 (December 1978), 1112-1118.

11. Clack, C. and Peyton-Jones, S. L. The Four-Stroke Reduction Engine. Proceedings of the 1986 ACM Conference on Lisp and Functional Programming, Association for Computing Machinery, August, 1986, pp. 220-232.

12. Crowley, W. P., C. P. Hendrickson, and T. E. Rudy. The SIMPLE Code. Internal Report UCID-17715, Lawrence Livermore Laboratory, Livermore, CA, February, 1978.

13. Darlington, J. and M. Reeve. ALICE: A Multi-Processor Reduction Machine for the Parallel Evaluation of Applicative Languages. Proceedings of the 1981 Conference on Functional Programming Languages and Computer Architecture, Portsmouth, NH, 1981, pp. 65-76.

14. Dennis, J. B. *Lecture Notes in Computer Science*. Volume 19: First Version of a Data Flow Procedure Language. In *Programming Symposium: Proceedings, Colloque sur la Programmation*, B. Robinet, Ed., Springer-Verlag, 1974, pp. 362-376.

15. Dennis, J. B. "Data Flow Supercomputers". *Computer 13*, 11 (November 1980), 48-56.

16. Eckert, J. P., J. C. Chu, A. B. Tonik & W. F. Schmitt. Design of UNIVAC - LARC System: 1. Proceedings of the EJCC, 1959, pp. 59-65.

17. Edler, J., A. Gottlieb, C. P. Kruskal, K. P. McAuliffe, L. Rudolph, M. Snir, P. J. Teller & J. Wilson. Issues Related to MIMD Shared-Memory Computers: The NYU Ultracomputer Approach. Proceedings of the 12th Annual International Symposium On Computer Architecture, Boston, June, 1985, pp. 126-135.

18. Ellis, J. R.. *Bulldog: a Compiler for VLIW Architectures*. The MIT Press, 1986.

19. Fisher, J. A. Very Long Instruction Word Architectures and the ELI-512. Proc. of the 10th, International Symposium on Computer Architecture, IEEE Computer Society, June, 1983.

20. Gajski, D. D. & J-K. Peir. "Essential Issues in Multiprocessor Systems". *Computer 18*, 6 (June 1985), 9-27.

21. Gurd, J. R., C. C. Kirkham, and I. Watson. "The Manchester Prototype Dataflow Computer". *Communications of ACM 28*, 1 (January 1985), 34-52.

22. Hennessey, J. L. "VLSI Processor Architecture". *IEEE Transactions on Computers C-33*, 12 (December 1984), 1221-1246.

23. Hiraki, K., S. Sekiguchi, and T. Shimada. System Architecture of a Dataflow Supercomputer. Computer Systems Division, Electrotechnical Laboratory, Japan, 1987.

24. Iannucci, R. A. *A Dataflow / von Neuamnn Hybrid Architecture*. Ph.D. Th., Dept. of Electrical Engineering and Computer Science, MIT, Cambridge, Mass., (in preparation) 1987.

25. Jordan, H. F. Performance Measurement on HEP - A Pipelined MIMD Computer. Proceedings of the 10th Annual International Symposium On Computer Architecture, Stockholm, Sweden, June, 1983, pp. 207-212.

26. Kuck, D., E. Davidson, D. Lawrie, and A. Sameh. "Parallel Supercomputing Today and the Cedar Approach". *Science Magazine 231* (February 1986), 967-974.

27. Lampson, B. W. and K. A. Pier. A Processor for a High-Performance Personal Computer. Xerox Palo Alto Research Center, January, 1981.

28. Li, Z. and W. Abu-Sufah. A Technique for Reducing Synchronization Overhead in Large Scale Multiprocessors. Proc. of the 12th, International Symposium on Computer Architecture, June, 1985, pp. 284-291.

29. Moon, D. A. Architecture of the Symbolics 3600. Proceedings of the 12th Annual International Symposium On Computer Architecture, Boston, June, 1985, pp. 76-83.

30. Nikhil, R. S., K. Pingali, and Arvind. Id Nouveau. Computation Structures Group Memo 265, Laboratory for Computer Science, MIT, Cambridge, Mass., Cambridge, MA 02139, July, 1986.

31. Papadopoulos, G. M. *Implementation of a General Purpose Dataflow Multiprocessor*. Ph.D. Th., Dept. of Electrical Engineering and Computer Science, MIT, Cambridge, Mass., (in preparation) 1987.

32. Patterson, D. A. "Reduced Instruction Set Computers". *Communications of ACM 28*, 1 (January 1985), 8-21.

33. Pfister, G. F., W. C. Brantley, D. A. George, S. L. Harvey, W. J. Kleinfelder, K. P. McAuliffe, E. A. Melton, V. A. Norton, and J. Weiss. The IBM Research Parallel Processor Prototype (RP3): Introduction and Architecture. Proceedings of the 1985 International Conference on Parallel Processing, Institute of Electrical and Electronics Engineers, Piscataway, N. J., 08854, August, 1985, pp. 764-771.

34. Radin, G. The 801 Minicomputer. Proceedings of the Symposium on Architectural Support for Programming Languages and Operating Systems, ACM, March, 1982.

35. Rau, B., D. Glaeser, and E. Greenwalt. Architectural Support for the Efficient Generation of Code for Horizontal Architectures. Proceedings of the Symposium on Architectural Support for Programming Languages and Operating Systems, March, 1982. Same as Computer Architecture News 10,2 and SIGPLAN Notices 17,4.

TOWARD A DATAFLOW / VON NEUMANN HYBRID ARCHITECTURE

Robert A. Iannucci

IBM Corporation
- and -
MIT Laboratory for Computer Science
545 Technology Square
Cambridge, Massachusetts 02139

ABSTRACT

Dataflow architectures offer the ability to trade program level parallelism in order to overcome machine level latency. Dataflow further offers a uniform synchronization paradigm, representing one end of a spectrum wherein the unit of scheduling is a single instruction. At the opposite extreme are the von Neumann architectures which schedule on a task, or process, basis.

This paper examines the spectrum by proposing a new architecture which is a *hybrid* of dataflow and von Neumann organizations. The analysis attempts to discover those features of the dataflow architecture, lacking in a von Neumann machine, which are essential for tolerating latency and synchronization costs. These features are captured in the concept of a *parallel machine language* which can be grafted on top of an otherwise traditional von Neumann base. In such an architecture, the units of scheduling, called *scheduling quanta*, are bound at compile time rather than at instruction set design time. The parallel machine language supports this notion via a large synchronization name space.

A prototypical architecture is described, and results of simulation studies are presented. A comparison is made between the MIT Tagged-Token Dataflow machine and the subject machine which presents a model for understanding the cost of synchronization in a parallel environment.

Key Words and Phrases: architecture, context switching, dataflow, hybrid, I-structure storage, latency, multiprocessor, name space, process state, split transaction, synchronization, von Neumann

1. Introduction

It is becoming increasingly apparent that the lessons learned in 40 years of optimizing von Neumann uniprocessor architectures do not necessarily carry over to multiprocessors. Compiler technology coupled with simple pipeline design is now used effectively [20, 25, 26, 28] to cover bounded memory latency in uniprocessors. Unfortunately, the situation is qualitatively different for multiprocessors, where large and often unpredictable latencies in memory and communications systems cannot be tolerated by using similar techniques. This is attributable at the architectural level to poor support for inexpensive dynamic synchronization [4]. Specifically, latency cost is incurred on a per-instruction basis, but synchronization on a per-instruction basis is impractical. A scalable, general purpose multiprocessor architecture must address these issues. Traditional compile time sequencing is too weak a paradigm for general purpose machines (*c.f.*, ELI-512 [15], the ESL Polycyclic processor [27]), and traditional run time sequencing mechanisms are not sufficiently flexible (*c.f.*, The IBM 360 Model 91 [1, 31], the Cray-1 [28]).

The overall goal of this study is to discover the critical hardware structures which must be present in multiprocessor architectures to effectively tolerate latency and synchronization costs. This investigation is based on demonstrating that a tradeoff exists between von Neumann instruction sequencing simplicity and dataflow sequencing generality. To explore this tradeoff, a new architecture is developed as a synthesis of the best features of von Neumann and dataflow ideas. Evaluation of this architecture is based on characterizing the differences in various architectural figures of merit (*e.g.*, number of instructions executed, instruction complexity) between the new machine and the well-studied MIT Tagged Token Dataflow Architecture (TTDA) [2, 5, 11, 14].

The remainder of this paper provides technical justification for, and details of, the new architecture. Section 2 describes the work leading up to this proposal, including a brief discussion of von Neumann and dataflow architectures and the ways they address the issues of latency and synchronization. Section 3 discusses how these two apparently dissimilar architectures may be combined into a new architecture. The architecture and instruction set of the new machine are described. Using a newly-developed code generator and simulator for the architecture, Section 4 presents results of the first set of experiments along with relevant comparisons to the TTDA.

2. Background

2.1. Two Fundamental Issues

In [4] we argue that architects of any scalable, general purpose multiprocessor must face two very basic issues in order to exploit parallelism in programs. The first issue is *latency*: the time which elapses between making a request (*e.g.*, a memory reference) and receiving the associated response. Latency often incurs a cost in the form of induced processor idle time and is directly attributable to *physical partitioning of the machine*. The second issue is *synchronization*: the time correlation of related activities. Synchronization also incurs a cost in the form of the fixed time required to perform a synchronization operation plus the time lost to waiting or context switching, and is directly attributable to *logical partitioning of the program*. That is, in order to exploit parallelism in a program it must be *decomposed* into fragments which communicate. Managing this communication while preserving precedence constraints is one primary job of a multiprocessor's synchronization mechanism.

These issues are not only fundamental, they also appear to be strongly related. For example, one possible solution to idling the processor during a long-latency remote memory reference is to switch the processor to another task in the same manner that an operating system will switch contexts when an input/output (I/O) operation is begun. Unfortunately, this requires a highly efficient synchronization mechanism to manage the matching of memory responses with idled, or deferred, tasks.

It was our conclusion that satisfactory solutions to the problems raised for von Neumann architectures can only be had by altering the architecture of the processor itself. Questions raised in this study regarding the near-miss behavior of certain von Neumann multiprocessors (*e.g.*, the Denelcor HEP [22, 30]) led to the belief that dataflow machines and von Neumann machines actually represent two points on a continuum of architectures.

Arvind has suggested that an architecture formed on the principles of *split transaction* I-Structure memory references in a von Neumann framework coupled with data driven rescheduling of suspended instructions in the local memory of each processor would be interesting. Such a machine has the potential of tolerating memory latency and of supporting fine-grained synchronization, and yet (in the strict sense) is neither a von Neumann machine nor a dataflow machine. This suggestion has led me to develop the hybrid architecture presented here. In order to better understand the motivations, the next sections re-examine the strengths and weaknesses of von Neumann and dataflow architectures.

Reprinted from *IEEE International Symposium on Computer Architecture*, 1988, pages 131-140.

0-8186-2642-9/92 $3.00 © 1988 IEEE

2.2. von Neumann Architectures

Advocates of non-von Neumann architectures (including the author) have argued that the notion of sequential instruction execution is the antithesis of parallel processing. This criticism is actually slightly off the mark. Rather, a von Neumann machine in a multiprocessor configuration does poorly because it fails to provide efficient synchronization support at a low level. Why is this so?

The participants in any one synchronization event require a common ground, a *meeting place*, for the synchronization to happen. This may take the form of a semaphore [9], a register [28, 22], a buffer tag [31], an interrupt level, or any of a number of similar devices. In all cases, one can simply think of the common ground as being the *name* of the resource used (*e.g.*, register number, tag value, etc.). The participants also require a mechanism to trigger synchronization action.

When viewed in this way, it should be clear that the number of simultaneously pending synchronization events is bounded by the size of this name space as well as by the cost of each synchronization operation. More often than not, this name space is tied to a physical resource (*e.g.*, registers) and is therefore quite small, thereby limiting support for low level dynamic synchronization. For most existing von Neumann machines, synchronization mechanisms are inherently larger grain (*e.g.*, interrupts) or involve busy waiting (*e.g.*, the HEP[1] [22, 30]). Therefore, the cost of each event is quite high. Such mechanisms are unsuitable for controlling latency cost. Moreover, since task suspension and resumption typically involve expensive context switching, exploitation of parallelism by decomposing a program into many small, communicating tasks may not actually realize a speed-up.

It is important to observe that these arguments favor the alteration of the basic von Neumann mechanism, and not its total abandonment. For situations where instruction sequencing and data dependence constraints can be worked out at compile time, there is still reason to believe that a von Neumann style sequential (deterministic time order) interpreter provides better control over the machine's behavior than does a dynamic scheduling mechanism and, arguably, better cost-performance. It is *only* in those situations where sequencing cannot be so optimized at compile time, *e.g.*, for long latency operations, that dynamic scheduling and low-level synchronization are called for. One must also keep in mind that, despite any desire to revolutionize computer architecture, von Neumann machines will continue to be the best understood base upon which to build for many years.

2.3. Dataflow Architectures

The MIT Tagged Token Dataflow Architecture, and other dataflow architectures like it, provide well-integrated synchronization at a very basic level. By using an encoded dataflow graph for program representation, machine instructions become self-sequencing. One strength of the TTDA is that each datum carries its own context identifying information. By this mechanism, program parallelism can be easily traded for latency because there is no additional cost above and beyond this basic mechanism for switching contexts on a per-instruction basis.

However, it is clear that not all of the distinguishing characteristics of the TTDA contribute towards efficient toleration of latency and synchronization costs. One very sound criticism is that intra-procedure communication is unnecessarily general. Intuitively, it should not be necessary to create and match tokens for scheduling *every* instruction within the body of a procedure - some scheduling can certainly be done by the compiler. In a dataflow machine, however, data driven scheduling is *de rigueur*. This implies, for instance, that the time to execute the instructions in a graph's critical path is the product of the critical path length and the pipeline depth. One is left to wonder if it might not be possible, even desirable, to optimize this by performing the *necessary* synchronization explicitly, and relying on more traditional (read: *well-understood*) mechanisms for instruction sequencing in the remainder of the cases. The uncertainties in this argument are the fraction of time wherein synchronization is necessary, and the complexity of the mechanisms required.

3. Synthesis

A simple view is that von Neumann and dataflow machines are not, in fact, orthogonal but rather sit at opposite ends of a spectrum of architectures. One might speculate that there are families of machines along this spectrum which trade instruction scheduling simplicity for better low level synchronization. One might further speculate that for some figure of architectural merit, taking into account hardware complexity, instruction scheduling flexibility, and synchronization support, that there exists some optimum point between the two extremes, *i.e.*, a hybrid architecture which synergistically combines features of von Neumann and Dataflow.

Starting with the observation that the costs associated with dataflow instruction sequencing in many instances are excessive, others have suggested that dataflow ideas should be used only at the inter-procedural level [23] thereby avoiding dataflow inefficiencies while seemingly retaining certain advantages. This view is almost correct, but ignores the importance of the fundamental issues discussed above. Restricting architectures to this "macro dataflow" concept would amount to giving up what is possibly a dataflow machine's biggest feature - the ability to context switch efficiently at a low level to cover memory latency.

Given this, one is led to ask the following question: *what mechanisms at the hardware level are essential for tolerating latency and synchronization costs?* Based on various studies of parallel machines [2, 7, 12, 22] the following conclusions are drawn:

- In general, on a machine capable of supporting multiple simultaneous threads of computation, executing programs expressed as a total ordering of instructions will incur more latency cost than will executing a logically equivalent partial ordering of the same instructions. In fact, for a class of programming languages which are *non-sequential* [33], expressing programs as a partial ordering is a necessary condition for avoiding deadlock. It is assumed, therefore, that the machine language must be able to express partial ordering.

- In any multiprocessor architecture, certain instructions will take an unbounded amount of time to complete (*e.g.*, those involving communication). Such operations can be either atomic, single phase operations or split, multiphase operations[2]. Multiphase processing will always minimize latency cost over single phase processing because the potential exists for covering processor idle time. Based on the frequency of the occurrence of such long latency operations [2] in all but the most trivial parallel computations, efficient multiphase operation requires specific hardware mechanisms [3, 12]. Multiphase instructions are commonly referred to as *split transactions*.

The remainder of this section describes a new, hybrid architecture along with its instruction set and programming model. The architecture can be viewed as either an evolution of dataflow architectures in the direction of more explicit (*i.e.*, compiler directed) control over instruction execution order, or as an evolution of von Neumann machines in the direction of better hardware support for synchronization and better tolerance of long latency operations. The study of this architecture will focus on the frequency of unavoidable run-time synchronization and, therefore, the applicability of compiler-directed control over instruction scheduling in a general-purpose multiprocessor.

3.1. Scheduling Quanta

The central idea of this new architecture involves some reconsideration of the basic unit of work in both dataflow and von Neumann architectures. The unit of parallel computation in a von Neumann machine is the *task*. Inter-task synchronization is typically expensive when it relies on software-implemented mechanisms. Such cost favors large tasks which synchronize infrequently. Within a task, synchronization of *producer* and *consumer* instructions is entirely implicit in the ordering of instructions. Between tasks, barrier synchronization is done explicitly with guards, semaphores, or some other similar mechanism. Context switching is usually done when necessary at the synchronization points, so an important performance metric is the *run length*, or number of instructions between synchronization operations. During such a run, instructions from the same context can enter the pipe at each pipe beat. This kind of locality can often be exploited at the hardware level; however, increasing the locality may imply a loss of parallelism.

---

[1]The HEP also exhibited several synchronization namespace problems: the register space was too small (2K), there was a limit of one outstanding memory request per process, and there was a very serious limit of 128 process status words per processor.

---

[2]A *multiphase* operation is one which can be divided into parts which separately *initiate* the operation and later *synchronize* prior to using the result.

This is in sharp contrast to the dataflow model where the basic unit of parallel computation is the instruction. Inter-task (*i.e.*, inter-instruction) synchronization is performed implicitly by the hardware; the single instruction "task" is not awakened until its operands are available. Context switching can and does occur at each pipe beat; any instruction n' which is enabled as a result of the completion of instruction n may not enter the pipeline for a number of cycles equal to the pipeline depth. The intervening cycles must be filled by instructions from another thread of execution, possibly but not necessarily from a related context. Not surprisingly, this model is highly parallel, but the parallelism comes at the expense of some lost locality.

3.1.1. Repartitioning Dataflow Graphs

Consider a graph for a simple code block (Figure 1). Note that there is some potential parallelism (lack of interdependence between instructions) in this graph. For example, instructions I1 and I5 do not depend on one another. They depend only on the availability of the values a, b, and c.

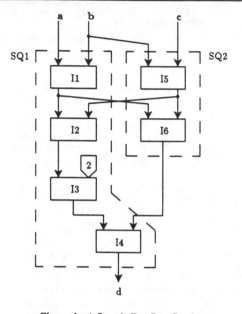

Figure 1: A Sample Dataflow Graph

More pertinent to this discussion are the instructions of the graph which *directly* depend on one another. Instructions I2 and I3, for example, have an interesting dependence. Having executed I2, it is known from the graph that instruction I3 can be executed because it only depends on I2 and a compile time constant. In some sense, then, the pair (I2 , I3) form a new instruction which has the same input and output characteristics as any other instruction, and which has similar synchronization requirements.

There has been some suggestion within the dataflow community that such aggregation be exploited, if only to improve performance. There is a danger in doing this by altering the machine instruction set, because any statistically beneficial aggregation will have been highly dependent on compilation and code generation techniques used while collecting said statistics. That is, the choice of aggregated instructions may vary as improvements are made to the compiler(s). This suggests that the issues of synchronization should be separated from the issues of opcode semantics.

A slightly more sophisticated view is to permit the compiler to aggregate an *arbitrary* collection of instructions according to any criterion of optimality into a unit of schedulability. Each such unit is called a *scheduling quantum*, or *SQ*. Their size, inter-SQ dependences, and content are determined at compile time. In the Figure, two SQ's are shown, but many other aggregations are possible.

3.1.2. Partitioning Strategies

Although the present discussion is oriented toward machine architectures, it is illuminating to look briefly at methods of partitioning programs expressed as graphs into SQ's, partly to lend credibility to the approach, and partly to better understand the relationship between the static and dynamic scheduling requirements of programs. Starting with a dataflow graph, partitioning may be done in a number of ways. Issues of concern include

- **Maximization of exploitable parallelism:** Poor partitioning can obscure inter-procedural and inter-iteration parallelism. The desire to aggregate instructions does not imply any interest in restricting or limiting parallelism - in fact, those cases where instructions may be grouped into SQ's are quite often places where there is little or no easily exploitable parallelism.

- **Maximization of run length:** Longer SQ's will ultimately lead to longer intervals between context switches (run length). Coupled with proper runtime support for suspension and resumption, this can lead to increased locality. Run lengths which are long compared to the pipeline depth have a positive effect on shortening critical path time. Short run lengths (frequent instruction aborts due to suspension of a frame reference) tend to bubble the pipeline.

- **Minimization of explicit synchronization:** Each arc which crosses SQ boundaries will require dynamic synchronization. Since synchronization operations are pure overhead[3], it is desirable to minimize them.

- **Deadlock avoidance:** Non-sequentiality implies that instruction execution order cannot be made independent of program inputs or, said another way, instruction execution order cannot be determined *a priori*. It is necessary to understand where this dynamic ordering behavior will manifest itself in the generated code. Such dynamic ordering must be viewed as a constraint on partitioning since two instructions whose execution order is dynamically determined cannot be statically scheduled in a single SQ.

- **Maximization of machine utilization:** Given a set of costs for instruction execution, context switching, synchronization, and operand access, partitions can be compared on the basis of how well they "keep the pipeline full." This metric is fairly machine specific and is in that sense less general than those previously described but no less important.

Extant partitioning algorithms [6, 13, 21] can be classified as *depth-first* or *breadth-first*. Depth-first algorithms [6] partition by choosing a path from an input to an output of a graph and making it into an SQ, removing the corresponding instructions from the graph in the process. The algorithm is repeated until no instructions remain unpartitioned. Such partitionings tend to be best at minimizing critical path time and rely heavily on pipeline bypassing since, by definition, instruction n depends directly on instruction $n-1$. Breadth-first algorithms [13, 21] tend to aggregate instructions which have similar input dependences but only weak mutual dependences. The *method of dependence sets* as presented in [21] is discussed in the next section.

3.1.3. The Method of Dependence Sets

In order to guarantee liveness of the partitioned graph, it is essential no cycle be introduced which cannot be resolved. Such cycles can be either static or dynamic.

> **Definition 1:** An *unresolvable static cycle* is a directed cycle of SQ's in a partitioned dataflow graph for which no schedule of SQ executions can terminate.

An example of how partitioning can give rise to a static cycle is shown in Figure 2. It can be shown [21] that a graph interpretation rule which includes *suspension* and *resumption*, *i.e.*, partial execution of SQ's, is a sufficient condition for preventing such static cycles from becoming unresolvable. Sarkar and Hennessy [29] avoid the unresolvability issue entirely by imposing a *convexity constraint* on the partitioning - static cycles can therefore never arise.

A much harder problem is that of preventing unresolvable dynamic cycles. Dynamic cycles arise due to the *implicit* arcs between STORE and FETCH instructions which refer to identical elements. Such arcs are implicit because they are generally input-dependent.

---

[3]Coming from a von Neumann uniprocessor mind set where explicit synchronization is virtually unheard of except in situations which require multitasking, it is natural to view synchronization in this way. Coming from the dataflow world where synchronization is unavoidable in every instruction execution, and where there is no opportunity to "optimize it out," it is also reasonable to view explicit synchronization instructions as overhead. In a later section, these perspectives are reconciled with the view that explicit synchronization instructions are both necessary and, in some sense, beneficial.

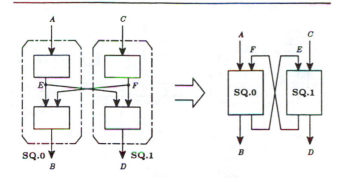

Figure 2: Partitioning which Leads to a Static Cycle

Definition 2: An *unresolvable dynamic cycle* is a directed cycle of SQ's in a partitioned dataflow graph, augmented with all possible input-specific dynamic arcs, for which no schedule of of SQ executions can terminate.

It is necessary to constrain partitioning such that unresolvable dynamic cycles provably cannot arise for any possible set of program inputs. An example will make this clearer. Consider the following Id program fragment:

```
{    a = vector (0,2);
     a[0] = 0;
     a[1] = a[i] + 1;
     a[2] = a[j] - 2;

     in a[1] - a[2]}
```

and its associated graph[4,5] in Figure 3. Such a graph *would* terminate under a dataflow instruction execution rule. However, without exercising some care, partitioning this graph into SQ's can lead to deadlock. Putting all of these instructions into a single partition won't work, nor will a partitioning such as that shown in Figure 4. Such partitionings result in code which can never terminate, despite the adherence to static dependences in deriving the individual SQ schedules.

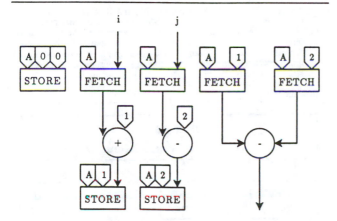

Figure 3: Program Graph Fragment

The problem, of course, is that the actual instruction execution order in the dataflow case depends on the indices used in the structure operations, where no such dependence is allowed in the partitioned case. Figure 5 shows two instruction execution orderings which must be possible in any correctly compiled version of this program. These orderings demonstrate the

---

[4]The descriptor for vector A is depicted as a constant to simplify the drawings. This is done without loss of generality.

[5]In the sequel, it is assumed that global storage is read by multiphase operations, and that the memory controller implements I-Structure-like synchronization [18]. In that sense, **FETCH** and **STORE** behave as **I-FETCH** and **I-STORE**.

---

dynamic dependences between **STORE**s and **FETCH**es. If these dependences were fixed, and if it were possible to determine them at compile time, SQ partitioning to avoid deadlock would be straightforward. Since this is not the case, the problem is one of developing a safe partitioning strategy which is insensitive to the arrangement of dynamic arcs. One approach is to make each partition exactly one instruction long, *i.e.*, the dataflow method. This, of course, is at odds with the desire to exploit static scheduling.

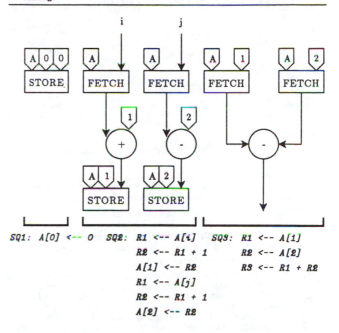

SQ1: A[0] <-- 0   SQ2: R1 <-- A[i]   SQ3: R1 <-- A[1]
                        R2 <-- R1 + 1   R2 <-- A[2]
                        A[1] <-- R2   R3 <-- R1 + R2
                        R1 <-- A[j]
                        R2 <-- R1 + 1
                        A[2] <-- R2

Figure 4: Partitioning which Leads to Deadlock

Another method is to give names to *sets of dependences*. The following definitions are in order:

Definition 3: A **FETCH**-*like output* of an instruction is one which is associated with a dynamic dependence. An instruction itself is **FETCH**-like if at least one of its outputs is **FETCH**-like, implying that the instruction initiates a split transaction (long latency) operation.

Definition 4: The *input dependence set* for an instruction in a well-connected graph [32] is the union of the output dependence

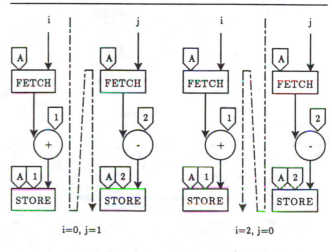

i=0, j=1   i=2, j=0

Figure 5: Input Dependent Execution Order

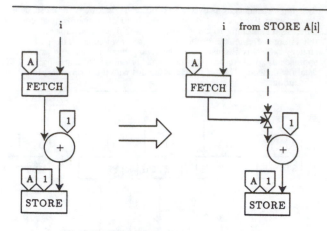

Figure 6: Gating Effect of FETCH-like Instructions

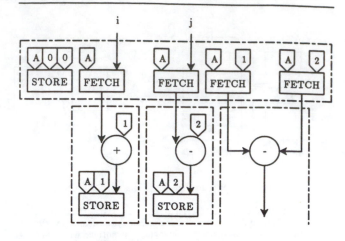

Figure 7: Properly Partitioned Graph

sets of all instructions from which it receives input. The input dependence set of the root instruction is defined as { α }.

Definition 5: The *output dependence set* for a given output of an instruction is either the instruction's input dependence set if the output is not FETCH-like, or the union of the instruction's input dependence set with a singleton set which uniquely names the given output if it is.

Note that it is a FETCH-like instruction's *output*, and not the instruction itself, with which is associated a change of dependence set. The intuition is that FETCH-like instructions themselves can never suspend while waiting for their output. Rather, the instructions which receive the FETCH-like instruction's output are the ones which will suspend. Figure 6 makes this clearer. A FETCH-like instruction can be viewed as gating the value of a STORE-like operation; the dynamic arc terminates on the virtual gate. It has the effect of suspending the "+" instruction until both the STORE and the FETCH have completed.

Applying the definitions to the graph in Figure 3 and using β, γ, and δ (in that order) for unique names results in the following assignments of input dependence sets to instructions (assume that vector *A* and the indices *i,j* are derived from the root with dependence set {α}):

Instruction	Input Dependence set
STORE(0)	{ α }
FETCH(i)	{ α }
FETCH(j)	{ α }
FETCH(1)	{ α }
FETCH(2)	{ α }
+1	{ α β }
STORE(1)	{ α β }
-2	{ α γ }
STORE(2)	{ α γ }
-	{ α δ }

The assignment of instructions to SQ's is now straightforward: an SQ is associated with each unique dependence set. Instructions are assigned to the SQ corresponding to their input dependence set in an order corresponding to their topological ordering in the unpartitioned graph. Since each distinct combination of dynamic arcs denotes a single SQ, dynamic scheduling can change to match the dynamic dependences. The correctly partitioned graph is shown in Figure 7. The determination of synchronization points is also straightforward: each dependence (arc) which crosses SQ boundaries must be explicitly synchronized by the consumer, or *sink*, SQ. Consumers in the same SQ as the instruction producing a value need not perform synchronization - it is implicit in the static scheduling of instructions within the SQ.

In [21], the deadlock-avoidance property of this algorithm is proved. Moreover, if procedure calls are compiled as FETCH-like operations, the method of dependence sets naturally allows inter-procedural parallelism. A simple extension to *k-bounded loops* [10] also allows inter-iteration parallelism. Run length, explicit synchronization, and machine utilization properties of this algorithm are studied in a later section.

3.2. Parallel Machine Language

Let's review the essential conclusions so far. Latency and synchronization have been shown to be fundamental issues in the development of scalable, general purpose multiprocessors, and the issues seem related in fairly incestuous ways. Basic changes to traditional architecture are necessary for dealing with them. One such change is that the execution time for any given instruction must be independent of latency (giving rise to split transactions). A second change is that synchronization mandates hardware support: each synchronization event requires a unique name. The name space is necessarily large, and name management must be efficient. To this end, a compiler should generate code which calls for synchronization when and only when it is necessary. A natural approach is to extend instruction sets to express the concepts of *both* implicit and explicit synchronization. Such an instruction set, which captures the notions of bounded instruction execution time, a large synchronization name space, and means of trading off between explicit and implicit synchronization is called a *parallel machine language* (PML).

It has been shown that adding partitioning to a dataflow graph is tractable. Doing so moves dataflow graphs into the realm of parallel machine languages. The question remains of how to organize a machine to efficiently implement a PML. One method would be to start with the explicitly-synchronized dataflow paradigm and to augment it with facilities for compiler-directed instruction scheduling (*e.g.*, *Monsoon* [24]). Another approach, described below, would be to start with the implicitly-synchronized von Neumann paradigm and to augment it with facilities for dynamic instruction scheduling.

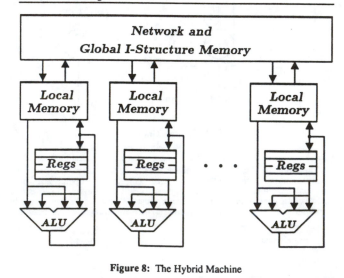

Figure 8: The Hybrid Machine

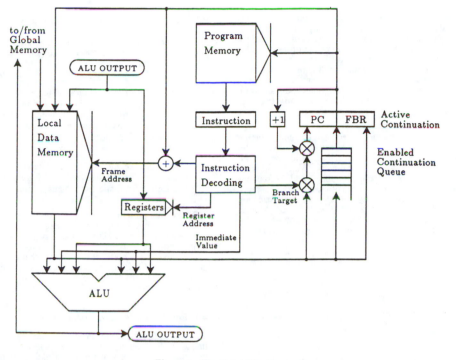

Figure 9: The Hybrid Processor

3.3. The Hybrid Multiprocessor

The architecture is modeled as an array of *n* identical processors, connected through a suitable switching network to a globally addressed I-Structure memory[6]. Each processor is made up of a pipelined datapath, a collection of high speed registers, and a local memory. Instructions are provided which allow movement of data between local and global memories, and between registers and local memories. All inter-processor communications can be thought of as going through *global memory*[7]. The *local memory* is both physically and logically local to a processor. For each invocation of each code block, a *frame* is allocated in the local memory of *exactly one processor* to hold local variables[8]. References to frame slots can be synchronizing or non-synchronizing.

3.3.1. Processor Hardware

The hardware which makes up a hybrid processor is strongly similar to that of a von Neumann machine, but with a few important differences (Figure 9). The datapath (ALU, etc.) and registers are conventional. The hardware datatypes are integers, floating point numbers, memory addresses, and the like. The most significant new datatype is the *continuation* which is a tuple of a program counter (PC) and a frame base register (FBR). Logical continuation states are depicted in Figure 10 and are encoded by the *location* of the continuation. *Enabled* continuations reside in the Enabled Continuation Queue. The *running* continuation resides in the Active Continuation Register. *Suspended* continuations reside in frame slots[8]. *Uninitiated* and *terminated* continuations are not explicitly represented.

The PC of the running continuation denotes the instruction to be dispatched next. Instructions may make operand references to the registers or

---

---

to slots in the local data memory. The local memory's behavior is similar to I-Structure storage in that each slot has several presence bits associated with it. A *non-synchronizing* reference to a slot behaves as a normal memory read operation. *Synchronizing* references invoke suspension of the running continuation if the slot being read is marked as EMPTY. Synchronizing reads of a WRITTEN slot behave just the same as nonsynchronizing reads.

The key hardware extension lies in the efficient state-transition management for continuations. Because continuations are word-sized objects, they can be easily fabricated when an SQ is invoked. When the running continuation encounters a blockage (via a synchronizing reference to an empty frame slot), the hardware simply stores the running continuation into the slot, marking it as now containing a continuation. An enabled continuation can then be selected from the queue. Upon satisfaction of the blockage (some other continuation writes into the slot), the suspended continuation is extracted and re-queued. A continuation may be suspended a number of times between initiation and termination. This behavior is reminiscent of the traditional *task* in a demand paged system which, upon encountering a missing memory page, becomes suspended until the page is made available.

Registers may be used freely *between* instructions which make suspensive references to the frame, but since no register saving takes place when a suspension occurs, register contents cannot be considered valid across potentially suspensive instructions. The cost of a register reference (maximum two per pipeline beat) is less than a local memory reference (maximum one per pipeline beat) which is, in turn, less than a global I-Structure reference (split transaction, possibly with an explicit address arithmetic instruction). Local memory is referenced relative to the FBR in the current continuation. I-Structure address space is global and is shared.

One can imagine a number of implementations of suspension which incur costs ranging from nothing to many tens or hundreds of instructions. In order to keep the implementation from distorting the kinds of code a com-

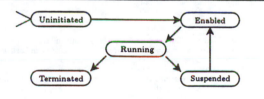

Figure 10: Continuation States

piler might generate, it is imperative that the cost of performing a context switch must be exceedingly low - on the order of a single pipe beat. To make this practical and general, context state must be easily saved in a single cycle. Moreover, it must be nearly trivial to create or destroy such context states as SQ's are initiated and terminated. Lastly, the number of such extant contexts cannot be bounded by some small hardware resource. For these reasons, context state *at suspension points* is represented solely by the continuation and its associated frame. By making the continuations no larger than a frame slot, saving and restoring becomes nearly trivial (a single memory reference) compared to schemes wherein registers are also saved[9].

The simple minded *dispatch instructions sequentially until blocked* paradigm works well, and has a very positive effect on locality. Other approaches are possible, however. The high-level goal is to dispatch instructions so as to keep the pipeline full of useful work. *Non-useful* work includes execution of NO-OPs (*i.e.*, pipeline bubbles) and instructions which suspend. Each processor maintains a queue of enabled continuations. One may view each continuation as logically contributing one instruction (the one pointed to by its PC) to the set of *enabled instructions*. At each time step, the processor's instruction dispatcher can freely choose one instruction from among this set. Optimal dispatching of instructions is impossible without foreknowledge of which instructions in the set *will* suspend. However, simple decoding of instructions allows the dispatcher to know if the instruction *cannot* suspend (*e.g.*, those which only reference registers or which make nonsuspensive references to frame memory) or if it *might possibly* suspend. A good strategy, then, is to divide the set of enabled instructions along these lines and to dispatch first from the subset of those which cannot suspend, delaying as long as possible execution of instructions which might suspend (thereby reducing the probability of suspension in many cases)[10].

3.3.2. Instruction Set

The instruction set is simple and regular in structure, with addressing modes and instruction functions being largely orthogonal. Instructions are readily implemented in a single cycle. The basic addressing modes are IMMEDIATE, REGISTER, FRAME NONSUSPENSIVE, and FRAME SUSPENSIVE. All unary and binary ops for arithmetic and logicals can take immediate, register, or frame slot operands and produce register or frame slot results. The MOVE opcode encodes all intra-process data movement. It is capable of moving an immediate, register, or frame slot to a register or frame slot. The MOVE-REMOTE opcode initiates movement of a value to a remote (non-local) frame slot. This instruction is used for procedure linkage, and is the only way one procedure can store into another's frame. The LOAD-FRAME-INDEX opcode and its variants initiate an indexed read from I-structure memory to the frame. STORE and its variants initiate a store to I-Structure memory. The TEST and RESET opcodes are provided for explicit synchronization and frame slot re-use, respectively. RESETs occur within the body of a multiple SQ loop to re-enable synchronization prior to iteration. The BRANCH and BRANCH-FALSE opcodes do the obvious things, causing the PC in the continuation to be replaced (conditionally in BRANCH-FALSE). The CONTINUE opcode causes a fork by creating and queueing a new continuation. The corresponding join operation is implemented implicitly through frame slots. A number of other instructions unique to TTDA-style program graphs have been implemented. The simplest are the CLOSURE ops which construct and manipulate closures as word-sized objects (rather than memory-bound structures). These are arguably easy to implement in single machine cycles. The remainder are instructions which form manager message packets to allocate and deallocate various resources.

In translating program graphs to machine language, arcs are mapped to frame slots. Slots may be re-used within a code block but it is the responsibility of the compiler to guarantee that all reading of a slot is complete before it is re-written. Synchronizing operand reads are used to implement inter-SQ communication including the synchronization associated with FETCH-like instructions. Note that it is the *reader* of the slot which chooses to synchronize or not; it is not a property of the slot itself. Each slot may have multiple readers, some synchronizing and some non-synchronizing.

---

[9]Intuition leads one to believe that such a scheme results in degraded performance in the form of additional memory references. As discussed in [21], this is an oversimplification because frame storage can be cached easily *without* a coherence problem. See Section 5. Experience generating code from dataflow graphs shows this strategy to work. More sophisticated code generation techniques can make even better use of such non-saved registers.

[10]This scheme is not ideal, however. Consider the case of having postponed execution of a long-latency but potentially suspensive FETCH. If executing the instruction does not, in fact, cause suspension, delaying it will give up cycles which could otherwise have been used to mask the latency.

4. Characterization of the Hybrid Architecture

Using the method of dependence sets, a new code generator for the Id compiler [32] has been constructed to generate PML code. A heavily instrumented simulation model of the hybrid machine has been built which allows study of the following, using compiled Id programs:

- the effects of architectural assumptions (*e.g.*, code partitioning) on program behavior. This *idealized* model imposes only very weak physical constraints, *i.e.*, the number of processors is assumed unbounded, all instructions are assumed to execute in unit time, and communication latency is assumed zero. Continuations execute when and only when the synchronization constraints are satisfied.

- the effects of physical constraints on otherwise idealized program behavior. To the idealized model are added *realistic* limits such as nonzero communication latency, finite processors, and realizable scheduling.

This section presents experimental results from the first set of simulation studies of the hybrid architecture along with a comparison to similar results from studies of the TTDA. One very interesting metric is the dynamic instruction count. Because synchronization is not entirely implicit in the hybrid model, it is reasonable to expect that compiling for and executing a program on the hybrid machine should result in more instructions executed than in the case of the same program compiled for and executed on the TTDA. By experimental results, it is shown that this is not necessarily so.

4.1. Power of a Hybrid Instruction

In the TTDA model, each invoked instruction constitutes its own continuation. Each instruction can *synchronize* or *join* two threads of computation and can *fork* two new threads in addition to performing some computation. In the hybrid model, each instruction is typically one of many in a single SQ. As in the TTDA, each instruction can join two threads of computation by making two suspensive references in the frame. However, each instruction can *continue* only a single thread of computation - forks are done explicitly by the CONTINUE instruction and therefore represent additional overhead. Assuming all other things equal, *e.g.*, the opcode set, hybrid instructions are strictly less powerful than TTDA instructions.

An interesting question, as alluded to earlier, is whether the full generality of TTDA instructions is used frequently or infrequently. By using the identical program graphs in generating code for both the TTDA and the hybrid machine, it has been possible to study this question in some detail.

Figure 11 shows some dynamic instruction counts for various Id benchmark programs. These numbers were derived from simulation programs written specifically for the TTDA and the hybrid architecture, and count only program, not system or manager, instructions[11,12]. The counts do not favor either architecture but rather show that, for a variety of program types, instruction counts are comparable to first order. If hybrid instructions are less powerful, how can this be?

One part of the answer lies in the reduced number of overhead operators in the hybrid code resulting from fewer independent threads. In the TTDA, termination detection is done via trees of IDENTITY instructions. The leaves of these trees are the instructions which otherwise produce no tokens, *e.g.*, STORE operations. In the hybrid model, it is only necessary to test for termination of the SQ in which such instructions reside. Hence, *n* STOREs in one SQ imply only *one* explicit synchronization operation instead of a binary tree of *n-1* IDENTITY instructions.

Another part of the answer is elimination of the need to perform explicit fan-out of FETCHed values; the associated frame slots can simply be re-read. In the TTDA, however, FETCH operations can have only a single destination instruction. Multiple destinations imply the need for an IDENTITY instruction as the destination for the FETCH.

Because, in general, it would take two hybrid instructions to mimic the function of a single TTDA instruction (join two threads, compute, continue two threads), one might expect the hybrid count to be roughly double the TTDA count, yet the counts are nearly the same. The effects described above, when combined, represent roughly 30% of this discrepancy. It is

---

[11]In neither case is the type of simulation model (idealized or not) relevant for instruction counts. Instruction counts do not vary across these models.

[12]Programs in the Procedure Calling Overhead section are essentially trivial routines enclosed in the standard procedure call framework. List programs (implemented with CONS, CAR, and CDR) are memory intensive. Vector programs (implemented with ARRAYs) include both a significant amount of memory traffic and ALU operations.

	Problem Size	Dynamic Instruction Counts	
		TTDA	*Hybrid*
Procedure calling overhead:			
CONS		14	14
CAR		9	4
CDR		9	4
Fibonacci	10th	3,708	3,265
Lists:			
Reverse	9	497	585
Compute Length	9	506	439
Multiplicative Reduction	9	1,014	909
Vectors and Matrices:			
Trivial Sum	500	5,023	3,513
Sum of Squares	500	19,072	23,058
Linear Recurrence	500	18,047	15,275
Pointwise Product	20	290	445
Inner Product	20	285	359
Matrix Multiplication	10x10	20,716	26,255

Figure 11: TTDA and Hybrid Instruction Count Comparison

likely that the remainder is attributable to the fact that it does *not* in general take two hybrid instructions to displace a single TTDA instruction. There are many instances of TTDA instructions in typical programs where the full generality and power of the instruction is not being used in the sense that the hybrid partitioning strategy chooses to eliminate it rather than mimic it. This conclusion is borne out by comparing the dynamic instruction mixes (instruction types) executed by the two architectures when running the same program. In the hybrid model, parallelism is retained in the machine code only when dictated by dynamic arc constraints. According to this view, the remainder of the parallelism in TTDA code is superfluous. In the next section, we examine the effect of this reduced parallelism in terms of the hybrid machine's ability to tolerate latency.

4.2. Parallelism and Latency

No amount of "optimization" by packing instructions into larger chunks is worth much if it negates the architecture's ability to synchronize efficiently or to tolerate latency. It is reasonably clear that the hybrid architecture provides the necessary synchronization support at a basic level for the purposes of program decomposition. But what about the hybrid machine's tolerance of long latency operations?

Consider as an example the recursive Fibonacci program of the previous section. Running this program under the idealized model yields a *parallelism profile* (Figure 12) showing the number of concurrently executable continuations as a function of time. This is more a characteristic of the program than of the machine - it shows the available parallelism subject to the chosen partitioning. In such an experiment, the cost of communicating across processor boundaries is the same as the cost of communicating within a processor: results of executing an instruction are available in the

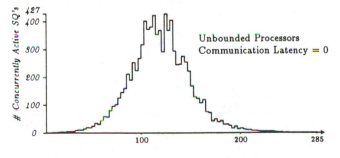

Figure 12: Idealized Parallelism Profile for FIBONACCI(14)

following cycle. The parallelism profile is a metric of the method of *logically decomposing* a program.

The effect of *physical partitioning*, or distributing a program can be estimated by assigning a cost to each inter-processor communication in terms of a delay between production and use of results (*i.e.*, a latency), by setting a limit on the number of processors (each processor can execute at most one instruction at any time *t*), and by allocating procedure invocations to individual processors by some rule. Note that this is more restrictive than a simple "finite processor" limit which simply forces *k* instructions on *p* processors to take ⌈k/p⌉ time. The top profile of Figure 13 shows the effect of these assumptions with the latency still zero, using a random policy for assigning invocations to processors. By increasing the latency and measuring the increase in execution time, it is possible to quantify the architecture's ability to use excess parallelism to cover the latency. In the lower half of Figure 13, the inter-processor latency has been increased from 0 to 10 pipe steps, yet the increase in critical path time is only 13.2%.

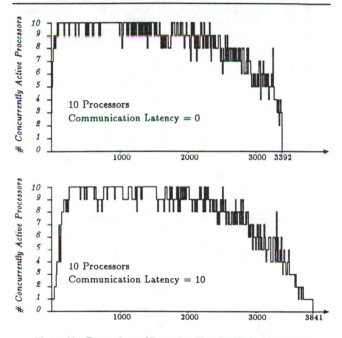

Figure 13: Comparison of Execution Time for Various Latencies

4.3. Dynamic Run Length

An important issue in partitioning as addressed earlier is the *dynamic run length*, or number of instructions successfully executed between suspensions. Figure 14 shows the instruction counts (from Figure 11 - this is the number of instructions which ran to completion), the number of aborted instructions (aborted instructions are not included in instruction count), the ratio of aborts to instructions expressed as a percentage, and the mean dynamic run length. With the exception of CAR, CDR, and CONS, aborted instructions are 8 to 16% of instructions successfully executed, and run lengths of 2.4 to 6.5 are typical.

5. Conclusion

A new architecture has been described which supports a parallel machine language, capturing the notions of split transaction operations, a large synchronization namespace, and means for trading between implicit and explicit synchronization. It has been demonstrated that the architecture is capable of effectively exploiting parallelism in partitioned dataflow graphs, of trading program parallelism for latency cost, and of enabling a compiler to control locality to first order.

From the preliminary results presented above, it appears that little of the full power of the TTDA's synchronization mechanism is actually used in typical programs. This leads to the observation that *explicit* synchronization instructions, used when necessary, may in some sense be cheaper than paying the full cost of synchronization at each instruction. This is, perhaps, the equivalent of the RISC argument applied to multiprocessing.

	Problem Size	Instr Count	Aborts	%	Run Length
Procedure calling overhead:					
CONS		14	4	28.57	1.3
CAR		4	1	25.00	1.0
CDR		4	1	25.00	1.0
Fibonacci	10th	3,265	265	8.12	3.4
Lists:					
Reverse	9	585	67	11.45	3.3
Compute Length	9	439	68	15.49	2.4
Multiplicative Reduction	9	909	121	13.31	2.7
Vectors and Matrices:					
Trivial Sum	500	3,513	2	0.06	585
Sum of Squares	500	23,058	3,004	13.03	3.8
Linear Recurrence	500	15,275	2	0.01	2,182
Pointwise Product	20	445	42	9.44	6.5
Inner Product	20	359	41	11.42	5.4
Matrix Multiplication	10x10	26,255	2,445	9.31	5.0

Figure 14: Hybrid Instruction Aborts and Run Length

As yet unanswered is the question of the effectiveness of the hybrid architecture, or architectures like it, for other parallel programming models (*e.g.*, Halstead's MultiLisp [16]). It is conjectured that simple extensions to the frame slot synchronization mechanism can effectively support demand-driven, or EVAL-when-touched scheduling. Of considerable practical interest is the possibility of targeting FORTRAN compilers to the hybrid paradigm.

Work from the present project reported elsewhere [21] includes integration of a local memory cache into the processor's design. Since local memory can only be read by the local processor, there is no issue of global coherence. Such a cache can lift the restriction of a single frame access per pipe beat. Many improvements to code generation have also been made including the *k-bounded* loop schema [10], while others have only been briefly considered, *e.g.*, peephole optimization and other criteria for SQ partitioning.

It is encouraging to see how the research efforts of various groups are converging on hybrid models such as the one presented here. Space constraints prohibit review of these projects; the interested reader is directed to the the work of Buehrer and Ekanadham [8], Halstead and Fujita [17], Papadopoulos [24] Sarkar and Hennessy [29], and Bic [6].

6. Acknowledgments

The author wishes to thank Andrew Chien, Ken Traub, Steve Heller, and the anonymous referees for their criticisms and suggestions for improvement of this manuscript. Special thanks go to Arvind for encouraging me to explore ideas of a hybrid architecture. The author also wishes to thank Lee Howe, Ev Shimp, Bobby Dunbar, Bill Hoke, Lucie Fjeldstad, Frank Moore, Dick Case, Hum Cordero, Bob Corrigan, Carl Conti, John Karkash and his other sponsors at IBM who made this work possible.

This report describes research done at the Laboratory for Computer Science of the Massachusetts Institute of Technology. Funding for the Laboratory is provided in part by the Advanced Research Projects Agency of the Department of Defense under Office of Naval Research contracts N00014-83-K-0125 and N00014-84-K-0099. The author is employed by the International Business Machines Corporation.

REFERENCES

1. Anderson, D. W., F. J. Sparacio, and R. M. Tomasulo. "The IBM System/360 Model 91: Machine Philosophy and Instruction-Handling". *IBM Journal 11* (January 1967), 8-24.

2. Arvind, S. A. Brobst, and G. K. Maa. Evaluation of the MIT Tagged-Token Dataflow Architecture. Computation Structures Group Memo 281, MIT, Laboratory for Computer Science, Cambridge, MA 02139, December, 1987.

3. Arvind and R. A. Iannucci. A Critique of Multiprocessing von Neumann Style. Proceedings of the 10th Annual International Symposium on Computer Architecture, June, 1983.

4. Arvind and R. A. Iannucci. Two Fundamental Issues in Multiprocessing. Proceedings of DFVLR - Conference 1987 on Parallel Processing in Science and Engineering, Bonn-Bad Godesberg, June, 1987.

5. Arvind, G. K. Maa, and D. E. Culler. Parallelism in Dataflow Programs. Computation Structures Group Memo 279, MIT, Laboratory for Computer Science, Cambridge, MA 02139, December, 1987.

6. Bic, L. A Process-Oriented Model for Efficient Execution of Dataflow Programs. Proc. of the 7th International Conference on Distributed Computing, Berlin, West Germany, September, 1987.

7. Bouknight, W. J., S. A. Denenberg, D. E. Mcintyre, J. M. Randall, A. H. Sameh, and D. L. Slotnick. "The ILLIAC IV System". *Proceedings of the IEEE 60*, 4 (April 1972).

8. Buehrer, R. and K. Ekanadham. "Incorporating Data Flow Ideas into von Neumann Processors for Parallel Execution". *IEEE Transactions on Computers C-36*, 12 (December 1987), 1515-1522.

9. Cox, G. W., W. M. Corwin, K. K. Lai, and F. J. Pollack. "Interprocess Communication and Processor Dispatching on the Intel 432". *ACM Transactions on Computer Systems 1*, 1 (February 1983), 45-66.

10. Culler, D. E. Resource Management for the Tagged-Token Dataflow Architecture - S.M. Thesis. Technical Report 332, MIT, Laboratory for Computer Science, Cambridge, MA 02139, January, 1985.

11. Culler, D. E. and Arvind. Resource Requirements of Dataflow Programs. Proceedings of the 15th Annual International Symposium on Computer Architecture, IEEE Computer Society, Honolulu, Hawaii, June, 1988.

12. Deminet, J. "Experience with Multiprocessor Algorithms". *IEEE Transactions on Computers C-31*, 4 (April 1982), 278-288.

13. Ekanadham, K. Multi-Tasking on a Dataflow-like Architecture. Tech. Rept. RC 12307, IBM T. J. Watson Research Laboratory, Yorktown Heights, NY, November, 1986.

14. Ekanadham, K., Arvind, and D. E. Culler. The Price of Parallelism. Computation Structures Group Memo 278, MIT, Laboratory for Computer Science, Cambridge, MA 02139, November, 1987.

15. Fisher, J. A. Very Long Instruction Word Architectures and the ELI-512. Proc. of the 10th, International Symposium on Computer Architecture, IEEE Computer Society, June, 1983.

16. Halstead, R. H., Jr. "MultiLisp: A Language for Concurrent Symbolic Computation". *ACM Transactions on Programming Languages and Systems 7*, 4 (October 1985), 501-538.

17. Halstead, R. H., Jr., and T. Fujita. MASA: A Multithreaded Processor Architecture for Parallel Symbolic Computing. Proceedings of the 15th Annual International Symposium on Computer Architecture, IEEE Computer Society, Honolulu, Hawaii, June, 1988.

18. Heller, S. K. An I-Structure Memory Controller (ISMC). MIT Department of Electrical Engineering and Computer Science, Cambridge, MA 02139, JUNE, 1983.

19. Heller, S. K. and Arvind. Design of a Memory Controller for the MIT Tagged-Token Dataflow Machine. Computation Structures Group Memo 230, MIT, Laboratory for Computer Science, Cambridge, MA 02139, October, 1983. Proceedings of IEEE ICCD '83 Port Chester, NY.

20. Hennessey, J. L. "VLSI Processor Architecture". *IEEE Transactions on Computers C-33*, 12 (December 1984), 1221-1246.

21. Iannucci, R. A. *A Dataflow / von Neuamnn Hybrid Architecture*. Ph.D. Th., MIT Department of Electrical Engineering and Computer Science, May 1988.

22. Jordan, H. F. Performance Measurement on HEP - A Pipelined MIMD Computer. Proceedings of the 10th Annual International Symposium On Computer Architecture, Stockholm, Sweden, June, 1983, pp. 207-212.

23. Kuck, D., E. Davidson, D. Lawrie, and A. Sameh. "Parallel Supercomputing Today and the Cedar Approach". *Science Magazine 231* (February 1986), 967-974.

24. Papadopoulos, G. M. *Implementation of a General Purpose Dataflow Multiprocessor*. Ph.D. Th., MIT Department of Electrical Engineering and Computer Science, May 1988.

25. Patterson, D. A. "Reduced Instruction Set Computers". *Communications of the ACM 28*, 1 (January 1985), 8-21.

26. Radin, G. The 801 Minicomputer. Proceedings of the Symposium on Architectural Support for Programming Languages and Operating Systems, ACM, March, 1982. Same as Computer Architecture News 10,2 and SIGPLAN Notices 17,4.

27. Rau, B., D. Glaeser, and E. Greenwalt. Architectural Support for the Efficient Generation of Code for Horizontal Architectures. Proceedings of the Symposium on Architectural Support for Programming Languages and Operating Systems, March, 1982. Same as Computer Architecture News 10,2 and SIGPLAN Notices 17,4.

28. Russell, R. M. "The CRAY-1 Computer System". *Communications of the ACM 21*, 1 (January 1978), 63-72.

29. Sarkar, V., and J. Hennessy. Partitioning Parallel Programs for Macro Dataflow. Proceedings of the ACM Conference on Lisp and Functional Programming, ACM, August, 1986, pp. 202-211.

30. Smith, B. J. A Pipelined, Shared Resource MIMD Computer. Proceedings of the 1978 International Conference on Parallel Processing, 1978, pp. 6-8.

31. Tomasulo, R. M. "An Efficient Algorithm for Exploiting Multiple Arithmetic Units". *IBM Journal 11* (January 1967), 25-33.

32. Traub, K. R. A Compiler for the MIT Tagged-Token Dataflow Architecture - S.M. Thesis. Technical Report 370, MIT, Laboratory for Computer Science, Cambridge, MA 02139, August, 1986.

33. Traub, K. R. *Sequential Implementation of Lenient Programming Languages*. Ph.D. Th., MIT Department of Electrical Engineering and Computer Science, May 1988.

An Architecture of a Dataflow Single Chip Processor

Shuichi SAKAI, Yoshinori YAMAGUCHI, Kei HIRAKI,

Yuetsu KODAMA and Toshitsugu YUBA

Electrotechnical Laboratory

1-1-4 Umezono, Tsukuba, Ibaraki 305, JAPAN

ABSTRACT

A highly parallel (more than a thousand) dataflow machine **EM-4** *is now under development. The* **EM-4** *design principle is to construct a high performance computer using a compact architecture by overcoming several defects of dataflow machines. Constructing the* **EM-4,** *it is essential to fabricate a processing element (PE) on a single chip for reducing operation speed, system size, design complexity and cost. In the* **EM-4,** *the PE , called* **EMC-R,** *has been specially designed using a 50,000-gate gate array chip. This paper focuses on an architecture of the* **EMC-R.** *The distinctive features of it are: a strongly connected arc dataflow model; a direct matching scheme; a RISC-based design; a deadlock-free on-chip packet switch; and an integration of a packet-based circular pipeline and a register-based advanced control pipeline. These features are intensively examined, and the instruction set architecture and the configuration architecture which exploit them are described.*

1. Introduction

A dataflow architecture is supposed to be the most suitable architecture for highly parallel computers. The reasons are: it can naturally extract the maximum available concurrency in a computation; it is suitable for VLSI implementation since a large number of identical processing elements (PEs) and repetitive data networks can be used in its construction; and dataflow languages provide an elegant solution for writing concurrent programs. There are, however, many technical problems involved in realizing a practical dataflow computer. Feasibility studies in the practical use of dataflow computers are essential.

Several architectures based on the dataflow concept have been proposed[1,2,3,4,5,8,9], some of which have been implemented in experimental machines. Among them the **SIGMA-1** [5], which is a large-scale dataflow supercomputer for numerical computations, shows the possibility to surpass the conventional von Neumann computers. It consists of 128 PEs and has a processing performance of more than 100 MFLOPS. A **SIGMA-1** PE is implemented by several gate array chips and a large memory. To construct a highly parallel machine, direct extension by merely adding more **SIGMA-1** PEs is not practical because the architectural design is complicated and too much hardware is required to implement all the PEs and the network. To realize a highly parallel machine, one or more PEs should be implemented on a single chip and the network structure must be simplified. The total architecture including computation model must be reconsidered.

The **EM-4**[10], whose target structure is more than 1000 PEs, is also being developed at the Electrotechnical Laboratory on the basis of the **SIGMA-1** project. The design principles of the **EM-4** are as follows.

1. Simplify the total architecture of a dataflow machine, e.g. interconnection network with O(N) hardware, a RISC-based single-chip PE design, and a direct matching scheme.
2. Improve machine performance by integrating a packet-based circular pipeline and a register-based advanced control pipeline.
3. Afford versatile resource management facilities, which current dataflow machines do not have, by introducing a strongly connected arc dataflow model.

The **EM-4**'s single-chip processor, called the **EMC-R**, realizes these principles. This paper focuses on the architecture of the **EMC-R**.

Section 2 describes design features of the **EMC-R**. Defects of current dataflow architectures are listed and distinctive features of the **EMC-R** (or the **EM-4**) for conquering them are shown. In section 3, the instruction set architecture of the **EMC-R** which reflects the above principles is described. Features of an instruction set, instruction formats and a packet format are shown there. Section 4 describes the configuration architecture of the **EMC-R** which realizes all of the above.

2. Design Features of the EMC-R

2.1. Defects of Current Dataflow Architectures

In order to design an efficient parallel machine, we closely examined the defects of current dataflow architectures. They are summarized as follows.

D1. A circular pipeline [4] does not work well as a "pipeline" for less parallel execution.

This is because current dataflow execution models have no advanced control mechanism. In the case of highly parallel execution ($\geq N \times S$, where N is the number of PEs and S is the number of pipeline stages in each PE), all the stages of a circular pipeline can be filled with tokens. In other cases, it may occur that only one token is going round the pipeline cycle, and that PE throughput is less than one per a pipeline circulation time.

D2. Simple packet-based architecture cannot exploit registers or a register file efficiently.

If you always realize a token as a packet, and if you make each of the packets enter a PE whenever possible, it is nonsense to reserve tokens in registers for the future node operation. This is one of the main reasons why a fine pitch pipeline is difficult to implement in a dataflow machine.

D3. Time complexity and hardware complexity for matching are heavy if you adopt the colored token style.

Color matching needs special hardware like associative memory or hashing hardware. They both require complex control logics and matching takes considerable time.

D4. Packet flow traffic is too heavy.

With a simple packet architecture, packet flow traffic is too heavy and a high-bandwidth low-delay interconnection network must be implemented. However, network performance is limited by current device technology.

D5. Current dataflow concepts cannot provide flexible and efficient resource management mechanisms.

If you realize mutual exclusion for resource management in a dataflow machine, you should provide some serialization mechanism (e.g. waiting queue). Its implementation is difficult, however, because the access to a concerned section can be violated by anyone else.

D6. It takes much time to eliminate garbage tokens.

If a program uses switch operations for conditional computations, there may occur a lot of garbage tokens. At the end of the execution, they must be collected to allow the working space to be reused. Time overhead for such operations is usually considerably large.

To overcome these defects, several novel facilities and mechanisms are introduced in the EMC-R, which are described in the following subsections.

2.2. Strongly Connected Arc Model

Although the basic EM-4 architecture is based on the dataflow model, a new model called a *strongly connected arc model* [7] has been introduced to compensate for the pure dataflow architecture. The strongly connected arc model can solve all the problems described in the previous subsection.

In this model, dataflow graph arcs are divided into two categories: the normal arcs and the strongly connected arcs. A dataflow subgraph whose nodes are connected by strongly connected arcs is called a strongly connected block. The control strategy of the modified dataflow model in which this model is introduced is that the operation nodes are executed exclusively in a strongly connected block. Figure 1 shows an example of strongly connected blocks. In this figure, there are two strongly connected blocks, A and B. When node 5 or node 6 is fired, block A or block B is executed exclusively. This has the effect of giving the nodes in a strongly connected block the highest priorities if nodes are executed depending on priorities. A strongly connected block acts as a macro node which includes several instructions and is executed as if it were a single basic node. In the EM-4, each strongly connected bock is executed by a single PE.

There are several advantages in the strongly connected arc model, which are shown below.

A1. This model makes it easy to introduce an advanced control pipeline to dataflow architecture, because the exclusion of the outer block instructions causes more deterministic execution of codes. This solves the problem of **D1**.

A2. Instruction execution cycles can be reduced by introducing a strongly connected register file which is used for storing tokens in a strongly connected block. This is possible as the registered data in the concerned block are not violated by any other data. This overcomes the defect **D2**.

A3. In an intra-block execution, matching can be realized much more easily and efficiently because it is not necessary to match function identifiers (i.e. colors) if the block is included in the function. This solves the inefficiency problem of **D3**.

These A1, A2 and A3 enable the EMC-R to have a fine pitch execution pipeline.

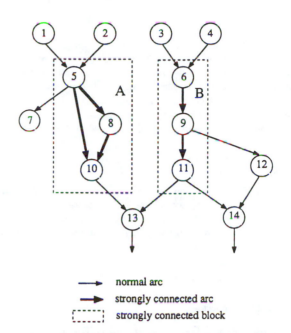

Legend:
→ normal arc
➤ strongly connected arc
⌐--- strongly connected block

Figure 1 An Example of a Strongly Connected Block.

A4. There are no packet transfers in a strongly connected block. This reduces the defect **D4**.

A5. It can provide flexible resource management facilities by constructing an indivisible instruction sequence (e.g. test and set). This overcomes the defect **D5**.

A6. It can simplify the problem of remaining garbage tokens. This is because only the flag resets of a strongly connected register file are needed for eliminating the garbage tokens. The operation can be performed simultaneously with the result data transfer, i.e. with no overhead. This reduces the defect **D6**.

2.3. Direct Matching Scheme

To remove the defect **D3**, a fast and simple data matching scheme is needed. A strongly connected model solves this problem within a block but matching overhead on a normal dataflow node is not solved. We have designed a simple new data matching scheme, called a *direct matching scheme*. This scheme is implemented using ordinary memories. Since the logic for realizing the scheme is fairly simple, it can be easily implemented by wired logic on the EMC-R.

When a function is invoked, an instance of storage is allocated to a group of PEs. This instance is called an *operand segment*. It is used for waiting and matching of operands. An operand segment has memory words whose number is equal to or larger than that of two operand instructions in the concerned function. The compiled codes for the function are stored in another area, which is called a *template segment*. The address of the instruction in the template segment has a one-to-one simple correspondence with that of the matching. Binding of an operand segment and a template segment is also performed at the function invocation time.

The matching is executed by checking the stored data in an operand segment and by storing new data if its partner is absent. The matching location for each dataflow node is uniquely given as an absolute memory address in an operand segment. Thus matching can be carried out without using the associative memory or a hashing mechanism.

2.4. Processor Connected Omega Network

The EM-4 uses a processor connected omega network as its interconnection network. Figure 2 illustrates an example of its topology. The advantages of this network are: the average distance from any PE to any other PE is order log(N), while N is the total number of PEs; the number of connection links from a PE is a small constant even if there are many PEs; and total number of switching elements is O(N) which is smaller than that of a multi-stage network (O(Nlog(N))).

The precise routing algorithm of the network will be reported in another paper.

The EMC-R contains an element of the processor connected omega network. One reason for this is to reduce the packet transfer time between a switch and a PE. The other reasons are the low hardware cost and the design simplicity. This element and processing function can work independently and concurrently.

3. Instruction Set Architecture

3.1. RISC Architecture

We adopt a RISC architecture for the EMC-R for simplicity and execution efficiency. Current dataflow architectures are not suited to RISC because defects D2, D3, and D4 in 2.1 obstruct its implementation. The EMC-R is suited to RISC for its features in 2.2 and 2.3. It can exploit a fine pitch pipeline, each stage of which is simple. It has a register file whose member is the strongly connected register described in 2.2.

The EMC-R is a dataflow RISC chip due to the following features: it has only 26 instructions; there are only four kinds of instruction formats; it has only two memory addressing modes; it has a register file; it uses no microprograms; its packet size is fixed; there are only a few packet types; and it has simple synchronization mechanisms (direct matching and a register-based sequencing).

Among them, the latter three should be regarded as the features of a *RISC PE for a parallel computer*.

In the following subsections, the features of EMC-R instruction set architecture are described.

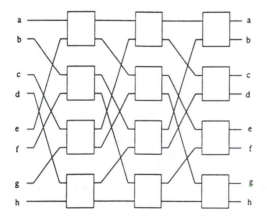

Figure 2 Processor Connected Omega Network.

3.2. Instruction Set

Table 1 shows an instruction set of the EMC-R. It has twenty-six kinds of instructions, each of which is executed in a single clock cycle (except continuous-memory-word-access instructions).

Details of an operation are afforded by the AUX field. For instance, the SHF instruction left or right shifts according to the contents of the AUX field.

In the EMC-R, a complex instruction can be performed by a strongly connected bock which contains simpler instructions. This is called a *macro instruction*. For instance, an integer division operation, a function call operation and complex structure operations are provided as macro instructions.

The following instructions are the characteristic instructions of the EMC-R.

(1) Branch Instructions

In the EMC-R, an action of a data switch operation in a strongly connected block is to fire one of the adequate nodes of its destination, without flowing any data. For this reason, the word BRANCH is used instead of SWITCH in the EMC-R for representing a data switch. There are six BRANCH instructions as shown in the Table 1. In order to simplify sequencing, they are implemented in a delayed branch style.

The EMC-R can provide a normal dataflow switch by strongly connecting the BRANCH instruction and the MKPKT instructions described below. In a good program, however, almost all of the switches are realized in a strongly connected block, because a packet flow overhead and a garbage token collection overhead are removed with this method (see 2.2).

(2) MKPKT

In the EMC-R, all of the instructions, except those of memory access and branch instructions, can make a packet for sending their results. In addition, it has a MKPKT instruction dedicated to packet

Table 1 Instruction Set

CATEGORY	INSTRUCTION	ACTION
Arithmetic and Logic	ADD	integer add
	SUB	integer subtract
	MUL	integer multiply
	DIV0	preparation of division
	DIV1	element of division
	DIV2	correction of division 0
	DIVR	remainder of division 0
	DIVQ	quotient of division 0
	SHF	shift
	AND	bitwise AND
	OR	bitwise OR
	EOR	bitwise exclusive OR
	NOT	bitwise NOT
	ALUTST	ALU test
Branch	BEQ	branch by equality
	BGT	branch by greaterness
	BGE	branch by greaterness or equality
	BTYPE	branch by data type
	BTYPE2	branch by 2 data types
	BOVF	branch by overflow
Memory or Register Read or Write	L	load from memory
	S	store to memory
	LS	load and store from/to memory
	LDR	load from register
Others	GET	send packet for remote operation
	MKPKT	make packet by two operands

generation. The **MKPKT** sends a packet whose address part is its first operand and whose data part is its second operand. Continuous **MKPKT**s perform the efficient distribution of the same data. Moreover, **MKPKT** supplies two special operations: an inter-function data transfer and a global data transfer such as a structure data transfer.

(3) GET

GET is an instruction for remote operations. It sends a return address to the address represented as its operand. For instance, CAR, CDR and sending a return address of a function are performed by the GET.

3.3. Instruction Format

The EMC-R has four types of instruction formats. Two of them are shown in Figure 3 (the other two are the immediate attached ones). Both of them are stored in a single memory word where each memory word is 38 bits long.

The OP field holds an operation code. AUX is a secondary field of the OP. If the concerned strongly connected block ends with the next instruction execution, then the M field (mode field) contains zero. R0 and R1 are the strongly connected registers used for the *next* instruction, if this instruction is strongly connected to other instructions. In this way, register-based advanced control is implemented in the EMC-R.

OUT is a tag field indicating whether the instruction generates a packet or not. If OUT is zero (Figure 3 (a)), then no packets are generated and the result is stored in R2. In this case, BC is a branch condition field which describes a branching style and DPL contains the displacement of a branching address. The latter two fields are used only in branch instructions.

If the OUT field contains one (Figure 3 (b)), then a packet is generated. The address part of the output packet is made up of the WCF, M2, CA, and DPL fields, and the operand segment identifier of the concerned function. The data part of the packet is the operation result.

A typical instruction execution is illustrated in more detail in 4.1 and 4.2.

3.4. Packet Format

A typical packet format is illustrated in Figure 4. Each packet consists of an address part and a data part, both of which have 39 bits.

(1) Address Part

HST field indicates whether this packet is bound for a normal destination or a host. PT is a packet type field. WCF is a waiting condition flag field, which indicates a type of matching. M is also a flag which indicates a type of dataflow arc. If it is zero, then the packet will fire a normal node; otherwise it will fire a strongly connected block. (GA, CA, MA) are the destination address fields. GA is a destination PE group address, CA is its column (i.e. member) address, and MA is a memory address. If this is a normal data packet, then MA is the matching address.

(2) Data Part

C is a cancel bit field indicating that the packet is a nonsense packet. DT and D are the data type and the data, respectively, which this packet carries.

3.5. Special Packets

A normal data packet has a NORM packet type, but packets for function control, structure access, remote memory access, etc. have special types. These special packets have no operand segment number, i.e. they are colorless. A special packet is generated by a MKPKT instruction or by a GET instruction. It is executed by a special strongly connected block named SP Monitor. A system manager can set the SP Monitor in any way desired during the system initialization, so the effect of a special packet can be properly determined by the manager. Thus the special packet execution in the EMC-R is completely flexible.

3.6. Program Examples

Figure 5 illustrates two FIBONACCI programs. Figure 5 (a) is a pure dataflow program and Figure 5 (b) is a program with strongly connected blocks. In the latter one, type checking and data switching

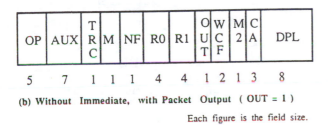

OP	AUX	T R C	M	NF	R0	R1	O U T	R2	BC	DPL
5	7	1	1	1	4	4	1	4	2	8

(a) Without Immediate, without Packet Output (OUT = 0)

OP	AUX	T R C	M	NF	R0	R1	O U T	W C F	M 2	C A	DPL
5	7	1	1	1	4	4	1	2	1	3	8

(b) Without Immediate, with Packet Output (OUT = 1)

Each figure is the field size.

Figure 3 Two Typical Types of Instruction Format.

H S T	PT	W C F	M	GA	CA	MA
1	5	2	1	7	3	20

(a) Address Part

C	*	DT	D
1	3	3	32

(b) Data Part

Each figure is the field size.

Figure 4 Typical Packet Format.

```
FIB:      (COPY   <EQ1 imml> <SW1 r>)          FIB:      [BEQ '1 (LEAF)  (R0:NL)]
                                                         [SUB '1 R1 (R0:NL) (NL:NL $)]
EQ1:      (EQ '1 <SW1 l>)                                [BEQ '2 (LEAF)  (R0:NL)]
                                                         [SUB '2 R2 (SEG:R1) (NL:NL $)]
SW1:      (SWITCH (T <CNST imml>)                        [MKPKT <CALL0 s> (SEG:R2 $)]
                  (F <EQ2 imml> <SW2 r>))                [MKPKT <CALL1 s> (NL:NL)]
                                               LEAF:     [MKPKT '1 <RETV r> (NL:NL)]
EQ2:      (EQ '2 <SW2 l>)

SW2:      (SWITCH (T <CNST imml>)
                  (F <SUB1 imml> <SUB2 imml>))

CNST:     (COPY '1 <RETV r>)

SUB1:     (SUB '1 <CALL0 s>)

SUB2:     (SUB '2 <CALL1 s>)
```

```
CALL0:    {*GCALL 'FIB <ADD l>}          CALL0:    {*GCALL 'FIB <ADD l>}

CALL1:    {*GCALL 'FIB <ADD r>}          CALL1:    {*GCALL 'FIB <ADD r>}

ADD:      (ADD <RETV r>)                 ADD:      (ADD <RETV r>)

RETV:     {*PASSVAL <KILL s>}            RETV:     {*PASSVAL <KILL s>}

KILL:     {*KILL}                        KILL:     {*KILL}
```

(a) A Normal Dataflow Program   **(b) A Strongly Connected Dataflow Program**

Figure 5 FIBONACCI Program.

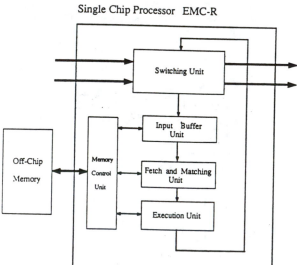

Figure 6 Block Diagram of the EMC-R.

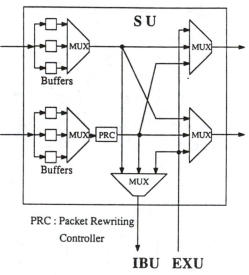

PRC : Packet Rewriting Controller

Figure 7 Switching Unit Organization.

are strongly connected to a single block illustrated as a rectangle in Figure 5 (b). It takes twenty-three clocks to execute the rectangular part if you select the former program (in the case of occurring recursive calls). If you select the latter program, it only takes nine clocks. This means that the strongly connected method can execute this subprogram about two and half times as fast as the pure dataflow method.

Remark that, in the above comparison, a **SWITCH** instruction and a **COPY** instruction were supposed to exist in the **EMC-R**. And remark that all the normal nodes of the EMC-R are executed in the same clock cycles with the pure dataflow machine **SIGMA-1**.

4. Configuration Architecture

4.1. EMC-R Architecture

Figure 6 shows a block diagram of the **EMC-R** which realizes all of the features described in the previous sections. The **EMC-R** consists of a Switching Unit (SU), an Input Buffer Unit (IBU), a Fetch and Matching Unit (FMU), an Execution Unit (EXU), a Memory Control Unit (MCU), and Maintenance Circuits.

(1) Switching Unit

The Switching Unit (SU) is a three-by-three packet switch which is an element of a processor connected omega network. It switches data independently of and concurrently with the other units. Each input port of the network has structured buffers. Organization of the SU is illustrated in Figure 7.

When a processor connected omega network is used in a buffered manner, store-and-forward deadlock prevention facilities must be supplied. In the EMC-R, a three bank buffer is provided in each input port. Firstly, a packet is buffered in the least level bank. When the packet arrives at the zeroth stage of the network, it is pushed into the one-upper-level bank. Because of the topological property of the processor connected omega network, any packet never covers three rounds of this network, so the logical structure of a packet transfer cannot make loops. This three bank strategy thus removes all store-and-forward deadlocks from the network.

Another feature of the SU is the function level dynamic load balancing facility. In the EM-4, special packets which monitor the load of PEs travel through the network. The SU rewrites these packets within the time period required by a normal packet transfer, i.e. with no overhead, and performs the load balancing. This rewriting is made by the **PRC** in Figure 7.

(2) Input Buffer Unit

The Input Buffer Unit (IBU) is a buffer for packets waiting for execution. A 32-word FIFO type buffer is implemented using a dual port RAM on chip. If this buffer is full, a part of the off-chip memory is used as a secondary buffer.

(3) Fetch and Matching Unit

The Fetch and Matching Unit (FMU) is used for matching tokens and fetching instructions. It performs a direct matching for a packet and a sequencing for a strongly connected block. It controls the pipelines of the processor, especially integrating two types of pipelines (see 4.2). The FMU contains an instruction address register, a packet data register, a register for matching data, several multiplexers, and control circuits.

(4) Execution Unit

The Execution Unit (EXU) is an instruction executor. Figure 8 illustrates its organization. The EXU contains an instruction register, two operand registers, a register file, an ALU, a barrel shifter, a multiplier, a versatile comparator, packet generation circuits, and control

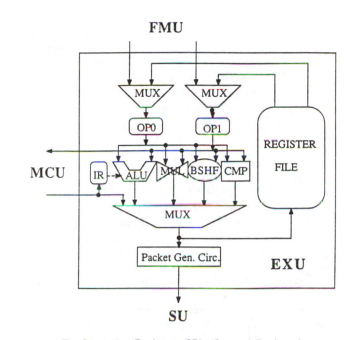

IR : Instruction Register   OPi : Operand Register i

Figure 8 Execution Unit Organization.

circuits.

In an execution cycle, the contents of operand registers are sent to the ALU, etc. Then the operation is carried out according to the **OP** and **AUX** fields of the instruction register. The result is sent in a packet or stored in a register file. All of these actions are made in a single clock, and, in the same clock, fetch and decode of the next instruction and data load from the FMU or a register file are performed (see 4.2).

(5) Memory Control Unit and Off-Chip Memory

The Memory Control Unit (MCU) arbitrates memory access requests from the IBU, the FMU, and the EXU, and sends data between the off-chip memory and the EMC-R. The MCU consists of a data multiplexer, an address multiplexer, and an arbitration controller.

The off-chip memory size can be up to 5 megabytes. It is used for a secondary packet buffer, a matching store, an instruction store, an area for the SP monitor (see 3.5), a structure store, and a working area.

(6) Maintenance Circuits

The Maintenance Circuits make initialization of the chip and memory words, handle many kinds of errors and provide the dynamic monitor which reports a system performance and the system status such as processor load, an active function number and structure area used. We will report the concept and the construction method of the Maintenance Circuits in another paper.

4.2. Pipeline Organization

Figure 9 illustrates the pipeline organization of the EMC-R. Basically, the pipeline has four stages, some of which have two substages. Each stage has a rectangle which represents a single clock action, or a bypass line which means no clock action. A small rectangle represents a half clock action.

Each packet from a network is buffered in the IBU if necessary (the far left side of the figure). Then the concerned template segment number (see 2.3) is fetched from the off-chip memory in the first stage (TNF). The number is stored at the top of the operand segment at the function invocation time. The first stage is bypassed when the packet is not a normal data packet.

The second stage is the matching stage. In the case of matching with the immediate, an immediate fetch (IMF) occurs. In the case of matching with data in the matching store, data at the concerned address is read in the former half clock (RD). If a partner exists, the flag at the address is eliminated in the latter half clock (EL); else a new packet data is written in the latter half clock (WR). This read-modify-write action is completed in a single clock cycle. The second stage is omitted if a new token fires a single operand instruction.

The third stage is an instruction fetch (IF) and decode (DC) stage. Each operation is performed in a half clock.

The fourth stage is an execution stage. Transfer of the result packet can be overlapped with the execution. If the next instruction is strongly connected with the current instruction, instruction fetch and data load of the next instruction are overlapped with the execution. The third stage and the fourth stage are repeated in the overlapped manner until there are no executable instructions in the concerned strongly connected block. If the instruction is a normal mode instruction or the last instruction of the strongly connected block, its execution can be overlapped with the instruction fetch and decode of a next packet processing. Thus, an integration of two types of pipelines, a packet-based circular pipeline (illustrated as thin lines in Figure 9) and a register-based advanced control pipeline (illustrated as thick lines in Figure 9), is realized.

During each stage, the TNF, the IMF, the RD, the WR, the EL and the IF are performed by the FMU with the assistance of the MCU. The DC and the EX are performed by the EXU.

The register-based advanced control pipeline is a fast and simple pipeline exploited by strongly connected blocks. Its throughput is at most six times as high as that of the packet-based circular pipeline.

Each PE has a peak processing performance of more than 12 MIPS.

4.3. Implementation

The EMC-R is a real processor chip, so its implementation is limited by current chip fabrication technology. Our chip contains 50,000 CMOS gates and 256 signal lines.

Table 2 shows the gate usage and pin usage of each EMC-R unit. The Switching Unit is complex as it has three bank buffers and their multiplexer at each port. The Execution Unit is also complex because it has many large modules such as a register file, a multiplier, a barrel shifter, and a packet generator. The Fetch and Matching Unit requires a little hardware, because the direct matching reduces the hardware cost of it.

As for pins, almost all of them are used for data buses of the network and the off-chip memory.

The EMC-R will be fabricated by June 1989. Then the EM-4 prototype which has 80 PEs will be constructed. It will consist of 16 processor boards, each of which will have five PEs and a mother board which the network will be implemented on. The EM-4 prototype hardware will be operational in 1990. Peak performance of this prototype is expected to be more than 1 GIPS. Construction of an efficient real machine of 1,000 PEs is the next program, which is the goal of the EM-4 project.

Table 2 Hardware Complexity

UNIT	Gates	Pins
Switching Unit	10,112	176
Input Buffer Unit	9,238	-
Fetch and Matching Unit	3,504	-
Execution Unit	19,692	-
Memory Control Unit	1,518	67
Maintenance Circuits	1,589	12
Total	45,653	255

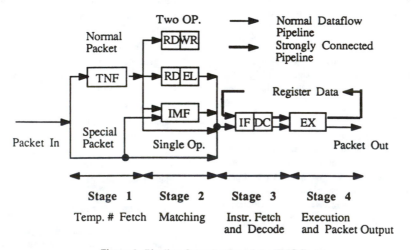

Figure 9 Pipeline Organization of the EMC-R.

5. Conclusion

This paper describes the architecture of the EMC-R, a single-chip dataflow processor which is a PE of the EM-4. The distinctive features of the EMC-R are:

(1) a strongly connected arc dataflow model;
(2) a direct matching scheme;
(3) a RISC-based design;
(4) a deadlock-free on-chip packet switch; and
(5) an integration of a packet-based circular pipeline and a register-based advanced control pipeline.

These features were examined, and the instruction set architecture and configuration architecture which exploit them were described.

The schedule of the hardware implementation is written in 4.3. As for softwares, a high level language and an optimizing compiler are currently under development. The latter has a node labeling scheduler for the intra-function load balancing [6] and a block constructor for automatically making strongly connected blocks. The optimization schemes and algorithms will be reported in another paper.

Future problems are as follows.
(1) Close consideration and expansion of a strongly connected arc dataflow model.
(2) Consideration of a chip design using much highly-integrated VLSI.

Acknowledgement

We wish to thank Dr. Hiroshi Kashiwagi, Deputy Director-General of the Electrotechnical Laboratory, Dr. Akio Tojo, Director of the Computer Science Division and Mr. Toshio Shimada, Chief of the Computer Architecture Section for supporting this research, and the staff of the Computer Architecture Section for the fruitful discussions.

References

[1] Amamiya,M., Takesue,M., Hasegawa,R. and Mikami,H.: Implementation and Evaluation of a List-Processing-Oriented Data Flow Machine, Proc. the 13th Annu. Symp. on Computer Architecture, pp.10-19 (June 1986).

[2] Arvind, Dertouzos,M.L. and Iannucci,R.A.: A Multiprocessor Emulation Facility, MIT-LCS Technical Report 302 (Sep. 1983).

[3] Dennis,J.B., Lim,W.Y.P. and Ackerman,W.B.: The MIT Dataflow Engineering Model, Proc. IFIP Congress 83, 553-560 (1983).

[4] Gurd,J., Kirkham,C.C. and Watson,I.: The Manchester Prototype Dataflow Computer, Commun. ACM, 21, 1, pp.34-52 (1985).

[5] Hiraki,K., Sekiguti,S. and Shimada,T.: System Architecture of a Dataflow Supercomputer, TENCON87, Seoul (1987).

[6] Otsuka,Y., Sakai,S. and Yuba,T.: Static Load Allocation in Dataflow Machines, Proc. of Technical Group on Computer Architecture, IECE Japan, CAS86-136, in Japanese (1986).

[7] Sakai,S., Yamaguchi,Y., Hiraki,K. and Yuba,T.: Introduction of a Strongly-Connected-Arc Model in a Data Driven Single Chip Processor EMC-R, Proc. Dataflow Workshop 1987, IECE Japan, pp.231-238, in Japanese (1987).

[8] Shimada,T., Hiraki,K., Nishida,K. and Sekiguchi,S.: Evaluation of a Prototype Data Flow Processor of the SIGMA-1 for Scientific Computations, Inf. Process. Lett.,16, 3, pp.139-143 (1983).

[9] Yamaguchi,Y., Toda,K. and Yuba,T.: A Performance Evaluation of a Lisp-Based Data-Driven Machine(EM-3), Proc. 10th Annual Symposium on Computer Architecture, pp.163-169 (1983).

[10] Yamaguchi,Y., Sakai,S., An Architectural Design of a Highly Parallel Dataflow Machine, to appear in IFIP'89 (1989).

Chapter 3: Coarse-Grained and Massively Parallel Architectures

Coarse-grained parallel architectures exploit parallelism by connecting together multiple copies of relatively independent processors. The architectures presented in this chapter differ primarily in how they communicate and in the structure of the interconnection network. Independent operations to be executed concurrently in these systems can be entire loop iterations or subroutines, instead of individual instructions. Similarly, massively parallel SIMD architectures connect together multiple copies of identical processors, but the processors are not independent. Instead, parallelism is exploited by having each processor simultaneously perform the same operation on a different data element.

Shared-memory multiprocessors

In a "typical" shared-memory multiprocessor, p identical processors are connected to an equal number of memory modules via some interconnection network[1-10] through which each processor can access any memory location in the shared-memory space. Critical problems in these systems are how to partition a program into independent tasks and how to schedule the execution of the tasks onto the processors. Partitioning Fortran Do loops into independent iterations produces a useful granularity of parallelism for shared-memory multiprocessors. The loop-scheduling strategy then determines which iterations will execute on which processors.

Static scheduling, such as Doacross scheduling,[11] assigns loop iterations to execute on specific processors at compile-time or load-time. With dynamic scheduling,[12,13*,14] also called "self-scheduling," idle processors assign iterations to themselves at run-time by accessing and incrementing a shared iteration-counter variable. Dynamic scheduling introduces some run-time overhead, but it can reduce processor load imbalances caused by the random execution time of different iterations. Iterations can have different execution times due to different outcomes of conditional branches within the iteration, unpredictable network delays, different patterns of cache misses, and other stochastic effects.

The loop blocking factor, l, is the number of consecutive iterations executed by each processor. With static scheduling, iterations 1 to l will execute on processor 0, iterations $l + 1$ to $2l$ will execute on processor 1, and so on. With dynamic scheduling, the loop blocking factor determines how many iterations the processor will execute between accesses to the shared iteration-counter. When a processor allocates the next block of iterations to itself, it increments the iteration-counter variable by l so that it will execute the next l consecutive iterations. Small values of l tend to increase the scheduling overhead in dynamic scheduling, because more accesses to the single shared iteration-counter are required, but they provide better load balancing. Larger values of l tend to decrease the scheduling overhead, at the expense of poorer load balancing.

Guided self-scheduling (GSS)[13*] combines dynamic scheduling with a variable loop blocking factor in an attempt to compromise between the good load balancing of small values of l and the low scheduling overhead of larger values of l. In the simplest form of GSS, the number of iterations allocated to a processor is $[R_i /p]$, where R_i is the number of iterations remaining to be executed at time T_i and p is the number of processors. This scheduling strategy assigns large blocks of iterations to processors near the beginning of a loop's execution to reduce the scheduling overhead. As fewer iterations remain toward the end of the execution of the loop, smaller blocks of iterations are assigned to processors to provide good load balancing.

An interesting enhancement to loop scheduling collects a history of execution behavior and uses this information to guide the scheduling of future executions of the program.[15] Besides loop scheduling, other program partitionings are possible,[16] such as finding independent subroutines to execute concurrently on different processors.

In addition to partitioning and scheduling, another important problem in shared-memory multiprocessors is synchronization, which ensures that processors do not violate program dependences by executing operations in an incorrect order.[17,18*-20] A wide variety of synchronization primitives have been suggested[21-28] to coordinate the execution of the processors and to restrict the order in which they access shared data. It has been pointed out that the need for all processors to simultaneously access synchronization variables in the shared memory can lead to hot-spots[29-32] that can severely degrade the system's performance.

Related to synchronization is the problem of cache coherence. In a shared-memory multiprocessor with private caches, multiple copies of a memory location can reside simultaneously in several caches. When a processor updates its cached copy of a shared-memory location, the fact that a change has occurred must be propagated to the other processors to ensure that no processor uses an old copy of the memory location. Schemes for maintaining coherence among the caches and memory have used a shared bus,[33-42] a central directory,[43-48] and a combination of simple hardware and sophisticated compiler analysis.[49-57]

The popularity of the shared-memory approach can be seen in the number of research and commercial machines that have been both proposed and built. These include the New York University Ultracomputer,[58] the IBM RP3,[31] the University of Illinois Cedar,[59,60*-62] the Horizon[63,64] and Tera[65*] machines, the BBN Butterfly[66] and Monarch,[67] the Alliant FX series,[68] and the Sequent Balance[69] and Symmetry.[70] The Orthogonal Multiprocessor[71*] is a partially shared-memory architecture that combines the benefits of a contention-free network with a significantly reduced hardware cost. Each of these machines solves the problems of scheduling, synchronization, and cache coherence using a slightly different approach.

Distributed-memory multicomputers

Distributed-memory multicomputers consist of several independent processors connected via dedicated communication links.[72*,73*] In distributed-memory multicomputers — in contrast with shared-memory multiprocessors — all of the memory is local to the individual processors. An explicit message must be sent between processors in order for one processor to access data stored in another's memory. The Cosmic Cube,[74] the Inmos Transputer,[75,76] the N-cube,[77,78] the FPS hypercube,[79] and the Intel iPSC hypercube[80] are examples of distributed-memory multicomputers. Several matrix algorithms for manipulating linear systems have been implemented for these machines.[81,82*] The Warp computer[83*] can be considered a hybrid distributed-memory multicomputer. It consists of multiple VLIW processors connected with point-to-point communication links, but the processors usually run in lockstep in a systolic array mode of operation.

Because it can be difficult for a programmer to explicitly encode the interprocessor communication into a program, a distributed-memory system may be more difficult to program than a shared-memory multiprocessor. To hide the communication — and thereby simplify the programmer's task — there are several systems[84-89,90*-92] that implement a virtual shared memory on top of a distributed system so that the distributed system appears to be a shared-memory system. These systems offer the scalability benefits of the distributed architecture, along with the more familiar programming model of the shared-memory systems. There also has been a great deal of interest[93-103] in exploiting the potential parallelism available in networks of heterogeneous workstations and personal computers using techniques such as remote procedure calls.

Reconfigurable and massively parallel architectures

Massively parallel SIMD architectures exploit parallelism by recognizing that, in many application programs, multiply nested loops frequently are used to execute the same operation on every element of a large data structure, such as a multiply dimensioned array. Instead of sequentially executing each iteration of the loop, or instead of executing independent iterations on separate processors, the SIMD machines execute a single instruction that performs the same operation on every element of the data structure simultaneously. These machines may consist of thousands of relatively simple processors, all controlled by a single instruction-sequencer. They may have very good performance on regularly structured problems, but they may be very inefficient on random serial sections of code. Typically, a front-end host machine executes these serial portions of the program.

Early examples of SIMD machines, also known as "array processors," include the Illiac IV,[104] the Texas Reconfigurable Array Computer (TRAC),[105,106*,107] and the Massively Parallel Processor (MPP).[108,109] The Partitionable SIMD/MIMD (PASM) System prototype machine[110] is a collection of SIMD processors that can be altered between SIMD, MIMD (multiple-instruction stream, multiple-data stream), and multiple SIMD modes. With the greater density of integrated circuit technology available today, compared to a few years ago, there has been a recent resurgence of interest in massively parallel architectures, as evidenced by the development of the Connection Machine,[111*] BLITZEN,[112*,113] and the MasPar MP-1.[114,115*,116] The SPLASH system[117] is an array processor that fits inside a Sun workstation. For some sequence comparison problems — such as speech recognition, data retrieval, or genetic analysis — this system has been shown to outperform several supercomputers. The Task-Flow architecture,[118*] which was developed with wafer-scale integration in mind, presents an interesting variation of the data flow idea for a massively parallel configuration. The MERLIN system[119] attempts to create a massively parallel system by connecting together heterogeneous machines via a high-speed interconnection network.

References (Chapter 3)

An asterisk following a reference citation below indicates the inclusion of that paper in this tutorial.

Shared-memory multiprocessors

Interconnection networks

1. L.N. Bhuyan, "Interconnection Networks for Parallel and Distributed Processing," *Computer*, Vol. 20, No. 6, June 1987, pp. 9-12.

2. D.M. Dias and J.R. Jump, "Analysis and Simulation of Buffered Delta Networks," *IEEE Trans. Computers*, Vol. C-30, No. 4, Apr. 1981, pp. 273-282.

3. G.R. Goke and G.J. Lipovski, "Banyan Networks for Partitioning Multiprocessor Systems," *Int'l Symp. Computer Architecture*, 1973, pp. 21-28.

4. C.P. Kruskal and M. Snir, "The Performance of Multistage Interconnection Networks for Multiprocessors," *IEEE Trans. Computers*, Vol. C-32, No. 12, Dec. 1983, pp. 1091-1098.

5. D.H. Lawrie, "Access and Alignment of Data in an Array Processor," *IEEE Trans. Computers*, Vol. C-24, No. 12, Dec. 1975, pp. 1145-1155.

6. J.H. Patel, "Processor-Memory Interconnections for Multiprocessors," *Int'l Symp. Computer Architecture*, 1979, pp. 168-177.

7. J.H. Patel, "Performance of Processor-Memory Interconnections for Multiprocessors," *IEEE Trans. Computers*, Vol. C-30, No. 10, Oct. 1981, pp. 771-780.

8. M.C. Pease, "The Indirect Binary n-Cube Microprocessor Array," *IEEE Trans. Computers*, Vol. C-26, No. 5, May 1977, pp. 458-473.

9. H.J. Siegel, "Interconnection Networks for SIMD Machines," *Computer*, Vol. 28, No. 6, June 1979, pp. 57-65.

10. C.L. Wu and T.-Y. Feng, "On a Class of Multistage Interconnection Networks," *IEEE Trans. Computers*, Vol. C-29, No. 8, Aug. 1980, pp. 694-702.

Scheduling

11. R. Cytron, "Doacross: Beyond Vectorization for Multiprocessors (Extended Abstract)," *Int'l Conf. Parallel Processing*, 1986, pp. 836-844.

12. Z. Fang et al., "Dynamic Processor Self-Scheduling for General Parallel Nested Loops," *Int'l Conf. Parallel Processing*, 1987, pp. 1-10.

13.* C.D. Polychronopoulos and D.J. Kuck, "Guided Self-Scheduling: A Practical Scheduling Scheme for Parallel Supercomputers," *IEEE Trans. Computers*, Vol. C-36, No. 12, Dec. 1987, pp. 1425-1439.

14. P. Tang and P.C. Yew, "Processor Self-Scheduling for Multiple-Nested Parallel Loops," *Int'l Conf. Parallel Processing*, 1986, pp. 528-535.

15. P.A. Suhler, "Heuristic Tuning of Parallel Loop Performance," *Int'l Conf. Parallel Processing, Vol. II: Software*, 1989, pp. 184-191.

16. B. Kruatrachue and T. Lewis, "Grain Size Determination for Parallel Processing," *IEEE Software*, Vol. 5, No. 1, Jan. 1988, pp. 23-32.

Synchronization

17. M. Dubois, C. Scheurich, and F. Briggs, "Memory Access Buffering in Multiprocessors," *Int'l Symp. Computer Architecture*, 1986, pp. 434-442.

18.* M. Dubois, C. Scheurich, and F.A. Briggs, "Synchronization, Coherence, and Event Ordering in Multiprocessors," *Computer*, Vol. 21, No. 2, Feb. 1988, pp. 9-21.

19. L. Lamport, "Time, Clocks, and the Ordering of Events in a Distributed System," *Comm. ACM*, Vol. 21, No. 7, July 1978, pp. 558-565.

20. L. Lamport, "How to Make a Multiprocessor Computer That Correctly Executes Multiprocess Programs," *IEEE Trans. Computers*, Vol. C-28, No. 9, Sept. 1979, pp. 690-691.

21. T.E. Anderson, "The Performance of Spin Lock Alternatives for Shared-Memory Multiprocessors," *IEEE Trans. Parallel and Distributed Systems*, Vol. 1, No. 1, Jan. 1990, pp. 6-16.

22. H. Dietz et al., "Static Synchronization Beyond VLIW," *Supercomputing '89*, Nov. 1989, pp. 416-425.

23. J. Goodman, M. Vernon, and P. Woest, "A Set of Efficient Synchronization Primitives for a Large-Scale Shared-Memory Multiprocessor," *Third Int'l Conf. Architectural Support Programming Languages and Operating Systems*, Apr. 1989, pp. 64-73.

24. C.P. Kruskal, L. Rudolph, and M. Snir, "Efficient Synchronization on Multiprocessors with Shared Memory," *ACM Symp. Principles Distributed Computing*, 1986, pp. 218-228.

25. Z. Li and W. Abu-Sufah, "On Reducing Data Synchronization in Multiprocessed Loops," *IEEE Trans. Computers*, Vol. C-36, No. 1, Jan. 1987, pp. 105-109.

26. S.P. Midkiff and D.A. Padua, "Compiler Algorithms for Synchronization," *IEEE Trans. Computers*, Vol. C-36, No. 12, Dec. 1987, pp. 1485-1495.

27. H. Su and P. Yew, "On Data Synchronization for Multiprocessors," *Int'l Symp. Computer Architecture*, 1989, pp. 416-423.

28. C. Zhu and P. Yew, "A Scheme to Enforce Data Dependence on Large Multiprocessor Systems," *IEEE Trans. Software Eng.*, Vol. SE-13, No. 6, June 1987, pp. 726-739.

29. G. Lee, C.P. Kruskal, and D.J. Kuck, "The Effectiveness of Combining in Shared Memory Parallel Computers in the Presence of Hot Spots," *Int'l Conf. Parallel Processing*, 1986, pp. 35-39.

30. G.F. Pfister and V.A. Norton, "Hot-Spot Contention and Combining in Multistage Interconnection Networks," *IEEE Trans. Computers*, Vol. C-34, No. 10, Oct. 1985, pp. 943-948.

31. G.F. Pfister et al., "The IBM Research Parallel Processor Prototype (RP3): Introduction and Architecture," *Int'l Conf. Parallel Processing*, 1985, pp. 764-771.

32. P.-C. Yew, N.-F. Tzeng, and D.H. Lawrie, "Distributing Hot-Spot Addressing in Large-Scale Multiprocessors," *IEEE Trans. Computers*, Vol. C-36, No. 4, Apr. 1987, pp. 388-395.

Cache coherence

33. J.K. Archibald, "A Cache Coherence Approach for Large Multiprocessor Systems," *Int'l Conf. Supercomputing*, 1988, pp. 337-345.

34. L.N. Bhuyan, B.-C. Liu, and I. Ahmed, "Analysis of MIN-Based Multiprocessors with Private Cache Memories," *Int'l Conf. Parallel Processing, Vol. I: Architecture*, 1989, pp. 51-58.

35. J.R. Goodman, "Using Cache Memory to Reduce Processor-Memory Traffic," *Int'l Symp. Computer Architecture*, 1983, pp. 124-131.

36. J.R. Goodman and P.J. Woest, "The Wisconsin Multicube: A New Large-Scale Cache-Coherent Multiprocessor," *Int'l Symp. Computer Architecture*, 1988, pp. 422-431.

37. R. Katz et al., "Implementing a Cache Consistency Protocol," *Int'l Symp. Computer Architecture*, 1985, pp. 276-283.

38. D.E. Marquardt and H.S. AlKhatib, "C2MP: A Cache-Coherent, Distributed Memory Multiprocessor-System," *Proc. Supercomputing '89*, 1989, pp. 466-475.

39. E.M. McCreight, "The Dragon Computer System, an Early Overview," *NATO Advanced Study Inst. Microarchitecture VLSI Computers*, July 1984, pp. 83-101.

40. M.S. Papamarcos and J.H. Patel, "A Low-Overhead Coherence Solution for Multiprocessors with Private Cache Memories," *Int'l Symp. Computer Architecture*, 1984, pp. 348-354.

41. C.P. Thacker, L.C. Stewart, and E.H. Satterthwaite, "Firefly: A Multiprocessor Workstation," *IEEE Trans. Computers*, Vol. 37, No. 8, Aug. 1988, pp. 909-920.

42. A.W. Wilson, "Hierarchical Cache/Bus Architecture for Shared Memory Multiprocessors," *Int'l Symp. Computer Architecture*, 1987, pp. 244-252.

43. D.V. James et al., "Scalable Coherent Interface," *Computer*, Vol. 23, No. 6, June 1990, pp. 74-77.

44. A. Agarwal et al., "An Evaluation of Directory Schemes for Cache Coherence," *Int'l Symp. Computer Architecture*, 1988, pp. 280-289.

45. J. Archibald and J.-L. Baer, "An Economical Solution to the Cache Coherence Problem," *Int'l Symp. Computer Architecture*, 1984, pp. 355-362.

46. L.M. Censier and P. Feautrier, "A New Solution to Coherence Problems in Multicache Systems," *IEEE Trans. Computers*, Vol. C-27, No. 12, Dec. 1978, pp. 1112-1118.

47. C.K. Tang, "Cache Design in the Tightly Coupled Multiprocessor System," *AFIPS Nat'l Computer Conf.*, 1976, pp. 749-753.

48. W.C. Yen, D.W.L. Yen, and K.-S. Fu, "Data Coherence Problem in a Multicache System," *IEEE Trans. Computers*, Vol. C-34, No. 1, Jan. 1985, pp. 56-65.

49. W.C. Brantley, K.P. McAuliffe, and J. Weiss, "RP3 Processor-Memory Element," *Int'l Conf. Parallel Processing*, 1985, pp. 782-789.

50. H. Cheong and A.V. Veidenbaum, "A Cache Coherence Scheme with Fast Selective Invalidation," *Int'l Symp. Computer Architecture*, 1988, pp. 299-307.

51. H. Cheong and A. Veidenbaum, "A Version Control Approach to Cache Coherence," *ACM Int'l Conf. Supercomputing*, 1989, pp. 322-330.

52. H. Cheong and A.V. Veidenbaum, "Compiler-Directed Cache Management in Multiprocessors," *Computer*, Vol. 23, No. 6, June 1990, pp. 39-47.

53. J. Edler et al., "Issues Related to MIMD Shared-Memory Computers: The NYU Ultracomputer Approach," *Int'l Symp. Computer Architecture*, 1985, pp. 126-135.

54. D.J. Lilja and P.-C. Yew, "Combining Hardware and Software Cache Coherence Strategies," *ACM Int'l Conf. Supercomputing*, 1991, pp. 274-283.

55. S.L. Min and J.-L. Baer, "A Timestamp-Based Cache Coherence Scheme," *Int'l Conf. Parallel Processing, Vol. I: Architecture*, 1989, pp. 23-32.

56. A.J. Smith, "CPU Cache Consistency with Software Support and Using 'One Time Identifiers,'" *Proc. Pacific Computer Comm.*, 1985, pp. 153-161.

57. A.V. Veidenbaum, "A Compiler-Assisted Cache Coherence Solution for Multiprocessors," *Int'l Conf. Parallel Processing*, 1986, pp. 1029-1036.

Shared-memory multiprocessor machines

58. A. Gottlieb et al., "The NYU Ultracomputer — Designing a MIMD, Shared-Memory Parallel Machine," *Int'l Symp. Computer Architecture*, 1982, pp. 27-42.

59. D.J. Kuck et al., "Parallel Supercomputing Today and the Cedar Approach," *Science*, Vol. 231, Feb. 28, 1986, pp. 967-974.

60.* J. Konicek et al., "The Organization of the Cedar System," *Int'l Conf. Parallel Processing, Vol I: Architecture*, 1991, pp. 49-56.

61. R. Eigenmann et al., "Restructuring Fortran Programs for Cedar," *Int'l Conf. Parallel Processing, Vol I: Architecture*, 1991, pp. 57-66.

62. P.A. Emrath et al., "The Xylem Operating System," *Int'l Conf. Parallel Processing, Vol I: Architecture*, 1991, pp. 67-70.

63. J.T. Kuehn and B.J. Smith, "The Horizon Supercomputing System: Architecture and Software," *Proc. Supercomputing '88*, Nov. 1988, pp. 28-34.

64. M.R. Thistle and B.J. Smith, "A Processor Architecture for Horizon," *Proc. Supercomputing '88*, Nov. 1988, pp. 35-41.

65.* R. Alverson et al., "The Tera Computer System," *Int'l Conf. Supercomputing*, 1990, pp. 1-6.

66. R.J. Thomas, "Behavior of the Butterfly Parallel Processor in the Presence of Memory Hot Spots," *Int'l Conf. Parallel Processing*, 1986, pp. 46-50.

67. R.D. Rettberg et al., "The Monarch Parallel Processor Hardware Design," *Computer*, Vol. 23, No. 4, Apr. 1990, pp. 18-30.

68. R. Perron and C. Mundie, "The Architecture of the Alliant FX/8 Computer," *IEEE Digest of Papers-CompCon*, Feb. 1986, pp. 390-393.

69. S.S. Thakkar, P.R. Gifford, and G.F. Fieland, "The Balance Multiprocessor System," *IEEE Micro*, Vol. 8, No. 1, Feb. 1988, pp. 57-69.

70. T. Lovett and S. Thakkar, "The Symmetry Multiprocessor System," *Int'l Conf. Parallel Processing, Vol. I: Architecture*, 1988, pp. 303-310.

71.* K. Hwang, P.-S. Tseng, and D. Kim, "An Orthogonal Multiprocessor for Parallel Scientific Computations," *IEEE Trans. Computers*, Vol. 38, No. 1, Jan. 1989, pp. 47-61.

Distributed-memory multicomputers

72.* W.C. Athas and C.L. Seitz, "Multicomputers: Message-Passing Concurrent Computers," *Computer*, Vol. 21, No. 8, Aug. 1988, pp. 9-24.

73.* J.P. Hayes and T. Mudge, "Hypercube Supercomputers," *Proc. IEEE*, Vol. 77, No. 12, Dec. 1989, pp. 1829-1841.

74. C.L. Seitz, "The Cosmic Cube," *Comm. ACM*, Vol. 28, No. 1, Jan. 1985, pp. 22-33.

75. A.J.G. Hey, "Supercomputing with Transputers — Past, Present, and Future," *Int'l Conf. Supercomputing*, 1990, pp. 479-489.

76. C. Whitby-Strevens, "The Transputer," *Int'l Symp. Computer Architecture*, 1985, pp. 292-300.

77. J.P. Hayes et al., "Architecture of a Hypercube Supercomputer," *Int'l Conf. Parallel Processing*, 1986, pp. 653-660.

78. J.P. Hayes et al., "A Microprocessor-Based Hypercube Supercomputer," *IEEE Micro*, Vol. 6, No. 5, 1986, pp. 6-17.

79. J.L. Gustafson, S. Hawkinson, and K. Scott, "The Architecture of a Homogeneous Vector Supercomputer," *Int'l Conf. Parallel Processing*, 1986, pp. 649-652.

80. R. Arlauskas, "iPSC/2 System: A Second Generation Hypercube," *Third Conf. Hypercube Concurrent Computers and Applications, Vol. I,* 1988, pp. 38-42.

81. C. Aykanat et al., "Iterative Algorithms for Solution of Large Sparse Systems of Linear Equations on Hypercubes," *IEEE Trans. Computers,* Vol. 37, No. 12, Dec. 1988, pp. 1554-1568.

82.* C. Moler, "Matrix Computation on Distributed Memory Multiprocessors," *First SIAM Conf. Hypercube Multiprocessors,* 1986, pp. 181-195.

83.* M. Annaratone et al., "The Warp Computer: Architecture, Implementation, and Performance," *IEEE Trans. Computers,* Vol. C-36, No. 12, Dec. 1987, pp. 1523-1538.

Virtual shared memory

84. S. Ahuja et al., "Matching Language and Hardware for Parallel Computation in the Linda Machine," *IEEE Trans. Computers,* Vol. 37, No. 8, Aug. 1988, pp. 921-929.

85. R. Bisiani, A. Nowatzyk, and M. Ravishankar, "Coherent Shared Memory on a Distributed System," *Int'l Conf. Parallel Processing, Vol. I.: Architecture,* 1989, pp. 133-141.

86. K. Li and P. Hudak, "Memory Coherence in Shared Virtual Memory Systems," *Proc. Ann. ACM Symp. Principles Distributed Computing,* 1986, pp. 229-239.

87. K. Li, "IVY: A Shared Virtual Memory System for Parallel Computing," *Int'l Conf. Parallel Processing, Vol. II: Software,* 1988, pp. 94-101.

88. K. Li and R. Schaefer, "A Hypercube Shared Virtual Memory System," *Int'l Conf. Parallel Processing, Vol I: Architecture,* 1989, pp. 125-132.

89. S. Lucco, "A Heuristic Linda Kernel for Hypercube Multiprocessors," *1986 Workshop Hypercube Multiprocessors,* 1986, pp. 32-38.

90.* B. Nitzberg and V. Lo, "Distributed Shared Memory: A Survey of Issues and Algorithms," *Computer,* Vol. 24, No. 8, Aug. 1991, pp. 52-60.

91. M. Stumm and S. Zhou, "Algorithms Implementing Distributed Shared Memory," *Computer,* Vol. 23, No. 5, May 1990, pp. 54-64.

92. K.-L. Wu and W.K. Fuchs, "Recoverable Distributed Shared Virtual Memory," *IEEE Trans. Computers,* Vol. 39, No. 4, Apr. 1990, pp. 460-469.

Heterogeneous systems

93. A.D. Birrell and B.J. Nelson, "Implementing Remote Procedure Calls," *ACM Trans. Computer Systems,* Vol. 2, No. 1, Feb. 1984, pp. 39-59.

94. D.R. Cheriton and W. Zwaenepoel, "The Distributed V Kernel and Its Performance for Diskless Workstations," *ACM Operating Systems Rev.,* Vol. 17, No. 5, 1983, pp. 129-140.

95. E. Cooper, "Replicated Distributed Programs," *ACM Symp. Operating Systems Principles,* Dec. 1985, pp. 63-78.

96. M. Faci and G.C. Shoja, "A Distributed Kernel for Support of Transparent Communication between Tasks," *Phoenix Conf. Computers and Comm.,* 1986, pp. 625-631.

97. R. Haggmann, "Process Server: Sharing Processing Power in a Workstation Environment," *Int'l Conf. Distributed Computing Systems,* 1986, pp. 260-267.

98. G.C. Shoja and R.G. Gurr, "Parallel Processing in Local Networks," *Int'l Conf. Parallel Processing,* 1986, pp. 1048-1051.

99. G.C. Shoja, G. Clarke, and T. Taylor, "REM: A Distributed Facility for Utilizing Idle Processing Power of Workstations," *Proc. IFIP WG 10.3 Working Conf. Distributed Processing,* Oct. 1987, pp. 205-218.

100. R.J. Souza and S.P. Miller, "Unix and Remote Procedure Calls: A Peaceful Coexistence?" *Int'l Conf. Distributed Computing Systems*, 1986, pp. 268-277.

101. A. Tanenbaum and R. van Renesse, "Distributed Operating Systems," *Computing Surveys*, Dec. 1985, pp. 419-463.

102. M. Theimer, K. Lantz, and D. Cheriton, "Preemptable Remote Execution Facilities for the V-System," *ACM Symp. Operating Systems Principles*, Dec. 1985, pp. 2-12.

103. B. Walker et al., "The LOCUS Distributed Operating System," *ACM Operating Systems Rev.*, Vol. 17, No. 5, 1983, pp. 49-70.

Reconfigurable and massively parallel architectures

104. W.J. Bouknight et al., "The Illiac IV System," *Proc. IEEE*, Vol. 60, No. 4, 1972, pp. 369-379.

105. G.J. Lipovski and A. Tripathi, "A Reconfigurable Varistructure Array Processor," *Int'l Conf. Parallel Processing*, 1977, pp. 165-174.

106.* M.C. Sejnowski et al., "An Overview of the Texas Reconfigurable Array Computer," *AFIPS Nat'l Computer Conf.*, 1980, pp. 631-641.

107. U.V. Premkumar et al., "Design and Implementation of the Banyan Interconnection Network in TRAC," *AFIPS Nat'l Computer Conf.*, 1980, pp. 643-653.

108. K.E. Batcher, "Design of a Massively Parallel Processor," *IEEE Trans. Computers*, Vol. C-29, No. 9, Sept. 1980, pp. 836-840.

109. A.P. Reeves and M. Gutierrez, "On Measuring the Performance of a Massively Parallel Processor," *Int'l Conf. Parallel Processing, Vol. I: Architecture*, 1988, pp. 261-270.

110. H.J. Siegel et al., "PASM: A Partitionable SIMD/MIMD System for Image Processing and Pattern Recognition," *IEEE Trans. Computers*, Vol. C-30, No. 12, Dec. 1981, pp. 934-947.

111.* L.W. Tucker and G.G. Robertson, "Architecture and Applications of the Connection Machine," *Computer*, Vol. 21, No. 8, Aug. 1988, pp. 26-38.

112.* D.W. Blevins et al., "BLITZEN: A Highly Integrated Massively Parallel Machine," *J. Parallel and Distributed Computing*, Vol. 8, No. 2, Feb. 1990, pp. 150-160.

113. E.W. Davis and J.M. Jennings, "Evaluation of New Architectural Features in a Massively Parallel SIMD Machine," *Int'l Conf. Parallel Processing, Vol. I: Architecture*, 1990, pp. 149-152.

114. T. Blank, "The MasPar MP-1 Architecture," *IEEE Digest of Papers-CompCon*, Feb. 1990, pp. 20-24.

115.* J.R. Nickolls, "The Design of the MasPar MP-1: A Cost-Effective Massively Parallel Computer," *IEEE Digest of Papers-CompCon*, Feb. 1990, pp. 25-28.

116. P. Christy, "Software to Support Massively Parallel Computing on the MasPar MP-1," *IEEE Digest of Papers-CompCon*, Feb. 1990, pp. 29-33.

117. M. Gokhale et al., "SPLASH: A Reconfigurable Linear Logic Array," *Int'l Conf. Parallel Processing, Vol. I: Architecture*, 1990, pp. 526-532.

118.* R.W. Horst, "Task Flow Computer Architecture," *Int'l Conf. Parallel Processing, Vol. I: Architecture*, 1990, pp. 533-540.

119. L. Wittie and C. Maples, "MERLIN: Massively Parallel Heterogeneous Computing," *Int'l Conf. Parallel Processing, Vol I: Architecture*, 1989, pp. 142-150.

Shared-memory multiprocessors

Guided Self-Scheduling: A Practical Scheduling Scheme for Parallel Supercomputers

CONSTANTINE D. POLYCHRONOPOULOS, MEMBER, IEEE, AND DAVID J. KUCK, FELLOW, IEEE

Abstract—This paper proposes *guided self-scheduling*, a new approach for scheduling arbitrarily nested parallel program loops on shared memory multiprocessor systems. Utilizing loop parallelism is clearly most crucial in achieving high system and program performance. Because of its simplicity, guided self-scheduling is particularly suited for implementation on real parallel machines. This method achieves simultaneously the two most important objectives: load balancing and very low synchronization overhead. For certain types of loops we show analytically that guided self-scheduling uses minimal overhead and achieves optimal schedules. Two other interesting properties of this method are its insensitivity to the initial processor configuration (in time) and its parameterized nature which allows us to tune it for different systems. Finally we discuss experimental results that clearly show the advantage of guided self-scheduling over the most widely known dynamic methods.

Index Terms—Parallel Fortran programs, parallel loops, parallel supercomputers, run-time overhead, self-scheduling, synchronization.

I. INTRODUCTION

AS technology approaches physical limitations, parallel processor systems offer a promising and powerful alternative for high performance computing. In principle, parallelism offers performance that can increase without bounds and depends only on the application at hand. In reality, however, parallelism does have its limitations [6], [19], [27]. Technology is still unable to support the realization of parallel machines with large numbers of general purpose processors. An even greater obstacle is our inability to efficiently utilize such massively parallel systems. Problems such as specifying parallelism, mapping or scheduling parallel programs on a given architecture, synchronizing the execution of a parallel program, memory management in parallel processing environments, and compiling for parallel machines remain areas for much future work.

In this paper we propose a practical method that can be used to obtain very efficient schedules of parallel loops on shared memory parallel machines. The problem of mapping or assigning different tasks of the same program to different processors (otherwise known as "scheduling") has only recently attracted considerable attention with the introduction

Manuscript received January 30, 1987; revised May 29, 1987. This work was supported in part by the National Science Foundation under Grants NSF DCR84-10110 and NSF DCR84-06916, the U.S. Department of Energy under Grant DOE DE-FG02-85ER25001, and the IBM Donation.

The authors are with the Center for Supercomputing Research and Development, University of Illinois at Urbana-Champaign, Urbana, IL 61801.

IEEE Log Number 8717030.

Reprinted from *IEEE Transactions on Computers*, Vol. C-36, No. 12, December 1987, pages 1425-1439. Copyright © 1987 by The Institute of Electrical and Electronics Engineers, Inc. All rights reserved.

of many parallel machines in the market. Although scheduling is an old, notorious problem with numerous versions and has attracted the attention of many researchers in the past [4], [5], [9], [12], [24], the results known to date offer little help when dealing with real parallel machines.

Existing methods are not adequate because they consider an idealized form of the problem where task execution times are fixed and known in advance, and they ignore "side-effects" (interprocessor communication and synchronization) [21], [23]. In reality, however, branching statements in programs, memory access interference, random processor latencies, and other "random events" make task execution times impossible to predict accurately in general. Furthermore, side-effects have a very important impact on scheduling.

The complexity of the scheduling problem has led the computing community to adopt heuristic approaches for each new machine. In many cases [6] the problem is entirely left to the user, and it is well known that hand-coding and manually inserting system calls in a program are necessary to achieve maximum performance. Worse yet this manual approach is different from machine to machine and is highly empirical. One could say that programming parallel machines is anything but "user friendly." Unless a systematic solution to the problem is found, only experts will be able to code for the parallel machines of the future, or these machines will be confined to a few processors and simple architectures.

On the other hand, it is difficult or impossible to find a universal solution for problems such as scheduling, minimization of interprocessor communication, and synchronization. This is so because these problems are often architecture dependent. Thus, a solution which is efficient for one machine organization may be inefficient for another. We believe, however, that more general solutions can be found for large classes of machine architectures. It is also clear that such problems must be solved automatically by the compiler, the operating system, or by the hardware.

This paper proposes guided self-scheduling (GSS), a new method for executing parallel loops on parallel processor systems. Even though we use Fortran loops in this presentation, the concepts and the proposed method are valid for parallel loops coded in any other language. The GSS method not only generates efficient (load balanced) schedules, but it also reduces substantially (and often minimizes) the number of synchronized accesses to loop indexes, an expensive operation on many shared memory parallel machines [30]. As shown later, GSS can be easily automated and should be efficient for most shared memory parallel processor systems.

The rest of the paper is organized as follows. Section II

gives some background information and the necessary definitions. Section III discusses alternatives for the parallel execution of programs and identifies the main advantages and disadvantages of each scheme. Section IV presents the guided self-scheduling method in detail and its application to a simple parallel loop. Different versions of GSS are discussed in Section IV-B. The results of experimental work that was performed with GSS are presented in Section V. Finally, the conclusion is given in Section VI.

II. BACKGROUND

The machine model used for this paper is a *shared memory parallel processor* system. It consists of p homogeneous and autonomous processors connected through an interconnection network to a set of memory modules, such that each memory module is accessible by all p processors. Commercial systems such as the Cray X-MP, Alliant FX/8, IBM 3090, and experimental machines such as the Cedar and the RP3 fit this model. High performance on shared memory parallel processor machines is achieved by executing a single program on more than one processor concurrently. During parallel execution, the data dependences must be observed in order for the semantics of the program to be preserved.

Data dependences [3], [13], [16], define a partial order or precedence relation on the statements of a program. There are three major types of data dependences, flow, anti, and output dependences. A *flow* dependence is defined between two (not necessarily different) program statements s_1 and s_2 (denoted $s_1 \delta s_2$), if a scalar or array variable assigned by s_1 is used in s_2. An *antidependence* $s_1 \bar{\delta} s_2$ between the two statements occurs if a variable used in s_1 is assigned by s_2, and s_1 lexically precedes s_2. If s_1 and s_2 assign values to the same variable, an *output* dependence $s_1 \delta^0 s_2$ is defined between the two statements. Dependences are also represented by arcs between nodes that represent statements. In the above definitions, arcs originating from s_1 and pointing to s_2 can be used to mark the corresponding dependences. A *forward* dependence is one whose arc points lexically forward. Similarly we define *backward* dependences.

The definition of dependences in Fortran loops is similar and requires the use of statement *instances*. A statement s_i that belongs to a loop of the form DO $I = 1, N$, has N different instances, one for each iteration of the loop. Statement instances are denoted by $s_i(I)$, $(1 \leq I \leq N)$. For two statements s_i and s_j that belong to a DO loop, a dependence $s_i \delta^* s_j$ is defined if and only if there are instances $s_i(I_1)$ and $s_j(I_2)$, such that $1 \leq I_1 \leq I_2 \leq N$ and $s_i(I_1) \delta^* s_j(I_2)$, where δ^* denotes any of the three types of data dependencies defined earlier. Such a dependence is called a *cross-iteration* dependence if the two statement instances involved in the dependence correspond to two different values of the loop index, i.e., $I_1 \neq I_2$. The difference $I_1 - I_2$ is called the *dependence distance*. The statement $s_i(I_1)$ is called the *dependence source* and the statement $s_j(I_2)$ the *dependence sink*.

A Fortran DO loop is of the form

DO $I = M, N, d$
  {B}
ENDO

where M and N are the lower and upper index bounds, d is the loop stride, and B is the loop body which can be straightline code or a loop itself. A DO loop can always be *normalized* to have $M = 1$ and $d = 1$ [29]. A DOALL loop is a DO loop without cross-iteration dependences. Obviously the iterations of DOALL loops are data independent. Thus, each iteration of a DOALL can be executed independently of the others. DO loops with cross-iteration dependences that are forward are called FORALL. FORALL loops can also be executed as DOALL's if synchronization is used to assure the correct order of execution of statements involved in a dependence. Index alignment can be used to convert some FORALL loops to DOALL's. Finally, we may have DO loops that also contain cross-iteration backward dependences. Such loops are called DOACR and they constitute the most complex case of parallel loops [7]. The DOACR loop covers the entire spectrum by determining the maximum amount of overlap between successive iterations. If total overlap is possible, then we have the DOALL case; in the zero overlap case, the DOACR loop is a serial or DOSERIAL loop.

Another type of parallelism arises from the concurrent execution of lexically disjoint program fragments (e.g., the parallel execution of two different subroutine calls). The act of allocating different program fragments to different processors is called *spreading*. Spreading can be done at the operation or statement level and is called *low-level spreading* (fine granularity), or it can be done at the loop and subroutine level and is called *high-level spreading* (coarse granularity).

In this paper we are primarily concerned with DOALL and FORALL loops. Since synchronization makes FORALL's appear as DOALL's we consider both types of loops to be DOALL's. A *one-way* nested loop with nest depth k, denoted by $L = (N_1, \cdots, N_k)$, has exactly one loop at each nest level, where N_i, $(i = 1, \cdots, k)$ is the number of iterations of the loop at the ith level. A *multiway* nested loop has at least two loops at some nest level. Nested loops that contain combinations of DOALL, DOACR, and DOSERIAL loops are called *hybrid*.

A compiler transformation called *loop coalescing* can be used to transform multiple one-way nested loops into singly nested loops. This transformation is useful for self-scheduling of parallel loops. The overhead associated with the access of loop indexes is reduced sharply in many cases when loop coalescing is applied. Coalescing transforms a multidimensional space into a linear space. All array indexes inside the loop code can now be expressed in terms of a single index. Another transformation that can be useful in our case is *loop distribution* [13], [18]. Loop distribution distributes a loop around each statement in its body, or around code modules inside the loop that form strongly connected components of the data dependence graph [18]. It is useful for transforming multiway nested loops to one-way nested. Thus, when coalescing is applied in conjunction with loop distribution, multiway nested loops can also be transformed into single loops. Another source transformation used in this paper is *loop interchange* [29]. Loop interchange permutes a pair of nested loops so that the outer becomes innerloop and vice versa. This transformation can be applied to improve in many aspects the parallel execution of Fortran loops on a particular machine. A detailed description of loop coalescing, loop distribution, and loop interchange can be found in the sources referenced above.

A program can be *partitioned* into a number of data dependent or independent tasks. A *task* is defined to be a program module that executes on one or more processors. Tasks can be *serial* or *parallel* depending on whether they can execute on one or more processors. A parallel task consists of a set of *processes* that can be defined by the compiler before execution, or dynamically during program execution. For example, a DOALL loop with N iterations is a task that can spawn up to N processes. Processes are serial and their execution is *nonpreemptive*. A *program task graph* is a directed graph whose nodes are tasks and arcs represent dependences between tasks. The program task graph can be constructed by the compiler.

The schemes used to schedule the tasks of a program on a parallel system can be broadly distinguished into two classes: *static* and *dynamic*. (In this paper the terms *scheduling*, *processor allocation*, and *processor assignment* are used interchangeably.) In static scheduling, processors are assigned tasks before execution starts. When program execution starts, each processor knows exactly which tasks to execute. A scheduling scheme is called *dynamic* when the actual processor allocation is performed by hardware or software mechanisms during program execution. Therefore, during dynamic scheduling, decisions for allocating processors are taken on-the-fly for different parts of the program, as the program executes. Dynamic scheduling can be performed through a *central* control unit or it can be *distributed*. A special case of scheduling through distributed control units is *self-scheduling* (SS) [26]. As implied by the term, there is no single control unit that makes global decisions for allocating processors, but rather the processors themselves are responsible for determining what task to execute next.

There are several factors (such as communication time and task granularity) that must be taken into account during scheduling. Implementations of pure versions of dynamic or self-scheduling that look at the instruction level for parallelism could be very inefficient and involve enormous overhead. There is no method that allows us to have some knowledge about the topology of the program at run time unless compiler support of some form is provided. Hybrid forms of dynamic or self-scheduling are possible by having the compiler help the control unit or the processors in making a scheduling decision. Guided self-scheduling is such a hybrid scheme that we discuss in this paper.

III. DESIGN RULES FOR RUN-TIME SCHEDULING SCHEMES

When static scheduling is used, the run-time overhead is minimal. With dynamic scheduling, however, the run-time overhead becomes a critical factor and may account for a significant portion of the total execution time of a program. This is a logical consequence of dynamic scheduling. While at compile time the compiler or an intelligent preprocessor is responsible for making the scheduling decisions, at run time this decision must be made in a case-by-case fashion, and the time spent for this decision-making process is reflected in the program's execution time.

One way to alleviate this problem is to have the scheduler make scheduling decisions for a chunk of the program while other parts of the program are already executing on the processors. This, however, implies advance knowledge about the structure of the program which cannot be available at run time. For example, we must know how to partition the program into a series of task sets so that during execution of a task set, decisions for the scheduling of the next task set can be overlapped. The execution time of the tasks in each task set should thus be long enough to allow the scheduler the necessary time to make the next decision. Moreover, if the scheduler is the operating system, the above overlapped scheduling is impossible since one or more processors must be "wasted" to execute the operating system itself. If a global control unit (GCU) is used and if the compiler is used to generate a substantial amount of scheduling information, we can decide on the number of processors for each specific task at run time. This can be done in many cases without additional overhead assuming the GCU can make decisions about a subset of tasks while the computational processors are working on another subset. In this case overlapped scheduling implies that the GCU is a stand-alone unit (a superprocessor) and, therefore, more costly than a traditional control unit which is essentially a sequencer. With parallel loops the problem is less complex since the structure of the loop is known as described later.

A. Complete Program Graphs

It has been shown [4] that, in certain cases of random task graphs, optimal schedules can be achieved by deliberately keeping one or more processors idle in order to better utilize them at a later point. This and other scheduling "anomalies" are reported in [12]. Detecting such anomalies, however, requires processing of the entire task graph in advance. Since this is not possible at run time, the luxury of deliberately keeping processors idle (with the *hope* that we may better utilize them later) should not be permitted. Even if we had a way of processing the task graph in its entirety at run time, the scheduling overhead of an intelligent heuristic could be enormous in many cases.

We believe that the following guideline for any run-time scheduling scheme should always be applied: make simple and fast scheduling decisions at run time. This principle implicitly forbids asking (and answering) questions of the form: "How many processors should we allocate to this task?" Answering such a question means, in general, that we are willing to hold up idle processors until they become as many as the number of processors requested by that task. This is true assuming that a task cannot start execution unless all processors allocated to it are available (and thus they all start executing that task at the same time). As explained later, the concept of processor allocation is very useful when it is used in a different context.

Since we want to avoid deliberate idling of processors as much as possible, any run-time scheduling scheme should rather be designed to ask (and answer) questions of the following type: "How much work should we give to this processor?" In other words, when a processor becomes idle, try to assign to it a new task as soon as possible making the best possible selection. As shown in [4] and [21], this policy is guaranteed to generate a schedule length (i.e., an execution time) which is at most twice as long as the optimal. Therefore, in our case, the entity of importance is the individual processor rather than the individual task.

More precisely, our approach to the scheduling problem can be outlined as follows. The program task graph (as defined in Section II) is constructed at compile time and contains two kinds of tasks (nodes): serial and parallel. (During execution, parallel tasks may be executed by more than one physical processor, while serial tasks are always executed by a single processor.) Parallel tasks are always composed of parallel loops. Note that very low granularity parallelism inside a serial task can be exploited by the different functional units of a single processor (if applicable). The next activity that occurs at compile time is the evaluation of the optimal number of *virtual* processors for each task. (Virtual processors are the processors *requested* by (but not necessarily granted to) each task.) This activity involves compile-time analysis of the anticipated run-time overhead incurred by the parallel execution of tasks. Therefore, only parallel tasks are considered during this phase. The optimal number of virtual processors gives an upper bound on the number of physical processors assigned to that task during execution. Methods for computing the optimal number of virtual processors and for performing compile-time overhead analysis are out of the scope of this paper [7], [20], [21]. During program execution, the request by a given task for the optimal number of processors may or may not be honored. In any case the number of physical processors used to concurrently execute a specific task is restricted to be less than or equal to the virtual processors attributed to that task at compile time.

Let us consider what happens during execution where the program is represented by the program task graph (with each node pointing to the appropriate fragment of code). Each node has as an attribute the number of virtual processors allocated to it. We assume that there is some kind of mechanism (e.g., in the operating system) that performs the bookkeeping, that is, determines which tasks have completed and which are ready to execute (based on the data dependence or precedence relations). Tasks ready to execute are queued in a shared pool of ready-to-execute tasks. When execution starts, individual processors (rather than tasks) become the central entity. During the execution phase, our approach is to consider each processor as it becomes idle, and decide the amount of work to be given to that processor. When an idle processor checks the first available task in the shared pool, it dispatches the entire task (if it is serial) or part of it (if it is parallel). The rest of this paper presents practical schemes for solving the scheduling problem for a very important class of parallel tasks, namely, arbitrarily nested parallel loops. Note that high-level spreading can be performed by organizing the queue of ready tasks appropriately, but again this is out of the scope of this work.

B. Parallel Loops

Because of the well-defined structure of loop tasks, scheduling of such constructs is less complicated. Furthermore, it has been shown that parallel loops account for the greatest percentage of program parallelism [17]. Therefore, designing low-overhead methods for the efficient allocation of parallel loops is crucial to machine performance.

Very little work has been done on this topic so far. This is partly due to the fact that one level (single loop) parallelism is enough to fully utilize the processors of most of the existing parallel machines. Also due to high run-time overhead, the first parallel processor machines (e.g., Cray X-MP with multitasking) looked for parallelism at the subroutine level; parallelism at the loop level was too expensive to exploit. Soon thereafter Cray systems employed microtasking [23] that now can be used to utilize parallelism at the loop level. The microtasking library is a tool supplied to the user, but how to use it effectively is again the user's responsibility. One of the few commercial systems that can schedule parallel loops automatically is the Alliant FX/8 multiprocessor. The machine consists of a set of computational processors each with pipelined arithmetic units. Thus, parallel loops with vector statements can fully utilize the concurrency features of this system. Different iterations of parallel loops are assigned to different processors. Below we show why this scheme is inefficient. Again up to two levels of parallelism can be utilized by the Alliant FX/8. On future systems with large numbers of processors, it will be necessary to exploit multidimensional parallelism, i.e., execute several nested loops concurrently.

A straightforward practice that has been widely discussed by users and system designers is exploiting the parallelism in DOALL loops by allocating successive iterations to successive processors. Depending on the implementation, this scheme can be anywhere from suboptimal to very inefficient. Thus, in a system with p processors it is common to execute a DOALL loop with $N > p$ iterations in the following way: iteration 1 is assigned to processor 1, iteration 2 to processor 2, $\cdots$, iteration p to processor p, iteration $p + 1$ to processor 1 and so on. Therefore, processor i will execute iterations $i, i + p, i + 2p, \cdots$. However, it is more efficient to make the assignment so that a block of successive iterations is allocated to the same processor. For example, in the above case it would be more wise to assign iterations $1, 2, \cdots, \lceil N/p \rceil$ to the first processor, iterations $\lceil N/p \rceil + 1, \lceil N/p \rceil + 2, \cdots, 2\lceil N/p \rceil$ to the second processor, and so on. Memory interleaving cannot be brought up as an argument against the latter approach since memory allocation can be done to best facilitate scheduling in either case.

There are several advantages that favor the second approach of assigning iterations to processors. When iterations of a parallel loop are assigned to processors by blocks of successive iterations, each processor does not have to check the value of the loop index each time it executes an iteration. Recall that the loop index is a shared variable and each processor must lock and unlock a semaphore in order to be granted access to it and get the next iteration. In case all processors finish simultaneously they will all access the loop index serially going through a time-consuming process. In the worst case, a time delay equivalent to the time required for N accesses to a shared variable will be added to at least one processor. If the assignment of blocks of iterations is performed instead, this worst case delay will be equivalent to only p accesses to the shared loop index. For a large N and a small p this will result in substantial savings, considering the fact that each access to the loop index will have to go through the processor-to-memory network. Note that the number of accesses to the loop index is independent of N in our case. Another advantage of this scheme is that when we execute FORALL loops in parallel, the block assignment can be done so that the cross-iteration dependences are contained within one block and the dependences are therefore satisfied by virtue of the assignment. Thus, synchronization needs to be used only selectively which, in certain cases, may result in shorter execution times. In what follows the second method is used, that is, whenever a parallel loop (excluding DOACR's) is executed on several processors, the allocation will be done so that each processor is assigned a block of successive iterations.

IV. SELF-SCHEDULING THROUGH IMPLICIT COALESCING

Most of the schemes that have been proposed so far [15], [28], implement self-scheduling by making extensive use of synchronization instructions. For example in [28] a barrier synchronization is associated with each loop in the construct. In addition all accesses to loop indexes are, by necessity, synchronized. Another common characteristic of these schemes is that they assign only one loop iteration to each incoming idle processor. Our scheme differs in all aspects discussed above. Only one barrier per serial loop is used. Furthermore, independently of the nest pattern and the number of loops involved we need synchronized access to only a single loop index. In contrast, the above schemes need synchronized access to a number of indexes which is equal to the number of loops in the construct.

Self-scheduling can become more effective by using loop coalescing [22]. The key characteristic of this transformation which is useful here, is its ability to express all indexes in a loop nest as a function of a single index. This makes it clear why synchronized access to each loop index is wasteful. We can always use a single index. If the loop bounds are known at run time just before we enter the loop, we may decide exactly how many iterations each processor will receive. Thus, when a processor accesses the single loop index to dispatch a range of consecutive iterations, it goes through a single synchronization point. Since the range of iterations is determined beforehand, each processor will dispatch all the work it is responsible for, the very first time it accesses the corresponding loop index. Therefore, only a total of p synchronization instructions will be executed. As a matter of comparison, in the schemes mentioned above, each processor executes a synchronization instruction for each loop in the nest, and each time it dispatches a new iteration. In a nested loop that consists of m separate loops we would then have a total of $m\Pi_{i=1}^{m} N_i$ synchronization instructions that will execute before the loop completes. The difference between p and $m\Pi_{i=1}^{m} N_i$ can obviously be tremendous. The schemes in [28] and [15] for example, involve an overhead which is unbounded on p. In the general case, however, where loops contain conditional statements, the assignment of $\lceil N/p \rceil$ iterations to each processor will compromise load balancing. Therefore, we

need something in between which will involve less overhead than self-scheduling, but it will also achieve load balancing.

A. The Guided Self-Scheduling (GSS(k)) Algorithm

In this section we present a simple, yet powerful algorithm for dynamic scheduling. The idea is to implement *guided self-scheduling* with bound k (GSS(k)), by "guiding" the processors on the amount of work they choose. The *bound* is defined to be the minimum number of loop iterations assigned to a given processor by GSS. The algorithm is discussed below in great detail and is summarized for $k = 1$ in Fig. 3. First we present the case of $k = 1$, GSS(1) or GSS for short, and later we discuss the general case for $k > 1$. The GSS algorithm achieves optimal execution times in many cases. Actually optimality is achieved in two dimensions. First, assuming that synchronization overhead is counted as part of a loop's execution time, GSS obtains optimal load balancing between processors and thus optimal execution time. At the same time GSS uses the minimum number of synchronization instructions that are needed to guarantee optimal load balancing.

1) Implicit Loop Coalescing and Interchange: Let us describe in more detail how self-scheduling through implicit loop coalescing works. First, assume that we have a perfectly (one-way) nested loop $L = (N_1, \cdots, N_m)$. Loop coalescing coalesces all m loops into a single loop $L' = (N = \Pi_{i=1}^{m} N_i)$ through a set of transformations f_i that map the index I of the coalesced loop L' to the indexes I_i, $(i = 1, 2, \cdots, m)$ of the original loop L such that $I_i = f_i(I)$, $(i = 1, 2, \cdots, m)$. This transformation is needed to express indexes of array subscripts, (that occur in the original loop body) as functions of the index I of the coalesced loop. This index transformation is universal, i.e., it is the same for all loops, perfectly nested or not and it is given by

$$I_k = f_k(I) = \left\lceil \frac{I}{\prod_{i=m}^{k-1} N_i} \right\rceil - N_k \left\lfloor \frac{I-1}{\prod_{i=m}^{k} N_i} \right\rfloor,$$

$$(k = 1, 2, \cdots, m). \quad (1)$$

Thus, a reference to an array element of the form $A(I_1, I_2, \cdots, I_m)$ in L can be uniquely expressed as $A(f_1(I), f_2(I), \cdots, f_m(I))$ in L' using the above transformation. (The introduction of complicated index expressions does not pose any performance "threat" since they are computed only once per processor or, in a different implementation, they may be completely ignored [21].) Therefore, each processor can compute locally f_i for a given I. Better yet, each processor can compute locally a range of values $f(x:y)$ for a range of $x \leq I \leq y$. The global index I is then kept in global memory as a shared variable. Each processor accesses I in a synchronized way and dispatches the next set of consecutive iterations of L along with a pointer to its code. Then inside each processor, mappings f_i as defined by (1) are used to compute the corresponding range for each index I_i of the original loop. After the index ranges are computed for each processor, execution proceeds in the normal mode. In case all loops in L are parallel and in the absence of conditional statements, no

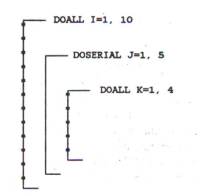

Fig. 1. Example loop for the application of GSS.

processor will ever go back to dispatch another range of iterations of I. This is obviously the minimum possible amount of synchronization that is needed with any self-scheduling scheme.

The process is more complicated with self-scheduling of hybrid loops. Let us look at the case of hybrid loops that consist of DOALL's and DOSERIAL loops, and in particular consider the example of Fig. 1. In this example the innermost and outermost loops are DOALL's and the second is a serial loop. Let us denote this loop with $L = (N_1, N_2, N_3) = (10, 5, 4)$. We have a total of $N = 200$ iterations. On a machine with an unlimited number of processors (200 in this case) each processor would execute five iterations of L, and this is the best possible that we can achieve. On a system with p processors, self-scheduling should be done such that iterations of L are evenly distributed among the p processors (assuming an equal execution time for all iterations). The presence of the serial loop in L, however, limits our ability to do this. It is noteworthy that the approach of assigning consecutive iterations of I to each processor would fail here. (This is true because after coalescing we have a single iteration space and assignments are done in blocks of consecutive iterations.) At most four successive iterations may be assigned at once. If all four are given to the same processor, the loop is executed serially. If each processor receives one iteration on the other hand, we can use only up to four processors.

This problem can be eliminated by permuting the indexes of the original loop, or equivalently, by applying implicit loop interchange [29]. Our goal is to permute the indexes so that the longest possible set of parallel iterations corresponds to successive values of the index I of L'. This can be done by permuting the indexes I and J so that the serial loop becomes the outermost loop or by permuting J and K so that the serial becomes the innermost loop. In general a serial loop can be interchanged with any DOALL that surrounds it, but it cannot be interchanged with a loop surrounded by it. Therefore, in the case of our example, we implicitly interchange loops I and J.

The interchange can be implemented trivially using implicit coalescing as follows. The mappings of I and J are permuted such that I is defined by the mapping of J and vice versa. No physical loop interchange takes place (neither physical coalescing). More specifically, if I_c is the global index of the coalesced loop for the example loop of Fig. 1, then the original indexes I, J, and K are mapped to I_c by (1) as follows.

$$I = \left\lceil \frac{I_c}{20} \right\rceil - 10 \left\lfloor \frac{I_c - 1}{200} \right\rfloor$$

$$J = \left\lceil \frac{I_c}{4} \right\rceil - 5 \left\lfloor \frac{I_c - 1}{20} \right\rfloor$$

$$K = I_c - 4 \left\lfloor \frac{I_c - 1}{4} \right\rfloor .$$

After implicit loop interchange, the mappings become

$$I = \left\lceil \frac{I_c}{4} \right\rceil - 10 \left\lfloor \frac{I_c - 1}{40} \right\rfloor$$

$$J = \left\lceil \frac{I_c}{40} \right\rceil - 5 \left\lfloor \frac{I_c - 1}{200} \right\rfloor$$

$$K = I_c - \left\lfloor \frac{I_c - 1}{4} \right\rfloor .$$

The result is that the first 40 successive values of I_c correspond now to 40 parallel iterations (instead of four iterations as previously). Therefore, up to 40 processors can be used in parallel. Extra synchronization is still needed, however. Each serial loop in L needs a barrier synchronization to enforce its seriality. The following proposition tells us when it is legal to apply loop interchange in order to maximize the number of consecutive parallel iterations.

Proposition 1: In a hybrid perfectly nested loop, any DOALL can be interchanged with any serial or DOACR loop that is in a deeper nest level. This loop interchange can be applied repeatedly and independently for any pair of (DOALL, DOSERIAL/DOACR) loops.

Proof: The proof is clear for the case of two loops. The general case follows by induction on the number of loops interchanged. ∎

The only case that remains to be discussed is nonperfectly (multiway) nested loops. This is identical to the one-way nested loop case, unless one of the following two conditions is met. 1) Loops at the same nest level have different loop bounds. 2) High-level spreading is to be applied to loops at the same nest level (i.e., loops at the same nest level are executed in parallel). In the first case, if k loops $N_{i+1}, N_{i+2}, \cdots, N_{i+k}$ happen to be at the ith nest level, the global index I_c is computed with N_i iterations for the ith level, which is given by

$$N_i = \max_{1 \le j \le k} \{N_{i+j}\}.$$

Then during execution, loop N_{i+j} at the ith level will have $N_i - N_{i+j}$ null iterations (which are not actually computed). Therefore, some of the processors execute only part of the code at level i. This corresponds to computing slices of each loop on the same processor. Thus, slices of the two loops corresponding to the same index values will be assigned to each idle processor. In general, if loops at the same nest level are independent or involve dependencies in only one direction, outer loops can be distributed [13] around them and each loop is considered separately (i.e., we coalesce each of them and consider them as separate tasks). When there are bidirectional dependences across loops at the same nest level, barrier synchronization can be used as mentioned above. If high-level spreading is to be applied, then implicit loop coalescing and a global index I_c will be computed for each loop that is spread.

2) The Scheduling Algorithm: So far we have seen how GSS coalesces the loops and assigns blocks of iterations to incoming (idle) processors. We have not mentioned, however, how the algorithm decides the number of iterations to be assigned to each idle processor. The schemes that have been proposed so far [2], [15], [26], [28] assign a single iteration at a time. For nested loops with many iterations, this approach involves a tremendous amount of overhead since several critical regions must be accessed each time a single iteration is dispatched. The GSS algorithm follows another approach by assigning several iterations (or an *iteration block*) to each processor. The size of each block varies and is determined by using a simple but powerful rule that is described below. Before we describe how block sizes are computed let us state our constraints.

Suppose that a parallel loop L (e.g., a DOALL) is to be executed on p processors. We assume that each of the p processors starts executing some iteration(s) of L at different times (i.e., not all p processors start computing L simultaneously). This is clearly a valid and practical assumption. If L, for example, is not the first loop in the program, the processors will be busy executing other parts of the program before they start on L. Therefore, in general, they will start executing L at different times which may vary significantly. (Of course one could force all p processors to start on L at the same time by enforcing a join (or barrier) operation before L; this would clearly be very inefficient.) Given now the assumption that the p processors will start executing L at arbitrary times, our goal is to dispatch a block of consecutive iterations of L to each incoming processor such that all processors terminate at approximately the same time. This is a very desirable property. If L_d, for example, is nested inside a serial loop L_s, then a barrier synchronization must be performed each time L_d completes (i.e., for each iteration of L_s). If the processors working on L_d do not terminate at the same time, a very significant amount of idle processor time (overhead) may be accumulated by the time L_s completes.

In general the best possible solution is that which guarantees that all p processors will terminate with at most B units of time difference from each other; where B is the execution time of the loop body of L. This goal can be achieved if blocks of iterations are assigned to idle processors following the next principle. An incoming processor p_i^x will dispatch a number of iterations x_i considering that the remaining $p - 1$ processors will also be scheduled at this (same) time. In other words p_i^x should leave enough iterations to keep the remaining $p - 1$ processors busy (in case they all decide to start simultaneously) while it will be executing its x_i iterations. If N is the total number of iterations, this can be easily done as follows. Since GSS coalesces loops, there will be a single index $I_c = 1$ $\cdots$ N, from which idle processors will dispatch blocks of

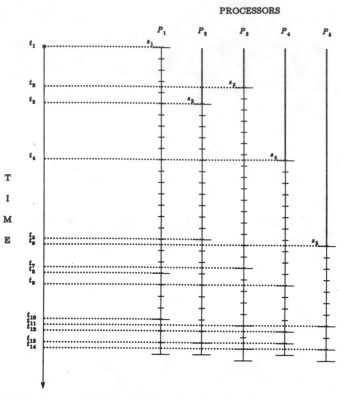

Fig. 2. An example of the application of the GSS algorithm for $N = 100$, $p = 5$.

iterations. Therefore, the assignment of iteration blocks is done by having each idle processor p_i perform the following operations:

$$x_i = \left\lceil \frac{R_i}{p} \right\rceil ; \qquad R_{i+1} \leftarrow R_i - x_i, \qquad (2)$$

and the range of iterations assigned to the ith processor is given by $[N - R_i + 1, \cdots, N - R_i + x_i]$, where $R_1 = N$. The detailed algorithm is described in Fig. 3.

As an example, consider the case of a DOALL L with $N = 100$ iterations that executes on five processors. All five processors start on L at different times. Each idle processor is assigned a block of consecutive iterations using the rule described above. The resulting execution profile is shown in Fig. 2. Even though the results presented in this section hold for the general case where different iterations of the same loop have different execution times, for this example we assume that all 100 iterations have equal execution times. Each vertical line segment in Fig. 2 represents the execution time of a loop iteration. The thick lines represent the execution of previous (unrelated to L) tasks on processors P_2, P_3, P_4, and P_5. The wider horizontal line segments mark the time when iteration blocks are actually dispatched by idle processors. For example, at time t_1 processor P_1 dispatches $\lceil 100/5 \rceil = 20$ iterations. The next processor to become available is P_3 which at time t_2 dispatches $\lceil (100 - 20)/5 \rceil = 16$ iterations. Processor P_1 will receive its next assignment at time t_8. The detailed assignment of iterations to processors for this example is shown in Table I. The events in the table are ordered by

Input An arbitrarily nested loop L, and p processors.

Output The optimal dynamic schedule of L on the p processors. The schedule is reproducible if the execution time of the loop bodies and the initial processor configuration (of the p processors) are known.

- Distribute the loops in L wherever possible.

- For each ordered pair of (DOALL, DOSERIAL/DOACR) loops, (where the DOALL is the outer loop) perform loop interchange.

- Apply implicit loop coalescing, and let I_c be the index of the coalesced iteration space.

- For each index i_h of the original loop define the index mapping as in (1),

$$i_h = f_{i_h}(I_c)$$

- If R_i is the number of remaining iterations at step i, then set $R_1 = N$, $i=1$, and for each idle processor do.

REPEAT

- Each idle processor (scheduled at step i) receives

$$z_i = \left\lceil \frac{R_i}{p} \right\rceil$$

iterations.

- $R_{i+1} = R_i - z_i$

- The range of the global index is $I_c \in [N-R_i+1,\dots, N-R_i+z_i] \equiv [l_i, \dots, u_i]$

- The range of each original loop index for that processor is given by

$$i_h \in [f_{i_h}(l_i),\dots, f_{i_h}(u_i)]$$

- $i = i + 1$

UNTIL $(R_i = 0)$

Fig. 3. The GSS algorithm.

TABLE I
THE DETAILED SCHEDULING EVENTS OF THE EXAMPLE OF FIG. 2
ORDERED BY TIME

Time	No. of unused iterations (I)	Next processor to be scheduled	No. of iterations assigned to this processor
t_1	100	P_1	20
t_2	80	P_3	16
t_3	64	P_2	13
t_4	51	P_4	11
t_5	40	P_2	8
t_6	32	P_5	7
t_7	25	P_3	5
t_8	20	P_1	4
t_9	16	P_4	4
t_{10}	12	P_1	3
t_{11}	9	P_3	2
t_{12}	7	P_5	2
t_{13}	5	P_4	1
t_{14}	4	P_4	1
t_{15}	3	P_2	1
t_{16}	2	P_3	1
t_{17}	1	P_3	1
		TOTAL= 100	

virtual time. From Fig. 2 we observe that although the five processors start executing L at different times, they all terminate within B units of time difference from each other. In general if p processors are assigned to a DOALL with N iterations using the above scheme, we have the following.

Lemma 1: Each of the *last $p - 1$* processors to be scheduled under the GSS algorithm is assigned exactly one iteration of L. These $p - 1$ processors are not necessarily physically distinct.

Proof: First we will show that there exists an i such that

R_i [as defined by (2)] is

$$R_i = p+1 \quad \text{or} \quad R_i = p \qquad (3)$$

where p is the number of processors. Suppose that such an i does not exist. Then there exists an i for which

$$R_i \geq p+2 \quad \text{and} \quad R_{i+1} \leq p-1.$$

But $R_{i+1} = R_i - \lceil R_i/p \rceil$ by definition. Thus, $\lceil R_i/p \rceil = R_i - R_{i+1} \geq p + 2 - (p - 1) = 3$, hence $R_i > 2p$.

Let $R_i = kp + r$ where $k \geq 2$ and $r > 1$. But $R_{i+1} = R_i - \lceil R_i/p \rceil < p$, or $kp + r - (k + 1) < p$, and since $r > 1$, $(k - 1)p - k < 0$ or finally $p < k/(k - 1)$. But since $k \geq 2$, it follows that $p < 2$ which contradicts the initial hypothesis that $p > 1$. Hence, (3) is true.

From (2) and (3) it follows directly that at least the last $p - 1$ and at most the last p assignments will involve iteration blocks of size 1. ∎

Theorem 1: Independently of the initial configuration (startup time) of the p processors that are scheduled under GSS, all processors finish executing L within B units of time difference from each other.

Proof: We will prove the theorem for the case where all p processors start executing L simultaneously. The proof for the general case is similar. By Lemma 1, at least the last $p - 1$, and at most the last p assignments will involve single iterations. Let us consider the latter case. The are two possible scenarios during the scheduling of L under GSS. In the first case each of the last p iterations is assigned to a different processor. Then by virtue of GSS it is easy to see that if t_i, t_j are the termination times for processors p_i, p_j, $i, j \in [1 \cdots p]$, respectively, we have $|t_i - t_j| < B$.

The second case is when the last p iterations of L are assigned to at most $p - 1$ different processors. Let p_i^x denote a processor whose last assignment was an iteration block of size x, and p_j^1 denote a processor that is assigned one or more of the last p iterations. Let t_i^x and t_j^1 be their corresponding completion times. Using the same argument as above we can show that all processors that received one of the last p iterations finish within B units of time apart from each other. It remains to show that any p_i^x and any p_j^1 terminate within B units of time from each other. We consider the case for $x = 2$. The general case is similar. We will prove that for any p_i^x and any p_j^1, $|t_i^x - t_j^1| \le B$.

Case 1: $t_i^x > t_j^1$, and suppose that $t_i^x - t_j^1 > B$ or equivalently, $t_i^x - 2B > t_j^1 - B$. The last inequality implies that p_j^1 was assigned a single iteration before the iteration block of size $x = 2$ was assigned to p_i^x. Clearly this contradicts the basic steps of the GSS algorithm. Therefore $t_i^x - t_j^1 \le B$.

Case 2: $t_i^x < t_j^1$ and suppose $t_j^1 - t_i^x > B$ or, $t_j^1 - B > t_i^x$ but the last inequality can never be true since p_i^x would have been assigned the last iteration instead of p_j^1. Therefore, $t_j^1 - t_i^x \le B$ and thus the statement of the theorem is true.

Note that if the p processors start executing L at different times $s_1 \le s_2 \le \cdots \le s_p$, the theorem still holds true under the following condition:

$$N > \frac{1}{B} \sum_{i=1}^{p} (s_p - s_i). \qquad \blacksquare$$

In reality B varies for different iterations (due to the presence of conditional statements) and $B \in \{b_1, b_2, \cdots, b_k\}$, where b_i, $(i = 1, \cdots, k)$ are all possible values of B. Suppose that B can assume any of its possible values with the same probability, i.e., $P[B = b_i] = 1/k$, $(i = 1, 2, \cdots, k)$. Then Lemma 1 and Theorem 1 are still valid. Of course a uniform distribution is not always a valid assumption. For example, in numerical software we often have exit IF's inside loops that test for some error condition. The loop is exited if the error condition arises. In such cases we can safely ignore the conditional statements. If the user or the compiler cannot make any assertion about the distribution of true/false branches, other heuristic tunnings can be used in GSS. For example, if we know that the probability of clustered true (false) branches (of a conditional statement inside a loop) is high, then we can make p artificially large to decrease the size of the iteration blocks assigned to each processor by GSS. Even though simulation results show that even in such cases GSS is still superior to self-scheduling, we can no longer prove that GSS is optimal. Under the above assumptions we also have the following.

Theorem 2: If iterations have constant execution time, the GSS algorithm obtains an optimal schedule under any initial processor configuration. GSS also uses the minimum possible number of synchronization points necessary to achieve optimal load balancing.

By synchronization points we mean the number of times processors enter critical regions (i.e., loop indexing). An implementation of GSS can be done so that when q (out of the p) processors become simultaneously available at step i, the first $q - 1$ receive $\lceil R_i/p \rceil$ iterations and the qth processor receives min $(\lceil (R_i - (q - 1)\lceil R_i/p \rceil)/p \rceil, \lceil R_i/p \rceil)$ iterations, where R_i is the number of unassigned iterations at the ith step of GSS. In general, when GSS is applied using (2) the number of synchronized accesses to loop indexes is given by the following theorem.

Theorem 3: The number of synchronization points required by GSS is p in the best case, and $O(pH_{\lceil N/p \rceil})$ in the worst case, where H_n denotes the nth harmonic number and $H_n \approx \ln (n) + \gamma + 1/2n$ (γ is Euler's constant).

Proof: The best case is obvious from the above discussion. In general it is clear that the number of iterations assigned to each processor will be (possibly multiple) occurrences of (some of) the integers

$$\left\lceil \frac{N}{p} \right\rceil, \left\lceil \frac{N}{p} \right\rceil - 1, \left\lceil \frac{N}{p} \right\rceil - 2, \cdots, 1$$

in this order. Obviously there will be at least $p - 1$ and at most p assignments of exactly one iteration. It can be also observed that the number of different assignments of iteration blocks of size $\lceil N/p \rceil - k$, $(k = 1, 2, \cdots, \lceil N/p \rceil - 2)$ depend on the relative values of p and $\lceil N/p \rceil - k$. More precisely, we can have at most

$$\left\lceil \frac{p}{\lceil N/p \rceil - k} \right\rceil, \qquad (k = 1, 2, \cdots, \lceil N/p \rceil - 2)$$

different assignments of iteration blocks of size $\lceil N/p \rceil - k$. Therefore, the total number of different assignments and thus the total number σ of synchronization points in the worst case is given by

$$\sigma \le p + \sum_{i=2}^{\lceil N/p \rceil} \left\lceil \frac{p}{i} \right\rceil = \sum_{i=1}^{\lceil N/p \rceil} \left\lceil \frac{p}{i} \right\rceil .$$

For computing the order of magnitude we can ignore the ceiling and finally have

$$\sigma \approx \sum_{i=1}^{\lceil N/p \rceil} \frac{p}{i} = p \sum_{i=1}^{\lceil N/p \rceil} \frac{1}{i} = pH_{\lceil N/p \rceil}$$

Therefore, the number of synchronization points in the worst case is $\sigma = O(pH_{\lceil N/p \rceil})$. $\blacksquare$

Thus, GSS goes through $O(p \ln (N/p))$ synchronization points in the worst case compared to $O(mN)$ synchronization points used by the schemes in [15] and [28]. Note that if barriers are used, GSS can coalesce all loops, serial and parallel. Consider for example a DOALL loop with $\Pi_{i=1}^{m} N_i$ iterations which is the result of coalescing m DOALL's. Suppose now that this DOALL is nested inside a serial loop with M iterations. GSS works fine on this doubly nested loop but it still must access two shared variables (loop indexes) for each assignment. The other alternative is to implicitly coalesce the serial and parallel loops into a single *block-parallel* loop or BDOALL with MN iterations. To do this a barrier synchronization must be executed every N iterations. If $I_c = 1 \cdots MN$, the number of remaining iterations R_i [in (2)] still assumes an initial value N. The difference here is that each time ($I_c \bmod N = 0$) a barrier synchronization is executed and R is reinitialized to N. This happens M times before the entire loop completes execution.

It should be noted that since GSS is a dynamic scheme the assumption that loop bounds are known is a realistic one. The index bounds of DO loops must be known just before we enter the loop.

B. Further Reduction of Synchronization Operations

Another interesting feature of the GSS algorithm is that it can be tuned to further reduce the number of synchronization operations that are required during scheduling. As mentioned above, the last $p - 1$ allocations performed by GSS assigned exactly one iteration to each processor. The synchronization overhead involved in these $p - 1$ allocations may still be very high, especially when p is very large and the loop body is small.

We shall see now how to eliminate the last $p - 1$ assignments of single iterations of GSS. In fact we can eliminate all assignments of iteration blocks of size k ($< \lceil N/p \rceil$) or less. Let us discuss first the problem of eliminating assignments of single iterations from GSS. We show how this can be done by means of an example. Consider the application of GSS to a DOALL with $N = 14$ iterations on $p = 4$ processors. The assignment of iterations to processors [using (2)] is shown below in detail.

$$\lceil 14/4 \rceil = 4, \; \lceil 10/4 \rceil = 3, \; \lceil 7/4 \rceil = 2, \; \lceil 5/4 \rceil = 2,$$
$$\lceil 3/4 \rceil = 1, \; \lceil 2/4 \rceil = 1, \; \lceil 1/4 \rceil = 1.$$

The seven successive assignments were done with iteration blocks of size 4, 3, 2, 2, 1, 1, 1. In this case the single iteration assignments account for almost half of the total assignments. We can eliminate the single iteration assignments by increasing the block size of the first $p - 1$ assignments by 1. The successive assignments in that case would be 5, 4, 3, and 2. Therefore, the total number of scheduling decisions (and thus synchronization operations) is reduced by $p - 1$. This reduction can be performed automatically by setting $R_1 = N + p$ in (2). Thus, the first assignment will dispatch $x_1 = \lceil (N + p)/p \rceil$ iterations. Otherwise, GSS is applied in precisely the same way. However, now it terminates not when the iterations are exhausted, but when for some i, $x_i < 2$. For the above example the application of GSS will generate the following assignments ($R_1 = \lceil (N + p)/p \rceil$).

$$\lceil 18/4 \rceil = 5, \; \lceil 13/4 \rceil = 4, \; \lceil 9/4 \rceil = 3, \; \lceil 6/4 \rceil = 2.$$

When the ratio N/p is rather small, GSS(k) for $k = 2$ may result in considerable savings. There is still a drawback, however, since the rule of making all the assignments of iteration blocks of size two or more is now always accurate. Consider again the previous example but now let $N = 15$. The assignments generated by GSS(2) will now be

$$\lceil 19/4 \rceil = 5, \; \lceil 14/4 \rceil = 4, \; \lceil 10/4 \rceil = 3, \; \lceil 7/4 \rceil = 2, \; \lceil 5/4 \rceil = 2.$$

But $5 + 4 + 3 + 2 + 2 = 16 > N = 15$, i.e., the number of iterations assigned by GSS(2) is more than the iterations of the loop. Fortunately the number of superfluous iterations in such cases cannot be more than one, and the termination problem can be easily corrected. The solution is given by the following theorem.

Theorem 4: Let k be the step in (2) such that $x_k = 2$ and $x_{k+1} = 1$. If $R_{k+1} = p$ then

$$\sum_{i=1}^{k} x_i = N$$

else, if $R_{k+1} = p - 1$ then

$$1 + \sum_{i=1}^{k-1} x_i = N.$$

Proof: The algorithm starts with a total of $N + p$ iterations, and it must assign a total of N iterations in blocks of size ranging from $\lceil (N + p)/p \rceil$ to 2. Since (for $p \geq 2$) at least one iteration block will be of size 2, and all assignments of iteration blocks of size 2 must be performed, it follows that the last assignment of GSS(2) will involve $R_k = p + 1$ or $R_k = p + 2$. In the latter case the last assignment will dispatch two iterations and the algorithm will terminate assigning, therefore, a total of $N + p - R_{k+1} = N$ iterations. If $R_k = p + 1$, the last assignment will also dispatch two iterations. In that case, however, the total number of iterations assigned will be $N + p - (p - 1) = N + 1$. Thus, $1 + \Sigma_{i=1}^{k-1} x_i = N$. ∎

Theorem 4 supplies the test for detecting and correcting superfluous assignments. The assignment and termination condition for GSS(2) is now given by

$$x_i = \left\lceil \frac{R_i}{p} \right\rceil ; \; R_{i+1} \leftarrow R_i - x_i$$

$$\text{if } (R_{i+1} \leq p) \text{ then}$$
$$\{ \text{stop};$$
$$\text{if } (R_{i+1} < p) \text{ then } x_i = 1 \}. \tag{4}$$

Using (4) now, the last assignment of GSS(2) for the last example will dispatch a single iteration. The same process can be applied to derive GSS(k) for any $2 < k < \lceil N/p \rceil$. The best value of k is machine and application dependent.

It should be emphasized that the GSS scheme can be implemented in hardware, it can be incorporated in the compiler, or it can be explicitly coded by the programmer. In the latter case the programmer may compute the iteration block size for each assignment, and force the assignment of such blocks by coding the corresponding loop appropriately. Consider for example the loop of Fig. 4(a). If array B holds the block size and S holds the starting iteration for each assignment, the loop of Fig. 4(a) can be coded as in Fig. 4(b).

```
        DOALL 1 I = 1, N
              . . .
              . . .
              . . .
        ENDOALL
                    (a)


        DOALL 1 I = 1, K
            DOSERIAL 2 J = S(I), S(I)+B(I)
                  . . .
                  . . .
                  . . .
                ENDOSERIAL
        ENDOALL
                    (b)
```

Fig. 4. Example of the application of GSS at the program level.

Assuming that self-scheduling (SS) is implemented in the target machine, the above loop will be executed as if GSS was supported by the machine (with some additional overhead involved with the manipulation of the bookkeeping arrays).

V. Simulation Results

A simulator was implemented to study the performance of self-scheduling (SS) and GSS (GSS(1)). In the SS scheme, loop scheduling was done by assigning a single iteration to each idle processor [2], [6], [28]. Idle processors access each loop index in a loop nest by using appropriate synchronization instructions. The simulator was designed to accept program traces generated by Parafrase, and it can be extended easily to implement other scheduling strategies. The experiments conducted for this work, however, used four representative loops which are shown in Fig. 5.

A. The Simulator

The simulator input consists of a set of tuples, where each tuple represents a single loop or a block of straight-line code [1]. Each tuple includes information such as number of iterations, execution time of basic blocks inside the loop, branching frequencies for the branches of each conditional statement inside a loop, dependence information, type of loop, etc. In the presence of conditional statements the conditions are "evaluated" separately for each iteration of the loop and the appropriate branch is selected. The user supplies the expected frequency with which each branch is selected. Otherwise, the simulator considers each branch equally probable. For this purpose a random number generator is used with a period of $2^{31} - 1$ [14]. Random numbers are generated using a uniform distribution and are normalized (in $[0 \cdots 1]$). For each conditional statement in the loop, the interval $[0 \cdots 1]$ is partitioned into a number of subintervals equal to the number of counted paths in that statement. The size of each subinterval is proportional to the expected frequency of that branch. For each iteration of the loop, a random number is generated and the subinterval to which it belongs is determined. Then the branch corresponding to that subinterval is taken.

The execution of arbitrary loops on multiprocessor systems with 2–4096 processors can be simulated. Processors can start on a loop at random times. The simulator also takes into

```
              DOALL 1 I1 = 1, 100
                 DOALL 2 I2 = 1, 50
                    DOALL 3 I3 = 1, 4
 L1:                   {20}
                       [if C then {10}]
                 ENDOALL
              ENDOALL
           ENDOALL
                    (a)


           DOALL 1 I1 = 1, 50
              {5}
              [if C then {10}]
              DOALL 2 I2 = 1, 40
                 {5}
                 DOALL 3 I3 = 1, 4
                    {10}
 L2:                [if C then {20}]
                 ENDOALL
              ENDOALL
           ENDOALL
                    (b)


           DOSERIAL 1 I1 = 1, 40
              DOALL 2 I2 = 1, 500
 L3:             {100}
                 [if C then {50}]
              ENDOALL
           ENDOSERIAL
                    (c)


           DOSERIAL 1 I1 = 1, 50

              DOALL 2 I2 = 1, 10
                 DOALL 3 I3 = 1, 10
                    DOALL 4 I4 = 1, 4
                       {10}
                       [if C then {50}]
                    ENDOALL
                 ENDOALL
              ENDOALL

                       |
                       v

              DOALL 5 I5 = 1, 100
 L4:             {50}
                 DOALL 6 I6 = 1, 5
                    {100}
                    [if C then {30}]
                 ENDOALL
              ENDOALL

                       |
                       v

              DOALL 7 I7 = 1, 20
                 DOALL 8 I8 = 1, 4
                    {30}
                 ENDOALL
              ENDOALL

           ENDOSERIAL
                    (d)
```

Fig. 5. Loops $L1$, $L2$, $L3$, and $L4$ used for the experiments.

account overhead incurred with operations on shared variables. For our purposes shared variables are considered to be only loop indexes. Although the current version of the simulator assumes a fixed memory access time, it can be easily extended to take into account random delays (due to network contention in shared memory systems). For each memory access, a random delay may be computed to fall within given upper and lower bounds. These bounds may be readjusted each time the number of processors (and thus the number of stages of the network) grows.

B. Experiments

The four loops $L1$, $L2$, $L3$, and $L4$ of Fig. 5 were used to conduct the experiments for this work. These loops are representative of those found in production numerical software. Serial and parallel loops are specified by the programmer, or are created by a restructuring compiler (e.g., Parafrase). The loops of Fig. 5 cover most cases since they include loops that are 1) all parallel and perfectly nested ($L1$), 2) hybrid and perfectly nested ($L3$), 3) all parallel and nonperfectly nested ($L2$), 4) hybrid nonperfectly nested ($L4$), 5) and finally one-way ($L2$), and multiway nested ($L4$). The arrows in $L4$ indicate flow dependences between adjacent loops. The numbers enclosed in brackets give the execution times of straight-line code in the corresponding positions.

Two sets of experiments were conducted, E_1 and E_2. The first set used the four loops of Fig. 5 ignoring the conditional statements which are enclosed in square brackets. Therefore, for E_1 all iterations of a particular loop had equal execution times. For E_2 the conditional statements were taken into account as well. Thus, in E_2 different iterations of a given loop had different execution times. The next step will be to consider loops with multiple and nested conditionals which were not included in these experiments.

Earlier in this paper we discussed the various types of overhead that are incurred during dynamic scheduling. One type of overhead is the time spent accessing and operating on a shared variable; in our case loop indexes. This time is not constant in practice and it depends on several factors such as network traffic, number of simultaneous requests for a particular index, and so on. For our experiments we chose this overhead to be constant and independent of the loop size or the number of processors. Since the purpose of our experiments is to study the relative (rather than the absolute) performance of GSS(1) and SS, the above assumption is not very restricting. For each scheduling decision the overhead is assumed to be a constant which represents, for instance, the number of clock cycles spent operating on a shared variable. Let o denote the overhead constant. We conducted the simulations for a best case (o_b), and a "worst" case (o_w) overhead. For the best case $o_b = 2$ since at least two clock cycles are needed to operate on a shared variable. For the worst case we chose $o_w = 10$. The value of 10 was chosen arbitrarily. In real parallel processor machines o_b and o_w can be much greater, but we are more interested in the difference $o_b - o_w$ rather than in their absolute values. E_1^b and E_1^w denote the set of experiments that ignored IF statements for $o_b = 2$ and $o_w = 10$, respectively. Similarly, E_2^b and E_2^w denote the set of experiments using $L1$, $L2$, $L3$, and $L4$ with IF statements, for $o_b = 2$ and $o_w = 10$, respectively.

The plots of Figs. 6 and 7 show the speedup of the four loops $L1$–$L4$ of Fig. 5, for different numbers of processors, for the experiment E_1 (E_1^b and E_1^w). There are four curves in each plot. Solid lines plot the speedup curves for GSS(1), and dashed lines plot the speedup curves for SS. More specifically the plot of Fig. 6(a) corresponds to loop $L1$. The upper and lower solid lines are the speedup curves resulting from the schedule of $L1$ under GSS(1) and for $o_b = 2$, $o_w = 10$, respectively. The upper and lower dashed lines are the

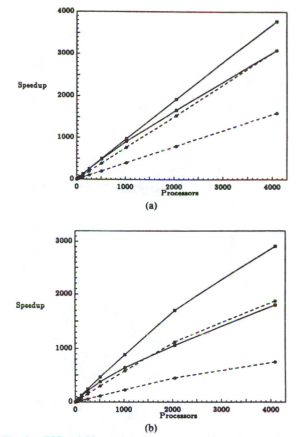

(a)

(b)

Fig. 6. GSS and SS speedups for (a) $L1$, and (b) $L2$ without IF's.

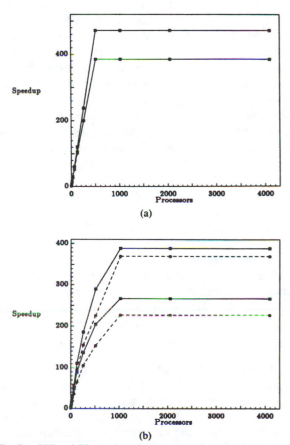

(a)

(b)

Fig. 7. GSS and SS speedups for (a) $L3$, and (b) $L4$ without IF's.

247

(a)

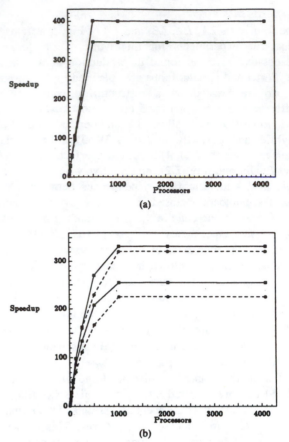

(a)

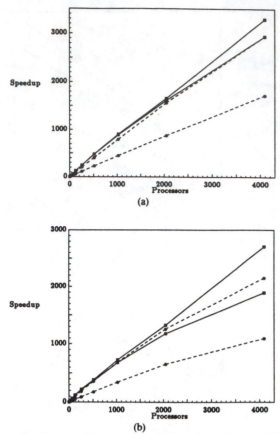

(b)

Fig. 8. GSS and SS speedups for (a) $L1$, and (b) $L2$ with IF's.

Fig. 9. GSS and SS speedups for (a) $L3$, and (b) $L4$ with IF's.

speedup curves of $L1$ under SS for $o_b = 2$, and $o_w = 10$. The plot of Fig. 6(b) shows the performance of GSS(1) and SS for $L2$ in E_1. Similarly Fig. 7(a) and (b) corresponds to $L3$ and $L4$ for E_1. In all plots, the upper solid and dashed lines correspond to GSS(1) and SS for $o_b = 2$, respectively. The lower solid and dashed lines correspond to GSS(1) and SS for $o_w = 10$.

In the same way Figs. 8 and 9 correspond to $L1$, $L2$, and $L3$, $L4$ respectively, for the E_2 experiments, i.e., with the IF statements taken into account. Therefore, in each plot we can see the relative performance of GSS(1), $o_b = 2$ versus GSS(1), $o_w = 10$; SS, $o_b = 2$ versus SS, $o_w = 10$; GSS(1), $o_b = 2$ versus SS, $o_b = 2$; and GSS(1) $o_w = 10$ versus SS, $o_w = 10$, for E_1 and E_2.

Except in the case of $L3$ where both GSS(1) and SS perform almost identically, we observe that in all other cases GSS(1) is better than SS by almost a factor of two in E_1 and E_2. In $L3$ for $p \geq 500$ we have the case of unlimited processors where each processor is assigned one iteration by both schemes. It is also clear from the plots that the difference in performance between GSS(1) and SS grows as the overhead grows. As it should be expected GSS(1) is less sensitive to scheduling overhead than SS.

The plots in Figs. 10, 11, 12, and 13 correspond to Figs. 6, 7, 8, and 9, respectively, and illustrate the speedup ratio GSS(1)/SS for each case for E_1 and E_2. The horizontal axis shows the log of the number of processors. In each plot there are two curves. The upper curve plots the speedup ratio GSS/SS for $o_b = 10$. The lower curve plots the same ratio for $o_w =$

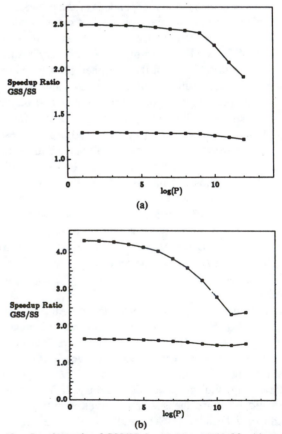

Fig. 10. Speedup ratio of GSS/SS for (a) $L1$, and (b) $L2$ without IF's.

248

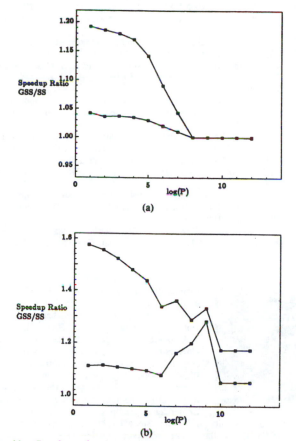

Fig. 11. Speedup ratio of GSS/SS for (a) $L3$, and (b) $L4$ without IF's.

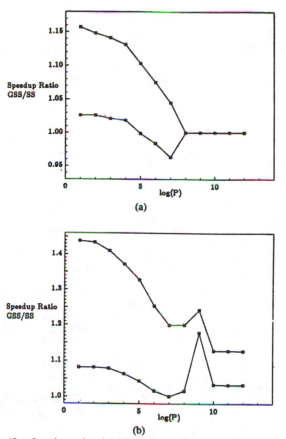

Fig. 13. Speedup ratio of GSS/SS for (a) $L3$, and (b) $L4$ with IF's.

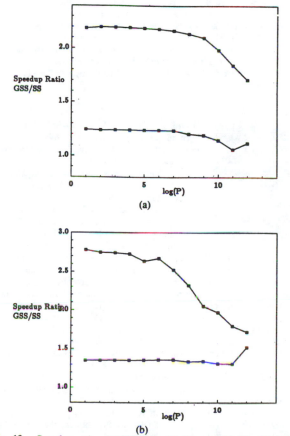

Fig. 12. Speedup ratio of GSS/SS for (a) $L1$, and (b) $L2$ with IF's.

2. The common characteristic of all ratio plots is that as the number of processors grows very large, the performance difference between GSS and SS becomes less significant. The large perturbations in the ratio curves can be explained by the fact that GSS is "logarithmically sensitive" while SS is "linearly sensitive" to scheduling overhead. Thus, the performance of SS tends to saturate much earlier (as the number of processors grows) than that of GSS. As the overhead grows the improvement offered by GSS becomes more significant. This is apparent in the plots of Figs. 10–13 where the ratio GSS(1)/SS is significantly larger for $o_w = 10$.

VI. CONCLUSIONS

Since parallel loops account for the greatest percentage of parallelism in numerical programs, the efficient scheduling of such loops is vital to program and system performance. In this paper we presented an efficient dynamic approach to solve the loop scheduling problem. The proposed method is general and can be easily incorporated into the compiler or the hardware.

Two important objectives are automatically satisfied: low overhead and load balancing. By guiding the amount of work given to each processor, very good (and often optimal) load balancing is achieved. The assignment of large iteration blocks, on the other hand, reduces the number of accesses to loop indexes and thus the run-time overhead.

If the GSS scheme is coupled with loop coalescing, the overhead can be further reduced, and by choosing the minimum unit of allocation, guided self-scheduling can be tuned to perform optimally for any given loop–system combination. Finally we showed that for certain types of loops the GSS scheme is optimal. Simulation results indicate that in general GSS is better than any other known dynamic method. Its simplicity and low overhead make it a good candidate for implementation on existing and future parallel processor machines.

ACKNOWLEDGMENT

We would like to thank the referees for their comments and suggestions that greatly enhanced the quality of the presentation of this work.

REFERENCES

[1] A. V. Aho and J. D. Ullman, *Principles of Compiler Design.* Reading, MA: Addison-Wesley, 1977.

[2] Alliant Computer Systems Corp., *FX/Series Architecture Manual,* Acton, MA, 1985.

[3] U. Banerjee, "Speedup of ordinary programs," Ph.D. dissertation, Univ. Illinois, Urbana-Champaign, DCS Rep. UIUCDCS-R-79-989, Oct. 1979.

[4] E. G. Coffman, Jr., Ed., *Computer and Job-Shop Scheduling Theory.* New York: Wiley, 1976.

[5] E. G. Coffman and R. L. Graham, "Optimal scheduling on two processor systems," *Acta Informatica,* vol. 1, no. 3, 1972.

[6] "Multitasking user guide," Cray Comput. Syst. Tech. Note SN-0222, Jan. 1985.

[7] R. G. Cytron, "Doacross: Beyond vectorization for multiprocessors," extended abstract, in *Proc. 1986 Int. Conf. Parallel Processing,* St. Charles, IL, Aug. 1986, pp. 836–844.

[8] J. R. Beckman Davies, "Parallel loop constructs for multiprocessors," M.S. Thesis, Univ. Illinois, Urbana-Champaign, DCS Rep. UIUCDCS-R-81-1070, May 1981.

[9] M. R. Garey and D. S. Johnson, *Computers and Intractability, A Guide to the Theory of NP-Completeness.* San Francisco, CA: Freeman, 1979.

[10] A. Gottlieb, R. Grishman, C. P. Kruskal, K. P. McAuliffe, L. Rudolph, and M. Snir, "The NYU Ultracomputer—Designing an MIMD shared-memory parallel machine," *IEEE Trans. Comput.,* vol. C-32, pp. 175–189, Feb. 1983.

[11] D. J. Kuck, E. S. Davidson, D. H. Lawrie, and A. H. Sameh, "Parallel supercomputing today and the cedar approach," *Science,* vol. 231, pp. 967–974, Feb. 28, 1986.

[12] R. L. Graham, "Bounds on multiprocessor scheduling anomalies and related packing algorithms," in *Proc. Spring Joint Comput. Conf.,* 1972.

[13] D. J. Kuck, R. Kuhn, D. Padua, B. Leasure, and M. Wolfe, "Dependence graphs and compiler optimizations," in *Proc. 8th ACM Symp. Principles Programming Languages,* Jan. 1981, pp. 207–218.

[14] H. Kobayashi, *Modeling and Analysis,* 2nd ed. Reading, MA: Addison-Wesley, 1981.

[15] C. Kruskal and A. Weiss, "Allocating independent subtasks on parallel processors," *IEEE Trans. Software Eng.,* vol. SE-11, Oct. 1985.

[16] D. J. Kuck, *The Structure of Computers and Computations, Vol. 1.* New York: Wiley, 1978.

[17] D. J. Kuck *et al.,* "The effects of program restructuring, algorithm change and architecture choice on program performance," in *Proc. Int. Conf. Parallel Processing,* Aug. 1984.

[18] D. A. Padua Haiek, "Multiprocessors: Discussions of some theoretical and practical problems," Ph.D. dissertation, Univ. Illinois, Urbana-Champaign, DCS Rep. UIUCDCS-R-79-990, Nov. 1979.

[19] C. D. Polychronopoulos and U. Banerjee, "Processor allocation for horizontal and vertical parallelism and related speedup bounds," *IEEE Trans. Comput.,* vol. C-36, Apr. 1987.

[20] C. D. Polychronopoulos, D. J. Kuck, and D. A. Padua, "Execution of parallel loops on parallel processor systems," in *Proc. 1986 Int. Conf. Parallel Processing,* St. Charles, IL, Aug. 1986, pp. 519–527.

[21] C. D. Polychronopoulos, "On program restructuring scheduling and communication for parallel processor systems," Ph.D. dissertation, Rep. 595, Center Supercomput. Res. Development, Univ. Illinois, Aug. 1986.

[22] ——, "Loop coalescing: A compiler transformation for parallel machines," in *Proc. 1987 Int. Conf. Parallel Processing,* St. Charles, IL, Aug. 1987.

[23] S. Reinhardt, "A data-flow approach to multitasking on CRAY X-MP computers," in *Proc. 10th ACM Symp. Oper. Syst. Principles,* Dec. 1985.

[24] S. Sahni, "Scheduling multipipeline and multiprocessor computers," *IEEE Trans. Compt.,* vol. C-33, July 1984.

[25] K. Schwan and C. Gaimon, "Automatic resource allocation for the Cm* multiprocessor," in *Proc. 1985 Int. Conf. Distributed Comput. Syst.,* 1985.

[26] B. Smith, "Architecture and applications of the HEP multiprocessor computer system," in *Real Time Processing IV, Proc. SPIE,* 1981, pp. 241–248.

[27] H. S. Stone, "Multiprocessor scheduling with the aid of network flow algorithms," *IEEE Trans. Software Eng.,* vol. SE-3, Jan. 1977.

[28] P. Tang and P. C. Yew, "Processor self-scheduling for multiple-nested parallel loops," in *Proc. 1986 Int. Conf. Parallel Processing,* Aug. 1986.

[29] M. J. Wolfe, "Optimizing supercompilers for supercomputers," Ph.D. dissertation, Univ. Illinois, Urbana-Champaign, DCS Rep. UIUC-CDCS-R-82-1105, 1982.

[30] C. Q. Zhu, P. C. Yew, and D. H. Lawrie, "Cedar synchronization primitives," Lab. Advanced Supercomput. Cedar Doc. 18, Sept. 1983.

Constantine D. Polychronopoulos (S'85–M'86) was born on April 5, 1958, in Patras, Greece. He received the Dipl. degree in mathematics from the University of Athens, Athens, Greece, in 1980, the M.S. degree in computer science from Vanderbilt University, Nashville, TN, in 1982, and the Ph.D. degree in computer science from the University of Illinois, Urbana-Champaign in 1986.

From 1982 to 1986 he was a Research Assistant in the Department of Computer Science and the Center for Supercomputing Research and Development at the University of Illinois. Since July 1986, he has been a Senior Software Engineer at the Center for Supercomputing Research and Development, and a Visiting Assistant Professor in the Department of Electrical and Computer Engineering at the University of Illinois. At CSRD he participates in the design of the Cedar compiler and the Parafrase II project. His primary research interests are in the areas of parallel processing, program restructuring, scheduling, synchronization, and interprocessor communication, and he has published a number of papers in these topics. He was a Fulbright Scholar in 1981–1982.

Dr. Polychronopoulos served on the program committee for the International Conference on Supercomputing, and he was coeditor of the proceedings. He is member of the ACM and the IEEE Computer Society.

David J. Kuck (S'59–M'69–SM'83–F'85), was born in Muskegon, MI, on October 3, 1937. He received the B.S.E.E. degree from the University of Michigan, Ann Arbor, in 1959, and the M.S. and Ph.D. degrees from Northwestern University, Evanston, IL, in 1960 and 1963, respectively.

From 1963 to 1965, he was a Ford Postdoctoral Fellow and Assistant Professor of Electrical Engineering at the Massachusetts Institute of Technology, Cambridge. In 1965, he joined the Faculty of the University of Illinois, Urbana. He is now a Professor of Computer Science and of Electrical and Computer Engineering and the Director of the Center for Supercomputing Research and Development, which he organized in 1984. He is currently engaged in the development of the Cedar parallel processing system. His research interests are in the coherent design of hardware and software systems, including the development of the Parafrase system, a program transformation facility for array and multiprocessor machines. He was a principal designer of the Burroughs Scientific Processor and the Illiac IV. In addition to serving as a consultant to a number of government and industrial organizations including Alliant Computer Systems, he was a founder of Kuck and Associates, Inc., which produces software that restructures programs for parallel and vector machines, as well as numerical software for such machines. Among his publications is *The Structure of Computers and Computations, Vol. 1.*

Dr. Kuck has served as an Editor for a number of professional journals, including the IEEE TRANSACTIONS ON COMPUTERS and the *Journal of the Association for Computing Machinery.*

Synchronization, Coherence, and Event Ordering in Multiprocessors

Michel Dubois and Christoph Scheurich

Computer Research Institute, University of Southern California

Fayé A. Briggs

Sun Microsystems

Reprinted from *Computer*, Vol. 21, No. 2, February 1988, pages 9-21. Copyright © 1988 by The Institute of Electrical and Electronics Engineers, Inc. All rights reserved.

Multiprocessors, especially those constructed of relatively low-cost microprocessors, offer a cost-effective solution to the continually increasing need for computing power and speed. These systems can be designed either to maximize the throughput of many jobs or to speed up the execution of a single job; they are respectively called *throughput-oriented* and *speedup-oriented multiprocessors*. In the first type of system, jobs are distinct from each other and execute as if they were running on different uniprocessors. In the second type an application is partitioned into a set of cooperating processes, and these processes interact while executing concurrently on different processors. The partitioning of a job into cooperating processes is called *multitasking*[1]* or *multithreading*. In both systems global resources must be managed correctly and efficiently by the operating system. The problems addressed in this article apply to both throughput-

*Multitasking is not restricted to multiprocessor systems; in this article, however, we confine our discussion, with no loss of generality, to multitasking multiprocessors.

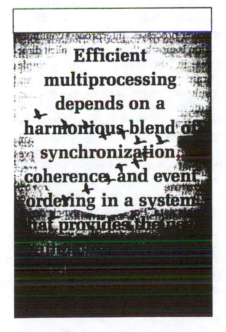

Efficient multiprocessing depends on a harmonious blend of synchronization, coherence, and event ordering in a system that provides the

and speedup-oriented multiprocessor systems, either at the user level or the operating-system level.

Multitasked multiprocessors are capable of efficiently executing the many cooperating numerical or nonnumerical tasks that comprise a large application. In general, the speedup provided by multitasking reduces the turnaround time of a job and therefore ultimately improves the user's productivity. For applications such as real-time processing, CAD/CAM, and simulations, multitasking is crucial because the multiprocessor structure improves the execution speed of a given algorithm within a time constraint that is ordinarily impossible to meet on a single processor employing available technology.

Designing and programming multiprocessor systems correctly and efficiently pose complex problems. Synchronizing processes, maintaining data coherence, and ordering events in a multiprocessor are issues that must be addressed from the hardware design level up to the programming language level. The goal of this article is not only to review these problems in some depth but also to show that in the design of multiprocessors these problems are intricately related. The definitions and concepts presented here provide a solid foundation on which to reason about the logical properties of a specific multiproces-

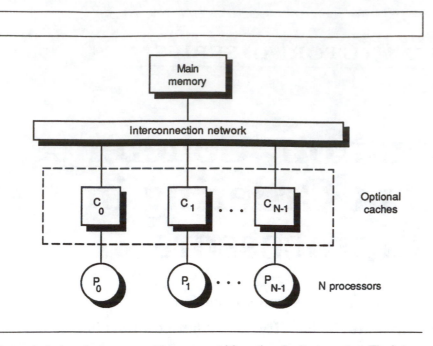

Figure 1. A shared-memory multiprocessor with optional private caches. The interconnection network may be either a simple bus or a complex network.

Basic definitions

The instruction set of a multiprocessor usually contains basic instructions that are used to implement synchronization and communication between cooperating processes. These instructions are usually supported by special-purpose hardware. Some primary hardware functions are necessary to guarantee correct interprocess communication and synchronization, while other, secondary hardware functions simplify the design of parallel applications and operating systems. The notions of synchronization and communication are difficult to separate because communication primitives can be used to implement synchronization protocols, and vice versa. In general, *communication* refers to the exchange of data between different processes. Usually, one or several sender processes transmit data to one or several receiver processes. Interprocess communication is mostly the result of explicit directives in the program. For example, parameters passed to a coroutine and results returned by such a coroutine constitute interprocess communications. *Synchronization* is a special form of communication, in which the data are control information. Synchronization serves the dual purpose of enforcing the correct sequencing of processes and ensuring the mutually exclusive access to certain shared writable data. For example, synchronization primitives can be used to

(1) Control a producer process and a consumer process such that the consumer process never reads stale data and the producer process never overwrites data that have not yet been read by the consumer process.

(2) Protect the data in a database such that concurrent write accesses to the same record in the database are not allowed. (Such accesses can lead to the loss of one or more updates if two processes first read the data in sequence and then write the updated data back to memory in sequence.)

In shared-memory multiprocessor systems, communication and synchronization are usually implemented through the controlled sharing of data in memory.

A second issue addressed in this article is *memory coherence*, a system's ability to execute memory operations correctly. Censier and Feautrier define a coherent memory scheme as follows: "A memory scheme is coherent if the value returned on a Load instruction is always the value given by the latest Store instruction with the same address."[5] This definition has been useful in the design of cache coherence mechanisms.[4] As it stands, however, the definition is difficult to interpret in the context of a multiprocessor, in which data accesses may be buffered and may not be atomic. Accesses are buffered if multiple accesses can be queued before reaching their destination, such as main memory or caches. An access by processor i on a variable X is atomic if no other processor is allowed to access any copy of X while the access by processor i is in progress. It has been shown that memory accesses need not be atomic at the hardware level for correct execution of concurrent programs.[6,7] Correctness of execution depends on the expected behavior of the machine. Two major classes of logical machine behavior have been identified because they are common in existing multiprocessor systems: the *strongly ordered* and the *weakly ordered* models of behavior.[7] The hardware of the machine must enforce these models by proper ordering of storage accesses and execution of synchronization and communication primitives. This leads to the third issue, the *ordering of events*.

The strictest logical model for the ordering of events is called *sequential consistency*, defined by Lamport. In a multiprocessor *sequential consistency* refers to the allowable sequence of execution of instructions within the same process and among different concurrent processes. Lamport defines the term more rigorously: "[A system is sequentially consistent if] the result of any execution is the same as if the operations of all the processors were executed in some sequential order, and the operations of each individual processor appear in this sequence in the order specified by its program."[8]

Since the only way that two concurrent processors can affect each other's execution is through the sharing of writable data and the sending of interrupt signals, it is

---

sor and to demonstrate that the hardware adheres to the logical model expected by the programmer. This foundation aids in understanding complex but useful architectures such as multiprocessors with private caches or with recombining interconnection networks (Figure 1).[2] Other important issues, such as scheduling and partitioning, have been addressed in a previous survey article.[3] Readers who are not familiar with the concept of cache memory should consult the survey by Smith.[4]

the order of these events that really matters. In systems that are sequentially consistent we say that events are strongly ordered.

However, if we look at many systems (transaction systems, for example), it becomes clear that sequential consistency is often violated in favor of a weaker condition. In many machines it is often implicitly assumed that the programmer should make no assumption about the order in which the events that a process generates are observed by other processes between two explicit synchronization points. Accesses to shared writable data should be executed in a mutually exclusive manner, controlled by synchronizing variables. Accesses to synchronizing variables can be detected by the machine hardware at execution time. Strong ordering of accesses to these synchronizing variables and restoration of coherence at synchronization points are therefore the only restrictions that must be upheld. In such systems we say that events are weakly ordered. Weak ordering may result in more efficient systems, but the implementation problems remain the same as for strong ordering: strong ordering must still be enforced for synchronizing variables (rather than for all shared writable data).

We can infer from this discussion that synchronization, coherence, and ordering of events are closely related issues in the design of multiprocessors.

Communication and synchronization

Communication and synchronization are two facets of the same basic problem: how to design concurrent software that is correct and reliable, especially when the processes interact by exchanging control and data information. Multiprocessor systems usually include various mechanisms to deal with the various granules of synchronizable resources. Usually, low-level and simple primitives are implemented directly by the hardware. These primitives are the basic mechanisms that enforce mutual exclusion for more complex mechanisms implemented in microcode or software.

Hardware-level synchronization mechanisms. All multiprocessors include hardware mechanisms to enforce atomic operations. The most primitive memory operations in a machine are Loads and

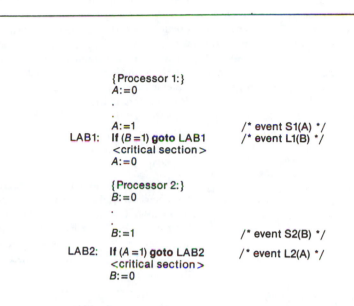

```
              {Processor 1:}
              A:=0
              .
              .
              A:=1                              /* event S1(A) */
       LAB1:  If (B=1) goto LAB1                /* event L1(B) */
              <critical section>
              A:=0

              {Processor 2:}
              B:=0
              .
              .
              B:=1                              /* event S2(B) */
       LAB2:  If (A=1) goto LAB2                /* event L2(A) */
              <critical section>
              B:=0
```

Figure 2. Synchronization protocol using two shared variables, *A* and *B*.

Stores. With atomic Loads and Stores complex synchronization protocols can be built. Figure 2 depicts a simple protocol. Before a processor can enter its critical section, it sets its control variable (*A* for processor 1 and *B* for processor 2) to 1. Hence, for both processors to be in their critical sections concurrently, both *A* and *B* must equal 1. But this is not possible, since a processor cannot enter its critical section if the other processor's control variable equals 1. Therefore, the two processors cannot execute their respective critical sections concurrently. This simple protocol can be deadlocked, but the problem can be remedied.[8] Such protocols are hard to design, understand, and prove correct, and in many cases they are inefficient.

More sophisticated synchronization primitives are usually implemented in hardware. If the primitive is simple enough, the controller of the memory bank can execute the primitive at the memory in the same way it executes a Load or a Store, at the added cost of a more complex memory controller. This is typically the case for the Test&Set and the Full/Empty bit primitives described below. Interprocessor interrupts are also possible hardware mechanisms for synchronization and communication. To send a message to another process currently

running on a different processor, a process can send an interrupt to that processor to notify the destination process.

A common set of synchronization primitives consists of Test&Set(lock) and Reset(lock). The semantics of Test&Set and Reset are

```
TEST&SET(lock)
  { temp ← lock; lock ← 1;
    return temp; }
RESET(lock)
  { lock ← 0; }
```

The microcode or software will usually repeat the Test&Set until the returned value is 0. Synchronization at this level implies some form of busy waiting, which ties up a processor in an idle loop and increases the memory bus traffic and contention. The type of lock that relies on busy waiting is called a *spin-lock*.

To avoid spinning, interprocessor interrupts are used. A lock that relies on interrupts instead of spinning is called a *suspend-lock* (also called *sleep-lock* in the C.mmp[1]). This lock is similar to the spin-lock in the sense that a process does not relinquish the processor while it is waiting on a suspend-lock. However, whenever it fails to obtain the lock, it records its status in one field of the lock and disables all interrupts except interprocessor interrupts. When a process frees the lock, it signals all waiting processors through an interprocessor interrupt. This mechanism prevents the excessive interconnection traffic caused by busy waiting but still consumes processor cycles. Spin-locks and suspend-locks can be based on primitives similar to Test&Set, such as Compare&Swap.

The Compare&Swap(r1,r2,w) primitive is a synchronization primitive in the IBM 370 architecture; r1 and r2 are two machine registers, and w points to a memory location. The success of the Compare&Swap is indicated by the flag z. The semantics of the Compare&Swap instruction are

COMPARE&SWAP(r1,r2,w)
{ $temp \leftarrow w$; if ($temp = $ r1)
    then {$w \leftarrow$ r2; $z \leftarrow 1$;}
    else {r1 $\leftarrow temp$; $z \leftarrow 0$;}
}

Test&Set and Compare&Swap are also called *read-modify-write* (RMW) primitives. A common performance problem associated with these basic synchronization primitives is the complexity of locking protocols. If N processes attempt to access a critical section at the same time, the memory system must execute N basic lock operations, one after the other, even if at most one process is successful. The NYU Ultracomputer[2] and the RP3 multiprocessor[9] use the Fetch&Add(x,a) primitive, where x is a shared-memory word and a is an increment. When a single processor executes the Fetch&Add on x, the semantics are

FETCH&ADD(x,a)
{ $temp \leftarrow x$; $x \leftarrow temp + a$;
    return $temp$; }

The implementation of the Fetch&Add primitive on the Ultracomputer is such that the complexity of an N-way synchronization on the same memory word is independent of N. The execution of this primitive is distributed in the interconnection network between the processors and the memory module. If N processes attempt to Fetch&Add the same memory word simultaneously, the memory is updated only once, by adding the sum of the N increments, and a unique value is returned to each of the N processes. The returned values correspond to an arbitrary serialization of the N requests. From the processor and memory point of view, the result is similar to a sequential execution of N Fetch&Adds, but it is performed in one operation. Consequently, the

Fetch&Add primitive is extremely effective in accessing sequentially allocated queue structures and in the forking of processes with identical code that operate on different data segments. For example, the following high-level parallel Fortran statement[10] can be executed in parallel by P processors if there is no dependency between iterations of the loop:

DOALL $N = 1$ **to** 100
    <code using N>
ENDDO

Each processor executes a Fetch&Add on N before working on a specific iteration of the loop. Each processor will return a unique value of N, which can be used in the code segment. The code for each processor is as follows (N is initially loaded with the value 1):

$n \leftarrow$ FETCH&ADD (N,1)
while ($n \leq 100$) **do**
    { <code using N>
        $n \leftarrow$ FETCH&ADD (N,1);
    }

In the HEP (Heterogeneous Element Processor) system, shared-memory words are tagged as *empty* or *full*. Loads of such words succeed only after the word is updated and tagged as full. After a successful Load, the tag can be reset to empty. Similarly, the Store on a full memory word can be prevented until the word has been read and the tag cleared. These mechanisms can be used to synchronize processes, since a process can be made to wait on an empty memory word until some other process fills it. This system also relies on busy waiting, and memory cycles are wasted on each trial. Each processor in the HEP is a multistream pipeline, and several process contexts are present in each processor at any time. A different process can immediately be activated when an attempt to synchronize fails. Very few processor cycles are wasted on synchronization. However, the burden of managing the tags is left to the programmer or the compiler. A more complex tagging scheme is advocated for the Cedar machine.[3]

Software-level synchronization mechanisms. Two approaches to synchronization are popular in multiprocessor operating systems: semaphores and message passing. We will discuss message passing in the next section. Operations on semaphores are P and V. A binary semaphore has the values 0 or 1, which signal acquisition and blocking, respectively. A counting semaphore can take any integer

value greater than or equal to 0. The semantics of the P and V operations are

$P(s)$
{ **if** ($s > 0$) **then**
    $s \leftarrow (s - 1)$;
        else
    { Block the process and append it
        to the waiting list for s;
        Resume the highest priority process in the READY LIST;}
}

$V(s)$
{ **if** (waiting list for s empty) **then**
    $s \leftarrow (s + 1)$;
        else
    { Remove the highest priority process blocked for s;
        Append it to the READY LIST;}
}

In these two algorithms shared lists are consulted and modified (namely, the Ready List* and the waiting list for s). These accesses as well as the test and modification of s have to be protected by spin-locks, suspend-locks, or Fetch&Adds associated with semaphore s and with the lists. In practice, P and V are processor instructions or microcoded routines, or they are operating system calls to the process manager. The process manager is the part of the system kernel controlling process creation, activation, and deletion, as well as management of the locks. Because the process manager can be called from different processors at the same time, its associated data structures must be protected. Semaphores are particularly well adapted for synchronization. Unlike spin-locks and suspend-locks, semaphores are not wasteful of processor cycles while a process is waiting, but their invocations require more overhead. Note that locks are still necessary to implement semaphores.

Another synchronization primitive implemented in software or microcode is Barrier, used to "join" a number of parallel processes. All processes synchronizing at a barrier must reach the barrier before any one of them can continue. Barriers can be defined as follows after the task counter Count has been initialized to zero:

BARRIER(N)
{ count := count + 1;
    if (count $\geq N$) **then**
    { Resume all processes on barrier
        queue;

---

*The Ready List is a data structure containing the descriptors of processes that are runable.

254

Table 1. Synchronization, communication, and coherence in various multiprocessors.

Multiprocessor	Number of processors	CPU architecture	Hardware primitives	Cache	Coherence scheme
IBM 3081	≤ 4	IBM 370	Compare&Swap (CS, CDS), Test&Set (TS)	Write-back	Central table
Synapse N + 1*	≤ 32	Motorola 68000	Compare&Swap (CAS), Test&Set (TAS)	Write-back	Distributed table/ bus watching
Denelcor HEP*	100s	Custom	Full/empty bit	No cache	
IBM RP3†	100s	IBM ROMP	Fetch&Op (e.g., Fetch&Add)	Write-back	No shared writable data in cache
NYU Ultracomputer†	100s		Fetch&Add	Write-back	No shared writable data in cache
Encore Multimax	≤ 20	National Semiconductor 32032	Test&Set ("interlocked" instructions)	Write-through (two processors share each cache)	Bus watching
Sequent Balance 8000	≤ 12	National Semiconductor 32032	Test&Set (spin-lock using lock cache and bus watching)	Write-through	Bus watching

*Commercial machines no longer in production.
†Experimental prototype.

Reset count; }
    else
    Block task and place in barrier queue;
}

The first N-1 tasks to execute Barrier would be blocked. Upon execution of Barrier by the Nth task, all N tasks are ready to resume. In the HEP each task that is blocked spin-locks on a Full/Empty bit. The Nth task that crosses the barrier writes into the tagged memory location and thereby wakes up all the blocked tasks. This technique is very efficient for executing parallel, iterative algorithms common in numerical applications.

Interprocess communication. In a shared-memory multiprocessor, interprocess communication can be as simple as one processor writing to a particular memory location and another processor reading that memory location. However, since these activities occur asynchronously, communication is in most cases implemented by synchronization mechanisms. The reading process must be informed at what time the message to be read is valid, and the writing process must know at what time it is allowed to write to a particular memory location without destroying a message yet to be read by another process. Therefore, communication is often implemented by mutually exclusive accesses to mailboxes. Mailboxes are configured and maintained in shared memory by software or microcode.

Message-based communication can be synchronous or asynchronous. In a synchronous system the sender transmits a message to a receiving process and waits until the receiving process responds with an acknowledgment that the message has been received. Symmetrically, the receiver waits for a message and then sends an acknowledgment. The sender resumes execution only when it is confirmed that the message has been received. In asynchronous systems the sending process does not wait for the receiving process to receive the message. If the receiver is not ready to receive the message at its time of arrival, the message may be buffered or simply lost. Buffering can be provided in hardware or, more appropriately, in mailboxes in shared memory.

A summary of synchronization and communication primitives for different processors is given in Table 1.

Coherence in multiprocessors

Coherence problems exist at various levels of multiprocessors. Inconsistencies (i.e., contradictory information) can occur between adjacent levels or within the same level of a memory hierarchy. For example, in a cache-based system with write-back caches, cache and main memory may contain inconsistent copies of data.[4] Multiple caches conceivably could possess different copies of the same memory block because one of the processors has modified its copy. Generally, this condition is not allowable.

In some cases data inconsistencies do not affect the correct execution of a program (for example, inconsistencies between memory and write-back caches may be tolerated). In the following paragraphs we identify the cases for which data

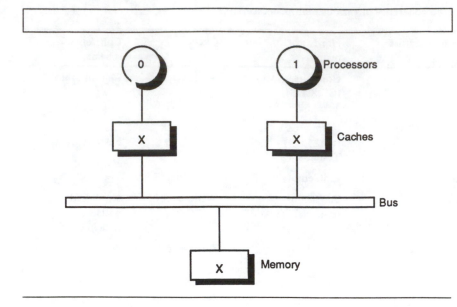

Figure 3. Cache configuration after a Load on X by processors 0 and 1. Copies in both caches are consistent.

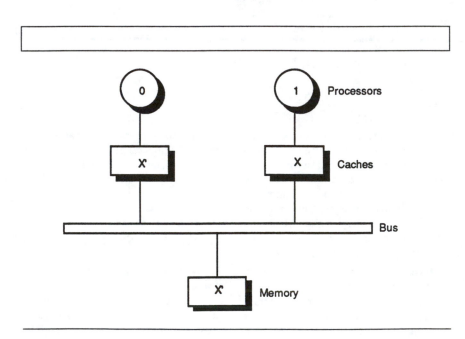

Figure 4. Cache configuration after a Store on X by processor 0 (write-through cache). The copies are inconsistent.

inconsistencies pose a problem and discuss various solutions.

Conditions for coherence. Data coherence problems do not exist in multiprocessors that maintain only a single copy of data. For example, consider a shared-memory multiprocessor in which each CPU does not have a private memory or cache (Figure 1 without optional caches). If Loads, Stores, and RMW cycles are atomic, then data elements are accessed and modified in indivisible operations. Each access to an element applies to the latest copy. Simultaneous accesses to the same element of data are serialized by the hardware.

Cache coherence problems exist in multiprocessors with private caches (Figure 1 with optional caches) and are caused by three factors: sharing of writable data, process migration, and I/O activity. To illustrate the effects of these three factors, we use a two-processor architecture with private caches (Figures 3-5). We assume that an element X is referenced by the CPUs. Let $L_j(X)$ and $S_j(X)$ denote a Load and a Store by processor j for element X in memory, respectively. If the caches do not contain copies of X initially, a Load of X by the two CPUs results in consistent copies of X, as shown in Figure 3. Next, if one of the processors performs a Store to X, then the copies of X in the caches become inconsistent. A Load by the other processor will not return the latest value. Depending on the memory update policy used in the cache, the cache level may also be inconsistent with respect to main memory. A write-through policy maintains consistency between main memory and cache. However, a write-back policy does not maintain such consistency at the time of the Store; memory is updated eventually when the modified data in the cache are replaced or invalidated. Figures 4 and 5 depict the states of the caches and memory for write-through and write-back policies, respectively.

Consistency problems also occur because of the I/O configuration in a system with caches. In Figure 6 the I/O processor (IOP) is attached to the bus, as is most commonly done. If the current state of the system is reached by an $L_0(X)$ and $S_0(X)$ sequence, a modified copy of X in cache 0 and main memory will not have been updated in the case of write-back caches. A subsequent I/O Load of X by the IOP returns a "stale" value of X as contained in memory. To solve the consistency problem in this configuration, the I/O processor must participate in the cache coherence protocol on the bus. The configuration in Figure 7 shows the IOPs sharing the caches with the CPUs. In this case I/O consistency is maintained if cache-to-cache consistency is also maintained; an obvious disadvantage of this scheme is the likely increase of cache perturbations and poor locality of I/O data, which will result in high miss ratios.

Some systems allow processes to migrate—i.e., to be scheduled in different processors during their lifetime—in order to balance the work load among the processors. If this feature is used in conjunction with private caches, data inconsistencies can result. For example, process A, which runs on CPU_0, may alter data contained in its cache by executing $S_0(X)$ before it is suspended. If process A migrates to CPU_1 before memory has been updated with the most recent value of X, process A may subsequently Load the stale value of X contained in memory.

It is obvious that a mere write-through policy will not maintain consistency in the system, since the write does not automatically update the possible copies of the data contained in the other caches. In fact, write-through is neither necessary nor sufficient for coherence.

Solutions to the cache coherence problem. Approaches to maintaining coherence in multiprocessors range from simple architectural principles that make incoherence impossible to complex memory coherence schemes that maintain coherence "on the fly" only when necessary. Here we list these approaches from least to most complex:

(1) A simple architectural technique is to disallow private caches and have only shared caches that are associated with the main memory modules. Every data access is made to the shared cache. A network interconnects the processors to the shared cache modules.

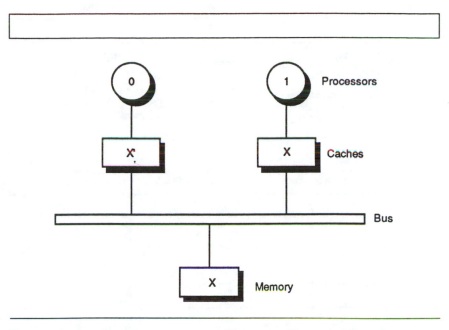

Figure 5. Same as Figure 4 but with write-back cache. The copies are inconsistent.

(2) For performance considerations it is desirable to attach a private cache to each CPU. Data inconsistency can be prevented by not caching shared writable data; such data are called *noncachable*. Examples of shared writable data are locks, shared data structures such as process queues, and any other data protected by critical sections. Instructions and other data can be copied into caches as usual. Such items are referred to as *cachable*. The compiler must tag data as either cachable or noncachable. The hardware must adhere to the meaning of the tags. This technique, apparently

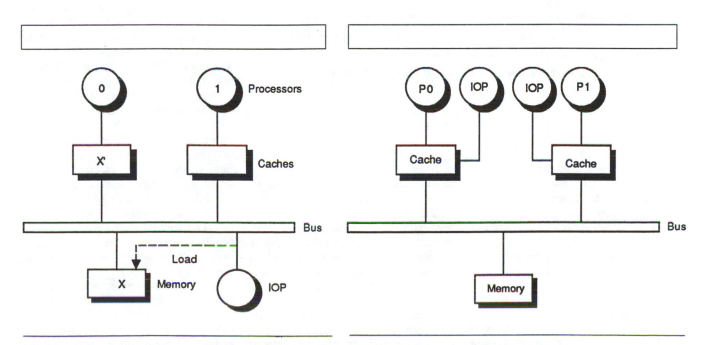

Figure 6. IOPs are attached to the bus and bypass the cache.   **Figure 7. IOPs are attached to the caches.**

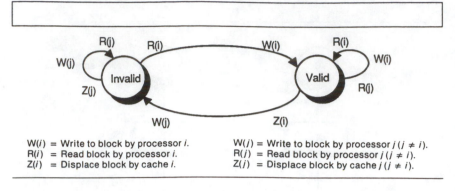

Figure 8. State diagram for a given block in cache *i* for a write-through coherence protocol.

W(*i*) = Write to block by processor *i*.
R(*i*) = Read block by processor *i*.
Z(*i*) = Displace block by cache *i*.

W(*j*) = Write to block by processor *j* (*j* ≠ *i*).
R(*j*) = Read block by processor *j* (*j* ≠ *i*).
Z(*j*) = Displace block by cache *j* (*j* ≠ *i*).

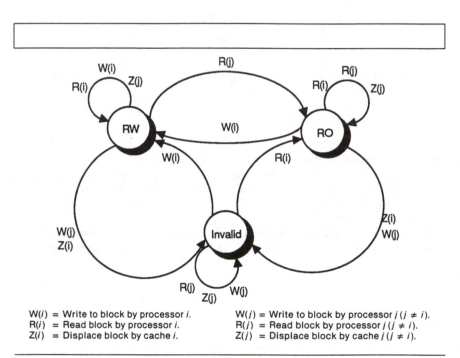

Figure 9. State diagram for a given block in cache *i* for a write-back coherence protocol.

W(*i*) = Write to block by processor *i*.
R(*i*) = Read block by processor *i*.
Z(*i*) = Displace block by cache *i*.

W(*j*) = Write to block by processor *j* (*j* ≠ *i*).
R(*j*) = Read block by processor *j* (*j* ≠ *i*).
Z(*j*) = Displace block by cache *j* (*j* ≠ *i*).

simple in principle, must rely on the detection within each CPU that a block is cachable or not. Such a detection can be made in a virtual memory environment by tagging each page. The tag is stored in entries in the CPU's translation buffers. Translation buffers (TBs) are similar to caches, but they store virtual-to-physical address translations.

(3) If all shared writable data are declared noncachable, the performance may be degraded appreciably. If accesses to shared writable data always occur in critical sections, then such data can be cached. Only the locks that protect the critical sections must remain noncachable. However, to maintain data consistency, all data modified in the critical section must be invalidated in the cache when the critical section is exited. This operation is often referred to as a *cache flush*. The flushing operation ensures that no stale data remain in the cache at the next access to the critical section. If another cache accesses the data via the acquisition of the lock, consistency is maintained. This scheme is adequate for transaction-processing systems in which a shared record is acquired,

updated in a critical section, and subsequently released. It works for write-through caches; for write-back caches, the design is more complex.

(4) A scheme allowing shared writable data to exist in multiple caches employs a centralized global table[5] and is used in many mainframe multiprocessor systems, such as the IBM 308x. The table stores the status of memory blocks so that coherence enforcement signals, called *cache cross-interrogates* (XI), can be generated on the basis of the block status. To maintain consistency, XI signals with the associated block address are propagated to the other caches either to invalidate or to change the state of the copies of the referenced block. An arbitrary number of caches can contain a copy of a block, provided that all the copies are identical. We refer to such a copy as a *read-only copy* (RO). To modify a block present in its cache, the processor must own the block with read and write access. When a block is copied from memory into cache, the block is tagged as exclusive (EX) if the cache is the only cache that has a copy of the block. A block is owned exclusively with read and write (RW) access when it has been modified. Only one processor can own an RW copy of a block at any time. The state IN (invalid) signals that the block has been invalidated.

The centralized table is usually located in the storage control element, which may also incorporate a crossbar switch that connects the CPUs to the main memory. To limit the accesses to the global table, local status flags can be provided in the cache directories for the blocks that reside in the cache. Depending on the status of the local flags and the type of request, the processor is allowed to proceed or is required to consult the global table.

(5) In bus-oriented multiprocessors the table that records the status of each block can be efficiently distributed among processors. The distributed-table scheme takes advantage of the broadcasting capability of the bus. Typically, consistency between the caches is maintained by a bus-watching mechanism, often called a *snoopy cache controller*, which implements a cache coherence protocol on the bus. In a simple scheme for write-through caches, all the snoopy controllers watch the bus for Stores. If a Store is made to a location cached in remote caches, then the copies of the block in remote caches are either invalidated or updated. This scheme also maintains coherence with I/O activity. Figure 8 depicts a state diagram of the block state changes depending on

the access type and the previous state of the block. A similar scheme was applied in the Sequent Balance 8000 multiprocessor, which can be configured with up to 12 processors.

The efficiency of the hardware that maintains coherence on the fly is vital. Recognizing that the Store traffic may contribute to bus congestion in a write-through system, Goodman proposed a scheme called *write-once*, in which the initial Store to a block copy in the cache also updates memory.[11] This Store also invalidates matching entries in remote caches, thereby ensuring that the writing processor has the only cached copy. Furthermore, Stores can be performed in the cache at the cache speed. Subsequent updates of the modified block are made in the cache only. A CPU or IOP Load is serviced by the unit (a cache or the memory) that has the latest copy of the block.

Multiprocessors with write-back caches rely on an ownership protocol. When the memory owns a block, caches can contain only RO copies of the block. Before a block is modified, ownership for exclusive access must first be obtained by a read-private bus transaction, which is broadcast to the caches and memory. If a modified block copy exists in another cache, memory must first be updated, the copy invalidated, and ownership transferred to the requesting cache. Figure 9 diagrams memory block state transitions brought about by processor actions. The first commercial multiprocessor with write-back caches was the Synapse N + 1.

Variants of the cache coherence bus protocols have been proposed. One scheme, proposed for the Spur project at the University of California, Berkeley, combines compile-time tagging of shared and private data and the ownership protocol. In another system, the Xerox Dragon multiprocessor, a write is always broadcast to other caches and main memory is updated only on replacement. These bus protocols are described and their performances compared in an article by Archibald and Baer.[12]

Advantages and disadvantages. Although scheme 1 provides coherence while being transparent to the user and the operating system, it does not reduce memory conflicts but only the memory access latency. Shared caches, by necessity, contradict the rule that processors and caches should be as close together as possible. I/O accesses must be serviced via the shared caches to maintain coherence.

Tagging shared writable data fails to alleviate the coherence problem caused by I/O accesses.

There are a number of disadvantages associated with scheme 2, which tags data as cachable or noncachable. The major one is the nontransparency of the multiprocessor architecture to the user or the compiler. The user must declare data elements as shared or nonshared if a concurrent language such as Ada, Modula-2, or Concurrent Pascal is used.[13] Alternatively, a multiprocessing compiler, such as Parafrase,[10] can classify data as shared or nonshared automatically. The efficiency of these approaches depends respectively on the ability of the language to specify data structures (or parts thereof) that are shared and writable and of the compiler to detect the subset of shared writable data. Since in practical implementations a whole page must be declared as cachable or not, internal fragmentation may result, or more data than the shared writable data may become noncachable.

Tagging shared writable data also fails to alleviate the coherence problem caused by I/O accesses. Either caches must be flushed before I/O is allowed to proceed, or all data subject to I/O must be tagged as noncachable as well. Depending on the frequency of I/O operations, both approaches reduce the overall hit rate of the caches and hence the speedup obtained by using caches.

Another common drawback of tagging shared writable data rather than maintaining coherence on the fly is the inefficiency caused by process migration. Caches must be flushed before each migration or process migration must be disallowed at the cost of limiting scheduling flexibility. Scheme 3—flushing caches only when synchronization variables are accessed—has performance problems. In practice the whole cache has to be flushed, or else the data accessed in a critical section must be tagged in the cache. I/O must also be preceded by cache flushing. Note that the programmer must be aware that coherence is restored only at synchronization points.

Scheme 3 appears to be attractive only for small caches.

Scheme 4 solves the problems caused by I/O accesses and process migration. However, a global table that must be accessed by all cache controllers can become a bottleneck, even when XIs are filtered by hardware. But the main problem of this coherence scheme is the distance between the processors and the global table. As processors become faster, the access latency of the table becomes a limiting factor of system performance; in particular, when cache access times are very fast, the time penalty for a miss (*miss penalty*) must be minimized.

By distributing the table among the caches, the last scheme partly solves the problems of table access contention and latency. However, the complexity of the bus interface unit is increased because it has to "watch" the bus. Furthermore, since the scheme relies on a broadcast bus, the number of processors that can be interconnected is limited by the bus bandwidth.

Ping-pong effect. In systems with caches employing scheme 4 or 5, the execution of synchronization primitives, such as atomic read-modify-write memory cycles, can create additional access penalties. If two or more processors are spinning on a lock, RMW cycles that cause the lock variable to bounce repeatedly from one cache to another are generated. This can be aggravated by clustering different locks into a given block of memory. However, if RMW operations are implemented carefully, spin-locks can be efficient.

Let us illustrate the ping-pong problem by an example and discuss techniques for reducing system performance degradations. In this example we will assume the use of the Test&Set(lock) instruction; however, the problem can occur with other primitives. The traditional segment of code executed to acquire access to a critical section via a spin-lock is the following:

while (TEST&SET(lock) = 1) **do** nothing;
  /* spin-lock with RMW cycles */
  < execute critical section >
RESET(lock);
  /* exit critical section */

Assume that each processor has a private write-back cache and that three or more processors attempt to access the critical section concurrently. If processor P_0 succeeds in acquiring the lock, the other processors (P_1 and P_2) will spin-lock and cause the modified lock variable to be invalidated in the other processors' caches for each access to the lock. As a result of the invalidation of the modified lock variable, the block is transferred to the requesting cache—a significant penalty. The modification is a result of the writing in the last part of the RMW memory cycle.

One technique for avoiding the ping-pong effect is to use the following segment of code in place of the while statement in the previous code segment:

```
repeat
    while (LOAD(lock) = 1) do nothing;
    /* spin without modification */
until (TEST&SET(lock) = 0);
```

In this segment of code the lock is first loaded to test its status. If available, a Test&Set is used to attempt acquisition. However, while a processor is attempting to acquire the lock, it "spins" locally in its cache, repeating the execution of a tight loop made of a Load followed by a Test. This spinning causes no invalidation traffic on the bus. On a subsequent release of the lock, the processors contend for the lock, and only one of them will succeed. The ping-pong problem is solved; spinlocks can therefore be implemented efficiently in cache-based systems.

Ping-ponging also occurs for shared writable variables. A typical example is the index N in the Doall loop described earlier, in the section on hardware-level synchronization mechanisms. Unless the implementation of Fetch&Add is carefully designed, accesses to the index N create a "hot spot,"[9] which in a cache-based system results in intense ping-ponging between the caches. The careful implementation of synchronization primitives and the creation of hot spots in cache-based systems are research topics that deserve more attention.

Strong and weak ordering of events

The mapping of an algorithm as conceived and understood by a human programmer into a list of machine instructions that correctly implement that algorithm is a complex process. Once the translation has been accomplished, however, it is relatively easy in the case of a uniprocessor to understand what modifications of the machine code can be made without altering the outcome of the execution. A compiler, for example, can resequence instructions to boost performance, or the processor itself can execute instructions

---

> **Local dependency checking is necessary, but it may not preserve the intended outcome of a concurrent execution.**

---

out of order if it is pipelined. This is allowable in uniprocessors, provided that hardware mechanisms (interlocks) exist to check data and control dependencies between instructions to be executed concurrently or out of program order.

If a processor is a part of a multiprocessor that executes a concurrent program, then such local dependency checking is still necessary but may not be sufficient to preserve the intended outcome of a concurrent execution. Maintaining correctness and predictability of the execution of concurrent programs is more complex for three reasons:

(1) The order in which instructions belonging to different instruction streams are executed is not fixed in a concurrent program. If no synchronization among instruction streams exists, then a very large number of different instruction interleavings is possible.

(2) If for performance reasons the order of execution of instructions belonging to the same instruction stream is different from the order implied by the program, then an even larger number of instruction interleavings is possible.

(3) If accesses are not atomic (for example, if multiple copies of the same data exist), as is the case in a cache-based system, and if not all copies are updated at the same time, then different processors can individually observe different interleavings during the same execution. In this case the total number of possible execution instantiations of a program becomes still larger.

To illustrate the possible types of interleavings, we examine the following three program segments to be executed concurrently by three processors (initially $A = B = C = 0$, and we assume that a Print statement reads both variables indivisibly during the same cycle):

P1	P2	P3
a: $A \leftarrow 1$	c: $B \leftarrow 1$	e: $C \leftarrow 1$
b: Print BC	d: Print AC	f: Print AB

If the outputs of the processors are concatenated in the order P1, P2, and P3, then the output forms a six-tuple. There are 64 possible output combinations. For example, if processors execute instructions in program order, then the execution interleaving a,b,c,d,e,f is possible and would yield the output 001011. Likewise, the interleaving a,c,e,b,d,f is possible and would yield the output 111111. If processors are allowed to execute instructions out of program order, assuming that no data dependencies exist among reordered instructions, then the interleaving b,d,f,e,a,c is possible and would yield the output 000000. Note that this outcome is not possible if processors execute instructions in program order only.

Of the 720 (6!) possible execution interleavings, 90 preserve the individual program order. We have already pointed out that of the 90 program-order interleavings not all six-tuple combinations can result (i.e., 000000 is not possible). The question remains whether out of the 720 non-program-order interleavings all six-tuple combinations can result. So far we have assumed that the memory system of the example multiprocessor is access atomic; this means that memory updates affect all processors at the same time. In a cache-based system such as depicted in Figure 1, this may not be the case; such a system can be nonatomic if an invalidation does not reach all caches at the same time.

In an atomic system it is easy to show that, indeed, not all six-tuple combinations are possible, even if processors need not adhere to program order. For example, the outcome 011001 implies the following: Processor P1 observes that C has been updated and B has not been updated yet. This implies that P3 must have executed statement e before P2 executed statement c. Processor P2 observes that A has been updated before C has been updated. This implies that P1 must have executed statement a before P3 executed statement e. Processor P3 observes that B has been updated but A has not been updated. This implies that P2 must have executed statement c before P1 executed statement a. Hence, e occurred before c, a occurred before e, and c occurred before a. Since this ordering is plainly impossible, we can conclude that in an atomic system, the outcome 011001 cannot occur.

The above conclusion does not hold true

in a nonatomic multiprocessor. Let us assume that the actual execution interleaving of instructions is a,c,e,b,d,f. Let us further assume the following sequence of events: When P1 executes b, P1's own copy of B has not been updated, but P1's own copy of C has been updated. Hence, P1 prints the tuple 01. When P2 executes d, P2's own copy of A has been updated, but P2's own copy of C has not been updated. Hence, P2 prints the tuple 10. When P3 executes f, P3's own copy of A has not been updated, but P3's own copy of B has been updated. Hence, P3 prints the tuple 01. The resulting six-tuple is indeed 011001. Note that all instructions were *executed* in program order, but other processors did not *observe* them in program order.

We might ask ourselves whether a multiprocessor functions incorrectly if it is capable of generating any or all of the above-mentioned six-tuple outputs. This question does not have a definitive answer; rather the answer depends on the expectations of the programmer. A programmer who expects a system to behave in a sequentially consistent manner will perceive the system to behave incorrectly if it allows its processors to execute accesses out of program order. The programmer will likely find that synchronization protocols using shared variables will not function. The difficulty of concurrent programming and parallel architectures stems from the effort to disallow all interleavings that will result in incorrect outcomes while not being overly restrictive.

Systems with atomic accesses. We have shown in an earlier work[14] that a necessary and sufficient condition for a system with atomic memory accesses to be sequentially consistent (the strongest condition for logical behavior) is that memory accesses must be performed in the order intended by the programmer—i.e., in program order. (A Load is considered performed at a point in time when the issuing of a Store from any processor to the same address cannot affect the value returned by the Load. Similarly, a Store on X by processor i is considered performed at a point in time when an issued Load from any processor to the same address cannot return a value of X preceding the Store.) In a system where such a condition holds, we say that storage accesses are *strongly ordered*.

In a system without caches a memory access is performed when it reaches the memory system or at any point in time

when the order of all preceding accesses to memory has become fixed. For example, if accesses are queued in a FIFO (first in, first out) buffer at the memory, then an access is performed once it is latched in the buffer. When a private cache is added to each processor, Stores can also be atomic in the case of a bus system because of the simultaneous broadcast capability of the buses; in such systems the invalidations generated by a Store and the Load requests broadcast by a processor are latched simultaneously by all the controllers (including possibly the memory controllers). As soon as each controller has taken the proper action on the invalidation, the access can be considered performed.

Buffering of access requests and invalidations also become possible if the rules governing sequential consistency are carefully observed. With extensive buffering at all levels, and provided that the interconnection and the memory system have sufficient bandwidth, the efficiency of all processors may be very high, even if the memory access latency is large compared to the processor cycle time. Two articles present more detailed discussions of the buffering of accesses and invalidations in cache-based multiprocessors.[7,15]

In a weakly ordered system the condition of strong ordering is relaxed to include accesses to synchronization variables only. Synchronization variables must be hardware-recognizable to enforce the specific conditions of strong ordering on them. Moreover, before a lock access can proceed, all previous accesses to nonsynchronization data must be allowed to "settle." This means that all shared memory accesses made before the lock operation was encountered must be completed before the lock operation can proceed. In systems that synchronize very infrequently, the relaxation of strong ordering

to weak ordering of data accesses can result in greater efficiency. For example, if the interconnection network is buffered and packet-switched, the interface between the processor and the network can send global memory requests only one at a time to the memory if strong ordering is to be enforced. The reason for this is that in such a network the access time is variable and unpredictable because of conflicts; in many cases waiting for an acknowledgment from the memory controller is the only way to ensure that global accesses are performed in program order. In the case of weak ordering the interface can send the next global access directly after the current global access has been latched in the first stage of the interconnection network, resulting in better processor efficiency. However, the frequency of lock operations will be higher in a program designed for a weakly ordered system.

Systems with nonatomic accesses. In a multiprocessor system with nonatomic accesses, it has been shown that the previous condition for strong ordering of storage accesses (and sequential consistency) is not sufficient.[14]

Example 1. In a system with a recombining network[2] the network can provide for access short-circuiting, which combines Loads and Stores to the same address within the network, before the Store reaches its destination memory module. For the parallel program in Figure 10—$S_i(X)$ and $L_i(X)$ represent global accesses "Store into location X by processor i" and "Load from location X by processor i," respectively—such short-circuiting can result in the following sequence of events:

(1) Processor 1 issues a command to store a value at memory location A.

Processor 1	Processor 2	Processor 3
$S_1(A)$	$L_2(A)$	$L_3(B)$
	$S_2(B)$	$L_3(A)$

Figure 10. Concurrent program for three processors accessing shared variables.

(2) Processor 2 reads the value written by processor 1 "on the fly" before A is updated.

(3) Because of the successful read of A in step 2, processor 2 issues a command to write a value at memory location B.

(4) Processor 3 reads the value written by processor 2; it reflects the updated B.

(5) Processor 3 reads memory location A and an old value for A is returned because the write to A by processor 1 has not propagated to A yet.

Each processor performs instructions in the order specified by the programmer, but sequential consistency is violated. Processor 2 implies that step 1 has been completed by processor 1 when it initiates step 3. In step 4 processor 3 recognizes that implication by successfully reading B. But when processor 3 then reads A, it does not find the implied new value but rather the old value. Consequently, processor 3 observes an effect of step 1 before it is capable of observing step 1 itself.

Example 2. In a cache-based system where memory accesses and invalidations are propagated one by one through a packet-switched (but not recombining) network, the same problem as in the previous example may occur. Initially, all processors have an RO copy of A in their cache.

(1) Processor 1 issues a command to store a value at memory location A. Invalidations are sent to each processor with a copy of A in its cache. (For simplicity we assume that the size of a cache block is one word.)

(2) Processor 2 reads the value of A as updated by processor 1, because the invalidation has reached its cache; processor 1 writes the data back to main memory and forwards a copy to processor 2.

(3) Because of the successful read of A in step 2, processor 2 issues a command to write a value at memory location B, sending invalidations for copies of B.

(4) Processor 3 reads the value written by processor 2; it reflects the updated B, because the associated invalidations have propagated to processor 3.

(5) Processor 3 reads memory location A and an old value for A is returned because the invalidation for A caused by processor 1 has not yet propagated to the third processor's cache.

Again each processor executes all instructions in program order. Furthermore, a processor does not proceed to issue memory accesses before all previous invalidations broadcast by the processor have been acknowledged. Yet the same problem occurs as in the previous example; sequential consistency is violated. This is the case because invalidations are essentially memory accesses. Because invalidations are not atomic, the system is not strongly ordered.

User interface

The discussion in this article shows that the issues of synchronization, communication, coherence, and ordering of events in multiprocessors are intricately related and that design decisions must be based on the environment for which the machine is destined. Coherence depends on synchronization in some coherence protocols because the user has to be aware that synchronization points are the only points in time at which coherence is restored. Strict ordering of events may be enforced all the time (strong ordering) or at synchronization points only (weak ordering).

At the user level most features of the physical (hardware) architecture are not visible. The instruction set of each processor and the virtual memory are the most important system features visible to the programs. Depending on the features of the physical architecture that are visible to the programmer, the task of programming the machine may be more difficult, and it may be more difficult to share the machine among different users.

Nontransparent coherence or ordering schemes. A sophisticated compiler may succeed in efficiently detecting and tagging the shared writable data to avoid the coherence problem. Such a compiler may also be able to make efficient use of synchronization primitives provided at different levels. The compiler may be aware of access ordering on a specific machine and generate code accordingly. It is not clear that compiler technology will improve to a point where efficient code can be generated for these different options.

If a program is written in a high-level concurrent language, the facility to specify shared writable data may not exist in the language, in which case we must still rely on the compiler for detecting the minimum set of data to tag as noncachable. It should be emphasized that perfectly legal programs in concurrent languages that allow the sharing of data, generally will not execute correctly in a system where events are weakly ordered.

User access to synchronization primitives. Programmers of concurrent applications may have in their repertoires different hardware- or software-controlled synchronization primitives. For performance reasons it may be advisable to let basic hardware-level synchronization instructions be directly accessible to users, who know their applications and can tailor the synchronization algorithm to their own needs. The basic drawback of such a policy is the increased possibility of deadlocks, resulting from programming errors or processor failure. Spin-locks and suspend-locks consume processor cycles and bus cycles. Therefore, such locks should never be held for a long time. Ideally, a processor should not be interruptible during the time that it owns a lock; for example, one or several processors may spin forever on a lock if the process that "owns" the lock has to be aborted because of an exception. In a virtual-machine environment the user process does not have any control over the interruptibility of the processor, and thus a process can be preempted while it is owning a lock. This will result in unnecessary, resource-consuming spinning from all other processes attempting to obtain the lock.

A solution to this problem is the task-force scheduling strategy,[1] in which all active processes of a multitask are always scheduled and preempted together. Another solution is the implementation of some kind of time-out on spinning. The drastic solution to all these problems is to involve the operating system in every synchronization or communication, so that it can include these mechanisms in its scheduling policy to maximize performance.

Making a multiprocessor function correctly can be a simple or an extremely difficult task. Basic synchronization mechanisms can be primitive or complex, wasteful of processor cycles or highly efficient. In any case the underlying hardware must support the basic assumptions of the logical model expected by the user. In a strongly ordered system such an assumption usually is that the system behaves in a sequentially consistent manner.

Increased transparency comes at the cost of efficiency and increased hardware complexity. But traditional and significant advantages such as the ability to protect users against themselves and other users, ease of programming, portability of programs, and efficient management of shared resources by multiple users are strong arguments for the designers of general-purpose computers to accept the hardware complexity and the negative effect on performance. The designers of general-purpose machines will probably prefer coherence enforcement on the fly in hardware, strong ordering of memory accesses, and restricted access to synchronization primitives by the user.

On the other hand, for machines with limited access by sophisticated users, such as supercomputers and experimental multiprocessor systems, the performance of each individual task may be of prime importance, and the increased cost of transparency may not be justified.

The challenge of the future lies in the ability to control interprocess communication and synchronization in systems without rigid structures. Efficient multiprocessing will be provided by systems in which synchronization, coherence, and logical ordering of events are carefully analyzed and blended together harmoniously in the context of efficient hardware implementations. It is necessary, however, to provide the programmer with a simple logical model of concurrency behavior. When multiprocessors do not conform to the concept of a single logical model, but rather must be viewed as a dynamic pool of processing, storage, and connection resources, the control in software over communication and synchronization becomes a truly formidable task. The concepts of strong and weak ordering as defined in this article correspond to two widely accepted models of multiprocessor behavior, and we believe that future designs will conform to one of the two models.□

Acknowledgment

Through many technical discussions, William Collier of IBM Poughkeepsie helped shape the content of this article.

References

1. A.K. Jones and P. Schwarz, "Experience Using Multiprocessor Systems—A Status Report," *Computing Surveys*, June 1980, pp. 121-165.

2. A. Gottlieb et al., "The NYU Ultracomputer—Designing an MIMD Shared Memory Parallel Computer," *IEEE Trans. Computers*, Feb. 1983, pp. 175-189.

3. D. Gajski and J.-K. Peir, "Essential Issues in Multiprocessor Systems," *Computer*, June 1985, pp. 9-27.

4. A.J. Smith, "Cache Memories," *Computing Surveys*, Sept. 1982, pp.473-530.

5. L.M. Censier and P. Feautrier, "A New Solution to Coherence Problems in Multicache Systems," *IEEE Trans. Computers*, Dec. 1978, pp.1112-1118.

6. W.W. Collier, "Architectures for Systems of Parallel Processes," IBM Technical Report TR 00.3253, Poughkeepsie, N.Y., Jan. 1984.

7. M. Dubois, C. Scheurich, and F. Briggs, "Memory Access Buffering In Multiprocessors," *Proc. 13th Int'l Symp. Computer Architecture*, June 1986, pp. 434-442.

8. L. Lamport, "How to Make a Multiprocessor Computer That Correctly Executes Multiprocess Programs," *IEEE Trans. Computers*, Sept. 1979, pp. 690-691.

9. G.F. Pfister et al., "The IBM Research Parallel Processor Prototype (RP3): Introduction and Architecture," *Proc. 1985 Parallel Processing Conf.*, pp. 764-771.

10. D.A. Padua, D.J. Kuck, and D.H. Lawrie, "High-Speed Multiprocessors and Compilation Techniques," *IEEE Trans. Computers*, Sept. 1980, pp. 763-776.

11. J.R. Goodman, "Using Cache Memory to Reduce Processor-Memory Traffic," *Proc. 10th Int'l Symp. Computer Architecture*, June 1983, Stockholm, Sweden, pp. 124-131.

12. J. Archibald and J.-L. Baer, "Cache Coherence Protocols: Evaluation Using a Multiprocessor Simulation Model," *ACM Trans. Computer Systems*, Nov. 1986, pp. 273-298.

13. G.R. Andrews and F.B. Schneider, "Concepts and Notations for Concurrent Programming," *Computing Surveys*, Mar. 1983, pp. 3-43.

14. M. Dubois and C. Scheurich, "Dependency and Hazard Resolution in Multiprocessors," Univ. of Southern Calif. Technical Report CRI 86-20.

15. C. Scheurich and M. Dubois, "Correct Memory Operation of Cache-Based Multiprocessors," *Proc. 14th Int'l Symp. Computer Architecture*, June 1987, pp. 234-243.

Michel Dubois has been an assistant professor in the Department of Electrical Engineering of the University of Southern California since 1984. Before that, he was a research engineer at the Central Research Laboratory of Thomson-CSF in Orsay, France. His main interests are computer architecture and parallel processing with an emphasis on high-performance multiprocessor systems. He has published more than 30 technical papers on multiprocessor architectures, performance, and algorithms, and he served on the program committee of the 1987 Architecture Symposium.

Dubois holds a PhD from Purdue University, an MS from the University of Minnesota, and an engineering degree from the Faculté Polytechnique de Mons in Belgium, all in electrical engineering. He is a member of the ACM and the Computer Society of the IEEE.

Christoph Scheurich is a doctoral student and research assistant in the Department of Electrical Engineering-Systems at USC. He received the BSEE in 1981 from the University of the Pacific, Stockton, California, and the MS degree in computer engineering in 1985 from USC. His current interests lie in computer architecture, specifically the design and implementation of multiprocessor memory systems.

Scheurich is a student member of the ACM and the Computer Society of the IEEE.

Fayé A. Briggs is in the Advanced Development Group at Sun Microsystems. He was an associate professor of electrical and computer engineering at Rice University, and prior to that he was on the faculty of Purdue University. He has also served as a consultant to IBM, TI, and Sun. His current research interests are multiprocessor and vector architectures, their compilers, operating systems, and performance. He has published more than 35 technical papers in these areas and is the coauthor of *Computer Architecture and Parallel Processing* (McGraw-Hill).

Briggs has a PhD from the University of Illinois and an MS from Stanford University, both in electrical engineering.

Readers may write to the authors c/o Michel Dubois, Dept. of Electrical Engineering, University of Southern California, University Park, Los Angeles, CA 90089-0781.

THE ORGANIZATION OF THE CEDAR SYSTEM

J. Konicek   T. Tilton   A. Veidenbaum   C. Q. Zhu   E. S. Davidson
R. Downing   M. Haney   M. Sharma   P. C. Yew   P. M. Farmwald
D. Kuck   D. Lavery   R. Lindsey   D. Pointer   J. Andrews   T. Beck
T. Murphy   S. Turner   N. Warter

Center for Supercomputing Research and Development *
University of Illinois at Urbana-Champaign
Urbana, Illinois, 61801

Abstract

The Cedar multiprocessor project at the Center for Supercomputing Research and Development at the University of Illinois is a research project to study issues in parallel processing. The goal of the project has been to design and study a scalable high-performance multiprocessor system for execution of parallel programs. This paper describes the organization of the major components of the Cedar system and their implementation, and demonstrates how the design objectives were met. The scalability of the shared memory system is also discussed.

Introduction

The Cedar multiprocessor project at the Center for Supercomputing Research and Development (CSRD) at the University of Illinois is a research project to study issues in parallel processing [1]. The goal of the project has been to design and study a scalable high-performance multiprocessor system for the execution of parallel programs. Currently, a 32-processor system is operational and is running Xylem, the Cedar operating system, and a Fortran restructuring compiler described in the companion papers.

The main objectives of the project can be summarized as follows:

1. Efficient execution of parallel programs

2. An architecturally scalable design

3. Use of memory and control hierarchy

4. Utilization of Omega networks [2] for high-bandwidth interconnect

5. Efficient synchronization

6. Integration of performance evaluation facilities into the system

Implementation of the Cedar architecture began in 1985 with the selection of the Alliant FX/8 system [3] as a building block for our machine. This system is used as a *cluster* of processors and a shared memory system is added linking 4 clusters together for a total of 32 vector processors. The high level organization of the Cedar system is shown in Figure 1.

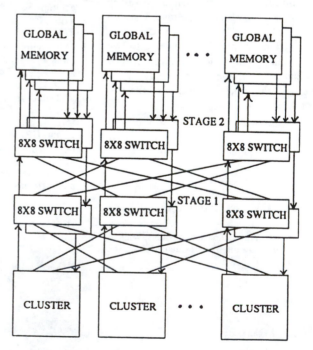

Figure 1: The Cedar System Organization.

The Cedar system has a memory hierarchy to

---

*At the time of this writing, T. Beck, E. S. Davidson, R. Downing, M. Haney, M. Sharma, and C. Q. Zhu are no longer with CSRD but have been included here because of their significant contributions to the implementation of the Cedar system while at CSRD.

"The Organization of the Cedar System" by J. Konicek et al. from *International Conference on Parallel Processing, Vol. 1: Architecture*, 1991, pages 49-56. Copyright © 1991 by CRC Press, Inc.

exploit locality and the varying degrees of sharing exhibited by instructions and data. The memory in each Alliant system forms one such level shared by 8 processors. The shared global memory of Cedar is the second level in the hierarchy and is shared by all processors. The control hierarchy is similarly divided into cluster and global components.

The shared memory bandwidth requirements of 32 vector processors are supported by a 32-way interleaved memory and the use of two unidirectional packet-switched Omega networks, called the forward and the reverse networks, for connecting the processors to the shared memory. The forward network routes requests from the processors to the memory modules, and the reverse network returns the responses.

The fast synchronization required by parallel programs is supported by implementing synchronization instructions in the memory modules. This provides indivisibility and saves multiple memory accesses on synchronization requests.

An integrated hardware and software performance analysis environment allows measurements to be made in both single-user and multi-user modes. Collected data is filtered and sent to workstations where visualization tools are used to display the data.

The remainder of this paper presents the organization of the major components of the Cedar system and their implementation. The following sections describe the processor cluster, the shared memory system, the implementation technology, and finally, the scalability of the shared memory system.

Processor Cluster

Each Cedar processor cluster consists of an Alliant FX/8 system augmented with the Global Interface hardware (described below). The cluster organization can be seen in Figure 2. In the remainder of this section, we will describe the pertinent features of the Alliant FX/8 architecture.

The FX/8 system is an 8-processor shared memory multiprocessor. Each processor has a vector unit with eight 32-word vector registers and multiple vector functional units. The processor is fully pipelined with a cycle of 170ns. The processor is rated at 11.8 MFLOPs peak (vector) performance.

The processors are connected through a crossbar switch to a 4-way interleaved, direct-mapped, shared, 512KB cache. The shared cache is connected to the interleaved cluster memory through a split transaction memory bus. The data busses

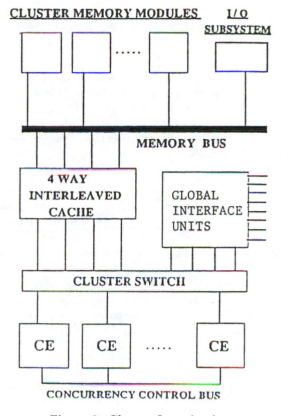

Figure 2: Cluster Organization.

are 64 bits wide. The I/O caches are also connected to the memory bus and are kept coherent with the shared cache by hardware.

Each processor contains a Concurrency Control Unit which is connected to the concurrency control bus. Instructions for starting and synchronizing the computation on multiple processors are implemented by this hardware. These instructions support execution of parallel Doall and Doacross style loops with self-scheduling of the processors.

The FX/8 supports data types ranging from 1 to 8 bytes. For reads, a processor can issue 2 requests before stalling the pipeline. Any number of writes can be outstanding. The memory is byte-addressable. Read requests always bring an 8-byte data word into the processor. Furthermore, unaligned memory accesses are allowed and the processor issues two requests if a word boundary is crossed.

The Shared Memory System

The four Cedar clusters are connected to the shared memory. The shared memory system includes the networks and the interleaved memory. Several major features of the shared memory system are described first, followed by a description of its major sub-systems.

Memory interleaving The Cedar shared memory consists of 32 independent modules. The word size in the shared memory is 8 bytes. The address interleaving is such that consecutive word addresses access successive memory modules. The memory is byte-addressable.

Address space partitioning The physical address space of each Cedar cluster is partitioned in two halves. The lower half describes the cluster memory address space and the upper half describes the shared memory space. Four separate cluster address spaces exist in the system but there is only one shared global address space. Bit 31 of the physical address distinguishes the global and cluster addresses. The virtual memory system maps the different parts of the physical address space accordingly.

Memory request ordering To utilize pipelining in the shared memory system weak ordering of memory accesses [4] is used on Cedar. Cedar can have multiple outstanding memory requests from each processor. The only thing guaranteed by the forward Omega network and memory is that requests from a processor to a given memory address are performed in the same order as issued by the processor. Requests to different addresses by the processor are satisfied by different memory modules and can occur in any order. Requests from different processors to a given address can reach the memory module in any order.

When a synchronization instruction to shared memory is executed, the processor is stalled and the synchronization request is not issued until all read and write requests by the processor have been performed by the requested memory modules.

Synchronization Cedar implements a set of fast, indivisible synchronization operations in shared memory based on the Zhu-Yew synchronization primitives [5]. The multiple disjoint paths in the interconnection network make it impossible to perform synchronization operations using a read-modify-write involving the processor. If the memory implemented only a TestAndSet instruction, a sequence of memory requests would be required to do the work of a Zhu-Yew primitive, increasing the time needed for synchronization and creating extra

memory traffic. For these reasons, the Cedar synchronization instructions are performed by a special processor in each memory module.

Data prefetch The restriction on the number of outstanding read requests by each Alliant processor makes it impossible to fully utilize the shared memory system pipeline. Data prefetching is implemented to overcome this limitation. It allows the processor to initiate a block move from the shared memory and continue the execution regardless of how many read requests are outstanding.

Interconnection Networks

Each Cedar network is a two-stage packet-switched Omega network composed of 8 crossbar switches and is shown in Figure 3. The network data path

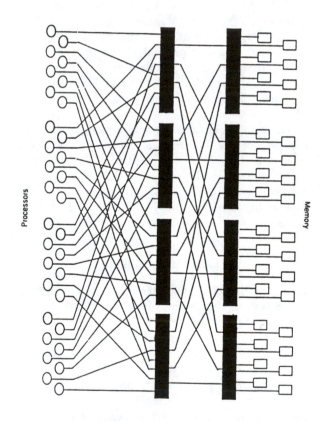

Figure 3: The Cedar Interconnection Network.

is one 64-bit word wide. A processor read request consists of one word in the forward network (address/control) and two words in the reverse network (address/control, and data). A write request is 2 words in the forward and 1 word in the reverse network. The synchronization request can be up to

3 words long in the forward and up to 2 words in the reverse network. A multiword request is sent as a single *packet* through the network.

The 8x8 crossbar switch has a 64-bit wide data path and provides a 2-deep queue per input port and a 2-deep queue per output port. Any crossbar input can be switched to any output in one system clock (85ns) when there are no conflicts. Each output port contains priority resolution logic for selecting which of the input ports simultaneously requesting the output port will be serviced.

The first word of a packet is an address/control (A/C) word. This word contains the destination address of the output port. A switch receives a packet and determines if any other input ports are requesting the same output port. If not, the packet is routed to the output port at the rate of one word per clock. The packet waits in the input queue if the requested output port is already used by another request or if this input port is not selected by priority resolution logic for routing. Once an input port queue is filled, the input port sends a *Busy* signal back to the sender until such time that the input queue has an empty slot.

For multiword packets the A/C word asserts a *Hold* signal which informs the switch to hold the route established by the A/C word for one more clock. In this way, multiple data words are transferred to the same destination. In general, for a packet of N words, *Hold* must be active for the first N-1 words. It should also be noted that a packet is indivisible. Should another request be received that requires the same output port, the current request must finish in its entirety before the new request can be honored.

A fixed-priority, non-blocking conflict resolution scheme is used in the crossbar. The priority of an input port is given by its number. When simultaneous requests conflict for a given output port, the highest priority request will be serviced first, then the next priority, and so on. However, all currently conflicting requests must be resolved before any new request can enter the arbitration. In this way, the highest priority input port cannot "starve" other input ports and prevent them from accessing a given output.

Global Interface Units

The Global Interface Unit (GIU) connects a processor to an input port of the forward network and to an output port of the reverse network. At each port, there is a queue on the GIU which can hold up to four requests. The GIU performs data prefetching and works together with the shared memory modules to execute the Cedar synchronization operations. Each GIU services one processor, so 8 GIUs are added to each cluster.

In the Alliant FX/8, memory requests are transferred between the eight processors and four cache banks by an 8 x 4 crossbar switch. For Cedar, this switch is expanded to an 8 x 8 crossbar. Each of the four new switch ports is shared by two GIUs.

Since each processor can have up to two pending requests, each GIU provides logic for managing two outstanding shared memory operations and works together with the Alliant cache to make sure that data transfers take place in the order requested by the processor. Read operations are completed when the GIU returns data to the processor. However, for write operations, the processor can continue as soon as the data is transferred to the GIU. Hence, there can be many outstanding writes in the shared memory system.

Vector Prefetch Unit   Each GIU contains a Vector Prefetch Unit (VPU). The VPU is a programmable address generator that fetches data from global memory into a direct-mapped 512-word memory called the prefetch data buffer. The VPU can issue a shared memory address every 170ns or two clocks and can have up to 512 outstanding requests.

The VPU receives the stride, mask, and length of the vector from the processor. Then the processor has to supply the starting address of the vector and the VPU fetches the specified vector into the data buffer. The processor can then read the vector using a vector instruction and the original shared memory address. The GIU detects that the shared memory operand is in the buffer and retrieves it from there.

The processor does the virtual address translation and sends physical addresses to the GIU. Therefore, when the VPU reaches a page boundary, it waits for the processor to emit the physical address of the first element to be fetched in the next page. Assuming that the processor will finish all accesses to the current page before issuing an address to the next page, the prefetch data buffer need only be one page long. For Cedar that size is 512 words or 4KB.

Each location in the prefetch data buffer has a valid bit associated with it. When data arrives from shared memory and is written to the buffer, the corresponding valid bit is set. Processor requests for elements which are not yet valid are held pending until the data arrives. All the data in the buffer for the current page is invalidated when the VPU starts to fetch the next page or when prefetching is turned off.

There are two ways for the processor to supply the starting address and begin the prefetch. It can be supplied implicitly by using a vector instruction to access the memory address of the first element in a vector. This access is held pending until the element arrives in the buffer and all successive shared memory accesses from the processor are directed to the data buffer. The second method is to supply the address explicitly using a special processor instruction. A vector instruction issued later will have its accesses directed to the data buffer. The advantage of explicit prefetching is that the processor is not held waiting until the data begins arriving from the shared memory. After starting the prefetch, it is free to do other work while waiting for the data buffer to fill. Thus, explicit prefetches can be moved up in the code to hide the shared memory latency.

Synchronization Control Unit   The Cedar synchronization instructions are performed in the shared memory. A memory module receives the instruction and operands from the processor. The result of the operation is returned to the processor. Controlling these data transfers is the job of the GIU's Synchronization Control Unit (SCU).

To initiate a synchronization operation, the opcode and operands are written to registers on the GIU by the processor. The writing of the opcode arms the SCU. Then, when the processor issues a TestAndSet instruction to a shared memory address, the SCU sends the opcode and the necessary operands to the shared memory, initiating the synchronization operation. It then waits for the result to come back. When the result returns, the processor is informed of the outcome (true or false) of the comparison operation performed by the shared memory module as described in the next section. Some synchronization operations also return additional data. This data is written to a register on the GIU for the processor to retrieve later. If the SCU is not armed when the TestAndSet is issued, then a simple TestAndSet request is sent to the shared memory.

To maintain weak ordering of memory requests, a synchronization operation cannot be initiated until all of the previously initiated writes have been completed. The GIU uses a counter to keep track of pending writes. Synchronization operations are held at the GIU until all writes have been acknowledged.

Shared Memory Modules

A memory module consists of a forward network (input) interface, memory control, a memory array with error correction circuitry, a synchronization processor, and a reverse network (output) interface. The memory has an 85ns cycle and is fully pipelined. The longest pipeline segment is the memory array which takes four 85ns cycles. Each memory module contains 2MB of memory.

The memory array and its control perform 64-bit reads, and 64-, 32-, 16-, or 8-bit writes. For unaligned or short writes it performs a read-modify-write access. Memory control also coordinates the execution of synchronization requests with the synchronization processor. Additional queuing is provided on the input and output of the memory array to buffer incoming or outgoing requests.

The input interface is responsible for receiving requests from the network, checking for errors, and queuing up to 2 words if the memory array is busy. The flow control between the forward network output port and the input interface is identical to the one used in the network.

The output interface receives a request from the memory array and sends it to the reverse network. It can queue up to 2 words if the network input port is busy.

Synchronization Processor   The processor consists of a 32-bit ALU, registers, and control. It has a cycle time of 85ns and can perform an addition, subtraction, or logical operation in one cycle. It performs the TestAndSet instruction and the Cedar synchronization instructions described below.

A Cedar synchronization instruction is an indivisible memory operation on either a 32-bit aligned word of Cedar shared memory called a *Key* or on a 64-bit word containing a *Key* and a 32-bit datum (*Key/Data* pair). Its indivisibility is due to the fact that the memory module in which the word resides is not available for other accesses until the synchronization operation is completed.

A synchronization operation is executed as follows:

1. Read the memory word at the specified address

2. Perform the specified logical test

3. If test fails terminate and notify the processor

4. Else perform the specified action

The actions can be a read or write for a *Key* or a *Key/Data* pair. An arithmetic or logical operation can be performed on a *Key* only.

The test is a comparison between a 32-bit operand (*OPERAND1*) sent by the GIU and the addressed memory word (*MWORD*). The test is *MWORD rel_op OPERAND1*, where *rel_op* can be one of the following: $<$, $<=$, $=$, $<>$, $>$, $>=$, TRUE (test always successful).

The instructions which specify an arithmetic or logical operation on the *Key* either return the *Key* value before the operation, after the operation, or just return an acknowledgment to the GIU, as specified by the instruction (e.g. pre-increment or post-increment is possible). The available synchronization processor operations are:

Arithmetic: Increment or decrement; add or subtract a 20-bit immediate value; add or subtract a 32-bit value.

Logical: OR, AND, XOR, XNOR (possibly after complementing one of the inputs) and NOT.

Other: IDENTITY (pass either operand through the ALU), SET to 0, SET to -1, NO-OP.

A synchronization instruction can have two formats: a 32-bit instruction word followed by one or two 32-bit operand words. The first operand is used in the test, the second operand is used in a 32-bit arithmetic or logical operation. The arithmetic operation can be performed without the second operand using a 20-bit immediate value. The advantage of this is that the synchronization packet from is GIU is only two words long, consisting of the address/control word plus a data word containing the instruction and first operand. 32-bit operations require a third word in the network.

Performance Monitoring

The Cedar performance monitoring system provides tracing and histogramming measurement tools for program and hardware performance analysis. It is composed of sub-systems each containing a Sun CPU board running UNIX and up to 18 CSRD-designed Tracers or Histogrammers. The GIUs, crossbar switches and memory modules have built-in performance monitoring points and can be connected to the Tracers and Histogrammers. Active probes allow connections to the cluster backplanes so that cluster performance measurements can be made. The performance monitoring hardware plugs into a VME bus [6] and is linked to the CSRD Ethernet.

The Tracer allows 20 bits of data to be collected and timestamped [7]. Tracing can be enabled or disabled through special control signals. Data can

be acquired at a rate of 20 bits every 170ns. The timestamp is 40 bits and is incremented every 50ns. The timestamps of multiple Tracers can be synchronized. Tracer modules can be used in parallel to increase the trace width. Up to 4 modules can be interleaved to increase the acquisition rate and/or trace buffer depth by a factor of 4.

The Histogrammer can count the number of occurrences of 64K events. A 64K by 32-bit static RAM array stores the number of occurrences of the events. Event detection logic accepts the module's 32 data inputs and 8 data enable inputs and performs a function which generates the RAM address associated with a specific event type. The data at that location is read from RAM, loaded into a 32-bit counter, incremented, and written back to RAM. Built-in functions for generating an address are selected by programming control registers through the VME interface. Histogramming events can be acquired every 170ns. Up to 4 histogrammer modules can be interleaved to increase the acquisition rate to 42.5ns.

Hardware Implementation

Cedar is designed using a synchronous approach. A system clock of 85ns is distributed to each cluster, memory module, GIU, and crossbar switch. The clock distribution logic is implemented using 100K ECL logic and guarantees minimum skew between different boards.

In order to build very fast networks that can be scaled up in size we use twisted pair cables and differential ECL to interconnect boards. ECL is also used in the crossbar switch construction and for the control logic in the memory module where speed is of essence. The rest of the logic is implemented in TTL.

Cedar is implemented using a mixture of surface-mounted and through-hole components. Printed-circuit boards of 11, 15, and 17 layers are used and are connected to passive backplanes using 300 and 400 pin connectors.

Diagnostic hardware on each board is connected to a set diagnostic processors for error monitoring. The errors are reported to a master console. A set of diagnostic routines can exercise and isolate errors in the shared memory hardware.

GIU   The GIU is implemented using mostly TTL technology with ECL used for cable drivers and receivers. The data buffer is implemented using fast SRAMs, with the valid bits stored in resetable

SRAMs. Each GIU is a single printed circuit board and resides in the modified Alliant chassis.

Crossbar Switch The crossbar is designed in 10KH ECL. Two boards implement the switch due to a large number of wires. The first switch board is designed to accept differential cable input (1280 wires) and present single-ended output (640). A second switch board provides one added level of buffering for total queue depth of 4 per stage and converts the single-ended outputs of the first board to differential cable drive.

Another component of the switch is a custom silicon device implementing the crossbar data path. This device, FXBAR, is roughly 2000 ECL gates packaged in a 148 pin PGA. It is a 4-bit wide slice of an 8x8 crossbar connection matrix with a 2-deep input queue and a one word output buffer (queue) on each port.

Memory Module Each memory module is a single printed circuit board containing 2MB of memory and the synchronization processor. The memory is implemented using 256K DRAMS and a standard single-bit-correct/double double-bit-detect error correction scheme. The synchronization processor is implemented using 4-bit wide ALUs. The data path is 64 bits wide except for the synchronization processor where it is 32 bits. The control logic and parts of input and output interface are implemented using the 10KH ECL logic. The remainder of the board is implemented using TTL logic.

Tracer and Histogrammer The Tracer is implemented on two boards; the Tracer board and the Tracer I/O board. The Tracer I/O board connects to the Tracer board through VME connectors. The Tracer board contains a VME interface and 3 tracer modules. The trace buffer of a module has 32-bit words and is populated with 1- or 4-megabit DRAMS, providing a 1- or 4-megaword trace buffer.

The Histogrammer is also implemented on two boards. Histogrammer I/O board receives and conditions all performance signals for the Histogrammer. The Histogrammer board contains a VME interface and 2 histogrammer modules.

Scalability Prediction

The performance scalability of the Cedar shared memory system can be gleaned from the simula-

tion results presented below. The simulator uses a register-transfer level description of the actual design and varies the number of processors [8].

The experiments were run using a traffic model which consists of vectors of 32 requests issued with stride one starting from a random base address. Two-thirds of the vectors are entirely read requests, with the other one-third write requests. Each processor issues 128 such vectors. While a vector request is outstanding in the network, processors do not issue any further requests. Once all outstanding words in a vector have been satisfied then a processor issues another vector request after waiting a length of time determined by a random number selected from an exponential distribution with mean given by $1/BIR$, where BIR is the burst issue rate and ranges from 0.001 to 1.0. The BIR approximates computational delays between vector requests. For BIR=1.0 there is no computation, just vector accesses.

The systems simulated are a close approximation of the Cedar shared memory system. The networks use 8x8 switches but in some cases a stage may only use 4 of the 8 crossbar ports. The sizes of the switches used in each stage of the forward network for different configurations are listed in Table 1. The configurations for the reverse network are the same except that the memories are connected to the first stage, and the processors to the last stage.

Table 1: Network Configurations for Simulation.

| Number of Processors | Switch Size | | | Number of Memories |
	1st Stage	2nd Stage	3rd Stage	
32	8x8	4x4		32
64	8x8	8x8		64
128	8x8	4x4	4x4	128
256	8x8	8x8	4x4	256
512	8x8	8x8	8x8	512

As can be seen in Figure 4, the observable memory bandwidth scales up almost linearly with the increase in the number of processors and memory modules. The slight loss of bandwidth that is observed is due to the limited queueing in the memory and network and can be further reduced by expanding the queues. Bandwidth increases with increasing BIR until the shared memory system is "saturated" at BIR values of .032 and higher.

The latency (Figure 5) and the interarrival time (Figure 6) represent the shared memory system

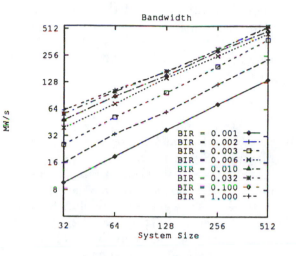

Figure 4: Bandwidth vs. System Size

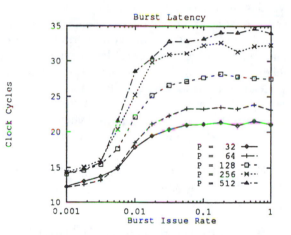

Figure 5: Burst Latency vs. Burst Issue Rate

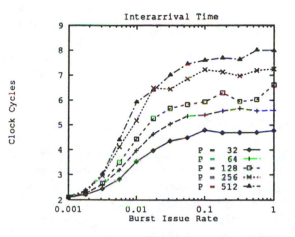

Figure 6: Interarrival Time vs. Burst Issue Rate

performance for a vector request. The latency is paid on the first element of the vector. Additional words requested arrive at intervals given by the interarrival time.

Acknowledgments

This work is supported in part by the National Science Foundation under Grant No. US NSF MIP84-10110, the U.S. Department of Energy under Grant No. US DOE DE-FG02-85ER25001.

The authors would like to thank Frank Dale, Greg Deffley, Steve Look, and Sally Hale for their excellent technical support during the construction of Cedar, and many others at CSRD who contributed directly or indirectly to the completion of this project.

References

[1] D. J. Kuck, E. S. Davidson, D. H. Lawrie, and A. H. Sameh, "Parallel supercomputing today and the Cedar approach," *Science*, vol. 231, pp. 967–974, Feb. 1986.

[2] D. H. Lawrie, "Access and alignment of data in an array processor," *IEEE Trans. Comput.*, vol. c-24, pp. 1145–1155, Dec. 1975.

[3] Alliant Computer Systems Corporation, Littleton, Massachusetts, *FX/Series Product Summary*, Oct. 1986.

[4] C. Scheurich and M. Dubois, "Correct memory operation of cached-based multiprocessors," in *Proc. 14th Annual Int'l Symp. on Computer Architecture*, June 1987.

[5] C.-Q. Zhu and P.-C. Yew, "A scheme to enforce data dependence on large multiprocessor systems," *IEEE Trans. Softw. Eng.*, vol. SE-13, no. 6, pp. 726–739, June 1987.

[6] IEEE Standard P1014, *The VMEbus Specification, Rev. C.1*, 1985.

[7] J. B. Andrews, "A hardware tracing facility for a multiprocessing supercomputer," CSRD Rep. 1009, University of Illinois, Urbana-Champaign, Illinois, May 1990.

[8] E. D. Granston, S. W. Turner, and A. V. Veidenbaum, "Design of a scalable, shared-memory system with support for burst traffic," in *Proc. 1st Annual Workshop on Scalable Shared-Memory Architectures*, Kluwer & Associates, Feb. 1991.

The Tera Computer System*

Robert Alverson   David Callahan   Daniel Cummings   Brian Koblenz
Allan Porterfield   Burton Smith

Tera Computer Company
Seattle, Washington USA

1   Introduction

The Tera architecture was designed with several major goals in mind. First, it needed to be suitable for very high speed implementations, *i. e.*, admit a short clock period and be scalable to many processors. This goal will be achieved; a maximum configuration of the first implementation of the architecture will have 256 processors, 512 memory units, 256 I/O cache units, 256 I/O processors, and 4096 interconnection network nodes and a clock period less than 3 nanoseconds. The abstract architecture is scalable essentially without limit (although a particular implementation is not, of course). The only requirement is that the number of instruction streams increase more rapidly than the number of physical processors. Although this means that speedup is sublinear in the number of instruction streams, it can still increase linearly with the number of physical processors. The price/performance ratio of the system is unmatched, and puts Tera's high performance within economic reach.

Second, it was important that the architecture be applicable to a wide spectrum of problems. Programs that do not vectorize well, perhaps because of a preponderance of scalar operations or too-frequent conditional branches, will execute efficiently as long as there is sufficient parallelism to keep the processors busy. Virtually any parallelism available in the total computational workload can be turned into speed, from operation level parallelism within program basic blocks to multiuser time- and space-sharing. The architecture even has strong support for implementing non-numeric languages like Lisp and Prolog and highly applicative languages like Sisal and Id.

A third goal was ease of compiler implementation. Although the instruction set does have a few unusual features, these do not seem to pose unduly hard problems for the code generator. There are no register or memory addressing constraints and only three addressing modes. Condition code setting is consistent and orthogonal. Although the richness of the instruction set often allows several ways to do something, the variation in their relative costs as the execution environment changes tends to be small. Because the architecture permits the free exchange of spatial and temporal locality for parallelism, a highly optimizing compiler may work hard improving locality and trade the parallelism thereby saved for more speed. On the other hand, if there is sufficient parallelism the compiler has a relatively easy job.

The Tera architecture is derived from that of Horizon [6, 9, 10]; although they are highly similar multistream MIMD systems, there are many significant differences between the two designs.

2   Interconnection Network

The interconnection network is a three-dimensional mesh of pipelined packet-switching nodes, each of which is linked to some of its neighbors. Each link can transport a packet containing source and destination addresses, an operation, and 64 data bits in both directions simultaneously on every clock tick. Some of the nodes are also linked to *resources*, *i. e.*, processors, data memory units, I/O processors, and I/O cache units. Instead of locating the processors on one side of the network and memories on the other (in what Robert Keller has called a "dancehall" configuration[5]), the resources are distributed more-or-less uniformly throughout the network. This permits data to be placed in memory units near the appropriate processor when that is possible and otherwise generally maximizes the distance between possibly interfering resources.

*This research was supported by the United States Defense Advanced Research Projects Agency under Contract MDA972-89-C-0002. The views and conclusions contained in this document are those of Tera Computer Company and should not be interpreted as representing the official policies, either expressed or implied, of DARPA or the U. S. Government.

The interconnection network of a 256 processor Tera system contains 4096 nodes arranged in a 16x16x16 toroidal mesh; that is, the mesh "wraps around" in all three dimensions. Of the 4096 nodes, 1280 are attached to the resources comprising 256 processors, 512 data memory units, 256 I/O cache units and 256 I/O processors. The 2816 remaining nodes do not have resources attached but still provide message bandwidth. To increase node performance, some of the links are missing. If the three directions are named X, Y, and Z, then X-links and Y-links are missing on alternate Z layers. This reduces the node degree from 6 to 4, or from 7 to 5 counting the resource link.

In spite of its missing links, the bandwidth of the network is very high. Any plane bisecting the network crosses at least 256 links, giving the network a data bisection bandwidth of one 64-bit data word per processor per tick in each direction. This bandwidth is needed to support shared memory addressing in the event all 256 processors are addressing memory on the other side of some bisecting plane simultaneously.

As the Tera architecture scales to larger numbers of processors p, the number of network nodes grows as $p^{3/2}$ rather than the $p\log(p)$ associated with the more commonly used multistage networks. For example, a 1024-processor system would have 32,768 nodes. The reason for the overhead per processor of $p^{1/2}$ instead of $\log(p)$ stems from the fact that the system is speed-of-light limited. One can argue that memory latency is fully masked by parallelism only when the number of messages being routed by the network is at least $p \times l$, where l is the (round-trip) latency. Since messages occupy volume, the network must have volume proportional to $p \times l$; since the speed of light is finite, the volume is also proportional to l^3 and therefore l is proportional to $p^{1/2}$ rather than $\log(p)$.

3 Memory

A full-sized system contains 512 data memory units of 128 megabytes each. Memory is byte-addressable, and is organized in 64-bit words. Four additional *access state* bits, more fully described in section 5, are associated with each word. Data and access state are each equipped with a separate set of single error correcting, double error detecting code bits. Data addresses are randomized in the processors using a scheme similar to that developed for the RP3[8]. The randomization is excellent for avoiding memory bank hotspots and network congestion, but makes it difficult to exploit memory locality using nearby memory units. In the Tera system, the randomization is combined with another notion called *distribution*. The processor data segment map has a distribution factor associated with each segment entry. Consecutive virtual addresses in a segment can be distributed among all 512 data memory units, a single unit, or any power of two in between.

Disk speeds have not kept pace with advances in processor and memory performance in recent years. The only currently reasonable solution to this problem is to lower the level of disks in the memory hierarchy by placing a large semiconductor memory between the disks and data memory. In a fully configured Tera system, the 70 gigabyte per second sustained bandwidth needed between secondary storage and data memory is supplied by 256 I/O cache units comprising a directly addressable memory of 256 gigabytes.

The I/O cache units are functionally identical to data memory. The only difference is that their latency is higher because their memory chips are slower (but denser). The fact that I/O cache has all of the attributes of main memory makes it possible to map I/O buffers directly into the address spaces of the application programs that access them. This is used to avoid copying by remapping segments.

A processor fetches instructions through a special path to a neighboring I/O cache unit. This avoids network traffic and network latency, but requires one copy of a program be made for every processor it is to run on.

4 Processors

Each processor in a Tera computer can execute multiple instruction streams simultaneously. In the current implementation, as few as one or as many as 128 program counters may be active at once. On every tick of the clock, the processor logic selects a stream that is ready to execute and allows it to issue its next instruction. Since instruction interpretation is completely pipelined by the processor and by the network and memories as well, a new instruction from a different stream may be issued in each tick without interfering with its predecessors. When an instruction finishes, the stream to which it belongs thereby becomes ready to execute the next instruction. As long as there are enough instruction streams in the processor so that the average instruction latency is filled with instructions from other streams, the processor is being fully utilized. Thus, it is only necessary to have enough streams to hide the expected latency (perhaps 70 ticks on average); once latency is hidden the processor is running at peak performance and additional streams do not speed the result.

If a stream were not allowed to issue its next instruction until the previous instruction completed then approximately 70 different streams would be required on each processor to hide the expected latency. The lookahead described in section 4.3 allows streams to issue multiple instructions in parallel, thereby reducing the number of streams needed to achieve peak performance.

4.1 Stream State

Each stream has the following state associated with it:

- 1 64-bit Stream Status Word (SSW)
- 32 64-bit General Registers (R0-R31)
- 8 64-bit Target Registers (T0-T7)

Context switching is so rapid that the processor has no time to swap the processor-resident stream state. Instead, it has 128 of everything, *i. e.*, 128 SSW's, 4096 general registers, and 1024 target registers. It is appropriate to compare these registers in both quantity and function to vector registers or words of cache in other architectures. In all three cases, the objective is to improve locality and avoid reloading data.

Program addresses are 32 bits long. Each stream's current program counter is located in the low half of its SSW. The upper half describes various modes (*e. g.* floating point rounding, lookahead disable), the trap disable mask (*e. g.* data alignment, floating overflow), and the four most recently generated condition codes. Most operations have a _TEST variant which emits a condition code, and branch operations can examine any subset of the last four condition codes emitted and branch appropriately.

Also associated with each stream are 32 64-bit general registers. Register R0 is special in that it reads as 0, and output to it is discarded. Otherwise, all general registers are identical.

The target registers are used as branch targets. The format of the target registers is identical to that of the SSW, though most control transfer operations only use the low 32 bits to determine a new PC. Separating the determination of the branch target address from the decision to branch allows the hardware to prefetch instructions at the branch targets, thus avoiding delay when the branch decision is made. Using target registers also makes branch operations smaller, resulting in tighter loops. There are also skip operations, which obviate the need to set targets for short forward branches.

One target register (T0) points to the trap handler, which is nominally an unprivileged program. When a trap occurs, the effect is as if a coroutine call to T0 had been executed. This makes trap handling extremely lightweight and independent of the operating system. Trap handlers can be changed by the user to achieve specific trap capabilities and priorities without loss of efficiency.

4.2 Horizontal Instructions

Processor effectiveness, the utilization of the instruction interpretation resources, has always been constrained by the difficulty of issuing more than one instruction per tick. This difficulty has become known as the Flynn Bottleneck[2]. Vector instructions sidestep this difficulty in part, but are not able to handle frequent conditional branches or heterogeneous scalar operations well. Processors with horizontal instructions, extreme examples of which are sometimes called Very Long Instruction Word (VLIW) architectures, offer a good alternative to vector instructions. In a horizontal instruction, several operations are specified together. Memory operations are usually simple loads and stores, and the others are two- or three-address register-to-register operations. If the overall architecture and organization are capable of achieving one instruction per tick, then every functional unit mentioned in the instruction is well-used. If the instructions are only moderately long, branches can be sufficiently frequent.

Tera instructions are mildly horizontal. They typically specify three operations: a memory reference operation like UNS_LOADB(yte), an arithmetic operation like FLOAT_ADD_MUL(tiply), and a control operation like JUMP. The control operation can also be a second arithmetic operation, FLOAT_ADD, or perhaps an INTEGER_ADD used in an address computation. Vectorizable loops can be processed at nominal vector rates (one flop per tick) using only horizontal instructions with these three kinds of operations. Matrix-vector multiplication attains nearly two flops per tick via the same technique used for its efficient vectorization.

4.3 Explicit-Dependence Lookahead

If there are enough streams executing on each processor to hide the average latency (about 70 ticks) then the machine is running at peak performance. However, if each stream can execute some of its instructions in parallel (*e. g.* 2 successive loads) then fewer streams and parallel activities are required to achieve peak performance.

The obvious solution to this problem is to introduce instruction lookahead; the only difficulty is controlling it. The traditional register reservation approach requires far too much scoreboard bandwidth in this kind of architecture. Either multi-streaming or horizontal instructions alone would preclude scoreboarding. The traditional alternative, exposing the pipeline, is also impractical because multi-streaming and unpredictable memory operation latency make it impossible to generate code that is both efficient and safe.

The Tera architecture uses a new technique called explicit-dependence lookahead. The idea is quite simple: each instruction contains a three bit lookahead field that explicitly specifies how many instructions from this stream will issue before encountering an instruction that depends on the current one. Since seven is the maximum possible lookahead value, at most eight instructions and twenty-four operations can be concurrently executing from each stream. A stream is ready to issue a new instruction when all instructions with lookahead values referring to the new instruction have completed. Thus, if each stream maintains a lookahead of seven then nine streams are needed to hide 72 ticks of latency.

Lookahead across one or more branch operations is handled by specifying the minimum of all distances involved. The variant branch operations JUMP_OFTEN and JUMP_SELDOM, for high- and low-probability branches respectively, facilitate optimization by providing a barrier to lookahead along the less likely path. There are also SKIP_OFTEN and SKIP_SELDOM operations. The overall approach is philosophically similar to exposed-pipeline lookahead except that the quanta are instructions, not ticks.

4.4 Protection Domains

Each processor supports as many as 16 active protection domains that define the program memory, data memory, and number of streams allocated to the computations using that processor. Each executing stream is assigned to a protection domain, but which domain (or which processor, for that matter) is not known to the user program. In this sense, a protection domain is a virtual processor and may be moved from one physical processor to another.

The protection domains share a single 64K data segment map and a 16K program page map. Each protection domain has two pairs of map base and limit registers that describe the region of each map available to it. The upper 2048 data segments and 1024 program pages are not relocated by the map bases, and are used by the operating system. Any active protection domain can use all of either or both maps. The map entries contain the physical address; the levels of privilege needed to read, write, or execute the segment or page; whether the segment or page was read, written, or executed, as appropriate; and the distribution (for the data map).

The number of streams available to a program is regulated by three quantities slim, scur, and sres associated with each protection domain. The current number of streams executing in the protection domain is recorded by scur; it is incremented when a stream is created and decremented when a stream quits. A create can only succeed when the incremented scur does not exceed sres, the number of streams reserved in the protection domain. The operations for reserving streams are unprivileged, and allow several streams to be reserved or released simultaneously. The stream limit slim is the operating system limit on the number of streams the protection domain can reserve.

When a stream executes a CREATE operation to create a new stream it increments scur, generates the initial SSW for the stream using one of its own target registers, copies the trap target T0 from its own T0 register, and loads three registers in the new stream from its own general purpose registers. The newly created stream can quickly begin executing useful work in cooperation with its creator as long as significant storage allocation is unnecessary. The QUIT operation terminates the stream that executes it, and decrements both sres and scur. The QUIT_PRESERVE operation only decrements scur, thereby giving up a stream without surrendering its reservation.

Each protection domain has a *retry limit* that determines how many times a memory reference can fail in testing a location's full/empty bit (see section 5) before it will trap. If a synchronization is not satisfied for a long time, then possibly a heavier weight mechanism that avoids busy waiting should be used to wait for the synchronization. The retry limit should be based on the amount of trap processing overhead, which varies depending on the run-time environment. The trap handler thus can invoke the heavier weight mechanism when appropriate.

4.5 Privilege Levels

The privilege levels apply to each stream independently. There are four levels of privilege: user, supervisor, kernel, and IPL. IPL level operates in absolute addressing mode and is the highest privilege level. User, supervisor, and kernel levels use the program and data maps for address translation, and represent increasing levels of privilege. The data map entries define the minimum levels needed to read and write each segment, and the program map entries define the *exact* level needed to execute from each page. The current privilege level of a stream is stored as part of the privileged stream state and is not available to a user-level stream.

Two hardware operations are provided to allow an executing stream to change its privilege level. The (LEVEL_ENTER *lev*) operation sets the current privilege level to the instruction map level if the current level is equal to *lev*. The LEVEL_ENTER operation is located at every entry point that can accept a call from a different privilege level. A trap occurs if the current level is not equal to *lev*. The (LEVEL_RETURN *lev*) operation is used to return to the original privilege level. A trap occurs if *lev* is greater than the current privilege level.

4.6 Exceptions

Exceptional conditions can occur in two ways. First, an instruction may not be executed due to insufficient privilege, as with a LEVEL_RETURN which attempts to raise the privilege level. This type of exception is quite easy to handle. More commonly, exceptions occur *while* executing instructions. With lookahead, further instructions may already be executing and overwriting registers which would be needed to restart instructions.

Rather than keep shadow copies of registers to support rollback, the Tera architecture defines certain exceptions as a side effect of instruction *completion*. In this model, exceptions are guaranteed to be signaled before they are needed, as indicated by the lookahead field. Thus, if instruction j depends on instruction i, all possible exceptions during the execution of instruction i will be signaled before instruction j begins execution.

To support diagnosis and recovery, certain state must be available to the trap handler. A trap can be caused by any of the three operations in an instruction. For each of the (at most eight) memory operations that trapped, the processor provides the trap handler with the trap reason and enough state to allow the operation to be retried (*e. g.* for demand paged virtual memory).

For arithmetic traps caused by the arithmetic operations no state is automatically provided to the trap handler. The decision to preserve operand values for possible use by the trap handler is made by the compiler. While the lookahead field normally only guards true dependence for registers, operand values may be preserved by limiting lookahead to guard antidependence as well.

5 Tagged Memory

Each memory location in the Tera computer system is equipped with four access state bits in addition to a 64-bit value. These access state bits allow the hardware to implement several useful modifications to the usual semantics of memory reference. The two data trap bits generate application-specific lightweight traps, the forward bit implements invisible indirect addressing, and the full/empty bit is used for lightweight synchronization. The influence of these access state bits can be suppressed by a corresponding set of bits in the pointer value used to access the memory.

The two trap bits in the access state are independent of each other and are available for use by the language implementer. If a trap bit is set in a location and the corresponding trap disable bit in the pointer is clear, a trap will occur. Uses for the trap bits include data breakpoints, demand-driven evaluation, run-time type exception signaling, implementation of "active" memory objects, and even stack limit checking.

The forward bit implements a kind of "invisible indirection". Unlike normal indirection, forwarding is controlled by both the pointer and the location pointed to. If the forward bit is set in the memory location and forwarding is not disabled in the pointer, the value found in the location is to be interpreted as a pointer to the target of the memory reference rather than the target itself. Dereferencing will continue until the pointer either disables forwarding or discovers that the addressed location has its forward bit reset. The primary use of forwarding is for on-the-fly modification of address-location bindings, for example in concurrent storage reclamation involving the copying of live structures from one space to another.

The full/empty bit controls the synchronizing behavior of memory references. Load and store operations can optionally use the full/empty bit in the addressed memory word by setting bits in the access control field. The four values for access control are shown below.

value	LOAD	STORE
0	read regardless	write regardless and set full
1	reserved	reserved
2	wait for full and leave full	wait for full and leave full
3	wait for full and set empty	wait for empty and set full

When access control is 2, loads and stores wait for the memory cell to be full before proceeding. In this context, it is sometimes useful to think of the full state as meaning "available" and the empty state as meaning "unavailable". The reading or writing of any part of an object is conveniently prevented by marking that part of it "unavailable". The access control value of 3 causes loads to be treated as "consume" operations and stores as "produce" operations. A load waits for full and then sets empty as it reads, and a store waits for empty and then sets full as it writes. A forwarded location that is not disabled and that has its full/empty bit set to empty is treated as "unavailable" until it fills again, irrespective of access control.

Additional operations exist to fetch the access state of a given memory location or to set the access state for a given location.

Although the full/empty bit provides a fast way of implementing arbitrary indivisible memory operations, the need for extremely brief mutual exclusion during "integer add to memory" is so important for scheduling applications that this function is done entirely within each memory unit by a single operation, FETCH_ADD. This is the Ultracomputer fetch-and-add operation[3], and differs from it only in that the network hardware does not combine fetch-and-add operations to the same memory location.

6 Arithmetic

The numeric data types directly supported by the Tera architecture include:

- 64 bit twos complement integers

- 64 bit unsigned integers

- 64 bit floating point numbers

- 64 bit complex numbers

Operations on these types include addition, subtraction, multiplication, conversion, and comparison. Reciprocation of unsigned and floating point quantities is provided for using Newton's method.

Other types are supported indirectly, including:

- 8, 16, and 32 bit twos complement integers

- 8, 16, and 32 bit unsigned integers

- arbitrary length unsigned integers

- 32 bit floating point numbers

- 128 bit "doubled precision" numbers

The shorter integers are sign- or zero-extended to 64 bit quantities as they are loaded from memory, and truncated to the appropriate length as they are stored. The fundamental support for arbitrary length integer arithmetic is provided by the operations INTEGER_ADD_MUL, UPPER_ADD_MUL, and CARRY_ADD_TEST that together implement $64 \times n$ bit unsigned multiply-add in approximately $2 \times n^2$ instructions.

The 32 bit floating point numbers are simply the real parts of the 64 bit complex type with imaginary parts set to zero. The 128 bit "doubled precision" type was pointed out to us by Kahan [1, 7, 4]; it represents a real number R as the unevaluated sum of two 64 bit floating point numbers r and ρ, where ρ is insignificant with respect to r and as near as possible to $R - r$. Support for this type is provided by FLOAT_ADD_LOWER which (with FLOAT_ADD) implements "doubled precision" addition in six instructions, and by FLOAT_MUL_ADD which rounds only once and is used to implement "doubled precision" multiplication in five instructions.

References

[1] T. J. Dekker. A floating-point technique for extending the available precision. *Numerische Math.*, 18:224–242, 1971.

[2] M. Flynn. Some computer organizations and their effectiveness. *IEEE Transactions on Computers*, C-21(9):948–960, September 1972.

[3] A. Gottlieb, R. Grishman, C. P. Kruskal, K. P. McAuliffe, L. Rudolph, and M. Snir. The NYU Ultracomputer - designing an MIMD shared memory parallel computer. *IEEE Transactions on Computers*, C-32(2):175–189, 1984.

[4] W. Kahan. Doubled-precision IEEE standard 754 floating-point arithmetic. Unpublished manuscript, February 1987.

[5] R. M. Keller. Rediflow: A proposed architecture for combining reduction & dataflow. In *PAW83: Visuals Used at the 1983 Parallel Architecture Workshop*, University of Colorado, Boulder, 1983.

[6] J. T. Kuehn and B. J. Smith. The Horizon supercomputer system: Architecture and software. In *Proceedings of Supercomputing '88*, Orlando, Florida, November 1988.

[7] S. Linnainmaa. Software for doubled-precision floating-point computations. *ACM Transactions on Mathematical Software*, 7:272–283, 1981.

[8] A. Norton and E. Melton. A class of boolean linear transformations for conflict-free power-of-two stride access. In *Proceedings of the 1987 International Conference on Parallel Processing*, pages 247–254, August 1987.

[9] Frank Pittelli and David Smitley. Analysis of a 3d toriodal network for a sihared memory architecture. In *Proceedings of Supercomputing '88*, Orlando, Florida, November 1988.

[10] M. R. Thistle and B. J. Smith. A processor architecture for Horizon. In *Proceedings of Supercomputing '88*, pages 35–41, Orlando, Florida, November 1988.

An Orthogonal Multiprocessor for Parallel Scientific Computations

KAI HWANG, FELLOW, IEEE, PING-SHENG TSENG, AND DONGSEUNG KIM, MEMBER, IEEE

Abstract—A new multiprocessor architecture, called *orthogonal multiprocessor* (OMP), is proposed in this paper. This OMP architecture has a simplified busing structure and partially shared memory, which compares very favorably over fully shared-memory multiprocessors using *crossbar switch*, *multiple buses*, or *multistage networks*. The higher performance comes mainly from significantly increased memory bandwidth, fully exploited parallelism, reduced communication overhead, and lower hardware control complexities. Parallel algorithms being mapped include matrix arithmetic, linear system solver, FFT, array sorting, linear programming, and parallel PDE solutions. In most cases, linear speedup can be achieved on the OMP system. The OMP architecture provides linearly scalable performance and is well suited for building special-purpose scientific computers such as for signal/image processing, machine sorting, linear system solvers, and PDE machines, etc.

Index Terms—Matrix algebra, multiprocessors, orthogonal memory access, parallel processing, parallel sorting, PDE machines, scientific computing, signal/image processing, supercomputers.

I. INTRODUCTION

VARIOUS shared-memory multiprocessor architectures have appeared in recent years; including *bus-structured* systems: Encore Multimax [12] and Elxsi 6400 [23], *crossbar connected* systems: Alliant FX/8 [36], *directly connected* systems: IBM 3090/400, Univac 1100/94, Cray X-MP [7], Cyberplus [10], and *multistage network* systems: IBM RP3 [28] and BBN Butterfly Processor [4]. Each architectural topology has its own merit in terms of supporting tightly-coupled MIMD operations using shared memory. However, each of them also has its own weakness in terms of hardware demand, arbitration control, effective memory bandwidth, and fault tolerance [14].

Recently, three research groups have independently developed a similar multiprocessor architecture for parallel processing [6], [18], [30]. These architectures use a two-dimensional array of partially shared memory, from which the processors access concurrently via dedicated memory buses. The interesting feature of such a shared-memory array is its capability to support *orthogonal memory access* without conflicts. Such a conflict-free memory architecture facilitates the implementation of a large class of parallel algorithms for matrix algebra, solving linear systems, linear programming, signal and image processing, sorting of large arrays, and parallel solution of PDE problems. We call such an architecture an *orthogonal multiprocessor* (OMP) system. Previously, this OMP architecture was called a *reduced-mesh multiprocessor with orthogonally shared memory* [18], or an *orthogonal memory-access multiprocessor* [30] or the *ETH-multiprocessor EMPRESS* [6].

The OMP architecture appeals very much to today's VLSI and busing technology. Sophisticated processors with built-in instruction cache and functional pipelines, 256K RAM's, and VME bus controllers are now available in monolithic chips. The access time of semiconductor memories has been significantly reduced to match with the cycle time of microprocessors or coprocessors. Furthermore, high-speed system buses are now available, such as the 100 Mbyte/s Nanobus used in Multimax system and the 320 Mbyte/s bus used in Elxsi 6400. These technological advances have inspired many computer architects to develop high-performance multiprocessors for parallel/vector processing [2], [11]–[14], [19]–[22]. The OMP architecture offers an *orthogonality* concept, which as we shall prove, plays a crucial role in delivering high performance. The OMP architecture is designed for a moderate degree of parallelism, say from 16 to 256 processors, based on state-of-the-art electronic technology [15], [33]. The hardware demand of an OMP is comparable to a crossbar multiprocessor or a multibus multiprocessor with fully shared memories. However, the control complexity of the OMP is significantly lower than that of any existing multiprocessor due to the restricted operating modes imposed by orthogonality.

The main contributions of the paper lie in the characterization of the OMP architecture, providing principles of orthogonal memory access, mapping parallel algorithms onto OMP, and analyzing multiprocessor performance. The results obtained should be useful to those who are involved in the development of efficient multiprocessor systems for scientific and engineering applications.

II. THE ORTHOGONAL MULTIPROCESSOR ARCHITECTURE

The logical architecture of an OMP system is depicted in Fig. 1. The system is constructed with *n processors P_i*, for $i = 0, 1, \cdots, n - 1$, and n^2 *memory modules M_{ij}* for $i, j = 0, 1, \cdots, n - 1$. These resources are interconnected with *n dedicated buses B_i* for $i = 0, 1, \cdots, n - 1$. Each bus is

Manuscript received November 20, 1985, revised June 25, 1987 and January 30, 1988. This research was supported in part by the NSF Grant DMC-84-21022, ONR Contract N14-86-K-0559, and the AFOSR Grant 86-0008.

K. Hwang and D. Kim are with the Department of Electrical Engineering-Systems, University of Southern California, Los Angeles, CA 90089.

P.-S. Tseng is with the Department of Electrical and Computer Engineering, Carnegie-Mellon University, Pittsburgh, PA 15213.

IEEE Log Number 8823537.

0-8186-2642-9/92 $3.00 © 1989 IEEE

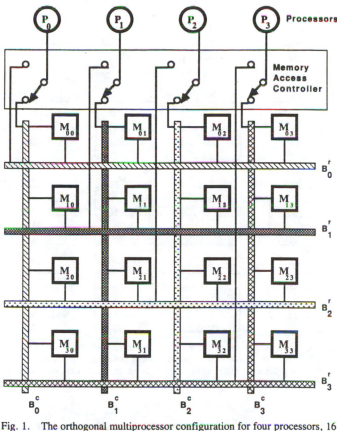

Fig. 1. The orthogonal multiprocessor configuration for four processors, 16 memory modules interconnected by four memory buses.

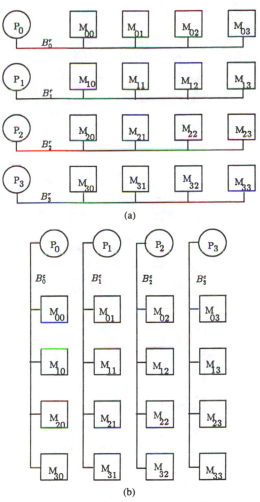

(a)

(b)

Fig. 2. Orthogonal memory access modes in OMP. (a) Row access mode. (b) Column access mode.

dedicated to one processor only; there is no time sharing of the buses by multiple processors. This will greatly reduce the memory access conflicts due to the lack of bus contention. The n buses can be functionally divided into two operational sets: n *row buses B_i^r* and *n column buses B_i^c* for $i = 0, 1, \cdots, n - 1$. Physically, the B_i^r and B_i^c are the same bus B_i. When B_i is used in a *row access mode*, the B_i^r is enabled and B_i^c is disconnected. Similarly, the B_i^c is enabled and B_i^r is disconnected, when B_i operates in a *column access mode*. The two access modes are mutually exclusive. This constraint simplifies the memory access control significantly. All arbiters in the memory modules use only two-way switches. The arbiters are coordinated by a *memory-access controller*, which has two control states; one for column access and the other for row access. If we remove the orthogonality constraint, we have to use n^2 independent arbiters which demand much higher control complexity.

We regard the OMP as a partially shared-memory system, because each memory module is shared by at most two processors. Each memory module M_{ij} has two access ports, one for B_i^r and the other for B_j^c. This implies that M_{ij} is only accessible by processor P_i and processor P_j. With the orthogonality and partial sharing of memory, possible memory access conflicts are significantly reduced. Hence, higher interprocessor–memory bandwidth can be established. The diagonal memory modules M_{ii} for $i = 0, 1, \cdots, n - 1$ are accessed by processor P_i exclusively. In other words, the diagonal modules are local memories to each processor. The off-diagonal modules are shared memories, each shared by two processors only.

The orthogonally accessed memory offers a number of attractive application potentials. Given any pair of processors (P_i, P_j), they can communicate with each other through the shared memory modules M_{ij} or M_{ji} in one or at most two memory cycles. Data or instruction broadcasting can be done in exactly two memory cycles. With n buses active at a time, the maximum memory bandwidth is n words per *major memory cycle*, which equals those systems using a crossbar switch or a multistage network. This implies that *n parallel reads/writes* can be carried out per each major cycle.

To characterize the orthogonal memory access patterns, let us denote $M_{ij}[k]$ as the kth word in the memory module M_{ij}. The ith *row memory M_i^r* consists of n memory modules M_{ij} for $j = 0, 1, \cdots, n - 1$, and similarly, the jth *column memory M_j^c* consists of M_{ij}, for $i = 0, 1, \cdots, n - 1$. The parallel accesses of M_i^r and of M_j^c are depicted in Fig. 2(a) and (b), respectively. Note that B_i^r is used to access M_i^r and B_j^c is used for M_j^c. Table I summarizes the notations used in the paper. In fact, the above memory access allows various row and column permutations as shown in Fig. 3. The following access rules must be observed: when row buses are used, only modules from distinct rows can form a legitimate access

279

TABLE I
LIST OF NOTATIONS USED

Notation	Meaning
P_i	Processor i, $0 \leq i \leq n-1$
B_j	Bus j, $0 \leq j \leq n-1$
B_i^c	Bus i used in column access mode
B_j^r	Bus j used in row access mode
M_{ij}	The (i,j)-th memory module, $0 \leq i, j \leq n-1$
M_i^c	All memory modules in the ith column
M_j^r	All memory modules in the jth row

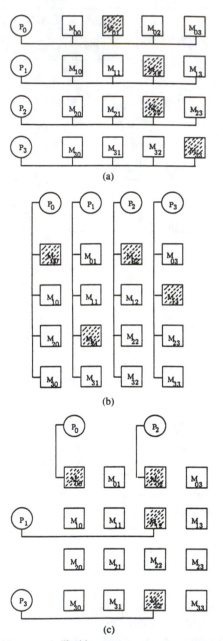

Fig. 3. Legitimate and illegitimate memory access patterns (accessed memory modules are shaded). (a) Legitimate row access. (b) Legitimate column access. (c) Illegitimate memory access using mixed modes.

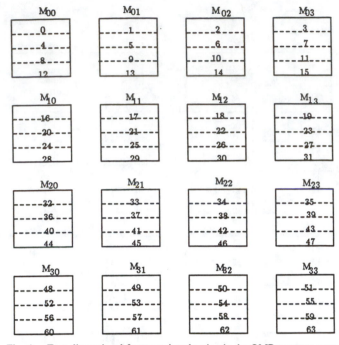

Fig. 4. Two-dimensional four-way interleaving in the OMP memory array. (The numbers inside each modules are memory addresses with stride distance 1 between modules in adjacent columns, and 16 between modules in adjacent rows.)

memory array. All modules belonging to the same row or the same column can be *n-way interleaved* to allow pipelined accesses with a *minor cycle*, which is $1/n$ of the major memory cycle. These row and column interleavings form the two-dimensional addressing illustrated in Fig. 4 for the case of $n = 4$ and $k = 4$ words per module. The row interleaving assumes a stride distance of one, while the column interleaving assumes a stride distance of $nk = 16$. With n-way interleaving per each row and per each column, the effective memory bandwidth can be increased from n words to n^2 words per major memory cycle. Usually, the *interleaved memory access* is for the execution of vector instructions or for access to regular data structures [19]. The *random access mode* is for randomly accessing scalar operands stored irregularly in the memory array.

The practice of random access mode (Fig. 3) and interleaved mode (Fig. 4) must not be mixed on the same memory bus at the same time. When an interleaved mode is used, only modules attached to the same row bus (or the same column bus) are accessed in an overlapped fashion using minor cycles. Theoretically, these two access modes can be applied on different row buses (or different column buses) at the same time. This may require a very complex addressing control. For our purpose, we restrict the access of memory to be either with a random-access mode or with an interleaved mode (but not both) for any given time period. Of course, this does not preclude the use of these two modes alternately at different time periods. Concurrent vector processing is done using multiple buses, each in an interleaved mode.

The OMP architecture is aimed at solving large-grain problems, where the data and programs are distributed over a large array of memory modules. The MIMD mode is adopted

pattern as shown in Fig. 3(a). Similarly, only modules from distinct columns can be accessed in parallel using the column buses as shown in Fig. 3(b). Mixed access patterns are forbidden as shown in Fig. 3(c).

To improve the memory bandwidth, one can consider the use of a *two-dimensional interleaving* scheme on the OMP

TABLE II
HARDWARE COMPLEXITIES OF VARIOUS MULTIPROCESSOR ARCHITECTURES

Architecture Features	Fully Shared-Memory Multiprocessors			OMP with Partially Shared Memory
	Crossbar Switch	Multiple-Buses	Multistage Network	
No. of Processors	n	n	n	n
Memory Modules	n	n	n	n^2
Module Capacity	C/n	C/n	C/n	C/n^2
Degree of Memory Sharing	n processors	n processors	n processors	2 processors
Switching Complexity	n^2 cross points	n shared buses	$n \log n$ switch boxes	n nonshared buses
Maximum Memory Bandwidth	n	n	n	n^2

for flexibility in applications. We shall compare the OMP to other shared-memory multiprocessor architectures in Section III. Mapping of various parallel algorithms onto the OMP system will be presented in Sections IV–VIII. Then we analyze the performance and design tradeoffs, and discuss programming and application issues.

III. COMPARISON TO OTHER MULTIPROCESSORS

The hardware demand of the OMP architecture is compared to known multiprocessor architectures in Table II. The comparison is based on using equal number of processors (n) and the same main memory capacity (C words). There are n memory modules for a fully shared-memory multiprocessor, each having a modular capacity of C/n words accessible by n processors. In the case of the OMP, there are n^2 memory modules, each having C/n^2 words accessible by at most two processors. The *multibus architecture* uses multiple time-sharing buses and multiported memory modules [25]. The major difference between the fully shared-memory system using multiple buses and the OMP architecture lies in the number of memory ports per module (n ports versus two ports), the modular capacity (C/n words versus C/n^2 words), and the effective memory bandwidth (n words versus n^2 words per major cycle). The *crossbar architecture* requires n^2 crosspoint switches and the *multistage network* demands the use of $n \log n$ 2×2 switches. The control complexity of these fully shared-memory architectures is much higher than that of an OMP as shown in Table II, especially in switching complexity and the degree of memory sharing.

The OMP requires an interconnection complexity of n buses with only two control states, which is much simpler than the crossbar switch and the multistage network. With the use of n buses and n^2 dual-ported memory modules, the OMP memory array should be able to operate with a faster memory cycle and simpler control than any of the fully shared-memory configurations. The bandwidth of the OMP memory varies between n and n^2 words depending on how frequently the interleaved mode is used on various buses. Of course, fully shared-memory multiprocessors have higher flexibility in supporting general-purpose applications. The OMP, with restricted memory access, is really meant for *special-purpose* applications in science, engineering, and high technology.

We analyze below the *effective memory bandwidth* of the OMP architecture. Let p be the probability that a processor requests a memory access (memory access rate). A memory access is performed with either a column access mode or a row access mode. Let q_c be the probability that a processor requests a column access. Then $q_r = 1 - q_c$ is the probability of requesting a row access. The memory bandwidth E is derived below as a function of n, p, and q_c.

Theorem 1: The orthogonal multiprocessor with n processors has the following effective memory bandwidth:

$$E = \sum_{j=1}^{n} \left\{ \binom{n}{j} p^j (1-p)^{n-j} \right.$$
$$\times \left[\sum_{k=1}^{\lceil j/2 \rceil - 1} (j-k) \binom{j}{k} q_c^k (1-q_c)^{j-k} \right.$$
$$\left. \left. + \sum_{k=\lceil j/2 \rceil}^{j} k \binom{j}{k} q_c^k (1-q_c)^{j-k} \right] \right\}. \quad (1)$$

Proof: The probability $\text{Prob}(k)$ that k processors request column accesses in the same memory cycle is

$$\text{Prob}(k) = \sum_{j=k}^{n} P_m(j) \cdot P_c(k|j) \quad (2)$$

where $P_m(j)$ is the probability that exactly j out of n processors request memory accesses. $P_c(k|j)$ is the conditional probability that k processors request column accesses and $j - k$ processors request row accesses, given that there are in total j memory requests. Using Bernoulli trial, $P_m(j)$ is written as

$$P_m(j) = \binom{n}{j} p^j (1-p)^{n-j}. \quad (3)$$

Similarly,

$$P_c(k|j) = \binom{j}{k} q_c^k (1-q_c)^{j-k}. \quad (4)$$

Suppose j processors request memory accesses. If k of them want the column access and $j - k$ the row access, we would carry on the access with a majority for the whole j requests due to the orthogonality. Hence, the number of successful memory accesses in each memory cycle is $\max(k, j - k)$. The bandwidth is thus obtained by including all possible values of j:

$$E = \sum_{j=1}^{n} P_m(j) \left[\sum_{k=0}^{\lceil j/2 \rceil - 1} (j-k)P_c(k|j) + \sum_{k=\lceil j/2 \rceil}^{j} kP_c(k|j) \right]$$
$$(5)$$

where the first term in the brackets corresponds to row accesses, and the second to column accesses. The proof is complete, after (3) and (4) are substituted into (5). Q.E.D.

For a multiprocessor with n processors and n^2 memory modules interconnected by an $n \times n$ crossbar switch network, the effective memory bandwidth has been formulated by

281

Bhuyan [5] as

$$E = n \left\{ 1 - (1-pq)\left(1 - p\,\frac{1-q}{n-1}\right)^{n-1} \right\} \qquad (6)$$

where q represents the probability of a request to access a *favorite memory*. A favorite memory is a memory module that a processor accesses more often than the rest. The probabilities of accessing the remaining modules were assumed equal in the above formulation.

For the sake of comparison, we consider the diagonal local memories as the favorite ones in the OMP architecture. This is due to the fact that processors access the local memories more frequently than the shared modules. Equal access probabilities are assumed for all off-diagonal memory modules. We divide the access probability q_c in (4) into two terms as follows:

$$q_c = q + \frac{1-q}{2} = \frac{1+q}{2}. \qquad (7)$$

The term q is for accessing the favorite memory and the term $(1-q)/2$ is for accessing the remaining modules in the same column or in the same row.

Fig. 5 shows the effective bandwidths of two multiprocessor architectures: the crossbar system versus the OMP. The curves are plotted as a function of the access probability p under two cases. The case in Fig. 5(a) corresponds to a higher probability of accessing the favorite memory ($q = 0.75$) and Fig. 5(b) for a lower value ($q = 0.5$). The plots demonstrate that the effective memory bandwidth of the OMP is comparable to that of the crossbar network.

In summary, we found that the OMP architecture requires much less control hardware by using dedicated memory buses (rather than time-sharing buses across many processors). The increased memory bandwidth is due to conflict-free access, lower degree of memory sharing, and two-dimensional memory interleaving. For the OMP, the resource conflict problems, such as hot spot and bus contention, are avoided by the synchronized orthogonality among multiple processors. All of these features are crucial in making OMP an attractive architecture for parallel scientific computations.

IV. MATRIX ALGEBRAIC COMPUTATIONS

Matrix algebra often demands operations such as matrix addition, transpose, multiplication, and LU decomposition, etc. These operations match perfectly with the architecture of the OMP. Let us use the matrix multiplication as an example.

Let A, B, and C be $n \times n$ matrices. A and B are distributed in the memory array in row-major order. The matrix multiplication ($C = A \cdot B = [c_{ij}]$) needs to perform n^2 inner product operations:

$$c_{ij} = A_i \cdot B_j^T = \sum_{k=0}^{n-1} a_{ik}b_{kj} \qquad (0 \le i, j \le n-1) \qquad (8)$$

where A_i is a row vector containing the ith row of A, and B_j^T is a column vector containing the jth column of B. The n elements ($c_{i0}, c_{i1}, \cdots c_{i,n-1}$) of the ith row of C are computed

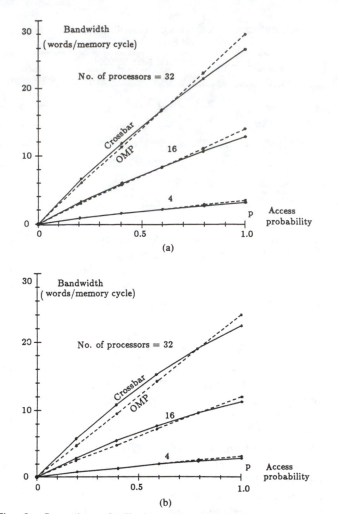

Fig. 5. Comparison of effective memory bandwidths of a crossbar-connected multiprocessor and an orthogonal multiprocessor of equal size. (a) Favorite memory access rate $q = 0.75$. (b) Favorite memory access rate $q = 0.5$.

concurrently as outlined below. Note that all n processors are involved in the parallel executions.

Parallel Computations of All Elements in the ith Row of Matrix C:

1) Read A_i by row access.

2) At the jth step ($j = 0, 1, \cdots, n-1$), B_j^T are read with a column access.

3) Multiply A_i and B_j^T term-by-term in parallel, generating all product terms $a_{ik}b_{kj}$, $k = 0, 1, \cdots, n-1$ for c_{ij}.

4) Store the product terms in the jth column memory M_j^c.

5) If $j < n$, then go to Step 2, else go to Step 6.

6) Now, all column memories contain product terms, one per each module. Perform parallel addition by column access to generate the ith row of C ($c_{i0}, c_{i1}, \cdots, c_{i,n-1}$).

The above procedure is formally specified in Algorithm 1. The parallel construct **forall** P_k, ($k = 0, 1, \cdots, n-1$) **doparallel** means that n processors run concurrently for parallel processing, where the index k corresponds to the kth processor. The end of this parallel process is indicated by **endforall**. The conventional **for** and **do** constructs still imply a sequential process. Each block of codes is delimited by the **begin** and **end** constructs.

Algorithm 1: Parallel Matrix Multiplication on OMP:

forall processors P_k, $(k = 0, 1, \cdots, n - 1)$ **doparallel**
  for $i = 0$ **to** $n - 1$ **do**
    begin
      Read a_{ik}
      for $j = 0$ **to** $n - 1$ **do**
        begin
          $c_{ij}^{[k]} = a_{ik}b_{kj}$ {$c_{ij}^{[k]}$ is a value associated with a
            processor P_k}
          Store $c_{ij}^{[k]}$ in M_{kj}.
        end(j)
      $c_{ik} = 0$
      for $m = 0$ **to** $n - 1$ **do**
        $c_{ik} = c_{ik} + c_{ik}^{[m]}$
    end(i)
  endforall.

Theorem 2: It takes $3n^2 + 2n$ time steps to perform a matrix multiplication on an OMP with n processors, where each multiplication, each addition, or each memory access is considered one time step.

Proof: The j-loop for generating the product terms requires $2n$ steps, and the m-loop requires n steps. Two steps are needed for reading A_i and resetting c_{ij}. Since there are n iterations (i-loop), the total time is $n(3n + 2)$.   Q.E.D.

Next, we consider the solution of a linear system equation characterized by $Ax = b$, where $A = [a_{ij}]$ is an $n \times n$ nonsingular matrix, $b = [b_j]$ is a column vector of coefficients, and $x = [x_j]$ is a column vector of unknown variables. Using Gaussian elimination, the problem can be solved by eliminating a_{ij}'s for $i > j$ in $n - 1$ steps (triangularization). The solutions for $x_n, x_{n-1}, \cdots, x_1$ are then obtained in a sequence of back substitutions. The triangularization procedure on OMP is specified in Algorithm 2, where $a_{ij}(t)$ and $b_{ij}(t)$ are the a_{ij} and b_{ij} at step t, respectively.

Algorithm 2: Parallel Triangularization of a Linear System:

for $t = 1$ **to** $n - 1$ **do**
  forall P_j, $(t < j \le n - 1)$ **doparallel**)
    for $i = t + 1$ **to** n **do**
      begin
        $m_{it} = a_{it}(t)/a_{tt}(t)$, $a_{tt}(t) \ne 0$
        Broadcast m_{it} to all processors.
        $a_{ij}(t + 1) = a_{ij}(t) - m_{it}a_{tj}(t)$
        $b_i(t + 1) = b_i(t) - m_{it}b_i(t)$
      end(i)
  endforall.

Theorem 3: It takes $O(n^2)$ time steps to solve a linear system of n equations on an OMP with n processors using Gaussian elimination, where each time step corresponds to a single arithmetic or a single memory access operation.

Proof: The i-loop of triangularization is repeated $n - 1$ times for each iteration t. Hence, it takes $C_1\{(n - 1) + (n - 2) + \cdots + 1\} = C_2n^2$ steps to perform the triangularization, where C_1 and C_2 are some constants. $n - i$ processors are used for concurrent substitutions at step i, $(i = 1, 2, \cdots, n - 1)$, immediately after the value x_{n-i} becomes known. Thus,

C_3n steps are needed on the OMP. The total time becomes $O(C_2n^2 + C_3n) = O(n^2)$.   Q.E.D.
Since a uniprocessor needs $O(n^3)$ time to solve a linear system of n equations [8], the OMP can achieve a linear speedup as shown in Theorem 3.

V. FAST FOURIER TRANSFORM

Shuffle-exchange network [34] and hypercube multicomputers [32] have been used for parallel FFT implementation. A parallel n^2-point FFT algorithm is developed below for the OMP system. The algorithm is then extended for FFT with kn^2 sample points, where $0 \le k \le m/2$, and m is the capacity of each memory module.

Initially the n^2 sample points $x(i)$, for $0 \le i \le n^2 - 1$, are stored in a column-major order, one element per each module. The FFT is derived from the discrete Fourier transform defined as follows:

$$X(k) = \sum_{i=0}^{n^2-1} x(i)w^{ki} \qquad 0 \le k \le n^2 - 1 \qquad (9)$$

where $w^{n^2} = 1$, $w = e^{j2\pi/n^2}$, $n^2 = 2^q$ (q: an integer), and $j = \sqrt{-1}$.

The FFT requires $\log n^2$ butterfly operations for each output sample data. The first $\log n$ of them have stride distances (the difference in data indexes of a butterfly operation pair) $n^2/2$, $n^2/4$, $n^2/8$, $\cdots$, n^2/n, which correspond to $n/2$, $n/4$, $n/8$, $\cdots$, n/n, respectively, in row stride distance. These are performed by row accesses on the OMP as specified in Algorithm 3. The remaining $\log n$ steps have stride distances $n/2$, $n/4$, $n/8$, $\cdots$, n/n, which correspond to $n/2$, $n/4$, $n/8$, $\cdots$, n/n, respectively, in column stride distance. They are executed by column accesses.

An example is given below for a 16-point FFT specified by the signal flow graph in Fig. 6. Initially, 16 samples $\{x(0), \cdots, x(15)\}$ are stored in column-major order, one in each memory module [Fig. 7(a)]. The entire process consists of four *stages* ($=\log 4^2$) [Fig. 7(a) and (b)]. A permutation must follow to sequence the result correctly [Fig. 7(c)]. Fig. 7(a) shows the first two *stages* using row accesses, and Fig. 7(b) illustrates the remaining two *stages* of column computation. A butterfly operation corresponds to each data pair joined by an arc in Fig. 7. The arc specifies the direction of data movement; the head receives data which are weighted products of the source data. Associated weights are shown on the arcs. Intermediate results after each *stage* t are denoted as $x(i)_t$, $i = 0, \cdots, n - 1$; $x(i)_0$ is the input sample $x(i)$, and $x(i)_4$ is the transformed data $X(j)$, where j is a bit-reversed representation of i. The permutation procedure consists of row exchange, column exchange, and row–column exchange [Fig. 7(c)].

Algorithm 3: Parallel One-Dimensional FFT on OMP:

procedure FFT
{ There are n^2 sample data and n processors. Input is in column-major order, stored one in each module. The output vector will be in bit-reversed column-major order.}
procedure *Butterfly* (i, j)
{ Compute the new value of $x[i]$ from $x[i]$ and $x[i$ XOR $2^j]$. This implementation assumes that the input vector is in correct order, and that the output vector will be in bit-

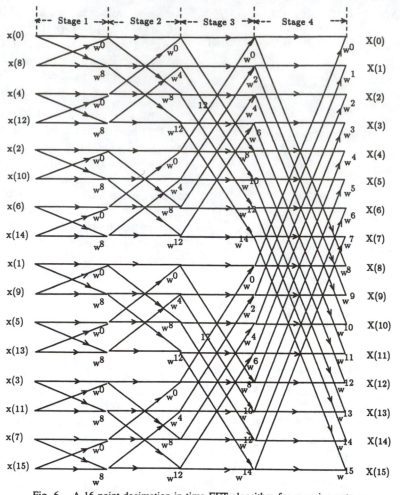

Fig. 6. A 16-point decimation-in-time FFT algorithm for mapping onto an
OMP with four processors in Fig. 7.

reversed order. Let $b_j(i)$ denote bit j of integer i, where bit
0 is the least-significant bit. Rev(i) produces an integer
which is the bit-reversal of i. }
begin
  if $b_j(i) = 0$
    then $x'[i] = x[i] + x[i + 2^j] W^{2^j \text{Rev}(i)}$
    else $x'[i] = x[i - 2^j] + x[i] W^{2^j \text{Rev}(i)}$
end*(Butterfly)*

forall P_k, $k = 0, \cdots, n - 1$ **doparallel**
  for $j = \log n^2 - 1$ **downto** $\log n$ **do** { row computation }
    begin
      for $i = 0$ **to** $n - 1$ **do**
        Butterfly $(k + in, j)$
      for $i = 0$ **to** $n - 1$ **do**
        $x[k + in] = x'[k + in]$ {x' is a temporary
          storage for the procedure *Butterfly*}
    end(j)
  for $j = (\log n) - 1$ **downto** 0 **do** { column computations }
    begin
      for $i = 0$ **to** $n - 1$ **do**
        Butterfly $(i + kn, j)$
      for $i = 0$ **to** $n - 1$ **do**
        $x[i + kn] = x'[i + kn]$
    end(j)
endforall.

To extend the FFT algorithm to kn^2 sample points, we
distribute k data points to each memory module. The sample
point $x_{(ln+j)n+i}$ is stored in $M_{ji}[l]$, where $0 \leq i, j < n, 0 \leq l$
$< k$. Logically, a $kn \times n$ array is stored in column-major
order. By this ordering, the data with stride distances 1, 2, 4,
$\cdots, n/2$ are reached through column accesses. The remaining
$n, 2n, 4n, \cdots, kn^2$ distances are reached by row accesses.
Once a stride distance is given, n butterfly operations are
performed in parallel without access conflict. Since the FFT
consists of $\log kn^2$ stages of butterfly operations, the first $\log$
$kn^2 - \log n$ butterfly operations are performed by row access
(k of them, whose stride distances are integer multiples of 2,
have their communication pairs in the same memory module),
and the remaining $\log n$ stages are carried out by column
accesses. We summarize the above results as follows.

Theorem 4: The kn^2-point FFT takes $O(kn \log kn)$ time
steps on an OMP of n processors, where each time step
corresponds to one butterfly operation or one permutation
operation.

Proof: In each stage, kn^2 butterfly operations are
performed in $O(kn)$ time, since n processors work concurrently. The row computation consists of $\log kn^2 - \log n$
stages with kn butterfly operations each, and the column
computation requires $\log n$ stages with kn butterfly operations
each. Permutation for ordering of the bit-reversed data needs

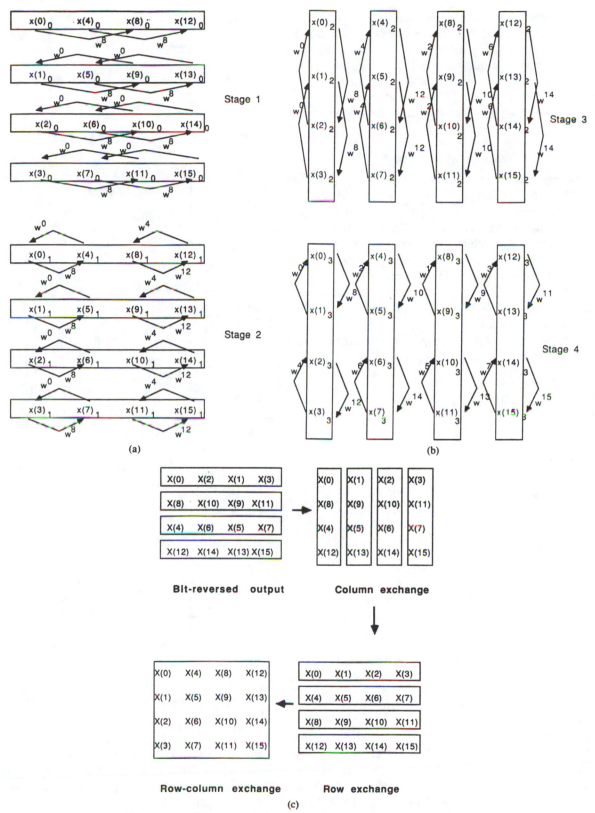

Fig. 7.   One-dimensional FFT on the OMP. (a) Row computations. (b)
Column computations. (c) Reordering of the output.

kn time. Hence, the total execution steps equal $O(kn \log kn)$. Q.E.D.

It takes $O(kn^2 \log kn)$ steps to perform the FFT on a uniprocessor [26]. Therefore, a linear speedup is achieved by the OMP as expected. The parallelism is exploited within each stage and successive stages must still be processed sequentially. To perform a two-dimensional FFT on the OMP, one can modify the above 1-D FFT algorithm by using two successive 1-D FFT processes: one using column memories and the other using row memories.

VI. PARALLEL SORTING USING OMP

An $O\{k^2 n (\log n) \log kn\}$ algorithm is developed for sorting $k^2 n^2$ numbers on an OMP, where $1 \le k^2 < m/2$. This sorting method results in an $O(n/\log n)$ speedup over the best known sequential sorting algorithm. The algorithm, called *orthogonal sorting*, combines the bitonic sort [3] with a sequential merge sort. The numbers are initially stored in column-major order in the memory array. The orthogonal sorting is specified recursively in Algorithm 4. The constructs **cobegin** and **coend** indicate that all statements within the block are to be executed concurrently.

Algorithm 4: Orthogonal Sorting of n^2 Numbers with One Number stored in Each Memory Module:

procedure *sort*(s, c, a)
  procedure *merge*(s, c, a)
  begin
    row-merge(s, c, a)
    col-merge(s, c, a)
  end (*merge*)

  begin
    if ($c = 1$) **then** *sortcol*(s, a) {performed by processor P_s}
      else
        cobegin
          sort(s, $c/2$, a)
          sort($s + c/2$, $c/2$, $-a$)
        coend
    merge(s, c, a)
end (*sort*).

The procedure *sort*(s, c, a) sorts data elements from column s to column $s + c - 1$, where a is a binary flag specifying either an ascending ($a = 1$) or a descending ($a = -1$) order of the sort. The sorting is initiated by *sort*(0, n, 1). The task *sortcol*(s, a) sorts data elements stored in a column memory M_s^c. This step uses a sequential *merge sort*. The procedure *merge*(s, c, a) merges a bitonic sequence of cn numbers from column s to $s + c - 1$ into a single sorted sequence. The task *row-merge*(s, c, a) does a merge within each row, producing c columns, each a bitonic sequence of length n. The task *col-merge*(s, c, a) merges bitonic sequences of cn numbers from column s to $s + c - 1$ into sorted sequences. Hence, *merge*(s, c, a) completes sorting of cn numbers in M_i^c modules, for $i = s, \cdots, s + c - 1$, using a bitonic merge.

We use an example to illustrate how to sort 16 numbers on an OMP with $n = 4$ processors. One number is stored in each

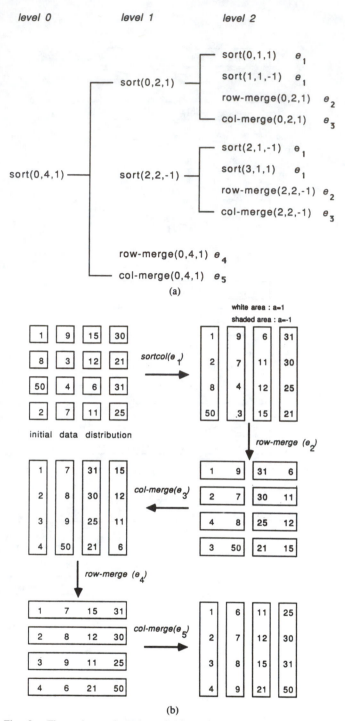

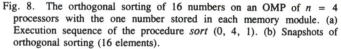

Fig. 8. The orthogonal sorting of 16 numbers on an OMP of $n = 4$ processors with the one number stored in each memory module. (a) Execution sequence of the procedure *sort* (0, 4, 1). (b) Snapshots of orthogonal sorting (16 elements).

memory module. The detailed execution sequence is shown in Fig. 8(a), which consists of three levels. It looks like an execution tree; however, all procedures at the same level may not be performed in parallel (because the procedure *merge* should follow the procedure *sortcol*). Procedures with the same execution label (e_i) will be executed concurrently. The whole sequence is executed in five steps [Fig. 8(b)].

By evenly distributing the numbers to all memory modules, the orthogonal sorting algorithm can be extended to sort $k^2 n^2$ numbers, where $1 \le k^2 < m/2$. Each of n^2 memory modules

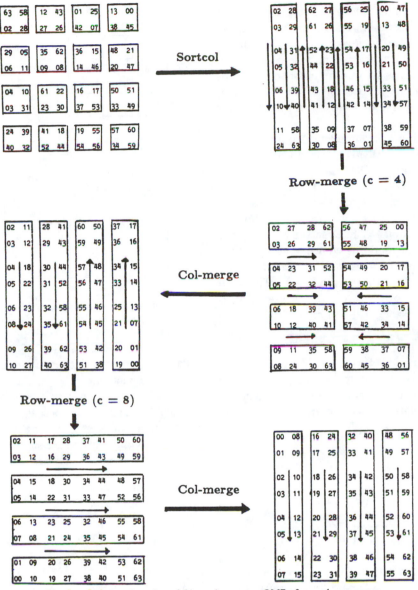

Fig. 9. Orthogonal sorting of 64 numbers on an OMP of $n = 4$ processors with four numbers stored in each memory module.

is initially loaded with k^2 numbers, as shown in Fig. 9 for the case of $k^2n^2 = 2^2 \times 4^2 = 64$. The sorting is done by initiating the procedure $sort(0, kn, k, 1)$. The task $sortcol(s, k, a)$ sorts k columns of data in a column memory of processor P_s using a sequential merge sort algorithm. The generalized orthogonal sorting is specified in Algorithm 5.

Theorem 5: The orthogonal sorting of k^2n^2 numbers requires $O\{k^2n(\log n) \log kn\}$ time steps on an OMP of n processors, where each step corresponds to the time required for one compare-and-exchange operation on a processor.

Proof: Due to the recursive decomposition by **cobegin** and **coend**, the sort has $\log n$ levels of execution [i.e., $sort(0, kn, k, a)$, $sort(0, kn/2, k, a)$, $sort(0, kn/4, k, a)$, $\cdots$, $sort(0, 2k, k, a)$, $sort(0, k, k, a)$]. The $sortcol$ takes $k \cdot kn \log kn$ steps. The task $row\text{-}merge$ uses at most $k \cdot kn \log n$ steps. The task $col\text{-}merge$ requires $k \cdot kn \log kn$ steps. It results in $k^2n \log kn$ steps to complete each level. Thus, the total execution time of the orthogonal sorting is $O\{k^2n(\log n) \log kn\}$.   Q.E.D.

Algorithm 5: Orthogonal Sorting of k^2n^2 Numbers with k^2 Numbers Stored in Each Memory Module:

procedure $sort(s, c, k, a)$
  procedure $merge(s, c, k, a)$
  begin
    $row\text{-}merge(s, c, a)$
    $col\text{-}merge(s, c, a)$
  end $(merge)$

begin
  if $(c = k)$ **then** $sortcol(s, k, a)$ {performed by
                                             processor P_s}
              else
                    cobegin
                       $sort(s, c/2, k, a)$
                       $sort(s + c/2, c/2, k, -a)$
                    coend
  $merge(s, c, k, a)$
end $(sort)$.

287

The best known sequential sorting algorithm requires $O(k^2n^2 \log kn)$ steps to sort k^2n^2 numbers. Therefore, the orthogonal sorting method can achieve a speedup of $O(n/\log n)$ over the sequential sort. For the special case of $k = 1$, it takes $O(n \log^2 n)$ time steps to sort n^2 numbers on an n-processor OMP. Because a uniprocessor needs $O(n^2 \log n)$ time steps to sort n^2 numbers, the $O(n/\log n)$ speedup holds also for the special case.

Parallel sorting methods are also implementable on a *mesh-connected computer* (MCC), that has n^2 processors. The MCC has a time complexity of $O(n)$ in sorting n^2 numbers [29], [37]. However, the $O(\log^2 n)$ speed gain in using an MCC is obtained at the expense of using n times more processors than the OMP. Further comparisons of OMP and MCC will be given in Section IX. In Scherson *et al.* [31], a *shear sort* is developed to sort n^2 numbers using a two-dimensional sorting network of n^2 *compare–exchange modules*, which is equivalent to using n^2 processors. The shear sort has a time complexity of $O(n\sqrt{\log n})$, but uses n times more processors than the orthogonal sort on an OMP.

VII. PARALLEL LINEAR PROGRAMMING

The *simplex method* [35] for linear programming is mapped onto the OMP. Consider the iterative part of the simplex method with p unknowns and q linear constraints. In each iteration, the computations involved are

Minimize $z = c_1x_{q+1} + c_2x_{q+2} + \cdots + c_px_{q+p} - z_0$, subject to the constraints

$$[I_{q \times q} A_{q \times p}]x_{(p+q) \times 1} \geq b_{q \times 1}$$

$$x_{(p+q) \times 1} \geq 0 \qquad (10)$$

where $x_{(p+q) \times 1} = [x_1 x_2 \cdots x_{q+p}]^T$, $A_{q \times p}$ is a coefficient matrix of constraints, and $I_{q \times q}$ is an identity matrix.

The variables x_1, x_2, $\cdots$, x_q are *basic variables*; x_{q+1}, x_{q+2}, $\cdots$, x_{q+p} are *free variables*; and $-z_0$ is the current minimal of the iterative process. The process terminates with the true minimal when all $c_i > 0$, $(1 \leq i \leq p)$. For a systematic computation, a coefficient matrix T is formulated as

$$T_{(q+1) \times (p+1)} = [t_{ij}] = \begin{bmatrix} A_{q \times p} & b_{q \times 1} \\ c_{1 \times p} & z_0 \end{bmatrix}. \qquad (11)$$

Initially, these are evenly distributed to the memory modules (Fig. 10). The following computations are performed in each iteration:

Step 1. Find a pivoting column s by $c_s = \min\{c_j \mid 1 \leq j \leq q\}$.
   If $c_s > 0$, then stop.
Step 2. Find a pivoting row r by $b_r/a_{rs} = \min\{b_i/a_{is} \mid b_i/a_{is} > 0, 1 \leq i \leq p\}$
Step 3. Perform the row eliminations as below:
   3a. $t_{rj} = t_{rj}/a_{rs}$ (for $1 \leq j \leq q + 1$)
   3b. $t_{is} = -t_{is}/a_{rs}$ (for $1 \leq i \leq p + 1$, $i \neq r$)
       $t_{ij} = t_{ij} - t_{is}t_{rj}$ (for $1 \leq i \leq p + 1$, $i \neq r$; $1 \leq j \leq q + 1$, $j \neq s$)
   3c. $t_{rs} = 1/a_{rs}$.

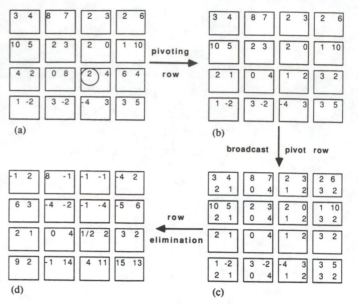

Fig. 10. Snapshots of one iteration of the simplex method on an OMP ($p = 7$ unknowns and $q = 3$ constraints). (a) Initial data distribution. (b) Pivot row converted. (c) Data after broadcast. (d) Result of one iteration.

Parallelizing Step 3 contributes to a linear speedup. The parallel computations in Step 3a are performed using column accesses. The data in row r are broadcast to the column memory modules. The processors then perform parallel computations in Step 3b using the row accesses. A few snapshots of one iteration are shown in Fig. 10 corresponding to the following numerical example ($p = 7$, $q = 3$):

$$3x_1 + 4x_2 + 8x_3 + 7x_4 + 2x_5 + 3x_6 + 2x_7 \geq 6$$

$$10x_1 + 5x_2 + 2x_3 + 3x_4 + 2x_5 + x_7 \geq 10$$

$$4x_1 + 2x_2 + 8x_4 + 2x_5 + 4x_6 + 6x_7 \geq 4$$

$$x_1 \geq 0, \ x_2 \geq 0, \ \cdots, \ x_7 \geq 0.$$

$$z = x_1 - 2x_2 + 3x_3 - 2x_4 - 4x_5 + 3x_6 + 3x_7 - 5. \qquad (12)$$

The circled location ($r = 3$, $s = 5$) is found by pivoting the row and column (Step 1 and 2). Step 3a is performed in Fig. 10(b). All pivoting row elements are broadcast in parallel [Fig. 10(c)] for the calculations of the second line of Step 3b. Fig. 10(d) shows the result after one iteration of the simplex method.

Theorem 6: Each iteration of the simplex method with p unknowns and q constraints can be computed in $O(pq/n)$ time steps on an OMP with n processors, where $p, q \gg n$, and each step corresponds to the time needed for one arithmetic operation or one comparison operation.

Proof: Step 1 requires $(q/n + \log n)$ operations since each processor has to perform q/n comparisons and then n processors cooperate to find a minimum among n of them. Similarly Step 2 needs $p/n + \log n$ operations. Step 3 consists of $(q + 1)/n$ steps for 3a, $p/n + 2pq/n$ steps for 3b, and a unit operation for 3c. Therefore, $O\{2(pq + p + q)/n + 2 \log n\} \approx O(2pq/n)$ operations, because $p \cdot q/n \gg p \gg \log n$. Q.E.D.

Without parallelization, the same iteration of the simplex

288

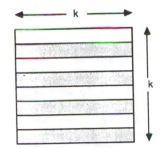

Fig. 11. The SLOR method implemented on an OMP for solving PDE problems.

TABLE III
TIME COMPLEXITIES OF MAPPING ALGORITHMS ONTO THE OMP AND A
UNIPROCESSOR

Algorithm	Time Complexity	
	OMP (n processors)	Uniprocessor
Matrix multiplication of size $n \times n$.	$O(n^2)$	$O(n^3)$
Linear System Solver for n unknowns.	$O(n^2)$	$O(n^3)$
1-D FFT over kn^2 elements.	$O(kn \log kn)$	$O(kn^2 \log kn)$
Sorting of $k^2 n^2$ numbers.	$O(k^2 n \log^2 n)$	$O(k^2 n^2 \log n)$
Linear programming of k_1 unknowns, and k_2 constraints. (simplex method)	$O(k_1 k_2/n)$ per iteration	$O(k_1 k_2)$ per iteration
PDE solver for $k \times k$ grids	$O(k^2/n)$ per iteration	$O(k^2)$ per iteration

method requires $p + q$ for Step 1 and 2, $q + p + 2pq + 1$ for Step 3, which becomes $O(pq + 2p + 2q + 1) \approx O(pq)$ time steps. Hence, a linear speedup is achieved on the OMP.

VIII. PARALLEL SOLUTION OF PDE'S

The OMP architecture can exploit parallelism embedded in iterative algorithms for solving partial differential equations (PDE), namely the *successive line overrelaxation* (SLOR) method or the *alternating direction implicit* (ADI) method [27], [29]. We choose the SLOR method to illustrate the parallelization process.

Consider the solution of a linear second-order PDE in a 2-D region:

$$A(x, y)\frac{\partial^2 u}{\partial x^2} + B(x, y)\frac{\partial u}{\partial x} + C(x, y)\frac{\partial^2 u}{\partial y^2}$$

$$+ D(x, y)\frac{\partial u}{\partial y} + E(x, y)u = F(x, y) \quad (13)$$

where A, B, C, D, E, and F are given functions. If the above equation is discretized on a mesh of $k \times k$ nodes, a difference equation is obtained for each node u_{pq}:

$$a_{pq}u_{p,q-1} + b_{pq}u_{p,q+1} + c_{pq}u_{p-1,q} + d_{pq}u_{p+1,q} + e_{pq}u_{pq}$$

$$= f_{pq} \quad (1 \le p, q \le k). \quad (14)$$

The SLOR method is based on Chebyshev overrelaxation as illustrated in Fig. 11. The points on the mesh are divided into odd and even sets of lines, as indicated by white and shaded strips, respectively. The method updates the odd and even lines alternatively using the following equations at the tth iteration:

$$a_{pq}u^*_{p,q-1} + e_{pq}u^*_{pq} + b_{pq}u^*_{p,q+1} = f_{pq} - c_{pq}u^{(t)}_{p-1,q} - d_{pq}u^{(t)}_{p+1,q}$$

$$(15)$$

$$u^{(t+1/2)}_{pq} = ru^*_{pq} + (1-r)u^{(t)}_{pq}. \quad (16)$$

The parameter r is a given relaxation factor, and $t = 1/2$, $1, 3/2, 2, \cdots$ with an increment of $1/2$ in successive values are used until u_{pq} converges. There are $k/2$ independent tridiagonal systems of length k along $k/2$ lines of the mesh which should be solved in every half iteration. The right-hand side depends on the known values from the lines above and below, which have been already computed in the very last half-iteration. If we distribute the 2-D mesh of points evenly in the memory, the communicational requirements of the SLOR method are well supported by the OMP architecture. In each half-iteration, all processors first compute the right-hand side using the column memory. Then, all processors solve $k/2$ tridiagonal systems in parallel using the row memory. Finally, all processors update the u values using the row memory accesses.

Theorem 7: Each iteration of the SLOR method on a mesh of $k \times k$ nodes can be performed in $O(k^2/n)$ time steps on an OMP with n processors, where each time step corresponds to a single arithmetic operation or a memory access operation.

Proof: The right-hand side of (15) needs four arithmetic operations using column access, resulting in $4 \cdot k^2/2 \cdot 1/n = 2k^2/n$ operations for all lines. Solving a tridiagonal system of length k needs $8k$ operations using a serial algorithm [29]. Since there are $k/2$ independent tridiagonal systems of length k, n of them are solved in parallel by n processors, which takes $k/(2n) \cdot 8k = 4k^2/n$. The updating process of (16) needs $3 \cdot k^2/(2n)$ arithmetic operations. Hence, the total time complexity for each iteration is $O(k^2/n)$. Q.E.D.

For a uniprocessor, it takes $2k^2$ steps to compute the right-hand side of (15), $k/2 \cdot 8k$ steps to solve the tridiagonal systems, and $3k^2/2$ steps in updating (16). The sequential SLOR method thus needs $O(k^2)$ steps. The above parallel method achieves again a linear speedup over the sequential method.

IX. PERFORMANCE AND CAPABILITY ANALYSIS

In this section, we analyze the performance and capability of the OMP as compared to other parallel computers such as MCC and hypercube systems. The time complexities of all the algorithms we have mapped onto the OMP are summarized in Table III as compared to those for a uniprocessor system [29]. All the algorithms result in a linear speedup, except the orthogonal sort which has a speedup of $O(n/\log n)$ over a uniprocessor. The results shown in Table III are indeed very impressive for the fact that only n processors are used to achieve appreciable speedups.

Many matrix and graph algorithms follow regularly structured data flow patterns. Most of these algorithms can be efficiently mapped onto the MCC [1], [9], [16], [24]. Other algorithms which demand global data transfers, such as sorting, FFT, and other arbitrary data movement operations can be mapped into the hypercube system efficiently. The OMP can simulate these architectures with a linearly scalable performance. We compare below an OMP of n processors with an MCC containing $kn \times kn$ processors. Note that k^2 memory modules of MCC are mapped into a single memory module in the OMP. Assume that each memory module in the MCC has a capacity of r words. Then each memory module of the OMP must have at least rk^2 words, i.e., $rk^2 \leq m$, where m is the capacity of each OMP memory module. When r and k are large, rk^2n^2 data points imply really large-grain computations. The following two theorems show that the OMP can be used effectively to simulate the MCC or the hypercube computers using only a small number of fast processors and memory modules.

Theorem 8: Any algorithm demanding T steps on an MCC of $kn \times kn$ processors can be executed in at most k^2nT steps on an OMP of n processors.

Proof: We map $kn \times kn$ blocks of data in the MCC onto the $n \times n$ memory modules of an OMP. Each $k \times k$ block is mapped onto k^2r consecutive words of an OMP memory module, i.e. the memory locations between $M_{i,j}[(pk + q)r]$ and $M_{i,j}[(pk + q + 1)r - 1]$ are the (I, J)th memory module of the MCC, where $(I, J) = (ik + p, jk + q)$ and $0 \leq i, j < n, 0 \leq p, q < k$. To simulate the operations of MCC, processor P_i of OMP performs local computations of the MCC processors in columns ik to $(i + 1)k - 1$. OMP processors simulate the north–south data movement through column access; similarly, east–west data transfer through row access. Each execution step in the MCC can be performed on an OMP in k^2n steps. Thus, an algorithm demanding T steps on an MCC requires at most k^2nT steps on an OMP. Q.E.D.

Next, we consider the simulation of a hypercube computer with kn^2 processors using an OMP of n processors, where kr data words of each k hypercube nodes are handled by each memory module of OMP. Note that the values of n and k must be chosen such that $kn^2 = 2^N$ for some integer N.

Theorem 9: An algorithm demanding T steps on a hypercube computer of kn^2 processors can be executed in at most knT steps on an OMP of n processors.

Proof: The hypercube memories are mapped into a rectangular array of $kn \times n$ blocks of r words each, i.e., $M_{i,j}[lr]$ to $M_{i,j}[(l + 1)r - 1]$ correspond to the local memory of node K, where $K = (jn + i)k + l, 0 \leq i, j \leq n - 1, 0 \leq l \leq k - 1$, and $kr \leq m$. Each OMP processor P_i simulates the local computations of node ikn to node $(i + 1)kn - 1$ in the hypercube computer. Processors rearrange data stored in their column memory modules to simulate data transfers of distances $1, 2, 4, \cdots, kn/2$, in the hypercube computer; similarly row memory modules are used for distances kn, $2kn, 4kn, \cdots, kn^2/2$. Each computing step and each routing step in the hypercube computer can be performed in kn steps on an OMP. Q.E.D.

The above methods indeed provide systematic ways of mapping onto the OMP architecture any parallel algorithm, which is originally designed for the MCC or for the hypercube

systems. The above time complexities (Theorems 8 and 9), as obtained by simulating an MCC or a hypercube computer on an OMP, are indeed upper bounds. In fact, all the parallel algorithms we have developed for the OMP have complexities which are lower than or equal to the upper bounds. For example, the orthogonal sort requires only $O(n \log^2 n)$ time steps, lower than the $O(n^2)$ obtained by mapping the Thompson–Kung sorting [complexity $O(n)$] [37] onto the OMP using Theorem 8. The mesh and hypercube multiprocessors are both popularly used in many scientific applications. This indicates that the OMP is indeed a powerful architecture for scientific and engineering computations.

X. Conclusions

We conclude by summarizing the advantages and shortcomings of the OMP architecture. Based on the results presented, the OMP architecture has the following distinct advantages.

1) The control complexity for parallel memory accesses in OMP is very simple as compared to fully shared-memory systems, because of synchronized orthogonality, smaller modular capacity, and lower memory access time.

2) With the orthogonal memory access and 2-D interleaved memory organization, the effective memory bandwidth is potentially n times higher than fully shared-memory multiprocessors using a crossbar switch, multiple buses, or a multi-stage network.

3) The OMP architecture has been demonstrated to be very powerful to implement a large class of scientific algorithms. Some of them have also been independently confirmed by Scherson and Ma [30], in which they prove that the performance of the OMP architecture compares favorably over the best known multiprocessor architecture within a factor of 3.

4) Many parallel algorithms are attractive candidates for efficient mapping onto the OMP architecture. Essentially, these are the algorithms which can exploit the orthogonal memory access property. We list the candidate algorithms in Table IV [9], [12], [14], [24], [27], [29]. However, not all of them have been thoroughly mapped onto the OMP. In [17] and [21], we have presented the use of the OMP for parallel image processing and pattern recognition.

Two obvious shortcomings of the OMP architecture are identified below. We point out these drawbacks in order to inspire continued research efforts to overcome the stated difficulties.

1) The orthogonal memory access principle prohibits possible memory accesses with mixed modes. This may prolong the communication between processors and reduce the flexibility in mapping those algorithms, which do not access the memory array in an orthogonal fashion.

2) The number of memory modules increases as the square of the number of processors, which makes the system expensive for massive parallelism. In other words, the proposed OMP architecture needs to be modified for fine-grain massively parallel processing as suggested in [11].

Despite a few shortcomings, the advantages of the OMP architecture are sufficiently strong to proclaim its efficiency, when the OMP is applied for matrix algebra, signal/image processing, sorting, linear programming, FFT, and parallel

TABLE IV

CANDIDATE ALGORITHMS FOR PARALLELIZATION USING THE
ORTHOGONAL MULTIPROCESSOR

Category	Algorithms and Computations
Vector/Matrix Arithmetic	Matrix Multiplication
	Sparse Matrix Operations
	Linear System Solution
	Eigenvalue Computations
	Least Squares Problems
Signal/Image Processing	Convolution and Correlation
	Digital Filtering
	Fast Fourier Transforms
	Feature Extraction
	Pattern Recognition
	Scene Labeling by Relaxation
Optimization Processes	Linear Programming
	Sorting and Searching
	Integer Programming
	Branch and Bound Algorithms
	Constrained Optimization
Partial Differential Equations	Ordinary Differential Equations
	Partial Differential Equations
	Finite-Element Analysis
	Domain Decomposition
	Numerical Integration
Special Functions and Graph Algorithms	Power Series and Functions
	Graph Matching
	Interpolation and Approximation

PDE solutions. The OMP architecture is well suited for modular construction using commercially available microprocessors, random-access memory chips, and off-the-shelf high-bandwidth buses. The two-dimensional architecture of the OMP has been generalized to the n orthogonal dimensions as reported in [11]. The generalized OMP can efficiently support massively parallel computations.

ACKNOWLEDGMENT

The authors appreciate the valuable suggestions made by the anonymous referees during the long reviewing process. The quality of the paper has been significantly improved in this process. We also appreciate the high professional standard set by the editor who handled the review of this submission.

REFERENCES

[1] M. J. Atallah and S. R. Kosaraju, "Graph problems on a mesh-connected processor array," *J. ACM*, vol. 31, no. 3, pp. 649–667, 1984.

[2] J. L. Baer, *Computer Systems Architecture*. Rockville, MD: Computer Science Press, 1980, ch. 10.

[3] K. E. Batcher, "Sorting networks and their applications," in *Proc. AFIPS Spring Joint Comput. Conf.*, 1968, pp. 307–314.

[4] BBN Labs., Inc., *Butterfly Parallel Processor Overview*, version 1, Mar. 1986.

[5] L. Bhuyan, "An analysis of processor–memory interconnection networks," *IEEE Trans. Comput.*, pp. 279–283, Mar. 1984.

[6] R. E. Buehrer *et al.*, "The ETH Multiprocessor EMPRESS: A dynamically reconfigurable MIMD system," *IEEE Trans. Comput.*, vol. C-31, pp. 1035–1044, Nov. 1982.

[7] S. S. Chen, "Cray X-MP-4 series," Cray Research presentations, Aug. 1985.

[8] G. Dahlquist and A. Bjeorck, *Numerical Methods*. Englewood Cliffs, NJ: Prentice-Hall, 1974, pp. 146–160.

[9] E. Dekel, D. Nassimi, and S. Sahni, "Parallel matrix and graph algorithms," *SIAM J. Comput.*, vol. 10, pp. 657–675, 1981.

[10] M. W. Ferrante, "Cyberplus and Map V interprocessor communications for parallel and array processor systems," in *Multiprocessors and Array Processors*, Karplus, Ed. San Diego, CA: Simulation Councils, Jan. 1987, pp. 45–54.

[11] K. Hwang and D. Kim, "Generalization of orthogonal multiprocessor for massively parallel computation," in *Proc. Frontiers Massively Parallel Computat.*, Fairfax, VA, Oct. 11-13, 1988.

[12] K. Hwang, "Advanced parallel processing with supercomputer architectures," *Proc. IEEE*, pp. 1348–1379, Oct. 1987.

[13] K. Hwang and F. Briggs, *Computer Architecture and Parallel Processing*. New York: McGraw-Hill, 1984.

[14] K. Hwang and D. DeGroot, Eds., *Parallel Processing for Supercomputers and Artificial Intelligence*. New York: McGraw-Hill, 1989.

[15] K. Hwang and J. Ghosh, "Hypernets: A communication-efficient architecture for constructing massively parallel computers," *IEEE Trans. Comput.*, pp. 1450–1466, Dec. 1987.

[16] S. L. Johnson, "Communication efficient basic linear algebra computations on hypercube architectures," *J. Parallel Distributed Comput.*, vol. 4, no. 2, pp. 133–172, 1987.

[17] K. Hwang and D. Kim, "Parallel pattern clustering on a multiprocessor with orthogonally shared memory," in *Proc. Int. Conf. Parallel Processing*, Aug. 1987, pp. 913–916.

[18] K. Hwang and P. S. Tseng, "An efficient VLSI multiprocessor for signal/image processing," in *Proc. Int. Conf. Comput. Design*, Oct. 1985, pp. 172–176.

[19] K. Hwang and Z. Xu, "Multipipeline networking for compound vector processing," *IEEE Trans. Comput.*, pp. 33–47, Jan. 1988.

[20] H. F. Jordan, "Structuring parallel algorithms in an MIMD, shared memory environment," *Parallel Comput.*, pp. 93–110, May 1986.

[21] D. Kim and K. Hwang, "Parallel image processing and pattern analysis on orthogonal multiprocessors," *IEEE Trans. Pattern Anal. Mach. Intell.*, submitted for publication.

[22] D. J. Kuck, E. S. Davidson, D. H. Lawrie, and A. H. Sameh, "Parallel supercomputing today and the Cedar approach," *Science*, vol. 231, pp. 967–974, Feb. 1986.

[23] S. K. McGrogan, "Modifying algorithms to achieve greater than linear performance improvements on the ELXSI 6400 multiprocessor," in *Multiprocessors and Array Processors*, Karplus, Ed. San Diego, CA: Simulation Councils, Jan. 1987, pp. 103–110.

[24] R. Miller and Q. Stout, "Geometric algorithms for digitized pictures on a mesh-connected computer," *IEEE Trans. Pattern Anal. Mach. Intell.*, vol. PAMI-7, pp. 216–228, Mar. 1985.

[25] T. N. Mudge, J. P. Hayes, and D. C. Winsor, "Multiple bus architectures," *IEEE Computer*, vol. 20, no. 6, pp. 42–48, June 1987.

[26] A. V. Openheim and R. W. Schafer, *Digital Signal Processing*. Englewood Cliffs, NJ: Prentice-Hall, 1975.

[27] J. M. Ortega and R. G. Voigt, "Solution of partial differential equations on vector and parallel computers," *SIAM Rev.*, pp. 149–240, June 1985.

[28] G. F. Pfister, W. C. Brantley, D. A. George, S. L. Harvey, W. J. Kleinfelder, K. P. McAuliffe, E. A. Melton, V. A. Norton, and J. Weiss, "The IBM Research Parallel Processor Prototype (RP3): Introduction and architecture," in *Proc. Int. Conf. Parallel Processing*, Aug. 1985, pp. 764–771.

[29] M. Quinn, *Designing Efficient Algorithms for Parallel Computers*. New York: McGraw-Hill, 1987, chs. 3 and 4.

[30] I. D. Scherson and Y. Ma, "Vector computations on an orthogonal memory access multiprocessing system," in *Proc. 8th Symp. Comput. Arithmetic*, May 1987, pp. 28–37.

[31] I. D. Scherson, S. Sen, and A. Schamir, "Shear sort: A true two-dimensional sorting technique for VLSI networks," in *Proc. Int. Conf. Parallel Processing*, 1986, pp. 903–908.

[32] C. L. Seitz, "The Cosmic Cube," *Commun. ACM*, vol. 28, no. 1, pp. 22–33, Jan. 1985.

[33] H. J. Siegel, *Interconnection Networks for Large-Scale Parallel Processing*. Boston, MA: Lexington, 1984.

[34] H. Stone, "Parallel processing with perfect shuffle," *IEEE Trans. Comput.*, vol. C-20, pp. 153–161, Feb. 1971.

[35] G. Strang, *Linear Algebra and Its Applications*. New York: Academic, 1980.

[36] J. Test, M. Myszewski, and R. C. Swift, "The Alliant FX/Series: Automatic parallelism in a multiprocessor mini-supercomputer," in Karplus, editor, *Multiprocessors and Array Processors*. San Diego, CA: Simulation Councils, Inc., Jan. 1987, pp. 35–44.

[37] C. D. Thompson and H. T. Kung, "Sorting on a mesh-connected

parallel computer," *Commun. ACM*, vol. 20, no. 4, pp. 263–271, Apr. 1977.

Kai Hwang (S'68–M'72–SM'81–F'86) received the B.S.E.E. degree from National Taiwan University, China, in 1966, the M.S.E.E. degree from the University of Hawaii, in 1969, and Ph.D. degree from the University of California at Berkely in 1972.

He is a Professor of Electrical Engineering and Computer Science at the University of Southern California, Los Angeles, where he has served as the Director of the Computer Research Institute. He has authored or coauthored over 100 scientific papers on computer organizations, parallel algorithms, supercomputers, multiprocessors, and AI-oriented computers. He has authored two books: *Computer Arithmetic* (New York: Wiley, 1979), and *Computer Architecture and Parallel Processing* (New York: McGraw-Hill, 1984), and edited *Supercomputer Design and Applications* (IEEE Computer Society Press, 1984), and *Parallel Processing for Supercomputers*, and *Artificial Intelligence* (New York: McGraw-Hill, 1989). He is the Editor-in-Chief of the *Journal of Parallel and Distributed Computing*. He has lectured worldwide on advanced computer topics and served as a scientific advisor or consultant for a number of federal, industrial, and international research organizations.

Dr. Hwang has served as an IEEE Computer Society Distinguished Visitor and was elected an IEEE Fellow for contributions to digital arithmetic, system architectures, and parallel processing. He has chaired the IEEE/ACM 1985 Seventh Symposium on Computer Arithmetic and the 1986 International Conference on Parallel Processing.

Ping-Sheng Tseng received the B.S. degree in electrical engineering from National Taiwan University, Taipei, Taiwan, in 1982, and the M.S. degree in computer engineering from University of Southern California, Los Angeles, in 1986.

He is presently a Ph.D. candidate in the Department of Electrical and Computer Engineering, Carnegie-Mellon University, Pittsburgh, PA. He is currently working on developing high-level programming tools for systolic computers. His research interests include high-performance computer architectures and their applications.

Dongseung Kim (S'86–M'88) received the B.S. degree in electronics engineering from Seoul National University, Seoul, Korea, in 1978, the M.S. degree in electrical and electronics engineering from the Korea Advanced Institute of Science and Technology, Seoul, Korea, in 1980, and the Ph.D. degree in computer engineering from the University of Southern California, Los Angeles, in 1988.

He was a full-time Instructor in the Department of Electronics Engineering, Kyung-book National University, Taegu, Korea, from 1980 to 1983. He was awarded a fellowship from the Korean government to continue his graduate study in the U.S.A. He is currently working as a Research Scientist in the Department of Electrical Engineering–Systems, University of Southern California, Los Angeles. His research interests include computer architecture, parallel algorithms, image processing, and neural networks.

Distributed-memory multicomputers

Multicomputers: Message-Passing Concurrent Computers

William C. Athas and Charles L. Seitz

California Institute of Technology

Reprinted from *Computer*, Vol. 21, No. 8, August 1988, pages 9-24. Copyright © 1988 by The Institute of Electrical and Electronics Engineers, Inc. All rights reserved.

Highly concurrent computers achieve remarkable performance on the broad class of computations that can be formulated and expressed as concurrent programs. This performance is scalable in the number of computing elements, open-ended with technology advances, and low in cost. Several highly concurrent or highly parallel systems are now commercially available, and innovative programmers are applying them successfully to a great variety of demanding computing problems.

This article provides a status report on the architecture and programming of a family of message-passing concurrent computers that have evolved out of the research of the DARPA-sponsored Submicron Systems Architecture Project in the Caltech Computer Science Department. These systems are organized as ensembles of small programmable computers, called nodes, connected by a message-passing network (see Figure 1). This multiple-computer structure has fittingly come to be known as a multicomputer.

First-generation multicomputers include the Cosmic Cube[1] and the well-known commercial hypercube multicom-

> **Attacking a large computing problem with a myriad of small programmable computers requires a combination of architecture, programming systems, and program formulation.**

puters; more than one hundred of these machines are currently in use. Second-generation multicomputers with faster nodes and much faster message-passing networks appeared during the past year. Configurations of these systems with as

few as 64 nodes exhibit performance comparable to that of conventional supercomputers on a wide variety of large computing problems.[2,3]

Multicomputer programming. The usual abstract unit in which a multicomputer computation is formulated, a *process,* is an instance of a program. Just as an electrical circuit might contain many instances of a certain type of component, and many types of components, a concurrent computation might contain many instances of one or more programs. The programs might be written in conventional programming notations, such as C, Fortran, Pascal, or Lisp, with a standard library of functions or subroutines that cause messages to be sent and received. Other functions that cause the creation and destruction of processes allow intermediate results to determine dynamically the distribution of a computation.

A process contains its own code and private variables, and coordinates its activities with other processes by sending and receiving messages. To support the process abstraction, each multicomputer node runs a multiprogramming operating system that allows multiple processes to coex-

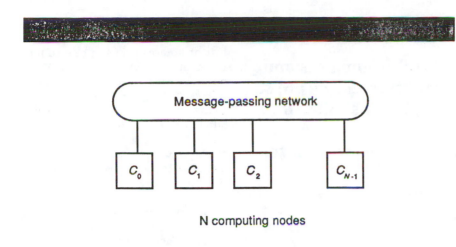

Figure 1. Programmer's model of a multicomputer.

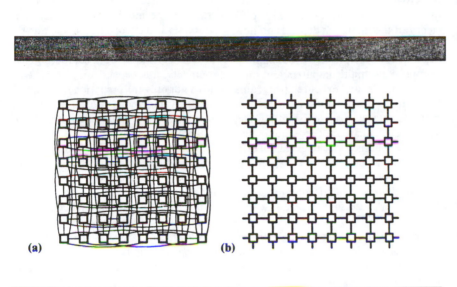

Figure 2. 64-node binary n-cube network (a), and two-dimensional mesh network (b).

ist within that node. Accordingly, the number of concurrent processes involved in a single computation can greatly exceed the number of nodes.

Physical architecture. Multiple-instruction, multiple-data parallel computers divide into two major types: shared-memory multiprocessors and message-passing multicomputers. We can uncover the reasons for many design choices used in multicomputers by comparing them with multiprocessors.

The logical structure of a shared-memory multiprocessor allows multiple processors to access memory in a single global address space. The aggregate demand on the global memory from a large number of processors dictates a number of memory elements comparable to the number of processors; hence, the shared global memory is a physically distributed memory that spans the global address space. Multiprocessors with large numbers of processors employ a switch network that allows any processor to connect to any memory. Some switch networks support a technique of combining references to, and operations on, the same storage location. Using a local or cache memory with each processor can reduce the volume of accesses through the switch network; however, use of a cache for global variables requires a mechanism that allows the cache memories to discover when a global variable has changed.

In contrast, the message-passing multicomputer is both logically and physically a distributed-memory system. The processor in each node computer is tightly coupled to a memory that is physically separate and logically private from the memories of the other node computers. A global memory address does not exist; rather, each node has its own private memory address space. The fixed numbering of the nodes, $0, 1, \ldots, N-1$, together with the unique numbering of the processes within each node, establishes globally unique identifiers for processes; hence, a global name space.

Interprocess communication in a multicomputer occurs by routing messages through a network such as a binary n-cube or mesh (see Figure 2). Regular networks simplify the routing. Their direct and bidirectional, as opposed to indirect,[4] structure allows process placement to exploit the locality of communications. The networks are also extensible, or scalable, to allow for systems with different numbers of nodes. The individual channels operate at rates comparable to the memory bandwidth of a node; the nodes cannot generate or absorb messages at a higher rate. The number of bits conveyed in parallel on a channel is typically less than the word length of the node memory, while messages are typically at least a few words long; hence, the message is serialized into a sequence of parallel-data units that we refer to as flow control units, or *flits*.

Latency issues. The *network latency* equals the time from when the head of a message enters the network at the source until the tail emerges at the destination. Since the flits move through the network in a pipeline fashion, the network latency equals the sum of two components:

- T_pD is the time associated with forming the path through the network, where T_p is the delay of the individual routing nodes encountered on the path, and D is the number of nodes traversed, or the distance.
- L/B is the time required for a message of length L to pass through the channels of bandwidth B.

Multicomputer message-passing networks and multiprocessor switch networks have a similar function. The multicomputer network provides a complete $N \times N$ connection between N nodes. The multiprocessor network provides an $N \times M$ connection between N processors and M memories, where N and M have comparable magnitudes. Although multicomputer and multiprocessor networks are optimized somewhat differently for their different operating environments, the latest designs of both run up against the same physical electronic and packaging limitations. As we describe later, it is practical to build networks of tens of nodes in which the path formation component of the network latency equals one or two instruction times for a processor fabricated using comparable technology. However, networks with thousands of nodes are much more difficult to build and can exhibit latencies of tens of instruction times.

The performance of conventional instruction processors is quite sensitive to *memory-access latency*, the delay from when the processor emits an address to when the data is returned from memory. Interprocess communication in a multiprocessor occurs through the shared global memory. If the memory-access latency exceeds about one instruction time, the processor must idle until the storage cycle completes. Unless multiprocessor designers can discover methods to implement switch networks with lower latency or develop processors that are less sensitive to the memory-access latency, scaling multiprocessors into the range of thousands of nodes will be impractical.

Separate mechanisms that distinguish the different requirements for processor-to-memory communication and interprocess communication save the multicomputer from this scaling dilemma. Because the processor and memory are physically localized in a node, the processor-to-memory communication is not a problem. Interprocess message communication takes place in larger units and less frequently than memory accesses, and accordingly can exhibit a larger latency. Thus, no serious physical obstacles prevent scaling message-passing networks to support communication between thousands of nodes.

Multicomputers and multiprocessors are so logically similar that each can run programs written for the other. Programs written in a process model with message-passing are routinely run on multiprocessors simply by implementing the message-passing operations in the global shared

---

Multicomputers and multiprocessors are so logically similar that each can run programs written for the other.

---

memory. Programs written in a process model with shared variables can be compiled to run on multicomputers by replacing assignments to shared variables with message-passing operations. The efficiency of this approach depends on how successfully the compiler can trace the data dependencies and manage the communications. Both multicomputers and multiprocessors can execute programs formulated for single-instruction, multiple-data message-passing parallel computers, such as the Connection Machine,[5] but such machines cannot efficiently execute programs that exploit the ability of multiple-instruction, multiple-data machines to run different programs on different processors.

Grain size. Although no single or perfect definition of grain size exists for multicomputers, the term loosely describes node size or complexity.[4] We refer to multicomputers whose nodes contain megabytes of memory as *medium-grain* machines, and to those whose nodes contain tens of kilobytes of memory as *fine-grain* machines.

Suppose we were to design a large-scale multicomputer with one gigabyte of primary storage. We might partition this storage into four-megabyte units for each of 256 nodes. We could package the integrated circuits for one node on a single circuit board or multichip carrier. Suitable programming environments for this medium-grain machine are directly compatible with programming environments hosted on workstations.

However, because multicomputers have few advantages over multiprocessors for small N, and because multiprocessors can simulate multicomputers more effectively than vice versa, consider the alternative of shifting N into a "niche" where multicom-

puters are still feasible but multiprocessors are not. For example, the same one gigabyte of storage might also be used for a fine-grain multicomputer with 32,768 nodes, each with 32 kilobytes of primary storage. This system could exhibit peak concurrency more than two orders of magnitude higher. A node would fit on a single very-large-scale-integration chip and would be extremely fast, given the advantage of processor-to-memory communication being localized to the chip.

Programming environments. A multicomputer includes one or more nodes with interfaces to a local area network, and/or one or more computers with interfaces to both the multicomputer's message-passing network and a local area network. Either of these configurations allows messages to be passed between processes in the multicomputer nodes and processes in network hosts, such as the user's workstation. Thus, multicomputers fit naturally into network computing environments and depend on the network hosts not only for preparing and compiling programs, but also for initiating and interacting with computations running on multicomputers.

The programming systems for medium-grain multicomputers have evolved through use for several years. Process code for an explicit concurrent formulation of a computing problem is written in familiar programming languages extended with a library of process-spawning and message-passing functions.

Our research group developed the Cosmic Environment and Reactive Kernel systems to support this multiple-process message-passing programming environment[6] on network hosts and medium-grain multicomputer nodes, respectively. The CE host runtime system consists of a set of daemon processes, utility programs, and libraries. It can serve as a stand-alone system for running message-passing programs on collections of .network-connected Unix hosts. It can also handle the allocation of, and interfaces to, one or more multicomputers. When interfaced to a multicomputer, it supports uniform communication between host and node processes. The RK node operating system supports multiprogramming, message-driven process scheduling, storage management, and system calls for message-passing and other functions on each node.

CE and RK together provide uniform communication between processes

Figure 3. Intel iPSC/2 node (top) and vector accelerator (bottom).

independent of the multicomputer node or network host on which they happen to be located. These systems allow message-passing programs to be run not only on multicomputers, but also on shared-memory multiprocessors, across networks of workstations, and on sequential computers. A principle and a formal property of the entire CE/RK system—within the limits of the computation being deterministic and not exceeding available storage sizes—is that the results of a computation do not depend on the distribution of the processes.

Programming systems that support fine-grain concurrency are in their early stages of development. These systems are based on new programming languages that provide constructs for expressing fine-grain concurrency. Although many programming languages and language constructs have been proposed, two general approaches for expressing fine-grain concurrency have emerged.

One approach is based upon a static process structure in which the number of processes and their connectivity is known before the program executes. In Occam,[7] for example, all processes and channels for a computation are denoted in the source program. Each channel connects exactly two processes, and communication through the channel is synchronous; that is, the completion of the send action at one end of the channel is synchronized with the completion of the receive action at the other end. The Occam compiler performs an operation analogous to macro expansion on processes and channels, resulting in the static process structure.

The other general approach is based upon dynamic process structures in which processes are created and destroyed on demand. Message passing is accomplished by reference to the destination process rather than to a channel, and is asynchronous and buffered. Because references to processes can be communicated in messages, the connectivity of the process structure can vary as the computation proceeds. The Actor model[8] and programming notations, and the Cantor programming system,[9] which we describe later, exemplify this approach.

Medium-grain multicomputers

Between 1981 and 1985, members of our research group designed, built several copies of, and developed the system software for the Cosmic Cube,[1] an experimental message-passing concurrent computer that became the archetype of the first-generation multicomputers. Commercial multicomputers that use the same organization and programming methods—the Intel iPSC/1, Ametek S/14, and N-Cube/10—were introduced in 1985. The size of a single node in these systems ranges from seven chips (one custom VLSI chip with processor and communications, plus six RAM chips) in the N-Cube to two circuit boards (a regular node board plus a vector accelerator board) in the Intel iPSC/1 VX.

All of these systems use software-controlled routing on a binary n-cube network to connect $N = 2^n$ nodes; hence, they are sometimes called cubes or hypercubes. The number of nodes in a single system ranges from four (two-dimensional cube) to 1,024 (10-dimensional cube). The Floating Point Systems T-Series and other machines based on the Inmos transputer[7] are also multicomputers, but they employ a computational model based on the Occam programming language.

These first-generation multicomputers have proven to be reasonably "general-purpose" concurrent computers. They have been applied to a wide range of easily partitioned and distributed computing problems, such as matrix operations, differential equation solvers, finite element analysis, finite difference methods, distant- or local-field many-body problems, fast Fourier transforms, ray tracing, heuristic searches, circuit simulation, and distributed simulation of systems composed of loosely coupled physical processes. Hundreds of research papers and reports have been published on the concurrent formulations and results of these computations.

Current status. Multicomputers currently stand at the threshold of a second generation of medium-grain machines. The nodes of these systems employ the same 32-bit processor and megabit RAM technology used in personal computers and workstations. In comparison with first-generation machines, node performance and memory capacity have improved by nearly an order of magnitude within the same physical size simply by tracking the advances in single-chip processor and RAM technology. However, second-generation multicomputers are most distinguished by message-routing hardware that makes the topology of the message-passing network practically invisible to the programmer.

The message-routing hardware employs a blocking variant of cut-through routing that we call *wormhole* routing.[10-12] A message consists of a sequence of flits, in which the flit at the head of the message governs the route. As the head flit advances along the specified route, the remaining flits follow in a pipeline fashion. If the head encounters a channel already in use, it is blocked until the channel is freed; the flow control within the network blocks the trailing flits.

This form of routing and flow control has two important advantages over the store-and-forward packet cut-through routing used in first-generation machines. First, it avoids using storage bandwidth in the nodes through which messages are routed. To the designer of a multicomputer, the storage bandwidth of a node is a precious resource that should be spent on computing cycles rather than message routing. Second, this routing technique makes the message latency largely insensitive to the distance in the message-passing network. The network latency, $T_pD + L/B$, is dominated by the second term in the sum for all but very short messages. For example, in one implementation in which $T_p \approx 80$ nanoseconds and $B \approx 25$ megabytes per second, a 40-byte message that traverses five nodes would require 0.4 microsecond for path formation, but 1.6 microseconds to convey the message. Also, the fixed software overhead of system calls and context switching is much larger than the network latency.

Another improvement in message performance results from using lower-dimension and higher-radix versions of the k-ary n-cube network.[4] We can think of a k-ary n-cube—a family of torus networks with k^n nodes—as constructed in n dimensions with k periodic coordinates in each dimension. This family includes the binary (2-ary) n-cube (see Figure 2) network on one extreme and the k-element ring network (k-ary 1-cube) at the opposite extreme, and spans a range of wirability and average distance between pairs of nodes.

An analysis of the cost and performance of these networks must take into account that the more wirable networks can afford to assign more parallel wires, hence a higher bandwidth, to each channel. The optimization to minimize latency simply minimizes $T_pD + L/B$. High-dimension networks reduce the first term at the expense of the second, while low-dimension networks reduce the second term at the expense of the first. An analysis[11] shows that a two-dimensional network minimizes latency for typical message lengths for $N \approx 256$.

The two-dimensional mesh (see Figure 2) is a variation on a k-ary 2-cube with the "end-around" cyclic connection eliminated. We prefer the mesh rather than the torus form of the cube because the mesh offers useful edge connectivity. Also, the mesh partitions into units that are still meshes, and the particular deadlock-free routing scheme used is simpler when the cyclic connection is eliminated.[10] Based on this reasoning, we expect that two-dimensional mesh networks will become the standard for second-generation machines.

Intel and Ametek recently introduced two early second-generation multicomputers. The Intel iPSC/2[2] is an upgraded Intel iPSC/1, with nodes based on the Intel 80386 processor and hardware wormhole message routing in the binary n-cube. Figure 3 shows an iPSC/2 node. The Ametek Series 2010[3] uses the Motorola 68020 as the node instruction processor, a microprogrammed second processor to manage the send and receive queues, and a two-dimensional wormhole routing mesh network. Figure 4 shows parts of two 4×4 submesh units of the Ametek Series 2010 and the way they are attached. Our research group developed the mesh routing chips[12]; MOSIS (Metal-Oxide Semiconductor Implementation Service) provided the fabrication. Both the iPSC/2 and the Series 2010 run the CE/RK programming environment.

In comparison with first-generation multicomputers, node performance has improved by nearly an order of magnitude, while the reduction in message latency for nonlocalized messages in the Series 2010 approaches three orders of magnitude. The relationship between communication and computing performance improved by two orders of magnitude. Faster communications extend the application span of multicomputers from easily partitioned and distributed problems to high-flux problems, such as searching, sorting, concurrent data structures,[11] graph problems, signal processing, image processing, and distributed simulation of systems composed of many tightly coupled physical processes. Making the message latency insensitive to message distance simplifies programming and allows more effective and less constrained dispersal of processes to achieve load balance.

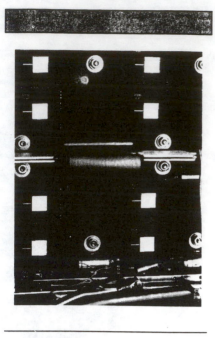

Figure 4. Close-up of a region of the Ametek Series 2010 backplane.

Configurations. We can scale and configure medium-grain multicomputers in several ways. The number of nodes, N, is the most important scaling. Node memory size is another configuration choice. The preferred node memory size will likely approximate that in workstation computers, with nodes operating as virtual memory computers.

Although the first-generation systems are homogeneous—that is, the nodes are nominally identical—we can construct multicomputers equally well as heterogeneous systems with a variety of specialized nodes for different computations, so long as all the nodes employ the same communication protocols. One form of heterogeneous multicomputer system already exists in the installation of different accelerators on different nodes, such as an Intel iPSC/1 configured with floating-point vector accelerators on half of the machine and memory expansion on the other half. We can also install I/O device controllers—such as those for disks, displays, and communications—on individual nodes or around the edges of the mesh. With disk interfaces, second-generation multicomputers support their own file systems and can even act as high-performance file servers for a network.

Third-generation systems. To place these developments into a long-term per-

Table 1. Medium-grain multicomputer history and projections.

Generation Years	First 1983-87	Second 1988-92	Third 1993-97
Typical node			
MIPS	1	10	100
Mflops scalar	0.1	2	40
Mflops vector	10	40	200
memory (Mbytes)	0.5	4	32
Typical system			
N (nodes)	64	256	1,024
MIPS	64	2,560	100K
Mflops scalar	6.4	512	40K
Mflops vector	640	10K	200K
memory (Mbytes)	32	1K	32K
Communication latency (100-byte msg)			
neighbor (microseconds)	2,000	5	0.5
nonlocal (microseconds)	6,000	5	0.5

```
% peek
Cube Daemon version 7.2, up 2 days 8 hours on host sol

{                     }   5d ipsc cube  , b:0000 [    mars iPSC d7]   5.4h
{CONCISE lena         }   5d ipsc cube  , b:0020 [    mars iPSC d7]   1.0h
{        TV wen-king  }   6d ipsc cube  , b:0040 [neptune iPSC d7]    1.3h
{                     }   3d cosmic cube, b:0000 [  venus fly trap ]  5.4h
{     orbits  dian    }   3d ghost cube , b:0000 [    mars :mimic ]  12.0m
{                     }   3d ghost cube , b:0008 [  saturn :mimic ]   1.2d
{     tester  jakov   }   6d cosmic cube, b:0000 [   ceres 6-cube ]   6.4m
{     optic  chuck    }  20n ginzu cube , b:0000 [  icarus ginzu d5] 20.0s
{                     }  12n ginzu cube , b:0000 [ hermes ginzu d5]  12.0h


GROUP {optic chuck} TYPE reactive IDLE 0.0s

( −1     0)   optichost   3s  3r 0q  [icarus 5049]  20.0s
( −1    −1)   SERVER      3s  1r 0q  [icarus 5051]  16.0s
( −1    −2)   FILE MGR    0s  0r 0q  [icarus 5052]  16.0s
(--- ---)     CUBEIFC     5s  3r 0q  [ ceres 8327]  18.0s
```

Figure 5. Cosmic Environment display showing how multicomputers on a network are allocated in "space-sharing."

spective, we observe that in accordance with the technology development model in the DARPA Strategic Computing program, the first-generation machines used relatively unaggressive technology to establish the computational model, programming methods, and applications. The second-generation systems achieve much higher performance by a combination of organizational refinement and VLSI technology.

Since multicomputers are scalable in size and technology, we expect that a third generation can develop with little organizational change from the second generation, requiring only the application of VLSI technology advances. The use of VLSI with smaller-sized features will scale processor and communication performance together. Thus, we do not expect the relationship between communication and computing performance to change significantly in the further evolution of these architectures. The most important organizational improvements in the third generation will be in the instruction processors, both in their performance and in their ability to switch context more efficiently than processors designed for use in personal computers and workstations.

Table 1 summarizes our projections of the evolution of medium-grain multicomputers.

Medium-grain concurrent programming

In preparation for an example of programming medium-grain multicomputers using a process model, we will describe several of the essential features of the Cosmic Environment and Reactive Kernel systems.[6] We will illustrate the user-interface functions and example using the C programming language.

Process groups. The entire set of processes involved in a single computation is called a process group. A CE utility program establishes the process group and allocates the multicomputer nodes, and thereafter manages the entry of the host process into the process group, the messages between them, and the messages to and from any node processes.

Multicomputers are normally not time-shared, but space-shared. A CE utility displays how all the multicomputers on a network are allocated, as well as the user's own host processes (see Figure 5). In this example, the 128-node iPSC d7 is allocated with one user (wen-king) running a computation on a 6d ipsc cube (64 nodes), another user (lena) on a 5d ipsc cube (32 nodes), and the remaining 5-cube free. Of course, the user with 64 nodes cannot distinguish these 64 nodes from a separate 64-node multicomputer. The logical node numbers will be 0, 1, . . . , 63, regardless of their physical location in the multicomputer.

Space-sharing has proven most appropriate for multicomputers because it allows a user to select a number of nodes appropriate to the number of processes and the load-balancing characteristics of a particular computation. It also produces predictable runtimes and does not allow one user's processes to upset the load balance of another process group.

The ghost cube in the display of Figure 5 is not a real multicomputer, but mimics one with a collection of 16 CE daemon processes distributed across a set of workstations on the local network. Using ghost cubes, sites that do not have regular access to a multicomputer have developed many multicomputer programs.

Process IDs, placement, and spawning. Every process within a process group has a unique identifier (ID), represented as an ordered pair: (node, pid). A value of the node parameter in the range $0 \ldots N-1$ designates a node process; otherwise, a host process. The pid part of the ID specifies a particular process within a node or within the host environment. The mynode, mypid, and nnode functions permit a process to determine its own ID and the number of nodes.

Processes in execution can freely spawn and kill other processes. The system's lowest-level process-spawning mechanisms give the programmer explicit control of process placement through the arguments of a dynamic process-creation function, spawn("filename", node, pid, "mode"). The node parameter determines process placement, and contrary to the usual practice in which the operating system assigns a pid, the pid is specified in the function. This scheme allows processes to build structures in which references to other processes are predetermined, rather than established by passing references in messages.

Process placement and IDs can also be decided dynamically during execution; other process-creation functions support this option. Functions also exist for creating a process in every node from the same "filename" specification. Fast process creation is crucial to the performance of many multicomputer computations. Accordingly, RK not only shares code segments for processes created from the same compiled program ("filename"), but also caches a copy of the initial data segment so that subsequent processes with the same "filename" specification can be created without accessing the file system.

Execution of spawn functions in host processes is how a computation that starts out as a process running on a host computer builds the process structure for a computation that runs on a multicomputer.

Once spawned, a process will not spontaneously migrate to another node; thus, it is most efficient to retain the physical

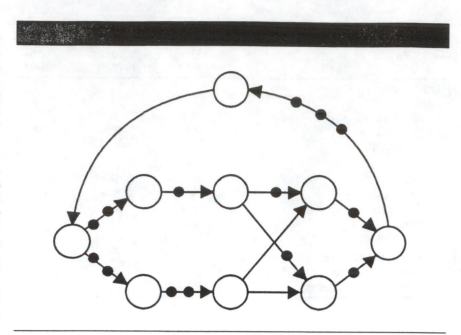

Figure 6. Example of a process-structure graph.

location of a process as a part of its unique ID. One of the implicit premises of multicomputer architectures is that costly communication mechanisms for dynamically binding computing resources to runable objects, as used in multiprocessors or in the dataflow model, are rarely necessary. It is instead sufficient for most problems to establish a binding of a process to a node that will persist for the life of the process. Although the CE/RK environment does not relocate processes, high-level programming systems that support dynamic relocation of processes are easily layered on top of the CE/RK environment.

Messages. A message is the logical unit of information exchange between processes. A message can be any number of bytes in length, from zero to any size that will fit in the memory of the nodes of the sending and receiving processes. Although message length or destination select different protocols for packetizing and routing messages, these differences are invisible to the application programmer.

Sending a message between processes requires that the sending process have reference to the receiving process. References are represented in message functions as IDs. The *process structure*—which we define as the set of processes within the process group, together with each

process's references to other processes—can be depicted as a directed graph with vertices representing processes and arcs representing references. We can also visualize the arcs as virtual communication channels, with messages traveling along the arcs (see Figure 6).

Messages are queued as necessary in the sending node, in transit, and in the receiving node. Accordingly, they have arbitrary delay from sender to receiver. However, message order is preserved between pairs of communicating processes; for example, if process *A* sends two messages in sequence to process *B*, they will arrive an arbitrary time later and in the same order as they were sent. Thus, we can think of the messages in Figure 6 as "traveling" at some arbitrary speed, but one message cannot pass another on a reference arc.

For the C-language user-interface routines to the CE/RK system, messages are sent and received from dynamically allocated storage accessed both by user processes and by the message system. Message buffers are blocks of memory with no presumed structure; thus, messages can convey arbitrary structures, such as simple variables, arrays, or user-defined types.

The xmalloc and xfree functions can allocate and free message space. These functions are semantically identical to the Unix malloc and free functions. When a

```c
#include <cube/cubedef.h>

typedef struct MESG MESG;                /* Message header structure.         */
struct MESG { int      pnode, ppid;      /* ID of the parent process.         */
              int      tbase    ;        /* Base for time-on-target tree.     */
              int      len      ;        /* Number of elements in the vector. */
              MESG   **type     ;} ;     /* Type field for filtering message. */
#define BUF(v) ((double *)(v + 1))       /* Data follows MESG immediately.    */

unsigned int this_node, this_pid, node_cnt;

main( )
{      MESG *v;

       this_node = mynode( );            /* node number of this process.      */
       this_pid  =  mypid( );            /* pid number of this process.       */
       node_cnt  = nnodes( );            /* number of nodes in this machine.  */
       v = (MESG *) xrecvb( );           /* Receive list from parent process. */
       mergesort(v);                     /* Sort the list.                    */
       xsend(v, v->pnode, v->ppid);      /* Send list back to parent.         */
}

mergesort(v)
       MESG *v ;
{      unsigned k1, k2, i, new_node;
       MESG *v1, *v2, *vtemp;
       double *d, *s, *b1, *b2;

       if(v->len <= 1) return;           /* len = 1 lists are already sorted. */
       k1 = ( v->len + 1 ) / 2;          /* Break the list into two lists.    */
       k2 = ( v->len     ) / 2;
       v1   = (MESG *) xmalloc(sizeof(MESG) + sizeof(double)*k1);
       v2   = (MESG *) xmalloc(sizeof(MESG) + sizeof(double)*k2);
       for(i = v1->len = k1, d = BUF(v1), s = BUF(v); i--; ) *d++ = *s++;
       for(i = v2->len = k2, d = BUF(v2)              ; i--; ) *d++ = *s++;

       new_node = this_node ^ v->tbase;          /* Next node in the tree.    */
       v1->tbase = v2->tbase = v->tbase << 1;    /* New base for building     */
                                                 /* the time-on-target tree.  */
       if (v1->len > 20 && new_node < node_cnt )
       {                                         /* If list is long enough    */
           spawn("msort",new_node,this_pid," ");  /* and next node exists,    */
           v1->pnode = this_node   ;             /* spawn a child process     */
           v1->ppid   = this_pid   ;             /* and send it a list.       */
           v1->type   = &v1        ;             /* The type field holds the  */
           xsend(v1,new_node,this_pid);          /* address of the msg ptr.   */
           v1 = 0;                               /* Msg ptr is set to nil.    */
       }
       else mergesort(v1);                       /* Sort v1 if can't split.   */

       mergesort(v2);                            /* Sort the second list.     */

       while(!v1) { vtemp = (MESG *) xrecvb( ); *vtemp->type = vtemp; }

       for(b1 = BUF(v1), b2 = BUF(v2), d = BUF(v); k1 || k2; )  /* Merge.     */
       {   while(k1 && (!k2 || (k2 && b1 <= *b2))) { k1--; *d++ = *b1++; }
           while(k2 && (!k1 || (k1 && b2 <= *b1))) { k2--; *d++ = *b2++; }
       }
       xfree(v1); xfree(v2);
}
```

Figure 7. Program text for a mergesort process.

message has been built in a message block pointed to by p, its contents can be sent as a message by the function xsend(p, node, pid). The xsend function also deallocates the message space; that is, xsend(p, ...) resembles xfree(p), except that it also sends a message. Thus, there is no need for blocking or for feedback that the message has been sent; when the function returns, the message block is gone.

The function xrecvb can receive messages and return a pointer to a new message. This blocking function does not return until a message has arrived for the process. The execution of the xrecvb function is just like allocating a message buffer with xmalloc, except that the message received determines the contents and length of the block allocated. Once the message contents are no longer needed, the allocated space should be freed. Of course, xfree(p) can free the message space, but so can xsend(p, ...) if there is a message of the same length to send. Frequently in message-passing programs, as in a later example, a message is received, modified by a computation, and then sent on to another process.

If process A calls xrecvb when the next message in the node's receive queue is for process B, RK might save the state of process A and start running process B. The appearance of xrecvb in the code marks choice points for switching the execution to another process; in this sense the scheduling is reactive or message driven. So long as a process makes progress, RK does not necessarily force a context switch unless some exceptional system event occurs.

Portability. The C-language primitives described here are system primitives, and not necessarily those the user would find most convenient. We selected these functions for reasons of portability, and because we can easily and efficiently layer other message primitives on top of them. For example, the usual interface routines for Fortran are expressed in terms of the x primitives (such as xsend and xrecvb), but include message types and can exercise discretion in receiving messages by type and sender ID. The CE/RK environment also includes a sizable library of other functions, including many compatible with Unix functions of the same name, such as the C-language standard I/O package.

A multicomputer interprets the x functions by allocating storage and by sending and receiving messages. A multiprocessor

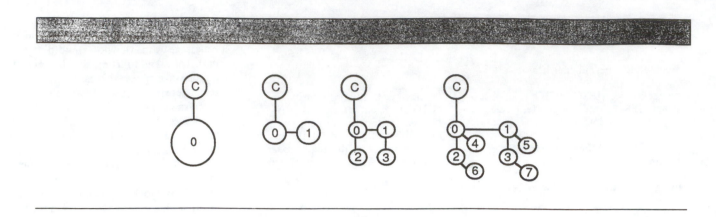

Figure 8. Sequence of building a time-on-target tree.

can interpret the same functions differently. The xmalloc and xfree functions allocate or free blocks in global shared memory. The xsend(p, node, pid) function passes ownership of the block pointed to by p to process (node, pid), and appends the pointer to the task queue of this process. The xrecvb function is the means by which a process can obtain a new task. This alternative operational interpretation allows CE/RK programs to run under native task systems on multiprocessors, and will also be a means of running the programs on future multicomputers that use multiprocessor nodes.

Programming example. Although we can use the functions in the low-level portable CE/RK environment as a compilation target for higher-level concurrent programming notations, the low-level environment is adequate for many purposes. This programming system has been used extensively in experiments with concurrent algorithms and in writing useful programs based on explicit concurrent formulations of computing problems typical of those in science and engineering. These application programs are based, for example, on concurrent adaptations of well-known sequential algorithms, on regular data-partitioning strategies, on the systolic algorithms developed for regular VLSI computational arrays, and on a wide variety of fundamental concurrent algorithms.

Our example uses the mergesort algorithm to sort a list of elements into ascending order. Briefly, we can describe mergesort as follows: A list of length 1 is already sorted and is returned. A list of length 2 or greater is split into two lists whose lengths differ at most by one. Mergesort is applied recursively to each of

these lists. The resulting two sorted lists are then merged into a sorted list that is returned. List elements are compared only in the merge operation. Mergesort requires $O(n \log n)$ comparisons for a list of length n, a minimum for sorting algorithms based on performing comparisons.

Figure 7 illustrates the complete C program for our example. With the omission of the code in the shaded areas, the mergesort function within this program implements the sequential form of this algorithm. Lists are represented with a defined type MESG followed by a list of double-precision floating-point elements; the program could easily be modified for any other built-in C type. The MESG structure contains a member for the length of the list (len), and several members for control of data distribution in the concurrent program. Input to the mergesort function points to a MESG, and the function returns when the list is sorted.

The adaptation of this program to a multicomputer exploits the recursive divide-and-conquer strategy of the mergesort algorithm for distributing the computation across the nodes of the multicomputer. Because the algorithm's recursion is twofold, a straightforward mapping of mergesort recursive calls to processes would build a binary-tree process structure dynamically. However, it is somewhat more elegant and efficient to distribute the effort in a scheme in which a mergesort process recursively keeps half of the work and gives away the other half. As illustrated in Figure 8 by a sequence of snapshots of the process structure, this scheme also builds a tree of processes, but of a form that we refer to as a *time-on-target* tree. The area of the circle for each process is proportional to the length of the

list it has to sort. We can systematically map this process structure onto $N = 2^n$ multicomputer nodes, as shown in the process labels.

The calling process, labeled C in Figure 8, invokes a sort by spawning the root mergesort process, labeled 0. The root mergesort process is nominally spawned in the same node as C (but potentially in any node). Process C then sends to process 0 a message in the format of the MESG structure followed by the list to be sorted. It includes in the members of the MESG structure its own ID (or some other ID to which the sorted list is to be returned), tbase equal to one, and the length of the message. Having handed off the sorting operation, process C can proceed concurrently with other computations until the sorted list is required, at which point it executes an xrecvb function.

The main function is an outer shell that allows the mergesort function to be used as a remote procedure. In the same fashion that C hands off the sort operation to the root mergesort process, the first shaded portion of the mergesort function hands off one of the two lists resulting from splitting the input list, but only if the list is long enough to justify it (v1 − > len > 20) and the multicomputer includes the target node (new_node < node_cnt). The distribution of the computation is inhibited when the individual sort operations are small or when all of the nodes are used. The new processes spawned are each identified in the MESG structure with a type in the form of a pointer to a v1 pointer. Returns from the recursive mergesort calls occur only after the computation has been completely distributed. The sorted lists from descendant processes can arrive in any order; thus, messages are

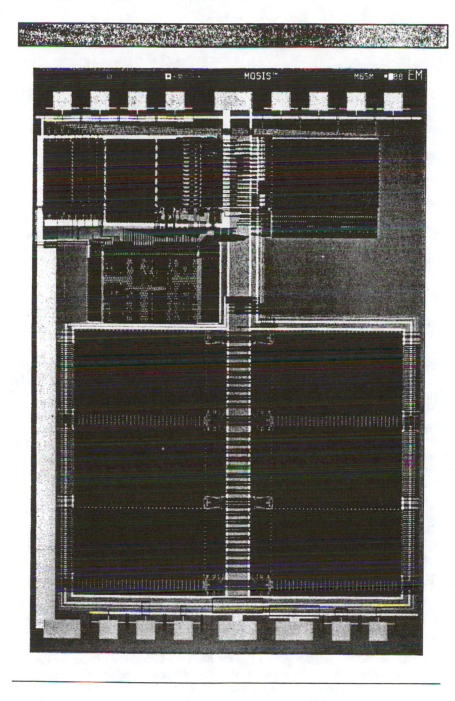

Figure 9. Photomicrograph of the Mosaic A single-chip node.

and programming. If a number of challenging problems can be solved, these machines might become the prevalent form of this architecture.

To understand some of the problems in the physical design and programming of such machines, members of our research group are developing a design and a programming system for a fine-grain multicomputer called Mosaic. Because medium-grain multicomputers can also host fine-grain computations, we have used medium-grain machines to develop fine-grain concurrent programs written in Cantor. We thus have a substantial collection of programs ready to run on Mosaic. Writing and instrumenting the execution of many diverse fine-grain Cantor programs was essential for establishing the requirements for the Mosaic design.

A stipulation of the Mosaic project has been that a node fit on a single chip. Our first attempt to design such a single-chip node resulted in the Mosaic A chip pictured in Figure 9. The bottom two-thirds of this chip is RAM—about the same fraction of the silicon complexity devoted to RAM in medium-grain nodes. The upper-left part of the chip includes a 16-bit instruction processor and program-controlled communication channels, and the upper right is ROM containing bootstrap and self-test programs. This processor ran at about six million instructions per second, and its four communication channels operated bit-serial at 2.5 megabytes per second.

The software-controlled routing is the most serious shortcoming in this design. It limits the effective channel bandwidth near the network bisection to about 0.25 megabyte per second, even if the nodes near the bisection spend all of their time routing messages. A machine with 1,024 nodes in a two-dimensional 32×32 mesh would have only 16 megabytes per second of bilateral message bandwidth across its network bisection to support 5,120 MIPS peak.

Our current node design, the Mosaic C, consists of a 14-MIPS 16-bit processor, 20-megabytes-per-second routing communication channels with $T_p = 50$ nanoseconds, and up to 16 kilobytes of RAM integrated onto a single VLSI chip using 1.2-micrometer complementary metal-oxide semiconductor technology. The major sections of this chip have been designed, fabricated separately through MOSIS, and shown to work correctly. We expect to build a full-size machine of 16,384 nodes in 1989, after assembling the

received and the pointers to them are stored into v1 pointers until the v1 pointer specific to this recursive call becomes non-0. Then the sorted v1 and v2 lists are merged and freed, and the mergesort function returns.

This programming paradigm of divide-and-conquer problems illustrates how a programmer can redesign a program or algorithm devised to run on a sequential computer so that, instead, it will distribute the computing to a collection of identical node processes. The mergesort algorithm performs a balanced splitting of a computing task, so that the computing load balances across the nodes of the multicomputer.

Fine-grain multicomputers

Fine-grain machines are the research frontier of multicomputer architectures sections into a single chip and building some smaller prototypes. The peak performance of this experimental fine-grain system should be quite phenomenal—200,000 MIPS for the 16,384-node machine—and the system will serve as a testbed for the development of programming systems and applications.

A two-dimensional 128×128 network would be inadequate for this machine, so we will organize it as a three-dimensional $32 \times 32 \times 16$ mesh. The network bisection for the two-dimensional network would include 128 channels, in contrast with 512 channels for the three-dimensional network, and the longest path would be 255 nodes instead of 78. The execution bandwidth of the Mosaic will be reasonably well balanced with its 20,480-megabytes-per-second bilateral message bandwidth across the network bisection. The average latency for a 20-byte message to a randomly selected destination node will be about 35 instruction cycles.

Since the implementation of low-latency networks becomes increasingly difficult for large N, how small must the message latency be for the message networks in fine-grain multicomputers? If the program sequences that execute between message operations in the formulation of a concurrent computation are reduced to only tens of instructions (or even less, as they often are for fine-grain program objects), is it not necessary to reduce the message latencies in proportion? Since this scaling in latency would be motivated by the same factors that cause N to be scaled up, the construction of fine-grain systems would be physically very difficult, indeed. However, one of the ways multicomputers accommodate message latency is by maintaining multiple processes or program objects in each node. When a process attempts to receive a message not yet in the node's pool of received messages, it switches context to another process that does have a message available. Maintaining many processes per node is also important to achieving load balance statistically.

As we observed in connection with future medium-grain multicomputers, a reduction in context-switching time is increasingly important. The Mosaic C was designed as a two-context processor; it has two program counters and two partially overlapping register banks to switch in one clock cycle between system and user contexts. Operations to memory are only one clock cycle longer than operations to registers. Registers are used principally as pointers into data structures maintained

Cantor objects strictly observe the reactive property; they are normally at rest until a message arrives.

by the Cantor runtime system, and are not saved following an object execution.

Programming systems such as Cantor can also help manage the network resource. Direct networks exhibit paths of different lengths, so Cantor can place processes to balance the computing load and localize message traffic for communication-intensive computations. Relatively localized message traffic helps to reduce the message latency as well as the congestion in the communication network. The Cantor compiler can often extract the process structure from the program text—so it can map processes systematically—or employ heuristics to compute a static placement with good properties for balancing the multicomputer's communication and computing resources.

Fine-grain concurrent programming

For highly regular or symmetric computations, such as grid-point calculations or systolic algorithms, we can view a fine-grain multicomputer as a collection of thousands of small computers. A second approach for computations with more complex behavior views the fine-grain multicomputer as a single computer. A partition is established between the tasks required of the program writer and the capabilities provided by the programming system. The program writer must express the computation in a way that exposes all of the concurrency that the system can use in execution. The programming system has complete responsibility for managing system resources.

In our experiments with this second approach, we express computations in terms of fine-grain objects that communicate only by message-passing. The capabil-

ities of objects are comparable in many ways to the capabilities of the processes of the CE/RK system. The semantics of message-passing are identical, but references and object creation are handled more carefully. An object consists of a code area and a private memory area. We have observed that the private memory area of objects in fine-grain message-driven programs is usually quite small, often less than one hundred bytes.

Cantor. The Cantor programming environment consists of a compiler, runtime system, and other programming tools that together manage the concurrent resources of the fine-grain machine. Cantor[9] is a programming notation for writing message-driven programs using concurrent objects. Each object is an independent computing agent that interacts with other objects solely by message-passing. The semantics of an object program are a form of Actor semantics, as defined by Agha.[8] Each object consists of a set of private variables that persist between receiving messages, a list of variables that describe the expected contents of the next message, and a sequence of actions that describe how the object will react to the next message.

Cantor objects strictly observe the reactive property; they are normally at rest until a message arrives. An object's response is determined by the contents of the message, the current contents of the private variables, and a sequence of procedural statements that define the object's fundamental actions, including creating new objects and sending more messages. An object in Cantor must process a message in a bounded number of steps. In earlier versions of Cantor, the syntax enforced this property. The current syntax has been liberalized to permit objects to run indefinitely; however, objects capable of this type of behavior can permanently block a computation from making progress.

The composition of a node number and local object number produces a unique identifier for an object. The object identifier, part of the value domain of Cantor's semantics, is called a reference. Message-passing is based on the sending object's possessing a reference to a destination object. An object acquires a reference upon creating a new object, or might receive a reference in a message.

After the sending object completes the send action, the message exhibits arbitrary delay in traveling from sender to destination. Likewise, the action of creating a new object exhibits arbitrary delay. While the send action requires no value to be produced, creating a new object yields a reference value for the new object. Thus, the generation of the reference value is immediate and can be used in a computation before the object is instantiated. For an object to process a message, the object must be instantiated.

Flow analysis. In the implementation of Cantor, the decoupling between the reference to an object and the instance of an object permits speculation about references before an object is required by a program. When the reference to an object exists, but the object has not yet been built, we call the reference value a *future*. Generating futures prior to executing a program, called *future flow*, can improve load balancing and preserve locality among communicating objects.

The problem of future flow during compilation parallels the problem of constant propagation in optimizing compilers. Value propagation graphs are constructed to denote the dependencies between the execution points where values become defined and the execution points where values are used. By generating a future for each of the definition vertices and propagating the reference value through the other vertices, a subset of the reference values used by a program is generated as futures at compile time. We can represent these futures as vertices of graphs that

```
qlist (row,col : int, next : ref) ::
*[ case (cmd : sym) of                                   % dispatch on message selector
    "check" : (rn,cn : int, caller : ref )               % check for conflict
            if rn = row or (cn − col) = abs (rn − row)   % if row or diagonal match then
              then send (false ) to caller               % reply false
              else if next = nil then send (true) to caller   % if no next then reply true
                    else send ("check",rn,cn,caller) to next  % else test next qlist element
                    fi
            fi
    "copy" : (caller : ref )                             % copy qlist
            if next = nil                                % if last element then copy and reply
              then send (qlist(row,col,nil )) to caller  % else forward copy request to next
              else send ("copy", self ) to next          % wait for copy list and add local copy
              [ (l : ref ) send (qlist(row,col,l)) to caller ]
            fi
]


queen (ql : ref, cn : int , out : ref ) ::               % ql — list of valid queen positions
                                                         % cn — column number
*[ (rn : int )                                           % receive test row number
   send ("check", rn, cn, self ) to ql                   % check for conflict of (rn,cn) in ql
   [ (reply : bool )
    if reply                                             % if no conflict then copy ql
      then send ("copy", self ) to ql                    % receive copy of ql
           [ (nql : ref )                                % add (rn,cn) to copy of ql
             nql = qlist(rn,cn,nql)                       % if last column
             if cn = 8 then send ("insert", nql) to out   % then enqueue result
                  else send (1) to queen(nql, cn + 1, out)  % else search next column
                  fi
           ]
    fi
   ]
   if rn < 8 then send (rn + 1) to self else exit fi     % if not last row
]                                                        % then search next row


make_q(out : ref ) ::
*[ (i : int) send (1) to queen(qlist (i,1,nil ),2,out)    % make initial set
          if i < 8 then send (i + 1) to self else exit fi  % of 8 queen objects
]
```

Figure 10. Concurrent eight-queens program.

show the connectivity and genealogy of objects.

The construction of the future graph is thwarted by data dependencies that cannot be resolved without running the program, and by nondeterminancy introduced by the message-passing semantics. A second type of flow analysis not obstructed by data dependencies and message nondeterminancy predicts how an object will be used based on its propensity to create new objects and send more messages. Based on the semantics of message-driven programs, concurrency is introduced only when an object sends more messages than it receives. The propensity to send more messages, called the *send factor* (*SF*), is defined as the maximum number of messages an object can send in response to processing a single message. The *new factor* (*NF*) is the maximum number of new objects the object can create in response to processing a message. *SF* and *NF* for each type of object can be calculated at compile time.

When creating a new object, for example, the object can generate concurrency (*SF* > 1), sustain concurrency (*SF* = 1), or reduce concurrency (*SF* < 1). If all objects for a program have *SF* ≤ 1, then the program is sequential. *SF* and *NF* assist heuristic decisions about the placement of new objects. For example, if *SF* and *NF* are greater than one, then the new object should be placed on a distant node to prevent excessive congestion of messages and objects within a small patch of the host multicomputer.

An example. To illustrate Cantor as a notation for expressing concurrent programs, and to demonstrate message-driven programming, let us examine the "eight-queens" problem. The task is to place eight queen pieces on an 8 × 8 chessboard so that no queen is in jeopardy of capture. The queen game piece captures any other piece that lies along the same row, column, or diagonal.

The search for the problem's 92 solutions is highly concurrent. From the capture rule, there will be only one queen per row and column. A concurrent search can therefore be organized either by row or by column. Assuming a column-by-column search, a queen is placed in a row of column 1. The rows of column 2 are then searched to find a safe position for the second queen. After a safe position has been found, the rows of column 3 are searched to find a safe position for the third queen. Each subsequent column search involves

checking the previous row and column pairs to be sure that the new position is safe. For the case where no safe row can be found, the partial solution is simply discarded.

A sequential search would involve backtracking once an impossible configuration is exposed. The backtracking step systematically removes the current emplacements of queens and then continues with a new placement. For the concurrent search, backtracking is not necessary, because all solutions are equally pursued. The only action taken in response to a detected impossible configuration is to discard the configuration.

The program fragment of Figure 10 performs the concurrent search. The names qlist, queen, and make_q denote object definitions and not objects. An object definition is a template for building an object; all objects result from object definitions. A program consists of a finite number of object definitions used to generate a possibly unbounded number of objects. The make_q object definition starts the concurrent search by creating eight new objects using the queen definition. Each of these objects searches for solutions starting with a different row number for column 1. The queen definition advances the search, column by column. The qlist definition maintains lists of partial solutions. The object definitions for starting the program and queueing the answers for display are not shown.

Performance analysis. The eight-queens program has been executed on sequential computers and such concurrent computers as the Cosmic Cube and Intel iPSC. The concurrent computers demonstrate the program's concurrency by exhibiting decreasing time to find the 92 solutions as more computing nodes are applied. These speedup curves are not themselves very revealing, so an alternate approach to studying the dynamics of the concurrency defines an abstract implementation for the execution environment and then measures the utilization of different resources.

Instrumented versions of the Cantor system allow a Cantor program to run under conditions ranging from infinite resources and zero latencies—the abstract implementation in which every opportunity for concurrency within a Cantor program is exploited—to specified numbers of nodes and message latencies. The only notable approximation in the measurements and analyses is that the processing of messages is assumed to be synchronized across all nodes. Each of these synchronized steps is called a *sweep*. Computations are organized into sweeps. For each sweep, every node that has one or more messages enqueued can process one message. All of the messages sent in response to processing a message are produced together. New objects are created initially as messages.

The instrumented execution of a program consists of a number of sweeps. For

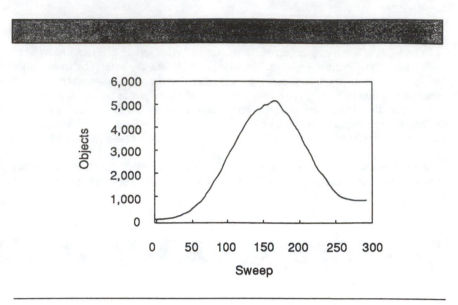

Figure 11. Object count for eight-queens (*N* = ∞).

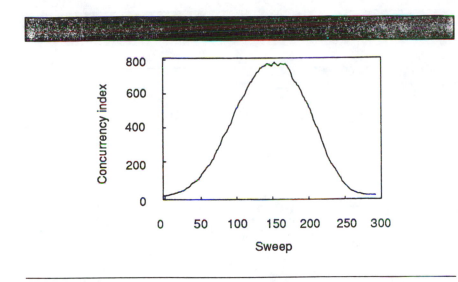

Figure 12. Concurrency index for eight-queens ($N = \infty$).

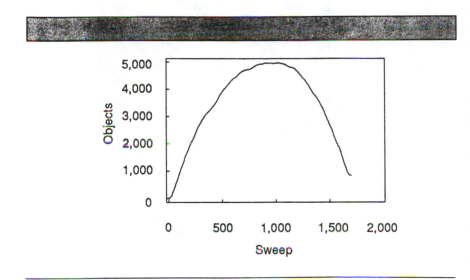

Figure 13. Object count for eight-queens ($N = 64$).

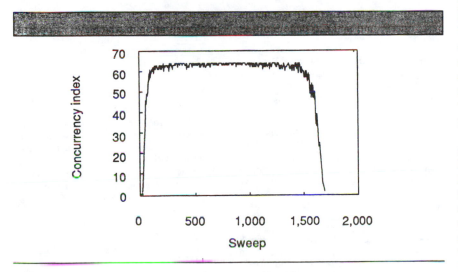

Figure 14. Concurrency index for eight-queens ($N = 64$).

each sweep the following data are tabulated:

- the total number of messages,
- the total number of active objects,
- the total number of objects, and
- the number of messages delivered this sweep.

An active object is defined as an object with one or more messages queued for it. The total number of object executions in a sweep, called the *concurrency index*, equals the number of active objects under the abstract implementation.

Figures 11 and 12 show the object count and concurrency index for the eight-queens program. The printing phase of the solutions was removed because it is entirely sequential. The program finds all 92 solutions in less than 300 sweeps. The cost for this performance is an immodest number of objects, peaking out at slightly over 5,000. Most of these objects, however, are purely transitory. The final object count, 830, includes the 92 solutions, requiring nine objects to represent each solution.

The abstract implementation represents a best case for the execution of the eight-queens program. A close similarity exists between message-driven programs and event-driven simulators, in which the only type of event is the processing of a message by an object. From this correspondence we expect any program that behaves poorly under the abstract implementation to perform poorly on any physically realizable implementation.

A variation on the abstract implementation fixes the number of nodes and evaluates program performance. Figures 13 and 14 show the object count and concurrency index graphs for the eight-queens program when the number of nodes is limited to 64. Because the mapping between objects and nodes is no longer one-to-one, a placement algorithm must assign objects to nodes. The algorithm attempts to balance the load of objects across the nodes by determining the node with the smallest object count and then placing the new object on this node.

The concurrency index graph for 64 nodes shows that nearly all nodes are utilized over a large interval of sweeps. By limiting the number of nodes to 64, the time to completion is increased by a factor of six. Because this program is deterministic (in the sense of performing exactly the same object executions on any execution), the area under the curves in Figures 12 and 14 is the same.

The placement algorithm used for Figures 13 and 14 required obtaining global information before placing a new object. Figure 15 compares the performance of three placement algorithms: the previous algorithm (o), a variation that uses the message count per node instead of the object count (m), and random placement (r). The figure plots the number of sweeps for each of the strategies against the number of nodes used to execute the program. The horizontal dashed line denotes the sweep count for the abstract implementation.

Random placement performs remarkably well and requires no global information. We can understand the performance of random placement by considering two cases. When the number of active objects is much smaller than the number of nodes, the probability that two or more objects are assigned to the same node is small. When the number of active objects is much greater than the number of nodes, then, by the weak law of large numbers, the probability that a node will be assigned an active object increases with the number of assignments made.

In our experiments with multicomputers over the past eight years, we have repeatedly underestimated their application span and overestimated the difficulty of writing programs. In fact, for certain applications the concurrent formulation for a problem has been simpler than the sequential formulation. Whether these machines will ever be considered general-purpose is debatable, but as message-passing performance improves relative to computing performance, the application span can only increase.

The next challenge for the architects of medium-grain multicomputers is to eliminate the software overhead of message-passing operations and to work with language and compiler developers to create programming environments that manage the system resources more completely.

Although we see the evolution of medium-grain multicomputers as a low-risk path, we are only cautiously optimistic about the practicality of fine-grain forms of the multicomputer architecture. However, it is clearly time to proceed to the full-scale experiment.□

Acknowledgments

The research described in this article was sponsored in part by the Defense Advanced Research Projects Agency, order number 6202, and monitored by the Office of Naval Research under contract number N00014-87-K-0745; and in part by grants from Intel Scientific Computers and Ametek Computer Research Division.

The architectures, designs, programming systems, and machines described in this article are the product of many years of effort by many creative, talented, and hard-working people, both in our Caltech Computer Science research group and in the industrial firms that have entered the multicomputer business. We wish to mention particularly the efforts of Wen-King Su, the designer and author of the Cosmic Environment system, and Jakov Seizovic, the author of the Reactive Kernel. We also wish to thank the MOSIS crew for their excellent service in fabricating message-routing chips and Mosaic elements.

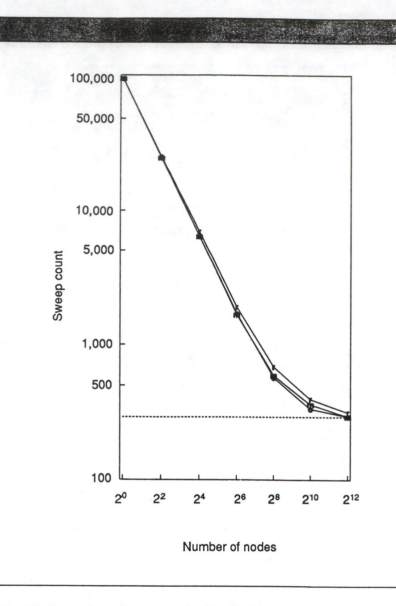

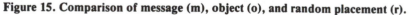

Figure 15. Comparison of message (m), object (o), and random placement (r).

References

1. C.L. Seitz, "The Cosmic Cube," *Comm. ACM,* Vol. 28, No. 1, Jan. 1985, pp. 22-33.

2. iPSC/2 brochures and application software reference material, Intel Scientific Computers, Beaverton, Ore., order number 280110-001.

3. Series 2010 brochures and application software reference material, Ametek Computer Research Division, Monrovia, Calif.

4. C.L. Seitz, "Concurrent VLSI Architectures," *IEEE Trans. Computers,* Vol. 33, No. 12, Dec. 1984, pp. 1247-1265.

5. W.D. Hillis, *The Connection Machine,* MIT Press, Cambridge, Mass., 1985.

6. C.L. Seitz, J. Seizovic, and W.-K. Su, "The

C Programmer's Abbreviated Guide to Multicomputer Programming,'' Caltech Computer Sci. Tech. Report 88-1, 1988.

7. Inmos, *The Occam Programming Manual,* Prentice-Hall, 1985.

8. G.A. Agha, *Actors: A Model of Concurrent Computation in Distributed Systems,* MIT Press, Cambridge, Mass., 1986.

9. W.C. Athas, ''Fine-Grain Concurrent Computation,'' Caltech Computer Sci. Tech. Report, 5242:TR:87, 1987.

10. W.J. Dally and C.L. Seitz, ''Deadlock-Free Message Routing in Multiprocessor Interconnection Networks,'' *IEEE Trans. Computers,* Vol. 36, No. 5, May 1987, pp. 547-553.

11. W.J. Dally, *A VLSI Architecture for Concurrent Data Structures,* Kluwer Academic Publishers, 1987.

12. C.M. Flaig, ''VLSI Mesh Routing Systems,'' Caltech Computer Sci. Tech. Report, 5241:TR:87, 1987.

William C. Athas received his BS degree in Computer Science from the University of Utah, and his MS and PhD degrees in Computer Science from the California Institute of Technology. He is currently a Caltech research fellow in Computer Science and is engaged in research in VLSI architecture and design, and programming systems for fine-grain concurrent computers.

Readers may write to Seitz at the California Institute of Technology, Computer Science 256-80, Pasadena, CA 91125.

Charles L. Seitz received his BS, MS, and PhD degrees from the Massachusetts Institute of Technology. He is now a professor of Computer Science at the California Institute of Technology. His research and teaching are in VLSI architecture and design, concurrent computation, and self-timed systems.

Seitz received the MIT Goodwin Medal and the Leonard G. Abraham Award of the IEEE Communications Technology Group. His research in concurrent computing was selected by *Science Digest* as one of the top 100 innovations of 1985.

Hypercube Supercomputers

JOHN P. HAYES, FELLOW, IEEE AND TREVOR MUDGE, SENIOR MEMBER, IEEE

The architecture and applications of the class of highly parallel distributed-memory multiprocessors based on the hypercube interconnection structure are surveyed. The history of hypercube computers from their conceptual origins in the 1960s to the recent introduction of commercial machines is briefly reviewed. The properties of hypercube graphs relevant to their use in supercomputers are examined, including connectivity, routing, and embedding. The hardware and software characteristics of current hypercubes are discussed, emphasizing the unique aspects of their operating systems and programming languages. A sample C program is presented to illustrate the single-code multiple-data programming style typical of distributed-memory machines in general, and hypercubes in particular. Two contrasting hypercube applications are presented and analyzed: image processing and branch-and-bound optimization. The paper concludes with a discussion of current trends.

I. INTRODUCTION

Parallel processing seeks to improve the speed with which a computation can be done by breaking it into subparts and concurrently executing as many of these as possible. The past few years have seen the emergence of commercial computers that employ hundreds of processors working in parallel to achieve the level of performance previously found only in multimillion-dollar supercomputers [1]. In many of these "massively" parallel machines, the processors are connected in a regular pattern called a hypercube. By using hundreds of low-cost microprocessors, the cost of these unconventional multiprocessors can be kept relatively low, putting them within reach of the single user. At the same time, extremely high computing performance can be achieved. To emphasize these points, one manufacturer has called its hypercube product a "personal supercomputer" [2]. This paper explores the origins, architecture, and applications of hypercube-based multiprocessors with performance at the supercomputer level.

The parallel computers of interest here consist of many processors and memory units which communicate via an interconnection network. The latter can range from a single shared bus to a complex multistage interconnection network [3]. Of particular significance in determining system performance is the manner in which the processors communicate with the memory subsystem. Two major approaches are found in contemporary parallel computers. The *shared-memory* approach employs a single central memory unit to which all processors have direct and rapid access. Contention for this shared memory, however, can result in serious performance loss. An alternative approach is to provide each processor with a local memory to which other processors have slow and indirect access. Such a *distributed-memory* scheme simplifies the interconnection of massive numbers of processors, but raises new problems in communication efficiency.

Most recently introduced multiprocessors have a few dozen processors connected to a shared memory over a common high-speed bus. Examples are the Sequent Balance [4] and the Encore Multimax [5]. Another class of shared-memory multiprocessors are massively parallel machines that provide a connection from each processor to a large multiport shared memory. Examples are the BBN Butterfly [6], one of the few commercially available machines in this category, and the RP3, an experimental machine developed at IBM [7]. A key feature of these machines is the omega-type multistage interconnection network that connects the processors to the shared memory [8].

Massively parallel multiprocessors are typically of the distributed-memory variety to avoid the contention problems associated with hundreds or thousands of processors sharing a very large global memory. Communication among the processors, however, requires an efficient interconnection network. Many proposals for such networks have been made, including meshes, pyramids, and multistage networks of the type mentioned above. Given the large variety of these proposals, it is interesting to note that the overwhelming majority of current commercial massively parallel machines are hypercube-connected.

Distributed-memory multiprocessors such as hypercubes eliminate most of the access contention problems associated with a large shared memory. They do so by partitioning the system memory into smaller local memories that are distributed among the available processors. Communication among these local memories then becomes a major design issue, since a relatively slow input-output operation is needed to access shared data assigned to a nonlocal memory. Such accesses take the form of messages passed between the local memories of the two processors. The management of this message-passing has major implications on all aspects of the system design, as well as on

Manuscript received August 5, 1988; revised June 5, 1989. This work was supported by the Office of Naval Research under Contract N00014-85-K-0531, by DoD Contract MDA904-87-C-4136, and by NSF Contract MIP-8802771.

The authors are with the Advanced Computer Architecture Laboratory, Dept. of Electrical Engineering and Computer Science, University of Michigan, Ann Arbor, MI 48109-2122, USA.

IEEE Log Number 8933020.

Reprinted from *Proceedings of the IEEE*, Vol. 77, No. 12, December 1989, pages 1829-1841. Copyright © 1989 by The Institute of Electrical and Electronics Engineers, Inc. All rights reserved.

applications software design. For example, a high-performance switching network or special interprocessor communication software (which usually is a part of the operating system resident in each node) is necessary. In addition, old algorithms must often be extensively restructured, as we will see later, to execute efficiently in the parallel environment created by these machines. This restructuring has also led to major extensions to traditional programming languages.

A hypercube is a generalization of the 3-dimensional cube graph to arbitrary numbers of dimensions. Just as a 3-dimensional cube has 2^3 nodes (vertices), so an n-dimensional cube has $N = 2^n$ nodes. Similarly, each node of a 3-cube has 3 edges (links) connected to it, and each node of an n-cube has n edges connected to it. Hypercube multiprocessors take this simple topology and use it to define the interconnection pattern among 2^n processors. Processors are placed at the nodes of the cube and are connected by links along the edges. Figure 1 illustrates hypercubes for small values of n.

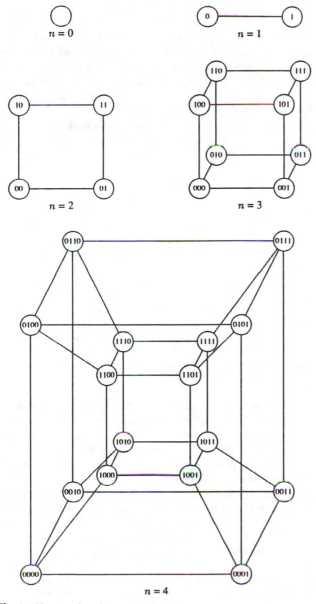

Fig. 1. Hypercubes for $n = 0, 1, 2, 3, 4$.

Hypercube topology has several attractive features. First, it is homogeneous or node-symmetric in the sense that the system appears the same from each node: There are no edges or boundaries where nodes may need to be treated as special cases. The hypercube achieves a good balance between the number of internode links used and their cost. It employs $nN/2$ links to connect $N = 2^n$ nodes, and each node processor has n links to manage. In all but a few recent hypercubes, nodes not directly connected must communicate via messages sent through intermediate nodes in store-and-forward fashion. The hypercube topology guarantees that no two nodes are more than n links apart. In addition, other useful computational structures, most notably meshes of arbitrary dimensions, can be embedded in a hypercube in such a way that adjacent nodes in the original structure are also adjacent in the hypercube. Thus for a wide class of useful applications, especially in scientific computing, the delays associated with interprocessor communication fall within acceptable limits. Another key factor in making hypercube computers practical from a commercial viewpoint is the fact that they can now be built economically with low-cost off-the-shelf microprocessor components [9]. Other proposals for massively parallel machines often require complex, expensive, and specially designed chips if they are to contain a reasonable number of integrated circuits (ICs). This is a more serious restriction than it might first appear, since a component count of more than a few tens of thousands of ICs puts air-cooled systems at the upper limits of acceptable reliability, regardless of the complexity of the subsystem within each IC.

The next section gives a brief history of hypercubes and outlines the main features of hypercube architectures. Section III discusses the structural properties of hypercubes and their influence on system design and application. Software design issues and a representative hypercube program are presented in Section IV. Section V examines two typical applications in depth: image processing and branch-and-bound optimization. Section VI concludes the survey with a brief discussion on current status and trends.

II. HYPERCUBE COMPUTERS

The earliest study of hypercube computers was published by Squire and Palais of the University of Michigan in 1963. Their stated goal was to design a computer "where the emphasis is on the programmability of highly parallel numerical computations," with hardware cost a secondary consideration [10], [11]. Among the reasons they cite for selecting the cube organization are the ease with which paths between nonadjacent nodes can be determined, and the fact that all nodes are identical and interchangeable. The proposed 12-dimensional (4096-node) Squire-Palais machine was estimated to require 20 times the hardware of the IBM Stretch, the largest supercomputer of the day, but a speedup of at least 100 was anticipated.

With the advent of the single-chip microprocessor in the early 1970s, several other proposals for microprocessor-based hypercubes were made. In 1975 IMS Associates, a manufacturer of personal computers, announced a 256-node commercial hypercube based on the Intel 8080 microprocessor, but it was never produced [12]. In 1977, Sullivan and his colleagues at Columbia University presented a proposal for a large hypercube called the Columbia Homogeneous Parallel Processor (CHOPP), which would have contained up to a million processors [13], [14]. Also in that year, Pease published an important study of the "indirect" binary n-cube architecture, for which he suggested a multistage interconnection network of the omega type for implementing the hypercube topology [15].

High hardware cost was clearly a major reason why these early hypercube designs were never implemented. The appearance of high-performance 32-bit microprocessor chips and dynamic RAM chips in the 1 M-bit range in the early 1980s made it economically feasible to construct practical hypercube computers of moderate size. The first such machine was the 64-node Cosmic Cube built by Seitz and his colleagues at Caltech, which became operational in 1983 [16]. This pioneering machine employed processor nodes based on the commercial Intel 8086/8087 microprocessor family. The Cosmic Cube was applied successfully to a variety of numerical computation tasks, often yielding significant speedups compared to conventional computers of similar cost. It was also the first of a series of experimental hypercube computers developed at Caltech [17], [18] and provided the main inspiration for the first generation of commercial hypercube computers.

In July 1985, Intel delivered the first production hypercube, the Intel Personal Supercomputer, or iPSC, which has a 80286/80287 CPU as its node processor and up to 128 nodes. Assuming a peak performance of 0.1 million floating-point operations per second (MFLOPS) per node, the 128-node iPSC has a potential or peak throughput of about 12 MFLOPS. (Note that a traditional vector supercomputer such as the Cray-1 has a peak throughput of 160 MFLOPS). Two other commercial hypercubes were introduced in 1985: NCUBE Corporation's NCUBE/ten and System 14/n from Ametek (subsequently Symult Systems). The System 14/n hypercube has up to 256 nodes, each employing an 80286/80287-based CPU similar to that of the iPSC, and an 80186 microprocessor for communication management. The NCUBE/ten can accommodate up to 1024 nodes, each based on a VAX-like 32-bit custom processor with a peak performance of around 0.4 MFLOPS. Thus, a fully configured NCUBE system has a peak throughput of about 400 MFLOPS. This high performance level is supported by extremely fast communication rates (both input/output and node-to-node), making the fully configured NCUBE/ten a true supercomputer. In 1988, researchers at Sandia National Laboratories using a 1024-node NCUBE/ten were the first to meet the widely publicized challenges posed by A. Karp and C. G. Bell to demonstrate the successful application of massive parallelism to large-scale practical problems in scientific computation [19]–[21]. This work, and that of many others, demonstrates convincingly that a properly programmed N-node hypercube can provide linear speedup—execution speeds that increase in proportion to N—for a wide range of computation problems.

Several new hypercubes with supercomputing performance have been built or announced since 1985, including the Caltech/JPL Mark III [18], the Floating Point Systems T Series [22], and the Intel iPSC/2 [23]. Some of these machines incorporate pipelined vector processors in their nodes, a feature of most earlier supercomputers. In some instances, they also employ special routing circuits to allow direct communication paths to be established between nonadjacent nodes. The second-generation Intel iPSC/2, for instance, has a vector-processing capability, as well as a circuit-switching internode communication network to replace the slower store-and-forward technique [24]. Peak performance figures in excess of 1000 MFLOPS (1 GFLOPS) are cited by the manufacturers of these newer hypercubes. The new communication hardware has reduced the time to pass a message between two nodes from a few milliseconds to a few microseconds. In fact, by effectively reducing the distance between all pairs of nodes to a small constant, a programmer can view the system as a pool of processors with a complete set of node-to-node connections. As a result, the requirement that the application algorithms have a hypercube-like communication structure is diminishing in importance. Furthermore, it raises the possibility of implementing a shared-memory architecture on a hypercube platform.

A few other recent supercomputers employ architectures that have been heavily influenced by the hypercube concept. The Connection Machine series manufactured by Thinking Machines Corporation employs up to 2^{16} or 65 536 simple processing nodes [25]. Sixteen nodes are placed on a chip with switching circuity that allows any node to be directly connected to any other node on the chip. The 2^{12} chips of the Connection Machine form the nodes of a 12-dimensional hypercube. The second-generation, CM-2 model of the Connection Machine announced in 1987 has a peak performance target of 2.5 GFLOPS [25]. The Symult Systems 2010 introduced in 1988 has up to 256 nodes interconnected as a toroidal mesh which, as we will see later, is closely related to a hypercube [26].

The basic architecture of a hypercube node processor is shown in Fig. 2. It is a self-contained computer with a CPU,

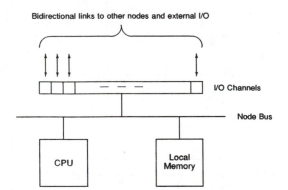

Fig. 2. Architecture of a typical node processor.

local memory for programs and data, and an input/output (I/O) subsystem. Its main distinguishing feature is the set of bidirectional I/O channels that link the node to its n immediate neighbors in the hypercube. These channels are used for interprocessor message passing and are typically implemented as bit-serial links with direct memory access (DMA) to the local memories of the nodes being linked. Processors not directly connected to one another by I/O links can communicate via intermediate nodes, which relay messages between the source and destination nodes. Additional links may be provided to connect each processor to a host computer and I/O devices such as secondary (disk) memories; in some instances all access to the I/O system is via the host computer. The host acts as a general system supervisor providing such operating system functions as

I/O management, as well as program editing and compilation facilities.

Communication issues play a central role in the architecture and performance of hypercubes and, indeed, of all distributed-memory computers. Hypercubes are typically configured so that the nodes execute the same application program on different data sets. Each node's program and data are stored in its local memory, so that most computation is within the individual nodes. When two nodes need to share information—for example, to exchange results—the shared data must be inserted in a message which is transmitted via a series of I/O transfers, possibly involving other nodes. The delay required for a node to obtain a data item in this fashion from one of its immediate neighbors is perhaps 1000 times the delay incurred when accessing data in the node's local memory. Thus great pains are taken to design hypercube application programs to minimize the need for message-passing, and to confine unavoidable message-passing to adjacent or nearly adjacent nodes.

The earliest hypercubes used store-and-forward communication schemes, which required of the order of 1 ms to transfer a message between adjacent nodes; k separate transfers or "hops" are necessary when source and destination are k links apart. Improvements in the efficiency of the message-passing software can reduce this delay by a factor of 10 or so [27]. However, to reduce the delay to a level comparable to the local memory access time (1 μs or less), hardware routing circuits have been devised. The Torus routing chip [28] and the Hyperswitch used in the JPL Mark III hypercube are examples of these [29].

The routing circuits proposed for hypercubes resemble crossbar switching networks and provide direct (circuit-switched) connections between arbitrary pairs of I/O channels associated with a single node. This permits a message to pass from source S to destination D without being stored at intermediate nodes. In effect, a direct high-speed circuit is established between S and D. Provided they do not contend for the same links, several separate circuits can pass through the same routing switch. A number of strategies have been devised for dealing with contention when it occurs. The "wormhole" approach of Dally and Seitz [28], versions of which are used in iPSC/2 and the Symult Systems 2010, allows a blocked message to retain control of the routing circuitry up to the blockage point: It is queued in the network until the blockage clears. Alternative "adaptive" strategies to the wormhole approach used in conjunction with the Hyperswitch attempt to find a free path around a blocked node [29]. Finally, there is a class of routing strategies that are adaptive only on their first hop as the message leaves S [30]. These reduce the likelihood of blockage and simplify deadlock avoidance, a concern with adaptive routing [31].

A hypercube computer is managed by an operating system (OS) which resides mainly in the host machine. The OS management functions peculiar to hypercubes include allocation of subcubes of nodes (smaller hypercubes formed by a subset of the available nodes) to multiple users, loading programs into the nodes (often done by a broadcasting operation), and managing processor–processor and processor–I/O communication. Communication functions such as message storing and forwarding may be assigned to the hypercube nodes in the form of a small node-resident OS kernel. It should be noted that node processes are inherently asynchronous, so that any necessary synchronization among processes in different nodes must be taken care of by the OS.

Because of the large numbers of nodes that may be present, packaging considerations are also very important in hypercube design in order to keep physical size, power consumption, and cooling needs within reasonable limits. The Connection Machine employs simple 1-bit processors and is therefore able to accommodate 16 node processors on a single custom IC. Thirty-two of these chips, their memories (4K bits per processor), and internode communication circuitry are placed in a single printed circuit board. Most commercial hypercube machines employ conventional 32-bit processors with much larger and expandable local memories. In a more typical case such as the Intel iPSC, the node consists of one or two small boards with several megabytes of local memory. An intermediate case represented by the NCUBE/ten has a 7-chip node comprising a custom 32-bit microprocessor chip and six memory chips with a combined storage capacity of 0.5 MB. Sixty-four nodes can be placed on a large (16 × 22-in.) board; however, this format does not allow for memory expansion. Figure 3 shows

Fig. 3. 64-node NCUBE/ten processor board.

a 64-node NCUBE/ten processor board, which functions as a 6-dimensional hypercube.

III. STRUCTURAL PROPERTIES

The graph properties of hypercubes that are relevant to their use in supercomputers [32], are examined next. An n-dimensional hypercube graph Q_n can be defined recursively as follows:

$$Q_1 = K_2$$
$$Q_n = K_2 \times Q_{n-1}$$

where K_2 is the 2-node complete graph, and $\times$ denotes the cartesian product of graphs. This definition implies that Q_n contains many subcubes of smaller dimensions, a property that may be exploited in several ways. For example, a hypercube Q_n can accommodate multiple users simultaneously by assigning each user a disjoint subcube Q_k within Q_n, where $k \leq n$. Furthermore, a measure of fault tolerance can be achieved by assigning to users only those subcubes that exclude known faulty nodes.

Q_n contains $N = 2^n$ nodes of degree n, and $n2^{n-1}$ edges. Thus, as the number of nodes N is increased to improve performance, the connection requirements of each node increase at a rate proportional to $n = \log_2 N$. This implies that practical limitations on the number of links per node can be met while allowance is made for the increased communication needs of a larger hypercube. Each node of Q_n is at distance one from n other nodes. The maximum internode distance or diameter of Q_n is n, which therefore defines the worst-case communication delay. The average internode distance is $(n2^{n-1})/(2^n - 1)$, which rapidly approaches $n/2$ as n is increased.

The nodes of Q_n may easily be labeled with n-bit addresses in such a way that nodes adjacent in the ith dimension differ only in the ith address bit (see Fig. 1). The resulting set of 2^n addresses $\{00..0, 00..1, \cdots, 11..1\}$ facilitate the implementation of key communication algorithms, including node-to-node routing and broadcasting from one node to the entire hypercube. Two basic programs for this purpose appear in Fig. 4. A copy of each is assumed to reside in every node of the hypercube as part of its resident OS. The program is executed whenever a message is generated locally or is received from another node for routing or broadcasting. The same basic communication algorithms are also implemented in the circuit-switching hardware discussed in Section II.

Figure 4(a) gives the basic node-to-node routing algorithm ROUTE which always selects a minimum-length path

```
procedure ROUTE;
  begin
    for next message from s_{n-1} s_{n-2}...s_0 to d_{n-1} d_{n-2}...d_0 do
      begin
        x_{n-1} x_{n-2}...x_0 := (s_{n-1} ⊕ d_{n-1})(s_{n-2} ⊕ d_{n-2})...(s_0 ⊕ d_0);
        for i := 0 to n-1 do
          if x_i = 1 then begin
            send message to i-th neighbor; exit;
          end;
      end;
  end.
```

(a)

```
procedure BROADCAST;
  begin
    if the current node is the source then C := 11...1
      else receive message and control word C := c_{n-1}c_{n-2}...c_0;
    for i := 0 to n - 1 do
      if c_i = 1 then begin
        c_i := 0;
        send message and C to i-th neighbor;
      end;
  end.
```

(b)

Fig. 4. Hypercube communication algorithms. (a) Node-to-node routing. (b) Broadcasting.

between the source node $S = s_{n-1}s_{n-2} \cdots s_0$ and the destination node $D = d_{n-1}d_{n-2} \cdots d_0$. ROUTE first computes $X = S \oplus D$ where $\oplus$ denotes the bitwise EXCLUSIVE-OR operation. It then scans X in a fixed direction, say, left to right. If ROUTE encounters some $x_i = 1$, it transmits the current message to its immediate neighbor along the ith dimension of Q_n (its ith neighbor). If $X = 00..0$, then the current node must also be the destination, and the message is retained for processing. By transmitting the message to a node whose ith address bit is 1 whenever it encounters

$x_i = 1$, ROUTE ensures that the ROUTE program in all subsequent nodes will find $x_i = 0$. Hence the message is always sent closer to the destination. It therefore travels the minimum possible distance from S to D, which is the number of ones in $S \oplus D$. An alternative routing algorithm developed by Valiant [33] routes each message to a randomly chosen node; from there the message is forwarded to its originally intended destination. The randomization assures that message congestion at nodes will be dispersed. Unfortunately, Valiant's router does not perform as well as the straightforward algorithm in many routine parallel processing tasks, and its more complex implementation requirements have discouraged its use.

A basic broadcasting algorithm, BROADCAST, is presented in Fig. 4(b). Assuming that each node can transmit the message to only one neighbor at a time, and that a single message transmission takes time τ, BROADCAST allows the message to be sent to all nodes in time $n\tau$, which is the minimum possible. A control word C is transmitted along with the message, and serves to tell each receiving node the dimensions along which it should retransmit the message. The first node S transmits the message and (and C) to a neighbor T in the first time period. In the second period, both S and T retransmit the message to two more nodes, and so on. Hence the number of copies of the messages being transmitted in successive time periods is 1, 2, 4, $\cdots$, 2^{n-1} so that all nodes are reached within n periods. Faster broadcasting can be achieved if a node transmits several copies of the message simultaneously.

Hypercubes have a very regular structure, which has several practical implications. As noted in Section I, they are homogeneous in the sense that the system structure looks the same from every node. In graph theoretic terms [34], Q_n is symmetric, meaning that every pair of nodes or lines can be interchanged without altering the graph structure. This property, combined with the fact that Q_n contains many easily identified subcubes of dimensions smaller than n, leads to the following conclusions.

1) A program can readily be designed to run unchanged on a hypercube of any dimension $k \geq 0$ by making k a parameter of the program. Thus, program development can be conducted on a small subcube, e.g., one with $n = 2$, while production runs can be executed by a larger hypercube.

2) A large hypercube computer can be efficiently shared by multiple users, each of whom is assigned a disjoint subcube by the OS. Such a scheme is implemented by the AXIS operating system of the NCUBE/ten, which allows a user to specify the dimension k of a desired hypercube. AXIS then allocates a Q_k from among the available free nodes, if it can find one. Several efficient methods for handling arbitrary sets of subcube allocation requests have recently been developed [35]. The subcube Q_k of Q_n can be viewed as a logical entity which can be relocated anywhere in Q_n by EXCLUSIVE-ORing the address of each node in Q_k with the address of the node in Q_n chosen as the logical origin. Broadcasting, and message transfers in general, can be performed using the logical node addresses. This simplifies many message transfer algorithms.

Hypercubes have many attractive and useful embedding properties, some of which have been studied by graph theorists for more than 20 years [36]. An (isomorphic) embedding of G into G' is a one-to-one mapping ϕ of nodes of G onto nodes of G', such that if (u, v) is an edge of G, $(\phi(u),$

$\phi(v))$ is an edge of G'. G is termed cubical if it has an embedding in the hypercube Q_n, for some n. Among the useful graphs that are cubical are trees (cycle-free graphs) and meshes of any dimension. The latter result is especially important since many large-scale numerical problems have data structures defined on d-dimensional meshes. Their solution—for example, by relaxation methods—requires efficient communication between neighboring nodes on the mesh. Thus, to solve such mesh-oriented problems on a massively parallel computer, it is very desirable that meshes be isomorphically embeddable into the structure of the host computer. This is underscored by the fact that at least one hypercube manufacturer has also introduced a product with a mesh rather than a hypercube interconnection structure [26].

Figure 5 illustrates how a 2-dimensional 4 × 4 mesh can be embedded in Q_4; the labels assigned to the mesh nodes

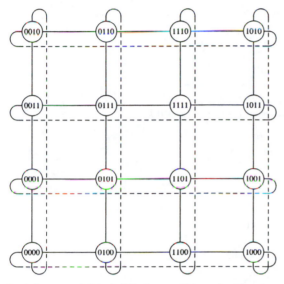

Fig. 5. A 4 × 4 mesh labeled for isomorphic embedding in Q_4.

correspond to the hypercube node labels in Fig. 1. Note that Q_4 can also accommodate a toroidal 4 × 4 mesh in which the edge nodes are connected in end-around fashion, as indicated by the dotted lines in Fig. 5. In general, a d-dimensional nontoroidal $k_1 \times k_2 \times \cdots \times k_d$ mesh M can be embedded in a hypercube Q_n of dimension $n \geq \Sigma_{i=1}^{d} \lceil \log_2 k_i \rceil$. If the dimension n of the available hypercube computer is too small, a mesh problem can often be partitioned efficiently into smaller mesh problems, each of which can be solved separately on the hypercube. An embedding of the $k_1 \times k_2 \times \cdots \times k_d$ mesh M into Q_n can easily be obtained by labeling the nodes of M so that the sequence of sublabels assigned to each dimension forms a Gray code [36]. For example, the nodes of the 4 × 4 mesh in Fig. 5 have labels $a_1a_0b_1b_0$ in which a_1a_0 and b_1b_0 assume the values G = 00, 01, 11, 10 along the vertical and horizontal dimensions of the mesh; G is a 2-bit reflected Gray code.

IV. SOFTWARE

The emergence of the commercial hypercube computer has demonstrated the feasibility of constructing low-cost massively parallel machines. The focus of research can now be expected to shift to the issue of how these machines can be programmed effectively. Indeed, a recent study concludes that the lack of appropriate parallel programming languages and software development tools is the single biggest impediment to the widespread use of parallel machines [37]. The operating system is also a major factor, as memory management, interprocess communication and other OS functions are critical to overall system operation. Three major software issues must be considered: the operating system used for developing application programs; the run-time operating system in the hypercube nodes, and the set of application programming languages to be used.

High-order parallel programming languages and support tools are essential if users of parallel systems are to develop machine-independent concurrent software [38]. Such software will hasten the day when reusable software becomes a reality for parallel machines, as it now is for conventional uniprocessors. The programming of hypercubes is normally done by writing a separate program to run on each processor. The programs communicate by low-level message-passing operations provided by the OS and available to the programmer through extensions to a sequential language such as C or FORTRAN. Typically, these programs are copies of a single program. The distinct copies will execute correctly regardless of their location in the hypercube. This style of programming is referred to as single code multiple data (SCMD) or single program multiple data (SPMD).

Two major problems with the SCMD style of programming are the lack of type checking in internode communications and the machine dependence of the code. These problems can be solved by using a suitable parallel language, that is, one whose units of concurrency are distributed across the processors and executed simultaneously. To be effective, such languages should be able to perform type checking across processor boundaries, provide language constructs for interprocess communications that can also function across processor boundaries, allow data sharing between processes to be specified at the language level, and provide for synchronous creation and termination of processes within a program. Languages that meet these criteria are discussed in [39]–[42].

UNIX provides an attractive OS environment for software development on both sequential and parallel machines. As a result, it is supported (in several different versions) by most of the hypercube manufacturers. The NCUBE/ten, for example, has a UNIX-like operating system called AXIS [9]. It provides the normal UNIX utilities for editing, debugging, and resource management which treat most system resources as files. The NCUBE/ten incorporates up to eight I/O subsystems to meet the high I/O bandwidth requirements of a supercomputer. These are organized, under AXIS, as one distributed file system to avoid having to deal with multiple separate file systems. AXIS manages a hypercube as a device file that can be opened, closed, and so forth, as if it were a normal file. It permits users to allocate subcubes that have the appropriate dimension for their application. Thus, one or two users with large problems or several users with small problems may share the hypercube. This flexibility greatly increases the system efficiency and gives a hypercube supercomputer a significant advantage over conventional supercomputers. Partitioning the main hypercube into subcubes is simplified in that each subcube is easily isolated logically from all other subcubes. A small OS nucleus called VERTEX is resident in each of the NCUBE/ten nodes. Its primary function is to provide communication between the nodes. It achieves this by, among other facilities, send and receive operations that transfer messages between any two nodes in the hypercube, using the ROUTE algorithm of Fig. 4(a), and by a "whoami" operation that allows a program to determine which logical node it is executing on and which I/O processor it is connected to.

We conclude this section with a sample SCMD program that calculates the maximum element of a vector of numbers v. More formally, the program calculates,

$$S = \max_{1 \le i \ge K} v[i]$$

where $K = n \cdot 2^{dim}$, n is the number of elements of v in each node of the cube, and dim is the dimension of the cube. A listing of the program, which is written in a parallel extension of the C language, appears in Fig. 6. This particular programming language is NCUBE's version of C, but other hypercube manufacturers use similar extensions to C (cf. Intel [43]). The extensions to C include internode send and receive operations implemented as function calls $nwrite$ and $nread$, respectively; and the whoami operation implemented by the function called $whoami$. These functions are part of the OS resident in the hypercube nodes. We assume that a copy of this program has been loaded into each of the nodes of a particular subcube that has been allo-

```
001    /*   NODE PROGRAM TO CALCULATE THE MAXIMUM OF A VECTOR v
002
003    pn    :    caller's logical processor number in subcube
004    proc  :    process number in node
005    host  :    node on Host for cube communication
006    dim   :    dimension of allocated cube                      */
007
008
009    whoami(&pn,&proc,&host,&dim);
010
011
012    /* Receive vector of length n from the host; VECLEN is the
013       possible length of the vector. (4 bytes per vector element) */
014
015    cf = 0;
016    type = DATA;
017    n = (nread((char *)v,VECLEN*4,&host,&type,&cf)/4);
018
019    /* Find m, the local maximum of v in this node */
020
021    m = MINF;
022    for (i = 0 ; i < n ; ++i) if (v[i] > m) m = v[i];
023
024    for (i = dim ; i > 0 ; --i) {
025
026    /* Execute once for each axis of the hypercube */
027
028        if (pn < power(2,i)) {
029
030        /* If this node is in the active part of the collapsed cube,
031           do the computation below, otherwise the node is done.
032           npn is the neighbor of pn on the i-th axis                 */
033
034           type = MAX;
035           npn = pn^power(2,(i-1));
036           if (npn < pn)
037
038           /* If neighbor's number is less, send the local maximum; otherwise
039              receive it and update its value.                              /*
040
041                   nwrite((char *)&m,4,npn,type,&cf);
042           else {
043                   nread((char *)&rm,4,&npn,&type,&cf);
044                   if (rm > m) m = rm;
045           }
046        }
047    }
048
049    /* send the final result back to the host */
050
051    if (pn == 0) {
052       type = RESULT;
053       nwrite((char *)&m,4,host,type,&cf);
054    }
```

Fig. 6. SCMD program to find the maximum element of a vector.

cated to this particular job. Execution of the program may be summarized as follows: It reads in equal numbers of the elements of v into each node, forms local maxima of these numbers, and then selects, in turn, the largest of these local maxima along successive dimensions of the hypercube. The selection process collapses the active part of the computation into smaller and smaller cubes.

The call to whoami on line 009 returns the calling program's logical node number (pn), the node on the host board used for I/O communications (host), and the order of the allocated subcube (dim). The call to nread on line 017 reads in an n-element slice of the vector v from the host. The for loop on line 022 finds the maximum element of the slice of v in the node (m is initially set to $-\infty$ on line 021). This is done in parallel in each node. During this phase of the computation, all 2^{dim} nodes are doing useful work and the utilization of the allocated cube approaches 100%. 2^{dim-1} new maxima are formed by comparing pairs of local maxima in nodes that are immediate neighbors in the dimth dimension. The new maxima are now confined to a (dim $-$ 1)-dimensional hypercube; in effect, the active cube is collapsed to half its initial size. This process of collapsing the active cube by half and selecting a new smaller set of maxima is repeated until the maximum of all the elements of v appear in logical node 0. The selection of the maximum among the nodes simulates a tree of comparators. Figure 7 illustrates this for a 3-cube.

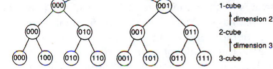

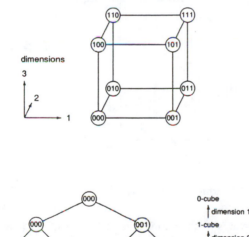

Fig. 7. Comparator tree to find the maximum.

The for loop that begins on line 024 starts at the highest dimension (dim) and finds the larger of each pair of local maxima in nodes that are adjacent in the highest dimension. It repeats this, stepping through all the dimensions. Line 028 selects the nodes (pns) in the part of the hypercube that remains active after collapsing along the (i + 1)st dimension. The neighboring nodes (npns) of the pns are those whose addresses differ in the ith bit position. Their addresses are calculated in the line 035 by performing the EXCLUSIVE-OR operation (^) on pn and $2^{(i-1)}$. Line 036 partitions the active nodes into two sets: those that are to receive local maxima (line 043) and those that send them (line 041). Line 044 finds the larger of the received value

and the local maxima already present in the node. Those nodes that send will not be active in the next iteration of the loop. Line 053 transmits the result from node 0 to the host.

V. APPLICATIONS

Figure 8 shows a representative list of applications of hypercube computers. This is by no means an exhaustive list, but it does illustrate the wide range of applications to

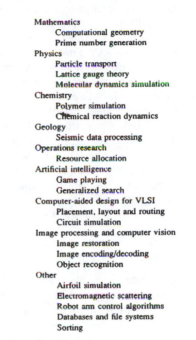

Fig. 8. List of applications.

which hypercubes are being applied. For a detailed picture of these applications, the reader is referred to [44], [45], the book by Fox *et al.* [46], and the book by Reed and Fujimoto [47]. Although the number of applications has grown rapidly, they are predominantly in the area of scientific computing in which the behavior of a physical system is being analyzed. For the majority of these applications, the parallelism can be determined at compile-time and depends on a simple partitioning of the problem domain which is often a physical space. For example, in the particle transport problems of photons in a fusion plasma [48], the underlying algorithm is a Monte Carlo method which divides physical space into equal subregions, then simulates particle behavior for each space independently, and finally averages the results obtained from the separate Monte Carlo experiments. Similarly, in the case of many image processing algorithms, as we will see below, the image is partitioned into subimages of equal size that are assigned to separate processors.

In contrast to the applications with compile-time parallelism, hypercubes are also beginning to be used in applications where the degree of parallelism cannot be determined before the program is run, and where, consequently, load balancing of work among the processors at run-time becomes an issue. Examples from Fig. 8 are database applications, where addition and deletion of records has the potential to cause some processors to be underutilized, and resource allocation algorithms, which are usually solved

317

using branch-and-bound algorithms, as will also be examined further. These algorithms are particularly "dynamic" in their behavior because they spawn work in an unpredictable fashion during their execution.

In the remainder of this section we review in detail two applications that typify both ends of the spectrum: obvious compile-time parallelism and dynamic or run-time parallelism. The first is an image processing application which has a large degree of natural parallelism. By making use of the embedding ideas of Section III, it can be implemented on a hypercube in a fairly straightforward fashion. The second is the 0-1 integer linear programming (ILP) problem. This is one of the simplest examples of a large class of algorithms called branch-and-bound methods, which are used in artificial intelligence and operations research. Unlike the majority of applications of hypercubes, in which the work of each node can be scheduled *a priori* by the programmer, branch-and-bound programs schedule processes dynamically at run-time. At first sight, this would seem to make them inappropriate for hypercubes because of the communications overhead associated with dynamic scheduling. Like the implementation of chess on a hypercube reported in [49], the branch-and-bound application shows that many problems hitherto considered unparallelizable have, in fact, a substantial content of exploitable parallelism.

A. Image Processing

The term image processing covers an important class of techniques that include the encoding/decoding of images for transmission, the enhancement and restoration of noisy images, the extraction of features such as edges, and the segmentation of images for the purposes of image understanding [50]. An image is a 2-dimensional mesh of elements (pixels) that can take on a finite number of values (typically 256). These values, or gray-levels, represent the light intensity at each point in the image.

A widely used image-processing technique is to convolve the image with a finite impulse response (FIR) function. Depending on the particular FIR function, this operation can be used for edge detection, template matching, noise removal, and general filtering. The FIR function is defined as an $m \times m$ matrix $K(\alpha, \beta)$ of constant coefficients referred to as the kernel. The kernel is moved across the image in one-pixel steps to implement the convolution function. At each step the pixel $P_{in}(i, j)$ coinciding with the center of the kernel is replaced by $P_{out}(i, j)$, such that,

$$P_{out}(i, j) = \sum_{\alpha = -\lfloor m/2 \rfloor}^{\alpha = \lfloor m/2 \rfloor} \sum_{\beta = -\lfloor m/2 \rfloor}^{\beta = \lfloor m/2 \rfloor} P_{in}(i, j) K(\alpha, \beta)$$

A typical example of an image-processing algorithm involving the convolution of the image with FIR functions is the Sobel edge detection algorithm [51]. The image is convolved with the each of the two FIR kernels shown in Fig. 9 (an integer approximation to the exact kernels is shown). The results of the convolution are the two images e_x and e_y where $e_x(i, j)$ is an $M \times M$ array of x-direction edge (gradient) strengths, and $e_y(i, j)$ is an $M \times M$ mesh of y-direction edge (gradient) strengths. These two arrays are then combined to form a combined edge strength array, E, and an edge direction array, Θ where

$$E(i, j) = \sqrt{e_x^2 + e_y^2}$$

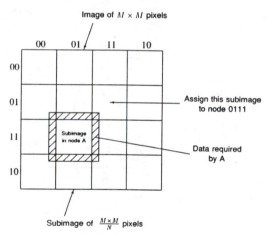

Fig. 9. The Sobel edge detector kernels.

and

$$\Theta(i, j) = \tan^{-1}\left(\frac{e_x}{e_y}\right) - \frac{\pi}{2}.$$

It can be seen from these equations that equal-size areas of the image require equal amounts of processing. Therefore, the natural approach to executing these algorithms on hypercubes is to partition the image into subimages of equal size and assign each subimage to a separate node processor. The subimages can be processed in parallel, using the mesh embedding technique of Section III to map adjacent subimages to adjacent nodes of the hypercube. Figure 10

Fig. 10. Partitioning the image.

illustrates this for an image of $M \times M$ pixels and a 4-cube; here the image is partitioned into 16 equal subimages.

In general, convolving with an FIR function is implemented in the SCMD mode of Section IV. The only potential contributor to inefficiency is the communication overhead that results from the need to exchange data around the edges of each subimage to allow the edge pixels to be convolved with the kernel. This is also illustrated in Fig. 10, which shows a subimage in processor A and the data (shaded) that have to be moved from adjacent processors. The number of pixels that has to be transferred is roughly $2Mm/\sqrt{N}$ if n is even, and $3Mm/\sqrt{2N}$ if n is odd. (Recall that $m \times m$ is the size of the kernel, $M \times M/N$ is the size of the subimage, and $N = 2^n$ is the number of processors). The communication time necessary to move the pixels is proportional to their number. However, as we have seen, communications are often performed as DMA operations and can be completely overlapped with processing. Of course, for large kernels and small subimages a point can be reached where overlap is impossible and communication times start

318

to dominate. This highlights the importance of having sufficiently large problems for a particular size of hypercube if its efficiency is to be maintained [52]. Results reported in [53] show that convolving with a simple FIR kernel can easily be performed at video frame rates (thirty 512×512 images per second).

It can be shown that if the discrete Fourier transform and its inverse are implemented by the FFT algorithm and if m is greater than about 10 [54], then it is more efficient to perform convolution in the frequency domain for a 512×512 image. The hypercube network is well suited to efficient implementation of the FFT, with communication occurring between pairs of adjacent nodes [55]. The data layout shown in Fig. 10 is also appropriate for calculating the FFTs, and for computing their product in the frequency domain. The FFT and its inverse require data to be communicated between subcubes, that is, between adjacent regions in Fig. 10. These, of course, are in adjacent processors.

B. Branch-and-Bound Algorithms

Our second representative application area for hypercubes concerns problems for which there exists no computationally efficient "direct" solution. A solution is often found via a heuristic search through a large solution space. Unguided search, however, can easily become inefficient as many of these problems are at least NP-complete. Several techniques have been developed to guide the search and improve its average efficiency. The most general of these techniques is the branch-and-bound (B&B) algorithm [56], which has been used to solve some well-known problems, including the traveling salesman problem [57], the knapsack problem [58], and many of the heuristic search algorithms in artificial intelligence such as A*, AO*, and alpha-beta [59].

The branching action of a B&B algorithm is performed by building a search tree, called a B&B tree, over the problem space of interest. The root of the B&B tree represents the complete problem space, and children nodes represent subspaces. The branching process proceeds from the root to the leaves of the tree, systematically partitioning subspaces into smaller ones. The leaf nodes represent subspaces that are small enough to be exhaustively searched for solutions. A subproblem P_i can be characterized by the value of an objective function f, which is defined as the value of the best solution that can be obtained from P_i. This value is not known, however, until the subtree rooted at P_i is completely expanded. Instead another function h, referred to as the lower bound function, is used as an estimate of f. In general, h is a heuristic function that is much easier to compute than f.

A B&B algorithm consists of four major procedures: 1) selection, 2) branching, 3) elimination, and 4) termination test. The selection procedure selects a subproblem from the set of subproblems that have been generated but not yet examined (the active subproblems). The selection is performed according to the heuristic selection function h which determines the order in which the subproblems are selected for expansion. A commonly used heuristic is best-first search, in which h is a lower bound estimate of the objective function f. Subproblems with smaller lower bounds are selected first. The branching procedure exam-

ines the currently selected subproblem and uses problem-specific methods to break it into smaller-sized subproblems. The elimination step examines these newly created subproblems and deletes the ones that cannot lead to better solutions than those already found. To accomplish this, a special subproblem referred to as the incumbent is used to store the best feasible solution discovered during the search. A subproblem is deleted if its lower bound is greater than or equal to that of the incumbent. Finally, the termination test procedure eliminates a new subproblem that cannot lead to feasible solutions. Again, problem-specific techniques are used to accomplish this.

We now describe a specific problem that uses the B&B algorithm, viz., the 0-1 ILP problem. This is an optimization problem in which it is desired to minimize the value of a linear objective function $f(x_1, x_2, \cdots, x_n)$ subject to a set of constraints. The variables $(x_1, x_2, \cdots, x_n)$, can take only the values 0 or 1. The problem can be more formally stated as follows:

$$\text{Minimize} \quad f = \sum_{j=1}^{n} c_j x_j$$

subject to the constraints

$$\sum_{j=1}^{n} a_{ij} x_j \geq b_i \quad i = 1, 2, \cdots, m$$

$$x_j \in \{0, 1\} \quad j = 1, 2, \cdots, n$$

It can be assumed, with no loss of generality, that the coefficients c_j, $j = 1, 2, \cdots, n$ are nonnegative. The solution method involves systematically assigning zeros and ones to some of the x_j variables to obtain subproblems. A subproblem which has the smallest lower bound is selected from the list of active subproblems. An unassigned variable is picked and is assigned the values 0 and 1 to create two new subproblems. Each subproblem is evaluated and, if it represents a feasible solution and its lower bound is less than that of the incumbent, then it becomes the new incumbent. Furthermore, all subproblems on the list with lower bounds greater than the new incumbent are deleted from the list. If the subproblem cannot lead to a feasible solution it is deleted. Finally, the subproblem is inserted back on the list if it is not presently feasible and its lower bound is less than that of the incumbent. The algorithm continues by selecting another subproblem from the list. The algorithm terminates when the list becomes empty.

We consider two parallel implementations of the foregoing B&B algorithm on hypercube multiprocessors. The first implementation, referred to as the Central List (CL) algorithm, consists of two major components: a master process which runs on the host and N slave processes which run on the nodes of the hypercube. The master process maintains the list of active subproblems and the incumbent, selects N subproblems from the list, and assigns one subproblem to each slave process. The N subproblems selected have the best bounds among the active subproblems. Each slave process then expands its subproblem, generates children subproblems and calculates their lower bounds. It also performs the lower bound, feasibility, and termination tests on the subproblems it generates. The results are then sent back to the master process, which inserts them on the list. The algorithm terminates when the list of active subproblems becomes empty and all the slave processes are idle.

The CL algorithm has the advantage of expanding subproblems whose bounds are the best globally. This is advantageous because subproblems that have smaller lower bounds are more likely to lead to solutions than others that have larger lower bounds. The algorithm, however, has some serious disadvantages. It requires two communication messages for each subproblem expansion. The first is required to send the subproblem from the host to the node for expansion. The second is needed to carry the newly created subproblems from the node to the host. Communication with the host becomes a bottleneck that reduces the performance of the algorithm.

The second B&B implementation, known as the Distributed List (DL) algorithm, attempts to put the resources of the hypercube to better use that the CL algorithm by distributing the list of active subproblems and a copy of the incumbent across the processing nodes. It employs $N + 1$ processes, each maintaining its own subset of the list. A supervisor process initiates the computation by generating N subproblems and assigning one to each of the remaining N processes. Each process then expands subproblems from its local list. It also performs the lower bound test, the feasibility and termination tests, and inserts the results back on its local list.

In our implementation on an NCUBE/ten [60], [61] the host runs the supervisor process while each of the N processing nodes run one of the other processes. A mechanism is employed by which the load can be balanced and the subproblems distributed across the processes. When a process becomes idle it requests subproblems from neighboring processes in the system. The process that receives the request examines its own list of active subproblems and either sends a portion of it to the requesting process or denies the request if its own list is too small to divide. In our implementation, a processor requests subproblems from one of its neighbors in the hypercube. It sends one half of its subproblems to an idle processor requesting subproblems.

Because the DL algorithm maintains multiple copies of the incumbent, processes can find feasible solutions independently and update their own incumbents. In the DL algorithm, once an incumbent is updated, its new value is broadcasted to all other processes. Figure 11 shows the

speedup measured for the two algorithms for various hypercube sizes. In the CL algorithm, the speedup is reasonable for up to 16 processors. Little is gained by increasing the number of processors beyond that. This can be attributed to host-to-node communication overhead which increases as the cube size increases, and to load imbalance resulting from communication delays. The performance of the DL algorithms shows that a distributed-list approach has better performance than the CL algorithm. This is expected since there is no bottleneck in communication; the communication bandwidth of the hypercube is utilized more efficiently. The performance of the two algorithms on a 64-process hypercube is compared to the performance of the corresponding serial algorithm on the VAX 11/780 and the IBM 3090 (single processor) in Fig. 12.

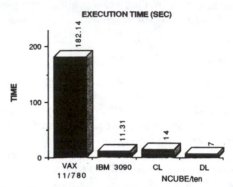

Fig. 12. Execution time for various systems.

VI. Discussion

As we have seen, hypercube multiprocessors are the realization of a concept that has been studied from a theoretical viewpoint for nearly 30 years. They represent one of the first applications of massive parallelism to commercial computers. Most of the current hypercubes can attain peak performance levels approaching those of traditional vector supercomputers. Success in reaching these levels for important practical applications has demonstrated not only the viability of hypercube supercomputers, but also the feasibility of massively parallel distributed-memory computers, in general. In particular, the assumptions underlying Amdahl's law[1] which places severe limits on the achievable speedup due to parallelism, are now seen as not applying to hypercube-class machines as they do to conventional vector architectures [52].

Nevertheless, several factors still make it difficult to achieve supercomputing performance with current hypercubes, including the small memory capacity and I/O bandwidth available in many of these machines. Most important, however, is the different style of programming required for hypercubes and other distributed-memory machines. It is not possible now to take an old sequential program (a so-called "dusty deck") and execute it directly on a hypercube computer. Such programs must be restructured, often

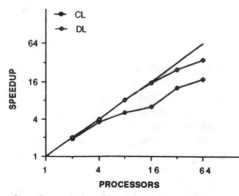

Fig. 11. Speedup of the CL and DL algorithms on the NCUBE/ten.

---

[1]Amdahl's law states that the speedup S of an n-processor system is $n/(1 + (n-1)f)$, where f denotes the fraction of nonparallelizible operations. Thus, no matter how large n becomes, S can never exceed $1/f$.

extensively, in order to achieve reasonable speedups. There are presently no "parallelizing" compilers or the like for automatic program restructuring, comparable to the vectorizing tools available for pipelined supercomputers. The design of automatic parallelizers for hypercubes, now in the early stages of research, is likely to provide a major impetus to the use of hypercube computers outside the scientific and research community, which accounts for most current hypercube usage. In addition, more user-friendly program development environments, standards for parallel programming languages and operating systems, and shareable software libraries are all likely to have a major positive influence on the use of these machines.

The rapid technological developments in VLSI that made hypercube computers feasible in the first place can be expected to continue to reshape these machines and lead to further improvements in their performance/cost ratio. New IC technologies will undoubtedly allow more powerful processors, larger memories, and more sophisticated interconnection techniques to be incorporated into future hypercubes. The most profound changes in the architecture of these machines seem likely to occur in their interconnection technology. The introduction of fast node-to-node routing circuits makes a hypercube computer seem to a programmer like a completely connected system in which each node is directly connected to all others, i.e., all nodes are neighbors. In such an environment, essentially any application graph can be embedded efficiently into the computer provided a sufficient number of nodes are available. This development is likely to expand the range of applications that can use these machines and to simplify their programming. If this occurs, then the hypercube will appear as merely the internal skeleton of an extremely general and flexible computer of essentially unlimited potential.

REFERENCES

[1] K. Hwang, "Advanced parallel processing with supercomputer architectures," in *Proc. IEEE*, pp. 1348–1379, Oct. 1987.
[2] Intel Scientific Computers. *iPSC System Overview*. Beaverton, Oregon, 1986.
[3] P. J. Denning, "Parallel computing and its evolution," *Communications of the ACM*, vol. 29, pp. 1163–1167, Dec. 1986.
[4] Sequent Computer Systems, Inc. *Balance Technology Summary*. Beaverton, OR 97006-6063, 1984.
[5] Encore Computer Corporation. *Multimax Technical Summary*, rev. ed. Marlboro, MA, May 1985.
[6] W. Crowther et al., "Performance measurements on a 128-node Butterfly parallel processor," in *Proc. 1985 Int. Conf. on Parallel Processing*, pp. 531–540, Aug. 1985.
[7] G. F. Pfister et al., "The IBM research parallel processor prototype (RP3): introduction and architecture," in *Proc. 1985 Int. Conf. on Parallel Processing*, pp. 764–771, Aug. 1985.
[8] H. J. Siegel, *Interconnection Networks for Large-Scale Parallel Processing: Theory and Case Studies*. Lexington, MA: Lexington Books, 1985.
[9] J. P. Hayes, T. N. Mudge, Q. F. Stout, S. Colley, and J. Palmer. "A microprocessor-based hypercube supercomputer," *IEEE MICRO*, pp. 6–17, Oct. 1986.
[10] J. S. Squire and S. M. Palais. "Physical and logical design of a highly parallel computer," Department of Electrical Engineering, University of Michigan, Ann Arbor, MI, Technical Report, Oct. 1962.
[11] ——, "Programming and design considerations for a highly parallel computer," in *Proc. Spring Joint Computer Conf.*, pp. 395–400, 1963.
[12] W. Millard, "Hyperdimensional μP collection seen functioning as mainframe," *Digital Design*, vol. 5, Nov. 1975.
[13] H. Sullivan and T. R. Bashkow, "A large scale, homogeneous, fully distributed parallel machine I, in *Proc. Computer Architecture Symp.*, pp. 105–117, 1977.
[14] H. Sullivan, T. R. Bashkow, and D. Klappholz, "A large scale, homogeneous, fully distributed parallel machine II, in *Proc. Computer Architecture Symp.*, pp. 118–124, 1977.
[15] M. C. Pease, "The indirect binary n-cube microprocessor array," *IEEE Trans. Computers*, vol. C-26, pp. 458–473, May 1977.
[16] C. L. Seitz, "The Cosmic Cube," *Communications ACM*, vol. 28, pp. 22–33, Jan. 1985.
[17] J. Tuazon, J. Peterson, M. Pniel, and D. Liderman, "Caltech/JPL Mark II hypercube concurrent processor," in *Proc. 1985 Int. Conf. on Parallel Processing*, pp. 666–671, Aug. 1985.
[18] J. Peterson, J. Tuazon, D. Liderman, and M. Pniel, "The Mark III hypercube-ensemble concurrent computer," in *Proc. 1985 Int. Conf. on Parallel Processing*, pp. 71–73, Aug. 1985.
[19] A. Karp, "What price multiplicity?" *Communications ACM*, vol. 30, pp. 7–9, Jan. 1986.
[20] G. R. Montry, J. L. Gustafson, and R. E. Benner, "Development of parallel methods for a 1024-processor hypercube," *SIAM J. Scientific and Statistical Computing*, vol. 9, pp. 1–32, July 1988.
[21] J. Dongarra, A. Karp, and K. Kennedy, "Winners achieve speedup of 400," *IEEE Software*, pp. 1–5, May 1988.
[22] J. Gustavson et al., "The architecture of a homogeneous multiprocessor," in *Proc. 1986 Int. Conf. on Parallel Processing*, pp. 649–652, Aug. 1986.
[23] Intel Scientific Computers. *Intel iPSC/2*. Beaverton, OR 97006, 1988.
[24] T. H. Dunigan. *Performance of a second-generation hypercube*. Oak Ridge National Lab., Oak Ridge, TN, Technical Report ORNL/TM-10881, Nov. 1988.
[25] Thinking Machines Corp., *Connection Machine Model CM-2 Technical Summary*. Technical Report HA87-4, April 1987.
[26] Ametek Corp. *Series 2010*. Monrovia, CA, 1988.
[27] T. N. Mudge, G. D. Buzzard, and T. S. Abdel-Rahman, "A high performance operating system for the NCUBE," in *Hypercube Multiprocessors 1987*, M. T. Heath, ed. Society for Industrial and Applied Mathematics, Philadelphia, PA, pp. 90–99, 1987.
[28] W. J. Dally and C. L. Seitz, "The torus routing chip," *Distributed Computing*, vol. 1, pp. 187–196, 1986.
[29] E. Chow et al., "Hyperswitch network for the hypercube computer," in *15th Ann. Int. Symp. on Computer Architecture*, pp. 90–99, May 1988.
[30] G. D. Buzzard, "High Performance Communications for Hypercube Multiprocessors." Ph.D. thesis, University of Michigan, 1988.
[31] W. J. Dally and C. L. Seitz, "Deadlock-free message routing in multiprocessor interconnection networks," *IEEE Trans. Computers*, vol. C-36, pp. 547–553, May 1987.
[32] F. Harary, J. P. Hayes, and H. J. Wu, "A survey of the theory of hypercube graphs," *Comput. Math. Applic.*, vol. 15, pp. 277–289, 1988.
[33] L. G. Valiant, "A scheme for parallel communication," *SIAM J. Computing*, vol. 11, pp. 350–361, May 1982.
[34] F. Harary. *Graph Theory*. Reading, MA: Addison-Wesley, 1969.
[35] S. Dutt and J. P. Hayes, "On allocating subcubes in a hypercube multiprocessor," in *Proc. 3rd Int. Conf. on Hypercube Concurrent Computers & Applications*, vol. I, pp. 801–810, Jan. 1989.
[36] M. Livingston and Q. F. Stout, "Embeddings in hypercubes," *Math. Comp. Modelling*, vol. 11, pp. 222–227, 1988.
[37] D. A. Buell et al., "Parallel algorithms and architectures: Report of a workshop," *J. Supercomputing*, pp. 301–325, 1988.
[38] ParaSoft Corp. *Programming Parallel Computers Using the EXPRESS System*, Mission Viejo, CA 92692, 1989.
[39] R. M. Clapp and T. N. Mudge, "ADA on a hypercube," in *Proc. 3rd Int. Conf. on Hypercube Concurrent Computers & Applications*, vol. I, pp. 399–408, Jan. 1989.
[40] D. Gelernter, "Generative communication in Linda," *ACM Trans. Prog. Lang. Syst.*, vol. 7, pp. 80–112, Jan. 1985.

[41] R. Pountain, *A Tutorial Introduction to Occam Programming*. Inmos Corp., Colorado Springs, CO, 1983.

[42] R. H. Perrott, *Parallel Programming*. Woking, England: Addison-Wesley, 1987.

[43] C. Moler and D. S. Scott. *Communication Utilities for the iPSC.* iPSC Technical Report 2, Intel Corp., Aug. 1986.

[44] *Hypercube Multiprocessors 1986*, M. T. Heath, ed. Philadelphia, PA: Society for Industrial and Applied Mathematics, 1986.

[45] *Hypercube Multiprocessors 1987*. M. T. Heath, ed. Philadelphia, PA: Society for Industrial and Applied Mathematics, 1987.

[46] G. Fox *et al.*, *Solving Problems on Concurrent Processors*. Englewood Cliffs, NJ: Prentice-Hall, 1988.

[47] D. A. Reed and R. M. Fujimoto, *Multicomputer Networks: Message-Based Parallel Processing.* Cambridge, MA: The MIT Press, 1987.

[48] W. R. Martin, T. C. Wan, T. S. Abdel-Rahman, and T. N. Mudge, "Monte Carlo photon transport on shared memory and distributed memory parallel processors," *Int. J. Supercomputer App.*, vol. 1, pp. 57–74, Fall 1987.

[49] E. W. Felten and S. W. Otto, "Chess on a hypercube," in *Proc. 3rd Int. Conf. on Hypercube Concurrent Computers & Applications, Vol. II*, pp. 1329–1341, Jan. 1989.

[50] A. Rosenfeld and A. C. Kak, *Digital Picture Processing*. New York: Academic Press, 1976.

[51] J. M. S. Prewitt, *Object enhancement and extraction*. New York: Academic Press, 1970.

[52] J. L. Gustafson, "Reevaluating Amdahl's law," *Communications ACM*, vol. 31, pp. 532–533, 1988.

[53] T. N. Mudge and T. S. Abdel-Rahman, "Vision algorithms for hypercube machines," *J. Parallel and Dist. Computing*, vol. 4, pp. 79–94, 1987.

[54] ——, *Specialized Computer Architecture for Robotics and Automation*, chapter Architecture for robot vision. New York, NY: Gordon and Breach Science Publishers, 1987, pp. 103–149.

[55] P. N. Swarztrauber, *Multiprocessor FFTs*. National Center for Atmospheric Research, Boulder, CO, 1986.

[56] E. L. Lawler and D. W. Wood, "Branch-and-bound methods: A survey," *Ops. Res.*, vol. 14, pp. 699–719, 1966.

[57] D. W. Sweeney, J. D. C. Little, K. G. Murty, and C. Karel, "An algorithm for the traveling salesman problem," *Ops. Res.*, vol. 11, pp. 972–989, 1963.

[58] G. Ingargiola and J. Korsh, "A general algorithm for one-dimensional knapsack problems," *Ops. Res.*, vol. 25, pp. 752–759, 1977.

[59] V. Kumar and L. Kanal, "A general branch and bound formulation for understanding and synthesizing AND/OR tree search procedures," *Artificial Intelligence*, vol. 21, pp. 179–198, 1983.

[60] T. S. Abdel-Rahman and T. N. Mudge, "Parallel branch and bound algorithms on hypercube multiprocessors," in *Proc. 3rd Conf. on Hypercube Concurrent Computers & Applications, vol. I*, pp. 1492–1499, Jan. 1989.

[61] T. S. Abdel-Rahman, "Parallel Processing of Best–First Branch and Bound Algorithms on Distributed Memory Multiprocessors," Ph.D. thesis, University of Michigan, 1989.

John P. Hayes (Fellow, IEEE) received the B.E. degree from the National University of Ireland, Dublin, in 1965, and the M.S. and Ph.D. degrees from the University of Illinois, Urbana, in 1967 and 1970, respectively, all in electrical engineering.

While at the University of Illinois he participated in the design of the ILLIAC III computer and carried out research in the area of fault diagnosis of digital systems. In 1970 he joined the Operations Research Group at the Shell Benelux Computing Center of the Royal Dutch Shell Company in The Hague, The Netherlands, where he was involved in mathematical programming and software development. From 1972 to 1982 he was a faculty member of the Departments of Electrical Engineering and Computer Science of the University of Southern California, Los Angeles. He is currently a Professor in the Electrical Engineering and Computer Science Department of the University of Michigan, Ann Arbor. His research interests include computer architecture; parallel processing; fault tolerance and reliability; and computer-aided design and testing of VLSI systems.

Dr. Hayes was Technical Program Chairman of the 1977 International Conference on Fault-Tolerant Computing. He is the author of over a hundred technical papers and several books, including *Digital System Design and Microprocessors* (McGraw-Hill, 1984) and *Computer Architecture and Organization*, 2nd Ed. (McGraw-Hill, 1988). He served as Editor of the Computer Architecture and Systems Department of *Communications of the ACM* from 1978 to 1981, and was Guest Editor of the June 1984 Special Issue of *IEEE Transactions on Computers*. He was the founding Director of the Advanced Computer Architecture Laboratory at the University of Michigan from 1985 to 1988. He is a member of the Association for Computing Machinery and Sigma Xi.

Trevor Mudge (Senior Member, IEEE) received the B.Sc. degree in cybernetics from the University of Reading, England, in 1969, and the M.S. and Ph.D. degrees in computer science from the University of Illinois, Urbana, in 1973 and 1977, respectively.

While at the University of Illinois he participated in the design of several special purpose computers and did research in computer architecture. Since 1977, he has been on the faculty of the University of Michigan, Ann Arbor where he has taught classes on logic design, CAD, computer architecture, and programming languages. He is presently an Associate Professor of Electrical Engineering and Computer Science, and Director of the Advanced Computer Architecture Lab. In addition to his position as a faculty member, he is a consultant for several computer companies in the areas of architecture and languages.

Dr. Mudge is the author of more than 80 papers on computer architecture, programming languages, VLSI design, and computer vision, and he holds a patent in computer aided design of VLSI circuits. He is a member of the ACM and of the British Computer Society.

Matrix Computation on Distributed Memory Multiprocessors

CLEVE MOLER*

Abstract: LINPACK style matrix computations on hypercubes and other distributed memory multiprocessor computer systems are considered. A *distributed matrix* data structure and two communication primitives, *gsend* and *gsum*, are proposed. Timing results for Gaussian elimination on a 64 processor hypercube are presented and analyzed.

Introduction

This paper is concerned with LINPACK and EISPACK style matrix computations on multiprocessor computer systems with distributed memories. LINPACK [1] and EISPACK [2,3] are widely used Fortran subroutine libraries for matrix computations on traditional single memory sequential computers. LINPACK is used for analyzing and solving systems of simultaneous linear equations, inverting matrices, solving least-squares problems and related calculations. EISPACK is used for analyzing and solving various matrix eigenvalue problems. Both libraries work with several different types of matrices, including symmetric and band matrices, and both handle real and complex matrices. But both libraries are limited to dense, stored matrices; they are not intended for the large, sparse matrix problems arising in elliptic partial differential equations and similar applications. In practice on most contemporary sequential computers, the orders of the matrices handled by LINPACK and EISPACK are limited to a few hundred.

In the "LINPACK Benchmark" [4], Dongarra has continued the compilation of performance data that was begun with the LINPACK User's Guide [1]. The benchmark lists the execution times of several dozen different computer systems for one program running on one specific matrix of order 100. Appendices in Dongarra's report give the execution times of a few large "supercomputers" using modifications of the LINPACK programs running on larger matrices. Although the data in [4] are only for one particular program and problem, the results are indicative of expected performance over a wide range of computationally intensive scientific and technical problems.

The type of multiprocessor computer system we are interested in is exemplified by the Intel iPSC hypercube, but our considerations are not limited to that machine, or even to hypercubes. The important architectural characteristics are:

---

* Intel Scientific Computers, Beaverton, Oregon 97006

- There are several dozen processors, say in the range from 8 to 256.

- Each processor has its own data memory with at least several thousand floating point words.

- Each processor can be controlled by its own program, although many applications will use multiple copies of a single program.

- Each processor has a powerful floating point arithmetic unit, possibly with vector or array oriented instructions.

- Processors communicate by message passing.

- It is possible to efficiently send a message from one processor to all other processors.

- There is no shared memory, no shared clock, no common sequencing control.

We refer to such computers as Distributed Memory Message Passing, or DMMP, machines. Hypercubes are one commercially viable way to manufacture such machines. For background on hypercubes, see Fox and Otto [5], Seitz [6], Rattner [7] and the iPSC System Overview [8].

Much of the published literature on parallel matrix computation has been concerned with systolic arrays, SIMD machines or shared memory multiprocessors, and is not directly applicable to DMMP machines. Other work on hypercube matrix computation has been done by groups at Caltech [9], Oak Ridge [10], and Yale [11].

One important way in which LINPACK and EISPACK will be used on such machines is in applications with many tasks involving matrices small enough to be stored on a single processor. The conventional subroutines can be used on the individual processors with no modification. We call such applications "embarrassingly parallel" to emphasize the fact that, while there is a high degree of parallelism and it is possible to make efficient use of many processors, the granularity is large enough that no cooperation between the processors is required within the matrix computations. We will not consider such uses further in this paper.

Design Goals

Our primary objective is to adapt the LINPACK and EISPACK libraries to the Distributed Memory Message Passing environment without extensive algorithmic or software modifications. It is of utmost importance to retain the numerical stability and accuracy attributes of the underlying algorithms that have been established by the error analyses of Wilkinson and others and by the decade of actual use. It is also desirable to retain as much as possible of the software structure and interface that is now familiar to many users.

We also want to have programs that execute efficiently. We are interested in effective utilization of the floating point power of all the processors, but not if it requires abandoning established numerical properties. We will not solve linear equations by Gauss-Jordan elimination without pivoting or compute eigenvalues from the explicit characteristic polynomial, even if such methods appear to be easily parallelizable. Fortunately, these two objectives do not seem to be in conflict. We do not know of any cases where numerically unreliable algorithms are significantly faster than reliable ones.

Distributed Matrices

With a distributed memory machine, the data in a large matrix should be distributed across the memory of all the of the processors. This will make it possible to fully utilize the large memory available and facilitate the load balancing task of keeping most of the processors busy doing useful arithmetic much of the time. There are many possible ways to distribute the data -- by submatrices, by rows or columns, by diagonals, etc. We believe that it is important to choose a single storage scheme for use over a wide range of matrix problems. The output of the eigenvector subroutine, for example, should be in the form expected as input to the linear equation solver.

In Fortran, two dimensional arrays are stored by columns; the element immediately following A(I,J) in memory is A(I+1,J), not A(I,J+1). This implies that column oriented algorithms are preferred on sequential machines with hierarchal memory hardware, such as caches or paging [12]. The innermost loops accessing A(I,J) should vary I and leave J fixed. LINPACK uses this strategy extensively; almost all the inner loops are carried out by the BLAS, or Basic Linear Algebra Subprograms [1], operating on one or two columns of a matrix. The original release of EISPACK placed little emphasis on memory access patterns, but a recent revision, known as EISPACK 3, gives a few of the frequently used EISPACK subroutines a column orientation.

We have chosen to generalize this column oriented matrix storage to the notion of a *distributed matrix* for DMMP machines. Throughout this paper, we use the following notation:

n = the order of the matrix,

p = the number of processors.

$m = \lceil n/p \rceil$ = the smallest integer $\geq n/p$

A distributed matrix allocates m or $m-1$ columns to each processor. We are primarily interested in problems with $n >> p$ so that each processor has several columns. If $n \approx p$, or $n < p$, our programs will still function correctly , but will not be particularly efficient.

If the columns are thought of as forming a deck of playing cards, and the processors as players in a card game, then the matrix is distributed by dealing the cards in order to the the players. Specifically, any column index j in the range from 1 to n can be expressed as

$$j = (l-1) \cdot p + k + 1$$

where $k = (j-1) \bmod p$ and $l = (j-1) \operatorname{div} p + 1$. The resulting indices k and l are in the ranges $0 \leq k \leq p-1$ and $1 \leq l \leq m$. A *distributed matrix* has column j stored on processor k in array position l. If n is exactly divisible by p then each processor has m columns, otherwise the later processors have only $m-1$ columns.

Several of the matrix factorization algorithms used in LINPACK and EISPACK have the following general structure.

for $k = 1$ to n do
    A_k = leading or trailing submatrix of order $n-k$
    modify A_k
end k loop

The modification of A_k can take many different forms, from the rank one update in Gaussian elimination, to the orthogonal similarity transformations in Hessenberg reduction. But all the algorithms work on submatrices of varying dimension formed from adjacent rows and columns. Moreover, it is possible to arrange the inner loops so that the algorithms are column oriented. For all such factorizations, our distributed matrix provides an automatic load balancing, because each of the submatrices A_k is also distributed in the same sense. This insures that during the k-th step, the active submatrix in each processor will have $n-k$ rows and either $\lceil (n-k)/p \rceil$ or $\lfloor (n-k)/p \rfloor$ columns. All processors will therefore have approximately the same amount of work to do. (Continuing the card game analogy, if the players take turns discarding their "columns", then they will always have within one of the same number.)

Global Operations

For the algorithms which we will consider, almost all of the data communication among the multiple processors can be expressed with two fundamental global operations, *gsend* and *gsum*.

- Global send -- send a vector from one processor to all other processors.

- Global sum -- form the vector sum of p vectors, one from each processor.

There are variants of these operations. For example, the sum may be needed by only one processor, or may be needed by all processors. Or, the addition may be replaced by other commutative element-wise arithmetic operation, such as multiplication or maximization.

To see how these operations might be used, consider a simple matrix-vector product. Let A be a large matrix, whose columns are distributed among the processors in the manner described above. Let x be a vector stored in one processor and suppose it is required to compute

$$y = Ax$$

On a conventional sequential processor, a column-oriented approach to computing this product involves forming a linear combination of the columns of A using the coefficients in x, rather than taking the inner product of the rows of A with x. In the first step on a DMMP machine, the processor containing x initiates a global send to make x available to all processors. Then each processor forms a linear combination of its columns of A, using the appropriate elements of x. Finally, all the processors participate in the global sum to accumulate y in the desired processor.

If $n >> p$, most of the time required to compute Ax is spent in the middle step, the linear combinations, where all processors have nearly the same amount of work to do, and can operate concurrently and independently. The initial communication step, and the final step which involves both communication and arithmetic, take only a small portion of the total time. As n grows with p remaining fixed, we expect the ratio of communication time to computation time to approach zero. (For this simple example, the details of our scheme for distributing the columns over the processors are not important. Any scheme which allocates the same number of columns to each processor would be satisfactory.)

A hypercube is one practical topology for DMMP machines which offers efficient implementations of $gsend$ and $gsum$. The technique is known as "use of spanning trees" or "induction on the dimension of subcubes" and is illustrated by the following figure.

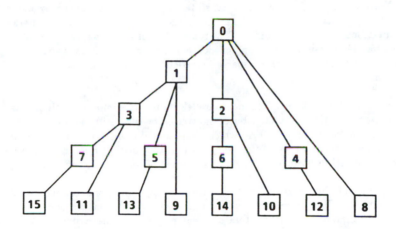

Suppose a message, such as the vector x, is to be sent from processor 0 to all other processors. At the first step, processor 0 sends it to processor 1. At the second step, 1 sends it to 3 and 0 sends it to 2. At the third step, processors 0 through 3 send it to processors 4 through 7, and so on. All communications between pairs of processors take place along direct hypercube connection paths. Any other processor could be made the root of this spanning tree by taking the bitwise exclusive or of the root processor number and the processor numbers shown in the figure. Clearly, the algorithm can be used on hypercubes of any dimension. The time required to send a message from any processor to all other processors is proportional to the dimension of the hypercube, which is $\log_2(p)$.

The global sum can be computed by following the spanning tree in the reverse order. Suppose each processor k has a scalar or vector quantity y_k and it is desired to form

$$y = \sum_{k=0}^{p-1} y_k$$

Consider forming y in processor 0 using the above spanning tree. At the first step each of the processors 8 through 15 sends their y_k to the processor above them in the tree and each of the processors 0 through 7 receives y_{k+8} and adds it to their y_k. At the next step, processors 4 through 7 send y's to 0 through 3, each of which does an addition. In the third step, 0 and 1 do additions. Then in the final step, processor 1, which has the sum of the y_k for odd k, sends it to processor 0, which has the sum for even k, and which then forms the desired result. Again, the elapsed time is proportional to $\log_2(p)$ and it is possible to form the result in any processor.

Software implementing *gsend* and *gsum* is described in detail in a report by Moler and Scott [13]. An interesting combination of these two algorithms which generates the sum in every processor, not just the root processor, in $\log_2(p)$ steps has been developed by Vance Faber [14].

Parallel Gaussian Elimination

We believe the notions discussed so far -- matrices distributed by columns, global sends, and global sums -- can serve as the basis for a wide range of parallel algorithms in computational linear algebra. The remainder of this paper concentrates on one such algorithm, Gaussian elimination for dense matrices. In future papers, we plan to consider other algorithms, including sparse matrices, orthogonal factorizations and eigenvalue problems.

Here is the outline of the our parallel Gaussian elimination algorithm, which computes the LU factorization of a distributed matrix. The algorithm is a direct generalization of the LINPACK subroutine DGEFA, which factors a double precision, general matrix. In fact, when there is only one processor, so $p = 1$, the algorithm reduces to the sequential, column-oriented algorithm used by LINPACK and some of its predecessors [12].

A copy of the program implementing this algorithm runs on each of the p processors in the machine. The processors are distinguished by their *id* numbers, which run from 0 to $p - 1$, and different processors store different columns of the matrix. (We have left out a few details, such as the actual interchange of elements determined by the pivoting and the handling of zero pivots. The actual implementation of this algorithm handles these details in the same way as DGEFA.)

$n\ =$ order of matrix

$p\ =$ number of processors

$id\ =$ individual processor index

$m\ =$ number of columns in id-th processor

$\quad = \lceil n/p \rceil$ or $\lfloor n/p \rfloor$ if $id <$ or $\geq (n \bmod p)$

$A\ =$ distributed matrix, stored in n by m array on each processor

328

$l = 1$

for $k = 1$ to n do

    if $id = (k-1)$ mod p then
        find *pivot* in l-th column of A
        $c = $ (portion of l-th column of A) / *pivot*
        $l = l + 1$
        initiate *gsend* of c
    else
        participate in *gsend* to obtain c
    endif

    for $j = l$ to m do
      $s = a_{k,j}$
      for $i = k+1$ to n do
        $a_{i,j} = a_{i,j} + s \cdot c_i$
      end i loop
    end j loop

end k loop

The outer loop of the algorithm involves k, the index of the variable to be eliminated. At the k-th step, the processor owning the k-th column of A assumes a temporary role as root processor for that step. The root processor determines the pivot element and divides elements $k+1$ through n of the pivot column by the pivot to form the vector c of multipliers. During this time the other $p-1$ processors are logically idle, although some of them may actually be finishing the previous step. We refer to this part of the computation as the *sequential* portion of the algorithm since only one processor is active.

After the root processor determines the multipliers, all the processors participate in the global send, so they all get copies of c. This is the *communication* portion.

Most of the time is spent in the nested j and i loops, where each processor adds scalar multiples of c to each of its remaining active columns. This is the *parallel* portion of the algorithm since all the processors are active with arithmetic operations. Some of the processors may have one more active column than some of the others, but all the columns are the same length, so the load balancing is quite good.

The inner loop on i is a fundamental operation in matrix computation -- add a scalar multiple of one vector to another vector. We look forward to the day when each processor will have a fast, vector oriented arithmetic unit and this operation can essentially be regarded as one machine instruction. In the meantime, the inner loop can be implemented with a carefully coded version of DAXPY [1].

It would be possible to have all the processors work on the selection of the pivot and the computation of the multipliers. This would reduce the amount of time spent in what we are calling the sequential portion of the algorithm, but would increase communication time. We have not pursued this idea because it violates our goal of making as few changes in the underlying LINPACK codes as possible, and because it is unlikely to lead to a significant improvement in overall performance.

Performance Measurement and Modeling

In this section, we discuss the performance of our LU factorization algorithm on the Intel iPSC hypercube, model d6, with 64 processors. The timing experiments were done in February, 1986, with version 1.9 of the node operating system, Intel FTN286 Fortran and assembly language BLAS.

The first figure shows the execution time for the LU factorization of a 100 by 100 double precision matrix using from 1 to 35 processors. The o's are the measured execution times. They range from 21.152 seconds for $p = 1$ to 4.000 seconds for $p = 32$.

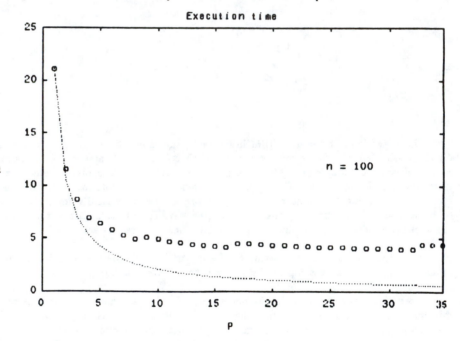

Most of the measurements involve values of p which are not powers of 2, and hence are not full subcubes of the hypercube. In these situations, only p processors are involved in the arithmetic and matrix storage, but all the processors in the next larger subcube are involved in spanning tree. Consequently, there small jumps in the overall trend when p crosses a power of 2.

The dotted line in the figure is the hyperbola, $t = t_1/p$, which would correspond to "perfect speedup" where the execution time for p processors is $1/p$ times the execution time for 1 processor. For this example, we obviously deviate from that ideal. In fact, after about

16 processors, adding more processors causes neither a significant decrease nor a significant increase in the execution time. The speedup is a factor a little over 5, no matter how many processors are used.

Factorization of a single matrix of order 100 must be regarded as a trivial, unrepresentative problem for a multiprocessor machine of this size. Such a problem can be easily solved by a single processor. To fully utilize the system, we must consider problems involving many matrices of this order, or matrices of larger order.

The performance is strongly dependent on the two parameters, n and p. For a given p, there is a maximum value of n determined by the amount of memory available. Let M be the number of floating point numbers that can be stored in one processor. We have taken $M = 30000$ for 64-bit arithmetic, even though a somewhat larger value could be used. On each processor, we must provide for $\lceil n/p \rceil$ columns of the distributed matrix and two additional vectors of length n. This leads to the inequality,

$$n \cdot \lceil n/p \rceil + 2n \leq M$$

and hence to the definition

$$n_{\max} = \sqrt{pM + (3p/2)^2} - (3p/2) \approx \sqrt{pM}$$

The values of $n_{\max}$ range from 171 for $p = 1$ to 1292 for $p = 64$.

The next figure shows the 128 pairs of n and p which were used in our primary timing experiment. The values of p range from 4 to 64 in steps of 4. For each p, there are 8 values of n, ranging from $n_{\max}/8$ to $n_{\max}$. So the smallest problem involves a matrix of order 43 distributed across 4 processors and the largest involves a matrix of order 1292 distributed across 64 processors.

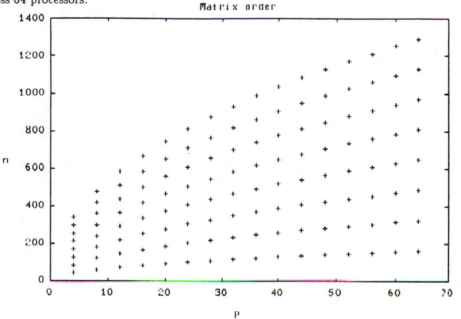

The LU factorization algorithm was timed for each of these n, p pairs. Here is a portion of the tabulated output showing the measured time, t, in seconds and a graph showing all 128 times. We see that the measured execution times range from slightly over 1 second for the smallest problem to slightly over 1000 seconds for the largest.

p	n	t
4	43	1.184
8	60	2.064
.....		
64	162	10.672
4	85	4.928
8	120	8.016
.....		
64	323	38.560
.....		
4	340	209.456
8	478	303.680
.....		
64	1292	1002.256

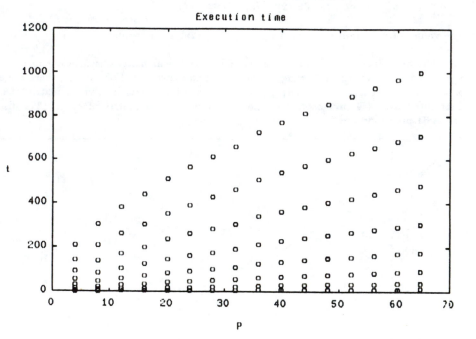

The data can be very accurately modeled by a linear combination of six functions of n and p. Let

$$d = \lceil \log_2(p) \rceil$$

denote the dimension of the subcube containing p processors. The six terms in the model are:

$$\frac{n^3}{p}, \quad \frac{n^2}{p}, \quad n^2, \quad nd, \quad n^2 d, \quad 1$$

The first two terms involve powers of n divided by p. They model the parallel portion of the algorithm, the nested loops on j and i which are executed concurrently by all the processors.

The third term does not involve p. It models the sequential portion of the algorithm, the pivot search and resulting scaling of the pivot column which is done by only a single processor at each step of the elimination.

The next two terms involve the dimension of the hypercube and model the communication time. The nd term is proportional to the total number of neighbor-to-neighbor messages sent by any one processor, and the $n^2 d$ term accounts for the lengths of the messages. (Since d is a discontinuous function of p, these terms also provide the jumps in the graph where p crosses a power of 2.)

We did a least-squares fit of the model to the data, using the LINPACK orthogonalization subroutines DQRDC and DQRSL, as embedded in PC-MATLAB [15]. (The graphs in this paper were also produced with PC-MATLAB.) The relative error in the resulting fit is well below 1% for all but a few of the observations involving small matrices.

The next two graphs show quantities derived directly from the original data with o's and quantities derived from the model with solid lines. The first graph shows floating point performance measured in megaflops, or millions of floating point operations per second.

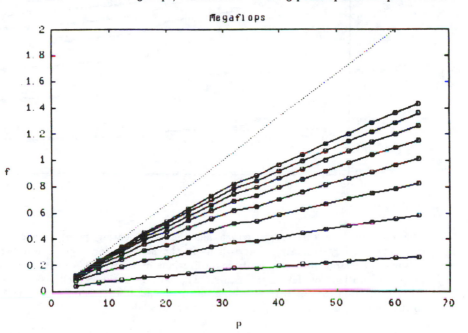

The megaflop rate is computed from the matrix order and the execution time by

$$f = \frac{2}{3}\frac{n^3}{t} \cdot 10^{-6}$$

The factor 2/3 comes from the fact that Gaussian elimination requires $1/3\ n^3$ multiplications and $1/3\ n^3$ additions. We see megaflop rates ranging up to 1.43 for the largest matrix and 64 processors.

The most interesting quantity is the *floating point utilization*. This is megaflops per processor, normalized to the megaflop rate of one processor with infinite memory. Specifically,

$$u = \frac{1}{\tau}\frac{f}{p}$$

where $\tau = 0.033$ is the assembly language DAXPY megaflop rate of a single Intel 80287 floating point arithmetic unit running at 8 Mhz. Values of floating point utilization near 1.0 correspond to having all of the processors busy doing floating point arithmetic all of the time. Values approaching 0.0 indicate that the floating point units are idle.

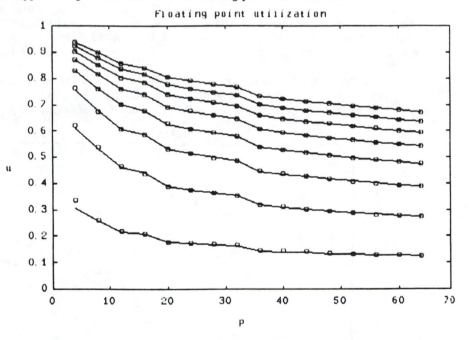

The top curve in this graph, which has the best floating point utilization, results from factoring the largest matrix that will fit in the memory for a given number of processors. Solving such large problems leads to utilizations of nearly 70% on 64 processors and even better utilizations on fewer processors. The bottom curve, which has the poorest floating point utilization, results from factoring matrices whose order is only 1/8-th of the maximum, so the memory used is only 1/64-th of the total available.

It turns out that, for this problem, floating point utilization significantly less than 1.0 is due more to the sequential nature of a portion of our algorithm, than it is due to hypercube communication times. To see this, we must take a closer look at the actual coefficients in the fit.

For the range of n and p considered in this experiment, three of the six terms in the model are dominant. The n^3/p term dominates the n^2/p term because the values of n are quite large. The nd term dominates the n^2d term because, for the version of the iPSC node operating system used here, the time required to send a message is only mildly dependent upon the length of the message. If we fit the timing data with just these three terms, the result is not quite as accurate as the six term fit, but it does simplify further analysis. The result obtained is

$$t \approx c_1 \frac{n^3}{p} + c_2 n^2 + c_3 nd$$

where $c_1 = 1.8361 \cdot 10^{-5}$, $c_2 = 2.1836 \cdot 10^{-4}$, $c_3 = 2.7024 \cdot 10^{-3}$

This leads to a manageable approximation of the floating point utilization.

$$u \approx \frac{1}{1 + \sigma \frac{p}{n} + \mu \frac{p \log p}{n^2}}$$

where $\sigma = \frac{c_2}{c_1} = 11.9$ and $\mu = \frac{c_3}{c_1} = 147.2$.

The σ term comes from the sequential portion of our version of parallel Gaussian elimination. For the range of n and p we are considering, it is the primary contributor to utilizations under 1.0. Modifications of the algorithm could reduce this term at the expense of increasing other terms, but we have chosen not to pursue such algorithms. Increasing the speed of the floating point processor should not alter this term, since it comes from the ratio of the sequential floating point processing to the parallel floating point processing.

The μ term comes from the message passing. Speeding up the communication hardware or the node operating system message handler would reduce this term. On the other hand, increasing the speed of the floating point processor would increase this term since it comes from a ratio of communication time to arithmetic time.

Matrix $n_{1/2}$

For modeling the performance of vector processors, Roger Hockney has introduced the parameter $n_{1/2}$, which he defines to be the vector length necessary to reach a floating point processing rate equal to one half of the maximum rate. Adapting this notion to matrix computation on parallel processors, we define the *matrix $n_{1/2}$* to be the matrix order, n, which, as a function of the number of processors, p, leads to the floating point utilization, u, equal to $1/2$. Using our simplified model, this leads to a quadratic equation for n.

$$u = \frac{1}{1 + \sigma \frac{p}{n} + \mu \frac{p \log p}{n^2}} = \frac{1}{2}$$

The solution is

$$n_{1/2} = \frac{\sigma p}{2} + \sqrt{(\frac{\sigma p}{2})^2 + \mu p \log p}$$

The following graph shows $n_{1/2}$ as a function of p for the parameter values obtained from the fit to the timing data described above.

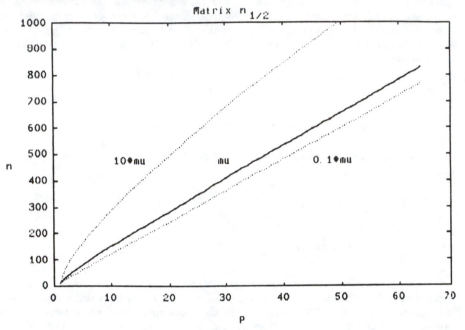

The graph also shows the functions which would result if μ were reduced or increased by factors of 10. We see that for the current system it is a reasonable approximation to ignore the communication term and obtain

$$n_{1/2} \approx \sigma p$$

This says that for the current system and algorithm, $n_{1/2}$ depends linearly on the number of processors, and on the sequential portion of the algorithm, but does not depend in a significant way on the communication parameters. However, for different systems or different algorithms, message passing costs might make substantial contributions to the value $n_{1/2}$.

References

[1] J. J. Dongarra, J. R. Bunch, C. B. Moler and G. W. Stewart, *LINPACK Users' Guide*, SIAM Publications, 368 pp., 1979.

[2] B. T. Smith, J. M. Boyle, J. J. Dongarra, B. S. Garbow, Y. Ikebe, V. C. Klema and C. B. Moler, *Matrix Eigensystem Routines -- EISPACK User's Guide*, Springer-Verlag, Lecture

Notes in Computer Science No. 6, First Edition, 388 pp., 1974. Second Edition, 552 pp., 1976.

B. S. Garbow, J. M. Boyle, J. J. Dongarra and C. B. Moler, *Matrix Eigensystem Routines -- EISPACK Guide Extension*, Springer Verlag, Lecture Notes in Computer Science No. 51, 343 pp., 1977.

[3] J. J. Dongarra and C. B. Moler, "EISPACK - A package for solving matrix eigenvalue problems," *Sources and Production of Mathematical Software*, (Wayne Cowell, editor), 68-87, Prentice Hall, 1984.

[4] Jack J. Dongarra, "Performance of Various Computers Using Standard Linear Equations Software in a Fortran Environment," Technical Memorandum No. 23, Mathematics and Computer Science Division, Argonne National Laboratory, issued periodically.

[5] Geoffrey Fox and Steve Otto, "Algorithms for Concurrent Processors," *Physics Today 37*, 50-59, 1984.

[6] Charles Seitz, "The Cosmic Cube," *Comm. A.C.M. 28*, 22-33, 1985.

[7] Justin Rattner, "Concurrent processing: A new direction is scientific computing," *Proc. National Computer Conference*, 1-9, 1985.

[8] *iPSC System Overview*, Order Number: 175278-002, Intel Scientific Computers, Beaverton, Oregon, 1986.

[9] Geoffrey Fox, Steve Otto and others, Series of recent technical reports, Physics Department, California Institute of Technology.

[10] George Davis, Al Geist, Esmond Ng and Mike Heath, Series of recent technical reports, Oak Ridge National Laboratory.

[11] Lennart Johnsson, Youcef Saad, Martin Schultz and others, Series of recent technical reports, Computer Science Department, Yale University.

[12] Cleve Moler, "Matrix computations with Fortran and paging," *Comm. A.C.M. 15*, 268-270, 1972.

[13] Cleve Moler and David S. Scott "Communication Utilities for the iPSC," technical report in preparation, Intel Scientific Computers, Beaverton, Oregon, 1986.

[14] Vance Faber, private communication, 1985.

[15] *PC-MATLAB User's Guide*, The MathWorks, Inc., Portola Valley, California, 1985.

Reprinted from *IEEE Transactions on Computers*, Vol.C-36, No. 12, December 1987, pages 1523-1538. Copyright © 1987 by The Institute of Electrical and Electronics Engineers, Inc. All rights reserved.

The Warp Computer: Architecture, Implementation, and Performance

MARCO ANNARATONE, EMMANUEL ARNOULD, THOMAS GROSS, MEMBER, IEEE, H. T. KUNG, MONICA LAM, ONAT MENZILCIOGLU, AND JON A. WEBB

Abstract—The Warp machine is a systolic array computer of linearly connected cells, each of which is a programmable processor capable of performing 10 million floating-point operations per second (10 MFLOPS). A typical Warp array includes ten cells, thus having a peak computation rate of 100 MFLOPS. The Warp array can be extended to include more cells to accommodate applications capable of using the increased computational bandwidth. Warp is integrated as an attached processor into a Unix host system. Programs for Warp are written in a high-level language supported by an optimizing compiler.

The first ten-cell prototype was completed in February 1986; delivery of production machines started in April 1987. Extensive experimentation with both the prototype and production machines has demonstrated that the Warp architecture is effective in the application domain of robot navigation as well as in other fields such as signal processing, scientific computation, and computer vision research. For these applications, Warp is typically several hundred times faster than a VAX 11/780 class computer.

This paper describes the architecture, implementation, and performance of the Warp machine. Each major architectural decision is discussed and evaluated with system, software, and application considerations. The programming model and tools developed for the machine are also described. The paper concludes with performance data for a large number of applications.

Index Terms—Computer system implementation, computer vision, image processing, optimizing compiler, parallel processors, performance evaluation, pipelined processor, scientific computing, signal processing, systolic array, vision research.

I. INTRODUCTION

THE Warp machine is a high-performance systolic array computer designed for computation-intensive applications. In a typical configuration, Warp consists of a linear systolic array of ten identical cells, each of which is a 10 MFLOPS programmable processor. Thus, a system in this configuration has a peak performance of 100 MFLOPS.

The Warp machine is an attached processor to a general purpose host running the Unix operating system. Warp can be accessed by a procedure call on the host, or through an interactive, programmable command interpreter called the Warp shell [8]. A high-level language called W2 is used to program Warp; the language is supported by an optimizing compiler [12], [23].

The Warp project started in 1984. A two-cell system was completed in June 1985 at Carnegie Mellon. Construction of two identical ten-cell prototype machines was contracted to two industrial partners, GE and Honeywell. These prototypes were built from off-the-shelf parts on wire-wrapped boards. The first prototype machine was delivered by GE in February 1986, and the Honeywell machine arrived at Carnegie Mellon in June 1986. For a period of about a year starting from early 1986, these two prototype machines were used on a daily basis at Carnegie Mellon.

We have implemented application programs in many areas, including low-level vision for robot vehicle navigation, image and signal processing, scientific computing, magnetic resonance imagery (MRI), image processing, radar and sonar simulation, and graph algorithms [3], [4]. In addition, we have developed an image processing library of over 100 routines [17]. Our experience has shown that Warp is effective in these applications; Warp is typically several hundred times faster than a VAX 11/780 class computer.

Encouraged by the performance of the prototype machines, we have revised the Warp architecture for reimplementation on printed circuit (PC) boards to allow faster and more efficient production. The revision also incorporated several architectural improvements. The production Warp machine is referred to as the PC Warp in this paper. The PC Warp is manufactured by GE, and is available at about $350 000 per machine. The first PC Warp machine was delivered by GE in April 1987 to Carnegie Mellon.

This paper describes the architecture of the Warp machine, the rationale of the design and the implementation, and performance measurements for a variety of applications. The organization of the paper is as follows. We first present an overview of the system. We then describe how the overall organization of the array allows us to use the cells efficiently. Next we focus on the cell architecture: we discuss each feature in detail, explaining the design and the evolution of the feature. We conclude this section on the cell with a discussion of hardware implementation issues and metrics. We then describe the architecture of the host system. To give the reader some idea of how the machine can be programmed, we describe the W2 programming language, and some general methods of partitioning a program onto a processor array that has worked well for Warp. To evaluate the Warp machine

Manuscript received February 2, 1987; revised June 15, 1987 and July 27, 1987. This work was supported in part by the Defense Advanced Research Projects Agency (DOD) monitored by the Space and Naval Warfare Systems Command under Contract N00039-85-C-0134, and in part by the Office of Naval Research under Contracts N00014-87-K-0385 and N00014-87-K-0533. Warp is a service mark of Carnegie Mellon. UNIX is a trademark of AT&T Bell Laboratories. Sun-3 is a trademark of Sun Microsystems.

M. Annaratone was with the Department of Computer Science, Carnegie Mellon University, Pittsburgh, PA 15213. He is now with the Institute for Integrated Systems, ETH Zentrum, 8092 Zurich, Switzerland.

E. Arnould, T. Gross, H. T. Kung, M. Lam, O. Menzilcioglu, and J. A. Webb are with the Department of Computer Science, Carnegie Mellon University, Pittsburgh, PA 15213.

IEEE Log Number 8717037.

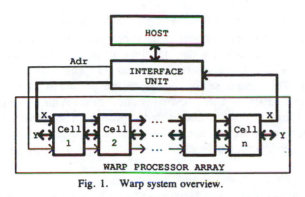

Fig. 1. Warp system overview.

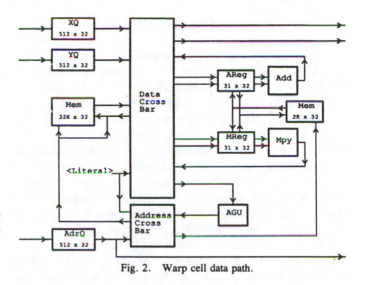

Fig. 2. Warp cell data path.

architecture, we present performance data for a variety of applications on Warp, and a comparison of the architecture of Warp to other parallel machines.

II. WARP SYSTEM OVERVIEW

There are three major components in the system—the Warp processor array (*Warp array*), the interface unit (*IU*), and the *host,* as depicted in Fig. 1. The Warp array performs the computation-intensive routines such as low-level vision routines or matrix operations. The IU handles the input/output between the array and the host, and can generate addresses (Adr) and control signals for the Warp array. The host supplies data to and receives results from the array. In addition, it executes those parts of the application programs which are not mapped onto the Warp array. For example, the host may perform decision-making processes in robot navigation or evaluate convergence criteria in iterative methods for solving systems of linear equations.

The Warp array is a linear systolic array with identical cells, called Warp cells, as shown in Fig. 1. Data flow through the array on two communication channels (X and Y). Those addresses for cells' local memories and control signals that are generated by the IU propagate down the Adr channel. The direction of the *Y* channel is statically configurable. This feature is used, for example, in algorithms that require accumulated results in the last cell to be sent back to the other cells (e.g., in back-solvers), or require local exchange of data between adjacent cells (e.g., in some implementations of numerical relaxation methods).

Each Warp cell is implemented as a programmable horizontal microengine, with its own microsequencer and program memory for 8K instructions. The Warp cell data path, as depicted in Fig. 2, consists of a 32-bit floating-point multiplier (Mpy), a 32-bit floating-point adder (Add), two local memory banks for resident and temporary data (Mem), a queue for each intercell communication channel (XQ, YQ, and AdrQ), and a register file to buffer data for each floating-point unit (AReg and MReg). All these components are connected through a crossbar. Addresses for memory access can be computed locally by the address generation unit (AGU), or taken from the address queue (AdrQ).

The Warp cell data path is similar to the data path of the Floating Point Systems AP-120B/FPS-164 line of processors [9], which are also used as attached processors. Both the Warp cell and any of these FPS processors contain two floating-point units, memory and an address generator, and are oriented

towards scientific computing and signal processing. In both cases, wide instruction words are used for a direct encoding of the hardware resources, and software is used to manage the parallelism (that is, to detect parallelism in the application code, to use the multiple functional units, and to pipeline instructions). The Warp cell differs from these earlier processors in two key aspects: the full crossbar of the Warp cell provides a higher intracell bandwidth, and the X and Y channels with their associated queues provide a high intercell bandwidth, which is unique to the Warp array architecture.

The host consists of a Sun-3 workstation that serves as the *master* controller of the Warp machine, and a VME-based multiprocessor *external host,* so named because it is external to the workstation. The workstation provides a Unix environment for running application programs. The external host controls the peripherals and contains a large amount of memory for storing data to be processed by the Warp array. It also transfers data to and from the Warp array and performs operations on the data when necessary, with low operating system overhead.

Both the Warp cell and IU use off-the-shelf, TTL-compatible parts, and are each implemented on a 15×17 in^2 board. The entire Warp machine, with the exception of the Sun-3, is housed in a single 19 in rack, which also contains power supplies and cooling fans. The machine typically consumes about 1800 W.

III. WARP ARRAY ARCHITECTURE

In the Warp machine, parallelism exists at both the array and cell levels. This section discusses how the Warp architecture is designed to allow efficient use of the array level parallelism. Architectural features to support the cell level parallelism are described in the next section.

The key features in the architecture that support the array level parallelism are simple topology of a linear array, powerful cells with local program control, large data memory for each cell, and high intercell communication bandwidth. These features support several program partitioning methods important to many applications [21], [22]. More details on the partitioning methods are given in Section VII-B, and a sample of applications using these methods is listed in Section VIII.

A linear array is easier for a programmer to use than higher dimensional arrays. Many algorithms in scientific computing and signal processing have been developed for linear arrays [18]. Our experience of using Warp for low-level vision has also shown that a linear organization is suitable in the vision domain as well. A linear array is easy to implement in hardware, and demands a low external I/O bandwidth since only the two end cells communicate with the outside world. Moreover, a linear array consisting of powerful, programmable processors with large local memories can efficiently simulate other interconnection topologies. For example, a single Warp cell can be time multiplexed to perform the function of a column of cells, so that the linear Warp array can implement a two-dimensional systolic array.

The Warp array can be used for both fine-grain and large-grain parallelism. It is efficient for fine-grain parallelism needed for systolic processing, because of its high intercell bandwidth. The I/O bandwidth of each cell is higher than that of other processors with similar computational power. Each cell can transfer 20 million 32-bit words (80 Mbytes) per second to and from its neighboring cells, in addition to 20 million 16-bit addresses. This high intercell communication bandwidth permits efficient transfers of large volumes of intermediate data between neighboring cells.

The Warp array is efficient for large-gain parallelism because it is composed of powerful cells. Each cell is capable of operating independently; it has its own program sequencer and program memory of 8K instructions. Moreover, each cell has 32K words of local data memory, which is large for systolic array designs. For a given I/O bandwidth, a larger data memory can sustain a higher computation bandwidth for some algorithms [20].

Systolic arrays are known to be effective for local operations, in which each output depends only on a small corresponding area of the input. The Warp array's large memory size and its high intercell I/O bandwidth enable it to perform *global* operations in which each output depends on any or a large portion of the input [21]. The ability of performing global operations as well significantly broadens the applicability of the machine. Examples of global operations are fast Fourier transform (FFT), image component labeling, Hough transform, image warping, and matrix computations such as LU decomposition or singular value decomposition (SVD).

Because each Warp cell has its own sequencer and program memory, the cells in the array can execute different programs at the same time. We call computation where all cells execute the same program *homogeneous,* and *heterogeneous* otherwise. Heterogeneous computing is useful for some applications. For example, the end cells may operate differently from other cells to deal with boundary conditions. Or, in a multifunction pipeline [13], different sections of the array perform different functions, with the output of one section feeding into the next as input.

IV. WARP CELL ARCHITECTURE

This section describes the design and the evolution of the architectural features of the cell. Some of these features were significantly revised when we reimplemented Warp on PC boards. For the wire-wrapped prototype, we omitted some architectural features that are difficult to implement and are not necessary for a substantial fraction of application programs [1]. This simplification in the design permitted us to gain useful experience in a relatively short time. With the experience of constructing and using the prototype, we were able to improve the architecture and expand the application domain of the production machine.

A. Intercell Communication

Each cell communicates with its left and right neighbors through point-to-point links, two for data and one for addresses. A queue with a depth of 512 words is associated with each link (XQ, YQ and AdrQ in Fig. 2) and is placed in the data path of the input cell. The size of the queue is just large enough to buffer one or two scan-lines of an image, which is typically of size 512 × 512 or 256 × 256. The ability to buffer a complete scan line is important for the efficient implementation of some algorithms such as two-dimensional convolutions [19]. Words in the queues are 34 bits wide; along with each 32-bit data word, the sender transmits a 2-bit control signal that can be tested by the receiver.

Flow control for the communication channels is implemented in hardware. When a cell tries to read from an empty queue, it is blocked until a data item arrives. Similarly, when a cell tries to write to a full queue of a neighboring cell, the writing cell is blocked until some data are removed from the full queue. The blocking of a cell is transparent to the program; the state of all the computational units on the data path freezes for the duration the cell is blocked. Only the cell that tries to read from an empty queue or to deposit a data item into a full queue is blocked. All other cells in the array continue to operate normally. The data queues of a blocked cell are still able to accept input; otherwise, a cell blocked on an empty queue will never become unblocked.

The implementation of run-time flow control by hardware has two implications. First, we need two clock generators—one for the computational units whose states freeze whenever a cell is blocked, and one for the queues. Second, since a cell can receive data from either of its two neighbors, it can block as a result of the status of the queues in either neighbor, as well as its own. This dependence on other cells adds serious timing constraints to the design since clock control signals have to cross board boundaries. This complexity will be further discussed in Section V.

The intercell communication mechanism is the most revised feature on the cell; it has evolved from primitive programmable delay elements to queues without any flow control hardware, and finally to the run-time flow-controlled queues. In the following, we step through the different design changes.

1) Programmable Delay: In an early design, the input buffer on each communication channel of a cell was a programmable delay element. In a programmable delay element, data are latched in every cycle and they emerge at the output port a constant number of cycles later. This structure is found in many systolic algorithm designs to synchronize or delay one data stream with respect to another. However, programmable high-performance processors like the Warp cells require a more flexible buffering mechanism. Warp programs do not usually produce one data item every cycle; a clocking discipline that reads and writes one item per cycle would be too restrictive. Furthermore, a constant delay through the buffer means that the timing of data generation must match exactly that of data consumption. Therefore, the programmable delays were replaced by queues to remove the tight coupling between the communicating cells.

2) Flow Control: Queues allow the receiver and sender to run at their own speeds provided that the receiver does not read past the end of the queue and the sender does not overflow the queues. There are two different flow control disciplines, run-time and compile-time flow-control. As discussed above, hardware support for run-time flow control can be difficult to design, implement, and debug. Alternatively, for a substantial set of problems in our application domain, compile-time flow control can be implemented by generating code that requires no run-time support. Therefore, we elected not to support run-time flow control in the prototype. This decision permitted us to accelerate the implementation and experimentation cycle. Run-time flow control is provided in the production machine, so as to widen the application domain of the machine.

Compile-time flow control can be provided for all programs where data only flow in one direction through the array and where the control flow of the programs is not data dependent. Data dependent control flow and two-way data flow can also be allowed for programs satisfying some restrictions [6]. Compile-time flow control is implemented by skewing the computation of the cells so that no receiving cell reads from a queue before the corresponding sending cell writes to it. For example, suppose two adjacent cells each execute the following program:

> **dequeue (X);**
> **output (X) ;**
> **dequeue (X);**
> **compute   ;**
> **compute   ;**
> **output (X) ;**

In this program, the first cell removes a data item from the X queue (**dequeue (X)**) and sends it to the second cell on **X** (**output (X)**). The first cell then removes a second item, and forwards the result to the second cell after two cycles of computation. For this program, the second cell needs to be delayed by three cycles to ensure that the **dequeue** of the second cell never overtakes the corresponding **output** of the first cell, and the compiler will insert the necessary **nops**, as shown in Fig. 3.

Run-time flow control expands the application domain of the machine and often allows the compiler to produce more efficient code; therefore, it is provided in the production machine. Without run-time flow control, WHILE loops and FOR loops and computed loop bounds on the cells cannot be implemented. That is, only loops with compile-time constant bounds can be supported. This restriction limits the class of

First cell	Second cell
dequeue(X);	nop ;
output(X) ;	nop ;
dequeue(X);	nop ;
compute ;	dequeue(X);
compute ;	output(X) ;
output(X) ;	dequeue(X);
	compute ;
	compute ;
	output(X) ;

Fig. 3.   Compile-time flow control.

programs executable on the machine. Moreover, many programs for the prototype machines can be made more efficient and easier to write by replacing the FOR loops with WHILE loops. For example, instead of executing a fixed number of iterations to guarantee convergence, the iteration can be stopped as soon as the termination condition is met. The compiler can produce more efficient code since compile-time flow control relies on delaying the receiving cell sufficiently to guarantee correct behavior, but this delay is not necessarily the minimum delay needed. Run-time flow control will dynamically find the minimum bound.

3) Input Control: In the current design, latching of data into a cell's queue is controlled by the sender, rather than by the receiver. As a cell sends data to its neighbor, it also signals the receiving cell's input queue to accept the data.

In our first two-cell prototype machine, input data were latched under the microinstruction control of the receiving cell. This implied that intercell communication required close cooperation between the sender and the receiver; the sender presented its data on the communication channel, and in the same clock cycle the receiver latched in the input. This design was obviously not adequate if flow control was supported at run time; in fact, we discovered that it was not adequate even if flow control was provided at compile time. The tight coupling between the sender and the receiver greatly increased the code size of the programs. The problem was corrected in subsequent implementations by adopting the design we currently have, that is, the sender provides the signal to the receiver's queue to latch in the input data.

In the above discussion of the example of Fig. 3, it was assumed that the control for the second cell to latch in input was sent with the output data by the first cell. If the second cell were to provide the input control signals, we would need to add an **input** operation in its microprogram for every **output** operation of the first cell, at exactly the cycle the operation takes place. Doing so, we obtain the following program for the second cell:

	nop ;
input (X)	;
	nop ;
	dequeue (X);
	output (X) ;
input (X),	dequeue (X);
	compute ;
	compute ;
	output (X) ;

Each line in the program is a microinstruction; the first column

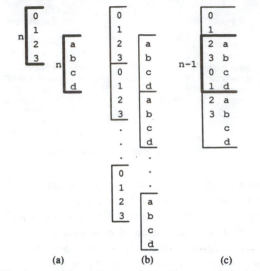

Fig. 4. Merging equal-length loops with an offset. (a) Original loops. (b) Execution trace. (c) Merged loop.

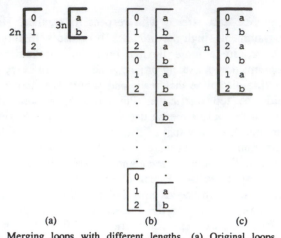

Fig. 5. Merging loops with different lengths. (a) Original loops. (b) Execution trace. (c) Merged loop.

contains the **Input** operations to match the **Output** operations of the first cell, and the second column contains the original program.

Since the input sequence follows the control flow of the sender, each cell is logically executing two processes: the input process, and the original computation process of its own. These two processes must be merged into one since there is only one sequencer on each cell. If the programs on communicating cells are different, the input process and the cell's own computation process are different. Even if the cell programs are identical, the cell's computation process may need to be delayed with respect to the input process because of compile-time flow control as described above. As a result, we may need to merge control constructs from different parts of the program. Merging two equal-length loops, with an offset between their initiation times, requires loop unrolling and can result in a threefold increase in code length. Fig. 4 illustrates this increase in code length when merging two identical loops of n iterations. Numbers represent operations of the input process, and letters represent the computation process. If two iterative statements of different lengths are overlapped, then the resulting code size can be of the order of the least common multiple of their lengths. For example, in Fig. 5, a two-instruction loop of $3n$ iterations is merged with a three-instruction loop of $2n$ iterations. Since 6 is the minimum number of cycles before the combined sequence of operations repeats itself, the resulting merged program is a six-instruction loop of n iterations.

4) Randomly Accessible Queues: The queues in all the prototype machines are implemented with RAM chips, with hardware queue pointers. Furthermore, there was a feedback path from the data crossbar back to the queues, because we intended to use the queues as local storage elements as well [1]. Since the pointers must be changed when the queue is accessed randomly, and there is only a single pair of queue pointers, it is impossible to multiplex the use of the buffer as a communication queue and its use as a local storage element. Therefore, the queues in the production machine are now implemented by a FIFO chip. This implementation allows us

to increase the queue size from 128 to 512 words, with board space left over for other improvements as well.

5) Queue Size: The size of the queues is an important factor in the efficiency of the array. Queues buffer the input for a cell and relax the coupling of execution in communicating cells. Although the average communication rate between two communicating cells must balance, a larger buffer allows the cells to receive and send data in bursts at different times.

The long queues allow the compiler to adopt a simple code optimization strategy [23]. The throughput for a unidirectional array is maximized by simply optimizing the individual cell programs provided that sufficient buffering is available between each pair of adjacent cells. In addition, some algorithms, such as two-dimensional convolution mentioned above, require large buffers between cells. If the queues are not large enough, a program must explicitly implement buffers in local memory.

B. Control Path

Each Warp cell has its own local program memory and sequencer. This is a good architectural design even if the cells all execute the same program, as in the case of the prototype Warp machine. The reason is that it is difficult to broadcast the microinstruction words to all the cells, or to propagate them from cell to cell, since the instructions contain a large number of bits. Moreover, even if the cells execute the same program, the computations of the cells are often skewed so that each cell is delayed with respect to its neighboring cell. This skewed computation model is easily implemented with local program control. The local sequencer also supports conditional branching efficiently. In SIMD machines, branching is achieved by masking. The execution time is equivalent to the sum of the execution time of the then-clause and the else-clause of a branch. With local program control, different cells may follow different branches of a conditional statement depending on their individual data; the execution time is the execution time of the clause taken.

The Warp cell is horizontally microcoded. Each component in the data path is controlled by a dedicated field; this orthogonal organization of the microinstruction word makes scheduling easier since there is no interference in the schedule of different components.

C. Data Path

1) Floating-Point Units: Each Warp cell has two floating-point units, one multiplier and one adder, implemented with commercially available floating-point chips [35]. These floating-point chips depend on extensive pipelining to achieve high performance. Both the adder and multiplier have five-stage pipelines. General purpose computation is difficult to implement efficiently on deeply pipelined machines because data-dependent branching is common. There is less data dependency in numerical or computer vision programs, and we developed scheduling techniques that use the pipelining efficiently. Performance results are reported in Section VIII.

2) Crossbar: Experience with the Programmable Systolic Chip showed that the internal data bandwidth is often the bottleneck of a systolic cell [11]. In the Warp cell, the two floating-point units can consume up to four data items and generate two results per cycle. Several data storage blocks interconnected with a crossbar support this high data processing rate. There are six input and eight output ports connected to the crossbar switch; up to six data items can be transferred in a single cycle, and an output port can receive any data item. The use of the crossbar also makes compilation easier when compared to a bus-based system since conflicts on the use of one or more shared buses can complicate scheduling tremendously.

Custom chip designs that combine the functionality of the crossbar interconnection and data buffers have been proposed [16], [28]. In the interconnection chip designed for polycyclic architectures [28], a "queue" is associated with each cross point of the crossbar. In these storage blocks, data are always written at the end of the queue; however, data can be read, or removed, from any location. The queues are compacted automatically whenever data are removed. The main advantage of this design is that an optimal code schedule can be readily derived for a class of inner loops [27]. In the Warp cell architecture, we chose to use a conventional crossbar with data buffers only for its outputs (the AReg and MReg register files in Fig. 2), because of the lower hardware cost. Near-optimal schedules can be found cheaply using heuristics [23].

3) Data Storage Blocks: As depicted by Fig. 2, the local memory hierarchy includes a local data memory, a register file for the integer unit (AGU), two register files (one for each floating-point unit), and a backup data memory. Addresses for both data memories come from the address crossbar. The local data memory can store 32K words, and can be both read and written every (200 ns) cycle. The capacity of the register file in the AGU unit is 64 words. The register files for the floating-point units each hold 31 usable words of data. (The register file is written to in every cycle so that one word is used as a sink for those cycles without useful write operations.) They are five-ported data buffers and each can accept two data items from the crossbar and deliver two operands to the functional units every cycle. The additional ports are used for connecting the register files to the backup memory. This backup memory contains 2K words and is used to hold all scalars, floating-point constants, and small arrays. The addition of the backup memory increases memory bandwidth and improves throughput for those programs operating mainly on local data.

4) Address Generation: As shown in Fig. 2, each cell contains an integer unit (AGU) that is used predominantly as a local address generation unit. The AGU is a self-contained integer ALU with 64 registers. It can compute up to two addresses per cycle (one read address and one write address).

The local address generator on the cell is one of the enhancements that distinguish the PC Warp machine from the prototype. In the prototype, data independent addresses were generated on the IU and propagated down the cells. Data dependent addresses were computed locally on each cell using the floating-point units. The IU of the prototype had the additional task of generating the loop termination signals for the cells. These signals were propagated along the Adr channel to the cells in the Warp array.

There was not enough space on the wire-wrapped board to include local address generation capability on each Warp cell. Including an AGU requires board space not only for the AGU itself, but also for its environment and the bits in the instruction word for controlling it. An AGU was area expensive at the time the prototype was designed, due to the lack of VLSI parts for the AGU functions. The address generation unit in the prototype IU uses AMD2901 parts which contain 16 registers. Since this number of registers is too small to generate complicated addressing patterns quickly, the ALU is backed up by a table that holds up to 16K precomputed addresses. This table is too large to replicate on all the cells. The address generation unit on the PC Warp cells is a new VLSI component (IDT-49C402), which combines the 64-word register file and ALU on a single chip. The large number of registers makes the backup table unnecessary for most addressing patterns, so that the AGU is much smaller and can be replicated on each cell of the production machine.

The prototype was designed for applications where all cells execute the same program with data independent loop bounds. However, not all such programs could be supported due to the size of the address queue. In the pipelining mode, where the cells implement different stages of a computation pipeline, a cell does not start executing until the preceding cell is finished with the first set of input data. The size of the address queue must at least equal the number of addresses and control signals used in the computation of the data set. Therefore, the size of the address queues limits the number of addresses buffered, and thus the grain size of parallelism.

For the production machine, each cell contains an AGU and can generate addresses and loop control signals efficiently. This improvement allows the compiler to support a much larger class of application. We have preserved the address generator and address bank on the IU (and the associated Adr channel, as shown in Fig. 1). Therefore, the IU can still support those homogeneous computations that demand a small set of complicated addressing patterns that can be conveniently stored in the address bank.

V. Warp Cell and IU Implementation

The Warp array architecture operates on 32-bit data. All data channels in the Warp array, including the internal data path of the cell, are implemented as 16-bit wide channels operating at 100 ns. There are two reasons for choosing a 16-

TABLE I		
IMPLEMENTATION METRICS FOR WARP CELL		
Block in Warp cell	Chip count	Area contribution (Percent)
Queues	22	9
Crossbar	32	11
Processing elements and registers	12	10
Data memory	31	9
Local address generator	13	6
Microengine	90	35
Other	55	20
Total for Warp cell	255	100

TABLE II		
IMPLEMENTATION METRICS FOR IU		
Block in IU	Chip count	Area contribution (Percent)
Data-converter	44	19
Address generator	45	19
Clock and host interface	101	31
Microengine	49	20
Other	25	11
Total for IU	264	100

bit time-multiplexed implementation. First, a 32-bit wide hardware path would not allow implementing one cell per board. Second, the 200 ns cycle time dictated by the Weitek floating-point chips (at the time of design) allows the rest of the data path to be time multiplexed. This would not have been possible if the cycle time of the floating-point chips were under 160 ns. The microengine operates at 100 ns and supports high and low cycle operations of the data path separately.

All cells in the array are driven from a global 20 MHz clock generated by the IU. To allow each cell to block individually, a cell must have control over the use of the global clock signals. Each cell monitors two concurrent processes: the input data flow (*I* process) and the output data flow (*O* process). If the input data queue is empty, the *I* process flow must be suspended before the next read from the queue. Symmetrically, the *O* process is stopped before the next write whenever the input queue of the neighboring cell is full. Stopping the *I* or *O* process pauses all computation and output activity, but the cell continues to accept input. There is only a small amount of time available between detection of the queue full/empty status and blocking the read/write operation. Since the cycle time is only 100 ns, this tight timing led to race conditions in an early design. This problem has been solved by duplicating on each cell the status of the I/O processes of the neighboring cells. In this way, a cell can anticipate a queue full/empty condition and react within a clock cycle.

A large portion of the internal cell hardware can be monitored and tested using built-in serial diagnostic chains under control of the IU. The serial chains are also used to download the Warp cell programs. Identical programs can be downloaded to all cells at a rate of 100 μs per instruction from the workstation and about 67 μs per instruction from the external host. Starting up a program takes about 5 ms.

The Warp cell consists of six main blocks: input queues, crossbar, processing elements, data memory, address generator, and microengine. Table I presents the contribution of these blocks to the implementation of the Warp cell. The microengine includes the program memory (8K instruction words of 272 bits, including parity). The Warp cell consumes 94 W (typical) and 136 W (maximum).

The IU handles data input/output between the host and the Warp array. The host–IU interface is streamlined by implementing a 32-bit wide interface, even though the Warp array has only 16-bit wide internal data paths. This arrangement is preferred because data transfers between the host and IU are

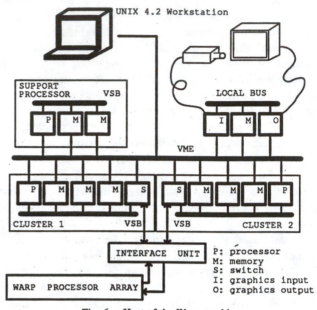
Fig. 6. Host of the Warp machine.

slower than the transfers between IU and the array. Data transfers between the host and IU can be controlled by interrupts; in this case, the IU behaves like a slave device. The IU can also convert packed 8-bit integers transferred from the host into 32-bit floating-point numbers for the Warp array, and vice versa.

The IU is controlled by a 96-bit wide programmable microengine, which is similar to the Warp cell controller in programmability. The IU has several control registers that are mapped into the host address space; the host can control the IU and hence the Warp array by setting these registers. The IU has a power consumption of 82 W (typical) and 123 W (maximum). Table II presents implementation metrics for the IU.

VI. HOST SYSTEM

The Warp host controls the Warp array and other peripherals, supports fast data transfer rates to and from the Warp array, and also runs application code that cannot easily be mapped on the array. An overview of the host is presented in Fig. 6. The host is partitioned into a standard workstation (the master) and an external host. The workstation provides a Unix programming environment to the user, and also controls the external host. The external host consists of two *cluster processors,* a subsystem called *support processor,* and some graphics devices.

Control of the external host is strictly centralized: the workstation, the master processor, issues commands to the cluster and support processors through message buffers local to each of these processors. The two clusters work in parallel, each handling a unidirectional flow of data to or from the Warp processor through the IU. The two clusters can exchange their roles in sending or receiving data for different phases of a computation, in a ping-pong fashion. An arbitration mechanism transparent to the user has been implemented to prohibit simultaneous writing or reading to the Warp array when the clusters switch roles. The support processor controls peripheral I/O devices and handles floating-point exceptions and other interrupt signals from the Warp array. These interrupts are serviced by the support processor, rather than by the master processor, to minimize interrupt response time. After servicing the interrupt, the support processor notifies the master processor.

The external host is built around a VME bus. The two clusters and the support processor each consist of a standalone MC68020 microprocessor (P) and a dual-ported memory (M), which can be accessed either via a local bus or via the global VME bus. The local bus is a VSB bus in the production machine and a VMX32 bus for the prototype; the major improvements of VSB over VMX32 are better support for arbitration and the addition of DMA-type accesses. Each cluster has a *switch* board (S) for sending and receiving data to and from the Warp array, through the IU. The switch also has a VME interface, used by the master processor to start, stop, and control the Warp array. The VME bus of the master processor inside the workstation is connected to the VME bus of the external host via a bus-coupler (bus repeater). While the prototype Warp used a commercial bus-coupler, the PC Warp employs a custom-designed device. The difference between the two is that the custom-designed bus repeater decouples the external host VME bus from the Sun-3 VME bus: intrabus transfers can occur concurrently on both buses.

There are three memory banks inside each cluster processor to support concurrent memory accesses. For example, the first memory bank may be receiving a new set of data from an I/O device, while data in the second bank are transferred to the Warp array, and the third contains the cluster program code.

Presently, the memory of the external host is built out of 1 Mbyte memory boards; including the 3 Mbytes of memory on the processor boards, the total memory capacity of the external host is 11 Mybtes. An expansion of up to 59 Mbytes is possible by populating all the 14 available slots of the VME card cage with 4 Mbyte memory boards. Large data structures can be stored in these memories where they will not be swapped out by the operating system. This is important for consistent performance in real-time applications. The external host can also support special devices such as frame buffers and high-speed disks. This allows the programmer to transfer data directly between Warp and other devices.

Except for the switch, all boards in the external host are off-the-shelf components. The industry standard boards allow us to take advantage of commercial processors, I/O boards, memory, and software. They also make the host an open system to which it is relatively easy to add new devices and interfaces to other computers. Moreover, standard boards provide a growth path for future system improvements with a minimal investment of time and resources. During the transition from prototype to production machine, faster processor boards (from 12 to 16 MHz) and larger memories have been introduced, and they have been incorporated into the host with little effort.

A. Host I/O Bandwidth

The Warp array can input a 32-bit word and output a 32-bit word every 200 ns. Correspondingly, to sustain this peak rate, each cluster must be able to read or write a 32-bit data item every 200 ns. This peak I/O bandwidth requirement can be satisfied if the input and output data are 8-bit or 16-bit integers that can be accessed sequentially.

In signal, image, and low-level vision processing, the input and output data are usually 16- or 8-bit integers. The data can be packed into 32-bit words before being transferred to the IU, which unpacks the data into two or four 32-bit floating-point numbers before sending them to the Warp array. The reverse operation takes place with the floating-point outputs of the Warp array. With this packing and unpacking, the data bandwidth requirement between the host and IU is reduced by a factor of two or four. Image data can be packed on the digitizer boards, without incurring overhead on the host.

The I/O bandwidth of the PC Warp external host is greatly improved over that of the prototype machine [5]. The PC Warp supports DMA and uses faster processor and memory boards. If the data transfer is sequential, DMA can be used to achieve the transfer time of less than 500 ns per word. With block transfer mode, this transfer time is further reduced to about 350 ns. The speed for nonsequential data transfers depends on the complexity of the address computation. For simple address patterns, one 32-bit word is transferred in about 900 ns.

There are two classes of applications: those whose input/output data are pixel values (e.g., vision), and those whose input/output data are floating-point quantities (e.g., scientific computing). In vision applications, data are often transferred in raster order. By packing/unpacking the pixels and using DMA, the host I/O bandwidth can sustain the maximum bandwidth of all such programs. Many of the applications that need floating-point input and output data have nonsequential data access patterns. The host becomes a bottleneck if the rate of data transfer (and address generation if DMA cannot be used) is lower than the rate the data are processed on the array. Fortunately, for many scientific applications, the computation per data item is typically quite large and the host I/O bandwidth is seldom the limiting factor in the performance of the array.

B. Host Software

The Warp host has a run-time software library that allows the programmer to synchronize the support processor and two clusters and to allocate memory in the external host. The run-time software also handles the communication and interrupts between the master and the processors in the external host.

The library of run-time routines includes utilities such as copying and moving data within the host system, subwindow selection of images, and peripheral device drivers. The compiler generates program-specific input and output routines for the clusters so that a user need not be concerned with programming at this level; these routines are linked at load time to the two cluster processor libraries.

The application program usually runs on the Warp array under control of the master; however, it is possible to assign subtasks to any of the processors in the external host. This decreases the execution time for two reasons: there is more parallelism in the computation, and data transfers between the cluster and the array using the VSB bus are twice as fast as transfers between the master processor and the array through the VME bus repeater. The processors in the external host have been extensively used in various applications, for example, obstacle avoidance for a robot vehicle and singular value decomposition.

Memory allocation and processor synchronization inside the external host are handled by the application program through subroutine calls to the run-time software. Memory is allocated through the equivalent of a Unix *malloc( )* system call, the only difference being that the memory bank has to be explicitly specified. This explicit control allows the user to fully exploit the parallelism of the system; for example, different processors can be programmed to access different memory banks through different busses concurrently.

Tasks are scheduled by the master processor. The application code can schedule a task to be run on the completion of a different task. Once the master processor determines that one task has completed, it schedules another task requested by the application code. Overhead for this run-time scheduling of tasks is minimal.

VII. PROGRAMMING WARP

As mentioned in the Introduction, Warp is programmed in a language called W2. Programs written in W2 are translated by an optimizing compiler into object code for the Warp machine. W2 hides the low-level details of the machine and allows the user to concentrate on the problem of mapping an application onto a processor array. In this section, we first describe the language and then some common computation partitioning techniques.

A. The W2 Language

The W2 language provides an abstract programming model of the machine that allows the user to focus on parallelism at the array level. The user views the Warp system as a linear array of identical, conventional processors that can communicate asynchronously with their left and right neighbors. The semantics of the communication primitives is that a cell will block if it tries to receive from any empty queue or send to a full one. This semantics is enforced at compile time in the prototype and at run time in the PC Warp, as explained in Section IV-A-2.

The user supplies the code to be executed on each cell, and the compiler handles the details of code generation and scheduling. This arrangement gives the user full control over

```
module MatrixMultiply (A in, B in, C out)
float A[10,10], B[10,10], C[10,10];

cellprogram (cid : 0 : 9)
begin
    function mm
    begin
        float col[10]; /* stores a column of the B matrix */
        float row;     /* accumulates the result of a row */
        float element;
        float temp;
        int i,j;

        /* first load a column of B in each cell */
        for i := 0 to 9 do begin
            receive (L, X, col[i], B[i,0]);
            for j := 1 to 9 do begin
                receive (L, X, temp, B[i,j]);
                send (R, X, temp);
            end;
            send (R, X, 0.0);
        end;

        /* calculate a row of C in each iteration */
        for i := 0 to 9 do begin
            /*  each cell computes the dot product
                between its column and the same row of A */
            row := 0.0;
            for j := 0 to 9 do begin
                receive (L, X, element, A[i,j]);
                send (R, X, element);
                row := row + element * col[j];
            end;

            /*  send out the result of each row of C */
            receive (L, Y, temp, 0.0);
            for j := 0 to 8 do begin
                receive (L, Y, temp, 0.0);
                send (R, Y, temp, C[i,j]);
            end;
            send (R, Y, row, C[i,9]);
        end;
    end
    call mm;
end
```

Fig. 7.   Example W2 program.

computation partitioning and algorithm design. The language for describing the cell code is Algol-like, with iterative and conditional statements. In addition, the language provides receive and send primitives for specifying intercell communication. The compiler handles the parallelism both at the system and cell levels. At the system level, the external host and the IU are hidden from the user. The compiler generates code for the host and the IU to transfer data between the host and the array. Moreover, for the prototype Warp, addresses and loop control signals are automatically extracted from the cell programs; they are generated on the IU and passed down the address queue. At the cell level, the pipelining and parallelism in the data path of the cells are hidden from the user. The compiler uses global data flow analysis and horizontal microcode scheduling techniques, software pipelining and hierarchical reduction to generate efficient microcode directly from high-level language constructs [12], [23].

Fig. 7 is an example of a 10 × 10 matrix multiplication program. Each cell computes one column of the result. We first load each cell with a column of the second matrix operand, then we stream the first matrix in row by row. As each row passes through the array, we accumulate the result for a column in each cell, and send the entire row of results to the host. The loading and unloading of data are slightly complicated because all cells execute the same program. **Send** and **receive** transfer data between adjacent cells; the first parameter determines the direction, and the second parameter selects the hardware channel to be used. The third parameter specifies the source (send) or the sink (receive). The fourth parameter, only applicable to those channels communicating with the host, binds the array input and output to the formal parameters of the cell programs. This information is used by the compiler to generate code for the host.

B. Program Partitioning

As discussed in Section III, the architecture of the Warp array can support various kinds of algorithms: fine-grain or large-grain parallelism, local or global operations, homogeneous or heterogeneous. There are three general program partitioning methods [4], [22]: *input partitioning, output partitioning*, and *pipelining*.

1) Input Partitioning: In this model, the input data are partitioned among the Warp cells. Each cell computes on its portion of the input data to produce a corresponding portion of the output data. This model is useful in image processing where the result at each point of the output image depends only on a small neighborhood of the corresponding point of the input image.

Input partitioning is a simple and powerful method for exploiting parallelism—most parallel machines support it in one form or another. Many of the algorithms on Warp make use of it, including most of the low-level vision programs, the discrete cosine transform (DCT), singular value decomposition [2], connected component labeling [22], border following, and the convex hull. The last three algorithms mentioned also transmit information in other ways; for example, connected components labeling first partitions the image by rows among the cells, labels each cell's portion separately, and then combines the labels from different portions to create a global labeling.

2) Output Partitioning: In this model, each Warp cell processes the entire input data set or a large part of it, but produces only part of the output. This model is used when the input to output mapping is not regular, or when any input can influence any output. Histogram and image warping are examples of such computations. This model usually requires a lot of memory because either the required input data set must be stored and then processed later, or the output must be stored in memory while the input is processed, and then output later. Each Warp cell has 32K words of local memory to support efficient use of this model.

3) Pipelining: In this model, typical of systolic computation, the algorithm is partitioned among the cells in the array, and each cell performs one stage of the processing. The Warp array's high intercell communication bandwidth and effectiveness in handling fine-grain parallelism make it possible to use this model. For some algorithms, this is the only method of achieving parallelism.

A simple example of the use of pipelining is the solution of elliptic partial differential equations using successive overrelaxation [36]. Consider the following equation:

$$\frac{\partial^2 u}{\partial x^2} + \frac{\partial^2 u}{\partial y^2} = f(x, y).$$

The system is solved by repeatedly combining the current values of u on a two-dimensional grid using the following recurrence.

$$u'_{i,j} = (1 - \omega)u_{i,j} + \omega \frac{f_{i,j} + u_{i,j-1} + u_{i,j+1} + u_{i+1,j} + u_{i-1,j}}{4},$$

where ω is a constant parameter.

In the Warp implementation, each cell is responsible for one relaxation, as expressed by the above equation. In raster order, each cell receives inputs from the preceding cell, performs its relaxation step, and outputs the results to the next cell. While a cell is performing the kth relaxation step on row i, the preceding and next cells perform the $k - 1$st and $k + 1$st relaxation steps on rows $i + 2$ and $i - 2$, respectively. Thus, in one pass of the u values through the ten-cell Warp array, the above recurrence is applied ten times. This process is repeated, under control of the external host, until convergence is achieved.

VIII. Evaluation

Since the two copies of the wire-wrapped prototype Warp machine became operational at Carnegie Mellon in 1986, we have used the machines substantially in various applications [2]–[4], [10], [13], [22]. The application effort has been increased since April 1987 when the first PC Warp machine was delivered to Carnegie Mellon.

The applications area that guided the development of Warp most strongly was computer vision, particularly as applied to robot navigation. We studied a standard library of image processing algorithms [30] and concluded that the great majority of algorithms could efficiently use the Warp machine. Moreover, robot navigation is an area of active research at Carnegie Mellon and has real-time requirements where Warp can make a significant difference in overall performance [32], [33]. Since the requirements of computer vision had a significant influence on all aspects of the design of Warp, we contrast the Warp machine with other architectures directed towards computer vision in Section VIII-B.

Our first effort was to develop applications that used Warp for robot navigation. Presently mounted inside of a robot vehicle, Warp has been used to perform road following and obstacle avoidance. We have implemented road following using color classification, obstacle avoidance using stereo vision, obstacle avoidance using a laser range-finder, and path planning using dynamic programming. We have also implemented a significant image processing library (over 100 programs) on Warp [30], to support robot navigation and vision research in general. Some of the library routines are listed in Table IV.

A second interest was in using Warp in signal processing and scientific computing. Warp's high floating-point computation rate and systolic structure make it especially attractive for these applications. We have implemented singular value decomposition (SVD) for adaptive beam forming, fast two-dimensional image correlation using FFT, successive overrelaxation (SOR) for the solution of elliptic partial differential equations (PDE), as well as computational geometry al-

TABLE III
MEASURED SPEEDUPS ON THE WIRE-WRAPPED PROTOTYPE WARP
MACHINE

Task (All images are 512×512. All code compiler generated.)	Time (ms)	Speedup over Vax 11/780 with floating-point accelerator
Quadratic image warping	400	100
Warp array generates addresses using quadratic form in 240 ms.		
Host computes output image using addresses generated by Warp.		
Road-following	6000	200
Obstacle avoidance using ERIM, a laser range-finder	350	60
Time does not include 500 ms for scanner I/O.		
Minimum-cost path, 512×512 image, one pass	500	60
Host provides feedback.		
Detecting lines by Hough Transform	2000	387
Host merges results.		
Minimum-cost path, 350-node graph	16000	98
Convex hull, 1,000 random nodes	18	74
Solving elliptic PDE by SOR, 50,625 unknowns (10 iterations)	180	440
Singular value decomposition of 100×100 matrix	1500	100
FFT on 2D image	2500	300
Warp array takes 600 ms. Remaining time is for data shuffling by host.		
Image correlation using FFT	7000	300
Data shuffling in host.		
Image compression with 8×8 discrete cosine transforms	110	500
Mandelbrot image, 256 iterations	6960	100

Task All images are 512×512. All code compiler generated.	Time (ms)	MFLOPS (Upper bound)	MFLOPS (Achieved)
100×100 matrix multiplication.	25	100	79
3×3 convolution.	70	94	66
11×11 symmetric convolution.	367	90	59
Calculate transformation table for non-linear warping.	248	80	57
Generate matrices for plane fit for obstacle avoidance using ERIM scanner.	174	62	49
Generate mapping table for affine image warping.	225	67	43
Moravec's interest operator.	82	60	36
3×3 maximum filtering.	280	67	30
Sobel edge detection.	206	77	30
Label color image using quadratic form for road following.	308	87	27
Image magnification using cubic spline interpolation.	8438	66	25
7×7 average gray values in square neighborhood.	1090	51	24
5×5 convolution.	284	52	23
Calculate quadratic form from labelled color image.	134	58	22
Compute gradient using 9×9 Canny operator.	473	92	21
Discrete cosine transform on 8×8 windows.	175	94	21
3×3 Laplacian edge detection.	228	94	20
15×15 Harwood-style symmetric edge preserving smoothing.	32000	50	16
Find zero-crossings.	179	78	16
Calculate (x,y,z) coordinates from ERIM laser range scanner data.	24	75	13
Histogram.	67	50	12
Coarse-to-fine correlation for stereo vision.	12	77	11
3×3 median filter.	448	50	7
Levialdi's binary shrink operation.	180	71	7
31×31 average gray values in square neighborhood.	444	61	5
Convert real image to integer using max, min linear scaling.	249	66	4
Average 512×512 image to produce 256×256.	150	58	3

gorithms such as convex hull and algorithms for finding the shortest paths in a graph.

A. Performance Data

Two figures of merit are used to evaluate the performance of Warp. One is overall system performance, and the other is performance on specific algorithms. Table III presents Warp's performance in several systems for robot navigation, signal processing, scientific computation, and geometric algorithms, while Table IV presents Warp's performance on a large number of specific algorithms. Both tables report the performance for the wire-wrapped Warp prototype with a Sun-3/160 as the master processor. The PC Warp will in general exceed the reported performance, because of its improved architec-

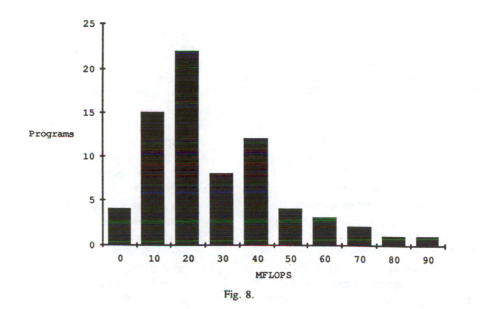

Fig. 8.

ture and increased host I/O speed as described earlier. Table III includes all system overheads except for initial program memory loading. We compare the performance of Warp to a VAX 11/780 with floating-point accelerator because this computer is widely used and, therefore, familiar to most people.

Statistics have been gathered for a collection of 72 W2 programs in the application areas of vision, signal processing, and scientific computing [23]. Table IV presents the utilization of the Warp array for a sample of these programs. System overheads such as microcode loading and program initialization are not counted. We assume that the host I/O can keep up with the Warp array; this assumption is realistic for most applications with the host of the production Warp machine. Fig. 8 shows the performance distribution of the 72 programs. The arithmetic mean is 28 MFLOPS, and the standard deviation is 18 MFLOPS.

The Warp cell has several independent functional units, including separate floating-point units for addition and multiplication. The achievable performance of a program is limited by the most used resource. For example, in a computation that contains only additions and no multiplications, the maximum achievable performance is only 50 MFLOPS. Table IV gives an upper bound on the achievable performance and the achieved performance. The upper bound is obtained by assuming that the floating-point unit that is used more often in the program is the most used resource, and that it can be kept busy all the time. That is, this upper bound cannot be met even with a perfect compiler if the most used resource is some other functional unit, such as the memory, or if data dependencies in the computation prevent the most used resource from being used all the time.

Many of the programs in Tables III and IV are coded without fine tuning the W2 code. Optimizations can often provide a significant speedup over the times given. First, the W2 code can be optimized, using conventional programming techniques such as unrolling loops with few iterations, replacing array references by scalars, and so on. Second, in some cases in Table III the external host in the prototype Warp

is a bottleneck, and it is possible to speed up this portion of the Warp machine by recoding the I/O transfer programs generated by the W2 compiler in MC68020 Assembly language. Moreover, the external host for the PC Warp is faster and supports DMA, so that even with the compiler generated code it will no longer be the bottleneck. Third, since restrictions on using the Warp cells in a pipeline are removed in PC Warp as explained in Section IV-B-4, it will be possible to implement many of the vision algorithms in a pipelining fashion. This can lead to a threefold speedup, since input, computation, and output will be done at the same time. Fourth, in a few cases we have discovered a better algorithm for the Warp implementation than what was originally programmed.

In Table III, the speedup ranges from 60 to 500. With the optimizations we discuss above, all systems listed should show at least a speedup of about 100 over the VAX 11/780 with a floating-point accelerator.

B. Architectural Alternatives

We discuss the architectural decisions made in Warp by contrasting them with the decisions made in bit-serial processor arrays, such as the Connection Machine [34] and MPP [7]. We chose these architectures because they have also been used extensively for computer vision and image processing, and because the design choices in these architectures were made significantly differently than in Warp. These differences help exhibit and clarify the design space for the Warp architecture.

We attempt to make our comparison quantitative by using benchmark data from a DARPA Image Understanding ("DARPA IU") workshop held in November 1986 to compare various computers for vision [29]. In this workshop, benchmarks for low and midlevel computer vision were defined and programmed by researchers on a wide variety of computers, including Warp and the Connection Machine [25].

We briefly review salient features of the Connection Machine, called CM-1, used in these benchmarks. It is a SIMD machine, consisting of an array of 64K bit-serial processing elements, each with 4K bits of memory. The processors are connected by two networks: one connects each processor to four adjacent processors, and the other is a 12-dimensional hypercube, connecting groups of 16 processors. The array is controlled by a host, which is a Symbolics 3640 Lisp machine. CM-1 is programmed in an extension to Common Lisp called *Lisp [24], in which references to data objects stored in the CM-1 array and objects on the host can be intermixed.

Although our intention is to illustrate architectural decisions made in Warp, not to compare it to the Connection Machine, we should not cite benchmark performance figures on two different computers without mentioning two critical factors, namely cost and size. CM-1 is approximately one order of magnitude more expensive and larger than Warp.

1) Programming Model: Bit-serial processor arrays implement a *data parallel* programming model, in which different processors process different elements of the data set. In the Connection Machine, the programmer manipulates data objects stored in the Connection Machine array by the use of primitives in which the effect of a Lisp operator is distributed over a data object.

In systolic arrays, the processors individually manipulate words of data. In Warp, we have implemented data parallel programming models through the use of input and output partitioning. We have encapsulated input partitioning over images in a specialized language called Apply [14]. In addition to these models, the high interprocessor bandwidth of the systolic array allows efficient implementation of pipelining, in which not the data, but the algorithm is partitioned.

2) Processor I/O Bandwidth and Topology: Systolic arrays have high bandwidth between processors, which are organized in a simple topology. In the case of the Warp array, this is the simplest possible topology, namely a linear array. The interconnection networks in the Connection Machine allow flexible topology, but low bandwidth between communicating processors.

Bit-serial processor arrays may suffer from a serious bottleneck in I/O with the external world because of the difficulty of feeding a large amount of data through a single simple processor. This bottleneck has been addressed in various ways. MPP uses a "staging memory" in which image data can be placed and distributed to the array along one dimension. The I/O bottleneck has been addressed by a new version of the Connection Machine, called CM-2 [31]. In this computer, a number of disk drives can feed data into various points in the array simultaneously. The CM-1 benchmark figures do not include image I/O: the processing is done on an image which has already been loaded into the array, and processing is completed with the image still in the array. Otherwise, image I/O would completely dominate processing time. In many cases it is necessary to process an image which is stored in a frame buffer or host memory, which is easier in Warp because of the high bandwidth between the Warp array and the Warp host. All the Warp benchmarks in this section include I/O time from the host.

The high bandwidth connection between processors in the Warp array makes it possible for all processors to see all data in an image, while achieving useful image processing time. (In fact, because of the linear topology, there is no time advantage to limit the passage of an image through less than all processors.) This is important in global image computations such as Hough transform, where any input can influence any output. For example, the transform of a 512×512 image into a 180×512 Hough space takes 1.7 s on Warp, only 2.5 times as long as on CM-1. The ratio here is far less than for a simple local computation on a large image, such as Laplacian and zero crossing.

In some global operations, processing is done separately on different cells, then combined in a series of pairwise merge operations using a "divide and conquer" approach. This type of computation can be difficult to implement using limited topology communications as in Warp. For example, in the Warp border following algorithm for a 512×512 image, individual cells trace the borders of different portions of the image, then those borders are combined in a series of merge operations in the Warp array. The time for border following on Warp is 1100 ms, significantly more than the 100 ms the algorithm takes on CM-1.

3) Processor Number and Power: Warp has only ten parallel processing elements in its array, each of which is a powerful 10 MFLOPS processor. CM-1, on the other hand, has 64K processing elements, each of which is a simple bit-serial processor. Thus, the two machines stand at opposite ends of the spectrum of processor number and power.

We find that the small number of processing elements in Warp makes it easier to get good use of the Warp array in problems where a complex global computation is performed on a moderate-sized data set. In these problems, not much data parallelism is "available." For example, the DARPA IU benchmarks included the computation of the two-dimensional convex hull [26] of a set of 1000 points. The CM-1 algorithm used a brush-fire expansion algorithm, which led to an execution time of 200 ms for the complete computation. The same algorithm was implemented on Warp, and gave the 18 ms figure reported in Table III. Similar ratios are found in the times for the minimal spanning tree of 1000 points (160 ms on Warp versus 2.2 s on CM-1) and a triangle visibility problem for 1000 three-dimensional triangles (400 ms on Warp versus 1 s on CM-1).

Simple algorithms at the lowest level of vision, such as edge detection computations, run much faster on large arrays of processors such as the Connection Machine than Warp. This is because no communication is required between distant elements of the array, and the large array of processors can be readily mapped onto the large image array. For example, the computation of an 11×11 Laplacian [15] on a 512×512 image, followed by the detection of zero crossings, takes only 3 ms on CM-1, as opposed to 400 ms on Warp.

The floating-point processors in Warp aid the programmer in eliminating the need for low-level algorithmic analysis. For example, the Connection Machine used discrete fixed-point approximation to several algorithms, including Voronoi diagram and convex hull. The use of floating-point made it unnecessary for the Warp programmer to make assumptions about the data range and distribution.

In conclusion, we see that bit-serial processor arrays excel in the lowest level of vision, such as edge detection. The CM-1's performance at this level exceeded Warp's by two orders of magnitude. However, specialized hardware must be used to eliminate a severe I/O bottleneck to actually observe this performance. The use of the router in the Connection Machine allows it to do well also at higher levels of vision, such as border following. We also see that the more general class of programming models and use of floating-point hardware in Warp give it good actual performance in a wide range of algorithms, especially including complex global computations on moderately sized data sets.

IX. CONCLUSIONS

The Warp computer has achieved high performance in a variety of application areas, including low-level vision, signal processing, and scientific computation. Currently produced by our industrial partner (GE), Warp is much more powerful and programmable than many other machines of comparable cost.

The effectiveness of the Warp computer results from a balanced effort in architecture, software, and applications. The simple, linear topology of the Warp array naturally supports several useful program partitioning models; the Warp cells' high degree of programmability and large local memory make up for the lack of higher dimensional connectivity. The high-computation rate on each cell is matched by an equally high inter- and intracell bandwidth. The host system provides the Warp array with high I/O bandwidth. The optimizing W2 compiler maps programs from a high-level language to efficient microcode for the Warp array. Integration of the Warp array into Unix as an attached processor makes the Warp machine easily accessible to users. A sizable application library has been implemented to support development of research systems in vision.

The development of a compiler is essential in designing the architecture of a machine. Designing and implementing a compiler require a thorough study of the functionality of the machine; the systematic analysis of the machine allows us to uncover problems that may otherwise be undetected by writing sample programs. The compiler is also an excellent tool for evaluating different architectural alternatives. The development of the W2 compiler has significantly influenced the evolution of the architecture of Warp.

An early identification of an application area is essential for the development of an experimental machine such as Warp whose architecture is radically different from conventional ones. Including the application users in the early phase of the project—the vision research group at Carnegie Mellon in our case—helped us focus on the architectural requirements and provided early feedback.

Prototyping is important for architecture development. An early prototype system gives the designers realistic feedback about the constraints of the hardware implementation and provides a base for the software and application developers to test out their ideas. To speed up implementation of the prototype, we used off-the-shelf parts. To concentrate our efforts on the architecture of the Warp array, we developed the host from industry standard boards.

The Warp machine has demonstrated the feasibility of programmable, high-performance systolic array computers. The programmability of Warp has substantially extended the machine's application domain. The cost of programmability is limited to an increase in the physical size of the machine; it does not incur a loss in performance, given appropriate architectural support. This is shown by Warp, as it can be programmed to execute many well-known systolic algorithms as fast as special-purpose arrays built using similar technology.

ACKNOWLEDGMENT

We appreciate the contributions to the Warp project by our colleagues and visitors at Carnegie Mellon: D. Adams, F. Bitz, C. Bono, M. Browne, B. Bruegge, C. H. Chang, E. Clune, R. Cohn, R. Conde, J. Deutch, P. Dew, B. Enderton, L. Hamey, P. K. Hsiung, K. Hughes, T. Kanade, G. Klinker, P. Lieu, P. Maulik, D. Morris, A. Noaman, T. M. Parng, H. Printz, J. Race, M. Ravishankar, J. Rendas, H. Ribas, C. Sarocky, K. Sarocky, J. Senko, Y. Shintani, B. Siegell, H. Sohn, P. Steenkiste, Y. B. Tsai, P. S. Tseng, R. Wallace, J. K. Wang, I. C. Wu, D. Yam, and A. Zobel. We thank our industrial partners GE and Honeywell for their contribution towards the construction of the wire-wrapped prototypes. We appreciate the continued collaboration with GE for the development of the production Warp machine. In particular, we thank R. Barned, S. Carmel, J. Cokus, J. Condon, D. Crump, R. A. Field, R. Gaus, N. Gearhart, J. Iannuzzi, A. Lock, C. Pickering, A. Pfueller, M. Sarig, S. Sillich, T. Stark, W. Tates, A. Toll, C. Walrath, and J. Weimar of GE in Syracuse for their efforts.

REFERENCES

[1] M. Annaratone, E. Arnould, T. Gross, H. T. Kung, M. S. Lam, O. Menzilcioglu, K. Sarocky, and J. A. Webb, "Warp architecture and implementation," in *Proc. 13th Annu. Int. Symp. Comput. Architecture,* IEEE/ACM, June, 1986, pp. 346–356.

[2] M. Annaratone, E. Arnould, H. T. Kung, and O. Menzilcioglu, "Using Warp as a supercomputer in signal processing," in *Proc. ICASSP 86,* Apr. 1986, pp. 2895–2898.

[3] M. Annaratone, F. Bitz, E. Clune, H. T. Kung, P. Maulik, H. Ribas, P. Tseng, and J. Webb, "Applications and algorithm partitioning on Warp," in *Proc. Compcon Spring 87,* San Francisco, CA, Feb., 1987, pp. 272–275.

[4] M. Annaratone, F. Bitz, J. Deutch, L. Hamey, H. T. Kung, P. C. Maulik, P. Tseng, and J. A. Webb, "Applications experience on Warp," in *Proc. 1987 Nat. Comput. Conf.,* AFIPS, Chicago, IL, June 1987, pp. 149–158.

[5] M. Annaratone, E. Arnould, R. Cohn, T. Gross, H. T. Kung, M. Lam, O. Menzilcioglu, K. Sarocky, J. Senko, and J. Webb, "Architecture of Warp," in *Proc. Compcon Spring 87,* San Francisco, CA, Feb. 1987, pp. 274–267.

[6] ——, "Warp architecture: From prototype to production," in *Proc. 1987 Nat. Comput. Conf.,* AFIPS, Chicago, IL, June, 1987, pp. 133–140.

[7] K. E. Batcher, "Design of a massively parallel processor," *IEEE Trans. Comput.,* vol. C-29, pp. 836–840, 1980.

[8] B. Bruegge, C. Chang, R. Cohn, T. Gross, M. Lam, P. Lieu, A. Noaman, and D. Yam, "The Warp programming environment," in *Proc. 1987 Nat. Comput. Conf.,* AFIPS, Chicago, IL, June 1987, pp. 141–148.

[9] A. E. Charlesworth, "An approach to scientific array processing: The architectural design of the AP-120B/FPS-164 family," *Computer,* vol. 14, pp. 18–27, Sept. 1981.

[10] E. Clune, J. D. Crisman, G. J. Klinker, and J. A. Webb, "Implementation and performance of a complex vision system on a systolic array machine," in *Proc. Conf. Frontiers Comput.*, Amsterdam, Dec. 1987.

[11] A. L. Fisher, H. T. Kung, and K. Sarocky, "Experience with the CMU programmable systolic chip," *Microarchitecture VLSI Comput.*, pp. 209–222, 1985.

[12] T. Gross and M. Lam, "Compilation for a high-performance systolic array," in *Proc. SIGPLAN 86 Symp. Compiler Construction*, ACM SIGPLAN, June, 1986, pp. 27–38.

[13] T. Gross, H. T. Kung, M. Lam, and J. Webb, "Warp as a machine for low-level vision," in *Proc. 1985 IEEE Int. Conf. Robot. Automat.*, Mar. 1985, pp. 790–800.

[14] L. G. C. Hamey, J. A. Webb, and I. C. Wu, "Low-level vision on warp and the apply programming model," in *Parallel Computation and Computers for Artificial Intelligence*, J. Kowalik, Ed. Hingham, MA: Kluwer Academic, 1987.

[15] R. M. Haralick, "Digital step edges from zero crossings of second directional derivatives," *IEEE Trans. Pattern Anal. Machine Intell.*, vol. PAMI-6, pp. 58–68, 1984.

[16] F. H. Hsu, H. T. Kung, T. Nishizawa, and A. Sussman, "Architecture of the link and interconnection chip," in *Proc. 1985 Chapel Hill Conf., VLSI*, Comput. Sci., Dep., Univ. North Carolina, May, 1985, pp. 186–195.

[17] T. Kanade and J. A. Webb, "End of year report for parallel vision algorithm design and implementation," Tech. Rep. CMU-R1 TR-87-15 Robot. Instit., Carnegie Mellon Univ., 1987.

[18] H. T. Kung, "Why systolic architectures?," *Computer*, vol. 15, pp. 37–46, Jan. 1982.

[19] ——, "Systolic algorithms for the CMU Warp processor," in *Proc. Seventh Int. Conf. Pattern Recognition*, Int. Ass. Pattern Recognition, 1984, pp. 570–577.

[20] ——, "Memory requirements for balanced computer architectures," *J. Complexity*, vol. 1, pp. 147–157, 1985.

[21] H. T. Kung and J. A. Webb, "Global operations on the CMU warp machine," in *Proc. 1985 AIAA Comput. Aerosp. V Conf.*, Amer. Instit. Aeronaut. Astronaut., Oct., 1985, pp. 209–218.

[22] ——, "Mapping image processing operations onto a linear systolic machine," *Distributed Comput.*, vol. 1, pp. 246–257, 1986.

[23] M. S. Lam, "A systolic array optimizing compiler," Ph.D. dissertation, Carnegie Mellon Univ., May 1987.

[24] C. Lasser, *The Complete *Lisp Manual*, Thinking Machines Corp., Cambridge, MA, 1986.

[25] J. J. Little, G. Gelloch, and T. Cass, "Parallel algorithms for computer vision on the connection machine," in *Proc. Image Understanding Workshop*, DARPA, Feb., 1987, pp. 628–638.

[26] F. P. Preparata and M. I. Shamos, *Computational Geometry—An Introduction.* New York: Springer-Verlag, 1985.

[27] B. R. Rau and C. D. Glaeser, "Some scheduling techniques and an easily schedulable horizontal architecture for high performance scientific computing," in *Proc. 14th Annu. Workshop Microprogramming*, Oct., 1981, pp. 183–198.

[28] B. R. Rau, P. J. Kuekes, and C. D. Glaeser, "A statistically scheduled VLSI interconnect for parallel processors," *VLSI Syst. Comput.*, Oct. 1981, pp. 389–395.

[29] A. Rosenfeld, "A report on the DARPA image understanding architectures workshop," in *Proc. Image Understanding Workshop*, DARPA, Los Angeles, CA, Feb., 1987, pp. 298–301.

[30] H. Tamura, S. Sakane, F. Tomita, N. Yokoya, K. Sakaue, and N. Kaneko, *SPIDER Users' Manual*, Joint System Development Corp., Tokyo, Japan, 1983.

[31] Thinking Machines Corp., *Connection Machine Model CM-2 Technical Summary HA 87-4*, Thinking Machines Corp., Apr. 1897.

[32] R. Wallace, A. Stentz, C. Thorpe, W. Whittaker, and T. Kanade, "First results in robot road-following," in *Proc. IJCAI*, 1985, pp. 1089–1093.

[33] R. Wallace, K. Matsuzaki, Y. Goto, J. Crisman, J. Webb, and T. Kanade, "Progress in robot road-following," in *Proc. 1986 IEEE Int. Conf. Robot. Automat.*, Apr., 1986, pp. 1615–1621.

[34] D. L. Waltz, "Applications of the connection machine," *Computer*, vol. 20, pp. 85–97, Jan. 1987.

[35] B. Woo, L. Lin, and F. Ware, "A high-speed 32 bit IEEE floating-point chip set for digital signal processing," in *Proc. ICASSP 84*, IEEE, 1984, pp. 16.6.1–16.6.4.

[36] D. Young, *Iterative Solution of Large Linear Systems.* New York: Academic, 1971.

Marco Annaratone received the Dott.Ing. degree in computer science and electrical engineering from Politecnico di Milano, Milan, Italy, in 1980.

From 1982 to 1984 he was Visiting Scientist in the Department of Computer Science at Carnegie Mellon University, Pittsburgh, PA. From 1984 to 1987 he was a faculty member in the same department, first as a Research Associate and then as a Research Computer Scientist. He is the author of *Digital CMOS Circuit Design* (Hingham, MA: Kluwer Academic), a book on VLSI design methodologies. His current research interests include computer architecture, parallel computer architecture, and parallel implementation of algorithms in the field of scientific computation. He is now an Assistant Professor of Computer Science at the Swiss Federal Institute of Technology (ETH), Zurich and can be reached at the Institute for Integrated Systems, ETH Zentrum, 8092 Zurich, Switzerland.

Emmanuel Arnould was born in Paris, France. He received the M.S. degree in electrical engineering from the Universite des Sciences, Paris, France, in 1981, and the M.S. degree in computer science from the Ecole Nationale Superieure des Telecommunications, Paris, France, in 1983.

Since February 1984, he has been a Research Engineer in the Department of Computer Science, Carnegie Mellon University, Pittsburgh, PA, where he actively participated in the design of the Warp computer. His research interests include computer system architecture, supercomputing, and supercomputer networks.

Thomas Gross (S'79–M'83) received the M.S. degree in computer science from Stanford University, Stanford, CA, the Diplom-Informatiker degree from the Technical University, Munich, Germany, and the Ph.D. degree in electrical engineering from Stanford University, Stanford, CA, in 1983, where he participated in the MIPS project.

He joined the faculty of the Department of Computer Science, Carnegie Mellon University, in 1984. His current research interests include practical aspects of high-performance computer systems: computer architecture, processor design, optimizing compilers, and the software systems that are needed to make high-performance computers usable.

Dr. Gross received an IBM Faculty Development Award in 1985.

H. T. Kung received the Ph.D. degree from Carnegie Mellon University, Pittsburgh, PA, in 1974.

He joined the faculty of Carnegie Mellon University in 1974 and was appointed to Professor in 1982. He is currently holding the Shell Distinguished Chair in Computer Science at Carnegie Mellon. He was Guggenheim Fellow in 1983–1984, and a full time Architecture Consultant to ESL, Inc., a subsidiary of TRW, in 1981. His current research interests are in high-performance computer architectures and their applications.

Dr. Kung has served on editorial boards of several journals and program committees of numerous conferences in VLSI and computer science.

Monica Lam received the Ph.D. degree in computer science from Carnegie Mellon University, Pittsburgh, PA, in 1987, and the B.S. degree in computer science from the University of British Columbia, Vancouver, B.C. in 1980.

She is currently a Research Associate in the Department of Computer Science at Carnegie Mellon University. Her research interests include parallel architectures and optimizing compilers.

Onat Menzilcioglu received the B.S. degree in electrical engineering from Middle East Technical University, Ankara, Turkey, in 1980, and the M.S. degree in computer engineering from Carnegie Mellon University, Pittsburgh, PA, in 1982.

He is a Ph.D. degree candidate in the Department of Electrical and Computer Engineering, Carnegie Mellon University. He has been working on programmable systolic array architectures since 1983. His research interests include computer architecture and design, and fault tolerance.

Jon A. Webb received the B.A. degree in mathematics from The University of South Florida, Tampa, in 1975, the M.S. degree in computer science from The Ohio State University, Columbus, in 1976, and the Ph.D. degree in computer science from The University of Texas, Austin, in 1980.

Since 1981 he has worked on the faculty of the Department of Computer Science at Carnegie Mellon University, where he is currently a Research Computer Scientist. His research interests include the theory of vision and parallel architectures for vision. He has published papers on the recovery of structure from motion, the shape of subjective contours, the design and use of a parallel architecture for low-level vision, and experiments in the visual control of a robot vehicle.

Dr. Webb is a member of the IEEE Computer Society and the Association for Computing Machinery.

Distributed Shared Memory: A Survey of Issues and Algorithms

Bill Nitzberg and Virginia Lo, University of Oregon

Reprinted from *Computer*, Vol. 24, No. 8, August 1991, pages 52-60. Copyright © 1991 by The Institute of Electrical and Electronics Engineers, Inc. All rights reserved.

Distributed shared-memory systems implement the shared-memory abstraction on multicomputer architectures, combining the scalability of network-based architectures with the convenience of shared-memory programming.

As we slowly approach the physical limits of processor and memory speed, it is becoming more attractive to use multiprocessors to increase computing power. Two kinds of parallel processors have become popular: tightly coupled shared-memory multiprocessors and distributed-memory multiprocessors. A tightly coupled multiprocessor system — consisting of multiple CPUs and a single global physical memory — is more straightforward to program because it is a natural extension of a single-CPU system. However, this type of multiprocessor has a serious bottleneck: Main memory is accessed via a common bus — a serialization point — that limits system size to tens of processors.

Distributed-memory multiprocessors, however, do not suffer from this drawback. These systems consist of a collection of independent computers connected by a high-speed interconnection network. If designers choose the network topology carefully, the system can contain many orders of magnitude more processors than a tightly coupled system. Because all communication between concurrently executing processes must be performed over the network in such a system, until recently the programming model was limited to a message-passing paradigm. However, recent systems have implemented a shared-memory abstraction on top of message-passing distributed-memory systems. The shared-memory abstraction gives these systems the illusion of physically shared memory and allows programmers to use the shared-memory paradigm.

As Figure 1 shows, distributed shared memory provides a virtual address space shared among processes on loosely coupled processors. The advantages offered by DSM include ease of programming and portability achieved through the shared-memory programming paradigm, the low cost of distributed-memory machines, and scalability resulting from the absence of hardware bottlenecks.

DSM has been an active area of research since the early 1980s, although its foundations in cache coherence and memory management have been extensively studied for many years. DSM research goals and issues are similar to those of research in multiprocessor caches or networked file systems, memories for nonuniform memory access multiprocessors, and management systems for distributed or replicated databases.[1] Because of this similarity, many algorithms and lessons learned in these domains can be transferred to DSM systems and vice versa.

However, each of the above systems has unique features (such as communication latency), so each must be considered separately.

The advantages of DSM can be realized with reasonably low runtime overhead. DSM systems have been implemented using three approaches (some systems use more than one approach):

(1) hardware implementations that extend traditional caching techniques to scalable architectures,

(2) operating system and library implementations that achieve sharing and coherence through virtual memory-management mechanisms, and

(3) compiler implementations where shared accesses are automatically converted into synchronization and coherence primitives.

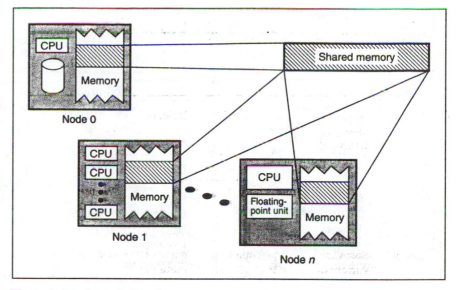

Figure 1. Distributed shared memory.

These systems have been designed on common networks of workstations or minicomputers, special-purpose message-passing machines (such as the Intel iPSC/2), custom hardware, and even heterogeneous systems.

This article gives an integrated overview of important DSM issues: memory coherence, design choices, and implementation methods. In our presentation, we use examples from the DSM systems listed and briefly described in the sidebar on page 55. Table 1 compares how design issues are handled in a selected subset of the systems.

Design choices

A DSM system designer must make choices regarding structure, granularity, access, coherence semantics, scalability, and heterogeneity. Examination of how designers handled these issues in several real implementations of DSM shows the intricacies of such a system.

Structure and granularity. The structure and granularity of a DSM system are closely related. Structure refers to the layout of the shared data in memory. Most DSM systems do not structure memory (it is a linear array of words), but some structure the data as objects, language types, or even an associative memory. Granularity refers to the size of the unit of sharing: byte, word, page, or complex data structure.

Ivy,[2] one of the first transparent DSM systems, implemented shared memory as virtual memory. This memory was unstructured and was shared in 1-Kbyte pages. In systems implemented using the virtual memory hardware of the underlying architecture, it is convenient to choose a multiple of the hardware page size as the unit of sharing. Mirage[3] extended Ivy's single shared-memory space to support a paged segmentation scheme. Users share arbitrary-size regions of memory (segments) while the system maintains the shared space in pages.

Hardware implementations of DSM typically support smaller grain sizes. For example, Dash[4] and Memnet[5] also support unstructured sharing, but the unit of sharing is 16 and 32 bytes respectively — typical cache line sizes. Plus[6] is somewhat of a hybrid: The unit of replication is a page, while the unit of coherence is a 32-bit word.

Because shared-memory programs provide locality of reference, a process is likely to access a large region of its shared address space in a small amount of time. Therefore, larger "page" sizes reduce paging overhead. However, sharing may also cause contention, and the larger the page size, the greater the likelihood that more than one process will require access to a page. A smaller page reduces the possibility of *false sharing*, which occurs when two unrelated variables (each used by different processes) are placed in the same page. The page appears shared, even though the

original variables were not. Another factor affecting the choice of page size is the need to keep directory information about the pages in the system: the smaller the page size, the larger the directory.

A method of structuring the shared memory is by data type. With this method, shared memory is structured as objects in distributed object-oriented systems, as in the Emerald, Choices, and Clouds[7] systems; or it is structured as variables in the source language, as in the Shared Data-Object Model and Munin systems. Because with these systems the sizes of objects and data types vary greatly, the grain size varies to match the application. However, these systems can still suffer from false sharing when different parts of an object (for example, the top and bottom halves of an array) are accessed by distinct processes.

Another method is to structure the shared memory like a database. Linda,[8] a system that has such a model, orders its shared memory as an associative memory called a *tuple space*. This structure allows the location of data to be separated from its value, but it also requires programmers to use special access functions to interact with the shared-memory space. In most other systems, access to shared data is transparent.

Coherence semantics. For programmers to write correct programs on a shared-memory machine, they must understand how parallel memory updates are propagated throughout the

Table 1. DSM design issues.

System Name	Current Implementation	Structure and Granularity	Coherence Semantics	Coherence Protocol	Sources of Improved Performance	Support for Synchro-nization	Hetero-geneous Support
Dash	Hardware, modified Silicon Graphics Iris 4D/340 worksta-tions, mesh	16 bytes	Release	Write-invalidate	Relaxed coherence, prefetching	Queued locks, atomic incre-mentation and decrementation	No
Ivy	Software, Apollo workstations, Apollo ring, modified Aegis	1-Kbyte pages	Strict	Write-invalidate	Pointer chain collapse, selec-tive broadcast	Synchronized pages, sema-phores, event counts	No
Linda	Software, variety of environments	Tuples	No mutable data	Varied	Hashing		?
Memnet	Hardware, token ring	32 bytes	Strict	Write-invalidate	Vectored in-terrupt support of control flow		No
Mermaid	Software, Sun workstations DEC Firefly multiprocessors, Mermaid/native operating system	8 Kbytes (Sun), 1 Kbyte (Firefly)	Strict	Write-invalidate		Messages for semaphores and signal/ wait	Yes
Mirage	Software, VAX 11/750, Ether-net, Locus dis-tributed operat-ing system, Unix System V interface	512-byte pages	Strict	Write-invalidate	Kernel-level implementa-tion, time window coherence protocol	Unix System V semaphores	No
Munin	Software, Sun workstations, Ethernet, Unix System V kernel and Presto paral-lel programming environment	Objects	Weak	Type-specific (delayed write update for read-mostly protocol)	Delayed update queue	Synchronized objects	No
Plus	Hardware and software, Motorola 88000, Caltech mesh, Plus kernel	Page for sharing, word for coherence	Processor	Nondemand write-update	Delayed operations	Complex synchronization instructions	No
Shiva	Software, Intel iPSC/2, hypercube, Shiva/native operating system	4-Kbyte pages	Strict	Write-invalidate	Data structure compaction, memory as backing store	Messages for semaphores and signal/ wait	No

system. The most intuitive semantics for memory coherence is *strict consistency*. (Although "coherence" and "consistency" are used somewhat inter-changeably in the literature, we use coherence as the general term for the semantics of memory operations, and consistency to refer to a specific kind of memory coherence.) In a system with strict consistency, a read operation re-turns the most recently written value. However, "most recently" is an ambig-uous concept in a distributed system. For this reason, and to improve perfor-mance, some DSM systems provide only a reduced form of memory coherence. For example, Plus provides processor consistency, and Dash provides only release consistency. In accordance with the RISC philosophy, both of these systems have mechanisms for forcing coherence, but their use must be explicitly specified by higher level software (a compiler) or perhaps even the programmer.

Relaxed coherence semantics allows more efficient shared access because it requires less synchronization and less data movement. However, programs that depend on a stronger form of coherence may not perform correctly if executed in a system that supports only a weaker form. Figure 2 gives brief definitions of strict, sequential, processor, weak, and release consistency, and illustrates the hierarchical relationship among these types of coherence. Table 1 indicates the coherence semantics supported by some current DSM systems.

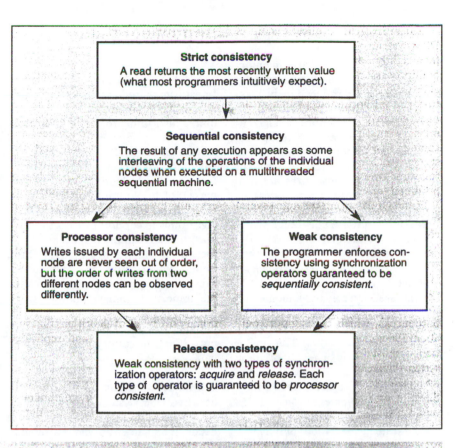

Figure 2. Intuitive definitions of memory coherence. The arrows point from stricter to weaker consistencies.

DSM systems

This partial listing gives the name of the DSM system, the principal developers of the system, the site and duration of their research, and a brief description of the system. Table 1 gives more information about the systems followed with an asterisk.

Agora (Bisiani and Forin, Carnegie Mellon University, 1987-): A heterogeneous DSM system that allows data structures to be shared across machines. Agora was the first system to support weak consistency.

Amber (Chase, Feeley, and Levy, University of Washington, 1988-): An object-based DSM system in which sharing is performed by migrating processes to data as well as data to processes.

Capnet (Tam and Farber, University of Delaware, 1990-): An extension of DSM to a wide area network.

Choices (Johnston and Campbell, University of Illinois, 1988-): DSM incorporated into a hierarchical object-oriented distributed operating system.

Clouds (Ramachandran and Khalidi, Georgia Institute of Technology, 1987-): An object-oriented distributed operating system where objects can migrate.

Dash* (Lenoski, Laudon, Gharachorloo, Gupta, and Hennessy, Stanford University, 1988-): A hardware implementation of DSM with a directory-based coherence protocol. Dash provides release consistency.

Emerald (Jul, Levy, Hutchinson, and Black, University of Washington, 1986-1988): An object-oriented language and system that indirectly supports DSM through object mobility.

Ivy* (Li, Yale University, 1984-1986): An early page-oriented DSM on a network of Apollo workstations.

Linda* (Carriero and Gelernter, Yale University, 1982-): A shared associative object memory with access functions. Linda can be implemented for many languages and machines.

Memnet* (Delp and Farber, University of Delaware, 1986-1988): A hardware implementation of DSM implemented on a 200-Mbps token ring used to broadcast invalidates and read requests.

Mermaid* (Stumm, Zhou, Li, and Wortman, University of Toronto and Princeton University, 1988-1991): A heterogeneous DSM system where the compiler forces shared pages to contain a single data type. Type conversion is performed on reference.

Mether (Minnich and Farber, Supercomputing Research Center, Bowie, Md., 1990-): A transparent DSM built on SunOS 4.0. Mether allows applications to access an inconsistent state for efficiency.

Mirage* (Fleisch and Popek, University of California at Los Angeles, 1987-1989): A kernel-level implementation of DSM. Mirage reduces thrashing by prohibiting a page from being stolen before a minimum amount of time (Δ) has elapsed.

Munin* (Bennett, Carter, and Zwaenepoel, Rice University, 1989-): An object-based DSM system that investigates type-specific coherence protocols.

Plus* (Bisiani and Ravishankar, Carnegie Mellon University, 1988-): A hardware implementation of DSM. Plus uses a write-update coherence protocol and performs replication only by program request.

Shared Data-Object Model (Bal, Kaashoek, and Tannenbaum, Vrije University, Amsterdam, The Netherlands, 1988-): A DSM implementation on top of the Amoeba distributed operating system.

Shiva* (Li and Schaefer, Princeton University, 1988-): An Ivy-like DSM system for the Intel iPSC/2 hypercube.

Scalability. A theoretical benefit of DSM systems is that they scale better than tightly coupled shared-memory multiprocessors. The limits of scalability are greatly reduced by two factors: central bottlenecks (such as the bus of a tightly coupled shared-memory multiprocessor), and global common knowledge operations and storage (such as broadcast messages or full directories, whose sizes are proportional to the number of nodes).

Li and Hudak[2] went through several iterations to refine a coherence protocol for Ivy before arriving at their dynamic distributed-manager algorithm, which avoids centralized bottlenecks. However, Ivy and most other DSM systems are currently implemented on top of Ethernet (itself a centralized bottleneck), which can support only about 100 nodes at a time. This limitation is most likely a result of these systems being research tools rather than an indication of any real design flaw. Shiva[9] is an implementation of DSM on an Intel iPSC/2 hypercube, and it should scale nicely. Nodes in the Dash system are connected on two meshes. This implies that the machine should be expandable, but the Dash prototype is currently limited by its use of a full bit vector (one bit per node) to keep track of page replication.

Heterogeneity. At first glance, sharing memory between two machines with different architectures seems almost impossible. The machines may not even use the same representation for basic data types (integers, floating-point numbers, and so on). It is a bit easier if the DSM system is structured as variables or objects in the source language. Then a DSM compiler can add conversion routines to all accesses to shared memory. In Agora, memory is structured as objects shared among heterogeneous machines.

Mermaid[10] explores another novel approach: Memory is shared in pages, and a page can contain only one type of data. Whenever a page is moved between two architecturally different systems, a conversion routine converts the data in the page to the appropriate format.

Although heterogeneous DSM might allow more machines to participate in a computation, the overhead of conversion seems to outweigh the benefits.

Implementation

A DSM system must automatically transform shared-memory access into interprocess communication. This requires algorithms to locate and access shared data, maintain coherence, and replace data. A DSM system may also have additional schemes to improve performance. Such algorithms directly support DSM. In addition, DSM implementers must tailor operating system algorithms to support process synchronization and memory management. We focus on the algorithms used in Ivy, Dash, Munin, Plus, Mirage, and Memnet because these systems illustrate most of the important implementation issues. Stumm and Zhou[1] give a good evolutionary overview of algorithms that support static, migratory, and replicated data.

Data location and access. To share data in a DSM system, a program must be able to find and retrieve the data it needs. If data does not move around in the system — it resides only in a single static location — then locating it is easy. All processes simply "know" where to obtain any piece of data. Some Linda implementations use hashing on the tuples to distribute data statically. This has the advantages of being simple and fast, but may cause a bottleneck if data is not distributed properly (for example, all shared data ends up on a single node).

An alternative is to allow data to migrate freely throughout the system. This allows data to be redistributed dynamically to where it is being used. However, locating data then becomes more difficult. In this case, the simplest way to locate data is to have a centralized server that keeps track of all shared data. The centralized method suffers from two drawbacks: The server serializes location queries, reducing parallelism, and the server may become heavily loaded and slow the entire system.

Instead of using a centralized server, a system can broadcast requests for data. Unfortunately, broadcasting does not scale well. All nodes — not just the nodes containing the data — must process a broadcast request. The network latency of a broadcast may also require accesses to take a long time to complete.

To avoid broadcasts and distribute the load more evenly, several systems use an owner-based distributed scheme.

This scheme is independent of data replication, but is seen mostly in systems that support both data migration and replication. Each piece of data has an associated owner — a node with the primary copy of the data. The owners change as the data migrates through the system. When another node needs a copy of the data, it sends a request to the owner. If the owner still has the data, it returns the data. If the owner has given the data to some other node, it forwards the request to the new owner.

The drawback with this scheme is that a request may be forwarded many times before reaching the current owner. In some cases, this is more wasteful than broadcasting. In Ivy, all nodes involved in forwarding a request (including the requester) are given the identity of the current owner. This collapsing of pointer chains helps reduce the forwarding overhead and delay.

When it replicates data, a DSM system must keep track of the replicated copies. Dash uses a distributed directory-based scheme, implemented in hardware. The Dash directory for a given cluster (node) keeps track of the physical blocks in that cluster. Each block is represented by a directory entry that specifies whether the block is *unshared remote* (local copy only), *shared remote*, or *shared dirty*. If the block is shared remote, the directory entry also indicates the location of replicated copies of the block. If the block is shared dirty, the directory entry indicates the location of the single dirty copy. Only the special node known as the *home cluster* possesses the directory block entry. A node accesses nonlocal data for reading by sending a message to the home cluster.

Ivy's dynamic distributed scheme also supports replicated data. A *ptable* on each node contains for each page an entry that indicates the probable location for the referenced page. As described above, a node locates data by following the chain of probable owners. The copy-list scheme implemented by Plus uses a distributed linked list to keep track of replicated data. Memory references are mapped to the physically closest copy by the page map table.

Coherence protocol. All DSM systems provide some form of memory coherence. If the shared data is not replicated, then enforcing memory coherence is trivial. The underlying network automatically serializes requests in the order they

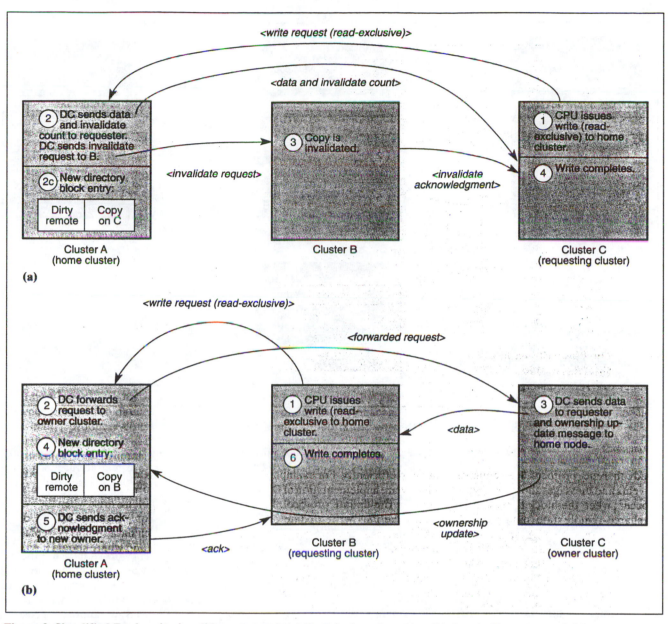

Figure 3. Simplified Dash write-invalidate protocol: (a) Data is shared remote; (b) data is dirty remote (after events depicted in Figure 3a). (DC stands for directory controller.)

occur. A node handling shared data can merely perform each request as it is received. This method will ensure strict memory consistency — the strongest form of coherence. Unfortunately, serializing data access creates a bottleneck and makes impossible a major advantage of DSM: parallelism.

To increase parallelism, virtually all DSM systems replicate data. Thus, for example, multiple reads can be performed in parallel. However, replication complicates the coherence protocol. Two types of protocols — write-invalidate and write-update protocols — handle replication. In a write-invalidate protocol, there can be many

copies of a read-only piece of data, but only one copy of a writable piece of data. The protocol is called write-invalidate because it invalidates all copies of a piece of data except one before a write can proceed. In a write-update scheme, however, a write updates all copies of a piece of data.

Most DSM systems have write-invalidate coherence protocols. All the protocols for these systems are similar. Each piece of data has a status tag that indicates whether the data is valid, whether it is shared, and whether it is read-only or writable. For a read, if the data is valid, it is returned immediately. If the data is not valid, a read request is

sent to the location of a valid copy, and a copy of the data is returned. If the data was writable on another node, this read request will cause it to become read-only. The copy remains valid until an invalidate request is received.

For a write, if the data is valid and writable, the request is satisfied immediately. If the data is not writable, the directory controller sends out an invalidate request, along with a request for a copy of the data if the local copy is not valid. When the invalidate completes, the data is valid locally and writable, and the original write request may complete.

Figure 3 illustrates the Dash directory-

359

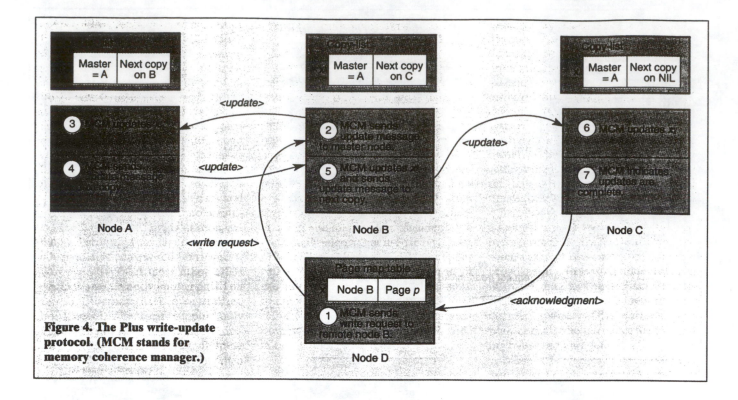

Figure 4. The Plus write-update protocol. (MCM stands for memory coherence manager.)

based coherence protocol. The sequence of events and messages shown in Figure 3a occurs when the block to be written is in shared-remote state (multiple read-only copies on nodes A and B) just before the write. Figure 3b shows the events and messages that occur when the block to be written is in shared-dirty state (single dirty copy on node C) just before the write. In both cases, the initiator of the write sends a request to the home cluster, which uses the information in the directory to locate and transfer the data and to invalidate copies. Lenoski et al.[4] give further details about the Dash coherence protocol and the methods they used to fine-tune the protocol for high performance.

Li and Hudak[2] show that the write-invalidate protocol performs well for a variety of applications. In fact, they show superlinear speedups for a linear equation solver and a three-dimensional partial differential equation solver, resulting from the increased overall physical memory and cache sizes. Li and Hudak rejected use of a write-update protocol at the onset with the reasoning that network latency would make it inefficient.

Subsequent research indicates that in the appropriate hardware environment write-update protocols can be imple-

mented efficiently. For example, Plus is a hardware implementation of DSM that uses a write-update protocol. Figure 4 traces the Plus write-update protocol, which begins all updates with the block's master node, then proceeds down the copy-list chain. The write operation is completed when the last node in the chain sends an acknowledgment message to the originator of the write request.

Munin[11] uses *type-specific memory coherence*, coherence protocols tailored for different types of data. For example, Munin uses a write-update protocol to keep coherent data that is read much more frequently than it is written (read-mostly data). Because an invalidation message is about the same size as an update message, an update costs no more than an invalidate. However, the overhead of making multiple read-only copies of the data item after each invalidate is avoided. An eager paging strategy supports the Munin producer-consumer memory type. Data, once written by the producer process, is transferred to the consumer process where it remains available until the consumer process is ready to use it. This reduces overhead, since the consumer does not request data already available in the buffer.

Replacement strategy. In systems that allow data to migrate around the system, two problems arise when the available space for "caching" shared data fills up: Which data should be replaced to free space and where should it go? In choosing the data item to be replaced, a DSM system works almost like the caching system of a shared-memory multiprocessor. However, unlike most caching systems, which use a simple least recently used or random replacement strategy, most DSM systems differentiate the status of data items and prioritize them. For example, priority is given to shared items over exclusively owned items because the latter have to be transferred over the network. Simply deleting a read-only shared copy of a data item is possible because no data is lost. Shiva prioritizes pages on the basis of a linear combination of type (read-only, owned read-only, and writable) and least recently used statistics.

Once a piece of data is to be replaced, the system must make sure it is not lost. In the caching system of a multiprocessor, the item would simply be placed in main memory. Some DSM systems, such as Memnet, use an equivalent scheme. The system transfers the data item to a "home node" that has a statically allocated space (perhaps on disk) to store a copy of an item when it is not needed elsewhere in the system. This method is simple to implement, but it wastes a lot of memory. An improvement is to have the node that wants to delete the item simply page it out onto disk. Although this does not waste any memory space, it is time consuming. Because it may be faster to transfer something over the network than to transfer it to disk, a better solution (used in Shiva) is to keep track of free memory in the system and to simply page the item out to a node with space available to it.

Thrashing. DSM systems are particularly prone to thrashing. For example, if two nodes compete for write access to a single data item, it may be transferred back and forth at such a high rate that no real work can get done (a Ping-Pong effect). Two systems, Munin and Mirage, attack this problem directly.

Munin allows programmers to associate types with shared data: write-once, write-many, producer-consumer, private, migratory, result, read-mostly, synchronization, and general read/write. Shared data of different types get different coherence protocols. To avoid thrashing with two competing writers, a programmer could specify the type as write-many and the system would use a delayed write policy. (Munin does not guarantee strict consistency of memory in this case.)

Tailoring the coherence algorithm to the shared-data usage patterns can greatly reduce thrashing. However, Munin requires programmers to specify the type of shared data. Programmers are notoriously bad at predicting the behavior of their programs, so this method may not be any better than choosing a particular protocol. In addition, because the type remains static once specified, Munin cannot dynamically adjust to an application's changing behavior.

Mirage[3] uses another method to reduce thrashing. It specifically examines the case when many nodes compete for access to the same page. To stop the Ping-Pong effect, Mirage adds a dynamically tunable parameter to the coherence protocol. This parameter determines the minimum amount of time (Δ) a page will be available at a node. For example, if a node performed a write to a shared page, the page would be writable on that node for Δ time. This solves the problem of having a page stolen away after only a single request on a node can be satisfied. Because Δ is tuned dynamically on the basis of access patterns, a process can complete a write run (or read run) before losing access to the page. Thus, Δ is akin to a time slice in a multitasking operating system, except in Mirage it is dynamically adjusted to meet an application's specific needs.

Related algorithms. To support a DSM system, synchronization operations and memory management must be specially tuned. Semaphores, for example, are typically implemented on shared-memory systems by using spin locks. In a DSM system, a spin lock can easily cause thrashing, because multiple nodes may heavily access shared data. For better performance, some systems provide specialized synchronization primitives along with DSM. Clouds provides semaphore operations by grouping semaphores into centrally managed segments. Munin supports the synchronization memory type with distributed locks. Plus supplies a variety of synchronization instructions, and supports delayed execution, in which the synchronization can be initiated, then later tested for successful completion. Dubois, Scheurich, and Briggs[12] discuss the relationship between coherence and synchronization.

Memory management can be restructured for DSM. A typical memory-allocation scheme (as in the C library malloc()) allocates memory out of a common pool, which is searched each time a request is made. A linear search of all shared memory can be expensive. A better approach is to partition available memory into private buffers on each node and allocate memory from the global buffer space only when the private buffer is empty.

R esearch has shown distributed shared memory systems to be viable. The systems described in this article demonstrate that DSM can be implemented in a variety of hardware and software environments: commercial workstations with native operating systems software, innovative customized hardware, and even heterogeneous systems. Many of the design choices and algorithms needed to implement DSM are well understood and integrated with related areas of computer science.

The performance of DSM is greatly affected by memory-access patterns and replication of shared data. Hardware implementations have yielded enormous reductions in communication latency and the advantages of a smaller unit of sharing. However, the performance results to date are preliminary. Most systems are experimental or prototypes consisting of only a few nodes. In addition, because of the dearth of test programs, most studies are based on a small group of applications or a synthetic workload. Nevertheless, research has proved that DSM effectively supports parallel processing, and it promises to be a fruitful and exciting area of research for the coming decade. ∎

Acknowledgments

This work was supported in part by NSF grant CCR-8808532, a Tektronix research fellowship, and the NSF Research Experiences for Undergraduates program. We appreciate the comments from the anonymous referees and thank the authors who verified information about their systems. Thanks also to Kurt Windisch for helping prepare this manuscript.

References

1. M. Stumm and S. Zhou, "Algorithms Implementing Distributed Shared Memory," *Computer*, Vol. 23, No. 5, May 1990, pp. 54-64.

2. K. Li and P. Hudak, "Memory Coherence in Shared Virtual Memory Systems," *ACM Trans. Computer Systems*, Vol. 7, No. 4, Nov. 1989, pp. 321-359.

3. B. Fleisch and G. Popek, "Mirage: A Coherent Distributed Shared Memory Design," *Proc. 14th ACM Symp. Operating System Principles*, ACM, New York, 1989, pp. 211-223.

4. D. Lenoski et al., "The Directory-Based Cache Coherence Protocol for the Dash Multiprocessor," *Proc. 17th Int'l Symp. Computer Architecture*, IEEE CS Press, Los Alamitos, Calif., Order No. 2047, 1990, pp. 148-159.

5. G. Delp, *The Architecture and Implementation of Memnet: A High-Speed Shared Memory Computer Communication Network*, doctoral dissertation, Univ. of Delaware, Newark, Del., 1988.

6. R. Bisiani and M. Ravishankar, "Plus: A Distributed Shared-Memory System," *Proc. 17th Int'l Symp. Computer Archi-*

tecture, IEEE CS Press, Los Alamitos, Calif., Order No. 2047, 1990, pp. 115-124.

7. U. Ramachandran and M.Y.A. Khalidi, "An Implementation of Distributed Shared Memory," *First Workshop Experiences with Building Distributed and Multiprocessor Systems*, Usenix Assoc., Berkeley, Calif., 1989, pp. 21-38.

8. N. Carriero and D. Gelernter, *How to Write Parallel Programs: A First Course*, MIT Press, Cambridge, Mass., 1990.

9. K. Li and R. Schaefer, "A Hypercube Shared Virtual Memory System," *Proc. Int'l Conf. Parallel Processing*, Pennsylvania State Univ. Press, University Park, Pa., and London, 1989, pp. 125-132.

10. S. Zhou et al., "A Heterogeneous Distributed Shared Memory," to be published in *IEEE Trans. Parallel and Distributed Systems*.

11. J. Bennett, J. Carter, and W. Zwaenepoel, "Munin: Distributed Shared Memory Based on Type-Specific Memory Coherence," *Proc. 1990 Conf. Principles and Practice of Parallel Programming*, ACM Press, New York, N.Y., 1990, pp. 168-176.

12. M. Dubois, C. Scheurich, and F.A. Briggs. "Synchronization, Coherence, and Event Ordering in Multiprocessors," *Computer*, Vol. 21, No. 2, Feb. 1988, pp. 9-21.

Bill Nitzberg is a PhD student in the Department of Computer and Information Science at the University of Oregon. In the AT&T-sponsored ACM International Programming Contest, Nitzberg was a member of the 1990 team and coached the 1991 team, which placed eighth and sixth, respectively.

Nitzberg received a BS in mathematics and an MS in computer science, both from the University of Oregon. He is a member of ACM.

Virginia Lo is an assistant professor in the Department of Computer and Information Science at the University of Oregon. Her research interests include distributed operating systems and the mapping of parallel algorithms to parallel architectures.

Lo received a BA from the University of Michigan, an MS in computer science from Pennsylvania State University, and a PhD in computer science from the University of Illinois at Urbana-Champaign. She is a member of the IEEE, the IEEE Computer Society, and the ACM.

Readers can reach the authors at the Department of Computer Science. University of Oregon, Eugene, OR 97403; e-mail [last name]@cs.uoregon.edu.

Reconfigurable and massively parallel architectures

An overview of the Texas Reconfigurable Array Computer*

by MATTHEW C. SEJNOWSKI, EDWIN T. UPCHURCH, RAJAN N. KAPUR,
DANIEL P. S. CHARLU and G. JACK LIPOVSKI
University of Texas at Austin
Austin, Texas

1.0 OVERVIEW

This paper presents an overview of TRAC and then discusses the system's suitability for some promising applications: Monte Carlo techniques, numerical solutions to linear systems, and data base applications.

1.1 Introduction

The Texas Reconfigurable Array Computer (TRAC) is an experimental computer system currently being built at the University of Texas at Austin. It is a multiprocessor system intended to utilize existing microprocessor technology and yet provide performance that promises to be superior to current state-of-the-art processor capabilities. The uniqueness and the potential capabilities of TRAC arise from its interconnection network: a dynamically reconfigurable banyan network.[1] The banyan network serves to partition and to configure the processor, memory and I/O resources of the system into different architectural organizations as demanded for efficient application formulation and solution. Although it was originally formulated as a high capacity scientific computer, it has been shown to perform well in both numerical and non-numerical applications.

A high-performance microprocessor-based system has some definite advantages over other large-scale computer designs. Chip count tends to be low, and microprocessors are very competitive in the "cost per computing power" sense, and should continue to be increasingly cost-effective in the future. Therefore, an obvious possibility for high-performance design is to include in the system as many microprocessors as needed to achieve the performance level desired. A major stumbling block in such a multi-processor system has been the nature of the interconnection network. In fact, the interconnection network may be much more expensive and complex than the rest of system.

It is well-known how a program can be run on a set of processors such that the data operated on consist of multiple-precision vector elements with the entire vector accessed simultaneously. This is done by connecting n processors to each of n independent memories with common address space, so that a given address across the memories contains one vector. Each CPU then processes one piece of the vector in parallel with all the others. Carry logic is used to interconnect processors acting upon different fragments of the same vector element, to achieve multi-precision arithmetic. For example, Figure 1 shows a system that operates on 2-element vectors where each element is 3 bytes long (each processor handles one byte).

The major drawback to such a machine is its lack of flexibility. The machine is essentially "hardwired" to operate on a specific type of data. When other data types are operated upon, gross inefficiencies result; the machine either ends up underpowered, overpowered, or just poorly configured for the task (for example, using the machine in Figure 1 to process 7-element vectors of 8 bits per element is clearly inefficient).

A logical way to improve the situation is to introduce switches into the bus structure, under control of software. One general way of doing this is the crossbar arrangement as shown in Figure 2.[2] Now the machine can be dynamically configured to adapt itself to the needs of the task. The big disadvantage here is that the number of switches required is proportional to the square of the number of resources in the system. For large systems (for example, a 1000-processor system), the switch count is then prohibitively large.

The TRAC system being built is a form of switched network in which the number of switches required goes up as $n * \log n$ with respect to the number of resources to connect. The major unique features of the TRAC computer are space sharing, reconfigurability, varistructuring, inter-task communication ability and the fact that its design makes it a virtual machine to the user. Space sharing implies that independent or interacting tasks can all be running simultaneously on the same computer, as opposed to the time sharing where tasks must await their allotted time-slot to execute. Reconfigurability is the ability of TRAC to dynamically partition its processors and resources (primary and secondary memories, I/O devices) under software control to obtain optimal utilization and minimal waste for the set of tasks to be run. Within a partition, TRAC is varistructured in that regardless of the data structure requirements for the task, any data width or architecture may be used; flexible microcode makes the exact processor configuration transparent to the software for the task. The machine is virtual

* This research is supported under NSF Grant MCS77-15968.

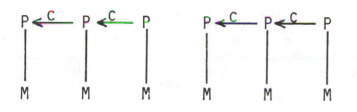

P = processors, 8-bit

M = memories

c = carry linkages

Figure 1—A two-element 24-bit/element vector computer.

in that user programs can be oblivious of the specific set of memory and processor modules used. Memories have space-page registers which allow them to be combined in any way to form address spaces. An extension of the virtual nature of the machine is TRAC's modularity. Without changing operating system software, resources and processors can be added on to the system in a building-block fashion to expand the machine to meet the needs of the user.

We now review the concepts which TRAC uses to achieve these goals. It is important to realize that these concepts are each more general in potential than in their realization in TRAC. They are currently the topics of extensive research by TRAC personnel at the University of Texas.

1.2 Concepts

The most fundamental concept in the system is the use of an SW-banyan network[3] to interconnect the set of processors

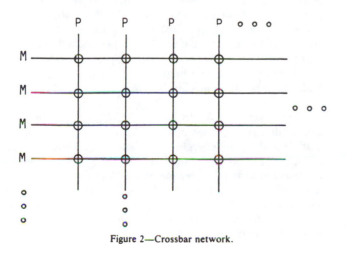

Figure 2—Crossbar network.

with the set of resources. A banyan is represented by a graph in which nodes are divided into three types: apex, base and intermediate nodes. In TRAC, apex nodes represent processors, base nodes represent memory or I/O or combined memory-I/O resources and other nodes represent switch nodes. It has the property that there is a unique path between any apex (processor) and base (resource) node pair through the intermediate nodes (switches). Furthermore, the graph may be regular in that all apex nodes look alike, all intermediate nodes look alike, and all base nodes are either memory nodes or I/O nodes or combined memory I/O nodes. Note the potential for mass production of the components; in fact, only four types of LSI IC's would be needed to build a very large and powerful computer. The intermediate nodes have a fixed number of arcs going toward apex nodes ("spread") and going toward base nodes ("fanout"). Figure 3 shows a typical SW banyan network. A characteristic of SW-banyans is that each level of intermediate nodes has $O(n)$ nodes, and there are $O(\log n)$ levels, hence $O(n*\log n)$ switches.

Each switch in the network is capable of interconnecting an incoming arc to any subset of the outgoing arcs and vice versa. Initializing the switches is done in hardware and is transparent to user programs.

For a given task, three types of subtrees can be established using the switch nodes[1]: data trees, instruction trees, and

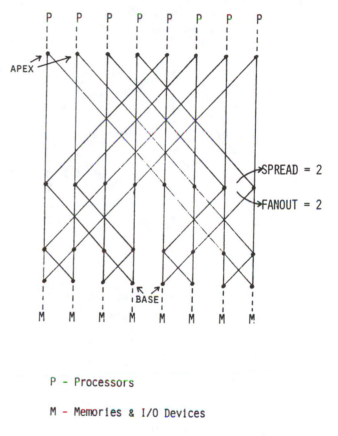

P - Processors

M - Memories & I/O Devices

• - Switches

Figure 3—A typical SW-banyan.

shared memory trees. Physically these are actually trees, but once formed they logically and electrically perform as busses. The data tree is used as a data bus to connect a processor with appropriate memory modules. The instruction tree is used as an instruction bus to broadcast instructions to a set of processors performing the same task (SIMD mode). Shared memory trees connect a set of processors to a single memory module for the purpose of sharing data; parts of the shared memory tree are used to extend a data bus from time to time in order to share a memory. The operation of these subtrees is shown later. Figure 4 shows examples of these trees. Following the paths of instruction trees and shared-memory trees is a GPC (generate-propagate-carry) bus used to interconnect processors all working on the same multi-precision data element. The GPC bus is also used for synchronization of processors, distributing status information and arbitration over control of shared memories.

In addition to the primary memories, TRAC has self-managing secondary memory (SMSM).[4] These modules are in-

cluded in the system network as resources. They are low cost, medium speed memory devices which may initially be implemented using CCD's, bubble memory or MOS RAM technology. The data within the SMSM is organized as segments and accessed by means of segment labels, making it act like an associative memory over the labels only. Since the directory structure is implemented in hardware, the burden of locating specific sets of data is taken from the software. A key use of SMSM's in the TRAC architecture is to virtualize the memory. If a processor accesses memory data which is not currently in one of the memory modules attached to the processor, the SMSM is used to page out current data in one of the modules, and then read in the desired page of data into the now-free memory module.

The concept of index registers located in memory nodes is used in TRAC. Instead of having processors supply a complete address and data bus to all resources (which would have to be replicated on each arc of the SW-banyan), a smaller 8-bit bus is used. References to locations in memory modules are made by specifying one of the index registers which reside on the memory modules themselves. This technique allows a short (8-bit) macro-instruction to be sent through the switches rather than a longer (16-bit) address. This includes the program counter and data stack pointers, as well as other special-purpose registers. The modules also have built-in hardware to increment or decrement the registers. Thus, in straight-line code, there is never any need, for example, for a processor to take part in the incrementing of the program counter (other than instructing the memory module to do so). Stack operations, also, typically require only incrementing and decrementing operations on the stack pointers.

Now that we have touched upon the concepts in use by TRAC, we describe the prototype implementation now in progress at the University of Texas at Austin and the configuration of architectures for tasks and task execution.

1.3 Operation

The TRAC system will initially consist of a four-level SW-banyan network with a fanout of 3 and spread of 2 (this amounts to 211 switch nodes). The network will connect 16 processors to 81 memory-I/O nodes. The base nodes will all (except for the switch control node and the port to external computer systems) have uniform interfaces which may support a memory module (of 4K byte capacity), an SMSM of 64K bytes or both. The banyan arcs consist of 23 signals, 8 of which are the data bus and three the carry-lookahead logic.

Given a set of tasks to run on TRAC, sets of resources can be allocated to each of the tasks in such a way that the partitions all are independent of one another. Thus the tasks "space share" the machine; see Figure 5. Each task has exclusive control of its resources and does not have to contend with other machines for the use of these resources. In addition, while the tasks are running, the system is dynamically reconfigurable, allowing specialized task structures to be created on demand.

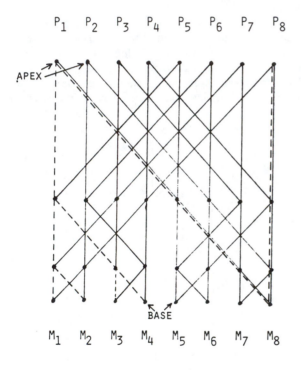

P_1 P_2 P_3 P_4 P_5 P_6 P_7 P_8

APEX

BASE

M_1 M_2 M_3 M_4 M_5 M_6 M_7 M_8

/ — Data Subtree connecting P_1 with M_1, M_2, M_3, M_4

// — Instruction Broadcast Tree connecting P_1 with P_8

— Also Shared Memory Tree allowing P_1 and P_8 to share M_8

Figure 4—Subtree examples.

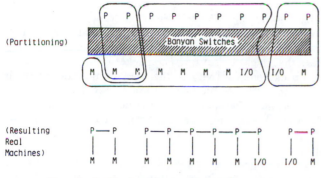

(Partitioning)

Banyan Switches

(Resulting
Real
Machines)

Figure 5—Partitioning and space sharing of resources.

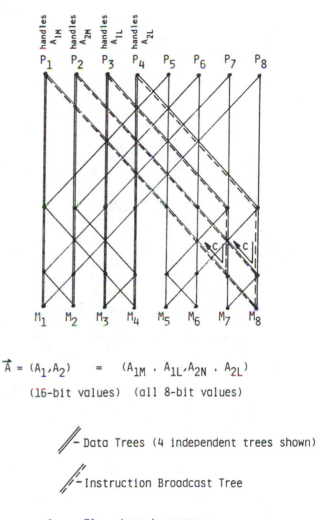

$$\vec{A} = (A_1, A_2) \quad = \quad (A_{1M} \cdot A_{1L}, A_{2N} \cdot A_{2L})$$

(16-bit values) (all 8-bit values)

 - Data Trees (4 independent trees shown)

- Instruction Broadcast Tree

Carry Flow shown by arrows

Figure 6—A subcomputer that handles 2-element vectors, 2 bytes per vector.

Each processor in the TRAC system operates with 8-bit operands. To achieve parallelism in processing multi-precision data, TRAC uses multiple processors. First we consider processing vectors of v elements of p bytes precision per element, using $v*p$ processors (later we show how less processors can be used by "folding" the array and/or its elements). Since all the processors will perform nearly the same operation on their respective bytes of a vector simultaneously, an instruction tree connects all processors together during an instruction-fetch cycle. The task's code thus needs to exist in only one of the processor's memory spaces. That memory fetches an instruction, then broadcasts the instruction through the data bus and over the instruction bus in one memory cycle to all the other processors in the partition. Figure 6 shows an example of a subcomputer that processes 2-element vectors, 16 bits per element. Note that the instruction subtree is totally independent of the data subtree. The GPC bus included in the instruction subtree provides carry-lookahead capability as well as other synchronization functions as described above.

Thus the entire array can be accessed simultaneously. In many cases, the number of available processors is limited, or the size of the vector is too large to allow completely parallel processing of the elements. This is where TRAC's varistructured capability comes into play.[5] When a task is to be loaded and run, it passes information to the scheduler for TRAC concerning the type of data structure the task uses as well as a the urgency of the task (the more urgent a task is, the more processors it is allocated). The scheduler arbitrates between all the tasks and performs a partitioning of processors and resources in order to best satisfy all the tasks' needs.

When a task is allocated a number of processors fewer than the full width of its vector elements, the elements are "folded" into the available memory width. For example, Figure 7 shows to different ways in which a 4-element vector with 2-byte elements can be packed into the memory modules of 6 processors (naturally, if 8 processors are available, the packing would be much more straightforward). The microcode in the processors makes the packing algorithm transparent to the user; for example, adding two vectors together would be accomplished by the same machine-language instruction regardless of which of the two alternative packings shown in Figure 7 is used.

More generally, logical vectors can be packed into a fixed memory width (as specified by the number of processors allocated for the task) as shown in Figure 8. In the figure, each horizontal row of data is capable of being accessed simultaneously by the microcode; a reference to a vector at the machine language level translates to sequentially accessing each of the rows of the memory. The processors

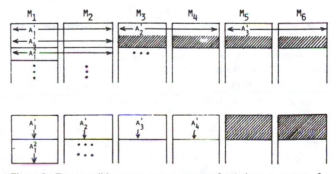

Figure 7—Two possible memory arrangements for 4-element vectors, 2-byte elements, in 6 memory modules.

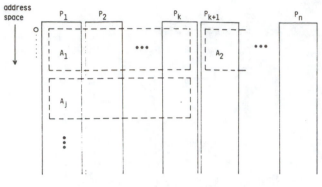

Figure 8—Varistructured processing of multi-byte precision
vectors.

once again perform identical operations; furthermore, they repeat the identical operations at each row of memory until the entire segment is accessed. The only differences are when handling most-significant or least-significant bytes; the processor microcodes handle these automatically.

A data tree always has a processor at its root and one or more of the resources at its leaves. It is important to realize that though the interconnections are electrically tree-structured, it is used as a conventional bus through which the memories at the leaves of the tree are logically all mapped into the root processor's memory space which is always one byte wide, and potentially 64K bytes long. Each of the memory modules is 4K bytes long, and is divided into four 1K pages, each of which has an onboard page register telling where the page fits into the processor's memory space. The four pages may be dedicated separately as any of program space (instruction space), control space (which contains a stack for descriptor and control information), operand space (containing a task data stack) data space (containing task global data).[6] Each of the four data spaces have associated with them two pointer registers as previously discussed.

An instruction tree is, orientation-wise, upside-down with respect to the data tree. Its root is a dummy (i.e. unused) memory module, while all its leaves are processor nodes. Anything sent over this tree by one of the processors is broadcast to all attached processors in order to implement SIMD mode processing. The carry tree is the same structurally as the instruction tree. However, as discussed earlier, by forcing the generate and propagate to zero, the propagation of carry signals can be broken up allowing vector parallelism.

A third type of subtree, the shared memory tree, allows multiple processors to be simultaneously connected to a memory module. A shared memory tree is identical in form to an instruction tree. Attached processors may all be part of the same task or may be from different tasks. At any particular point in time, only one processor can have access to the memory. Arbitration for access rights to the memory are done round-robin style using the carry lookahead as a priority circuit, so that no processor can lock out other processors from access to the memory indefinitely. Shared memory provides a good means of communicating large amounts of intertask or intratask data.

Another means of processor-processor communication is packet switching.[7] Packet segments travel from memory node to processor node by hopping between adjoining switch nodes, one hop per memory cycle, independently of any trees that might be set up. The packet transmissions occur as a background activity so that they do not interfere with other activity. Destination information contained in the packets route the packet through the nodes. Packets may be explicitly sent and received through TRAC machine language or implicitly sent as part of certain microcoded instructions.

Since registers residing within the processors are of fixed width, but data can in general be of any width, TRAC machine language instructions that perform data manipulation do not explicitly involve processor registers (such as load and store accumulator instructions found on many other machines). Instead, the instructions tend to be the memory-memory type. Stack operations are supported, with the on-memory index registers used as stack pointers. For example, the add instruction takes the top two elements on the stack and replaces them with their vector sum, adjusting stack pointers accordingly.

TRAC subsystems can be architectured to implement each of the types of parallel execution structures described in the literature.[8] In one type of asynchronous parallelism (MIMD), a task may, at some point in its execution, fork into multiple subtasks operating independently of one another. Once the fork occurs, subtasks may have to communicate data and status information with other subtasks. Another occurrence of asynchronous parallelism is the concept of task pipelining. In this scheme, a subtask operates on a set of input data and produces a set of output data. This output is then used as input to the next subtask in the chain, which likewise produces output. All processes operate asynchronously except for the necessary synchronization of inputs and outputs. A third form of asynchronous parallelism is the data-flow concept; extending the concept of operators to subroutines and functions (which are subtasks), a subtask is allowed to run only when all of its input parameters are present (the parameters may be outputs from other subtasks).

Asynchronous parallelism is easily achieved in the TRAC system. Because of the ability of subtasks to have completely separate and independent sets of processors and resources (space sharing), asynchronism and non-interference is assured. Several methods of inter-subtask communication are available, including shared memory modules, packet switching, and dynamic reconfiguration to physically transfer memory modules between subtasks.

Another mode of parallelism is vector parallelism, as discussed earlier. We have seen that the varistructured nature of TRAC allows it to intrinsically support this mode.

Synchronous parallelism includes situations in which subtasks may have different instruction flows, but must all operate such that simultaneous events are well-defined. For example, the addition of floating-point values might employ two subtasks; one to handle the mantissa and one to handle the exponent. If the mantissa subtask shifts the mantissa, the other subtask must simultaneously increment the exponent. Other examples include matrix inversions and string or set searches. In the TRAC system, tasks running on different processors can be in synchronization with each other if care is taken by the system programmer to control task startup and interrupts. Inter-subtask communication could be implemented through shared memories.

The TRAC interconnection network also implements parallelism in data movement as well as computation. The many paths from apex and base nodes represent potentially active data paths for memory and instruction fetches. The use of the network for packet movement in its phases of inactivity for bus service offers a potentially vast bandwidth for asynchronous data movement.

2.0 APPLICATIONS

We now examine some typical application areas which could take advantage of TRAC's architecture. Each of these applications demonstrate the power of TRAC to support several forms of parallel execution, to be configured for a given application and to reconfigure during the phases of execution of an application and to utilize high-volume data transfers through the network. A crucial role for TRAC will be to serve as a focus for the analysis of applications and algorithms for parallel formulations. The existence of a system which can serve as an experimental facility for execution of parallel algorithms should be a strong stimulus for this significant problem area.

2.1 Iterative solutions of linear systems

We will describe the configuration of systems for the solution of large sparse linear systems of the type

(1) $Au = b$
where
A is an $N \times N$ coefficient matrix,
u is N element vector,
b is a known N element vector and
N is of the order of $10^{**}3$ to $10^{**}6$.

Such systems are frequently encountered in the numerical solution of partial differential equations arising from problems in areas such as oil recovery, nuclear reactor design, scientific weather prediction and many others. Partial differential equations (PDEs) can be converted into simultaneous linear equations using finite element methods or finite difference methods.[9] The conversion method, as well as the nature of the physical system described by the PDEs influences the structure of the matrix A.[10] Two types of procedures used to solve large sparse linear systems are *direct* methods and *iterative* methods. In general for large systems, iterative methods require less storage and may require fewer arithmetic operations than direct methods.

Iterative methods work by breaking up the system into subsystems. A number of different groupings are feasible: point row-wise, wavefront, submatrix etc. Let us consider some block iterative methods. Here the matrix A is parti-

Figure 9—Linear system $Au = b$ block partitioned with $q = 4$.

tioned into submatrices $A(i,j)$ (Figure 9); the resulting subsystems are solved and the results are merged. The subsystems are often selected such that their solution is trivial, e.g. the submatrices may be lower triangular; if this is not the case other techniques can be used. This is repeated until some stopping criterion is fulfilled.

In the Jacobi method, one solves g subsystems during each iteration as follows:

(2) $A(i,i)*Ui(n+1) = -\Sigma A(i,j)*Ui(n) + Bi$ for all $j.NE.i$
$j = 1,q$
where
$A(i,j)$: submatrix i,j
$Ui(n)$: solution subvector i at nth iteration,
Bi: subvector B.

For a dense matrix or a sparse matrix without structure, for subsystem i to compute $Ui(n+1)$ it must have all $Uj(n)$ where $j.NE.i$. Thus $g - 1$ transfers are required for computing a subvector and $q*(q - 1)$ transfers are required in computing the result vector per iteration. However, a knowledge of the structure of matrix A can be used to reduce the number of transfers.

Consider the data flow graph of the iterations (Figure 10)— each node in the graph represents the solution of a subsystem; the directed arcs represent data transfers from a subsystem to another subsystem. Data must be present on all the input arcs at a subsystem before that solution can proceed. In this case q subsystems at the nth iteration must be solved before any of the solutions at the $(n + 1)$th iteration can proceed. Again, a knowledge of the structure of matrix A can be used to permit those subsystems to proceed, whose input arcs are full.

Consider the case where each subsystem is assigned to a partition. Each partition can operate in one of 3 modes:

1. Computation mode: Intrapartition computation. This can involve intrapartition synchronous packet transmission, e.g., as in a matrix multiply.
2. Communicating mode: Receiving/transmitting data from/ to another partition.
3. Idle: Not (1) or (2).

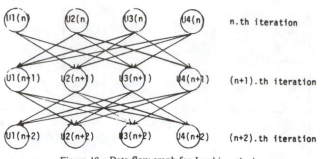

Figure 10—Data flow graph for Jacobi method.

The current version of TRAC does not support the overlapped operation of (1) and (2) although there is no intrinsic reason in the TRAC architecture which will prevent its extension to this further dimension of parallel execution.

For the Jacobi method the computation for an iteration of subsystem solution is according to equation (2). This computation can be performed using a matrix multiply and a vector add.

The Gauss Seidel method (which is structurally similar to several other methods) is a better technique on the basis of convergence criteria: it requires the solution of q subsystems of the form:

$$(3) \quad A(i,i).Ui(n+1) = -\Sigma A(i,j)*Uj(n+1)$$
$$j=1.i-1$$
$$-\Sigma A(i,j)*Uj(n)+Bi$$
$$j=i+1.q$$

The corresponding data flow graph is shown in Figure 11. The dependencies in this graph indicate that only one node can be active at a given time. Prepaging techniques based on[11] can be realized using structures similar to that shown in Figure 12. This can result in up to 50 percent reduction in processing time.

An analysis of the dataflow within each node indicates that all the inputs are not necessary for the operation of the node to commence (Figure 13)! We can still assign a subsystem per partition, but by permitting each subsystem to proceed when it has sufficient input data, utilization is enhanced (Figure 14). This can give up to a $(q-1)$ fold improvement on a q partition (with one subsystem per partition) system. We are currently studying these and other structures.

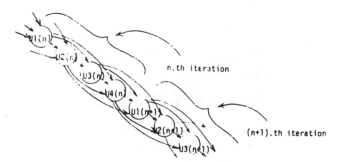

Figure 11—Data flow graph for Gauss Seidel method.

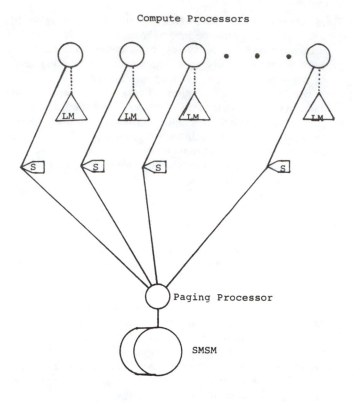

LM:Local Memory   S:Shared Memory SMSM:Secondary memory

Figure 12—Structure for prepaged Gauss Seidel method.

2.2 Monte Carlo method

The Monte Carlo method consists of constructing a probabilistic model of a problem in which the problem solution is a statistical parameter of the model that is determined by repeated, independent random sampling. As with any statistical process, a large number of trials must be made in order to obtain accurate results. This method generally converges slowly as $1/(SQRT\ n)$ where n is the number of trials performed (convergence acceleration techniques are known but are not included in this discussion). Because of this slow convergence, the Monte Carlo method is seldom used if the problem is amenable to other numerical techniques. A major advantage of this method however in terms of parallel processing, is that the solution at each point can be estimated independently (in parallel) and the method can easily be extended to higher dimensional problems with linear increase in computational complexity.

The Monte Carlo method was selected for evaluation on TRAC for the following reasons:

1. it is computationally intense;
2. it contains considerable inherent asynchronous parallelism;
3. its algorithms tend to be simple;
4. the method is useful in numerical applications.

Initially a very simple numerical integration problem to find the area of a unit circle is used to benchmark TRAC. This problem, though extremely simple, contains the essential elements of the Monte Carlo technique. First, the mathematical problem is described, then an organization to compute the results that exploits as much inherent parallelism as possible is given. Finally, a mapping of this task structure onto TRAC is discussed including the potential performance of the system.

The mathematical model of the problem is shown in Figure 15 where the area has been normalized to the unit square for convenience. Generally speaking, one can describe a probabilistic model of the problem in which "darts" (represented by pseudo-random number pairs) are thrown at the square and the area of the circle determined by counting the number of times a dart hits inside the circle (successes) compared to the total number of throws. The area of the circle is then given by:

$$AREA = HITS/TOTAL\ THROWS.$$

As more and more "darts" are thrown the area of the circle is determined more accurately. Of course, the problem can be reduced by symmetry to consideration of the first quadrant only and the resulting area multiplied by four. Mathematically two independent sequences of random variables Xi and Yi are generated. The points (Xi, Yi) are tested to see if they lie within the circle by determining if $Xi**2 + Yi**2 < 1$.

The steps of the algorithm can logically be partitioned between two task types which can run independently. Tasks

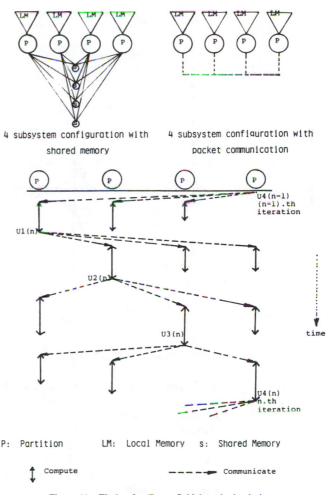

4 subsystem configuration with   4 subsystem configuration with
      shared memory   packet communication

P: Partition   LM: Local Memory   s: Shared Memory

↕ Compute   - - - - - Communicate

Figure 14—Timing for Gauss Seidel method solution.

of type A perform the calculations of the individual trials, and determine if the trial was a success (hit) or a failure. Tasks of type B check the prescribed convergence criteria and terminate the whole process when satisfied. Generally one would like to have a large number of type A tasks running in parallel and a single type B task checking their results.

The steps of tasks A and B are outlined as follows:

Task A

begin
  generate pseudo-random number pair (Xi, Yi)
    if $Xi**2 + Yi**2 < 1$
      success: = success + 1
      total: = total + 1
end

Task B

begin
  newarea: = success/total
    if (newarea − oldarea)$<e$ stop.
    oldarea = newarea
end

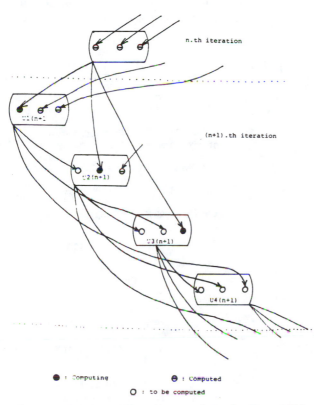

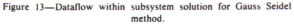

● : Computing   ⊖ : Computed

○ : to be computed

Figure 13—Dataflow within subsystem solution for Gauss Seidel method.

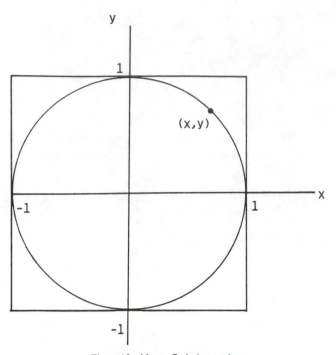

Figure 15—Monte Carlo integration.

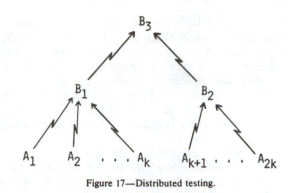

Figure 17—Distributed testing.

A conceptual TRAC configuration is shown in Figure 16. Identical machines $A1, A2....An$ would be configured and operate asynchronously reporting the results of their experiments by packets sent to task B. Task B would monitor the convergence and determine when to terminate the processing. Although this process organization fits the problem well and offers a potential reduction in processing time by very nearly $1/n$ there are two problems:

1. Counter bottleneck. If n is very large (as one would hope for a full-scale TRAC machine), task B may become a bottleneck due to the large number of packets received from the A tasks. A possible solution is illustrated in Figure 17 in which a small number of additional B processes are introduced forming a tree to reduce the message traffic to each Bi. When a total counter in a Bi task overflows the next higher counter is updated. The updating process could be skewed to avoid bursts of updates caused by the A tasks running very nearly in lock step.
2. Parallel pseudo-random number generation. It was assumed that each task Ai generates its own pseudo-random numbers (PRN). This is a non-trivial assumption, since one must be sure that the parallel sequences of PRN are independent. A method has been developed

to guarantee that the sequences are independent. This method assumes a PRN sequence in which one has confidence. Given this sequence generated by a multiplicative PRN algorithm then each Ai is assigned a seed from the assumed PRN sequence (see Figure 18). An offset constant, c, is used by each Ai to generate its next PRN. More details and extensions of this method are found in[12]. Once the n seeds, Xi and c are computed and sent to the corresponding Ai tasks, each task can generate its PRN's in parallel independent of the other tasks.

2.3 Database management

The design and implementation of special machine architectures for database management has been receiving increasing attention in recent years. A major reason for this

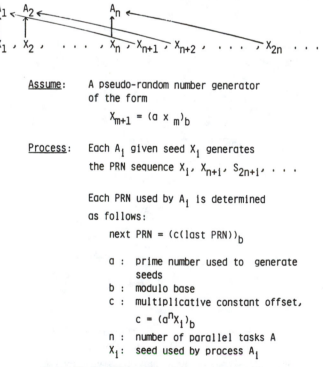

Assume: A pseudo-random number generator of the form

$$X_{m+1} = (a \; x_m)_b$$

Process: Each A_i given seed X_i generates the PRN sequence $X_i, X_{n+i}, S_{2n+i}, \ldots$

Each PRN used by A_i is determined as follows:

next PRN $= (c(\text{last PRN}))_b$

a : prime number used to generate seeds
b : modulo base
c : multiplicative constant offset,
    $c = (a^n X_i)_b$
n : number of parallel tasks A
X_i: seed used by process A_i

Figure 18—Parallel pseudo-random number generation.

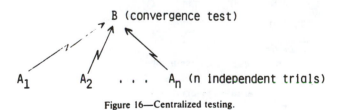

Figure 16—Centralized testing.

interest is the rapidly growing size of databases and the high frequency of query processing. Hsiao[13] in his description of data utilities, suggests a future database capacity requirement of over 10**12 bytes and a peak query frequency of a million requests/second.

A number of different approaches have been taken toward solving the very large database processing problem.[14,15,16] Reconfigurable machines are becoming feasible primarily due to the appearance of low cost microprocessors. The flexibility of such machines may permit a synthesis of the previously described database machine approaches with the additional capability for highly efficient concurrent query processing through configuration to match individual or groups of queries. In effect, special purpose sub-computers can be created to process each query and a number of these machines can run concurrently.

2.3.1 Approach

One approach suitable for the hierarchical data base management system is to consider TRAC as a potential backend machine to process indices to a large data file. The database data file will reside on a general purpose host system on a conventional mass storage device with secondary index files (inverted file and record association file) being searched and updated in the the backend, and implemented so as to take advantage of the backend's novel architectural features. A key file consisting of a key type, keys and a trace (logical identifier) for each record occurrence in the database is maintained on the backend. Traces described by Lowenthal[17] are tuples which represent record occurrences and the logical positioning of a record in a hierarchically structured database. Operations on the key file are functionally equivalent to operations on an inverted file. This file may be segmented by key type and paged into fast access SMSM memories[4] and searched to determine a set of traces which are then passed along to a set operation pipeline where they are combined with other trace sets to generate a response set for complex queries. Queries may be represented in a disjunctive form:

$$A(1).op.A(2).op. ....A(i) ... .op. A(n)$$

where each $A(i)$ represents conjunctions of relational expressions defined on key items and values within a single record type and ".op." represents a set operation, such as union, intersection and difference. For example, consider the query:

Find name SMITH where salary is greater than $20,000 and location is Austin.

Where name, salary and location are key items. Suppose each of these keys are on separate key files, then

$A(1)$: (name. = .SMITH)
$A(2)$: (salary.>.20000)
$A(3)$: (location. = .Austin)

and the query is of the form:

(name, = ,SMITH) .and. (salary,>,20000) .and. (location, = ,Austin).

Processors are configured to search the corresponding key file for each of the $A(i)$'s. The $A(i)$'s have been constructed as simple operations so that a single pass through the file is sufficient to determine the response set. As a result of these searches, the average data traffic through the pipeline is greatly reduced.

A principal focus of this investigation is the development of efficient algorithms for sorting and set operations on indices. Efficient set operation algorithms are necessary to combine trace sets to determine the response for complex queries. Sorting is required to arrange the key file by trace value so that each trace set entering the pipeline will be sorted to facilitate set operations for individual queries. Sorting could be performed during slack periods or during updating sessions and could use the large number of processors that would be available at that time. Separating the sorting from individual query processing eliminates much redundant sorting.

While other architectures also offer potential for very large data base management, the inherent parallel but flexible TRAC structure promises to be a viable alternative to, or a useful addition to, those other techniques.

2.3.2 System configuration

Based on the approach described in the previous section the backend system is configured into multiple pipelines of the type shown in Figure 19. For the set operation stages it is assumed that in general the size of the trace sets will be large relative to the memory available for individual pipelines. Furthermore, traces will only be available page by page from the search stage. Under these constraints a pipeline approach is valid. It is expected that on the average several hundred pipelines could exist simultaneously on a machine with 6000 or more processing elements. Note that this is an average figure and the peak query concurrency could be higher.

High input bandwidth to the pipeline is required to avoid a possible I/O bottleneck. The approach taken is to page the key file, segmented by key type, from secondary memory to high speed SMSM. These memories output continuously, and the data can be read by attaching processors dynamically to the desired bytes of the key. Figure 20 shows an example input. The key portion and trace are read in parallel by the attached processors. Key bytes are compared with a comparand register slice in each processor, and if the query

Figure 19—System functional pipeline.

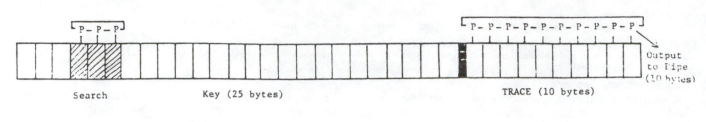

Search Key (25 bytes) TRACE (10 bytes) Output to Pipe (10 bytes)

—: carry linkage

Figure 20—Pipeline input.

condition is satisfied, the associated trace is pushed into RAM buffers attached to the proper pipeline. More than one processor can be attached at the same time to a byte of memory so that a number of pipelines can be serviced concurrently by the same input module.

There is also the possibility of overlapping or time sharing stages of the pipeline. For example, set intersection may result in diminished output while set union will result in increased output. The flow through the network, therefore may not be smooth resulting in idle time that could be shared with other processes. Resources can be released as the pipeline begins to empty.

The interesting possibility of performance improvement through query lookahead and Boolean tree height reduction for optimizing the configuration and scheduling of the query pipelines is under investigation. Algorithms discussed by Kuck[18] and Ramamoorthy[19] for tree height reduction in arithmetic expressions may be applicable in this context.

3.0 CONCLUSIONS

TRAC offers the potential for a great amount of parallelism. We are studying the approaches to best utilize the computer, and preliminary results are positive. This paper summarized the architecture and its uses. The following papers on TRAC in these proceedings show more detail on how the hardware is built. Though not presented in depth in these proceedings, a joint effort between the University of Texas Electrical Engineering Department and the Computer Science Department has yielded extensive research and development in the areas of operating systems, system simulation and other software areas.

4.0 ACKNOWLEDGMENTS

The authors would like to gratefully acknowledge J. C. Browne, M. M. Malek, H. L. Taylor and the members of the TRAC team whose extensive works are reflected in this paper.

BIBLIOGRAPHY

1. Lipovski, G. J. and Tripathi, A., "A Reconfigurable Varistructure Array Processor," *Proc. of the 1977 International Conference on Parallel Processing,* August 1977, pp. 165-174.
2. Wulf, W. A. and Bell, C. G., "C.mmp—A Multi-Miniprocessor," *AFIPS Proceedings,* Vol. 41, FJCC, 1972, pp. 122-131.
3. Goke, R. and Lipovski, G. J., "Banyan Networks for Partitioning on Multiprocessor Systems," *Proceedings of the First Annual Symposium on Computer Architecture,* 1973, pp. 21-30.
4. Lipovski, G. J., Su, S. Y., and Watson, J. K., "A Self-Managing Secondary Memory System," *Proceedings of the Third Annual Symposium on Computer Architecture,* January 1976.
5. Premkumar, U. V., "TRAC: Principles of Operation," Technical Report TRAC-3, University of Texas at Austin, January 15, 1979.
6. Smullen, J. R., "Memory Management of TRAC," Technical Report TRAC-2, University of Texas at Austin, May 1979.
7. Tripathi, A. R. and Lipovski, G. J., "Packet Switching in Banyan Networks," Symposium on Computer Architecture, 1979.
8. DeGroot, R. D., "Introduction to the Architecture of TRAC," Technical Report TRAC-1, University of Texas at Austin, January 1977.
9. Young, D. M. and Gregory, T., *A Survey of Numerical Mathematics,* Vol. II, Academic Press, 1972.
10. Young, D. M., *Iterative Techniques in Numerical Analysis,* Academic Press, 1971.
11. Trivedi, K. S., "An Analysis of Prepaging," CS-1977-7, Department of Computer Science, Duke University, August 1977.
12. Upchurch, E. T. and Lipovski, G. J., "Parallel Pseudorandom Number Generation and Monte Carlo Methods on TRAC," TRAC Technical Report, in preparation.
13. Hsiao, D. X. and Madnick, D. K., "Data Base Machine Architecture in the Context of Information Technology Revolution," *Proceedings, Third Very Large Database Conference,* October 1977.
14. Berra, P. B., "Recent Developments in Data Base and Information Retrieval Hardware and Architecture," *COMPSAC,* November 1978, pp. 698-703.
15. Dewitt, D. J., "DIRECT- A Multiprocessor Organization Supporting Relational Data Base Management Systems," *Proceedings of the Fifth Symposium on Computer Architecture,* April 1976.
16. Lipovski, G. J., "Architectural Features of CASSM: A Context Addressed Segment Sequential Memory," *Proceedings of the Fifth Annual Symposium on Computer Architecture,* April 1978, pp. 31-38.
17. Lowenthal, E. I., "A Functional Approach to the Design of Storage Structures for Generalized Data Management Systems," Ph.D. Dissertation, Computer Science Department, University of Texas at Austin, August 1971.
18. Kuck, D. J., et al., "On the Number of Operations Simultaneously Executable in FORTRAN-like Programs and their Resulting Speedup," *IEEE Transactions on Computers,* December 1972, pp. 1293-1310.
19. Ramamoorthy, C. V., et al., "Compilation Techniques for Recognition of Parallel Processable Tasks in Arithmetic Expressions," *IEEE Transactions on Computers,* November 1973, pp. 986-998.

Architecture and Applications of the Connection Machine

Lewis W. Tucker and George G. Robertson

Thinking Machines Corp.

Reprinted from *Computer*, Vol. 21, No. 8, August 1988, pages 26-38. Copyright © 1988 by The Institute of Electrical and Electronics Engineers, Inc. All rights reserved.

As the use of computers affects increasingly broader segments of the world economy, many of the problems to which people apply computers grow continually larger and more complex. Demands for faster and larger computer systems increase steadily. Fortunately, the technology base for the last twenty years has continued to improve at a steady rate—increasing in capacity and speed while decreasing in cost for performance. However, the demands outpace the technology. This raises the question, can we make a quantum leap in performance while the rate of technology improvement remains relatively constant?

Computer architects have followed two general approaches in response to this question. The first uses exotic technology in a fairly conventional serial computer architecture. This approach suffers from manufacturing and maintenance problems and high costs. The second approach exploits the parallelism inherent in many problems. The parallel approach seems to offer the best long-term strategy because, as the problems grow, more and more opportunities arise to exploit the parallelism inherent in the data itself.

Where do we find the inherent parallelism and how do we exploit it? Most computer programs consist of a control sequence (the instructions) and a collection of data elements. Large programs have tens of thousands of instructions operat-

Massively parallel computer architectures have come of age. We describe here the architecture, evolution, and applications of the Connection Machine system.

ing on tens of thousands or even millions of data elements. We can find opportunities for parallelism in both the control sequence and in the collection of data elements.

In the control sequence, we can identify threads of control that could operate independently, thus on different processors. This approach, known as *control parallelism*, is used for programming most multiprocessor computers. The primary problems with this approach are the diffi-

culty of identifying and synchronizing these independent threads of control.

Alternatively, we can take advantage of the large number of independent data elements by assigning one processor to each data element and performing all operations on the data in parallel. This approach, known as *data parallelism*,[1] works best for large amounts of data. For many applications, it proves the most natural programming approach, leading to significant decreases in execution time as well as simplified programming.

Massively parallel architectures containing tens of thousands or even millions of processing elements support this "data-parallel" programming model. Early examples of this kind of architecture are ICL's Distributed Array Processor (DAP),[2] Goodyear's Massively Parallel Processor (MPP),[3] Columbia University's Non-Von,[4] and others.[5] Each of these machines has some elements of the desired architecture, but lacks others. For example, the MPP has 16K (K = 1,024) processing elements arranged in a two-dimensional grid, but interprocessor communication is supported only between neighboring processors.

The Connection Machine provides 64K physical processing elements, millions of virtual processing elements with its *virtual processor* mechanism, and general-purpose, reconfigurable communications networks. The Connection Machine

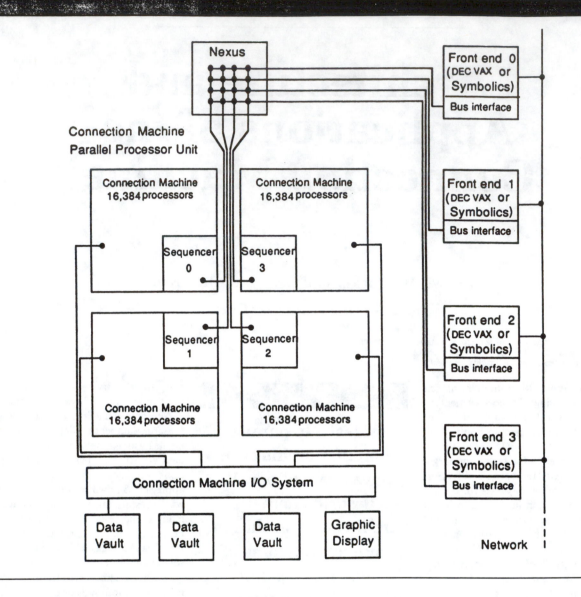

Figure 1. Connection Machine system organization.

encompasses a fully integrated architecture designed for data-parallel computing.

Architecture of the Connection Machine

The Connection Machine is a data-parallel computing system with integrated hardware and software. Figure 1 shows the hardware elements of the system. One to four front-end computer systems (right side of Figure 1) provide the development and execution environments for system software. They connect through the nexus (a 4×4 cross-point switch) to from one to four sequencers. Each sequencer controls up to 16,384 individual processors executing parallel operations. A high-performance, data-parallel I/O system (bottom of Figure 1) connects processors to peripheral mass storage (the DataVault) and graphic display devices.

System software is based upon the operating system or environment of the front-end computer, with minimal visible software extensions. Users can program using familiar languages and programming constructs, with all development tools provided by the front end. Programs have normal sequential control flow and do not need new synchronization structures.

Thus, users can easily develop programs that exploit the power of the Connection Machine hardware.

At the heart of the Connection Machine system lies the parallel-processing unit consisting of thousands of processors (up to 64K), each with thousands of bits of memory (four kilobits on the CM-1 and 64 kilobits on the CM-2). As well as processing the data stored in memory, these processors when logically interconnected can exchange information. All operations happen in parallel on all processors. Thus, the Connection Machine hardware directly supports the data-parallel programming model.

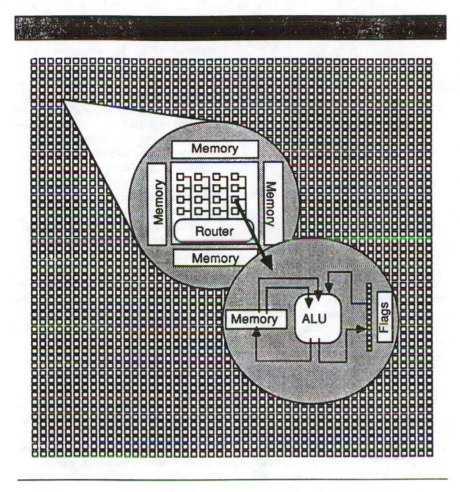

Figure 2. CM-1 data processors.

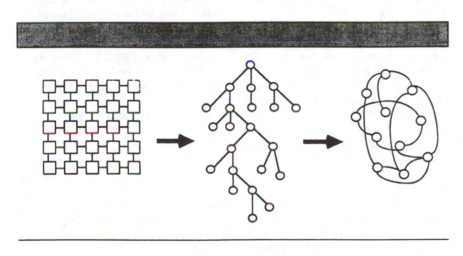

Figure 3. Complex problems change topology.

CM-1: First implementation of CM concept. Hillis originally conceived the Connection Machine architecture while at MIT and described it in his thesis.[6] The design of the Connection Machine began in 1980 at the MIT AI Laboratory, where the basic architectural design and prototype custom integrated circuits were developed. It became clear that private enterprise would have to get involved to actually build the machine, so Thinking Machines was founded in 1983.

The Connection Machine Model CM-1 was designed at Thinking Machines during 1983 and the first half of 1984. By the end of 1984, with funding from the Defense Advanced Research Projects Agency, Thinking Machines had built the first 16K-processor CM-1 prototype. A demonstration of its capabilities took place in May 1985, and by November the company had constructed and successfully demonstrated a full 64K-processor machine. Thinking Machines commercially introduced the machine in April 1986. The first machines went to MIT and Perkin-Elmer in the summer of 1986.

As illustrated in Figure 1, the CM-1 contains the following system components:

- up to 64K data processors,
- an interprocessor communications network,
- one to four sequencers, and
- one to four front-end computer interfaces.

Although part of the original Connection Machine design, the I/O system was not implemented until the introduction of the CM-2.

CM-1 data processors and memory. The CM-1 parallel-processing unit contains from 16K to 64K data processors. As shown in Figure 2, each data processor contains

- an arithmetic-logic unit and associated latches,
- four kilobits of bit-addressable memory,
- eight one-bit flag registers,
- a router interface, and
- a two-dimensional-grid interface.

The data processors are implemented using two chip types. A proprietary custom chip contains the ALU, flag bits, and communications interface for 16 data processors. Memory consists of commercial static RAM chips, with parity protection. A fully configured parallel-processing unit contains 64K data processors, consisting of 4,096 processor chips and 32 megabytes of RAM.

A CM-1 ALU consists of a three-input, two-output logic element and associated latches and memory interface (see Figure 2). The basic conceptual ALU cycle first reads two data bits from memory and one data bit from a flag. The logic element then computes two result bits from the three input bits. Finally, one of the two results is stored in memory and the other result, in a flag. The entire operation is conditional on the value of a context flag; if the flag is zero, then the results for that data processor are not stored.

The logic element can compute any two Boolean functions on three inputs. This simple ALU suffices to carry out all the operations of a virtual-machine instruction set. Arithmetic is carried out in a bit-serial fashion, requiring 0.75 microsecond per bit plus instruction decoding and overhead. Hence, a 32-bit Add takes about 24 microseconds. With 64K processors computing in parallel, this yields an aggregate rate of 2,000 million instructions per second (that is, two billion 32-bit Adds per second).

The CM processing element is a reduced-instruction-set-computer processor. Each ALU cycle breaks down into subcycles. On each cycle, data processors execute one low-level instruction (called a *nanoinstruction*) issued by the sequencer, while the memories can perform one read or write operation. The basic ALU cycle for a two-operand integer Add consists of three nanoinstructions: LoadA to read memory operand A, LoadB to read memory operand B, and Store to store the result of the ALU operation. Other nanoinstructions direct the router and NEWS (northeast-west-south) grid, and perform diagnostic functions.

CM-1 communications. Algorithm designers typically use data structuring techniques to express important relationships between data elements. For example, an image-understanding system usually employs a two-dimensional grid to represent the individual pixels of the image. At a later stage in the processing, however, a tree data structure or relational graph might represent more abstract relationships such as those between objects and their parts (see Figure 3).

On a serial machine with sufficient random access memory, pointers to memory elements are used to implement complex data structures. In a data-parallel architecture, however, individual data elements are assigned to individual processors and interprocessor communication expresses the relationships between the elements of very large data structures.

The CM-1 was designed with flexible interprocessor communication in mind and supports several distinct communication mechanisms:

• *Broadcast communications* allow immediate data to be broadcast from the

> ## The CM-1 was designed with flexible interprocessor communication in mind.

front-end computer or the sequencer to all data processors at once.

• *Global OR* is a logical OR of the ALU carry output from all data processors, which makes it possible to quickly discover unusual or termination conditions.

• *Hypercube communication* forms the basis for the router and numerous parallel primitives supported by the virtual-machine model. The topology of the network consists of a Boolean *n*-cube. For a fully configured CM-1, the network is a 12-cube connecting 4,096 processor chips (that is, each 16-processor chip lies at the vertex of a 12-cube). An example of a parallel primitive implemented with the Hypercube is Sort, which runs in logarithmic time; sorting 64K 32-bit keys takes about 30 milliseconds.

• The *router* directly implements general pointer following with switched message packets containing processor addresses (the pointers) and data. The router controller, implemented in the CM processor chips, uses the Hypercube for data transmission. It provides heavily overlapped, pipelined message switching with routing decisions, buffering, and combining of messages directed to the same address, all implemented in hardware.

• The *NEWS grid* is a two-dimensional Cartesian grid that provides a direct way to perform nearest-neighbor communication. Since all processors communicate in the same direction (north, east, west, or south), addresses are implicit and no collisions occur, making NEWS communication much faster (by about a factor of six) than router communication for simple regular message patterns.

CM-1 sequencer, nexus, and front-end interface. The CM-1 sequencer—a spe-

cially designed microcomputer used to implement the CM virtual machine—is implemented as an Advanced Micro Devices 2901/2910 bit-sliced machine with 16K 96-bit words of microcode storage. A Connection Machine contains from one to four sequencers. The sequencer's input is a stream of high-level, virtual-machine instructions and arguments, transmitted on a synchronous 32-bit parallel data path from the nexus. The sequencer outputs a stream of nanoinstructions that controls the timing and operation of the CM data processors and memory.

The CM-1 nexus—a 4×4 cross-point switch—connects from one to four front-end computers to from one to four sequencers. The connections to front-end computers are via high-speed, 32-bit, parallel, asynchronous data paths, while the connections to sequencers are synchronous. The nexus provides a partitioning mechanism so that the CM can be configured as up to four partitions under front-end control. This allows isolation of parts of the machine for different users or purposes (such as diagnosis and repair of a failure in one partition while other partitions continue to run). When more than one sequencer is connected to the same front-end through the nexus, they are synchronized by a common clock generated by the nexus.

The front-end bus interface supports a 32-bit, parallel, asynchronous data path between the front-end computer and the nexus. The FEBI is the only part of the CM-1 that lies outside of the main cabinet. It resides as a board in the system bus of the front end (any DEC VAX containing a VAXBI I/O bus and running Ultrix, or any Symbolics 3600 series Lisp machine).

CM virtual-machine model. The CM virtual-machine parallel instruction set, called Paris, presents the user with an abstract machine architecture very much like the physical Connection Machine hardware architecture, but with two important extensions: a much richer instruction set and a virtual-processor abstraction.

Paris. Paris provides a rich set of parallel primitives ranging from simple arithmetic and logical operations to high-level APL-like reduction (parallel prefix) operations,[7] sorting, and communications operations. The interface to Paris between the front end and the rest of the Connection Machine reduces to a simple stream of operation codes and arguments. The argu-

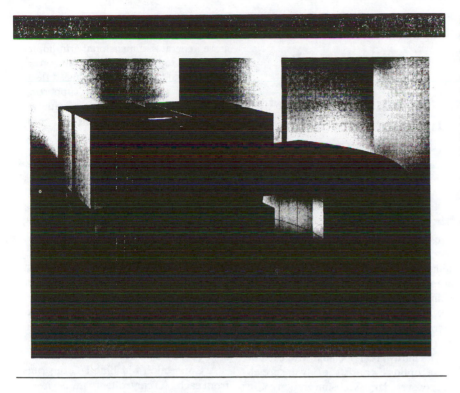

Figure 4. Connection Machine Model CM-2 and DataVault.

ments usually describe fields to operate on, in the form of a start address and bit length. Arguments can also be immediate data, broadcast to all data processors.

Most of Paris is implemented in firmware and runs on the sequencers, where the opcode/argument stream is parsed and expanded to the appropriate sequence of nanoinstructions for the data processors. Since Paris defines the virtual-machine instruction set, we use the same name for the assembly language of the Connection Machine.

Virtual processors. Data-parallel applications often call for many more individual processors than are physically available on a given machine. Connection Machine software provides for this through its virtual-processor mechanism, supported at the Paris level and transparent to the user. When we initialize the Connection Machine system, the number of virtual processors required by the application is specified. If this number exceeds the number of available physical processors, the local memory of each processor splits into as many regions as necessary, with the processors automatically time-sliced among the regions.

For example, if an application needed to process a million pieces of data, it would request $V = 2^{20}$ virtual processors. Assume the available hardware to have $P = 2^{16}$ physical processors, each with $M = 2^{16}$ bits of memory (the size for CM-2 memory; $M = 2^{12}$ bits of memory for the CM-1). Then each physical processor would support $V/P = 16$ virtual processors.

This ratio V/P, usually denoted N, is called the *virtual-processor ratio,* or *VP-ratio.* In this example, each virtual processor would have $M/N = 2^{12}$ bits of memory and would appear to execute code at about $1/N = 1/16$ the speed of a physical processor. In fact, virtual processors often exceed this execution rate, since instruction decoding by the sequencer can be amortized over the number of virtual processors.

CM software environment. The Connection Machine system software uses existing programming languages and environments as much as possible. Languages are based on well-known standards. Minimal extensions support data-parallel constructs so that users need not learn a new programming style. The Connection Machine front-end operating system (either Unix or Lisp) remains largely unchanged.

Fortran on the Connection Machine system uses the array extensions in the draft Fortran 8x standard (proposed by American National Standards Institute Technical Committee X3J3) to express data-parallel operations. The remainder of the language is the standard Fortran 77. No extension is specific to the Connection Machine; the Fortran 8x array extensions map naturally onto the underlying data-parallel hardware.

The *Lisp and CM-Lisp languages are data-parallel dialects of Common Lisp (a version of Lisp currently being standardized by ANSI Technical Committee X3J13). *Lisp gives programmers fine control over the CM hardware while maintaining the flexibility of Lisp. CM-Lisp is a higher-level language that adds small syntactic changes to the language interface and creates a powerful data-parallel programming language.

The C* language is a data-parallel extension of the C programming language (as described in the draft C standard proposed by ANSI Technical Committee X3J11). C* programs can be read and written like serial C programs. The extensions are unobtrusive and easy to learn.

The assembly language of the Connection Machine, Paris, is the target language of the high-level-language compilers. Paris logically extends the instruction set of the front end and masks the physical implementation of the CM processing unit.

Evolution of the CM-2. Experience gained during the first year of in-house use of the CM-1 led to the initiation of a project to build an improved version of the machine: the Connection Machine Model CM-2.

The design team established several goals for the CM-2: increasing memory capacity, performance, and overall reliability while maintaining or improving ease of manufacturing. To continue to support the CM-1 customer base, the designers wanted the CM-2 to be program compatible with the previous machine. Finally, the designers wanted the CM-2 to incorporate a high-speed I/O system for peripheral data storage and display devices.

To satisfy these goals, CM-2 kept the basic architecture of the CM-1 (see Figure 1). To increase performance, the CM-2 incorporates a redesigned sequencer and CM processor chip and an optional floating-point accelerator. A four-fold increase in microcode storage in the sequencer allowed for improvements in performance and functionality in the virtual-machine implementation. A sixteen-fold increase in memory capacity brought total memory capacity up to 512 megabytes. Enhanced reliability resulted from adding error correction to the memory system, and diagnostic capability was improved by increasing the number of data paths with error detection (parity). A redesigned NEWS grid increased functionality and ease of manufacture. CM-2 implemented an I/O system to support a massively parallel disk system (called the DataVault) and a high-speed color graphics system.

The CM processor chip underwent redesign in late 1985 and early 1986. The first prototype of the CM-2 was working by the end of 1986. The company commercially introduced the CM-2 (see Figure 4) in April 1987, and delivered about a dozen machines to customers in the fall of 1987. The first DataVault was delivered at the end of 1987.

CM-2 data processors and memory. The CM-2 data processor strongly resembles the CM-1 data processor. The major differences are

- 64 kilobits of bit-addressable memory instead of four kilobits,
- four one-bit flag registers instead of eight,
- an optional floating-point accelerator,
- a generalized NEWS-grid interface to support n-dimensional grids,
- an I/O interface, and
- increased error-detection circuitry.

The CM-2 data processors are implemented using four chip types. A proprietary custom chip contains the ALU, flag bits, router interface, NEWS-grid interface, and I/O interface for 16 data processors, and part of the Hypercube network controller. The memory consists of commercial dynamic RAM chips, with single-bit error correction and double-bit error detection. The floating-point accelerator consists of a custom floating-point interface chip and a floating-point execution chip; one of each is required for every 32 data processors. A fully configured 64K-processor system contains 4,096 processor chips, 2,048 floating-point interface chips, 2,048 floating-point execution chips, and half a gigabyte of RAM.

CM-2 floating-point accelerator. In addition to the bit-serial data processors described above, the CM-2 parallel-processing unit has an optional floating-point accelerator closely integrated with the processing unit. This accelerator has

The DataVault combines high reliability with fast transfer rates for large blocks of data.

two options: single precision or double precision. Both options support IEEE standard floating-point formats and operations, and increase the rate of floating-point calculations by a factor of more than 20. Taking advantage of this speed increase requires no change in user software.

The hardware associated with each of these options consists of two special-purpose very-large-scale-integration chips: a memory-interface unit and a floating-point execution unit for each pair of CM-2 processor chips. Because the floating-point units access memory in an orthogonal manner to the CM-2 processors, the memory-interface unit transposes 32-bit words before passing them to the floating-point unit.

Firmware that drives the floating-point accelerator stages the data through the memory-interface unit to the floating-point execution unit. In general, it takes $5N$ stages to implement a floating-point operation, for a virtual-processor ratio of N. However, the firmware is pipelined so as to require only $3N + 2$ stages instead of $5N$ stages.

CM-2 communications. The CM-2 communications are basically the same as those of the CM-1 with two exceptions. First, we redesigned the router to improve reliability, diagnostic capability, and performance. For example, we enhanced its performance by providing hardware for en route combining of messages directed to the same destination. The combining operations supported include Sum, Logical OR, Overwrite, Max, and Min.

The second major difference lies in the nature of grid communications. We completely redesigned grid communications for the CM-2. We wanted to increase flexibility and functionality while simplifying the overall system architecture and increasing manufacturing ease and relia-

bility. We accomplished this by replacing the two-dimensional NEWS grid with a more general n-dimensional grid implemented on top of the Hypercube (by grey-encoding addresses). We enhanced flexibility and functionality by supporting high-level-language concepts with n-dimensional-grid nearest-neighbor communication. Thus, programmers can employ one-dimensional to sixteen-dimensional nearest-neighbor grid communication according to the requirements of the task. Manufacturing ease and reliability are enhanced because we removed the separate set of cables for the NEWS grid.

CM-2 I/O structure. The Connection Machine I/O structure moves data into or out of the parallel-processing unit at aggregate peak rates as high as 320 megabytes per second using eight I/O controllers. All transfers are parity-checked on a byte-by-byte basis.

A Connection Machine I/O bus runs from each I/O controller to the devices it controls. This bus is 80 bits wide (64 data bits, eight parity bits, and eight control bits). The I/O controller multiplexes and demultiplexes between 256-bit processor chunks and 64-bit I/O-bus chunks. The controller also acts as arbitrator, allocating bus access to the various devices on the bus.

DataVault. Since standard peripheral devices do not operate at the speeds that the CM system itself can sustain, we had to design a mass-storage system capable of operating at very high speed. The DataVault combines high reliability with fast transfer rates for large blocks of data. It holds five gigabytes of data, expandable to ten gigabytes, and transfers data at a rate of 40 megabytes per second. Eight DataVaults, operating in parallel, offer a combined data transfer rate of 320 megabytes per second and hold up to 80 gigabytes of data.

The design philosophy followed for the Connection Machine architecture served for the DataVault as well: we used standard technology in a parallel configuration. Each DataVault unit stores data spread across an array of 39 individual disk drives. Each 64-bit data chunk received from the Connection Machine I/O bus is split into two 32-bit words. After verifying parity, the DataVault controller adds seven bits of error-correcting code and stores the resulting 39 bits on 39 individual drives. Subsequent failure of

Table 1. Example applications.

Field	Application
Geophysics	Modeling geological strata using reverse time migration techniques
VLSI Design	Circuit simulation and optimization of cell placement in standard cell or gate array circuits
Particle Simulation	*N*-body interactions, such as modeling defect movement in crystals under stress and modeling galaxy collisions
Fluid-Flow Modeling	Cellular autonoma and Navier-Stokes-based simulation, such as turbulance simulation in helicopter rotor-wake analysis and fluid flow through pipes
Computer Vision	Stereo matching, object recognition, and image processing
Protein-Sequence Matching	Large database searching for matching protein sequences
Information Retrieval	Document retrieval from large databases, analysis of English text, and memory-based reasoning
Machine Learning	Neural-net simulation, conceptual clustering, classifier systems, and genetic algorithms
Computer Graphics	Computer-generated graphics for animation and scientific visualization

Conservative engineering throughout ensures that the machine is manufacturable, maintainable, and reliable. The power of the machine arises from its novel architecture rather than from exotic engineering. It incorporates few types of boards; one board in particular—the matrix board—is replicated 128 times in a 64K machine. The matrix board is a 10-layer board with 9-mil trace widths.

The chip technology is also current state of the art and conservative. The CM-1 chip was implemented on a 10,000-gate, two-micron, complementary-metal-oxide-semiconductor gate array. The CM-2 chip is implemented on two-micron CMOS standard cells and has about 14,000 gate equivalents.

The massive parallelism of the machine makes it possible to provide a particularly powerful and fast set of hardware diagnostics. For example, the entire memory (which accounts for a large percentage of the silicon area of the machine) can be tested in parallel. Diagnostics can isolate a failure to a particular chip or pair of chips and one wire connecting them more than 98 percent of the time. Diagnostics, in combination with the error-detection hardware on all data paths, leads to a reliable and maintainable system, with mean time to repair well under one hour.

any one of the 39 drives does not impair reading of the data, since the ECC allows detection and correction of any single-bit error.

Although operation is possible with a single failed drive, three spare drives can replace failed units until repaired. The ECC provides 100-percent recovery of the data on the failed disk, allowing a new copy of this data to be reconstructed and written onto the replacement disk. Once this recovery is complete, the database is considered healed. This mass-storage system architecture leads to high transfer rates, reliability, and availability.

Graphics display. Visualization of scientific information is becoming increasingly important in areas such as modeling fluid flows or materials under stress. The enormous amount of information resulting from such simulations is often best communicated to the user through high-speed graphic displays. We therefore designed a real-time, tightly coupled graphic display for the Connection Machine. This system consists of a $1,280 \times 1,024$-pixel frame-buffer module with 24-bit color and four overlays (with hardware pan and zoom)

and a high-resolution, 19-inch color monitor. The frame buffer is a single module that resides in the Connection Machine backplane in place of an I/O controller. This direct backplane connection allows the frame buffer to receive data from the Connection Machine processors at rates up to one gigabit per second.

CM-2 engineering and physical characteristics. The cube-shaped Connection Machine measures 1.5 meters a side and is made up of eight subcubes. Each subcube contains 16 matrix boards, a sequencer board, and two I/O boards, arranged vertically. This vertical arrangement allows air cooling of the machine. Power dissipation is 28 kilowatts. Each matrix board has 512 processors and four megabytes of memory. The matrix board has 32 custom chips implementing the processors and router, 16 floating-point chips, 16 custom floating-point memory-interface chips, and 176 RAM chips. The nexus board occupies the space between the subcubes. Each front end has one front-end interface board. Red lights on the front and back, with one light for each CM chip (4,096 altogether), assist troubleshooting.

CM-2 performance. We can measure the Connection Machine's performance in a number of ways. Since the machine uses bit-serial arithmetic, the speed of integer arithmetic and logical operations will vary with word length; the languages implemented on the machine take advantage of this and use small fields whenever possible. For example, 32-bit integer arithmetic and logical operations run at 2,500 million instructions per second, while eight-bit arithmetic runs at 4,000 MIPS.

The speed of the machine also depends on how many processors take part in a particular calculation, and on the virtual-processor ratio. In some cases, higher virtual-processor ratios lead to higher instruction rates because the physical processors are better utilized.

Sustained floating-point performance has been shown to exceed 20 gigaflops (billions of floating-point operations per second) for polynomial evaluation using 32-bit floating-point-precision operands. When the function to be computed involves interprocessor communication such as a $4K \times 4K$-element matrix multiply, sustained performance typically exceeds five gigaflops.

We can express the performance of the Connection Machine communications systems in either of two ways: bandwidth or time per operation. Grid communications performance varies with the choice of grid dimensionality, grid shape, and virtual-processor ratio. A two-dimensional-grid Send operation takes about three microseconds per bit. For 32-bit, two-dimensional grid operations, that translates into 96 microseconds or 20 billion bits per second of communications bandwidth.

Router communications performance is somewhat harder to measure because it depends on the complexity of the addressing pattern in the message mix, and thus the number of message collisions. For a typical message mix, 32-bit general Send operations take about 600 microseconds. This translates into about three billion bits per second of communications bandwidth for typical message mixes (peak bandwidth exceeds 50 billion bits per second).

The performance of the Connection Machine I/O system depends on the number of channels in use. Each of up to eight I/O channels has a bandwidth of 40 million bytes per second, for a total bandwidth of 320 million bytes per second. This peak bandwidth has been observed on an installed DataVault disk system. The typical sustained bandwidth on the DataVault is 210 million bytes per second, which makes it possible to copy the entire contents of the Connection Machine memory (512 megabytes) to disk in about 2.4 seconds.

The preceding discussions show that the Connection Machine achieves significant gains in performance over conventional computers through the use of a data-parallel model in a fine-grained, massively parallel architecture without using any exotic technology. But, how broadly applicable is this data-parallel model? In the remainder of this article, we will illustrate the breadth of applications by describing a range of applications already developed on the Connection Machine.

Applications of the Connection Machine

Performance measures of massively parallel architectures tell only part of the story. One of the significant revelations that occurred with the introduction of the Connection Machine concerned the surprising number of different application areas suitable for this technology.

The general-purpose nature of the Connection Machine permits it to be applied equally well to numeric and symbolic processing.

Although data-parallel programming requires a different approach towards computation, programmers quickly adapted. In fact, they often found that many systems are naturally expressed in a data-parallel programming model. Fears that parallel programming would require a massive reeducation effort proved unfounded.

The partial list of applications given in Table 1 illustrates the range of applications developed for the Connection Machine. In general, most applications required less than a person-year of effort and were prototyped in a matter of months. The list includes examples from engineering, materials science, geophysics, artificial intelligence, document retrieval, and computer graphics. Far from being an architecture designed for special domains, the general-purpose nature of the Connection Machine permits it to be applied equally well to numeric and symbolic processing.

We include here discussions of three applications from the fields of VLSI design, materials science, and computer vision. These examples illustrate the use of parallelism in a range of areas and the role interprocessor communication plays in supporting the data-structure requirements of each application. Grid-based communication finds primary application in regularly structured problems such as particle simulations, while general routing supports the differing topologies of circuit simulation and computer vision. Consult Waltz[8] for detailed descriptions of several other applications.

Molecular dynamics. Since the 1960s, materials science has been a key technology in designing jet-engine turbine blades and other high-technology products. To understand materials more fully, designers often perform simulation studies. Unfortunately, macro-level experiments, whether direct or computer-simulated, have not successfully explained important behaviors such as metal fatigue. That requires simulation at the molecular level. Here a major problem arises. Studies of perfect crystals generally offer little help in understanding real-world materials, as evidenced by the fact that the strengths predicted by such studies often exceed those measured in actual metals by twenty to fifty times. Defects in the crystalline structure alter its properties and dramatically increase the computational complexity of simulation studies. Often the interactions of ten thousand to one million atoms need to be simulated to accurately represent the real-world behavior of materials.

Molecular-dynamics simulation is extremely computation-intensive, and the necessity of computing high-order interactions on systems of millions of particles poses major problems for conventional machines. Data-parallel architectures permit the investigator to see in minutes what would take hours on traditional hardware. The Connection Machine virtual-processor mechanism allows the investigator to simulate systems many times larger than would a physical-processor system alone.

A commonly used model for molecular dynamics uses the Lennard-Jones 6/12 potential to describe the interactions between uncharged, nonbonded atoms. Two approaches permit the study of this behavior on the Connection Machine. In both cases, processors are assigned to individual particles. Each processor contains the (x,y,z) position of the particle, the velocity, and the force on the particle from a previous time step of the simulation. All calculations are performed using 32-bit floating-point precision.

In the first approach, we consider interactions between all particles. Particles are arbitrarily assigned to processors. The NEWS grid circulates the information about each particle throughout the CM such that each processor can compute the force its particle receives from every other particle in the system. All processors use the result of these forces to update their own (x,y,z) position in parallel. Depending upon the purpose of the simulation, we might observe several hundred time steps. For large systems, each processor computes tens of thousands of force calculations during a single time step.

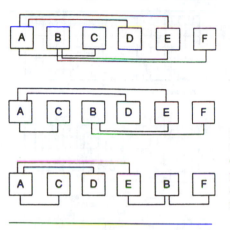

Circuit Placement

Figure 5. VLSI cell placement. Given an initial placement of cells, individual cells swap positions to reduce the total wire length.

This approach makes no assumption about which particles lie near others and hence dominate the overall force calculation. Dramatic improvements in execution time are possible if we know the location of nearby particles in advance. If we assume that the particles of the simulation have a regular structure and do not drift far from their initial relative positions (as in modeling solid-phase materials at low temperatures), we can take an alternative approach.

In the second approach, particles are assigned to processors according to their spatial configuration. In a manner akin to convolution, nearest-neighbor communication is used to calculate the forces from a surrounding $K \times K$ neighborhood of particles. Particles are free to drift, but we assume they stay roughly ordered relative to each other. Since the force calculation is dominated by these near neighbors, we can impose a cutoff in the force calculation. We simply ignore interactions of distant particles.

Even in large-scale simulations, the number of near neighbors remains relatively small. Thus, we need to compute only a fraction of the total number of force calculations. As expected, this results in a significant reduction in the time required for simulation. Systems as large as a million molecules when tested showed sustained execution rates in excess of 2.6 gigaflops.

Researchers have applied this data-parallel approach to studying defect motion in two-dimensional crystals of 16,384 atoms. They introduce stress by gradually shifting the top and bottom rows of atoms in opposite directions. They then observe the resulting movement, or percolation, of the defects. This work has contributed greatly to the study of stress-failure modes in various materials.

VLSI design and circuit simulation. Computer-aided design tools are routinely used in VLSI design, but as the size of circuits increases, two aspects of the design process become increasingly important and computationally expensive: cell placement and circuit simulation.

Cell placement. Semicustom VLSI circuits with more than 10,000 cells or parts have become quite common. Placing this number of parts on a chip while simultaneously minimizing the area taken up by interconnecting wire has proved a difficult and time-consuming problem. Minimization of area occupied is important because in general the smaller the area, the higher the expected yield. Designers have applied various automated methods to this problem. One method, employing *simulated annealing,*[9] produces good optimization results on a broad spectrum of placement problems. Unfortunately, for circuits having 15,000 parts, simulated annealing may require 100 to 360 hours on a conventional computer. On a 64K-processor Connection Machine, the time required reduces to less than two hours.

Simulated annealing is an optimization procedure related to an analogous process in materials science wherein the strength of a metal is improved by first raising it to a high temperature and then allowing it to cool slowly. When the metal is hot, the energy associated with its molecules causes them to roam widely. As the metal cools, molecules lose their energy and become more restricted in their movements, settling into a compact, stable configuration. This general optimization procedure, already applied to a variety of problems, supports parallel implementation.

Designers apply simulated annealing to VLSI placement in the following way. Given an initial arbitrary placement of cells for a VLSI circuit, the designer first computes the size of the silicon chip required. Improvement in the layout results from swapping cells to reduce the total wire length (see Figure 5). If the only

exchanges permitted are those that reduce total wire length, the placement pattern would seek a local minimum—not necessarily optimal.

Simulated annealing, however, accepts a certain percentage of "bad" moves in order to expose potentially better solutions, avoiding the classic trap of local minimums. The percentage of such "bad" moves the system will accept is governed by a parameter usually expressed as a temperature. Starting with a high temperature, a large number of cells are permitted to change position over great distances. Gradually, the temperature parameter is lowered, restricting the movement of cells and the number of exchanges. Ultimately, the system converges to a near-optimal solution as only nearby "good" exchanges are permitted.

Implementation of simulated annealing in parallel on the Connection Machine is straightforward. Individual cells, potential locations for cells, and nodes where wires between cells connect are represented in individual processors. The need to exchange information between cells at arbitrary locations illustrates the utility of the general router-based communications mechanism of the Connection Machine.

Simulated annealing takes place as follows. According to the given temperature parameter, a certain percentage of cells initiate a swap, calculate the expected change in wire length, and accept or reject the move. Potential exchanges are chosen by randomly generating the addresses of other cells. (Exchanges in general are not independent when performed in parallel, so restrictions on cell movements are enforced to ensure the consistency of the cell rearrangement.) This process repeats as the temperature parameter slowly lowers, restricting cell movement until the solution is acceptable to the designer.

Circuit simulation. A second area of importance to the electronics industry is VLSI circuit simulation. Unfortunately, our ability to simulate large circuits has not kept pace with the increasing number of components. Again, this results from the computation-intensive nature of simulation. Consequently, often only circuits with several hundred transistors are simulated at a time. Just as computer-aided design tools have become essential for successful implementation of VLSI, designers need simulation at the level of analog waveforms to verify circuit design.

Real circuits operate according to the characteristics of each component and

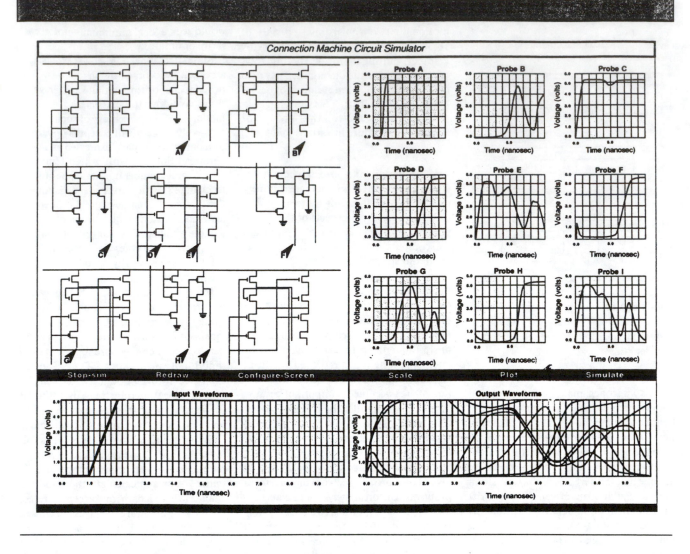

Figure 6. Simulation output of VLSI circuit. Waveforms from multiple probe points are displayed for a given input.

through enforcement of Kirchoff's law, which states that at each node the current entering the node is exactly balanced by the current leaving the node. In computer simulation, this leads to the application of an iterative relaxation method at each time step, which brings the circuit into equilibrium.

A Gauss-Jacobi relaxation algorithm for solving a system of nonlinear differential equations has been employed to simulate VLSI circuits.[10] As implemented on a Connection Machine, individual components (such as transistors, resistors, or capacitors) and nodes are each assigned to individual processors. Pointers express the connectivity of the circuit. During simulation, the pattern of communication directly reflects the topology of the circuit.

A simulation time step starts with all nodes sending their voltages to the terminals of the components to which they connect. In the initial time step, we know only the potentials at the power supply and ground nodes (others are assumed zero). Each element computes its response and sends this information back to connecting nodes. Each node processor checks to see if all currents balance. If so, the time step is complete; otherwise, each node processor updates its expected potential according to the relaxation rule, and the cycle repeats. In practice, each time step typically requires three to four iterations and accounts for one-tenth of a nanosecond simulated time. Figure 6 shows a typical simulation.

Because all operations take place in par-

allel, simulations of circuits with more than 10,000 devices can run in a few minutes on a 64K-processor Connection Machine. Simulations of circuits having more than 100,000 transistors have run in less than three hours.

Computer vision. Problems in computer vision pose a major challenge for today's systems not only because the problem is large (256K pixels in a typical video image), but also because we need a variety of data structures to meet the differing representational requirements of vision. We can easily see how to apply massively-parallel systems to pixel-level image processing, but it is often less clear how parallelism applies to higher-level concerns, as in the recognition of objects in a scene.

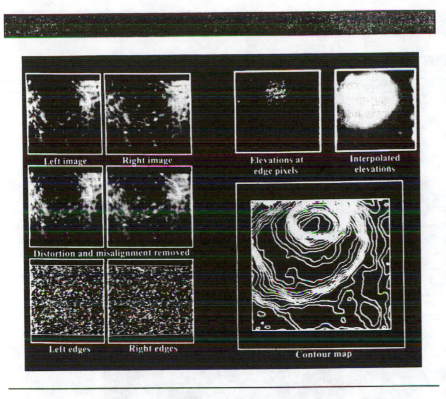

Figure 7. Using a stereo pair of left and right terrain images, the system corrects for any geometric distortions, detects edge points, computes elevations, and generates a contour map for the given terrain.

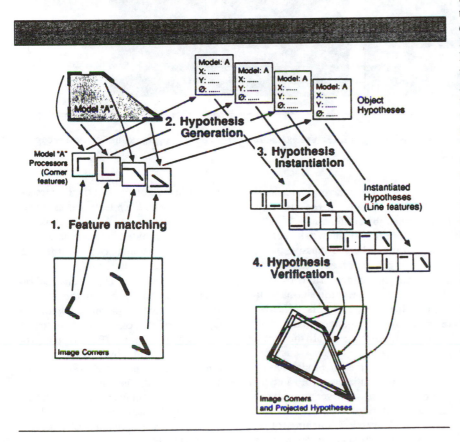

Figure 8. Parallel object-recognition steps.

Therefore, we show here two examples in computer vision: production of a depth map from stereo images, and two-dimensional-object recognition.

Depth map from binocular stereo. Binocular stereo is a method for determining three-dimensional distances based on comparisons between two different views of the same scene. It is used by biological and machine vision systems alike. Drumheller and Poggio[11] have implemented a program that solves this problem in near-real time and illustrates aspects of performing image analysis on the Connection Machine.

Given a stereo image pair, the program produces a depth map expressed in the form of a topographic display. First, two images (left and right) are digitized and loaded into the Connection Machine, with pixel pairs from right and left images assigned to individual processors. Next, a difference-of-Gaussians filter is applied to each image to detect edge points, which form the primitive tokens to be matched in the two images. All pixels perform this difference-of-Gaussians convolution in parallel.

To determine the disparity of features between left and right images, the Connection Machine system performs a local cross-correlation between the two images. It slides the right image over the left using NEWS communications. At a given relative shift, the two edge-point patterns are ANDed in parallel, producing a new image that has the Boolean value t only at points where the left and right images both contain an edge.

Then each processor counts the number of t's in a small neighborhood, effectively computing the degree of local correlation at each point. This occurs at several relative shifts, with each processor keeping a record of the correlation score for each shift.

Finally, each processor selects the shift (disparity) at which the maximum correlation took place.

Since the above process determines disparity (and distance) only at edge pixels, we must "fill in" the non-edge pixels by interpolation using a two-dimensional heat-diffusion model. The resulting depth map is displayed either as a gray-scale image with density as a function of height from the surface, or in standard topology map format. The entire process, from loading in a pair of 256 × 256-pixel stereo images to production of a contour map, completes in less than two seconds on a

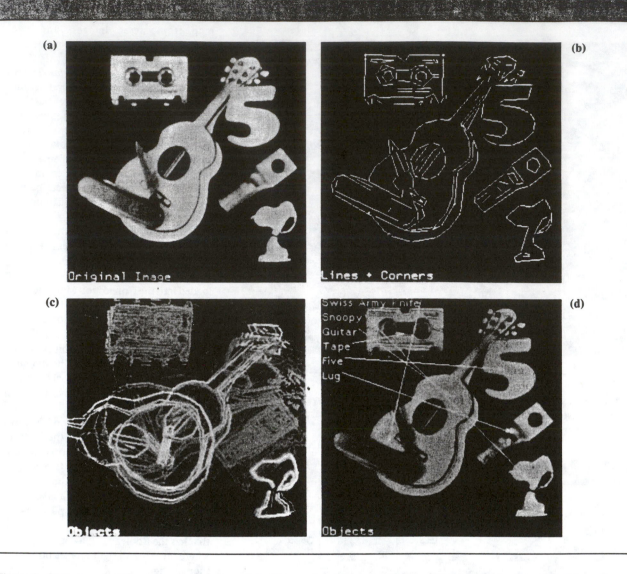

(a) Original Image
(b) Lines + Corners
(c) Objects
(d) Swiss Army Knife / Snoopy / Guitar / Tape / Five / Lug — Objects

Figure 9. Object recognition example showing original image (a), feature extraction (b), hypothesis generation (c), and recognition and labeling of objects (d).

64K-processor Connection Machine (see Figure 7).

Object recognition. Recognition of objects in natural scenes remains an unsolved problem in computer science despite attracting research interest for many years. It is important in many applications, including robotics, automated inspection, and aerial photo-interpretation.

In contrast to many of the systems designed to date, the object-recognition system described in this section was designed to work with object databases containing hundreds of models and to search each scene in parallel for instances of each model object.[12] While this system is limited to recognition of two-

dimensional objects having rigid shapes, it is being extended to the three-dimensional object domain.

The general framework for the approach taken here is massive parallel hypothesis generation and test. Whereas object-recognition algorithms traditionally use some form of constraint-based tree search, here searching is effectively replaced by hypothesis generation and parameter space clustering. In this scheme, image features in the scene serve as events, while features of each model serve as expectations waiting to be satisfied. Hypotheses arise whenever an event satisfies an expectation.

On the Connection Machine, objects known to the system are represented simply as a collection of features—generally

straight line-segments and their intersections at corners. Each feature is assigned to its own processor. A single object is therefore distributed over a number of processors, enabling each feature to actively participate in the solution.

Features useful for hypothesis generation are those that constrain the position and orientation of a matching model object. A single point, line, or patch of color is by itself not sufficient. In a two-dimensional world, however, the intersection of two lines that matches an expected model corner can be used to generate a hypothesis that an instance of the model object exists—albeit translated and rotated such that the corresponding features come into alignment.

Figure 8 illustrates this parallel hypothesis generation and verification method. An unknown scene is first digitized and loaded into the Connection Machine memory as an array of pixels, one per processor. Edge points are marked and straight line segments are fitted to edge points using a least-squares estimate. Intersecting lines are grouped into corner features and matched in parallel with corresponding corner features in the model database.

Whenever a match between an image and model feature occurs, a hypothetical instance of the corresponding model object is created and projected into the image plane. A hypothesis-clustering scheme, related to the Hough transform, is next applied to order hypotheses according to the support offered by mutually supporting hypotheses. Although this still leaves many possible interpretations for each image feature, the Connection Machine can quickly accept or reject thousands of hypotheses in parallel using a template-like verification step.

Verification results from having each instance check the image for evidence supporting each of its features in parallel. Hypotheses having strong support for their expected features are accepted over those with little support. Expected features of an object that are occluded or obscured in the scene do not rule out the hypothesis, they only weaken the confidence the system has in the object's existence. Competitive matching between instances for each image feature finally resolves any conflicts that arise in the overall scene interpretation. Results appear in Figure 9.

The time required from initial image acquisition to display of recognized objects is approximately six seconds on a 64K-processor Connection Machine. Experiments have shown this time to be constant over a range of object database sizes from 10 to 100. We expect optimization of this task to reduce the time to less than one second.

T he Connection Machine represents an exciting approach to dealing with the large and complex problems that a growing number of people wish to solve with computer systems. The size of problems has grown at a rate faster than improvements in technology, forcing us to find innovative ways of using current technology to achieve quantum leaps in performance.

We have described the architecture and evolution of the Connection Machine, which directly implements a data-parallel model in hardware and software. From the applications described here and elsewhere, it seems clear to us that data-level parallelism has broad applicability. We expect that its applicability will continue to grow as people continue to require solutions to larger and more complex problems. □

References

1. W.D. Hillis and G.L. Steele, "Data-Parallel Algorithms," *Comm. ACM,* Vol. 29, No. 12, 1986, pp. 1,170-1,183.
2. P.M. Flanders et al., "Efficient High Speed Computing with the Distributed Array Processor," *High-Speed Computer and Algorithm Organization,* Kuch, Lawrie, and Sameh, eds., Academic Press, New York, 1977.
3. K.E. Batcher, "Design of a Massively Parallel Processor," *IEEE Trans. Computers,* Vol. C-29, No. 9, 1980.
4. D.E. Shaw, *The Non-Von Supercomputer,* tech. report, Dept. of Computer Science, Columbia Univ., New York, August 1982.
5. L.S. Haynes et al., "A Survey of Highly Parallel Computing," *Computer,* Vol. 15, No. 1, 1982, pp. 9-24.
6. W.D. Hillis, *The Connection Machine,* MIT Press, Cambridge, Mass., 1985.
7. G.E. Blelloch, "Scans as Primitive Parallel Operations," *Proc. Int'l Conf. Parallel Processing,* Aug. 1986, pp. 355-362.
8. D.L. Waltz, "Applications of the Connection Machine," *Computer,* Vol. 20, No. 1, 1987, pp. 85-97.
9. C.D. Kirkpatrick, C.D. Gelatt, and M.P. Vecchi, "Optimization by Simulated Annealing," *Science,* Vol. 220, May 1983, pp. 671-680.
10. R.A. Newton, and A.L. Sangiovanni-Vincentelli, "Relaxation-Based Electrical Simulation," *IEEE Trans. Computer-Aided Design,* Vol. CAD-3, No. 4, 1984.
11. M. Drumheller and T. Poggio, "On Parallel Stereo," *Proc. 1986 IEEE Int'l Conf. on Robotics and Automation,* April 1986, pp. 1,439-1,488.
12. L.W. Tucker, C.R. Feynman, and D.M. Fritzsche, "Object Recognition Using the Connection Machine," *Proc. IEEE Conf. Computer Vision and Pattern Recognition,* June 1988, pp. 871-877.

Acknowledgments

Numerous people have contributed to the development of the architecture and applications of the Connection Machine. We wish to offer special thanks to Danny Hillis, Brewster Kahle, Guy Steele, Dick Clayton, Dave Waltz, Rolf-Dieter Fiebrich, Bernie Murray, and Mike Drumheller for their help in preparing this article.

This work was partially sponsored by the Defense Advanced Research Projects Agency under contract no. N00039-84-C-0638.

Lewis W. Tucker is a senior scientist at Thinking Machines Corp., where he is engaged in the application of parallel architectures to machine vision. His interests include image understanding, parallel algorithms, computer architecture, and machine learning.

Tucker earned his BA from Cornell University in 1972 and a PhD in computer science from the Polytechnic Institute of New York in 1984.

George G. Robertson is a principal engineer at Xerox PARC, working on user interface research and artificial intelligence. Previously, at Thinking Machines, he worked on massively parallel systems and artificial intelligence. His publications are primarily in the areas of user interfaces, programming language design, operating systems design, distributed systems, and machine learning.

Robertson received an MS in computer science from Carnegie Mellon University and a BA in mathematics from Vanderbilt University.

Readers may write to Tucker at Thinking Machines Corp., 245 First St., Cambridge, MA 02142.

BLITZEN: A Highly Integrated Massively Parallel Machine*

DONALD W. BLEVINS

The Microelectronics Center of North Carolina, Research Triangle Park, North Carolina 27709-2889

EDWARD W. DAVIS

Department of Computer Science, North Carolina State University, Raleigh, North Carolina 27695-8206

ROBERT A. HEATON

The Microelectronics Center of North Carolina, Research Triangle Park, North Carolina 27709-2889

AND

JOHN H. REIF

Department of Computer Science, Duke University, Durham, North Carolina 27706

The goal of the BLITZEN project is to construct a physically small, massively parallel, high-performance machine. This paper presents the architecture, organization, and feature set of a highly integrated SIMD array processing chip which has been custom designed and fabricated for this purpose at the Microelectronics Center of North Carolina. The chip has 128 processing elements (PEs), each with 1K bits of static RAM. Unique local control features include the ability to modify the global memory address with data local to each PE, and complementary operations based on a condition register. With a 16K PE system (only 128 custom chips are needed for this), operating at 20 MHz, data I/O can take place at 10,240 megabytes per second through a new method using a 4-bit bus for each set of 16 PEs. A 16K PE system can perform IEEE standard 32-bit floating-point multiplication at a rate greater than 450 megaflops. Fixed-point addition on 32-bit data exceeds the rate of three billion operations per second. Since the processors are bit-serial devices, performance rates improve with shorter word lengths. The BLITZEN chip is one of the first to incorporate over 1.1 million transistors on a single die. It was designed with 1.25-μm, two-level metal, CMOS design rules on an 11.0 by 11.7-mm die. © 1990 Academic Press, Inc.

* This work was supported in part by NASA Goddard Space Flight Center under Contract Number NAG-5-966 to the Microelectronics Center of North Carolina. Professor Reif is also supported by Contracts ONR N00014-80-C-0647, Air Force AFOSR-87-0386, ONR N00014-87-K-0310, NSF CCR-8696134, DARPA/ARO DAAL03-88-K-0195, and DARPA/ISTO N00014-88-K-0458.

1. OVERVIEW AND MOTIVATION

Parallel machines make use of multiple processing elements (PEs) executing simultaneously to speed up computation. For the purposes of this paper, we will consider a *massively* parallel machine to be a parallel machine with at least 10,000 processors. A number of massively parallel machines have been constructed, including the Massively Parallel Processor (MPP) built for NASA Goddard Space Flight Center by Goodyear Aerospace Corp. (now LORAL Defense Systems—Akron) [1, 12], the Distributed Array Processor (DAP) built by the British firm ICL [7, 15], and the Connection Machine (CM) built by Thinking Machines, Inc. [11, 16]. These projects have demonstrated the feasibility of constructing machines with massive parallelism. Nevertheless, only a relatively small number of the machines have been built so far and they have been utilized almost exclusively by *research* branches of government agencies and academic and industrial organizations.

1.1. *Miniaturization of Sequential Computing Machines*

The situation now may be very similar to the development of the first mainframe computers in the late 1940s: only a few general purpose computers existed. At that time, IBM made an early study which indicated that the worldwide use of computers would require only a few dozen mainframes (the rest of the computing equipment being calculators or special purpose machines). Nevertheless, a combination of advantageous engineering and economic factors resulted in the proliferation of computers. Central among these factors was the use of advanced electronic techniques to reduce the physical size, that is, to *miniaturize* computing machines. By miniaturization, we mean a high level of integration of the hardware onto VLSI components. Note that the process of miniaturizing sequential architectures has not necessarily degraded the computing power available to users. Miniaturization first allowed mainframe computing machines to be economically manufactured; and later, further improvements in integrated circuit technology allowed personal computing machines to be physically placed within the working environment of office workers, engineers, and scientists. In fact the development, for example, of miniaturized RISC architectures has actually *improved* performance in many cases, by allowing higher execution rates.

1.2. *BLITZEN: A Miniaturized Massively Parallel Machine*

The central goal of the BLITZEN project is to develop a miniaturized massively parallel machine. The machine will be physically small while providing the performance associated with massively parallel processing. A highly integrated VLSI processing array chip (the BLITZEN chip) has been designed and fabricated as the fundamental building block for this machine. We are convinced that the development of such a miniaturized machine will have the same benefits as discussed above for conventional sequential machines:

(1) These miniaturized machines should be much more economical, allowing a much larger market for massively parallel machines.

(2) The miniaturized machines could be backplaned with conventional workstations, making the capabilities of massively parallel computation easily accessible to engineers and scientists.

(3) A miniaturized machine could potentially be used in environments that require very small size and power consumption, such as on space flights. For example, NASA is proposing to have such a machine as a component of the Space Station computing system.

This paper provides rationale for design decisions, many of which have the dual benefit of both ensuring miniaturization and improving performance.

The BLITZEN project involves a number of institutions in the Research Triangle area of North Carolina, including Duke University, North Carolina State University (NCSU), and the Microelectronics Center of North Carolina (MCNC). Project personnel in addition to the authors included Jonathan Rosenberg, Jonathan Becher, Nigel Hooke, and Lars Nyland of the Computer Science Department of Duke.

Team effort to date has resulted in development of the processing element architecture [4, 5], custom design and fabrication of the PE array chip [9, 10], development of a full-scale PE array simulator [14], microcode for selected arithmetic operations, and the specification of an assembler language and architecture for the BLITZEN controller [13]. We are in the process of developing a prototype system and a high-level parallel programming environment for the BLITZEN machine.

1.3. *Organization of the Paper*

In the next section, BLITZEN Systems, we provide an overview of system architecture concepts and software for this machine. Section 3 is a description of the bit-serial processing element. Some comparisons with the MPP and Connection Machine are given. Local control features and methods for memory access are emphasized. Following the discussion of the individual PE architecture we describe in Section 4, PE Array Chip Architecture, the organization of PEs on the custom chip with emphasis on our interconnection and I/O schemes. Section 5, Chip Feature Set, has details of the custom chip design and instruction pipeline.

2. BLITZEN SYSTEMS

2.1. *System Architecture Overview*

A top-level view of the system architecture is presented in Fig. 1. Massive SIMD processing takes place in the processing array. Subsequent sections of this paper are concerned with the architecture of PEs in the processing array and with the custom chip that has been designed and fabricated for the array. Data in the on-chip local memory is supplied from off-chip, video random access memory (VRAM) data memory, with the transfers considered I/O operations with respect to the array.

Instructions are broadcast from the control unit to all PEs in the array. More specifically, operation codes originate in microcoded routines stored in control memory, and local memory addresses are generated from a register set. Together they form an array instruction. Control logic manages the register set and sequences the microinstructions. A scalar microprocessor can be included for use as the proces-

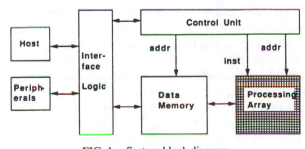

FIG. 1. System block diagram.

sor running an application program. It executes scalar instructions and sends calls for array instructions to the sequencing logic in the control unit.

Two external interfaces are planned. The host interface is a narrow path that matches the host word length. It is used for downloading programs (both application and microcode) and transferring data at low bandwidth between BLITZEN and the host with its peripherals. High-speed peripherals communicate with BLITZEN through custom peripheral interface logic. This path accesses the data memory and is potentially very wide for very high bandwidth.

2.2. *Data Memory*

Each BLITZEN processing element has 1K bits of RAM on-chip for holding data. It is known that many applications can benefit from additional memory, but the 1K amount was governed by chip size and density limits. In BLITZEN, the on-chip memory is supported by off-chip data memory that is accessed across the I/O buses. The use of VRAM for this purpose was mentioned earlier. Data memory can be viewed as the primary data memory of the system with on-chip RAM treated as registers or data cache.

Using the high-bandwidth I/O buses it is possible to change the content of all or part of the on-chip RAM very quickly. In one instruction cycle, 32 bits (eight 4-bit items) can be transferred between VRAM and each array chip. If the system is operating at 20 MHz, the total transfer rate is (4 bytes/chip)*(128 chips) per 50 ns, or 10.24 gigabytes per second. In 128 instruction cycles, a 32-bit data item can be transferred into (or out of) the on-chip RAM of each PE. In 4096 instruction cycles the entire 1K per PE RAM can be loaded. In 8192 cycles the contents of on-chip RAM for the entire array can be swapped with the data memory. Operating at 20 MHz, the time required to transfer an array of 32 bit items is 6.4 μs, and the time to swap the total contents is 409.6 μs.

2.3. *Programmer's Model*

BLITZEN is a computing system whose primary computational resource is a single instruction stream, multiple data stream array processor with a massive number of processing elements. This massively parallel array operates in conjunction with several other major system components.

Programming BLITZEN takes place at several levels. At the lowest level is the machine language for the array. The hardware instruction set is specified in [4]. Since the instruction set is concerned with bit-serial manipulation and register transfers, it is not expected to be used by application programmers. Rather, it is the basis for a microcode development language, named Blitz [13], that couples array operations with control unit register transfers and sequencing operations. Commonly used routines corresponding to as-

sembly language instructions such as load, store, add, floating-point add, etc., are being written in Blitz for inclusion in a microcode library whose routines can be called from a higher-level language. An object-oriented language based on C++ is being developed for application programming. High-level language statements will be compiled into parallel assembly language statements that result in calls to microcode routines which are executed on the array hardware.

2.4. *Parallel PE Array Simulator*

Prior to the existence of hardware, a software behavioral simulator known as "Zyglotron" was developed [14]. It is a "full-scale" simulator in that it can simulate the entire 16,384 PE array with very high performance. Zyglotron is being used for microcode development, and can allow the development of algorithms and high-level software to proceed concurrently with hardware system development. As noted in the abstract of [14], "The simulator has achieved such high performance by taking advantage of a natural mapping that exists between massively parallel bit-serial machines and the vector architecture used in many high performance scientific supercomputers." The simulator runs on CONVEX C-1 and C-220 vector processing machines, and is written in C and in the CONVEX assembly language.

3. PROCESSING ELEMENT ARCHITECTURE

Each processing element in BLITZEN is a bit-serial processor, with a variable length shift register and random access memory. The BLITZEN design used the MPP PE architecture described by Batcher, the chief architect of the MPP [2], as a starting point. The existence of the MPP has provided experience with massively parallel processing such as that reported by the MPP Working Group to the NASA Associate Administrator for Space Science and Applications [6] and by Batcher [3].

Our group has designed various improvements on the MPP PE architecture into BLITZEN:

(1) Incorporation of RAM *on-chip* for each PE. *Motivation:* This enables implementation of masked memory writes and allows the PE to access memory without off-chip delays.

(2) *Bus oriented I/O* with a 4-bit path for each set of 16 PEs. *Motivation:* This gives BLITZEN a total I/O capability of 4096 bits per cycle. (In comparison, the MPP has a total I/O capability of 256 bits per cycle, and the Connection Machine has an I/O capability of 1024 bits per cycle.)

(3) *Local* modification of RAM addressing. *Motivation:* This provides local indirect addressing for table lookup and indexing by allowing on-chip memory accesses to be determined by the contents of each PE's shift register.

(4) *Local* conditional control of arithmetic and logic

functions. *Motivation:* This improves the performance of various arithmetic operations.

(5) *Bidirectional* shift register. *Motivation:* This allows more flexible data movement.

(6) An *X-grid interconnect,* allowing eight neighbors per PE. *Motivation:* This gives a factor of two improvement over a four-neighbor NEWS grid in diagonal data movement.

Note that (3) and (4) give the BLITZEN PE a degree of MIMD control, which can improve the flexibility and efficiency of the machine.

Figure 2 presents the functional elements of one BLIT-ZEN PE and shows a similarity to the PE in the MPP. Blocks with double line boundaries are storage devices. There are six single-bit registers labeled A, B, C, G, K, and P. Two devices hold multiple bits. One is a variable length shift register which, in conjunction with registers A and B, has a capacity of 32 bits. The remaining storage device is a 1024-bit random access memory. Arithmetic and logical operations are performed by a full adder and a logic block. The above elements communicate primarily over a single-bit data bus. A 4-bit I/O bus provides a path to pads of the chip for connection to external storage devices. An I/O bus is shared among 16 PEs on a chip. A functional description of the BLITZEN PE is given in the following paragraphs, and then subsequent sections discuss innovative features that represent significant departures of BLIT-ZEN from the MPP.

3.1. *Functional Description*

Data Bus. Elements of a PE communicate over the data bus. In one processing cycle it can transfer 1 bit of data from any one of its sources to one or more of its destinations. Several of these destinations may be specified in one instruction.

Logic. The P register is central to arithmetic and logical operations in the PE. It is also used for inter-PE routing. For logic, an operation is performed between the state of P at the beginning of a processing cycle and the value of the data bit on the data bus. The result of the operation is stored in P at the end of the cycle. All 16 Boolean functions of two variables are implemented.

Arithmetic. A full adder performs bit-serial arithmetic in each PE by forming the 2-bit sum of the 3 bits stored in registers A, P, and C at the beginning of a processing cycle. The result is output from the adder as a sum bit, which is stored in the B register, and a carry bit, which is stored in the C register. Addition of n-bit operands is performed by a microprogram loop which loads operand bits into registers A and P, performs the full add, and then stores the sum from register B into the shift register or memory.

A half add operation is also provided, which forms the 2-bit sum of the 2 bits stored in registers A and C. The state of P is not involved. The result is output from the adder circuit as a sum bit and carry bit, which are stored in registers B and C, respectively.

Two's complement subtraction is implemented by add-

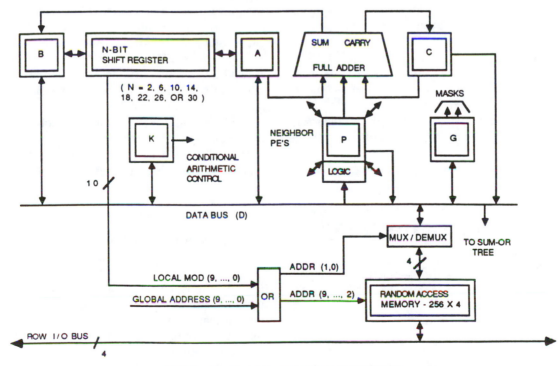

FIG. 2. Functional elements of one BLITZEN PE.

ing the two's complement of the subtrahend. It is readily formed by initially setting the carry bit in register C and then using logic at register P to form the logical (one's) complement of the operand.

Shifting. The shift register is a variable length device with bidirectional shift paths. It is logically positioned between registers A and B in the path for recirculating a sum back to the adder input. The shift register has N stages, where N can be set to 2, 6, 10, 14, 18, 22, 26, or 30. Registers A and B add two stages to the path length, providing a total length ranging from 4 to 32 in multiples of 4.

Figure 3 is a diagram of the shift register with the A and B registers on either end, showing the structure with groups of stages that can be bypassed to achieve variation in the shift path length. Stages in the shift path for the length currently set are considered to be active stages while stages that are bypassed are inactive. Shifting occurs only in the active stages. Data are maintained in position in the inactive stages.

In one processing cycle the register shifts one place, either right or left. A right shift is from register B toward register A. In a right shift, the leftmost active stage is loaded with the value in B at the beginning of the cycle and the rightmost active stage is shifted to A. The shift register can be cleared.

3.2. *On-Chip Memory*

An on-chip, static random access memory is associated with each PE. From a processing point of view it is a 1024 by 1-bit RAM. A memory read operation reads the single bit specified by a 10-bit address and places the value on the data bus. A memory write operation writes the value from the data bus into the location specified by a 10-bit address.

Input/output operations view memory as a 256 by 4-bit RAM. I/O operations access memory using the 8 most significant bits of the 10-bit address, and transfer 4 bits between the I/O bus and the memory.

Masking, the local control feature that can be used to enable or disable certain operations, is possible on all write memory accesses.

3.3. *Local Address Modification*

In a SIMD machine, identical control signals and addresses are distributed from a control unit to all PEs. In the absence of local control, all PEs would perform the same operation and access the same memory location in their respective RAMs. Performing the same operation in all PEs is the essence of SIMD parallel architectures. However, a certain amount of local control is almost essential, and other local features can enhance performance. In BLITZEN we have provided the typical masking features plus two innovative features: local address modification and local conditional operation.

Batcher [3] reported many problems where one would like to address the local memory with local, independent addresses rather than a single global address. In BLITZEN, independent addressing is available since the global address can be modified at each PE. Conventional processors generally modify an address that appears in an instruction by adding index or base register values, or extracting an address from some location for indirect use. In a SIMD machine, logic that handles local modification of addresses must appear at each PE and be locally decoded. That is, the logic must appear at each of the 128 PEs on this chip. To conserve chip area the modification chosen is the logical OR of the global address with 10 bits from the shift register. This can simulate indexing when data structures begin on appropriate power of two boundaries where the least significant bits are zeros. When normal (unmodified) memory operations are issued, the global address is unchanged.

Figures 2 and 3 show the 10-bit bundle of signals from the shift register that are the source of address modification bits. The 10 most significant bits of the 16-bit section of the shift register are used for this purpose.

We believe BLITZEN is the first massively parallel machine with the ability to modify the global SIMD memory address in every PE. This means that BLITZEN has addressing logic with every PE. Previously, a SIMD machine developed by DEC [8], and the Connection Machine 2, allowed a large group of processors to share indirect addressing logic. Shared logic imposes a sequentiality on the processing, contradicting the massive parallelism that is desired.

3.4. *Conditional Operations*

BLITZEN provides additional new local control of PEs through the use of a programmable conditional operation test involving register K. When using the conditional feature, operations which are strictly logical complements of each other can be performed at the same time in different PEs. The feature applies to operations involving logic at register P and loading a value into register C. When a conditional operation is issued, processing is normal in all PEs where $K = 0$. In those PEs where $K = 1$ the results are com-

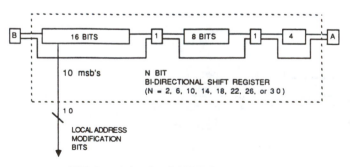

FIG. 3.   Bidirectional shift register structure.

plemented. Since both normal and complemented operations take place, based on testing a condition, this is like a restricted form of the high-level IF-THEN-ELSE concept with both the THEN and the ELSE clauses happening concurrently. On a parallel machine the concept is generalized to WHERE, indicating that it applies to all PEs where the condition applies. Flow of control with conditional operations occurs as shown in Fig. 4. When a conditional operation instruction is not used by the programmer, register K is available to hold a temporary value.

This conditional operation feature can be used to improve performance, by a factor near two, in nonrestoring division algorithms where an iterative step depends on the result of the previous step, as shown in Fig. 5. If the previous step produced a negative partial remainder, then during the current iteration a quotient bit of zero is generated and the divisor is added to the existing partial remainder. If the previous step produced a positive partial remainder, a quotient bit of one is generated and the divisor is subtracted from the existing partial remainder.

An SIMD machine with many processors is likely to have both situations at every iteration, and need to logically follow both paths of the flowchart. The approach to following both paths concurrently is to use conditional execution with the sign bit of the partial remainder as the condition flag in K. If the written conditional code assigns one to the quotient and performs subtraction, that will happen in those PEs where the partial remainder is equal to or greater than zero. In all other PEs, the complementary result will occur: zero is assigned to the quotient and addition is performed, as desired.

Additional features of BLITZEN apply to the larger view that involves a multiplicity of PEs rather than a single PE. Thus we consider the array of PEs on a chip in the next section.

4. PE ARRAY CHIP ARCHITECTURE

4.1. *Organization of PEs and Functional Components*

The above PE architecture is used as the basis for the BLITZEN VLSI processor array chip. A single chip con-

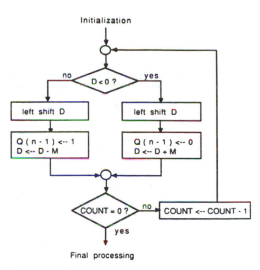

FIG. 5. The iterative loop in nonrestoring division. D is the partial remainder, M is the divisor, and Q is the quotient.

tains 128 PEs, each with 1K bits of locally addressable memory.

By placing 128 PEs and their local memory on a single chip, we make a major step toward miniaturization of the BLITZEN machine. Only 128 of these PE array chips are required for an entire 16,384 PE BLITZEN machine. (In comparison the MPP processing element array chip contains 8 PEs without the local memory, and the system requires a total of 2048 such chips. The Connection Machine has 16 PEs per chip, again without local memory.)

A single PE is a building block for the chip architecture. PEs are organized into an 8 by 16 array on the chip. They are interconnected with a two-dimensional grid for communication between PEs, as discussed in the next section. Data are moved on and off the chip over a set of eight I/O buses, each with 16 PEs attached, as described in Section 4.4, BLITZEN I/O Scheme. The value on each PE data bus can be sent to an on-chip sum-OR tree to form an inclusive-OR of data bus values from all PEs. This value is brought to a chip pad for output. The sum-OR value is useful in associative processing algorithms.

Figure 6 shows the organization of PEs on the chip, including the X-grid interconnections, I/O buses, and some logic and control signals that are common to all PEs on the chip.

4.2. *Message Routing Capability on the BLITZEN Machine*

One major design decision was *not* to use a logarithmic diameter interconnection network, such as the hypercube used by the Connection Machine. Instead we use a variant of the two-dimensional grid, an eight-neighbor X-grid suggested to us by C. Fiduccia, with diameter 128, which is the square root of the number of processors. In spite of our

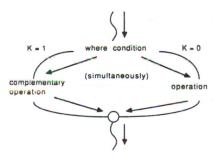

FIG. 4. Flow of control with conditional operations.

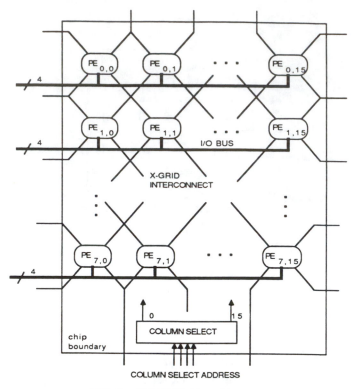

FIG. 6.   BLITZEN chip architecture.

background in theoretical computer science, we concluded that a logarithmic diameter network would be impractical for our needs. The key problems with logarithmic diameter networks, such as the hypercube, are:

(1) The number of I/O pads (namely 896) that would be required for hypercube edges exiting a processing element chip with 128 PEs is impossibly large.

(2) The inter-PE wiring requires large amounts of area, both on-chip and between chips.

A decision to use a hypercube interconnection network would make it very difficult to highly integrate our machine. Because of pin count and network area requirements, we would have been limited to only 16 PEs per chip, and even then only have 1/16 of the I/O pins required for a full hypercube interconnect. The results would be an interconnect with perhaps no greater communication capabilities than a two-dimensional grid.

Another argument in favor of the grid interconnect is the empirical experience that a very large class of applications naturally requires the grid interconnect.

The Connection Machine has some impressive built-in hardware for performing permutation message routing. Unfortunately, this routing circuitry uses a large fraction of their processor chip area and decreases the step rate of their machine. We decided that our need for high-performance, miniaturized architecture was more important than the

need for message routing circuitry (which can be replaced by software routing routines that are nearly as efficient).

4.3. X-Grid Interconnection

Processing elements are interconnected in two ways on a chip: a grid interconnection for routing and a bus structure for I/O. Figure 6 shows the X-grid nearest-neighbor routing network. PEs are arranged in a two-dimensional grid with interconnection paths to neighbors in the eight compass directions N, NE, E, SE, S, SW, W, and NW. A routing operation transfers the state of P to the P register of a neighboring PE and accepts a new state from the PE in the opposite compass direction.

Four bidirectional routing connections are brought out of each PE from the four logical corners: NE, SE, SW, and NW. The connections intersect between PEs. A routing path is established by an operation which sends data out in one direction and accepts data in from one of the remaining directions. As an example, routing to the north direction can be achieved by sending the value of the P register out to the NE and accepting a value into P from the SE. The data value on the SE input originated in the PE to the south. All PEs route the same direction in one processing cycle.

Eight paths can be established with four wires out of each PE by sending data on one wire, receiving data on one of the other three wires, and placing the remaining two wires in the high impedance state. This X-grid interconnects PEs on a chip and extends across chip boundaries so that an array of chips can be uniformly interconnected. Additional off-chip logic can provide various treatments of edges of the total array, as was done in the MPP system. The use of the X-grid allows a factor of two improvement in the frequently occurring case of diagonal data movement.

4.4. BLITZEN I/O Scheme

Data I/O is the critical path in any parallel machine. The MPP's I/O scheme is simple—data are shifted in from the west edge of the array using the S-plane, and shifted out simultaneously along the east edge. In a BLITZEN system the array would be segmented along chip boundaries. So, a natural extension to the MPP I/O scheme would be to have data flow in one side of a chip and out the other using the same S-plane idea. thus BLITZEN would have data I/O occurring every 16 PEs, from west to east, using 32 pins.

At that time in the chip design activity, floorplanning predicted that the local static RAM should have a 256 by 4 aspect ratio. The RAM would have a 4-bit interface, with further demultiplexing and multiplexing for the 1-bit PE data bus. Since there were four data wires available per row of PEs on a chip, an alternative I/O approach was presented. The approach was to move, conceptually, the 16 output S-plane connections from the east edge to the west edge, and combine them with the 16 input S-plane connections to form eight bidirectional, 4-bit I/O buses on each chip. Each 4-bit bus is shared by the 16 PEs in a row. This scheme has several advantages, such as very high bandwidth, an easier interface for extending memory off-chip, the ability to broadcast data to all PEs simultaneously, fast data movement across the chip, and elimination of the S-plane.

Each chip has column select logic that is used in conjunction with the I/O buses. For normal I/O transfers, one PE in each row is active. The PE column index is the same for all rows and is given by a 4-bit address to the column select logic. In broadcast mode, data can be input to all PEs on a row; thus column selection is not used.

High system I/O bandwidth is thus provided by the eight 4-bit I/O buses per chip. Figure 6, presented earlier, shows the chip architecture with the I/O buses. In one processing cycle, 32 bits can be accessed at a column of eight PEs on each chip. The column is randomly addressable on each cycle. Motivation for this scheme is based on the desire to bring the I/O rate into reasonable balance with the processing rate.

In a system with 16K PEs, 128 chips are arranged in a 16 by 8 array. Each column of 16 chips is a 128 by 16 array of PEs presenting 512 I/O bus lines. The total array, with eight columns, has 4096 I/O lines for data movement into and out of the array as shown in Fig. 7.

Video RAM chips are available with very high block data transfer rates, matching the rates of our PE I/O buses, and with 4-bit outputs, matching our 4-bit I/O buses. We plan to use 1-megabit VRAM chips, organized as 256K by 4, to augment the PE memory by 64K bits for each PE. We will allow the 16 PEs along an I/O bus to share a vertically packaged VRAM chip as indicated in Fig. 8.

4.5. Operation Codes

BLITZEN is an SIMD machine. All PEs receive the same instruction from a control unit. An instruction contains an operation code and address information for accessing memory and performing I/O transfers. Operations performed in the PEs in one processing cycle are governed by a single operation code. Figure 9 is the 23-bit format of this code.

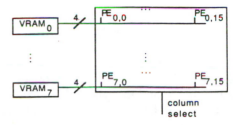

FIG. 8. Video RAMs attached to I/O buses at a chip.

The format shows several distinct fields specifying operations to be performed. This allows several operations to occur simultaneously in one processing cycle. When a register is both the source of a data bit and the target of an assignment which can change the register state, the original value of the register is used as the source value. State changes occur late in the processing cycle.

Most of the fields represent operations. The last field is special. It represents individual bits that identify local operations. Code bit L identifies masked P register operations, both logic and routing. Code bit M identifies masked operations involving the adder, shift register, registers A, B, and C, memory write, and input. Code bit N is used to select conditional operations on P and C. The final code bit, O, identifies memory operations with local address modification.

Operation code bits 0, 1, and 2 identify the source of data for the data bus. The data bus source can be any of the single-bit registers in a PE, or a bit from memory. When memory is the source, a single-bit memory read operation is performed at the addressed location.

Code bits 3 through 7 specify the logic operation to be performed at P, or specify the routing operation to one of the eight nearest neighbors. This field is also used to set the length of the shift register. Operations coded in a single field cannot be performed concurrently. An instruction which sets the shift register length prevents the simultaneous assignment of values to P.

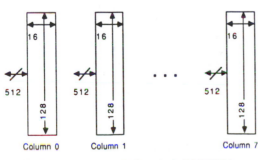

FIG. 7. Total array I/O paths in BLITZEN.

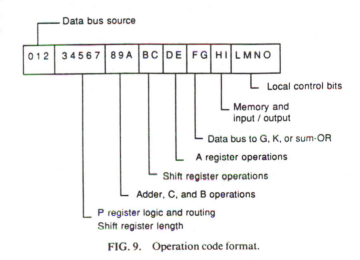

FIG. 9. Operation code format.

Code bits 8, 9, and A specify the operation to be performed by the adder, resulting in assignment of sum and carry values to B and C. This field is also used to assign values to registers B and C.

Code bits B and C specify shift register operations. Code bits D and E assign values to register A. Code bits F and G specify the transfer of the data bus to register G, register K, or the sum-OR tree.

Code bits H and I specify memory and I/O operations. Memory transfers to or from the data bus are considered read or write operations. Transfers to or from the I/O bus are considered output and input operations.

A total of 59 operations are defined. Of these, 41 are maskable, 18 can be conditionally executed, and 5 allow local memory address modification.

Up to seven operations can be combined into a single instruction, representing seven concurrent activities. As an example of combining operations into one instruction, consider a step in an addition process where one operand is in memory, the other is in the shift register, and the result is being placed in the shift register. Operations possible in one processing cycle are (1) perform a full add using the values in A, P, and C at the start of the cycle and placing the sum in B and the carry in C; (2) read memory and place the bit on the data bus; (3) load P with the value from the data bus; (4) move the starting value of B into the shift register while shifting right; and (5) transfer the shift register's rightmost bit into A.

5. CHIP FEATURE SET

The BLITZEN PE array chip was designed by the Microelectronics Center of North Carolina with two orthogonal constraints: maximize both integration and speed. The chip incorporates over 1.1 million transistors on a die 11.0 by 11.7 mm. It was designed with MCNC's 1.25-μm, two-level metal, CMOS process. It is packaged in a 168-pin PGA and is designed for the JEDEC 3.3-V power supply standard. The operating frequency is 20 MHz worst case, and power dissipation is less than 1.0 W.

The chip contains 128 PEs positioned in an 8 by 16 array. Internally, a three-stage pipeline enables BLITZEN to execute an instruction every cycle, as shown in Fig. 10. During the first cycle a 23-bit SIMD instruction from the control

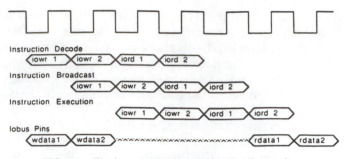

FIG. 11. The instruction pipeline for I/O bus transfers.

unit is latched and decoded into a fully horizontal 59-bit microinstruction. During the second stage of the pipeline the microinstruction is broadcast to all 128 PEs. In the final stage the instruction is executed. By issuing a fully horizontal microinstruction, no additional decoding logic was needed in the PEs. The encoding of the 23-bit instruction was optimized to minimize the amount of internal decoding.

Data transfers on the I/O bus take place in a single cycle as shown in the timing diagram in Fig. 11. If the I/O buses are used as an interface to high-density video RAMs, blocks of data can be transferred quickly to and from the chip. Routing communication on the X-grid also takes place in a single cycle.

Figure 12 is the floorplan of a single PE. Each PE has access to its own 1K bits of memory, which are internally organized as 32 by 32 bits. Multiplexing is provided to select 4 out of 32 bits for interfacing to that PE's I/O bus. When a PE accesses memory for an operand, further selection of 1 out of 4 bits is needed. Address calculation logic (predecode) is also needed at each PE to support the indirect addressing mode provided by local modification of the global address. The execution unit of a PE, including the shifter and ALU, contains approximately 1130 transistors.

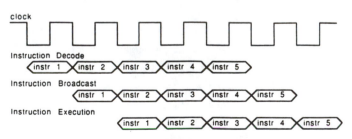

FIG. 10. The instruction pipeline.

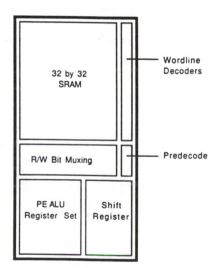

FIG. 12. VLSI design floorplan for one PE.

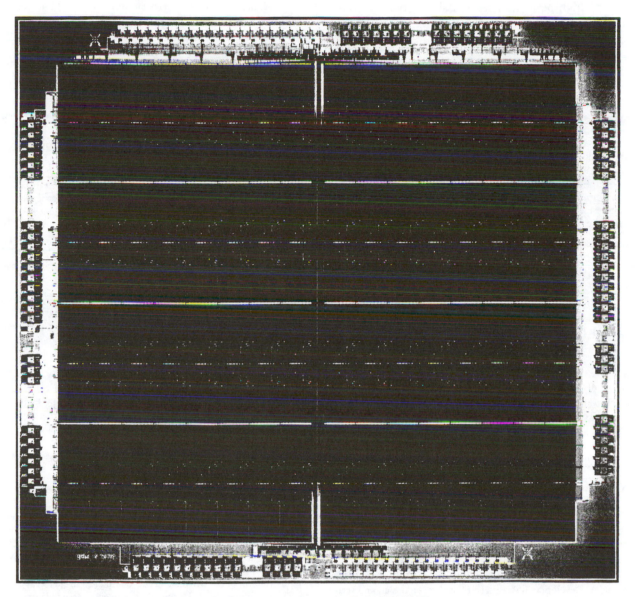

FIG. 13. Photomicrograph of a BLITZEN chip.

The PE design represents a modular functional block which is replicated 128 times on a chip. In addition there are grid interconnection signals, a sum-OR tree, instruction decode and pipeline logic, I/O pads, power distribution, and other frame logic necessary to produce an operational chip. A photomicrograph of the complete chip is shown in Fig. 13. A summary of pin requirements for the BLITZEN chip is given in Table I.

A total of 117 pins is needed for logic signals to the 8 by 16 array of PEs on a chip. This does not include power or clock signals.

6. CONCLUSION

The architecture and VLSI design of a new massively parallel processing array chip have been described. The BLIT-ZEN PE array chip, containing 1.1 million transistors, is being fabricated by the Microelectronics Center of North Carolina. The chips are the basis for a highly integrated,

TABLE I

Logic Pin Requirements

Function	Pins	Direction
Operation code	23	In
Memory address	10	In (two pins also used for column select)
Column select	2	In
Valid	1	In
I/O bus	32	In/out
Neighbor interconnects	48	In/out
Sum-OR	1	Out

miniaturized, high-performance, massively parallel machine, also known as BLITZEN, that is currently under development.

ACKNOWLEDGMENTS

The work reported in this paper resulted from our efforts as an interinstitutional research group participating with the support of the Microelectronics Center of North Carolina and of NASA Goddard SFC. We also benefited from discussions with Kenneth Batcher of LORAL Defense Systems—Akron concerning architecture of the MPP and local address modification schemes; with John Dorband of NASA Goddard SFC concerning conditional operations; and with Charles Fiduccia of General Electric who described their cross-omega machine with an eight-neighbor grid interconnect. The interest and support of Milt Halem, NASA Goddard SFC, has been crucial to the success of this project.

REFERENCES

1. Batcher, K. E. Design of a massively parallel processor. *IEEE Trans. Comput.* **C-29**, 9 (Sept. 1980), 836–840.

2. Batcher, K. E. Array unit. In Potter, J. L. (Ed.), *The Massively Parallel Processor.* MIT Press, Cambridge, MA, 1985.

3. Batcher, K. E. The architecture of tomorrow's massively parallel computer. *Proc. First Symposium on the Frontiers of Massively Parallel Scientific Computation,* 1986.

4. Blevins, D. W., Davis, E. W., and Reif, J. H. Processing element and custom chip architecture for the BLITZEN massively parallel processor. MCNC Tech. Rep. TR87-22, 1987.

5. Davis, E. W., and Reif, J. H. Architecture and operation of the BLITZEN processing element. *Proc. Third International Conference on Supercomputing,* Boston, MA, May 1988.

6. Fischer, J. R., *et al.* Report from the MPP Working Group to the NASA Associate Administrator for Space Science and Applications. NASA Tech. Memorandum 87819, November, 1987.

7. Forest, B. M., Roweth, D., Stroud, N., Wallace, D. J., and Wilson, G. V. Implementing neural network models on parallel computers. *Comput. J.* **30**, 5 (1987), 413–419.

8. Grondalski, R. A VLSI chip set for a massively parallel architecture. *Proc. International Solid State Circuits Conference (ISSCC 87),* 1987.

9. Heaton, R. A. Development of Blitzen tools: Blitzen design and verification methodology. MCNC Tech. Bulletin, Vol. 4, No. 4, 1988.

10. Heaton, R. A., and Blevins, D. W. BLITZEN: A VLSI array processing chip. *Proc. Custom Integrated Circuits Conference,* May, 1989.

11. Hillis, W. D. *The Connection Machine.* MIT Press, Cambridge, MA, 1985.

12. Potter, J. L. (Ed.). *The Massively Parallel Processor.* MIT Press, Cambridge, MA, 1985.

13. Rosenberg, J. B., and Davis, E. W. BLITZ: Blitzen's microcode assembly language design document. MCNC Tech. Rep. TR88-14, 1988.

14. Rosenberg, J. B., Becher, J., and Hooke, N. Vectorization enables full scale simulation of massively parallel (SIMD) architectures. *Proc. Third International Conference on Supercomputing.* Boston, MA, 1988.

15. Sharp, J. A. *An Introduction to Distributed and Parallel Processing.* Blackwell Scientific Publications, Oxford, 1987.

16. Tucker, L. W., and Robertson, G. G. Architecture and applications of the connection machine. *Computer* **21**, 8 (Aug. 1988). 26–38.

Received February 1, 1989; revised July 27, 1989

DONALD W. BLEVINS received his M.S. degree in electrical engineering from Rutgers University in 1986. In 1984 he became a Member of Technical Staff at AT&T Bell Laboratories. At the Laboratories he worked on the design of the WE 32301 Memory Management Unit and a graphics processor. In August of 1984 Don became a Member of Technical Staff with the Microelectronics Center of North Carolina. Don currently works for Precision Products Corp.

EDWARD W. DAVIS received his Ph.D. in computer science from the University of Illinois in 1972. He worked for Goodyear Aerospace Corp. (now LORAL Defense Systems—Akron) on the STARAN parallel processor. He is currently an associate professor of computer science at North Carolina State University in Raleigh, North Carolina, with interests in computer architecture and parallel processing.

ROBERT (FRED) HEATON received his M.S. degree in electrical engineering from Carnegie–Mellon University in 1982. In 1980 he became a Member of Technical Staff at AT&T Bell Laboratories. While there he did design for the CRISP microprocessor and AT&T's WE 32000 microprocessor and 32101 Memory Management Unit. Fred has been a Member of Technical Staff with the Microelectronics Center of North Carolina since June 1987.

JOHN HENRY REIF was born August 4, 1951, in Madison, Wisconsin. He received his B.S. degree (magna cum laude) in applied mathematics and computer science from Tufts University, Medford, Massachusetts, in 1973 and his M.S. and Ph.D. degrees in applied mathematics from Harvard University, Cambridge, Massachusetts, in 1975 and 1977, respectively. From 1975 to 1978, Dr. Reif held research positions at Harvard University and the University of Rochester. As a faculty member, Dr. Reif was an assistant professor at the University of Rochester (1978–1979) and at Harvard University (1979–1983), and then moved to associate professor at Harvard (1983–1986). Since the summer of 1986, Dr. Reif has been a tenured professor of computer science at Duke University. Durham, North Carolina, where he develops and manipulates theoretical computer science problems involving efficient algorithms, parallel computation, robotics, and optical computing.

The Design of the MasPar MP-1:
A Cost Effective Massively Parallel Computer

John R. Nickolls

MasPar Computer Corporation
749 North Mary Avenue
Sunnyvale, CA 94086

Abstract

By using CMOS VLSI and replication of components effectively, massively parallel computers can achieve extraordinary performance at low cost. Key issues are how the processor and memory are partitioned and replicated, and how interprocessor communication and I/O are accomplished. This paper describes the design and implementation of the MasPar MP-1, a general purpose massively parallel computer system that achieves peak computation rates beyond a billion floating point operations per second, yet is priced like a minicomputer.

Massively Parallel System

Massively parallel computers use more than 1,000 processors to obtain computational performance unachievable by conventional processors [1,2,3]. The MasPar MP-1 system is scalable from 1,024 to 16,384 processors and its peak performance scales linearly with the number of processors. A 16K processor system delivers 30,000 MIPS peak performance where a representative instruction is a 32-bit integer add. In terms of peak floating point performance, the 16K processor system delivers 1,500 MFLOPS single precision (32-bit) and 650 MFLOPS double precision (64-bit), using the average of add and multiply times.

To effectively apply a high degree of parallelism to a single application, the problem data is spread across the processors. Each processor computes on behalf of one or a few data elements in the problem. This approach is called "data-level parallel" [4] and is effective for a broad range of compute-intensive applications.

Partitioning the computational effort is the key to high performance, and the simplest and most scalable method is data parallelism. The architecture of the MP-1 [5] is scalable in a way that permits its computational power to be increased along two axes: the performance of each processor, and the number of processors. This flexibility is well matched to VLSI technology where circuit densities continue to increase at a rapid rate. The scalable nature of massively parallel systems protects the customers' software investment while providing a path to increasing performance in successive products [6].

Because its architecture provides tremendous leverage, the MP-1 implementation is conservative in terms of circuit complexity, design rules, IC geometry, clock rates, margins, and power dissipation. A sufficiently high processor count reduces the need to have an overly aggressive (and thus expensive) implementation. Partitioning and replication make it possible to use low cost, low power workstation technology to build very high performance systems. Replication of key system elements happily enables both high performance and low cost.

Array Control Unit

Because massively parallel systems focus on data parallelism, all the processors can execute the same instruction stream. The MP-1 has a single instruction stream multiple data (SIMD) architecture that simplifies the highly replicated processors by eliminating their instruction logic and instruction memory, and thus saves millions of gates and hundreds of megabytes of memory in the overall system. The processors in a SIMD system are called processor elements (PEs) to indicate that they contain only the data path of a processor.

The MP-1 array control unit (ACU) is a 14 MIPS scalar processor with a RISC-style instruction set and a demand-paged instruction memory. The ACU fetches and decodes MP-1 instructions, computes addresses and scalar data values, issues control signals to the PE array, and monitors the status of the PE array. The ACU is implemented with a microcoded engine to accommodate the needs of the PE array, but most of the scalar ACU instructions execute in one 70 nsec clock. The ACU occupies one printed circuit board.

Processor Array

The MP-1 processor array (figure 1) is configurable from 1 to 16 identical processor boards. Each processor board has 1,024 processor elements (PEs) and associated memory arranged as 64 PE clusters (PECs) of 16 PEs per cluster. The processors are interconnected via the X-Net neighborhood mesh and the global multistage crossbar router network.

The processor boards are approximately 14" by 19" and use a high density connector to mate with a common backplane. A processor board dissipates less than 50 watts; a full 16K PE array and ACU dissipate less than 1,000 watts.

A PE cluster (figure 2) is composed of 16 PEs and 16 processor memories (PMEM). The PEs are logically arranged as a 4 by 4 array for the X-Net two-dimensional mesh interconnection. Each PE has a large internal register file shown in the figure as PREG. Load and store instructions move data between PREG and PMEM. The ACU broadcasts instructions and data to all PE clusters and the PEs all contribute to an inclusive-OR reduction

0-8186-2642-9/92 $3.00 © 1990 IEEE

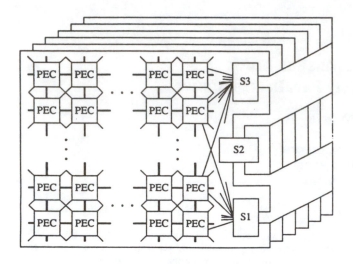

Figure 1. Array of PE Clusters

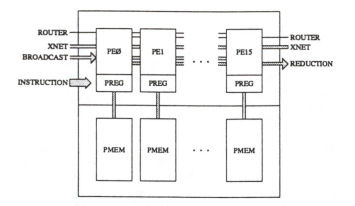

Figure 2. PE Cluster

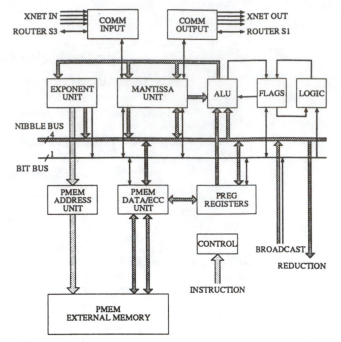

Figure 3. Processor Element and Processor Memory

tree received by the ACU. The 16 PEs in a cluster share an access port to the multistage crossbar router.

The MP-1 processor chip is a full-custom design that contains 32 identical PEs (2 PE clusters) implemented in two-level metal 1.6μ CMOS and packaged in a cost effective 164 pin plastic quad flat pack. The die is 11.6 mm by 9.5 mm, and has 450,000 transistors. A conservative 70 nsec clock yields low power and robust timing margins.

Processor memory, PMEM, is implemented with 1 Mbit DRAMs that are arranged in the cluster so that each PE has 16 Kbytes of ECC-protected data memory. A processor board has 16 Mbytes of memory, and a 16 board system has 256 Mbytes of memory. The MP-1 instruction set supports 32 bits of PE number and 32 bits of memory addressing per PE, so the memory system size is limited only by cost and market considerations.

As an MP-1 system is expanded, each increment adds PEs, memory, and communications resources, so the system always maintains a balance between processor performance, memory size and bandwidth, and communications and I/O bandwidth.

Processor Elements

The MP-1 processor element (PE) design is different than that of a conventional processor because a PE is mostly data path logic and has no instruction fetch or decode logic. SIMD system performance is the product of the number of PEs and the speed of each PE, so the performance of a single PE is not as important as it is in conventional processors. Present VLSI densities and the relative tradeoffs between the number of processors and processor complexity encourage putting many PEs on one chip. The resulting design tradeoff between PE area and PE performance tends to reduce the PE architecture to the key essentials.

Each PE (figure 3) is designed to deliver high performance floating point and integer computation together with high memory bandwidth and communications bandwidth, yet have minimal complexity and silicon area to make it feasible to replicate many PEs on a single high-yield chip.

Like present RISC processors, each PE has a large on-chip register set (PREG) and all computations operate on the registers. Load and store instructions move data between the external memory (PMEM) and the register set. The register architecture substantially improves performance by reducing the need to reference external memory. The compilers optimize register usage to minimize load/store memory traffic.

Each PE has 40 32-bit registers available to the programmer and an additional 8 32-bit registers that are used internally to implement the MP-1 instruction set. With 32 PEs per die, the resulting 48 Kbits of register occupy about 30% of the die area, but represent 75% of the transistor count. Placing the registers on-chip yields an aggregate PE/PREG bandwidth of 117 gigabytes per second with 16K PEs. The registers are bit and byte addressable.

Each PE provides floating point operations on 32 and 64 bit IEEE or VAX format operands and integer operations on 1, 8, 16, 32, and 64 bit operands. The PE floating point/integer hardware has a 64-bit MANTISSA unit, a 16-bit EXPONENT unit, a 4-bit ALU, a 1-bit LOGIC unit, and a FLAGS unit; these units perform floating point, integer, and boolean computations. The floating point/integer unit uses more than half of the PE silicon area but provides substantially better performance than the bit-serial designs used in earlier massively parallel processors.

Most data movement within each PE occurs on the internal PE 4-bit NIBBLE BUS and the BIT BUS (figure 3). During a 32-bit or 64-bit floating point or integer instruction, the ACU microcode engine steps the PEs through a series of operations on successive 4-bit nibbles to generate the full precision result. For example, a 32-bit integer add requires 8 clocks: during each clock a nibble is fetched from a PREG register, a nibble is simultaneously obtained from the MANTISSA unit, the nibbles are added in the ALU, and the sum is delivered to the MANTISSA unit. At the same time, the ALU delivers a carry bit to the FLAGS unit to be returned to the ALU on the next step. The ALU also updates bits in the FLAGS unit that indicate overflow and zeroness.

The different functional units within the PE can be simultaneously active during each micro-step. For example, floating point normalization and de-normalization steps use the EXPONENT, MANTISSA, ALU, FLAGS, and LOGIC units together. The ACU issues the same micro-controls to all PEs, but the operation of each PE is locally enabled by the E-bit in its FLAGS unit. During a floating point operation, some micro-steps are data-dependent, so the PEs locally disable themselves as needed by the EXPONENT and MANTISSA units.

Because the MP-1 instruction set focuses on conventional operand sizes of 8, 16, 32, and 64 bits, MasPar can implement subsequent PEs with smaller or larger ALU widths without changing the programmer's instruction model. The internal 4-bit nature of the PE is not visible to the programmer, but does make the PE flexible enough to accommodate different front-end workstation data formats. The PE hardware supports both little-endian and big-endian format integers, VAX floating point F, D, and G format, and IEEE single and double precision floating point formats.

Along with the PE controls, the ACU broadcasts 4 bits of data per clock onto every PE nibble bus to support MP-1 instructions with scalar source operands. The PE nibble and bit bus also drive a 4-bit wide inclusive-OR reduction tree that returns to the ACU. Using the OR tree, the ACU can assemble a 32-bit scalar value from the OR of 16,384 32-bit PREG values in 8 clocks plus a few clocks of pipeline overhead.

Processor Memory

Because only load and store instructions access PMEM processor memory, the MP-1 overlaps memory operations with PE computation. When a load or store instruction is fetched, the ACU queues the operation to a separate state machine that operates independently of the normal instruction stream. Up to 32 load/store instructions can be queued and executed while PE computations proceed, as long as the PREG register being loaded or stored is not used by the PE in a conflicting way. A hardware interlock mechanism in the ACU prevents PE operations from using a PREG register before it is loaded and from changing a PREG register before it is stored. The optimizing compilers move loads earlier in the instruction stream and delay using

registers that are being stored. The 40 registers in each PE assist the compilers in obtaining substantial memory/execution overlap.

The PMEM processor memory can be directly or indirectly addressed. Direct addressing uses an address broadcast from the ACU, so the address is the same in each PE. Using fast page mode DRAMS, a 16K PE system delivers memory bandwidth of over 12 gigabytes per second. Indirect addressing uses an address computed locally in each PE's PMEM ADDRESS UNIT and is a major improvement over earlier SIMD architectures[7] because it permits the use of pointers, linked lists, and data structures in a large processor memory. Indirect addressing is about one third as fast as direct addressing.

X-Net Mesh Interconnect

The X-Net interconnect directly connects each PE with its 8 nearest neighbors in a two-dimensional mesh. Each PE has 4 connections at its diagonal corners, forming an X pattern similar to the Blitzen[8] X grid network. A tri-state node at each X intersection permits communications with any of 8 neighbors using only 4 wires per PE.

Figure 1 shows the X-Net connections between PE clusters. The PE chip has two clusters of 4 by 4 PEs and uses 24 pins for X-Net connections. The cluster, chip, and board boundaries are not visible and the connections at the PE array edges are wrapped around to form a torus. The torus facilitates several important matrix algorithms and can emulate a one-dimensional ring with two X-Net steps.

All PEs have the same direction controls so that, for example, every PE sends an operand to the North and simultaneously receives an operand from the South. The X-Net uses a bit-serial implementation to minimize pin and wire costs and is clocked synchronously with the PEs; all transmissions are parity checked. The PEs use the shift capability of the MANTISSA unit to generate and accumulate bit-serial messages. Inactive PEs can serve as pipeline stages to expedite long distance communication jumps through several PEs. The MP-1 instruction set [5] implements X-Net operations that move or distribute 1, 8, 16, 32, and 64 bit operands with time proportional to either the product or the sum of the operand length and the distance. The aggregate X-Net communication rate in a 16K PE system exceeds 20 gigabytes per second.

Multistage Crossbar Interconnect

The multistage crossbar interconnection network provides global communication between all the PEs and forms the basis for the MP-1 I/O system. The MP-1 network uses three router stages shown as S1, S2, and S3 in figure 1 to implement the function of a 1024 by 1024 crossbar switch. Each cluster of 16 PEs shares an originating port connected to router stage S1 and a target port connected to stage S3. Connections are established from an originating PE through stages S1, S2, S3, and then to the target PE. A 16K PE system has 1024 PE clusters, so each stage has 1024 router ports and the router supports up to 1024 simultaneous connections.

Originating PEs compute the number of a target PE and transmit it to the router S1 port. Each router stage selects a connection to the next stage based on the target PE number. Once established, the connection is bidirectional and can move data between the originating and target PEs. When the connection is closed, the target PE returns an acknowledgement. Because the router ports are multiplexed among 16 PEs, an arbitrary communication pattern takes 16 or more router cycles to complete.

The multistage crossbar is well matched to the SIMD architecture because all communication paths are equal length, and therefore all communications arrive at their targets simultaneously. The router connections are bit-serial and are clocked synchronously with the PE clock; all transmissions are parity checked. The PEs use the MANTISSA unit to simultaneously generate outgoing router data and assemble incoming router data.

The MP-1 router chip implements part of one router stage. The router chip connects 64 input ports to 64 output ports by partially decoding the target PE addresses [9]. The full-custom design is implemented in two-level metal 1.6μ CMOS and packaged in a 164 pin plastic quad flat pack. The die is 7.7 mm by 8.1 mm, and has 110,000 transistors. Three router chips are used on each processor board.

A 16K PE system has an aggregate router communication bandwidth in excess of 1.5 gigabytes per second. For random communication patterns the multistage router network is essentially equivalent to a 1024 by 1024 crossbar network with far fewer switches and wires.

Conclusion

Through a combination of massively parallel architecture, design simplicity, cell replication, CMOS VLSI, conservative clock rates, surface mount packaging, and volume component replication, the MasPar MP-1 family delivers very high performance with low power and low cost. The massively parallel design provides cost effective computing for today and a scalable growth path for tomorrow.

References

[1] S. F. Reddaway, "DAP, A Distributed Array Processor", *First Annual Symposium on Computer Architecture*, IEEE/ACM, Florida, 1973.

[2] Kenneth E. Batcher, "Design of a Massively Parallel Processor", *IEEE Transactions on Computers*, vol C-29, pp. 836-840, Sept 1980.

[3] W. Daniel Hillis, *The Connection Machine*, MIT Press, 1985.

[4] David L. Waltz, "Applications of the Connection Machine", *Computer*, pp. 85-97, January 1987.

[5] Tom Blank, "The MasPar MP-1 Architecture", *Proceedings of IEEE Compcon Spring 1990*, IEEE, February 1990.

[6] Peter Christy, "Software to Support Massively Parallel Computing on the MasPar MP-1", *Proceedings of IEEE Compcon Spring 1990*, IEEE, February 1990.

[7] Ken Batcher, "The Architecture of Tomorrow's Massively Parallel Computer", *Frontiers of Massively Parallel Scientific Computing*, NASA CP 2478, September 1986.

[8] Edward W. Davis and John H. Reif, "Architecture and Operation of the BLITZEN Processing Element", *3rd Intl. Conf. on Supercomputing*, vol III, pp. 128-137, May 1988.

[9] Robert Grondalski, "A VLSI Chip Set for a Massively Parallel Architecture", *International Solid State Circuits Conference*, February 1987.

Task Flow Computer Architecture

Robert W. Horst
Center for Reliable and High Performance Computing
University of Illinois
Urbana, IL 61801

Abstract -- This paper introduces a parallel computer architecture known as *task flow*. Simple replicated cells contain both memory packets and processing logic. Each memory packet contains a data field, the next instruction, and a link. Execution of each task is accomplished by following a linked list of memory packets. Register values are communicated as part of the transmission packet. Variations in the instruction set, synchronization, interconnection topology, and hardware implementation are discussed. Wafer scale integration is suggested as a potential technology for implementing task flow machines. A matrix-vector multiplication program illustrates the flow of tasks between cells.

1. Overview of Task Flow

This paper introduces a new approach to parallel computation called *task flow* architecture. The major difference from current machines is the concept of sending computations to stationary data objects, rather than sending data from memory to stationary processors. Task flow machines do not contain separate processors and memories, instead there are multiple *cells* which contain both computing and memory elements. Data is partitioned across the simple identical interconnected cells. Computation is performed by a set of tasks flowing through the network. Each task is executed by following a linked-list of *memory packets* (MPs), each of which contains a data element, the next instruction to perform, and a link to the next MP.

A high level block diagram of a task flow machine is shown in Figure 1. Each cell contains input queues, a wide shallow memory and one arithmetic unit. The state of each executing task is transmitted between cells as a *transmission packet* (TP). The TP contains data register values, the instruction to perform at the destination, and the link to the next MP. A single instruction may have its instruction fetch and execution performed in two different cells. A cell receives a *RCV* TP, uses the embedded address to address the MP, and performs the indicated operation producing a new *SND* TP. The SND packet may be sent to another cell or routed back to the same cell. New tasks are forked by instructions which create both a SND TP and a *SEQ* (sequential) TP. The SEQ packet continues task execution at the next MP address in the current cell.

An example may help to illustrate the way in which the flow of tasks accomplishes program execution. Consider a vector, V which is distributed among the cells in such a way that V_i resides in the cell i. A program to sum the vector elements would proceed as follows. First a TP is sent to V_1 in Cell 1. The instruction in the TP is a LOAD instruction which specifies that the data field of the addressed MP is to be fetched and placed into one of the register fields of the outgoing TP. The MP also has a link to the location of V_2, and the first ADD instruction which

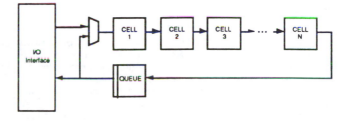

Figure 1. Unidirectional ring task flow machine

will be performed at V_2. After the LOAD has been executed in Cell 1, the task continues by sending a new TP to Cell 2. This TP contains V_1 in a register field, the address of V_2 in the link field, and the first ADD in the instruction field. At Cell 2, fetching the addressed MP retrieves V_2, the address of V_3, and the second ADD instruction. V_2 is added to the incoming register field and the sum is directed to a register field of the outgoing TP. The task continues to flow from cell to cell accumulating the sum in a register field.

The assignment of data to cells determines whether a task will spend its time local to one cell or distributed across many cells. Data is assigned to cells in such a way that performance loss due to remote communication is minimized. Many tasks may be simultaneously active in the machine. Tasks which flow between neighboring cells execute in roughly the same time as tasks which remain local to a single cell.

The following sections will contrast task flow with other parallel architectures, and will discuss the trade-offs in designing a task flow computer. Some of the design aspects considered include the instruction set, interconnection network, hardware implementation, and potential applications.

2. Task flow, control flow and data flow

Current approaches to parallel processing include Single Instruction Multiple Data (SIMD) machines, parallel processors, systolic arrays, and data flow machines. SIMD machines use a single sequential instruction stream to control parallel arithmetic units [1, 2]. Multiple Instruction Multiple Data (MIMD) computers have a large number of sequential processors which are connected to memory elements through a routing network. Examples of massively parallel MIMD machines include the IBM RP3 project and University of Illinois Cedar project.

In systolic arrays, data is passed through a 1 or 2 dimensional communications network in such a way that operands simultaneously arrive at a processing element.

At each processing element, the algorithm is stored in memory or is implemented directly in hardware control. Newer variations of systolic arrays, such as WARP [3] and iWARP [4], provide queuing at each stage to relax the constraints of simultaneous arrival of all operands. These machines behave much like MIMD multi-processors with a fast interconnection network. Each processing element has one thread of control. Systolic arrays may be designed to support several computational models: local, domain partition, pipeline, multi-function pipeline, and ring [5].

Data flow machines pass data tokens to processing elements which "fire" when all operands have arrived. Each processing element asynchronously fires when all operand tokens have arrived, and then generates a new result token. Data flow machines are most naturally programmed using a single-assignment language. This allows data dependencies to be easily detected, and allows statements to be processed in any order [6].

A comparison of different classes of computer architectures is shown in Figure 2. Serial and SIMD machines have a single thread of control. In MIMD machines and systolic arrays, the number of control threads is determined by the number of processors. The number of threads in a task flow machine is determined by the number of tasks executing. This number is bounded by the total amount of TP queuing available in the system.

Architecture	Control Threads	Next op Trigger	Multi-thread Interactions	Native Data Structure	Grain Size
Serial Control Flow	1	Instruct Fetch	Sequential	Scalar	-
SIMD Control Flow	1	Instruct Fetch	Synchronous Parallel	Vector	Fine
MIMD Control Flow	N	Instruct Fetch	Asynchronous	Multiple Vectors	Medium - Coarse
Systolic Array	N	Clock Pulse	Synchronous Pipelined	Dense Matrix	Fine
Data Flow	<= N	Operand Arrival	Asynchronous	Data Flow Graph	Medium - Coarse
Task Flow	<= NQ	TP Arrival	Synchronous or Asynch	Sparse Matrix	Fine - Coarse

Figure 2. Comparison of control flow, data flow, and task flow. N = number of processing elements, Q = maximum number of queued transmission packets (TP) in each cell of a task flow machine.

The table also contrasts the architectures for the event which triggers the next operation, the way multiple threads pass data to each other, the data structure which is most naturally processed, and the typical grain size of parallel operations. Task flow lends itself to computations which require frequent synchronous or less frequent asynchronous task communications. The natural linked-list structure of MPs is especially effective in sparse matrix computation, with no scatter-gather required to expand and compress the sparse structures into dense vectors. The grain size of a task flow machine may vary from extremely fine (with the execution of each instruc-

tion distributed across two cells) to coarse (with long procedures executed entirely within a single cell).

When a program is written for a task flow machine, each appearance of a variable on the right hand side of a statement constitutes one "visit" to that variable. The MP storing that variable has a link to the next variable to visit. Since there is only one link per MP, the same variable should not appear more than once on the right hand side of a statement -- otherwise, there would be two different successors to the access of the variable. Therefore, programming of a pure task flow machine would be done in a *single-retrieval* language. If a single retrieval language is used, there is a simple correspondence between an assembly language program and the memory layout of the memory packets. Each memory packet includes a link to the next variable to be visited and the instruction to be performed on that variable.

Several different techniques may be used to relax the strict requirement of using a single retrieval language. When a variable must be read more than once, there may be enough registers in the architecture to keep one variable in a register. Another solution is for multiple copies of the variable to be stored at the time the variable is computed. Finally, a "GET" instruction may be used to fetch a data value without sending the control thread to the fetched variable.

It is interesting to note that task flow is the opposite of data flow in many respects. Operations begin when the instructions reach the data values rather than when the data reaches the processing elements. Programming is done most naturally with a single-retrieval language rather than a single-assignment language. Task flow machines operate on large arrays of shared data, where fine-grain data flow machines have no concept of shared data storage.

Task flow encourages a flatter memory hierarchy than standard MIMD machines. In task flow, forwarding tasks to memory elements substitutes for passing large arrays between processors and memory. There is less need to cache data close to the processor using the data, making it more feasible to use a flat memory hierarchy. The elimination of caches reduces area requirements for each cell, and eliminates performance penalties for filling the caches and maintaining cache coherence.

Compiler optimization for MIMD machines involves optimal assignment of variables to registers to avoid memory references, while task flow optimization involves optimizing the placement of variables in memory. The compiler should assign variables to memory locations in a way which balances cell utilization and minimizes links to other than the current or neighboring cells.

3. Instruction Set Architecture

A description of the operation of some representative task flow instructions is shown in Figure 3. Instructions in a task flow machine are fetched from the memory of a sending cell, then transmitted to the receiving cell. Each instruction has the opportunity to cause actions at both cells. In general, the data manipulation operations of the instruction are performed at the receiving cell, while generation of new tasks is performed at the sending cell. It would be possible to design instruction sets which perform multiple memory references at the destination cell, but the implementation is simplified if each instruction is limited to at most one memory reference.

Operands available to arithmetic instructions include the register values transmitted from sender to receiver, and the data field of the memory packet fetched at the receiver. For instance, the ADD instruction adds the memory data value to one of the registers and stores the result in a register. Different types of operands (fixed, floating point, strings, etc.) would be handled by different instructions. For simplicity in explaining the concepts of task flow, this paper assumes a single operand type.

Instructions are provided to fork a task into multiple tasks. The simplest FORK instruction sends one task to the receiving cell (addressed by the link field of the memory packet), and another task to the next sequential MP in the same cell. Variations of fork instructions could combine the fork with arithmetic operations to provide the destination cell with an operation in addition to the fork (which is executed as a no-operation instruction at the receiver).

When storing data in a memory location, it is usually undesirable to continue the execution of the current task at the MP containing the data being stored. The Store-via-Forked-task (STF) instruction sends data to the MP addressed by the link, but continues the task at the next sequential instruction. Temporarily, two tasks are generated. At the receiver, the data field of the addressed MP is written with the store data and the forked task is terminated.

Registers associated with an executing task are part of the transmission packet sent from cell to cell. The width of the data path between cells is dependent on the number of registers -- adding one 32-bit register to the architecture requires an additional 64 connections to a cell for the input and output paths. It is possible to design an instruction set with a single register and all other operands located in memory. A single register instruction set was created for an early task flow design, but it required many instructions to be defined with multiple memory accesses. Adding a second register helps to simplify the instruction definitions and sequences. The following discussion assumes two registers, but it would be possible to define machines with many more registers. The width of registers has been simulated with 32-bit variables, but scientific machines may require 64-bit registers.

GET is an instruction which has no direct corresponding instruction in other types of machines. GET places a return address in one of the register fields and sends the packet to a receiver. The receiver fetches the data, places it in one of the register fields, and forwards the task to the return location rather than the target of the link field at the MP.

GET allows a MP to have multiple possible successors. The most frequent successor is specified by the link field, and others must use the GET instruction, which requires a round-trip delay for sending the request and returning the data. In the future, trace-scheduling compilers may automatically code the most frequent paths in native mode task flow code while programming the less frequent paths using GET. Note that GET allows the emulation of a "normal" architecture which suspends execution until data is returned to the same processor which requested it.

In the examples below, GET always sends a no-operation instruction back with the data (the instruction stored at the MP would be for a different execution path). A more complicated instruction set could have a set of GET operators such as GET-and-ADD which would return the data along with an arithmetic opcode.

NOP — No Operation, Goto next link
Sender actions:
Receiver actions: Create SND packet

-Packet-	-Instr-	-Ra-	-Rb-	-Cell-	-Adr-
SND	MEM.instr	RCV.Ra	RCV.Rb		MEM.link

LOAD Ra — Load Ra from memory
Sender actions:
Receiver actions: Create SND packet

-Packet-	-Instr-	-Ra-	-Rb-	-Cell-	-Adr-
SND	MEM.instr	MEM.data	RCV.Rb		MEM.link

Add Ra — Ra = Ra + memory
Sender actions:
Receiver actions: SUM = RCV.Ra + MEM.data; Create SND packet

-Packet-	-Instr-	-Ra-	-Rb-	-Cell-	-Adr-
SND	MEM.instr	SUM	RCV.Rb		MEM.link

Add Rb — Ra = Rb + memory
Sender actions:
Receiver actions: SUM = RCV.Rb + MEM.data; Create SND packet

-Packet-	-Instr-	-Ra-	-Rb-	-Cell-	-Adr-
SND	MEM.instr	SUM	RCV.Rb		MEM.link

FORK — Fork a new task
Sender actions: Create SEQ packet
Receiver actions: Create SND packet

-Packet-	-Instr-	-Ra-	-Rb-	-Cell-	-Adr-
SND	MEM.instr	RCV.Ra	RCV.Rb		MEM.link
SEQ	NOP	RCV.Ra	RCV.Rb	LocCell	LocAdr+1

STF Ra — Store Ra to memory via Forked task
Sender actions: Create SEQ packet
Receiver actions: MEM.data = RCV.Ra

-Packet-	-Instr-	-Ra-	-Rb-	-Cell-	-Adr-
SEQ	NOP	RCV.Ra	RCV.Rb	LocCell	LocAdr+1

GET Rb — Send task to get data and return to next
Sender actions: Override SND.Rb with LocCell, LocAdr+1
Receiver actions: Create SND packet

-Packet-	-Instr-	-Ra-	-Rb-	-Cell-	-Adr-
SND	NOP	RCV.Ra	MEM.data		RCV.Rb

BZERO Ra — Branch if Ra == 0, else sequential
Sender actions:
Receiver actions: If (RCV.Ra == 0) create SND else create SEQ

-Packet-	-Instr-	-Ra-	-Rb-	-Cell-	-Adr-
SND	MEM.instr	RCV.Ra	RCV.Rb		MEM.link
SEQ	NOP	RCV.Ra	RCV.Rb	LocCell	LocAdr+1

LLOAD Rb — Locked Load Rb from memory
Sender actions:
Receiver actions: Retry if MEM.lock!=1; Create SND; MEM.lock=0

-Packet-	-Instr-	-Ra-	-Rb-	-Cell-	-Adr-
SND	MEM.instr	RCV.Ra	MEM.data		MEM.link

LSTF Ra — Locked Store Rb to memory via Forked task
Sender actions: Create SEQ packet
Receiver actions: Retry if MEM.lock!=0; MEM.data,.lock=RCV.Ra,1

-Packet-	-Instr-	-Ra-	-Rb-	-Cell-	-Adr-
SEQ	NOP	RCV.Ra	RCV.Rb	LocCell	LocAdr+1

Figure 3. Partial instruction set description for a 2-register task flow machine.

The partial instruction set description shows the BZERO instruction as an example of a conditional branch. Conditional branches cause either a normal SND packet to be sent to the target of the link field, or a SEQ packet to be sent to the next sequential location in the same cell.

The locked instructions, LLOAD and LSTF are example of instructions which allow synchronization between tasks. Several alternatives for synchronization are discussed in the following section.

4. Synchronization primitives

Synchronization is required in order to share data between tasks. Most of the synchronization instructions suggested for shared memory multi-processors could be adapted to a task flow machine. For instance, a test-and-set instruction could be sent by multiple tasks to a MP containing a lock value. If the lock was not zero, the task would be re-issued to the same MP; otherwise, the lock value would be set to one and the task continued at the target of the MP. This would implement a critical section at the target location. At the end of the critical section, an STF instruction would clear the lock value and allow another task to enter the critical section.

The drawback of such a simple locking scheme is that all tasks to be synchronized converge at a single cell. The current design instead incorporates a locking scheme similar to the one used in the HEP processor [7, 8]. The scheme includes a lock bit to indicate the validity of each MP. Each instruction which generates or consumes the data field has a bit which indicates whether the lock bit of the MP is to be honored or ignored. If the lock is to be honored, instructions generating data must wait for the lock bit to be cleared before proceeding. Instructions consuming data must wait for the lock bit to be set before proceeding. The finer degree of locking has the advantage of distributing the synchronization across many different cells. Tasks which share data use the lock instructions to guarantee that execution will proceed correctly regardless of whether the producer or consumer of the data arrives first.

5. Interconnection Networks

The simplest interconnection network for a task flow machine is a unidirectional ring, as shown in Figure 1. Tasks may flow around the ring, or remain local to one cell. Bypass logic is provided to allow packets to bypass cells between the sender and receiver, even if the intermediate cells are busy. Input queues at each cell provide some buffering of packets. When a queue is nearly full, a busy signal is propagated to the previous cell to temporarily halt the transmission of additional packets. The ring requires no logic for arbitration or routing. Neighboring cells of the ring can be arranged to be physically adjacent, in order to improve the cycle time.

The disadvantage of the ring for large numbers of cells is that communication to non-adjacent cells can cause saturation of the communications paths at the intermediate cells. For this reason, a ring is not feasible for standard MIMD machines which require round-trip delays to perform all remote reads. In contrast, task flow

programs may accomplish work on the way to the destination cell. Also, the low cost of task migration may allow data to be placed in such a way that fewer accesses to remote data are required. This should allow simple networks, such as the ring, to have high performance at low cost and complexity. Performance studies will determine whether this is possible for certain classes of problems. This paper assumes a simple unidirectional ring network.

More complex networks are possible. Some of the possibilities include the bi-directional ring, chordal ring, mesh, torus, hypercube, and crossbar. At each increment of complexity, there is likely to be some loss in performance of a single path due to arbitration, additional multiplexing, and longer distances between communicating cells. It remains an open issue to determine the appropriate tradeoffs in single path performance versus interconnection flexibility.

6. Hardware Implementation

The most attractive feature of task flow architecture is that most of the machine consists of fairly simple identical cells. Each cell may be built as a single integrated circuit with wide input and output busses to transmit packets. In a two-register machine, each transmission packet includes two registers (32 or 64 bits each), the link to the next MP (approx 32 bits), the instruction (approx 8 bits), and a few control bits (clock, busy, parity, etc.). Thus each TP is approximately 110-174 bits. Doubling this for input and output busses totals 220-388 signal pins if the signals are not multiplexed. This number barely falls into the feasible range of current packaging technology. The number of pins could be reduced through time-multiplexing, but at some cost in performance.

A more cost-effective alternative may be to take advantage of increased circuit densities possible with wafer scale integration (WSI). The usual difficulty in using an entire undiced wafer is that there are always some number of defects, and these cannot be allowed to disable the entire wafer. Many different wafer architectures have been proposed for configuring 2-D meshes and trees out of the non-defective cells on a wafer. A few techniques have also been proposed for configuring linear arrays on a wafer. The linear array techniques generally offer better "harvest" of good cells, and require less configuration hardware than more complex 2-D topologies.

The author has developed a new wafer scale interconnection architecture to allow linear arrays to be configured from the working cells on a partially good wafer [9]. The technique uses four multiplexers per cell to communicate with the four nearest neighbors. A simple algorithm is used to set configuration latches controlling the multiplexers in such a way that all working and reachable cells are configured in a linear chain. The technique guarantees that the delay between the output of one cell and the input of the next cell in the chain is exactly four multiplexer delays. The clock is sent through the same multiplexers as the data to reduce clock skew. The fixed delay between cells and the clocking scheme allow the system to be run at extremely high clock rates.

Assuming 1μ CMOS technology, the maximum clock frequency for data transfers is estimated at about 200 Mhz (5 ns). Instructions take multiple clocks, typically ranging from four clocks for a simple LOAD, up to 17 clocks for MPY. There may be an additional one or two clocks of latency for instructions which flow to the next cell in the ring. The extra time spent in communications affects the time for a single task, but does not reduce the peak processing throughput. In many applications, enough tasks may be added to keep the cells fully utilized. Average processing power of each task may reach 30 MIPs. Floating point performance depends on the amount of floating point hardware devoted to each cell.

The optimal mix of memory and processing power of each cell is yet to be investigated. A reasonable choice may be to devote half of each cell to processing and half to memory. With current 1 micron CMOS technology, there could be approximately 1 Mbit of memory per cell. Total cell area would be about 100 mm^2, and 140 cells would fit on a 6" wafer. Assuming typical defect densities and some form of memory error correction or deallocation, the total yield of usable cells per wafer is estimated at 100.

A block diagram of a single cell is shown in Figure 4. Incoming TPs are first loaded into a pipeline register. The cell compares its local cell number with the destination cell of the TP. If they do not match, the TP passes through the bypass queue to the output pipeline register. An instruction which is just completing may create a new SND packet which is destined for another cell. If this is the case, the new SND packet has priority for the output register and any bypass packets are queued.

If the received TP cell number matches the current cell, the TP is forwarded through the receive queue to the execution logic. If the cell is busy, several packets may be queued until the current instruction completes. The address field addresses the memory while the received instruction is being decoded. The data field of the addressed MP may be modified by a store instruction, or may be used

as an operand of a load or arithmetic instruction. The memory data may be sent to the ALU along with one of the received registers. When the operation has been completed, the output latch is loaded and the outgoing instruction is decoded in order to determine whether a new task is to be started. The cell address of the destination is compared to the current cell to determine whether the task is to remain in the current cell or is to be passed to the next cell.

Overflow of the queues is prevented by propagating a busy signal to the previous cell. The busy signal is sent at the point where there is just enough room left in the queues to save the maximum number of packets which could be generated by the previous cell before it responds to the busy signal. A busy cell continues to forward packets not bound for it. Instructions which fail to complete, either due to a busy destination or due to attempted access of a locked variable, are sent back to the queue for later execution. The cell cycles through the instructions in its input queue looking for instructions which may successfully complete.

Instruction fetch is automatically overlapped with data fetch, since the same MP holds both the data for one instruction and the instruction opcode for the next. There is effectively a two stage pipeline (fetch, execute) which is spread across any two successive cells visited by a task.

The design shown in the block diagram is not internally pipelined. An instruction must complete its memory access and ALU operation before the next memory access can begin. More complex implementations could include a pipeline stage between the memory and ALU, or could have pipelined arithmetic units. The added area devoted to pipelining would reduce the total number of cells per wafer, but would allow more than one task to be simultaneously active at each cell. It is not clear whether

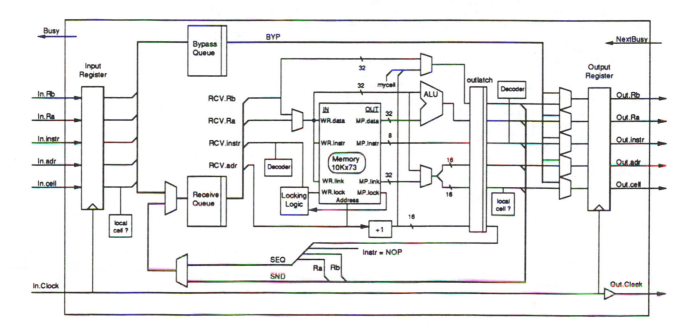

Figure 4. Block diagram of one cell of a 2-register task flow machine.

or not this is a good tradeoff. The simpler design is presented here in order to explain the basic concepts more clearly.

The implementation presented here makes no attempt to minimize the memory required to store link and instruction fields. It would be possible, for instance, to use relative rather than absolute addressing to reduce the number of bits required for the cell number and address offsets. Variable length MPs would also be a way of reducing memory requirements, allowing only the required fields to be included.

The block diagram indicates that the destination cell and address are derived by extracting bitfields from the MP link field. This "physical addressing" requires cell assignments of variables to be fixed at compile time. Virtual addressing could be added by placing a virtual-physical address translation table between the memory link field and the output latch. The translation memory would be accessed in parallel with the ALU operation. Virtual addressing would allow relocation of data, and would permit the paging of memory packets to bulk RAM or disk storage. At this time, only physical addressing is assumed, as it is sufficient for solving a variety of interesting problems.

7. Task Flow Execution

An example of task flow execution is shown in Figure 5. This example assumes the two-register instruction set of Figure 3 and the hardware block diagram of Figure 4. The particular cells for this example are intended to show the flexibility in data placement, not necessarily the optimal assignment.

Time flows from the top to the bottom of the diagram. The program is solving the sum of a multiplication and a division for a particular set of values. At each time step, the value of relevant memory locations is shown, as well as the TPs sent to the next cell to be encountered in the flow of the task.

Note that the STF (store-and-fork) instruction creates a second task which sends the intermediate value of B*C to a location which will later be picked up by the main task. If the communications network always delivers packets in order, there is no chance that the B*C store will not be completed by the time the main tasks tries to load the value because the STF must arrive at cell 11 before the ADD. If the B*C value had been generated by a separate task (started from an earlier FORK instruction), it would not have been possible to guarantee the order of arrival at cell 11. In that case, B*C would have been stored using the LSTF instruction, and the addition would have used the LADD instruction to force the addition to be queued until the store had been completed.

8. Applications

Potential applications of task flow include a wide range of scientific and engineering problems. In particular, problems involving sparse matrices and other fine-grain parallelism are of interest. Further study will be required before knowing whether task flow is applicable to a wide range of problems, or is better suited for special

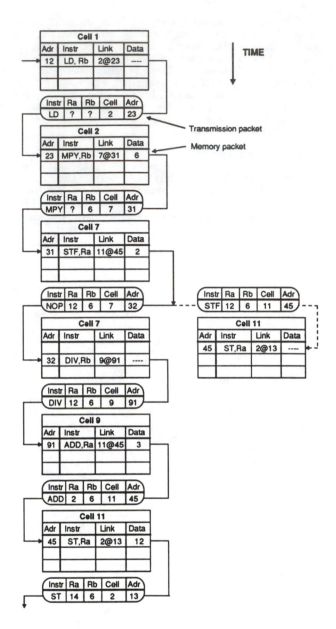

Figure 5. Task flow execution example. Computation of A = B*C + B/D for B = 6, C= 2, D = 3

purpose architectures. Improved programming tools must be developed before it will be possible to evaluate performance on real applications.

To date, only a few small problems have been hand-assembled and run on a simulator. One such problem is the product of a sparse matrix and a vector. This calculation is of interest because of its importance in scientific problems and in neural network simulations.

To illustrate how a matrix-vector product would be computed on a task flow machine, consider a 3-cell 2-register machine solving the following equation:

$$\begin{bmatrix} U_0' \\ U_1' \\ U_2' \end{bmatrix} = \begin{bmatrix} 0 & W_{01} & W_{02} \\ W_{10} & 0 & W_{12} \\ W_{20} & W_{21} & W_{22} \end{bmatrix} \cdot \begin{bmatrix} U_0 \\ U_1 \\ U_2 \end{bmatrix}$$

In a neural network simulation, the U's correspond to the current state of activation of the neurons, and the W's are the weights between neurons. The problem is computed by three tasks. Each task first multiplies one of the vector elements by each of the matrix elements in a column, and then accumulates the products for one row. Placement of the weights determines which operations are performed locally, and which require a task to migrate between cells.

Figure 6 is a simplified flow diagram which shows the path traversed by each of the tasks when one column of the weight matrix is assigned to each cell. The rectangles

show only the data field of the memory packets encountered, and the rounded rectangles show only the instruction field of the transmission packets. Solid lines show the primary task flow and dotted lines show the flow of store-and-fork subtasks. For this data assignment, each task remains local until its multiplies are completed, then flows from cell to cell accumulating products. Non-local communication requirements can be determined by counting each time a line crosses a cell boundary. In the diagram, MPs whose data fields are unused have been omitted. One extra MP would be required at each point on the diagram where there are two sequential TPs.

If the matrix had been assigned with one row in each cell, the multiply phase would flow from cell to cell, and the accumulate phase would remain local. Other data assignments would cause both phases to flow between cells. Unlike systolic arrays, there is no need for an exact correspondence between the dimensions of the matrix

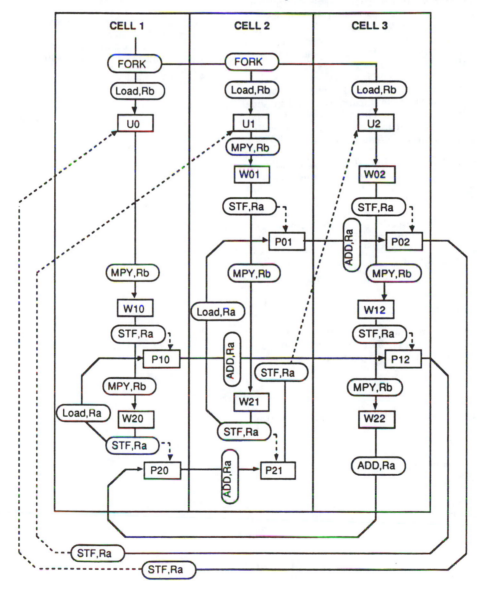

Figure 6. Matrix-vector multiply in a 3-cell 2-register task flow machine.

and the number of cells. Rows may be split between cells, or multiple rows may be assigned to each cell.

Theoretically, the simple example can be scaled up to large matrices and a large number of cells without communications becoming a bottleneck. Future work will involve simulating the performance of task flow machines while varying the number of cells, size of the matrices, density of the matrices, and the data assignment.

9. Conclusions

This paper has examined some of the issues involved in the design of task flow computers. Many variations of task flow are possible by varying the instruction set, synchronization, interconnection topology, and hardware implementation.

Some of the major ideas presented in this paper include: 1) An architecture which reduces the need for remote data access through tasks which can be easily migrated to cells containing the referenced data, 2) A reduction in task migration time by storing the current data, the next instruction, and the link address in the same memory packet, 3) A new type of instruction set consisting of a small instruction field, a field containing either instruction constants or variable data, and a field providing both data addresses and branch addresses, 4) Cost-effective implementation alternatives using new wafer scale techniques and a simplified memory hierarchy.

With wafer-scale integration, it may be feasible to build 100-cell wafers with aggregate processing power of over 3,000 MIPs each. 1000-wafer systems with 100,000 cells are within the realm of economic feasibility. Systems built around wafer scale task flow machines have the potential to be some of the fastest and most cost effective systems for certain applications. Continuing work will be required to determine the difficulty and efficiency of porting real applications to task flow architectures.

10. Acknowledgements

The author wishes to thank Janak Patel for many helpful discussions and ideas. This research was supported by Tandem Computers Incorporated.

References

[1] E. W. Kozdrowicki, D. J. Theis, "Second Generation of Vector Supercomputers," *IEEE Computer*, pp. 71-83, November 1980.

[2] D. Hillis, *The Connection Machine*, Cambridge, MA: MIT Press, 1987.

[3] M. Annaratone, E. Arnould, T. Gross, et al., "The Warp Computer: Architecture, Implementation, and Performance," *IEEE Trans Computers*, vol. C-36, no. 12, pp. 1523-1538, Dec. 1987.

[4] S. Borkar, R. Cohn, G. Cox, et al., "iWarp: An Integrated Solution to High-Speed Parallel Computing," in *proc. Supercomputing '88*, Kissimmee, Florida, Nov. 1988.

[5] H. T. Kung, "WARP Experience: We Can Map Computations Onto a Parallel Computer Efficiently," in *proc. Int'l Conference on Supercomputing*, pp. 668-675, July 1988.

[6] P. C. Treleaven, I. G. Lima, "Future Computers: Logic, Data Flow, ... Control Flow?," *IEEE Computer*, pp. 47-56, March 1984.

[7] H. F. Jordan, "Experience with Pipelined Multiple Instruction Streams," *Proc. IEEE*, vol. 72, no. 1, pp. 113-123, 1984.

[8] B. J. Smith, "Architecture and Applications of the HEP Multiprocessor Computer System," *SPIE*, vol. 298, pp. 241-248, 1981.

[9] R. Horst, "A Linear-Array WSI Architecture for Improved Yield and Performance," in *proc. International Conference on Wafer Scale Integration*, San Francisco, CA, Jan. 1990.

Chapter 4: Architectural Comparisons

It is difficult to predict the performance of different parallel architectures when a specific application program is being executed since the architectures have significant differences in memory delay, instruction scheduling constraints, synchronization overhead, implementation details, and a variety of other parameters. For instance, pipelined processors and multiple instruction-issue processors have a single program counter that eliminates the need for explicit synchronization, while the multiple, independent program counters in a shared-memory multiprocessor introduce complex synchronization requirements. How these architectural differences translate into differences in cost and performance is not readily apparent.

Comparing parallelism extraction techniques

The performance potential of multiple-instruction issuing, and the interaction of multiple-instruction issuing with pipelining, have been investigated by several researchers.[1*-5,6*] Their work has shown that — at the basic block level — pipelining and multiple-instruction issuing are essentially equivalent in their abilities to exploit fine-grained parallelism. However, some studies[7,8*] have shown that there is an optimal pipeline length that is a function of the dependences in the instruction trace and of the skews and delays in the pipeline circuitry itself. Similarly, there may be an optimal instruction width for the multiple instruction-issue architectures.[9]

Studies using matrix multiplication on the PASM prototype[10] indicate that the MIMD configuration may be outperformed by the SIMD organization.[11,12] Using a fast Fourier transform application with the PASM prototype machine, researchers[13,14*] discovered that the performance difference of the SIMD mode and the MIMD mode is very dependent on the synchronization scheme. Matrix multiplication and matrix inversion have been used to compare the performance of the SM3 machine to that of a hypercube.[15] It has been suggested[16] that — for very parallel programs — the instruction-level parallelism of a superscalar processor may have approximately the same performance potential as the loop-level parallelism of a shared-memory multiprocessor. However, the superscalar processor requires extensive register renaming and very accurate branch prediction to match the performance of the multiprocessor, while the multiprocessor has to contend with the cache coherence problem. The best architectural choice may be a combined architecture that exploits the advantages — while compensating for some of the disadvantages — of both the fine-grained and coarse-grained architectures.

Other studies have focused on the incremental performance improvements of some hardware parallelism extraction techniques[17] and on the incremental improvements of some compiler techniques.[18] While these and other studies[19] have shed some light on the differences among parallelism extraction techniques, clearly more work needs to be done to understand the cost and performance trade-offs among the various architectures and to understand the circumstances under which the different approaches can be applied most effectively.

Finally, a great many more issues are involved in building a parallel machine than those discussed in this tutorial. For instance, it has been suggested[20] that system reliability may fundamentally limit parallel performance. In order to create truly large-scale parallel systems, computer architects must incorporate into multiprocessor machine designs the ability to tolerate hardware failures. Without this ability, the performance of the machines will be limited by the reliability of the underlying hardware.

References (Chapter 4)

An asterisk following a reference citation below indicates the inclusion of that paper in this tutorial.

Comparing parallelism extraction techniques

1.* N.P. Jouppi and D.W. Wall, "Available Instruction-Level Parallelism for Superscalar and Superpipelined Machines," *Third Int'l Conf. Architectural Support Programming Languages and Operating Systems*, Apr. 1989, pp. 272-282.

2. N.P. Jouppi, "The Nonuniform Distribution of Instruction-Level and Machine Parallelism and Its Effect on Performance," *IEEE Trans. Computers*, Vol. 38, No. 12, Dec. 1989, pp. 1645-1658.

3. W. Mangione-Smith, S.G. Abraham, and E.S. Davidson, "Architectural vs. Delivered Performance of the IBM RS/6000 and the Astronautics ZS-1," *Hawaii Int'l Conf. System Sciences, Vol. I: Architecture*, 1991, pp. 397-408.

4. A.R. Pleszkun and G.S. Sohi, "The Performance Potential of Multiple Functional Unit Processors," *Int'l Symp. Computer Architecture*, 1988, pp. 37-44.

5. M.D. Smith, M. Johnson, and M.A. Horowitz, "Limits on Multiple Instruction Issue," *Third Int'l Conf. Architectural Support Programming Languages and Operating Systems*, Apr. 1989, pp. 290-302.

6.* G.S. Sohi and S. Vajapeyam, "Tradeoffs in Instruction Format Design for Horizontal Architectures," *Third Int'l Conf. Architectural Support Programming Languages and Operating Systems*, Apr. 1989, pp. 15-25.

7. P.G. Emma and E.S. Davidson, "Characterization of Branch and Data Dependencies in Programs for Evaluating Pipeline Performance," *IEEE Trans. Computers*, Vol. C-36, No. 7, July 1987, pp. 859-875.

8.* S.R. Kunkel and J.E. Smith, "Optimal Pipelining in Supercomputers," *IEEE Int'l Symp. Computer Architecture*, 1986, pp. 404-411.

9. S. Ho and L. Snyder, "Balance in Architectural Design," *Int'l Symp. Computer Architecture*, 1990, pp. 302-310.

10. H.J. Siegel et al., "PASM: A Partitionable SIMD/MIMD System for Image Processing and Pattern Recognition," *IEEE Trans. Computers*, Vol. C-30, No. 12, Dec. 1981, pp. 934-947.

11. S.A. Fineberg, T.L. Casavant, and T. Schwederski, "Mixed-Mode Computing with the PASM System Prototype," *Allerton Conf. Communication, Control, and Computing*, 1987, pp. 258-267.

12. S.A. Fineberg et al., "Non-Deterministic Instruction Time Experiments on the PASM System Prototype," *Int'l Conf. Parallel Processing, Vol. I: Architecture*, 1988, pp. 444-451.

13. E.C. Bronson, T.L. Casavant, and L.H. Jamieson, "Experimental Application-Driven Architecture Analysis of an SIMD/MIMD Parallel Processing System," *Int'l Conf. Parallel Processing, Vol. I: Architecture*, 1989, pp. 59-67.

14.* E.C. Bronson, T.L. Casavant, and L.H. Jamieson, "Experimental Application-Driven Architecture Analysis of an SIMD/MIMD Parallel Processing System," *IEEE Trans. Parallel and Distributed Systems*, Vol. 1, No. 2, Apr. 1990, pp. 195-205.

15. S.Y.W. Su and A.K. Thakore, "Matrix Operations on a Multicomputer System with Switchable Main Memory Modules and Dynamic Control," *IEEE Trans. Computers*, Vol. C-36, No. 12, Dec. 1987, pp. 1467-1484.

16. D.J. Lilja and P.-C. Yew, "The Performance Potential of Fine-Grain and Coarse-Grain Parallel Architectures," *Hawaii Int'l Conf. System Sciences, Vol. I: Architecture*, 1991, pp. 324-333.

17. A.K. Uht, "Incremental Performance Contributions of Hardware Concurrency Extraction Techniques," *First Int'l Conf. Supercomputing*, June 1987, pp. 355-376.

18. W.W. Hwu and P.P. Chang, "Exploiting Parallel Microprocessor Microarchitectures with a Compiler Code Generator," *Int'l Symp. Computer Architecture*, 1988, pp. 45-53.

19. K. Hwang, "Advanced Parallel Processing with Supercomputer Architectures," *Proc. IEEE*, Vol. 75, No. 10, Oct. 1987, pp. 1348-1379.

20. V.F. Nicola and A. Goyal, "Limits of Parallelism in Fault-Tolerant Multiprocessors," *Int'l Working Conf. Dependable Computing Critical Applications*, 1991, pp. 65-72.

Comparing parallelism extraction techniques

Available Instruction-Level Parallelism for Superscalar and Superpipelined Machines

Norman P. Jouppi
David W. Wall

Digital Equipment Corporation
Western Research Lab

Abstract

Superscalar machines can issue several instructions per cycle. Superpipelined machines can issue only one instruction per cycle, but they have cycle times shorter than the latency of any functional unit. In this paper these two techniques are shown to be roughly equivalent ways of exploiting instruction-level parallelism. A parameterizable code reorganization and simulation system was developed and used to measure instruction-level parallelism for a series of benchmarks. Results of these simulations in the presence of various compiler optimizations are presented. The *average degree of superpipelining* metric is introduced. Our simulations suggest that this metric is already high for many machines. These machines already exploit all of the instruction-level parallelism available in many nonnumeric applications, even without parallel instruction issue or higher degrees of pipelining.

1. Introduction

Computer designers and computer architects have been striving to improve uniprocessor computer performance since the first computer was designed. The most significant advances in uniprocessor performance have come from exploiting advances in implementation technology. Architectural innovations have also played a part, and one of the most significant of these over the last decade has been the rediscovery of RISC architectures. Now that RISC architectures have gained acceptance both in scientific and marketing circles, computer architects have been thinking of new ways to improve uniprocessor performance. Many of these proposals such as VLIW [12], superscalar, and even relatively old ideas such as vector processing try to improve computer performance by exploiting instruction-level parallelism.

They take advantage of this parallelism by issuing more than one instruction per cycle explicitly (as in VLIW or superscalar machines) or implicitly (as in vector machines). In this paper we will limit ourselves to improving uniprocessor performance, and will not discuss methods of improving application performance by using multiple processors in parallel.

As an example of instruction-level parallelism, consider the two code fragments in Figure 1-1. The three instructions in (a) are independent; there are no data dependencies between them, and in theory they could all be executed in parallel. In contrast, the three instructions in (b) cannot be executed in parallel, because the second instruction uses the result of the first, and the third instruction uses the result of the second.

```
Load   C1<-23(R2)     Add    R3<-R3+1
Add    R3<-R3+1       Add    R4<-R3+R2
FPAdd  C4<-C4+C3      Store  0[R4]<-R0

(a) parallelism=3     (b) parallelism=1
```

Figure 1-1: Instruction-level parallelism

The amount of instruction-level parallelism varies widely depending on the type of code being executed. When we consider uniprocessor performance improvements due to exploitation of instruction-level parallelism, it is important to keep in mind the type of application environment. If the applications are dominated by highly parallel code (e.g., weather forecasting), any of a number of different parallel computers (e.g., vector, MIMD) would improve application performance. However, if the dominant applications have little instruction-level parallelism (e.g., compilers, editors, event-driven simulators, lisp interpreters), the performance improvements will be much smaller.

In Section 2 we present a machine taxonomy helpful for understanding the duality of operation latency and parallel instruction issue. Section 3 describes the compilation and simulation environment we used to measure the parallelism in benchmarks and its exploitation by different architectures. Section 4 presents the results of these simulations. These results confirm the duality of superscalar and superpipelined machines, and show serious limits on the instruction-level parallelism available in most applications. They also show that most classical code optimizations do nothing to relieve these limits. The importance of cache miss latencies, design complexity, and technology constraints are considered in Section 5. Section 6 summarizes the results of the paper.

2. A Machine Taxonomy

There are several different ways to execute instructions in parallel. Before we examine these methods in detail, we need to start with some definitions:

operation latency
> The time (in cycles) until the result of an instruction is available for use as an operand in a subsequent instruction. For example, if the result of an Add instruction can be used as an operand of an instruction that is issued in the cycle after the Add is issued, we say that the Add has an operation latency of one.

simple operations
> The vast majority of operations executed by the machine. Operations such as integer add, logical ops, loads, stores, branches, and even floating-point addition and multiplication are simple operations. Not included as simple operations are instructions which take an order of magnitude more time and occur less frequently, such as divide and cache misses.

instruction class
> A group of instructions all issued to the same type of functional unit.

issue latency
> The time (in cycles) required between issuing two instructions. This can vary depending on the instruction classes of the two instructions.

2.1. The Base Machine

In order to properly compare increases in performance due to exploitation of instruction-level parallelism, we define a base machine that has an execution pipestage parallelism of exactly one. This base machine is defined as follows:

- Instructions issued per cycle = 1
- Simple operation latency measured in cycles = 1
- Instruction-level parallelism required to fully utilize = 1

The one-cycle latency specifies that if one instruction follows another, the result of the first is always available for the use of the second without delay. Thus, there are never any operation-latency interlocks, stalls, or NOP's in a base machine. A pipeline diagram for a machine satisfying the requirements of a base machine is shown in Figure 2-1. The execution pipestage is cross-hatched while the others are unfilled. Note that although several instructions are executing concurrently, only one instruction is in its execution stage at any one time. Other pipestages, such as instruction fetch, decode, or write back, do not contribute to operation latency if they are bypassed, and do not contribute to control latency assuming perfect branch slot filling and/or branch prediction.

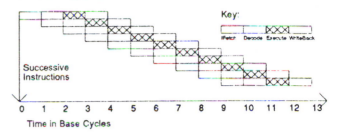

Figure 2-1: Execution in a base machine

2.2. Underpipelined Machines

The single-cycle latency of simple operations also sets the base machine cycle time. Although one could build a base machine where the cycle time was much larger than the time required for each simple operation, it would be a waste of execution time and resources. This would be an *underpipelined machine*. An underpipelined machine that executes an operation and writes back the result in the same pipestage is shown in Figure 2-2.

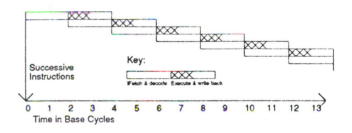

Figure 2-2: Underpipelined: cycle > operation latency

The assumption made in many paper architecture proposals is that the cycle time of a machine is many times larger than the add or load latency, and hence several adders can be stacked in series without affecting the cycle time. If this were really the case, then something would be wrong with the machine cycle time. When the add latency is given as one, for example, we assume that the time to read the operands has been piped into an earlier pipestage, and the time to write back the result has been pipelined into the next pipestage. Then the base cycle time is simply the minimum time required to do a fixed-point add and bypass the result to the next instruction. In this sense machines like the Stanford MIPS chip [8] are underpipelined, because they read operands out of the register file, do an ALU operation, and write back the result all in one cycle.

Another example of underpipelining would be a machine like the Berkeley RISC II chip [10], where loads can only be issued every other cycle. Obviously this reduces the instruction-level parallelism below one instruction per cycle. An underpipelined machine that can only issue an instruction every other cycle is illustrated in Figure 2-3. Note that this machine's performance is the same as the machine in Figure 2-2, which is half of the performance attainable by the base machine.

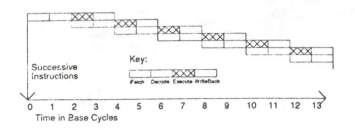

Figure 2-3: Underpipelined: issues < 1 instr. per cycle

In summary, an underpipelined machine has worse performance than the base machine because it either has:

- a cycle time greater than the latency of a simple operation, or

- it issues less than one instruction per cycle.

For this reason underpipelined machines will not be considered in the rest of this paper.

2.3. Superscalar Machines

As their name suggests, superscalar machines were originally developed as an alternative to vector machines. A superscalar machine of degree n can issue n instructions per cycle. A superscalar machine could issue all three parallel instructions in Figure 1-1(a) in the same cycle. Superscalar execution of instructions is illustrated in Figure 2-4.

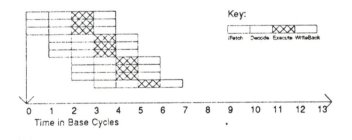

Figure 2-4: Execution in a superscalar machine ($n=3$)

In order to fully utilize a superscalar machine of degree n, there must be n instructions executable in parallel at all times. If an instruction-level parallelism of n is not available, stalls and dead time will result where instructions are forced to wait for the results of prior instructions.

Formalizing a superscalar machine according to our definitions:

- Instructions issued per cycle = n

- Simple operation latency measured in cycles = 1

- Instruction-level parallelism required to fully utilize = n

A superscalar machine can attain the same performance as a machine with vector hardware. Consider the

operations performed when a vector machine executes a vector load chained into a vector add, with one element loaded and added per cycle. The vector machine performs four operations: load, floating-point add, a fixed-point add to generate the next load address, and a compare and branch to see if we have loaded and added the last vector element. A superscalar machine that can issue a fixed-point, floating-point, load, and a branch all in one cycle achieves the same effective parallelism.

2.3.1. VLIW Machines

VLIW, or *very long instruction word*, machines typically have instructions hundreds of bits long. Each instruction can specify many operations, so each instruction exploits instruction-level parallelism. Many performance studies have been performed on VLIW machines [12]. The execution of instructions by an ideal VLIW machine is shown in Figure 2-5. Each instruction specifies multiple operations, and this is denoted in the Figure by having multiple crosshatched execution stages in parallel for each instruction.

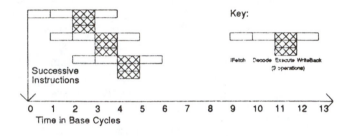

Figure 2-5: Execution in a VLIW machine

VLIW machines are much like superscalar machines, with three differences.

First, the decoding of VLIW instructions is easier than superscalar instructions. Since the VLIW instructions have a fixed format, the operations specifiable in one instruction do not exceed the resources of the machine. However in the superscalar case, the instruction decode unit must look at a sequence of instructions and base the issue of each instruction on the number of instructions already issued of each instruction class, as well as checking for data dependencies between results and operands of instructions. In effect, the selection of which operations to issue in a given cycle is performed at compile time in a VLIW machine, and at run time in a superscalar machine. Thus the instruction decode logic for the VLIW machine should be much simpler than the superscalar.

A second difference is that when the available instruction-level parallelism is less than that exploitable by the VLIW machine, the code density of the superscalar machine will be better. This is because the fixed VLIW format includes bits for unused operations while the superscalar machine only has instruction bits for useful operations.

A third difference is that a superscalar machine could be object-code compatible with a large family of non-parallel machines, but VLIW machines exploiting different amounts of parallelism would require different instruction sets. This is because the VLIW's that are able to exploit more parallelism would require larger instructions.

In spite of these differences, in terms of run time exploitation of instruction-level parallelism, the superscalar and VLIW will have similar characteristics. Because of the close relationship between these two machines, we will only discuss superscalar machines in general and not dwell further on distinctions between VLIW and superscalar machines.

2.3.2. Class Conflicts

There are two ways to develop a superscalar machine of degree n from a base machine.

1. Duplicate all functional units n times, including register ports, bypasses, busses, and instruction decode logic.

2. Duplicate only the register ports, bypasses, busses, and instruction decode logic.

Of course these two methods are extreme cases, and one could duplicate some units and not others. But if all the functional units are not duplicated, then potential class conflicts will be created. A class conflict occurs when some instruction is followed by another instruction for the same functional unit. If the busy functional unit has not been duplicated, the superscalar machine must stop issuing instructions and wait until the next cycle to issue the second instruction. Thus class conflicts can substantially reduce the parallelism exploitable by a superscalar machine. (We will not consider superscalar machines or any other machines that issue instructions out of order. Techniques to reorder instructions at compile time instead of at run time are almost as good [6, 7, 17], and are dramatically simpler than doing it in hardware.)

2.4. Superpipelined Machines

Superpipelined machines exploit instruction-level parallelism in another way. In a superpipelined machine of degree m, the cycle time is $1/m$ the cycle time of the base machine. Since a fixed-point add took a whole cycle in the base machine, given the same implementation technology it must take m cycles in the superpipelined machine. The three parallel instructions in Figure 1-1(a) would be issued in three successive cycles, and by the time the third has been issued, there are three operations in progress at the same time. Figure 2-6 shows the execution of instructions by a superpipelined machine.

Formalizing a superpipelined machine according to our definitions:

- Instructions issued per cycle = 1, but the cycle time is $1/m$ of the base machine

- Simple operation latency measured in cycles = m
- Instruction-level parallelism required to fully utilize = m

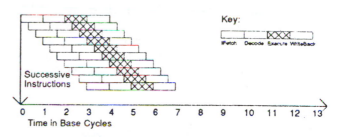

Figure 2-6: Superpipelined execution (m=3)

Superpipelined machines have been around a long time. Seymour Cray has a long history of building superpipelined machines: for example, the latency of a fixed-point add in both the CDC 6600 and the Cray-1 is 3 cycles. Note that since the functional units of the 6600 are not pipelined (two are duplicated), the 6600 is an example of a superpipelined machine with class conflicts. The CDC 7600 is probably the purest example of an existing superpipelined machine since its functional units are pipelined.

2.5. Superpipelined Superscalar Machines

Since the number of instructions issued per cycle and the cycle time are theoretically orthogonal, we could have a superpipelined superscalar machine. A superpipelined superscalar machine of degree (m,n) has a cycle time $1/m$ that of the base machine, and it can execute n instructions every cycle. This is illustrated in Figure 2-7.

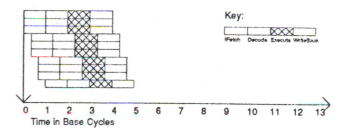

Figure 2-7: A superpipelined superscalar (n=3,m=3)

Formalizing a superpipelined superscalar machine according to our definitions:

- Instructions issued per cycle = n, and the cycle time is $1/m$ that of the base machine

- Simple operation latency measured in cycles = m

- Instruction-level parallelism required to fully utilize = $n*m$

2.6. Vector Machines

Although vector machines also take advantage of (unrolled-loop) instruction-level parallelism, whether a machine supports vectors is really independent of whether it is a superpipelined, superscalar, or base machine. Each of these machines could have an attached vector unit. However, to the extent that the highly parallel code was run in vector mode, it would reduce the use of superpipelined or superscalar aspects of the machine to the code that had only moderate instruction-level parallelism. Figure 2-8 shows serial issue (for diagram readability only) and parallel execution of vector instructions. Each vector instruction results in a string of operations, one for each element in the vector.

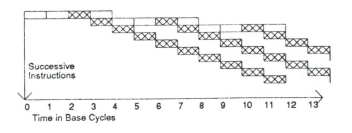

Figure 2-8: Execution in a vector machine

2.7. Supersymmetry

The most important thing to keep in mind when comparing superscalar and superpipelined machines of equal degree is that they have basically the same performance.

A superscalar machine of degree three can have three instructions executing at the same time by issuing three at the same time. The superpipelined machine can have three instructions executing at the same time by having a cycle time 1/3 that of the superscalar machine, and issuing three instructions in successive cycles. Each of these machines issues instructions at the same rate, so superscalar and superpipelined machines of equal degree have basically the same performance.

So far our assumption has been that the latency of all operations, or at least the simple operations, is one base machine cycle. As we discussed previously, no known machines have this characteristic. For example, few machines have one cycle loads without a possible data interlock either before or after the load. Similarly, few machines can execute floating-point operations in one cycle. What are the effects of longer latencies? Consider the MultiTitan [9], where ALU operations are one cycle, but loads, stores, and branches are two cycles, and all floating-point operations are three cycles. The MultiTitan is therefore a slightly superpipelined machine. If we multiply the latency of each instruction class by the frequency we observe for that instruction class when we perform our benchmark set, we get the *average degree of superpipelining*. The average degree of superpipelining is computed in Table 2-1 for the MultiTitan and the CRAY-1. To the extent that some operation latencies are greater than one base machine cycle, the remaining amount of exploitable instruction-level parallelism will be reduced. In this example, if the average degree of instruction-level parallelism in slightly parallel code is

around two, the MultiTitan should not stall often because of data-dependency interlocks, but data-dependency interlocks should occur frequently on the CRAY-1.

Instr. class	Frequency	MultiTitan latency	CRAY-1 latency
logical	10%	x 1 = 0.1	x 1 = 0.1
shift	10%	x 1 = 0.1	x 2 = 0.2
add/sub	20%	x 1 = 0.2	x 3 = 0.6
load	20%	x 2 = 0.4	x11 = 2.2
store	15%	x 2 = 0.3	x 1 = 0.15
branch	15%	x 2 = 0.3	x 3 = 0.45
FP	10%	x 3 = 0.3	x 7 = 0.7
Average Degree of Superpipelining		1.7	4.4

Table 2-1: Average degree of superpipelining

3. Machine Evaluation Environment

The language system for the MultiTitan consists of an optimizing compiler (which includes the linker) and a fast instruction-level simulator. The compiler includes an intermodule register allocator and a pipeline instruction scheduler [16, 17]. For this study, we gave the system an interface that allowed us to alter the characteristics of the target machine. This interface allows us to specify details about the pipeline, functional units, cache, and register set. The language system then optimizes the code, allocates registers, and schedules the instructions for the pipeline, all according to this specification. The simulator executes the program according to the same specification.

To specify the pipeline structure and functional units, we need to be able to talk about specific instructions. We therefore group the MultiTitan operations into fourteen classes, selected so that operations in a given class are likely to have identical pipeline behavior in any machine. For example, integer add and subtract form one class, integer multiply forms another class, and single-word load forms a third class.

For each of these classes we can specify an operation latency. If an instruction requires the result of a previous instruction, the machine will stall unless the operation latency of the previous instruction has elapsed. The compile-time pipeline instruction scheduler knows this and schedules the instructions in a basic block so that the resulting stall time will be minimized.

We can also group the operations into functional units, and specify an issue latency and multiplicity for each. For instance, suppose we want to issue an instruction associated with a functional unit with issue latency 3 and multiplicity 2. This means that there are two units we might use to issue the instruction. If both are busy then the machine will stall until one is idle. It then issues the instruction on the idle unit, and that unit is unable to issue another instruction until three cycles later. The issue latency is independent of the operation latency; the former affects later operations using the same functional unit, and the latter affects later instructions using the result of this one. In either case, the pipeline instruction scheduler tries to minimize the resulting stall time.

Superscalar machines may have an upper limit on the number of instructions that may be issued in the same cycle, independent of the availability of functional units. We can specify this upper limit. If no upper limit is desired, we can set it to the total number of functional units.

Our compiler divides the register set into two disjoint parts. It uses one part as temporaries for short-term expressions, including values loaded from variables residing in memory. It uses the other part as home locations for local and global variables that are used enough to warrant keeping them in registers rather than in memory. When number of operations executing in parallel is large, it becomes important to increase the number of registers used as temporaries. This is because using the same temporary register for two different values in the same basic block introduces an artificial dependency that can interfere with pipeline scheduling. Our interface lets us specify how the compiler should divide the registers between these two uses.

4. Results

We used our programmable reorganization and simulation system to investigate the performance of various superpipelined and superscalar machine organizations. We ran eight different benchmarks on each different configuration. All of the benchmarks are written in Modula-2 except for yacc.

ccom   Our own C compiler.

grr   A PC board router.

linpack   Linpack, double precision, unrolled 4x unless noted otherwise.

livermore The first 14 Livermore Loops, double precision, not unrolled unless noted otherwise.

met   Metronome, a board-level timing verifier.

stan   The collection of Hennessy benchmarks from Stanford (including puzzle, tower, queens, etc.).

whet   Whetsones.

yacc   The Unix parser generator.

Unless noted otherwise, the effects of cache misses and systems effects such as interrupts and TLB misses are ignored in the simulations. Moreover, when available instruction-level parallelism is discussed, it is assumed that all operations execute in one cycle. To determine the actual number of instructions issuable per cycle in a specific machine, the available parallelism must be divided by the average operation latency.

4.1. The Duality of Latency and Parallel Issue

In section 2.7 we stated that a superpipelined machine and an ideal superscalar machine (i.e., without class conflicts) should have the same performance, since they both have the same number of instructions executing in parallel. To confirm this we simulated the eight benchmarks on an ideal base machine, and on superpipelined and ideal superscalar machines of degrees 2 through 8. Figure 4-1 shows the results of this simulation. The superpipelined machine actually has less performance than the superscalar machine, but the performance difference decreases with increasing degree.

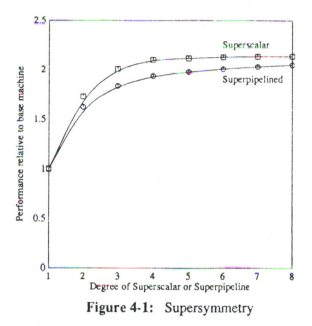

Figure 4-1: Supersymmetry

Consider a superscalar and superpipelined machine, both of degree three, issuing a basic block of six independent instructions (see Figure 4-2). The superscalar machine will issue the last instruction at time t_1 (assuming execution starts at t_0). In contrast, the superpipelined machine will take 1/3 cycle to issue each instruction, so it will not issue the last instruction until time $t_{5/3}$. Thus although the superscalar and superpipelined machines have the same number of instructions executing at the same time in the steady state, the superpipelined machine has a larger startup transient and it gets behind the superscalar machine at the start of the program and at each branch target. This effect diminishes as the degree of the superpipelined machine increases and all of the issuable instructions are issued closer and closer together. This effect is seen in Figure 4-1 as the superpipelined performance approaches that of the ideal superscalar machine with increasing degree.

Another difference between superscalar and superpipelined machines involves operation latencies that are non-integer multiples of a base machine cycle time. In particular, consider operations which can be performed in less time than a base machine cycle set by the integer add latency, such as logical operations or register-to-register moves. In a base or superscalar machine these operations would require an entire clock because that is by definition the smallest time unit. In a superpipelined machine these instructions might be executed in one superpipelined cycle. Then in a superscalar machine of degree 3 the latency of a logical or move operation might be 2/3 longer than in a superpipelined machine of degree 3. Since the latency is longer for the superscalar machine, the superpipelined machine will perform better than a superscalar machine of equal degree. In general, when the inherent operation latency is divided by the clock period, the remainder is less on average for machines with shorter clock periods. We have not quantified the effect of this difference to date.

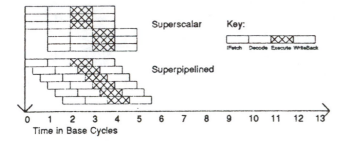

Figure 4-2: Start-up in superscalar vs. superpipelined

4.2. Limits to Instruction-Level Parallelism

Studies dating from the late 1960's and early 1970's [14, 15] and continuing today have observed average instruction-level parallelism of around 2 for code without loop unrolling. Thus, for these codes there is not much benefit gained from building a machine with super-pipelining greater than degree 3 or a superscalar machine of degree greater than 3. The instruction-level parallelism required to fully utilize machines is plotted in Figure 4-3. On this graph, the X dimension is the degree of superscalar machine, and the Y dimension is the degree of superpipelining. Since a superpipelined superscalar machine of only degree (2,2) would require an instruction-level parallelism of 4, it seems unlikely that it would ever be worth building a superpipelined superscalar machine for moderately or slightly parallel code. The superpipelining axis is marked with the average degree of superpipelining in the CRAY-1 that was computed in Section 2.7. From this it is clear that vast amounts of instruction-level parallelism would be required before the issuing of multiple instructions per cycle would be warranted in the CRAY-1.

Unfortunately, latency is often ignored. For example, every time peak performance is quoted, maximum bandwidth independent of latency is given. Similarly, latency is often ignored in simulation studies. For example, instruction issue methods have been compared for the CRAY-1 assuming all functional units have 1 cycle latency [1]. This results in speedups of up to 2.7 from parallel issue of instructions, and leads to the mistaken conclusion that the CRAY-1 would benefit substantially from concurrent instruction issuing. In reality, based on Figure 4-3, we would expect the performance of the CRAY-1 to benefit very little from parallel in-

struction issue. We simulated the performance of the CRAY-1 assuming single cycle functional unit latency and actual functional unit latencies, and the results are given in Figure 4-4.

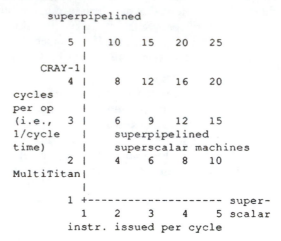

```
     superpipelined
          |
      5 |   10   15   20   25
          |
  CRAY-1|
      4 |    8   12   16   20
cycles    |
per op    |
(i.e., 3 |    6    9   12   15
1/cycle   |    superpipelined
time)     |    superscalar machines
      2 |    4    6    8   10
MultiTitan|
          |
      1 +-------------------- super-
        1    2    3    4    5 scalar
      instr. issued per cycle
```

Figure 4-3: Parallelism required for full utilization

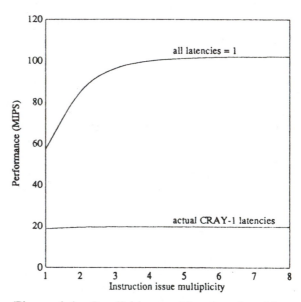

Figure 4-4: Parallel issue with unit and real latencies

As expected, since the CRAY-1 already executes several instructions concurrently due to its average degree of superpipelining of 4.4, there is almost no benefit from issuing multiple instructions per cycle when the actual functional unit latencies are taken into account.

4.3. Variations in Instruction-Level Parallelism

So far we have been plotting a single curve for the harmonic mean of all eight benchmarks. The different benchmarks actually have different amounts of instruction-level parallelism. The performance improvement in each benchmark when executed on an ideal superscalar machine of varying degree is given in Figure 4-5. Yacc has the least amount of instruction-level parallelism. Many programs have approximately two instructions executable in parallel on the average, including the C compiler, PC board router, the Stanford collection, metronome, and whetstones. The Livermore loops approaches an instruction-level parallelism of 2.5. The official version of Linpack has its inner loops unrolled four times, and has an instruction-level parallelism of 3.2. We can see that there is a factor of two difference in the amount of instruction-level parallelism available in the different benchmarks, but the ceiling is still quite low.

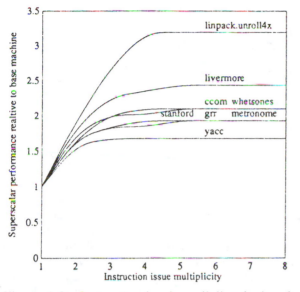

Figure 4-5: Instruction-level parallelism by benchmark

4.4. Effects of Optimizing Compilers

Compilers have been useful in detecting and exploiting instruction-level parallelism. Highly parallel loops can be vectorized [3]. Somewhat less parallel loops can be unrolled and then trace-scheduled [5] or software-pipelined [4, 11]. Even code that is only slightly parallel can be scheduled [6, 7, 17] to exploit a superscalar or superpipelined machine.

The effect of loop-unrolling on instruction-level parallelism is shown in Figure 4-6. The Linpack and Livermore benchmarks were simulated without loop unrolling and also unrolled two, four, and ten times. In either case we did the unrolling in two ways: *naively* and *carefully*. Naive unrolling consists simply of duplicating the loop body inside the loop, and allowing the normal code optimizer and scheduler to remove redundant computations and to re-order the instructions to maximize parallelism. Careful unrolling goes farther. In careful unrolling, we reassociate long strings of additions or multiplications to maximize the parallelism, and we analyze the stores in the unrolled loop so that stores from early copies of the loop do not interfere with loads in later copies. Both the naive and the careful unrolling were done by hand.

The parallelism improvement from naive unrolling is mostly flat after unrolling by four. This is largely because of false conflicts between the different copies of an unrolled loop body, imposing a sequential framework on some or all of the computation. Careful unrolling gives us a more dramatic improvement, but the parallelism available is still limited even for tenfold unrolling.

One reason for this is that we have only forty temporary registers available, which limits the amount of parallelism we can exploit.

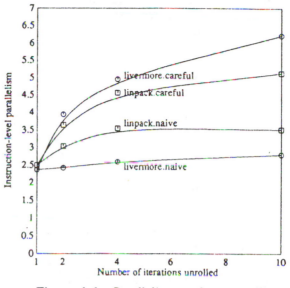

Figure 4-6: Parallelism vs. loop unrolling

In practice, the peak parallelism was quite high. The parallelism was 11 for the carefully unrolled inner loop of Linpack, and 22 for one of the carefully unrolled Livermore loops. However, in either case there is still a lot of inherently sequential computation, even in important places. Three of the Livermore loops, for example, implement recurrences that benefit little from unrolling. If we spend half the time in a very parallel inner loop, and we manage to make this inner loop take nearly zero time by executing its code in parallel, we only double the speed of the program.

In all cases, cache effects were ignored. If limited instruction caches were present, the actual performance would decline for large degrees of unrolling.

Although we see that moderate loop-unrolling can increase the instruction-level parallelism, it is dangerous to generalize this claim. Most classical optimizations [2] have little effect on the amount of parallelism available, and often actually decrease it. This makes sense; unoptimized code often contains useless or redundant computations that are removed by optimization. These useless computations give us an artificially high degree of parallelism, but we are filling the parallelism with makework.

In general, however, classical optimizations can either add to or subtract from parallelism. This is illustrated by the expression graph in Figure 4-7. If our computation consists of two branches of comparable complexity that can be executed in parallel, then optimizing one branch reduces the parallelism. On the other hand, if the computation contains a bottleneck on which other operations wait, then optimizing the bottleneck increases the parallelism. This argument holds equally well for most global optimizations, which are usually just combinations of local optimizations that require global information to detect. For example, to move invariant code out of a loop, we just remove a large computation and replace it with a reference to a single temporary. We also insert a large computation before the loop, but if the loop is executed many times then changing the parallelism of code outside the loop won't make much difference.

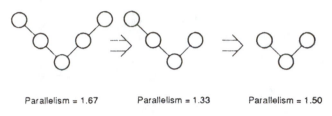

Parallelism = 1.67   Parallelism = 1.33   Parallelism = 1.50

Figure 4-7: Parallelism vs. compiler optimizations

Global allocation of registers to local and global variables [16] is not usually considered a classical optimization, because it has been widespread only since the advent of machines with large register sets. However, it too can either increase or decrease parallelism. A basic block in which all variables reside in memory must load those variables into registers before it can operate on them. Since these loads can be done in parallel, we would expect to reduce the overall parallelism by globally allocating the variables to registers and removing these loads. On the other hand, assignments of new values to these variables may be easier for the pipeline scheduler to re-order if they are assignments to registers rather than stores to memory.

We simulated our test suite with various levels of optimization. Figure 4-8 shows the results. The leftmost point is the parallelism with no optimization at all. Each time we move to the right, we add a new set of optimizations. In order, these are pipeline scheduling, intra-block optimizations, global optimizations, and global register allocation. In this comparison we used 16 registers for expression temporaries and 26 for global register allocation. The dotted and dashed lines allow the different benchmarks to be distinguished, and are not otherwise significant.

Doing pipeline scheduling can increase the available parallelism by 10% to 60%. Throughout the remainder of this paper we assume that pipeline scheduling is performed. For most programs, further optimization has little effect on the instruction-level parallelism (although of course it has a large effect on the performance). On the average across our test suite, optimization reduces the parallelism, but the average reduction is very close to zero.

The behavior of the Livermore benchmark is anomalous. A large decrease in parallelism occurs when we add optimization because the inner loops of these benchmarks contain redundant address calculations that are recognized as common subexpressions. For example, without common subexpression elimination the address of A[I] would be computed twice in the expression "A[I]

= A[I] + 1". It happens that these redundant calculations are not bottlenecks, so removing them decreases the parallelism.

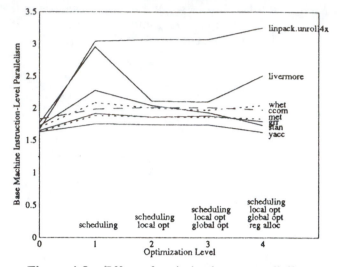

Figure 4-8: Effect of optimization on parallelism

Global register allocation causes a slight decrease in parallelism for most of the benchmarks. This is because operand loads can be done in parallel, and are removed by register allocation.

The numeric benchmarks Livermore, Linpack, and Whetstones are exceptions to this. Global register allocation increases the parallelism of these three. This is because key inner loops contain intermixed references to scalars and to array elements. Loads from the former may appear to depend on previous stores to the latter, because the scheduler must assume that two memory locations are the same unless it can prove otherwise. If global register allocation chooses to keep a scalar in a register instead of memory, this spurious dependency disappears.

In any event, it is clear that very few programs will derive an increase in the available parallelism from the application of code optimization. Programs that make heavy use of arrays may actually lose parallelism from common subexpression removal, though they may also gain parallelism from global register allocation. The net result seems hard to predict. The single optimization that does reliably increase parallelism is pipeline scheduling itself, which makes manifest the parallelism that is already present. Even the benefit from scheduling varies widely between programs.

5. Other Important Factors

The preceding simulations have concentrated on the duality of latency and parallel instruction issue under ideal circumstances. Unfortunately there are a number of other factors which will have a very important effect on machine performance in reality. In this section we will briefly discuss some of these factors.

5.1. Cache Performance

Cache performance is becoming increasingly important, and it can have a dramatic effect on speedups obtained from parallel instruction execution. Figure 5-1 lists some cache miss times and the effect of a miss on machine performance. Over the last decade, cycle time has been decreasing much faster than main memory access time. The average number of machine cycles per instruction has also been decreasing dramatically, especially when the transition from CISC machines to RISC machines is included. These two effects are multiplicative and result in tremendous increases in miss cost. For example, a cache miss on a VAX 11/780 only costs 60% of the average instruction execution. Thus even if every instruction had a cache miss, the machine performance would only slow down by 60%! However, if a RISC machine like the WRL Titan [13] has a miss, the cost is almost ten instruction times. Moreover, these trends seem to be continuing, especially the increasing ratio of memory access time to machine cycle time. In the future a cache miss on a superscalar machine executing two instructions per cycle could cost well over 100 instruction times!

```
Machine cycles cycle mem   miss    miss
        per    time  time  cost    cost
        instr  (ns)  (ns)  cycles  instr
-----------------------------------------
VAX11/780 10.0  200   1200    6       .6
WRL Titan  1.4   45    540   12      8.6
       ?   0.5    5    350   70    140.0
-----------------------------------------
```

Table 5-1: The cost of cache misses

Cache miss effects decrease the benefit of parallel instruction issue. Consider a 2.0cpi (i.e., 2.0 cycles per instruction) machine, where 1.0cpi is from issuing one instruction per cycle, and 1.0 cpi is cache miss burden. Now assume the machine is given the capability to issue three instructions per cycle, to get a net decrease down to 0.5cpi for issuing instructions when data dependencies are taken into account. Performance is proportional to the inverse of the cpi change. Thus the overall performance improvement will be from 1/2.0cpi to 1/1.5cpi, or 33%. This is much less than the improvement of 1/1.0cpi to 1/0.5cpi, or 100%, as when cache misses are ignored.

5.2. Design Complexity and Technology Constraints

When machines are made more complicated in order to exploit instruction-level parallelism, care must be taken not to slow down the machine cycle time (as a result of adding the complexity) more than the speedup derived from the increased parallelism. This can happen in two ways, both of which are hard to quantify. First, the added complexity can slow down the machine by adding to the critical path, not only in terms of logic stages but in terms of greater distances to be traversed when crossing a more complicated and bigger machine. As we have seen from our analysis of the importance of

latency, hiding additional complexity by adding extra pipeline stages will not make it go away. Also, the machine can be slowed down by having a fixed resource (e.g., good circuit designers) spread thinner because of a larger design. Finally, added complexity can negate performance improvements by increasing time to market. If the implementation technologies are fixed at the start of a design, and processor performance is quadrupling every three years, a one or two year slip because of extra complexity can easily negate any additional performance gained from the complexity.

Since a superpipelined machine and a superscalar machine have approximately the same performance, the decision as to whether to implement a superscalar or a superpipelined machine should be based largely on their feasibility and cost in various technologies. For example, if a TTL machine was being built from off-the-shelf components, the designers would not have the freedom to insert pipeline stages wherever they desired. For example, they would be required to use several multiplier chips in parallel (i.e., superscalar), instead of pipelining one multiplier chip more heavily (i.e., superpipelined). Another factor is the shorter cycle times required by the superpipelined machine. For example, if short cycle times are possible though the use of fast interchip signalling (e.g., ECL with terminated transmission lines), a superpipelined machine would be feasible. However, relatively slow TTL off-chip signaling might require the use of a superscalar organization. In general, if it is feasible, a superpipelined machine would be preferred since it only pipelines existing logic more heavily by adding latches instead of duplicating functional units as in the superscalar machine.

6. Concluding Comments

In this paper we have shown superscalar and superpipelined machines to be roughly equivalent ways to exploit instruction-level parallelism. The duality of latency and parallel instruction issue was documented by simulations. Ignoring class conflicts and implementation complexity, a superscalar machine will have slightly better performance (by less than 10% on our benchmarks) than a superpipelined machine of the same degree due to the larger startup transient of the superpipelined machine. However, class conflicts and the extra complexity of parallel over pipelined instruction decode could easily negate this advantage. These tradeoffs merit investigation in future work.

The available parallelism after normal optimizations and global register allocation ranges from a low of 1.6 for Yacc to 3.2 for Linpack. In heavily parallel programs like the numeric benchmarks, we can improve the parallelism somewhat by loop unrolling. However, dramatic improvements are possible only when we carefully restructure the unrolled loops. This restructuring requires us to use knowledge of operator associativity, and to do interprocedural alias analysis to determine when memory references are independent. Even when we do this, the performance improvements are limited by the non-parallel code in the application, and the improvements in parallelism are not as large as the degree of unrolling. In any case, loop unrolling is of little use in non-parallel applications like Yacc or the C compiler.

Pipeline scheduling is necessary in order to exploit the parallelism that is available; it improved performance by around 20%. However, classical code optimization had very little effect on the parallelism available in non-numeric applications, even when it had a large effect on the performance. Optimization had a larger effect on the parallelism of numeric benchmarks, but the size and even the direction of the the effect depended heavily on the code's context and the availability of temporary registers.

Finally, many machines already exploit most of the parallelism available in non-numeric code because they can issue an instruction every cycle but have operation latencies greater than one. Thus for many applications, significant performance improvements from parallel instruction issue or higher degrees of pipelining should not be expected.

7. Acknowledgements

Jeremy Dion, Mary Jo Doherty, John Ousterhout, Richard Swan, Neil Wilhelm, and the reviewers provided valuable comments on an early draft of this paper.

References

1. Acosta, R. D., Kjelstrup, J., and Torng, H. C. "An Instruction Issuing Approach to Enhancing Performance in Multiple Functional Unit Processors." *IEEE Transactions on Computers C-35*, 9 (September 1986), 815-828.

2. Aho, Alfred V., Sethi, Ravi, and Ullman, Jeffrey D.. *Compilers: Principles, Techniques, and Tools.* Addison-Wesley, 1986.

3. Allen, Randy, and Kennedy, Ken. "Automatic Translation of FORTRAN Programs to Vector Form." *ACM Transactions on Programming Languages and Systems 9*, 4 (October 1987), 491-542.

4. Charlesworth, Alan E. "An Approach to Scientific Array Processing: The Architectural Design of the AP-120B/FPS-164 Family." *Computer 14, 9* (September 1981), 18-27.

5. Ellis, John R. *Bulldog: A Compiler for VLIW Architectures.* Ph.D. Th., Yale University, 1985.

6. Foster, Caxton C., and Riseman, Edward M. "Percolation of Code to Enhance Parallel Dispatching and Execution." *IEEE Transactions on Computers C-21*, 12 (December 1972), 1411-1415.

7. Gross, Thomas. Code Optimization of Pipeline Constraints. Tech. Rept. 83-255, Stanford University, Computer Systems Lab, December, 1983.

8. Hennessy, John L., Jouppi, Norman P., Przybylski, Steven, Rowen, Christopher, and Gross, Thomas. Design of a High Performance VLSI Processor. Third Caltech Conference on VLSI, Computer Science Press, March, 1983, pp. 33-54.

9. Jouppi, Norman P., Dion, Jeremy, Boggs, David, and Nielsen, Michael J. K. MultiTitan: Four Architecture Papers. Tech. Rept. 87/8, Digital Equipment Corporation Western Research Lab, April, 1988.

10. Katevenis, Manolis G. H. Reduced Instruction Set Architectures for VLSI. Tech. Rept. UCB/CSD 83/141, University of California, Berkeley, Computer Science Division of EECS, October, 1983.

11. Lam, Monica. Software Pipelining: An Effective Scheduling Technique for VLIW Machines. SIGPLAN '88 Conference on Programming Language Design and Implementation, June, 1988, pp. 318-328.

12. Nicolau, Alexandru, and Fisher, Joseph A. "Measuring the Parallelism Available for Very Long Instruction Word Architectures." *IEEE Transactions on Computers C-33*, 11 (November 1984), 968-976.

13. Nielsen, Michael J. K. Titan System Manual. Tech. Rept. 86/1, Digital Equipment Corporation Western Research Lab, September, 1986.

14. Riseman, Edward M., and Foster, Caxton C. "The Inhibition of Potential Parallelism by Conditional Jumps." *IEEE Transactions on Computers C-21*, 12 (December 1972), 1405-1411.

15. Tjaden, Garold S., and Flynn, Michael J. "Detection and Parallel Execution of Independent Instructions." *IEEE Transactions on Computers C-19*, 10 (October 1970), 889-895.

16. Wall, David W. Global Register Allocation at Link-Time. SIGPLAN '86 Conference on Compiler Construction, June, 1986, pp. 264-275.

17. Wall, David W., and Powell, Michael L. The Mahler Experience: Using an Intermediate Language as the Machine Description. Second International Conference on Architectural Support for Programming Languages and Operating Systems, IEEE Computer Society Press, October, 1987, pp. 100-104.

TRADEOFFS IN INSTRUCTION FORMAT DESIGN
FOR HORIZONTAL ARCHITECTURES

Gurindar S. Sohi and Sriram Vajapeyam

Computer Sciences Department
University of Wisconsin-Madison
1210 W. Dayton Street
Madison, WI 53706.

Abstract

With recent improvements in software techniques and the enhanced level of fine grain parallelism made available by such techniques, there has been an increased interest in horizontal architectures and large instruction words that are capable of issuing more that one operation per instruction. This paper investigates some issues in the design of such instruction formats. We study how the choice of an instruction format is influenced by factors such as the degree of pipelining and the instruction's view of the register file. Our results suggest that very large instruction words capable of issuing one operation to each functional unit resource in a horizontal architecture may be overkill. Restricted instruction formats with limited operation issuing capabilities are capable of providing similar performance (measured by the total number of time steps) with significantly less hardware in many cases.

1. INTRODUCTION

To exploit fine grain parallelism, a high-performance processor must provide a set of functional units that comprise an underlying *resource architecture* and an operation issuing mechanism to provide work to the functional units. Fine grain parallelism amongst operations of different types can be exploited by using multiple functional units, each of which performs a different arithmetic/logic operation and by issuing operations to these functional units in parallel. Fine grain parallelism amongst operations of the same type can be exploited by pipelining the functional unit (used by the operations) to a greater extent or by providing multiple copies of the same functional unit.

The resource architecture is driven by an operation issuing mechanism that reads source operands from a set of registers (*register file*) and routes them to the functional units via a datapath (*input interconnect*). Once the results of the operations are available at the output of the functional units, they are routed back to the register file via another datapath (*output interconnect*).

Traditionally, the operation issuing mechanism in most machines has been limited to issuing at most one operation[1] (a single instruction) in a single clock cycle in spite of the presence of multiple functional units that could accept more than one operation per clock cycle [1, 14]. This is sometimes referred to as the *Flynn bottleneck* [6]. For many years this bottleneck was not considered to be very significant because of the limited amounts of fine-grain parallelism that could be detected in most applications [13, 16]. In the absence of sophisticated compiler techniques to detect and enhance the available fine-grain parallelism and the enormous hardware required to do the same, a peak operation issue rate of 1 operation per cycle seemed adequate.

However, recent work, has suggested that the amount of fine-grain parallelism that is available in an application could be enhanced considerably by the use of software techniques, especially for computation-intensive scientific programs [9]. With an enhanced level of fine-grain parallelism in the application programs, operation issuing mechanisms that allow for the initiation of several operations simultaneously may be in order.

Architectures with enhanced operation issuing capabilities have aroused considerable interest in the computer architecture community and several have appeared recently. These include VLIW machines such as the ELI-512[5] and its follow-on TRACE family of machines [3], the ESL Polycyclic processor[11] and its follow-on Cydrome Cydra 5 Departmental Supercomputer [12], and decoupled architectures such as the ZS-1 [15]. Even some single-chip microarchitectures attempt to issue more than one operation in a clock cycle [10].

VLIWs and the Cydra 5 provide instruction formats where each instruction is capable of issuing several operations in a single clock cycle. Such architectures are also called *horizontal architectures* and their instructions are called *horizontal instructions*. Proposed horizontal architectures make extensive use of software support to detect parallelism and pack several independent operations into a horizontal instruction. A horizontal instruction provides the basic multiple operation issuing mechanism. Architectures such as the ZS-1 use more traditional instruction formats that issue only one operation per instruction; multiple operation issue is achieved by issuing more than one operation per cycle at run time.

---

[1] In this paper, we distinguish between "operations" and "instructions". An instruction consists of one or more operations.

In this paper, we study horizontal architectures whose instruction formats are capable of issuing multiple operations with a single instruction. In designing such architectures, one of the first questions that a computer architect must answer concerns the number of operations that each instruction should be capable of issuing. There are several tradeoffs to consider. Let us illustrate this with the help of an example.

Suppose that a machine has to be designed for a hypothetical task that consists of 3 independent floating-point ADD operations and 2 independent floating-point MUL operations. Assume that the floating-point ADD and MUL operations take 5 and 6 clock cycles to execute, respectively. Using a resource architecture of 3 adders and 2 multipliers and an instruction format capable of issuing 5 operations simultaneously, one could achieve a best-case execution time of 6 clock cycles. To support this execution, the register file and the input interconnect would have to be capable of supplying 10 operands per cycle to the functional units. However, an execution time of 6 clock cycles could be achieved even with 2 multipliers, 2 adders, an instruction format capable of issuing 4 operations simultaneously and a register file/input interconnect capable of supplying 8 operands per cycle if the adders are pipelined and are able to accept a new request on every clock cycle. Continuing further, an execution time of 7 (10) clock cycles could be achieved with only one pipelined multiplier, one pipelined adder, an instruction format capable of issuing 2 (1) operations and a register file capable of supplying 4 (2) operands per cycle.

The above example serves to illustrate one major tradeoff in the design of a horizontal instruction format, namely the capabilities of an instruction format (and the associated hardware needed to support it) versus the number of time steps taken to execute a task using the instruction format. As we shall see, the tradeoff is complicated further by several factors. While the choice of an appropriate instruction format is clearly a very important one, it has not been studied widely in the literature. Previous studies have concentrated on full-fledged instruction formats that are capable of issuing one operation to every functional unit in the resource architecture in a single instruction [4]. This may be due to the fact that the machines capable of issuing more than one operation per instruction that have been built so far use full-fledged horizontal instruction formats [2, 3, 5, 12].

In this paper, we are interested in determining if full-fledged horizontal instruction formats (and the enormous amount of hardware needed to support them) are indeed worthwhile or might restricted instruction formats that can issue only a few operations at once be adequate. To do so, we study various horizontal instruction formats and see how they are influenced by and how they impact other architectural factors and decisions. Our studies use a hypothetical horizontal architecture that resembles (though not exactly) some recently announced horizontal architectures. The factors that we consider include the degree of pipelining of each resource, the view of the registers presented to the operations, and the parallelism available in the programs.

The outline of this paper is as follows. Section 2 discusses our machine model, the benchmarks that we use and our evaluation methodology. Section 3 discusses the maximum performance potential. Section 4 presents a detailed study of several horizontal instruction formats. Finally, section 5 presents a summary and some concluding remarks.

2. MACHINE MODEL AND EVALUATION METHODOLOGY

2.1. Machine Architecture and Instruction Format Considerations

The basic operation set of most horizontal architectures consists of "simple" load/store, register-register operations. Simple operations are used because more complex operations can be broken into a sequence of simpler operations that allow the software more flexibility in optimization. Each operation is simple in that it can be examined, decoded and issued in a single clock cycle. However, it may take several clock cycles to actually complete execution. We use a similar operation set in our machine model. Arithmetic operations use a 3-address format; 2 source operand addresses and 1 destination operand address. Load and store operations use a 2-address format. The operation set includes floating point operations as well as integer operations. All operations have scalar operands; no vector operations are used.

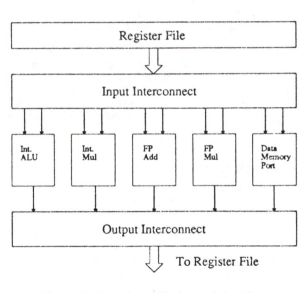

Figure 1: The Model Horizontal Architecture

The resource architecture that we consider in this paper consists of an integer adder/logical unit, an integer multiplier, a floating point adder, a floating point multiplier and a port to the data memory (Figure 1). We study two degrees of pipelining for each resource: (i) a modest degree of pipelining which we shall refer to as *modest pipelining* and (ii) a greater degree of pipelining which we shall refer to as *deep pipelining*. The number of pipeline stages in each of the functional units for the two cases is given below.

Functional Unit	Modest Pipelining	Deep Pipelining
Load	6	12
Int. Add	1	2
Int. Mul.	4	8
FP Add	3	6
FP Mul.	4	8

The number of pipeline stages for a system with modest pipelining are taken from [4] and are representative of moderately pipelined machines such as the TRACE family; the number of pipeline stages for deep pipelining are twice that of modest pipelining and are representative of highly pipelined machines such as the CRAY class of machines.

The computational units in Figure 1 are used in the obvious manner. Only memory data references proceed through the memory port; instruction references access an instruction cache and, to simplify matters, we assume that all instruction references hit in the instruction cache (not shown).

Fine-grain parallelism amongst operations that use distinct functional units can be exploited easily with the resource architecture of Figure 1. Fine-grain parallelism amongst operations that use the same functional unit can be exploited by providing more copies of the functional units, by increasing the number of pipeline stages in each unit, or by both. We do not consider multiple copies of each functional unit for two reasons. First, as we shall see in Section 3, the best-case performance of the resource architecture of Figure 1 is not substantially different from the best-case performance of a machine with unlimited resources *for our benchmark programs*, especially if the degree of pipelining is high. Second, the resource architecture of Figure 1 provides an excellent starting point for any study of horizontal architectures. Unless we understand the issues involved in exploiting the resource architecture of Figure 1, the study of more complex resource architectures can be quite frustrating. Finally, the resource architecture of Figure 1 is of significant current interest (notice the similarities between it and the resource architectures of the TRACE 7/200 and Cydra 5).

To provide operands to the operations in a horizontal instruction, the register file must be designed accordingly. Important factors include: (i) the view of the registers presented to the operations/instructions, and (ii) the number of read and write *ports* that must be provided.

The registers could be organized so that the instruction set views them either as a set of *shared* registers that are used both for integer and floating-point operations or as a *split* register file with a distinct set of registers for integer and floating-point operands. A shared register file is used in the Cydra 5 whereas a split register file is used in the TRACE machines. Apart from the splitting of registers, another issue that must be considered is the *partitioning* of registers of a particular type. Partitioning is needed to reduce the number of read and write ports for very long instruction formats [3]. However, the partitioning of a set of registers is important only if there is more than one functional unit of each type and we shall not consider it in this paper.

A shared register file has three distinct advantages over a split register file. First, a shared register file provides the best opportunity for a compiler to schedule operations in parallel since operations can be scheduled without being constrained by their type. More on this in section 4. Second, a shared register file is able to achieve a better utilization of registers. Third, a compiler's job is easier if it is presented with a unified view of the registers [17].

Unfortunately, the number of ports that must be provided (and consequently the complexity of the interconnects) is increased if a shared register file is used in conjunction with a horizontal instruction format. The number of register read and write ports that must be provided is dictated by the horizontal instruction format. If P independent operations are packed into a horizontal instruction, the register file must have $2P$ read ports to provide the operands and P write ports[2] to accept results from the functional units (note that loads and stores require fewer ports). Once the design of the register file and the horizontal instruction format has been fixed, the design of the input and output interconnects is determined automatically since the interconnects must be capable of routing as many operations from and to the register file(s) as is specified by the instruction format.

We use 2 metrics to measure the "goodness" of a horizontal instruction format. They are: (i) the number of time steps (clock cycles) taken to execute a program, and (ii) the code density of the program using the horizontal instruction format. The code density (a static measure) is the average number of useful (non-NOP) operations that are present in a horizontal instruction. NOPs must be used if no useful operation can be found to fill an operation slot in a horizontal instruction. Less dense code implies wasted memory space, unless an encoding of the horizontal instructions is used (as is the case in the TRACE machines). More importantly, the code density is an indicator of how well the capabilities of the instruction format are actually being used. More on this in section 4.

2.2. Experimental Methodology, Benchmark Programs and Performance Metrics

To evaluate the different performance tradeoffs, we carried out several experiments using a set of benchmark programs. The benchmark programs that we use are the original 14 Lawrence Livermore loops [8]. (Also see[7] for related experiments using some more benchmarks). These benchmarks are easily understood and have been used widely in the evaluation of high-performance numeric processing machines. We assume that the reader is familiar with these benchmarks. The programs are hand-compiled into our 3-address operation set assuming that only one operation can be issued per instruction and assuming an unlimited number of registers[3]. An unlimited number of registers is assumed because we did not want our results to be influenced by the spilling operations introduced due to a limited number of registers. Furthermore, the number of architectural registers that one provides are always subject to debate.

Loop unrolling is used to enhance the available fine-grain parallelism. More loop unrolling implies more fine-grain parallelism. After unrolling, the benchmarks are fed into a scheduler (discussed in the next section). The scheduler compacts the operations into a horizontal instruction format subject to resource and instruction format constraints.

Using the resulting code we calculate (i) the *per iteration* execution time, (ii) the *code density* of the resulting code and (iii) the *total execution time* which is the sum of the individual execution times of each of the benchmarks. We assume that an instruction can be issued in a single clock cycle, irrespective of its width. All our results for the execution times are presented in clock cycles. We do not attempt to convert clock cycles into actual times since many of the factors that influence the clock

---

[2] Providing additional read ports can be accomplished by a simple replication of the registers. Providing additional write ports is more complex. We shall not discuss ways of providing additional write ports in this paper; suffice it to say that providing additional write ports can be quite cumbersome in most technologies.

[3] This assumption has also been made in [4].

are highly dependent upon the technology and the implementation. Keep in mind, however, that the clock cycle for a deeply pipelined system is smaller than the clock cycle for a modestly pipelined system.

2.3. The Scheduler

All our experiments are driven by a *scheduler* that schedules operations in the benchmark subject to the constraints of the horizontal instruction format and compacts the operations into horizontal instructions. The scheduler uses algorithms similar to those used in the Bulldog compiler [4]. It attempts to generate an optimal compaction of operations into horizontal instructions; however, optimality is not guaranteed.

The scheduler first builds a DAG representing the dependencies in the basic block. The nodes of the graphs are the individual operations and the edges are the dependencies. Each node is then assigned a *depth*. The depth of a node is the longest path to the node from any entry point of the DAG, plus the time taken to execute the operation in the node itself. The depths are used as priorities in scheduling the instructions.

After the depths have been assigned, operations are scheduled bottom-up, i.e., starting from the exit points in the DAG, and propagating up to the entry points. Scheduling is done on a first-come first-served basis, with the depths used to assign priorities to operations that are ready to be scheduled at the same time. Constraints are placed on the scheduler by the number of operations of each type that can be issued simultaneously (this is dictated by the number of read ports in the register file that supplies operand values and the number of functional units of each type) and also by the number of operations that can complete execution simultaneously (number of write ports in the register file).

3. MAXIMUM PERFORMANCE POTENTIAL

Before evaluating various horizontal instruction formats, let us consider the best-case performance that can be achieved with the parallelism available in the benchmarks. Table 1 presents the best-case per iteration execution time (in time steps or clock cycles) for the benchmarks for various degrees

of unrolling both for modest (Mod.) and deep (Deep) pipelining. An unrolling of 1 implies no loop unrolling. Unrollings greater than 10 have not been shown because they did not result in significant additional improvement in the *total execution time* (though individual loops with none or very few loop-carried dependencies did benefit from additional unrolling with unlimited resources in some cases).

The results of Table 1 assume an *unlimited* number of functional unit resources, unlimited number of read and write ports, and a horizontal instruction format capable of issuing an unlimited number of operations. Hence the best-case execution time is determined solely by the length of the critical path. Since the length of the critical path (in terms of clock cycles) is doubled in the case of deep pipelining with unlimited resources, the execution times for deep pipelining are exactly twice the execution times for modest pipelining. The total execution time is the sum of the time taken to execute all iterations of all the loops (implicit in this calculation is a multiplication of the per-iteration execution times by the number of iterations in each loop).

Table 2 presents the best-case execution times for the horizontal architecture of Figure 1 for the cases of modest and deep pipelining using a full-fledged horizontal instruction format capable of issuing one operation to each functional unit in a single instruction (a total of 5 operations). Figures 2(a) and 2(b) compare the execution times of the model architecture of Figure 1 and an ideal horizontal architecture capable of issuing an unlimited number of operations to an unlimited number of functional units in a single instruction. Bar charts are used in Figure 2 because of their visual appeal. Unless shown otherwise, subsequent results in this paper will use bar charts to present the results as a total or an average for all the benchmarks.

As we can see from Table 1, Table 2 and Figure 2, the limited resource architecture of Figure 1 is not a major impediment to the exploitation of the parallelism available in the benchmark programs (even with a high degree of loop unrolling), especially if the degree of pipelining is high. In some cases, additional performance could be obtained by providing

Table 1: Execution Times with an Unlimited Resource

Architecture and Unlimited Operation Issue

Loop	Iterations Unrolled							
	1		2		5		10	
	Mod.	Deep	Mod.	Deep	Mod.	Deep	Mod.	Deep
1	22	44	11.5	23.0	5.2	10.4	3.1	6.2
2	21	42	11.0	22.0	5.0	10.0	3.0	6.0
3	14	28	8.5	17.0	5.2	10.4	4.1	8.2
4	14	28	7.5	15.0	3.6	7.2	2.3	4.6
5	28	56	24.5	49.0	22.4	44.8	21.7	43.4
6	29	58	25.0	50.0	22.6	45.2	21.8	43.6
7	32	64	16.5	33.0	7.2	14.4	4.1	8.2
8	34	68	17.5	35.0	7.6	15.2	4.3	8.6
9	26	52	13.5	27.0	6.0	12.0	3.5	7.0
10	35	70	17.5	35.0	7.6	15.2	4.3	8.6
11	10	20	6.5	13.0	4.4	8.8	3.7	7.4
12	11	22	6.0	12.0	3.0	6.0	2.0	4.0
13	51	102	26.0	52.0	11.0	2.0	6.0	12.0
14	50	100	25.5	51.0	10.8	21.6	5.9	11.8
Total (x1000)	94	188	58.1	116.2	36.7	73.3	29.5	59.0

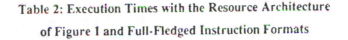

Loop	Iterations Unrolled							
	1		2		5		10	
	Mod.	Deep	Mod.	Deep	Mod.	Deep	Mod.	Deep
1	24	45	14.5	25.0	8.8	13.0	7.2	9.0
2	30	50	21.0	31.0	17.0	20.2	16.2	17.6
3	15	29	9.0	17.5	5.4	10.6	4.2	8.3
4	15	29	9.5	16.5	6.4	9.0	6.0	6.7
5	28	56	24.5	49.0	22.4	44.8	21.7	43.4
6	29	58	25.0	50.0	22.6	45.2	21.8	43.6
7	33	64	23.0	34.0	19.6	22.0	18.5	19.6
8	48	71	45.0	48.5	41.0	43.0	37.7	38.7
9	30	53	21.0	30.5	15.6	18.8	13.5	14.8
10	36	70	24.0	37.0	22.0	23.6	22.0	22.1
11	10	20	6.5	13.0	4.4	8.8	4.0	7.4
12	11	22	7.0	12.5	5.0	6.8	5.0	5.1
13	51	102	26.5	52.0	20.0	22.2	20.0	20.1
14	51	101	27.0	52.0	16.0	23.2	14.8	15.7
Total (x1000)	98.8	191.4	66.2	121.2	49.7	81.0	46.1	69.8

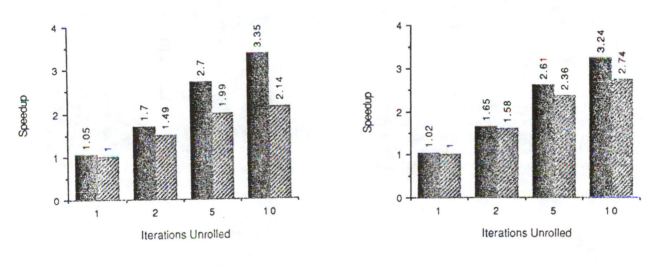

(a) Modest Pipelining   (b) Deep Pipelining

Solid Bars : Ideal Architecture

Hatched Bars : Model Architecture

Figure 2: Comparative Performance of an Ideal and the Model Architectures

more resources (for example loops 2 and 7). Overall, the performance could be improved by a factor of 1.56 by providing additional resources if the resources are moderately pipelined and each loop is unrolled 10 times to enhance the available parallelism (it is interesting to compare this number with a factor of 1.48 for the TRACE 14/200 versus the TRACE 7/200 for all 24 Livermore loops[3]). If the resources are deeply pipelined, this factor is only 1.18.

To support execution of a full-fledged instruction format for the architecture of Figure 1, a shared register file needs 10 read ports and 5 write ports. If the register file was split into separate floating-point and integer register files, the floating point register file would need 5 read ports (4 for arithmetic operations and 1 for a store) and 3 write ports (2 for arithmetic operation results and 1 for the destination of a store). The integer register file would need 6 read ports (4 for arithmetic operations, 1 for the address of a memory operation and 1 for the store of an integer register) and 3 write ports (2 arithmetic operations plus 1 integer load).

A full-fledged horizontal instruction format will work very well in executing a program that has *precisely the same number of independent operations of each type*. However, such a format could be quite wasteful of instruction space and interconnection datapaths if the operations are unbalanced (more operations of one type) and if similar performance could be achieved with more restricted formats. Therefore, we consider restricted instruction formats for the resource architecture of Figure 1.

4. RESTRICTED HORIZONTAL INSTRUCTION FORMATS

4.1. One Operation Per Instruction

A first step would be to issue only a single operation per clock cycle as in any conventional machine. By doing so, we are exploiting the available fine-grain parallelism by pipelining alone. However, by studying the performance with a single operation issue per clock, we can establish a good lower bound on the performance of the resource architecture of Figure 1.

Shared Register File

To support the issue of one operation per cycle, a register file needs to provide 2 operands per cycle to the functional units and be able to accept 1 result from them, i.e., have 2 read ports and 1 write port. The input interconnect needs to be capable of routing two operands from the register file to the inputs of an arbitrary functional unit in every clock cycle and the output interconnect needs to be capable of routing a single result from the output of the functional units back to the register file. This configuration of the interconnects is standard in most conventional processor designs. Figure 3 presents the total execution time for the benchmarks for varying degrees of loop unrolling both for modest and deep pipelining.

Split Register File

Now consider a register file partitioned into distinct integer and floating point registers. If the input and output interconnects are similar to the case of a shared register file, i.e., a set of buses for the input operands of all the functional units and a single result bus for the result of all the functional units, a split register file is no different from a shared register file and, with no constraints on the size of either set of registers, the performance of the two architectural organizations will be the same.

However, partitioning the register file allows for a modification of the interconnect. The input interconnect can be partitioned into two input interconnects - one that connects the integer registers to the inputs of the integer functional units and another that connects the inputs of the floating point registers to the inputs of the floating point functional units (with appropriate connections to the memory port). Likewise, the output interconnect can be partitioned into separate interconnects for the integer and floating-point components. If the output interconnect is partitioned, an integer and floating-point operation can complete in the same clock cycle (even though only one operation is issued in a clock cycle). This flexibility allows for a slightly better performance than what could be achieved with a shared register file.

Figure 4 presents the results for a split register file with separate input and output interconnect for the integer and floating-point components. Comparing with Figure 3, we see that we can achieve slightly better performance by partitioning the interconnect mainly due to the scheduling flexibility provided by the additional data path. However, there is room for improvement both for split and shared register files (compare the results of Figures 3 and 4 with the results of Table 2).

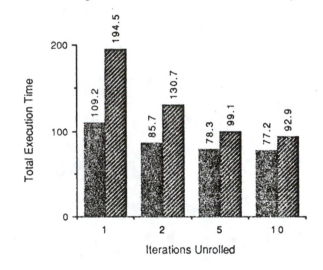

Solid Bars : Modest Pipelining
Hatched Bars : Deep Pipelining

Figure 4: Total Execution Time (in thousands of clock cycles) with a Split Register File and 1 Operation Per Instruction

For the reader interested in comparing our results with the results presented in [4], the results of Figures 3 and 4 correspond to the "sequential ELI" (but with a different resource architecture), those of Table 1 correspond to an "ideal ELI" and those of Table 2 correspond to a "single cluster ELI". Our results follow trends similar to the results of [4]. In some cases, speedups greater than 20 over a simple pipelined execution[4] can be achieved with an enhanced level of fine grain parallelism and multiple operation issue (loop 8 is one such case) whereas in other cases the speedup is not so significant (loops 5 and 6 show this behavior).

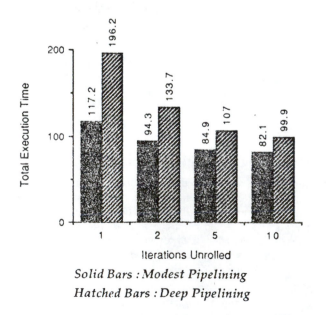

Solid Bars : Modest Pipelining
Hatched Bars : Deep Pipelining

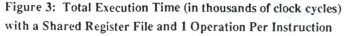

Figure 3: Total Execution Time (in thousands of clock cycles) with a Shared Register File and 1 Operation Per Instruction

---

[4]Note that a simple pipelined execution with limited fine grain parallelism already allows for some overlap. The results for a purely serial machine have not been presented because that would not provide a realistic lower bound for comparing horizontal architectures.

From Table 2 and Figures 3 and 4 we see that, for the resource architecture of Figure 1, speedups of 2.54 and 2.81 can be achieved for modest and deep pipelining, respectively, by making use of loop unrolling to enhance fine grain parallelism and by using pipelining and multiple operation issue to exploit this parallelism (going from rolled loops and the issue of one operation per instruction in Figure 3 to unrolled loops and the issue of 5 operations per instruction in Table 2). However, in the case of deep pipelining, most of this performance improvement can be obtained simply by enhancing the fine grain parallelism (loop unrolling) and by using pipelining to exploit it, without the need to issue more than one operation per instruction. This can be seen from Figure 3 where, with a loop unrolling of 10 and pipeline scheduling, a speedup of 1.96 can be achieved even with the issue of a single operation per instruction. This leaves only a factor of 1.44 to be gained by the issue of more than 1 operation per instruction. For modest pipelining where pipelining alone is not sufficient to exploit the available fine grain parallelism, multiple operation issue must also be used. Therefore, while the use of instruction formats capable of issuing more than one operation simultaneously will clearly improve the number of time steps required to execute a program, the need for such instruction formats is less compelling if the degree of pipelining in the machine is greater.

4.2. Two Operations Per Instruction

Now we consider a horizontal instruction format that allows two operations to be issued simultaneously.

Shared Register File

To allow two operations to issue per cycle with a shared register file, the input interconnect must be capable of delivering 4 operands from the register file to the functional units in every cycle. This requires the register file to have 4 read ports. Similarly, since 2 results can be generated in each cycle, the register file needs to have 2 write ports and the output interconnect needs to be able to deliver the results from the outputs of the functional units to the register file write ports. With this configuration, operations can be submitted to any two functional units with a single instruction.

Figures 5 and 6 present the total execution times and the average code densities for the benchmark programs for the cases of modest and deep pipelining. The code density is the average of the code densities of all the benchmarks (the code densities were not presented for the results of Figures 3 and 4 because the code density is 1 if there is only 1 operation per instruction). Since the code density is an indicator of a static phenomenon, namely the efficiency of a horizontal instruction format, the average has not been weighted by the number of iterations in the benchmarks.

By issuing two operations per cycle in a horizontal instruction, we can obtain a significant performance improvement especially if the level of pipelining is modest (compare the results of Figures 5 and 6 with the results of Figure 3). However, the code density suffers. This is because several horizontal instructions can not issue 2 operations. When two useful operations cannot be packed into a horizontal instruction, a NOP must be inserted. Notice that the code density improves as more loop unrolling is used. This is because by increasing the parallelism available (more loop unrolling) the same number of operations can be compacted into a fewer horizontal instructions.

Comparing the results of Figures 5 and 6 with the results of Table 2, we see that the *total* execution time that can be achieved by issuing 2 operations per instruction is quite close (a 13% difference for modest pipelining and a 6% difference for deep pipelining) to the best-case execution time that can be achieved by using a full-fledged instruction format, but the former requires significantly smaller amount of hardware to support it. We note again that for some individual loops (for example loops 3 and 8) the execution time could be improved by issuing more operations per instruction (see Table 3).

In Table 3, we show the code densities (CD) and per-iteration execution times (T) for each of the individual loops for a loop unrolling of 10 both for modest and deep pipelining. We notice that loops which could benefit from issuing more operations per instruction have comparatively high code densities for this restricted horizontal format. That is, the restricted format is being utilized well and a wider instruction format may be more appropriate. But loops with code densities near

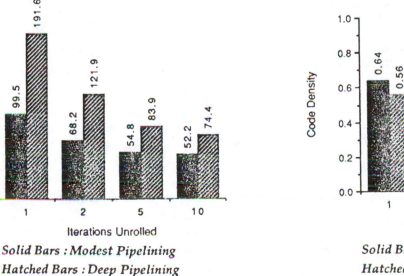

Solid Bars : *Modest Pipelining*

Hatched Bars : *Deep Pipelining*

Figure 5: Total Execution Time (in thousands of clock cycles) with a Shared Register File and 2 Operations Per Instruction

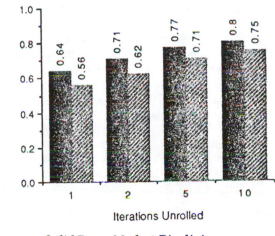

Solid Bars : *Modest Pipelining*

Hatched Bars : *Deep Pipelining*

Figure 6: Average Code Density with a Shared Register File and 2 Operations Per Instruction

0.5 are able to achieve close to the best-case performance with this restricted instruction format. Note that code densities can not be less than 0.5 for this instruction format since that would imply the presence of instructions with no operations at all.

Table 3: Performance of the Individual Loops with a Shared Register File and Two Operations Per Instruction

Loop	Modest		Deep	
	T	CD	T	CD
1	10.0	0.76	10.4	0.74
2	21.3	0.82	21.5	0.82
3	4.9	0.80	8.3	0.56
4	7.1	0.79	7.5	0.76
5	21.7	0.66	43.4	0.62
6	21.8	0.68	43.6	0.64
7	26.4	0.81	26.2	0.82
8	50.1	0.93	50.9	0.92
9	19.2	0.76	19.7	0.76
10	27.4	0.75	28.2	0.73
11	4.0	0.75	7.4	0.58
12	5.0	0.80	5.3	0.77
13	22.6	0.95	23.3	0.93
14	17.6	0.94	18.6	0.89

Split Register File

If the register file is partitioned, then we have a choice of two horizontal instruction formats to support the issue of more than one operation per instruction. The first format (free format) allows the issue of two operations to arbitrary functional units in a single instruction. As with a shared file, this would require the use of 4 read ports and 2 write ports in each of the register files. The second format (constrained format) is constrained to allow at most one integer and one floating point operation per instruction[5]. Because the constrained horizontal format places additional restrictions on the scheduler, programs compiled into a constrained format horizontal instruction set will have a greater execution time than programs compiled into a free format instruction set. But supporting the constrained horizontal instruction format poses fewer demands on the register files and the interconnects. To support the constrained horizontal format, each register file needs to have only 2 read ports and 1 write port and the input and output interconnects have the same complexity as in the case of the single operation instruction format of Section 4.1.

The total execution times and the average code densities for the benchmark programs using split register files and a constrained horizontal instruction format are presented in Figures 7 and 8. For these results, our scheduler was constrained to use a split register file with 2 read ports and 1 write port on either file. Comparing the results of Figures 7 and 8 with the results of Figure 4, we see that the performance improvement by issuing 1 integer and 1 floating-point operation per instruction in a constrained format is significant, though not spectacular (20.2% and 12.9%, respectively, for modest and deep pipelining). Furthermore, as expected, the constrained format is not able to accomplish the same performance as the free format

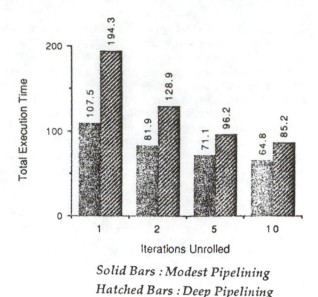

Solid Bars : Modest Pipelining
Hatched Bars : Deep Pipelining

Figure 7: Total Execution Time (in thousands of clock cycles) with a Split Register File and 2 Operations Per Instruction

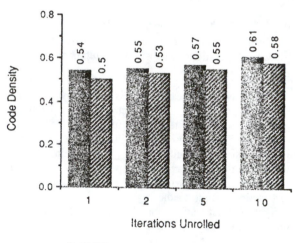

Solid Bars : Modest Pipelining
Hatched Bars : Deep Pipelining

Figure 8: Average Code Density with a Split Register File and 2 Operations Per Instruction

(compare Figures 5 and 7) but it requires less hardware (fewer register ports and less complex interconnect) to support it. Also, the code density is worse with a split register file because of the additional constraints placed on the scheduler (compare Figures 6 and 8).

4.3. Three Operations Per Instruction

Continuing further, we now consider horizontal instruction formats capable of issuing 3 operations per instruction.

Shared Register File

To support the issue of 3 operations per instruction cycle, the register file needs to have 6 read ports and 3 write ports. Also, the sizes of the input and output interconnects increase in proportion to the increased number of register file ports.

---

[5]Load and store operations are classified specially. Both need to access an integer register read port to obtain an address when they are issued. For a store, the other source operand accessed when it is issued could either be a floating point or an integer register. Likewise, loads would require a write port to the appropriate register file when they complete. Special case situations for loads and stores are automatically handled by our scheduler.

Figures 9 and 10 present the total execution times and the average code densities for the cases of modest and deep pipelining, respectively. As expected, the code density is lower than in the case of a 2-operation horizontal instruction format because of the large number of NOPs. Furthermore, little performance improvement over a 2-operation instruction format can be achieved since there is little room for improvement. For modest levels of pipelining and a loop unrolling of 10, the capability to issue 3 operations per instruction results in only a 9-10% improvement over the capability to issue 2 operations per instruction. For deep pipelining, this figure is about 5%. Therefore, if the hardware needed to provide the additional register ports and the additional interconnect degrades the clock cycle by as little as 5% in the deep pipelining case, the utility of the wider horizontal instruction format for the given functional unit resources (and benchmarks) is questionable.

Split Register File

With a split register file, we can have three different horizontal instruction formats that can support the issue of 3 operations: a free format that allows the issue of up to 3 operations of either type, a constrained format that allows the issue of two floating point and one integer operation (CONS1) and a constrained format that allows the issue of two integer and one floating point operation (CONS2) per instruction. As before, loads and stores are classified accordingly.

We do not consider a free format for the same reasons as Section 4.2. If an application has more floating point operations than integer operations, the CONS1 format is more suitable. On the other hand, if the application has more integer operations than floating point operations, the CONS2 format is more suitable. We evaluated both restricted formats and both had a similar overall performance for our benchmark programs, though one was somewhat better than the other in individual cases. For brevity, we present only the results for the CONS1 format (in Figures 11 and 12). Surprisingly, issuing 3

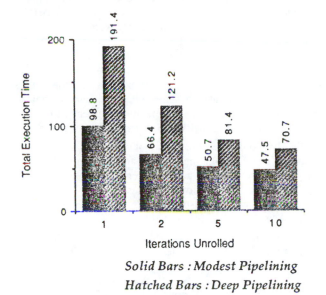

Solid Bars : Modest Pipelining
Hatched Bars : Deep Pipelining

Figure 9: Total Execution Time (in thousands of clock cycles) with a Shared Register File and 3 Operations Per Instruction

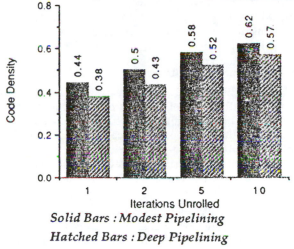

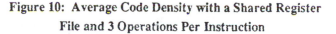

Solid Bars : Modest Pipelining
Hatched Bars : Deep Pipelining

Figure 10: Average Code Density with a Shared Register File and 3 Operations Per Instruction

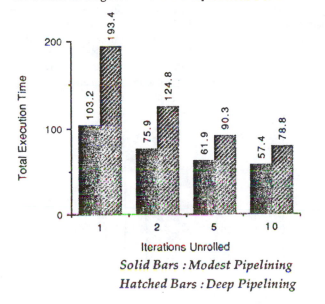

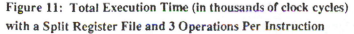

Solid Bars : Modest Pipelining
Hatched Bars : Deep Pipelining

Figure 11: Total Execution Time (in thousands of clock cycles) with a Split Register File and 3 Operations Per Instruction

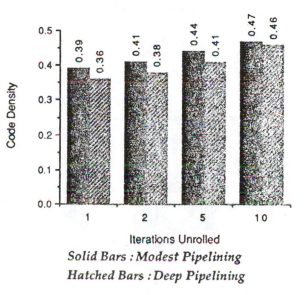

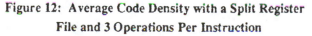

Solid Bars : Modest Pipelining
Hatched Bars : Deep Pipelining

Figure 12: Average Code Density with a Split Register File and 3 Operations Per Instruction

operations in a restricted format with a split register file has worse performance than a 2-operation instruction format with a shared register file even though the former requires more hardware. Remember, however, that the latter format file is able to support 2 operations of *either type* in a single instruction. This is not possible with the former instruction format.

The somewhat disappointing total execution time results of Figure 11 suggest that a shared register file may be preferable to a split register file if a restricted instruction format is to be used. For a full-fledged instruction format capable of issuing one operation to every functional unit, splitting the registers clearly saves on the number of register ports and reduces the complexity of the interconnects. However, if restricted instruction formats (and simpler interconnects) are to be used, splitting the register file may pose unnecessary constraints on the scheduling of operations, thereby resulting in worse performance as compared to a shared register file.

Since the performance of restricted instruction formats capable of issuing 2-3 operations per instruction is quite close to the performance of a full-fledged instruction format especially with a shared register file, we do not consider other restricted instruction formats, for example, formats capable of issuing 4 operations.

4.4. Comparative Results

Figures 13(a) and 13(b) summarize our results by comparing the performance of different horizontal instruction formats for our model architecture, both with modest and deep pipelining. Maximum performance (minimum number of clock cycles) is achieved when we can issue an operation to each functional unit in a single clock cycle with a wide instruction. Issuing only one operation per instruction with a shared register file results in minimum performance.

The figures also show the performance when issuing one operation per instruction with a split register file, and two and three operations per instruction with a shared register file. (The register file organizations chosen here are the ones which give the better performance for the corresponding instruction formats). We notice that for both modest and deep pipelining, issuing 3 operations per instruction results in very little additional speedup as compared to issuing 2 operations per instruction. Issuing 2 operations per instruction has a significant advantage over issuing just one operation per instruction if the degree of pipelining is modest and has a modest performance advantage if the degree of pipelining is high.

5. SUMMARY AND CONCLUDING REMARKS

The choice of an appropriate horizontal instruction format is crucial to the design of horizontal architectures. Horizontal architectures that have been proposed in the literature have full-fledged instruction formats capable of issuing an operation to each functional in the resource architecture unit with a single instruction. We felt that a horizontal architecture with a full-fledged instruction format (or to coin a term, a "complex horizontal architecture") is overkill since it is appropriate only for some programs and also requires an enormous amount of register file and interconnect hardware. Keeping this in mind, we studied horizontal architectures with restricted instruction formats (or "reduced horizontal architectures") and saw how this choice was influenced by factors such as the degree of pipelining and an instruction's view of the register file.

Our results suggest that, if the degree of pipelining is high, there is less need to issue more operations in parallel. Even with moderate levels of pipelining, restricted horizontal instruction formats capable of issuing operations only to a few functional units are competitive with full-fledged instruction formats capable of issuing one operation to each functional unit. While restricted instruction formats may perform worse than full-fledged formats on some programs, overall they are able to execute programs in a comparable number of time steps with much better code density and much less hardware.

We also considered the choice of a register file organization. A register file split into integer and floating point registers is clearly superior to a shared register file when a full-fledged horizontal instruction format is supported. However, for restricted horizontal instruction formats, a shared register file may be better and deserves attention.

An issue that we have ignored in this paper is the impact of the additional hardware needed to support a wider horizontal instruction format on the clock cycle. We assumed that an instruction is issued in a single clock cycle and that the clock cycle is the same for the various instruction formats, irrespective of the amount of hardware needed to support it. This is not true and machines with wider instruction formats typically have larger clock periods. As an example, compare the ZS-1 whose instruction formats can issue only one operation per instruction and the TRACE 7/200 whose instruction formats can issue several operations per instruction. Both machines are implemented in similar TTL technology but the clock period of the ZS-1 is 45ns and that of the TRACE 7/200 is 130ns. When the clock period is taken into account, the need to use wider instruction formats is even less compelling.

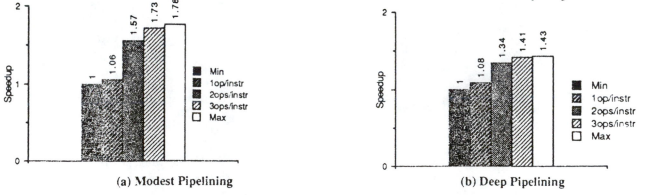

(a) Modest Pipelining   (b) Deep Pipelining

Figure 13: Comparative Speedups for various Horizontal Instruction Formats, using the Model Architecture of Figure 1 (10 Iterations Unrolled for each Loop)

In conclusion, horizontal architectures provide an excellent paradigm for exploiting fine-grain parallelism. However, a good architecture for exploiting fine-grain parallelism must make use of both pipelining and parallel operation issue. Unless the computer architect pays adequate attention to pipelining also, the architect is bound to get caught up in a vicious circle. To issue more operations simultaneously, additional register file and interconnect hardware must be provided. This additional hardware will penalize the clock cycle which in turn will reduce the number of pipeline stages in the functional units. With a reduced number of pipeline stages, more operations must be issued in parallel to exploit the available parallelism. A good horizontal architecture design must attempt to use both pipelining and parallel operation issue and must provide adequate instruction formats that enhance the ability of the architecture to exploit both pipelining and multiple operation issue without penalizing either.

Acknowledgments

This work has benefited from discussions with Jim Goodman and Jim Smith and was supported in part by NSF Grant CCR-8706722.

References

[1] D. W. Anderson, F. J. Sparacio, and R. M. Tomasulo, "The IBM System/360 Model 91: Machine Philosophy and Instruction-Handling," *IBM Journal of Research and Development*, pp. 8-24, January 1967.

[2] A. E. Charlesworth, "An Approach to Scientific Array Processing: The Architectural Design of the AP-120B/FPS-164 Family," *Computer*, vol. 14, September 1981.

[3] R. P. Colwell, R. P. Nix, J. J. O'Donnell, D. B. Papworth, and P. K. Rodman, "A VLIW Architecture for a Trace Scheduling Compiler," *IEEE Transactions on Computers*, vol. 37, pp. 967-979, August 1988.

[4] J. R. Ellis, "Bulldog: A Compiler for VLIW Architectures," Research Report YALE/DCS/RR-364, Department of Computer Science, Yale University, Seattle, WA 98195, February 1985.

[5] J. A. Fisher, "Very Long Instruction Word Architectures and the ELI-512," *Proc. 10th Annual Symposium on Computer Architecture*, pp. 140-150, June 1983.

[6] M. J. Flynn, "Very High-Speed Computing Systems," *Proceedings of the IEEE*, vol. 54, pp. 1901-1909, December 1966.

[7] N. P. Jouppi and D. W. Wall, "Available Instruction-Level Parallelism for Superscalar and Superpipelined Machines," in *Proc. ASPLOS III*, Boston, MA, April 1989.

[8] F. H. McMahon, *FORTRAN CPU Performance Analysis*. Lawrence Livermore Laboratories, 1972.

[9] A. Nicolau and J. A. Fisher, "Measuring the Parallelism Available for Very Long Instruction Work Architectures," *IEEE Transactions on Computers*, vol. C-33, pp. 968-976, November 1984.

[10] Y. N. Patt, W.-M. Hwu, and M. Shebanow, "HPS, A New Microarchitecture: Rationale and Introduction," in *Proc. 18th Annual Workshop on Microprogramming*, Pacific Grove, CA, pp. 103-108, December 1985.

[11] B. R. Rau, C. D. Glaeser, and R. L. Picard, "Efficient Code Generation For Horizontal Architectures: Compiler Techniques and Architectural Support," *Proc. 9th Annual Symposium on Computer Architecture*, pp. 131-139, April 1982.

[12] B. R. Rau, "Cydra 5 Directed Dataflow Architecture," *Digest of Papers, COMPCON Spring 1988*, pp. 106-113, February 1988.

[13] E. M. Riseman and C. C. Foster, "The Inhibition of Potential Parallelism by Conditional Jumps," *IEEE Transactions on Computers*, vol. C-21, pp. 1405-1411, December 1972.

[14] R. M. Russel, "The CRAY-1 Computer System," *CACM*, vol. 21, pp. 63-72, January 1978.

[15] J. E. Smith, et al, "The ZS-1 Central Processor," *Proc. ASPLOS II*, pp. 199-204, October 1987.

[16] G. S. Tjaden and M. J. Flynn, "Detection and Parallel Execution of Independent Instructions," *IEEE Transactions on Computers*, vol. C-19, pp. 889-895, October 1970.

[17] W. A. Wulf, "Compilers and Computer Architecture," *IEEE Computer*, vol. 14, pp. 41-47, July 1981.

Experimental Application-Driven Architecture Analysis of an SIMD/MIMD Parallel Processing System

EDWARD C. BRONSON, STUDENT MEMBER, IEEE, THOMAS L. CASAVANT, MEMBER, IEEE, AND
LEAH H. JAMIESON, MEMBER, IEEE

Abstract—Experimental analysis of the architecture of an SIMD/MIMD parallel processing system is presented. Detailed implementations of parallel fast Fourier transform programs were used to examine the performance of the prototype of the PASM parallel processing system. Detailed execution time measurements using specialized timing hardware were made for the complete FFT and for components of SIMD, MIMD, and barrier synchronized MIMD implementations. The component measurements isolated the effects of floating-point arithmetic operations, interconnection network transfer operations, and program control overhead. These detailed component measurements allow an accurate extrapolation of the execution time, speedup, and efficiency of the MIMD, SIMD, and barrier synchronized MIMD programs to a full 1024-processor PASM system. This constitutes one of the first results of this kind, in which controlled experiments on fixed hardware were used to make comparisons of these fundamental modes of computing. Overall, the experimental results demonstrate the value of mixed-mode SIMD/MIMD computing and its suitability for computationally intensive algorithms such as the FFT.

Index Terms—Barrier synchronization, fast Fourier transform, parallel architecture evaluation, PASM, performance analysis, signal processing, SIMD/MIMD computation

I. INTRODUCTION

THIS paper describes the detailed experimental analysis of the architecture of an SIMD/MIMD parallel processing system by executing detailed applications programs. Experiments were performed on the prototype of the PASM parallel processing system at Purdue University. *PASM* (Partitionable SIMD MIMD) is a dynamically reconfigurable architecture designed to allow both SIMD and MIMD operation, and to provide the flexible computation and communications capability needed for the wide range of algorithms as found in image and speech processing applications [16], [17].

In this paper, we use the *fast Fourier transform* (FFT) algorithm as a vehicle to examine and evaluate the architecture performance and to compare the SIMD and MIMD modes of operation. Our results also provide insight into multimicroprocessor implementation of SIMD/MIMD architectures and the

usefulness of this mixed mode as a paradigm for structuring computations in general. The FFT programs exercise PASM's floating-point hardware for arithmetic operations [11] and the multistage cube interconnection network [1] for interprocessor communication. The programs and execution times presented in this paper are among the first applications executing on the PASM system [6] and are the first floating-point program results obtained on the system. Precise experimental execution times are measured for small FFT's using specialized timing circuitry on the prototype hardware. These results are adjusted using a novel normalization scheme and then extrapolated to obtain execution time, speedup, and efficiency figures for a full 1024-processor PASM system. The extrapolation technique and the measurements used for the components of the extrapolation are verified experimentally using four-processor and eight-processor programs.

While one aspect of benchmarking involves execution of a well-understood application on a machine in order to obtain execution time information, there are many other aspects as well. A primary goal of benchmarking is to *compare* different machines along some well-defined set of architectural variations and computational characteristics. This work should *not* be considered a benchmarking study for several reasons.

1) We consider only one architecture. In fact, for our hybrid SIMD/MIMD programs, PASM is the *only* machine which supports their direct execution.

2) We are interested in studying the various modes of a novel architecture, not providing a judgment of this machine relative to several architectures.

3) Signal processing computations, such as the FFT, were a target application in the design of PASM. Our interest in conducting these experiments was explicitly to understand the interaction between computation of FFT's and the PASM architecture.

In the experiments reported, three implementations of a 4-processor 8-point FFT algorithm are studied in detail. An SIMD version performs all FFT operations in SIMD mode. An MIMD version performs arithmetic operations in MIMD mode and polls the network to determine the network status during data transfer operations. A third program uses barrier synchronization [9] to align the operations of the processing elements just prior to the network transfer operation in place of polling to test the status of the network. This program can be considered a *hybrid* of the SIMD and MIMD

Manuscript received April 21, 1989; revised December 15, 1989. This work was supported by the National Science Foundation under Grant CCR-8704826, CCR-8809600, and in part by the NSF Software Engineering Research Center (SERC), and the Supercomputing Research Center (SRC).

E. C. Bronson and L. H. Jamieson are with the School of Electrical Engineering, Purdue University, West Lafayette, IN 47907.

T. L. Casavant is with the Department of Electrical and Computer Engineering, University of Iowa, Iowa City, IA 52242.

IEEE Log Number 8934121.

0-8186-2642-9/92 $3.00 © 1990 IEEE

modes of computation for PASM: the arithmetic calculations and the network transfers are performed in MIMD mode, while the barrier synchronization operation is performed by using special-purpose hardware designed for SIMD operation. This barrier synchronized MIMD (BMIMD) mode gave the best execution time, 9% faster than the SIMD implementation and 39% faster than the MIMD version. Measurements of the components of the implementations isolate the effects of the floating-point arithmetic operations, network transfers, and program control overhead, and allow interpretation of the differences in the three overall execution times. Effects due to the number of memory wait states, movement to and from the floating-point coprocessor, masking to enable and disable processing elements, network setup and data transfer, and mode switching are analyzed. Finally the detailed component measurements are used to project a speedup of 760 for a 1024-processor 2048-point BMIMD FFT program. In this calculation, since the problem size per processing element remains constant, these results represent very modest "scaled speedups" [7] and are therefore quite promising.

The following section presents a brief overview of the PASM system and its prototype. The FFT algorithm and its implementations are described in Section III. Section IV presents the measurement techniques used. The experimental results are presented in Section V and discussed in Section VI. More details about this work can be found in [3].

II. PASM AND THE PASM PROTOTYPE

PASM is a reconfigurable architecture in which the processors can be dynamically partitioned to form independent virtual SIMD and/or MIMD machines of various sizes. This section discusses relevant characteristics of the PASM architecture in addition to motivating some of the design characteristics. Further details can be found in [16] and [17].

Much has been written concerning design motivations for PASM since 1981 [16]. The computer architect's job is always made easier when the generality of the requirements for a machine are reduced. Early in the design phase of PASM, image and signal processing were identified as an important target application area. As it turns out, this led to a very general-purpose architecture, but along the way design decisions were guided by the characteristics of image and signal processing. Two notable ones were the following.

1) Some algorithms were well-suited to an MIMD model, others were suited to an SIMD model, while still a third group exhibited segments of each model. This led to the hybrid SIMD/MIMD architecture.

2) Many applications exhibited static interprocess communication *patterns* for well-defined "phases" of the computation. This led to the choice of a circuit-switched multistage cube implementation for the interconnection network.

These design decisions are reflected in the overall PASM architecture.

The PASM parallel computation unit contains N *processing elements* (PE's) (numbered from 0 to $N-1$) and an interconnection network. Each PE is a processor and memory pair. PE memory is used by the PE CPU for data storage in SIMD mode and both data and instruction storage in MIMD mode.

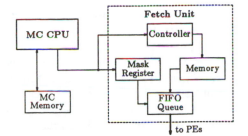

Fig. 1. Simplified MC structure with emphasis on the Fetch Unit.

The *microcontrollers* (MC's) are a set of Q microprocessors that act as the control units for the PE's in SIMD mode and orchestrate the activities of the PE's in MIMD mode. Each MC controls N/Q PE's. A set of MC's and their associated PE's form a virtual machine. In SIMD mode, each MC fetches instructions and common data from its memory, executes the control instructions (e.g., branches), and broadcasts the data processing instructions to its PE's. In MIMD mode, each MC may coordinate its PE's using instructions and data from its memory.

The experiments described in this paper were performed on a 4-MC 16-PE prototype of PASM. The PE and MC CPU's are Motorola MC68000 microprocessors operating at 8 MHz. Each PE contains a Motorola MC68881 floating-point coprocessor [11] operating at 8 or 16 MHz. Communication with the coprocessor in the PE during floating-point operations proceeds as with any peripheral.

Each PE contains special purpose hardware timing circuitry. A Motorola MC68230 timer, enhanced with additional TTL counting logic to improve resolution, was used to count processor clock cycles with an accuracy of ± 125 ns. The timer can be started or stopped by writing to a timer control register.

A simplified diagram of the structure of an MC is shown in Fig. 1. The MC contains memory from which the MC CPU reads instructions and data. Whenever the MC needs to broadcast SIMD instructions to its associated PE's, it first sets the Mask Register in the Fetch Unit to specify which PE's will execute the instructions to follow. The MC then writes a control word to the Fetch Unit Controller to specify the location and size of a block of SIMD instructions in the Fetch Unit Memory. The Fetch Unit Controller moves this block into the Fetch Unit FIFO Queue. The current value in the Mask Register is enqueued along with each SIMD instruction.

A PE obtains SIMD instructions by performing an instruction fetch from a reserved PE memory area called the *SIMD instruction space*. Whenever logic in the PE's detects an access to this memory, a request for an SIMD instruction is sent by the PE to the Fetch Unit. When all enabled PE's have issued a request, the instruction is released by the Fetch Unit and the PE's can execute the instruction. Disabled PE's do not receive the instruction and remain idle until an instruction is broadcast for which they are enabled. Switching from MIMD to SIMD mode only requires the execution of a jump instruction from an address in memory where MIMD instructions are stored to the PE SIMD instruction space. A switch from SIMD to MIMD mode is performed by the MC broadcasting a jump instruction with a target address in the PE's MIMD space.

The SIMD instruction broadcast mechanism can also be utilized for *barrier synchronization* [9], [12] of MIMD programs. When a program requires the PE's to synchronize, the MC, instructs the Fetch Unit Controller to enqueue an arbitrary data word. When the PE's executing the MIMD program need to synchronize (e.g., before a network transfer), they execute a memory read operation to the SIMD instruction space. Because the PE hardware treats SIMD instruction fetches and data reads identically, the PE's will be allowed to proceed only after the Fetch Unit has released the enqueued data and all active PE's have read it from their SIMD instruction space. This synchronizes the PE's. Thus, the same hardware that provides for SIMD synchronization among PE's also provides a fast mechanism for barrier synchronization because each barrier operation requires only a single PE data read from the SIMD instruction space, regardless of the number of PE's involved in the barrier.

The MC68000 processor can execute instructions from memory with different access times. The minimum memory read or write cycle time is four clock periods. Accessing slower memory will cause the generation of one or more processor *wait states* which will increase the instruction cycle time. Each wait state requires an additional clock cycle to perform a 16-bit read or write. Each PE contains 28 kilobytes of 0 or 1 wait state static RAM and 2 megabytes of dynamic RAM that operates at about three wait states. The Fetch Unit delivers data instructions to the PE's with a delay of two wait states due simply to the component delays of the hardware comprising the Fetch Unit's FIFO queue.

The interconnection network for the PASM prototype is a circuit-switched Extra-Stage Cube network [1], which is a fault-tolerant variation of the multistage cube network. The network is capable of operating in both point-to-point and broadcast modes. In order to communicate with another PE, the initiating PE must set up a path through the network. A path is established by first writing a PE routing tag to the network *data transfer register* (DTR). The PE then sets a bit in a control register to instruct the network interface to interpret the value in the DTR as a routing tag. Byte or word data values written to the DTR will now be automatically sent through the network. The receiving PE reads the transferred data from its DTR. Upon completion, the sending PE writes to the network control register to close the path and free the network.

III. ALGORITHM SELECTION

In this paper, the FFT algorithm was used as a vehicle for comparing the SIMD, MIMD, and BMIMD modes of operation on the PASM prototype. The FFT was chosen to study because it has a very regular, data-independent control structure. The well-understood algorithm organization makes it useful for realistically exercising the parallel hardware while being able to isolate the effects of the algorithm implementation from the architecture under study. Other examples of common data-independent algorithms having regular control flow include digital filtering, power spectrum estimation, convolution, and histogramming. The FFT programs exercise PASM's floating-point hardware for arithmetic operations, the multistage Cube

interconnection network, and the specialized timing hardware. Six different coprocessor operations are used in the various calculations: floating-point addition, subtraction, and multiplication, single-precision moves to and from the coprocessor, and moves between the floating-point registers. In this section, the FFT algorithm is derived and its program implementations are discussed.

Fast Fourier Transform

The *discrete Fourier transform* (DFT) of a complex M-point sequence, s_m, $0 \leq m < M$, is defined as

$$\mathfrak{F}_k = \sum_{m=0}^{M-1} s_m e^{-j(2\pi/M)mk}, \qquad 0 \leq k < M, \qquad (1)$$

where $j^2 = -1$ [14]. The direct calculation of the radix 2 DFT using (1) requires $O(M^2)$ operations. The FFT computes the DFT of a sequence in $O(M \log_2 M)$ serial operations. One FFT formulation is the radix 2 *decimation-in-time* (DIT) algorithm. In this algorithm, the M-point input sequence, s_m, is divided into two $M/2$-point subsequences

$$s_m^a = s_{2m}, \qquad m = 0, 1, \cdots, M/2 - 1, \qquad (2)$$

and

$$s_m^b = s_{2m+1}, \qquad m = 0, 1, \cdots, M/2 - 1. \qquad (3)$$

The DFT of the sequence s_m can now be written using the two subsequences as

$$\mathfrak{F}_k = \sum_{m=0}^{\frac{M}{2}-1} s_m^a W_M^{2mk} + \sum_{m=0}^{\frac{M}{2}-1} s_m^b W_M^{(2m+1)k},$$

$$k = 0, 1, 2, \cdots, M - 1 \quad (4)$$

where $W_M = e^{-j(2\pi/M)}$ and is called a *twiddle factor*. Equation (4) can be rewritten as

$$\mathfrak{F}_k = S_k^a + W_M^k S_k^b, \qquad 0 \leq k < M/2, \qquad (5)$$

and

$$\mathfrak{F}_{k+M/2} = S_k^a - W_M^k S_k^b, \qquad M/2 \leq k < M \qquad (6)$$

where S_k^a and S_k^b are the $M/2$-point DFT's of s_m^a and s_m^b, respectively. Equations (5) and (6) show that an M-point DFT can be computed from two $M/2$-point DFT's. By halving the number of points in the transform at each stage of the FFT, the DFT of an M-point sequence can be computed in $O(M \log_2 M)$ operations.

Fig. 2 is a signal flow graph of an 8-point radix 2 DIT FFT algorithm mapped to four PE's. The algorithm consists of $\log_2 M$ stages. At each stage, $M/2$ *butterfly* operations are executed. A butterfly operation is shown in Fig. 3. For each butterfly operation the input consists of two complex values, A and B. One complex multiplication and two complex additions are performed, and two complex outputs, X and Y, are generated. The twiddle factor, W_M^k, used in the calculation of each butterfly is marked in Fig. 2 and the value differs

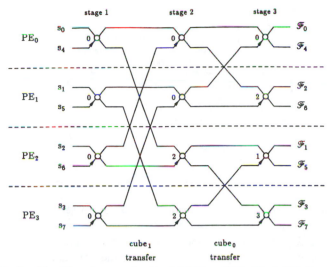

Fig. 2. Signal flow diagram of an 8-point FFT on 4 PE's. The twiddle factor for each butterfly is W_8^k, where k is the number adjacent to each arrow.

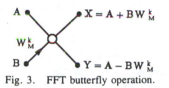

Fig. 3. FFT butterfly operation.

from stage to stage and within the stages. It should be noted that $W_M^0 = 1$ and $W_M^{M/4} = j$. Therefore, the first and second stages of the algorithm require no multiplications [14]. The $M/2$ butterfly operations performed within each stage are independent and can be executed in parallel. Parallel algorithms to perform an M-point FFT in $M/2$ PE's include those presented in [2], [8], [13], and [18].

Between stages, the PE's must exchange data items before performing the next set of butterfly operations. This exchange can be performed by the cube interconnection function. The *Cube* interconnection function, cube_c, $0 \leq c < \log_2 M/2$, is defined as

$$\text{cube}_c (p_{n-1} \cdots p_{c+1} p_c p_{c-1} \cdots p_0)$$
$$= p_{n-1} \cdots p_{c+1} \overline{p_c} p_{c-1} \cdots p_0 \quad (7)$$

where $p_{n-1} \cdots p_0$ is the binary representation of an arbitrary logical PE address, and $\overline{p_c}$ is the complement of p_c [15]. The complexities of the M-point radix 2 DIT serial and parallel FFT algorithms are given in Table I.[1]

Programs

Three 4-PE parallel FFT programs, one 8-PE parallel FFT program, and two serial FFT programs were implemented and executed on PASM to study the architecture and examine the tradeoffs between the different modes of parallel computation. The experimental results are presented and discussed in Sections V and VI.

---

[1] Parallel FFT algorithms using fewer than $M/2$ PE's are presented in [8]. In the experiments described here, we consider only the M-point, $M/2$ PE case. Because of the similarity of the algorithms using fewer PE's to those examined here, similar execution characteristics and speedups can be projected.

TABLE I
COMPLEXITY OF THE M-POINT RADIX 2 DIT FFT ALGORITHMS

PEs	Multiplication Steps	Addition Steps	Cube Transfer Steps
1	$(M/2)(\log_2 M - 2)$	$M \log_2 M$	
$M/2$	$\log_2 M - 2$	$2 \log_2 M$	$\log_2 M/2$

One 4-PE 8-point SIMD program performs all FFT operations in SIMD mode. A 4-PE MIMD version calculates the butterfly operations in MIMD mode and polls the network to determine the status during network transfer operations. A 4-PE BMIMD program uses barrier synchronization to align the operations of the PE's just prior to a network transfer in place of polling to test network status. The execution times for the component parts of these three 4-PE 8-point FFT programs and an additional serial 8-point FFT program were measured. Values obtained for the component parts of these programs were used to project the execution time of larger FFT's executing on a greater number of PE's and allows accurate extrapolation of the results to a 1024-PE PASM system.

An 8-PE SIMD 16-point FFT program and a serial 16-point FFT program were also implemented. The execution times measured for these programs were used to verify the projected performance measures.

Implementation

All of the programs were written in MC68000 Assembly language [10] as straight in-line code with no loops. This generated the fastest possible code and eliminated issues of programming style from the architecture studies.

Detailed analysis of the architecture was possible by carefully implementing the algorithm so as not to obscure architecture performance. Each program consists of an *initialization phase*, an *FFT algorithm phase*, and an *output phase*. Execution time measurements were made on the FFT algorithm phase of each program. In the initialization phase, the MC and each PE precompute and store all necessary data in preparation for the timing of the FFT algorithm phase. The execution time and the transformed data are printed during the output phase.

The FFT programs perform all computations that are not dependent on the operations of the FFT in the initialization phase. This optimization includes: ordering and initializing the input data in PE memory; precalculating the PE masks used by the MC; precalculating the logical PE number, cube function network routing tags, and FFT twiddle factors in each PE. Each PE has internal access to its own physical PE number. For a fixed PASM partition size, the logical PE number can be determined from the physical PE number. The order of the FFT input data is determined using the logical PE number. The values of the PE masks vary with the number of PE's. The routing tags for each network operation are computed using the physical PE number and MC numbers. The PE twiddle factor values are dependent upon the size of the FFT, the stage number of the FFT, and the logical PE number. These values are calculated during initialization by each PE and stored in memory. No preloaded register values are assumed.

In the FFT algorithm phase, each PE obtains the input data from PE memory, computes the FFT, and stores the transformed data back to PE memory. The storage location of intermediate data during program execution differs between the parallel and serial program implementations. For the parallel FFT programs, each PE contains only two complex data values. So, during the butterfly calculations, all of the data can reside in floating-point coprocessor registers. Each interstage network operation transfers only one complex value. The data that are not transferred remain in each PE's coprocessor registers. In the serial FFT programs, all of the data reside within a single PE. Since there are not enough data registers and coprocessor floating-point registers to store all of the intermediate data, most of the intermediate data are stored in memory. This requires many extra operations to move both of the complex data values to coprocessor registers for each butterfly operation.

The FFT programs use floating-point arithmetic. A PE floating-point operation is initiated by writing an instruction word to the floating-point coprocessor. Depending upon the operation to be performed, this is followed by successive reads or writes to coprocessor registers. Typically the main processor will poll the coprocessor to determine if the operation has completed. Efficient interface procedures were written to perform the floating-point operations by waiting a constant delay in lieu of polling the coprocessor. With these procedures, SIMD mode floating-point operations can be executed efficiently because the MC does not need to coordinate coprocessor polling responses from all PE's. These procedures were more efficient than code that polled the coprocessor and were used in all program implementations.

Each network transfer required sending two 32-bit single precision floating-point numbers (the real and imaginary parts of the complex X or Y). In this work, only 8-bit network transfers were used, therefore transferring each number requires four network writes and four network reads. The cube functions are nonblocking and the entire network circuit is configured within a few clock cycles after the last PE requests a network path.

IV. Measurement Techniques

This section describes the techniques used to obtain the experimental execution times. Use of the specialized PE timing hardware and normalization of instruction execution are described.

Specialized Timing Hardware

Execution times were measured in clock cycles using the specialized PE timing hardware described in Section II. Measurements were made by inserting instructions to start and stop the timers in the code before program assembly. The execution time of a parallel program is the greatest amount of time required by the MC and any one PE to complete execution. When measuring the execution time of a complete FFT program the timers were always started and stopped simultaneously in SIMD mode. The measured times for SIMD mode operations agreed within 1 clock cycle across all PE's. In MIMD mode, since each PE timer was started and stopped

TABLE II
Average PE Execution Times ($\bar{x}$) and Standard Deviations (σ) in Microseconds for 100 NOP Instructions Executed from Various Instruction Stream Origins

Instruction Stream Origin	Execution Time		Clock Cycles per Instruction
	$\bar{x}$	σ	
dynamic RAM	89.161	0.389	7.13
Fetch Unit queue	75.003	0.021	6.00
1 wait state static RAM	62.479	0.047	5.00
0 wait state static RAM	50.000	0.000	4.00

independently, the measured execution times across the PE's varied.

All execution times were measured for a single pass through the program. If repeated executions of the program resulted in varying execution times, the measurement was repeated until a clear dominant value was established. This variance in execution times was observed only when executing SIMD mode programs and was less than 3% of the total program execution time. In MIMD mode, repeated execution time measurements were always within 1 clock cycle. The variation in SIMD execution times is due to synchronization of instructions in PE's with processor clocks that are not always in phase. In the prototype, each PE has its own internal independent 16 MHz clock. The 8 MHz clock signal used to operate the MC68000 processor is obtained by dividing the output of a 16 MHz clock. There is no circuitry to synchronize PE clocks. Therefore, the phase of any two 8 MHz PE clocks may differ by as much as one clock cycle of the 16 MHz clock (0.063 ns). The relative phase of any two PE clocks will change during the program as different sets of PE's are enabled and disabled by the MC's.

The time required to start and stop the timers will vary according to the mode of computation, the number of PE's enabled, and the origin of the PE instruction stream. This *timer overhead* was measured and subtracted from the experimental program execution times.

Normalization of Instruction Execution

On the PASM prototype, the origin of PE instructions influences the execution time of a parallel program. For example, measurements have shown that PE instructions will execute faster when processing in MIMD mode and when fetched from 0 wait state memory than when in processing in SIMD mode and fetched from the Fetch Unit Queue. Table II gives the measured PE execution times for 100 NOP instructions when fetched from various instruction stream origins. These execution times are linearly related as can be clearly seen from Fig. 4. This variation in instruction execution time is an artifact of the prototype hardware implementation and is not a general characteristic of the architecture or mode of processing. In the experiments performed, the MIMD programs with instructions fetched from static memory enjoyed an artificial speed advantage over SIMD programs. Since the hardware timing circuitry can discern a performance variation as small as a single clock cycle, it was necessary to normalize

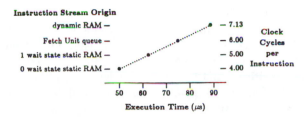

Fig. 4. PE execution times for 100 NOP instructions executed from various instruction stream origins.

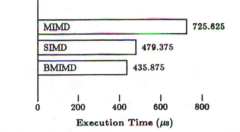

Fig. 5. Execution time for 8-point FFT programs on 4 PASM PE's.

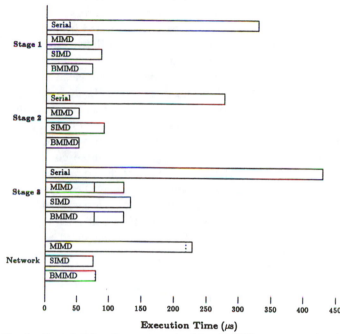

Fig. 6. Execution time for components of 8-point FFT programs on 1 and 4 PE's.

all program execution times, to make meaningful timing comparisons between different programming modes. A different hardware implementation could easily equalize the execution time of instructions fetched from different instruction stream origins.

The memory access time for all instructions was normalized to two wait states (six clock cycles). This is equivalent to the PE SIMD instruction space access time and no normalization was necessary for SIMD instruction fetches. In the results presented in Section V, all other memory access cycles were normalized. During program execution, only static RAM memory was used within each PE. For SIMD mode, the static RAM was used only for data storage. To obtain the normalized execution time of any program component, the execution time was measured once using 0 wait state static RAM and again using 1 wait state static RAM. The difference between these two execution times is the time required for a single wait state per memory cycle. Adding the difference between these two execution times to the 1 wait state execution time is equivalent to the program executing from 2 wait state memory. By using this 2 wait state normalized execution time, the time of an instruction fetch in SIMD mode from the Fetch Unit Queue is equivalent to an instruction access in MIMD mode from memory. Direct comparison of program times was then possible.

An indication of the accuracy of the measurement techniques presented here can be seen in Table II in the execution time for instructions fetched from the PEs' dynamic RAM. This memory has a 3 wait state access time and requires seven clock cycles for each memory read. The small additional time (0.13 clock cycle) per instruction is due to the PE processor being forced to wait while the dynamic RAM memory periodically refreshes.

V. EXPERIMENTAL RESULTS

Execution time of the complete FFT algorithm was measured for the three 4-PE 8-point parallel implementations, for the 8-PE 16-point SIMD program, and for the single PE 8- and 16-point serial programs. The execution times for the 4-PE programs are shown in Fig. 5. The serial 8-point FFT executed in 1045.000 μs.

The components of the 4-PE parallel programs and the single PE 8-point FFT program were also studied. These measurements included the execution time of register initialization, program control overhead, FFT stage 1, cube$_1$ interconnection function, FFT stage 2, cube$_0$ function, and FFT stage 3. The execution times for the components of each of the 8-point FFT programs are shown in Fig. 6. The length of each

TABLE III
EXECUTION TIMES IN MICROSECONDS FOR COMPONENTS OF 8-POINT FFT PROGRAMS ON 1 AND 4 PE'S. NA INDICATES THAT THIS COMPONENT DOES NOT APPLY TO THIS PROGRAM

Component	Serial	Parallel		
		MIMD	SIMD	BMIMD
Initialization	9.0	19.500	15.750	19.500
Control	NA	7.500	NA	7.500
Stage 1	329.0	72.750	86.875	72.750
Stage 2	277.0	52.000	91.500	52.000
Stage 3	430.0			
PEs 0, 1		76.750	133.500	76.750
PEs 2, 3		122.750		122.750
Network $\bar{x}$		223.094	75.375	78.828
σ		3.185	0.000	0.634

bar in Fig. 6 indicates the maximum execution time for each program component. The times corresponding to each bar are also given Table III. The *FFT stage execution time* includes the time required to compute the floating-point butterfly operation plus the time required to move floating-point data to, from, and within the coprocessor. The *network execution time* is the time to transfer a complex floating-point value from the MC68000 data registers of the sending PE to the data registers of the receiving PE. This includes the time to write the routing tag to the network, request a network path, transfer the data one byte at a time, reconstruct the transferred data, and drop the network path. A solid line across a bar (MIMD and BMIMD Stage 3) indicates that while some of the PE's executed the program component at the maximum time indicated by the length of the bar, other PE's only required the time indicated by the solid line. This is due to the specific implementation of the FFT algorithm and will be described later. A dotted line across a bar (MIMD and BMIMD Network) indicates the minimum execution time for the program component. The measured execution times across all PE's for this component lie between the time indicated by the length of the bar and the time indicated by the dotted line. Table III gives the average PE execution times ($\bar{x}$) and the standard deviations (σ) for the network program components.

The times presented in Fig. 6 and Table III are quite accurate. The program components in Fig. 6 account for a minimum of 93% of the execution time of each FFT program. The remaining execution time is required for program initialization and control. Measured values for these components are given in Table III. Summing all of the component times for each program gives execution times of 720.688 μs for the MIMD version, 478.375 μs for the SIMD program, 432.156 μs for the BMIMD program, and 1045.000 μs for the serial version. These sums differ from the measured execution times for the complete FFT programs by -0.68%, -0.21%, -0.85%, and 0.00%, respectively. The measured execution times are discussed in the next section.

VI. DISCUSSION

The high precision measurement techniques used in this study permitted a detailed analysis of the PASM architecture during execution of the components of each program. In this section, the differences in execution time for each of the program components are discussed. These measured component execution times are then used to project execution time, speedup, and efficiency.

Execution Times

Fig. 5 shows that the MIMD program has the longest execution time for any of the 4-PE parallel programs. This parallel implementation of the FFT algorithm has a speedup of 1.44 over the serial FFT program. The SIMD program requires 34% less time than the MIMD program with a speedup over the serial FFT of 2.18. The execution time of the BMIMD program is 9% less than the execution time of the SIMD program. The speedup for this program with respect to the serial program is 2.40. The reasons for the variation in execution times can be explained by examining the individual program components.

In stage 1, each program executes a W_8^0 butterfly. In all modes, the butterfly requires two additions and two subtractions. The difference in the measured execution time for stage 1 is a result of the data movement from the coprocessor after the butterfly calculation. In the cube$_1$ network transfer that follows stage 1, PE's 0 and 1 transfer Y while PE's 2 and 3 transfer X. In MIMD and BMIMD modes, all PE's move the appropriate complex X or Y value from the coprocessor regis-

ters to the MC68000 data registers at roughly the same time. This requires two floating-point move operations. In SIMD mode, PE's 0 and 1 must first be enabled while PE's 2 and 3 are disabled and the complex Y value is moved from the coprocessor. PE's 0 and 1 are then disabled while PE's 2 and 3 are enabled and the complex X value is moved. The SIMD mode program requires two more move operations than the MIMD and BMIMD implementations.

In stage 2, the difference in measured execution time between the SIMD and MIMD programs is even greater than for stage 1. One half of the PE's perform a $W_8^0 = 1$ butterfly while the other half compute an $W_8^2 = j$ butterfly. Both of these butterfly operations require two floating-point additions and two floating-point subtractions. In the MIMD and BMIMD versions, calculation of this stage is straightforward. Each PE moves the recently transferred data values to the coprocessor registers, computes the butterfly, and moves a single complex data item from the coprocessor in preparation for the cube$_0$ network transfer. The SIMD stage 2 operation is much more complex. Although $W_8^0 = 1$ and $W_8^2 = j$ butterflies require the same number of arithmetic operations, the butterfly operations combine the A and B data values in a different order. However, it is possible to move the data into coprocessor registers in a sequence that allows the addition and subtraction operations to be performed simultaneously in all PE's. Additional masking and data movement is then necessary to prepare for the network transfer. Another reason for the longer stage 2 SIMD execution time is the necessity for an SIMD stage computation to leave the data that are not transferred in the correct floating-point registers across all PE's. This data movement is not necessary for the MIMD or BMIMD programs since each PE computes the stages independently and knows the storage locations of the data from the previous stage.

In stage 3, PE's 2 and 3 compute butterflies with nontrivial twiddle factors requiring multiply operations. PE's 0 and 1 compute the less complex W_8^0 and W_8^2 butterflies. For MIMD and BMIMD mode, the execution time for the butterflies computed by PE's 2 and 3 is indicated by the length of the bar in Fig. 6. The execution time for PE's 0 and 1 is indicated by the solid line across the bar. In SIMD mode, all of the PE's execute butterflies using multiply operations. Since half of the PE's transferred the A value in the preceding cube$_0$ function and the other half transferred the B data item, extra processing is required by the SIMD stage 3 to enable and disable the two sets of PE's and move the data values to different PE coprocessor registers.

The execution time required for the interconnection network transfers varies widely among the three program implementations. The SIMD network operation requires the least amount of processing time. Since all PE's execute the network operations in lock-step fashion, the data transfers are synchronized with no need to test the network for data availability. In MIMD mode, each PE executes each butterfly independently and no implicit synchrony can be assumed when reaching the network transfer component of the program. Therefore, it is necessary for each PE to test the network (in a software polling loop) before transferring a data item and to wait on the network

Mode	J	R	A	C	S_1	S_2	S_m	S_f
MIMD	4.000	19.500	3.500	223.125	72.750	52.000	99.500	122.750
SIMD	NA	15.750	NA	75.375	86.875	91.500	125.500	133.500
BMIMD	4.000	19.500	3.500	78.875	72.750	52.000	99.500	122.750

for a data item to become available. This testing and waiting (in software) results in high end-to-end network transfer times. Like the MIMD program, each PE executes each butterfly stage independently in the BMIMD version. However, the BMIMD version performs a barrier synchronization just prior to the network transfer. Once all of the PE's are synchronized, the data are sent and received without testing the status of the network. The execution time for the BMIMD version is slightly greater than for the SIMD version. The difference is the time required for all PE's to read from the SIMD instruction space and synchronize.

Since the execution time for the SIMD network transfer is less than the time for the barrier synchronization network transfer used in the BMIMD program, it would appear that a faster program could be constructed by using the SIMD network transfer. This is not the case. The overhead incurred by jumping to SIMD instruction space before the transfer and back to MIMD program space for the next butterfly stage exceeds the expected time savings. In addition, each time MIMD operation is resumed, it is necessary to test and branch in order for each PE to determine which butterfly operation it is to perform. The execution time overhead for these test and branch operations exceeds the time for testing and branching of an MIMD program that remains in MIMD mode and uses barrier synchronization.

Projecting Program Execution Times

Using the measured FFT components execution times, an expression for the execution time of an M-point FFT program running on $M/2$ PASM PE's, $M \geq 8$, in MIMD, SIMD, or BMIMD mode was derived. The expression is a sum of the execution times of the components of an FFT program. For an M-point FFT, the number of each component to sum is either fixed for all size FFT's or can be expressed as a function of M. The expression presented is used to predict the execution times for larger size FFT's using a greater number of PE's and allows us to extrapolate our results to a full 1024-PE PASM system. For $M/2$ PE's and M data items, the execution time of an FFT program can be expressed as

$$T_P(M) = J + R + (A + C) \log_2 (M/2) + S \qquad (8)$$

where the component execution times are defined as

J   program control overhead
R   data and address register initialization
A   a single MIMD test and branch operation
C   cube interconnection network transfer
S   execution of all FFT butterfly stages.

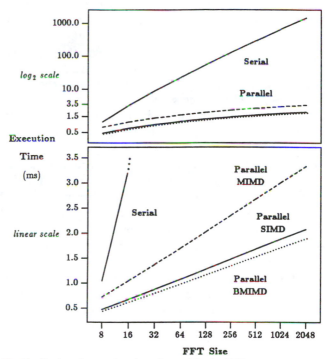

Fig. 7.   Projected execution times for an M-point FFT program on 1 (serial) and $M/2$ (parallel) PASM PE's, $8 \leq M \leq 2048$, M a power of 2.

The total time to execute all of the butterfly stages can be expressed as

$$S = S_1 + S_2 + (\log_2 M - 3) S_m + S_f, \qquad (9)$$

where the component execution times are defined as

S_1 stage 1 (W_M^0; input obtained from memory)
S_2 stage 2 (W_M^0 and $W_M^{M/4}$)
S_m intermediate stage (multiplication butterfly)
S_f final stage (results stored in memory).

The execution time, $T_P(M)$, for an M-point FFT program executing on $M/2$ PASM PE's, $M/2 \geq 4$, can be projected using the data in Table IV. Equation (8) can be used to project execution times for programs operating in MIMD, SIMD, or BMIMD modes because the terms in (8) that do not apply to SIMD mode have no entries in Table IV. The execution times for the intermediate stage, S_m, were obtained from measurements on the final stage of modified programs in which the butterfly results were stored in registers instead of PE memory.

The graphs in Fig. 7 illustrate the projected execution times for an M-point FFT program on a single PE and on $M/2$ PE's for $M = 8$ to $M = 2048$. The same projected execution times for the parallel programs are shown in both graphs but different horizontal scales are used. These times are extrapolated with high confidence. For the 4-PE cases, the expression yields execution times of 724.250 μs for MIMD, 478.375 μs for SIMD, and 435.750 μs for BMIMD. These values differ from the measured execution times for the complete FFT's by -0.19%, -0.21%, and -0.03%, respectively.

With the exception of the network transfer components, the component times are independent of the size of the FFT being computed so the effects of computing larger size FFT's on the component times are nil. In the case of network operations, the possibility of increased delay should be considered. However, in the case of the multistage cube, the latency grows only at a logarithmic rate as compared to the growth of the problem size. In fact, the effect is even less than logarithmic because with any size network, the contributions to latency come from two sources—network access and propagation time. As the network becomes larger, the propagation is the only aspect which grows logarithmically while the access times are unaffected.

An extrapolation expression was also derived to predict the serial FFT execution times for larger size FFT's. For an 8-point FFT, this expression yields an execution time of 1047.250 μs which differs from the measured execution time by 0.21%. For a 16-point FFT, the predicted execution time was 3313.750 μs which differs by 0.48% from the measured execution time of 3297.750 μs.

Equation (8) was also validated for the 8-PE 16-point SIMD FFT program. In order to obtain measurements on 8 fully-functional PE's, it was necessary to operate the MC68881 floating-point coprocessors with a clock frequency of 8 MHz instead of 16 MHz. The data for execution times of the program components used for this validation were similar to the data presented in Table IV. The FFT stage times were larger since floating-point operations required more time. With the slower floating-point coprocessor, the expression yields an execution time for a 4-PE 8-point FFT of 647.750 μs which differs by 0.29% from the measured execution time of 649.625 μs. For the 8-PE 16-point FFT, the predicted execution time was 923.125 μs which differs from the measured execution time of 937.625 μs by -1.55%.

For the parallel programs, as the number of points in the FFT (and number of PE's) increase, the effect of MIMD network operations (the main difference between the BMIMD and MIMD versions) causes the gap between the performance of the MIMD version and both the SIMD and BMIMD versions to widen. Note the general logarithmic growth in execution time as the number of points in the FFT increases. Equations (8) and (9) are both dominated by logarithmic terms, as is clearly shown in the upper graph of Fig. 7. The execution times of the serial FFT increase at a rate proportional to the FFT size. The rate of increase is slightly greater for smaller FFT's because adding more points requires that more and more intermediate data be stored in PE memory rather than in registers. For the parallel programs, the number of PE's increases along with the FFT size and the execution time required for data storage remains the same in each stage, independent of M.

The projections in Fig. 7 are based on the assumption that

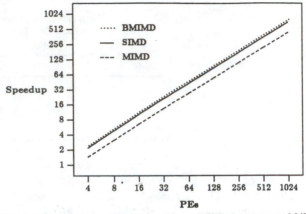

Fig. 8. Projected speedup for an M-point FFT program on $M/2$ PE's, $8 \le M \le 2048$, M a power of 2.

the speed of the hardware of a larger PASM system would be equivalent to that of the prototype hardware. This is a very conservative assumption. Implementation of a full 1024-PE PASM would certainly be built using much faster state-of-the-art microprocessors. For Motorola processors in the MC68000 family, the projected execution times can be directly adjusted to account for higher clock rates. These adjusted projected times will still be quite conservative since enhanced microprocessors will use wider data paths and have faster and more sophisticated floating-point hardware. The results that are therefore of most interest are the detailed comparison of the serial, SIMD, MIMD, and BMIMD implementations rather than the actual execution times.

Projection of Speedup and Efficiency

To further analyze the performance of the architecture executing MIMD, SIMD, and BMIMD programs, the projected serial execution times were used along with the projected parallel execution times to obtain estimates of speedup and efficiency for the parallel programs. These measures are less dependent on hardware speed than the execution time figures.

Fig. 8 illustrates the projected speedups for system sizes up to 1024 PE's. These figures are based on the projected execution times of the parallel programs obtained with (8) and (9), and a comparable analytic prediction of the execution times of M-point serial FFT's, $T_S(M)$. The projected efficiency, $E(M)$, for an $M/2$-PE M-point FFT program is defined as

$$E(M) = \frac{T_S(M)}{(M/2)T_P(M)}. \tag{10}$$

Fig. 9 illustrates the projected efficiency for the parallel FFT programs. Note that for 1024 PE's in SIMD and BMIMD modes, the projected efficiency is almost 76%. Hence, the overhead of communication remains low. This is significant and has even greater positive implications for a similar system with a message or packet-switched network: the FFT is nearly worst case with respect to network configuration overheads in a circuit-switched system.

VII. CONCLUSIONS

This work focused on the evaluation of an SIMD/MIMD parallel architecture by obtaining performance measurements

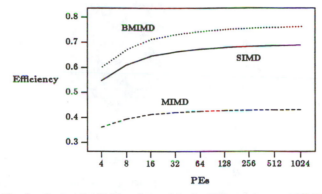

Fig. 9. Projected efficiency for an M-point FFT program on $M/2$ PE's, $8 \leq M \leq 2048$, M a power of 2.

for various implementations of the FFT algorithm. The experiments were performed on the prototype PASM parallel processing system. Detailed execution time measurements were possible using specialized timing hardware. These measurements, along with a novel normalization scheme, allowed evaluation of the effects of a number of aspects of the architecture on the performance of the FFT programs. Most notable is the significant performance advantage of the SIMD implementation over the MIMD implementation, and the even further improvement attained with a barrier synchronized MIMD implementation. The difference between the SIMD and MIMD implementations can be attributed primarily to interconnection network time; the improvement gained with the BMIMD version is principally due to MIMD execution of arithmetic operations combined with barrier synchronization at the points at which data transfers occur. This constitutes one of the first results of this kind, in which controlled experiments on fixed hardware were used to make comparisons of these fundamental modes of computing. The results demonstrate the importance of a fast and efficient MIMD hardware synchronization capability.

Also notable are the projections in which the information obtained by executing the FFT programs on a small number of processors is used to extrapolate performance for larger FFT's on a larger system. Although 8-point FFT's are used as the basis for these projections, these algorithms contain all of the basic components of larger FFT programs. The detailed measurements of the components of the implementations allow us to do a very accurate construction of the execution times and speedups for larger size problems. The projections accurately model many aspects of the architecture including interconnection network access, data transfers, floating-point arithmetic, coprocessor access, use of registers and memory, and program control overhead. These extrapolations are verified to within 2% by comparing the predicted 16-point 8-PE time to the actual measured time for a 16-point 8-PE implementation. The projections indicate a widening of the gap between the performance of the MIMD version and the SIMD and BMIMD implementations due to network operation costs.

All of the programs were written in MC68000 Assembly language. Many of the interesting comparisons between the various implementations of the FFT would not have been observed if the programs had not been written at this fine level of detail. The detailed experiments reported here provided significant insight into many aspects of the PASM architecture and prototype implementation. This knowledge will be useful for optimizing high-level parallel language compilers designed to produce code for executing on PASM.

ACKNOWLEDGMENT

The authors thank S. Fineberg, W. Nation, P. Pero, T. Schwederski, and H. J. Siegel for their many helpful discussions.

Preliminary versions of portions of this work were published in the Proceedings of the 1989 IEEE International Conference on Acoustics, Speech, and Signal Processing [4] and in the Proceedings of the 1989 International Conference on Parallel Processing [5].

REFERENCES

[1] G. B. Adams III and H. J. Siegel, "The extra stage cube: A fault-tolerant interconnection network for supersystems," *IEEE Trans. Comput.*, vol. C-31, pp. 443–454, May 1982.

[2] G. D. Bergland, "Fast Fourier transform hardware implementations—An overview," *IEEE Trans. Audio Electroacoust.*, vol. AU-17, pp. 104–108, June 1969.

[3] E. C. Bronson, T. L. Casavant, and L. H. Jamieson, "Experimental analysis of multi-mode fast Fourier transforms on the PASM parallel processing system prototype," Tech. Rep. EE 88-27, Purdue Univ., West Lafayette, IN, May 1988.

[4] ——, "Experimental analysis of multi-mode fast Fourier transforms on the PASM parallel processing system," in *Proc. 1989 IEEE Int. Conf. Acoust., Speech, Signal Processing*, May 1989, pp. 2540–2543.

[5] ——, "Experimental application-driven architecture analysis of an SIMD/MIMD parallel processing system," in *Proc. 1989 Int. Conf. Parallel Processing*, Aug. 1989, pp. 159–167.

[6] T. L. Casavant, H. J. Siegel, T. Schwederski, L. H. Jamieson, S. A. Fineberg, M. J. McPheters, E. C. Bronson, W. Disch, K. Schurecht, E. H. Loh, C. Ringer, B. Cox, and C. A. Toomey, "Experimental benchmarks and initial evaluation of the performance of the PASM system prototype," Tech. Rep. EE 88-2, Purdue Univ., West Lafayette, IN, Jan. 1988.

[7] J. L. Gustafson, G. R. Montry, and R. E. Benner, "Development of parallel methods for a 1024-processor hypercube," *SIAM J. Scientif. Statist. Comput.*, vol. 9, pp. 609–638, July 1988.

[8] L. H. Jamieson, P. T. Mueller, Jr., and H. J. Siegel, "FFT algorithms for SIMD parallel processing systems," *J. Parallel Distributed Comput.*, vol. 3, pp. 47–71, Mar. 1986.

[9] S. F. Lundstrom and G. H. Barnes, "A controllable MIMD architecture," in *Proc. 1980 Int. Conf. Parallel Processing*, Aug. 1980, pp. 165–173.

[10] Motorola, *MC68000 16/32-Bit Microprocessor Programmer's Reference Manual*, 4th ed., Englewood Cliffs, NJ: Prentice-Hall, 1984.

[11] Motorola, *MC68881 Floating-Point Coprocessor User's Manual*, 1st

ed. Austin, TX: MC68881UM/AD, Motorola MOS Integrated Circuits Division, 1985.

[12] M. O'Keefe and H. Dietz, "Performance analysis of hardware barrier synchronization, Tech. Rep. EE 89-51, Purdue University, West Lafayette, IN, Aug. 1989.

[13] M. C. Pease, "The indirect binary n-cube microprocessor array," *IEEE Trans. Comput.*, vol. C-26, pp. 458–473, May 1977.

[14] L. R. Rabiner and B. Gold, *Theory and Application of Digital Signal Processing*. Englewood Cliffs, NJ: Prentice-Hall, 1975.

[15] H. J. Siegel, *Interconnection Networks for Large-Scale Parallel Processing: Theory and Case Studies*. Lexington, MA: Lexington Books, 1985.

[16] H. J. Siegel, L. J. Siegel, F. C. Kemmerer, P. T. Mueller, Jr., H. E. Smalley, Jr., and S. D. Smith, "PASM: A partionable SIMD/MIMD system for image processing and pattern recognition," *IEEE Trans. Comput.*, vol. C-30, pp. 934–947, Dec. 1981.

[17] H. J. Siegel, T. Schwederski, J. T. Kuehn, and N. J. Davis IV, "An overview of the PASM parallel processing system," in *Computer Architecture*, D. D. Gajski, V. M. Milutinovic, H. J. Siegel, and B. P. Furht, Eds. Washington, DC: IEEE Comput. Soc. Press, 1987, pp. 387–407.

[18] H. S. Stone, "Parallel processing with the perfect shuffle," *IEEE Trans. Comput.*, vol. C-20, pp. 153–161, Feb. 1971.

Thomas L. Casavant (S'85–M'86) received the B.S. degree in computer science in 1982 from the University of Iowa, Iowa City, and the M.S. and Ph.D. degrees in electrical and computer engineering from the University of Iowa in 1983 and 1986, respectively.

From 1986 to 1989 he was on the faculty of the School of Electrical Engineering at Purdue University where he also served as the Director of the EE School's Parallel Processing Laboratory. In August, 1989, he joined the faculty of the Department of Electrical and Computer Engineering at the University of Iowa as an Assistant Professor. His research interest include design and analysis of parallel/distributed computing systems, programming environments, algorithms, and programs.

Dr. Casavant is a member of IEEE Computer Society and the Association for Computing Machinery.

Edward C. Bronson (S'90) received the B.S. degree in 1975, the M.S. degree in 1981, and the Ph.D. degree in 1990, all in electrical engineering from Purdue University, West Lafayette, IN.

From 1975 to 1977 he worked in research on physiological signal processing for pharmaceutical drug testing as a bioengineer for the Interdisciplinary Drug Engineering and Assessment Laboratory in the School of Pharmacy at Purdue University. He continued this research from 1977 to 1984 at Pharmadynamics Research, Inc., West Lafayette, IN, a company that he co-founded. From 1984 to 1987 he worked for AT&T Bell Laboratories as a member of the Technical Staff on speech signal processing techniques directed toward the development of low bit-rate speech coding algorithms. He holds two patents in this area. His current research interests include computer architectures and algorithms, parallel and distributed processing, speech analysis and recognition, and signal processing.

Dr. Bronson is a member of the IEEE Computer Society, the Association for Computing Machinery, and the Association for Computational Linguistics (ACL).

Leah H. Jamieson (S'75–M'77) received the S.B. degree in mathematics in 1972 from the Massachusetts Institute of Technology, Cambridge, the M.A. and M.S.E. degrees in 1974, and the Ph.D. degree in 1977, all in electrical engineering and computer science from Princeton University, Princeton, NJ.

Since 1976 she has been on the faculty at Purdue University, West Lafayette, IN, where she is currently Professor of Electrical Engineering. Her research interests include the design and analysis of parallel processing algorithms; the application of parallel processing to the areas of digital speech, image, and signal processing; the modeling of parallel processes; and speech analysis and recognition. She co-edited books on *Algorithmically-Specialized Parallel Computers* (New York: Academic, 1985) and *The Characteristics of Parallel Algorithms* (Cambridge, MA: MIT Press, 1987).

Dr. Jamieson has served as Associate Editor for the IEEE TRANSACTIONS ON ACOUSTICS, SPEECH, AND SIGNAL PROCESSING, the *Journal of Parallel and Distributed Computing*, and *The Journal of VLSI Signal Processing*. She has served as a member of the National Research Council Advisory Committee to the Army Research Office and as a member of the Advisory Committee for the NSF Division of Microelectronics Information Processing Systems. She is a member of the IEEE Technical Activities Board Awards and Recognition Committee. From 1981 to 1983 she was a member of the Administrative Committee of the IEEE Acoustics, Speech, and Signal Processing Society. She is currently an ASSP Distinguished Lecturer.

About the Author

David J. Lilja is a member of the electrical engineering faculty at the University of Minnesota, Minneapolis. Previously, he worked as a research assistant in the Center for Supercomputing Research and Development at the University of Illinois at Urbana-Champaign and as a development engineer in the processor and memory design group at Tandem Computers Incorporated in Cupertino, California. His main research interests currently are in computer architecture, parallel processing, and supercomputing. He received a B.S. in computer engineering from Iowa State University, Ames, and an M.S. and a Ph.D., both in electrical engineering, from the University of Illinois at Urbana-Champaign. He is a member of the IEEE Computer Society and the ACM and is a registered professional engineer.

IEEE Computer Society

OTHER IEEE COMPUTER SOCIETY PRESS TITLES

MONOGRAPHS

Analyzing Computer Architectures
Written by J.C. Huck and M.J. Flynn
(ISBN 0-8186-8857-2); 206 pages

Branch Strategy Taxonomy and Performance Models
Written by Harvey G. Cragon
(ISBN 0-8186-9111-5); 150 pages

**Desktop Publishing for the Writer:
Designing, Writing, and Developing**
Written by Richard Ziegfeld and John Tarp
(ISBN 0-8186-8840-8); 380 pages

Digital Image Warping
Written by George Wolberg
(ISBN 0-8186-8944-7); 340 pages

Integrating Design and Test—CAE Tools for ATE Programming
Written by K.P. Parker
(ISBN 0-8186-8788-6); 160 pages

**JSP and JSD—The Jackson Approach to Software Development
(Second Edition)**
Written by J.R. Cameron
(ISBN 0-8186-8858-0); 560 pages

National Computer Policies
Written by Ben G. Matley and Thomas A. McDannold
(ISBN 0-8186-8784-3); 192 pages

Physical Level Interfaces and Protocols
Written by Uyless Black
(ISBN 0-8186-8824-2); 240 pages

**Protecting Your Proprietary Rights in Computer
and High-Technology Industries**
Written by Tobey B. Marzouk, Esq.
(ISBN 0-8186-8754-1); 224 pages

X.25 and Related Protocols
Written by Uyless Black
(ISBN 0-8186-8976-5); 304 pages

TUTORIALS

Advanced Computer Architecture
Edited by D.P. Agrawal
(ISBN 0-8186-0667-3); 400 pages

Advances in Distributed System Reliability
Edited by Suresh Rai and Dharma P. Agrawal
(ISBN 0-8186-8907-2); 352 pages

**Autonomous Mobile Robots:
Perception, Mapping, and Navigation—Volume 1**
Edited by S.S. Iyengar and A. Elfes
(ISBN 0-8186-9018-6); 552 pages

**Autonomous Mobile Robots:
Control, Planning, and Architecture—Volume 2**
Edited by S.S. Iyengar and A. Elfes
(ISBN 0-8186-9116-6); 536 pages

**Broadband Switching:
Architectures, Protocols, Design, and Analysis**
Edited by C. Dhas, V.K. Konangi, and M. Sreetharan
(ISBN 0-8186-8926-9); 528 pages

Computer and Network Security
Edited by M.D. Abrams and H.J. Podell
(ISBN 0-8186-0756-4); 448 pages

Computer Architecture
Edited by D.D. Gajski, V.M. Milutinovic, H. Siegel, and B.P. Furht
(ISBN 0-8186-0704-1); 602 pages

Computer Arithmetic I
Edited by Earl E. Swartzlander, Jr.
(ISBN 0-8186-8931-5); 398 pages

Computer Arithmetic II
Edited by Earl E. Swartzlander, Jr.
(ISBN 0-8186-8945-5); 412 pages

**Computer Communications: Architectures,
Protocols and Standards (Second Edition)**
Edited by William Stallings
(ISBN 0-8186-0790-4); 448 pages

Computer Graphics Hardware: Image Generation and Display
Edited by H.K. Reghbati and A.Y.C. Lee
(ISBN 0-8186-0753-X); 384 pages

Computer Graphics: Image Synthesis
Edited by Kenneth Joy, Nelson Max, Charles Grant,
and Lansing Hatfield
(ISBN 0-8186-8854-8); 380 pages

Computer Vision: Principles
Edited by Rangachar Kasturi and Ramesh Jain
(ISBN 0-8186-9102-6); 700 pages

Computer Vision: Advances and Applications
Edited by Rangachar Kasturi and Ramesh Jain
(ISBN 0-8186-9103-4); 720 pages

Digital Image Processing (Second Edition)
Edited by Rama Chellappa
(ISBN 0-8186-2362-4); 400 pages

Digital Private Branch Exchanges (PBXs)
by Edwin Coover
(ISBN 0-8186-0829-3); 394 pages

Distributed Computing Network Reliability
Edited by Suresh Rai and Dharma Agrawal
(ISBN 0-8186-8908-0); 357 pages

Distributed Software Engineering
Edited by Sol Shatz and Jia-Ping Wang
(ISBN 0-8186-8856-4); 294 pages

Domain Analysis and Software Systems Modeling
Edited by Ruben Prieto-Diaz and Guillermo Arango
(ISBN 0-8186-8996-X); 312 pages

**DSP-Based Testing of Analog and
Mixed Signal Circuits**
Edited by Matthew Mahoney
(ISBN 0-8186-0785-8); 272 pages

Fault Tolerant Computing
Edited by V. Nelson and B. Carroll
(ISBN 0-8186-8677-4); 428 pages

Formal Verification of Hardware Design
Edited by Michael Yoeli
(ISBN 0-8186-9017-8); 340 pages

Hard Real-Time Systems
Edited by J.A. Stankovic and K. Ramamritham
(ISBN 0-8186-0819-6); 624 pages

**Integrated Services Digital Networks (ISDN)
(Second Edition)**
Edited by William Stallings
(ISBN 0-8186-0823-4); 406 pages

For Further Information Call 1-800-CS-BOOKS or Write:

IEEE Computer Society Press, 10662 Los Vaqueros Circle, PO Box 3014,
Los Alamitos, California 90720-1264, USA

IEEE Computer Society, 13, avenue de l'Aquilon,
B-1200 Brussels, BELGIUM

IEEE Computer Society, Ooshima Building, 2-19-1 Minami-Aoyama,
Minato-ku, Tokyo 107, JAPAN

Local Network Technology (Third Edition)
Edited by William Stallings
(ISBN 0-8186-0825-0); 512 pages

Microprogramming and Firmware Engineering
Edited by V. Milutinovic
(ISBN 0-8186-0839-0); 416 pages

Modeling and Control of Automated Manufacturing Systems
Edited by A. A. Desrochers
(ISBN 0-8186-8916-1); 384 pages

Nearest Neighbor Pattern Classification Techniques
Edited by Belur V. Dasarathy
(ISBN 0-8186-8930-7); 464 pages

New Paradigms for Software Development
Edited by William Agresti
(ISBN 0-8186-0707-6); 304 pages

Object-Oriented Computing, Volume 1: Concepts
Edited by Gerald E. Petersen
(ISBN 0-8186-0821-8); 214 pages

Object-Oriented Computing, Volume 2: Implementations
Edited by Gerald E. Petersen
(ISBN 0-8186-0822-6); 324 pages

Parallel Architectures for Database Systems
Edited by A.R. Hurson, L.L. Miller, and S.H. Pakzad
(ISBN 0-8186-8838-6); 478 pages

Reduced Instruction Set Computers (RISC)
(Second Edition)
Edited by William Stallings
(ISBN 0-8186-8943-9); 448 pages

Software Engineering Project Management
Edited by R. Thayer
(ISBN 0-8186-0751-3); 512 pages

Software Maintenance and Computers
Edited by D.H. Longstreet
(ISBN 0-8186-8898-X); 304 pages

Software Quality Assurance: A Practical Approach
Edited by T.S. Chow
(ISBN 0-8186-0569-3); 506 pages

Software Reusability
Edited by Peter Freeman
(ISBN 0-8186-0750-5); 304 pages

Software Reuse—Emerging Technology
Edited by Will Tracz
(ISBN 0-8186-0846-3); 400 pages

Software Risk Management
Edited by B.W. Boehm
(ISBN 0-8186-8906-4); 508 pages

**Standards, Guidelines and Examples on System
and Software Requirements Engineering**
Edited by Merlin Dorfman and Richard H. Thayer
(ISBN 0-8186-8922-6); 626 pages

System and Software Requirements Engineering
Edited by Richard H. Thayer and Merlin Dorfman
(ISBN 0-8186-8921-8); 740 pages

Test Access Port and Boundary-Scan Architecture
Edited by C. M. Maunder and R. E. Tulloss
(ISBN 0-8186-9070-4); 400 pages

Test Generation for VLSI Chips
Edited by V.D. Agrawal and S.C. Seth
(ISBN 0-8186-8786-X); 416 pages

Visual Programming Environments: Paradigms and Systems
Edited by Ephraim Glinert
(ISBN 0-8186-8973-0); 680 pages

Visual Programming Environments: Applications and Issues
Edited by Ephraim Glinert
(ISBN 0-8186-8974-9); 704 pages

Visualization in Scientific Computing
Edited by G.M. Nielson, B. Shriver, and L. Rosenblum
(ISBN 0-8186-8979-X); 304 pages

VLSI Testing and Validation Techniques
Edited by H. Reghbati
(ISBN 0-8186-0668-1); 616 pages

Volume Visualization
Edited by Arie Kaufman
(ISBN 0-8186-9020-8); 494 pages

REPRINT COLLECTIONS

**Distributed Computing Systems:
Concepts and Structures**
Edited by A. Ananda and B. Srinivasan
(ISBN 0-8186-8975-0); 416 pages

**Expert Systems: A Software Methodology
for Modern Applications**
Edited by Peter Raeth
(ISBN 0-8186-8904-8); 476 pages

Milestones in Software Evolution
Edited by Paul W. Oman and Ted G. Lewis
(ISBN 0-8186-9033-X); 332 pages

Object-Oriented Databases
Edited by Ez Nahouraii and Fred Petry
(ISBN 0-8186-8929-3); 256 pages

Validating and Verifying Knowledge-Based Systems
Edited by Uma G. Gupta
(ISBN 0-8186-8995-1); 400 pages

ARTIFICIAL NEURAL NETWORKS TECHNOLOGY SERIES

Artificial Neural Networks—Concept Learning
Edited by Joachim Diederich
(ISBN 0-8186-2015-3); 160 pages

Artificial Neural Networks—Electronic Implementation
Edited by Nelson Morgan
(ISBN 0-8186-2029-3); 144 pages

Artificial Neural Networks—Theoretical Concepts
Edited by V. Vemuri
(ISBN 0-8186-0855-2); 160 pages

SOFTWARE TECHNOLOGY SERIES

Computer-Aided Software Engineering (CASE)
Edited by E.J. Chikofsky
(ISBN 0-8186-1917-1); 110 pages

**Software Reliability Models:
Theoretical Development, Evaluation and Applications**
Edited by Y.K. Malaiya and P.K. Srimani
(ISBN 0-8186-2110-9); 136 pages

MATHEMATICS TECHNOLOGY SERIES

Computer Algorithms
Edited by Jun-ichi Aoe
(ISBN 0-8186-2123-0); 154 pages

Multiple-Valued Logic in VLSI Design
Edited by Jon T. Butler
(ISBN 0-8186-2127-3); 128 pages

COMMUNICATIONS TECHNOLOGY SERIES

Multicast Communication in Distributed Systems
Edited by Mustaque Ahamad
(ISBN 0-8186-1970-8); 110 pages

ROBOTICS TECHNOLOGY SERIES

Multirobot Systems
Edited by Rajiv Mehrotra and Murali R. Varanasi
(ISBN 0-8186-1977-5); 122 pages

PUBLISH WITH IEEE COMPUTER SOCIETY PRESS

TODAY'S COMPUTER SCIENCE PROFESSIONALS ARE TURNING TO US TO PUBLISH THEIR TEXTS

BENEFITS OF IEEE COMPUTER SOCIETY PRESS PUBLISHING :

- ❑ Timely publication schedules
- ❑ Society's professional reputation and recognition
- ❑ High-quality, reasonably priced books
- ❑ Course classroom adoption
- ❑ Open options on the type and level of publication to develop
- ❑ Built-in mechanisms to reach a strong constituency of professionals
- ❑ Peer review and reference

Enjoy the personal, professional, and financial recognition of having your name in print alongside other respected professionals in the fields of computer and engineering technology. Our rapid turnaround (from approved proposal to the published product) assures you against publication of dated technical material, and gives you the potential for additional royalties and sales from new editions. Your royalty payments are based not only on sales, but also on the amount of time and effort you expend in writing original material for your book.

Your book will be advertised to a vast audience through IEEE Computer Society Press catalogs and brochures that reach over 500,000 carefully chosen professionals in numerous disciplines. Our wide distribution also includes promotional programs through our European and Asian offices, and over-the-counter sales at 50 international computer and engineering conferences annually.

IEEE Computer Society Press books have a proven sales record, and our tutorials enjoy a unique niche in today's fast moving technical fields and help us maintain our goal to publish up-to-date, viable computer science information.

Steps for Book Submittals:

1- Submit your proposal to the Editorial Director of IEEE Computer Society Press. It should include the following data: title; your name, address, and telephone number; a detailed outline; a summary of the subject matter; a statement of the technical level of the book, the intended audience, and the potential market; a table of contents including the titles, authors, and sources for all reprints; and a biography.

2- Upon acceptance of your proposal, prepare and submit copies of the completed manuscript, including xerox copies of any reprinted papers and any other pertinent information, and mail to the Editorial Director of IEEE Computer Society Press.

3- The manuscript will then be reviewed by other respected experts in the field, and the editor-in-charge.

4- Upon publication, you will receive an initial royalty payment with additional royalties based on a percentage of the net sales and on the amount of original material included in the book.

We are searching for authors in the following computer science areas:

ADA
ARCHITECTURE
ARTIFICIAL INTELLIGENCE
AUTOMATED TEST EQUIPMENT
CAD / CAE
COMPUTER GRAPHICS
COMPUTER LANGUAGES
COMPUTER MATHEMATICS
COMPUTER WORKSTATIONS
DATABASE ENGINEERING
DIGITAL IMAGE PROCESSING
DISTRIBUTED PROCESSING
EXPERT SYSTEMS
FAULT-TOLERANT COMPUTING
IMAGING

LOCAL AREA NETWORKS
OPTICAL STORAGE DATABASES
PARALLEL PROCESSING
PATTERN RECOGNITION
PERSONAL COMPUTING
RELIABILITY
ROBOTICS
SOFTWARE ENGINEERING
SOFTWARE ENVIRONMENTS
SOFTWARE MAINTENANCE
SOFTWARE TESTING AND
   VALIDATION
AND OTHER AREAS AT THE
FOREFRONT OF
COMPUTING TECHNOLOGY !

Interested ?

For more detailed guidelines please contact:

Editorial Director, c/o IEEE Computer Society Press,
10662 Los Vaqueros Circle, Los Alamitos, California 90720-1264.

 IEEE COMPUTER SOCIETY

 THE INSTITUTE OF ELECTRICAL AND ELECTRONICS ENGINEERS, INC.